Market Efficiency: Stock Market Behaviour in Theory and Practice
Volume II

The International Library of Critical Writings in Financial Economics

Series Editor: Richard Roll

Allstate Professor of Economics
The Anderson School at UCLA, US

This major series presents by field outstanding selections of the most important articles across the entire spectrum of financial economics – one of the fastest growing areas in business schools and economics departments. Each collection has been prepared by a leading specialist who has written an authoritative introduction to the literature. Wherever possible, the articles in these volumes have been reproduced as originally published using facsimile reproduction, inclusive of footnotes and pagination to facilitate ease of reference.

1. The Theory of Corporate Finance (Volumes I and II)
   Michael J. Brennan

2. Futures Markets (Volumes I, II and III)
   A.G. Malliaris

3. Market Efficiency: Stock Market Behaviour in Theory and Practice (Volumes I and II)
   Andrew W. Lo

Future titles will include:

The Debt Market
Stephen A. Ross

Empirical Corporate Finance
Michael J. Brennan

Options Markets

Emerging Markets

International Securities

Continuous Time Finance

For a list of all Edward Elgar published titles visit our site on the World Wide Web at
http://www.e-elgar.co.uk

Market Efficiency: Stock Market Behaviour in Theory and Practice Volume II

Edited by

Andrew W. Lo

Harris & Harris Group Professor
Sloan School of Management
Massachusetts Institute of Technology, US

THE INTERNATIONAL LIBRARY OF CRITICAL WRITINGS IN FINANCIAL ECONOMICS

An Elgar Reference Collection
Cheltenham, UK • Lyme, US

© Andrew W. Lo 1997. For copyright of individual articles, please refer to the Acknowledgements

All rights reserved. No part of this publication may be reproduced, stored in a retrieval system or transmitted in any form or by any means, electronic, mechanical or photocopying, recording, or otherwise without the prior permission of the publisher.

Published by
Edward Elgar Publishing Limited
8 Lansdown Place
Cheltenham
Glos GL50 2HU
UK

Edward Elgar Publishing, Inc.
1 Pinnacle Hill Road
Lyme
NH 03768
US

A catalogue record for this book
is available from the British Library

Library of Congress Cataloging-in-Publication Data
Market efficiency : stock market behaviour in theory and practice /
    edited by Andrew W. Lo.
        (International library of critical writings in
    financial economics : 3) (An Elgar reference collection)
        Includes bibliographical references.
        1. Stocks—Prices—Mathematical models. 2. Efficient market
theory—Mathematical models. I. Lo, Andrew W. (Andrew Wen-Chuan)
II. Series. III. Series: An Elgar reference collection.
HG4636.M367 1997
332.63'222—dc21   97-3805
                                                                                                          CIP

ISBN 1 85898 161 1 (2 volume set)

Printed and bound in Great Britain by
Hartnolls Limited, Bodmin, Cornwall

Contents

Acknowledgements ix
Foreword by Richard Roll xi
Introduction to both volumes by Andrew W. Lo xiii

PART I VARIANCE BOUNDS TESTS

1. John Y. Campbell and Robert J. Shiller (1989), 'The Dividend-Price Ratio and Expectations of Future Dividends and Discount Factors', *Review of Financial Studies*, **1** (3), 195–228 — 3
2. Marjorie A. Flavin (1983), 'Excess Volatility in the Financial Markets: A Reassessment of the Empirical Evidence', *Journal of Political Economy*, **91** (6), 929–56 — 37
3. Christian Gilles and Stephen F. LeRoy (1991), 'Econometric Aspects of the Variance-Bounds Tests: A Survey', *Review of Financial Studies*, **4** (4), 753–91 — 65
4. Sanford J. Grossman and Robert J. Shiller (1981), 'The Determinants of the Variability of Stock Market Prices', *American Economic Review*, **71** (2), May, 222–7 — 104
5. Allan W. Kleidon (1986), 'Variance Bounds Tests and Stock Price Valuation Models', *Journal of Political Economy*, **94** (5), October, 953–1001 — 110
6. Stephen F. LeRoy and Richard D. Porter (1981), 'The Present-Value Relation: Tests Based on Implied Variance Bounds', *Econometrica*, **49** (3), May, 555–74 — 159
7. Terry A. Marsh and Robert C. Merton (1986), 'Dividend Variability and Variance Bounds Tests for the Rationality of Stock Market Prices', *American Economic Review*, **76** (3), June, 483–98 — 179
8. Robert C. Merton (1987), 'On the Current State of the Stock Market Rationality Hypothesis', in Rudiger Dornbusch, Stanley Fischer and John Bossons (eds), *Macroeconomics and Finance: Essays in Honor of Franco Modigliani*, Chapter 5, Cambridge, MA: MIT Press, 93–124 — 195
9. Ronald W. Michener (1982), 'Variance Bounds in a Simple Model of Asset Pricing', *Journal of Political Economy*, **90** (1), February, 166–75 — 227
10. Robert J. Shiller (1981), 'Do Stock Prices Move Too Much to be Justified by Subsequent Changes in Dividends?', *American Economic Review*, **71** (3), June, 421–36 — 237
11. Kenneth D. West (1988), 'Dividend Innovations and Stock Price Volatility', *Econometrica*, **56** (1), January, 37–61 — 253

PART II OVERREACTION AND UNDERREACTION

12. Ray Ball and Philip Brown (1968), 'An Empirical Evaluation of Accounting Income Numbers', *Journal of Accounting Research*, **6** (2), Autumn, 159–78 — 281
13. Victor L. Bernard and Jacob K. Thomas (1990), 'Evidence that Stock Prices do not Fully Reflect the Implications of Current Earnings for Future Earnings', *Journal of Accounting and Economics*, **13**, 305–40 — 301
14. K.C. Chan (1988), 'On the Contrarian Investment Strategy', *Journal of Business*, **61** (2), April, 147–63 — 337
15. Navin Chopra, Josef Lakonishok and Jay R. Ritter (1992), 'Measuring Abnormal Performance: Do Stocks Overreact?', *Journal of Financial Economics*, **31**, 235–68 — 354
16. Werner F.M. De Bondt and Richard Thaler (1985), 'Does the Stock Market Overreact?', *Journal of Finance*, **XL** (3), July, 793–805 — 388
17. Bruce N. Lehmann (1990), 'Fads, Martingales, and Market Efficiency', *Quarterly Journal of Economics*, **CV** (1), February, 1–28 — 401
18. Andrew W. Lo and A. Craig MacKinlay (1990), 'When are Contrarian Profits Due to Stock Market Overreaction?', *Review of Financial Studies*, **3**(2), 175–205 — 429

PART III ANOMALIES

19. Rolf W. Banz (1981), 'The Relationship between Return and Market Value of Common Stocks', *Journal of Financial Economics*, **9**, 3–18 — 463
20. S. Basu (1977), 'Investment Performance of Common Stocks in Relation to Their Price-Earnings Ratios: A Test of the Efficient Market Hypothesis', *Journal of Finance*, **XXXII** (3), June, 663–82 — 479
21. Stephen J. Brown, William Goetzmann, Roger G. Ibbotson and Stephen A. Ross (1992), 'Survivorship Bias in Performance Studies', *Review of Financial Studies*, **5** (4), 553–80 — 499
22. Thomas E. Copeland and David Mayers (1982), 'The Value Line Enigma (1965–1978): A Case Study of Performance Evaluation Issues', *Journal of Financial Economics*, **10**, 289–321 — 527
23. Donald B. Keim (1983), 'Size-Related Anomalies and Stock Return Seasonality: Further Empirical Evidence', *Journal of Financial Economics*, **12**, 13–32 — 560
24. Josef Lakonishok and Seymour Smidt (1988), 'Are Seasonal Anomalies Real? A Ninety-Year Perspective', *Review of Financial Studies*, **1** (4), 403–25 — 580
25. Andrew W. Lo and A. Craig MacKinlay (1990), 'Data-Snooping Biases in Tests of Financial Asset Pricing Models', *Review of Financial Studies*, **3** (3), 431–67 — 603

26. Richard Roll (1983), 'Vas Ist Das? The Turn-of-the-Year Effect and the Return Premia of Small Firms', *Journal of Portfolio Management*, **9**, Winter, 18–28 — 640
27. Richard Roll (1984), 'Orange Juice and Weather', *American Economic Review*, **74**, 861–80 — 651
28. Barr Rosenberg, Kenneth Reid and Ronald Lanstein (1985), 'Persuasive Evidence of Market Inefficiency', *Journal of Portfolio Management*, **11**, 9–16 — 671
29. Michael S. Rozeff and William R. Kinney, Jr (1976), 'Capital Market Seasonality: The Case of Stock Returns', *Journal of Financial Economics*, **3**, 379–402 — 679

Name Index — 703

Acknowledgements

The editor and publishers wish to thank the authors and the following publishers who have kindly given permission for the use of copyright material.

American Economic Association for articles: Sanford J. Grossman and Robert J. Shiller (1981), 'The Determinants of the Variability of Stock Market Prices', *American Economic Review*, **71** (2), May, 222–7; Robert J. Shiller (1981), 'Do Stock Prices Move Too Much to be Justified by Subsequent Changes in Dividends?', *American Economic Review*, **71** (3), June, 421–36; Richard Roll (1984), 'Orange Juice and Weather', *American Economic Review*, **74**, 861–80; Terry A. Marsh and Robert C. Merton (1986), 'Dividend Variability and Variance Bounds Tests for the Rationality of Stock Market Prices', *American Economic Review*, **76** (3), June 483–98.

American Finance Association for articles: S. Basu (1977), 'Investment Performance of Common Stocks in Relation to Their Price-Earnings Ratios: A Test of the Efficient Market Hypothesis', *Journal of Finance*, **XXXII** (3), June, 663–82; Werner F.M. De Bondt and Richard Thaler (1985), 'Does the Stock Market Overreact?', *Journal of Finance*, **XL** (3), July, 793–805.

The Econometric Society for articles: Stephen F. LeRoy and Richard D. Porter (1981), 'The Present-Value Relation: Tests Based on Implied Variance Bounds', *Econometrica*, **49** (3), May, 555–74; Kenneth D. West (1988), 'Dividend Innovations and Stock Price Volatility', *Econometrica*, **56** (1), January, 37–61.

Elsevier Science B.V. for article: Victor L. Bernard and Jacob K. Thomas (1990), 'Evidence that Stock Prices do not Fully Reflect the Implications of Current Earnings for Future Earnings', *Journal of Accounting and Economics*, **13**, 305–40.

Elsevier Science SA for articles: Thomas E. Copeland and David Mayers 1982), 'The Value Line Enigma (1965–1978): A Case Study of Performance Evaluation Issues', *Journal of Financial Economics*, **10**, 289–321; Donald B. Keim (1983), 'Size-Related Anomalies and Stock Return Seasonality: Further Empirical Evidence', *Journal of Financial Economics*, **12**, 13–32; Michael S. Rozeff and William R. Kinney, Jr (1976), 'Capital Market Seasonality: The Case of Stock Returns', *Journal of Financial Economics*, **3**, 379–402; Navin Chopra, Josef Lakonishok and Jay R. Ritter (1992), 'Measuring Abnormal Performance: Do Stocks Overreact?', *Journal of Financial Economics*, **31**, 235–68; Rolf W. Banz (1981), 'The Relationship between Return and Market Value of Common Stocks', *Journal of Financial Economics*, **9**, 3–18.

Institute of Professional Accounting for article: Ray Ball and Philip Brown (1968), 'An Empirical Evaluation of Accounting Income Numbers', *Journal of Accounting Research*, **6** (2), Autumn, 159–78.

Institutional Investor, Inc. for articles: Richard Roll (1983), 'Vas Ist Das? The Turn-of-the-Year-Effect and the Return Premia of Small Firms', *Journal of Portfolio Management*, **9**, Winter, 18–28; Barr Rosenberg, Kenneth Reid and Ronald Lanstein (1985), 'Persuasive Evidence of Market Inefficiency', *Journal of Portfolio Management*, **11**, 9–16.

MIT Press Journals for article: Bruce N. Lehmann (1990), 'Fads, Martingales, and Market Efficiency', *Quarterly Journal of Economics*, **CV** (1), February, 1–28.

MIT Press for excerpt: Robert C. Merton (1987), 'On the Current State of the Stock Market Rationality Hypothesis', in Rudiger Dornbusch, Stanley Fischer and John Bossons (eds), *Macroeconomics and Finance: Essays in Honor of Franco Modigliani*, Chapter 5, 93–124.

Oxford University Press for articles: Josef Lakonishok and Seymour Smidt (1988), 'Are Seasonal Anomalies Real? A Ninety-Year Perspective', *Review of Financial Studies*, **1** 403–25; John Y. Campbell and Robert J. Shiller (1989), 'The Dividend-Price Ratio and Expectations of Future Dividends and Discount Factors', *Review of Financial Studies*, **1** (3), 195–228; Andrew W. Lo and A. Craig MacKinlay (1990), 'When are Contrarian Profits Due to Stock Market Overreaction?', *Review of Financial Studies*, **3** (2), 175–205; Andrew W. Lo and A. Craig MacKinlay (1990), 'Data-Snooping Biases in Tests of Financial Asset Pricing Models', *Review of Financial Studies*, **3** (3), 431–67; Christian Gilles and Stephen F. LeRoy (1991), 'Econometric Aspects of the Variance-Bounds Tests: A Survey', *Review of Financial Studies*, **4** (4), 753–91; Stephen J. Brown, William Goetzmann, Roger G. Ibbotson and Stephen A. Ross (1992), 'Survivorship Bias in Performance Studies', *Review of Financial Studies*, **5** (4), 553–80.

University of Chicago Press for article: K.C. Chan (1988), 'On the Contrarian Investment Strategy', *Journal of Business*, **61** (2), April, 147–63; Ronald W. Michener (1982), 'Variance Bounds in a Simple Model of Asset Pricing', *Journal of Political Economy*, **90** (1), February, 166–75; Marjorie A. Flavin (1983), 'Excess Volatility in the Financial Markets: A Reassessment of the Empirical Evidence', *Journal of Political Economy*, **91** (6), 929–56; Allan W. Kleidon (1986), 'Variance Bounds Tests and Stock Price Valuation Models', *Journal of Political Economy*, **94** (5), October, 953–1001.

Every effort has been made to trace all the copyright holders but if any have been inadvertently overlooked the publishers will be pleased to make the necessary arrangement at the first opportunity.

In addition the publishers wish to thank the Library of the London School of Economics and Political Science and the Marshall Library of Economics, Cambridge University, for their assistance in obtaining these articles.

Foreword

Richard Roll

Professor Lo's superb introductory essay for these two volumes on Market Efficiency concludes, 'If, as [Nobel Laureate] Paul Samuelson has suggested, financial economics is the crown jewel of the social sciences then the EMH [Efficient Market Hypothesis] must account for half the facets'. Lo and Samuelson are lauding the quality of the scientific debate in this very important field of research. These past three decades of intensive scholarship are epitomized by the papers collected in these volumes, yet the debate rages on, perhaps, as Professor Lo intimates, because it can never be answered in the absolute.

The idea of an *informationally* efficient financial market is disarmingly simple, yet fraught with subtleties and frightfully hard to prove one way or the other. Stated in its most elementary form, the EMH asserts 'there is no free lunch', particularly in financial markets. In other words, prices should fluctuate unpredictably, costless trading schemes should earn no economic rent [excess profit], persons without special skills should earn no more by speculating in financial markets than they would earn in an alternative occupation.

Why are financial markets likely to exhibit these properties? Greed, pure and simple; the strenuous efforts of millions to make money. Nowhere in human affairs is competition so ardent, pure and unhindered as in financial markets. When competition is inescapable, it drives down prices, reduces profits to a bare minimum, and renders the marginal competitor just indifferent between continuing and seeking another vocation.

To most financial economists, it seems evident that if competition is effective in any market, it must reach its highest refinement in financial markets. In the first place, entry is perfectly unfettered. Anyone can pick up a telephone and become an 'investor' within a few minutes. Even traditionally competitive occupations such as farming and hair styling have far greater entry costs. Second, information is abundant and virtually free. The financial press, both printed and electronic, contains daily and real time news about thousands of assets and economic events. Third, professional services are profuse – there are stock brokers in every hamlet and thousands of investment advisors easily reachable. In most developed nations, virtually every family owns financial assets, though often indirectly through pension and other funds; in some countries, stock market speculation is a national pastime.

Given these realities, scientific research has focused on the resulting prices. What should be their characteristics under competition? What are their characteristics in reality? As Professor Lo so eloquently explains, the early literature adopted the procedure of (1) specifying a stochastic process for prices that would preclude everyone from easy profits and (2) testing whether actual prices followed such a process. The earliest and simplest process studied was the 'random walk', i.e. price changes are purely random and thus completely unforecastable. In a shock to market professionals, early empirical literature found little reason to reject such a process for many well-known assets. A closely related generalization, the 'martingale' process, was also studied empirically with similar findings.

But this early work ran headlong into some serious objections, both theoretical and empirical. Theoretically, the random walk hypothesis asks too much. If it were literally true, no speculator would cover costs; but significant costs are, in fact, widely incurred in the process of analysing, trading and managing investments. A large portion of the financial industry would cease to exist if prices actually followed a random walk and everyone believed it. Hence, at least some *infra*-marginal competitors must be earning persistent profits before costs, else they would disappear. Professor Lo has selected the important papers that formalized this idea. Their basic conclusion was: an asset's price cannot and should not reflect all information known to anyone. Price changes must be somewhat predictable with sophisticated skills.

With larger databases and faster computers, empirical scholars began to uncover many suspicious patterns in prices. Professor Lo discusses several categories: 'variance bounds tests' that revealed what might be excessive volatility, departures from pure randomness in price movements, and anomalies, 'a regular pattern in an asset's return which is reliable, widely known, and inexplicable'. An example of the latter is the famous 'small firm effect', higher returns from investments in smaller companies than in larger companies, even risk-adjusted.

Every puzzling empirical finding has elicited one or more rejoinders in support of the EMH; bid/ask spreads for short-term non-randomness, accounting practices for variance bound violations, inappropriate risk adjustment for the small firm effect, data mining for everything! As Professor Lo correctly argues, such give and take could last forever; it must finally be settled in the marketplace itself. Many academics have followed exactly that strategy, reportedly with mixed results. It may not be so easy to exploit an alleged market inefficiency.

Yet this widely-appreciated difficulty is a pitiful impediment in the face of greed, which continues unabated. More individuals than ever are trying their hand at getting rich quick. It's the modern gold rush. The only difference is that transport is electronic rather than maritime or equine. Financial markets are, if anything, more competitive than ever. They are globally integrated.

But are prices becoming more efficient? Have the scholars overlooked forces, perhaps behavioural, that mitigate the supposed influence of competition? What instrument can measure Professor Lo's *relative* degree of efficiency? These are fascinating, scientifically important, and possibly lucrative issues.

Richard Roll

Introduction

Andrew W. Lo

There is an old joke, widely told among economists, about an economist strolling down the street with a companion when they come upon a $100 bill lying on the ground. As the companion reaches down to pick it up, the economist says 'Don't bother – if it were a real $100 bill, someone would have already picked it up'.

This humorous example of economic logic gone awry strikes dangerously close to home for students of the Efficient Markets Hypothesis (EMH), one of the most controversial and well-studied propositions in all the social sciences. It is disarmingly simple to state, has far-reaching consequences for academic pursuits and business practice, and yet is surprisingly resilient to empirical proof or refutation. Even after three decades of research and literally thousands of journal articles, economists have not yet reached a consensus about whether markets – particularly financial markets – are efficient or not.

This happy state of intellectual turmoil has launched many distinguished careers, leaving in its wake a rich legacy of economic thought that still challenges us today. Much of that legacy, and some of the more recent research, is collected here in these two volumes. The fact that there are two volumes, not one, reflects the breadth and depth of the EMH. The first volume begins with the theoretical foundations of the EMH, from Paul Samuelson's (1965) seminal piece to Fischer Black's (1986) bold challenge. These influential articles define the EMH and lay the groundwork on which the rest of the articles in these two volumes, and much of the extant EMH literature, are built.

The next set of articles concerns the Random Walk Hypothesis (RWH), one of the earliest economic models of financial market prices. For quite some time the RWH was taken to be equivalent to the EMH, and although it is now recognized that the two are indeed distinct – one neither necessary nor sufficient for the other – nevertheless, the RWH literature occupies a central role in empirical investigations of the EMH.

The second volume covers three other aspects of the EMH: variance bounds tests, overreaction and underreaction, and anomalies. Each of these topics concerns some kind of alleged empirical inconsistency with the EMH: stock prices are too volatile; stock prices overreact to past price changes; stock prices underreact to earnings announcements; and stock prices exhibit regularities that can be profitably exploited. These are 'alleged' inconsistencies in the sense that a verdict has not yet been returned, and despite what some consider to be damning evidence against the EMH, the prosecution has yet to eliminate all reasonable doubt.

In this respect, the articles contained in these two volumes may be viewed as the exhibits and minutes of an ongoing trial in which each new generation of economists and businessmen can participate, as jurors, witnesses and even barristers, arguing one side of the case or the other. The EMH will no doubt hold the fascination and stimulate the imagination of social scientists for years to come.

1 Theoretical Foundations

As with so many of the ideas of modern economics, the origins of the EMH can be traced back to Paul Samuelson (1965), whose contribution is neatly summarized by the title of his article 'Proof that Properly Anticipated Prices Fluctuate Randomly'. In an informationally efficient market – not to be confused with an allocationally or Pareto-efficient market – price changes must be unforecastable if they are properly anticipated, i.e. if they fully incorporate the expectations and information of all market participants. Fama (1970) operationalizes this hypothesis, which he summarizes in the well-known epithet 'prices fully reflect all available information', by placing structure on various information sets available to market participants.

This concept of informational efficiency has a wonderfully counter-intuitive and seemingly contradictory flavour to it: the more efficient the market, the more random the sequence of price changes generated by such a market, and the most efficient market of all is one in which price changes are completely random and unpredictable. This, of course, is not an accident of Nature but is the direct result of many active participants attempting to profit from their information. Unable to curtail their greed, an army of investors aggressively pounce on even the smallest informational advantages at their disposal, and in doing so, they incorporate their information into market prices and quickly eliminate the profit opportunities that gave rise to their aggression. If this occurs instantaneously, which it must in an idealized world of 'frictionless' markets and costless trading, then prices must always fully reflect all available information and no profits can be garnered from information-based trading (because such profits have already been captured).

Such compelling motivation for randomness is unique among the social sciences and is reminiscent of the role that uncertainty plays in quantum mechanics. Just as Heisenberg's uncertainty principle places a limit on what we can know about an electron's position and momentum if quantum mechanics holds, this version of the EMH places a limit on what we can know about future price changes if the forces of economic self-interest hold.

However, one of the central tenets of modern financial economics is the necessity of some trade-off between risk and expected return, and although this version of the EMH places a restriction on expected returns, it does not account for risk in any way. In particular, if a security's expected price change is positive, it may be the reward needed to attract investors to hold the asset and bear the corresponding risks. Indeed, if an investor is sufficiently risk averse, he might gladly *pay* to avoid holding a security which has unforecastable returns.

In such a world, the RWH and Martingale Model – two statistical models of unforecastable returns (see below) – need not be satisfied even if prices do fully reflect all available information. This was demonstrated conclusively by LeRoy (1973) and Lucas (1978), who construct explicit examples of well-functioning markets in which the EMH holds but where returns are not completely random.

Grossman (1976) and Grossman and Stiglitz (1980) go even further. They argue that perfectly informationally efficient markets are an *impossibility*, for if markets are perfectly efficient, the return to gathering information is nil, in which case there would be little reason to trade and markets would eventually collapse. Alternatively, the degree of market *inefficiency* determines the effort investors are willing to expend to gather and trade on information, hence a non-degenerate market equilibrium will arise only when there are sufficient profit opportunities, i.e. inefficiencies, to compensate investors for the cost of trading and information-gathering. The profits earned by these attentive investors may be viewed as economic rents that accrue to those willing to engage in such activities. Who are the providers of these rents? Black (1986) gives us a provocative answer: noise traders, individuals who trade on what they think is information but is in fact merely noise.

These articles provide the theoretical foundations on which the rest of the EMH literature is built. The remaining articles in these two volumes are empirical studies that attempt to test the EMH in one form or another.

2 The Random Walk Hypothesis

Much of the EMH literature before LeRoy (1973) and Lucas (1978) revolved around the RWH and the Martingale Model, two statistical descriptions of unforecastable price changes that were taken to be implications of the EMH. One of the first tests of the RWH was developed by Cowles and Jones (1937) which compared the frequency of *sequences* and *reversals* in historical stock returns, where the former are pairs of consecutive returns with the same sign, and the latter are pairs of consecutive returns with opposite signs. Cootner (1962), Fama (1965), Fama and Blume (1966), Osborne (1959) perform related tests of the RWH, and with the exception of Cowles and Jones (who subsequently acknowledged an error in their analysis), all of these articles indicate support for the RWH using historical stock price data.

More recently, Lo and MacKinlay (1988) exploit the fact that return variances scale linearly under the RWH – the variance of a two-week return is twice the variance of a one-week return if the RWH holds – and construct a variance ratio test which rejects the RWH for weekly US stock returns indexes from 1962 to 1985. In particular, they find that variances grow faster than linearly as the holding period increases, implying positive serial correlation in weekly returns. Oddly enough, Lo and MacKinlay also show that individual stocks generally do satisfy the RWH, a fact that we shall return to in Section 4.

French and Roll (1986) document a related phenomenon: stock return variances over weekends and exchange holidays are considerably lower than return variances over the same number of days when markets are open. This difference suggests that the very act of trading creates volatility, which may well be a symptom of Black's (1986) noise traders.

For holding periods much longer than one week, e.g. three to five years, Fama and French (1988) and Poterba and Summers (1988) find negative serial correlation in US stock returns indexes using data from 1926 to 1986. Although their estimates of serial correlation coefficients seem large in magnitude, there is insufficient data to reject the RWH at the usual levels of significance. Moreover, a number of statistical artifacts documented by Kim, Nelson, and Startz (1991) and Richardson (1993) cast serious doubt on the reliability of these longer-horizon inferences.

Finally, Lo (1991) considers another aspect of stock market prices long thought to have been a departure from the RWH: long-term memory. Time series with long-term memory exhibit an unusually high degree of persistence, so that observations in the remote past are non-trivially correlated with observations in the distant future, even as the time span between the two observations increases. Nature's predilection towards long-term memory has been well-documented in the natural sciences such as hydrology, meteorology and geophysics, and some have argued that economic time series must therefore also have this property.

However, using recently developed statistical techniques, Lo (1991) constructs a test for long-term memory that is robust to short-term correlations of the sort uncovered by Lo and MacKinlay (1988), and concludes that despite earlier evidence to the contrary, there is little support for long-term memory in stock market prices. Departures from the RWH can be fully explained by conventional models of short-term dependence.

3 Variance Bounds Tests

The variance bounds literature begins with the observation that in a world without uncertainty, the market price of a share of common stock must equal the present value of all future dividends, discounted at the appropriate cost of capital. In an uncertain world, one can generalize this *dividend-discount model* or *present-value relation* in the natural way: the market price equals the conditional expectation of the present value of all future dividends, discounted at the appropriate risk-adjusted cost of capital, and conditional on all available information. This generalization is explicitly developed by Grossman and Shiller (1981).

LeRoy and Porter (1981) and Shiller (1981) take this as their starting point in comparing the variance of stock market prices to the variance of *ex post* present values of future dividends. If the market price is the conditional expectation of present values, then the difference between the two, i.e. the forecast error, must be uncorrelated with the conditional expectation by construction. But this implies that the variance of the *ex post* present value is the sum of the variance of the market price (the conditional expectation) and the variance of the forecast error. Since volatilities are always non-negative, this variance decomposition implies that the variance of stock prices cannot exceed the variance of *ex post* present values. Using annual US stock market data from various sample periods, LeRoy and Porter (1981) and Shiller (1981) find that the variance bound is violated dramatically. Although LeRoy and Porter are more circumspect about the implications of such violations, Shiller concludes that stock market prices are too volatile and the EMH must be false.

These two papers ignited a flurry of responses which challenged Shiller's controversial conclusion on a number of fronts. For example, Flavin (1983), Kleidon (1986) and Marsh and Merton (1986) show that statistical inference is rather delicate for these variance bounds, and that even if they hold in theory, for the kind of sample sizes Shiller uses and under plausible data-generating processes, the sample variance bound is often violated purely due to sampling variation. These issues are well summarized in Gilles and LeRoy (1991), Merton (1987) and West (1988).

More importantly, on purely theoretical grounds, Marsh and Merton (1986) and Michener (1982) provide two explanations for violations of variance bounds that are perfectly consistent with the EMH. Marsh and Merton (1986) show that if managers smooth dividends – a well-known empirical phenomenon documented in several studies of dividend policy – and if earnings follow a geometric random walk, then the variance bound is violated in theory, in which case the empirical violations may be interpreted as *support* for this version of the EMH.

Alternatively, Michener constructs a simple dynamic equilibrium model along the lines of Lucas (1978) in which prices do fully reflect all available information at all times but where individuals are risk averse, and this risk aversion is enough to cause the variance bound to be violated in theory as well.

These findings highlight an important aspect of the EMH that had not been emphasized in earlier studies: tests of the EMH are always tests of joint hypotheses. In particular, the phrase 'prices fully reflect all available information' is a statement about two distinct aspects of prices: the information content and the price-formation mechanism. Therefore, any test of this proposition must concern the *kind* of information reflected in prices, and *how* this information comes to be reflected in prices.

Apart from issues regarding statistical inference, the empirical violation of variance bounds may be interpreted in many ways. It may be a violation of EMH, or a sign that investors are risk averse, or a symptom of dividend smoothing. To choose among these alternatives, more evidence is required.

4 Overreaction and Underreaction

A common explanation for departures from the EMH is that investors do not always react in proper proportion to new information. For example, in some cases investors may overreact to performance, selling stocks that have experienced recent losses or buying stocks that have enjoyed recent gains. Such overreaction tends to push prices beyond their 'fair' or 'rational' market value, only to have rational investors take the other side of the trades and bring prices back in line eventually. An implication of this phenomenon is price reversals: what goes up must come down, and vice-versa. Another implication is that *contrarian* investment strategies – strategies in which 'losers' are purchased and 'winners' are sold – will earn superior returns.

Both of these implications were tested and confirmed using recent US stock market data. For example, using monthly returns of NYSE stocks from 1926 to 1982, DeBondt and Thaler (1985) document the fact that the winners and losers in one 36-month period tend to reverse their performance over the next 36-month period. Curiously, much of these reversals occur in January [see the discussion below on the 'January effect']. Chopra, Lakonishok and Ritter (1992) reconfirm these findings after correcting for market risk and the size effect. And Lehmann (1990) shows that a zero-net-investment strategy in which long positions in losers are financed by short positions in winners almost always yields positive returns for monthly NYSE/AMEX stock returns data from 1962 to 1985.

However, Chan (1988) argues that the profitability of contrarian investment strategies cannot be taken as conclusive evidence against the EMH because there is typically no accounting for risk in these profitability calculations (although Chopra, Lakonishok and Ritter (1992) do provide risk adjustments, their focus was not on specific trading strategies). By risk-adjusting the returns of a contrarian trading strategy according to the Capital Asset Pricing Model, Chan (1988) shows that the expected returns are consistent with the EMH.

Moreover, Lo and MacKinlay (1990) show that at least half of the profits reported by Lehmann (1990) are not due to overreaction but rather the result of positive cross-autocorrelations between stocks. For example, suppose the returns of two stocks A and B are both serially uncorrelated but are positively cross-autocorrelated. The lack of serial correlation implies no overreaction (which is characterized by negative serial correlation), but positive cross-autocorrelations yields positive expected returns to contrarian trading strategies. The existence of several economic rationales for positive cross-autocorrelation that are consistent with EMH suggests that the profitability of contrarian trading strategies is not sufficient evidence to conclude that investors overreact.

The reaction of market participants to information contained in earnings announcements also has implications for the EMH. In one of the earliest studies of the information content of earnings, Ball and Brown (1968) show that up to 80 per cent of the information contained in the earnings 'surprises' is anticipated by market prices.

However, the more recent article by Bernard and Thomas (1990) argues that investors sometimes underreact to information about future earnings contained in current earnings. This is related to the 'post-earnings announcement drift' puzzle first documented by Ball and Brown (1968), in which the information contained in earnings announcement takes several days to become fully impounded into market prices. Although such effects are indeed troubling for the EMH, their economic significance is often questionable – while they may violate the EMH in frictionless markets, very often even the smallest frictions, e.g. positive trading costs, taxes, can eliminate the profits from trading strategies designed to exploit them.

5 Anomalies

Perhaps the most common challenge to the EMH is the anomaly, a regular pattern in an asset's returns which is reliable, widely known and inexplicable. The fact that the pattern is regular and reliable implies a degree of predictability, and the fact that the regularity is widely known implies that many investors can take advantage of it.

For example, one of the most enduring anomalies is the 'size effect', the apparent excess expected returns that accrue to stocks of small-capitalization companies – in excess of their risks – which was first discovered by Banz (1981). Keim (1983), Roll (1983) and Rozeff and Kinney (1976) document a related anomaly: small capitalization stocks tend to outperform large capitalization stocks by a wide margin over the turn of the calendar year. This so-called 'January effect' seems robust to sample period, and is difficult to reconcile with the EMH because of its regularity and publicity. Other well-known anomalies include the Value Line enigma (Copeland and Mayers, 1982), the profitability of return-reversal strategies (Rosenberg, Reid and Lanstein, 1985), the relation between price/earning ratios and expected returns (Basu, 1977), the volatility of orange juice futures prices (Roll, 1984), and calendar effects such as holiday, weekend, and turn-of-the-month seasonalities (Lakonishok and Smidt, 1988).

What are we to make of these anomalies? On the one hand, their persistence in the face of public scrutiny seems to be a clear violation of the EMH. After all, most of these anomalies can be exploited by relatively simple trading strategies, and while the resulting profits may not be riskless, they seem unusually profitable relative to their risks (see, especially, Lehmann, 1990).

But on the other hand, EMH supporters might argue that such persistence is in fact evidence in favour of EMH or, more to the point, that these anomalies cannot be exploited to any significant degree because of factors such as risk or transactions costs. Moreover, although some anomalies are currently inexplicable, this may be due to a lack of imagination on the part of academics, not necessarily a violation of the EMH. For example, recent evidence now suggests that the January effect is largely due to 'bid-ask bounce', i.e. closing prices for the last trading day of December tend to be at the bid price and closing prices for the first trading day of January tend to be at the ask price. Since small-capitalization stocks are also often low-price stocks, the effects of bid-ask bounce in percentage terms are much more pronounced for these stocks – a movement from bid to ask for a $5.00 stock on the NYSE (where the minimum bid-ask spread is $0.125) represents a 2.5 per cent return.

Whether or not one can profit from anomalies is a question unlikely to be settled in an academic setting. While calculations of 'paper' profits of various trading strategies come easily to academics, it is virtually impossible to incorporate in a realistic manner important features of the trading process such as transactions costs (including price impact), liquidity, rare events, institutional rigidities and nonstationarities. The economic value of anomalies must be decided in the laboratory of actual markets by investment professionals, over long periods of time, and even in these cases superior performance and simple luck are easily confused.

In fact, luck can play another role in the interpretation of anomalies: it can account for anomalies that are not anomalous. Regular patterns in historical data can be found even if no regularities exist, purely by chance. Although the likelihood of finding such spurious regularities is usually small (especially if the regularity is a very complex pattern), it increases dramatically with the number of 'searches' conducted on the same set of data. Such *data-snooping* biases are illustrated in Brown *et al.* (1992) and Lo and MacKinlay (1990) – even the smallest biases can translate into substantial anomalies such as superior investment returns or the size effect.

6 The Current State of Efficient Markets

In light of the studies included in these two volumes, and the extensive literature from which they are drawn, what can we conclude about the EMH? Amazingly, there is still no consensus among financial economists. Despite the many advances in the statistical analysis, databases and theoretical models surrounding the EMH, the main effect that the large number of empirical studies have had on this debate is to harden the resolve of the proponents on each side.

One of the reasons for this state of affairs is the fact that the EMH, by itself, is not a well-defined and empirically refutable hypothesis. To make it operational, one must specify additional structure, e.g. investors' preferences, information structure. But then a test of the EMH becomes a test of several auxiliary hypotheses as well, and a rejection of such a joint hypothesis tells us little about which aspect of the joint hypothesis is inconsistent with the data. Are stock prices too volatile because markets are inefficient, or is it due to risk aversion, or dividend smoothing? All three inferences are consistent with the data. Moreover, new statistical tests designed to distinguish among them will no doubt require auxiliary hypotheses of their own which, in turn, may be questioned.

More importantly, tests of the EMH may not be the most informative means of gauging the efficiency of a given market. What is often of more consequence is the *relative* efficiency of a particular market, relative to other markets, e.g. futures vs. spot markets, auction vs. dealer markets. The advantages of the concept of relative efficiency, as opposed to the all-or-nothing notion of absolute efficiency, are easy to spot by way of an analogy. Physical systems are often given an efficiency rating based on the relative proportion of energy or fuel converted to useful work. Therefore, a piston engine may be rated at 60 per cent efficiency, meaning that on average 60 per cent of the energy contained in the engine's fuel is used to turn the crankshaft, with the remaining 40 per cent lost to other forms of work, e.g. heat, light, noise.

Few engineers would ever consider performing a statistical test to determine whether or not a given engine is perfectly efficient – such an engine exists only in the idealized frictionless world of the imagination. But measuring relative efficiency – relative to the frictionless ideal – is commonplace. Indeed, we have come to expect such measurements for many household products: air conditioners, hot water heaters, refrigerators, etc. Therefore, from a practical point of view, and in light of Grossman and Stiglitz (1980), the EMH is an idealization that is economically unrealizable, but which serves as a useful benchmark for measuring relative efficiency.

A more practical version of the EMH is suggested by another analogy, one involving the notion of thermal equilibrium in statistical mechanics. Despite the occasional 'excess' profit opportunity, on average and over time, it is not possible to earn such profits consistently without some type of competitive advantage, e.g., superior information, superior technology, financial innovation. Alternatively, in an efficient market, the only way to earn positive profits *consistently* is to develop a competitive advantage, in which case the profits may be viewed as the economic rents which accrue to this competitive advantage. The consistency of such profits is an important qualification – in this version of the EMH, an occasional free lunch is permitted, but free lunch plans are ruled out.

To see why such an interpretation of the EMH is a more practical one, consider for a moment applying the classical version of the EMH to a non-financial market, say, the market for biotechnology. Consider, for example, the goal of developing a vaccine for the AIDS virus. If the market for biotechnology is efficient in the classical sense, such a vaccine can *never* be developed – if it could, someone would have already done it! This is clearly a ludicrous presumption since it ignores the difficulty and gestation lags of research and development in biotechnology. Moreover, if a pharmaceutical company does succeed in developing such a vaccine, the profits earned would be measured in the billions of dollars. Would this be considered 'excess' profits, or economic rents that accrue to biotechnology patents?

Financial markets are no different in principle, only in degree. Consequently, the profits that accrue to an investment professional need not be a market *inefficiency*, but may simply be the fair reward to breakthroughs in financial technology. After all, few analysts would regard the hefty profits of Amgen over the past few years as evidence of an inefficient market for pharmaceuticals – Amgen's recent profitability is readily identified with the development of several new drugs (Epogen, for example, a drug that stimulates the production of red blood cells), some considered breakthroughs in biotechnology. Similarly, even in efficient financial markets there are very handsome returns to breakthroughs in financial technology.

Of course, barriers to entry are typically lower, the degree of competition is much higher, and most financial technologies are not patentable (though this may soon change) hence the 'half life' of the profitability of financial innovation is considerably smaller. These features imply that financial markets should be relatively more efficient, and indeed they are. The market for used securities is considerably more efficient than the market for used cars. But to argue that financial markets must be perfectly efficient is tantamount to the claim that an AIDS vaccine cannot be found. In an efficient market, it is difficult to earn a good living, but not impossible.

In light of the various issues raised in these two volumes, the EMH is likely to be debated for quite some time. And despite the continuing lack of consensus in academia and industry, the ongoing dialogue has given us many new insights into the economic structure of financial markets. If, as Paul Samuelson has suggested, financial economics is the crown jewel of the social sciences, then the EMH must account for half the facets.

Note

* This is an introductory chapter to two volumes of collected papers on the Efficient Markets Hypothesis, to be published by Edward Elgar Publishing Co. I thank John Cox, Bruce Lehmann, Craig MacKinlay, Jay Ritter, Dick Roll, Christian Sheridan and Jiang Wang for helpful discussions in preparing this introduction and selecting the articles included in these volumes. This research was partially supported by the MIT Laboratory for Financial Engineering and an Alfred P. Sloan Research Fellowship.

Part I
Variance Bounds Tests

[1]

The Dividend-Price Ratio and Expectations of Future Dividends and Discount Factors

John Y. Campbell
Princeton University

Robert J. Shiller
Yale University

A dividend-ratio model is introduced here that makes the log of the dividend-price ratio on a stock linear in optimally forecast future one-period real discount rates and future one-period growth rates of real dividends. If ex post discount rates are observable, this model can be tested by using vector autoregressive methods. Four versions of the linearized model, differing in the measure of discount rates, are tested for U.S. time series 1871–1986 and 1926–1986: a version that imposes constant real discount rates, and versions that measure discount rates from real interest rate data, aggregate real consumption data, and return variance data. The results yield a metric to judge the relative importance of real dividend growth, measured real discount rates, and unexplained factors in determining the dividend-price ratio.

What accounts for the variation through time in the dividend-price ratio on corporate stocks? The dividend-

---

An earlier version of this paper was circulated as NBER Working Paper 2100. This research was supported by the NSF and the John M. Olin Fellowship at the NBER (Campbell). Any opinions expressed here are those of the authors and do not necessarily represent the views of the institutions with which they are affiliated. We are grateful to Michael Brennan, Steve Brown, David Hendry, Greg Mankiw, Sam Ouliaris, Peter Phillips, Mark Watson, and anonymous referees for helpful comments. We are particularly grateful to Jim Poterba for assistance with the data and to Andrea Beltrati for correcting an error in our unit roots test program. Address reprint requests to John Y. Campbell, Woodrow Wilson School, Princeton University, Princeton, NJ 08544.

price ratio is often interpreted as reflecting the outlook for dividends: when dividends can be forecast to decrease or grow unusually slowly, the dividend-price ratio should be high. Alternatively, the ratio is interpreted as reflecting the rate at which future dividends are discounted to today's price: when discount rates are high, the dividend-price ratio is high. In principle, the dividend-price ratio ought to have both of these interpretations at once. Yet their relative importance has never been established, and it is not clear whether these two interpretations together can account for time variation in the dividend-price ratio if one assumes that market expectations are rational. We address these questions by using long historical time series on broad stock indexes in the United States.

Our method is to test a dividend-ratio model relating the dividend-price ratio D/P to the expected future values of the one-period rates of discount r and one-period growth rates of dividends g over succeeding periods. The model might be described as a dynamic version of the Gordon (1962) model, $D/P = r - g$, which was derived under the assumption that dividends will grow at a constant rate forever, and that the discount rate will never change. This article fills a significant gap in the literature by permitting an analysis of the variation *through time* in the dividend-price ratio in relation to predictable changes in discount rates and dividend growth rates. Most previous studies of the dividend-price ratio have been concerned with the *cross-sectional* relationship between dividend-price ratios and average returns [e.g., Black and Scholes (1974)], while our own previous work on the time-series behavior of dividends and stock prices [e.g., Shiller (1981) and Campbell and Shiller (1987)] relies for the most part on the assumption that discount rates are constant.

The dividend-ratio model opens up important new avenues for econometric work. In this article we use it as follows. We think of log dividends and discount rates as two elements in a possibly large vector of variables that summarize the state of the economy at any point in time. The state vector evolves through time as a multivariate linear stochastic process with constant coefficients.[1] Stock market participants observe the state vector contemporaneously and know the process that it follows; they use this knowledge to forecast future log dividends and discount rates.

If dividends and discount rates are observable ex post, then this structure, together with the dividend-ratio model, implies restrictions on the joint time-series behavior of dividends, discount rates, and stock prices. In particular, the difference between the ex post stock return and the ex post discount rate should not be predictable from a linear regression on infor-

---

[1] This structure is consistent with models in which managers determine dividends without reference to stock prices, and also with "dividend-smoothing" models in which managers react to prices in setting dividends [Marsh and Merton (1986, 1987)].

The Dividend-Price Ratio

mation known in advance, and the log dividend-price ratio should be an optimal linear forecaster of the present value of future dividend growth rates and discount rates. These propositions can be tested formally, and they can also be evaluated informally: for example, by comparing the history of the actual log dividend-price ratio with that of an optimal forecast from a linear vector autoregressive model.

The measurement of dividends is straightforward, but the measurement of discount rates is not. Indeed, one view is that the only source of information on discount rates is the stock price itself. Our approach can be useful even if this view is correct; as discussed further below, we can use the dividend-ratio model to obtain a better estimate of the long-term discount rate by correcting the stock price for dividend expectations. However, we begin by using several simple models which imply that discount rates can be measured outside the stock market. We recognize that these models are unlikely to be able to account for all variation in stock prices, but it is worth knowing how far they can take us toward a complete explanation. We do not attempt to provide any formal theoretical justification for the measures we use, but we note that they have been the subject of some attention in the recent finance literature [see, for example, Fama and French (1988); French, Schwert, and Stambaugh (1987); Hansen and Singleton (1983); Marsh and Merton (1986); and Poterba and Summers (1986, 1988)].

We study several versions of the basic model, which differ in their measure of ex ante discount rates. In what we will call version 1 of the model, the one-period real discount rate on stock is assumed to be constant through time. In version 2, the discount rate is assumed to be the one-period ex ante real return on short debt (Treasury bills or commercial paper), plus a constant risk premium. In version 3, the ex ante discount rate is given by the expected growth rate of real aggregate consumption per capita multiplied by the coefficient of relative-risk aversion, plus a constant risk premium.[2] In these three versions of the model, the discount rate on stock varies because the riskless real rate of interest varies, while the risk premium on stock is assumed to be constant. In version 4, by contrast, the ex ante discount rate is the sum of a constant riskless rate and a time-varying risk premium given by the conditional variance of stock returns times the coefficient of relative-risk aversion.

All four versions of the model have implications for returns—version 1, for example, implies that expected real stock returns are constant, while version 2 implies that expected excess returns on stock over short debt

---

[2] For a theoretical justification, see Breeden (1979), Grossman and Shiller (1981), and Hansen and Singleton (1983).

are constant—and these implications have been studied in the literature.[3] The main contribution of this article is to derive the implications of these discount rate models for stock prices, using the dividend-ratio model.

We also use the dividend-ratio model in a slightly different way. The model allows us to study the term structure of expected real stock returns implied by aggregate stock prices. The dividend-price ratio is in effect a long-term expected real return on stock, but it is contaminated in that it is also influenced by expected changes in real dividends. We can use the dividend-ratio model to purge the dividend-price ratio of expected changes in dividends, so that we derive a sort of real consol yield. This is of interest whether or not our measures of one-period discount rates, discussed above, are satisfactory.

The organization of this article is as follows. Section 1 derives the dividend-ratio model as a linear approximation to an exact relationship between stock prices, stock returns, and dividends. Section 2 discusses the stock market data and discount rate data that we use. Section 3 outlines our vector autoregressive method for analyzing movements in the dividend-price ratio, and Section 4 applies it to the data. Section 5 concludes. In the Appendix we study the approximation error in the dividend-ratio model, finding that it appears to be small in practice.

1. The Dividend-Ratio Model

We start by writing the real price of a stock or stock portfolio, measured at the beginning of time period t, as P_t. The real dividend paid on the portfolio during period t will be written D_t. The realized log gross return on the portfolio, held from the beginning of time t to the beginning of time $t + 1$, is written

$$h_t \equiv \log (P_{t+1} + D_t) - \log (P_t) \qquad (1)$$

We would like to obtain a linear relationship between log returns, log dividends, and log prices. The exact relationship in Equation (1) is nonlinear, since it involves the log of the *sum* of the price and the dividend. It turns out, however, that h_t can be well approximated by the variable ξ_t, $h_t \simeq \xi_t$, where ξ_t is defined as follows:

---

[3] Version 1 of the model has been the subject of considerable controversy. A partial list of references is: Campbell and Shiller (1987); Fama and French (1988); Keim and Stambaugh (1986); Kleidon (1986); LeRoy and Porter (1981); Mankiw, Romer, and Shapiro (1985); Marsh and Merton (1986); Poterba and Summers (1988); Shiller (1981); and West (1987, 1988). With regard to version 2, several of the above authors have asked whether the variance of short-term interest rates might help explain the variance of stock market prices. Version 3 of the model has been analyzed extensively, following the original theoretical work of Lucas (1978) and Breeden (1979), by Grossman and Shiller (1981); Grossman, Melino, and Shiller (1987); Hansen and Singleton (1983); Hall (1988); Mankiw, Rotemberg, and Summers (1985); and Mehra and Prescott (1985), among others. Version 4 has been proposed, following an exploratory analysis by Merton (1980), by Pindyck (1984, 1986), who argues that much of the variability in stock prices can be explained by the variability of the volatility of stock returns. Against this, Poterba and Summers (1986) have argued that volatility is not persistent enough to account for much variation in stock prices. French, Schwert, and Stambaugh (1987) and Campbell (1987) also examine the relationship between volatility and expected stock returns.

The Dividend-Price Ratio

$$\xi_t \equiv k + \rho \log(P_{t+1}) + (1 - \rho) \log(D_t) - \log(P_t)$$
$$= k + \rho p_{t+1} + (1 - \rho) d_t - p_t \qquad (2)$$

Here, lowercase letters denote logs of the corresponding uppercase letters. The parameter ρ is close to but a little smaller than 1, and k is a constant term.

Equation (2) differs from Equation (1) in that the log of the sum of the price and the dividend is replaced by a constant k, plus a weighted average of the log price and the log dividend with weights ρ and $(1 - \rho)$. Below, we will justify this approximation rigorously as a first-order Taylor expansion of Equation (1). But first we will explain intuitively why the approximation works.

It is easiest to begin by explaining why the *difference* $\rho \Delta \log(P_{t+1}) + (1 - \rho) \Delta \log(D_t)$ approximates the *difference* $\Delta \log(P_{t+1} + D_t)$. Having done this, we can derive the constant k that makes the approximation hold in levels. By a standard argument, the change in the log of $(P_{t+1} + D_t)$ is approximately equal to the proportional change in the level:

$$\Delta \log(P_{t+1} + D_t) \simeq \frac{P_{t+1} + D_t - P_t - D_{t-1}}{P_t + D_{t-1}}$$

$$= \frac{P_{t+1} - P_t}{P_t + D_{t-1}} + \frac{D_t - D_{t-1}}{P_t + D_{t-1}}$$

If now we suppose that the ratio of the price to the sum of price and dividend is approximately constant through time at the level ρ, whereby $P_t \simeq \rho(P_t + D_{t-1})$ and $D_{t-1} \simeq (1 - \rho)(P_t + D_{t-1})$, then we have the relationship we need:

$$\Delta \log(P_{t+1} + D_t) \simeq \frac{\rho(P_{t+1} - P_t)}{P_t} + \frac{(1 - \rho)(D_t - D_{t-1})}{D_{t-1}}$$

$$\simeq \rho \Delta \log(P_{t+1}) + (1 - \rho) \Delta \log(D_t)$$

This explanation makes it clear that ρ is the average ratio of the stock price to the sum of the stock price and the dividend. In the static Gordon (1962) world—where the log stock return $h_t = h$, a constant, and the dividend growth rate $\Delta d_t = g$, a constant—the ratio $P_t/(P_t + D_{t-1})$ is also constant and equals $\exp(g - h)$.[4] In our empirical work below we will construct ρ by using the formula $\rho = \exp(g - h)$, setting h equal to the sample mean stock return and g equal to the sample mean dividend growth rate.

The above argument shows that the change in $\log(P_{t+1} + D_t)$ is approximated by the change in $\rho \log(P_{t+1}) + (1 - \rho) \log(D_t)$. But we want our approximation to work in levels as well as changes. The constant term k in Equation (2) ensures that our approximation holds exactly for levels in the static world of constant stock returns and dividend growth rates. The

---

[4] To see this, just note that $\exp(g) = D_t/D_{t-1} = P_t/P_{t-1}$ and that $\exp(h) = (P_t + D_{t-1})/P_{t-1}$, so that $\exp(g - h) = P_t/(P_t + D_{t-1})$. We must have $g < h$ if stock prices are to be finite.

value of k can be expressed most simply if we define $\delta_t \equiv d_{t-1} - p_t$, the log dividend-price ratio. In the static world δ_t is a constant: $\delta_t = \delta = \log(1/\rho - 1)$. Then we have

$$k = -\log(\rho) - (1-\rho)\delta \qquad (3)$$

With this definition of k, the approximate return (which is also constant in the static world) is

$$\begin{aligned}\xi &= (1-\rho)(d_t - p_{t+1}) + (p_{t+1} - p_t) + k \\ &= (1-\rho)\delta + g - \log(\rho) - (1-\rho)\delta \\ &= g - \log(\rho) = h\end{aligned}$$

where the last equality follows from the formula for ρ given above. Thus, ξ and h are equal in the static world and Equation (2) holds exactly.

When stock returns and dividend growth rates are not constant, but vary through time, then Equation (2) does not hold exactly. It holds as a first-order Taylor approximation of Equation (1).[5] The higher-order terms in the Taylor expansion of Equation (1), which are neglected in Equation (2), create an approximation error. In the Appendix, however, we present evidence that in practice the error is small and almost constant. (It is worth noting that a constant approximation error would not affect any of our empirical results since we do not test any restrictions on the means of the data.)

So far we have written our equations in terms of the log levels of dividends and prices, d_t and p_t. It will be convenient to rewrite them in terms of the dividend-price ratio $\delta_t \equiv d_{t-1} - p_t$ and the dividend growth rate Δd_t. Rewriting Equation (2) and substituting h_t for ξ_t, we get

$$h_t \simeq k + \delta_t - \rho\delta_{t+1} + \Delta d_t \qquad (2')$$

Equation (2') can be thought of as a difference equation relating δ_t to δ_{t+1}, Δd_t, and h_t. We can solve this equation forward, and if we impose the terminal condition that $\lim_{i\to\infty}\rho^i\delta_{t+i} = 0$, we obtain

$$\delta_t \simeq \sum_{j=0}^{\infty} \rho^j(h_{t+j} - \Delta d_{t+j}) - \frac{k}{1-\rho} \qquad (4)$$

This equation says that the log dividend-price ratio δ_t can be written as a discounted value of all future returns h_{t+j} and dividend growth rates Δd_{t+j}, discounted at the constant rate ρ less a constant $k/(1-\rho)$. It is important to note that all the variables in Equation (4) are measured ex post; (4) has been obtained *only* by the linear approximation of h_t and the imposition of a condition that δ_{t+i} does not explode as i increases. There is no economic content to Equation (4).

We can obtain an economic model of the dividend-price ratio if we are

---

[5] More precisely, if we rewrite the right-hand side of Equation (1) as a nonlinear function of dividend-price ratios and dividend growth rates δ_t, δ_{t+1}, and Δd_t and take a first-order Taylor expansion around the point $\delta_t = \delta_{t+1} = \delta$ and $\Delta d_t = g$, then we obtain Equation (2).

The Dividend-Price Ratio

willing to impose some restriction on the behavior of h_t. In particular, suppose that we have a theory that provides an "ex post discount rate" r_t satisfying

$$E_t h_t = E_t r_t + c \qquad (5)$$

Here E_t denotes a rational expectation formed by using the information set I_t that is available to market participants at the *beginning* of period t, and h_t and r_t are measured at the end of period t. Equation (5) says that there is some variable whose beginning-of-period rational expectation, plus a constant term c, equals the ex ante return on stock over the period. As an example, consider the hypothesis that the expected real return on stock equals the expected real return on commercial paper, plus a constant. Then the ex post real return on commercial paper can be used as the ex post discount rate in Equation (5).

If we can observe the ex post discount rate r_t, then Equations (4) and (5) together yield a testable economic model of the dividend-price ratio.[6] To see this, note that we can take expectations of the left- and right-hand sides of Equation (4), conditional on agents' information I_t at the beginning of period t. The left-hand side of (4) is unchanged because δ_t is known at the beginning of period t (it is in I_t).[7] The right-hand side becomes the discounted value of all expected future h_{t+j} and Δd_{t+j}, conditional on I_t. But Equation (5) implies that $E_t h_{t+j} = E_t r_{t+j} + c$, so we can substitute in expected future discount rates r_{t+j} to obtain

$$\delta_t \simeq E_t \sum_{j=0}^{\infty} \rho^j (r_{t+j} - \Delta d_{t+j}) + \frac{c-k}{1-\rho} \qquad (6)$$

Equation (6) is what we will call the dividend-ratio model, or dynamic Gordon model. It explains the log dividend-price ratio as an expected discounted value of all future one-period "growth-adjusted discount rates," $r_{t+j} - \Delta d_{t+j}$. It represents the combined effect on the log dividend-price ratio of expected future discount rates and dividends that we noted in the opening paragraph of this article.

The original Gordon model, $D_t/P_t = r - g$, can be obtained as a special case of our dividend-ratio model when discount rates and dividend growth rates are constant through time and when the constant term c equals zero. Unlike Gordon, however, we will not use our model to try to explain the mean level of the dividend-price ratio; rather, we will allow a free constant term c (representing a constant risk premium in stock returns), which means that our model restricts only the dynamics of the dividend-price ratio and not its mean level.

The dividend-ratio model has some important advantages when com-

---

[6] In fact, we can also test the model if we observe not r_t but some unknown coefficient times r_t. We show how to do this in Section 3, but at this stage we assume that r_t itself is observable.

[7] This is true because we defined the log dividend-price ratio δ as the difference between last year's log dividend and the log stock price at the beginning of the year.

pared with earlier empirical models. First, it is linear in logs. This makes it easy to combine with log-linear models of dividends and prices. As stressed by Kleidon (1986) and others, log-linear models are appealing on a priori grounds, and they appear to fit the data better than linear ones do.

Second, Δd_{t+j} and r_{t+j} enter symmetrically in Equation (6); all that matters for the dividend-price ratio is their difference, that is, the growth-adjusted discount rate. This offers a significant advantage when we come to do empirical work. The original model [Equations (1) and (5)] concerns *real* prices, *real* dividends, and *real* discount rates. However, price indices used to convert nominal values to real values are measured much more poorly than are nominal dividends, share prices, and interest rates. Neither δ_t nor $\Delta d_{t+j} - r_{t+j}$ depends on the price index used,[8] so if we are willing to treat $\Delta d_{t+j} - r_{t+j}$ as a single variable, we can work in nominal terms throughout and reduce our vulnerability to measurement error. Unfortunately, if we want to study forecasts of Δd_{t+j} and r_{t+j} separately, we must rely on a measured price deflator.

The usefulness of the dividend-ratio model depends on the quality of the approximation used to derive it. This, in turn, will vary from one data set to another. The next section discusses the data sets used in this article, and the Appendix presents some measures of the approximation error in Equations (2) and (4) for these data.

2. Data on Prices, Dividends, and Discount Rates

The two main data sets used in this article are described in Table 1. The first consists of annual observations on prices and dividends for the Standard & Poors Composite Stock Price Index (S&P 500), extended back to 1871 by using the data in Cowles (1939).[9] The corresponding discount rate measures and price deflators are summarized in Table 1.

Our second data set is taken from the Center for Research in Security Prices (CRSP) series of monthly returns on the value-weighted New York Stock Exchange (NYSE) index from 1926 to 1985. Returns are reported both inclusive and exclusive of dividends, and this makes it possible to compute the levels of dividends and prices up to an arbitrary scale factor. The CRSP data incorporate careful corrections for stock splits, noncash distributions, mergers, delisting, and other potential problems [Fisher and

---

[8] Strictly speaking, this result assumes (as implied by the timing convention in our definition of h_t) that dividends are paid at the end of the time period t and that real interest rates r_t are measured from the beginning of t to the end of t.

[9] This data set is also used in Campbell and Shiller (1987) and is very similar to the data used by Shiller (1981); Mankiw, Romer, and Shapiro (1985); West (1988); and other contributors to the "volatility" literature. Kleidon (1986) also studied the Standard & Poors data from 1926, and Wilson and Jones (1987) have analyzed in some detail the properties of the pre-1926 Cowles data.

The Dividend-Price Ratio

Table 1
Description of data sets

Cowles/S&P 500, 1871-1986

Nominal stock price: January S&P Composite Index, spliced to series in Cowles (1939). 1871-1986.
Nominal dividend: Total dividend per share accruing to index. 1871-1985.
  Price deflator, model versions 1, 2, and 4: January Producer Price Index (annual average before 1900). 1871-1986.
  Price deflator, model version 3: Consumption deflator, as used in Grossman and Shiller (1981). 1889-1985.
  Nominal discount rate, model version 2: Annual return on four- to six-month prime commercial paper (six-month starting in 1979), rolled over in January and July. Interest rate data starting in 1938 are from the Board of Governors of the Federal Reserve System, with pre-1938 data from Macaulay (1938). 1871-1985.
  Nominal discount rate, model version 3: Nominal growth in aggregate per capita consumption of nondurables and services, as used in Grossman and Shiller (1981). 1889-1985.
  Real discount rate, model version 4: Squared ex post annual real return on the stock index. 1871-1985.

Value-weighted NYSE index, 1926-1986

Nominal stock price: January 1 value-weighted NYSE index, from CRSP Stock Index File. 1926-1986.
Nominal dividend: Value-weighted NYSE index, total dividends for year, from CRSP Stock Index File. 1926-1985.
  Price deflator: January consumer price index, from Ibbotson Associates (1987). 1926-1986.
  Nominal discount rate, model version 2: Annual return on one-month Treasury bills, rolled over monthly, from Ibbotson Associates (1987). 1926-1985.
  Nominal discount rate, model version 3: Nominal growth in aggregate per capita consumption of nondurables and services, as used in Grossman and Shiller (1981). 1926-1985.
  Real discount rate, model version 4: Squared ex post annual real return on the stock index. 1926-1985.

Lorie (1977)].[10] Corresponding monthly nominal Treasury bill rates and CPI inflation rates are from Ibbotson Associates (1987).

Although the raw CRSP data are available monthly, we follow Marsh and Merton (1987) and aggregate to an annual data interval. The main reason for doing this is that individual firms tend to change dividends no more frequently than once a year, so that aggregate dividends display seasonals within the year.[11]

In Table 2 we present some statistics that summarize the behavior of the nominal stock market variables in our two data sets. The most striking result in the table is the similarity in the period of overlap, 1926-1986. For example, the log dividend-price ratios on Cowles/S&P 500 stocks and the value-weighted NYSE index have a correlation of 0.985 over this period.

---

[10] These data have been used by Marsh and Merton (1987) in their study of aggregate dividend behavior, by Fama and French (1988) and Poterba and Summers (1987) in analyses of mean reversion in stock returns, and by many other writers in finance. CRSP data are also available for the equal-weighted New York Stock Exchange index. We obtained empirical results for this series, but they are qualitatively similar to those for the value-weighted index and to save space we do not report them here. These results are available from the authors on request.

[11] In aggregating the data to an annual interval, we assumed that dividends paid each month are accumulated through the year without receiving interest. The annual dividend is then the sum of monthly dividend payments, while the annual price is formed as the previous year's price times the one-year return excluding dividends, compounded monthly.

203

Table 2
Summary statistics for stock market data

	Data set and sample period			Correlation of Cowles/S&P and NYSE, 1926–1986
Statistic	Cowles/S&P, 1871–1986	Cowles/S&P, 1926–1986	NYSE, 1926–1986	
Δp_t:				
Mean	0.032	0.044	0.042	
Standard deviation	0.178	0.200	0.208	0.972
Δd_t:				
Mean	0.030	0.041	0.040	
Standard deviation	0.132	0.131	0.134	0.958
δ_t:				
Mean	−3.053	−3.121	−3.143	
Standard deviation	0.277	0.294	0.290	0.985

All variables in this table are nominal and measured annually. p_t is the log stock price, d_t is the log dividend, and δ_t is the log dividend-price ratio $d_{t-1} - p_t$.

It would seem that these indices reflect the same broad movements in prices and dividends.

In Table 3 we complete our review of the data by testing for unit roots in the various nominal and real series. This is important for two related reasons. First, the standard theory of inference in regressions with stochastic regressors requires that all variables be stationary. If we regress stock returns on variables with unit roots, the conventional standard errors may be seriously misleading. Second, when we use Equation (6) to characterize the behavior of the dividend-price ratio that is implied by a model of stock-price behavior, the results are likely to be sensitive to the stationarity assumption we make.

The test statistic used in Table 3 is one of a class recently proposed by Phillips (1987) and Phillips and Perron (1988). It is a modification of the F-statistic in the Dickey-Fuller (1981) regression of the change in a variable on a constant, a time trend, and the lagged level of the variable. Under the null hypothesis that the variable has a unit root, this regression has no explanatory power asymptotically since the change in the variable is stationary while the trend and level are not. However, the F-statistic has a nonstandard distribution, which is calculated numerically by Dickey and Fuller for the case where the change in the variable is white noise. Phillips and Perron's modification to the F-statistic enables one to apply the same distribution even when the change in the variable is serially correlated.

The main results in Table 3 are as follows. The null hypothesis of a unit root is generally not rejected for levels of prices and dividends, whether these are measured in nominal terms or real terms. The exception is that the null of a unit root can be rejected for the real dividend on Cowles/

The Dividend-Price Ratio

Table 3
Univariate tests for unit roots

	Data set and sample period	
Variable	Cowles/S&P, 1871–1986	NYSE, 1926–1986
Nominal		
p_t	2.890	3.622
d_t	3.194	4.972
Δp_t	49.578***	22.969***
Δd_t	33.012***	14.342***
r_t	3.916	4.173
$\Delta d_t - r_t$	30.794***	13.410***
δ_t	10.711***	6.250**
π_t	28.442***	7.359**
Real		
p_t	4.124	2.670
d_t	7.089**	3.532
Δp_t	47.831***	25.436***
Δd_t	33.438***	17.422***
r_t	26.113***	5.346*

Variables are defined as follows: p_t is the log stock price, d_t is the log dividend, δ_t is the log dividend-price ratio $d_{t-1} - p_t$, π_t is the measured inflation rate, and r_t is the commercial-paper rate (1871–1986) or Treasury-bill rate (1926–1986).
This table presents tests of the null hypothesis that a series has a unit root. The test statistic is $Z\Phi_3$ from Phillips and Perron (1988) and as used in Perron (1988). The statistic is formed from the F-statistic in the regression $\Delta y_t = \mu + \beta t + \alpha y_{t-1}$, corrected for serial correlation in the equation error by using a fourth-order Newey-West (1987) correction. The critical values for the statistic are as reported in Fuller (1976): 1% 8.27 (*** in the table), 2.5% 7.16, 5% 6.25 (** in the table), and 10% 5.34 (* in the table).

S&P 500 stocks at the 5 percent level. This presumably reflects some negative autocorrelations in the growth rate of this series.[12] The unit root null is strongly rejected for growth rates of stock market variables and for the log dividend-price ratio.

The unit root tests in Table 3 are univariate and do not take account of the "adding up" constraint that the sum of stationary processes must be stationary. Accordingly, there are some internally inconsistent results in the table. For example, in the Cowles/S&P data it cannot be true that the log dividend-price ratio and the log real dividend are stationary while the log real price has a unit root. It is also inconsistent that inflation and real interest rates, and nominal dividend growth corrected or uncorrected for nominal interest rates, seem to be stationary in all data sets, but the unit root null is not rejected for nominal interest rates.

We proceed under the assumption that the log dividend-price ratio and growth rates of real dividends and prices are stationary, so that log divi-

---

[12] It is possible that the series is genuinely stationary around a trend, but it is also possible that our tests are falsely rejecting the null hypothesis because the series has negative autocorrelations in growth rates arising from an autoregressive-moving-average (ARMA) representation in growth rates with a large (but not unit) moving-average root. Such series tend to revert, not to a trend, but to a long moving average of their past history. Schwert (1988) presents Monte Carlo results in which false rejection of a unit root null occurs for this reason.

dends and prices are cointegrated processes.[13] Econometric techniques have been developed for processes of this sort by Engle and Granger (1987), Phillips and Durlauf (1986), and Stock (1987). Our model is particularly straightforward to deal with since the cointegrating vector is specified in the model and does not require estimation. Ordinary theory of estimation of stationary vector autoregressions is applicable here.

3. Vector Autoregressions and the Dividend-Ratio Model

In this section we propose a method for analyzing the historical movements of stock prices in relation to dividends and alternative measures of discount rates. The method is an extension of that developed in Campbell and Shiller (1987).

Our approach uses the dividend-ratio model derived in Section 1. As we showed there, a linear approximation to the log stock return implies that the log dividend-price ratio can be written as a discounted value of expected future dividend growth rates and discount rates. We would like to test the adequacy of some popular measures of the ex post discount rate on stock. We can do this by comparing the log dividend-price ratio with the forecast of dividend growth and discount rates obtained from an unrestricted econometric model: in practice, we will use a log-linear vector autoregression, or VAR. We can make the comparison in a formal statistical way, or informally by looking at the historical movements of these two variables.

Our approach is different from the regression methods commonly used to test a model of expected stock returns. The standard way to proceed would be to regress the one-period ex post stock return less the ex post discount rate, $h_t - r_t$, on a constant term and on some variables known at the start of period t. If the coefficients on these variables are jointly significant, then the model is rejected statistically.

Our approach has two potential advantages over the standard approach. First, it may have more power to detect long-lived deviations of stock prices from the "fundamental value" implied by the model. As Shiller (1984) and Summers (1986) have argued, single-period returns regressions have extremely low power against this alternative. Second, even if the regression approach does reject the model, the rejection can be hard to interpret. The regression results do not tell us whether the behavior of the dividend-price ratio is quite different from that implied by the model or whether it is rather similar. We do not know whether we reject the model because it is entirely wrong or because the dividend-price ratio is affected by some economically minor, but statistically detectable, factor. Our approach explicitly compares movements in the dividend-price ratio with the movements that are implied by the model.

---

[13] We note that this is a conservative assumption in the sense that it leads to greater variability in the rational forecast of expected future dividends, and less evidence of excess volatility in stock prices, than does the assumption that dividends and prices are stationary around a deterministic trend.

The Dividend-Price Ratio

It might seem that our approach does not take proper account of extra information that market participants may have. If the market knows a great deal about the future paths of dividends and discount rates, then how can our unrestricted econometric model reproduce the market's forecast?

The answer is that we include the log dividend-price ratio itself as one variable in the vector autoregression. This enables the VAR to generate a forecast of dividends and discount rates that exactly equals the log dividend-price ratio. Intuitively, even though we do not observe everything that market participants do, we do observe the log dividend-price ratio, and that variable summarizes the market's relevant information.

Another way to make the same point is that those restrictions on the VAR which ensure that the unrestricted forecast equals the dividend-price ratio are algebraically equivalent to those which ensure that the one-period stock return cannot be predicted by the lagged variables included in the VAR. Adding extra variables cannot make stock returns unpredictable if they were found to be predictable using fewer variables; similarly, adding extra variables cannot make the log dividend-price ratio equal the unrestricted forecast of dividends and discount rates if these series differ when fewer variables are used.

In order to explain our approach precisely, we will now introduce some more notation. To keep the exposition as simple as possible, we will redefine all variables as deviations from means; this enables us to drop constant terms, which, as explained in Section 1, are not the focus of our inquiry and are not restricted by our model.

We assume that at the start of period t, market participants observe a vector of state variables y_t; their information set I_t is just the history $\{y_t, y_{t-1}, \ldots\}$. We assume that y_t follows a linear stochastic process with constant coefficients that are known to market participants. It follows from this assumption that any subset of the variables in y_t (where linear combinations of variables can be included) also follows a linear stochastic process with constant coefficients.

We now define a vector x_t that includes the variables in y_t that we econometricians observe. Our information set H_t is the history $\{x_t, x_{t-1}, \ldots\}$. A parsimonious choice for x_t is the vector $[\delta_t, r_{t-1} - \Delta d_{t-1}]'$, where we remove the means from the data since these are unrestricted, and we lag the growth-adjusted discount rate by one period to ensure that it is known to the market by the start of period t. This vector x_t is the smallest that allows us to test the restrictions of the dividend-ratio model. We could of course choose a larger vector [see, for example, Campbell and Shiller (1988a)], but as noted above this could only strengthen a rejection of the model.

We assume that the linear process for x_t can be written as a vector autoregression (VAR) with p lags: $x_t = C_1 x_{t-1} + C_2 x_{t-2} + \cdots + C_p x_{t-p} + u_t$, where C_i for $i = 1 \cdots p$ are each 2×2 matrices. Since p can be large, this assumption involves little further loss of generality. We will write the (j, k) element of C_i as C_{ijk}; thus, C_{ijk} is the coefficient of the jth variable in x_t on the kth variable lagged i times.

It will be convenient for us to rewrite the VAR in first-order, or companion, form along lines first suggested for rational expectations models by Sargent (1979). Doing this enables us to convert a pth-order autoregression into a first-order autoregression, for which the formula for conditional expectations has a simple form. This is done by defining a new vector z_t, which includes $2p$ rather than 2 elements: δ_t and $(p-1)$ lags, and $r_{t-1} - \Delta d_{t-1}$ and $(p-1)$ lags. For example, if $p = 2$, then we can write $z_t = [\delta_t, \delta_{t-1}, r_{t-1} - \Delta d_{t-1}, r_{t-2} - \Delta d_{t-2}]'$, $v_t = [u_{1t}, 0, u_{2t}, 0]'$. The vector z_t then follows a first-order VAR, where the rows corresponding to δ_t and Δd_{t-1} are stochastic and the others are deterministic:

$$\begin{bmatrix} \delta_t \\ \delta_{t-1} \\ r_{t-1} - \Delta d_{t-1} \\ r_{t-2} - \Delta d_{t-2} \end{bmatrix} = \begin{bmatrix} C_{111} & C_{211} & C_{112} & C_{212} \\ 1 & 0 & 0 & 0 \\ C_{121} & C_{221} & C_{122} & C_{222} \\ 0 & 0 & 1 & 0 \end{bmatrix} \begin{bmatrix} \delta_{t-1} \\ \delta_{t-2} \\ r_{t-2} - \Delta d_{t-2} \\ r_{t-3} - \Delta d_{t-3} \end{bmatrix} + \begin{bmatrix} u_{1t} \\ 0 \\ u_{2t} \\ 0 \end{bmatrix}$$

The VAR system can be written more parsimoniously as

$$z_t = A z_{t-1} + v_t \tag{7}$$

The vector z_t has the useful property that to forecast it ahead k periods, given our information set H_t, we simply multiply z_t by the kth power of the matrix A: $E[z_{t+k} \mid H_t] = A^k z_t$.

As a final investment in notation, we define a vector $e1$ such that $e1'z_t \equiv \delta_t$, and a vector $e2$ such that $e2'z_t \equiv r_{t-1} - \Delta d_{t-1}$. That is, $e1$ and $e2$ "pick out" the elements δ_t and $r_{t-1} - \Delta d_{t-1}$ from the vector z_t. In the example above, $e1 = [1\ 0\ 0\ 0]'$ and $e2 = [0\ 0\ 1\ 0]'$.

We are now in a position to state the restrictions of the dividend-ratio model (6) on the vector autoregression (7). We note first that a very weak implication of the dividend-ratio model is that the log dividend-price ratio δ_t should Granger-cause $r_t - \Delta d_t$. The reason is that δ_t embodies the market's information about the full vector of state variables y_t. Unless y_t contains only $r_{t-1} - \Delta d_{t-1}$ and its lags, so that market forecasts are based only on the history of this variable, δ_t will have incremental explanatory power for $r_t - \Delta d_t$. And we can rule out the case in which y_t contains only $r_{t-1} - \Delta d_{t-1}$ and lags by noting that it implies, counterfactually, that δ_t should be an exact linear function of current and lagged $r_{t-1} - \Delta d_{t-1}$. This point is discussed at greater length in Campbell and Shiller (1987).

Of course, the dividend-ratio model also imposes a tight set of cross-equation restrictions on the VAR. To derive these, we take expectations of Equation (6), conditional on the VAR information set H_t. The left-hand side is unchanged since δ_t is in H_t. The right-hand side becomes an expected discounted value conditional on H_t [since H_t is a subset of the market's information set I_t that defines the expectations in Equation (6)]. Thus, we have

$$\delta_t \simeq E\left[\sum_{j=0}^{\infty} \rho^j (r_{t+j} - \Delta d_{t+j}) \mid H_t\right] \equiv \delta'_t \tag{8}$$

The Dividend-Price Ratio

where we have dropped constant terms, as discussed above. Equation (8) says that δ_t should equal the unrestricted VAR forecast of the discounted value of $r_{t+j} - \Delta d_{t+j}$, which we call δ'_t. We can rewrite this equation, using the multiperiod VAR forecasting formula given above, as

$$\delta_t = e1'z_t = \sum_{j=0}^{\infty} \rho^j e2' A^{j+1} z_t \equiv \delta'_t \qquad (9)$$

Since Equation (9) is to hold for all realizations of z_t, we must have

$$e1' = \sum_{j=0}^{\infty} \rho^j e2' A^{j+1} = e2'A(I - \rho A)^{-1} \qquad (10)$$

where the second equality follows by evaluating the infinite sum, noting that it must converge because the elements of z_t are stationary.

Equation (10) defines a set of $2p$ nonlinear restrictions on the VAR coefficients. These can be tested by using a nonlinear Wald test. If we write the estimated vector of VAR coefficients as γ, the estimated variance-covariance matrix of these coefficients as Θ, and the vector of deviations of the estimated system from the model as λ, then the Wald test statistic is $\lambda'(\partial \lambda/\partial \gamma' \Theta \partial \lambda/\partial \gamma)^{-1}\lambda$. Under the null hypothesis, it is distributed χ^2, with degrees of freedom equal to the number of restrictions (the number of elements of λ). In the case of Equation (10), $\lambda = e1' - e2'A(I - \rho A)^{-1}$ and has $2p$ elements. The derivatives of λ with respect to the VAR parameters can be calculated numerically.[14]

The more usual regression approach to the model can also be expressed as a Wald test of restrictions on the VAR. If we postmultiply the restrictions in Equation (10) by $(I - \rho A)$, we get $2p$ linear restrictions, one for each column of the matrix A:

$$e1'(I - \rho A) - e2'A = 0 \qquad (11)$$

One can show that Equation (11) states the restrictions of the model in returns form: $E(\xi_t - r_t \mid H_t) = 0$, where ξ_t is as defined in Equation (2).[15] A Wald test of Equation (11) on the VAR, using the formula above with $\lambda = e1'(I - \rho A) - e2'A$, is numerically equivalent to a test that there are $2p$ zero coefficients when $\xi_t - r_t$ is regressed on the variables in z_t.

It is important to note, however, that a Wald test of the restrictions (10) is not equivalent to a test of (11), even though (10) and (11) are algebraically equivalent. Formally, the reasons are that (10) and (11) are related

---

[14] A similar approach can be used to calculate standard errors for diagnostic statistics, such as the correlation between δ'_t and δ_t. This correlation is a function of the VAR coefficients γ (and also of the variance-covariance matrix of the VAR explanatory variables, but we treat this as fixed). For any such function $f(\gamma)$, we can obtain a standard error as $\sqrt{\partial f/\partial \gamma' \Theta \partial f/\partial \gamma}$, where the derivatives are calculated numerically.

[15] The constant term c does not appear here because in this section we have defined all variables as deviations from their means. Means are not restricted by our model. To see how Equation (11) is equivalent to the restriction on returns, rewrite it as $e1'z_t - e1'\rho(Az_t) - e2'(Az_t) = 0$. Note that $Az_t = E_t z_{t+1}$. Then $e1'z_t = \delta_t$, $e1'\rho(Az_t) = \rho E_t \delta_{t+1}$, and $e2'(Az_t) = E_t(r_t - \Delta d_t)$. Combining these elements and using the definition of ξ_t in Equation (2) gives us the restriction on returns.

by a nonlinear transformation and that Wald tests are not invariant to such transformations. As we have already argued, it may be easier to detect departures from the null by looking at the behavior of the dividend-price ratio than by looking at one-period stock returns. In our empirical work we will present tests of both the dividend-price ratio restriction (10) and the one-period stock return restriction (11).

The approach outlined above is appealingly simple, since it involves a VAR with only two variables. It enables us to test a model of expected stock returns by using Equation (10) or (11) and to compute the implications of predictable excess returns for the log dividend-price ratio by using Equation (9).

Unfortunately, the two-variable approach does not allow us to judge the relative importance for the log dividend-price ratio of expectations of future dividends and discount factors, since it treats the discount rate adjusted for dividend growth as a single variable. To address this question, we need to expand the vector of variables we observe, x_t, to include Δd_{t-1} and r_{t-1} separately. Redefining z_t and A in the obvious manner, and defining $e1$, $e2$, and $e3$ to pick out δ_t, Δd_{t-1}, and r_{t-1}, respectively, we now have the following equation instead of (9):

$$e1'z_t = \sum_{j=0}^{\infty} \rho^j (e3' - e2') A^{j+1} z_t \qquad (12)$$

or $\delta_t = \delta'_t \equiv \delta'_{rt} + \delta'_{dt}$. δ'_t is now defined to equal the right-hand side of Equation (12), while δ'_{rt} is the component of δ'_t that forecasts future discount rates and δ'_{dt} is the component that forecasts (the negative of) dividend growth rates: $\delta'_{rt} \equiv e3'A(I - \rho A)^{-1} z_t$, and $\delta'_{dt} \equiv -e2'A(I - \rho A)^{-1} z_t$.

We can use the three-variable system to see whether expectations of dividend growth, measured by δ'_{dt}, or of discount rates, measured by δ'_{rt}, have historically been more important in determining the dividend-price ratio. As discussed in the introduction, we can also construct an implicit long-term expected real return on stock by purging the log dividend-price ratio of the influence of expected future dividends. From Equation (4), if we remove the present value of expected future dividend growth, δ'_{dt}, from δ_t, what we are left with is a present value of expected future stock returns, $E_t \sum_{j=0}^{\infty} \rho^j h_{t+j}$. The sum of the weights in this expression is $1/(1 - \rho)$, so if we multiply by $(1 - \rho)$ we get a weighted average of expected future stock returns. This has the same form as Shiller's (1979) expression for a consol yield as a weighted average of expected future short-term interest rates. Accordingly, we will call $(1 - \rho)(\delta_t - \delta'_{dt})$ a long-term expected real stock return.[16]

The restrictions (12) can again be rewritten in returns form to get

---

[16] The discussion here omits constant terms. The long-term expected real stock return can be adjusted to have the correct mean by adding the unconditional mean log stock return.

The Dividend-Price Ratio

$e1'(I - \rho A) - (e3' - e2')A = 0$, which corresponds to $E(\xi_t \cdot r_t \mid H_t) = 0$, as before.

Our discussion so far has assumed that we observe the ex post discount rate r_t itself. But in version 3 of the model we observe instead real consumption growth Δc_t, which is related to r_t by $r_t = \alpha \Delta c_t$, where α is the coefficient of relative-risk aversion.[17] Similarly, in version 4 we observe V_t, the squared ex post stock return, and our model is that $r_t = \alpha V_t$. Since α is not known, but must be estimated from the data, our methods require some modification in this case.

Taking version 3 as an example, we define $x_t = [\delta_t, \Delta d_{t-1}, \Delta c_{t-1}]'$. We redefine z_t, A, $e1$, $e2$, and $e3$ appropriately ($e3$ picks out Δc_{t-1} from z_t). Then the model implies

$$\delta_t = \delta'_t \equiv \delta'_{rt} + \delta'_{dt} \equiv \alpha e3'A(I - \rho A)^{-1}z_t - e2'A(I - \rho A)^{-1}z_t \quad (13)$$

and

$$e1'(I - \rho A) - (\alpha e3' - e2')A = 0 \quad (14)$$

We can estimate α, the coefficient of relative-risk aversion, by using the restrictions (14). One might at first think that a unique value for α could be found by postmultiplying (14) by $A^{-1}e3$ and solving the resulting expression for α in terms of estimated coefficients. However, the restrictions (14) imply that α is overidentified. When $p > 1$, the matrix A is singular because of its special structure. Defining $e4$ as the vector that is 0 except for the second element, which is 1, then $(\rho e1' + \alpha e3' - e2' - e4')A = 0$.

Our approach was, instead, to use a method-of-moments estimator for α [Hansen (1982)]. Recall that we write γ as the vector of VAR coefficients, Θ as its variance-covariance matrix, and λ as the vector of deviations of the estimated VAR from the model. In this case, $\lambda = \lambda(\alpha, \gamma) = e1 - (\rho A)'e1 - A'(\alpha e3 - e2)$. We choose α to minimize the Wald test statistic for the model $\lambda(\alpha, \gamma)'(\partial \lambda / \partial \gamma' \Theta \partial \lambda / \partial \gamma)^{-1}\lambda(\alpha, \gamma)$. We do this in two steps, first evaluating the derivatives $\partial \lambda / \partial \gamma$ at $\alpha = 1$, and then evaluating them at the first round estimate of α. The minimized Wald statistic is distributed χ^2 under the null, with $3p - 1$ degrees of freedom.

The resulting estimate of α has the following interpretation. Equation (14) asserts that the prediction at time t of the linearized return ξ_t equals (a constant plus) α times the predicted change in log consumption. Our estimate of α is thus analogous to other estimates in the literature that rely on making forecast returns correspond to forecast changes in consumption. In Grossman and Shiller (1981), estimation of α along these lines was suggested (in the context of a plot of stock prices and their ex post rational

---

[17] Once again we have dropped constant terms. The implicit assumption here is that the consumption data for each year represent consumption on December 31 of the year. Thus, in January of each year (the month in which our stock-price data are drawn), Δc_{t-1} is known but Δc_t is not. There is no fully satisfactory way to handle the unit-averaged consumption data in the context of a theoretical model involving point-of-time consumption data without going to the continuous-time econometrics format, as in Grossman, Melino, and Shiller (1987). We did experiment with the model $r_t = \alpha \Delta c_{t+1}$, with results that are discussed below.

counterpart), but the discussion was couched in levels; the simple method used here of dealing with nonstationarity (dividing by lagged dividend) was not used, and formal estimation in such terms was not attempted.

4. Empirical Results

In this section we apply the methods worked out in the previous section to our two stock market data sets. We begin by analyzing versions 1 and 2 of the model—in which expected real stock returns and expected excess returns on stock over short debt, respectively, are constant through time—since in these versions no unknown parameter needs to be estimated from the VAR system.

We study version 1 of the model by using a two-variable system that includes the log dividend-price ratio and the real dividend growth rate. (In this version the dividend growth rate is the only component of the growth-adjusted discount rate that varies through time, so it is the only component that needs to be included in the VAR.) We study version 2 by using a similar two-variable system that includes the log dividend-price ratio and the return on short debt less the dividend growth rate. We then move to a three-variable system in which real dividend growth and the real return on short debt are included separately.

For each data set, the parameter ρ, which is taken as known in our analysis, was formed as the exponential of the difference between the sample average change in log dividends and the log of the sample average real return on stocks. The parameter ρ therefore differs slightly across data sets; it is 0.937 for the Cowles/S&P data and 0.933 for the NYSE data. In order to check for robustness, we also estimated models with ρ fixed at 0.90, 0.95, and 0.975. The results were very similar to those reported.[18]

Table 4 displays detailed results for version 1 of the model, based on a VAR system with a single lag ($p = 1$). While this lag length may be too short (we try longer lags below), it has the advantage that we can give full details of the results in a single table. We report results for the Cowles/S&P and New York Stock Exchange data in separate panels.

At the top of each panel of Table 4, we report regressions of the exact log stock return h_t and the approximate log stock return ξ_t on two variables known at the start of period t: the dividend-price ratio δ_t and the lagged dividend growth rate Δd_{t-1}. These are the variables that enter the first-order VAR system. If version 1 of our model is correct, so that expected real stock returns are constant through time, then the regression coefficients of returns on these variables should equal zero. We can test the

---

[18] One might think that changing the discount factor ρ would dramatically affect the standard deviation of the series δ'_t. The discount rate did indeed have an important effect in our earlier paper [Campbell and Shiller (1987)]. But recall that here δ_t and δ'_t are defined in log terms, so their movements represent percentage changes in the dividend-price ratio. As the discount rate changes, it affects both the absolute variability of the dividend-price ratio and its absolute mean level. The net effect on the percentage variability of the dividend-price ratio is small.

212

The Dividend-Price Ratio

Table 4
Testing constant expected real returns

Dependent variable	Explanatory variable δ_t	Δd_{t-1}	R^2	Joint significance of coefficients

Cowles/S&P, 1871–1986
Regressions of returns on information:

h_t	0.129 (0.057)	−0.013 (0.121)	0.043	0.078
ξ_t	0.141 (0.057)	−0.012 (0.120)	0.053	0.045

VAR estimation:

δ_{t+1}	⎡ 0.706 (0.066)	0.259 (0.139) ⎤	0.515	0.000
Δd_t	⎣ −0.197 (0.039)	0.231 (0.083) ⎦	0.227	0.000

Implications of VAR estimates:
$\delta'_t = 0.636 \delta_t - 0.097 \Delta d_{t-1}$
   (0.123)   (0.106)

$\sigma(\delta'_t)/\sigma(\delta_t) = 0.637$ corr $(\delta'_t, \delta_t) = 0.997$
           (0.124)   (0.006)
Significance level for Wald test that $\delta'_t = \delta_t$: 0.005

Dependent variable	Explanatory variable δ_t	Δd_{t-1}	R^2	Joint significance of coefficients

Value-weighted NYSE, 1926–1986
Regressions of returns on information:

h_t	0.154 (0.087)	−0.385 (0.213)	0.108	0.031
ξ_t	0.170 (0.086)	−0.374 (0.209)	0.120	0.021

VAR estimation:

δ_{t+1}	⎡ 0.689 (0.094)	0.570 (0.229) ⎤	0.500	0.000
Δd_t	⎣ −0.187 (0.047)	0.157 (0.115) ⎦	0.246	0.000

Implications of VAR estimates:
$\delta'_t = 0.471 \delta_t + 0.109 \Delta d_{t-1}$
   (0.114)   (0.131)

$\sigma(\delta'_t)/\sigma(\delta_t) = 0.470$ corr $(\delta'_t, \delta_t) = 0.995$
           (0.114)   (0.011)
Significance level for Wald test that $\delta'_t = \delta_t$: 0.000

Variables are defined as follows: p_t is the log stock price, d_t is the log dividend, δ_t is the log dividend-price ratio $d_{t-1} - p_t$, h_t is the log one-period stock return, and ξ_t is the approximation of h_t defined in Equation (2). The variable δ'_t is the unrestricted forecast of the present value of future growth-adjusted discount rates from a VAR (equivalent to the negative of the present value of future dividend growth rates in this version of the model), defined in Equations (8) and (9). The VAR includes the log dividend-price ratio and the dividend growth rate.

Standard errors are reported in parentheses under each coefficient. The matrix of VAR coefficients is the matrix A defined in Equation (7), except for a sign switch in the off-diagonal elements due to the fact that results are reported for dividend growth rather than for the negative of dividend growth. The constant-expected-return model is tested in two different ways: by regressing the exact and approximate log stock returns h_t and ξ_t on the lagged variables that appear in the VAR and testing the joint significance of the coefficients, and by a VAR Wald test of the hypothesis that $\delta'_t = \delta_t$ [Equation (10)]. The approximate stock-return regression test is equivalent to a VAR Wald test of Equation (11).

model by testing the joint significance of these coefficients.[19] We use both exact and approximate returns as a way to evaluate the accuracy of our approximation. If the approximation error is constant, then the regression test of the model will give the same result whether exact or approximate returns are used.

The returns regressions show that stock returns are somewhat predictable. The lagged log dividend-price ratio has a positive effect on stock returns, while the lagged real dividend growth rate has a negative effect. This pattern holds across both data sets, although in the Cowles/S&P data the log dividend-price ratio is more highly significant, while in the NYSE data both variables are about equally significant. The two variables are jointly significant at about the 5 percent level in each data set, which rejects the constancy of expected real stock returns at this level. The results are similar whether exact or approximate returns are used, although the rejections are slightly stronger with approximate returns.

The ability of the dividend-price ratio to predict returns has been noted before [for example, by Shiller (1984) and by Flood, Hodrick, and Kaplan (1986)]. The special feature of our approach is that we can use the dividend-ratio model to compute the implications of this predictability for the behavior of the dividend-price ratio. To do this, we start from the VAR estimates, which are reported in Table 4 below the returns regressions. The coefficients reported are the elements of the matrix A (except that the off-diagonal elements have a sign switch because results are reported for dividend growth rather than for the negative of dividend growth). We use these coefficients, and Equation (9), to compute the variable δ'_t, a linear combination of the explanatory variables in the VAR.

If the constant-expected-return model were true, the variable δ'_t would place a unit weight on δ_t and a zero weight on Δd_{t-1}. In fact, we can reject at the 0.5 percent level the hypothesis that δ'_t equals δ_t.[20] In both data sets the weight of δ'_t on Δd_{t-1} is close to zero, as it should be under the null, but the weight on δ_t is considerably less than unity. In the Cowles/S&P data, for example, it is 0.636 with an asymptotic standard error of 0.13. This means that δ'_t, the unrestricted forecast of the present value of future real dividend growth, has a standard deviation about two-thirds that of the log dividend-price ratio δ_t; in other words, the log dividend-price ratio moves about 50 percent too much.

One way to understand this result is to consider what it means for the dividend-price ratio to have a positive effect on subsequent stock returns. The dividend-price ratio is high when prices are low, and the effect on returns implies that prices tend to rise subsequently. To eliminate the

---

[19] As we noted in the previous section, the regression test that uses the approximate stock return is numerically equivalent to a VAR Wald test of Equation (11). The reported standard errors and test statistics are not corrected for heteroskedasticity. We also computed standard errors using White's (1984) heteroskedasticity correction and found them to be similar or slightly smaller.

[20] We test this hypothesis by using a nonlinear Wald test of the restrictions given in Equation (10).

The Dividend-Price Ratio

Table 5
Testing constant expected real and excess returns

| | Model version 1 (constant expected real returns) ||| Model version 2 (constant expected excess returns) |||
| | Lag length ||| Lag length |||
	1	3	5	1	3	5
Cowles/S&P, 1871-1986						
h_t regression test	0.078	0.056	0.083	0.100	0.007	0.014
ξ_t regression test	0.045	0.035	0.055	0.073	0.005	0.009
Test that $\delta'_t = \delta_t$	0.005	0.000	0.000	0.009	0.000	0.000
$\sigma(\delta'_t)/\sigma(\delta_t)$	0.637	0.370	0.382	0.674	0.434	0.402
	(0.124)	(0.129)	(0.073)	(0.111)	(0.143)	(0.060)
corr (δ'_t, δ_t)	0.997	0.837	0.326	0.999	0.856	0.431
	(0.006)	(0.246)	(0.565)	(0.004)	(0.200)	(0.583)
Value-weighted NYSE, 1926-1986						
h_t regression test	0.031	0.063	0.042	0.111	0.097	0.042
ξ_t regression test	0.021	0.043	0.024	0.081	0.069	0.023
Test that $\delta'_t = \delta_t$	0.000	0.000	0.000	0.005	0.001	0.000
$\sigma(\delta'_t)/\sigma(\delta_t)$	0.470	0.290	0.365	0.544	0.360	0.528
	(0.114)	(0.079)	(0.130)	(0.140)	(0.115)	(0.284)
corr (δ'_t, δ_t)	0.995	0.616	−0.089	1.000	0.119	−0.353
	(0.011)	(0.432)	(0.505)	(0.002)	(0.767)	(0.392)

Variables are defined as follows: δ_t is the log dividend-price ratio, h_t is the log one-period stock return, and ξ_t is the approximation to h_t defined in Equation (2). The variable δ'_t is the unrestricted forecast of the present value of future growth-adjusted discount rates from a VAR, defined in Equations (8) and (9). The VAR includes the log dividend-price ratio and the dividend growth rate (for model version 1) or the short-term real interest rate less the dividend growth rate (for model version 2).

The constant-expected-return model is tested in two different ways: by regressing the exact and approximate log stock returns h_t and ξ_t (or excess returns $h_t - r_t$ and $\xi_t - r_t$ in model version 2) on the lagged variables that appear in the VAR and testing the joint significance of the coefficients, and by a VAR Wald test of the hypothesis that $\delta'_t = \delta_t$ [Equation (10)]. The approximate stock-return regression test is equivalent to a VAR Wald test of Equation (11).

predictability of returns, the stock price would have to be less variable around the dividend.

It is striking that the model is rejected at about the 5 percent level when using a one-period-return regression test [equivalently, a Wald test of Equation (11) on the VAR], but is rejected at the 0.5 percent level when using a test of the hypothesis that $\delta'_t = \delta_t$ [a nonlinear Wald test of Equation (10) on the VAR]. Campbell and Shiller (1988a) relate this fact to the observation made by Fama and French (1988) and others that returns are more predictable over many periods than over a single period.

The results in Table 4 are conditional on the one-lag specification of the system (although, of course, adding lags in a fixed sample can never reduce the R^2 of the equation explaining stock returns). In the left-hand part of Table 5 (the "Model version 1" columns) we summarize the results for VAR lag lengths 1, 3, and 5. (In the pth-order VAR, the independent variables are $\delta_t, \ldots, \delta_{t-p+1}$ and $\Delta d_{t-1}, \ldots, \Delta d_{t-p}$.) In both data sets the second lag variables raise the R^2 for the dividend growth equation (not reported in the table) by at least 10 percentage points. Little further improvement occurs thereafter. The significance level at which we reject the constant-expected-real-return model fluctuates between 2 and 10 percent when we use a one-period-return regression test, and it is always 0.5 percent or better when we test that $\delta'_t = \delta_t$. The result that the dividend-price ratio moves too much seems very robust; indeed, as the lag length increases, the ratio $\sigma(\delta'_t)/\sigma(\delta_t)$ tends to fall. It is estimated quite precisely, even in the high-order VAR systems.

The main effect of increasing lag length is that the estimated correlation of δ_t and δ'_t falls. It seems likely that the extremely high correlation in the first-order model is an artifact of the information set, which contains only δ_t and Δd_{t-1}. The variable Δd_{t-1} is not highly persistent or smooth, so δ'_t does not place a large weight on it and instead moves closely with δ_t. It is also possible that the higher-order models are picking up the tendency of real dividends to revert to a long average of past dividends; when we compute the correlation of δ'_t with a detrended real dividend, it rises with lag length. However, the correlation coefficients are very imprecisely estimated, so strong conclusions are unwarranted.

The estimates in Tables 4 and 5 are derived from vector autoregressions over the whole sample period for each data set. We also estimated VAR systems with one and two lags over subsamples 1871–1925, 1926–1955, and 1956–1986. The constant-real-returns model is rejected more strongly in the later subsamples. Thus, in the Cowles/S&P data, the approximate return regression test (with lag length 2) rejects at the 41 percent level in 1871–1925, the 28 percent level in 1926–1955, and the 7.1 percent level in 1956–86. The test that $\delta'_t = \delta_t$ rejects at the 29 percent level in 1871–1925, the 5.1 percent level in 1926–1955, and the 0.1 percent level in 1956–1986. In every case the ratio $\sigma(\delta'_t)/\sigma(\delta_t)$ is estimated to be less than 1.

In the right-hand part of Table 5 we move on to consider version 2 of the model, in which expected excess returns on stock over commercial paper or Treasury bills are constant through time. We begin with a two-variable system including δ_t and $r_{t-1} - \Delta d_{t-1}$; this has the advantage that the price deflator cancels from both variables, so our results are not dependent on the accuracy of the measured deflator.

The results for excess returns in Table 5 are qualitatively very similar to those for real returns. Excess stock returns are slightly less predictable than real returns in low-order systems, but as we increase lag length this difference disappears. Once again the test that $\delta'_t = \delta_t$ rejects more strongly than the return regression test, and the dividend-price ratio seems to move too much. The ratio $\sigma(\delta'_t)/\sigma(\delta_t)$ is never higher than 0.678 in any of the systems we estimate, and the difference between this ratio and unity is almost always statistically significant at the 5 percent level or better. The correlation between δ_t and δ'_t again falls with lag length, but it is imprecisely estimated.[21]

---

[21] When we estimated VAR systems over the subsamples used for model version 1, we again found the strongest evidence against the model in the period 1956–1986. The dividend-price ratio again appeared to "move too much" in every subsample.

The Dividend-Price Ratio

Table 6
Testing constant expected excess returns by using interest rates and dividend growth rates

	Lag length 1	Lag length 3
Cowles/S&P, 1871–1986		
h_t regression test	0.179	0.011
ξ_t regression test	0.135	0.008
Test that $\delta'_t = \delta_t$	0.019	0.000
$\sigma(\delta_t - \delta'_{dt})/\sigma(\delta_t)$	0.395	0.761
	(0.113)	(0.201)
$\sigma(\delta'_{rt})/\sigma(\delta_t)$	0.186	0.253
	(0.062)	(0.111)
corr $(\delta_t - \delta'_{dt}, \delta'_{rt})$	0.395	0.383
	(0.538)	(0.703)
Value-weighted NYSE 1926–1986		
h_t regression test	0.055	0.051
ξ_t regression test	0.036	0.032
Test that $\delta'_t = \delta_t$	0.003	0.000
$\sigma(\delta_t - \delta'_{dt})/\sigma(\delta_t)$	0.537	0.946
	(0.114)	(0.171)
$\sigma(\delta'_{rt})/\sigma(\delta_t)$	0.237	0.245
	(0.091)	(0.150)
corr $(\delta_t - \delta'_{dt}, \delta'_{rt})$	0.001	−0.707
	(0.434)	(0.346)

Variables are defined as follows: δ_t is the log dividend-price ratio, h_t is the log one-period stock return, and ξ_t is the approximation to h_t defined in Equation (2). The variable δ'_t is the unrestricted forecast of the present value of future growth-adjusted discount rates from a VAR, defined in Equations (8) and (9). The VAR includes the log dividend-price ratio, the dividend growth rate, and the short-term real interest rate. The variable δ'_{dt} is the unrestricted forecast of the present value of the negative of future dividend growth rates from the VAR, defined in Equation (12). The variable δ'_{rt} is the unrestricted forecast of the present value of future discount rates from the VAR, defined in Equation (12).

The constant-expected-excess-return model is tested in two different ways: by regressing the exact and approximate excess log stock returns $h_t - r_t$ and $\xi_t - r_t$ on the lagged variables that appear in the VAR and testing the joint significance of the coefficients, and by a VAR Wald test of the hypothesis that $\delta'_t = \delta_t$ [Equation (10)]. The approximate stock-return regression test is equivalent to a VAR Wald test of Equation (11).

The similarity between the results for excess and real stock returns in Table 5 suggests that time variation in short-term real interest rates is not particularly helpful in explaining the movements of the dividend-price ratio. In Table 6 we present some results, based on a three-variable system including real dividend growth and real interest rates separately, that confirm this view. Systems of lag length 1 and 3 are estimated; we do not go up to lag 5 since the number of variables in the system now grows more rapidly with lag length. For each data set, the table gives the following numbers: significance levels for the predictability of exact and approximate excess returns; a rejection significance level for the hypothesis that $\delta'_t = \delta_t$; the standard deviation of the implied long-term expected real return $\delta_t - \delta'_{dt}$ as a ratio to the standard deviation of δ_t; the standard deviation of the unrestricted forecast of the discounted value of future short-term real interest rates δ'_{rt} as a fraction of the standard deviation of δ_t; and the correlation

217

between $\delta_t - \delta'_{dt}$ and δ'_{rt}. If the predictability of real returns were entirely due to time-varying short-term real interest rates, so that excess stock returns were unpredictable, then we should not reject that $\delta'_t = \delta_t$, and we should find $\delta_t - \delta'_{dt}$ equal to δ'_{rt} with the same standard deviation and a correlation of unity.

In fact, the hypothesis that $\delta'_t = \delta_t$ is strongly rejected. The results in Table 6 show that δ'_{rt} has a much smaller standard deviation than $\delta_t - \delta'_{dt}$ does (the difference in variability increases as we increase lag length) and that the correlation between the two variables is small. In about half the systems we estimate, in fact, the correlation is actually negative.

This finding can be traced back to the following features of the data. The ex post short-term real interest rate, used here as a measure of the discount rate r_t, is not highly variable; in the Cowles/S&P data, for example, it has a standard deviation of 0.091, while real dividend growth and the log dividend-price ratio have standard deviations of 0.278 and 0.132, respectively. In the NYSE data the standard deviation of the ex post real interest rate is even lower, at 0.045, while the other two series are about as variable as in the Cowles/S&P data. Furthermore, in the VAR systems we estimate, the real rate is forecastable largely because of its own serial correlation. We find that it is not even Granger-caused by the log dividend-price ratio at the 10 percent level. It seems that short-term real interest rates are not sufficiently variable, and do not have the appropriate correlation with stock prices, to explain big movements in the log dividend-price ratio.

In Table 7 we move on to evaluate real consumption growth and the volatility of stock returns as measures of time-varying discount rates on stock (versions 3 and 4 of the model, respectively). As discussed in the previous section, these versions of the model have a free parameter α which can be interpreted as the coefficient of relative-risk aversion and which we estimate from the unrestricted VAR coefficients by using the method of moments. The format of Table 7 is similar to that of Table 6, except that we report the estimate of α with its standard error.

The results in Table 7 are discouraging for the view that real consumption growth is an adequate measure of the one-period discount rate on stock. The estimates of the coefficient of relative-risk aversion always have the wrong sign, and this version of the model is rejected about as strongly as are previous versions in VAR systems that have more than one lag. Once again the expected present value of future discount rates, δ'_{rt}, has too little variability and a correlation with $\delta_t - \delta'_{dt}$ that falls with lag length.

Inspection of the equation for consumption growth in the underlying VAR system reveals why α is always estimated to be negative. In all the equations we estimate, the log dividend-price ratio Granger-causes consumption growth at conventional significance levels, but a high ratio at the start of a year forecasts low consumption growth over the year. This

The Dividend-Price Ratio

Table 7
Testing consumption- and volatility-based models of the discount rate

	Model version 3 (consumption)		Model version 4 (volatility)	
	Lag length		Lag length	
	1	3	1	3
Cowles/S&P, 1871–1986				
Estimate of α	−2.191	−0.423	2.552	0.960
(standard error)	(1.399)	(0.818)	(2.549)	(0.985)
ξ_t regression test	0.072	0.038	0.170	0.096
Test that $\delta'_t = \delta_t$	0.012	0.000	0.039	0.007
$\sigma(\delta_t - \delta'_{dt})/\sigma(\delta_t)$	0.484	0.711	0.368	0.724
	(0.100)	(0.216)	(0.122)	(0.211)
$\sigma(\delta'_{rt})/\sigma(\delta_t)$	0.227	0.038	0.077	0.095
	(0.149)	(0.081)	(0.116)	(0.148)
corr $(\delta_t - \delta'_{dt}, \delta'_{rt})$	0.910	−0.024	0.339	0.660
	(0.073)	(0.788)	(1.415)	(0.525)
Value-weighted NYSE, 1926–1986				
Estimate of α	−3.423	−0.332	1.810	1.318
(standard error)	(1.926)	(1.067)	(2.614)	(1.261)
ξ_t regression test	0.259	0.046	0.052	0.162
Test that $\delta'_t = \delta_t$	0.168	0.000	0.000	0.000
$\sigma(\delta_t - \delta'_{dt})/\sigma(\delta_t)$	0.526	0.811	0.538	0.857
	(0.108)	(0.175)	(0.111)	(0.178)
$\sigma(\delta'_{rt})/\sigma(\delta_t)$	0.396	0.035	0.107	0.151
	(0.170)	(0.120)	(0.322)	(0.215)
corr $(\delta_t - \delta'_{dt}, \delta'_{rt})$	0.930	0.190	0.731	0.187
	(0.087)	(0.709)	(0.453)	(1.140)

Variables are defined as follows: δ_t is the log dividend-price ratio, h_t is the log one-period stock return, and ξ_t is the approximation to h_t defined in Equation (2). The variable δ'_t is the unrestricted forecast of the present value of future growth-adjusted discount rates from a VAR, defined in Equation (13). The VAR includes the log dividend-price ratio, the dividend growth rate, and the consumption growth rate (for model version 3) or the squared ex post stock return (for model version 4). The variable δ'_{dt} is the unrestricted forecast of the present value of the negative of future dividend growth rates from the VAR, and the variable δ'_{rt} is the unrestricted forecast of the present value of future discount rates from the VAR; both are defined in Equation (13).
In these versions of the model the discount rate includes a free parameter α. This is estimated from the VAR by using Equation (14) and a method-of-moments estimator. The model is tested in two ways: by using a Wald test of Equation (14) (ξ_t regression test) and by using a nonlinear Wald test of Equation (13) (test that $\delta'_t = \delta_t$).

means that low consumption growth is associated with a high one-period discount rate on stock, which requires α to be negative.[22]

The results for version 4 of the model are somewhat better, but still discouraging. The estimates of α now have the right sign, but they are very imprecisely estimated. The variable δ'_{rt} has very low variability, and in the

---

[22] We also estimated version 3 of the model assuming that consumption is measured at the beginning of the year, so that $r_t = \alpha \Delta c_{t+1}$. With this timing assumption, the estimate of α is no longer negative, but it is still insignificantly different from zero. The dividend-price ratio no longer Granger-causes the discount rate measure, and the model is more strongly rejected.

219

VAR forecasting equation for volatility, the squared ex post stock return is not Granger-caused by the log dividend-price ratio at the 10 percent level. The model is rejected almost as strongly as before in systems with more than one lag.

5. Conclusion

This article has examined time variation in corporate stock prices relative to dividends. As a framework for analyzing stock-price movements, we have proposed a dividend-ratio model that expresses the log dividend-price ratio as the rational expectation of the present value of future dividend growth rates and discount rates. We have used the equation in combination with a vector autoregression to break down movements in the log dividend-price ratio into components attributable to expected future dividend growth, expected future discount rates, and unexplained factors.

Our main results are three. First, there is some evidence that the log dividend-price ratio does move with rationally expected future growth in dividends. The log dividend-price ratio Granger-causes real dividend growth in all the systems we estimated, and the unrestricted forecast of the present value of future dividend growth rates from a VAR, δ'_{dt}, has a standard deviation that is generally about half that of the actual log dividend-price ratio δ_t. The correlation between δ'_{dt} and δ_t is extremely high in first-order VAR systems, falling dramatically as we increase the VAR lag length. It generally remains positive in high-order systems but is imprecisely estimated.

Second, the various measures of short-term discount rates that we used—short-term interest rates, consumption growth, and the volatility of stock returns themselves—are unhelpful in explaining stock-price movements. One of the weakest implications of the model is that the log dividend-price ratio should help forecast measured discount rates if, in fact, expectations of future discount rates drive stock prices. But neither short-term real interest rates nor squared ex post real stock returns are Granger-caused by the log dividend-price ratio at conventional significance levels. The log dividend-price ratio does Granger-cause real consumption growth, but the correlation between Δc_t and δ_t has the wrong sign. When we compute the rational expectation of the present value of future discount rates, δ'_{rt}, we find that it is far less variable than the component of the log dividend-price ratio that is not explained by dividends, $\delta_t - \delta'_{dt}$.

Third, there is substantial unexplained variation in the log dividend-price ratio. The unexplained part of δ_t is roughly equal to $\delta_t - \delta'_{dt}$, since measured discount rates contribute little to the explanation of δ_t, and the variable $\delta_t - \delta'_{dt}$ has a standard deviation about half that of δ_t.

To give an idea of what remains to be explained, we present an estimate of the long-term expected real stock return in Table 8. The variable reported is the unconditional mean log stock return plus $(1 - \rho)(\delta_t - \delta'_{dt})$. As discussed in Section 3, this variable is a weighted average of expected future discount rates on stock; it is the stock market equivalent of a consol

The Dividend-Price Ratio

Table 8
Dividend-price ratio and long-term expected real stock return

Date	D_{t-1}/P_t	Long-term expected return	Date	D_{t-1}/P_t	Long-term expected return
1929	0.034	0.068	1958	0.047	0.081
1930	0.046	0.078	1959	0.033	0.068
1931	0.063	0.096	1960	0.031	0.061
1932	0.093	0.118	1961	0.033	0.061
1933	0.067	0.109	1962	0.028	0.056
1934	0.035	0.079	1963	0.033	0.060
1935	0.041	0.077	1964	0.030	0.059
1936	0.033	0.067	1965	0.029	0.055
1937	0.040	0.076	1966	0.029	0.054
1938	0.071	0.097	1967	0.034	0.061
1939	0.037	0.076	1968	0.029	0.057
1940	0.046	0.084	1969	0.028	0.052
1941	0.058	0.093	1970	0.033	0.059
1942	0.076	0.109	1971	0.033	0.061
1943	0.061	0.102	1972	0.029	0.056
1944	0.051	0.094	1973	0.026	0.049
1945	0.047	0.087	1974	0.034	0.059
1946	0.036	0.072	1975	0.053	0.083
1947	0.045	0.076	1976	0.041	0.081
1948	0.055	0.092	1977	0.038	0.074
1949	0.065	0.102	1978	0.048	0.081
1950	0.063	0.104	1979	0.052	0.089
1951	0.064	0.105	1980	0.050	0.089
1952	0.054	0.095	1981	0.045	0.085
1953	0.051	0.092	1982	0.052	0.087
1954	0.055	0.094	1983	0.048	0.088
1955	0.041	0.082	1984	0.042	0.080
1956	0.038	0.074	1985	0.045	0.081
1957	0.039	0.072			

This table reports the dividend-price ratio D_{t-1}/P_t for each year in our sample, together with an estimate of the required long-term real rate of return on stocks for that year. This estimate is formed as the unconditional mean real rate of return on stocks, plus $(1 - \rho)$ times $(\delta_t - \delta'_{dt})$, the component of the demeaned log dividend-price ratio that cannot be accounted for by expected dividend growth. The variable δ'_{dt} is the unrestricted forecast of the present value of the negative of future dividend growth rates from a VAR, defined in Equation (12). The estimated VAR includes two lags of the log dividend-price ratio and the log real dividend growth rate.

yield in the bond market. The estimate is based on a VAR system that includes two lags of the log dividend-price ratio and the real dividend growth rate. (The system is similar to the ones reported in Table 5.) Prices and dividends are taken from the CRSP value-weighted New York Stock Exchange index. After allowing for the lags in the model, our series runs from 1929 to 1985. For comparison, we also report the raw-dividend-price ratio D_{t-1}/P_t.

It is clear from Table 8 that the long-term expected real return on stock is highly variable (recall that it is not a one-period expected return, but a long-term average of expected returns). Also, it does not move in parallel with the short-term real interest rate. Short-term real rates were unusually low in the late 1970s, but there is no sign of matching behavior in $(1 - \rho) \cdot (\delta_t - \delta'_{dt})$—which, instead, was unusually low throughout the 1960s.

We have reached these conclusions by using a methodology that is significantly more general and robust than any previously available. In particular, we have not assumed that dividends are stationary around a fixed time trend [as Shiller (1981) did] or that they follow a linear process with a unit root [as Mankiw, Romer, and Shapiro (1985) and West (1987, 1988) did]. Rather, we have been able to model dividends as a *log*-linear process with a unit root. This incorporates the geometric random walk model of Kleidon (1986) and LeRoy and Parke (1987) and the dividend-smoothing model of Marsh and Merton (1986, 1987) as special cases. We have also been able to incorporate some simple and popular models of discount rate variation into our analysis.

There are, of course, a number of caveats that need to be taken into account in evaluating our results. Our approach relies on the accuracy of a first-order Taylor approximation to the log return on stocks. This approximation is essential if we are to be able to solve forward for the price implications of a returns model. We have presented evidence in the Appendix that the approximation is quite accurate for our data, but approximation error could have some influence on our results.

Our measures of discount rates are applicable only under certain assumptions, which might be questioned. In one version of the model a constant risk premium is assumed; in another, a constant riskless rate—rather extreme assumptions. And of course, even under these assumptions, there is a question whether we measure the risk-free rate or the risk premium accurately with our data. Theory suggests that the discount rate should be a function of the leverage of the firm, which changes through time as the price of the firm changes [Black (1976)], a factor not taken into account in our analysis.

Throughout, we have also assumed that stable, linear stochastic processes drive log dividends, log prices, and discount rates. Some of our procedures are robust to failures of this assumption. Notably, when we test the hypothesis that dividends and measured discount rates can fully explain stock-price movements, our test is either a regression of ex post stock returns on information or a nonlinear test of algebraically equivalent restrictions. The return regression should give zero coefficients whether the information variables follow stable or unstable, linear or nonlinear processes. The nonlinear test will find that $\delta'_t = \delta_t$ if the return regression gives zero coefficients, so it is equally robust.

On the other hand, the qualitative comparison of δ_t and δ'_t, which we use to characterize a failure of the null hypothesis, may be vulnerable to a misspecification of the processes for prices, dividends, and discount rates. However, we believe that this comparison is fairly reliable in our data, since we obtain similar results over various subsamples.

Our econometric methods are based on asymptotic distribution theory. It is possible that they are subject to some bias in finite samples. Mankiw and Shapiro (1986) and Stambaugh (1986) have studied bias in regression tests, while Flavin (1983), Kleidon (1986), and Mattey and Meese (1986) have pointed out that volatility tests can suffer from this problem. We have conducted our own Monte Carlo study of the methods used in this article

The Dividend-Price Ratio

[Campbell and Shiller (1988b)]. While we do find some bias toward rejection of the model, and some downward bias in the estimates of $\sigma(\delta'_t)/\sigma(\delta_t)$, the bias is not sufficient to explain our empirical findings.

Our results are also conditional on an adequate specification of lag length in the VAR systems we estimate. We try lag lengths up to 5 in two-variable systems and 3 in three-variable systems. The main effect of altering lag length is that the correlation between δ_t and δ'_{dt} falls, particularly when we move from one to two lags. As argued above, we suspect that the extremely high correlation in the first-order system is to some extent spurious.

Our conclusions might also be affected by adding more lagged variables to our information set H_t. We note, however, that adding more variables could only increase the explanatory power of regressions explaining stock returns. Given the risk of overfitting regressions in finite samples, we have chosen to consider a relatively small set of information variables in this article. In Campbell and Shiller (1988a), we have extended the set of variables somewhat by including corporate earnings data. We obtain results for one-lag systems including earnings that are similar to the results reported here for higher-order systems.

There is an interesting parallel between our results and those of Fama and French (1988) and Flood, Hodrick, and Kaplan (1986). These authors find that stock returns are more highly predictable when measured over several years than when measured over one year. The predictability of returns seems to cumulate over time. Our dividend-ratio model can be seen as a way to compute the effects of single-period predictability of returns when they are cumulated over infinite time. We find that moderate predictability of one-year stock returns can have dramatic implications for the log dividend-price ratio. In particular, the log dividend-price ratio has a standard deviation that is at least 50 percent higher than it would be if stock returns were unpredictable.

Appendix: Approximation Error of the Dividend-Ratio Model

In this Appendix we evaluate in several different ways the approximation error in the dividend-ratio model, Equation (6). We do this by studying the error in the underlying Equations (2) and (4) and by directly comparing δ'_t as given in Equation (9) with an exact log dividend-price ratio in a simple model. The evaluations proceed as follows:

1. We compare exact return h_t to approximate return ξ_t.
2. We compare the log dividend-price ratio δ_t with the right-hand side of Equation (4), using a terminal condition.
3. We compare an exact log dividend-price ratio where the price is the present value of expected dividends with the approximate log dividend-price ratio δ'_t.
4. We compare regression results when h_t or ξ_t are regressed on information.

Table A1
Evaluation of approximation error: Log-linear approximation to stock return

	Variable		
Data set, sample period, and statistic	Exact return h_t	Approximate return ξ_t	Error, $\xi_t - h_t$
Cowles/S&P, 1871–1986:			
Mean	0.081	0.076	−0.005
Standard deviation	0.170	0.169	0.005
Correlation with exact return	1.0000	0.9996	−0.3108
Value-weighted NYSE, 1926–1986:			
Mean	0.089	0.081	−0.008
Standard deviation	0.201	0.199	0.006
Correlation with exact return	1.0000	0.9995	−0.3394

All variables in this table are nominal. h_t is the log one-period stock return, and ξ_t is the approximation to h_t defined in Equation (2).

The first, second, and fourth comparisons use actual data, the third uses a Monte Carlo experiment in which data are generated by a known vector autoregressive model. The first two comparisons relate to ex post data, and the second two relate to conditional expectations.

1. Table A1 compares the approximate nominal stock return ξ_t, defined in Equation (2), with the exact nominal return h_t.[23] The approximation error is quite small and, most important for our purposes, is almost constant. (Constant approximation error will not affect our results since our models do not restrict mean returns.)

2. Even though the approximation error is small for one-period returns, it might cumulate when we solve forward to obtain Equation (4). To check this possibility, we constructed an approximate log dividend-price ratio δ_t^A by using Equation (4), the time series of ex post stock returns h_t and dividend growth rates Δd_t, and a terminal condition $\delta_T^A = \delta_T$.[24] In Table A2 we compare this variable with the actual log dividend-price ratio δ_t. If our approximation held exactly in Table A1 (that is, if we had $\xi_t = h_t$ for all t), then there would also be no error in Table A2. In order to reduce the influence of the terminal condition, we use only the first 30 years of each sample in computing the summary statistics. The approximation error is again quite small and not highly variable.

3. For our Monte Carlo experiment, we first generated 1000 replications of the vector z_t by using a normal random-number generator and the estimated parameters of the one-lag vector autoregressive model estimated here in Table 4, top panel. We then computed the corresponding 1000

---

[23] Real stock returns are obtained by subtracting the inflation rate from nominal returns, and excess stock returns are obtained by subtracting ex post nominal discount rates from nominal returns. Therefore, the approximation error for these return concepts is the same as for nominal stock returns.

[24] This terminal condition is used only for evaluating the approximation in Equation (4), not in the empirical work of the article.

The Dividend-Price Ratio

Table A2
Evaluation of approximation error: Log-linear approximation to dividend-price ratio

Data set, sample period, and statistic	Variable δ_t	δ_t^A	$\delta_t^A - \delta_t$
Cowles/S&P, 1871–1986:			
Mean	−3.007	−2.935	0.072
Standard deviation	0.242	0.238	0.011
Correlation with δ_t	1.000	0.982	0.044
Value-weighted NYSE, 1926–1986:			
Mean	−2.989	−2.877	0.112
Standard deviation	0.263	0.266	0.027
Correlation with δ_t	1.000	0.995	0.063

Summary statistics are computed only over the first 30 years of each sample. δ_t is the log dividend-price ratio, and δ_t^A is an approximate log dividend-price ratio constructed by using Equation (4), the time series of ex post stock returns h_t and dividend growth rates Δd_t, and a terminal condition $\delta_T^A = \delta_T$.

observations of δ'_t by using the right-hand side of Equation (9). The variable δ'_t is what the log dividend-price ratio should be if discount rates are constant through time (version 1 of our model) and if our approximation holds exactly.

If dividends are generated by the lognormal VAR system and if discount rates are constant through time, then, without using any approximation, the log dividend-price ratio should equal δ_t^{LN} as defined by

$$\delta_t^{LN} = -\log\left(\sum_{j=1}^{\infty} \exp(m_j)\right) \qquad (A1)$$

where

$$m_j = e2'\bigg\{j\mu + (I-A)^{-1}(A - A^{j+1})(z_t - \mu)$$
$$+ 0.5 \sum_{k=1}^{j} (I-A)^{-1}(I-A^k)\Omega(I-A^k)'(I-A)^{-1'}e2\bigg\}$$

Table A3
Monte Carlo evaluation of approximation error: Log-linear approximation to dividend-price ratio

Statistic	Exact log dividend-price ratio δ_t^{LN}	Approximate log dividend-price ratio δ'_t	Error, $\delta'_t - \delta_t^{LN}$
Mean	−2.867	−2.710	0.157
Standard deviation	0.179	0.176	0.003
Correlation with δ_t^{LN}	1.000	0.99997	−0.896

The results in this table are based on simulated, not actual, data. We generated 1000 replications of a vector z_t, including the log dividend-price ratio and the dividend growth rate, by using a normal random-number generator and the estimated parameters of the one-lag vector autoregressive model estimated in Table 4, top panel. We then computed the corresponding observations of δ'_t by using the right-hand side of Equation (9). These are compared with observations of δ_t^{LN}, defined in Equation (A1). If our approximation (2) is accurate, then δ'_t should equal δ_t^{LN}.

where μ is defined as the mean of the vector $z_t = x_t$, where Ω is the variance matrix of the error term $u_t = v_n$ and where the other symbols are as described in the text of this article.[25]

It follows that we can test the accuracy of our approximation by comparing δ'_t with δ_t^{LN}. Comparisons of this sort are given in Table A3. The correlation of δ'_t with δ_t^{LN} is extremely high at 0.99997, and the other measures also show very close correspondence. There is thus no need to use the more complicated nonlinear expression (A1) instead of (9) for the log dividend-price ratio.

4. Even though ξ_t and h_t are highly correlated, it does not automatically follow that the approximation does not pose problems for our Wald tests of the dividend-ratio model. We therefore compared regressions of ξ_t and h_t on information. A detailed comparison is presented in Table 4; comparative significance levels for rejection of the dividend-ratio model are presented also in Tables 5 and 6. The significance tends to be slightly stronger for approximate returns, indicating that there is some correlation of the approximation error with the explanatory variables. However, the difference is small and should not affect the broad conclusions we get from our approximate model.

References

Black, F., 1976, "Studies of Stock Price Volatility Changes," *Proceedings of the Business and Economic Statistics Section, American Statistical Association*, 177–181.

Black, F., and M. Scholes, 1974, "The Effects of Dividend Yield and Dividend Policy on Common Stock Prices and Returns," *Journal of Financial Economics*, 1, 1–22.

Breeden, D. T., 1979, "An Intertemporal Asset Pricing Model with Stochastic Consumption and Investment Opportunities," *Journal of Financial Economics*, 7, 265–296.

Campbell, J. Y., 1987, "Stock Returns and the Term Structure," *Journal of Financial Economics*, 18, 373–399.

Campbell, J. Y., and R. J. Shiller, 1987, "Cointegration and Tests of Present Value Models," *Journal of Political Economy*, 95, 1062–1088.

Campbell, J. Y., and R. J. Shiller, 1988a, "Stock Prices, Earnings, and Expected Dividends," *Journal of Finance*, 43, 661–676.

Campbell, J. Y., and R. J. Shiller, 1988b, "The Dividend Ratio Model and Small Sample Bias: A Monte Carlo Study," forthcoming in *Economics Letters*.

Cowles, A., 1939, *Common Stock Indexes* (2d ed.), Principia Press, Bloomington, Ind.

Dickey, D. A., and W. A. Fuller, 1981, "Likelihood Ratio Statistics for Autoregressive Time Series with a Unit Root," *Econometrica*, 49, 1057–1072.

Engle, R. F., and C. W. J. Granger, 1987, "Cointegration and Error-Correction: Representation, Estimation and Testing," *Econometrica*, 55, 251–276.

Fama, E. F., and K. R. French, 1988, "Permanent and Temporary Components of Stock Prices," *Journal of Political Economy*, 96, 246–273.

---

[25] The first element δ_1 in the vector z, need not satisfy Equation (A1), of course, since the estimated VAR model from Table 4 does not exactly satisfy the assumptions of the nonlinear expectations model.

The Dividend-Price Ratio

Fisher, L., and J. H. Lorie, 1977, *A Half Century of Returns on Stocks and Bonds*, Graduate School of Business, University of Chicago.

Flavin, M. A., 1983, "Excess Volatility in the Financial Markets: A Reassessment of the Empirical Evidence," *Journal of Political Economy*, 91, 929-956.

Flood, R. P., R. J. Hodrick, and P. Kaplan, 1986, "An Evaluation of Recent Evidence on Stock Market Bubbles," Working Paper 1971, National Bureau of Economic Research, Cambridge, Mass.

French, K. R., G. W. Schwert, and R. F. Stambaugh, 1987, "Expected Stock Returns and Volatility," *Journal of Financial Economics*, 19, 3-29.

Fuller, W. A., 1976, *Introduction to Statistical Time Series*, Wiley, New York.

Gordon, M. J., 1962, *The Investment, Financing and Valuation of the Corporation*, Irwin, Homewood, Ill.

Grossman, S. J., A. Melino, and R. J. Shiller, 1987, "Estimating the Continuous-Time Consumption-Based Asset-Pricing Model," *Journal of Business and Economic Statistics*, 5, 315-327.

Grossman, S. J., and R. J. Shiller, 1981, "The Determinants of the Variability of Stock Market Prices," *American Economic Review*, 71, 222-227.

Hall, R. E., 1988, "Intertemporal Substitution in Consumption," *Journal of Political Economy*, 96, 339-357.

Hansen, L. P., 1982, "Large Sample Properties of Generalized Method of Moments Estimators," *Econometrica*, 50, 1029-1054.

Hansen, L. P., and K. J. Singleton, 1983, "Stochastic Consumption, Risk Aversion, and the Temporal Behavior of Asset Returns," *Journal of Political Economy*, 91, 249-265.

Ibbotson Associates, 1987, *Stocks, Bonds, Bills and Inflation: 1987 Yearbook*, Ibbotson Associates, Chicago.

Keim, D. B., and R. F. Stambaugh, 1986, "Predicting Returns in the Stock and Bond Markets," *Journal of Financial Economics*, 17, 357-390.

Kleidon, A. W., 1986, "Variance Bounds Tests and Stock Price Valuation Models," *Journal of Political Economy*, 94, 953-1001.

LeRoy, S. F., and W. R. Parke, 1987, "Stock Price Volatility: A Test Based on the Geometric Random Walk," unpublished paper, University of California, Santa Barbara.

LeRoy, S. F., and R. D. Porter, 1981, "The Present-Value Relation: Tests Based on Implied Variance Bounds," *Econometrica*, 49, 97-113.

Lucas, R. E., 1978, "Asset Prices in an Exchange Economy," *Econometrica*, 46, 1429-1445.

Macaulay, F., 1938, *Some Theoretical Problems Suggested by the Movements of Interest Rates, Bond Yields and Stock Prices in the United States Since 1856*, National Bureau of Economic Research, New York.

Mankiw, N. G., D. Romer, and M. D. Shapiro, 1985, "An Unbiassed Reexamination of Stock Market Volatility," *Journal of Finance*, 40, 677-687.

Mankiw, N. G., J. Rotemberg, and L. Summers, 1985, "Intertemporal Substitution in Macroeconomics," *Quarterly Journal of Economics*, 100, 225-251.

Mankiw, N. G., and M. D. Shapiro, 1986, "Do We Reject Too Often? Small Sample Properties of Tests of Rational Expectations Models," *Economics Letters*, 20, 139-145.

Marsh, T. A., and R. C. Merton, 1986, "Dividend Variability and Variance Bounds Tests for the Rationality of Stock Market Prices," *American Economic Review*, 76, 483-498.

Marsh, T. A., and R. C. Merton, 1987, "Dividend Behavior for the Aggregate Stock Market," *Journal of Business*, 60, 1-40.

Mattey, J., and R. Meese, 1986, "Empirical Assessment of Present Value Relations," *Econometric Reviews*, 5, 171-234.

Mehra, R., and E. Prescott, 1985, "The Equity Premium: A Puzzle," *Journal of Monetary Economics*, 15, 145-162.

Merton, R. C., 1980, "On Estimating the Expected Return on the Market," *Journal of Financial Economics,* 8, 323–361.

Newey, W. K., and K. D. West, 1987, "A Simple, Positive Definite, Heteroscedasticity and Autocorrelation Consistent Covariance Matrix," *Econometrica,* 55, 703–708.

Perron, P., 1988, "Trends and Random Walks in Macroeconomic Time Series: Further Evidence from a New Approach," *Journal of Economic Dynamics and Control,* 12, 297–332.

Phillips, P. C. B., 1987, "Time Series Regression with a Unit Root," *Econometrica,* 55, 277–302.

Phillips, P. C. B., and S. N. Durlauf, 1986, "Multiple Time Series with Integrated Variables," *Review of Economic Studies,* 53, 473–496.

Phillips, P. C. B., and P. Perron, 1988, "Testing for Unit Roots in Time Series Regression," forthcoming in *Biometrika.*

Pindyck, R. S., 1984, "Risk, Inflation, and the Stock Market," *American Economic Review,* 74, 335–351.

Pindyck, R. S., 1986, "Risk Aversion and the Determinants of Stock Market Behavior," working paper 1921, National Bureau of Economic Research, New York.

Poterba, J. M., and L. H. Summers, 1986, "The Persistence of Volatility and Stock Market Fluctuations," *American Economic Review,* 76, 1142–1151.

Poterba, J. M., and L. H. Summers, 1988, "Mean Reversion in Stock Prices: Evidence and Implications," forthcoming in *Journal of Financial Economics.*

Sargent, T. J., 1979, "A Note on the Estimation of the Rational Expectations Model of the Term Structure," *Journal of Monetary Economics,* 5, 133–143.

Schwert, G. W., 1988, "Tests for Unit Roots: A Monte Carlo Investigation," forthcoming in *Journal of Business and Economic Statistics.*

Shiller, R. J., 1979, "The Volatility of Long-Term Interest Rates and Expectations Models of the Term Structure," *Journal of Political Economy,* 87, 1190–1219.

Shiller, R. J., 1981, "Do Stock Prices Move Too Much to be Justified by Subsequent Changes in Dividends?" *American Economic Review,* 71, 421–436.

Shiller, R. J., 1984, "Stock Prices and Social Dynamics," *Brookings Papers on Economic Activity,* 457–498.

Stambaugh, R. F., 1986, "Bias in Regressions with Lagged Stochastic Regressors," unpublished paper, Graduate School of Business, University of Chicago.

Stock, J. H., 1987, "Asymptotic Properties of Least Squares Estimates of Cointegrating Vectors," *Econometrica,* 55, 1035–1056.

Summers, L. H., 1986, "Does the Stock Market Rationally Reflect Fundamental Values?" *Journal of Finance,* 41, 591–601.

West, K. D., 1987, "A Specification Test for Speculative Bubbles," *Quarterly Journal of Economics,* 102, 553–580.

West, K. D., 1988, "Dividend Innovations and Stock Price Volatility," *Econometrica,* 56, 37–61.

White, H., 1984, *Asymptotic Theory for Econometricians,* Academic Press, Orlando, Fla.

Wilson, J. W., and C. P. Jones, 1987, "A Comparison of Annual Common Stock Returns: 1871–1925 with 1926–85," *Journal of Business,* 60, 239–258.

# [2]
Excess Volatility in the Financial Markets: A Reassessment of the Empirical Evidence

Marjorie A. Flavin
University of Virginia

> Numerous authors, including Shiller, LeRoy and Porter, and Singleton, have reported empirical evidence that stock prices and long interest rates are more volatile than can be justified by standard asset-pricing models. This paper shows that in small samples the "volatility" or "variance-bounds" tests tend to be biased, often severely, toward rejection of the null hypothesis of market efficiency. Thus the apparent violation of market efficiency may be reflecting the sampling properties of the volatility measures, rather than a failure of the market efficiency hypothesis itself. The paper also reports some unbiased estimates of the bounds on holding period yields and long interest rates. Much of the evidence of excess volatility disappears when the tests are corrected for small sample bias.

In recent papers, Shiller (1979) and LeRoy and Porter (1981) have reported empirical evidence that stock prices and long interest rates are more volatile than can be justified within the standard asset-pricing models. Further empirical evidence on excess volatility in the financial markets has been reported in numerous studies, including Pesando (1979), Amsler (1980), Singleton (1980), Grossman and Shil-

I am grateful for comments and suggestions received during workshops at the Board of Governors, Brown, Chicago, CUNY, Duke, Michigan, University of Rochester, and Virginia Polytechnic Institute. For helpful discussions and comments on earlier drafts I also thank Richard Ashley, Robert Barro, Edwin Burmeister, Matthew Cushing, Wake Epps, Robert Hall, James Hamilton, Lars Hansen, Stephen LeRoy, Ronald Michener, Richard Porter, Robert Shiller, Kenneth Singleton, Jonathan Skinner, James Stock, William Poole, and Charles Whiteman. Earlier versions of the paper were circulated under the title "Small Sample Bias in Tests of Excess Volatility in the Financial Markets."

ler (1981), Shiller (1981a, 1981b, 1981c), and Blanchard and Watson (1982). According to the empirical evidence reported in these papers, the variance of stock prices, holding yields on long-term bonds, and long interest rates exceed the upper bounds implied by the variance of dividends and short interest rates. Further, the variances of stock prices and long interest rates exceed their estimated upper bounds by very large margins in many cases.

This paper argues that in small samples the "volatility" or "variance-bounds" tests tend to be strongly biased toward rejection of the null hypothesis of no excess volatility. Thus the apparent violation of the market efficiency hypothesis may be reflecting the sampling properties of the volatility measures in small samples rather than a failure of the market efficiency hypothesis.

The innovative tests developed by Shiller and LeRoy and Porter are formulated according to the following line of reasoning. If stock prices are modeled as the present discounted value of rationally forecasted future dividends, the volatility, or variance, of the stock price is limited by the volatility, or variance, of the dividend series. Similarly, under the expectations theory of the term structure of interest rates, which asserts that the long-term interest rate is equal to an average of rationally expected future short-term interest rates, the variance of the long rate is limited by the variance of the short rate. The upper bound on the volatility of long rates, or stock prices, has been tested either (1) by comparing a point estimate of the upper bound with a point estimate of the variance being bounded or (2) by calculating both point estimates and the asymptotic covariance matrix of the estimates and testing whether the estimated variance of long rates or stock prices exceeds the estimated upper bound by an amount that is statistically significantly greater than zero. In either procedure, the test statistics may be misleading if, for samples of the size typically used in the variance-bounds tests, the point estimates are biased or, more generally, if the asymptotic distributions are not close approximations to the finite sample distributions. This paper argues that the estimate of the upper bound in these tests is biased downward in small samples and that the magnitude of the bias is large enough to provide a potential explanation of the apparent violation of the bounds.

To see intuitively why the variance-bounds tests tend to be biased against the null hypothesis, consider the basic bound on the volatility of long interest rates: var (R_t) < var (R_t^*), where R_t is the actual long rate and R_t^* is the perfect-foresight long rate, defined as the value the long rate would take if agents had perfect foresight concerning the path of the short rate. Under the market efficiency hypothesis, R_t is equal to the expectation of R_t^* conditional on currently available in-

EXCESS VOLATILITY

formation and therefore must have a variance smaller than the variance of R_t^*. If the population means of R_t and R_t^* were known a priori, unbiased estimates of var (R_t) and var (R_t^*) could be obtained by taking squared deviations of R_t and R_t^* from their population means. The empirical applications of the variance-bounds tests have relied on sample variances of R_t and R_t^* that were computed by taking deviations from sample means. Taking deviations from the sample mean induces downward bias in the sample variance, however, since the sample mean has the following property: the sample variance of a data series, expressed in deviations from some constant, is minimized when that constant is set equal to the sample mean. The greater the variance of the sample mean, the greater is the extent to which the sample mean will "fit" some of the stochastic components of the data series and the greater is the bias in the sample variance. Because R_t^* is a long moving average of a variable (the short rate), which is itself highly serially correlated, the variance of $\bar{R}_t^*$ tends to exceed the variance of $\bar{R}_t$, and as a result the sample variance of R_t^* tends to be more strongly downward biased than the sample variance of R_t. Since var (R_t^*) is the upper bound on var (R_t), the net effect is that the difference vâr (R_t^*) − vâr (R_t) is biased toward rejection of the null hypothesis of no excess volatility. This bias toward rejection of the null hypothesis also arises in tests of the upper bound on the variance of stock prices and the variance of holding period yields on long-term bonds.

Section I considers an economy in which the short rate is generated by an AR1 process with the autoregressive parameter equal to 0.95 for quarterly observations. Investors are risk neutral and form expectations of future short rates rationally, with the result that yields on 20-year discount bonds are generated exactly as hypothesized by the pure (i.e., no liquidity premium) expectations hypothesis. The exact finite sample distributions of the sample statistics, vâr (R_t), vâr (R_t^*), and vâr (R_t^*) − vâr (R_t), are calculated for a sample of size 100 in such an economy.

In Section II, some of the test procedures implemented in Shiller (1979, 1981b) and Singleton (1980) are reviewed in light of the findings concerning the small sample distributions of the variance-bounds statistics. Depending on the bound being tested and the estimation method used, the bias toward rejection of no excess volatility ranges from modest to strong to severe. Section II also reports some unbiased estimates of the bounds on the variances of holding period yields and long interest rates. Much of the evidence of excess volatility in the bond market disappears when the tests are corrected for small sample bias.

I. Comparison of Small Sample and Asymptotic Distributions in an Efficient-Market Economy

In order to keep the problem as simple as possible, the model economy studied in this section is one in which the short rate follows a first-order autoregressive (AR1) process:

$$r_t = \rho r_{t-1} + \epsilon_t, \tag{1}$$

where r_t is the short-term interest rate, expressed in deviations from the mean, and ϵ_t is an independently and identically distributed disturbance; $\epsilon \sim N(0, \sigma_\epsilon^2)$.

According to the expectations hypothesis of the term structure, the linearized long rate on a pure discount bond is simply the average of current and future expected short rates:

$$R_t = \frac{1}{n} \sum_{j=0}^{n-1} {}_t r_{t+j}, \tag{2}$$

where R_t is the n-period long rate and ${}_t r_{t+j}$ is the expectation, in period t, of r_{t+j}. Note that the long rate does not include a liquidity premium.

Using the assumption that the short rate follows an AR1 process, we see that all expected future short rates are proportional to the current short rate:

$${}_t r_{t+j} = \rho^j r_t = \rho^j \sum_{i=0}^{\infty} \rho^i \epsilon_{t-i}. \tag{3}$$

Thus the long rate is also proportional to the short rate:

$$R_t = \frac{1 - \rho^n}{n(1 - \rho)} r_t = \frac{1 - \rho^n}{n(1 - \rho)} \sum_{i=0}^{\infty} \rho^i \epsilon_{t-i}. \tag{4}$$

Define the "perfect-foresight" long rate, R_t^*, as the value the long rate would take if agents had perfect foresight concerning the path of the short rate:[1]

$$R_t^* = \frac{1}{n} \sum_{j=0}^{n-1} r_{t+j}. \tag{5}$$

By straightforward but tedious manipulation, the perfect-foresight long rate can be expressed as a linear combination of past, current, and future disturbances:

---

[1] Shiller uses the terminology "ex post rational" long rate in referring to this variable.

EXCESS VOLATILITY

$$R_t^* = \frac{1}{n(1-\rho)} \sum_{j=1}^{n-1} (1 - \rho^{n-j})\epsilon_{t+j} + \frac{1-\rho^n}{n(1-\rho)} \sum_{i=0}^{\infty} \rho^i \epsilon_{t-i}. \quad (6)$$

Equation (6) reflects the basic hypothesis of efficiency in the bond market: the actual long rate, R_t, is the expectation of the perfect-foresight long rate, R_t^*, conditional on all available information.

Substituting equation (4) into equation (6) yields

$$R_t^* = R_t + \theta_t, \quad (7)$$

where

$$\theta_t = \frac{1}{n(1-\rho)} \sum_{j=1}^{n-1} (1 - \rho^{n-j})\epsilon_{t+j}.$$

R_t, which depends only on current and past disturbances, and θ_t, which depends only on future disturbances, are distributed independently, with the implication that

$$\text{var}(R_t^*) = \text{var}(R_t) + \text{var}(\theta_t). \quad (8)$$

Since the variance of the forecast error must be nonnegative, the variance of R_t^* constitutes an upper bound on the variance of R_t:

$$\text{var}(R_t^*) \geq \text{var}(R_t). \quad (9)$$

The upper bound on the variance of the long rate, equation (9), is, of course, a restriction on the population moments of R_t^* and R_t. Assuming that r_t, and therefore R_t^* and R_t, are stationary and ergodic time-series processes, the population variances of R_t^* and R_t can be consistently estimated from a single realization of the process over time.[2]

The upper bound on the volatility of long rates, or stock prices, has been tested either by comparing point estimates of var (R_t^*) and var (R_t) or by calculating both point estimates of var (R_t^*) and var (R_t) and the asymptotic covariance matrix of the estimates and testing whether the difference vâr (R_t^*) − vâr (R_t) is significantly less than zero. In either procedure, the test statistics may be misleading if, for samples of the size typically used in the variance-bounds tests, the point estimates are biased or, more generally, if the asymptotic distributions are not close approximations to the finite sample distributions.

---

[2] If the short rate is nonstationary (i.e., if $\rho \geq 1$), the variances of r_t, R_t, and R_t^* are undefined and the theoretical variance bounds must be reformulated. Almost all of the empirical volatility literature, including LeRoy and Porter (1981), Shiller (1979, 1981b), and Singleton (1980), has been based on the assumption that the short rate (or dividends) is a stationary process.

This section of the paper studies the properties of the variance-bounds statistics in samples of 100 quarterly observations on the yields of 20-year discount bonds and 3-month bills. These observations are assumed to be drawn from an efficient-market economy in which the short rate is generated by an AR1 process with $\rho = 0.95$. The exact small sample distributions that the sample statistics, vâr (R_t^*), vâr (R_t), and vâr (R_t^*) − vâr (R_t), would have in such an economy are then calculated and compared to the asymptotic distributions.

Calculation of the Small Sample Distributions[3]

In order to avoid having to refer to "the variance of the variance of R_t," the following notation will be used: $V = $ vâr (R_t), $V^* = $ vâr (R_t^*), and $D = $ vâr (R_t^*) − vâr (R_t).

In equations (1)–(6), the first observation on the short rate, r_1, was expressed as a function of disturbances from the infinite past. For the purpose of calculating the small sample distributions, it is more convenient to model the first observation on the short rate as a random draw from the stationary distribution of the short rate:

$$r_1 = \frac{\epsilon_1}{\sqrt{1 - \rho^2}}, \qquad (10)$$

where $\epsilon_1 \sim N(0, \sigma_\epsilon^2)$. By modeling r_1 as a drawing from the stationary distribution of the short rate, a sample of T observations on r can be expressed as a function of T disturbances rather than an infinite number. For the purpose of characterizing the distributions of V, V^*, and D, the stochastic specification of r_1 given by equation (10) is completely equivalent to the specification of r_1 as a function of disturbances from the infinite past.

With this modification, each of the random variables V, V^*, and D can be expressed as a quadratic form in the disturbance of the short-rate process, ϵ. To construct the quadratic form representing the variance of the long rate, V, recall that in this example the long rate is proportional to the short rate,

$$R_t = \alpha r_t, \qquad (11)$$

where $\alpha = (1 - \rho^n)/n(1 - \rho)$. The vector of T observations on the short rate can be expressed as a linear transformation of the disturbances:

---

[3] I am grateful to Robert Hall for suggesting this approach for computing the exact finite sample distributions of the variances.

EXCESS VOLATILITY

$$\begin{bmatrix} r_1 \\ r_2 \\ r_3 \\ \cdot \\ \cdot \\ \cdot \\ r_T \end{bmatrix} = \begin{bmatrix} \frac{1}{\sqrt{1-\rho^2}} & 0 & 0 & 0 & \cdots & 0 \\ \frac{\rho}{\sqrt{1-\rho^2}} & 1 & 0 & 0 & \cdots & 0 \\ \frac{\rho^2}{\sqrt{1-\rho^2}} & \rho & 1 & 0 & \cdots & 0 \\ \cdot & \cdot & & & & \\ \cdot & \cdot & & & & \\ \cdot & \cdot & & & & \\ \frac{\rho^{T-1}}{\sqrt{1-\rho^2}} & \rho^{T-2} & \rho^{T-3} & \rho^{T-4} & \cdots & 1 \end{bmatrix} \begin{bmatrix} \epsilon_1 \\ \epsilon_2 \\ \epsilon_3 \\ \cdot \\ \cdot \\ \cdot \\ \epsilon_T \end{bmatrix}. \quad (12)$$

Using the notation S (for short rate) for the $T \times T$ matrix in equation (12) and ϵ for the T-element column vector of disturbances, the sample variance of the long rate, V, can be expressed as a quadratic form in ϵ,

$$V = \epsilon' A \epsilon, \quad (13)$$

where A is the $T \times T$ symmetric matrix, $A = \alpha^2 T^{-1} S'S$. At this point, the mean of the short rate, which is also the mean of the long rate, is assumed to be known a priori; the quadratic form A represents the variance of R_t around the population mean. The variance of R_t around its sample mean will be studied later.

The quadratic form representing the sample variance of the perfect-foresight long rate, V^*, will be of order $T + n - 1$, where n is the number of periods in the long rate, because the last observation on R_t^* depends on r_T and $n - 1$ subsequent observations on the short rate. Let L denote the $T \times T + n - 1$ matrix that transforms the $T + n - 1$ observations on the short rate into T observations on the perfect-foresight long rate:

$$\begin{bmatrix} R_1^* \\ R_2^* \\ R_3^* \\ \cdot \\ \cdot \\ \cdot \\ R_T^* \end{bmatrix} = \frac{1}{n} \begin{bmatrix} 1 & 1 & 1 & \cdots & 1 & 0 & 0 & 0 & \cdots & 0 \\ 0 & 1 & 1 & 1 & \cdots & 1 & 0 & 0 & \cdots & 0 \\ 0 & 0 & 1 & 1 & 1 & \cdots & 1 & 0 & \cdots & 0 \\ \cdot & & & & & & & & & \\ \cdot & & & & & & & & & \\ \cdot & & & & & & & & & \\ 0 & 0 & 0 & \cdots & 0 & 1 & 1 & 1 & \cdots & 1 \end{bmatrix} \begin{bmatrix} r_1 \\ r_2 \\ r_3 \\ \cdot \\ \cdot \\ \cdot \\ r_{T+n-1} \end{bmatrix}, \quad (14)$$

where the width of the band of ones is n.

The sample variance of R_i^* around its population mean can be expressed as the quadratic form of order $T + n - 1$,

$$V^* = \epsilon'B\epsilon, \qquad (15)$$

where $B = T^{-1}S'L'LS$; S is the lower-triangular matrix defined as in equation (12), except with order $T + n - 1$ instead of T, and ϵ is the $T + n - 1$ element column vector of disturbances.

The difference between the variances, $D = V^* - V$, is given by the difference of the quadratic forms for V^* and V:

$$D = \epsilon'[B - A]\epsilon. \qquad (16)$$

(Of course the $T \times T$ matrix A as defined above must be augmented by adding $n - 1$ rows and $n - 1$ columns of zeros so that it conforms with the matrix B.)

The problem now becomes one of calculating the distribution of a quadratic form in normal deviates. Let Λ denote the diagonal matrix with the eigenvalues of the quadratic form A on the main diagonal, and P the matrix of eigenvectors; $P'AP = \Lambda$. Since $PP' = I$, $\epsilon'A\epsilon = \epsilon'PP'APP'\epsilon = \epsilon'P\Lambda P'\epsilon$. Define a new disturbance term η such that $\eta = P'\epsilon$. Since P is an orthonormal matrix, the new disturbances are independently distributed, $\eta \sim N(0, \sigma_\epsilon^2)$, with the same variance as the original disturbance, ϵ. Thus the sample variance of the long rate, V, is a weighted sum of squared normal deviates:

$$V = \epsilon'A\epsilon = \eta'\Lambda\eta = \sum_{j=1}^{T} \lambda_j \eta_j^2, \qquad (17)$$

where λ_j are the eigenvalues of the quadratic form A. The characteristic function of $\sum_{j=1}^{T} \lambda_j \eta_j^2$ is

$$\phi(t) = \prod_{1}^{T}(1 - 2i\lambda_j \sigma_\epsilon^2 t)^{-1/2}. \qquad (18)$$

By inverting the characteristic function, one can obtain the cumulative distribution function of the random variable, V. The value of the distribution function, evaluated at x, is given by

$$F(x) = \frac{1}{2} - \frac{1}{\pi}\int_0^\infty t^{-1}I[e^{-itx}\phi(t)]dt, \qquad (19)$$

where $I[\cdot]$ denotes the imaginary part of the expression in the brackets.

All of the small sample distributions reported in the next section were computed by the following procedure: (1) The symmetric matrix defining the quadratic form was generated, after assigning numerical values to the parameters T, n, and ρ; (2) the eigenvalues of the matrix were obtained using numerical methods; and (3) the inversion

EXCESS VOLATILITY

formula (eq. [19]), which is a function of the eigenvalues, was integrated numerically.[4]

Asymptotic Distributions

Unlike the small sample distributions, the asymptotic distributions can be derived analytically. Let V, V^*, and D denote the sample statistics calculated by taking deviations from the population mean, and V_s, V_s^*, and D_s denote the corresponding statistics computed by taking deviations from the sample mean. The bias induced in V_s, V_s^*, and D_s by taking deviations from the sample mean is of order $1/T$ (Anderson 1971, p. 463). Similarly, $T \cdot \text{var}(V_s)$, $T \cdot \text{var}(V_s^*)$, and $T \cdot \text{var}(D_s)$ differ from $T \cdot \text{var}(V)$, $T \cdot \text{var}(V^*)$, and $T \cdot \text{var}(D)$, respectively, by terms of order $1/T$ (Anderson 1971, p. 471). Thus, in deriving the means and variances of the asymptotic distributions of V_s, V_s^*, and D_s, we can analyze the simpler case in which the statistics are calculated by taking deviations from the population mean.

Using equations (4) and (6) for R_t and R_t^*, respectively, we see that straightforward calculation of the means of the asymptotic distributions of V, V^*, and D yields

$$\mu_V = E(R_t^2) = \frac{\alpha^2 \sigma_\epsilon^2}{1 - \rho^2},$$

$$\mu_{V^*} = E(R_t^{*2}) = \left(\frac{\alpha^2}{1 - \rho^2} + \sum_{i=1}^{n-1} \alpha_i^2\right)\sigma_\epsilon^2, \qquad (20)$$

$$\mu_D = E[(R_t^* - R_t)^2] = \sigma_\epsilon^2 \sum_{i=1}^{n-1} \alpha_i^2,$$

where $\alpha = (1 - \rho^n)/n(1 - \rho)$ and $\alpha_i = [1 - \rho^{(n-i)}]/n(1 - \rho)$.

Singleton (1980) showed that the sample statistics V, V^*, and D are consistent estimators of μ_V, μ_{V^*}, and μ_D. Further, V, V^*, and D are asymptotically normally distributed, with variances given by

$$\lim_{T \to \infty} T \text{ var }(V) = 2 \sum_{s=-\infty}^{\infty} [E(R_t R_{t+s})]^2,$$

$$\lim_{T \to \infty} T \text{ var }(V^*) = 2 \sum_{s=-\infty}^{\infty} [E(R_t^* R_{t+s}^*)]^2, \qquad (21)$$

$$\lim_{T \to \infty} T \text{ var }(D) = 2 \sum_{s=-\infty}^{\infty} [E(\theta_t \theta_{t+s})]^2.$$

(Recall that $\theta_t = R_t^* - R_t$.)

[4] The eigenvalues were computed using the International Math and Science Library (IMSL) routine EIGRS; the numerical integration was performed using IMSL routine DCADRE.

Evaluating these variances for the model posited in this paper gives

$$\text{var}(V) = \frac{2\alpha^4(1+\rho^2)}{T(1-\rho^2)^3}\sigma_\epsilon^4,$$

$$\begin{aligned}\text{var}(V^*) = \frac{2}{T}\Bigg\{&\bigg(\frac{\alpha^2}{1-\rho^2} + \sum_{i=1}^{n-1}\alpha_i^2\bigg)^2 \\ &+ 2\sum_{j=1}^{n-2}\bigg(\sum_{i=1}^{n-1-j}\alpha_i\alpha_{i+j} + \frac{\rho^j\alpha^2}{1-\rho^2}\\ &+ \sum_{i=1}^{j}\alpha\alpha_i\rho^{j-1}\bigg)^2 \\ &+ \frac{2}{1-\rho^2}\bigg[\frac{\rho^{(n-1)}\alpha^2}{1-\rho^2} + \sum_{i=1}^{n-1}\alpha\alpha_i\rho^{(n-1-i)}\bigg]^2\Bigg\}\sigma_\epsilon^4,\end{aligned} \quad (22)$$

$$\text{var}(D) = \frac{2}{T}\bigg[\bigg(\sum_{i=1}^{n-1}\alpha_i^2\bigg)^2 + 2\sum_{j=1}^{n-2}\bigg(\sum_{i=1}^{n-1-j}\alpha_i\alpha_{i+j}\bigg)^2\bigg]\sigma_\epsilon^4.$$

Comparison of Small Sample and Asymptotic Distributions

Recall that the numerical example was constructed to mimic quarterly data in which the short rate was a 3-month rate and the term of the long rate was 20 years. The autoregressive parameter of the short-rate process, ρ, was set at 0.95.[5] For the small sample distributions, the sample size, T, was set at 100 (quarterly) observations. Table 1 reports the means of the asymptotic distributions of V, V^*, and D, for $\rho = 0.95$, $T = 100$, and $n = 80$. The variance of the short-rate innovation is normalized at one ($\sigma_\epsilon^2 = 1$).

The asymptotic standard deviations reported in table 1 were obtained by evaluating the expressions (22) for the asymptotic variances of V, V^*, and D for a sample size of 100. Before turning to the calculations of the actual small sample distributions, it should be noted that table 1 itself contains some evidence that the asymptotic distributions are not close approximations to the small sample distributions for samples of 25 years of quarterly data. Because V and V^* are both sample variances, neither random variable can take on negative values. Using asymptotic distribution theory to approximate the distribution of V^*, however, one would conclude that V^* is normally distributed with mean 3.802 and standard deviation 4.619, implying that V^* is less than zero for over 20 percent of its distribution.

[5] In a first-order autoregression of quarterly observations on 3-month Treasury bill yields (sample period 1950:I–1982:I), the estimated autoregressive parameter was 0.953, with a standard error of .03. (These data were obtained from Salomon Brothers, Inc. 1982.)

EXCESS VOLATILITY

TABLE 1

Means and Standard Deviations of Asymptotic Distributions

Variable	Mean	Asymptotic Standard Deviation
V^*	3.802	4.619
V	.620	.150
D	3.182	3.139

The actual small sample distributions of V, V^*, and D are plotted in figure 1. In each of the three panels of figure 1, the distributions labeled a represent the small sample distributions of V^*, V, and D, assuming that the mean of the short-rate process is known a priori. The distributions labeled b represent the small sample distributions of V_s^*, V_s, and D_s when R_t and R_t^* are each expressed in deviations from their respective sample means instead of the population mean. The distributions labeled c in panels 1 and 3 represent the small sample distributions of V_s^* and D_s, respectively, when R_t^* is calculated using a terminal condition R_T^* and both R_t^* and R_t are expressed in deviations from the sample mean. The distributions labeled d represent the small sample distributions of spectral estimates. The distributions b, c, and d are explained more fully below.

Consider the distributions labeled a. If the mean of the underlying process is known, the sample variance is an unbiased estimate of the population variance (Anderson 1971, p. 448).[6] However, even when the mean is known, the sample variances are not closely approximated by the normal distribution. All three random variables have strongly skewed small sample distributions; the probability that V will take on a value less than its mean is 60 percent, and V^* and D each have a 65 percent probability of taking on values less than their respective means.

It is important to keep in mind that two unrealistically strong assumptions concerning the information available to the econometrician have been maintained in computing the small sample distributions represented by the a curves. First, the mean of the short-rate process has been assumed to be known a priori. Second, the perfect-foresight variance V^* has been calculated assuming that all of the $n-1$ postsample observations on the short rate, r_{T+1} to r_{T+n-1}, are available, enabling the econometrician to construct the perfect-foresight

---

[6] The means of the small sample distributions of V, V^*, and D were calculated making use of the fact that the mean of a quadratic form in normal deviates is equal to the sum of the eigenvalues of the quadratic form. For each of the three quadratic forms, the sum of the eigenvalues matched the analytically derived population mean (reported in table 1) to four decimal places.

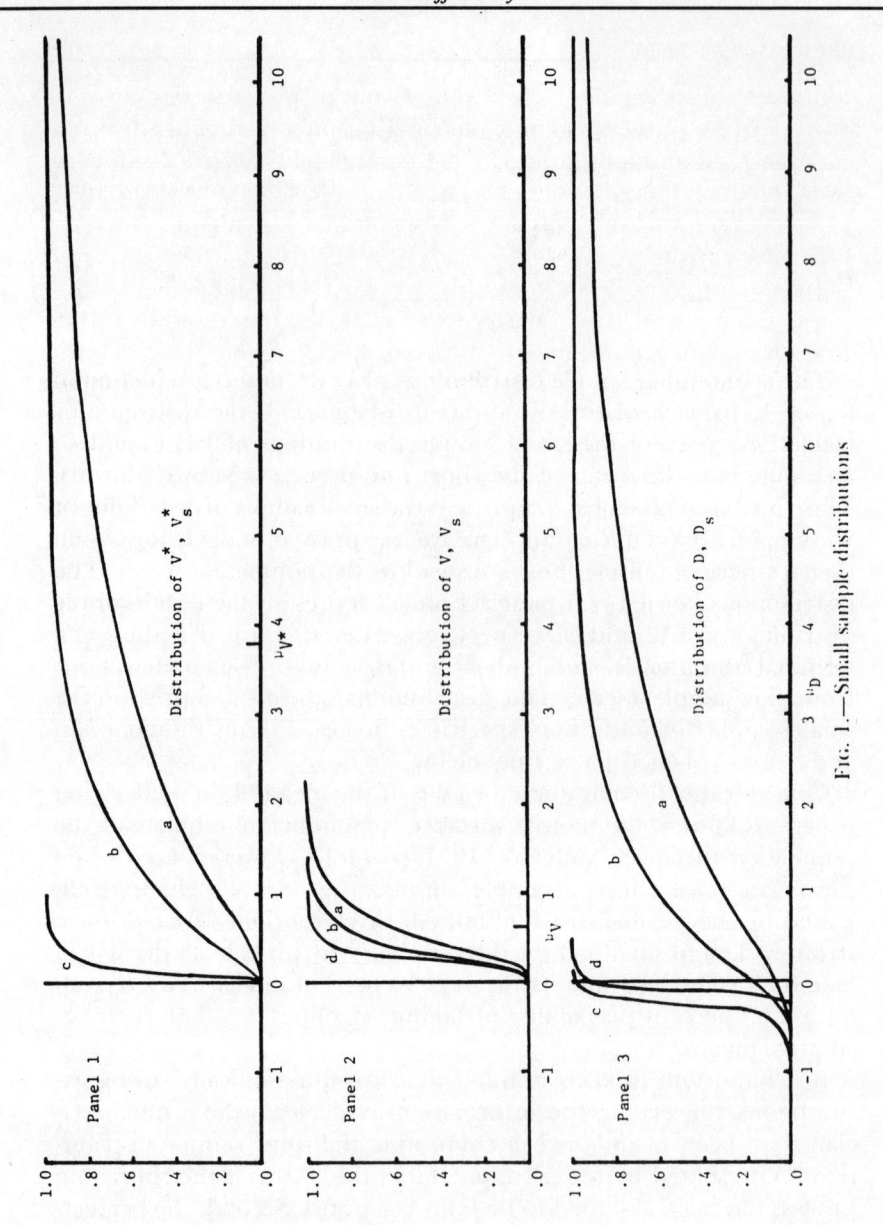

Fig. 1.—Small sample distributions

EXCESS VOLATILITY

long-rate series, R_1^* to R_T^*, without having to resort to any form of extrapolation of the short-rate data. Even under these unrealistically favorable assumptions concerning the availability of prior information and data, there is a 6.6 percent chance that the sample variance, V, will exceed its upper bound, V^*, if the null hypothesis of market efficiency is true.

In practice, the variance-bounds tests have been implemented using data on r_t and R_t in deviations from their sample means rather than deviations from population means. Let A_s denote the quadratic form representing the variance of R_t expressed in deviations from its sample mean.[7] The distribution of $V_s = \epsilon'A_s\epsilon$ is given by curve b in panel 2 of figure 1. When the population mean of R_t is not known a priori and the sample variance is expressed in deviations from the sample mean, the sample variance is a downward biased estimator of the population mean of var (R_t); the mean of V_s is 0.4251, as compared to the population mean of var (R_t) of 0.6200.

Similarly, the curve labeled b in panel 1 is the small sample distribution of V_s^* in which the vector of observations on the short rate is expressed in deviations from the sample mean before constructing the series on R_t^*. Again, expressing the data in deviations from the sample mean creates a downward bias: the mean of the distribution b is 1.537, less than half the value of the population moment, var (R_t^*), of 3.802. Because V_s^* is more strongly downward biased than V_s, expressing the data in deviations from sample means results in a net downward bias to $D_s = V_s^* - V_s$. When the data are expressed in deviations from sample means, D_s has a mean of 1.112, as compared to a population value of var (R_t^*) − var (R_t) of 3.182. Further, there is a 16.8 percent chance that the sample variance, V_s, will exceed its upper bound, V_s^*, if the null hypothesis of market efficiency is true.

II. Review of Previous Tests of Excess Volatility

In this section some of the test procedures implemented by Shiller and Singleton are reviewed in light of the findings concerning the small sample distributions of the variance-bounds test statistics.

---

[7] To construct the quadratic form A_s, take the matrix S and calculate the sum of the elements in each column. Denote the sum of the elements in the jth column as $m(j)$. Subtract $m(j)/100$ from each element of the jth column of the original matrix S, for $j = 1, 2, \ldots, 100$. Premultiplying this matrix by its transpose and multiplying by the scalar $\beta^2 T^{-1}$ gives the quadratic form A_s. In modifying A to form A_s, the degrees of freedom correction is automatically incorporated into A_s, since the rank of the quadratic form is reduced by one by the modification. Thus A has T nonzero eigenvalues, while A_s has $T - 1$ nonzero eigenvalues.

Shiller's Approach

In his empirical work on the volatility of stock prices and long interest rates (Shiller 1979, 1981a, 1981b, 1981c; Grossman and Shiller 1981), Shiller not only examines the basic upper bound on the variance of the long interest rate or stock prices, var (R_t) < var (R_t^*), but also formulates and presents empirical evidence on an upper bound on the variance of holding period yields.

In illustrating the apparent excess volatility of long interest rates in his 1979 paper, Shiller graphs actual AAA utility bond yields against a perfect-foresight long rate constructed from data on the 4–6-month prime commercial paper rate. In these graphs, the perfect-foresight long rate moves smoothly and remains within the band between 6.25 percent and 6.75 percent, while the actual long rate moves sharply and varies between 4.5 percent and 11.5 percent over the same period (1966:I–1977:III). Since the variance of the perfect-foresight long rate places an upper bound on the variance of the actual long rate, these graphs do appear to "stand in glaring contradiction" (p. 1213) to the efficient markets model.

In the absence of actual data on the postsample values of the short rate, Shiller computed the perfect-foresight long-rate series, R_t^*, recursively from an assumed terminal value, R_T^*,

$$R_t^* = \gamma R_{t+1}^* + (1 - \gamma)r_t, \tag{23}$$

where γ is a constant close to but less than one.[8] In the case of a pure discount bond, $\gamma = (n - 1)/n$. The terminal value, R_T^*, was assumed to be equal to the average short rate over the sample period. It is a simple matter to grind out the distribution of Shiller's approximation to the perfect-foresight long rate using the methods of the previous section. Let $\tilde{R}_t^*$ denote Shiller's approximation to R_t^* and $\tilde{V}^*$ the sample variance of $\tilde{R}_t^*$ expressed in deviations from the sample mean; $\tilde{V}^* = \epsilon'\tilde{B}_s\epsilon$, where $\tilde{B}_s$ is a symmetric matrix of order 100.[9]

---

[8] The parameter γ arises in Shiller's linearization of the basic term structure equation relating the long rate to future expected short rates. If a coupon bond is selling near par, the mean of the long rate ($\bar{R}$) will be approximately equal to the coupon rate (C). Shiller takes Taylor series expansions around $R_t = \bar{R} = C$ and $r_{t+j} = \bar{R} = C, j = 0, 1, \ldots, n - 1$, to obtain $R_t = [(1 - \gamma)/(1 - \gamma^n)] \sum_{j=0}^{n-1} \gamma^j r_{t+j}$, where $\gamma = 1/(1 + R_0)$ and R_0 is the point around which the equation is linearized. In practice, Shiller sets $R_0 = \bar{R}$ and thus linearizes around the mean of the long rate. For a pure discount bond, $C = 0$ and $\gamma = 1$ so that the long rate is a simple (unweighted) average of future short rates in the linearized model: $R_t = (1/n) \sum_{j=0}^{n-1} r_{t+j}$ (see Shiller 1979, pp. 1194–99).

[9] The quadratic form representing V^* was generated in the following way. The 100 × 100 matrix, $\tilde{L}$, which transforms the 100 observations on the short rate into 100 observations on R_t^*, was constructed by setting its first 21 rows equal to the first 21 rows of the previously defined matrix L. (This reflects the fact that the first 21 observations on R_t^* do not depend on the assumed terminal value $\tilde{R}_T^*$.) The assumption that R_T^* is equal to the average short rate over the sample period is imposed by setting each

EXCESS VOLATILITY

The distribution of the quadratic form $\epsilon'\bar{B}_s\epsilon$, which represents the sample variance of the perfect-foresight long rate constructed using Shiller's assumption concerning the terminal value of R_t^*, is given by the curve c in panel 1 of figure 1. The small sample variance $\epsilon'\bar{B}_s\epsilon$ has a mean of 0.1521 and a zero probability of taking on values greater than 1.1. As illustrated in panel 1, Shiller's method of obtaining an approximate series for R_t^*, when applied to this numerical example, results in an estimated variance of R_t^* that is severely biased downward. Not only is the expectation of $\epsilon'\bar{B}_s\epsilon$ far below the population mean of var (R_t^*) of 3.802, there is a zero probability that $\epsilon'\bar{B}_s\epsilon$ will take on a value even one-third the value of the population mean of var (R_t^*).

Curve c in panel 3 shows the distribution of $\epsilon'[\bar{B}_s - A_s]\epsilon$, which represents the difference between Shiller's approximation to the variance of R_t^* and the variance of R_t, both expressed in deviations from sample means. The measure of the perfect-foresight variance is more strongly biased than the sample variance of R_t, and the difference between the sample variances is negative throughout 99.9 percent of its distribution. The mean of $\epsilon'[\bar{B}_s - A_s]\epsilon$ is -0.2729, as compared to the population mean of the difference var (R_t^*) − var (R_t) of 3.182. Thus, even though markets are efficient in this example and the *population* variance of R_t^* is several times the population variance of R_t, *estimating* the variance of R_t^* by imposing the terminal condition that R_T^* equal the sample mean of the short rate induces so much downward bias that the sample variance of R_t exceeds its estimated upper bound with probability .999.

It is important to point out that Shiller's 1979 paper uses the constructed variable $\tilde{R}_t^*$ only for the purpose of illustrating the notion of excess volatility of long interest rates; none of his formal statistical tests of market efficiency in the bond market use the constructed variable. In his subsequent paper addressing the volatility of stock prices (1981b), however, Shiller does use a perfect-foresight stock price variable that parallels $\tilde{R}_t^*$ in its construction. That is, the perfect-foresight stock price variable is constructed by assuming a terminal value equal to the sample mean of the (detrended) actual stock price

---

element of the last (100th) row equal to 0.01. Using $\tilde{L}(i, j)$ to denote the element in the ith row and the jth column of $\tilde{L}$, rows 99–22 were generated recursively by setting $\tilde{L}(i, j) = (79/80)\tilde{L}(i + 1, j)$ for $i \neq j$ and $\tilde{L}(i, j) = (79/80)\tilde{L}(i + 1, j) + (1/80)$ for $i = j$. The 100 observations on $\tilde{R}_t^*$ are given by $\tilde{R}_t^* = \tilde{L}S\epsilon$, where S is the previously defined matrix that transforms the vector of disturbances into the vector of realizations on the short rate. In order to reflect the fact that $\tilde{R}_t^*$ is expressed in deviations from the sample mean, take the matrix product $\tilde{L}S$ and calculate, for each column, the sum of the elements in the column. Denote the sum of the elements in the jth column as $m(j)$. Subtract $m(j)/100$ from each element of the jth column of the original matrix product $\tilde{L}S$, for $j = 1, 2, \ldots, 100$. Premultiplying this matrix by its transpose and dividing by T gives the matrix $\bar{B}_s$.

series and solving backward recursively. While the numerical values in this paper were chosen with the bond market rather than the stock market in mind, the two problems are similar enough that the evidence of downward bias in Shiller's estimate of the perfect-foresight long rate may indicate that his estimate of the standard deviation of the perfect-foresight stock price index could be seriously downward biased as well.

The formal statistical evidence of excess volatility of long interest rates presented in Shiller's 1979 paper was based primarily on a comparison of the variance of the holding period return of a long-term bond with the variance of the short interest rate. As derived by Shiller, the linearized holding yield ($\tilde{H}_t$) is given by

$$\tilde{H}_t = \frac{R_t - \gamma_n R_{t+1}}{1 - \gamma_n}, \qquad (24)$$

where $\gamma_n = \gamma(1 - \gamma^{n-1})/(1 - \gamma^n)$, γ is as previously defined, and n is the number of periods in the long-term bond. Directly from equation (24), var $(\tilde{H}_t)$ can be expressed as a function of var (R_t) and cov (R_t, R_{t+1}). The cov (R_t, R_{t+1}) term is then substituted out to obtain an expression for var $(\tilde{H}_t)$ in terms of var (R_t), var (r_t), γ_n, and ρ_{rR} (the correlation coefficient between R_t and r_t). The upper bound on var $(\tilde{H}_t)$ is obtained by maximizing this expression with respect to var (R_t); thus the bound itself is not a function of var (R_t):

$$\max_{\text{var}(R_t)} \text{var}(\tilde{H}_t) = \frac{\text{var}(r_t)\rho_{rR}^2}{1 - \gamma_n^2}. \qquad (25)$$

Since ρ_{rR}^2 must be less than one, the variance of the short rate places an upper bound on the variance of $\tilde{H}_t$. Shiller's basic inequality restriction is

$$\sigma(\tilde{H}_t) \leq a\sigma(r_t), \qquad (26)$$

where $a = 1/\sqrt{1 - \gamma_n^2}$.

Using the fact that $\tilde{H}_t$ is approximately serially uncorrelated (and assuming that $\tilde{H}_t$ is normally distributed), Shiller uses the χ^2 distribution to compute a one-sided 95 percent confidence interval for the sample statistic $\hat{\sigma}(\tilde{H}_t)$. A lower bound on $\hat{\sigma}(\tilde{H}_t)$, denoted $\sigma_m(\tilde{H}_t)$, is then calculated from the confidence interval. Since the small sample distribution of the estimated standard deviation of the short rate, $\hat{\sigma}(r_t)$, is not known, Shiller does not conduct a formal statistical test of the hypothesis that the standard deviation of the holding period return satisfies the upper bound in equation (26). However, comparison of the point estimates of the standard deviation of the short rate with the lower bound on the holding period yield seems discouraging from

EXCESS VOLATILITY

the point of view of proponents of market efficiency. In four of the six data sets studied by Shiller, the lower bound on the variability of holding period yields, $\sigma_m(\tilde{H}_t)$, was twice as large as the point estimate of its upper bound. For the other two data sets, $\sigma_m(\tilde{H}_t)$ was narrowly within the estimated upper bound.[10]

To see that inequality (26) will tend to be biased toward rejection of the null hypothesis of market efficiency, note that under Shiller's assumptions an unbiased estimate of the variance of the holding period yield can be obtained simply by taking the sum of squares of the deviations of $\tilde{H}_t$ from its sample mean and dividing by degrees of freedom $(T - 1)$ rather than sample size (T). However, the short rate, r_t, is highly serially correlated, so that the same correction for degrees of freedom will not eliminate the downward bias in the sample variance of r_t. Recall that in the numerical example studied in this paper the actual long rate is proportional to the short rate. Thus the small sample distribution of the variable $V = \epsilon' A_s \epsilon$ characterizes the sample variances of either R_t or r_t, under different normalizations of the error variance, σ_ϵ^2. For the numerical values examined above, the downward bias was substantial even for a sample of 25 years worth of data; the sample standard deviation of r_t is $\sqrt{.4251/.6200} = 82.8$ percent of the population standard deviation of r_t.

Using the notation var (r_t) for the population variance of r_t and vâr (r_t) for the sample variance of r_t (computed by taking deviations from the sample mean and dividing by T), we denote the relative bias of vâr (r_t) by[11]

$$\frac{E[\text{vâr } (r_t)]}{\text{var } (r_t)} = 1 - \frac{\text{var } (\bar{r}_t)}{\text{var } (r_t)}, \qquad (27)$$

where var $(\bar{r}_t)$ is the variance of the sample mean of r_t. If the short rate is generated by an AR1 process, equation (27) can be evaluated by straightforward algebra:

$$\frac{E[\text{vâr } (r_t)]}{\text{var } (r_t)} = 1 - \frac{1 + \rho}{(1 - \rho)T} + \frac{2\rho(1 - \rho^T)}{(1 - \rho)^2 T^2}. \qquad (28)$$

---

[10] In the paper discussed above, Shiller's long-term interest rate data consisted of data on bonds with very long terms to maturity; in some data sets, the bonds were 25-year bonds, in other data sets, the bonds were consols. In a subsequent paper (1981c), Shiller reports the sample standard deviations of the 6-month Treasury bill rate and the holding period yield on medium term bonds (1-year–4.5-year Treasury notes). For the sample period 1955:II–1972:II, the sample standard deviation of the holding period yield did not exceed the point estimate of its upper bound for Treasury notes with 1 year or 1.5 years to maturity. For Treasury notes with 2–4.5 years to maturity, the sample standard deviation of the holding period yield did exceed the point estimate of the upper bound, but the violation was smaller in magnitude than the violations reported in Shiller (1979), based on the very long-term bonds.

[11] I am grateful to James H. Stock for suggesting the closed-form expressions (eqq. [27] and [28]) for the bias of the sample variance of the short rate.

TABLE 2

Data Set	T (1)	n (2)	γ_n (3)	ρ (4)	$\hat{\sigma}(r)$ (5)	$a\hat{\sigma}(r)$ (6)	k (7)	$\frac{a\hat{\sigma}(r)}{k}$ (8)	$\hat{\sigma}(\hat{H})$ (9)	$\sigma_m(\hat{H})$ (10)
1. U.S., quarterly 1966:I–1977:II	46	100	.978	.95	1.78	8.55	.70	12.21	19.5	16.5
2. U.S., monthly 1969:1–1974:1	61	288	.992	.983	1.77	14.03	.53	26.47	27.4	23.6
3. U.S., annual 1960–76	17	25	.925	.815	1.39	3.66	.79	4.63	9.82	7.65
4. U.S., annual 1919–58	40	25	.940	.815	1.86	5.44	.90	6.04	5.48	4.58
5. U.K., quarterly 1956:I–1977:II	86	∞	.980	.95	2.84	14.3	.81	17.65	34.4	30.4
6. U.K., annual 1824–1929	106	∞	.968	.815	1.17	4.66	.96	4.85	4.95	4.43

NOTE.—Explanation of symbols: T = sample size; n = number of periods in the long-term bond; γ_n = constant involved in the linearization of the model; ρ = autoregressive parameter in the short-rate process; $\hat{\sigma}(r)$ = estimated standard deviation of the short rate, calculated by taking deviations from the sample mean and dividing by $T - 1$; $a\hat{\sigma}(r)$ = estimated upper bound, where $a = 1/(1 - \gamma_n^2)^{1/2}$; k = relative bias of $\hat{\sigma}(r)$; $\hat{\sigma}(\hat{H})$ = estimated standard deviation of the linearized holding period yield; $\sigma_m(\hat{H})$ = critical value for the lower 5 percent tail of $\hat{\sigma}(\hat{H})$, assuming that $\hat{\sigma}^2(\hat{H})$ is distributed χ^2.

Using equation (28) we can calculate and correct for the bias to the upper bound of the holding period yield. The accuracy of the bias calculation depends, of course, on the validity of the assumption concerning the time-series process generating the short rate. Table 2 calculates the bias to the upper bound on the holding period yield for each of the six data sets studied in Shiller's 1979 paper. In calculating the bias, I retain the assumption that quarterly data on short-term interest rates (3–6-month maturities) are well approximated by an AR1 process with an autoregressive parameter of 0.95. I also assume that the AR1 parameter for monthly, as opposed to quarterly, observations on the short rate is $0.95^{1/3} = 0.983$ and that the AR1 parameter for annual observations is $(0.95)^4 = 0.815$.

Columns 2, 3, 5, 6, 9, and 10 of table 2 reproduce certain columns of table 1 in Shiller (1979).[12] Column 7 reports the value of k, the relative bias of $\hat{\sigma}(r)$; $E[\hat{\sigma}(r)] = k\sigma(r)$, which was calculated as

$$k = \left\{\left(\frac{T}{T-1}\right)\left[1 - \frac{1+\rho}{(1-\rho)T} + \frac{2\rho(1-\rho^T)}{(1-\rho)^2 T^2}\right]\right\}^{1/2}. \quad (29)$$

As indicated by column 7, the small sample bias in $\hat{\sigma}(r)$ ranges from trivial for the data set with a sample period of 100 years ($k = 0.96$) to substantial for the monthly data set with a sample period of 5 years

---

[12] Shiller also reports a "tighter" upper bound on $\sigma(\hat{H})$ as well as bounds that are applicable when r_t is nonstationary in his table 1.

EXCESS VOLATILITY

($k = 0.53$). Column 8 reports the estimated upper bound, corrected for small sample bias: $a\hat{\sigma}(r)/k$.

Without the bias correction, the upper bound on the volatility of holding period yields was violated on the basis of the sample statistics, that is, $\sigma_m(\tilde{H}) > a\hat{\sigma}(r)$, for four of the six data sets. Further, in the four data sets that violate the bound, $\sigma_m(\tilde{H})$ is roughly twice its estimated upper bound.

The bias correction changes the result of only one data set (data set 2) from violation to nonviolation of the bound. However, the three data sets that still violate the bound are not independent observations against the null hypothesis since they cover substantially the same historical period: each of the three contains the period 1966–76.

After the upper bound has been corrected for bias, the evidence of excessive volatility of holding period yields is considerably less dramatic: for three virtually nonoverlapping sample periods (U.S., 1969–74; U.S., 1919–58; and U.K., 1824–1929), the standard deviation of holding period yields is narrowly within the upper bound. The standard deviation of holding period yields exceeds the upper bound by a margin of 35–75 percent for the three data sets that contain the period 1966–76.[13]

Singleton's Approach

While Singleton (1980) reports some results based on holding period returns, his paper focuses primarily on the upper bound on the long interest rate:

$$\text{var}(R_t) \leq \text{var}(R_t^*). \tag{30}$$

Using spectral analysis, Singleton computes consistent estimates not only of var (R_t) and var (R_t^*) but also of the covariance matrix of the estimates of var (R_t) and var (R_t^*). Like Shiller, Singleton finds that his point estimates of var (R_t) exceed the point estimates of the upper bound, var (R_t^*). Further, Singleton conducts asymptotic tests of whether the variance of the long rate satisfies the upper bound. For

[13] When the bound on the volatility of holding period yields is applied to the stock market, Shiller finds that the estimated standard deviation of the holding period yield is more than five times the upper bound, even with a sample period of over one hundred years (Shiller 1981b). Considering the sample size, correcting for the bias induced by eliminating the sample mean will not substantially change the magnitude of the violation. However, the exponential trend in the stock price series had been removed from the stock price data as well as the dividend data in order to achieve stationarity. One would have to assess the biases potentially induced by the detrending in order to reliably interpret the strength of the evidence against the market efficiency hypothesis in the context of the stock market. Shiller emphasized that the results could be sensitive to detrending, stating that "assumptions about public knowledge or lack of knowledge of the long run growth path are important" (1981b, p. 421, n. 2).

each of the three data sets analyzed, the violation of the upper bound is statistically significant at the 5 percent level.

Singleton does not use postsample data on the short rate to literally construct a data series on the perfect-foresight long rate R_t^*. Instead, his estimates of var (R_t^*) are computed on the basis of observations on the short rate and on the theoretical relationship between the short rate and the perfect-foresight long rate. The perfect-foresight long rate in Shiller's linearized model is given by

$$R_t^* = \delta \sum_{s=0}^{n-1} \gamma^s r_{t+s}, \qquad (31)$$

where γ is a constant (see n. 8), and $\delta = (1 - \gamma)/(1 - \gamma^n)$. Based on the known linear relationship between R_t^* and r_t,[14] the spectral density of R_t^* can be expressed as a function of the spectral density of r_t:

$$S_{R*}(\lambda) = g^2(\lambda) S_r(\lambda), \quad |\lambda| \leq \pi, \qquad (32)$$

where $g^2(\lambda) = \delta^2[1 - 2\gamma^n \cos(n\lambda) + \gamma^{2n}]/[1 + \gamma^2 - 2\gamma \cos(\lambda)]$ and $S_{R*}(\lambda)$ and $S_r(\lambda)$ are the spectral density functions of R_t^* and r_t, respectively. The variance of R_t^* is equal to the integral of the spectral density of R_t^*:

$$\text{var } R_t^*) = \int_{-\pi}^{\pi} S_{R*}(\lambda) d\lambda. \qquad (33)$$

Singleton estimated the variance of the perfect-foresight long rate by estimating $S_r(\lambda)$ from the short-rate data, calculating the function $S_{R*}(\lambda)$ implied by equation (32), and integrating the estimate of $S_{R*}(\lambda)$ over the interval $-\pi$ to π. Before computing the spectral densities of r_t and R_t, Singleton removed the sample mean and sample (linear) trend from the data, which consisted of monthly observations over the sample period 1959:1–1971:6.

In his appendix, "Model Restrictions on the Spectral Densities of Interest Rates," Shiller discusses the theoretical relationship (eq. [32]) between the spectral densities of R_t^* and r_t in the limiting case in which the long bond is a consol. He notes that $g^2(\lambda)$ is equal to one at $\lambda = 0$ and declines monotonically as λ increases. Further, $g^2(\lambda)$ drops rapidly as λ increases for γ close to one.

The fact that $g^2(\lambda)$ declines monotonically implies that the low fre-

---

[14] For purposes of illustration, I assume that the parameters as well as the form of the relationship between R_t^* and r_t are known. In the context of the term structure of interest rates, treating γ as known is, in my view, a sensible interpretation of the model, since γ is defined as $\gamma = 1/(1 + R_0)$, where R_0 is the point around which the linearization is taken. In practice, both Shiller and Singleton set $R_0 = \bar{R}_t$ and linearize around the sample mean of the long rate. Empirical results reported below indicate that the results are perceptibly but not dramatically affected by varying the value of γ.

EXCESS VOLATILITY

quency components of $S_r(\lambda)$ account for a greater proportion of the variance of R_t^* than of the variance of r_t. A sample mean and sample trend will tend to "fit" much of the low frequency movement in a small sample of time-series data. Thus, taking deviations from the sample mean and trend will bias a sample variance downward by underestimating the low frequency movements of the series. This downward bias in the sample variance of the short rate will be "amplified" by the filter function $g^2(\lambda)$ to create a (proportionally) greater downward bias in the estimate of var (R_t^*).[15] Elimination of the sample mean and sample trend will also create a downward bias in the sample variance of the actual long rate, R_t. However, because the spectrum of the actual long rate is much less concentrated at the low frequencies than the perfect-foresight long rate, the bias in the sample variance of R_t will tend to be smaller than the bias to the estimated variance of R_t^*.

The Appendix describes a procedure for constructing quadratic forms that represent the sample statistics calculated by applying the spectral estimators to 100 quarterly observations generated by the model economy specified in Section I.[16] The finite sample distributions of these quadratic forms are plotted in figure 1. The distribution of the spectral estimate of var (R_t^*) was so close to the distribution of Shiller's estimator that it could not be plotted distinctly from curve c in panel 1. The mean of the spectral estimate of var (R_t^*) was 0.183, as compared to the population value of var (R_t^*) of 3.802. The curve labeled d in panel 2 gives the small sample distribution of the spectral estimate of var (R_t), which has mean 0.288, as compared to the population value of var (R_t) of 0.62. The small sample distribution of the spectral estimate of the difference is given by curve d in panel 3. In the numerical example, $\mu_D =$ var (R_t^*) − var (R_t) = 3.2. However, because of the severe bias to the spectral estimate of var (R_t^*), the spectral estimate of D has mean −0.104 and has a 92.12 percent probability of taking on values less than zero. That is, the estimated variance of R_t exceeds the estimated upper bound 92 percent of the time, even though the null hypothesis of market efficiency holds, by construction, in the numerical example.

---

[15] The point that Singleton's estimate of the upper bound was biased downward by the detrending is stated in Shiller (1981c): "Perhaps [Singleton's] more dramatic results stem from his decision to subtract linear trends from the data, and in effect assume the trends were known by the market in advance. Any such assumption has the effect of reducing the uncertainty about future interest rates and thus reducing the permissible volatility of long rates according to the expectations model. Ultimately the inequality tests must hinge on our priors as to the reasonableness of such assumptions" (p. 76).

[16] Because the long rate in the numerical example is assumed to be the yield on a pure discount bond, the parameters in the linearized term structure relation (eq. [31]) can be specified a priori; $\gamma = 1$ and $\delta = 1/n$.

TABLE 3
Estimated Noncentral Second Moment of R_t^* and R_t

Term of Long Bond	Sample Period	Estimated Noncentral Second Moment of R_t^*	Estimated Noncentral Second Moment of R_t
10 years	1950:I–1973:I	22.03	19.00
20 years	1950:I–1963:I	17.79	10.90

Note.—Noncentral second moments were calculated as $(1/T) \sum_{t=1}^{T} x_t^2$, where T denotes the number of observations.

Some Unbiased Estimates

The paper closes by reporting some unbiased estimates of the variance-bounds statistic var (R_t^*) − var (R_t). Following a suggestion of Richard Porter, the noncentral second moments of R_t^* and R_t were calculated. Assuming that the long rate does not contain a liquidity premium, R_t^* and R_t have the same mean, μ. Since

$$E(R_t^{*2}) = \text{var}(R_t^*) + \mu^2$$

and (34)

$$E(R_t^2) = \text{var}(R_t) + \mu^2,$$

the difference between the noncentral moments is an unbiased estimate of var (R_t^*) − var (R_t).

Data series on R_t^* for 10- and 20-year Treasury bonds were constructed from data on the 3-month Treasury bill rate using Shiller's linearized term structure relation:

$$R_t^* = \frac{1-\gamma}{1-\gamma^n} \sum_{s=0}^{n-1} \gamma^s r_{t+s}, \quad \gamma = \frac{1}{1+R_0}, \quad (35)$$

where $n = 40$ for the 10-year bond and $n = 80$ for the 20-year bond. The term structure equation was linearized around the point $R_0 = 0.01$. Data were available on the short rate for 1950:I–1982:IV.[17] In order to avoid using a terminal condition, the R_t^* series for the 10-year bond was calculated for $t = 1950:I–1973:I$ and the R_t^* series for the 20-year bond was calculated for $t = 1950:I–1963:I$. The estimated noncentral second moments of R_t^* and R_t are reported in table 3.[18]

---

[17] The data were from Salomon Brothers, Inc. (1982).
[18] If the term structure relation is linearized around $R_0 = 0.02$ instead of 0.01, the sample noncentral second moment of R_t^* is 21.19 for the 10-year bond and 15.22 for the 20-year bond. With quarterly data, R_0 is a quarterly (nonannualized) interest rate.

EXCESS VOLATILITY

According to table 3, the difference between the estimated noncentral second moments of R_t^* and R_t, which is an unbiased estimate (assuming no liquidity premium) of var (R_t^*) − var (R_t), is 3.03 for the 10-year bonds and 6.89 for the 20-year bonds.[19] The empirical finding that var (R_t) is within the upper bound imposed by var (R_t^*) will not be reversed if the model is generalized to include a (constant) positive liquidity premium in the long rate. If R_t does contain a liquidity premium, the population mean of R_t would exceed the population mean of R_t^*. Thus the assumed absence of a liquidity premium biases the estimate of var (R_t^*) − var (R_t) downward.

The average of the squared observations on the short rate for the sample, 1950:I–1982:IV, was 34.53. Since r_t, R_t, and R_t^* all have the same population mean in the absence of a liquidity premium, these estimates of the noncentral second moments imply that the variances are in the order predicted by the efficient markets model:

$$\text{var } (r_t) > \text{var } (R_t^*) > \text{var } (R_t). \tag{36}$$

Since var (R_t^*) − var (R_t) = var (θ_t), table 3 provides estimates of the market's standard error in predicting R_t^*. For the 10-year bonds, the market's standard error in forecasting R_t^* was 174 basis points; for 20-year bonds, the standard error was 262 basis points.

The postwar quarterly data on the 3-month Treasury bill rate, 10-year Treasury bond yield, and perfect-foresight Treasury bond yield are plotted in figure 2. The perfect-foresight 10-year bond yield, denoted by the dotted line, starts to rise steeply in the early 1970s, reflecting the unusually high short rates in 1979–82. The rise in the long rate may have appeared, in 1969, to indicate overreaction to the contemporaneous rise in short rates, or excess volatility. However, history has clearly exonerated the sharp rise in the long rate in the late 1960s and early 1970s. In studying figure 2, one is struck, not by the volatility of the long rate, but by the accuracy of the long rate in predicting the explosion of short rates in the early 1980s.

---

[19] In calculating the noncentral second moment of R_t, the sample period was limited to the exact sample available for the corresponding perfect-foresight long rate; i.e., the 1973:II–1982:IV data on the 10-year long rate and the 1963:II–1982:IV data for the 20-year long rate were not used. If the noncentral second moment of R_t itself were of primary interest, using all of the available data would be efficient. However, in the variance-bounds problem, one is primarily interested in obtaining a precise estimate of the *difference* of the two moments. The sampling variability of the difference of the two sample moments is an increasing function of the variance of the sample second moment of R_t and a decreasing function of the covariance of the sample second moments of R_t and R_t^*. Including the additional data on R_t reduces the variance of the sample moment of R_t but also reduces the covariance of the two sample moments. Based on the conjecture that the effect of the covariance term dominates, the additional observations available for R_t were excluded.

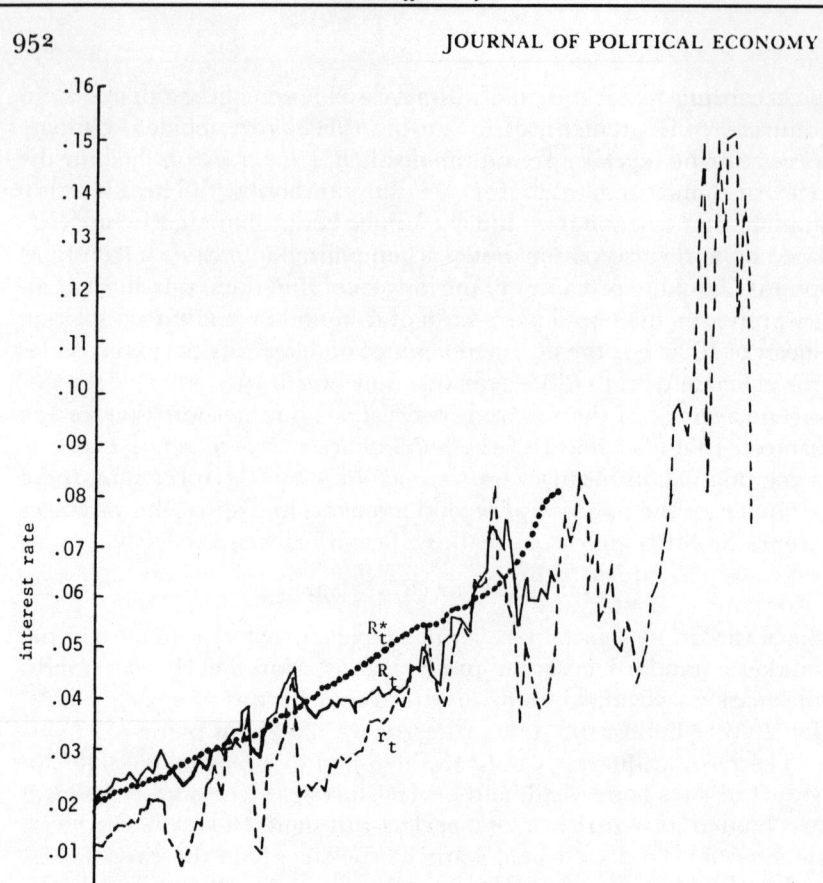

FIG. 2.—Plot of r_t, R_t, and R_t^*, U.S. Treasury securities: r_t = 3-month Treasury bill rate, denoted by dashed line; R_t = 10-year Treasury bond yield, denoted by solid line; R_t^* = perfect-foresight 10-year rate, denoted by dotted line. The sample period for the short-rate data is 1950:I–1982:IV. The perfect-foresight long rate was computed using Shiller's linearized term structure relation, $R_t^* = [(1 - \gamma)/(1 - \gamma^n)] \sum_{i=0}^{n-1} \gamma^i r_{t+i}$, for $\gamma = 1/(1 + R_0)$, where R_0 is the point around which the term structure relation is linearized. For the R_t^* series plotted in figure 2, $R_0 = 0.01$ and $n = 40$. The series on R_t^* was computed only up to 1973:I, the last observation for which the necessary postsample data were available. The data, from Salomon Brothers (1982), consist of observations taken during January, April, July, and October of each year.

III. Conclusions

The basic problem addressed by this paper—that the upper bound on the volatility of long interest rates or stock prices is difficult to measure in small samples—was certainly recognized by the authors who formulated the variance-bounds tests. In fact, Shiller refrains from conducting formal statistical tests of the hypothesis that the holding period yield on long interest rates is within its upper bound

EXCESS VOLATILITY

on the grounds that the small sample distribution of the upper bound is unknown. In the conclusion to his 1979 paper, Shiller acknowledges that he cannot rule out the possibility that the population variance of the short rate exceeds the sample variance by a sufficiently large margin to exonerate the market efficiency hypothesis, "since we have no real information in small samples about possible trends or long cycles in interest rates. Indeed, some would claim that short-term interest rates may be unstationary and hence have infinite variance. The fact that the lower bound on the left-hand side exceeds the sample value of the right-hand side may be interpreted as safely telling us, then, that we must rely on such unobserved variance or expected explosive behavior of short rates if we wish to retain expectations models" (pp. 1213–14).

Shiller's subsequent papers on long interest rate volatility (1981a, 1981c) reach the same general conclusion: the observed volatility of long interest rates can be justified as the rational response to new information about future short-term interest rates only if the population variance of short interest rates is much larger than the sample variance. In addition to random sampling error, Shiller cites several situations in which the population variance of the short rate would tend to exceed the sample variance: the short-rate process is nonstationary; the short-rate process is stationary but inappropriately detrended;[20] or the short-rate data suffer from what Krasker (1980) has termed the "peso problem"—market participants rationally perceived the possible occurrence of a major disturbance that was not realized within the sample period.[21]

---

[20] LeRoy and Porter (1981) also recognized the importance of the treatment of trends. They write, "The question remains whether the resulting series [earnings and price data for Standard and Poor's Composite Index, ATT, GE, and GM, corrected for inflation and earnings retention] can be assumed to obey the stationarity requirement. There appears to be some evidence of downward trends, although they are not clearly significant. We have decided to neglect such evidence and simply assume that the series are stationary since otherwise it is necessary to address such difficult questions as ascertaining to what degree stockholders can be assumed to have foreseen the assumed trend in earnings. It seems preferable to assume instead that there exist long cycles in the earnings series, implying that a sample of only a few decades may well appear nonstationary.... We do not argue that this treatment is entirely adequate, nor do we in any way minimize the problem of nonstationarity; the dependence of our results on the assumption of stationarity is probably their single most severe limitation" (pp. 568–69).

[21] Krasker (1980) examines an "apparent" failure of market efficiency in which the forward rate for Mexican pesos persistently underpredicted the future spot rate. Krasker argued that market participants rationally perceived a significant probability that the peso would be devalued. Since the devaluation did not occur within the sample period, the rational discounting of the peso in forward contracts gave rise to strong serial correlation in the spot-rate forecast errors.

This paper is focused primarily on the small sample properties of the variance-bounds test when the variances are expressed in deviations from the sample mean rather than the population mean. Even in the absence of other problems, such as nonstationarity, inappropriate detrending, and the peso problem, the results of the paper indicate that the variance-bounds test statistics tend to be seriously biased toward rejection of the null hypothesis of market efficiency when the variances are computed in deviations from sample means. For samples of the size typically used in the variance-bounds tests, the magnitude of the bias is substantial. The strategy of focusing on the consequences of taking deviations from the sample mean was not motivated by a judgment that other potential problems with the data, such as the peso problem, are empirically unimportant. To the contrary, my guess is that, for some data sets, the peso problem is probably very important. However, the effects of the peso problem are extremely difficult to assess empirically since by definition it involves the effects of unrealized possible outcomes.

By taking into account the small sample properties of the variance-bounds statistics, the evidence of excess volatility of holding period returns and long rates is attenuated along several dimensions. First, the upper bound on the variance of 10- and 20-year long rates is not violated in the postwar U.S. quarterly data. Second, the violation of the upper bound on holding period yields is not robust with respect to sample period. Third, in data sets for which the variance of holding period yields still exceeds the upper bound, the magnitude of the violation is smaller, and no evidence has been presented that the violation of the upper bound is statistically significant.

Appendix

Procedure for Obtaining the Small Sample Distributions of the Spectral Estimates

A vector of 101 observations on the short rate is given by $S\epsilon$, where S is a square matrix of order 101 as given in equation (12) and ϵ is a vector of 101 observations on the disturbance. Before computing the spectra, Singleton transformed the data by removing the sample mean and sample trend and by prewhitening by the filter $1 - .85L$. Defining X as the 101×2 matrix consisting of a column of ones and the column vector $[1, 2, 3, \ldots, 101]'$, and I the 101×101 identity matrix, construct $M = [I - X(X'X)^{-1}X']$. Construction of a 100×101 matrix, denoted H, which quasi differences the data with the filter $1 - .85L$ is straightforward. A vector of 100 observations on the transformed short-rate data is represented as $HMS\epsilon$. Denote the matrix product HMS as the 100×101 matrix D: $D = HMS$.

EXCESS VOLATILITY

Construct the complex-valued matrix P,

$$P = \frac{1}{\sqrt{2\pi T}} \begin{bmatrix} e^{i1\lambda_0} & e^{i2\lambda_0} & \cdots & e^{iT\lambda_0} \\ e^{i1\lambda_1} & e^{i2\lambda_1} & \cdots & e^{iT\lambda_1} \\ \vdots & \vdots & & \vdots \\ e^{i1\lambda_{T-1}} & e^{i2\lambda_{T-1}} & \cdots & e^{iT\lambda_{T-1}} \end{bmatrix}, \qquad (A1)$$

where T is the sample size (in this case 100) and $\lambda_j = 2\pi j/T, j = 0, \ldots, T - 1$. The Fourier transform of the data is given by $PD\epsilon$.

The unweighted sum of the periodogram ordinates could be obtained by computing $\epsilon' D' \bar{P}' PD\epsilon$, where $\bar{P}$ is the conjugate of P. Singleton's estimates were weighted averages of the periodogram ordinates, however; he first smoothed the ordinates with an inverted V window (of width nine ordinates) and multiplied by a filter function, denoted $f(\lambda)$. The filter function is used to "recolor" the data and, in the case of the perfect-foresight long rate, also incorporates the theoretical filter $g^2(\lambda)$ given in equation (32). Denote the column vector of T periodogram ordinates as $\mathbf{z}$. Applying the window can be represented by premultiplying $\mathbf{z}$ by a square matrix V of order T. Define a diagonal matrix F, also of order T, in which the kth diagonal element is $f(\lambda_j)$, $\lambda_j = 2\pi(k - 1)/T$. The sum of the weighted periodogram ordinates is given by $\mathbf{u}FV\mathbf{z}$, where $\mathbf{u}$ is a T-element row vector of ones. Denote the T-element row vector $\mathbf{u}FV$ as $\mathbf{w}$ and construct the $T \times T$ diagonal matrix W, in which the ith diagonal element of W is the ith element of the vector $\mathbf{w}$. Thus the weighted sum of periodogram ordinates is given by

$$\epsilon' D' \bar{P}' WPD\epsilon. \qquad (A2)$$

Multiply the matrix product $D'\bar{P}'WPD$ by the scalar $2\pi/T$ and denote the resulting matrix as C:

$$C = \frac{2\pi}{T} D'\bar{P}'WPD. \qquad (A3)$$

The matrix C is a real, symmetric matrix of order 101.

Thus the sum of the weighted spectral density function can be expressed as a quadratic form in normal deviates. The small sample distributions of the spectral estimates of the variances can be obtained by applying the procedure described in Section I to the quadratic form $\epsilon' C \epsilon$.

All that remains is to specify the filters used to weight the smoothed periodogram ordinates. In the case of the spectral estimate of var (R_t^*), the filter was

$$f_{v^*}(0) = \frac{1}{(1 - .85)^2},$$

$$f_{v^*}(\lambda_j) = \frac{1 - \cos(n\lambda_j)}{n^2(1 - \cos \lambda_j)[1 - 2(.85)\cos \lambda_j + (.85)^2]}, \qquad (A4)$$

where $\lambda_j = 2\pi j/T, j = 1, 2, \ldots, T - 1$, and $n = 80$.

To obtain the spectral estimate of var (R_t), the filter was

$$f_v(\lambda_j) = \frac{\alpha^2}{1 - 2(.85)\cos \lambda_j + (.85)^2}, \qquad (A5)$$

where $\lambda_j = 2\pi j/T, j = 0, 1, \ldots, T - 1$, and α is the factor of proportionality between the short rate and the long rate in the numerical example; $\alpha = (1 - \rho^n)/n(1 - \rho)$.

References

Amsler, Christine. "The Term-Structure of Interest Rates in an Expanded Market Model." Ph.D. dissertation, Univ. Pennsylvania, 1980.
Anderson, Theodore W. *The Statistical Analysis of Time Series.* New York: Wiley, 1971.
Blanchard, Olivier J., and Watson, Mark W. "Bubbles, Rational Expectations, and Financial Markets." Working Paper no. 945. Cambridge, Mass.: Nat. Bur. Econ. Res., July 1982.
Flavin, Marjorie A. "Time Series Evidence on the Expectations Hypothesis of the Term Structure." *Carnegie-Rochester Conference Series on Public Policy,* vol. 20. Amsterdam: North-Holland, in press.
Grossman, Sanford J., and Shiller, Robert J. "The Determinants of the Variability of Stock Market Prices." *A.E.R. Papers and Proc.* 71 (May 1981): 222–27.
Krasker, William. "The 'Peso Problem' in Testing the Efficiency of Forward Exchange Markets." *J. Monetary Econ.* 6 (April 1980): 269–76.
LeRoy, Stephen F., and Porter, Richard D. "The Present-Value Relation: Tests Based on Implied Variance Bounds." *Econometrica* 49 (May 1981): 555–74.
Michener, Ronald W. "Variance Bounds in a Simple Model of Asset Pricing." *J.P.E.* 90 (February 1982): 166–75.
Nerlove, Marc; Grether, David M.; and Carvalho, José L. *Analysis of Economic Time Series: A Synthesis.* New York: Academic Press, 1979.
Pesando, James. "Time Varying Term Premiums and the Volatility of Long-Term Interest Rates." Unpublished manuscript. Toronto: Univ. Toronto, Dept. Econ., July 1979.
Salomon Brothers, Inc. *Analytical Record of Yields and Yield Spreads.* New York: Salomon Brothers, April 1982.
Shiller, Robert J. "The Volatility of Long-Term Interest Rates and Expectations Models of the Term Structure." *J.P.E.* 87 (December 1979): 1190–1219.
———. "The Use of Volatility Measures in Assessing Market Efficiency." *J. Finance* 36 (May 1981): 291–304. (*a*)
———. "Do Stock Prices Move Too Much to Be Justified by Subsequent Changes in Dividends?" *A.E.R.* 71 (June 1981): 421–36. (*b*)
———. "Alternative Tests of Rational Expectations Models: The Case of the Term Structure." *J. Econometrics* 16 (May 1981): 71–87. (*c*)
Singleton, Kenneth J. "Expectations Models of the Term Structure and Implied Variance Bounds." *J.P.E.* 88 (December 1980): 1159–76.

[3]
Econometric Aspects of the Variance-Bounds Tests: A Survey

Christian Gilles
Board of Governors of the Federal Reserve System

Stephen F. LeRoy
University of Minnesota

We survey the variance-bounds tests of asset-price volatility, stressing the econometric aspects of these tests. The first variance-bounds tests of the present-value relation reported apparently striking evidence of excess volatility of asset prices. The statistical significance of the results, however, was either marginal or, in the case of model-free tests, impossible to assess. Moreover, the tests were soon criticized for a number of biases. Various other tests of the present-value relation were later developed, avoiding in different degrees the econometric problems attending the first-generation tests. The majority of these second-generation tests also found excess volatility, though sometimes of borderline statistical significance. This finding of excess volatility is robust and is difficult to explain within the representative-consumer, frictionless-market model.

The variance-bounds debate—whether asset prices are more volatile than traditional models imply—has

---

We have received helpful comments from Marjorie Flavin, Wayne Joerding, Hashem Pesaran, Richard Porter, Gary Shea, Robert Shiller, Jon Sonstelie, Douglas Steigerwald, and Kenneth West. This article should not be interpreted as reflecting the views of the Board of Governors of the Federal Reserve System or its staff.

engaged a number of economists over the past decade. At first glance, the variance-bounds controversy seems rooted in ideological considerations: as in debates in other areas of economics, it raises questions about the rationality of markets. In all such debates, the issue is the success of current neoclassical theory in explaining economic phenomena. Some argue for fundamental departures from the neoclassical program.

Fortunately, the variance-bounds debate has largely avoided the meaningless verbal exchanges that are typical of ideological disagreements. Genuine scientific differences, which are resolvable by further theoretical and empirical work, characterize this debate. As a result, progress has been rapid and a convergence of opinion appears to be occurring. While it is an exaggeration to characterize the variance-bounds debate as a model of how scientific work should proceed, the case could be made.

Econometric, not ideological or theoretical, issues have dominated the variance-bounds debate. As a consequence, evaluating the empirical evidence of excess volatility is difficult. Further, the debate is based on simulations in settings where straightforward analytical demonstrations are available. In many cases, these simulations obscure rather than clarify the main lines of development. As things stand, the time required to gain a foothold in this literature is excessive.

In this article, we introduce the variance-bounds debate and stress econometric issues—unlike LeRoy (1984, 1989) and West (1988b) who focus on theoretical issues. While the exposition is intended to be self-contained, readers should consult the original papers.

The theory and first-generation tests due to Shiller (1979, 1981) and LeRoy and Porter (1981) are reviewed in Section 1. Discussion of theory is brief to avoid duplication of LeRoy (1984, 1989) and West (1988b), and because those readers who wish to master the econometric aspects of the debate will already be familiar with the underlying theory. In Section 2, we present Flavin's (1983) and Kleidon's (1986b) econometric critiques of the Shiller–LeRoy–Porter findings of excess volatility. Here theoretical analysis of the econometric properties of two-observation samples drawn from the autoregressive dividend model replaces the simulation methods used by Flavin and Kleidon. By relying on analytical methods, readers should see the intuition underlying Flavin and Kleidon's claim that the original tests are biased toward rejection. In Section 3, we turn to the "second-generation" variance-bounds tests, which also found excess volatility of asset prices using alternative econometric methods. We believe that these second-generation tests reinforce the conclusion based on the first-generation tests; asset-price volatility exceeds that predicted by the simplest present-value model. Granted this provisional conclusion, the question becomes why asset-price volatility is high. Here the literature has not arrived at even a provisional conclusion. Several possibilities are discussed in Section 4. Conclusions are offered in Section 5.

1. First-Generation Tests

1.1 The variance-bounds theorems

The variance-bounds inequalities are implications of the present-value relation. In our usage, this means that an asset's price is equal to the expected present value of the asset's payments, discounted at a constant rate.[1] Two questions arise: (i) Why focus on testing the present-value relation rather than consumption-based asset pricing more generally? (ii) Why test only the volatility implications of the present-value relation, rather than all its implications for the covariances between asset yields and prices? With regard to (i), whether yields of financial assets are sufficient to explain their prices is an important substantive question. If so, the principle of parsimony can be invoked in future modeling to justify ignoring the aggregate effects of risk aversion.

With regard to (ii), the same question—Why focus on one particular implication of the theory to the exclusion of all others?—could be directed equally well to tests of market efficiency that focus on return autocorrelations. The answer then would be that if, contrary to the present-value relation, future price changes can be inferred from past prices, analysts can recommend trading rules that outperform buy and hold in expected return. With regard to the variance-bounds tests, the alternative to the present-value relation might be that stock prices are driven by protracted waves of optimism or pessimism. The impli-

---

[1] The constancy assumption has caused misinterpretation: in the finance literature, it is not customary to include constancy of the discount rate in the definition of the present-value relation [e.g., Merton (1987)]. This element of generality in the finance literature's definition of the present-value relation is an outgrowth of the practice in elementary finance instruction of portraying net present value as the single unambiguously correct way to think about all problems in finance (in preference to such alternatives as internal rate of return as a criterion for capital budgeting, for example). In practice, the important problem in applying the present-value relation is to determine the magnitude of the adjustment for risk that is appropriate in the setting under consideration.

The problem of determining asset prices generally and that of determining what discount rate to use in the present-value relation are related tautologically. In general equilibrium, it makes no difference whether the analyst determines the price of financial assets directly, or indirectly from the present-value relation after determining the equilibrium discount factor. We follow here the practice, common among nonfinancial economists, of analyzing asset pricing without explicit reference to the present-value relation, and then formulating the present-value relation as a falsifiable special case by assuming constancy of the discount rate. Empirical testing then determines whether the present-value relation appears in fact to be false.

The difference between these two usages is entirely semantic—our purpose is not to urge one framework or the other, but only to alert readers to a possible source of misunderstanding.

cation of excessive volatility is tested directly by variance-bounds tests. Such informal discussion suggests that variance-bounds tests have different power than regression-based tests under different alternative hypotheses and therefore merit independent study.

The main variance-bounds theorem is now reviewed. Define p_t^*, the ex post rational price of stock at date t (the term is Shiller's), as the present discounted value of future dividends:[2]

$$p_t^* \triangleq \sum_{i=1}^{\infty} \beta^i d_{t+i}. \tag{1}$$

The present-value relation says that actual stock price is the conditional expectation of ex post rational price

$$p_t = E(p_t^* | I_t), \tag{2}$$

where I_t is investors' information.

Under assumptions to be specified, the variance of ex post rational price and that of actual price are related by

$$V(p_t^*) = V(p_t) + \frac{\beta^2 V(r_t)}{1 - \beta^2}, \tag{3}$$

where r_t represents excess return:

$$r_t \triangleq d_t + p_t - E(d_t + p_t | I_{t-1}). \tag{4}$$

(Note our terminology: we use "return" and "rate of return" where others sometimes use "payoff" and "return," respectively.) To derive (3), note that (1) and (2) imply

$$p_t = \beta E(d_{t+1} + p_{t+1} | I_t)$$

or

$$p_t = \beta(d_{t+1} + p_{t+1} - r_{t+1}), \tag{5}$$

using (4). Now update (5) by one period and use the result to substitute out p_{t+1} in (5). Iterating and using (1), there results

$$p_t = p_t^* - \sum_{j=1}^{\infty} \beta^j r_{t+j}.$$

Assume now that $V(r_t)$ is constant over time, as occurs, for example, under a linear covariance-stationary dividends process when information revelation is regular (as in the example below). Shifting the

---

[2] We let the symbol $\triangleq$ denote the defining equality.

Variance-Bounds Tests

rightmost term to the left side and taking variances (noting that the r_{t+j}'s are mutually uncorrelated), there results

$$V(p_t) + 2\operatorname{Cov}\left(p_t, \sum_{j=1}^{\infty} \beta^j r_{t+j}\right) + \frac{\beta^2 V(r_t)}{1-\beta^2} = V(p_t^*). \quad (6)$$

Because rational forecasting implies in addition that p_t and r_{t+j} have zero covariance, (6) implies (3). Dropping subscripts, the latter equation becomes

$$V(p^*) = V(p) + \frac{\beta^2 V(r)}{1-\beta^2}. \quad (7)$$

Equation (7) underlies all the variance-bounds tests discussed in this paper. It says that the variance of ex post rational price equals the sum of the variance of actual price and that of returns (where the latter is multiplied by a constant which depends on the discount rate). If investors have little information about future dividends, then the variance of price is low. Returns, however, buffeted by the largely unexpected realizations of dividends, are highly volatile. In the opposite case in which agents can accurately predict dividends into the distant future, the variance of price is almost as high as that of ex post rational price. Returns, on the other hand, are very smooth.

LeRoy and Porter outlined two types of volatility tests: bounds tests and orthogonality tests [the terms are due to Durlauf and Hall (1989)]. The simplest bounds test is

$$V(p) \leq V(p^*),$$

a direct consequence of (7). A less straightforward bounds test is the LeRoy-Porter lower bound on $V(p)$. Define H_t to be the information set consisting of current and past dividends alone and take $\hat{p}_t$ to be the price that would prevail under H_t:

$$\hat{p}_t \triangleq E(p_t^* | H_t).$$

Then, assuming that I_t is at least as informative as H_t, the rule of iterated expectations implies that

$$\hat{p}_t = E(p_t | H_t),$$

but the conditional expectation of any random variable x is less volatile than x itself, implying

$$V(\hat{p}_t) \leq V(p_t)$$

or, assuming stationarity,

$$V(\hat{p}) \leq V(p). \quad (8)$$

This lower bound on $V(p)$ is of interest primarily because it is equivalent to West's inequality on return volatility, discussed below.

The simplest orthogonality test of asset-price volatility determines whether $V(p^*)$, $V(p)$, and $V(r)$ are consistent with (7). If instead $V(p)$ and $V(r)$ are too large to be consistent with (7), the orthogonality of price and returns is rejected in favor of the hypothesis that these variables are negatively correlated [in view of (6), if $V(p_t) + \beta^2 V(r_t)/(1 - \beta^2)$ exceeds $V(p_t^*)$, the covariance term must be negative].

1.2 An example
An extended example will facilitate understanding of the variance-bounds theorems and will aid in the exposition of the sampling problems that attend their empirical implementation. Suppose that dividends follow a first-order Markov process

$$d_{t+1} = \lambda d_t + \epsilon_{t+1}, \qquad (9)$$

where $E(\epsilon_t) = 0$, $V(\epsilon_t) = 1$, $|\lambda| < 1$, and the ϵ_t are serially independent. Here the mean of the dividend process is set to zero since a nonzero mean would drop out of all variance expressions. Further, agents are assumed to have sufficient information to forecast dividends perfectly up to m periods in advance. However, agents have no information about dividends beyond $t + m$ other than the information conveyed by dividends up to $t + m$. This all-or-nothing specification is restrictive if taken literally; its advantage is to provide a simple parameterization of the amount of information available to investors. As a consequence, comparison of actual and ex post rational stock prices is very easy, since the ex post rational stock price process is a limiting case ($m = \infty$) of the class of actual stock price processes.

The present-value relation yields

$$p_t^m = \beta d_{t+1} + \cdots + \beta^m d_{t+m} + \beta^{m+1} E_{t+m}(d_{t+m+1}) + \beta^{m+2} E_{t+m}(d_{t+m+2}) + \cdots, \qquad (10)$$

where p_t^m is the actual price of stock. Using (9) to form expectations and simplifying, (10) becomes

$$p_t^m = \frac{\beta\lambda}{1 - \beta\lambda} d_t + \sum_{i=1}^{m} \frac{\beta^i \epsilon_{t+i}}{1 - \beta\lambda}. \qquad (11)$$

We now can compute the variance of p_t^m:

$$V(p_t^m) = \frac{\beta^2 \lambda^2}{(1 - \lambda^2)(1 - \beta\lambda)^2} + \frac{\beta^2 - \beta^{2(m+1)}}{(1 - \beta^2)(1 - \beta\lambda)^2}. \qquad (12)$$

$V(p_t^m)$ rises with m toward an asymptote,

Variance-Bounds Tests

$$V(p_t^\infty) = \frac{\beta^2(1+\beta\lambda)}{(1-\lambda^2)(1-\beta\lambda)(1-\beta^2)}, \quad (13)$$

which is just the variance of the ex post rational stock price.

Now we evaluate the variance of the one-period returns. Equation (5) implies that

$$r_{t+1}^m = d_{t+1} + p_{t+1}^m - \beta^{-1}p_t^m.$$

Substituting (11) for p_t^m and p_{t+1}^m and taking the variance, we get

$$V(r_t^m) = \frac{\beta^{2m}}{(1-\beta\lambda)^2}. \quad (14)$$

Notice that $V(p_t^\infty)$, $V(p_t^m)$, and $V(r_t^m)$ as given by (13), (12), and (14), respectively, satisfy

$$V(p_t^\infty) = V(p_t^m) + \frac{\beta^2 V(r_t^m)}{1-\beta^2},$$

agreeing with (7).

1.3 Implementation

Shiller's (1981) implementation of an operational test of the inequality $V(p_t) \le V(p_t^*)$ was simple and direct—more so than that of LeRoy and Porter, as will be seen below. To correct for trend, Shiller divided through by constant growth rate trends. To understand Shiller's resolution of the problem that p_t^* is not observable, notice that the ex post rational price (1) is the solution to the recursion

$$p_t^* = \beta(p_{t+1}^* + d_{t+1}) \quad (15)$$

that satisfies the condition

$$\lim_{t\to\infty} \beta^t p_t^* = 0. \quad (16)$$

Shiller simply replaced p_t^* by the solution to (15) that satisfies instead the terminal condition

$$p_T^* = \frac{1}{T}\sum_{t=1}^{T} p_t. \quad (17)$$

Denote by $p_{t|\bar{p}}^*$ the observable version of p_t^* generated by (15) and (17).

Shiller constructed sample estimates of the variances of p_t and $p_{t|\bar{p}}^*$ in the usual way as the average squared deviation of each variable from its own mean. Using a century-long data set, Shiller found that the standard deviation of actual stock prices exceeded that of the ex post rational stock prices by a factor of 5.59. Although no significance tests were reported, he interpreted this result as constituting rejection of the variance-bounds inequalities.

As noted in Section 1.1, LeRoy and Porter defined their null hypothesis from the equality version (7) of the variance-bounds relation. They assumed that dividends and stock prices, adjusted for trend as described below, were generated by a covariance-stationary bivariate linear process, with parameters restricted by (7). A simplified and intuitive version of the LeRoy–Porter implementation goes as follows: (i) estimate a linear autoregressive model for dividends and estimate β as the reciprocal of 1 plus the average rate of return on stock; (ii) estimate $V(p_t^*)$ by applying the present-value relation (1) directly to the model for dividends (thus avoiding the problem that p_t^* is unobservable); (iii) estimate $V(r_t)$ from the observable series of one-period returns; and (iv) estimate $V(p_t)$ from a linear model for p_t. It was found that the point estimate of each of the two terms on the right-hand side of (7) by itself exceeds the term on the left-hand side, indicating rejection of the variance bounds. However, the associated confidence intervals based on asymptotic distributions were so wide that the rejection of (7) was of borderline statistical significance.

LeRoy and Porter corrected for trend, not by implementing a mechanical trend adjustment, but by reversing the effect of the variables which cause the trend: inflation and corporate retained earnings.[3] Assuming that the returns per unit of capital are covariance stationary, the LeRoy–Porter algorithm should produce stationary series for price and dividends. Instead, LeRoy and Porter noted (1981, p. 569) that the adjusted series showed some evidence of a downward trend, but the LeRoy–Porter implementation of the trend correction was flawed, as Kleidon (1986b, note 4) pointed out.[4]

---

[3] Specifically, inflation was removed from the data by dividing a commodity price index into dividends, earnings, and prices. To reverse the effect of earnings retention, it was assumed that the value of stock equals the product of a quantity index representing the amount of physical capital held by firms and a price index representing the dollar value per unit of this capital. If it is assumed that the physical capital acquired with retained earnings is purchased at the same price as currently available capital is valued, and is equally productive, then data on retained earnings can be used to compute recursively the price and quantity variables.

[4] In the 1988 version of this paper, we provided a corrected exposition of the algorithm and LeRoy and Parke implemented it in the 1988 version of their 1990 paper, using the 112-year sample of Shiller instead of the LeRoy–Porter postwar sample. The downward trend in the supposedly trend-adjusted series that LeRoy and Parke reported was even more pronounced in the 112-year sample than that which LeRoy and Porter had reported. We do not know the reason for this downward trend, but it clearly invalidates the LeRoy–Porter trend correction and renders it of secondary interest (except, perhaps, to researchers interested in investigating the cause of the downward trend, which is worthy of study in its own right). Because the trend correction failed at its assigned task, detailed description of it was deleted from this paper and that of LeRoy and Parke (the earlier versions of these papers are available from the authors).

Variance-Bounds Tests

2. The Critics

2.1 Flavin[5]

Flavin's (1983) paper made two criticisms of Shiller's econometric tests. The first was that both the variance of p_t and that of p_t^* are estimated with downward bias in small samples. Further, the effect is more severe for p_t^* than for p_t, implying possible reversal of the empirical counterpart of the variance-bounds inequalities even if the present-value relation is true. The second is that Shiller's procedure for calculating an observable version of p_t^* also induces bias toward rejection.

To understand Flavin's first criticism, we review the elementary statistics involved in estimating the variance of a population. If a sample $\{x_1, x_2, \ldots, x_n\}$ is drawn from a common distribution with known mean μ, the average squared deviation around the population mean yields an unbiased estimator of the variance:

$$\frac{E\left[\sum_{i=1}^{n}(x_i - \mu)^2\right]}{n} = \sigma^2. \tag{18}$$

Note that it is not necessary to assume that the x_i are mutually uncorrelated.

If the mean must be estimated, however, the variance estimator constructed by substituting the sample mean for the population mean in (18) is biased toward zero. The standard remedy is to reduce the degrees of freedom by 1:

$$\hat{\sigma}^2 = \sum_{i=1}^{n} \frac{(x_i - \bar{x})^2}{n - 1}.$$

The resulting estimator is unbiased only under the additional assumption that the x_i are uncorrelated. Flavin pointed out that both p_t and p_t^* are autocorrelated positively. Therefore reducing degrees of freedom by 1 will not provide an unbiased estimator of the variance of either p_t or p_t^*. Further, p_t^* is more strongly autocorrelated than p_t, implying that the variance of p_t^* is estimated with a greater downward bias than that of p_t. Flavin's argument suggests that if the present-value model is rejected when the volatility statistic $\hat{V}(p^*) - \hat{V}(p)$ is negative, type I error (rejecting the null when it is true) will occur with high probability. Therefore, the rejection region should be chosen smaller. Ideally, one would prespecify the probability of type I error and choose the rejection region accordingly. Under model-free

---

[5] Kleidon's (1986a) paper, written contemporaneously with Flavin's (1983) paper, made independently many of the same points as Flavin.

tests, however, this is impossible because the distribution of the volatility statistic is unspecified.

To illustrate these assertions, we consider the sampling distribution of the sample variance of p_t^* and p_n based on samples of size 2, from the example in Section 1.2. The assumption of two-element samples is less restrictive than it might seem: a sample of size 2, but with observations separated by n periods, is qualitatively similar to a consecutive sample of size n. This is so because for large n, p_{t+n} is virtually independent of p_t, and similarly for p_{t+n}^* and p_t^*. We follow Flavin in assuming that the discount rate β is known. One would like to avoid this restrictive assumption, but the calculations to be presented would be rendered intractable if sampling variability of the estimate of β were considered. It is also assumed that p_t^* is measured correctly, pending discussion below.

Assume, as in Section 1.2, that individuals can forecast dividends up to m periods in the future. The sample variance of p_t^m is given by

$$\hat{V}_n(p_t^m) = (p_{t+n}^m - \bar{p})^2 + (p_t^m - \bar{p})^2, \tag{19}$$

where $\bar{p} = (p_{t+n}^m + p_t^m)/2$. Expression (19), which reflects the usual correction for degrees of freedom (the sum of squares is divided by the number of observations, 2, less 1) simplifies to

$$\hat{V}_n(p_t^m) = \frac{(p_{t+n}^m - p_t^m)^2}{2}.$$

We wish to take the expectation of the sample variance under the assumption that dividends follow (9). To do so, use (11) to write p_{t+n}^m as

$$p_{t+n}^m = \frac{\beta\lambda d_{t+n} + \sum_{i=1}^m \beta^i \epsilon_{t+n+i}}{1 - \beta\lambda}$$

$$= \frac{\beta\lambda(\epsilon_{t+n} + \cdots + \lambda^{n-1}\epsilon_{t+1} + \lambda^n d_t) + \sum_{i=1}^m \beta^i \epsilon_{t+n+i}}{1 - \beta\lambda}.$$

Using (11) again to obtain an expression for p_t^m, subtracting this from p_{t+n}^m, squaring, taking the expectation, and dividing by 2, we obtain

$$E[\hat{V}_n(p_t^m)] = \left[\frac{\beta^2\lambda^2(\lambda^n - 1)^2}{1 - \lambda^2} + \sum_{i=1}^n (\beta\lambda^{n+1-i} - \beta^i)^2 \right.$$

$$\left. + \sum_{i=n+1}^m (\beta^{i-n} - \beta^i)^2 + \sum_{i=m+1}^{m+n} \beta^{2(i-n)}\right]$$

$$\times [2(1 - \beta\lambda)^2]^{-1}, \tag{20}$$

Variance-Bounds Tests

for $n \leq m$, and

$$E\left[\hat{V}_n(p_t^m)\right] = \left[\frac{\beta^2\lambda^2(\lambda^n - 1)^2}{1 - \lambda^2} + \sum_{i=1}^{m} (\beta\lambda^{n+1-i} - \beta^i)^2 \right.$$

$$\left. + \sum_{i=m+1}^{n} (\beta\lambda^{n+1-i})^2 + \sum_{i=n+1}^{m+n} \beta^{2(i-n)}\right]$$

$$\times \left[2(1 - \beta\lambda)^2\right]^{-1}, \tag{21}$$

for $n > m$, and

We now use these expressions for the expectation of the sample variance to verify some properties of the bias of the variance estimators. First, in large samples, the variance of p_t^m is estimated without bias:

$$\lim_{n \to \infty} E\left[\hat{V}_n(p_t^m)\right] = V(p_t^m),$$

for all m and λ [let n go to infinity in (21) and observe that the result coincides with (12)]. It makes sense for the sample variance of p_t^m (corrected for degrees of freedom) to be an asymptotically unbiased estimator of $V(p_t^m)$ since p_{t+n}^m is approximately independent of p_t^m when n is large, even when λ is high (but less than unity).

Second, we have as a special case ($m = \infty$) of (20)

$$\lim_{n \to \infty} E\left[\hat{V}_n(p_t^*)\right] = V(p_t^*),$$

so the sample variance of p_t^* gives an asymptotically unbiased estimate of its population variance as well. With both actual and ex post rational stock price estimated without bias, there is no bias problem in large-sample tests.

For small samples and unrestricted m and λ, the sample variance of p_t^m underestimates its population variance for two reasons. First, with $\lambda > 0$, the positive autocorrelation of dividends induces a corresponding positive correlation between nearby values of p_t^m. The simple correction for degrees of freedom takes no account of this dependence. Second, since agents can foresee dividends up to m periods ahead, the dividend realizations upon which p_{t+n}^m is based overlap those on which p_t^m is based if $m > n$. Hence again bias results. If both of these conditions are absent (i.e., if $\lambda = 0$ and $m < n$), the sample variance is unbiased for any sample size:

$$E[\hat{V}_n(p_t^m)] = V(p_t^m)$$

---

[6] The (unavoidably tedious) verification of these equations involves isolating the coefficient of d_t and each of the $\epsilon_{t,n}$, squaring term-by-term, and using the facts (i) $E[(\epsilon_t)^2] = 1$; (ii) $E[(d_t)^2] = 1/(1 - \lambda^2)$; and (iii) d_t is independent of the $\epsilon_{t,r}$.

[verify the equality of the appropriately restricted versions of (21) and (12)].

Even if these conditions are met, the test statistic of the variance-bounds inequality is biased toward rejection—$V(p_t^n)$ is estimated without bias, but with n finite, $V(p_t^*)$ is underestimated as a result of the second effect noted above.[7] Thus, rejection of the variance-bounds inequality is likely in finite samples even if the null hypothesis is true. We see that whether dividends are autocorrelated or not, and however many periods ahead agents can forecast dividends, the sample variances provide an unbiased estimate of the corresponding population variances only in large samples, and that in finite samples this problem is more severe for the ex post rational price than for the actual price.

We turn now to Flavin's second criticism of Shiller's empirical implementation of the variance-bounds tests: bias is induced in the test statistic when an observable proxy is substituted for the unobservable p_t^* series [see also Shea (1989)]. As noted in Section 1, Shiller generated an observable version $p_{t|\bar{p}}^*$ of the p_t^* series from the recursion (15), supplying the remaining degree of freedom by imposing terminal condition (17). For each t, $p_{t|\bar{p}}^*$ in general gives a biased estimate of p_t^*, conditional on the realization of the sample. To show this, compare $p_{t|\bar{p}}^*$ to the series $p_{t|T}^*$ constructed as the solution to the recursion (15) satisfying the terminal condition $p_{T|T}^* = p_T$. By (2), $p_{T|T}^* = E(p_T^*|I_T)$. And if at any date $t \leq T$, $p_{t|T}^* = E(p_t^*|I_T)$, then

$$p_{t-1|T}^* = \beta(d_t + p_{t|T}^*) = \beta[d_t + E(p_t^*|I_T)] = E(p_{t-1}^*|I_T),$$

where the last equality follows from (15). This proves that at each date t in the sample, $p_{t|T}^* = E(p_t^*|I_T)$, but if $p_{t|T}^*$ is an unbiased estimate of p_t^*, then $p_{t|\bar{p}}^*$ must be biased to the extent that the two series differ. The fact that $p_{t|T}^*$ is a better proxy for p_t^* than $p_{t|\bar{p}}^*$ is now well understood and more recent variance-bounds papers, such as Mankiw, Romer, and Shapiro (1985) and Durlauf and Hall (1989), use the unbiased series.

We just established that $p_{t|T}^*$ estimates p_t^* without bias, but this does not mean that the sample variance of $p_{t|T}^*$ estimates the expectation of the sample variance of p_t^* without bias.[8] To see that the sample variance of $p_{t|T}^*$ will not be closely related to the expected sample variance of p_t^*, it suffices to observe that (except in the trivial

---

[*] For example, (13) implies that $V(p_t^*) = \beta^2/(1 - \beta^2)$, while (20) implies that $E[\hat{V}_n(p_t^*)] = \beta^2(1 - \beta^n)/(1 - \beta^2)$, which is smaller than $V(p_t^*)$.

[8] The latter, rather than the population variance of p_t^*, is the relevant parameter for comparison if we wish to separate the bias induced by incorrect measurement of p_t^*, under discussion here, from the general problem of small-sample bias discussed above.

Variance-Bounds Tests

certainty case) the population variance of $p^*_{t|T}$ is not constant over time even if the population variance of p^*_t is constant. Because $p^*_{T|T} = p_T$, we have $V(p^*_{T|T}) = V(p_T) < V(p^*_T)$, by the variance-bounds theorem, but $\lim_{t \to -\infty} V(p^*_{T-t|T}) = V(p^*_T)$ since the $p^*_{T-t|T}$ series converges toward the true p^*_t going backward in time.[9]

It is clear intuitively why substituting the observable $p^*_{t|T}$ for the unobservable p^*_t will reduce the estimated variance of ex post rational price. The two variables are equal, except that in $p^*_{t|T}$ the innovations in dividends occurring after the end of the sample are set equal to zero, which can only reduce the variance of ex post rational price. Of course, the effect is strongest near the end of the sample. It follows that in long samples the downward bias induced by substituting $p^*_{t|T}$ for p^*_t will be negligible since at most dates $p^*_{t|T}$ will be very close to p^*_t. For smaller samples, however, the effect may be far from negligible.

Flavin restricted her discussion to Shiller (1979, 1981) and Singleton (1980); therefore it remains to determine whether her criticisms apply to LeRoy and Porter (1981). The criticism just discussed does not apply since LeRoy and Porter made no use of an observable proxy for p^*_t. However, Flavin's first criticism of Shiller, that autocorrelation between successive elements of p^*_t induces downward bias in the variance estimate, does have an analog that applies to LeRoy and Porter. Suppose that dividends follow the first-order autoregression (9). In small samples, the estimated value of the autoregression parameter will be biased toward zero. The first-order term of the bias is $2/n$. This bias induces a corresponding downward small-sample bias in the estimated variance of p^*_t.

However, the bias problem is more complicated than this. As (13) indicates, the variance of p^*_t is a convex function of λ, but then, by Jensen's inequality, the expectation of the sample variance will be greater than the value indicated by (13), with the expected sample value substituted for the population value of each parameter. In sum then, the bias will depend on two effects: λ is estimated with downward bias, inducing downward bias in $V(p^*_t)$; sample variability in the estimated λ will induce upward bias in $V(p^*_t)$ because of the convexity of the variance expression. The outcome will depend on which effect is stronger.

Thus, about the LeRoy–Porter estimation procedure, Flavin's analysis tells us only what is in any case evident from first principles: any nonlinear estimation procedure will in general be subject to bias, with the sign of the bias impossible to determine *a priori*.

---

[9] Shea (1989) pointed out that the population variance of $p^*_{t|T}$ is nonconstant.

2.2 Kleidon

Kleidon's (1986b) criticism focused on Grossman and Shiller's (1981) contention that the smoothness of a time-series plot of p_t^* relative to p_t contradicts the variance-bounds theorems. To Kleidon such a conclusion is completely unwarranted. The variance-bounds inequalities refer to cross sections, not time series. That is, if we could run a large number of replications of the economy, the variance-bounds theorems imply that we would find that

$$\hat{V}(p_t) = \frac{\Sigma_i (p_{it} - \bar{p}_t)^2}{n-1} \leq \hat{V}(p_t^*) = \frac{\Sigma_i (p_{it}^* - \bar{p}_t^*)}{n-1}, \quad (22)$$

for each t, where i runs over replications of the economy, not time. Unfortunately, history occurs only once, so we have only a single value for i. The time-series inequality

$$\hat{V}(p) = \frac{\Sigma_t (p_t - \bar{p})^2}{n-1} \leq \hat{V}(p^*) = \frac{\Sigma_t (p_t^* - \bar{p}^*)^2}{n-1}, \quad (23)$$

for a single economy is what the data appear to contradict, but (22) and (23) are very different. Kleidon observed that nothing about the variance-bounds theorems guarantees that (23) will be satisfied, even in large samples. Hence reversal of (23) does not contradict the present-value relation.

To see Kleidon's point, we present two examples. The first is adapted from Kleidon (1986b, pp. 975–976). Suppose that a stock pays a dividend d_T only at some terminal date T. Take d_T to equal $\Sigma_{i=1}^{T} \epsilon_i$, where ϵ_i is an identically and independently distributed random variable with mean zero and variance unity (as above, the mean is suppressed). Assuming no discounting, we have

$$p_t^* = d_T = \sum_{i=1}^{T} \epsilon_i,$$

for all t, so

$$V(p_t^*) = T, \quad \text{for } t = 1,2,...,T.$$

Actual price is given by

$$p_t = E_t(p_t^*) = \sum_{i=1}^{t} \epsilon_i,$$

implying that

$$V(p_t) = t, \quad \text{for } t = 1,2,...,T.$$

Since $V(p_t) = t \leq V(p_t^*) = T$, if we look across economies, the variance-bounds inequality is satisfied at each date.

766

Variance-Bounds Tests

But imagine that only one replication of this experiment is available. The distributions of p_t and p_t^* corresponding to time-series plots of these variables are those conditional on the one realization of d_T. Since $p_t^* = d_T$, for all t, the conditional variance of p_t^* is zero, while p_t evolves randomly from $p_0 = 0$ to $p_T = d_T$. Plainly, p_t^* appears smoother than p_t.[10]

The second example is less transparent, but is nonetheless useful because it aids in the interpretation of Kleidon's simulations. Suppose that dividends follow a geometric random walk,

$$\ln(d_{t+1}) = \ln(d_t) + \epsilon_{t+1},$$

or, equivalently,

$$d_{t+1} = d_t \times \exp(\epsilon_{t+1}), \qquad (24)$$

where ϵ_{t+1} is distributed independently as normal with mean μ and variance σ^2 and $d_0 = 1$. Further, if $\mu + \sigma^2/2 = 0$, then $E(d_{t+1}|d_t) = d_t$, for all t, so that d_t is a martingale without trend.[11] Now take as a measure of ex post rational price the variable $p_t^*(1)$, defined by

$$p_t^*(1) \triangleq \beta(p_{t+1} + d_{t+1}), \qquad (25)$$

so that ex post rational price equals the present value of the position next year. Set p_t in the usual way:

$$p_t = E(p_t^*(1)|d_t, d_{t-1}, \ldots). \qquad (26)$$

Using the rule of iterated expectations, (25) and (26) imply that

$$p_t = \frac{\beta}{1-\beta} d_t, \qquad (27)$$

where we have assumed away bubbles and have used the fact that dividends have an expected growth rate of zero. Therefore p_t is a martingale as well. Because of (26), the variance-bounds theorem implies that p_t has lower volatility than $p_t^*(1)$ for each t. If we take the second moment around zero, we therefore have

$$E[p_t^2] < E[(p_t^*(1))^2],$$

---

[10] Analytically, we have $V(p_t^*|d_T) = 0$, for all t. As to the actual price, its conditional variance is given by

$$V(p_t|d_T) = V(p_t) - \frac{[\text{Cov}(p_t, d_T)]^2}{V(d_T)} = t - \frac{t^2}{T}.$$

This parabola has zeros at $t = 0$ and $t = T$, and is positive between the two.

[11] This is so because (24) implies that $E(d_{t+1}|d_t) = d_t E[\exp(\epsilon_{t+1})]$. The lognormal distribution has the property that $E[\exp(\epsilon_{t+1})] = \exp(\mu + \sigma^2/2) = 1$ if $\mu + \sigma^2/2 = 0$.

for each t, implying that if $\hat{\theta}$ is defined by

$$\hat{\theta} \triangleq \frac{\sum_{t=1}^{T} (p_t^*(1))^2}{T} - \frac{\sum_{t=1}^{T} p_t^2}{T},$$

then

$$E(\hat{\theta}) > 0. \tag{28}$$

The variance-bounds test associated with this inequality—check whether $\hat{\theta}$ is in fact positive—appears straightforward. Neither of Flavin's criticisms applies: by taking second moments around zero instead of the sample mean her first criticism is avoided,[12] while defining ex post rational price so that it is observable avoids her second criticism as well. Further, dividends have a constant mean by assumption, so it would seem that trend adjustment is not a problem. Yet if the variance-bounds test is conducted on simulated data, $\hat{\theta}$ turns out to be negative in almost every sample which has at least 50 or 100 draws.

Joerding (1986), who originated this example, interpreted it as reflecting a problem with random number generators [see also Joerding (1988), Kleidon and Koski (1992), and Joerding (1992)]. We take a different line. Note that, from (25) and (27), we have $p_t^*(1) = p_{t+1}$. Therefore $\hat{\theta}$ takes the simple form

$$\hat{\theta} = \frac{p_{T+1}^2 - p_1^2}{T}.$$

Because p_t is a martingale, the martingale convergence theorem [Billingsley (1979, p. 416)] implies that p_t will approach a constant on almost every sample path. In view of

$$p_{t+1} = p_t \exp(\epsilon_{t+1})$$

[an implication of (24) and (27)], the only way p_{t+1} can equal p_t is for the constant to which they converge to be zero. Thus the martingale convergence theorem implies that, in a sufficiently large sample, $T\hat{\theta}$ will be arbitrarily close to $-p_1^2$ with arbitrarily high probability. Even though the variance-bounds inequality is satisfied in the population, its sample counterpart is reversed with arbitrarily high probability in large samples.

The preceding examples give ample indication that a single time series, no matter how long, may fail to provide reliable estimates of the relevant population variances, but both examples were constructed under the assumption that dividends are nonstationary, a

---

[12] This device was used by Mankiw, Romer, and Shapiro (1985); see Section 3.

Variance-Bounds Tests

specification explicitly excluded by Shiller, and LeRoy and Porter. We have already seen that if dividends are generated by (9) with $|\lambda| < 1$, then the sample variances $\hat{V}(p)$ and $\hat{V}(p^*)$ based on a single time series are asymptotically unbiased estimates of $V(p)$ and $V(p^*)$. However, suppose that $\lambda = 1$, so that dividends are a random walk. Analysis of the geometric version of this case occupies the bulk of Kleidon's article.

Two preliminary points: first, a difference equation such as (9) does not completely characterize dividends, whatever the value of λ. Also needed is an initial condition. In taking $V(p_t)$ and $V(p_t^*)$ as constants, we adopted tacitly the usual convention that the drawing d_0 of dividends at some initial date is from the limiting distribution to which d_t converges. Under this convention, d_t is stationary, implying that its variance is constant. In the random-walk case, however, there is no limiting distribution. It follows that no matter what distribution d_0 is drawn from, d_t is not stationary. Accordingly, $V(p_t)$ and $V(p_t^*)$, although finite, are functions of time. Thus by taking $\lambda = 1$, Kleidon undertook to analyze the robustness of Shiller's conclusions when the underlying assumption of stationarity is a misspecification. This approach is in sharp contrast to Flavin, who accepted Shiller's stationarity assumption and analyzed small-sample problems.

Second, nonstationarity does not invalidate the variance-bounds theorems. The equation $p_t = E(p_t^*|I_t)$ implies that $V(p_t) \leq V(p_t^*)$, for each t, whether or not dividends are stationary. Rather, it is the assumption that these variances are constant over time, which is adopted in econometric implementation of the variance-bounds theorems, that is violated if stationarity fails.

Now we return to Kleidon's discussion of the Grossman–Shiller contention that the smoothness of p^* relative to p indicates violation of the variance-bounds inequalities. We have seen that if dividends are a random walk, the sample variances of p and p^* over a single time series do not correspond to the (nonconstant) cross-section variances that enter the variance-bounds theorems. Hence, the apparent smoothness of p^* relative to p is uninformative about whether the variance bounds are satisfied.

Sample variances from a single time series, as we have seen, are not good estimators of the corresponding (unconditional) population variances, but that does not mean that they are uninterpretable. We now prove that in small samples

$$E[\hat{V}_n(p_t^m)] > E[\hat{V}_n(p_t^*)] \tag{29}$$

is true if and only if

$$V(p_{t+n}^m|p_t^m) > V(p_{t+n}^*|p_t^*) \tag{30}$$

is true.[13] Thus, loosely, sample unconditional variances behave like population conditional variances.[14]

To prove the above assertion, recall that in two-element samples we have

$$\hat{V}_n(p_t^m) = \frac{(p_{t+n}^m - p_t^m)^2}{2}.$$

Taking expectations, using the fact that $V(p_{t+n}^m) = V(p_t^m)$, and simplifying, this becomes

$$E[\hat{V}_n(p_t^m)] = \gamma_0^m - \gamma_n^m, \qquad (31)$$

where $\gamma_n^m \triangleq \text{Cov}(p_t^m, p_{t+n}^m)$. Now, by the linearity of the dividend process and the present-value relation, the variance of p_{t+n}^m conditional on p_t^m is given by

$$V(p_{t+n}^m | p_t^m) = \gamma_0^m - \frac{(\gamma_n^m)^2}{\gamma_0^m}, \qquad (32)$$

the formula for residual variance from linear regression theory. Dividing (31) for finite m by (31) for $m = \infty$ and applying the same procedure to (32), we get

$$\frac{E[\hat{V}_n(p_t^m)]}{E[\hat{V}_n(p_t^*)]} = \frac{V(p_{t+n}^m | p_t^m)}{V(p_{t+n}^* | p_t^*)} \times A,$$

where $A \triangleq \gamma_0^m(\gamma_0^\infty + \gamma_n^\infty)/\gamma_0^\infty(\gamma_0^m + \gamma_n^m)$.

For small samples, γ_n^m/γ_0^m (the regression coefficient of p_{t+n}^m on p_t^m) is approximately equal to unity, leading to $A \cong 1$. Note here that "small samples" means that n is vanishingly small, not just finite. We conclude that

$$\frac{E[\hat{V}_n(p_t^m)]}{E[\hat{V}_n(p_t^*)]} \cong \frac{V(p_{t+n}^m | p_t^m)}{V(p_{t+n}^* | p_t^*)},$$

for all m and λ, and small n, implying that (30) is true if and only if (29) is true, as asserted.

Returning to Kleidon, consider the population inequality

$$V(p_{t+n} | p_t) > V(p_{t+n}^* | p_t^*), \qquad (33)$$

corresponding to the observed choppiness of p relative to p^*. In view of the result just reported, this inequality is consistent with the vari-

---

[13] This is a new result, the only one in this paper.

[14] In early drafts of his paper, Kleidon provided informal discussion along these lines, but deleted this material from the published version; see Kleidon (1986b, p. 967, note 9).

Variance-Bounds Tests

ance-bounds theorems, which state that the variance of p is less than that of p^* only if the respective variances are conditioned on the same information set. In (33), the conditioning sets are different, so the variance-bounds theorems do not contradict (33). In particular, the variance of p^*_{t+n} conditional on p^*_t has no economic meaning since agents cannot observe p^*_t at t (or, for that matter, at any later date).

Since the variance-bounds theorems do not apply to conditional variances, the inequality (33) must be studied from scratch. This analysis is done easily using the linear autoregression model for dividends. Explicit evaluation of the conditional variances shows that for small n, the inequality (33) is exactly what one should expect. Essentially because the recursion $p^*_t = \beta(d_{t+1} + p^*_{t+1})$ has no error, nearby values of p^* are much more highly correlated than nearby values of p [see LeRoy (1984, pp. 185–186)], leading to conditional variances lower for p^* than for p. If $\lambda = 0.99$, this effect persists for n as high as 50, while if $\lambda = 1$, any finite-sized sample will have the qualitative properties of a small sample.

The foregoing considerations suggest that if dividends follow a random walk, the sample variance of p is likely to exceed the sample variance of p^* for samples of any size, but is the random-walk model consistent with a sample standard deviation of p which exceeds that of p^* by a factor as high as 5.59, the value Shiller reported? To gauge the meaning of the coefficient reported by Shiller, Kleidon ran Monte Carlo studies in which the present-value relation holds by construction and where dividends are generated by a geometric random walk with parameters chosen to give the best fit to Shiller's data. The variance inequality was deemed violated by the sample if the sample variance of p_t exceeded that of p^*_t, and to be "grossly violated" if the ratio of sample variances exceeded 5. Kleidon reported a frequency of violations of about 90 percent (when following Shiller's detrending procedure); the frequency of gross violations varied from 4.6 percent, for a rate of interest of 0.075, to almost 40 percent, for a rate of interest of 0.05.

Shiller (1988) responded that when the rate of interest varies, so does the dividend–price ratio if the dividend growth rate μ stays constant. The combination of the rate of growth μ chosen by Kleidon and a rate of interest of 5 percent implies an implausible value of the dividend–price ratio. Shiller ran experiments similar to those of Kleidon, but specified μ to vary with the rate of interest in order to leave the implied dividend–price ratio at its average historical level. He obtained much lower frequencies of gross violations.

Note that in the debate between Kleidon and Shiller about the appropriate parameter values to assume in Monte Carlo experiments, we have completely lost contact with the variance-bounds theorems.

If dividends follow a random walk (whether arithmetic or geometric), the sample variance bears no relation to any simple unconditional population parameter. Consequently, the robustness of the original variance-bounds theorems is sacrificed. For example, Kleidon and Shiller assumed that agents have no information beyond current dividends. How would their rejection frequencies be affected if this unrealistic assumption were relaxed? In the absence of any underlying theory, it is impossible to say.

Kleidon's paper emphasized that the first-generation empirical tests of the variance-bounds relation depended on the stationarity of the underlying series. The Shiller and LeRoy-Porter papers were clear about this dependence, so the question becomes whether the trend adjustment used in each case in fact produced a stationary series. Shiller's trend removal—take residuals from a constant growth rate path—will produce a stationary series only if the original series is trend stationary. The empirical evidence for the existence of unit roots in dividends—i.e., against the stationarity of dividends—is weaker than for most macroeconomic time series; thus, based on the evidence on dividends alone, the stationarity question remains open. However, in most macroeconomic models, dividends are cointegrated with variables such as GNP, investment, consumption, and so forth. Therefore the relevant evidence is that concerning unit roots for macroeconomic variables generally, not just dividends. The evidence now indicates that most macroeconomic variables do have unit roots. Of course, even if so, it remains open whether the bias induced by nonstationarity is sufficient to explain the variance-bounds violations.

2.3 Summary
The reason Shiller's rejections of the variance-bounds inequality were so striking is that the results did not depend on a particular specification of the model for dividends (as noted above, the LeRoy-Porter version did not share this attractive "model-free" property). Flavin and Kleidon pointed out that, while it is true that the variance-bounds inequality itself is model free, the properties of any econometric test of that inequality can only be investigated conditional on a particular dividends model. They argued that under reasonable specifications of the dividends model, variance-bounds tests will reject with high probability even if the present-value model is true. There can be no doubt that, at a minimum, the critics established that econometric problems with variance-bounds tests are potentially severe. Whether these problems are severe enough to account for the extent of the apparent excess volatility, however, remained controversial.

Variance-Bounds Tests

3. Second-Generation Tests

3.1 West

West (1988a) derived a variance-bounds test that (i) is valid even if dividends are nonstationary, and (ii) does not require a proxy for p_t^*. To understand West's test, recall the definition of H_t as the information set consisting of current and past dividends. West defined x_{tH} as the expectation of the cum dividend ex post rational price conditional on H_t, and x_{tI} as the corresponding variable for investors' actual information set I_t:

$$x_{tH} \triangleq \sum_{i=0}^{\infty} \beta^i E(d_{t+i}|H_t), \quad x_{tI} \triangleq \sum_{i=0}^{\infty} \beta^i E(d_{t+i}|I_t).$$

West's result was that under the weak assumption that I_t contains H_t, the innovation variance of x_{tH} exceeds that of x_{tI}:

$$E[(x_{t+1,H} - E[x_{t+1,H}|H_t])^2] \geq E[(x_{t+1,I} - E[x_{t+1,I}|I_t])^2].$$

The meaning of West's inequality becomes apparent when we recast it in more familiar notation. Recalling the definitions of the ex dividends price series $\hat{p}_t$ and p_t,

$$\hat{p}_t \triangleq \sum_{i=1}^{\infty} \beta^i E(d_{t+i}|H_t), \quad p_t \triangleq \sum_{i=1}^{\infty} \beta^i E(d_{t+i}|I_t),$$

we have

$$x_{t+1,H} = \hat{p}_{t+1} + d_{t+1} \quad \text{and} \quad E(x_{t+1,H}|H_t) = \beta^{-1}\hat{p}_t.$$

Similarly,

$$x_{t+1,I} = p_{t+1} + d_{t+1} \quad \text{and} \quad E(x_{t+1,I}|I_t) = \beta^{-1}p_t.$$

Thus the innovations in x_{tH} and x_{tI} are recognized as just the returns

$$\hat{r}_{t+1} = \hat{p}_{t+1} + d_{t+1} - \beta^{-1}\hat{p}_t \quad \text{and} \quad r_{t+1} = p_{t+1} + d_{t+1} - \beta^{-1}p_t,$$

and West's inequality reduces to

$$V(\hat{r}_t) \geq V(r_t). \tag{34}$$

Thus, investors' actual returns must have lower variance than the returns that would obtain if investors' information consisted of H_t.

West's upper bound on return variance is a direct implication of the LeRoy–Porter lower bound on price variance. To see this, observe that the LeRoy–Porter equality (3) holds for any information set. Therefore it holds for H_t, implying

$$V(p_t^*) = V(\hat{p}_t) + \frac{\beta^2 V(\hat{r}_t)}{1 - \beta^2}. \qquad (35)$$

The LeRoy–Porter lower bound (8) on price variance, combined with (3) and (35), yields West's inequality (34).

West argued in favor of his test that, unlike the first-generation variance-bound tests, it is valid whether or not dividends are stationary. Even if dividends are generated by a linear process with a unit root, so that dividends and prices are cointegrated rather than stationary, the population return variances will be constant. Therefore their sample counterparts provide consistent estimates of population values. This argument is correct, but it must be remembered that it applies only for nonstationary dividend processes that are linear. We believe that a more natural treatment of trend is to specify a log-linear, rather than linear, dividend process, so that dividend growth rates are stationary. Although West's variance-bounds test does not apply directly, it can be adapted to the log-linear case; see LeRoy and Parke (1990), discussed below.

3.2 Mankiw, Romer, and Shapiro

Mankiw, Romer, and Shapiro (1985, 1991) (hereafter MRS) claimed to have provided an unbiased volatility test. The derivation is as follows: Let p_t^0 be any variable that can be constructed from information available to agents at t, and let $p_{t|T}^*$, as in Section 2.1, be the observable version of p_t^*. Consider the identity

$$p_{t|T}^* - p_t^0 \equiv (p_{t|T}^* - p_t) + (p_t - p_t^0). \qquad (36)$$

Under unbiased forecasting, $p_{t|T}^* - p_t$ must be uncorrelated with any variable observable at t; in particular, with $p_t - p_t^0$. Hence by squaring both sides of (36), taking expectations, and making use of $E[(p_{t|T}^* - p_t)(p_t - p_t^0)] = 0$, we get

$$S \triangleq E[(p_{t|T}^* - p_t^0)^2] - E[(p_{t|T}^* - p_t)^2] - E[(p_t - p_t^0)^2] = 0. \qquad (37)$$

The last equality is valid for any definition of p_t^0, but if p_t^0 is interpreted as a "naive forecast" of $p_{t|T}^*$, then the actual price must outperform p_t^0 as a forecast of $p_{t|T}^*$, which implies (37).

The sample counterpart of (37) is defined in the obvious way:

$$\hat{S} \triangleq \frac{1}{T} \left\{ \sum_{t=1}^{T} (p_{t|T}^* - p_t^0)^2 - \sum_{t=1}^{T} (p_{t|T}^* - p_t)^2 - \sum_{t+1}^{T} (p_t - p_t^0)^2 \right\}.$$

MRS set p_t^0 as a constant multiple of dividends in the preceding year. They found that $\hat{S}$ was negative, indicating excess volatility.

Variance-Bounds Tests

MRS claimed that because this volatility test uses noncentral rather than central variances, it is unbiased.[15] To evaluate this claim, we first point out a redefinition of terms that crept into the variance-bounds literature with Flavin's paper. By "test," econometricians ordinarily mean something very precise. Besides specifying a test statistic, it is necessary to identify a rejection region such that, if the null hypothesis is true, it will be rejected with preassigned probability α. A test is biased toward rejection if the probability of rejection exceeds α.

In the variance-bounds literature, however, the terms "test" and "unbiased test" have been used more loosely. Because of the difficulty of evaluating small-sample distributions, many have dispensed with any formal attempt to specify a rejection region as defined above. The variance-bounds inequalities are then rejected if the sample variance of p_t is much higher than that of p_t^*, with no attempt to define "much." In the variance-bounds literature, a test is said to be biased toward rejection if the expected value of the test statistic is in the direction of excess volatility, relative to the corresponding population parameter. Because this property concerns only the first moment of the distribution of the test statistic, it is usually easy to investigate. For example, the equality $E(\hat{S}) = S = 0$ is the basis for MRS's claim to have provided an unbiased test. However, the result that $\hat{S}$ gives an unbiased estimate of S does not establish that the test is unbiased in the usual sense.

Given the difficulty in evaluating type I error probabilities, the redefinitions of the terms "test" and "unbiased test" that have taken place are understandable. The two definitions are related: in showing small-sample bias (as redefined), Flavin created a strong presumption that the apparently dramatic rejections of the variance-bounds inequalities that Shiller reported are suspect, but when MRS went on to report the results of what they called an unbiased test, it is important to note that by this they meant only that the expectation of their test statistic equals the corresponding population parameter.

Shea (1989) pointed out two major problems with MRS's tests, both attributable to the use of $p_{t|T}^*$ in place of p_t^*. First, the outcome of the tests is very sensitive to the choice of terminal date. Second, because of the nonstationarity induced by the dependence of both population parameters and statistics on $p_{t|T}^*$ (which is nonstationary even if p_t^* is stationary), there is no prospect of using asymptotic theory to derive confidence intervals for the tests. To avoid both problems, Shea suggested using a rolling terminal date. Under Shea's

---

[15] Flavin had already noted that noncentral variances have this property and had reported the results of such tests. She credited Richard Porter with the insight that use of noncentral variances provides a way around her criticism of Shiller's tests (1983, p. 950).

recommended procedure, for each time period the same value of τ is used to calculate the ex post rational price

$$p^*_{t|\tau} \triangleq \sum_{i=1}^{\tau} \beta^i d_{t+i} + \beta^\tau p_{t+\tau},$$

instead of defining τ as $T - t$. However, the estimates of $p^*_{t|\tau}$ calculated in this way are not equal to the expectation of p^*_t conditional on the entire sample, lessening the appeal of Shea's procedure. Also, Shea's procedure is wasteful of data: with sample size T, a rolling terminal date τ allows construction of the price series only until $t = T - \tau$ since $p^*_{t|\tau}$ requires an observation of $p_{t+\tau}$. A larger value of τ reduces the observation error in the series $p^*_{t|\tau}$, but also reduces its length. In any case, Shea's results were much more favorable to the variance-bounds theorems than MRS's.

As noted above, in their 1985 paper, MRS made no attempt to determine whether their rejection of the present-value model was statistically significant—they concluded only that their point estimates suggested excess volatility. However, in their 1991 paper, MRS calculated asymptotic standard errors, using the rolling horizon to assure stationarity. They concluded that the excess volatility was of moderate but not overwhelming statistical significance. This was exactly the conclusion LeRoy and Porter had reached, also based on asymptotic standard errors.

Marsh and Merton (1986) and Merton (1987) observed that dividend smoothing by management could bias variance-bounds tests in general, and MRS's test in particular, toward rejection. If dividends are slow to reflect changes in underlying profitability, measured dividend volatility could give an impression that fundamentals had remained stable even when the opposite was the case. To illustrate the problem, Merton (1987) analyzed an example in which dividends were assumed to be zero within the sample and showed that econometric problems with the MRS test would result. Merton's example is a hybrid of models analyzed by Flavin and Kleidon. The nonstationarity of prices implied by the zero-dividend assumption results in econometric problems, as Kleidon showed; the substitution of the observable $p^*_{t|T}$ for the unobservable p^*_t induces small-sample bias, as Flavin showed. In fact, the latter problem is magnified in the context of Merton's example as a consequence of his assumption that within-sample dividends are zero. This observation formed the basis for MRS's (1991) response to Merton's criticism. They noted that, empirically, end-of-sample price is a small contributor to within-sample price relative to within-sample dividends at most dates of a hundred-year sample. Therefore, they argued, the econometric problem Merton pointed out is of little practical importance.

Variance-Bounds Tests

Merton's criticism and MRS's reply failed to distinguish between two separate phenomena: low dividends and smoothed dividends. It is true that firms retain a large fraction of their earnings, implying that capital gains typically exceed dividends, but that does not necessarily cause problems for model-based variance-bounds tests (since these estimate the variance of ex post rational price directly from dividends, rather than relying on some observable version of p_t^*). For example, if dividends follow a geometric random walk, variance-bounds tests can be constructed by estimating the mean and variance of the dividend growth rate and comparing the implied volatility of ex post rational price with that of actual price [see LeRoy and Parke (1990), discussed below]. Nothing about Merton's example suggests that these parameters are more difficult to estimate when the mean dividend growth rate is high (as will occur when corporations retain most of their earnings) than when it is low. Thus low dividend payout rates, even though they imply that stock prices depend mostly on out-of-sample dividends, do not necessarily cause problems for variance-bounds tests. Smoothed dividends, however, are another story. If dividend growth rates have important low-frequency components, small-sample problems are exacerbated. MRS's reply did not address this aspect of Merton's criticism.

3.3 Scott, and Durlauf and Hall

Scott (1985) observed that nothing about the hypothesized equality between p_t and $E(p_t^*|I_t)$ requires that this equality be tested by comparing variances. Under the null hypothesis, the error e_t in

$$p_t^* = a + bp_t + e_t$$

is uncorrelated with the explanatory variable, so the present value model can be tested equally well by determining whether a equals zero and b equals unity in an ordinary least squares regression. Scott argued that such regression tests of the present-value model are essentially free of the econometric problems associated with volatility tests. He found empirically that b was near zero rather than unity, implying that p_t^* and p_t are virtually uncorrelated, conflicting with the present-value model.

Recent work by Durlauf and Hall (1989) clarified the relation between Scott's regression test and the volatility tests of the present-value relation. Continuing along the line initiated by Scott, Durlauf and Hall pointed out that it is possible to translate the restriction on parameters implied by volatility tests into a corresponding coefficient restriction in regression tests. To achieve this translation, Durlauf and Hall modeled stock prices p_t as the sum of q_t, the expected value of discounted dividends, and a noise variable s_t, which is unrestricted.

As usual, p_t^* is written as q_t plus an orthogonal forecast error f_t. We have

$$p_t = q_t + s_t, \qquad p_t^* = q_t + f_t, \tag{38}$$

where the left-hand side variables are observed by the econometrician and the right-hand side variables are unobserved. The present-value model corresponds to $s_t = 0$. Now consider the regression

$$p_t = \theta(p_t - p_t^*) + u_t.$$

We wish to obtain the restriction on θ implied by $V(p) \leq V(p^*)$. To do so, write θ as $\text{Cov}(p_t, p_t - p_t^*)/V(p_t - p_t^*)$ and use (38) to eliminate p_t and p_t^*:

$$\theta = \frac{\text{Cov}(q_t + s_t, s_t - f_t)}{V(s_t - f_t)}$$

$$= \frac{\text{Cov}(q_t, s_t) + V(s_t) - \text{Cov}(s_t, f_t)}{V(s_t) - 2\text{Cov}(s_t, f_t) + V(f_t)} \tag{39}$$

[using the orthogonality condition $\text{Cov}(q_t, f_t) = 0$]. Similarly, express the variance bounds inequality $V(p_t) \leq V(p_t^*)$ in terms of the moments of s_t, q_t, and f_t:

$$V(q_t) + 2\,\text{Cov}(q_t, s_t) + V(s_t) \leq V(q_t) + V(f_t). \tag{40}$$

Combining (39) and (40), Durlauf and Hall obtained $\theta \leq \tfrac{1}{2}$.

Thus, rejection of $V(p) \leq V(p^*)$ is equivalent to rejecting $\theta \leq \tfrac{1}{2}$, but the present-value model should be rejected for any θ that differs significantly from zero, not just for values of θ that significantly exceed $\tfrac{1}{2}$. Durlauf and Hall argued that regression-based tests such as that of Scott, which reject for any nonzero value of θ, are likely to be superior to volatility tests, which do not detect small amounts of model noise.[16]

This argument is incorrect. The reason is that so far we have been vague about the choice of rejection region. If in a model-based variance-bounds test the rejection region is computed via simulation, then the rejection region associated with the chosen probability of type I error depends on the variance of the forecast error. In the Durlauf–Hall regression context, the same statistic, θ, is involved in both the (bounds) test of the inequality $\theta \leq \tfrac{1}{2}$ and the (orthogonality) test of the equality $\theta = 0$. Therefore type I error can be set equal in the two cases only if both tests have the same rejection region, but then the probability of type II error will also be equal under any

---

[16] LeRoy and Porter (1981, p. 561), Frankel and Stock (1987), and Froot (1989), reasoning similarly, also concluded that bounds tests have lower power than orthogonality tests.

Variance-Bounds Tests

alternative hypothesis so that, contrary to the Durlauf–Hall argument, in the regression context orthogonality tests do not have greater power than bounds tests.

The main purpose of the Durlauf–Hall paper was not to compare bounds and orthogonality tests of stock price volatility, but to measure the variance of model noise as a contributor to the total variance of stock prices. The fact that noise cannot be assumed to be orthogonal to any of the variables causes ambiguity in the measurement of noise variance. However, Durlauf and Hall showed that there exist lower bounds on the amount of model noise consistent with the data. Durlauf and Hall showed that at least 84 percent of the variance of prices can be attributed to noise under the estimator associated with the bounds test $V(p) \leq V(p^*)$.[17] Under the noise variance estimator associated with the more stringent orthogonality test, noise variance is essentially equal to that of stock prices. Durlauf and Hall concluded from these results that "movements in expected discounted dividends, with a constant discount rate, have essentially nothing to do with the actual movements of the stock market" (p. 17).

3.4 Campbell and Shiller

In three recent papers, Campbell and Shiller (1987, 1988a, 1988b) introduced material not found in Shiller's early papers on asset-price volatility. Campbell and Shiller noted that if the present-value model is true, (i) an optimal prediction of the present value of future expected dividends can be formed using current price alone and (ii) this optimal prediction coincides with current price. It follows that the present-value model implies testable restrictions of the coefficients of a bivariate vector autoregression of stock prices and dividends. This insight was not new to the variance-bounds literature (the LeRoy–Porter volatility test consisted exactly of tests of restrictions on the coefficients of a bivariate autoregression).[18] However, in implementing their tests, Campbell and Shiller (1988a) introduced a method for trend correction that, although not perfect, is superior to anything that went before. Campbell and Shiller assumed that dividends and whatever other variables predict dividends form a multivariate log-

---

[17] Apparently, Durlauf and Hall did not correct for trend in any way. Therefore, given that the forecast error is a martingale (facing toward the past), if the price process has a unit root, then spurious correlation will result, implying upward bias in the Durlauf–Hall estimate of noise variance. We are indebted to Douglas Steigerwald for pointing this out.

[18] In 1987, Campbell and Shiller observed that "there are several [procedures for testing the present-value relation] in the literature: these include single-equation regression tests, tests of cross-equation restrictions on a vector autoregression (VAR), and variance bounds tests" (p. 1063). In taking the latter two categories to be distinct, Campbell and Shiller appeared to be unaware that the idea of testing the volatility implications of the present-value relation by investigating the validity of cross-equation restrictions in a bivariate autoregression had already been introduced into the variance-bounds literature.

linear model. To reconcile the log-linearity of the dividend model with the linearity of the present-value relation, Campbell and Shiller log-linearized the expression defining the rate of return (the opposite procedure, linearizing the dividend model, would introduce heteroskedasticity). Comparison of the actual rate of return with its log-linearized counterpart—the two are correlated almost perfectly—allowed Campbell and Shiller to argue that the error introduced by the log-linearization is negligible. The present-value model that results from iterating the log-linearized version of the definition of the rate of return expresses the log price–dividend ratio as the present value of the discounted expected dividend growth rates. All these variables are essentially free of trend, implying that the econometric problems attending the first-generation volatility tests by reason of the nonstationarity of the underlying series are avoided.

Campbell and Shiller reported the results of a variety of tests of the equality of the log price–dividend ratio and the present value of future dividend growth rates, and for the most part found evidence of significant violation. Most relevant for the variance-bounds question, for example, Campbell and Shiller compared the standard deviation of the log actual price–dividend ratio with the standard deviation of the present value of future expected dividend growth rates. If the present value model is correct, it must be the case that, since these variables are the same, their standard deviations are equal. In fact, Campbell-Shiller found that the standard deviation of the actual price–dividend ratio was twice that of its theoretical counterpart, indicating significant excess volatility.

In 1988, Campbell and Shiller (1988b) added corporate earnings to the price–dividend autoregression. They found that earnings is a strong predictor of dividend growth even conditional on the current log price–dividend ratio. This finding contradicts the present-value model, according to which current price is a sufficient statistic for future dividend growth. This article also contains a valuable discussion of the relation between the variance-bounds tests and the return autocorrelation tests conducted by Fama and French (1988), Poterba and Summers (1988), and others. Recall that LeRoy and Porter had based their variance-bounds test on the fact that the forecast error for ex post rational price equals a weighted average of future total returns, so rejection of the variance-bounds inequality implies that returns are autocorrelated. Consequently, in the language of Campbell and Shiller, "excess volatility and predictability of multiperiod returns are not two phenomena, but one" (p. 663).

Unfortunately, direct comparison between the first-generation variance-bounds tests and the return autocorrelation results is impossible because the former tests imply autocorrelatedness of total return,

Variance-Bounds Tests

whereas the latter tests imply autocorrelatedness of the rate of return (i.e., total return per dollar of stock value). However, under the Campbell–Shiller linearization, the analog of total return is exactly the rate of return. Thus, since the same return measure is involved in both variance-bounds and return autocorrelation tests, one can go beyond the mere observation that rejection of the variance-bounds inequality implies returns are autocorrelated. In addition, one can translate any pattern of autocorrelation of rates of return into the implied correlation between the log actual price–dividend ratio and the forecast error for log ex post rational price–dividend ratio. Further, rejection of the orthogonality of the log ex post rational price–dividend ratio and the log actual price–dividend ratio implies exactly that a weighted average of future rates of return, with weights that decline geometrically according to a factor related to the average price–dividend ratio, is forecastable. Given the numerical value of this weighting factor, it turns out that the variance-bounds violations correspond to the finding that long-term (five- and ten-year) rates of return are highly autocorrelated. This was exactly the finding of Fama and French and Poterba and Summers.

3.5 LeRoy and Parke, and Cochrane

LeRoy and Parke (1990), in work initially conducted independently of the Campbell–Shiller research discussed above, proposed correcting for the trend in stock prices by dividing prices by dividends. They assumed that dividends follow a geometric random walk, their purpose being to derive variance-bounds tests that would be valid in the setting used by Kleidon to criticize Shiller. LeRoy and Parke began by reporting a model-free bounds test of the volatility of the price–dividend ratio along the lines of Shiller (1981), and also a model-based bounds test as developed by LeRoy and Porter. Taking the rejection region to be defined by a negative value of the volatility statistic $\hat{V}(p^*) - \hat{V}(p)$, they found that the model-free bounds test rejected the model, whereas the model-based test accepted it. This discrepancy reflected primarily the radically different estimates of ex post rational price volatility generated under the two procedures: the volatility estimate produced by the model-free procedure [using $p^*_{t|T}$, the observable version of ex post rational price obtained from the recursion (15) and the terminal condition $p^*_{T|T} = p_T$] was less than one-quarter that produced by the model-based procedure (estimating the discount factor and the mean and variance of the dividend growth rate and entering these as arguments in the expression for the variance of ex post rational price).

781

The obvious explanation for the disparity between model-free and model-based estimates of ex post rational price volatility is estimation bias. Flavin's arguments established the strong presumption that the model-free estimates are biased downward. The model-based estimates are also subject to bias: even though the mean and variance of the dividend growth rate and discount factor can be estimated without bias, sampling variance in the estimates of these parameters will generally induce bias in the estimated variance of ex post rational price because of the nonlinearity of the variance expression.

This differential effect of estimation bias suggests that type I error is much higher under model-free tests than under model-based tests. This reflects the arbitrary specification that the rejection region consists of negative values of $\hat{V}(p^*) - \hat{V}(p)$ regardless of sampling error. A better procedure would be to use the Monte Carlo simulations to specify a rejection region that fixes the estimated probability of type I error at some constant like 10 percent. LeRoy and Parke found that the 10 percent rejection region (based on the Monte Carlo experiments) depended critically on how much information agents are assumed to have, which is not restricted under the null hypothesis. The first conclusion of LeRoy and Parke, therefore, was that the inequality test of the variance-bounds relation, being subject to a "nuisance parameter" problem, is uninformative about the null hypothesis. This is true of both the model-free and model-based versions.

LeRoy and Parke went on to consider orthogonality tests. The orthogonality test (7), devised by LeRoy and Porter, takes the form of an equality, not an inequality. Because under the null hypothesis this equality is valid for any specification of agents' information, there is no nuisance parameter problem (at least with regard to population parameters; there remains the possibility that sampling distributions depend on agents' information). The problem with (7) is that its derivation depends on the assumption that dividends are generated by a linear process, which is inconsistent with the log-linear geometric random walk. To get around this problem, LeRoy and Parke derived an analog to (7) that is valid under log-linear dividend processes. The associated null hypothesis was significantly rejected for any specification of agents' information.

Finally, LeRoy and Parke considered West's test. The Campbell–Shiller log-linearization implies that West's inequality takes a particularly simple form under the geometric random walk: it says that the variance of the rate of return on stock is bounded above by the variance of the dividend growth rate. As an inequality test, West's test is in principle subject to the same nuisance parameter problem as the price variance inequality test. In practice, however, it turned out that

Variance-Bounds Tests

there was no nuisance parameter problem. The Monte Carlo tests showed that, as with the orthogonality test, West's inequality was significantly rejected for any specification of agents' information.[19]

The LeRoy-Parke results depend on two restrictive assumptions: that dividends follow a geometric random walk and that the discount rates are constant. Neither assumption can be justified except as a crude approximation. However, the problem with more complex and realistic models for dividends and discount factors is that under such specifications the rational expectations assumption becomes less plausible. For example, it is easy to verify that dividend growth rates have nonzero autocorrelations, contrary to the LeRoy-Parke specification, but it strains one's credulity to assume that agents know a sequence of autocorrelation coefficients for dividend growth rates and price stock taking account of these deviations from randomness.

Perhaps it is a matter of taste whether one prefers simple models that are not descriptively accurate or more complex models that, because of their complexity, put the rational expectations assumption to harder use. In any case, Cochrane (1990) derived a version of the LeRoy-Parke bound on the variance of the price-dividend ratio that is consistent with time-varying discount rates and autocorrelated dividend growth rates. To evaluate the bound, Cochrane used a linear approximation similar (but not identical) to that of Campbell and Shiller. Cochrane found that the variance bound was satisfied. This result is analogous to the LeRoy-Parke finding that the model-based point estimate of the variance of the price-dividend ratio was less than its upper bound. As discussed above, LeRoy and Parke concluded that in the absence of an attempt to control the probability of type I error, this result cannot be construed as favoring the present-value relation. The same observation applies to Cochrane's finding.

Cochrane also estimated decompositions of the variance of the price-dividend ratio into the sum of expected dividend growth rates and discount factors along the lines of Campbell and Shiller. Finally, he derived bounds on the mean and standard deviation of discount factors, as in Hansen and Jagannathan (1991). This material, being related only indirectly to variance bounds, is not discussed here.

3.6 Summary
The critics had established that, as attractive as Shiller's model-free variance-bounds test was by reason of its generality, it had the defect that its econometric properties cannot be investigated. Further, under dividend models that were (represented as) reasonable, these prop-

---

[19] See LeRoy (1990) for a nontechnical exposition and for a plot of the rate of return on stock against the dividend growth rate.

erties are very unsatisfactory. The emphasis in the second-generation variance-bounds tests was on developing tests that had acceptable econometric properties under realistic dividend models. In this they largely succeeded. With the exception of Mankiw, Romer, and Shapiro (1991) and Cochrane (1990), the second-generation tests found statistically significant excess volatility. However, it is important to recall that any model-based test is necessarily a test of a joint hypothesis that includes an assumption about the process generating dividends. Consequently, there remains the possibility that the appearance of excess price volatility may be caused by misspecification of the dividend model.

4. Possible Explanations

In this section, we review the suggested explanations for excess volatility of asset prices. First, investors may overreact to dividend news. That is, market participants may not be perfectly rational and have rational expectations. According to this view, stock prices are moved by fads [Shiller (1984), DeBondt and Thaler (1985)]; or, as Keynes described it, the stock market is a beauty contest in which one wins by "anticipating what average opinion expects the average opinion to be" (1936, p. 156). DeLong et al. (1988) showed that if "noise traders" have irrationally optimistic expectations, there is an equilibrium in which stock prices are more volatile than under the present-value model. Moreover, this equilibrium is stable in the sense that noise traders do not necessarily suffer losses.

Within the paradigm of neoclassical economics, rationality is part of the inner core, insulated from falsification. Explanations for price volatility that involve irrationality are therefore inadmissible. Before jettisoning the neoclassical paradigm to explain one (admittedly important) phenomenon, one should consider explanations that do not rely on irrationality.

If stock prices have greater volatility than expected values of discounted future dividends, the reason may be rational speculative bubbles.[20] The theory and evidence on bubbles was reviewed in West (1988b) and Flood, Hodrick, and Kaplan (1986). If the price of a security contains a deterministic bubble, then the value of the bubble

---

[20] See Gilles and LeRoy (1990) for a discussion of rational speculative bubbles within a context of general equilibrium. Flood and Hodrick (1986) observed that model-free variance-bounds tests include bubbles in the null hypothesis because of the way the observable version of ex post rational price is constructed. Therefore a finding of excess volatility in a non-model-based test cannot be attributed to bubbles. Flood, Hodrick, and Kaplan (1986) noted that the model-based tests of LeRoy and Porter did not use the observable version of ex post rational price, implying that in this case the presence of bubbles could cause rejection of the variance-bounds inequality.

Variance-Bounds Tests

will grow at the rate of interest, inducing nonstationarity of the price even when dividends are stationary. The data on price–dividend ratios, however, show no evidence of the implied nonstationarity [Diba and Grossman (1988)].

Stochastic bubbles are more interesting. They grow, then collapse. A stochastic bubble, once having burst, cannot be reborn; if there exists such a bubble, it must have been present from the asset's inception. However, there may exist many stochastic bubbles on the same price, and they may start so small that they do not noticeably affect the price of the asset for a long period before taking off and then bursting. To the observer, the price will exhibit swings. If bubble bursts are independent of dividends, stock prices are more volatile than the present-value relation predicts. If bursts are correlated negatively with dividends, still greater excess price volatility results and markets appear to overreact to dividend news.

West (1987) at first favored the bubble explanation of stock-price volatility. Upon reviewing the evidence in West (1988b), however, he reversed his conclusion. One of the reasons he gave for disqualifying rational bubbles is that they cannot be the source of excess volatility in bond prices. Bubbles, whether deterministic or stochastic, can only occur when the horizon is infinite, at least in discrete-time models. With a finite horizon, a backward induction annihilates any bubble at its inception. Shiller (1979) and Singleton (1980) reported evidence of excess volatility of bond prices. Because bonds have finite maturity, such excess volatility cannot be due to bubbles. It seems likely, West argued, that stock prices show too much variability for the same reason that bond prices do; if so, the culprit is not bubbles. Against this argument, however, is the new evidence [Campbell and Shiller (1987)] that the Shiller–Singleton finding of excess volatility in the bond market is due to incorrect trend adjustment. If so, the apparent excess volatility of stock prices, even under correct trend adjustment, favors the bubble explanation.

The present-value relation as we defined it assumes that the rate of discount is constant (see note 1). Since this assumption does not necessarily hold, it is natural to study the effect of discount rate variability on asset-price volatility. To see the connection, assume that there is a single consumption good and that the representative consumer maximizes $E(\Sigma_j \beta^j u(c_{t+j}) | I_t)$ with u of the constant relative risk aversion class $u(c) = c^{1-\rho}/(1-\rho)$. Let r_{it} denote the gross one-period rate of return (1 plus the rate of return) on asset i, and let m_t be the marginal rate of substitution of consumption at $t+1$ for consumption at t [i.e., $m_t = \beta u'(c_{t+1})/u'(c_t)$]. Assuming interior maxima, the following relation will hold [Grossman and Shiller (1981)]:

$$1 = E(m_t \times r_{it} | I_t). \tag{41}$$

If the consumer is risk neutral ($\rho = 0$), then (41) yields the constant expected rate of return (the same for all securities) $E(r_{it}) = 1/\beta$, and hence we get the present-value relation that the data reject. In this model, excess volatility (relative to that predicted by the present-value model) implies that the consumer is not risk neutral.

Grossman and Shiller (1981), LeRoy and LaCivita (1981), and Michener (1982) worked out the implications of (41) for the volatility of asset prices. All found that risk aversion implies greater price volatility than in the present-value model. These results seem encouraging, but for the utility index $\ln(c)$ to produce violation of the variance bounds of the observed magnitude, the aggregate consumption series must be much more volatile than it actually is. The very smooth actual post WWII consumption series implies an implausibly high estimated value of the coefficient of relative risk aversion ρ [Grossman and Shiller (1981)].

The Grossman–Shiller finding of a high value of ρ is consistent with that of Mehra and Prescott (1985), who based their approach on the average covariance between the marginal rate of intertemporal substitution and stock returns. They considered the implications of (41) for the equity premium, defined as the difference between the average rate of return on a diversified portfolio of stocks and the risk-free rate. Mehra and Prescott found that the average real annual yield on the Standard and Poors 500 Index was 7 percent, while that on short-term debt was less than one percent. Let the latter of these yields stand in for the risk-free rate r^* and note that (41) implies

$$r_t^* = 1/E(m_t|I_t). \qquad (42)$$

We can then rewrite (41) as

$$\frac{E(r_t|I_t) - r_t^*}{r_t^*} = -\mathrm{Cov}(m_t, r_t|I_t),$$

where r_t is the gross return on the Standard and Poors 500 Index. Mehra and Prescott constructed an artificial economy parameterized so that the growth rate of consumption is a stationary random process with the same mean, variance, and serial correlation as those observed in the U.S. economy. They concluded that an elasticity of substitution between the year t and year $t + 1$ consumption good sufficiently low to yield the 6 percent average equity premium also yields real interest rates far in excess of those observed. Because the elasticity of intertemporal substitution is the reciprocal of ρ, an equity premium equal to six times the risk-free rate implies a high value of ρ, precisely the Grossman–Shiller finding. The main conclusion of Mehra and Prescott was that, even if one were to accept a high value of ρ as plausible,

Variance-Bounds Tests

the model (41) is not saved because (42) then implies too high a value for the risk-free rate.

Mehra and Prescott calibrated an artificial economy, rather than using standard econometric techniques. It is, however, possible to modify methods used in the present-value model to test the specific model with time-varying discount rates [Campbell and Shiller (1988a)]. Singleton (1987) reviewed the literature on consumption-based asset-pricing models and reported on the results of a large number of studies besides those noted here. He concluded from these results that the U.S. aggregate data reject the model. This conclusion is robust to changes in the specification of the utility function and in the number of goods assumed to be present.

Progress on these issues will almost certainly require introducing either frictions or non-von Neumann–Morgenstern preferences. Mehra and Prescott and others suggested that the equity premium puzzle points to the importance of frictions. Bewley (1982), following up on this suggestion, showed that if consumers are liquidity constrained, or can only imperfectly insure wealth fluctuations, then individual consumption streams do not fluctuate in sympathy with each other, so the aggregate consumption series will be smoother than the individual series. A definitive test of Bewley's model would require panel data on consumption, asset holdings, and income of individuals, data that are not readily available.

The main problem for the representative-agent expected-utility model is that the smoothness of the aggregate consumption series suggests a low elasticity of intertemporal substitution. A variety of other evidence suggests that the coefficient of relative risk aversion is also low (or moderate), but within the expected-utility, time-separable framework, the intertemporal elasticity of substitution is the reciprocal of the coefficient of relative risk aversion, so we cannot have both. It is possible that uncoupling risk aversion and intertemporal substitution holds the key to the volatility and equity-premium puzzles. Relaxing time separability while preserving expected utility gives enough flexibility to distinguish behavior due to temporal substitution from that due to risk aversion. However, as explained in Epstein and Zin (1989), nonseparable utility leads an expected-utility maximizer to choose consumption plans that are dynamically inconsistent: a plan chosen as optimal in one period becomes suboptimal later. Preferences that do not vary in this fashion and also induce behavior toward risk that is divorced from intertemporal choice cannot satisfy von Neumann–Morgenstern axioms; a consumer with such preferences cannot be indifferent to the timing of the resolution of uncertainty [Kreps and Porteus (1978)], as expected utility implies.

However, Kreps–Porteus or still more general preferences could reconcile the low degree of intertemporal substitution indicated by aggregate consumption with the moderate degree of risk aversion that economists consider reasonable. Epstein and Zin (1989) showed that in such a setting, the risk premium on a particular asset depends on the correlation of the asset's return both with the market portfolio—as in the capital asset pricing model—and with consumption—as in (41). Epstein and Zin (1991) conducted an empirical study with mildly encouraging results: their stock market and aggregate consumption data rejected a von Neumann–Morgenstern specification of preferences, but could not reject a Kreps–Porteus specification. Weil (1989), however, showed that Kreps–Porteus preferences did not solve the risk-premium puzzle, but instead uncover two puzzles that Mehra and Prescott could not distinguish in the expected-utility framework. In addition to the risk-premium puzzle (the risk premium is too high, in view of the evidence on risk aversion), there is a risk-free rate puzzle (the risk-free rate is too low, in view of the evidence on intertemporal substitution). To explain these puzzles, Weil concluded, a proper specification of preferences is probably less important than market frictions.

5. Conclusion

In its 15-year history, the variance-bounds literature has evolved on a circuitous path. Shiller's first-generation model-free tests provided point estimates of price variances that suggested excess volatility, but the question of statistical significance remained open. This was necessarily the case because, in the absence of an assumed model for dividends, there was no way to investigate the econometric properties of the volatility statistics. The critics remedied this deficiency by supplying models for dividends and deriving the econometric properties of the variance-bounds statistics under the joint assumption that the present-value model is correct and that the dividends equation is well specified. They identified various sources of bias in the model-free variance-bounds tests, suggesting that the apparent excess volatility of asset prices was spurious. The second-generation tests took the obvious next step: expand the null hypothesis to include a model for dividends and then specify a variance-bounds test that performs well if the null hypothesis is true. The model-based tests that resulted—for example, those of Campbell and Shiller and LeRoy and Parke—have much in common with the first-generation model-based tests.

If in some respects the variance-bounds literature evolved toward a point near to where it started; in other respects it evolved into new territory. For example, adequate solutions to the problem of detrend-

Variance-Bounds Tests

ing price data, which had been the downfall of both the first-generation papers, were offered in the second-generation papers. Also, the second-generation papers brought to the forefront several critical distinctions that, although present in the first-generation papers, were not emphasized adequately or developed there. Besides the distinction between model-based and model-free tests, one thinks of the distinction between bounds and orthogonality tests.

The evidence is in: asset prices are more volatile than is implied by the present-value equation. Because of the vast improvement in our understanding of the econometric issues attending the variance-bounds tests, there is no longer any room for reasonable doubt about the statistical significance of the excess volatility. Several possible explanations for the excess volatility were reviewed in the preceding section. The authors of this paper are not in complete agreement about how promising these lines of research are. The first author expects that taking adequate account of frictions will go a long way toward resolving the excess volatility, particularly under parameterizations of preferences that are more general than those considered so far in the variance-bounds literature. The second author hopes this is correct, but expects that when the explanation of excess volatility is found, the critical ideas will lie farther from the neoclassical paradigm.

References

Bewley, T. F., 1982, "Thoughts on Tests of the Intertemporal Asset Pricing Model," working paper, Northwestern University, July.

Billingsley, P., 1979, *Probability and Measure* (2nd ed.), Wiley; New York.

Campbell, J. Y., and R. J. Shiller, 1987, "Cointegration and Tests of Present Value Models," *Journal of Political Economy*, 95, 1062-1088.

Campbell, J. Y., and R. J. Shiller, 1988a, "The Dividend-Price Ratio and Expectations of Future Dividends and Discount Factors," *Review of Financial Studies*, 1, 195-228.

Campbell, J. Y., and R. J. Shiller, 1988b, "Stock Prices, Earnings, and Expected Dividends," *Journal of Finance*, 43, 661-676.

Cochrane, J. C., 1990, "Explaining the Variance of Price-Dividend Ratios," working paper, University of Chicago.

DeBondt, W. F. M., and R. Thaler, 1985, "Does the Stock Market Overreact?" *Journal of Finance*, 40, 793-808.

DeLong, J. B., et al., 1988, "Noise Trader Risk in Financial Markets," Discussion Paper 1416, Harvard Institute of Economic Research, December.

Diba, B., and H. Grossman, 1988, "Explosive Rational Bubbles in Stock Prices," *American Economic Review*, 78, 520-530.

Durlauf, S. N., and R. E. Hall, 1989, "Measuring Noise in Stock Prices," working paper, Stanford University.

Epstein, L. G., and S. E. Zin, 1989, "Substitution, Risk Aversion, and Temporal Behavior of Consumption and Asset Returns: A Theoretical Framework," *Econometrica*, 57, 937-969.

Epstein, L. G., and S. E. Zin, 1991, "Substitution, Risk Aversion, and the Temporal Behavior of Consumption and Asset Returns: An Empirical Analysis," *Journal of Political Economy*, 99, 263-286.

Fama, E. F., and K. R. French, 1988, "Permanent and Temporary Components of Stock Prices," *Journal of Political Economy*, 96, 246-273.

Flavin, M. A., 1983, "Excess Volatility in the Financial Markets: A Reassessment of the Empirical Evidence," *Journal of Political Economy*, 91, 929-956.

Flood, R. P., and R. J. Hodrick, 1986, "Asset Price Volatility, Bubbles, and Process Switching," *Journal of Finance*, 41, 831-842.

Flood, R. P., R. J. Hodrick, and P. Kaplan, 1986, "An Evaluation of Rècent Evidence on Stock Market Bubbles," working paper, Northwestern University.

Frankel, J. A., and J. Stock, 1987, "Regression vs. Volatility Tests of Foreign Exchange Markets," *Journal of International Money and Finance*, 6, 49-66.

Froot, K. A., 1989, "Tests of Excess Forecast Volatility in the Foreign Exchange and Stock Markets," working paper, MIT.

Gilles, C., and S. F. LeRoy, 1990, "Bubbles and Charges," working paper, University of California, Santa Barbara; forthcoming in *International Economic Review*.

Grossman, S. J., and R. J. Shiller, 1981, "The Determinants of the Variability of Stock Market Prices," *American Economic Review*, 71, 222-227

Hansen, L. P., and R. Jagannathan, 1991, "Implications of Security Market Data for Models of Dynamic Economies," *Journal of Political Economy*, 99, 225-262.

Joerding, W., 1986, "Variance Bounds Tests and Simulated Stock Prices," working paper, Washington State University.

Joerding, W., 1988, "Are Stock Prices Excessively Sensitive to Current Information?" *Journal of Economic Behaviour and Organization*, 9, 71-85.

Joerding, W., 1992, "Are Stock Prices Excessively Sensitive to Current Information?: Reply," *Journal of Economic Behaviour and Organization*, forthcoming.

Keynes, J. M., 1936, *The General Theory of Employment, Interest, and Money*, Harcourt, Brace & World, New York.

Kleidon, A. W., 1986a, "Bias in Small Sample Tests of Stock Price Rationality," *Journal of Business*, 59, 237-261.

Kleidon, A. W., 1986b, "Variance Bounds Tests and Stock Price Valuation Models," *Journal of Political Economy*, 94, 953-1001.

Kleidon, A. W., and J. L. Koski, 1992, "Are Stock Prices Excessively Sensitive to Current Information?: Comment," *Journal of Economic Behaviour and Organization*, forthcoming.

Kreps, D. M., and E. L. Porteus, 1978, "Temporal Resolution of Uncertainty and Dynamic Choice Theory," *Econometrica*, 46, 185-200.

LeRoy, S. F., 1984, "Efficiency and the Variability of Asset Prices," *American Economic Review*, 74, 183-187.

LeRoy, S. F., 1989, "Efficient Capital Markets and Martingales," *Journal of Economic Literature*, 27, 1583-1621.

LeRoy, S. F., 1990, "Capital Market Efficiency: An Update," *Economic Review, Federal Reserve Bank of San Francisco*.

Variance-Bounds Tests

LeRoy, S. F., and C. J. LaCivita, 1981, "Risk Aversion and the Dispersion of Asset Prices," *Journal of Business*, 54, 535-547.

LeRoy, S. F., and W. R. Parke, 1990, "Stock Price Volatility: Tests Based on the Geometric Random Walk," working paper, University of California, Santa Barbara.

LeRoy, S. F., and R. D. Porter, 1981, "The Present-Value Relation: Tests Based on Implied Variance Bounds," *Econometrica*, 49, 555-574.

Mankiw, N. G., D. Romer, and M. D. Shapiro, 1985, "An Unbiased Reexamination of Stock Market Volatility," *Journal of Finance*, 40, 677-687.

Mankiw, N. G., D. Romer, and M. D. Shapiro, 1991, "Stock Market Forecastability and Volatility: A Statistical Appraisal," *Review of Economic Studies*, 58, 455-477.

Marsh, T. A., and R. C. Merton, 1986, "Dividend Variability and Variance Bounds Tests for the Rationality of Stock Market Prices," *American Economic Review*, 76, 483-498.

Mehra, R., and E. C. Prescott, 1985, "The Equity Premium: A Puzzle," *Journal of Monetary Economics*, 15, 145-161.

Merton, R. C., 1987, "On the Current State of the Stock Market Rationality Hypothesis," in S. Fischer (ed.), *Macroeconomics and Finance: Essays in Honor of Franco Modigliani*, MIT, Cambridge, Mass.

Michener, R. W., 1982, "Variance Bounds in a Simple Model of Asset Pricing," *Journal of Political Economy*, 90, 166-175.

Poterba, J., and L. H. Summers, 1988, "Mean Reversion in Stock Prices: Evidence and Implications," *Journal of Financial Economics*, 22, 27-59.

Scott, L., 1985, "The Present Value Model of Stock Market Prices: Regression Tests and Monte Carlo Results," *Review of Economics and Statistics*, 57, 599-605.

Shea, G. S., 1989, "Ex-Post Rational Price Approximations and the Empirical Reliability of the Present-Value Relation," *Journal of Applied Econometrics*, 4, 139-159.

Shiller, R. J., 1979, "The Volatility of Long Term Interest Rates and Expectations Models of the Term Structure," *Journal of Political Economy*, 87, 1190-1209.

Shiller, R. J., 1981, "Do Stock Prices Move Too Much to be Justified by Subsequent Changes in Dividends?" *American Economic Review*, 71, 421-436.

Shiller, R. J., 1984, "Stock Prices and Social Dynamics," *Brookings Papers on Economic Activity*, 457-498.

Shiller, R. J., 1988, "The Probability of Gross Violations of a Present Value Variance Inequality," *Journal of Political Economy*, 96, 1089-1092.

Singleton, K. J., 1980, "Expectations Models of the Term Structure and Implied Variance Bounds," *Journal of Political Economy*, 88, 1159-1176.

Singleton, K. J., 1987, "Specification and Estimation of Intertemporal Asset Pricing Models," in B. Friedman and F. Hahn (eds.), *Handbook of Monetary Economics*, North-Holland, Amsterdam.

Weil, P., 1989, "The Equity Premium Puzzle and the Risk-Free Rate Puzzle," *Journal of Monetary Economics*, 24, 401-421.

West, K. D., 1987, "A Specification Test for Speculative Bubbles," *Quarterly Journal of Economics*, 102, 553-580.

West, K. D., 1988a, "Dividend Innovations and Stock Price Volatility," *Econometrica*, 56, 37-61.

West, K. D., 1988b, "Bubbles, Fads and Stock Price Volatility Tests: A Partial Evaluation," *Journal of Finance*, 43, 636-656.

[4]
The Determinants of the Variability of Stock Market Prices

By SANFORD J. GROSSMAN AND ROBERT J. SHILLER*

The most familiar interpretation for the large and unpredictable swings that characterize common stock price indices is that price changes represent the efficient discounting of "new information." It is remarkable given the popularity of this interpretation that it has never been established what this information is about. Recent work by Shiller, and Stephen LeRoy and Richard Porter, has shown evidence that the variability of stock price indices cannot be accounted for by information regarding future dividends since dividends just do not seem to vary enough to justify the price movement. These studies assume a constant discount factor. In this paper, we consider whether the variability of stock prices can be attributed to information regarding discount factors (i.e., real interest rates), which are in turn related to current and future levels of economic activity.

The appropriate discount factor to be applied to dividends which are received k years from today is the marginal rate of substitution between consumption today and consumption k periods from today. We use historical data on per capita consumption from 1890–1979 to estimate the realized value of these marginal rates of substitution. Theoretically, as LeRoy and C. J. La Civita have also noted independently of us, consumption variability may induce stock price variability whose magnitude depends on the degree of risk aversion.

Robert Hall also studied these marginal rates of substitution and concluded that consumption is a random walk. We show that if current consumption and dividends are the best predictors of future consumption and dividends in Hall's sense, then the discount factor applied to stock prices would not vary. The variability of stock prices implies they do vary, so we conclude that consumers must have a better method for forecasting future consumption than using only current consumption (for example, consumers may know when the economy is in a recession).

I. Stock Returns and the Marginal Rate of Substitution

Consider a consumer who can freely buy or sell asset i and whose utility can be written as the present discounted value of utilities of consumption in future years $U_t = \sum_{k=0}^{\infty} \beta^k u(C_{t+k})$, where $\beta = 1/(1+r)$ and r is the subjective rate of time preference. A necessary condition for his holdings of the asset at t to be optimal, given that the consumer maximizes the expectation at time t, of this utility function is

$$(1) \quad u'(C_t)P_{it} = \beta E[u'(C_{t+1})(P_{it+1} + D_{it+1})|I_t]$$

where P_{it} is the real price (in terms of the single consumption good or "market basket" C_t) of asset i and D_{it+1} is the real dividend paid at $t+1$ to holders of record at t. The term E denotes mathematical expectation, conditional here on I_t which is all the information about the future which the agent possesses at time t. The left-hand side of (1) is the cost in terms of foregone current consumption of buying a unit of the asset, while the right-hand side gives the expected future consumption benefit derived from the dividend and capital value of the asset. This relation plays a central role in modern theoretical models of optimal dynamic consumption and portfolio decisions, such as those of Robert Lucas.

*University of Pennsylvania and National Bureau of Economic Research, respectively. This research was supported by the National Science Foundation under grants SOC79-07651 and SOC79-13429. The views expressed here are not necessarily those of the supporting agency. Roger Huang provided research assistance.

Since $u'(C_t)$ and P_{it} are known at time t (in contrast to P_{it+1}, D_{it+1}, and C_{t+1} which are not), we can rewrite (1) as

(2) $$1 = E(R_{it}S_t | I_t)$$

where $S_t = \beta u'(C_{t+1})/u'(C_t)$ is the marginal rate of substitution between present and future consumption (the reciprocal of the usual measure), and $R_{it} = (P_{it+1} + D_{it+1})/P_{it}$ is the return (or rather one plus the rate of return as it is usually calculated). Note that the expectation in (2) conditional on information I_t is always 1. Hence it does not depend on I_t. Therefore, it equals the unconditional or simple expectation

(3) $$1 = E(R_{it}S_t)$$

Thus, the proper stochastic interpretation of the familiar two-period diagram is that the expected product of the uncertain return and the uncertain marginal rate of substitution is one. This means that $E(R_{it})$ needn't equal the subjective rate of time preference nor need it be the same for all assets ("expected profit opportunities" may exist). Instead, (3) says that a *weighted* expectation of returns, with weights corresponding to marginal rates of substitution, is the same for all assets. Returns which come in periods of low marginal utility of consumption (i.e., when consumption is high) are given little weight, because they do little good in terms of utility. Returns which come in periods of high marginal utility are given a lot of weight. The same expression can also be written another way, using the fact that the expected product of two variables is the product of their means plus their covariance:

(4) $$E(R_{it}) = E(S_t)^{-1} \cdot (1 - cov(R_{it}, S_t))$$

Equation (4) states that the expected return of an asset depends on the covariance of the asset's return with the marginal rate of substitution. An asset is very "risky" if its payoff has a high negative covariance with S. (Douglas Breeden has recently persuasively argued for the use of consumption correlatedness as the appropriate measure of risk.)

The theory of asset returns embodied in each of expressions (1) through (4) is very powerful because it can be applied so generally. It holds for *any* asset, or portfolio of assets. It holds for *any* individual consumer who has the option of investing in stocks (even if he chooses not to hold stocks) and thus it must hold for aggregate consumption so long as some peoples' consumption is well represented by the aggregate consumption. It holds even if the individual's choices regarding other assets are constrained (for example, the individual cannot trade in his or her "human capital," is constrained by institutional factors in housing investment, or is unable to borrow money) so long as such constraints do not affect his ability to change his saving rate through stock purchases or sales. It incorporates all sorts of uncertainty that people consider in making investment decisions, since these factors are reflected in consumption. The model holds for any time interval, whether a month, a year, or a decade.

II. Perfect Foresight Stock Prices

By iterating (1), we find that price P_{it} at time $t < n$ is the expected present value of dividends and a terminal price P_{in} discounted by the marginal rates of substitution:

(5) $$P_{it} = E\left[\sum_{j=1}^{n-t} \beta^j \frac{u'(C_{t+j})}{u'(C_t)} D_{it+j} \right. $$
$$\left. + \beta^{n-t} \frac{u'(C_n)}{u'(C_t)} P_{in} \Big| I_t \right]$$

It is useful to define the perfect foresight stock price P_{it}^*, which is the price at t given that the consumer knows the whole future time path of consumption, dividends, and the terminal price P_{in}:

(6) $$P_{it}^* = \sum_{j=1}^{n-t} \beta^j \frac{u'(C_{t+j})}{u'(C_t)} D_{it+j}$$
$$+ \beta^{n-t} \frac{u'(C_n)}{u'(C_t)} P_{in}$$

Clearly (5) states that $P_{it} = E[P^*_{it}|I_t]$. Further, we assume that $u(C)$ is of the constant relative risk aversion form

(7) $$u(C) = \frac{1}{1-A} C^{1-A} \quad 0 < A < \infty$$

where A is the "coefficient of relative risk aversion," which is a measure of the concavity of the utility function or the disutility of consumption fluctuations.

Figure 1 shows a plot of P_t from 1889 to 1979, where P_t is the annual average Standard and Poor's Composite Stock Price Index divided by the consumption deflator. On the same figure, we plot the perfect foresight real price P_t^* for $A = 0$ and $A = 4$ using (6) and (7), where we use actual realized real annual dividends for the Standard and Poor series, the Kuznets-Kendrick-US NIA per capita real consumption on nondurables and services and the terminal date $n = 1979$. For each A, we generate a value of β so that (3) holds, as estimated by the sample mean. The case $A = 0$ is revealing; this is the case of risk neutrality, and of a constant discount factor. Notice that with a constant discount factor, P_t^* just grows with the trend in dividends; it shows virtually none of the short-term variation of actual stock prices. The larger A is, the bigger the variations of P_t^* and $A = 4$ was shown here because for this A, P, and P^* have movement of very similar magnitude. Irwin Friend and Marshall Blume estimated A to be about 2 under the assumption that the only stochastic component of wealth is stock returns. Irwin Friend and Joel Hasbrouck estimated A to be about 6 when stock returns and human capital are the stochastic components of wealth. We also computed a P^* series using after-tax returns. It did not look much different from the P^* shown here in the first half of the sample when income taxes were generally unimportant, and did not seem to fit P any better in the second half.

The rough correspondence between P^* and P (except for the recent data) shows that if we accept a coefficient of relative risk aversion of 4, we can to some extent reconcile the behavior of P with economic theory even under the assumption that future price movements are known with certainty. In a world of certainty, the marginal rate of substitution S_t would equal the inverse of one plus the real interest rate, ρ_t. Hence our equilibrium condition becomes $(P_{t+1} + D_{t+1}) \div P_t = 1 + \rho_t$. Thus it can be shown that real stock prices as well as real prices of other assets whose dividend is stable in real terms will rise dramatically over periods when real interest rates are very high. Real interest rates will be high when C_{t+1} is high relative to C_t, for example, in periods of depression when C_t is abnormally low. Hence it is an equilibrium for P_t to be low (relative to P_{t+1}) because otherwise people will desire to dissave (for example, by selling stock at t) in order to maintain their consumption level. Movements in real interest rates which are necessary to equilibrate desired savings to actual savings will lead to changes in stock prices even if dividends are unchanged. It is these movements which are brought out in the figure when P^* with $A = 4$ is compared with P^* with $A = 0$.

The correlation between P^* and P is perhaps not altogether surprising, given the correlation between the stock market and aggregate economic activity over the business cycle noted long ago by many people (see, for example, Arthur Burns and Wesley Mitchell). However, P_t^* is not merely a proxy for aggregate economic activity or consumption at time t. If we assume, as an approximation, that dividends follow a growth path $D_t = D_0 \delta^t$ and if we set $n = \infty$ in (6) to ignore the terminal price, then P_t^* is given by $P_t^* = D_0 \delta^t [C_t^A \sum_{k=0}^{\infty} (\beta \delta)^k C_{t+k}^{-A}]$. This says that P_t^* follows a growth path times the ratio of C_t^A to a weighted harmonic average of future C^A. The weights decline exponentially into the future. Thus, for example, P^* declines gradually between 1907 and 1919 not because consumption declined, since real per capita consumption remained more or less level over this period, but because the gap between current consumption and the longer-run outlook widened. In other words, P^* fell at this time because the perfect-foresight individual, knowing his economic fortune would eventually improve following

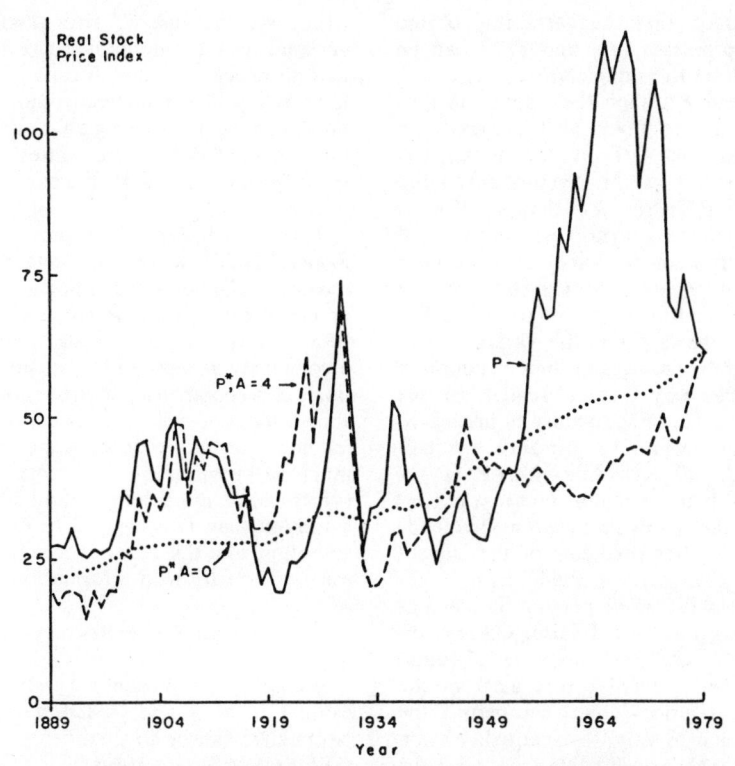

FIGURE 1. ACTUAL AND PERFECT FORESIGHT STOCK PRICES, 1889–1979

Note: The solid line P_t is the real Standard and Poor Composite Stock Price Average. The other lines are: P_t^* (as defined by expression (6) and (7), the present value of actual subsequent real dividends using the actual stock price in 1979 as a terminal value. With $A=0$ (dotted line) the discount rates are constant, while with $A=4$ (dashed line) they vary with consumption.

the war period, wished to try to smooth his consumption over this period. This kind of relationship between P and C would not have been visible by looking at raw stock price and economic activity index series alone, as the earlier scholars did. On the other hand, the short-run correspondence between P and P^* around such episodes as the panics of 1893 or 1907 was in effect noted by these authors.

Our construction implies that P^* (as well as P) is a leading indicator of future levels of economic activity, but it does not suggest the conventional notion of a fixed lead of a few months to a year between P and aggregate economic activity. However, such a fixed lead has never been quantitatively established (see C. W. J. Granger and M. Hatanaka).

Once we drop the assumption of perfect foresight, there need not be a close relationship between P_t and P_t^*. If consumers have no information about P_t^*, then P_t will be a constant and P_t^* will vary. We can write $P_t^* = P_t + U_t$ where $U_t = P_t^* - E[P_t^*|I_t]$ is a forecast error. Since P_t is in the information set I_t, U_t must be uncorrelated with P_t, so that the variability of the stochastic process $\{P_t^*\}$ will be *larger* than that of the stochastic process $\{P_t\}$. Further, if we consider any subset of the information set at t, say I_t^s, then $Var(P_t^*|I_t^s) > Var(P_t|I_t^s)$. If we make the assumption that the variability of the stochastic processes $\{P_t\}$ and $\{P_t^*\}$ can be estimated from the sample variability of observed P_t and P_t^*, then the figure can give some evidence in favor of the hypothesis that A is at least 4. From the figure, it is clear that with $A=0$ the variance inequality is reversed: P_t^* varies *less* than P_t. This is evidence against the hypothesis that the discount factory does not vary. Once we raise A to, say, $A=4$, then the variability of the discount factor forces P_t^* to vary a lot. The larger A is, the larger is the variability induced in P_t^* by changes in the consumption path. Another way that the reader can see that discount factor variability is important is to apply the above variance inequality with $I_t^s = D_t$, yielding $Var(P_t^*|D_t) > Var(P_t|D_t)$. If the discount factor was constant, then this states that current dividends should be a better predictor of the current stock price than current dividends can predict weighted future dividends. Casual observation suggests this is false. Current dividends are a very good forecaster of future dividends, and a terrible forecaster of the current stock price. Once we permit the discount factor to vary, the inequality has a much greater chance of being true, since the current dividend is a poor forecaster of future discount factors.

If it is accepted that the variability of the discount factor is important, then we can use this to provide evidence against Hall's assertion that short-term movements in consumption are not forecastable by consumers. To see this, write the jth term in the summation in (5) as $E(\beta^j u'(C_{t+j})/u'(C_t)|I_t) E(D_{t+j}|I_t) + cov(\beta^j u'(C_{t+j})/u'(C_t), D_{t+j}|I_t)$. If neither the expectation of $\beta^j u'(C_{t+j})/u'(C_t)$ nor its covariance with dividends is forecastable (depends on I_t), then this term varies only due to changes in the expectation of D_{t+j}, i.e., due to information about dividends. If, moreover, $E(\beta^j u'(C_{t+j})/u'(C_t)|I_t) = \gamma^j$ (as might be suggested by Hall's random walk hypothesis), then P_t equals $E(\hat{P}_t^*|I_t)$ where $\hat{P}_t^* = \Sigma \gamma^j D_{t+j}$ (plus a deterministic term due to the covariance). $\hat{P}_t^*$ has a *constant* discount factor and is proportional to P^* in Figure 1 with $A=0$. Because P_t^* with $A=0$ fails the variance test as mentioned previously, we tend to reject models with constant discount factors. Hence we conclude that consumption changes are forecastable. This implies that expected real interest rates vary (contrary to the claims of Eugene Fama and others).

This conclusion does not contradict Robert Hall's assertions that (i) to an *econometrician* who does not know as much as consumers, the marginal utility of consumption is a random walk, and (ii) that income may be a proxy for lagged consumption in econometric models which have shown that consumption is very sensitive to income. The fact that stock prices vary so much with consumption suggests that consumers have more information about consumption than is contained in current consumption, and this leads expected real interest rates to vary with information.

III. Further Research

We have some preliminary results on the estimation of A and β. Estimates of both parameters can be derived using expression (3) for two different assets, which we took as stocks and short-term bonds. Unfortunately, the estimates of A for the more recent subperiods seem implausibly high. This breakdown of the model mirrors the divergence between P^* and P since the early 1950's, as well as the extremely low real return on short-term bond rates in this period. There was an enormous rise in stock prices in that period which cannot be explained by changes in realized dividends or in marginal rates of substitution. Preliminary results show that it cannot be explained by taxes. Friend and Blume noticed an extremely high excess return of stocks over bonds in this period relative to all other subperiods from 1890 to date. Their estimated market price of risk was twice as high in the decade 1952–61 as the highest of any other decade. While the divergence between P_t and P_t^* might be considered an enormous forecast error, we don't have any idea as to why $E(P_t^*|I_t)$ should have changed so much.

REFERENCES

D. Breeden, "An Intertemporal Asset Pricing Model With Stochastic Consumption and Investment Opportunities," *J. Financ. Econ.*, Sept. 1979, 7, 265–96.

Arthur F. Burns and Wesley C. Mitchell, *Measuring Business Cycles*, New York 1956.

E. Fama, "Short-Term Interest Rates as Predictors of Inflation," *Amer. Econ. Rev.*, June 1975, 65, 269–82.

I. Friend and M. Blume, "The Demand for Risky Assets," *Amer. Econ. Rev.*, Dec. 1975, 65, 900–23.

_____ and J. Hasbrouck, "Effect of Inflation on the Profitability and Valuation of U.S. Corporations," Univ. Pennsylvania 1980.

C. W. J. Granger and M. Hatanaka, *Spectral Analysis of Economic Time Series*, Princeton 1964.

R. Hall, "Stochastic Implications of the Life Cycle-Permanent Income Hypothesis," *J. Polit. Econ.*, Dec. 1978, 6, 971–88.

S. LeRoy and R. Porter, "The Present Value Relation: Tests Based on Implied Variance Bounds," *Econometrica*, Mar. 1981.

_____ and C. J. La Civita, "Risk Aversion and the Dispersion of Asset Prices," *J. Bus., Univ. Chicago*, 1981 forthcoming.

R. E. Lucas, "Asset Prices in an Exchange Economy," *Econometrica*, Nov. 1978, 46, 1429–45.

R. Shiller, "Do Stock Prices Move Too Much to be Justified by Subsequent Changes in Dividends?," *Amer. Econ. Rev.*, June 1981, 71.

[5]

Variance Bounds Tests and Stock Price Valuation Models

Allan W. Kleidon
Stanford University

> Previous use of plots of stock prices and "perfect-foresight" prices p_t^* as evidence of either "excess volatility" or nonconstant discount rates is invalid since by construction p_t^* will differ from and be much smoother than rational prices if discount rates are constant. Further, prices appear nonstationary, which can account for the previously reported gross violations of variance bounds. Conditional variance bounds that are valid under nonstationarity are not violated for Standard and Poor's data. The results are consistent with changes in expectations of future cash flows causing changes in stock prices.

I. Introduction

The question what determines changes in stock prices has long intrigued economists. The suggested answers cover the range from the "animal spirits" of Keynes (1936, p. 161) to models of market efficiency and rational expectations, for example, in Fama (1970b). A fundamental problem in testing rational expectation models is the well-known identification issue: If the implications of a particular model are not supported empirically, is it the fault of the assumptions of market efficiency and rational expectations, the fault of the particular model being tested, or both?

I am grateful for the assistance and encouragement of my dissertation committee, Merton Miller (chairman), Craig Ansley, George Constantinides, Eugene Fama, John Gould, Jon Ingersoll, and Richard Leftwich, and the others who have given helpful comments on this paper, especially Fischer Black, Michael Gibbons, Robert Korajczyk, David Modest, Paul Pfleiderer, Myron Scholes, and the referees (particularly Stephen LeRoy). Partial financial support was provided by the Program in Finance, Stanford University.

Another possibility is that the model has not been adequately tested either because additional assumptions required to conduct the tests are violated empirically or because the data used simply do not correspond to the theory. It is argued here that these problems are found in much of a recent literature that has led to a resurgence in stated opposition to the belief that stock prices represent a rational valuation of future cash flows. Tobin (1984, p. 26), for example, cites Shiller (1981b) as showing that "asset markets [do not] in fact generate fundamental valuations. The speculative content of market prices is all too apparent in their excessive volatility." He continues: "Keynes's classic description of equity markets as casinos where assessments of long-term investment prospects are overwhelmed by frantic short-term guesses about what average opinion will think average opinion will think . . . rings as true today as when he wrote it" (see also Ackley 1983, p. 13; Arrow 1983, p. 12). These are strong statements; however, this paper will argue that they are not justified by the work offered in their support.

The variance bounds literature referred to by Tobin uses a deceptively simple idea to test stock price valuation models based on Miller and Modigliani (1961), with an assumption of constant discount rates. As shown in Miller and Modigliani, there are several equivalent representations in terms of dividends, earnings, and investments. Shiller uses the following dividend model:[1]

$$p_t = \sum_{\tau=1}^{\infty} \frac{E\{d_{t+\tau}|\Phi_t\}}{(1+r)^\tau}, \qquad (1)$$

where r is an assumed constant discount rate, d_t is dividends in time t, and $\{X|\Phi\}$ denotes the conditional distribution of the random variable X given the information Φ. The "perfect-foresight price" p_t^{*}[2] is defined as

$$p_t^* \equiv \sum_{\tau=1}^{\infty} \frac{d_{t+\tau}}{(1+r)^\tau}. \qquad (2)$$

A comparison of (1) and (2) shows that

$$p_t = E\{p_t^*|\Phi_t\}, \qquad (3)$$

which forms the basis for the variance bound

$$\text{var}(p_t) \leq \text{var}(p_t^*). \qquad (4)$$

---

[1] Grossman and Shiller (1981) and Shiller (1981a, 1981b, 1981c) work with this model, while LeRoy and Porter (1981) use the earnings stream approach.

[2] See Shiller (1981c, p. 292). The term "perfect-foresight price" is unfortunate since p_t^* as defined in (2) will not necessarily be the price that would prevail under certainty. See Sec. IV below for futher comment.

VARIANCE BOUNDS TESTS.

The logic behind the bound is the simple and general notion that the variance of the conditional mean of a distribution is less than that of the distribution itself. Since the price p_t is a forecast of p_t^*, the variance of the forecast p_t should be less than that of the variable being forecast.

Figure 1 plots Standard and Poor's (1980) annual composite stock price index 1926–79 augmented with the Cowles et al. (1938) common stock index 1871–1925 (the solid line) and p_t^* calculated from the following recursion implied by definition (2):

$$p_t^* = \frac{p_{t+1}^* + d_{t+1}}{1 + r}, \qquad (5)$$

subject to a condition that equates the terminal p_T^* to the terminal price p_T. It seems obvious from figure 1 that the bound in (4) is grossly violated, with the consequent implication that prices cannot be set by the model (1). Since (1) implies that changes in price are driven by changes in expectations of future cash flows, it seems reasonable to infer that something else must be causing the large variation in prices. Tobin relies on speculation unrelated to fundamental values.

The data shown in figure 1 were used in Shiller (1981b), but similar characteristics are apparent in other data as well. Consider figure 2, which also plots prices p_t (the solid line) and corresponding p_t^* series. The relevant characteristics are very similar to those in figure 1.

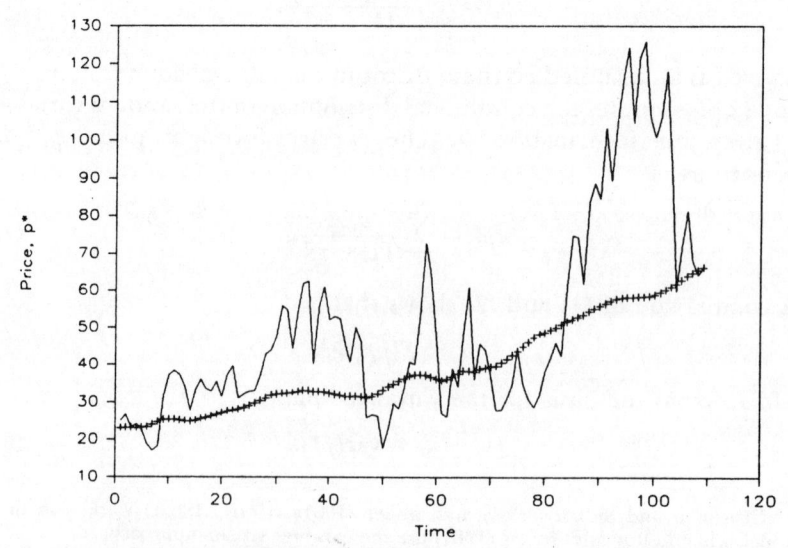

FIG. 1.—Standard and Poor's (real) annual composite stock price index 1926–79 augmented with Cowles Commission common stock index 1871–1925 (solid line) and corresponding perfect-foresight series, including terminal condition $p_T^* = p_T$.

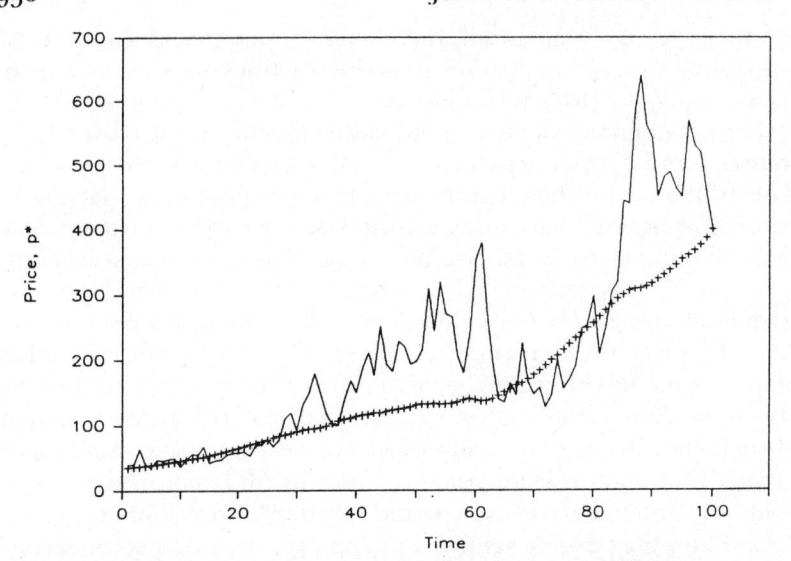

FIG. 2.—Nonstationary (geometric random walk) price series (solid line) and corresponding perfect-foresight series, including terminal condition $p_T^* = p_T$.

Again, it seems obvious that the bound (4) is violated and that consequently the valuation model (1) is empirically untenable.

However, such conclusions based on figure 2 are absolutely unfounded. This figure is based not on real data but on simulated data that by construction are generated by the rational valuation model (1). The variance bound (4) is *not* violated, and absolutely nothing can be inferred from the plots about the validity of the model (1).

This seems startling at first glance. Much of the impact of the variance bounds literature has come from the apparent clear violation of the inequality (4) by plots such as figure 1. Indeed, it has been claimed that an inspection of these plots provides such obvious evidence against the inequality (4) and the valuation model (1) that formal empirical tests of (4) need not be relied on (see Shiller 1981a, pp. 4, 7; 1984). Tirole (1985, p. 1085) also claims: "Simply by looking at Figures 1 and 2 in Shiller [1981b], this inequality [i.e., (4)] is not satisfied." This interpretation is clearly false if plots virtually identical to figure 1 can be readily created when (1) holds by construction.

More important, the price process used in figure 2 is not an unusual or artificial construct, but rather is the (geometric) random walk traditionally regarded in finance as an excellent empirical description of the price process in actual data.[3] This paper examines Standard and

---

[3] For construction details, see Sec. IIA below, particularly n. 7. Note also that the primary characteristics of time-series plots such as figs. 1 and 2 do not depend on the nonstationarity assumption and are present even in stationary AR(1) processes for prices, as demonstrated in Sec. II below. See Kleidon (1986) for more detail on the stationary case.

Poor's series in some detail and demonstrates empirically that the traditional process used to construct figure 2 is consistent with Standard and Poor's price series in figure 1.

The economic intuition behind the compatibility of plots such as figures 1 and 2 with the variance bound (4) is simple, once one sees it. The fundamental flaw in the current interpretation is that the inequality (4) is essentially a *cross-sectional* relation across different economies, but figures 1 and 2 give time-series plots for a single economy. The bound (4) is derived with respect to values of p^* that differ from each other at date t because different realizations of future dividends have different present values at date t. These different realizations occur across the different economies or worlds that may possibly occur in the future, looking forward from date t. If future realizations of dividends are unexpectedly good, the realized value of p_t^* will be greater than what is expected at t, which by (3) is simply the current price p_t. If the future is unexpectedly bad, p_t^* is less than p_t.

Consider the possible values of p^* and price that may occur at some particular date t. If the price p_t predicts p_t^*, the theory given by (4) states that there should be greater variation across all possible realizations of p_t^* than in p_t. The problem with using real data is that ex post we can observe only one of the ex ante possible economies, and so we cannot look across different values of p^*, each corresponding to a different economy, to see if the theory is correct. We can do this by simulation, however, and it is shown below that precisely the predicted relation across different possible economies holds for the process used to construct figure 2, which is a time-series plot of only one of the ex ante possible outcomes.

Given that we observe only one world in practice, it is important to examine what should be expected in plots of time series of price and p^* for a single economy. First, note that we would not expect the series to look like each other if there is uncertainty at t about future dividends since the price p_t will be the expected value of p_t^* across possible economies and the ex post value of p_t^* once the future is revealed will in general differ from its expected value at t. How much difference will exist between plots of p_t^* and p_t depends on the amount of information available when prices are set, and it is shown below that figures 1 and 2 are consistent with a reasonable assumption about information available when Standard and Poor's prices are set.

The second insight, which is crucial to an interpretation of plots such as figures 1 and 2, is that the dividend stream being forecast at dates $t - 1, t - 2, \ldots$ and $t + 1, t + 2, \ldots$ is essentially identical to the stream forecast at t, and hence the present value of the ex post realizations will be highly correlated. Consequently the time series of p_t^* will be highly correlated, which translates into the "smooth" time-series path given in figures 1 and 2.

Of course, since p_t^* depends on information about future dividends not known at t, it is not part of the information used to set p_t or, indeed, any other price. At each date the best available information is used to set prices, and as information changes, the price will change. If, for example, the information Φ_t comprises current and past dividends, any change in dividends at t will in general imply changes in all future dividends, and the price will change by the present value of the change in expected dividends. Empirically, changes in dividends tend to persist for a very long time, and so the implied revisions in price can be very large relative to the change in current dividends.

But since by construction p_t^* is always calculated using all realized future dividends, there are no unexpected changes in dividends with implications for changes in p_t^* as there are for prices. In fact, the ex post return from both dividends and capital gains will always exactly equal the discount rate r for the p_t^* series, by the definition (2). Therefore, the possible change in consecutive values of p_t^* is limited to the capital gain required to give the ex post return r, which is another way of stating why the time series p_t^* can be much smoother than that of price. Consequently, one should expect time-series plots of p_t^* and p_t for a single economy to look like figures 1 and 2, even if *across possible economies* the variability of p_t^* exceeds that of p_t.

These arguments are established more rigorously in Section II, which demonstrates that plots such as figures 1 and 2 cannot be used to replace more formal tests of the inequality (4). Further, it is clear that, since (4) is derived by considering alternative possible economies, extra assumptions must be made to test (4) using time-series data for only one economy. Section III shows empirically that the traditional assumption in finance of nonstationary (random walk) prices is not rejected for Standard and Poor's series and that the gross violations of (4) currently reported in the literature are consistent with incorrect assumptions of stationarity in the time-series tests conducted. Section III also derives and tests inequalities similar to (4) that are implied by the (geometric random walk) time-series process for prices. It is shown that Standard and Poor's price and dividend data do not violate these bounds. Section IV contains a summary and concluding remarks.

II. Interpretation of Plots of Price and p_t^*

The current interpretation of plots such as figures 1 and 2 is that they demonstrate that prices are not set by the valuation model (1). Although the literature is not always clear on the reasoning, there appear to be two related arguments based on these plots. The first, examined in Section II*A*, relies on the undisputed smoothness of a time-series plot of p_t^* relative to prices as evidence against (1). Section IIB discusses the second, which attempts to infer the plausibility of the model from the degree of correspondence between the series p_t and p_t^*. The argument based on smoothness is clearly a less stringent test than that based on correspondence since two series may be drawn from similar stochastic processes and hence show similar time-series properties, yet not show correspondence between the observations. The conclusion reached here is that neither argument is valid.

A. *Variance Bounds and "Short-Term Variation"*

The characteristic of the time-series plots of price p_t and p_t^* that seems most at odds with the claim that $\text{var}(p_t^*) \geq \text{var}(p_t)$ is the striking "smoothness" of p_t^* compared with the price series. The current interpretation in the literature is that this is evidence against the inequality. However, this interpretation is incorrect, and in fact the bound does not address the issue of how smooth one time series is compared with the other. The literature has incorrectly identified the variances used in the inequality (4) with smoothness or "short-term variation" in time-series plots of price and p_t^*.

Examples of this argument occur frequently in the variance bounds literature. For example, Shiller (1981b, p. 421) states that "one is struck by the smoothness and stability of the *ex post* rational price series p_t^* when compared with the actual price series." Grossman and Shiller (1981), in one of the most influential papers using the argument, assume a constant relative risk aversion utility of consumption function,

$$U(c) = \frac{1}{1-A} c^{1-A}, \quad 0 < A < \infty, \qquad (6)$$

and calculate (p. 223) the "perfect-foresight stock price" p_t^{*1} with constant and nonconstant discount rates. Under the assumption that investors know the whole future path of consumption (p. 223), they calculate implied discount rates from (6) for different values of the risk aversion parameter and attempt to infer the parameter value that makes the observed stock price series consistent with market efficiency (p. 224). The risk neutrality case ($A = 0$) gives constant discount rates (assuming constant time preference), and p_t^* appears much closer to the actual price series for $A = 4$ (nonconstant rates), at least for the period up to about 1950. Their results are reproduced here as figure 3.

---

[1] Some papers use the notation P_t^* and P_t, as in Grossman and Shiller (1981), while others use the lower-case notation p_t^* and p_t, which is used throughout this paper.

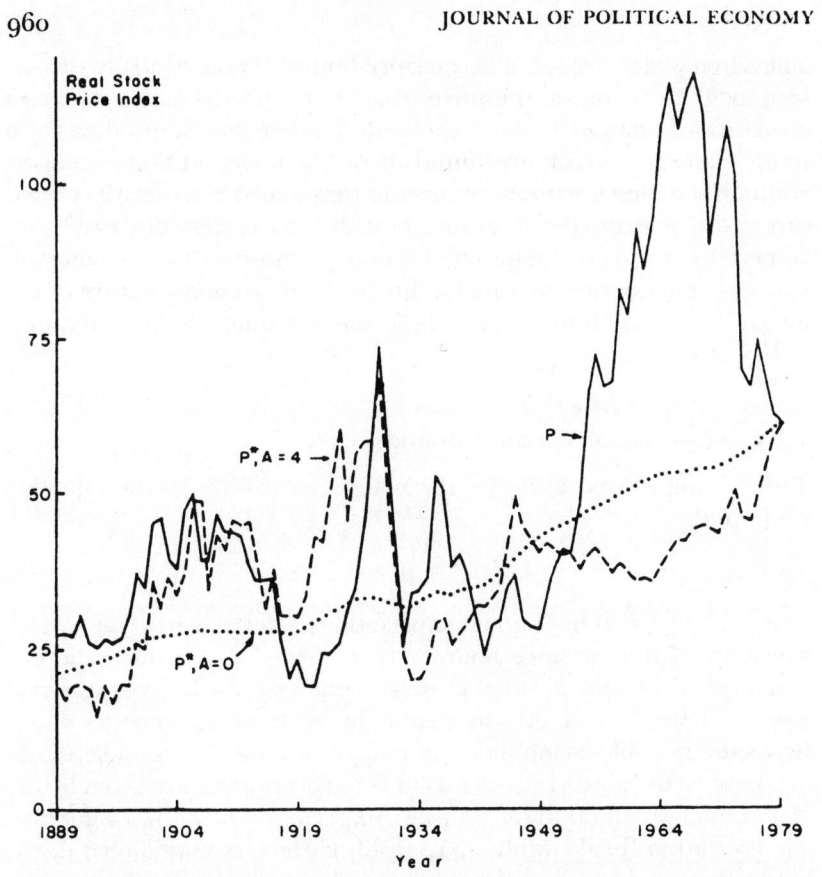

FIG. 3.—Grossman and Shiller's (1981) series of actual and perfect-foresight stock prices, 1889–1979 (reproduced from p. 225). The solid line P_t is the real Standard and Poor's composite stock price average. The other lines are: P_t^* (as defined by their expressions 6 and 7), the present value of actual subsequent real dividends using the actual stock price in 1979 as a terminal value. With $A = 0$ (dotted line) the discount rates are constant, while with $A = 4$ (dashed line) they vary with consumption.

Grossman and Shiller select the risk aversion parameter $A = 4$ in figure 3 (1981, p. 224) because of the smoothness of p_t^* when discount rates are assumed constant: "Notice that with a constant discount factor, P_t^* just grows with the trend in dividends; it shows virtually none of the *short-term variation* of actual stock prices. The larger A is, the bigger the variations of P_t^* and $A = 4$ was shown here because for this A, P, and P^* have movements of very similar magnitude" (emphasis added)

It has been shown in figure 2 that p_t^* is much smoother than price even if the constant discount rate model (1) holds by construction. The primary cause of the confusion shown in the current literature is related to the construction of p_t^* using ex post information not avail-

VARIANCE BOUNDS TESTS.

able when prices are set. The variance bound (4) is essentially a cross-sectional restriction on the prices that would prevail across different economies at date t. Tests of the bound using time-series data for a single economy, which are found throughout the literature, require additional strong assumptions beyond those needed to derive (4), and care must be exercised to ensure that the "variances" discussed with respect to time-series data correspond to those in the variance inequality. This section first highlights the cross-sectional nature of the inequality, then shows exactly how the argument in the literature fails.

1. Cross-sectional Variance Bounds

The equations used to derive the bound are (1)–(3) above. Equation (3) implies

$$p_t^* = p_t + \xi_t, \tag{7}$$

where $E\{\xi_t|p_t\} = 0$ by rational expectations. Clearly $\text{var}(p_t^*) \geq \text{var}(p_t)$, which gives the variance bound (4) in terms of the unconditional variances of p_t^* and p_t. This illustrates the essentially cross-sectional nature of the bound. At any date t the realized information Φ_t restricts the possible economies that may occur, and the possible values of the present value of dividends in those economies are given by the conditional distribution $\{p_t^*|\Phi_t\}$, with expectation p_t by (3). Each possible realization for Φ_t implies a (possibly different) conditional distribution for p_t^*, including the conditional expectation p_t. Integration over all possible economies results in the distribution of prices with variance $\text{var}(p_t)$ used in the bound (4) and the unconditional distribution of p_t^*.

This argument also applies to distributions other than the unconditional distributions that result when all possible realizations of Φ_t are considered. For example, knowledge of Φ_{t-1} may restrict the possible economies at t relative to the total set. More generally, (7) implies that

$$\begin{aligned} \text{var}\{p_t^*|\Phi_{t-k}\} &= \text{var}\{p_t|\Phi_{t-k}\} + \text{var}\{\xi_t|\Phi_{t-k}\} \\ &\geq \text{var}\{p_t|\Phi_{t-k}\}, \quad k = 0, \ldots, \infty, \end{aligned} \tag{8}$$

where information at $t - k$ is included in information at t (traders do not forget), and rational expectations require that $\text{cov}\{\xi_t, p_t|\Phi_{t-k}\} = 0$. The inequalities in (8) are clearly useful if conditional variances ($k < \infty$) are defined but unconditional variances ($k = \infty$) are not—for example, for the case of a random walk in prices, which is shown below to be empirically relevant. Further, it is shown below that confusion in interpretation of time-series plots of price and p_t^* stems from comparing the conditional variance of price, $\text{var}\{p_t|p_{t-k}\}$, with an inappropriate conditional variance of p_t^*, $\text{var}\{p_t^*|p_{t-k}^*\}$, which does not limit the conditioning information to information available to traders at time $t - k$.

To illustrate the distinctions, consider the following dividend process (which ignores irrelevant means for current purposes):

$$d_t = \rho d_{t-1} + \eta_t, \tag{9}$$

where η_t is independently and identically distributed (i.i.d.) $(0, \sigma_\eta^2)$. Then we have the following proposition.

PROPOSITION 1. If prices are set by (1) and information comprises current and past dividends given by (9), then

$$\begin{aligned} p_t &= a d_t \\ &= \rho p_{t-1} + a \eta_t, \end{aligned} \tag{10}$$

where $a \equiv \rho/(1 + r - \rho)$.

Proof. Follows directly from substitution in (1) for expected future dividends given (9), with simplification of the resulting infinite series. Q.E.D.

This process includes both stationary dividends ($|\rho| < 1.0$) and nonstationary random walk dividends ($\rho = 1.0$). We proceed by giving the variances of the conditional distributions $\{p_t|\Phi_{t-k}\}$ and $\{p_t^*|\Phi_{t-k}\}$, where Φ_{t-k} is limited to current and past dividends or, equivalently from (10), to p_{t-k}. The limit as $k \to \infty$ gives the unconditional distributions. The variances of the appropriate conditional distributions verify (8), but for the random walk case when $\rho = 1.0$, the conditional variances are well defined but the unconditional variances are not.

PROPOSITION 2. Assume prices are set by (1) with current and past dividends given by (9) as information. Then

$$\begin{aligned} \text{var}\{p_t|\Phi_{t-k}\} &= \text{var}\{p_t|p_{t-k}\} \\ &= \sigma_\eta^2 a^2 \left(\frac{1 - \rho^{2k}}{1 - \rho^2} \right). \end{aligned} \tag{11}$$

Proof. Given the dividend process (9), the result follows directly from (10) conditioned on p_{t-k} with simplification of the resulting infinite series. Q.E.D.

PROPOSITION 3. Assume that prices are set by (1) with current and past dividends given by (9) as information and that $|1/(1 + r)| < 1.0$.

Then

$$\text{var}\{p_t^*|\Phi_{t-k}\} = \text{var}\{p_t^*|p_{t-k}\}$$

$$= \sigma_\eta^2 a^2\left[\left(\frac{1-\rho^{2k}}{1-\rho^2}\right) + \frac{(1+r)^2}{\rho^2(2r+r^2)}\right] \quad (12)$$

$$= \text{var}\{p_t|p_{t-k}\} + \frac{\sigma_\eta^2 a^2(1+r)^2}{\rho^2(2r+r^2)}.$$

Proof. Follows from the definition (2) and the dividend process (9), conditioning on d_{t-k}, and simplifying the resulting infinite series. Q.E.D.

Note that in (12) the difference between the conditional variances $\text{var}\{p_t^*|\Phi_{t-k}\}$ and $\text{var}\{p_t|\Phi_{t-k}\}$, which by (8) equals $\text{var}\{\xi_t|\Phi_{t-k}\}$, is for this case a constant equal to $\text{var}\{p_t^*|\Phi_t\}$. Note also that the restriction on r in proposition 3 prohibits $-2 \leq r \leq 0$, which ensures that the denominator in the expression for $\text{var}\{p_t^*|\Phi_t\}$ in (12) is positive.[5]

It can be verified that the limits (as $k \to \infty$) of the conditional variances in (11) and (12) equal the corresponding unconditional variances:

$$\text{var}(p_t) = \frac{\sigma_\eta^2 a^2}{1-\rho^2}, \quad (13)$$

$$\text{var}(p_t^*) = \frac{\sigma_\eta^2(1+r+\rho)}{(1+r-\rho)(1-\rho^2)(2r+r^2)}. \quad (14)$$

Further, for the random walk case ($\rho = 1.0$), we have

$$\lim_{\rho \to 1} \text{var}\{p_t|p_{t-k}\} = \frac{\sigma_\eta^2 k}{r^2} \quad (15)$$

and

$$\lim_{\rho \to 1} \text{var}\{p_t^*|p_{t-k}\} = \frac{\sigma_\eta^2}{r^2}\left[k + \frac{(1+r)^2}{2r+r^2}\right]. \quad (16)$$

This shows that the unconditional variances of p_t and p_t^* are not defined for the random walk, so that strictly speaking the bound (4) involves undefined terms. However, the corresponding variances satisfy inequality (8).

Throughout this section, the interpretation of the variances has been in the cross-sectional sense of (unobserved) variances at t across different possible economies. To illustrate this notion, we now show

---

[5] See Kleidon (1986) for an interpretation of this condition in terms of the time-series process for p_t^*.

the values for p_1 and p_1^* for 20 replications of the simulated economy used to generate figure 2. The model used is the (geometric) random walk for prices traditionally used in finance, and it is shown in Section III below that this model is consistent with Standard and Poor's prices used in figures 1 and 3. The dividend process is[6]

$$\ln d_t = \mu + \ln d_{t-1} + \epsilon_t, \qquad (17)$$

where ϵ_t is i.i.d. $N(0, \sigma^2)$. We then have the following proposition.

PROPOSITION 4. Assume that prices are generated by (1) with current and past dividends given by (17) as information. Then the implied price is

$$p_t = \left(\frac{1+g}{r-g}\right)d_t, \qquad (18)$$

where $1 + g \equiv \exp[\mu + (\sigma^2/2)]$.

Proof. From (17), the lognormality of $\exp(\mu + \epsilon_t)$ and the standard result for its expectation, and the independence of $\epsilon_t, \epsilon_\tau, \tau \neq t$, we have

$$E\{d_{t+\tau}|d_t\} = d_t(1 + g)^\tau,$$

where g is defined in (18). Substitution into (1) gives (18) directly. Q.E.D.

Figure 4 shows price and p^* *at the same date* $t = 1$ across 20 economies that were identical at $t = 0$ but are different at $t = 1$. In each economy the starting price is set as $p_0 = 40.0$, and the same dividend process given by (17) is used in each replication—all that change are the random innovations ϵ_t.[7] The first seed chosen arbitrarily for the random number generator produces the observations for "economy 1" used for figure 2, and subsequent seeds are produced internally by the IMSL generator.

From (8), we know that the variance of p_1 given p_0 should be less than the variance of p_1^* given p_0, and figure 4 shows precisely this result. Values of p_1 vary across the 20 economies from a low of 30.48 for economy 10 to a high of 61.35 for economy 17. Much greater variability across economies is seen in p_1^*, as the theory predicts, and values range from 8.99 (economy 4) to 477.83 (economy 6).

To complete the picture, figure 5 shows *time-series* plots of 100

---

[6] No dividend smoothing is assumed, which is conservative since Standard and Poor's dividend series since about 1950 appears much smoother than either prices or (accounting) earnings. Section III discusses the implications of dividend smoothing in more detail.

[7] The values for the drift μ and the innovation variance σ^2 are estimated from first differences of logs of Standard and Poor's (real) price series for 1926–79, and Standard and Poor's (real) price index in 1926 is approximately 40.0. The series ϵ_t are generated using the IMSL subroutine GGNPM. For more details, see Kleidon (1983).

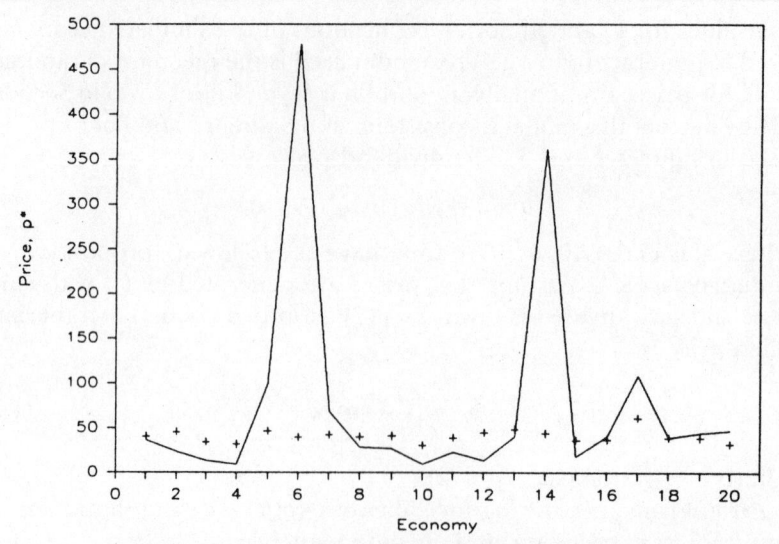

FIG. 4.—Distribution of p^* (solid line) and prices at time 1 across 20 economies that are identical at time 0. Note that this is not a time-series plot for one economy but the values at time $t = 1$ across 20 different economies.

observations of p_t and p_t^* for three of the 20 economies shown in figure 4.[8] The three economies are 2, 4, and 6; the latter two are chosen because they give the lowest and highest values of p_t^*, respectively. It is obvious from figure 5 that the wide variation in p_t^* is simply the result of different ex post draws of dividends over time for the different economies. Each is possible at time 0 since the same stochastic process and same initial price p_0 prevail in each economy. Ex post, quite different worlds could be encountered, and each implies its own value of p_t^*. The variance bounds hold across these different economies.

Although figures 4 and 5 show clearly the notion underlying variance bounds tests, the luxury of observing different worlds that may unfold through time is limited to theory or simulation. In reality we observe only one world. I now consider the properties one should expect to find in time-series plots for one economy.

2. Resolution of the Apparent Paradox

The current consensus has interpreted "smoothness" or lack of "short-term variation" in p_t^* relative to price as evidence against the

---

[8] The first economy is shown in fig. 2, and plots for the first 10 economies are given in Kleidon (1983, app. A).

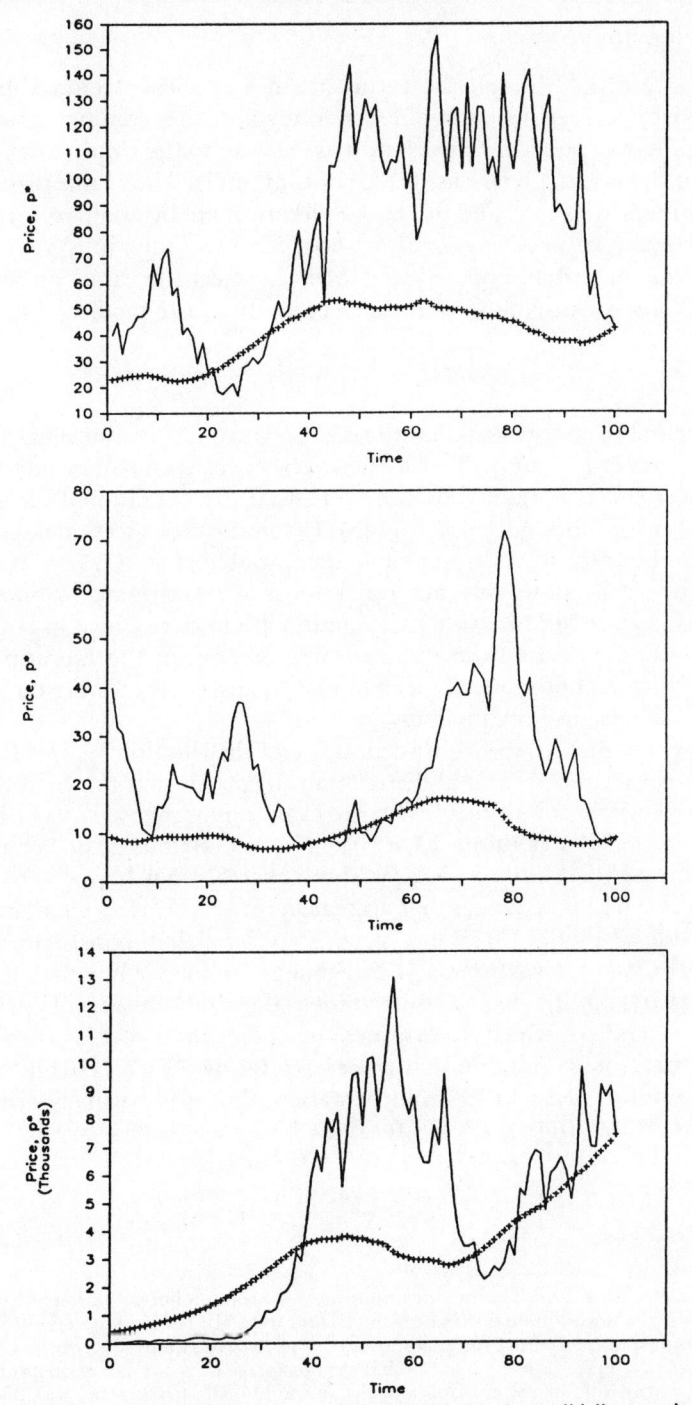

FIG. 5.—Plots of time series of nonstationary price series (solid line) and corresponding p_t^* series, for economies 2, 4, and 6 from 20 replications shown in fig. 4.

inequality (4). Although the terms are not explicitly defined in the literature, it seems reasonable to interpret the comments about smoothness or short-term variation as relating to the conditional variance of the series, given past values of that series. Thus I interpret the smoothness of price and p_t^* to be determined by $\text{var}\{p_t|p_{t-k}\}$ and $\text{var}\{p_t^*|p_{t-k}^*\}$, respectively. Lack of short-term variation in p_t^* versus p_t, which led Grossman and Shiller (1981) to reject the valuation model (1), is consequently defined here to mean that, for small k,

$$\text{var}\{p_t^*|p_{t-k}^*\} < \text{var}\{p_t|p_{t-k}\}. \tag{19}$$

Since the issue concerns conditional variances, it is natural to examine the general bound (8), which is written in terms of conditional variances.[9] It is immediately apparent that the conditional distribution $\{p_t^*|p_{t-k}^*\}$ does not appear in (8)! Given the cross-sectional nature of these bounds, it could not since the variable p_t^* by (2) uses future dividend realizations that are not known at t and hence cannot be used as part of conditioning information at t to derive a valid bound. Consequently, despite the numerous references in the literature to the relative smoothness of price and p_t^*, this is a red herring with respect to variance inequalities.

It is clear that as $k \to \infty$ the conditional distribution $\{p_t^*|p_{t-k}^*\}$ approaches the unconditional distribution of p_t^*, so that the bound (4) will indeed hold for sufficiently large k (assuming the variances of the unconditional distributions exist). What is not obvious is the behavior of $\{p_t^*|p_{t-k}^*\}$ for k small. We now show exactly what happens to the three conditional variances that appear in (8) and (19) as k changes for the dividend model (9). We have already seen that, consistent with (8), $\text{var}\{p_t|p_{t-k}\} < \text{var}\{p_t^*|p_{t-k}\}$. It remains to show the relation between $\text{var}\{p_t|p_{t-k}\}$, which determines the smoothness of prices, and $\text{var}\{p_t^*|p_{t-k}^*\}$, which determines the smoothness of p_t^*.

PROPOSITION 5. Assume that prices are set by (1) with current and past dividends given by (9) as information, that η_t is normally distributed, and that $|1/(1 + r)| < 1.0$. Then

$$\text{var}\{p_t^*|p_{t-k}^*\} = \text{var}(p_t^*)(1 - \rho_k^2), \tag{20}$$

---

[9] An earlier version of this paper distinguished between conditional variances similar to (19) and the unconditional variances in (4), and this argument is adopted in LeRoy (1984) using the conditional variances in (19). The current comparison of the conditional variances in (8) with those in (19) has the advantage of showing that the problem is not primarily with the use of conditional vs. unconditional variances, but with the use of incorrect conditional variances in (19).

where

$$\rho_k \equiv \frac{\text{cov}(p_t^*, p_{t-k}^*)}{\text{var}(p_t^*)}$$

$$= \frac{\rho^{k+1}(2r + r^2) - (1 - \rho^2)(1 + r)^{1-k}}{(1 + r + \rho)(\rho + r\rho - 1)}.$$

Proof. Equation (20) follows directly from the normality of p_t^*, the definition of var(p_t^*) is given in (14) above, and cov(p_t^*, p_{t-k}^*) is straightforward to calculate given the definition (2) and the dividend process (9). Q.E.D.

It can be verified that the limit (as $k \to \infty$) of var$\{p_t^*|p_{t-k}^*\}$ in (20) is var(p_t^*) and that for the random walk case ($\rho = 1.0$)

$$\lim_{\rho \to 1} \text{var}\{p_t^*|p_{t-k}^*\} =$$

$$\frac{\sigma_\eta^2[(k+1)(2r + r^2) - (1+r)(3+r) + 2(1+r)^{1-k} + 1]}{r^2(2r + r^2)}. \quad (21)$$

Again in this case, the conditional variances var$\{p_t^*|p_{t-k}^*\}$ are well defined for $k < \infty$.

Figure 6 shows the relevant conditional variances var$\{p_t|p_{t-k}\}$, var$\{p_t^*|p_{t-k}\}$, and var$\{p_t^*|p_{t-k}^*\}$, assuming $r = 0.065$ and $\sigma_\eta^2 = 1$. Parts *a*, *b*, and *c* each show the three conditional variances for k from 0 to 100, for values of $\rho = 0.80, 0.99$, and 1.0, respectively. As k increases, both var$\{p_t|p_{t-k}\}$ and var$\{p_t^*|p_{t-k}\}$ increase, and by (12) the difference is the constant var$\{p_t^*|p_t\}$. The inequalities in (8) are never violated, although for the random walk in part *c* of figure 6 both variances increase without bound.

Particularly interesting is the behavior of var$\{p_t^*|p_{t-k}^*\}$ relative to var$\{p_t|p_{t-k}\}$, which determines the relative smoothness of the series. Both equal zero at $k = 0$, and for some value k (which increases in ρ) it must be the case that var$\{p_t^*|p_{t-k}^*\} > $ var$\{p_t|p_{t-k}\}$ since we know that eventually the unconditional variances of p_t^* and p_t satisfy this inequality (assuming they exist). The key result, however, is that short-term variances show the opposite result, just as noted by Grossman and Shiller (1981). For k small, we see that var$\{p_t^*|p_{t-k}^*\} < $ var$\{p_t|p_{t-k}\}$, and this can hold for quite large k depending on the parameter ρ in the dividend process.

This implies that plots such as figures 1 and 3 above *should* show greater smoothness in p_t^* than in the price series if prices are given by (1). Such smoothness provides no evidence against either the bound (4) or the valuation model (1) but, on the contrary, is to be expected. Consequently the evidence used by Grossman and Shiller (1981) to

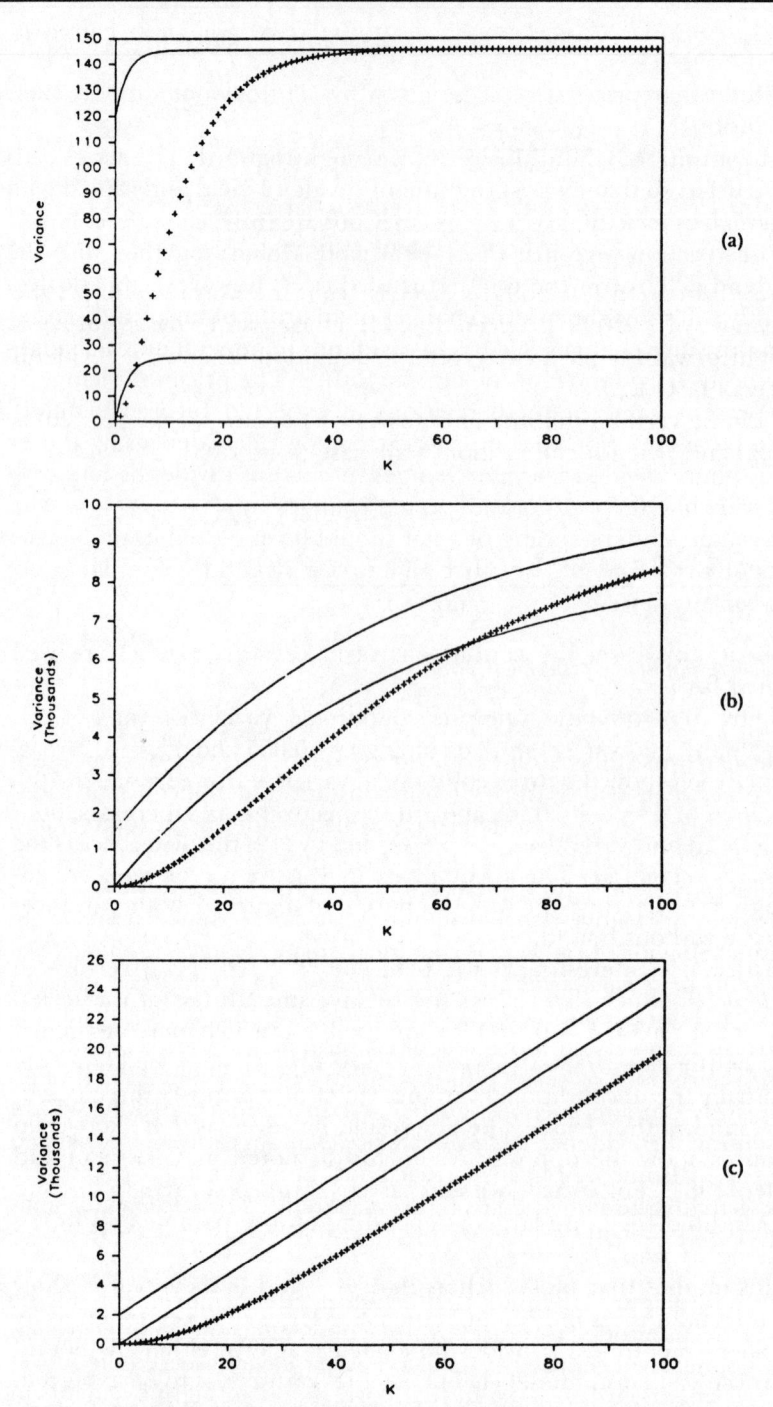

FIG. 6.—Conditional variances var$\{p_t^*|p_{t-k}\}$ (upper solid line), var$\{p_t|p_{t-k}\}$ (lower solid line), and var$\{p_t^*|p_{t-k}^*\}$ (broken line), $k = 0, \ldots, 100$, for AR(1) prices and dividends with (a) $\rho = 0.80$, (b) $\rho = 0.99$, and (c) $\rho = 1.0$.

conclude that prices cannot be given by (1) does not support their conclusion.

The intuition behind this result is straightforward. The series p_t^* is constructed so that ex post the sum of dividend yield and capital gain always gives exactly the rate r by (2). Consequently, changes in p_t^* will by construction give just the capital gain, which, together with the dividend d_t, ensures the total return r. Prices, however, can and frequently will show short-term changes of an order of magnitude larger than this since changes in current dividends in general imply changes in expected dividends for the infinite future. The price will change by the present value of these revisions in expected future dividends. Since by assumption the series p_t^* is already calculated using the ex post infinite dividend series, changes in current dividends imply no new information and no unexpected changes in p_t^*.

Given an understanding of what should be expected in time-series plots of price and p_t^*, we turn now to the issue of correspondence between the series.

B. Correspondence between p_t^* and p_t

1. The Argument

Grossman and Shiller (1981) rely on the relative degree of correspondence between two p_t^* series (with constant and nonconstant rates) and the price series p_t to determine which model is preferable, and they argue (p. 224) that "the rough correspondence between [p_t^*, $A = 4$] and [p_t] (except for the recent data) shows that if we accept a coefficient of relative risk aversion of 4, we can to some extent reconcile the behavior of [p_t] with economic theory *even under the assumption that future price movements are known with certainty*" (emphasis added).

The statement concerning a certainty assumption is crucial, and we return to it shortly. A more recent claim that the price series should correspond to the p_t^* series is one of the strongest. Shiller (1984) relies exclusively on plots such as figure 3 as a "particularly striking way of presenting the evidence" that stock price changes cannot be explained in terms of "some new information about future earnings" (p. 30). He uses virtually the same plot as figure 3 (extended to 1981) and claims (p. 31):

> [Figure 3] shows that actual dividend movements of the magnitude "forecast" by price movements never appeared in nearly a century of data. We *might* have observed big movements in [p_t^*, $A = 0$] that correspond to big movements in [p_t] and that would mean that movements in [p_t] really did appropriately forecast movements in future dividends. On

the other hand, this just did not happen. Look, for example, at the stock market decline of the Great Depression, from 1929 to 1932. $[p_t^*, A = 0]$ did go down then, but only very slightly, far less than the decline in $[p_t]$. The reason is that real dividends declined substantially only for the few worst years of the Depression. These few lean years have little impact on $[p_t^*, A = 0]$, which depends in effect on the longer-run outlook for stocks.

2. Analysis

Section IIA demonstrates that, even if cross-sectional variance bounds are satisfied, time-series plots of price and p_t^* will frequently show the series p_t^* as being much smoother than the price series if there is uncertainty about future dividends when prices are set. Consequently, it is not surprising that the series do not correspond to each other. What is crucial is how much information is available, which determines the degree of correspondence that should be expected. It is clear from the simulations in figures 2 and 5 that the amount of uncertainty about future cash flows implicit in the traditional geometric random walk is sufficient to imply the degree of divergence between p_t^* and p_t shown in Standard and Poor's series in figure 1.

Shiller's (1984) argument that the stock price should not have declined as much as it did between 1929 and 1932 because dividends declined substantially only in the few worst years of the depression assumes that stockholders knew that the lower dividends they were seeing would not last far into the future. Grossman and Shiller (1981) are more explicit and add an assumption of certainty about future prices. This assumption is not part of the model ostensibly being tested. The original model, given as (1) above, writes price in terms of expected future dividends, in contrast to p_t^*, which uses the ex post outcomes. In a world of certainty we would expect p_t^* to correspond to the actual price series—if discount rates were estimated correctly and the price series were rational, they should be identical.

But of course the actual stock prices shown in figure 3 were not set in a world of omniscience. If Grossman and Shiller's p_t^* series with nonconstant discount rates exactly corresponded to the actual price series, it would be misleading to claim that the series were consistent with economic theory "even under the assumption that future prices are known with certainty." Rather, there would be consistency with economic theory *only* under certainty since the price series will follow the ex post series exactly only if shareholders have perfect information about the future dividend series. If they do not—which is surely the state of things—then one should expect deviation between ex ante and ex post prices.

The question then is not whether the p_t and p_t^* series deviate, but rather how much they deviate. It is initially tempting to regard the p_t^*, $A = 4$ series as preferable to the $A = 0$ series because it more closely resembles actual prices p_t. But until we specify how much the p_t^* series *should* deviate from the price series—that is, until we specify the amount of uncertainty in the market about future cash flows—we cannot decide which plot deviates by the correct amount. The issue is addressed by Shiller (1984, p. 35), but he does not present sufficient evidence to allow inference about the degree of divergence to be expected: "Of course, people do not have perfect foresight, and so actual stock prices [p_t] need not equal [p_t^*]. We [i.e., Grossman and Shiller (1981)] argue that even under imperfect information we might expect [p_t] to resemble [p_t^*], though if information is very bad the resemblance could be very weak." This illustrates precisely the difficulty in examining plots such as figures 1 and 3. Until we know how imperfect the information is, we cannot interpret how weak the resemblance should be. A fundamental misinterpretation of such figures has been to make inferences about the validity of the valuation model (1) without specifying the yardstick necessary to allow such inferences.

To see whether the degree of correspondence between p_t^* and price in figure 1 is consistent with the valuation equation (1), we need a model that specifies the information available to the market about future cash flows. One possibility—favored by Grossman and Shiller—is to assume that shareholders have a large amount of information about future dividends. Then the only way prices could be rational is if discount rates vary greatly because of changes in aggregate consumption, which is their solution. Unfortunately, as discussed in more detail below, this solution fails when applied to other data.

An alternative explanation is much more consistent with the data. Using the (geometric) random walk for prices traditionally used in finance and assuming that the only information available at time t is the past history of dividends, we see in figures 2 and 5 that there is sufficient uncertainty about future cash flows to imply the large divergence between prices and p_t^* seen in Standard and Poor's data in figures 1 and 3. The procedures used to construct figures 2 and 5 are conservative since discount rates are strictly constant by construction and no dividend smoothing is assumed.[10]

---

[10] Hence Marsh and Merton (1984a, p. 19) are incorrect in claiming that "[fig. 3] can be interpreted as implying that the p_t^* series has 'too little' volatility to be consistent with a dividend process which is not smoothed."

C. Conclusion

This section has demonstrated that plots such as figures 1 and 3 cannot be regarded as inconsistent with the valuation model (1), although at first they appear to be convincing evidence against its validity. It is tempting to look at the p_t^* series as the "true" price, which does not vary much through time, and the actual price as (correlated) deviations from the true price. Such an interpretation is incorrect because the price at t can only be assessed relative to the information Φ_t. Thus in figure 2 the actual price series is by construction the conditional expectation of p_t^* given Φ_t, and by construction the prediction error ξ_t in (7) (i.e., the difference between this conditional expectation and the ex post outcome for p_t^*) is uncorrelated with p_t or with past prices, which are also in Φ_t.

What is potentially misleading from figure 2 is that successive prediction errors are highly correlated with each other, which appears to contradict the previous statement. Again, however, the problem lies in the information that is implicitly being used for conditioning. Previous forecast errors ξ_{t-k} are not in the information set at t since previous p_{t-k}^* that depend on the ex post outcomes for future dividends are unknown at t. Clearly the errors will be correlated since almost the same future set of dividends are being forecast at, say, t and $t + 1$.[11] As seen in figures 4 and 5, the errors across economies at time t are indeed unrelated to prices at t.

Despite the potential for confusion in plots such as figure 3, they have been heavily relied on in the literature and have even been treated as stronger evidence against (1) than formal tests of the bound (4). Shiller (1981a, pp. 4, 7; 1984) claims that figure 3 alone is sufficient to show that stock prices are inconsistent with the valuation model (1), as does Tirole (1985). This is simply incorrect. However (as Shiller [1981a] points out), the more formal tests of (4) based on time-series data for a single economy are also problematic, and I now turn to them.

III. Time-Series Tests of Variance Bounds

The assumption typically made to test the bound (4) using time-series data is that the relevant variables (namely, dividends and prices for the dividend discount model being discussed here) follow stationary and ergodic processes. If this is true, then the sample moments are consistent estimators for the moments of the unobservable distribu-

---

[11] The issue of overlapping forecast errors also arises in other contexts, e.g., spot and forward foreign exchange rates (see Hansen and Hodrick 1980).

tions used in the inequality, assuming a sufficiently long time series of realizations from those distributions.[12]

Shiller (1981*b*, 1981*c*) tests the bound (4) with Standard and Poor's and Dow Jones Industrial Average indexes of annual stock prices and dividends (1981*b*, pp. 434–35), using sample variances of price and p_t^* as estimators of unconditional population variances. He reports that the bound appears grossly violated but does not conduct formal significance tests. LeRoy and Porter (1981) also test (4) but derive it from Miller and Modigliani's (1961) model based on future earnings X_t and investments I_t:

$$p_t = \sum_{\tau=1}^{\infty} \frac{E\{(X_{t+\tau} - I_{t+\tau})/n_t|\Phi_t\}}{(1 + r)^\tau}, \qquad (22)$$

where r is an assumed constant discount rate and n_t is the number of shares outstanding at t.[13] LeRoy and Porter conduct formal tests of the bound under the assumption of stationarity of their series. The point estimates imply violation for Standard and Poor's data, but sampling error is sufficiently high that the bound is not rejected at conventional significance levels (p. 557). Tests on individual stocks indicate rejection.

However, there are at least two important reasons to question whether the extra assumptions underlying these tests are valid empirically. First, as documented in Section IIIC below, the data used in many of the variance bounds tests are consistent with the assumption that prices follow a nonstationary random walk. If so, the unconditional variances in (4) do not exist, and the use of sample variances of p_t and p_t^* as estimators of population unconditional variances is invalid. Section IIIA shows that the apparent gross violations of the variance bound (4) reported in the current literature using sample variances of p_t and p_t^* are consistent with an incorrect assumption of stationarity of prices and dividends. However, it is valid to estimate conditional variances even if prices are nonstationary, and Section

---

[12] See Fuller (1976, p. 230). Just how long is "sufficient" in this context, even assuming stationarity and ergodicity, is investigated in detail in Kleidon (1983, chap. 5; 1986). See also Flavin (1983).

[13] They do not use exactly this model but use $n_{t+\tau}$ as the divisor, which implicitly assumes that the net benefits of future investments do not accrue to current shareholders. In private correspondence, Stephen LeRoy indicates that this adjustment makes little difference. Two other issues are of greater potential significance. First, LeRoy and Porter (1979, pp. 2, 3) adjust prices and earnings to account for earnings retention. Although this is feasible under certain conditions, their procedure uses an incorrect timing assumption that violates the dividend irrelevance proposition. Second, their results are based on incorrect data since in effect they create an artificial Standard and Poor's price series with a spurious seasonal at lag 4, as shown in their table 4 (1981, p. 570). For details, see Kleidon (1983, chap. 3).

IIIB shows that Standard and Poor's data do not violate the conditional variance inequalities in (8).

LeRoy and Porter discuss the assumption of stationarity of earnings and prices in some detail and make adjustments for earnings retention. Shiller (1981c, p. 293) claims that "the resulting series appear stationary," but LeRoy and Porter report that, after their adjustments, there remains evidence of nonstationarity.[14] They continue (1981, p. 569): "We have decided to neglect such evidence and simply assume that the series are stationary. . . . We do not argue that this treatment is entirely adequate, nor do we in any way minimize the problem of nonstationarity; the dependence of our results on the assumption of stationarity is probably their single most severe limitation."

The second problem, that of dividend smoothing, has important implications for all research that attempts to infer the properties of an infinite stream of future dividends from some finite ex post set of dividends that are under some control of management. Empirical evidence suggests that management takes care to create a smooth short-run dividend series that may not reflect one for one the fortunes of the firm as determined primarily by its earnings and investment opportunities.[15] Ceteris paribus, the less variable the dividend stream, the more variable will be the price series that comprises the present value of future dividends. For example, a firm seeking to finance expansion internally may withhold all dividends over some finite period, with an implicit promise of some future (perhaps liquidating) dividend.[16]

If dividends are smoothed, the time series may be covariance nonstationary and violate the assumption of ergodicity necessary to allow estimation of valid cross-sectional variance bounds with time-series data. To illustrate, suppose that at t there exists a firm that has future cash flows per share D composed of earnings (paid out fully as dividends) at only one period, say T, and suppose for convenience that the discount rate $r = 0$.[17] This implies that the conditional distribution $\{p_t^*|\Phi_t\}$ is just the conditional distribution $\{D|\Phi_t\}$. Clearly the bound (4) holds at t assuming that the relevant variances are defined.

---

[14] Since LeRoy and Porter attempt to correct for nonstationarity, the results in this section based on original data apply to their work only to the extent that nonstationarity remains.

[15] See, e.g., Lintner (1956) and Fama and Babiak (1968). This does not deny that dividends may contain some information, as in the signaling hypotheses of Ross (1977) and Bhattacharya (1980).

[16] Note that Marsh and Merton's (1984a) definition of dividend smoothing does not deal with this case since it does not allow firms to pay zero dividends in any period when the price is positive (see their eq. [7], p. 13).

[17] Paul Pfleiderer suggested this example, say for the case of a firm drilling for oil.

However, the ex post time series p_t^*, calculated from the recursion (5) and based on the terminal payment, will be a constant with zero sample variance. The price series will show positive variance if information about the terminal payment becomes available through time so that the bound (4) will appear violated if estimated by sample variances.

The problem is more severe for inequalities that, unlike (4) or (8), are invalid if an assumption of ergodicity of dividends is violated. The variance inequality that has received most attention in the literature is (4), but others exist. Some, such as LeRoy and Porter's bound (1981, p. 560) on the coefficient of dispersion (i.e., the ratio of the standard deviation to the mean), are similar to (4) in that they rely on stationarity and ergodicity assumptions for testing, but not for the intrinsic validity of the bound. Others such as in Shiller (1981c) are based on the time series of prices and dividends, and so rely on some form of stationarity for their validity, even aside from issues of testing. Shiller's alternate bounds are given as (1981c, p. 296, eqq. I-2, I-3)

$$\sigma(\Delta p) \leq \frac{\sigma(d)}{\sqrt{2r}}, \tag{23}$$

$$\sigma(\Delta p) \leq \frac{\sigma(\Delta d)}{\sqrt{2r^3/(1 + 2r)}}, \tag{24}$$

where $\sigma(\cdot)$ is standard deviation, Δp and Δd are first differences of price and dividends, respectively, and r is the (assumed constant) one-period discount rate. The derivation of (23) assumes joint covariance stationarity of the time series p_t and d_t, while that of (24) assumes joint stationarity of Δp_t and Δd_t, with information variables contained in the information set (Shiller 1981c, pp. 295–97). Only (24) is consistent with nonstationary (random walk) prices and dividends, and only (24) is not violated by point estimates.[18] However, the assumptions underlying both (23) and (24) may be violated if dividends are smoothed.

The issue of dividend smoothing can have striking implications for some more recent tests that attempt to overcome criticisms of early variance bounds tests. For example, West (1984) derives and tests the inequality that the variance of changes through time in the present value of expected dividends will be greater when the information set comprises current and past dividends than when it comprises a larger set. Although he regards the necessary assumption that dividends

---

[18] See Shiller (1981c, p. 297). He continues: "Of course, we do not expect the data to violate all inequalities even if the model is wrong" and notes that, although this inequality is not violated for first differences of the data, the relevant bound is violated when the data are differenced using an interval of 10 years (i.e., $x_t - x_{t-10}$). Section IIIB discusses this claim in the context of comparable results based on conditional variances.

follow an autoregressive integrated moving average (ARIMA) process as "relatively mild" (p. 3), this can be violated if dividend smoothing implies changes in a future residual dividend that do not show up in the currently observed dividend series. In the extreme, if the finite and observed dividend series were constant, the use of only this stream to predict future dividends would imply constant future dividends, and so the present value would be constant through time and the innovation zero. In West's terminology, this would appear to be evidence that 100 percent of price changes could be attributed to speculative bubbles—in fact, the violation of the assumption of an ARIMA process for dividends simply means that the theoretical inequality is invalid.[19]

Although the issue of dividend smoothing is potentially very important in interpreting the results from any particular test, the remainder of this section assumes nonsmoothed dividends as in figures 2 and 5 to highlight the implications of nonstationarity, which is most crucial in the current context. First, Section IIIA discusses the nonstationary price model used in figure 2, derives consistent dividend and earnings models, and shows that the current gross violations of the bound (4) are not surprising if prices follow this process with parameters corresponding to Standard and Poor's price data. Section IIIB derives conditional variance inequalities that are valid for the nonstationary price process and demonstrates that Standard and Poor's series do not violate these bounds. Section IIIC completes the argument by showing empirically that the assumed process is consistent with Standard and Poor's data.

A. Nonstationary Prices and Tests of Unconditional Variances

Stationarity of stock prices is vital to the validity of much of the variance bounds literature. The cited tradition in finance for treating stock prices as nonstationary random walks goes back to at least 1934 when it was recognized "that stock prices resemble cumulations of purely random changes" (Working [1934]; cited in Roberts [1959, p. 2]). Annual accounting earnings also appear to be well described as

---

[19] Similar issues arise in recent attempts to account for nonconstant discount rates in (1). For example, Scott (1984) uses Hansen's (1982) generalized method of moments estimator and assumes in one specification that dividends are not mean-reverting to avoid criticisms concerning assumed stationarity of dividends. However, in this case he assumes (p. 8) that "the percentage change in dividends and stock prices as well as the price-dividend ratio ($\Delta D/D$, $\Delta P/P$, P/D) are stationary." Such an assumption may be violated if dividends are smoothed.

random walks.[20] However, most variance bounds tests assume stationarity of stock prices, dividends, or earnings, usually after deflation by some price index to account for inflation, and "detrending" to remove a perceived deterministic time trend. Nelson and Plosser (1982) compare these two approaches and cannot reject that stock prices (as well as several other macroeconomic variables) are "nonstationary stochastic processes with no tendency to return to a trend line" (p. 139).[21]

The simplest random walk model, (10) above with $\rho = 1.0$, implies a zero expected capital gain component in stock returns, which historically is not true given less than full payout of earnings as dividends. An alternate model,

$$p_t = \mu + p_{t-1} + \epsilon_t, \quad (25)$$

where ϵ_t is i.i.d. with mean zero and variance σ^2, implies an expected capital gain rate that varies inversely with the price level. The most plausible economic model in this context is a geometric random walk,

$$\ln p_t = \mu + \ln p_{t-1} + \epsilon_t, \quad (26)$$

or

$$p_t = p_{t-1} \exp(\mu + \epsilon_t). \quad (27)$$

If the capital gain rate is defined as $(p_t - p_{t-1})/p_{t-1}$, then the (conditional) expected capital gain rate (g) is constant and is given by

$$\begin{aligned} g &\equiv E\left\{\frac{p_t - p_{t-1}}{p_{t-1}} \bigg| p_{t-1}\right\} \\ &= \exp\left(\mu + \frac{\sigma^2}{2}\right) - 1.0, \end{aligned} \quad (28)$$

assuming lognormality of $\exp(\mu + \epsilon_t)$ in (27). Expected capital gain rates are calculated below using (28).

1. Consistent Price, Dividend, and Earnings Processes

The valuation models based on dividends (1) and earnings or net cash flows (22) preclude any necessary one-to-one relation between the time-series process for price and the time-series process for earnings or dividends. As discussed with respect to dividend smoothing, any

---

[20] For empirical studies on annual earnings as a random walk, see, e.g., Little (1962), Ball and Watts (1972), Albrecht, Lookabill, and McKeown (1977), and Watts and Leftwich (1977). For quarterly earnings see Foster (1978).

[21] They note the implications of nonstationarity for variance bounds tests (pp. 142, 143), as do Black (1980) and Copeland (1983). See also Kling (1982).

particular set of observations may be unrepresentative of the total expected dividend stream. In principle, the same phenomenon could occur in the earnings stream (net cash flow) approach since the pattern of net cash flows does not necessarily correspond to changes in the present value of expected future net cash flows through time. Further, we do not observe the requisite "economic earnings" but accounting earnings. One cannot infer that a rational price series must be generated by a particular stochastic process just because dividends or earnings follow the process in a finite set of observations, or vice versa. However, one can infer a (nonunique) process for dividends or earnings that is compatible with the observed price series and see if the process is confirmed in dividend/earnings data.

This section assumes that prices follow the geometric random walk (26), defines consistent dividend and earnings processes, and discusses the underlying economic models. We have seen from proposition 4 above that one dividend process consistent with the price process (26) is

$$\ln d_t = \mu + \ln d_{t-1} + \epsilon_t, \tag{17}$$

where μ and ϵ_t are identical to those in (26), since

$$p_t = \left(\frac{1+g}{r-g}\right) d_t. \tag{18}$$

Not surprisingly, one consistent earnings process also has constant expected growth and is analogous to the price (26) and dividend per share (17) processes. However, the earnings stream approach involves investment as well as earnings. To specify the expected growth rate in earnings and its relation to that in prices and dividends per share, two issues are important: Is investment financed internally (via retained earnings) or externally (via new capital issues), and how profitable are the investments?

PROPOSITION 6. If investment is a constant proportion δ of earnings each period, is financed internally, and earns the rate of return r, then an earnings per share process consistent with the price process (26) and the dividend per share process (17) is

$$\ln e_t = \mu + \ln e_{t-1} + \epsilon_t, \tag{29}$$

and the relation between p_t and e_t is given by

$$p_t = \frac{1}{r} E\{e_{t+1}|e_t\}$$
$$= \frac{1+g}{r} e_t, \tag{30}$$

where $e_t \equiv X_t/n_t$ and $1 + g \equiv \exp[\mu + (\sigma^2/2)]$.

Proof. Equation (29) follows from (26) if (30) holds, and the expected growth rate in earnings is g. But given the assumed investment process, $g = \delta r$ (cf. Copeland and Weston 1983, p. 485). Further, since all financing is internal, $d_t = (1 - \delta)e_t$, and substitution into (18) gives (30).[22] Q.E.D.

Note that, although consistent processes for price and dividends were derived in terms of an unspecified empirical growth rate g, the earnings and investment model defines this rate in terms of fundamental variables, $g = \delta r$.

2. Tests of Unconditional Variances: Simulation Results

I now demonstrate that gross violations of bounds based on unconditional variances can result if the procedures of, say, Shiller (1981*b*) are applied to a series that by construction is rationally set by Miller-Modigliani valuation models with constant discount rates but that is nonstationary. This section reports the results of Monte Carlo simulations of the nonstationary price and dividend processes given above. The parameter values $\mu = .0095$, $\sigma = .218$, and $p_0 = 40.0$ are set to correspond to estimates for Standard and Poor's (deflated) annual price series, 1926–79. A series of disturbances ϵ_t are generated by the IMSL subroutine GGNPM, and the dividend and corresponding rational price series are generated by (17) and (18). The p_t^* series is generated recursively by (5) with the terminal condition $p_T^* = p_T$.[23] The sample variances of the price series p_t and the p_t^* series are then calculated, and the variance bound (4) is deemed violated if for sample variances $\text{var}(p_t) > \text{var}(p_t^*)$. The procedure is carried out for two different but related price series. The first is the series constructed by (18), and the second "detrends" prices and dividends before calculating the corresponding p_t^* series following Shiller (1981*b*, p. 432).

Table 1 gives the percentage (across 100 replications) of violations of the variance bound (4) for the simulated price series (18) and its

---

[22] If external financing (from new securities) is raised for the investment, the growth rate in earnings will exceed g, the growth rate for prices and dividends per share (see Miller and Modigliani 1961, pp. 421–26). The assumption of normal returns on investment is less likely to be violated for the economy as a whole, as reflected in Standard and Poor's index, than for some particular "growth company." If investment earns abnormal returns, compare Miller and Modigliani (1961, p. 423, eq. 25).

[23] Marsh and Merton (1984*a*) show that, if the terminal value p_T^* is set equal to the average sample price, the bound (4) is always violated if prices follow (26). This result does not hold for the terminal condition imposed by Grossman and Shiller (1981) and examined here (although Marsh and Merton [1984*b*, p. 12, n. 4] state the contrary). Their analysis does not show whether the "gross violations" of the bound that are reported in the literature can be explained by nonstationarity of prices, which is examined in table 2 below.

TABLE 1

PERCENTAGE OF VIOLATIONS OF VARIANCE BOUNDS CALCULATED FROM: (i) SIMULATED RATIONAL (GEOMETRIC) RANDOM WALK SERIES, (ii) THE SAME SERIES WITH EXPONENTIAL "DETRENDING," AND (iii) THE MATCHING CONSTRUCTED "PERFECT-FORESIGHT" PRICE SERIES

	VIOLATIONS (%) OF VARIANCE BOUND: var(p^*) ≥ var(p)						DURBIN-WATSON STATISTIC FOR RESIDUALS FROM DETRENDING IN (ii)	
	(i) Random Walk Series			(ii) "Detrended" Random Walk Series				
SAMPLE SIZE (T)	$r = .05$	$r = .065$	$r = .075$	$r = .05$	$r = .065$	$r = .075$	Mean	Standard Deviation
5	100	100	100	95	95	95	2.37	.54
10	100	100	100	97	99	99	1.44	.52
50	83	83	88	89	90	90	.38	.19
100	86	87	87	90	92	92	.20	.10
200	86	87	88	92	92	93	.10	.05
1,000	95	95	95	100	100	100	.02	.01
2,000	91	91	91	96	96	96	.01	.006
3,000	72	71	71	99	99	99	.007	.005

NOTE.—Based on 100 replications. The relevant processes are: (i) $\ln p_t = \mu_p + \ln p_{t-1} + \epsilon_t$, ϵ_t i.i.d. $N(0, \sigma^2)$. $\ln d_t = \mu_p + \ln d_{t-1} + \epsilon_t$, $p_t = ad_t$, where $a = (1 + g)/(r - g)$, $(1 + g) = \exp[\mu_p + (\sigma^2/2)]$, and r = a constant discount rate. Parameter values are $\mu_p = 0.0095$, $\sigma = 0.218$, and $p_i(0) = 40.0$. (ii) The series are "detrended" (following Shiller [1981b, p. 432]): $\hat{d}_t = d_t/e^{b(t-T)}$, $\hat{p}_t = p_t/e^{b(t-T)}$, where T is the base year, and b is estimated as the coefficient on time in a regression of the log of price on a constant and time. (iii) The "perfect-foresight" series corresponding to cases i and ii are defined as $p_t^* = (p_{t+1}^* + D_{t+1})/(1 + r)$, where D_{t+1} = the dividend from i or ii, and $p_T^* = p_T$, the terminal price in i or ii.

detrended counterpart. Results are shown for three different (real) discount rates r, namely 0.05, 0.065, and 0.075. Over 1926–81, Ibbotson and Sinquefield (1982, p. 15, exhibit 3) report an arithmetic mean nominal return per annum on the Center for Research in Security Prices (CRSP) file of common stocks of 0.114, with mean inflation of 0.031 per annum. Over the same period, the mean return for small stocks was 0.181, and Standard and Poor's index is composed of larger stocks. Shiller (1981b, p. 431, table 2) uses a discount rate of 0.048 per annum (in real terms) for detrended data or 0.063 per annum (p. 430) for nondetrended data. The rate 0.075 is given for comparison.

The most striking result of table 1 is the very high number of violations of the variance bound (4). The detrending procedure appears to exacerbate the tendency to reject the inequality, but the discount rates examined here do not appear to have much effect on the frequency of violation.[24] Table 1 also gives the mean and standard deviation (across replications) of the Durbin-Watson statistic from ordinary least squares (OLS) regression of prices on time, which is part of the detrending procedure. As noted below (n. 33), the average value for sample size 50 is almost identical to that obtained for the actual Standard and Poor's price series.

Although table 1 establishes that the variance bounds test procedures overwhelmingly result in violations of the bound (4) when applied to a nonstationary series generated by (1), it does not show whether gross violations are likely to occur. For 1,000 Monte Carlo replications for the sample size 100, which corresponds to Shiller (1981b, 1981c) and Grossman and Shiller (1981), table 2 gives both the number of violations of (4) (i.e., when the ratio of the sample standard deviation of price to the sample standard deviation of p_t^* exceeds 1.0) and the number of gross violations (when the ratio exceeds 5.0). Shiller (1981b, p. 341, table 5) reports a gross violation ratio of 5.59 for Standard and Poor's data. For rational, nonstationary series that are detrended, 397 replications out of 1,000 (or about 40 percent) give violation ratios greater than 5.0 using a discount rate r of 0.05, and 148 replications (almost 15 percent) for $r = 0.065$. Even for $r = 0.075$, almost 5 percent of the replications result in gross violations.

In short, the results of table 2 show that the gross violations of the bound (4) are not surprising if test procedures that assumed the existence of population unconditional variances were incorrectly applied

---

[24] As Joerding (1984) points out, the discount rate can in principle affect the frequency of violation. Further, table 2 shows that the discount rates examined here do affect the average amount by which the bound is violated.

TABLE 2

SUMMARY STATISTICS OF THE DISTRIBUTION OF THE RATIO OF SAMPLE STANDARD DEVIATION OF PRICE TO SAMPLE STANDARD DEVIATION OF "PERFECT-FORESIGHT" PRICE, ACROSS 1,000 REPLICATIONS FOR SAMPLE SIZE 100, FOR (i) SIMULATION RATIONAL (GEOMETRIC) RANDOM WALK SERIES AND (ii) THE SAME SERIES WITH EXPONENTIAL "DETRENDING"

	NUMBER OF VIOLATIONS (Ratio > 1.0)	NUMBER OF "GROSS VIOLATIONS" (Ratio > 5.0)	RATIO MEAN*	RATIO STANDARD DEVIATION	MINIMUM RATIO	MAXIMUM RATIO	PERCENTILE 50th (Median)	PERCENTILE 90th	PERCENTILE 95th
Case i, random walk:									
$r = .05$	855	307	3.56	2.70	.51	15.59	2.62	7.22	8.40
$r = .065$	865	62	2.65	1.50	.53	8.46	2.55	4.55	5.25
$r = .075$	869	21	2.33	1.15	.57	7.48	2.39	3.75	4.31
Case ii, "detrended" random walk:									
$r = .05$	894	397	4.29	3.04	.49	14.65	3.31	8.53	9.62
$r = .065$	915	148	3.30	1.66	.51	8.86	3.42	5.39	6.09
$r = .075$	925	46	2.90	1.24	.52	6.89	2.98	4.44	4.94

NOTE.—The relevant processes are defined in table 1.
* All summary statistics are for the distribution across 1,000 replications.

to nonstationary price data. Note that the parameter values used in these simulations are chosen as those estimated for Standard and Poor's price series, 1926–79, and that the nonstationary process (26) used here is consistent with the data. Note also that the simulations assume a dividend process with the same innovation variance as the price series, in (17) and (26). At least since 1950, Standard and Poor's dividend series is much smoother than the corresponding price or earnings series. Consequently, the simulation results are biased against finding gross violations relative to a dividend series with a lower sample innovation variance, and one would expect even greater rejection in actual empirical tests.

B. Tests of Inequalities Based on Conditional Variances

This subsection tests the conditional variance inequalities given by (8), which are valid for nonstationary price series. The results show that the conditional bounds are not violated by Standard and Poor's data and provide both confirmation and interpretation of tests of inequality (24) above based on differences of prices and dividends.

We test variances of p_t and p_t^* conditional on past prices p_{t-k}, for $k = 1, 2, 5,$ and 10. The assumed price process is the geometric random walk (26), which implies that

$$\operatorname{var}\{p_{t+k}|p_t\} = \operatorname{var}\{p_t \exp(\mu + \epsilon_{t+1})\exp(\mu + \epsilon_{t+2}) \ldots \exp(\mu + \epsilon_{t+k})|p_t\}$$

$$= p_t^2 \operatorname{var}\left[\exp\left(k\mu + \sum_{n=1}^{k} \epsilon_{t+n}\right)\right]$$

$$\equiv p_t^2 c_k,$$

where c_k is constant through time given ϵ_t i.i.d. $N(0, \sigma^2)$.[25] Hence the conditional variances are constant through time except for scaling by p_t^2, and to avoid the resulting heteroscedasticity the inequality tested here is

$$\operatorname{var}\left\{\frac{p_{t+k}}{p_t}\bigg|p_t\right\} \leq \operatorname{var}\left\{\frac{p_{t+k}^*}{p_t}\bigg|p_t\right\}. \tag{31}$$

---

[25] As noted by Gary Chamberlain, more general distributional assumptions that allow conditional heteroscedasticity (i.e., nonconstant c_k) are consistent with the tests conducted here, although in that case the bounds are in terms of the expected value of the conditional variances.

VARIANCE BOUNDS TESTS

The population variances in (31) are constant through time for the price and dividend processes (26) and (17).[26] Note the equality of the conditional means,

$$E\left\{\frac{p_{t+k}}{p_t}\bigg|p_t\right\} = E\left\{\frac{p^*_{t+k}}{p_t}\bigg|p_t\right\}$$
$$= (1 + g)^k, \tag{32}$$

where $1 + g$ is the growth rate in prices as above. The conditional variances in (31) are estimated by the corresponding sample mean square deviations from the conditional means, using the sample estimated growth for the conditional means of p_{t+k} and p^*_{t+k} by (32).[27]

Table 3 reports the ratio of the conditional standard deviation of price to the conditional standard deviation of p^*_t for Standard and Poor's series, 1926–79, together with a sampling distribution for a sample size of 54, for discount rates of 0.05, 0.065, and 0.075. This distribution was constructed as in Section IIIA by simulation (here over 2,000 replications) of the price and dividend processes given by equations (26), (17), and (18), for parameter values corresponding to Standard and Poor's series.

There are two main results of interest in table 3. First, comparison of Standard and Poor's statistics with the corresponding sampling distribution shows that none of the inequalities given by (31) is violated at even a 10 percent significance level. Second, note that the point estimates do not violate (31) for $k = 1, 2$, or 5 but do violate for $k = 10$. It is significant that Shiller (1981c, p. 297) reports that the bound (24), which is consistent with nonstationary prices and dividends, is not violated when the data are differenced with a lag (k) of 1 but are violated when $k = 10$. Although he treats this as an important rejection, he presents no formal significance tests. The simulation results here show that violation of the bound (31) by point estimates for $k = 10$ is consistent with the valuation model (1).

Again, note that this sampling distribution is generated under the assumption of no dividend smoothing and, consequently, is conservative if dividends are smoothed. Even if smoothing is ignored, however, these tests show that Standard and Poor's price and dividend

---

[26] The use of a sample p^*_t that is constructed subject to a terminal condition such as $p_T = p^*_T$ implies that the conditional variances are equal at T, but the estimation in this section does not explicitly account for this time dependence. However, the sampling distribution constructed by Monte Carlo simulation implicitly accounts for this since the same procedures are carried out there as for Standard and Poor's data.

[27] The sensitivity of results to the use of sample growth rates was checked in the simulations by repeating the analysis using the true (known) growth rate, and the results were essentially unchanged.

TABLE 3

RATIO OF CONDITIONAL STANDARD DEVIATION OF PRICE TO CONDITIONAL STANDARD DEVIATION OF p^* BY DIFFERENT CONDITIONING LAGS k, FOR STANDARD AND POOR'S SERIES 1926–79, AND SUMMARY STATISTICS OF THE DISTRIBUTION OF THIS RATIO IN 2,000 REPLICATIONS OF SIMULATED GEOMETRIC RANDOM WALK WITH SAMPLE SIZE 54

			SIMULATION						
		Number of		Ratio				Percentile	
	STANDARD AND	Simulation	Ratio	Standard	Minimum	Maximum	50th		
LAG	POOR'S RATIO	Violations (Ratio > 1.0)	Mean*	Deviation	Ratio	Ratio	(Median)	90th	95th
Rate $r = .05$:									
$k = 1$	.46	0	.38	.15	.01	.92	.38	.57	.64
$k = 2$	.64	31	.53	.20	.01	1.23	.53	.79	.87
$k = 5$	.83	435	.78	.30	.02	2.09	.76	1.16	1.29
$k = 10$	1.17	816	.98	.41	.04	4.24	.91	1.48	1.76
Rate $r = .065$:									
$k = 1$	.59	0	.41	.15	.02	.93	.41	.60	.66
$k = 2$	.81	32	.56	.20	.02	1.26	.57	.82	.90
$k = 5$	.96	495	.82	.29	.03	2.11	.80	1.19	1.30
$k = 10$	1.21	888	1.00	.38	.06	3.12	.95	1.49	1.73
Rate $r = .075$:									
$k = 1$	.58	0	.43	.15	.02	.94	.43	.62	.68
$k = 2$	.79	34	.58	.20	.02	1.26	.59	.84	.90
$k = 5$	.92	528	.83	.28	.04	2.04	.83	1.19	1.30
$k = 10$	1.13	924	1.02	.37	.07	2.76	.97	1.48	1.69

NOTE.—The conditional variances at lag k are: $\text{var}(p_{t+k}/p_t|p_t) = E\{[p_{t+k} - E(p_{t+k}|p_t)]/p_t\}^2$, $\text{var}(p^*_{t+k}/p_t|p_t) = E\{[p^*_{t+k} - E(p^*_{t+k}|p_t)]/p_t\}^2$, where $E(p_{t+k}|p_t) = E(p^*_{t+k}|p_t) = p_t(1 + g)^k$. The growth rate g is estimated as $\hat{g} = \exp[\hat{\mu} + (\hat{\sigma}^2/2)]$, where μ and σ are mean and standard deviation of the series $\ln p_t - \ln p_{t-1}$. The relevant processes are defined in table 1. No detrending is done here.

* All summary statistics are for the distribution across 2,000 replications.

series do not violate the well-defined conditional variance inequalities implied by the valuation model (1). I now complete the argument by showing the empirical validity of the nonstationary price process used to derive these tests.

C. Evidence on Nonstationarity of Prices, Earnings, and Dividends

This subsection applies the tests in Nelson and Plosser (1982) for nonstationarity of various macroeconomic variables to prices, earnings, and dividends used in variance bounds tests. First, autocorrelation functions for levels and first differences of random walks, and for residuals ("deviations from trend") from a regression of a random walk on time, are compared with the sample autocorrelations. Second, two different specifications of the autoregressive representation are tested directly for unit roots, as discussed in Fuller (1976) and Dickey and Fuller (1979).[28] The first specification is the simple autoregression (Dickey and Fuller 1979, p. 428, eq. 2.1)

$$Y_t = \mu + \rho Y_{t-1} + e_t, \qquad (33)$$

where e_t is assumed i.i.d. $N(0, \sigma^2)$ and $\rho = 1.0$ under the null hypothesis. Fuller (1976, pp. 371, 373) tabulates empirical distributions for two test statistics for this model under the null hypotheses $\rho = 1.0$ and $\mu = 0.0$. The first statistic is $n(\hat{\rho}_\mu - 1)$, where $\hat{\rho}_\mu$ is the least-squares estimate of ρ in (33) and n is the sample size. The second test statistic, $\hat{\tau}_\mu$, is the "t-statistic" under the null hypothesis $\rho = 1$.[29] The second specification (Dickey and Fuller 1979, p. 428, eq. 2.2) includes time as a regressor:

$$Y_t = \mu + \beta t + \rho Y_{t-1} + e_t. \qquad (34)$$

The statistics are similar to those for (33) and are denoted $n(\hat{\rho}_\tau - 1)$ and $\hat{\tau}_\tau$ for the model (34) (Fuller 1976, pp. 371, 373).

1. Stock Prices

The primary price data used here are Standard and Poor's annual composite stock price index for 1926–79 and quarterly composite

---

[28] Other procedures for testing for the existence of more than one unit root are discussed in Hasza and Fuller (1979) and applied in Meese and Singleton (1982). The hypothesis of multiple unit roots is rejected for the series examined here.

[29] For a given significance level the critical value of the statistic $\hat{\tau}_\mu$ is larger (in absolute value) than for the usual t-distribution since the sampling distribution of $\hat{\rho}_\mu$ is centered at values less than 1.0 in finite samples. Dickey and Fuller (1979, pp. 429–30) indicate that, if $\mu \neq 0.0$ in (33), the statistic $\hat{\tau}_\mu$ will imply acceptance of the hypothesis $\rho = 1$ with probability greater than the nominal level, although they do not indicate the amount of discrepancy.

stock price index for 1947:I to 1978:IV (1980, pp. 134–37). Diagnostic plots of both levels and first differences show that the raw (nominal) data reflect price level changes in later periods. Consequently the series are deflated by the gross national product (GNP) implicit price deflator, and diagnostic checks indicate that this procedure seems adequate. Unless otherwise stated, p_t here refers to deflated prices.[30]

Tables 4 and 5 give results for autocorrelation and Dickey and Fuller (1979) tests, respectively. Section A in table 4 gives results for sample autocorrelations for the levels of seven series. The first three series are taken from Nelson and Plosser (1982, table 2). Series 1 and 2 are constructed as a random walk and a time-aggregated random walk,[31] and the autocorrelations are those expected in a sample of size T (here, 100). The third series is the log of nominal stock price. Series 4 and 5 (6 and 7) are deflated price and log of deflated price for Standard and Poor's annual (quarterly) series cited above. Section B in table 4 gives corresponding autocorrelations for first differences of the series, while section C gives autocorrelations for the residuals from a regression of the series on time, following Nelson and Kang (1981).

The major result from table 4 is that the autocorrelation functions for the stock price data show marked similarity to those for the constructed random walks. Several other results are also apparent. First, there seems little difference in the autocorrelation functions of the deflated price series, P_t/GNP_t, and its logarithm, $\ln(P_t/\text{GNP}_t)$. Second, the sample size affects the degree to which the first-order sample autocorrelation coefficient r_1 is less than 1.0 in levels of the series. For the constructed random walk, r_1 is 1.0 with infinite observations but 0.95 for sample size 100. For Standard and Poor's annual data (series 4, 5) r_1 is approximately 0.90 ($T = 54$), while for quarterly data (series 6, 7) r_1 is 0.97 ($T = 128$). Third, although first differences of Nelson and Plosser's nominal series (table 4, series 10) indicate large first-order autocorrelation ($r_1 = 0.22$, standard error .10), which is consistent with time aggregation, the deflated annual and quarterly Standard and Poor's data do not show such high first-order autocorrelation.[32]

---

[30] The stock price series in Nelson and Plosser (1982) is not deflated, and their results are reported in table 4 for comparison.

[31] That is, the series is constructed by averaging sets of observations from a random walk with a smaller observation interval than the resulting series. Working (1960) demonstrates that, as the number of shorter interval observations averaged to produce the resultant time-aggregated series becomes large, the first-order serial correlation in the latter series approaches .25.

[32] For the annual data, r_1 is virtually zero, while the quarterly series shows $r_1 = 0.14$ with a standard error of .09. The autocorrelation in the nominal series may reflect price level changes rather than temporal aggregation.

Section C in table 4 shows that not only do the stock price series match the constructed random walk data, but OLS regression of stock prices on time is very poorly specified. For series 19 (ln P_t/GNP_t, annual data), the Durbin-Watson statistic is only 0.38,[33] reflecting the very high autocorrelation in the residuals. Nelson and Kang (1981) show that this is to be expected if a random walk is inappropriately regressed on time, and the results are consistent with those of Nelson and Plosser (1982).

Table 5 gives the results of the Fuller (1976) and Dickey and Fuller (1979) tests for prices. In no case is the null hypothesis $\rho = 1$ rejected at the 10 percent level, and especially for the quarterly data the test statistics are well above the 10 percent critical value (rejection is indicated by small values of the statistics). Further, when time is included as a regressor (eq. [34] above), the null hypothesis $\beta = 0$ is not rejected at conventional significance levels.[34] Although the intercept $\hat{\mu}$ from (33) to (34) is not statistically far from zero in table 5, the implied economic magnitudes are very large, which is consistent with sample values of the slope coefficient $\hat{\rho}$ less than 1.0 if the true coefficient equals 1.0. For example, the estimated intercept for series 2 (annual data, ln P_t/GNP_t) is 0.44, which implies an expected capital gain rate of over 0.44 per annum (in real terms). If one imposes the null hypothesis $\rho = 1$ from the geometric random walk model (26), $\hat{\mu}$ is given by the sample mean of the first differences in log of price ($\nabla \ln p_t \equiv \ln p_t - \ln p_{t-1}$). For Standard and Poor's annual index, 1926–79, $\hat{\mu}$ is 0.0095, and the point estimate of σ^2 (the sample variance of $\nabla \ln p_t$) is 0.048. This implies using (28) a (real) expected capital gain rate of 0.033 per annum, which is reasonable.

In short, tables 4 and 5 show that the random walk models (25) and (26) cannot be rejected for Standard and Poor's price series.

2. Earnings and Dividends

We examine whether the nonstationarity of dividends and earnings implied by (17) and (29) is supported empirically. The earnings per share and dividend per share series are Standard and Poor's annual series corresponding to the composite stock price index, 1926–79. Note that the accounting earnings series is only a proxy for the eco-

---

[33] Table 1 above gives the average Durbin-Watson statistic across 100 replications, for different sample sizes, of the regression of a (geometric) random walk on time. For samples of size 50 (table 4, series 19, has 54 observations), the average Durbin-Watson statistic is 0.375.

[34] For table 5, series 6 (ln P_t/GNP_t, annual data), although the "t-statistic" is 2.26, this statistic does not have a true t-distribution for the sample size 54. For the corresponding quarterly series ($T = 128$), the "t-statistic" is -1.05.

TABLE 4

Sample Autocorrelations for Levels, First Differences, and Deviations from Time Trend for Random Walks and Stock Prices
(Annual and Quarterly Data)

SERIES*	PERIOD	T	r_1†	r_2	r_3	r_4	r_5	r_6	S.E.‡	ADJUSTED R^2	DURBIN-WATSON
A. Sample autocorrelations: levels:											
1. Random walk		100	.95	.90	.85	.81	.76	.70	...	...	...
2. Time-aggregated random walk		100	.96	.91	.86	.82	.77	.73	...	...	...
3. Log of price (ln P_t): annual	1871–1970	100	.96	.90	.85	.79	.75	.71	.10	...	...
4. Deflated price (P_t/GNP$_t$): annual	1926–79	54	.91	.82	.81	.77	.71	.63	.13	...	...
5. Log of deflated price (ln P_t/GNP$_t$): annual	1926–79	54	.89	.79	.75	.71	.68	.64	.13	...	...
6. Deflated price (P_t/GNP$_t$): quarterly	1947:1–1978:IV	128	.97	.93	.90	.86	.83	.79	.09	...	...
7. Log of deflated price (ln P_t/GNP$_t$): quarterly	1947:1–1978:IV	128	.97	.94	.91	.87	.84	.81	.09	...	...

B. Sample autocorrelations: first differences:

		r_1	r_2	r_3	r_4	r_5	r_6	r_7	r_8	r_9	r_{10}
8. Random walk		Large	.00	.00	.00	.00	.00	.00	…	…	…
9. Time-aggregated random walk		Large	.25	.00	.00	.00	.00	…	…	…	…
10. ln P_t: annual	1871–1970	100	.22	−.13	−.08	−.18	−.23	.02	.10	…	…
11. P_t/GNP_t: annual	1926–79	54	−.03	−.31	.06	.15	.00	−.08	.13	…	…
12. ln(P_t/GNP_t): annual	1926–79	54	.02	−.25	−.02	−.13	.01	.06	.13	…	…
13. P_t/GNP_t: quarterly	1947:I–1978:IV	128	.14	−.09	.01	−.02	−.01	−.05	.09	…	…
14. ln(P_t/GNP_t): quarterly	1947:I–1978:IV	128	.13	−.07	.02	.02	−.01	−.07	.09	…	…

C. Autocorrelations of residuals ("deviations from trend")—Model: $Y_t = \beta_0 + \beta_1 t + \epsilon_t$:

		r_1	r_2	r_3	r_4	r_5	r_6	r_7	r_8	r_9	r_{10}
15. Random walk		61	.85	.71	.58	.47	.36	.27	…	…	…
16. Random walk		101	.91	.82	.74	.66	.58	.51	.10	…	…
17. ln P_t: annual	1871–1970	100	.90	.76	.64	.53	.46	.43	.10	…	.33
18. P_t/GNP_t: annual	1926–79	54	.81	.63	.55	.46	.33	.19	.13	.45	.38
19. ln(P_t/GNP_t): annual	1926–79	54	.80	.57	.44	.33	.28	.22	.13	.46	.07
20. P_t/GNP_t: quarterly	1947:I–1978:IV	128	.95	.89	.83	.78	.72	.67	.09	.38	.05
21. ln(P_t/GNP_t): quarterly	1947:I–1978:IV	128	.95	.90	.85	.80	.75	.70	.09	.46	

* The source for series (1)–(3), (8)–(10), and (15)–(17) is Nelson and Plosser (1982) and references therein. The other series are Standard and Poor's annual (fourth quarter) and quarterly composite stock price indexes. GNP$_t$ is the gross national product implicit price deflator.
† r_n is the nth-order sample autocorrelation coefficient.
‡ S.E. gives the approximate standard error of r for the sample size T under the null hypothesis of zero autocorrelation.

TABLE 5
TEST STATISTICS FOR SMALL SAMPLE TESTS FOR RANDOM WALKS IN STANDARD AND POOR'S ANNUAL PRICE SERIES (1926–79) AND QUARTERLY PRICE SERIES (1947:I–1978:IV)

SERIES	$\hat{\mu}$ (t-Statistic)*	$\hat{\beta}$ (t-Statistic)*	$\hat{\rho}$	$n(\hat{\rho}-1)$†	t-STATISTIC‡ ($H_0: \hat{\rho}=1$)	ADJUSTED R^2	Durbin-Watson	r_1§	r_2	r_3	r_4
				Model A: $Y_t = \mu + \rho Y_{t-1} + e_t$							
Annual (4th quarter):											
1. Deflated price (P_t/GNP$_t$)∥	6.63 (1.62)	...	.90	−5.04	−1.65	.83	1.96	.01	−.25	.10	.18
2. Log of deflated price $\ln P_t$/GNP$_t$	.44 (1.75)	...	.89	−5.57	−1.72	.80	1.84	.07	−.19	.03	−.08
Quarterly:											
3. P_t/GNP$_t$	2.54 (1.70)	...	.97	−3.77	−.16	.96	1.69	.15	−.08	.01	−.02
4. $\ln(P_t/\text{GNP}_t)$	.12 (1.92)	...	.97	−3.56	−.19	.97	1.72	.13	−.07	.02	.02
				Model B: $Y_t = \mu + \beta t + \rho Y_{t-1} + e_t$							
Annual (4th quarter):											
5. P_t/GNP$_t$	3.42 (.81)	.28 (1.73)	.82	−9.22	−2.29	.84	1.93	.03	−.18	.20	.25
6. $\ln(P_t/\text{GNP}_t)$	.74 (2.60)	.006 (2.26)	.77	−11.59	−2.76	.83	1.86	.07	−.13	.18	.04
Quarterly:											
7. P_t/GNP$_t$	2.75 (1.77)	−.02 (−.81)	.98	−2.45	−.82	.96	1.72	.14	−.10	−.00	−.04
8. $\ln(P_t/\text{GNP}_t)$	.09 (1.13)	−.0003 (−1.05)	.98	−2.03	−.76	.97	1.77	.11	−.10	−.00	−.01

* Large sample t-statistics (in parentheses) under the null hypotheses that μ and β equal zero.
† The 10 percent critical values for this statistic under the null hypothesis $\hat{\rho}=1$ are −10.7 (−11.0) for $n=50$ (100) under model A (i.e., with no time regressor) and −16.8 (−17.5) under model B (which includes time as a regressor) (Fuller 1976, p. 371).
‡ The 10 percent critical values under the null hypothesis $\hat{\rho}=1$ are −2.60 (−2.58) for $n=50$ (100) under model A and −3.18 (−3.15) under model B (Fuller 1976, p. 373).
§ r_n is the nth-order autocorrelation coefficient. The approximate standard errors are .13 and .09 for annual and quarterly data, respectively, under the null hypothesis of zero correlation.
∥ GNP$_t$ is the gross national product implicit price deflator.

nomic earnings series X_t in the Miller-Modigliani valuation models. The deflation procedure and nonstationarity tests used for prices are applied to the earnings and dividend series.

Table 6 gives the results from the Fuller (1976) and Dickey and Fuller (1979) tests, and the autocorrelation tests give similar results. Section A tests directly for unit roots in the simple autoregression (33), and the null hypothesis $\hat{\rho} = 1$ is not rejected at even the 10 percent level for either earnings or dividends. Section B gives results for the autoregression (34), which includes time as an additional regressor. This model adds virtually no extra explanatory power over the simple autoregression (in terms of R^2), and for the dividend series (series 7 and 8, table 6) the null hypothesis $\hat{\rho} = 1$ is not rejected at the 10 percent level. However, the null hypothesis $\hat{\rho} = 1$ is rejected at the 5 percent level for both earnings series (5 and 6) when time is included.

The earnings results produce an interesting question in interpretation and are similar to results for a dividend series that Shiller (1981c) relies on to conclude that dividends are stationary. When looking just at the simple earnings autoregression without time, the random walk model fits well. When time is included, although there is virtually no increase in R^2, the coefficient on time appears significantly different from zero and the coefficient on lagged earnings seems significantly less than one. On balance, the simple autoregression seems preferable. First, it is consistent with the results of other studies of earnings per share, including those based on individual securities.[35] Second, it is consistent with the price process established above and economically seems more reasonable than (34).

The evidence relied on in Shiller (1981c, 1983) for stationarity of dividends (and consequently prices) is more tenuous. He considers a combination of the Standard and Poor's data used in table 6 with earlier Cowles Commission data, which together extend from 1871 to 1978. For this series, he reports (1981c, p. 299, n. 7) that the autoregression of log d_t, including time as a regressor, gives a coefficient on log d_{t-1} of 0.807 and a standard error of .058, which has a probability value of .05 using Fuller's (1976) tabulations. On the basis of this result, he concludes (1983, p. 237) that "we can reject a random walk at the 5 percent level in favor of stationary fluctuations around a trend."

There are several problems with this interpretation. First, table 6

---

[35] See the references in n. 20 above. Note also the result in Watts and Leftwich (1977) that, although for particular samples some ARIMA models apparently fit better than the simple random walk (e.g., to accommodate the residual autocorrelation in table 6), there is little evidence that such models are better at prediction.

TABLE 6
TEST STATISTICS FOR SMALL SAMPLE TESTS FOR RANDOM WALKS IN STANDARD AND POOR'S ANNUAL EARNINGS AND DIVIDENDS SERIES (1926–79)

SERIES	$\hat{\mu}$ (t-Statistic)*	$\hat{\beta}$ (t-Statistic)*	$\hat{\rho}$	$n(\hat{\rho}-1)$†	t-Statistic‡ $(H_0: \hat{\rho}=1)$	Adjusted R^2	Durbin-Watson	r_1§	r_2	r_3	r_4
					Model A: $Y_t = \mu + \rho Y_{t-1} + e_t$						
1. Deflated earnings (E_t/GNP_t)‖	.24 (.84)	...	.97	−1.54	−.51	.85	1.85	.06	−.14	−.14	−.11
2. Log of deflated earnings (ln E_t/GNP_t)	.12 (1.30)	...	.93	−3.78	−1.16	.81	1.64	.17	−.09	−.24	−.09
3. Deflated dividends (D_t/GNP_t)	.27 (1.61)	...	.91	−4.85	−1.49	.81	1.60	.19	−.19	−.05	−.02
4. Log of deflated dividends (ln D_t/GNP_t)	.12 (1.80)	...	.89	−6.09	−1.71	.77	1.63	.18	−.20	−.06	.01
					Model B: $Y_t = \mu + \beta t + \rho Y_{t-1} + e_t$						
5. E_t/GNP_t	.45 (1.72)	.05 (3.86)	.61	−19.86	−3.64	.88	1.72	.06	−.11	−.19	−.16
6. ln(E_t/GNP_t)	.26 (2.81)	.01 (3.76)	.61	−20.04	−3.84	.86	1.58	.15	−.09	−.30	−.13
7. D_t/GNP_t	.35 (2.06)	.0009 (2.28)	.78	−11.25	−2.59	.82	1.59	.17	−.24	−.09	.01
8. ln(D_t/GNP_t)	.13 (2.03)	.0004 (2.33)	.75	−12.71	−2.78	.79	1.62	.16	−.25	−.11	.02

* Large sample t-statistics (in parentheses) under the null hypotheses that μ and β equal zero.
† The 10 percent (5 percent) critical values for this statistic under the null hypothesis $\hat{\rho}=1$ are −10.7 (−13.3) for $n=50$ under model A (i.e., with no time regressor) and −16.8 (−19.8) under model B (which includes time as a regressor) (Fuller 1976, p. 371).
‡ The 10 percent (5 percent) critical values under the null hypothesis $\hat{\rho}=1$ are −2.60 (−2.93) for $n=50$ under model A and −3.18 (−3.50) under model B (Fuller 1976, p. 373).
§ r_n is the nth-order autocorrelation coefficient. The approximate standard error is .13 under the null hypothesis of zero correlation.
‖ GNP_t is the gross national product implicit price deflator.

shows that, even for the autoregression including time, the dividend series since 1926 does not reject the random walk. Although it is true that a longer data set gives greater power in such tests, it is likely that the very early data are less reliable than Standard and Poor's series. Second, the results for the longer dividend series are not as clear-cut as Shiller implies. Replication of his results (over 1871–1979) gives a value for $n(\hat{\rho}_\tau - 1)$ of -21.61, which barely rejects at the .05 level, and a value for $\hat{\tau}_\tau$ of -3.41, which in Fuller's tabulations is not significant at the .05 level. Further, the longer data do not reject the random walk in either prices or dividends using the simple autoregression (33) (without time as an additional regressor) at even the .10 level for either test statistic, and the price data do not reject the hypothesis $\hat{\rho} = 1$ at the .10 level even when time is included.

3. Conclusion

In summary, the price data never reject nonstationarity, even for long time series, and although there are some cases in which nonstationarity in earnings or dividends appears rejected when time is included as a regressor, there is no rejection of nonstationarity of these series for the simple autoregression (33). Of course, even if the series were stationary, this does not indicate that the price series should be stationary because of the possible dividend (and accounting earnings) smoothing discussed above. In fact, time-series plots show that the dividend series since 1950 is much smoother than either the price or earnings series. This is consistent with the argument that earnings (and investments) are the fundamental variables and that a finite set of derived dividends may not be representative of the information used to set stock prices.[36] Even when smoothing is ignored, however, Sections IIIA and IIIB demonstrate that, once nonstationarity of prices is accounted for, valid variance bounds tests are not rejected in Standard and Poor's price and dividend data.

IV. Conclusions

This paper demonstrates that reliance on plots of price and p_t^* to determine whether changes in expectations of future cash flows cause

---

[36] This argument casts some doubt on the procedures of Granger (1975), who combines a dividend smoothing model from Fama and Babiak (1968) with a random walk in earnings, to generate predictions of future dividends for use with the dividend valuation model (1). What is not verified in his example is that the short-run properties of his smoothed dividend series are sufficient to derive the price process implied by his earnings model. If the smooth dividend stream is not representative of all future dividends, then the use in (1) of optimal forecasts based on the smooth process will not necessarily give the true rational price.

price changes is very misleading since by construction p_t^* will not correspond to p_t and will be much smoother than p_t if prices are set by (1) and the future is not known with certainty. Further, it is shown empirically that one cannot reject the hypothesis that prices are nonstationary and that the "gross violations" of the bound (4) that have been reported in the literature are consistent with incorrect application of estimation techniques that assume stationarity to nonstationary series. The conditional variance bounds (8) derived and tested here are valid if prices are nonstationary and are not violated for Standard and Poor's price and dividend series.

The implications of these results can best be seen with reference to the conclusions drawn in the literature from plots of price and p_t^* and the apparent violations of the inequality (4). Early conclusions were that stock prices cannot be reconciled with rational valuation models, as in Shiller (1981b, p. 422). Although Shiller (1981b, 1981c) recognizes that discount rates need not be constant, he argues that there is so little variation in the cash flow variables in such valuation models that discount rate movements must be very large if prices are rational. Moreover, he regards this possibility as at least counter to generally held views and states (1981a, p. 1) that "most people feel that stock price changes are due primarily to changing expectations about future dividends rather than changing rates of discount."

Attempts have been made to explain stock price movements in terms of nonconstant discount rates. The most influential work is that of Grossman and Shiller (1981),[37] whose primary claim, as noted by Shiller (1981a, p. 2), is that "most of the variability of stock prices might be attributed to information about consumption," which causes changes in discount rates. However, subsequent work has not been successful in extending their results. Hansen and Singleton (1983), for example, are able to explain only a small portion of the variability of stock prices in terms of nonconstant discount rates. Shiller (1981a) notes that, if price changes are driven by changes in expectations about aggregate consumption, then changes across assets should show a degree of contemporaneous correlation that is absent for the assets he examines. In general, even within the same industry and with very clean stock price data, there are wide cross-sectional differences in returns for any given period that seem difficult to reconcile purely in terms of changes in expectations of aggregate consumption.

Given the discouraging evidence on the ability of changes in expectations about consumption to explain changes in asset prices, Shiller

---

[37] See also LeRoy and LaCivita (1981), Shiller (1981a), Michener (1982), Hansen and Singleton (1983), Joerding (1983), Litzenberger and Ronn (1985), and Mehra and Prescott (1985).

(1981a, p. 40) suggests that it might be possible to develop a "psychological model of asset prices" that preserves large discount rate movements, although he argues that it seems equally plausible that there are "temporary fads or speculative bubbles." He concludes: "If . . . the reader goes back to a rational expectations model in which information about potential dividend movements, rather than discount rate movements, causes stock prices to move, then since actual aggregate dividend movements of such magnitude have never been observed, what is the source of information about such potential movements? Can we be satisfied with a model which attributes stock price movements and their business cycle correlation to public rational expectations about movements in a variable which has, in effect, never yet been observed to move?"

This paper demonstrates a plausible solution to the apparent puzzle: The assertion that price changes cannot be attributed to changes in expectations of future cash flows, based on plots such as figure 3 and the results of tests of the bound (4), has simply not been established. Recall that figure 2 displays similar characteristics to Standard and Poor's data in figure 3, yet by construction prices in figure 2 are set by the valuation model (1). Further, Kleidon (1983, chap. 6) shows that a large part of observed price changes can be associated with changes in expectations of future cash flows, using simple models and a few information variables.

Nevertheless, the question whether or not discount rates are constant as in (1) is a different issue. The variance bounds methodology may not be very powerful in detecting departures from constancy, as shown in Stock (1982). Further, even if the constant rate model performs relatively well empirically, there are still important theoretical questions about the conditions under which (1) will hold exactly. Although (1) does not require risk neutrality, the derivation of temporally constant expected rates of return for discounting expected cash flows—"risk-adjusted" discount rates—requires restrictive conditions in models of expected return that allow for risk aversion, such as the capital asset pricing model (CAPM) of Sharpe (1964) and Lintner (1965) or more general models.[38]

One implication is that the construct p_t^* will not in general be the

---

[38] Although LeRoy (1973) demonstrates that discount rates are not necessarily constant with risk aversion, he does not show the converse. See Fama (1970a) and Constantinides (1980) for sufficient conditions for a constant discount rate (across time for a given security) with risk aversion, in the context of the CAPM. Note also that financial economists typically do not reserve the term "expected present value" model for (1) with constant discount rates but include the use of nonconstant risk-adjusted rates. More general models of asset pricing include Merton (1973), Rubinstein (1976), Lucas (1978), Breeden (1979), Brock (1982), and Grossman and Shiller (1982).

price that would prevail if investors had perfect foresight, and so the term "perfect-foresight" price is unfortunate. If investors were risk neutral, the rate r used to discount the uncertain flows in (1) would be the same as that used to discount the certain flows in (2), but in general the appropriate expected rates of return will be different. However, the analysis in this paper does not depend on whether p_t^* is truly the price that would prevail under perfect foresight or whether the definition (2) just gives the present value of the ex post dividends discounted at the (possibly risk-adjusted) rate r from (1).

The major impact of the variance bounds literature has been to suggest that virtually no stock price changes are related to changes in expectations of future cash flows and further that prices may be irrational. This impact has been widespread; for example, Arrow (1983) discusses the volatility of securities markets as compatible with "irrational judgements about uncertainty" (p. 13) and states (p. 12) that "[a] very rigorous analysis for the bond and stock markets (Shiller, 1979, 1981[b]) has shown the incompatibility of observed behavior with rational expectations models, at least in a simple form." At least one published paper explicitly presumes excess volatility in stock prices. Pakes (1985, p. 395, n. 3) states: "Note that the presence of the error term, $\eta_{1,t}$, implies that there may be more variance in stock market evaluations than can be justified by the variance in earnings (which accords with the results of LeRoy and Porter [1981] and Shiller [1981b])."

The results of this paper suggest that such modifications to our theories are, at best, premature.

References

Ackley, Gardner. "Commodities and Capital: Prices and Quantities." *A.E.R.* 73 (March 1983): 1–16.
Albrecht, W. Steve; Lookabill, Larry L.; and McKeown, James C. "The Time-Series Properties of Annual Earnings." *J. Accounting Res.* 15 (Autumn 1977): 226–44.
Arrow, Kenneth J. "Behavior under Uncertainty and Its Implications for Policy." Technical Report no. 399. Stanford, Calif.: Stanford Univ., Center Res. Organizational Efficiency, February 1983.
Ball, Ray, and Watts, Ross. "Some Time Series Properties of Accounting Income." *J. Finance* 27 (June 1972): 663–81.
Bhattacharya, Sudipto. "Nondissipative Signaling Structures and Dividend Policy." *Q.J.E.* 95 (August 1980): 1–24.
Black, Fischer. "Notes on 'The Determinants of the Variability of Stock Market Prices.'" Manuscript. Cambridge: Massachusetts Inst. Tech., Sloan School Management, October 1980.
Breeden, Douglas T. "An Intertemporal Asset Pricing Model with Stochastic Consumption and Investment Opportunities." *J. Financial Econ.* 7 (September 1979): 265–96.

VARIANCE BOUNDS TESTS

Brock, William A. "Asset Prices in a Production Economy." In *The Economics of Information and Uncertainty*, edited by John J. McCall. Chicago: Univ. Chicago Press (for N.B.E.R.), 1982.

Constantinides, George M. "Admissible Uncertainty in the Intertemporal Asset Pricing Model." *J. Financial Econ.* 8 (March 1980): 71–86.

Copeland, Basil L., Jr. "Do Stock Prices Move Too Much to Be Justified by Subsequent Changes in Dividends? Comment." *A.E.R.* 73 (March 1983): 234–35.

Copeland, Thomas E., and Weston, J. Fred. *Financial Theory and Corporate Policy*. 2d ed. Reading, Mass.: Addison-Wesley, 1983.

Cowles, Alfred, et al. *Common Stock Indexes, 1871–1937*. Cowles Commission Monograph no. 3. Bloomington, Ind.: Principia, 1938.

Dickey, David A., and Fuller, Wayne A. "Distribution of the Estimators for Autoregressive Time Series with a Unit Root." *J. American Statis. Assoc.* 74, pt. 1 (June 1979): 427–31.

Fama, Eugene F. "Efficient Capital Markets: A Review of Theory and Empirical Work." *J. Finance* 25 (May 1970): 383–417. (*a*)

———. "Multiperiod Consumption-Investment Decisions." *A.E.R.* 60 (March 1970): 163–74. (*b*)

Fama, Eugene F., and Babiak, Harvey. "Dividend Policy: An Empirical Analysis." *J. American Statis. Assoc.* 63 (December 1968): 1132–61.

Flavin, Marjorie A. "Excess Volatility in the Financial Markets: A Reassessment of the Empirical Evidence." *J.P.E.* 91 (December 1983): 929–56.

Foster, George. *Financial Statement Analysis*. Englewood Cliffs, N.J.: Prentice-Hall, 1978.

Fuller, Wayne A. *Introduction to Statistical Time Series*. New York: Wiley, 1976.

Granger, Clive W. J. "Some Consequences of the Valuation Model When Expectations Are Taken to Be Optimum Forecasts." *J. Finance* 30 (March 1975): 135–45.

Grossman, Sanford J., and Shiller, Robert J. "The Determinants of the Variability of Stock Market Prices." *A.E.R. Papers and Proc.* 71 (May 1981): 222–27.

———. "Consumption Correlatedness and Risk Measurement in Economies with Non-traded Assets and Heterogeneous Information." *J. Financial Econ.* 10 (July 1982): 195–210.

Hansen, Lars Peter. "Large Sample Properties of Generalized Method of Moments Estimators." *Econometrica* 50 (July 1982): 1029–54.

Hansen, Lars Peter, and Hodrick, Robert J. "Forward Exchange Rates as Optimal Predictors of Future Spot Rates: An Econometric Analysis." *J.P.E.* 88 (October 1980): 829–53.

Hansen, Lars Peter, and Singleton, Kenneth J. "Stochastic Consumption, Risk Aversion, and the Temporal Behavior of Asset Returns." *J.P.E.* 91 (April 1983): 249–65.

Hasza, David P., and Fuller, Wayne A. "Estimation for Autoregressive Processes with Unit Roots." *Ann. Statis.* 7 (September 1979): 1106–20.

Ibbotson, Roger G., and Sinquefield, Rex A. *Stocks, Bonds, Bills, and Inflation: The Past and the Future*. Charlottesville, Va.: Financial Analysts Res. Found., 1982.

Joerding, Wayne. "Variable Risk Factors and Excess Volatility in the Stock Market." Manuscript. Pullman: Washington State Univ., Dept. Econ., October 1983.

———. "Stock Market Volatility and a Finite Time Horizon." Manuscript. Pullman: Washington State Univ., Dept. Econ., February 1984.

Keynes, John Maynard. *The General Theory of Employment, Interest and Money.* London: Macmillan, 1936.

Kleidon, Allan W. "Stock Prices as Rational Forecasters of Future Cash Flows." Ph.D. dissertation, Univ. Chicago, 1983.

——. "Bias in Small Sample Tests of Stock Price Rationality." *J. Bus.* 59 (April 1986): 237–61.

Kling, Arnold. "What Do Variance Bounds Tests Show?" Manuscript. Washington: Bd. Governors, Fed. Reserve Sys., May 1982.

LeRoy, Stephen F. "Risk Aversion and the Martingale Property of Stock Prices." *Internat. Econ. Rev.* 14 (June 1973): 436–46.

——. "Efficiency and the Variability of Asset Prices." *A.E.R. Papers and Proc.* 74 (May 1984): 183–87.

LeRoy, Stephen F., and LaCivita, C. J. "Risk Aversion and the Dispersion of Asset Prices." *J. Bus.* 54 (October 1981): 535–47.

LeRoy, Stephen F., and Porter, Richard D. "The Present-Value Relation: Technical Supplement." Manuscript. Santa Barbara: Univ. California, 1979.

——. "The Present-Value Relation: Tests Based on Implied Variance Bounds." *Econometrica* 49 (May 1981): 555–74.

Lintner, John. "Distribution of Incomes of Corporations among Dividends, Retained Earnings, and Taxes." *A.E.R. Papers and Proc.* 46 (May 1956): 97–113.

——. "The Valuation of Risk Assets and the Selection of Risky Investments in Stock Portfolios and Capital Budgets." *Rev. Econ. and Statis.* 47 (February 1965): 13–37.

Little, Ian M. D. "Higgledy Piggledy Growth." *Bull. Oxford Univ. Inst. Econ. and Statis.* 24 (November 1962): 387–412.

Litzenberger, Robert H., and Ronn, Ehud I. "A Utility-based Model of Common Stock Price Movements." Working Paper no. 791. Stanford, Calif.: Stanford Univ., Grad. School Bus., May 1985.

Lucas, Robert E., Jr. "Asset Prices in an Exchange Economy." *Econometrica* 46 (November 1978): 1429–45.

Marsh, Terry A., and Merton, Robert C. "Dividend Variability and Variance Bounds Tests for the Rationality of Stock Market Prices." Working Paper no. 1584-84. Cambridge: Massachusetts Inst. Tech., Sloan School Management, August 1984. (*a*)

——. "Earnings Variability and Variance Bounds Tests for the Rationality of Stock Market Prices." Working Paper no. 1559-84. Cambridge: Massachusetts Inst. Tech., Sloan School Management, March 1984. (*b*)

Meese, Richard A., and Singleton, Kenneth J. "On Unit Roots and the Empirical Modeling of Exchange Rates." *J. Finance* 37 (September 1982): 1029–35.

Mehra, Rajnish, and Prescott, Edward C. "The Equity Premium: A Puzzle." *J. Monetary Econ.* 15 (March 1985): 145–61.

Merton, Robert C. "An Intertemporal Capital Asset Pricing Model." *Econometrica* 41 (September 1973): 867–87.

Michener, Ronald W. "Variance Bounds in a Simple Model of Asset Pricing." *J.P.E.* 90 (February 1982): 166–75.

Miller, Merton H., and Modigliani, Franco. "Dividend Policy, Growth, and the Valuation of Shares." *J. Bus.* 34 (October 1961): 411–33.

Nelson, Charles R., and Kang, Heejoon. "Spurious Periodicity in Inappropriately Detrended Time Series." *Econometrica* 49 (May 1981): 741–51.

Nelson, Charles R., and Plosser, Charles I. "Trends and Random Walks in

Macroeconomic Time Series: Some Evidence and Implications." *J. Monetary Econ.* 10 (September 1982): 139–62.

Pakes, Ariel. "On Patents, R & D, and the Stock Market Rate of Return." *J.P.E.* 93 (April 1985): 390–409.

Roberts, Harry V. "Stock-Market 'Patterns' and Financial Analysis: Methodological Suggestions." *J. Finance* 14 (March 1959): 1–10.

Ross, Stephen A. "The Determination of Financial Structure: The Incentive-Signalling Approach." *Bell J. Econ.* 8 (Spring 1977): 23–40.

Rubinstein, Mark. "The Valuation of Uncertain Income Streams and the Pricing of Options." *Bell J. Econ.* 7 (Autumn 1976): 407–25.

Scott, Louis O. "The Present Value Model of Stock Prices: Empirical Tests Based on Instrumental Variables Estimators." Manuscript. Urbana: Univ. Illinois, October 1984.

Sharpe, William F. "Capital Asset Prices: A Theory of Market Equilibrium under Conditions of Risk." *J. Finance* 19 (September 1964): 425–42.

Shiller, Robert J. "Consumption, Asset Markets and Macroeconomic Fluctuations." Paper presented at the Money and Banking Workshop. Chicago: Univ. Chicago, September 1981. (*a*)

———. "Do Stock Prices Move Too Much to Be Justified by Subsequent Changes in Dividends?" *A.E.R.* 71 (June 1981): 421–36. (*b*)

———. "The Use of Volatility Measures in Assessing Market Efficiency." *J. Finance* 36 (May 1981): 291–304. (*c*)

———. "Do Stock Prices Move Too Much to Be Justified by Subsequent Changes in Dividends? Reply." *A.E.R.* 73 (March 1983): 236–37.

———. "Theories of Aggregate Stock Price Movements." *J. Portfolio Management* 10 (Winter 1984): 28–37.

Standard and Poor's. *Security Price Index Record.* New York: Standard and Poor's, 1980.

Stock, James H. "Tests of Market Efficiency When Consumers Are Risk Averse." Manuscript. Berkeley: Univ. California, Dept. Econ., November 1982.

Tirole, Jean. "Asset Bubbles and Overlapping Generations." *Econometrica* 53 (September 1985): 1071–1100.

Tobin, James. "A Mean-Variance Approach to Fundamental Valuation." *J. Portfolio Management* 11 (Fall 1984): 26–32.

Watts, Ross L., and Leftwich, Richard W. "The Time Series of Annual Accounting Earnings." *J. Accounting Res.* 15 (Autumn 1977): 253–71.

West, Kenneth D. "Speculative Bubbles and Stock Price Volatility." Manuscript. Princeton, N.J.: Princeton Univ., Dept. Econ., 1984.

Working, Holbrook. "A Random-Difference Series for Use in the Analysis of Time Series." *J. American Statis. Assoc.* 29 (March 1934): 11–24.

———. "Note on the Correlation of First Differences of Averages in a Random Chain." *Econometrica* 28 (October 1960): 916–18.

ECONOMETRICA

THE PRESENT-VALUE RELATION: TESTS BASED ON IMPLIED VARIANCE BOUNDS[1]

By Stephen F. LeRoy and Richard D. Porter[2]

This paper investigates the implications for asset price dispersion of conventional security valuation models. Successively sharper variance bounds on asset prices are derived. Large-sample tests of the bounds are determined and applied to aggregated and disaggregated price and earnings data of U.S. corporations.

1. INTRODUCTION AND SUMMARY OF CONCLUSIONS

CONSIDER A SCALAR TIME SERIES $\{x_t\}$ which is generated jointly with a vector time series $\{\underline{z}_t\}$ as a stationary multivariate linear stochastic process. We then may define $\{y_t\}$ as another scalar time series related to $\{x_t\}$ and $\{\underline{z}_t\}$ by

$$(1) \quad y_t = \sum_{j=0}^{n} \beta^j x_t^e(j),$$

where $x_t^e(j)$ denotes $E(x_{t+j}|I_t)$, I_t is the realization of $\{x_t\}$ and $\{\underline{z}_t\}$ up to and including time t, and $\beta < 1$. The multivariate time series $\{x_t, \underline{z}_t\}$ may be labeled the independent-variable series, its distribution being taken as exogenous, and $\{y_t\}$ the dependent-variable series. Equation (1) is the present-value relation. It states that the distribution of the dependent-variable process is related to that of the independent-variable process in such a way that the current realization of the dependent-variable process equals the present discounted expected value of one element of the independent-variable process, (x_t), where the expectation is conditional on all information currently available.

The present-value relation is repeatedly encountered in economic theory. The most familiar application is to the theory of stock prices, where $\{x_t\}$ refers to some corporation's earnings, $\{\underline{z}_t\}$ to any variables other than past earnings which are used to predict its future earnings, $\{y_t\}$ to the price of stock, and β to the discount factor.[3] In expectations theories of the term structure of interest rates, the present-value relation also appears (with a finite upper limit in the summation in (1)), although its validity in such applications is based on a linear

---

[1] The analyses and conclusions set forth are those of the authors and do not necessarily indicate concurrence by other members of the research staffs, by the Board of Governors, or by the Federal Reserve Banks.

[2] We wish to thank Evelyn Flynn, Gregory Connor, Juan Perea, and Birch Lee for able assistance and William Barnett, Fischer Black, Christopher Sims, Michael Dooley, Donald Hester, Agustin Maravall, Bennett McCallum, Darrel Parke, David Pierce, William Poole, Jack Rutner, and especially Robert Shiller, and two anonymous referees for helpful criticism. Thanks are also due to Susan Fay Eubank for typing innumerable drafts.

[3] As is well known in the finance literature, the representation of stock prices as the present value of discounted earnings involves double counting if any earnings are retained, since in that case both retained earnings and the revenues generated subsequently by these retentions are counted. However, in our model the maintained hypothesis that earnings are stationary implicitly presumes no retention. In the empirical work examined below an adjustment to the data to correct for earnings retention will be required.

approximation (Shiller [15]). Finally, the permanent income hypothesis of Friedman [2] may also be cast in the framework of equation (1).

In Section 2 of the present paper we state and prove three theorems about the variance of the dependent-variable process as it relates to that of the independent-variable process. The theorems embody successively sharper restrictions on the parameters of the independent and dependent variable processes. Theorem 1 asserts that the coefficient of dispersion (i.e., the ratio of the standard deviation to the mean) of $\{y_t\}$ is less than that of $\{x_t\}$. The second theorem involves two new time series $\{\hat{y}_t\}$ and $\{y_t^*\}$ which are generated by altering the amount of information assumed available about the future innovations of $\{x_t\}$ from that implicit in the specified joint distribution of $\{x_t\}$ and $\{\underline{z}_t\}$. If it is assumed that there is no information about the future innovations in $\{x_t\}$, the derived present value series is defined to be $\{\hat{y}_t\}$. On the other hand, if the future innovations in $\{x_t\}$ are taken as known, the derived present value series is labeled $\{y_t^*\}$. The dependent-variable series of primary interest, $\{y_t\}$, is in a sense an intermediate case since the realizations of $\{\underline{z}_t\}$ may be viewed as in general providing some information about the innovations in the univariate process for $\{x_t\}$, but not complete information. Theorem 2 exploits this fact, asserting that the variances of $\{\hat{y}_t\}$ and $\{y_t^*\}$ constitute lower and upper bounds, respectively, on the variance of $\{y_t\}$. Theorem 3, unlike Theorems 1 and 2 which state that the variance of $\{y_t\}$ lies within an interval, is the basis for an asymptotic point test of the null hypothesis defined by the present-value relation. If $\{\pi_t\}$ is defined as the present value of the forecast errors for $\{x_t\}$, we show that $\text{var}(y_t) + \text{var}(\pi_t) = \text{var}(y_t^*)$. Theorem 3 asserts that the three terms of this variance decomposition can all be estimated from observations on x_t and y_t and, therefore, forms the basis for a large-sample test of the present-value equation.

These theorems furnish a basis for constructing tests of the validity of the present-value relation. Such theorems are necessary because the present-value relation cannot be tested directly without also specifying the variables $\underline{z}_t$ used to predict x_t and then determining the joint distribution of $\{x_t, \underline{z}_t\}$, since in the absence of such a procedure the $x_t^e(j)$ are not measurable. Consequently, direct tests of the present-value relation are always conditional on the specification of the set of variables used to predict x_t, and the difficulty of specifying these variables exhaustively greatly weakens the plausibility of any conclusions based on such direct tests. By contrast, our three theorems are valid for general specifications of the joint distribution of $\{x_t, \underline{z}_t\}$, and do not require identification of the distribution of $\{x_t, \underline{z}_t\}$, or even specification of what the variables $\underline{z}_t$ are. Thus even though we do not measure the expectations $x_t^e(j)$ or the discounted forecast errors π_t, our theorems constitute testable implications of the present-value relation. The fact that the maintained assumptions required for our indirect tests are so much weaker than those required for the direct tests adds to the appeal of our results. Statistical tests of the three theorems are derived in Section 3.

In Section 4 we consider the application of our results to the theory of stock prices. First it is shown that the efficient capital markets hypothesis as conventionally formulated implies (and is implied by) the present-value relation between earnings and stock prices. Consequently, the hypothesis of capital market efficiency implies the validity of the theorems, and the latter may therefore be used to construct tests of market efficiency. That capital market efficiency implies restrictions on the volatility of stock prices is at first surprising because the most commonly-cited implication of market efficiency is that stock prices should move instantaneously rather than gradually in response to news. However, the result that if markets are efficient the coefficient of dispersion of stock prices should be less than that of earnings (Theorem 1) makes sense if it is observed that the present-value equation defines stock prices as a kind of weighted average of earnings, and an average is generally less volatile than its components. Another consideration strengthens this conclusion. Since stock prices are an average of expected rather than actual earnings, and since expected earnings can plausibly be assumed to regress toward a mean (correcting for trend) in the increasingly distant future, it follows that expected earnings should show less dispersion than actual earnings, further reducing the anticipated dispersion of stock prices.

Our first data set is based on Standard & Poor's Composite Index of stock prices and the related earnings and dividends series. The observations are quarterly over the interval 1955 to 1973, and the data are corrected for trend.[4] The estimated coefficients of dispersion of earnings and stock prices are 0.172 and 0.452, indicating that the inequality of Theorem 1 is contradicted (Table III). The point estimates on which the tests of Theorems 2 and 3 are based imply an even more flagrant violation of the model; for example, the estimated variance of y_t is 4.89, whereas the estimated variance of y_t^*, which theoretically should exceed that of y_t, is 0.255. These results, while dramatic, are difficult to interpret in the absence of any indication of the reliability of the test statistics. To provide such an indication, we calculated formal tests based on the asymptotic distribution of the parameter estimates, as described in Section 3. Because the test statistics measuring departures from the null hypothesis are all insignificant, the derived confidence intervals suggest that our statistical tests may have very little power.

The outcome of these tests may reflect the fact that they are based on aggregate data, whereas the theory applies to individual firms; a simple argument (presented in detail in Section 2) demonstrates the possible existence of bias in our tests due to aggregation error across firms. If the earnings of each firm consist of a common factor and an individual uncorrelated term, and if the common factor is forecastable whereas the individual term is not, then our tests will be biased in favor of rejection of market efficiency. In the reverse case, our tests will be biased in favor of acceptance. We do not know which case, if either, is more plausible than the intermediate case under which these biases approximately cancel, but the example provides strong motivation to examine data for individual firms. We collected quarterly earnings and price data for three large

---

[4] For a detailed description of the data, the complete derivation of the statistical tests, and for the data themselves, see LeRoy and Porter [9]; this paper is available upon request from the authors.

corporations—American Telephone & Telegraph, General Electric, and General Motors—then adjusted them for trend in the same way as the aggregate data, and calculated the test statistics for the three theorems.

The empirical results for the firm data show, as might be expected, that sharper hypotheses are more often rejected than blunt hypotheses. The point estimates for the tests of Theorem 1 were somewhat closer to being consistent with the null hypothesis of market efficiency for the individual firms than for the aggregate data. For one firm (GM) the coefficient of dispersion of earnings exceeded that of stock prices, as implied by the theory, while for another (GE) the two were virtually identical. Only AT&T was similar to the aggregate data in that earnings were considerably less volatile than stock prices, although for AT&T as with the aggregate data the test statistic did not allow rejection of the null hypothesis of Theorem 1 at the usual significance levels. Contrary to the implication of Theorem 2, however, the variance of y_t exceeded that of y_t^* by a wide margin for each of the three firms as with the aggregate data. Further, the relevant test statistic was significant for one firm (GE) and of borderline significance for another (GM), although it was insignificant for the third (AT&T). Finally, the test statistics for the more restrictive Theorem 3 all indicated rejection of the null hypothesis at the one per cent level.

Comparison of the results for the three firms with those for the Standard & Poor's series gives no clear reason to suspect that aggregation over firms biases aggregate tests either way, although, of course, this conclusion is not unequivocal since the Standard & Poor's series cannot be viewed as a simple aggregate of the three firms alone. As with the aggregate data, the point estimates for the firms are not consistent with the efficient markets model, although they are somewhat closer to those expected from theory than those for the aggregate data. However, the confidence intervals for the firms are more prone to indicate rejection of the null hypothesis; the smaller confidence regions for the firm data suggest that tests based on firm data may be somewhat more powerful than those for aggregate data.

We see that based on both aggregated and disaggregated data, stock prices appear to be more volatile than is consistent with the efficient capital markets model. This conclusion differs from that of most studies of market efficiency, such as that of Fama [1]. In many studies of market efficiency, it is observed that the martingale assumption requires that measured rates of return be serially uncorrelated; consequently, the efficient capital markets model may be tested by determining whether it is possible to reject the joint hypothesis that all the autocorrelations of rates of return are zero. Typically this null hypothesis cannot be rejected at the usual significance levels; we show this to be the case also for the rates of return earned on the stock of our three firms. Since these tests of the nonautocorrelatedness of rates of return are derivable consequences of the same model used to generate our variance restrictions, we are led to inquire why the nonautocorrelatedness implication is apparently satisfied, whereas the variance implications are not. Although it is possible that the difference in the outcomes of the dispersion and autocorrelation tests is due to differing sensitivity to specification or measurement error, an explanation that appears more attractive to us is that the dispersion tests have greater power than the autocorrelation tests against the hypothesis of market efficiency, given that alternative hypothesis which actually generated the data. This argument suggests that a promising way to investigate the stock market would be to ascertain what kinds of structures in earnings and prices would lead to deviations from market efficiency that would be more readily detected by a dispersion test than by an autocorrelation test. We have not yet pursued this line, however.

It is not clear how to interpret our rejection of the hypothesis we have characterized as "market efficiency." It should be recognized that our theorems are actually tests of a joint hypothesis, some elements of which have only tenuous support. The most important elements in our joint hypothesis are (i) the present-value relation (or, in the stock market application, the equivalent martingale assumption), (ii) the assumption that the real conditional expected rate of return on stock is constant over time, and (iii) the assumption of rational expectations. If our tests are not subject to econometric or measurement difficulties, then our rejection of the theorems implies that one or more of these elements of the joint hypothesis must be rejected. There is no reason to doubt that with further work it will be possible to distinguish which of the components of the rejected joint hypothesis must be revised.

In an important recent paper, Shiller [16] has independently derived and conducted tests of expectations models of the term structure of interest rates based on implied restrictions on the admissible dispersion of long rates relative to short. These restrictions are similar to our Theorems 1 and 2; in addition, Shiller obtained some important frequency-domain implications of the model. Although Shiller's tests, unlike ours, are based on point estimates rather than confidence intervals, implying that there is no way to determine statistical significance, he finds that the expectations model of the term structure appears to be violated, long rates being too volatile relative to short rates. The fact that Shiller's results on interest rates so closely parallel ours on stock prices suggests that neither set of results can be dismissed as a statistical accident. Rather, in our view, the fact that asset prices appear to fluctuate more than is consistent with most financial models in current use should be regarded as a major challenge to those models. As yet, however, it is impossible to determine what changes in financial theory may turn out to be necessary to accommodate our results and those of Shiller.

2. THREE THEOREMS ON THE VARIANCE OF THE DEPENDENT-VARIABLE PROCESS[5]

It is assumed that the $p \times 1$ vector $\{x_t, \underline{z}_t\}$ follows a multivariate linearly regular stationary stochastic process:

(2) $\begin{bmatrix} x_t \\ \underline{z}_t \end{bmatrix} = \underline{c} + \underline{\epsilon}_t + D_1 \underline{\epsilon}_{t-1} + D_2 \underline{\epsilon}_{t-2} + \cdots = \underline{c} + D(B) \underline{\epsilon}_t,$

---

[5] In the remainder of this paper we let the upper limit (n) in the summation in (1) be infinite, as is appropriate for application to the stock market.

where the innovations sequence $\{\underline{\epsilon}_t\}$ is a set of serially uncorrelated vector random variables with zero mean and positive definite covariance matrix Σ, where $\underline{c}$ is a $p \times 1$ vector, the D_i are square matrices of order p, and where B is the lag operator, defined by $B^j\underline{\epsilon}_t = \underline{\epsilon}_{t-j}$.[6] If we delete all but the first element of the vector equation (2), we obtain

(3) $\quad x_t = c + \underline{\delta}'_0 \underline{\epsilon}_t + \underline{\delta}'_1 \underline{\epsilon}_{t-1} + \cdots = c + \underline{\delta}'(B)\underline{\epsilon}_t,$

where c is the first element of $\underline{c}$ and $\underline{\delta}'_i$ is the first row of D_i.[7] We incur no loss of generality by ignoring the distribution of $\underline{z}$ since the information content of current and past values of $\underline{z}$ is contained in the current and past values of $\underline{\epsilon}$, which are known. The conditional expected future values of x are given by

(4) $\quad x_t^e(j) = c + \underline{\delta}'_j \underline{\epsilon}_t + \underline{\delta}'_{j+1}\underline{\epsilon}_{t-1} + \cdots .$

In general, the forecasts $x_t^e(j)$ depend on the $\underline{z}_t$ as well as the x_t, since both are needed to construct the lagged $\underline{\epsilon}_t$. In this case the series $\{\underline{z}_t\}$ is said to be a leading indicator of $\{x_t\}$, in Pierce's [11] usage; see also Granger [3]. In the special case in which all the elements of $\underline{\delta}_j$ are zero except the first, efficient forecasts of $\{x_t\}$ can be constructed from past realizations of $\{x_t\}$ alone since in that case $\{\underline{z}_t\}$ is not a leading indicator of $\{x_t\}$. In this special case $\underline{\epsilon}_t$ and $\underline{\delta}_j$ can be taken as scalars without loss of generality. More generally, when $\underline{z}_t$ is a leading indicator of x_t, we can express the dependent-variable series in terms of the (vector) innovations in the independent-variable series. By substituting (4) into (1), it is easily verified that we have

(5) $\quad y_t = \dfrac{c}{1-\beta} + \displaystyle\sum_{j=0}^{\infty}\left[\sum_{k=j}^{\infty}\beta^{k-j}\underline{\delta}'_k\right]\underline{\epsilon}_{t-j} \equiv \dfrac{c}{1-\beta} + \underline{a}'(B)\underline{\epsilon}_t,$

where $\underline{a}'_j = \sum_{k=j}^{\infty}\beta^{k-j}\underline{\delta}'_k$.

We now state and prove the three theorems restricting the variance of $\{y_t\}$.

THEOREM 1: *The coefficient of dispersion of $\{y_t\}$ is less than that of $\{x_t\}$ for any distribution obeying* (2).

The proof of Theorem 1 is most conveniently presented later. At this point, it is useful to consider a special case in order to render Theorem 1 as intuitive as possible. Suppose that $\{\underline{z}_t\}$ is not a leading indicator of $\{x_t\}$ and that $\{x_t\}$ is distributed by a first-order autoregressive process,

$$x_t - c = \phi(x_{t-1} - c) + \epsilon_t, \quad |\phi| < 1,$$

which has the moving-average representation

$$x_t = c + \epsilon_t + \phi\epsilon_{t-1} + \phi^2\epsilon_{t-2} + \cdots .$$

---

[6] $D(B) = D_0 + D_1 B + D_2 B^2 + \cdots$, with $D_0 = I$.

[7] That is, $\delta(B) = \underline{\delta}_0 + \underline{\delta}_1 B + \underline{\delta}_2 B^2 + \cdots$ where $\underline{\delta}_0 = (1, 0, 0, \ldots, 0)$. See Rozanov [12] or Hannan [4] for a general discussion of the statistical properties of (2).

It is easily verified that the ratio of the coefficients of dispersion takes the simple form

$$\text{(6)} \quad \frac{CD(y_t)}{CD(x_t)} = \frac{1-\beta}{1-\beta\phi},$$

which is always less than one since β is bounded by zero and one. Equation (6) shows that the lower ϕ is and the higher β is, the lower will be the ratio of the coefficients of dispersion. The reason is that if ϕ is near zero, expected x_t regresses rapidly toward the trend value c, which means that y_t is approximately equal to current x_t plus the discounted value of a series of constants. The addition of constants to x_t raises the mean of y_t without increasing its standard deviation, thereby lowering its coefficient of dispersion. Similarly, if β is near 1, relatively more weight is given to future expected x_t than to current x_t, compared to the case when β is near zero. Since for any value of ϕ expected future x_t has less dispersion than current x_t, the effect of larger values of β is to lower the ratio of the coefficients of dispersion.

Depending on the actual distribution of $\{x_t\}$, the test implied by Theorem 1 may not be very powerful statistically. Thus, if β is near one in the population and the distribution of $\{x_t\}$ incorporates strong damping, the efficient markets model might imply that the coefficient of dispersion of $\{y_t\}$ is a small fraction of that of $\{x_t\}$, say, one-quarter. In that case, the test implied by Theorem 1 that the ratio of coefficients of dispersion is less than unity would with high probability indicate acceptance of the null hypothesis even when it should be rejected (for example, if in the population the ratio of coefficients of dispersion were 1/2 or 3/4). Again, it is impossible to test this conjecture directly without knowledge of the joint distribution of $\{x_t\}$ and $\{z_t\}$. We seek to derive restrictions on the dispersion of $\{y_t\}$ stronger than those implied by Theorem 1, but still without specifying the distribution of $\{z_t\}$.

To do so we observe that so far we have used only one function of the parameters of the marginal distribution of $\{x_t\}$: its coefficient of dispersion. It might be expected that stronger restrictions on the behavior of $\{y_t\}$ could be derived if all the parameters of the distribution of $\{x_t\}$ were employed. To show that this is in fact possible we consider once again the general leading indicator case under which there exist variables z_t which figure in the forecasts of future x_t, but which do not predict x_t perfectly. Now fix the marginal distribution of $\{x_t\}$ and consider two polar cases: one under which there exist variables z_t which in addition to past x_t allow perfect forecasting of x_t, and the other in which $\{z_t\}$ is not a leading indicator of $\{x_t\}$ (i.e., in which there are no variables other than lagged x_t which assist in the forecasting of future x_t). Define $\{y_t^*\}$ and $\{\hat{y}_t\}$ as the series generated when the present-value relation operates on $\{x_t\}$ in each of these cases, and note that the distributions of these hypothetical price variables, unlike that of $\{y_t\}$, are completely determined by the marginal distribution of $\{x_t\}$.

THEOREM 2: *When z_t is a leading indicator of $\{x_t\}$ the coefficient of dispersion of $\{y_t\}$ is greater than or equal to that of $\{\hat{y}_t\}$, and less than that of $\{y_t^*\}$.*[8]

Theorem 2 gives bounds on the variance of any series $\{y_t\}$ that is generated by some joint distribution of x_t and z_t, and these bounds can be calculated from the marginal distribution of $\{x_t\}$ alone, implying that, as required, the general leading indicator case be tested without actually estimating the joint distribution of $\{x_t\}$ and $\{z_t\}$.

The proof of Theorem 2 is direct. By definition, y_t^* is expressible as

$$(7) \quad y_t^* = x_t + \beta x_{t+1} + \beta^2 x_{t+2} + \cdots .$$

Now define π_t, the discounted value of forecast errors, as

$$(8) \quad \pi_t = \sum_{j=1}^{\infty} \beta^j (x_{t+j} - x_t^e(j)),$$

where the $x_t^e(j)$ are the forecasts made under the general leading indicator model, as before. Then we have

$$y_t^* = y_t + \pi_t.$$

Now y_t depends only on the innovations in x_t and z_t up to and including period t, while π_t depends only on the innovations occurring after period t. Accordingly, they are statistically independent, and we have

$$(9) \quad \text{var}(y_t^*) = \text{var}(y_t) + \text{var}(\pi_t).$$

Equation (9) shows that the higher the variance of the discounted sum of forecast errors, the lower the variance of $\{y_t\}$. Consequently, the variance of $\{y_t^*\}$ provides an upper bound for the variance of $\{y_t\}$. Also, assuming as throughout that the information set always contains at least the past history of $\{x_t\}$, the variance of $\{\hat{y}_t\}$ furnishes a lower bound for the variance of $\{y_t\}$, since the presence of forecasting variables z_t in the information set can never increase the variance of discounted forecasting errors. Stating this conclusion in terms of coefficients of dispersion, we have

$$CD(\hat{y}_t) \leq CD(y_t) < CD(y_t^*).$$

Note that the right-hand side strict inequality follows from the fact that the model is one in which uncertainty cannot be entirely eliminated.

---

[8] As Singleton [18] observed, the proof to follow applies without modification in the case when y_t is given by

$$(1') \quad \sum_{k=1}^{K} \sum_{j=0}^{\infty} \beta_k^j x_{kt}^e(j),$$

that is, when y_t is the sum of K terms of the form of (1). Since this vector extension is immediate, our proof is restricted to the case $K = 1$. Note also that in economic applications of the present-value relation discussed in this paper, equation (1) is sufficiently general.

PRESENT-VALUE RELATION

We are now in a position to prove Theorem 1. By virtue of Theorem 2, it is sufficient to show that the coefficient of dispersion of $\{y_t^*\}$ is less than that of $\{x_t\}$. But that result may be developed directly from equation (7). We have

$$\text{var}(y_t^*) = E\big[(x_t - c) + \beta(x_{t+1} - c) + \beta^2(x_{t+2} - c) + \cdots \big]^2$$

or

(10) $\quad \text{var}(y_t^*) = \dfrac{1}{1 - \beta^2}\big[\gamma_x(0) + 2\beta\gamma_x(1) + 2\beta^2\gamma_x(2) + \cdots \big],$

where $\gamma_x(i) \equiv \text{covariance }(x_t, x_{t-i})$ for all t. From the Cauchy-Schwartz inequality and stationarity, $\gamma_x(i) < \gamma_x(0)$ if $i > 0$, so

(11) $\quad \text{var}(y_t^*) < \gamma_x(0)\left[\dfrac{1}{1 - \beta^2} + \dfrac{2\beta}{(1 - \beta)(1 - \beta^2)}\right] = \dfrac{\gamma_x(0)}{(1 - \beta)^2}.$

From (11) it follows immediately that

$$\dfrac{\sqrt{\gamma_y^*(0)}}{c/(1 - \beta)} < \dfrac{\sqrt{\gamma_x(0)}}{c}.$$

THEOREM 3: *When $\{z_t\}$ is a leading indicator of $\{x_t\}$, the variance of $\{y_t^*\}$ is equal to the variance of $\{y_t\}$ plus the variance of $\{\pi_t\}$, the discounted forecast error. Further, all these variances may be estimated directly using only measurements on $\{x_t\}$ and $\{y_t\}$.*[9]

We have already proved the first part of Theorem 3 (see equation (9)). Thus the significant assertion of Theorem 3 is that equation (9) may be used to construct a point test of the efficient markets model which can be applied without specifying the variables z_t and estimating their joint distribution with x_t. This is not obvious since the forecasts $x_t^e(j)$ which are used to calculate the π_t are not directly observable, nor can they be calculated without knowledge of the joint distribution of $\{z_t\}$ and $\{x_t\}$. However, it happens that even though π_t is not directly observable, its variance can be calculated from the distribution of $\{x_t\}$ and $\{y_t\}$ alone, and this is the content of Theorem 3.

To show this, substitute (3) and (4) into (8) to obtain

$$\pi_t = \beta\underline{\delta}_0' \underline{\varepsilon}_{t+1} + \beta^2(\underline{\delta}_0' \underline{\varepsilon}_{t+2} + \underline{\delta}_1' \underline{\varepsilon}_{t+1})$$
$$+ \beta^3(\underline{\delta}_0' \underline{\varepsilon}_{t+3} + \underline{\delta}_1' \underline{\varepsilon}_{t+2} + \underline{\delta}_2' \underline{\varepsilon}_{t+1}) + \cdots .$$

---

[9] Singleton [18] also obtained a vector extension of Theorem 3; see footnote 8 supra. His extension, however, assumes that the $\beta_k (k = 1, 2, \ldots K)$ are known, whereas in our model β is estimable.

Collecting terms, squaring, and taking expectations gives

$$(12) \quad \mathrm{var}(\pi_t) = \frac{\beta^2 \underline{a}_0' \Sigma \underline{a}_0}{1 - \beta^2},$$

where $\underline{a}_0$ is as defined in (5). Although $\underline{a}_0$ is not directly estimable, its weighted length is. Equation (5) may be used to derive

$$(13) \quad \underline{a}_0' \underline{\epsilon}_{t+1} = y_{t+1} + \frac{x_t - y_t}{\beta},$$

from which we calculate an expression for $\underline{a}_0' \Sigma \underline{a}_0$:

$$(14) \quad \underline{a}_0' \Sigma \underline{a}_0 = \mathrm{var}\big[\, y_{t+1} + 1/\beta (x_t - y_t) \,\big].$$

Since Σ is positive definite, $\mathrm{var}(\pi_t) > 0$. Combining equations (12) and (14), we have

$$(15) \quad \mathrm{var}(\pi_t) = \frac{\mathrm{var}(\beta y_{t+1} + x_t - y_t)}{1 - \beta^2}$$

which is directly measurable. Since the variances of $\{\hat{y}_t\}$ and $\{y_t^*\}$ are functions of β and a univariate representation for $\{x_t\}$, they are, of course, directly estimable from observations on x_t and y_t.[10]

The theorems just proved apply to individual firms; can they be tested on cross-section averages? A simple example[11] shows that aggregation bias may be a problem, depending on the covariance of x_{it} among firms and on the assumption made about the forecastability of x_{it}. Suppose that x_{it} depends linearly on a common factor z_t, which is perfectly forecastable, and a white noise term w_{it}:

$$x_{it} = \alpha(z_t + w_{it}).$$

Further, suppose that w_{it} is independent across firms, is independent of z_t, has common variance across firms, and is not forecastable. Since the forecastable component of each x_{it} is identical across firms, we have $CD(y_t) = CD(y_{it})$ for all i, as is readily verified. However, upon aggregation, the cancellation of the white noise terms, w_{it}, implies that $CD(y_t^*) < CD(y_{it}^*)$ for all i. If $CD(y_t^*)$ were viewed as an estimate of $CD(y_{it}^*)$, it would be biased toward zero, and a test of the null hypothesis, $CD(y_{it}) < CD(y_{it}^*)$ based on the inequality $CD(y_t) < CD(y_t^*)$ would be biased toward rejection. More generally, the example suggests that our tests will be biased toward rejection if the common component of x_{it} is more forecastable than the independent components. We do not know if this assumption is more reasonable than its opposite, in which case our tests are biased

---

[10] Observe that $E(x_t) = c$ and $E(y_t) = c/(1 - \beta)$ so that β may be readily estimated from the means of the two observed processes.

[11] We are indebted to a referee for this example.

toward acceptance. However, since we do not wish to prejudge the question by presuming that the two components are equally forecastable, as must be implicitly assumed under tests based on aggregated data, we are motivated to conduct our tests on both disaggregated and aggregated data, and thereby to avoid the issue of aggregation error.

3. TEST STATISTICS

The three theorems developed in Section 2 impose nonlinear restrictions on the expected value and autocovariance function of the bivariate process for x_t and y_t. To restate these restrictions in a way that is convenient for testing, we first define

(16) $\quad \gamma_{xy}(k) = E[(x_t - c)(y_{t-k} - c/(1-\beta))]$

for $k = 0, \pm 1, \pm 2$, and so forth. Theorem 1 states that

(17) $\quad f_1 > 0,$

where

(18) $\quad f_1 = \dfrac{[\gamma_x(0)]^{1/2}}{c} - \dfrac{[\gamma_y(0)]^{1/2}}{c/(1-\beta)}.$

Theorem 3 imposes the restriction

(19) $\quad f_3 = 0,$

where

(20) $\quad f_3 = \gamma_y^*(0) - \gamma_y(0) - \gamma_\pi(0)$

$= \dfrac{1}{1-\beta^2}\left[\gamma_x(0) + 2\sum_{j=1}^{\infty} \beta^j \gamma_x(j)\right] - \gamma_y(0)$

$- \dfrac{1}{1-\beta^2}\left[(1+\beta^2)\gamma_y(0) + \gamma_x(0) + 2\beta\gamma_{xy}(-1) - 2\beta\gamma_y(1) - 2\gamma_{xy}(0)\right],$

in view of (10) and (15). The upper bound in Theorem 2 may be written as

(21) $\quad f_2^u > 0,$

where

(22) $\quad f_2^u = \dfrac{[\gamma_{y^*}(0)]^{1/2}}{c/(1-\beta)} - \dfrac{[\gamma_y(0)]^{1/2}}{c/(1-\beta)}$

$= \dfrac{(1-\beta)}{c(1-\beta^2)^{1/2}}\left[\gamma_x(0) + \sum_{k=1}^{\infty} 2\beta^k \gamma_x(k)\right]^{1/2} - \dfrac{[\gamma_y(0)]^{1/2}}{c/(1-\beta)}.$

Finally, the lower bound restriction in Theorem 2 is

(23) $\quad f_2^l > 0,$

where

(24) $\quad f_2^l = \dfrac{[\gamma_y(0)]^{1/2}}{c/(1-\beta)} - \dfrac{[\gamma_{\tilde{y}}(0)]^{1/2}}{c/(1-\beta)}$

and

$$\gamma_{\tilde{y}}(0) = \sum_{j=0}^{\infty} \left[\sum_{k=j}^{\infty} \beta^{k-j} b_k \right]^2 \sigma_v^2$$

where σ_v^2 and $b(B)(= 1 + b_1 B + b_2 B^2 + \cdots)$ may be obtained by factoring the autocovariance generating function of $\{x_t\}$.[12]

Large-sample tests of the nonlinear restrictions in (17), (19), (21), and (23) on the functions in (18), (20), (22), and (24), respectively, may be constructed in a straightforward manner. First, a bivariate stationary and invertible ARMA representation for x and y is specified.[13] To estimate the ARMA model parameters, Wilson's [20] quasi-maximum likelihood algorithm is used except that the means are estimated first and then treated as if they are known.[14] The form of the estimated model is thus

$$\begin{bmatrix} \phi_{11}(B) & \phi_{12}(B) \\ \phi_{21}(B) & \phi_{22}(B) \end{bmatrix} \begin{bmatrix} x_t - \bar{x} \\ y_t - \bar{y} \end{bmatrix} = \begin{bmatrix} \theta_{11}(B) & \theta_{12}(B) \\ \theta_{21}(B) & \theta_{22}(B) \end{bmatrix} \underline{\zeta}_t,$$

where $\phi_{ij}(B)$ and $\theta_{ij}(B)$ are polynomials of order p_{ij} and q_{ij}, respectively,

$$\phi_{ij}(B) = k_{ij} - \sum_{s=1}^{p_{ij}} \phi_{ij,s} B^s,$$

$$\theta_{ij}(B) = k_{ij} - \sum_{s=1}^{q_{ij}} \theta_{ij,s} B^s,$$

---

[12] That is, σ_v^2 and $b(B)$ are solutions to

$$\sigma_v^2 b(B) b(B^{-1}) = \sum_{j=-\infty}^{\infty} \gamma_x(j) B^j.$$

[13] See Wilson [19 and 20] for a description of multiple ARMA models. From (3) and (5) it will be seen that the bivariate process for y and x is a linear regular stationary process so that there exists an infinite order moving average representation (Wold decomposition). We assume that this representation can be approximated by a finite parameter bivariate ARMA representation; see Sims [17] for a proof that rational functions provide a mean square approximation to such linear regular processes. We also assume that under the alternative hypothesis, x and y are generated by a linear regular process which can be approximated as under the null hypothesis by a finite parameter ARMA model.

[14] Wilson's procedure maximizes the logarithm of the likelihood function under a normality assumption concerning the error, neglecting effects of initial conditions. The sample means x and y are used to estimate the population means c and $c/(1-\beta)$, respectively.

PRESENT-VALUE RELATION

$k_{ij} = 1$ if $i = j$ and is 0 otherwise, and $\{\underline{\zeta}_t\}$ is a set of serially uncorrelated bivariate random variables with zero mean and covariance matrix V. Let $\underline{\omega}$ be the vector of ARMA parameters (including intercepts and distinct elements of V) with $\hat{\underline{\omega}}$ denoting the estimate of $\underline{\omega}$. Under general conditions $\hat{\underline{\omega}}$ is asymptotically normally distributed with mean $\underline{\omega}$ and covariance matrix Ω.[15] Next, given $\hat{\underline{\omega}}$ and an estimate of Ω, the associated function $f_i(\underline{\omega})$, i.e., the functions in (18), (20), (22), and (24), and its asymptotic standard error may be evaluated. Since each of the test functions, f_i, is continuous, the ratio of $f_i(\hat{\underline{\omega}})$ to its estimated asymptotic standard error will have a $N(0, 1)$ distribution under the null hypothesis. That is,

$$\sqrt{T}(f_i(\hat{\underline{\omega}}) - f_i(\underline{\omega})) \to N(0, \underline{j}_i' \Omega \underline{j}_i),$$

where

$$\underline{j}_i = \frac{\partial f_i(\underline{\omega})}{\partial \underline{\omega}}$$

and T denotes the sample size.

4. APPLICATION TO THE EFFICIENT MARKETS MODEL OF STOCK PRICES

The efficient markets model may be characterized by the restriction that the (real) rate of return on stock $\{r_t\}$ is a time series obeying the relation

(25) $\quad E(r_t | I_t) = \rho$

for all I_t, where ρ is a positive constant. This relation is the basis for most empirical tests of market efficiency, since it implies that no information contained in I_t is of any assistance in predicting future expected rates of return.[16] The analytical justification for identifying such a restriction with some economic notion of market efficiency, such as Pareto-optimal resource allocation or costless dissemination of information, is not immediate. This point is not pursued here; see, however, LeRoy [6, 7, 8], Lucas [10], Rubinstein [13], and Woodward [21] for discussion. If all (real) earnings on stock x_t are paid out in dividends and the payout is assumed to occur at the beginning of the period, the rate of return

---

[15] See LeRoy and Porter [9] for a detailed examination of the conditions and our estimate of the Ω based on $\hat{\omega}$. We assume that the fourth cumulants of ζ_t are zero in estimating the covariance matrix of V.

[16] In Fama's review article on the efficient capital markets theory [1], the efficient markets model when $\{z_t\}$ is a leading indicator of x_t is termed the semi-strong-form constant-return model, while the case in which z_t is the empty set is called the weak-form constant return model. In his context, the terminology is appropriate since it appears to be natural to view a model in which the expected return is constant conditional on the broader set of information as involving a stronger restriction on reality. Here, however, these usages would be misleading since in fact neither model is generally a special case of the other. Further, we will derive results that apply over all multivariate stationary earnings distributions, and therefore a fortiori over all distributions in which z_t is not a leading indicator. Thus in Fama's terminology, some of our weak-form results follow as a special case of the strong-form results. We see that Fama's definition, while analytically equivalent to our usage, would be misleading in the present context.

is

(26) $$r_t = \frac{y_{t+1}}{y_t - x_t} - 1,$$

where y_t is the (real) price of stock. Taking expectations conditional on I_t and using (25), this becomes

$$y_t = x_t + \frac{y_t^e(1)}{1 + \rho}.$$

Repeating this procedure and assuming convergence, we obtain the present-value relation (1), with $\beta = (1 + \rho)^{-1}$.[17]

The fact that stock prices are expressible as the present value of expected earnings means that the theorems derived in Section 2 are consequences of capital market efficiency as defined by (25). These results provide insights into the functions of capital markets that are interesting and not altogether obvious. For example, Theorem 1 says that the coefficient of dispersion of stock prices is necessarily less than that of earnings; this fact was noted and interpreted in the introduction. Additionally, equations (9), (13), and (15) show that the greater the accuracy with which individuals are able to forecast earnings, the higher the variance of stock prices, but the lower the variance of the rate of return on stock. These results are surprisingly powerful considering the generality with which the distribution of earnings has been specified. However, our primary interest is in constructing statistical tests of market efficiency, and not in providing extended interpretation of the properties of efficient markets, so we turn now to the empirical implementation.

Earnings and price data for Standard & Poor's Composite Index, AT&T, GE, and GM were assembled, and an attempt was made to correct for trends induced by inflation and earnings retention.[18] The question remains whether the resulting

---

[17] This argument, of course, does no more than motivate the connection between equation (25) defining an efficient capital market and the present-value relation. A formal derivation is found in Samuelson [14]. Note that even though under certainty the present-value relation is an immediate consequence of the definition of the rate of return, under uncertainty the strong restriction (25) on the distribution of rates of return is required in order to derive the present-value relation from the definition of the rate of return. Under general conditions of uncertainty (i.e., without assuming (25)), the present-value relation does not obtain.

[18] To correct for inflation, we divided all variables by the GNP deflator. The correction for retained earnings was somewhat more involved. First, we calculated a new variable, k_t, which may be viewed as a quantity index of the physical capital to which corporate equity is title. This index was assumed to equal unity at the initial time period and was augmented in proportion to the amount of retained corporate earnings in each quarter:

$$k_t = \begin{cases} 1, & t = 1, \\ k_{t-1} + \dfrac{E_t - D_t}{P_0}, & t = 2, 3, \ldots, \end{cases}$$

where E_t is real earnings, D_t is real dividends, and P_t is real stock value. Finally, the adjusted earnings and equity value series, x_t and y_t, were calculated by dividing the actual earnings and equity value series by k_t:

$$x_t = E_t/k_t, \qquad y_t = P_t/k_t.$$

See LeRoy and Porter [9] for the original data and adjusted series.

series can be assumed to obey the stationarity requirement. There appears to be some evidence of downward trends, although they are not clearly significant. We have decided to neglect such evidence and simply assume that the series are stationary since otherwise it is necessary to address such difficult questions as ascertaining to what degree stockholders can be assumed to have foreseen the assumed trend in earnings. It seems preferable to assume instead that there exist long cycles in the earnings series, implying that a sample of only a few decades may well appear nonstationary. On this interpretation, no correction for nonstationarity is indicated, but we must expect that, as with any statistical test based on a small sample, high Type II error will occur. We do not argue that this treatment is entirely adequate, nor do we in any way minimize the problem of nonstationarity; the dependence of our results on the assumption of stationarity is probably their single most severe limitation.

Table I presents the bivariate ARMA estimates for the four different data sets as well as the large-sample standard errors.[19] Table II shows the chi-square statistics $C(i, j)$ for the overall adequacy of the bivariate model.[20] The results in Table II suggest that the overall specification is adequate. The lefthand panel of Table III displays estimates of the four statistics f_1, f_2^l, f_2^u, and f_3, and of the asymptotic standardized normal ratios (z ratios) for f_1, f_2^u, and f_3, namely:

$$z_1 = f_1 / \left(\hat{L}_1' \left(\frac{1}{T} \right) \hat{\Omega} \hat{L}_1 \right)^{1/2}, \quad z_2^u = f_2^u / \left(\hat{L}_2^{u\prime} \left(\frac{1}{T} \right) \hat{\Omega} \hat{L}_2^u \right)^{1/2},$$

$$z_3 = f_3 / \left(\hat{L}_3' \left(\frac{1}{T} \right) \hat{\Omega} \hat{L}_3 \right)^{1/2}.[21]$$

The middle and right panels of Table III present estimates of the variance and coefficients of dispersion, respectively, of y_t, $\hat{y}_t$, y_t^*, and π_t. For GM the coefficient of dispersion of earnings exceeds that of prices, as required by Theorem 1. However, for GE the two statistics are virtually identical, while for AT&T and the Standard & Poor's Index the coefficients of dispersion of prices are several times higher that those of earnings. Despite these apparently pronounced inequalities, none of the three z-statistics for the associated test $H_0: f_1 = 0$ are even nearly significant, so we can conclude that at the 5 percent level the data are consistent with Theorem 1. These results indicate that, as reported in the introduction, our tests have very wide confidence intervals. As expected, the hypothesis $H_0: f^l > 0$ that stock price variance exceeds its theoretical lower bound is accepted; since the point estimate indicates acceptance, it is unnecessary to calculate the z statistics associated with f^l.

---

[19] As indicated earlier, a circumflex over a parameter denotes an estimate. Only the nonzero lags are reported in Table I. Selection of the nonzero lags followed the identification procedures suggested by Haugh [5].

[20] See Wilson [19, 20].

[21] To conserve space we have listed the estimates of j_i and Ω in LeRoy and Porter [9]. The sample periods for the four data sets were 1955:1 to 1973:4 (Standard & Poor), 1955:1 to 1977:4 (AT&T), 1955:1 to 1978:2 (GE); and 1955:4 to 1977:4 (GM). To let starting transients damp out, the first ten observations in each sample were used to provide initial conditions; see Wilson [19]. The sample means $\bar{x}$ and $\bar{y}$ were also based on this truncated sample.

TABLE I
PARAMETER ESTIMATES OF THE BIVARIATE ARMA PROCESS

Firm or Aggregate	π	ρ	$\hat{\beta}$	$\hat{\sigma}_{11}$	$\hat{\sigma}_{12}$	$\hat{\sigma}_{22}$	\multicolumn{2}{c}{$\hat{\phi}_{11}$}	\multicolumn{2}{c}{$\hat{\theta}_{11}$}	\multicolumn{2}{c}{$\hat{\theta}_{12}$}	\multicolumn{2}{c}{$\hat{\theta}_{21}$}	\multicolumn{2}{c}{$\hat{\phi}_{22}$}	\multicolumn{2}{c}{$\hat{\theta}_{22}$}
							Lag	Coeff.	Lag	Coeff.	Lag	Coeff.	Lag	Coeff.	Lag	Coeff.	Lag	Coeff.
Standard and Poor																		
Estimate	.285	4.89	.942	$.542 \times 10^{-3}$	$.990 \times 10^{-2}$	.280	1	.814	4	−.182					1	.761	3	.158
Standard Error	.0343	3.79	.0456					.072		.082						.068		.062
Estimate							4	.099	5	.338					4	.240	4	.082
Standard Error								.068		.082						.072		.080
Estimate									12	−.237							5	.447
Standard Error										.072								.075
Estimate									17	.268							12	−.306
Standard Error										.076								.079
Estimate																	17	.246
Standard Error																		.086
American Telephone and Telegraph																		
Estimate	.783	46.8	.983	3.21×10^{-3}	-3.28×10^{-2}	1.09×10^{-2}	1	.988	7	.231			3	-4.85×10^{-2}	1	.966	1	−.298
Standard Error	.095	13.7	5.29×10^{-3}					.022		.086				1.64×10^{-2}		.032		.102
Estimate									13	−.179			14	-3.06×10^{-2}			3	−.265
Standard Error										.087				1.58×10^{-2}				.103
Estimate													16	3.67×10^{-2}				
Standard Error														1.61×10^{-2}				
General Electric																		
Estimate	.497	44.7	.989	.0139	.0416	18.1	1	.273	9	.288	8	−.008	3	12.16	1	.944	12	−.290
Standard Error	.00173	6.91	.00169					.090		.095		.002		3.63		.048		.100
Estimate									11	.194			5	5.37			13	.359
Standard Error										.100				3.48				.102
Estimate									12	−.451			10	5.04				
Standard Error										.094				3.36				
Estimate													11	9.75				
Standard Error														3.41				
General Motors																		
Estimate	1.37	69.5	.980	.217	.590	41.5	4	.632	1	−.144	2	−.0209			1	.965	6	−.147
Standard Error	.104	18.2	4.86×10^{-3}					.082		.114		.0082				.029		.105
Estimate									9	.262	3	−.0181					9	.066
Standard Error										.118		.0083						.102
Estimate									10	.178	16	−.0158						
Standard Error										.121		.0082						

PRESENT-VALUE RELATION

TABLE II
"Chi-Square" Statistics for Overall Adequacy of Bivariate Specification

Firm or Aggregate	$C(1, 1)$	$C(1, 2)$	$C(2, 1)$	$C(2, 2)$
Standard & Poor	49.3 (38)	32.2 (38)	28.7 (38)	20.7 (38)
AT&T	30.2 (46)	27.2 (46)	28.4 (46)	22.2 (46)
GE	35.2 (47)	35.8 (47)	27.1 (47)	21.8 (47)
GM	22.0 (44)	41.2 (44)	21.0 (44)	32.8 (44)

Note:

$$C(i,j) = T \left(\sum_{k=1}^{df} r_{ij}^2(k) \right)$$

where

$$r_{ij}(k) = \frac{1}{T} \left(\sum_{t=1}^{T-k} \hat{\varepsilon}_{it} \hat{\varepsilon}_{jt+k} \right)$$

and df, the degrees of freedom, is reported in parentheses beneath each "chi-square" statistic.

On the basis of point estimates, the Theorem 2 upper bound test, $\gamma_y(0) < \gamma_y^*(0)$, or, equivalently, $f_2^u > 0$, is flagrantly violated for all four data sets. However, as before, the asymptotic variances of the test statistics are very high—only for GE is rejection of the null hypothesis clearly called for. GM is a borderline case at the 5 per cent level, while for AT&T and the Standard & Poor's Index acceptance is indicated. Finally, for the more restrictive Theorem 3 test that $\gamma_y^*(0) = \gamma_y(0) + \gamma_\pi(0)$, the z statistic for the hypothesis $H_0: f_3 = 0$ indicates clear rejection of market efficiency for the three firms; for the aggregate index the test statistic was not significantly different from zero.

Our results may be summarized as follows: the point estimates corresponding to our three theorems all indicate that the bounds on price dispersion implied by the efficient markets model are dramatically violated empirically, although the confidence intervals on our tests are so wide that the departures are not always statistically significant. This conclusion differs from that of most tests of restriction (25), which generally indicate acceptance of the null hypothesis (Fama [1]).[22]

In order to interpret this discrepancy, we computed the standard autocorrelation test of the sort that has led to the acceptance of market efficiency (Table IV). The statistic appropriate for testing the joint hypothesis that the population autocorrelation of the rate of return up to lag k equal zero is

$$(27) \quad \chi^2(k) = T \sum_{i=1}^{k} [\hat{\gamma}_r(i)/\hat{\gamma}_r(0)]^2,$$

---

[22] It should be noted that we have tested the model in real terms in contrast to most work in which nominal magnitudes are examined.

TABLE III
Test Statistics, Variances, and Coefficients of Dispersion

Firm or Aggregate Index	Test Statistics f_1	f_2^1	f_2^2	f_3	Variances $\gamma_y(0)$	$\gamma_{\hat{y}}(0)$	$\gamma_{y^*}(0)$	Coefficients of Dispersion $CD(x)$	$CD(\hat{y})$	$CD(y)$	$CD(y^*)$
Standard & Poor	−.280	.396	−.348	−8.63	4.89	1.64×10^{-1}	.255	3.99	.172	8.28×10^{-2}	.452	.052
z Statistic	−.193		−.242	−.254								
AT&T	−.281	.420	−.314	−828.7	385.7	9.77×10^{-6}	24.6	467.6	.139	6.68×10^{-5}	.420	.106
z Statistic	−1.096		−1.223	−2.006								
GE	-6.84×10^{-4}	.288	−.264	−1478.4	165.9	3.81×10^{-4}	1.12	1313.6	.287	4.36×10^{-4}	.288	.024
z Statistic	−.0056		−2.57	−4.41								
GM	.103	.375	−.314	−1773.9	690.5	3.37×10^{-2}	19.90	1103.3	.481	2.64×10^{-3}	.378	.064
z Statistic	.596		−1.84	−2.76								

TABLE IV
Tests of Overall Market Efficiency

Firm or Aggregate	Chi-Square Statistics for Rates of Return $\chi^2(12)$	$\chi^2(24)$
Standard & Poor	88.0	155.4
American Telephone and Telegraph	9.4	15.2
General Electric	10.2	17.0
General Motors	10.8	14.4

where the term in brackets is the sample autocorrelation of rates of return, equation (26), at lag i. Under the null hypothesis of market efficiency, (27) is distributed as a chi-square statistic with k degrees of freedom. We calculated $\chi^2(k)$ for $k = 12$ and $k = 24$; for $k = 12$ ($k = 24$) the critical value of the chi-square statistic at the twenty-five per cent level is 14.8 (28.2), while at the one per cent level the critical value is 26.2 (43.0). Comparison of the sample statistics with the critical values indicates that the hypotheses that all lagged autocorrelations in rates of return are zero is accepted at the 25 per cent level for either $k = 12$ or $k = 24$ for the firm data, although it is rejected at the one per cent level for the Standard & Poor's Index for either $k = 12$ or $k = 24$.

As indicated earlier in Section 1, we are not able to resolve this difference between our results in which market efficiency is rejected with the standard results in which the opposite conclusion is reached. As suggested in the introduction, one possibility is that our test has greater power than the standard test for the particular dispersion restriction embodied in Theorem 3.[23]

University of California, Santa Barbara and Federal Reserve Board

Manuscript received March, 1978; revision received January, 1980.

---

[23] Both our test and the standard test may be derived from (13). Theorem 3 tests only one of the restrictions contained in (13), while the standard test is a simultaneous test of all the restrictions. The situation is analogous to a multivariate test that all the coefficients in a linear model are simultaneously zero versus a t test on an individual coefficient. If one particular coefficient is nonzero, the t test for that coefficient would have greater power than the multivariate test.

REFERENCES

[1] FAMA, EUGENE F.: "Efficient Capital Markets: A Review of Theory and Empirical Work," *Journal of Finance*, 25 (1970), 383–416.
[2] FRIEDMAN, MILTON: *A Theory of the Consumption Function*. Princeton: Princeton University Press, 1957.
[3] GRANGER, C. W. J.: "Investigating Causal Relations by Econometric Models and Cross-Spectral Methods," *Econometrica*, 37 (1969), 424–438.

[4] HANNAN, E. J.: *Multiple Time Series.* New York: John Wiley and Sons, 1970.
[5] HAUGH, LARRY D.: *The Identification of Time Series Interrelationships with Special Reference to Dynamic Regression Models,* Ph.D. Dissertation, Department of Statistics, University of Wisconsin, 1972.
[6] LEROY, STEPHEN F.: "Risk Aversion and the Martingale Property of Stock Prices," *International Economic Review,* 14 (1973), 436–446.
[7] ———: "Efficient Capital Markets: Comment," *Journal of Finance,* 31 (1976), 139–141.
[8] ———: "Securities Prices Under Risk-Neutrality and Near Risk-Neutrality," reproduced, University of Chicago, 1979.
[9] LEROY, STEPHEN F., AND RICHARD D. PORTER: "The Present-Value Relation: Tests Based on Implied Variance Bounds," Federal Reserve Board Special Studies Paper, 1980.
[10] LUCAS, ROBERT E., JR.: "Asset Prices in an Exchange Economy," *Econometrica,* 46 (1978), 1426–1446.
[11] PIERCE, DAVID A.: "Forecasting Dynamic Models with Stochastic Regressors," *Journal of Econometrics,* 3 (1975), 349–374.
[12] ROZANOV, YU. A.: *Stationary Random Processes,* Tr. by A. Feinstein. San Francisco: Holden-Day, 1963.
[13] RUBINSTEIN, MARK: "Securities Market Efficiency in an Arrow-Debreu Economy," *American Economic Review,* 65 (1975), 812–824.
[14] SAMUELSON, PAUL A.: "Proof that Properly Anticipated Prices Fluctuate Randomly," *Industrial Management Review,* 6 (1965), 41–49.
[15] SHILLER, ROBERT J.: *Rational Expectations and the Structure of Interest Rates,* unpublished Ph.D. dissertation, Department of Economics, M.I.T., 1972.
[16] ———: "The Volatility of Long-Term Interest Rates and Expectations of the Term Structure," *Journal of Political Economy,* 87 (1979), 1190–1219.
[17] SIMS, CHRISTOPHER A.: "Approximate Price Restrictions in Distributed Lag Estimation," *Journal of the American Statistical Association,* 67 (1972), 169–175.
[18] SINGLETON, KENNETH J.: "Expectations Models of the Term Structure and Implied Variance Bounds," *Journal of Political Economy,* 88 (1980), 1159–1176.
[19] WILSON, G. TUNNICLIFFE: Unpublished Ph.D. dissertation, Lancaster University, 1970.
[20] ———: "The Estimation of Parameters in Multivariate Time Series Models," *Journal of the Royal Statistical Society,* Series B, 35 (1973), 76–85.
[21] WOODWARD, S. E.: "Properly Anticipated Prices Do Not, In General, Fluctuate Randomly," reproduced, University of California, Santa Barbara, 1979.

[7]
Dividend Variability and Variance Bounds Tests for the Rationality of Stock Market Prices

By TERRY A. MARSH AND ROBERT C. MERTON*

Perhaps for as long as there has been a stock market, economists have debated whether or not stock prices rationally reflect the "intrinsic" or fundamental values of the underlying companies. At one extreme on this issue is the view expressed in well-known and colorful passages by Keynes that speculative markets are no more than casinos for transferring wealth between the lucky and unlucky. At the other is the Samuelson-Fama Efficient Market Hypothesis that stock prices fully reflect available information and are, therefore, the best estimates of intrinsic values. Robert Shiller has recently entered the debate with a series of empirical studies which claim to show that the volatility of the stock market is too large to be consistent with rationally determined stock prices. In this paper, we analyze the variance-bound methodology used by Shiller and conclude that this approach cannot be used to test the hypothesis of stock market rationality.

Resolution of the debate over stock market rationality is essentially an empirical matter. Theory may suggest the correct null hypothesis—in this case, that stock market prices are rational—but it cannot tell us whether or not real-world speculative prices as seen on Wall Street or LaSalle Street are indeed rational. As Paul Samuelson wrote in his seminal paper on efficient markets: "You never get something for nothing. From a nonempirical base of axioms, you never get empirical results. Deductive analysis cannot determine whether the empirical properties of the stochastic model I posit come close to resembling the empirical determinants of today's real-world markets" (1965, p. 42).

On this count, the majority of empirical studies report results that are consistent with stock market rationality.[1] There is, for example, considerable evidence that, on average, individual stock prices respond rationally to surprise announcements concerning firm fundamentals, such as dividend and earnings changes, and that prices do not respond to "noneconomic" events such as cosmetic changes in accounting techniques. Stock prices are, however, also known to be considerably more volatile than either dividends or accounting earnings. This fact, perhaps more than any other, has led many, both academic economists and practitioners, to the belief that prices must be moved by waves of "speculative" optimism and pessimism beyond what is reasonably justified by the fundamentals.[2]

---

*Sloan School of Management, MIT, Cambridge, MA 02139 and Hoover Institution, Stanford University; and Sloan School of Management, MIT, respectively. This paper is a substantial revision of a part of our 1983 paper which was presented in seminars at Yale and Harvard. We thank the participants for helpful comments. We also thank G. Gennotte, S. Myers, R. Ruback, and R. Shiller; and for his advice on the econometric issues, J. Hausman. We are especially grateful to F. Black, both for his initial suggestion to explore this topic, and for sharing with us his deep insights into the problem. We are pleased to acknowledge financial support from the First Atlanta Corporation for computer services. We dedicate the paper to the scientific contributions and the memory of John V. Lintner, Jr.

[1] To be sure, of the hundreds of tests of efficient markets, there have been a few which appear to reject market efficiency (see "Symposium on Some Anomalous Evidence on Capital Market Efficiency," *Journal of Financial Economics*, June-September 1978). For the most part, however, these studies are joint tests of both market efficiency and a particular equilibrium model of differential expected returns across stocks such as the Capital Asset Pricing Model and, therefore, rejection of the joint hypothesis may not imply a rejection of market efficiency. Even in their strongest interpretation, such studies have at most rejected market efficiency for select segments of the market. For further discussions, see Merton (1986).

[2] For example, in discussing the problems of Tobin's Q theory in explaining investment, Barry Bosworth

Until recently, the belief that stock prices exhibit irrationally high volatility had not been formally tested. In a series of papers (1981a, b, and 1982), Shiller uses seemingly powerful variance bounds tests to show that variations in aggregate stock market prices are much too large to be justified by the variation in subsequent dividend payments.[3] Under the assumption that the expected real return on the market remains essentially constant over time, he concludes that the excess variation in stock prices identified in his tests provides strong evidence against the Efficient Market Hypothesis. Even if the expected real return on the market does change over time, Shiller further concludes that the amount of variation in that rate necessary to "save" the Efficient Market Hypothesis is so large that the measured excess variation in stock prices cannot reasonably be attributed to this source.

We need hardly mention the significance of such a conclusion. If Shiller's rejection of market efficiency is sustained, then serious doubt is cast on the validity of this cornerstone of modern financial economic theory. Although often discussed in the context of profit opportunities for the agile and informed investor, the issue of stock market rationality has implications far beyond the narrow one of whether or not some investors can beat the market. As Keynes noted long ago (1936, p. 151), and as is evident from the modern Q theory of investment, changes in stock prices—whether rationally determined or not—can have a significant impact on real investment by firms.[4] To reject the Efficient Market Hypothesis for the whole stock market and at the level suggested by Shiller's analysis implies broadly that production decisions based on stock prices will lead to inefficient capital allocations. More generally, if the application of rational expectations theory to the virtually "ideal" conditions provided by the stock market fails, then what confidence can economists have in its application to other areas of economics where there is not a large central market with continuously quoted prices, where entry to its use is not free, and where shortsales are not feasible transactions?

The strength of Shiller's conclusions is derived from three elements: (i) the apparent robustness of the variance bound methodology; (ii) the length of the data sets used in the tests—one set has over 100 years of dividend and stock price data; and (iii) the large magnitude of the empirical violation of his upper bound for the volatility of rational stock prices. Shiller in essence relies upon elements (ii) and (iii) to argue that his rejection of the efficient market model cannot be explained away by "mere" sampling error alone.[5] Nevertheless, Marjorie Flavin (1983) and Allan Kleidon (1983a,b) have shown that such sampling error can have a nontrivial effect on the variance bound test statistics.

In this paper, we focus exclusively on element (i) and conclude that Shiller's variance bound methodology is wholly unreliable for the purpose of testing stock market rationality. Thus, even if his estimates contained no sampling error at all, his findings do not constitute a rejection of the efficient market model. To support our claim, we present an alternative variance bound test which has the feature that observed prices will, *of necessity*, be judged rational if they fail the

---

writes: "Nor does it seem reasonable to believe that the present value of expected corporate income actually fell in 1973–1974 by the magnitude implied by the stockmarket decline of that period, when q declined by 50 percent. ...As long as management is concerned about long-run market value and believes that this value reflects 'fundamentals,' it would not scrap investment plans in response to the highly volatile short-run changes in stock prices" (1975, p. 286).

[3] Using the variance bound methodology, Stephen LeRoy and Richard Porter (1981) claim to show that stock prices are "too volatile" relative to accounting earnings. For a similar discussion of their analysis, see our 1984 paper.

[4] For a recent discussion of the "causal" effect of stock price changes on investment, see Stanley Fischer and Merton (1984).

[5] Shiller notes on this general point: "The lower bound of a 95 percent one-sided χ^2 confidence interval for the standard deviation of annual changes in real stock prices is over five times higher than the upper bound allowed by our measure of the observed variability of real dividends. The failure of the efficient markets model is thus so dramatic that it would seem impossible to attribute the failure to such things as data errors, price index problems, or changes in tax laws" (1981a, p. 434).

Shiller test. That is, if observed stock prices were to satisfy Shiller's variance bound test, then they would be deemed irrational by our test. It would seem, therefore, that for any set of stock market price data, the hypothesis of market rationality can be rejected by some variance bound test.

This seeming paradox arises from differences in assumptions about the underlying stochastic processes used to describe the evolution of dividends and rational stock prices. Affirmative empirical evidence in support of the class of aggregate dividend processes postulated in our variance bound test is presented in our forthcoming article. The specific model derived and tested in that paper significantly outperforms the univariate autoregressive model associated with the Shiller analysis.

The Shiller variance bound test and our alternative test share in common the null hypothesis that stock prices are rational, but differ as to the assumed stochastic process for dividends. Since Shiller's data sets strongly reject the joint hypothesis of his test and sustain our's, we conclude that his variance bound test results might better be interpreted as an impressive rejection of his model of the dividend process than as a rejection of stock market rationality.

I. On the Reliability of the Dividend Variance Bound Test of Stock Market Rationality

In his 1981a article, Shiller concludes that:

> measures of stock price volatility over the past century appear to be far too high—five to thirteen times too high—to be attributed to new information about future real dividends if uncertainty about future dividends is measured by the sample standard deviation of real dividends around their long-run exponential path. [p. 434]

In reaching this conclusion, he relies upon a variance bound test—hereafter called the "p^* test"—which establishes an upper bound on the variance of the level of detrended real stock prices in terms of the variance of a constructed "ex post rational" detrended and real price series.[6] In this section, we begin with a brief review of the development of his test and then present an alternative variance bound test which actually *reverses* the direction of the inequality established in the p^* test. That is, the *upper* bound on the variance of rationally determined stock prices in the Shiller test is shown to be the *lower* bound on that same variance in the alternative test.

The key assumptions underlying the p^* test can be summarized as follows:

(S1) Stock prices reflect investor beliefs which are rational expectations of future dividends.
(S2) The "real" (or inflation-adjusted) expected rate of return on the stock market, r, is constant over time.
(S3) Aggregate real dividends on the stock market, $\{D(t)\}$, can be described by a finite-variance stationary stochastic process with a deterministic exponential trend (or growth rate) which is denoted by g.

To develop the p^* test from these assumptions, Shiller defines an *ex post* rational detrended price per share in the market portfolio at time t:

$$(1) \qquad p^*(t) \equiv \sum_{k=0}^{\infty} \eta^{k+1} d(t+k),$$

where $d(s) \equiv D(s)/(1+g)^{s+1}$ is the detrended dividend per share paid at the end of period s and $\eta \equiv (1+g)/(1+r)$. $p^*(t)$ is called an *ex post* (detrended) rational price because it is the present value of *actual* subsequent (to time t) detrended dividends. If as posited in (S1), actual stock prices, $\{P(t)\}$, are *ex ante* rational prices, then it follows from (1) that

$$(2) \qquad p(t) = \varepsilon_t[p^*(t)],$$

---
[6]Shiller also develops a second variance bound test that establishes an upper bound on the variance of unanticipated changes in detrended real stock prices in terms of the variance of detrended real dividends. An analysis of this "innovations test" is presented later in this section.

for each t where $p(t) \equiv P(t)/(1+g)^t$ is the detrended real stock price per share of the market portfolio at the beginning of period t and ε_t is the expectation operator conditional on all information available to the market as of time t.

If, as Shiller (1981a, p. 422) points out, $p(t)$ is an *ex ante* rational price, then it is also an optimal forecast of $p^*(t)$. If $p(t)$ is such an optimal forecast, then the forecast error, $u(t) \equiv p^*(t) - p(t)$, should be uncorrelated with $p(t)$. It follows therefore that under this hypothesis, $\text{Var}[p^*(t)] = \text{Var}[p(t)] + \text{Var}[u(t)] > \text{Var}[p(t)]$. That is, in a set of repeated experiments where a forecast $p(t)$ and a sequence of subsequent dividends, $d(t+k)$, $k = 0,1,\ldots$, are "drawn," it should turn out that the sample variance of $p^*(t)$ exceeds the sample variance of the forecast $p(t)$.

If (detrended) dividends follow a regular stationary process, then rationally determined (detrended) stock prices must also. Hence, from assumption (S3), it follows by the Ergodic Theorem that time-series ensembles of $\{p(t)\}$ and $\{p^*(t)\}$ can be used to test the "cross-sectional" proposition that $\text{Var}[p^*(t)] > \text{Var}[p(t)]$.[7]

To compute an estimate of $p^*(t)$ with a finite sample time period, it is, of course, necessary to truncate the summation in (1). If, as Shiller (1981a, p. 425) notes, the time-series sample is "long enough," then a reasonable estimate of the variance of $p^*(t)$ can be obtained from that truncated summation. At the point of truncation, Shiller assigns a "terminal" value, $p^*(T)$, which is the average of the detrended stock prices over the sample period. That is,

$$(3) \qquad p^*(T) = \left[\sum_{t=0}^{T-1} p(t)\right]/T,$$

where T is the number of years in the sample period.

Under the posited conditions (S1)–(S3), the null hypothesis of the p^* test for rational stock prices can be written as

$$(4) \qquad \text{Var}[p^*] \geq \text{Var}[p],$$

where from (1) and (3), the constructed $p^*(t)$ series used to test the hypothesis is given by

$$(5) \qquad p^*(t) = \sum_{k=0}^{T-t-1} \eta^{k+1} d(t+k) + \eta^{T-t} p^*(T), \quad t = 0,\ldots,T-1.$$

As summarized by Shiller in the paragraph cited at the outset of this section, the results reported in his Table 2 (1981a, p. 431) show that the variance bound in (4) is grossly violated by both his Standard and Poor's 1871–1979 data set and his modified Dow Industrial 1928–79 data set.

Although widely interpreted as a rejection of stock market rationality (S1),[8] these findings are more precisely a rejection of the joint hypothesis of (S1), (S2), and (S3). As noted in our introduction, Shiller (1981, pp. 430–33) argues that a relaxation of (S2) to permit a time-varying real discount rate would not produce sufficient additional variation in prices to "explain" the large magnitude of the violation of the derived variance bound. However, even if (S2) were known to be true, this violation of the bound is not a valid rejection of stock market rationality unless (S3) is also known to be true. Nevertheless, to some, (S3) may appear to encompass such a broad class of stochastic processes that any plausible real-world time-series of dividends can be well-approximated by some process within its domain.[9] If this were so, then, of course, the p^* test, viewed as a test of stock market rationality, would be robust. In fact, however, this test is very sensitive to

---

[7] That is, the time-series estimator $\Sigma_0^{T-1}[p(t) - \bar{p}]^2/T$ can be used to estimate $\text{Var}[p(t)]$ and similarly for $p^*(t)$.

[8] As a recent example, see James Tobin (1984).

[9] Perhaps this belief explains why Shiller devotes 20 percent of his paper (1981a) to justifying the robustness of his findings with respect to assumption (S2) and virtually no space to justifying (S3).

the posited dividend process. We show this by deriving a variance bound test of rational stock prices that reverses the key inequality (4). While maintaining assumptions (S1) and (S2) of the p^* test, this alternative test replaces (S3) with the assumption of a different, but equally broad, class of dividend processes. As background for the selection of this alternative class, we turn now to discuss some of the issues surrounding dividend policy and the sense in which rational stock prices are a reflection of expected future dividends, this to be followed by the derivation of our test.

If the required expected real rate of return on the firm is constant, then its intrinsic value per share at time t, $V(t)$, is defined to be the present value of the expected future real cash flows of the firm that will be available for distribution to each of the shares currently outstanding. From the well-known accounting identity,[10] it follows that the firm's dividend policy must satisfy the constraint:

$$(6) \quad V(t) = \varepsilon_t \left[\sum_{k=0}^{\infty} D(t+k)/(1+r)^{k+1} \right].$$

Although management can influence the intrinsic value of its firm by its investment decisions, management has little, if any, control over the stochastic or unanticipated changes in $V(t)$. In sharp contrast, management has sole responsibility for, and control over, the dividends paid by the firm. There are, moreover, no important legal or accounting constraints on dividend policy. Hence, subject only to the constraint given in (6), managers have almost complete discretion and control over the choice of dividend policy.

This constraint on dividend choice is very much like the intertemporal budget constraint on rational consumption choice in the basic lifetime consumption decision problem for an individual. In this analogy, the intrinsic value of the firm, $V(t)$, corresponds to the capitalized permanent income or wealth of the individual, and the dividend policy of the firm corresponds to the consumption policy of the individual. Just as there are an uncountable number of rational consumption plans which satisfy the consumer's budget constraint for a given amount of wealth, so there are an uncountable number of distinct dividend policies that satisfy (6) for a given intrinsic value of the firm. Hence, like rational consumers in selecting their plans, rational managers have a great deal of latitude in their choice of dividend policy.[11]

If stock prices are rationally determined, then

$$(7) \quad P(t) = V(t) \quad \text{for all } t.$$

Hence, the only reason for a change in rational stock price is a change in intrinsic value. Since a manager can choose any number of different dividend policies that are consistent with a particular intrinsic value of the firm, the statement that "rational stock prices reflect expected future dividends" needs careful interpretation. It follows from (6) and (7) that rational stock prices will satisfy

$$(8) \quad P(t) = \varepsilon_t \left[\sum_{k=0}^{\infty} D(t+k)/(1+r)^{k+1} \right].$$

Thus, rational stock prices reflects expected future dividends through (8) in the same sense that an individual's current wealth reflects his expected future consumption through the budget constraint. Pursuing the analogy further: if because of an exogenous event (for example, a change in preferences), a consumer changes his planned pattern of

---

[10] The cash flow accounting identity applies only to dividends paid *net* of any issues or purchases of its outstanding securities. "Gross" dividends are, of course, subject to no constraint. Hence, all references to "dividends" throughout the paper are to "net" dividends paid.

[11] The fact that individual firms pursue dividend policies which are vastly different from one another is empirical evidence consistent with this view.

consumption, then it surely *does not* follow from the budget constraint that this change in the expected future time path of his consumption will cause his current wealth to change. Just so, it does not follow from (8) that a change in dividend policy by managers will cause a change in the current rationally determined prices of their shares.[12] For a fixed discount rate, r, it does however follow from (8) that an unanticipated change in a rationally determined stock price must necessarily cause a change in expected future dividends, and this is so for the same feasibility reason that with a constant discount rate, an unanticipated change in a consumer's wealth must necessarily cause a change in his planned future consumption. *In short, (8) is a constraint on future dividends and not on current rational stock price.*

Since management's choice of dividend policy clearly affects the time-series variation in observed dividends, the development of the relation between the volatility of dividends and rational stock prices requires analysis of the linkage between the largely controllable dividend process and the largely uncontrollable process for intrinsic value.

Unlike the theory of consumer choice, there is no generally accepted theory of optimal dividend policy.[13] Empirical researchers have, therefore, relied on positive theories of dividend policy to specify their models. The prototype for these models is John Lintner's model (1956) based on stylized facts first established by him in a classic set of interviews of managers about their dividend policies. Briefly, these facts are: (L1) Managers believe that their firms should have some long-term target payout ratio; (L2) In setting dividends, they focus on the change in existing payouts and not on the level; (L3) A major unanticipated and nontransitory change in earnings would be an important reason to change dividends; (L4) Most managers try to avoid making changes in dividends which stand a good chance of having to be reversed within the near future. In summary, managers set the dividends that their firms pay to have a target payout ratio as a long-run objective, and they choose policies which smooth the time path of the changes in dividends required to meet that objective.

As most textbook discussions seem to agree, these target payout ratios are measured in terms of long-run sustainable ("permanent") earnings rather than current earnings per share. In the special case where the firm's cost of capital r is constant in real terms, real permanent earnings at time t, $E(t)$, are related to the firm's intrinsic value per share by $E(t) = rV(t)$.

With this as background, we now develop a model of the dividend process as an alternative to the p^* test's (S3) process. A class of dividend policies which captures the behavior described in the Lintner interviews is given by the rule:

$$(9) \quad \Delta D(t) = gD(t) + \sum_{k=0}^{N} \gamma_k [\Delta E(t-k) - gE(t-k)],$$

where Δ is the forward difference operator, $\Delta X(t) \equiv X(t+1) - X(t)$, and it is assumed that $\gamma_k \geq 0$ for all $k = 0, 1, \ldots, N$. In words, managers set dividends to grow at rate g, but deviate from this long-run growth path in response to changes in permanent earnings that deviate from their long-run growth path. Describing the policies in terms of the

---

[12] By the accounting identity, net dividend policy (as described in fn. 10) cannot be changed without changing the firm's investment policy. However, changes in investment policy need not change the current intrinsic value of the firm. Managers can implement virtually any change in net dividends per share (without affecting the firm's intrinsic value) by the purchase or sale of financial assets held by the firm or by marginal changes in the amount of investment in any other "zero net present value" asset held by the firm (for example, inventories). Such transactions will change the composition of the firm's assets and the time pattern of its future cash flows, but not the present value of the future cash flows. Since these "trivial" changes in investment policy will not affect the intrinsic value of the firm, they will not affect the current level of rationally determined stock price. See our forthcoming article (Section 6.3) for further discussion of the difficulties of measuring net dividends.

[13] Indeed, the classic Miller-Modigliani (1961) theory of dividends holds that dividend policy is irrelevant, and hence, in this case, there is no optimal policy.

change in dividends rather than the levels, and having these changes depend on changes in permanent earnings, is motivated by Lintner's stylized facts (L2) and (L3). His behavioral fact (L4) is met in (9) by specifying the change in dividends as a moving average of current and past changes in permanent earnings over the previous N periods.

Equation (9) can be rewritten in terms of detrended real dividends and permanent earnings as

$$(10) \quad \Delta d(t) = \sum_{k=0}^{N} \lambda_k \Delta e(t-k),$$

where $e(s) \equiv E(s)/(1+g)^s$ and $\lambda_k \equiv \gamma_k/(1+g)^{k+1}$. By integrating (10),[14] we can express the level of detrended dividends at time t in terms of current and past detrended permanent earnings as

$$(11) \quad d(t) = \sum_{k=0}^{N} \lambda_k e(t-k).$$

By inspection of (11), the dividend policies in (9) satisfy Lintner's (L1) condition of a long-run target payout ratio where this ratio is given by $\delta \equiv \sum_{0}^{N} \lambda_k$.

Consider an economy in which the p^* test assumptions (S1) and (S2) *are known* to hold, but instead of (S3), assume that (9) describes the stochastic process for aggregate real dividends on the market portfolio. From the assumption of a constant discount rate (S2) and the definition of permanent earnings, we have from (11) that detrended real dividends at time t can be written as

$$(12) \quad d(t) = r \sum_{k=0}^{N} \lambda_k v(t-k)$$

$$= r\delta \sum_{k=0}^{N} \theta_k v(t-k)$$

where $v(s) \equiv V(s)/(1+g)^s$ is the detrended real intrinsic value per share of the firm at time s and $\theta_k \equiv \lambda_k/\delta \geq 0$ with $\sum_{0}^{N} \theta_k = 1$.

From (S1), stock prices are known to be rationally determined, and therefore, it follows from (7) that $p(t) = v(t)$ for all t. Hence, from (12), current detrended dividends can be expressed as a function of current and past detrended stock prices: namely,

$$(13) \quad d(t) = \rho \sum_{k=0}^{N} \theta_k p(t-k),$$

where $\rho = r\delta$ is the long-run or steady-state dividend-to-price ratio on the market portfolio.[15] Thus, from (S1), (S2), and (9), detrended aggregate real dividends are a moving average of current and past detrended real stock prices. Moreover, under these posited conditions, the *ex post* rational price series constructed for the sample period $[0, T]$ can be expressed as a convex combination of the observed detrended stock prices, $p(t)$, $t = -N, \ldots, 0, 1, \ldots, T-1$. That is, from (3) and (13), (5) can be rewritten as

$$(14) \quad p^*(t) = \sum_{k=-N}^{T-1} w_{tk} p(k),$$

$$t = 0, 1, \ldots, T-1,$$

where, as can be easily shown, the derived weights satisfy

$$\sum_{k=-N}^{T-1} w_{tk} = 1$$

and $w_{tk} \geq 0$ with $w_{tk} = 0$ for $k < t - N$.

THEOREM 1: *If, for each t, $p^*(t) = \sum_{k=0}^{T-1} \pi_{tk} p(k)$ where $\sum_{k=0}^{T-1} \pi_{tk} = 1$; $\sum_{t=0}^{T-1} \pi_{tk} \leq 1$ and $\pi_{tk} \geq 0$, then for each and every sample path of stock price realizations, $\text{Var}(p^*) \leq \text{Var}(p)$, with equality holding if and only if*

---

[14] The constant of integration must be zero since $e(t) = 0$ implies that $V(t) = 0$, which implies that $e(t+s) = 0$ and $d(t+s) = 0$ for all $s \geq 0$.

[15] The target payout ratio δ and the long-run growth rate g are related by $g = (1-\delta)r/[1+r\delta]$.

all realized prices are identical in the sample $t = 0,\ldots, T-1$.

The formal proof is in the Appendix. However, a brief intuitive explanation of the theorem is as follows: for each $t, t = 0,\ldots, T-1$, $p^*(t)$ is formally similar to a conditional expectation of a random variable p with possible outcomes $p(0),\ldots, p(T-1)$ where the $\{\pi_{tk}\}$ are interpreted as conditional probabilities. $\text{Var}(p^*)$ is, therefore, similar to the variance of the conditional expectations of p which is always strictly less than the variance of p itself (unless, of course, $\text{Var}(p) = 0$).

The variance inequality in Theorem 1 is the exact opposite of inequality (4) which holds that $\text{Var}(p^*) \geq \text{Var}(p)$. That is, if the *ex post* rational price series satisfies the hypothesized conditions of Theorem 1, then the p^* test inequality will be violated whether or not actual stock prices are *ex ante* rational. Because Theorem 1 applies to each and every time path of prices, its derived inequality $\text{Var}(p^*) \leq \text{Var}(p)$ holds *in-sample*. A fortiori, it will obtain for any distribution of prices. Thus, even for a "bad draw," $\text{Var}(p^*)$ will not exceed $\text{Var}(p)$.

Although the inequality in Theorem 1 is an analytic result, it does not strictly hold for all possible sample paths of the $p^*(t)$ series generated by the dividend process (9) and rational stock prices. By inspection of (3) and (14), for each $t, N \leq t \leq T$, $p^*(t)$ is a convex combination of the sample stock prices $\{p(0),\ldots, p(T-1)\}$ that satisfies the hypothesized conditions of Theorem 1. However, for $0 \leq t \leq N-1$, $p^*(t)$ will depend upon both the sample period's stock prices and one or more "out-of-sample" stock prices $\{p(-N),\ldots, p(-1)\}$. Hence, with the exception of one member of the class of processes given by (9),[16] $\text{Var}(p^*) \leq \text{Var}(p)$

[16] The exception is the polar case of (9) where $N = 0$ and mangers choose a dividend policy so as to maintain a target payout ratio in both the short and long run. In this case, with $d(t) = pp(t)$ for all t, we have the stronger analytic proposition that the Shiller variance bound inequality (4) must be violated in all samples if stock prices are rational.

need not obtain for each and every sample path of prices.[17] The problem created here by out-of-sample prices is similar to the general "start-up" problem in using a finite sample to estimate a moving average or distributed lag process. Because only the first N of the T sample elements in the p^* series depend on out-of-sample prices, the influence of these prices on the sample variance of p^* becomes progressively smaller as the length of the sample period is increased. Indeed, as proved in the Appendix, we have that

THEOREM 2: *If* (S1) *and* (S2) *hold and if the process for aggregate real dividends is given by* (9), *then in the limit as* $T/N \to \infty$, $\text{Var}(p^*)/\text{Var}(p) \leq 1$ *will hold almost certainly.*

As noted in the introduction, the Shiller variance bound theorem has been widely interpreted as a test of stock market rationality. However, as with Theorem 1, Theorem 2 concludes that $\text{Var}(p^*)$ is a *lower* bound on $\text{Var}(p)$ whereas, the corresponding Shiller theorem concludes that $\text{Var}(p^*)$ is an *upper* bound on $\text{Var}(p)$. Both Theorem 2 and the Shiller theorem are mathematically correct and both share in common the hypothesis (S1) that stock prices are rationally determined. Therefore, if these variance bound theorems are interpreted as tests of stock market rationality, then we have the empirical paradox that this hypothesis can always be rejected. That is, if observed stock prices were to satisfy the p^* test of stock market rationality, then this same sample of prices must fail our test, and conversely. This finding alone casts considerable doubt on the reliability of such variance bound theorems as tests of stock market rationality.

The apparent empirical paradox is, of course, resolved by recognizing that each of the variance bound theorems provides a test of a different joint hypothesis. In addition to

[17] For example, if all in-sample prices happened to be the same (i.e., $p(t) = \bar{p}, t = 0,\ldots, T-1$), but the out-of-sample prices were not, then for that particular sample path, $\text{Var}(p^*) > \text{Var}(p) = 0$.

(S1), both theorems also assume that the real discount rate is constant. Hence, neither (S1) nor (S2) of the respective joint hypotheses is the source of each theorem's contradictory conclusion to the other.[18] It therefore follows necessarily that the class of aggregate dividend processes (9) postulated in Theorem 2 is incompatible with the Shiller theorem assumption (S3) of a regular stationary process for detrended aggregate dividends.[19] That is, given that (S1) and (S2) hold, nonstationarity of the dividend process is a necessary condition for the validity of Theorem 2[20] whereas stationarity of the dividend process is a sufficient condition for the validity of the p^* test inequality (4). Thus, the diametrically opposite conclusions of these variance bound theorems follow directly from the differences in their posited dividend processes.

In this light, it seems to us that if the p^* test is to be interpreted as a test of any single element of its joint hypothesis, (S1), (S2), and (S3), then it is more appropriately viewed as a test of (S3) than of (S1). Viewed in this way, the previously cited empirical findings of a large violation of inequality (4) would appear to provide a rather impressive rejection of the hypothesis that aggregate real dividends follow a stationary stochastic process with a trend. As noted, Shiller has argued extensively that his results are empirically robust with respect to assumption (S2). In a parallel fashion, we would argue that they are also robust with respect to (S1). That is, even if stock prices were irrationally volatile, the amount of irrationality required to "save" the stationarity hypothesis (S3) is so large that the measured five-to-thirteen times excess variation in stock prices cannot reasonably be attributed to this source.

Perhaps the p^* test might still be saved as a test of stock market rationality if there were compelling a priori economic reasons or empirical evidence to support a strong prior belief that aggregate dividends follow a stationary process with a trend. We are, however, unaware of any strong theoretical or empirical foundation for this belief. Indeed, the standard models in the theoretical and empirical literature of both financial economics and accounting assume that stock prices, earnings, and dividends are described by nonstationary processes.[21] In his analyses of the Shiller and other variance bounds tests, Kleidon (1983a, b) uses regression and other time-series methods to show that the hypothesis of stationarity for the aggregate Standard and Poor's 500 stock price, earnings, and dividend series can be rejected.

We (in our forthcoming article) develop and test an aggregate dividend model based on the same Lintner stylized facts used to motivate (9) here. In this model, the dividend-to-price ratio follows a stationary process, but both the dividend and stock price

---

[18] Since the two theorems share the assumption (S2) and for any sample of prices, one must fail, they cannot reliably be used to test this hypothesis either. However, as Eugene Fama (1977) and Stewart Myers and Stuart Turnbull (1977) have shown, we note that a constant discount rate is inconsistent with a stationary process for dividends when investors are risk averse. Hence, the assumptions (S2) and (S3) are a priori mutually inconsistent.

[19] If $V(t)$ follows a stationary process and the dividend process is given by (9), then the innovations or unanticipated changes in intrinsic value, $\Delta V(t) + D(t) - rV(t)$, will not form a martingale as is required by (6). If, as is necessary for the validity of (9), the intrinsic value follows a nonstationary process, then from (6) and (7), both dividends and rational stock prices must also be nonstationary.

[20] If $p(t)$ and $d(t)$ follow nonstationary processes, the variances of the price and dividend are, of course, not well-defined in the time-series sense that they were used in Shiller's variance bound test. However, Var(p^*) and Var(p) can be simply treated as sample statistics constructed from the random variables $\{p(t)\}$ and $\{d(t)\}$, and for any finite T, the conditional moments of their distributions will exist. If, moreover, the processes are such that the dividend-to-price ratio converges to a finite-variance steady-state distribution, then the conditional expectation of the variance bound inequality as expressed in Theorem 2, $\varepsilon_0[\text{Var}(p^*)/\text{Var}(p)]$, will exist even in the limit as $T \to \infty$.

[21] In financial economics, the prototypical assumption is that the per period rates of return on stocks are independently and identically distributed over time. Together with limited liability on stock ownership, this implies a geometric Brownian motion model for stock prices which is not, of course, a stationary process. There is a long-standing and almost uniform agreement in the accounting literature that accounting earnings (either real or nominal) can best be described by a nonstationary process (see George Foster, 1978, ch. 4).

processes are themselves nonstationary. This model is shown to significantly outperform empirically the univariate autoregressive model (with a trend) normally associated with a stationary process. These results not only cast further doubt on the stationarity assumption, but also provide affirmative evidence in support of the class of dividend processes hypothesized in Theorems 1 and 2.

Our model can also be used to reinterpret other related empirical findings which purport to show that stock prices are too volatile. For example, to provide a more-visual (if less-quantitatively precise) representation of the "excess volatility" of stock prices, Shiller (1981a, p. 422) plots the time-series of the levels of actual detrended stock prices and the constructed *ex post* rational prices, $p^*(t)$. By inspection of these plots, it is readily apparent that $p(t)$ is more volatile than $p^*(t)$. Instead of implying "too much" stock price volatility, these plots can be interpreted as implying that the p^* series has "too little" volatility to be consistent with a dividend process which is not smoothed. They are, however, entirely consistent with rational and nonstationary stock prices and dividend policies like (9) which smooth the dividend process.

It also appears in these plots that the levels of actual prices "revert" toward the p^* trend line. In the context of (14), this apparent correspondence in trend should not be surprising since $p^*(t)$ is in effect a weighted sum of *future* actual prices that were, of course, not known to investors at time t. The *ex post* "mistakes" in forecasts of these future prices by the market at time t are, thus, "corrected" when the subsequent "right" prices (which were already contained in $p^*(t)$) are revealed.[22]

In his latest published remarks on the plots of these time-series, Shiller concludes:

> The near-total lack of correspondence, except for trend, between the aggregate stock price and its *ex post* rational counterpart (as shown in Figure 1 of my 1981a paper) means that essentially no observed movements in aggregate dividends were ever correctly forecast by movements in aggregate stock prices! [1983, p. 237]

This conclusion does not, however, appear to conform to the empirical facts. As shown in our forthcoming article, the single variable that provides, by far, the most significant and robust forecasting power of the subsequent year's change in aggregate dividends is the previous year's unanticipated change in aggregate stock price.[23]

Shiller (1981a, pp. 425-27) presents a second variance bound test of rational stock prices that uses the time-series of "price innovations" that he denotes by $\delta p(t) \equiv p(t) - p(t-1) + d(t-1) - \rho p(t-1)$. Under the assumption that detrended dividends have a stationary distribution, he derives as a condition for rational stock prices that

$$(15) \quad \text{Var}(d) \geq \text{Var}(\delta p)\left[(1+\rho)^2 - 1\right],$$

where $\text{Var}(d)$ and $\text{Var}(\delta p)$ denote the sample variances of the level of detrended dividends and the innovations of price changes, respectively. As reported in Shiller's cited Table 2, the null hypothesis of rational stock prices seems, once again, to be grossly violated by both his data sets.

If, however, dividends are generated by a process like (9) and rational stock prices follow a nonstationary process, then the inequality (15) is no longer valid. Moreover, in this case, it is likely that inequality (15) will be violated. Suppose, for example, that the innovations in (detrended) stock prices follow a geometric Brownian motion

---

[22] The strength of this apparent reversion to trend is further accentuated by using the *ex post* or in-sample trend of stock prices to detrend both the actual stock price and the $p^*(t)$ time-series.

[23] As shown in Fischer and Merton, in addition to predicting dividend changes, aggregate real stock price changes are among the better forecasters of future changes in business cycle variables including *GNP*, corporate earnings, and business fixed investment. These empirical findings might also be counted in the support of the hypothesis of stock market rationality.

given by

(16) $$\delta p(t) = \sigma p(t-1) Z(t),$$

where $\{Z(t)\}$ are independently and identically distributed random variables with $\varepsilon_{t-1}[Z(t)] = 0$; $\varepsilon_{t-1}[Z^2(t)] = 1$; σ, a positive constant and where ε_t is the expectation operator, conditional on information available at time t. It follows from (16) and the properties of $\{Z(t)\}$ that

(17) $$\varepsilon_0[\text{Var}(\delta p)] = \varepsilon_0\left[\sum_{t=0}^{T-1} \sigma^2 p^2(t)\right]/T,$$

$$= \sigma^2 \varepsilon_0\left[\text{Var}(p) + (\bar{p})^2\right],$$

where $\bar{p} = p^*(T)$ given in (3).

From the posited dividend process given in (13), $d(t)/\rho$ is a distributed lag of past stock prices where the distribution weights are nonnegative and sum to unity. Thus, the ensemble $\{d(t)/\rho\}$ satisfies the hypothesized conditions of Theorems 1 and 2. It follows, therefore, that $\text{Var}(d/\rho) \le \text{Var}(p)$. Factoring out the constant ρ and rearranging terms, the inequality can be rewritten as

(18) $$\text{Var}(d) \le \rho^2 \text{Var}(p),$$

with equality holding only in the special limiting case of (13) with $d(t) = \rho p(t)$. Combining (17) and (18) and rearranging terms, we have that

(19) $$\varepsilon_0[\text{Var}(d)] \le \rho^2 \varepsilon_0[\text{Var}(\delta p) - \sigma^2 \bar{p}^2]/\sigma^2.$$

In sharp contrast to the stationary dividend case in (15) where the variance of dividends provides an upper bound on the volatility of rational stock price innovations, inspection of (19) shows that this variance provides only a *lower* bound on that volatility for our dividend process.[24] Inequalities

---

[24] By inspection of (18) and (19), it is evident that the strength of the inequality (19) will depend on the degree of "dividend smoothing" undertaken by managers. Gen-

(15) and (19) are not, of course, mutually exclusive for all parameter values. However, using the estimated values of $\text{Var}(\delta p)$, $\bar{p}$, $\text{Var}(p)$, and ρ reported by Shiller for his 1871–1979 Standard and Poor's data set, and our equation (17), we have that $\hat{\rho} = 0.0480$ and $\hat{\sigma}^2 = \text{Var}(\delta p)/[\text{Var}(p) + \bar{p}^2] = 0.0276$. Substitution of these values in (15) implies that $\varepsilon_0[\text{Var}(d)] \ge .0983\,\varepsilon_0[\text{Var}(\delta p)]$ whereas the same values substituted in (19) implies that $\varepsilon_0[\text{Var}(d)] \le .0835\,\varepsilon_0[\text{Var}(\delta p)] - .0276(\bar{p})^2]$. Thus, given these parameter values it would appear that any recorded values for $\text{Var}(\delta p)$ and $\text{Var}(d)$ would violate one or the other variance bound inequalities for rational stock price innovations. Hence, the empirical finding that $\text{Var}(d) \ll .0983\,\text{Var}(\delta p)$—although inconsistent with the stationarity assumption (S3)— is entirely consistent with rational stock prices and the aggregate dividend process (9).

We are not alone in questioning the specification of the dividend process in the Shiller model. In addition to the cited Kleidon analyses, Basil Copeland (1983) has commented on the assumption of a deterministic trend. In his reply to Copeland, Shiller had this to say on the specification issue:[25] "Of course, we do not literally believe with certainty all the assumptions in the model which are the basis of testing. I did not intend to assert in the paper that I know dividends were indeed stationary around the historical trend" (1983, p. 236). We have shown, however, that variance bound inequality (4) is critically sensitive to the assumption of a stationary process for aggregate dividends. If aggregate dividend policy is described by a smoothing or averaging of intrinsic values that follow a nonstationary process, then the misspecification of stationarity in the dividend process does not

---

erally, the larger is N and the more evenly distributed the weights $\{\theta_k\}$ in (13), the smaller will be $\text{Var}(d)$ with no corresponding reduction in $\text{Var}(\delta p)$.

[25] We surely echo this view with respect to our own dividend model (9). We do not however, assert that the variance bound condition of Theorems 1 and 2 provides a reliable method for testing stock market rationality.

just weaken the power of this bound as a test of stock market rationality—it destroys it—because in that case the fundamental inequality is exactly reversed.

In summary, the story that dividends follow a stationary process with a trend leads to the empirical conclusion that aggregate stock prices are *grossly* irrational. It has, therefore, the deep and wide-ranging implications for economic theory and policy that follow from this conclusion. The majority of empirical tests of the efficient market theory do not, however, concur with this finding. Hence, to accept this dividend story, we must further conclude that the methodologies of these tests were sufficiently flawed that they failed to reject this hypothesis in spite of the implied substantial irrationality in stock prices. Similar flaws must also be ascribed to the extensive studies in finance and accounting that claim to show earnings, dividends, and stock prices follow nonstationary processes. If, however, this dividend story is rejected, then the empirical violation of inequalities (4) and (15) implies nothing at all about stock market rationality. In the spirit of Edward Leamer's (1983) discussion of hypothesis testing, we therefore conclude that the Shiller variance bound theorem is a wholly unreliable test of stock market rationality because, as Leamer said, "...there are assumptions within the set under consideration that lead to radically different conclusions" (p. 38).

II. Overview and Conclusion

In the previously cited reply to Copeland, Shiller proclaims:

> The challenge for advocates of the efficient markets model is to tell a convincing story which is consistent both with observed trendiness of dividends for a century and with the high volatility of stock prices. They can certainly tell a story which is within the realm of possibility, but it is hard to see how they could come up with the inspiring evidence for the model. [1983, p. 237]

We believe that the theoretical and empirical analysis presented here provides such "inspiring evidence."

In general, the statistical properties of estimators drawn from a nonstationary population are an important matter in evaluating the significance of variance bound inequality violations.[26] As it happens, our reconciliation of the gross empirical violations of Shiller's variance bound inequalities is not based on sampling arguments. That is, we do not merely show that it is *possible* to have a chance run of history where the measured volatility of dividends is greatly exceeded by the measured volatility of rational stock prices. Instead, our "reversals" of variance bound inequalities (4) and (15) are based on expected values over the population. Thus, over repeated runs of history, we expect that, on average, these inequalities would be violated.

If our results seem counterintuitive to some, then perhaps this indicates that such intuitions about volatility relations between optimal forecasts and realizations are implicitly based on the assumption of stationary and linear processes. If so, we hope that this analysis serves to illustrate the potential for cognitive misperceptions from applying such intuitions to nonstationary systems.

Economists have long known that fluctuations in stock prices are considerably larger than the fluctuations in aggregate consumption, national income, the money supply, and many other similar variables whose expected future values presumably play a part in the rational determination of stock prices. Indeed, as noted in the introduction, we suspect that the sympathetic view held by some economists toward the proposition of excess stock market volatility can largely be traced to this long-established observation. Those who make this inference implicitly assume that the level of variability observed in these economic variables provides the appropriate

---

[26] Kenneth West (1984) and N. Gregory Mankiw et al. (1985) derive variance bound inequalities which appear to apply to nonstationary processes for prices and dividends. Using the Shiller data, Mankiw et al. find their inequalities are grossly violated. By studying the statistical properties of their estimates, Merton (1986) shows that the Mankiw et al. tests cannot be reliably applied when stock prices follow diffusion processes such as the geometric Brownian motion.

frame of reference from which to judge the rationality of observed stock price volatility. Although quantitatively more precise, the Shiller analysis adopts this same perspective when it asks: "If stock prices are rational, then why are they so volatile (relative to dividends)?" The apparent answer is that stock prices are not rational.

Our analysis turns this perspective "on its head" by asking: "If stock prices are rational, then why do dividends exhibit so little volatility (relative to stock prices)?" Our answer is simply that managers choose dividend policies so as to smooth the effect of changes in intrinsic values (and hence, rational stock prices) on the change in dividends. The a priori economic arguments and empirical support presented for this conclusion surely need no repeating. We would note, however, that this explanation is likely to also apply to the time-series of other economic flow variables. There are, for example, good economic reasons for believing that aggregate accounting earnings, investment, and consumption have in common with dividends that their changes are smoothed either by the behavior of the economic agents that control them or by the statistical methods which are used to measure them. An initial examination of the data appears to support this belief. If a thorough empirical evaluation confirms this finding, then our analysis casts doubt in general over the use of volatility comparisons between stock prices and economic variables which are not also speculative prices, as a methodology to test stock market rationality.

In summary of our view of the current state of the debate over the efficient market theory, Samuelson said it well when he addressed the practicing investment managers of the financial community over a decade ago:

> Indeed, to reveal my bias, the ball is in the court of the practical men: it is the turn of the Mountain to take a first step toward the theoretical Mohammed....
>
> ...If you oversimplify the debate, it can be put in the form of the question, Resolved, that the best of money managers cannot be demonstrated to be able to deliver the goods of superior portfolio-selection performance.
> Any jury that reviews the evidence, and there is a great deal of relevant evidence, must at least come out with the Scottish verdict:
> Superior Investment performance is unproved. [1974, pp. 18–19]

Just so, our evidence does not prove that the market is efficient, but it does at least warrant the Scottish verdict:

Excess stock price volatility is unproved. The ball is once again in the court of those who doubt the Efficient Market Hypothesis.

APPENDIX

PROOF of Theorem 1:

Define Π as the $T \times K$ matrix of elements π_{tk} in Theorem 1, so that $p^* = \Pi p$. We show that the following three conditions

(A1) $\quad \pi_{tk} > 0$

(A2) $\quad \sum_{k=1}^{T} \pi_{tk} = 1 \quad$ for all $\quad t = 1, \ldots, T$

(A3) $\quad \sum_{t=1}^{T} \pi_{tk} \leq 1 \quad$ for all $\quad k = 1, \ldots, T$

are sufficient for

(A4) $\quad \text{Var}(\Pi p) \leq \text{Var}(p),$

where $\text{Var}(x)$ is defined as the *sample* variance operator applied to the elements of x.

LEMMA: *Any given p can be decomposed as $\bar{p}\iota + \tilde{p}$ where $\bar{p}$ is the sample mean, ι is a vector of ones, and $\tilde{p}$ is the vector of deviations of the elements of p about $\bar{p}$. Then,*

(A5) $\quad \tilde{p}'\Pi'\left(I - \frac{1}{T}\iota\iota'\right)\Pi\tilde{p} \leq \tilde{p}'\tilde{p}$

implies

$$(A6) \quad \text{Var}(\Pi p) = \left[\frac{p'\Pi'\left(I - \frac{1}{T}\iota\iota'\right)\Pi p}{T}\right]$$

$$\leq \left[\frac{p'\left(I - \frac{1}{T}\iota\iota'\right)p}{T}\right] = \text{Var}(p)$$

under condition (A2) where $\text{Var}(\Pi p)$ is computed with respect to the T elements of Πp, and $\text{Var}(p)$ is defined with respect to the T elements of p. If the matrix Π is rectangular of dimension $T \times X$, then the additional constraint $\sum_{t=1}^{T} \pi_{tk} \leq T/K$ is sufficient for equation (A6).

PROOF:
Substitute the decomposition $p = \bar{p}\iota + \tilde{p}$ into (A5) and realize that $(I - 1/T\iota\iota')\bar{p}\iota = 0$ and $(I - 1/T\iota\iota')\Pi\bar{p}\iota = 0$.

To prove Theorem 1, define the norm:

$$(A7) \quad \|\Pi\tilde{p}\|^2 = \sum_t \left(\sum_k \pi_{tk}\tilde{p}_k\right)^2.$$

Since the function $f(u) = u^2$ is convex, it follows that if $p_{tk} > 0$ and $\sum_k \pi_{tk} = 1$, then,

$$(A8) \quad \left(\sum_k \pi_{tk}\tilde{p}_k\right)^2 \leq \sum_k \pi_{tk}\tilde{p}_k^2,$$

so

$$(A9) \quad \|\Pi\tilde{p}\|^2 \leq \sum_t \sum_k \pi_{tk}\tilde{p}_k^2$$

$$= \sum_k \tilde{p}_k^2 \sum_t \pi_{tk} \leq \sum_k \tilde{p}_k^2.$$

(The last inequality in (A10) is strict if $\sum_t \pi_{tk} < 1$). Equation (A9) can be rewritten as

$$(A10) \quad \|\Pi\tilde{p}\| \leq \|\tilde{p}\|.$$

Also,

$$(A11) \quad \tilde{p}'\Pi'\left(I - \frac{1}{T}\iota\iota'\right)\Pi\tilde{p} \leq \|\Pi\tilde{p}\|.$$

(A10) and (A11) together imply (A5) which,

by the Lemma, implies (A6), that is,

$$(A12) \quad \text{Var}(\Pi p) \leq \text{Var}(p).$$

PROOF of Theorem 2:
Using the definition of the (detrended) *ex post* rational price, $p^*(t)$, given in (5), and allowing (detrended) dividends to be a general distributed lag of (detrended) prices as in (13), *ex post* rational prices can be expressed in terms of the observed and pre-sample (detrended) prices as

$$(A13) \quad \begin{bmatrix} p^*(T-1) p^*(T-2) \\ p(T-3) \\ \vdots \\ p^*(1) \end{bmatrix}$$

$$= \left\{ \frac{1}{T} \begin{bmatrix} \eta \ldots \eta & 0 \ldots 0 \\ \eta^2 \ldots \eta^2 & 0 \ldots 0 \\ \eta^3 \ldots \eta^3 & 0 \ldots 0 \\ \vdots & \vdots \\ \eta^T \ldots \eta^T & 0 \ldots 0 \end{bmatrix} \right.$$

$$+ \rho \begin{bmatrix} \eta & 0 & 0 \ldots 0 \\ \eta^2 & \eta & 0 \ldots 0 \\ \eta^3 & \eta^2 & \eta \ldots 0 \\ \vdots & \vdots & \vdots \\ \eta^T & \eta^{T-1} & \eta^{T-2} \ldots 0 \end{bmatrix}$$

$$\times \begin{bmatrix} \theta_0 & \theta_1 \ldots \theta_N & 0 \ldots 0 & 0 \ldots 0 \\ 0 & \theta_0 \ldots \theta_{N-1} & \theta_N & 0 & 0 \ldots 0 \\ \vdots & \vdots & & \theta_N & 0 & 0 \\ \vdots & \vdots & & \vdots & \vdots & \vdots \\ 0 & 0 & \theta_0\theta_1 & 0 \ldots 0 \\ 0 & 0 \ldots 0 & 0 \ldots \theta_0 & \theta_1 \ldots \theta_N \end{bmatrix} \right\}$$

$$\times \begin{bmatrix} p(T-1) \\ p(T-2) \\ \vdots \\ p(1) \\ p(-1) \\ \vdots \\ p(-N) \end{bmatrix}$$

where $\eta \equiv (1+g)/(1+r) \equiv 1/(1+r\delta) \equiv 1/(1+\rho)$ (the first identity follows from the definition of η in (1), the second from fn. 15, and the third from the definition of ρ in (15)) and the level of dividends is a distributed lag of the level of past prices, as in (13), that is, $d(t) = \rho \sum_{k=0}^{N} \theta_k p(t-k)$.

Equation (A13) may be conveniently rewritten as

(A14) $\quad p^* = [A_1 + A_2 \Theta] p$

where A_1 is the first matrix on the right-hand side of (A13), that is, the matrix that involves multiplication by the scalar $1/T$), A_2 is the next matrix, that involves multiplication by the scalar ρ, and Θ is the matrix that contains the elements $\theta_1, \theta_2, \ldots, \theta_N$. The weights in the matrix A_1 reflect the contribution $1/T$ of each of the observed prices $[p(T-1), \ldots p(0)]$ to $p^*(T)$ in accordance with (3), together with the weight $[1/(1+\rho)]^{T-t}$ attached to $p^*(T)$ in the determination of $p^*(t)$ in (5). The matrix A_2 contains the discount weights that (5) places on dividends as components of each $p^*(t)$, while Θ contains the distributed lag weights of dividends on past prices, as given in (13). Using these definitions of A_1, A_2, and Θ, (A14) is equivalent to

(A15) $\quad p^* = Wp$,

where $W = [w_{tk}]$, the w_{tk} being those defined in (14).

It may be verified that the component A_1 of the transformation matrix W is irrelevant to the application of Theorem 1 (because the proof proceeds in terms of $\tilde{p}$, the deviations of the elements of p about $\bar{p}$). The elements of $A_2 \Theta$ are positive and sum to unity or less across the rows, and if $\Theta = I$, or Θ is such that column elements of $A_2 \Theta$ sum to less that $T/(T+N)$ if $\Theta \neq I$, then the conditions of Theorem 1 are satisfied, and we have

(A16) $\quad \text{Var}(p^*) \leq \text{Var}(p)$.

In the market rationality tests, the variance of the *ex post* rational prices is compared not to the variance of the $(T+N)$ vector of T observed *and* N presample prices, but to the variance of only the T observed prices. Partitioning of the $(T+N)$ prices into in-sample and out-of-sample prices, it is straightforward to show that

(A17) $\quad \text{Var}(p^*)/\text{Var}(p_T) \leq 1$

$$+ \frac{T \cdot N}{(N+T)^2} \frac{(\bar{p}_T - \bar{p}_N)^2}{\text{Var}(p_T)}$$

$$- \frac{N}{(N+T)} \left[\frac{\text{Var}(p_T) - \text{Var}(p_N)}{\text{Var}(p_T)} \right],$$

where $\bar{p}_T = \sum_{t=0}^{T-1} p(t)/T$;

$$\bar{p}_N = \sum_{t=-N}^{-1} p(t)/N;$$

$$\text{Var}(p_T) = \sum_{t=0}^{T-1} [p(t) - \bar{p}_T]^2/T;$$

$$\text{Var}(p_N) = \sum_{t=-N}^{-1} [p(t) - \bar{p}_N]^2/N.$$

The sum of the last two terms on the right-hand side of (A17) can be positive for some sample paths. However, if N is finite, and the nonstationary process for prices is not degenerate, then it is clear that the start-up adjustment terms in (A17) converge in mean square to zero as $T \to \infty$.

REFERENCES

Bosworth, Barry, "The Stock Market and the Economy," *Brookings Papers on Economic Activity*, 2:1975, 257–300.

Copeland, Basil L., Jr., "Do Stock Prices Move Too Much to be Justified by Subsequent Changes in Dividends?: Comment," *American Economic Review*, March 1983, 73, 234–35.

Fama, Eugene F., "Risk-Adjusted Discount Rates and Capital Budgeting under Uncertainty," *Journal of Financial Economics*, August 1977, 5, 3–24.

Fischer, Stanley and Merton, Robert C., "Macroeconomics and Finance: The Role of the Stock Market," *Carnegie-Rochester Conference Series on Public Policy*, Vol. 21, *Essays on Macroeconomic Implications of Financial and Labor Markets and Political Processes*, Autumn 1984, 57–108.

Flavin, Marjorie A., "Excess Volatility in the Financial Markets: A Reassessment of the Empirical Evidence," *Journal of Political Economy*, December 1983, *91*, 929–56.

Foster, George, *Financial Statement Analysis*, Englewood Cliffs: Prentice-Hall, 1978.

Keynes, John Maynard, *The General Theory of Employment Interest and Money*, New York: Harcourt, Brace, 1936.

Kleidon, Allan W., (1983a) "Variance Bounds Tests and Stock Price Valuation Models," unpublished working paper, Graduate School of Business, Stanford University, January 1983.

_____, (1983b) "Bias in Small Sample Tests of Stock Price Rationality," unpublished paper, University of Chicago, 1983.

Leamer, Edward E., "Let's Take the Con Out of Econometrics," *American Economic Review*, March 1983, *73*, 31–43.

LeRoy, Stephen F. and Porter, Richard D., "The Present-Value Relation: Tests Based on Implied Variance Bounds," *Econometrica*, May 1981, *49*, 555–74.

Lintner, John, "Distribution of Incomes of Corporations Among Dividends, Retained Earnings, and Taxes," *American Economic Review Proceedings*, May 1956, *66*, 97–113.

Mankiw, N. Gregory, Romer, David and Shapiro, Matthew D., "An Unbiased Reexamination of Stock Market Volatility, *Journal of Finance*, July 1985, *40*, 677–78.

Marsh, Terry A. and Merton, Robert C., "Aggregate Dividend Behavior and Its implications for Tests of Stock Market Rationality," Working Paper 1475-83, Sloan School of Management, September 1983.

_____ and _____, "Earnings Variability and Variance Bounds Tests for the Rationality of Stock Market Prices," Working Paper 1559-84, Sloan School of Management, March 1984.

_____ and _____, "Dividend Behavior for the Aggregate Stock Market," *Journal of Business*, forthcoming.

Merton, Robert C., "On the Current State of the Stock Market Rationality Hypothesis," in Stanley Fischer et al., eds., *Macroeconomics and Finance: Essays in Honor of Franco Modigliani*, Cambridge: MIT Press, 1986.

Miller, Merton H. and Modigliani, Franco, "Dividend Policy, Growth and the Valuation of Shares," *Journal of Business*, October 1961, *34*, 411–33.

Myers, Stewart C. and Turnbull, Stuart M., "Capital Budgeting and the Capital Asset Pricing Model: Good News and Bad News," *Journal of Finance*, May 1977, *32*, 321–33.

Samuelson, Paul A., "Proof That Properly Anticipated Prices Fluctuate Randomly," *Industrial Management Review*, Spring 1965, *6*, 41–49.

_____, "Challenge to Judgment," *Journal of Portfolio Management*, Fall 1974, *1*, 17–19.

_____, "Optimality of Sluggish Predictors Under Ergodic Probabilities, *International Economic Review*, February 1976, *17*, 1–7.

Shiller, Robert J., (1981a) "Do Stock Prices Move Too Much to be Justified by Subsequent Changes in Dividends?," *American Economic Review*, June 1981, *71*, 421–36.

_____, (1981b) "The Use of Volatility Measures in Assessing Market Efficiency," *Journal of Finance*, May 1981, *36*, 291–311.

_____, "Consumption, Asset Markets, and Macroeconomic Fluctuations," *Carnegie-Rochester Conference Series on Public Policy*, Vol. 17, *Essays on Economic Policy in a World of Change*, 1982, 203–38.

_____, "Do Stock Prices Move Too Much to be Justified by Subsequent Changes in dividends?: Reply," *American Economic Review*, March 1983, *73*, 236–37.

Tobin, James, "On the Efficiency of the Financial System," Hirsch Memorial Lecture, New York, May 15, 1984.

West, Kenneth D., "Speculative Bubbles and Stock Price Volatility," Financial Research Center, Memo. No. 54, Princeton University, December 1984.

[8]

On the Current State of
the Stock Market
Rationality Hypothesis

Robert C. Merton

1 Introduction

The foundation for valuation in modern financial economics is the rational market hypothesis. It implies that the market price of a security is equal to the expectation of the present value of the future cash flows available for distribution to that security where the quality of the information embedded in that expectation is high relative to the information available to the individual participants in the market. As has been discussed at length elsewhere,[1] the question whether this hypothesis is a good approximation to the behavior of real-world financial markets has major substantive implications for both financial and general economic theory and practice.

The rational market hypothesis provides a flexible framework for valuation. It can, for example, accommodate models where discount rates are stochastic over time and statistically dependent on future cash flows. It can also accommodate nonhomogeneity in information and transactions costs among individual market participants. The theory is not, however, a tautology. It is not consistent with models or empirical facts that imply that either stock prices depend in an important way on factors other than the fundamentals underlying future cash flows and discount rates, or that the quality of information reflected in stock prices is sufficiently poor that investors can systematically identify significant differences between stock price and fundamental value.

Although the subject of much controversy at its inception more than two decades ago, the rational market hypothesis now permeates virtually every part of finance theory. It has even become widely accepted as the "rule" (to which one must prove the exception) for finance practice on Wall Street, LaSalle Street, and in courtrooms and corporate headquarters. However, recent developments in economic theory and empirical work have again cast doubts on the validity of the hypothesis. Representing one view, Summers (1985) sees much of the renewed controversy as little more than a case of financial economists and general economists engaging in a partisan diversion of intellectual effort over methodological questions instead of focusing on sound research on major substantive questions.[2] He sees this development as only hastening an apparent secular trend toward inefficient disjunction between the fields of finance and economics on subjects of conjoint research interest. Perhaps that is so. But I must confess to having quite the opposite view on these same research efforts with regard to both their substance and their presumed dysfunctional effects on the fields of finance and economics. However, to pursue this issue further would only be an exercise in self-refutation. Thus, it suffices to say that whether market rationality is viewed as a "hot topic" or as merely a "topic with too much heat," an analysis of the current state of research on this issue would appear timely—especially so on this occasion honoring Franco Modigliani, past president of both the American Economic Association and the American Finance Association and prime counterexample to the Summers doctrine.

This paper focuses on the central economic question underlying the issue of stock market rationality: Do real-world capital markets and financial intermediaries, as a practical matter, provide a good approximation to those ideal-world counterparts that are necessary for efficient investor risk bearing and efficient allocation of physical investment? Although satisfaction of the rational market hypothesis is surely not sufficient to ensure efficient allocations, its broad-based rejection is almost certainly sufficient to rule out efficient allocations.[3]

From this perspective on the issue, it matters little whether or not real-world dealers and deal makers can "scalp" investors and issuers as long as their profits are a small fraction of aggregate transactions in important and well-established markets. Similarly, it matters little for this issue whether, as suggested by Van Horne (1985), promoters often make large-percentage profits during the transient period of time between the inception of a new financial product (or market) and the widespread acceptance (or rejection) of the product by investors and issuers.

In evaluating market rationality as it bears on economic efficiency, it matters very much whether stock prices generally can be shown to depend in an important way on factors other than fundamentals. It also matters very much whether it can be shown that either academic economists or practitioners systematically provide better forecasts of fundamental values than stock prices do. Thus, this analysis focuses on empirical work on aggregate stock price behavior, and especially the new volatility test methodologies, which appear to provide evidence of this very sort.

Although these empirical findings have had the most immediate effect in reviving the controversy over stock market rationality, some of the emerging developments in theory may prove, in the longer run, to be more important in resolving the controversy. Before proceeding with the analysis of empirical work, therefore, I pause briefly to comment on two of the more promising candidates to supersede the rational market theory.

Grounded in the sociological behavioral theory of the self-fulfilling prophecy, the theory of rational expectations speculative bubbles[4] in effect provides a theoretical foundation for answering the "If you are so smart, why aren't you rich?" question underlying the rational market argument that fullyrecognized, sizable, and persistent deviations between market price and fundamental value must necessarily provide "excess profit" opportunities for either investors or issuers. As we know, however, from the work of Tirole (1982), the interesting conditions under which such rational bubble equilibria can exist are still to be determined. In particular, if the theory is to be applied to the aggregate stock market in realistic fashion, then it must accommodate both "positive" and "negative" bubbles in a rational expectations framework. Such application would seem to require a satisfactory process to explain both the limits on share repurchase by firms when prices are persistently below marginal production cost and the limits on the creation of new firms with "instant profits" for the promoters in periods when general stock market prices significantly exceed that marginal cost.

Although few economists would posit irrational behavior as the foundation of their models, many, of course, do not subscribe to the sort of "super-rational" behavior implied by the rational expectations theory (with or without bubbles). Based on the pioneering work of Kahneman and Tversky (1979, 1982), the theory of cognitive misperceptions (by which I mean the observed set of systematic "errors" in individual decision making under uncertainty) may become a base from which economic theory formally incorporates nonrational (or as some economists have described it, "quasi-rational") behavior.

As discussed in Arrow (1982), the empirical findings of such systematic misperceptions in repeated laboratory experiments appear sound, and there would also appear to be many test cases within economics. In terms of the current state of empirical evidence in both cognitive psychology and financial economics, it would seem somewhat premature, however, to conclude that cognitive misperceptions are an important determinant of aggregate stock market behavior. Specifically, the same sharp empirical findings of cognitive misperceptions have not (at least to my knowledge) been shown to apply to individual decision making *when the individual is permitted to interact with others (as a group) in analyzing an important decision and when the group is repeatedly called upon to make similar types of important decisions.* But, this is, of course, exactly the environment in which professional investors make their stock market decisions.

If professional investors are not materially affected by these cognitive misperceptions, then it would seem that either competition among professional investors would lead to stock prices that do not reflect the cognitive errors of other types of investors, or professional investors should earn substantial excess returns by exploiting the deviations in price from fundamental value. Unlike the theory of rational expectations bubbles with its self-fulfilling prophecy, there is no a priori reason in this theory to believe that investment strategies designed to exploit significant deviations of price from fundamental value will not be successful. However, as shown in the following section, rather robust evidence indicates that professional investors do not earn substantial excess returns.

These two theories, along with Shiller's (1984) theory of fads, explicitly incorporate in an important way positive theories of behavior derived from other social sciences. In doing so, they depart significantly from the "traditional" approach of mainstream *modern* economic theory: namely, to derive the positive theories of "how we do behave" almost exclusively from normative economic theories of "how we should behave." Whether these theories throw light on the specific issue of aggregate stock market rationality, it will surely be interesting to follow the impact on economic theory generally from these attempts to bring economics "back into line" with the rest of the social sciences.

2 Empirical Studies of Stock Market Rationality

In his seminal 1965 paper proving the martingale property of rationally determined speculative price changes, Paul Samuelson was careful to warn readers against interpreting conclusions drawn from his model about markets as empirical statements: "You never get something for nothing. From a nonempirical base of axioms, you never get empirical results. Deductive analysis cannot determine whether the empirical properties of the stochastic model I posit come close to resembling the empirical determinants of today's real-world markets" (p. 42). One can hardly disagree that the question whether stock market rationality remains a part of economic theory should be decided empirically. There is, however, a complication: we have no statute of limitations for rejecting a theory. To the extent that one assumes the advancement of knowledge, it is the fate of all theory to be encompassed, superseded, or outright rejected in the long run. Nevertheless, at any moment, one must choose: either to continue to use the theory or to discard it. It is with this choice in mind that I examine the empirical evidence to date on stock market rationality.

As economists have cause to know well, the "long run" in economic behavior can indeed be long. Having already sustained itself for at least twenty years,[5] the rational market theory exemplifies this same fact—here in the history of economic science instead of in the history of economic behavior. The longevity of the theory can surely not be attributed to neglect on the part of economists bent on putting it to empirical test. I have not made any formal comparisons, but I suspect that over these twenty years, few, if any, maintained hypotheses in economic theory have received as much empirical attention as the rational market hypothesis. Indeed, there have probably been *too many* such tests. Although it is likely that this claim could be supported on the grounds of optimal resource allocation alone, the case is made here solely on statistical grounds. In preparation for this and other matters that bear on the testing of market rationality, I briefly review the history of these tests.

2.1 Early Tests of Stock Market Returns

About the time that Samuelson's fundamental paper appeared in print, what has since become the Chicago Center for Research in Security Pricing completed the construction of a file of prices and related data on all New York Stock Exchange-listed stocks from 1926 to 1965. This file has been periodically updated and expanded to include other exchanges so that there are now available almost sixty years of monthly data and more than twenty years of daily data on thousands of stocks. In addition, Robert Shiller of Yale has created a return file for the aggregate stock market with data going back to 1872.

There had been some earlier empirical studies of the randomness of speculative price changes, but the availability of a large-scale, easily accessible data base caused a flurry of such studies beginning in the mid-1960s. From simple runs and serial correlation tests to sophisticated filtering and spectral analysis, the results were virtually uniform in finding no significant serial dependencies in stock returns. The few cases of significant serial correlation were small in magnitude and short-lived (disappearing over a matter of a few days), and they could largely be explained by specialist activities for individual stocks or "non-contemporaneous trading effects" for portfolios of stocks. These findings were, of course, consistent with the Samuelson martingale property as a necessary condition for rationally determined prices.

Financial researchers at this time were aware of the possibility that a significant part of this randomness could be from random "animal spirits," which would cause prices to deviate from fundamental values. There was, however, a widespread belief that the empirical evidence did not support this alternative to market rationality. The foundation for this belief was the assumption that even with animal spirits, in the long run, stock prices will converge in the statistical equilibrium sense to their fundamental values. From this assumption, it follows that deviations from fundamental values will, by necessity, induce serial dependences in stock returns.[6] If such deviations were significant, then these dependences should be detectable as, for example, systematic patterns in the long-wave frequencies of the spectral analysis of stock returns. Moreover, there had been empirical studies of "relative strength" portfolio strategies that should do well if the market "underreacts" to information and of "relative weakness" (contrary opinion) portfolio strategies that should do well if the market tends to "overreact" to information. Neither of these produced significant results.[7] Working along similar lines were the studies of stocks that appear on the most active trading list or that had moved up or down by unusually large amounts, designed to look for evidence of under- or overreaction. Once again, no significant findings. Thus, it appeared at the time that the empirical evidence not only gave support to Samuelson's necessary condition for rationally determined prices, but also failed to lend support to the alternative hypothesis of random animal spirits.

As we know today from the work of Summers (1986) and others, many of these studies provided rather weak tests for detecting the types of generalized serial correlations that random animal spirits might generate, especially when the speed of reversion to fundamental values is slow. However, the concern in the 1960s was over another issue surrounding the power of these tests: the selective bias inherent in "secret models."

2.2 Tests of Professional Investor Performance

As the cynical version of the story goes, one could not lose by testing market rationality. If, indeed, significant empirical violations were found, one could earn gold, if not glory, by keeping this discovery private and developing portfolio strategies to be sold to professional money managers who would take advantage of these violations. If, instead, one found no significant violations, then this (financial) "failure" could be turned into academic success by publishing the results in the scientific journals. Thus, while each study performed might represent an unbiased test, the collection of such studies *published* were likely to be biased in favor of not rejecting market rationality. Unlike the more generally applicable claim for "quality" bias that studies that are consistent with the accepted theory are subject to less scrutiny by reviewers than ones that purport to reject it, the potential for material effects from "profit-induced" biases is probably specialized within economic analyses to studies of speculative prices.

One need not, however, accept this cynical characterization of academic financial researchers to arrive at much the same conclusion. The portfolio strategies tested by academics were usually simple and always mechanical; therefore, the fact that they yielded no evidence of significant profit opportunities is perhaps no great surprise. However, real-world professional investors with significant resources might well have important information sources and sophisticated models (be they of fundamentals or market psychology) that are used to beat the market systematically. As this version of the story goes, *if only* the academics could gain access to these proprietary models, they would quickly be able to reject the rational market hypothesis. Unfortunately, one assumes that few successful professional investors are likely to reveal their hypothetically profitable models, and thereby risk losing their source of income, simply to refute publicly the rationally determined price hypothesis of economists (which by hypothesis they have, of course, already determined privately to be false). Thus, it would seem that the possibility of proprietary models would, at least, significantly weaken, and in all likelihood, bias, the academic tests of market rationality.

Concern over the "secret model" problem led to the next wave of empirical tests for which the pioneering study of the mutual fund industry by Jensen (1968) serves as a prototype. The basic assumptions underlying these tests hold that if such models exist, then professional investors have them, and if they have them, then the results should show themselves in superior performance (at least, before expenses charged to investors) of the funds they managed. Tracking the performance of 115 investment companies over the period 1945-1964, Jensen found no significant evidence of superior performance for the fund industry as a whole. Later work by Jensen and others also found no evidence that individual investment companies within the industry had superior performance. That is, it was found that for any fund which had outperformed the naive market strategy of investing in the past, the odds of the same fund doing so in the future were essentially fifty-fifty. Similar studies subsequently made of the performance of other professional investor groups (e.g., insurance company equity funds, bank trust departments) came to much the same results. Moreover, as I have indicated in my preliminary remarks, these findings have remained robust to date.[8]

To be sure, the variances of the returns on these managed portfolios are sufficiently large that although the point estimates of the excess returns in these studies support the null hypothesis of no superior performance, they cannot reject the alternative null hypothesis that the managers do provide sufficient performance to earn the 25–100 basis points they charge. This fact may be important to the economics of the money management industry, but is inconsequential for the broader question of market rationality as a good approximation to the real-world stock market. That is, the undiscovered existence of proprietary models is not likely to provide an important explanation for the rational market hypothesis having remained unrejected for so long a time.

2.3 Anomalous Evidence on Stock Market Rationality

During the period of the 1960s and early 1970s, the overwhelming majority of empirical findings continued to support the market rationality theory (cf. Fama, 1970). Indeed, editors of both finance and broader economic journals, quite understandably, became increasingly reluctant to allot scarce journal space to yet another test that did not reject market rationality. Despite the mountain of accumulated evidence in support of the hypothesis, there were a relatively few of the empirical studies conducted during this period that did not seem to fit the rational market model. For example, low-price-to-earnings-ratio stocks seem systematically to earn higher average returns (even after correcting for risk differences) than high-price-to-earnings-ratio stocks. This "PE effect," later renamed the "small stock effect" after it was shown to be more closely associated with firm size than PE ratios, still remains a puzzle. Some other anomalies were the finding of various seasonal regularities such as the "January effect" and "the-day-of-the-week effect," and still another is the behavior of stock returns after a stock split. As the number of such puzzles gradually accumulated, the apparently closed gate on the empirical issue of market rationality began to reopen. Indeed, by 1978, even the *Journal of Financial Economics* (with its well-known editorial view in support of market rationality) devoted the entire June–September issue to a symposium on anomalous evidence bearing on market efficiency.

During this period, there were a number of empirical findings in the general economics literature that also cast doubt on the hypothesis of market rationality. Time series calculations of Tobin's Q appeared to suggest that stock market prices were too high at times while much too low at others, to be explained by economic fundamentals alone. Modigliani and Cohn (1979) presented a theory and empirical evidence that stock prices were irrationally low during the 1970s because investors failed to take correct account of the radically increased levels of the inflation rate in assessing expected future corporate profits and the rate at which they should be discounted.

Collectively these findings raised questions about the validity of stock market rationality, but they were hardly definitive. Some were found to be significant in one time period, but not in another. Others, such as Long's (1978) study on the market valuation of cash dividends, focused on a small sample of obscure securities. Virtually all shared the common element of testing a joint hypothesis with other important and unproven assumptions in addition to stock market rationality. There is, for example, the common joint hypothesis of stock market rationality *and* prices that are formed according to (one or another tax version of) the Capital Asset Pricing Model. Thus, at most, these tests rejected a hypothesis including stock market rationality but also other assumptions that, on a priori grounds, could reasonably be argued as less likely to obtain than market rationality.

During the past five years, a series of tests based upon the volatility of stock prices has produced seemingly new evidence of market non-rationality that some consider relatively immune to these criticisms of the earlier apparent rejections. One group of these tests pioneered by LeRoy and Porter (1981) and Shiller (1981) has focused on the volatility of aggregate stock market price relative to either aggregate earnings or dividends over long time periods (in the case of the former for the postwar period, and in the latter since before the turn of the century). Their findings have been interpreted as confirming the long-felt-but-unproved belief among some economists that stock prices are far more volatile than could ever be justified on fundamental evaluations alone.

A second group of tests examines the short-run volatility of stock price changes from one trading day to the next. It was known in the 1960s that the measured variance rate on stock returns is significantly lower over short time periods including weekends and holidays when the market is closed than over the same-length time periods when the market is open every day. The "rational" explanation given for this "seasonal" observation on volatility held that with businesses and many government activities closed, less new information is produced on these nontrading days than on trading days when they are open. However, using a period in the 1960s when the stock market was closed on every Wednesday, French and Roll (1984) show that the previously identified lower stock return volatility over short time periods that include a nontrading day applied to the Wednesday closings as well. Because nonspeculative market activities were generally open on these Wednesdays, the earlier presumed explanation was thus plainly inadequate. It would appear that market trading itself seems to cause increased volatility in market prices, and some interpret this finding as evidence against market prices being based on fundamentals alone.[9]

2.4 Ex Ante and Ex Post Predictions of the Theory

Explaining why rationally determined speculative price changes would exhibit the martingale property even though the underlying economic variables upon which these prices are formed may have considerable serial dependences, Samuelson (1965, p. 44) writes, "We would expect people in the market place, in pursuit of avid and intelligent self-interest, to take account of those elements of future events that in a probability sense may be discerned to be casting their shadows before them." The empirical evidence to date has been remarkably robust in finding no important cases of either lagged variables explaining stock price returns or of real-world investors (who make their decisions without benefit of even a peek into the future) being able to beat the market. This impressive success in confirming the *ex ante* component of the theory's prophecy has not, however, been matched in confirming its *ex post* component: namely, one should be able to find current or future economic events related to the fundamentals that, on average, explain current and past changes in stock prices.

As has been discussed elsewhere (cf. Fama, 1981; Fischer and Merton, 1984; Marsh and Merton, 1983, 1985), the change in aggregate stock prices is an important leading indicator of macro economic activity. Indeed, it is the best single predictor of future changes in business fixed investment, earnings, and dividends. Moreover, the forecast errors in the realization of future earnings changes are significantly correlated with the then-contemporaneous changes in stock prices. Nevertheless, although the writers for the popular financial press try hard, they often cannot identify the specific economic events that are important enough to cause the aggregate value of the stock market to change by as much as 2% in a single day.

At the micro level, the accounting and finance literatures are populated with studies of the behavior of individual stock prices, on, before, and after, the date of some potentially important event such as an earnings or tender offer announcement. These "event" studies lend some support to the *ex post* component of market rationality by showing that stock price changes predict many such events, respond quickly and in an unbiased fashion to surprises, and do not respond to seemingly important events that, in fact, should be affect the fundamentals (e.g., "cosmetic" changes in accounting earnings that have no impact on current or future cash flows). However, some of these studies (cf. Ohlson and Penman, 1985, who find that stock price return volatility appears to increase significantly after a stock split) provide conflicting evidence that indicates that stock prices may be affected by factors other than fundamentals.

Just as the strong empirical support for the *ex ante* component of market rationality has moved the focus of theoretical research from models of differential information to models of rational expectations bubbles, animal spirits, and fads, so the relative lack of closure on the *ex post* component seems to be the driving force behind the methodological focus of current empirical tests of the hypothesis. Finance specialists seem to favor short-term volatility or event studies, while general economists favor long-term studies, but both appear to agree that the statistical properties of volatility tests make them the most promising approach for rejecting the hypothesis of aggregate stock market rationality. The bulk of the formal analysis in this paper is focused on the long-term volatility tests, leaving for another occasion the examination of the event-study approach. Before undertaking that task, I digress to comment on a few, perhaps prosaic, but nevertheless important issues that frame the testing of this hypothesis.

2.5 Some Methodological Problems in Testing the Theory

As we all know, what the stock market actually did from 1872 to 1985 is an enumerable fact. As such, those numbers do not change even as the number of tests of the rational market hypothesis on these same data continues to grow. As we also know, the standard test statistics used in these studies do not reflect that fact. While, of course, the same comment could be made about virtually every area of economic model testing (cf. Leamer, 1983), it perhaps warrants more than usual attention in this case because of the unusually large number of studies, the large number of observations in the data set, and the magnitudes of unexplained volatility in stock prices.

As a case study of the problem, let us consider the regression study of the hypothesis that the expected real rate of return on the market is a constant, which is discussed in the Summers (1985) article. He writes, "Simple regression of real ex post stock returns on lagged dividend yields find that the null hypothesis that the real ex ante rate is constant can be rejected at almost any confidence level" (p. 635). Although hardly a proponent of this null hypothesis in either theory or practice (cf. Merton, 1973, 1980), I would nevertheless argue that in making his statement for apparently clear rejection, Summers does not take account of the number of regressions, *collectively*, researchers have run of stock returns on various contemporaneous and lagged variables. That some adjustment for this fact could have material implications for the strength of his conclusion is readily apparent from the negligible R^2 or explanatory power of these lagged yields. While one could perhaps argue on a priori grounds that dividend yield is a reasonable surrogate variable for expected return, I can report that much the same statistical significance results obtain (on the same data set, of course) if one regresses returns on the reciprocal of current stock price alone, omitting the dividend series altogether.[10]

If knowledge is to advance, we must seek out the exceptions, the puzzles, the unexplained residuals and attempt to explain them. But, before problem solution must come problem identification. Thus, economists place a premium on the discovery of puzzles, which in the context at hand amounts to finding apparent rejections of a widely accepted theory of stock market behavior. All of this fits well with what the cognitive psychologists tell us is our natural individual predilection to focus, often disproportionately so, on the unusual. As I have hinted earlier, this emphasis on the unusual has been institutionalized by responsible and knowledgeable journal editors who understandably look more favorably upon empirical studies that find anomalous evidence with respect to a widely accepted theory than upon studies that merely serve to confirm that theory yet again. This focus, both individually and institutionally, together with little control over the number of tests performed, creates a fertile environment for both unintended selection bias and for attaching greater significance to otherwise unbiased estimates than is justified.

To clarify the point, consider this parable on the testing of coin-flipping abilities. Some three thousand students have taken my finance courses over the years, and suppose that each had been asked to keep flipping a coin until tails comes up. At the end of the experiment, the winner, call her A, is the person with the longest string of heads. Assuming no talent, the probability is greater than a half that A will have flipped 12 or more straight heads. As the story goes, there is a widely believed theory that no one has coin-flipping ability, and, hence, a researcher is collecting data to investigate this hypothesis. Because one would not expect everyone to have coin-flipping ability, he is not surprised to find that a number of tests failed to reject the null hypothesis. Upon hearing of A's feat (but not of the entire environment in which she achieved it), the researcher comes to MIT where I certify that she did, indeed, flip 12 straight heads. Upon computing that the probability of such an event occurring by chance alone is 2^{-12}, or .00025, the researcher concludes that the widely believed theory of no coin-flipping ability can be rejected at almost any confidence level.

Transformed to the context of tests of stock market rationality, what empirical conclusion about the theory can be reached if we are told of a certified discovery of a particular money manager who outperformed the market in each and every year for twelve years? Even if the individual researcher can further certify that the discovery of this apparently gifted manager was by a random drawing, the significance of the finding cannot be easily assessed. We know that the population size of (past and present) money managers is quite large. We also know that the number of researchers (past and present) studying professional money management performance is not small. However, as indicated, for quite legitimate individual and institutional reasons, results that simply confirm the "norm" (of no significant performance capability) tend not to be reported. Thus, the number of such random drawings undertaken *collectively* by researchers is unknown, and this makes the assessment of significance rather difficult.

As we surely could do in the case of A's purported coin-flipping talent, we might try to resolve this problem by testing the money manager's talent "out of sample." Because of survivorship bias, this cannot be done easily with data from years prior to the money manager's run. If the run is still current, then we must wait many years to accumulate the new data needed to test the hypothesis properly.

The problem of assessing significance becomes, therefore, especially acute for testing theories of stock market behavior where very long observation periods (e.g., fifty to one hundred years) are required. One such class of examples is theories where price and fundamental value deviate substantially and where it is further posited that the speed of convergence of price to value is slow.

If, as is not unusual (cf. Shiller, 1984), a theory is formulated as a possible solution for an empirical puzzle previously found in the data, then the construction of a proper significance test of the theory on these same data becomes quite subtle.

Consider, for example, the following sequence of empirical studies and theories, which followed the finding in the early 1970s, that low-price-to-earnings-ratio stocks seem significantly to outperform high-price-to-earnings-ratio stocks when performance is adjusted for risk according to the Capital Asset Pricing Model. Because there was already theory and evidence to suggest that the CAPM was inadequate to explain all the cross-sectional differentials in average security returns and because price-to-earnings ratios are not statistically independent of other firm characteristics (e.g., industry, dividend yield, financial and business risks), early explanations of the puzzle centered on additional dimensions of risk as in the arbitrage pricing and intertemporal capital asset pricing theories and on the tax effects from the mix of the pretax returns between dividends and capital gains. Further empirical analysis of the same data suggested that the aberration was more closely related to the size of the firm than to price-to-earnings ratios, although this claim is still subject to some dispute. Although firm size is also not statistically independent of other firm characteristics, this finding added the prospect of market segmentation or "tiering" to the original list of possible explanations for the puzzle.

Still further empirical analysis of the same data found a "seasonal" effect in stock returns that appeared to produce systematically larger returns on the market in the month of January. Closer inspection of these data pinpointed the source in place and time to be smaller firms in the early part of January. Moreover, by combining these two studies, it seems that the original PE/small-firm puzzle is almost entirely the result of stock price behavior in January. This result shifted the emphasis of theoretical explanation from risk factors and segmentation to "temporary" depressions in prices caused by year-end tax-loss sales of stocks that have already declined in price.

In the growing list of theoretical explanations of this puzzle (followed by tests on the same data set), perhaps the most recent entry is the "overreaction behavioral theory" of DeBondt and Thaler (1985) which implies that a "contrary opinion" portfolio strategy will outperform the market. It is particularly noteworthy because it also represents an early attempt at a formal test of cognitive misperceptions theories as applied to the general stock market.[11] To test their theory, they construct two portfolios (each containing 35 stocks): one contains extreme winners based on past returns and the other extreme losers. They find that in a series of nonoverlapping three-year holding periods, the "winners," on average, underperformed the market by 1.7% per year and the "losers" overperformed the market by 6.5% per year. The difference between the two, 8.2% per year, was judged to be significant with a t-statistic of 2.20.

Do the empirical findings of DeBondt and Thaler, using over a half-century of data, really provide significant evidence for their theory? Is it reasonable to use the standard t-statistic as a valid measure of significance when the test is conducted on the same data used by many earlier studies whose results influenced the choice of theory to be tested? As it happens in this particular case, the former substantive question can be answered without addressing the latter methodological one. That is, Franco Modigliani is fond of the saying, "If, for a large number of observations, you have to consult the tables to determine whether or not your t-statistic is significant, then it is not significant." This expressed concern over the delicate issue of balancing type I and type II errors would seem to apply here. Moreover, consider the additional findings of the study as described by the authors (p. 799): "First, the overreaction effect is asymmetric; it is much larger for losers than for winners. Secondly, consistent with previous work on the turn-of-the-year effect and seasonality, most of the excess returns are realized in January." As the authors later put it. (p. 804), "Several aspects of the results remain without adequate explanation." It is at this moment difficult to see a clear theoretical explanation for overreaction being asymmetric and, even more so, for the excesses tending to be corrected at the same time each year.

Suppose, however, that the authors had found no such unexplained anomalies with respect to their theory and a larger t-statistic. Would their test, considered in methodological terms, have fulfilled their expressed goal? Namely, "... our goal is to test whether the overreaction hypothesis is *predictive* [their emphasis]. In other words, whether it does more for us than merely to explain, ex post, the P/E effect or Shiller's results on asset price dispersion" (p. 795). When a theory is formulated as an explanation of a known empirical puzzle and then tested on the same data from which the puzzle arose, it would appear that the distinction between "prediction" and "ex post explanation" can be quite subtle.

These same concerns, of course, apply equally to the many empirical studies that do not reject market rationality. The early tests of serial dependences in stock returns that used the newly created data bases in the 1960s may have been sufficiently independent to satisfy the assumptions underlying the standard test statistics. It is, however, difficult to believe in the same level of independence for the practically countless subsequent runs used to test closely related hypotheses on the same data.

Although there is no obvious solution to these methodological problems in testing the rational market hypothesis, it does not follow that the controversies associated with the hypothesis cannot be empirically resolved. It does follow, however, that the reported statistical significance of the evidence, both for and against the hypothesis, is likely to overstate—perhaps, considerably so—the proper degree of precision to be attached to these findings. As noted at the outset, although common to all areas of economic hypothesis testing, these methodological problems appear to be especially acute in the testing of market rationality. Thus, it would seem that in evaluating the evidence on this matter, "more-than-usual" care should be exercised in examining the substantive economic assumptions and statistical methodologies used to present the evidence. In this spirit, I try my hand at examining the recent volatility tests of aggregate stock market rationality.

2.6 Volatility Tests of Stock Market Rationality

Having already expressed my views on the LeRoy and Porter (1981) and Shiller (1981) variance bound studies as tests of stock market rationality,[12] I provide only a brief summary of those views as background for the discussion of more recent volatility tests that have evolved from their work.

In formulating his variance bound tests, Shiller (1981) makes three basic economic assumptions: (S.1) stock prices reflect investor beliefs, which are rational expectations of future dividends; (S.2) the real expected rate of return on the stock market is constant over time; (S.3) aggregate real dividends on the stock market can be described by a finite-variance stationary stochastic process with a deterministic exponential growth rate. From these assumptions, Shiller derives two variance bound relations: the first is that the variance of real and detrended stock prices is bounded above by the variance of real and detrended "perfect-foresight" stock prices constructed by discounting *ex post* the realized stream of dividends at the estimated average expected rate of return on the stock market. The second is that the variance of the innovations (or unanticipated changes) in stock prices is bounded from above by the product of the variance of dividends and a constant that parametrically depends on the long-run or statistical equilibrium expected dividend-to-price ratio. Using 109 years of data, Shiller found that the sample statistics violated by a very large margin both of his variance bounds on stock price behavior. Although he did not derive the sampling properties of his estimates, Shiller argued that the magnitude of the violations together with the long observation period make sampling error an unlikely candidate to explain these violations. Nevertheless, subsequent simulations by Flavin (1983) and Kleidon (1983a,b) have shown that sampling error, and, in addition, sample bias, could be important factors.

Some economists interpret the Shiller findings as strong evidence against the theory that stock prices are based upon fundamentals alone. Others, most recently Summers (1985) and Marsh and Merton (1986), are more careful in noting that even if the results are "true" rejections, then they reject the joint hypothesis (S.1), (S.2), and (S.3), which need not, of course, imply rejection of (S.1).[13] As noted earlier in this section, there are a priori economic reasons as well as empirical evidence leading us to reject the hypothesis (S.2) that the expected real rate is constant. While these are perhaps sufficient to reconcile the test findings with market rationality, some economists (including Shiller, 1981, 1982) have presented analyses suggesting that fluctuations in the expected real rate might have to be "unreasonably large" to make this accommodation.

If (S.2) were modified to permit the expected real rate to follow a stochastic but stationary process, then, together with (S.3), detrended rational stock prices must follow a stationary process. The prototype processes for stock prices and dividends used by both finance academics and practitioners are not stationary, and this raises a priori questions about assumption (S.3). Kleidon (1983a,b) reports time series evidence against stationarity for both stock prices and dividends, and, using simulations, shows that Shiller's findings can occur for nonstationary dividend processes and rationally determined stock prices.

Marsh and Merton (1986) show that if the stationarity assumption is replaced by a Lintner-like dividend model where the dividend is a positive distributed lag of past stock prices, then the inequality in Shiller's first variance bounds test is exactly reversed. Thus, for any given time series of stock prices, this variance bound will always be violated by one or the other assumption about the dividend process. Hence, they conclude that the bound is wholly unreliable as a test of stock market rationality. They further show that for this class of dividend processes, there is no easily identified bound between the variance of dividends and the variance of stock price innovations.

Judging from these studies, the amount of light that these variance bounds tests can shed on the issue of market rationality seems to depend critically on the way in which we model the uncertainty surrounding future economic fundamentals. That is, if the underlying economic fundamentals are such that the levels of rationally determined, real (and detrended) stock prices can be described by a stationary process, then they have power. If, instead, it is the percentage change in stock prices that is better described by a stationary process, then they have no power. This observation was surely one of the important driving forces in the development of the "second-generation" volatility tests beginning with West (1983, 1984) and represented most recently by Mankiw, Romer, and Shapiro (1985). Although closely related to the original Shiller-LeRoy-Porter formulations, these tests appear to be far more robust because they do not require the stationarity assumption. Since the Mankiw, Romer, and Shapiro (MRS) study is the most recent version of these tests, the analysis here focuses on it.

As with the original Shiller variance bound test, which derived an inequality between the variance of rational stock prices $\{P(t)\}$ and the variance of ex post, perfect-foresight stock prices $\{P^*(t)\}$, MRS also use these series, together with a time series of "naive forecast" stock prices $\{P^0(t)\}$, to test the following derived bounds [p. 679, (11') and (12')]:

$$E_0[P^*(t) - P^0(t)]^2 \geq E_0[P^*(t) - P(t)]^2 \tag{1}$$

and

$$E_0[P^*(t) - P^0(t)]^2 \geq E_0[P(t) - P^0(t)]^2, \tag{2}$$

where E_0 denotes the expectation operator, conditional on initial conditions at $t = 0$. Although MRS do retain what has been called here Shiller's assumptions (S.1) and (S.2), they do not make the stationarity assumption (S.3). Hence, this conditioning of the expectations is necessary to make sense of (1) and (2) when the series are not stationary processes.

To test the bounds (1) and (2), they form the test statistics [p. 683, (16), (17)],

$$S_1 = \frac{1}{T}\sum_{t=1}^{T} [P^*(t) - P^0(t)]^2 - \frac{1}{T}\sum_{t=1}^{T} [P^*(t) - P(t)]^2 \tag{3}$$

and

$$S_2 = \frac{1}{T}\sum_{t=1}^{T} [P^*(t) - P^0(t)]^2 - \frac{1}{T}\sum_{t=1}^{T} [P(t) - P^0(t)]^2, \tag{4}$$

and show that $E[S_1] \geq 0$ and $E[S_2] \geq 0$. With the same data set used by Shiller (1981) but now extended to run from 1872 to 1983, and a "naive forecast" $\{P^0(t)\}$ based on the current dividend, MRS find that these second moment inequalities are substantially violated by the point estimates of both (3) and (4).

The MRS analysis appears to address all the cited criticisms of the first-generation volatility tests with two exceptions, both of which they point out (p. 686): the assumption of a constant discount rate and the statistical significance of their estimates. Since the former has already been discussed in the literature on the first-generation tests, I examine only the latter here.

As with the original Shiller analysis, it is understandable that MRS did not examine the significance issue formally. After all, it is no easy task to derive the necessary mathematical relations for general processes. In the Shiller case, the assumption of stationarity for the underlying processes make somewhat credible the heuristic argument that with a 109-year observation period, the sample statistic is not likely to differ from its expected value by the large magnitudes necessary to void his apparent rejection. Such creditability does not, however, extend to nonstationary processes. Because the extension to include nonstationary processes is the most important contribution of the MRS and other second-generation volatility tests, it is appropriate to examine the sampling properties of their statistics in such an environment.

As noted, deriving these properties in general is no easy task. Thus, I focus here on a simple example that fits their conditions and is easy to solve for the sampling properties.

Suppose there is a rationally priced stock that we know as of today ($t = 0$) will not pay a dividend until at least time T in the future. Suppose (as is often assumed in representative finance models) the dynamics for stock price in real terms, $P(t)$, follows a geometric Brownian motion, which we can describe by the Itô stochastic differential equation:

$$\frac{dP}{P} = r\,dt + \sigma\,dZ, \qquad (5)$$

where r is the required expected real return on the stock; σ^2 is the instantaneous variance rate; and dZ is a Weiner process. r and σ^2 are positive constants.

Suppose further that we decide to perform an MRS type experiment using price data from today until year T in the future. Since none of us knows today what stock prices will be in the future, it is clear that the test statistic is conditional only on the current price, $P(0) = P_0$, and the date at which we end the test, T.

By the MRS definition, the ex post perfect-foresight stock price series,

$\{P^*(t)\}$, will be constructed according to the rule

$$dP^*(t) = rP^*(t)\,dt \tag{6}$$

with the further terminal or boundary condition that

$$P^*(T) = P(T). \tag{7}$$

From (6) and (7), it follows immediately that

$$P^*(t) = e^{-r(T-t)}P(T). \tag{8}$$

From the posited dynamics (5), we can represent the random variable for the stock price at time t in the future, conditional on $P(0) = P_0$, by

$$P(t) = P_0 \exp[\mu t + \sigma Z(t)], \tag{9}$$

where $\mu \equiv (r - \sigma^2/2)$ and $Z(t) = \int_0^t dZ(s)$ is a normally distributed random variable with the properties that

$$E_0[Z(t)] = 0,$$
$$E_0[Z(t)Z(s)] = \min(s, t). \tag{9a}$$

It follows from (9) and (9a) that ($0 \leq t \leq T$)

$$E_0[P(t)] = P_0 e^{rt} \tag{10a}$$

and

$$E_0[P^2(t)] = P_0^2 \exp[(2r + \sigma^2)t]. \tag{10b}$$

It follows from (8), (10a), and (10b) that

$$E_0[P^*(t)] = P_0 e^{rt} \tag{11a}$$

and

$$E_0\{[P^*(t)]^2\} = P_0^2 \exp[2rt + \sigma^2 T]. \tag{11b}$$

By comparison of (10) with (11), we see that the conditional expectation of the "forecast," $P(t)$, is equal to the conditional expectation of the "realization," $P^*(t)$, and the conditional noncentral second moment of the forecast is always less than the corresponding second moment of the realization. This verifies in this model the fundamental principle underlying both the first- and second-generation volatility tests, the principle that rational forecasts should exhibit less volatility than the realizations.

For analytic convenience, suppose that in performing this test, we choose our "naive forecast," $P^0(t)$, equal to zero for all t (which is acceptable within

The Stock Market Rationality Hypothesis

the MRS methodology). In this case, the MRS volatility bound statistic (3) can be rewritten as

$$E_0(X_1) \geq E_0(X_3) \tag{12}$$

and the MRS volatility bound statistic (4) can be rewritten as

$$E_0(X_1) \geq E_0(X_2), \tag{13}$$

where

$$X_1 \equiv \frac{1}{T} \int_0^T [P^*(t)]^2 \, dt,$$

$$X_2 \equiv \frac{1}{T} \int_0^T [P(t)]^2 \, dt, \tag{14}$$

$$X_3 \equiv X_1 + X_2 - \frac{2}{T} \int_0^T P^*(t) P(t) \, dt.$$

with the MRS $S_1 = X_1 - X_3$ and the MRS $S_2 = X_1 - X_2$.

Substituting from (8) and (9) and computing the conditional expectations, we have that

$$\begin{aligned} E_0[S_1] &= E_0[X_1 - X_3] \\ &= (P_0)^2 [e^{(2r+\sigma^2)T} - 1]/[2r + \sigma^2]T \end{aligned} \tag{15}$$

and

$$\begin{aligned} E_0[S_2] &= E_0[X_1 - X_2] \\ &= \frac{(P_0)^2 e^{\sigma^2 T}}{2r(2r + \sigma^2)T} [\sigma^2(e^{2rT} - 1) - 2r(1 - e^{-\sigma^2 T})]. \end{aligned} \tag{16}$$

By inspection of (15) and (16), we confirm the MRS inequalities $E_0[S_1] \geq 0$ and $E_0[S_2] \geq 0$, and moreover, we see that for $\sigma^2 > 0$, they are strict inequalities whose magnitudes grow without bound as the observation period T becomes large. Unfortunately, the standard deviations of both statistics also grow without bound as the observation period becomes large, and moreover, the rates of growth are at a larger exponential rate than the expected values. Hence, for large T, virtually any realized sample values for S_1 and S_2 are consistent with the ex ante inequalities (12) and (13).

In noting the upward trend in their series and the prospect for heteroskedasticity, MRS (pp. 685–686) attempt to correct for this possible inefficiency by weighting each observation by the inverse of the market price of the stock. However, such a scaling of the data does not rectify the sampling problem. For example, using their scheme, the new statistic S_2', replacing S_2 in (16), can be written as

$$S_2' = \frac{1}{T}\int_0^T \{[P^*(t)]/P(t)\}^2\,dt - \frac{1}{T}\int_0^T [P(t)/P(t)]^2\,dt. \tag{17}$$

Again computing expectations, we have

$$E_0[S_2'] = [e^{\sigma^2 T} - 1]/\sigma^2 T - 1, \tag{18}$$

which is positive and growing in magnitude without bound. Again, the standard deviation of S_2' also grows at a larger exponential rate than $E_0[S_2']$.

Because $E_0(S_1) \geq 0$ and $E_0(S_2) \geq 0$, it follows that $E_0(X_3)/E_0(X_1) \leq 1$ and $E_0(X_2)/E_0(X_1) \leq 1$. A perhaps tempting alternative method for testing the inequalities (12) and (13) would be to use the ratios X_3/X_1 and X_2/X_1 instead of the differences S_1 and S_2. However, as we now show, unless the real discount rate is considerably larger than the volatility parameter σ^2, the ex ante expected values of both these ratios produce exactly the reverse of the inequalities for the ratios of their individual expectations.

Define the statistics $Q_1 \equiv X_3/X_1$ and $Q_2 \equiv X_2/X_1$. By substituting from (8), (9), and (14), we can write the expressions for Q_1 and Q_2 as

$$Q_1 = 1 + Q_2 - 4r\left\{\int_0^T \exp[-(r+\mu)(T-t) - \sigma[Z(T)-Z(t)]]\,dt\right\}\Big/[1-e^{-2rT}] \tag{19}$$

and

$$Q_2 = 2r\left\{\int_0^T \exp[-2\mu(T-t) - 2\sigma[Z(T)-Z(t)]]\,dt\right\}\Big/[1-e^{-2rT}]. \tag{20}$$

Taking expectations and integrating (20), we have

$$E_0[Q_2] = 2r[1 - e^{-(2r-3\sigma^2)T}]/\{(2r-3\sigma^2)[1-e^{-2rT}]\}. \tag{21}$$

By inspection of (21), if $2r > 3\sigma^2$, then $E_0[Q_2] \to 2r/[2r - 3\sigma^2] > 1$ as T gets large. If $0 < r \leq 3\sigma^2$, then $E_0[Q_2] \to \infty$ as T gets large. Thus, for large T, the expectation of the ratio X_2/X_1 satisfies exactly the reverse of the inequality satisfied by the ratio of their expectations $E_0[X_2]/E_0[X_1]$, and this is the case for all positive parameter values r and σ^2.

Taking expectations in (19) and substituting from (21), we have

$$E_0[Q_1] = 1 + 2r\left\{\frac{[1 - e^{-(2r-3\sigma^2)T}]}{(2r - 3\sigma^2)} - \frac{2[1 - e^{-(2r-\sigma^2)T}]}{(2r - \sigma^2)}\right\}\bigg/[1 - e^{-2rT}]. \quad (22)$$

From (22), if $0 < 2r \leq 3\sigma^2$, then $E_0[Q_1] \to \infty$ as T gets large. For $2r > 3\sigma^2$ and large T, we have that $E_0[Q_1] \to 1 + 2r(5\sigma^2 - 2r)/(2r - 3\sigma^2)(2r - \sigma^2)$ which only becomes less than one if $2r > 5\sigma^2$. As described in Merton (1980, p. 353, table 4.8), the average monthly variance rate on the market between 1926 and 1978 was estimated to be 0.003467, which amounts to a $\sigma^2 = 0.0416$ in annual units. Hence, an expected annual real rate of return on the market of the order of 10% would be required to make $E_0[Q_1]$ satisfy the inequality $E_0[Q_1] < 1$. Thus, in addition to being indicative of the sampling problems, the expectation of these ratios are largely consistent with the empirical evidence reported by MRS.

The choice of $P^0(t) \equiv 0$ as the "naive forecast" in this example does not explain these findings. If, for example, we chose $P^0(t) = P_0 e^{rt}$, the "true" conditional expected value for both $P(t)$ and $P^*(t)$, the large T results will remain essentially unchanged because the ratios of second central and noncentral moments tend to one for both $P(t)$ and $P^*(t)$. Indeed, in this case, the MRS inequality just reduces to the original Shiller variance bound defined here in terms of conditional variances and using the "true" ex ante expected values for $P^*(t)$ and $P(t)$. For much the same reason, the selection of almost any naive forecast whose volatility is considerably less than that of stock price is unlikely to change these results. As shown by example in the appendix, the asymptotic distributions for S_1 and S_2 need not converge even if the naive forecast is unbiased and follows a nonstationary process quite similar to the one posited for stock prices.

The example presented here assumes that the underlying stock pays no interim dividends, and therefore one might wonder whether perhaps this polar case is also pathological with respect to the MRS analysis. Although unable to solve fully the dividend-paying case analytically, I offer the following analysis to suggest that the fundamental sampling problems identified by this example will not be significantly changed.

The MRS analysis appears to be impeccable with respect to bias (i.e., the expected value conditions on their inequalities). The problem is that the standard deviation of their estimate for the noncentral second moments grows at an exponential rate greater than the growth of the expected value of the estimate. Thus, the important characteristic to examine is the relation between the second moment and the square root of the fourth moment of future stock prices. Suppose that the dividend paid is a constant proportion ρ of the current stock price. The noncentral second moment of $P(T)$, given $P(0)$, can be written as $[P(0)]^2 \exp[2(r - \rho + \sigma^2/2)T]$. The square root of the noncentral fourth moment of $P(T)$ can be written as $[P(0)]^2 \cdot \exp[(2(r - \rho) + 3\sigma^2)T]$. Thus, as long as $2r + \sigma^2 > 2\rho$, the expected second-moment estimate grows exponentially. However, the ratio of the expected value of the estimate to its standard deviation will, for large T, always decline according to $\exp[-2\sigma^2 T]$, independently of the payout ratio, ρ. Because the MRS estimates involve simple averages of sums (or integrals) of squared stock prices, it thus seems unlikely that the sampling properties of the estimators for large T will be significantly affected by appending dividends to the model. To the extent that dividend changes are more sticky than proportional to stock price changes (which as an empirical matter, they seem to be),[14] the model presented here becomes an even better approximation.

In this light and given that Shiller (1981) had already found enormous empirical violations of the central second-moment bounds between actual stock prices and ex post perfect-foresight prices, it is not altogether surprising to find that the measured noncentral second moments of these same two series also exhibit large violations when estimated on the same data set. In that sense, the Mankiw-Romer-Shapiro study provides no important new empirical findings about the magnitudes of stock market volatility. Nevertheless, their study (together with the West, 1984, analysis) is central to the controversy over the rational market hypothesis because of its claim to rule out the interpretation of Shiller's empirical findings as simply a rejection of the assumption of a stationary process for dividends and stock prices. As shown here, this claim remains to be proved.

3 Conclusion

In summary, I believe that when the heat of the controversy dissipates, there will be general agreement that the rejection or acceptance of the rational market hypothesis as a good approximation to real-world stock market behavior will turn on how we model uncertainty. If, in fact, the levels of expected real corporate economic earnings, dividends, and discount rates in the future are, *ex ante*, well-approximated by a long average of the past levels (plus perhaps a largely deterministic trend), then it is difficult to believe that observed volatilities of stock prices, in both the long and not-so-long runs, are based primarily on economic fundamentals. This assertion can be confirmed by simulations using economic models of the nonfinancial sector with stationary processes for the levels of outputs generating the uncertainty.

Thus, if the well-informed view among economists and investors in the 1930–1934 period was that corporate profits and dividends for *existing*[15] stockholders would return in the reasonably near future to their historical average levels (plus say a 6% trend), then market prices in that period were not based upon fundamentals. If this were the view, then it is surely difficult to explain on a rational basis why the average standard deviation of stock returns during this period was almost three times the corresponding average for the forty-eight other years between 1926 and 1978 (cf. Merton, 1980, pp. 353–354). If once again in the 1962–1966 period, the informed view was that required expected returns and the levels and growth rates of real profits in the future would be the same as in the long past, then stock prices were (ex ante) too high.[16]

If, as is the standard assumption in finance, the facts are that the future levels of expected real corporate economic earnings, dividends, and discount rates are better approximated by nonstationary stochastic processes, then even the seemingly extreme observations from these periods do not violate the rational market hypothesis.

In light of the empirical evidence on the nonstationarity issue, a pronouncement at this moment that the rational market theory should be discarded from the economic paradigm can, at best, be described as "premature." However, no matter which way the issue is ultimately resolved, the resolution itself promises to identify fruitful new research paths for both the finance specialists and the general economist. Just as the break-throughs of more than two decades ago by Lintner, Markowitz, Miller, Modigliani, Samuelson, Sharpe, and Tobin dramatically changed every aspect of both finance theory and practice, so the rejection of market rationality together with the development of the new theory to supersede it would, once again, cause a complete revision of the field. If, however, the rationality hypothesis is sustained, then instead of asking the question "Why are stock prices so much more volatile than (measured) consumption, dividends, and replacement costs?" perhaps general economists will begin to ask questions like "Why do (measured) consumption, dividends, and replacement costs exhibit so little volatility when compared with rational stock prices?" With this reversed perspective may come the development of refined theories of consumer behavior (based upon intertemporally dependent preferences, adjustment costs for consumption, the nontradability of human capital, and cognitive misperceptions) that will explain the sluggish changes in aggregate consumption relative to permanent income. They may also see new ways of examining the question of sticky prices that has long been an important issue in the analysis of the business cycle.

Because rational speculative prices cannot be sticky, comparisons of the volatilities of such prices with nonspeculative prices may provide a useful yardstick for measuring the stickiness of nonspeculative prices and their impact on aggregate economic activity.

Appendix

In the text, it was shown that if rational stock prices follow a geometric Brownian motion and if the naive forecast $P^0(t) = 0$, then the MRS sample statistics, S_1 and S_2, will have asymptotic distributions whose dispersions are growing at an exponential rate greater than their expected values. As noted, the choice of a naive forecast that follows a stationary process with an exponential trend does not change this conclusion about the asymptotic distributions. Using the model of the text, we now show that selection of a naive forecast variable that is both unbiased and follows a nonstationary process very much like the rational stock price need not alter this conclusion. Thus, it would appear that conditions under which the MRS statistics will exhibit proper distributional properties for long observation periods are quite sensitive to the choice of the naive forecast variable and, therefore, are not robust.

Suppose that the naive forecast is given by $P^0(t) = \lambda(t)P(t)$, where $\{\lambda(t)\}$ are independently and identically distributed positive random variables with

$$E[\lambda(t)] = 1,$$
$$\text{var}[\lambda(t)] = \delta^2,$$
$$E[\lambda^3(t)] = m_3,$$
$$E[\lambda^4(t)] = m_4.$$
(A.1)

$\lambda(t)$ describes the "noise" component of the naive forecast relative to the optimal forecast, which by assumption is the stock price, $P(t)$. It is further assumed that the noise is independent of all stock prices [i.e., $\lambda(t)$ and $P(s)$ are independent for all t and s]. Therefore, $E[P^0(t)|P(t)] = P(t)$, and hence, $P^0(t)$ is an unbiased forecast. Because, moreover, the $\{\lambda(t)\}$ follow a stationary process, the nonstationary part of the process describing the naive forecast is perfectly correlated with the optimal forecast, $P(t)$.

Substituting for $P^0(T)$ in (3) and rearranging terms, we can write the continuous-time form for the MRS statistics S_1 as

$$S_1 = \frac{1}{T}\int_0^T P(t)[2[1 - \lambda(t)]P^*(t) - [1 - \lambda^2(t)]P(t)]\,dt. \tag{A.2}$$

From (A.1) and (A.2), we can write the expectation of S_1 conditional on the sample path $\{P(t)\}$, $\bar{S}_1$, as

$$\bar{S}_1 = \frac{\delta^2}{T}\int_0^T [P(t)]^2\,dt, \tag{A.3}$$

because $\lambda(t)$ is independent of both $\{P(t)\}$ and $\{P^*(t)\}$. Note: $\bar{S}_1$ does not depend

The Stock Market Rationality Hypothesis

on the sample path of $P^*(t)$. From (A.3) and (10.b), we have

$$E_0[S_1] = \delta^2 P_0^2 [e^{(2r+\sigma^2)T} - 1]/[(2r + \sigma^2)T], \tag{A.4}$$

which satisfies the MRS strict inequality $E_0[S_1] > 0$ provided the naive forecast is not optimal (i.e., $\delta^2 > 0$).

Define the random variable $Y_1 \equiv [S_1 - \bar{S}_1]^2$. From (A.2) and (A.3), we write Y_1 as

$$Y_1 = \frac{1}{T^2} \int_0^T \int_0^T P(t)P(s)[2[1 - \lambda(t)]P^*(t) - [1 + \delta^2 - \lambda^2(t)]P(t)] \cdot [2[1 - \lambda(s)]P^*(s) - [1 + \delta^2 - \lambda^2(s)]P(s)]\,ds\,dt. \tag{A.5}$$

Because $\lambda(t)$ is independent of $\lambda(s)$ for $t \neq s$, we have from (A.1) and (A.5) that the expectation of Y_1, conditional on the sample path $\{P(t)\}$, $\bar{Y}_1$, can be written as

$$\bar{Y}_1 = \frac{1}{T^2} \int_0^T P^2(t)[4\delta^2[P^*(t)]^2 + 4[1 + \delta^2 - m_3]P(t)P^*(t) + [m_4 - (1 + \delta^2)^2]P^2(t)]\,dt. \tag{A.6}$$

Note that the integrand of (A.6) is always positive. From (8) and (9), we have, for $k = 2, 3, 4$,

$$E_0\{[P(t)]^k[P^*(t)]^{4-k}\} = [P_0 e^{rt}]^4 \exp[6\sigma^2 T + \frac{\sigma^2}{2}k(k-7)(T-t)]. \tag{A.7}$$

Taking expectations in (A.6) and substituting from (A.7), we have that $E_0[Y_1] = E_0[\bar{Y}_1]$ grows exponentially as

$$E_0[Y_1] \sim \exp[(4r + 6\sigma^2)T]/T^2. \tag{A.8}$$

Therefore, the standard deviation of the MRS sample statistics S_1 given by $\sqrt{E_0[Y_1]}$ grows exponentially according to $\exp[(2r + 3\sigma^2)T]/T$. By inspection of (A.4), we have that the ratio of $E_0[S_1]$ to $\sqrt{E_0[Y_1]}$ declines exponentially at the rate $(-2\sigma^2 T)$. Thus, for large T, virtually any sample result for S_1 is consistent with the population condition $E_0[S_1] > 0$. By a similar analysis, the reader can verify that the same result obtains for the MRS statistic S_2.

In contrasting their tests with the earlier Shiller (1981) analysis, MRS (1985, p. 683) point out that their statistics do not require detrending "... because the 'naive forecast' P_t^0 can grow as dividends grow ...." On p. 684, they further their case for robustness by noting "... that the naive forecast need not be efficient in any sense." The naive forecast analyzed here does not seem to be pathological with respect to the conditions they set forth. Thus, it would appear that the naive forecasts necessary to provide proper asymptotic distributional properties for their statistics are anything but naive.

Notes

1. See Fischer and Merton (1984), Marsh and Merton (1983, 1986), and Merton (1983).

2. As may come as a great surprise to those financial economists who regularly publish papers on capital budgeting problems, earnings estimation, financing decisions, and dividend policy, Summers (1985, p. 634) finds it rather "... unfortunate that financial economists remain so reluctant to accept any research relating asset prices and fundamental values." In making this remark, perhaps Summers has in mind those financial economists who might select the closing price on the New York Stock Exchange of a ketchup company's common stock as a better estimate of that firm's fundamental value than an estimate provided by a general economist who computes a present value based on a linear regression model 1 of the supply and demand for ketchup; autoregressive forecasts of future costs of tomatoes, wages, prices of ketchup substitutes, and consumer incomes; and a "reasonable" discount rate.

3. As is well known, even with well-functioning (although not complete) markets and rational, well-informed consumer-investors, the competitive market solution may not be a pareto optimum, and thus, market rationality is not a sufficient condition for efficiency. Using the neoclassical model with overlapping generations, Tirole (1985) has shown that financial security prices that deviate from fundamentals can lead to better allocations than "rational" prices. However, I would argue that those cases in which stock prices both deviate substantially from fundamental values *and* lead to a pareto optimum allocation of investment are, at best, rare.

4. On the self-fulfilling prophecy, see R. K. Merton, (1948). On the rational expectations speculative bubble theory, see Blanchard (1979), Blanchard and Watson (1982), Tirole (1982), and Van Horne (1985).

5. This assumes as a "base date" the publication of Samuelson's 1965 paper, which first set forth the theory in rigorous form. There was, of course, the oral publication of his ideas for at least fifteen years before 1965, as well as many studies of speculative prices and their random properties, extending back as far as the early 1900s.

6. See, for example, the model analyzed in Merton (1971, pp. 403–406), which examines price behavior and optimal portfolio selection when instantaneous stock price changes are random, but the level of stock price regresses toward a "normal price level" with a trend.

7. As will be discussed, the recent study by DeBondt and Thaler (1985) presents evidence that seemingly contradicts these earlier findings.

8. Jensen (1968) found that the average "excess return" per year (including management expenses) across all funds in his sample and all the years from 1945 to 1964, was −1.1%, and 66% of the funds had negative average excess returns. When expenses were excluded, the corresponding statistics were −0.4% per year and 48%. As reported in a recent Business Week article (February 4, 1985, pp. 58–59), based on the industry standard data from SEI Funds Evaluation Services, 74% of managed equity portfolios underperformed the Standard & Poor's 500 Index in 1984; 68% underperformed for the period 1982–1984; 55% underperformed for 1980–1984; and 56% underperformed for 1975–1984.

The Stock Market Rationality Hypothesis

9. To the extent that stock market prices themselves are an important source of information for investors in calibrating and evaluating other data used to make their assessments of the fundamentals, the original argument that systematically less information is produced on days when the market is closed can be extended to include the Wednesday closings.

10. See Marsh and Merton (1985). Miller and Scholes (1982) find the same result for individual stock returns.

11. As perhaps some indication of the tentative nature of the evidence drawn to support behavioral theories of the stock market, we have, on the one hand, DeBondt and Thaler concluding that investors make cognitive mistakes that result in the underpricing of stocks that have declined (losers) and overpricing of stocks that have risen (winners) and, on the other, Shefrin and Statman (1985) concluding that the evidence supports (different) cognitive mistakes that cause investors to sell their winners "too early" and hold on to their losers "too long." It would seem, therefore, that even a "rational" investor, fully cognizant of his natural tendency to make these mistakes, would, nevertheless, find himself "convicted" by his actions of one or the other cognitive failures.

12. As junior author of Marsh and Merton (1983, 1986).

13. More precisely, Summers (1985, p. 635) refers to the joint hypothesis involving what has been called here "(S.1) and (S.2)." I do not know whether his failure to note the stationarity condition (S.3) as well was intended or not.

14. See Marsh and Merton (1985).

15. Some investors in 1930–1934 may have believed that there was a significantly changed probability of broad-based nationalization of industry than in the past. Given the substantially increased levels of business and financial leverage, there were perhaps others who saw a different prospect for widespread bankruptices than was the case in the past.

16. There were, however, some economists and professional investors who apparently believed that the government had finally found both the will and the means to avoid major macroeconomic disruptions from high unemployment, erratic growth rates, and unstable inflation. Their best guesses for the future may have been formulated with less weight on the distant past.

References

Arrow, K. J., 1982, "Risk Perception in Psychology and Economics," *Economic Inquiry* 20 (January), 1–9.

Blanchard, O., 1979, "Speculative Bubbles, Crashes, and Rational Expectations," *Economic Letters* 3, 387–389.

Blanchard, O., and M. W. Watson, 1982, "Bubbles, Rational Expectations, and Financial Markets," in *Crises in the Economic and Financial Structure*, P. Wachtel (ed.), Lexington Books, pp. 295–315.

DeBondt, W. F. M., and R. Thaler, 1985, "Does the Stock Market Overreact?" *Journal of Finance* 40(3) (July), 793–805.

Fama, E., 1970, "Efficient Capital Markets: A Review of Theory and Empirical Work," *Journal of Finance* 25 (May), 383–417.

Fama, E., 1981, "Stock Returns, Real Activity, Inflation and Money," *American Economic Review*, 71, 545–565.

Fischer, S., and R. C. Merton, 1984, "Macroeconomics and Finance: The Role of the Stock Market," in *Essays on Macroeconomic Implications of Financial and Labor Markets and Political Processes*, K. Brunner and A. H. Meltzer (eds.), Carnegie-Rochester Conference Series on Public Policy, Vol. 21 (Autumn), pp. 57–108.

Flavin, M. A., 1983, "Excess Volatility in the Financial Markets: A Reassessment of the Empirical Evidence," *Journal of Political Economy* 91 (December), 929–956.

French, K., and R. Roll, 1984, "Is Trading Self-Generating?" unpublished paper, Graduate School of Business, University of Chicago (February).

Jensen, M. C., 1968, "The Performance of the Mutual Funds in the Period 1945–1964," *Journal of Finance* 23 (May), 384–416.

Kahneman, D. and A. Tversky, 1979, "Prospect Theory: An Analysis of Decision under Risk," *Econometrica* 47 (March), 263–291.

Kahneman, D. and A. Tversky, 1982, "Intuitive Prediction: Biases and Corrective Procedures," in *Judgement under Uncertainty: Heuristics and Biases*, D. Kahneman, P. Slovic, and A. Tversky (eds.), Cambridge University Press.

Kleidon, A. W., 1983a, "Variance Bounds Tests and Stock Price Valuation Models," working paper, Graduate School of Business, Stanford University (January).

Kleidon, A. W., 1983b, "Bias in Small Sample Tests of Stock Price Rationality," unpublished, University of Chicago.

Leamer, E. E., 1983, "Let's Take the Con Out of Econometrics," *American Economic Review* 73(1), 31–43.

LeRoy, S. F., and R. D. Porter, 1981, "The Present-Value Relation: Tests Based on Implied Variance Bounds," *Econometrica* 49(3), 555–574.

Long, Jr., J. B., 1978, "The Market Valuation of Cash Dividends: A Case to Consider," *Journal of Financial Economics* 6(2/3) (June/September), 235–264.

Mankiw, N. G., D. Romer, and M. D. Shapiro, 1985, "An Unbiased Reexamination of Stock Market Volatility," *Journal of Finance* XL(3) (July), 677–687.

Marsh, T. A., and R. C. Merton, 1983, "Aggregate Dividend Behavior and Its Implications for Tests of Stock Market Rationality," working paper No. 1475–83, Sloan School of Management, MIT (September).

Marsh, T. A., and R. C. Merton, 1985, "Dividend Behavior for the Aggregate

Stock Market," working paper No. 1670–85, Sloan School of Management, MIT (May).

Marsh, T. A., and R. C. Merton, 1986, "Dividend Variability and Variance Bounds Tests for the Rationality of Stock Market Prices," *American Economic Review*. 76(3) (June), 483–498.

Merton, R. C., 1971, "Optimum Consumption and Portfolio Rules in a Continuous Time Model," *Journal of Economic Theory* 3 (December), 373–413.

Merton, R. C., 1973, "An Intertemporal Capital Asset Pricing Model," *Econometrica* 41 (September), 867–887.

Merton, R. C., 1980, "On Estimating the Expected Return on the Market: An Exploratory Investigation," *Journal of Financial Economics* 8, 323–361.

Merton, R. C., 1983, "Financial Economics," in *Paul Samuelson and Modern Economic Theory*, E. C. Brown and R. M. Solow (eds.), McGraw-Hill, pp. 105–138.

Merton, R. K., 1948, "The Self-Fulfilling Prophecy," *Antioch Review* (Summer), 193–210.

Miller, M. H., and M. S. Scholes, 1982, "Dividends and Taxes: Some Empirical Evidence," *Journal of Political Economy* (90), 1118–1142.

Modigliani, F., and R. Cohn. 1979, "Inflation, Rational Valuation and the Market," *Financial Analysts Journal* (March–April), 3–23.

Ohlson, J. A., and S. H. Penman, 1985, "Volatility Increases Subsequent to Stock Splits: An Empirical Abberation," *Journal of Financial Economics* 14(2) (June), 251–266.

Samuelson, P. A., 1965, "Proof That Properly Anticipated Prices Fluctuate Randomly," *Industrial Management Review* 6 (Spring), 41–49.

Shefrin, H., and M. Statman, 1985, "The Disposition to Sell Winners Too Early and Ride Losers Too Long: Theory and Evidence," *Journal of Finance* 40(3) (July), 777–790.

Shiller, R. J., 1981, "Do Stock Prices Move Too Much to be Justified by Subsequent Changes in Dividends?" *American Economic Review* 71 (June), 421–436.

Shiller, R. J., 1982, "Consumption, Asset Markets, and Macroeconomic Fluctuations," *Carnegie-Rochester Conference on Public Policy* 17, 203–250.

Shiller, R. J., 1984, "Stock Prices and Social Dynamics," *Brookings Papers on Economic Activity* 2, 457–498.

Summers, L. H., 1982, "Do We Really Know That Financial Markets are Efficient?" National Bureau of Economic Research, working paper No. 994 (September).

Summers, L. H., 1985, "On Economics and Finance," *Journal of Finance* XL(3) (July), 633–635.

Summers, L. H., 1986, "Does the Stock Market Rationally Reflect Fundamental Values?" *Journal of Finance* 41(3) (July), 591–600.

Tirole, J., 1982, "On the Possibility of Speculation Under Rational Expectations," *Econometrica* 59 (September), 1163–1181.

Tirole, J., 1985, "Asset Bubbles and Overlapping Generations," *Econometrica* 53(5) (September), 1071–1100.

Van Horne, J. C., 1985, "On Financial Innovations and Excesses," *Journal of Finance* XL(3) (July), 621–631.

West, K. D., 1983, "A Variance Bounds Test of the Linear-Quadratic Inventory Model," in *Inventory Models and Backlog Costs: An Empirical Investigation*, unpublished Ph.D. dissertation, Massachusetts Institute of Technology (May).

West, K. D., 1984, "Speculative Bubbles and Stock Price Volatility," Financial Research Center, Memorandum No. 54, Princeton University (December).

[9]
Variance Bounds in a Simple Model of Asset Pricing

Ronald W. Michener
University of Virginia

This paper presents a parametric example of a one-asset exchange economy in which the asset price is endogenously determined. It is demonstrated that the volatility of the asset's price uniformly violates the theoretical upper bound implied by the present value relation. In addition, the variance bounds may be violated by a significant margin at the same time the asset's price is almost a random walk. The example has a dual interpretation as a consumption function, and under this interpretation it is demonstrated that the permanent-income hypothesis does not necessarily restrict the time-series properties of consumption.

Recent work on asset pricing by Singleton (1980), LeRoy and Porter (1981), and Shiller (1981) has emphasized an apparent anomaly in the behavior of asset prices. If, as is widely maintained, the price of an asset is simply the discounted value of its dividends, discounted at a constant rate, that is,

$$\text{asset price} = \sum_{j=0}^{\infty} \left(\frac{1}{1+r}\right)^j E_t(\text{dividends}_{t+j}), \qquad (1)$$

then the variability of an asset's price ought to be systematically related to the variability of its dividend stream. Moreover, since an asset's price is a long moving average of its dividend series, asset prices should, theoretically, have small variances. Crude empiricism suggests that asset prices actually have large variances. The aforementioned

---

This paper has benefited from the helpful comments of Stephen LeRoy and Robert J. Shiller. Robert Lucas and Ken Singleton are responsible for bringing the problem, and the proposed solution, to my attention. Errors which remain are (alas!) my own.

work has been directed at developing statistical techniques to determine whether the variability of asset prices does indeed exceed that implied by the standard asset-pricing model. The answer is that asset prices do seem to show too much variability.

Shiller (1981) estimated the standard deviation of stock prices to be six to 12 times its theoretical upper limit. This is consistent with the findings of LeRoy and Porter (1981), who found a coefficient of dispersion of stock prices almost 10 times its theoretical upper limit. All such empirical tests, naturally, are actually joint tests of the economic model and the statistical model with which the econometrician describes the behavior of dividends. For this reason, there is still debate on the significance of this empirical work. However, if we accept the excessive volatility of asset prices as fact, where does this leave the theory of asset pricing?

One obvious route of reconciliation is to maintain that expectations are not rational. If investors, driven by "animal spirits," overreact to current information, it would explain the surprising volatility of asset prices. Such an explanation not only violates neoclassical tenets, it also clashes with the evidence which has been adduced in favor of the efficiency of asset markets. Hence the challenge to economic theory is clear. Theory must provide a model of asset pricing consistent with (1) rational expectations and optimizing behavior, (2) the empirical martingale property of stock prices, and (3) the high volatility of stock prices.

General equilibrium models of asset pricing by LeRoy (1973) and Lucas (1978) had already attacked the accuracy of the standard expectations model of asset prices (eq. [1]). Such work originally had, as a major objective, to establish that stock prices in a general equilibrium model need not have the martingale property except under risk neutrality. A natural extension is to ask whether such a general equilibrium model might provide an explanation for the volatility of stock prices. LeRoy and La Civita (1981) posed such a question in a simple two-state finite-horizon model and determined that, within their model, the volatility of stock prices increased without bound as the risk aversion of the utility function increased. As the matter now stands, general equilibrium models of asset pricing are known to be compatible with the martingale property of asset prices for risk neutrality; they are known to be consistent with the high volatility of stock prices for extreme risk aversion. One wishes they could be consistent with both. This paper contains a simple example which explores the possibility that the general equilibrium model might be consistent with both. The results are mildly encouraging. The martingale property may be very nearly true, while the volatility of asset prices may substantially exceed the theoretical upper bound.

The Model

Consider a representative consumer who maximizes a utility function given by:

$$\sum_{t=0}^{\infty} \beta^t \log c_t, \quad 0 < \beta < 1. \quad (2)$$

There is only one asset in this world, for example, shares in a fruit tree. It produces its nonstorable consumption good, y, according to the following first-order Markov process:

$$\ln y' = \alpha \ln y + \epsilon_t, \quad (3)$$

where $0 \leq \alpha < 1$ and $\epsilon_t \sim N(0,\sigma^2)$.

Since there is no storage and no investment, the real side of this model is trivial. In equilibrium, $c = y \cdot z$. However, the price of the asset must be determined so as to make it optimal for the consumer to hold his pro rata portion of the existing shares in the fruit tree. The consumer's budget constraint is given by:

$$y \cdot z + p(y) \cdot z = c + p(y) \cdot x, \quad (4)$$

where z is the beginning-of-period asset share, c is consumption, x is the end-of-period asset share, and $p(y)$ is the equilibrium price of the asset, in terms of y, the consumption good. Let the value function $V(y,z)$, be defined by

$$V(y,z) = \max_{(c,x)} \left[u(c) + \beta \int_\Omega V(y',x) dF(y'|y) \right], \quad (5)$$

subject to the constraint given by equation (4).

The questions of existence and uniqueness of the value function and the function $p(y)$ are dealt with in Lucas (1978). These properties can be established under quite general conditions (which, regrettably, are violated here by the choice of an unbounded utility function). One solution strategy is to "guess" $V(y,z)$ and $p(y)$ and then verify that they satisfy the functional equation given in (5) above. A good initial guess would be that $V(y,z)$ is linear in the logarithm of y and the logarithm of wealth. Hence, consider the candidate:

$$p(y) = a_1 y, \quad (6)$$

$$V(y,z) = k_0' + k_1' \log[y \cdot z + p(y) \cdot z] + k_2' \log y. \quad (7)$$

For $p(y) = a_1 y$, this is equivalent to

$$V(y,z) = k_0 + k_1 \log z + k_2 \log y. \quad (7')$$

VARIANCE BOUNDS

Provided $V(y,z)$ has the hypothesized form, (5) may be rewritten as:

$$k_0 + k_1 \log z + k_2 \log y = \max_x \Big\{\log[y \cdot z + a_1 y(z - x)] \qquad (5')$$

$$+ \beta \int_\Omega (k_0 + k_1 \log x + k_2 \log y') dF(y'|y)\Big\}.$$

The first-order condition for (5') is:

$$\frac{-a_1 y}{y \cdot z + a_1 y(z - x)} + \frac{\beta k_1}{x} = 0. \qquad (8)$$

Equation (8) can be solved for $x(y,z)$. When this is substituted into the functional equation, there are terms in log y, log z, and constants on both sides. Equating coefficients gives three conditions determining a_1, k_0, k_1, and k_2. The final condition comes from our definition of equilibrium: $x = z$. The solution is:

$$k_0 = 0, \qquad (9)$$

$$k_1 = \frac{1}{1 - \beta}, \qquad (10)$$

$$k_2 = \frac{1}{1 - \beta\alpha}, \qquad (11)$$

$$a_1 = \frac{\beta}{1 - \beta}. \qquad (12)$$

Our attention should center on the equilibrium price function, $p(y) = [\beta/(1 - \beta)]y$. Note that, even in the case when the dividend is an independent identically distributed random variable, the price of the asset responds to the current dividend. This occurs *despite* the facts that the price is the value of the asset *after* payment of the current period's dividend and that the current period's dividend provides no information about future dividends. This result occurs because of the concavity of the utility function. If the representative consumer were risk neutral, the asset's price would not respond to this information-less dividend (see Lucas 1978). The response occurs here because of the influence of the diminishing marginal utility of consumption. A meager dividend today leaves the representative consumer "hungry," and his attempt to convert his share of the asset into current consumption depresses its price. Conversely, an exceptionally generous dividend today prompts the consumer to try to spread his windfall into the future by increasing his asset holdings—thus driving up asset prices. This result coincides with the result derived by LeRoy and La Civita (1981). Risk aversion and diminishing marginal utility of consumption are inseparable properties of concave utility functions. Hence it is appropriate to attribute the variability of asset prices to risk aversion, as LeRoy and La Civita do. In casual usage, though, risk aversion is often associated with uncertainty. Uncertainty is not crucial to the volatility of asset prices. To take an extreme example, suppose the representative consumer knows with certainty that $y_t = 1$ for every $t \geq 1$, as would be the case if $\alpha = 0$ and $\epsilon \equiv 0$. The asset's period zero price would still vary with y_0 according to $[\beta/(1 - \beta)]y_0$. Hence, as an expositional matter, it seems more enlightening to attribute the sensitivity of asset prices to current dividends to the diminishing marginal utility of consumption. It is the desirability of smoothing consumption over time which creates the variability in asset prices, and this does not require uncertainty.

Variance Bounds

Suppose now that a time-series econometrician analyzes this world. What would he discover? To answer this question explicitly, we must make a modest compromise with rigor.

We have posited an AR(1) on the log of the dividend, y. Hence, strictly speaking, $\{y_t\}_{t=0}^{\infty}$ itself will not be a stationary time series. However, for y_0 sufficiently close to 1 and σ_ϵ^2 sufficiently small, we may obtain an excellent approximation to a stationary time series by using $\log y \approx y - 1$. Approximately, then, we would have:

$$y_t = (1 - \alpha) + \alpha y_{t-1} + \epsilon_t. \tag{13}$$

Our econometrician would posit that:

$$p(y) = \sum_{j=1}^{\infty} \left(\frac{1}{1+r}\right)^j E_t(y_{t+j}|I). \tag{14}$$

The sum starts at 1 since in our model the asset owner gets his dividend prior to the beginning of asset trading. Hence the new owner receives his first dividend in the next period. Here I includes current and past values of y as well as current and past values of some additional variables x. The x are completely independent of y, but this fact is unknown to the econometrician.

Following Singleton (1980), he would reason that conditional on (14), $\sigma_{p(y)}^2$ would satisfy the following inequalities:

$$\sigma_{p^*(y)}^2 \geq \sigma_{p(y)}^2 \geq \sigma_{\hat{p}(y)}^2, \tag{15}$$

where

$$\hat{p}(y) = \sum_{j=1}^{\infty} \left(\frac{1}{1+r}\right)^j E_t(y_{t+j}|y_t, y_{t-1}, \ldots), \tag{16}$$

VARIANCE BOUNDS

and

$$p^*(y) = \sum_{j=1}^{\infty} \left(\frac{1}{1+r}\right)^j y_{t+j}. \tag{17}$$

The inequalities, developed at length in Singleton (1980), follow from the fact that the optimum predictor of y_{t+j} will vary at least as much as a (potentially) suboptimal predictor which uses only past values but not more than the actual realization.

Since y_t follows the autoregressive process (13), we have that:

$$E_t(y_{t+j}|y_t, y_{t-1}, \ldots) = \alpha^j(y_t - 1) + 1, \tag{18}$$

so that

$$\hat{p}(y) = \sum_{j=1}^{\infty} \left(\frac{1}{1+r}\right)^j [\alpha^j(y-1) + 1]$$

$$= \left(\frac{\alpha}{1+r}\right)\left\{\frac{1}{1-[\alpha/(1+r)]}\right\}(y_t - 1) + \frac{1}{r(1+r)}. \tag{19}$$

Hence

$$\sigma^2_{\hat{p}(y)} = \left(\frac{\alpha}{1+r}\right)^2 \left\{\frac{1}{1-[\alpha/(1+r)]}\right\}^2 \sigma^2_y$$

$$= \left(\frac{\alpha}{1+r}\right)^2 \left\{\frac{1}{1-[\alpha/(1+r)]}\right\}^2 \frac{\sigma^2_\epsilon}{1-\alpha^2}. \tag{20}$$

Calculating $\sigma^2_{p^*(y)}$ is somewhat more complex. The quantity $p^*(y)$ can be compactly written as

$$p^*(y_t) = \frac{[1/(1+r)]F}{1-[1/(1+r)]F} y_t, \tag{21}$$

where $Fx_t = x_{t+1}$; that is, F is the forward shift operator. Hence the spectral density of $p^*(y)$ is given by

$$S_{p^*(y)}(\lambda) = \frac{[1/(1+r)]^2 S_y(\lambda)}{\{1-[1/(1+r)]e^{i\lambda}\}\{1-[1/(1+r)]e^{-i\lambda}\}}. \tag{22}$$

But $S_y(\lambda)$ is simply

$$S_y(\lambda) = \frac{\sigma^2_\epsilon}{2\pi(1-\alpha e^{i\lambda})(1-\alpha e^{-i\lambda})}, \tag{23}$$

so that

$$S_{p^*(y)}(\lambda) = \tag{24}$$

$$\frac{[1/(1+r)]^2 \sigma^2_\epsilon}{2\pi(1-\alpha e^{i\lambda})(1-\alpha e^{-i\lambda})\{1-[1/(1+r)]e^{i\lambda}\}\{1-[1/(1+r)]e^{-i\lambda}\}}.$$

This could be integrated to obtain the variance of $p^*(y)$; however, it is more convenient to note that this is the spectral density of an AR(2). Hence we can appeal to the well-known (Box and Jenkins 1976, p. 62) result for the variance of an AR(2). This yields

$$\sigma^2_{p^*(y)} = \left(\frac{1}{1+r}\right)^2 \tag{25}$$

$$\cdot \left\{\frac{1 + [\alpha/(1+r)]}{1 - [\alpha/(1+r)]}\right\} \frac{\sigma^2_\epsilon}{\{1 + [\alpha/(1+r)]\}^2 - \{\alpha + [1/(1+r)]\}^2}.$$

With some simplification, this becomes,

$$\sigma^2_{p^*(y)} = \left(\frac{1}{1+r}\right)^2 \left\{\frac{1 + [\alpha/(1+r)]}{1 - [\alpha/(1+r)]}\right\} \frac{\sigma^2_\epsilon}{(1 - \alpha^2)\{1 - [1/(1+r)]^2\}}. \tag{26}$$

For our time-series econometrician to estimate these variances, he would need an estimate of r, the real rate of return in the economy. A natural choice—indeed, the choice made by Shiller—would be to estimate r with the average over time of the dividend-to-price ratio. In this model, that is a constant:

$$r = \frac{y}{p(y)} = \frac{y}{[\beta/(1-\beta)]y} = \frac{1-\beta}{\beta}. \tag{27}$$

The actual variance of $p(y)$ is

$$\sigma^2_{p(y)} = \frac{\beta^2}{(1-\beta)^2}\sigma^2_y = \frac{\beta^2}{(1-\beta)^2(1-\alpha^2)}\sigma^2_\epsilon. \tag{28}$$

In terms of the original parameters, α and β,

$$\sigma^2_{p^*(y)} = \beta^2 \frac{(1+\alpha\beta)}{(1-\alpha\beta)} \frac{\sigma^2_\epsilon}{(1-\alpha^2)(1-\beta^2)}. \tag{29}$$

Hence:

$$\sigma^2_{p(y)} - \sigma^2_{p^*(y)} = \frac{\beta^2 \sigma^2_\epsilon}{(1-\beta)^2(1-\alpha^2)}\left[1 - \frac{(1+\alpha\beta)(1-\beta)^2}{(1-\alpha\beta)(1-\beta^2)}\right] \tag{30}$$

$$= \frac{\beta^2 \sigma^2_\epsilon}{(1-\beta)^2(1-\alpha^2)}\left[\frac{2\beta(1-\alpha)(1-\beta)}{(1-\alpha\beta)(1-\beta^2)}\right] > 0.$$

It can be shown that

$$\sigma^2_{p^*(y)} - \sigma^2_{\hat{p}(y)} = \frac{\beta^2 \sigma^2_\epsilon}{(1-\beta^2)(1-\alpha\beta)^2} > 0. \tag{31}$$

VARIANCE BOUNDS

This is a special case of a very general result. So the ordering of the variances, as determined by the econometrician, given infinite data, would be

$$\sigma^2_{p(y)} \geq \sigma^2_{p^*(y)} \geq \sigma^2_{\hat{p}(y)} \tag{32}$$

(cf. eq. [15]). This is the ordering many investigators have found in real data. It is doubly remarkable here, because in this model $\sigma^2_{\hat{p}(y)}$ marks the "appropriate" bound, in that only past y's are useful in predicting future y's.

The Martingale Property

If the martingale property held exactly, it would be the case that

$$\log[p(y') + y'] - \log[p(y)] = C_0 + \xi, \tag{33}$$

where C_0 is a constant and ξ is a white-noise error term. In fact, we have

$$\log[p(y') + y'] - \log[p(y)] = C'_0 - (1 - \alpha) \log[p(y)] + \epsilon, \tag{34}$$

where $C'_0 = -\alpha \log \beta - (1 - \alpha) \log(1 - \beta)$, and ϵ is white noise, as before. Only if $\alpha = 1$ will the martingale property hold exactly.[1] However, if α is near 1 it would be extremely difficult to distinguish (33) from (34) via a regression test without a very large sample.[2] It can be the case, though, even with α near 1, that the variance bounds are violated by a substantial margin. Let us denote the ratio of $\sigma^2_{p(y)}$ to $\sigma^2_{p^*(y)}$ by $f(\alpha,\beta)$. Then

$$f(\alpha,\beta) = \frac{(1 - \alpha\beta)(1 + \beta)}{(1 + \alpha\beta)(1 - \beta)} \tag{35}$$

The function f is increasing in β and decreasing in α. Shiller (1981, table 1), using modified Dow Industrial data, estimated a dividend-to-price ratio of .0456. The model presented here would generate a dividend-to-price ratio in this neighborhood for $\beta = .96$. Hence it is interesting to evaluate $f(\alpha,\beta)$ for α near 1 and β in the vicinity of .96.

From table 1 it is clear that the variance of $p(y)$ may exceed its theoretical upper bound by quite a margin at the same time that $p(y)$ is behaving very nearly as a random walk.

---

[1] Note that if $\alpha = 1$, the Taylor series expansion required to get eq. (13) need no longer be a good approximation. A nonstationary process on ln y will wander away from a neighborhood of $y = 1$ with probability 1.

[2] A reader skeptical of the contention that standard tests have very low power under the alternative hypothesis advanced here may consult the simulation study done for a similar problem in Box and Ljung (1978, table 3).

TABLE 1
$f(\alpha,\beta)$

α	β .94	.96	.98
.95	1.83	2.26	3.54
.90	2.70	3.58	6.21
.85	3.61	4.96	9.02

This reconciliation, while suggestive, is not as strong as one might hope for. Empirical point estimates suggest a standard deviation nine times the upper bound. Table 1 rationalizes a population parameter no more than three times the upper bound. More fundamentally, this model describes a pure exchange economy and, therefore, most likely exaggerates the volatility of asset prices. Asset prices fluctuate from the unsuccessful attempts of agents to smooth their consumption stream over time. In a production economy, where the supply of assets is not completely inelastic, it seems reasonable to assume that price fluctuations would be reduced. An extension of this paper and that of LeRoy and La Civita (1981) would be to explore the volatility of asset prices in the general equilibrium framework developed by Brock (1978, in press).

One further point is illustrated by this example. Note that

$$W = \text{wealth} = y \cdot z + p(y) \cdot z = \frac{1}{1-\beta} y \cdot z. \tag{36}$$

Equivalently,

$$c = y \cdot z = (1 - \beta)W, \tag{37}$$

which is a permanent-income consumption function! This shows the close relationship between the asset-pricing problem and the consumption function. It also shows that Hall's contention (1978), that a permanent-income model of consumption implies a random walk for consumption, is not necessarily true in general equilibrium. Furthermore, it suggests that the random walk of consumption and the random walk of asset prices could be intimately related phenomena. Here, both would require the same restriction on technology: $\alpha = 1$.

Finally, one might be tempted to correlate consumption and asset prices, interpreting a positive correlation as evidence in favor of the model of asset pricing advanced here. But it is clearly open to the interpretation that it is asset prices which influence consumption via the consumption function.

Given the many connections between the theory of the consumption function and the theory of asset pricing, there may well be opportunities for integrating the two.

References

Box, George E. P., and Jenkins, Gwilym M. *Time Series Analysis: Forecasting and Control.* Rev. ed. San Francisco: Holden-Day, 1976.

Box, George E. P., and Ljung, G. M. "On a Measure of Lack of Fit in Time Series Models." *Biometrika* 65, no. 2 (1978): 297–303.

Brock, William A. "An Integration of Stochastic Growth Theory and the Theory of Finance—Part I: The Growth Model." Report no. 7822, Univ. Chicago, Center Math. Studies Bus. and Econ., Dept. Econ. and Graduate School Bus., 1978.

———. "Asset Prices in a Production Economy." In *The Economics of Information and Uncertainty,* edited by John J. McCall. Chicago: Univ. Chicago Press (for Nat. Bur. Econ. Res.), in press.

Hall, Robert E. "Stochastic Implications of the Life Cycle–Permanent Income Hypothesis: Theory and Evidence." *J.P.E.* 86, no. 6 (December 1978): 971–87.

LeRoy, Stephen F. "Risk Aversion and the Martingale Property of Stock Prices." *Internat. Econ. Rev.* 14 (June 1973): 436–46.

LeRoy, Stephen F., and La Civita, C. J. "Risk Aversion and the Dispersion of Asset Prices." *J. Bus.* 92 (October 1981): 535–47.

LeRoy, Stephen F., and Porter, Richard D. "The Present-Value Relation: Tests Based on Implied Variance Bounds." *Econometrica* 49 (May 1981): 555–74.

Lucas, Robert E., Jr. "Asset Prices in an Exchange Economy." *Econometrica* 46 (November 1978): 1429–45.

Shiller, Robert J. "Do Stock Prices Move Too Much to Be Justified by Subsequent Changes in Dividends?" *A.E.R.* 71 (June 1981): 421–36.

Singleton, Kenneth J. "Expectations Models of the Term Structure and Implied Variance Bounds." *J.P.E.* 88, no. 6 (December 1980): 1159–76.

[10]
Do Stock Prices Move Too Much to be Justified by Subsequent Changes in Dividends?

By ROBERT J. SHILLER[*]

A simple model that is commonly used to interpret movements in corporate common stock price indexes asserts that real stock prices equal the present value of rationally expected or optimally forecasted future real dividends discounted by a constant real discount rate. This valuation model (or variations on it in which the real discount rate is not constant but fairly stable) is often used by economists and market analysts alike as a plausible model to describe the behavior of aggregate market indexes and is viewed as providing a reasonable story to tell when people ask what accounts for a sudden movement in stock price indexes. Such movements are then attributed to "new information" about future dividends. I will refer to this model as the "efficient markets model" although it should be recognized that this name has also been applied to other models.

It has often been claimed in popular discussions that stock price indexes seem too "volatile," that is, that the movements in stock price indexes could not realistically be attributed to any objective new information, since movements in the price indexes seem to be "too big" relative to actual subsequent events. Recently, the notion that financial asset prices are too volatile to accord with efficient markets has received some econometric support in papers by Stephen LeRoy and Richard Porter on the stock market, and by myself on the bond market.

To illustrate graphically why it seems that stock prices are too volatile, I have plotted in Figure 1 a stock price index p_t with its *ex post* rational counterpart p_t^* (data set 1).[1] The stock price index p_t is the real Standard and Poor's Composite Stock Price Index (detrended by dividing by a factor proportional to the long-run exponential growth path) and p_t^* is the present discounted value of the actual subsequent real dividends (also as a proportion of the same long-run growth factor).[2] The analogous series for a modified Dow Jones Industrial Average appear in Figure 2 (data set 2). One is struck by the smoothness and stability of the *ex post* rational price series p_t^* when compared with the actual price series. This behavior of p^* is due to the fact that the present value relation relates p^* to a long-weighted moving average of dividends (with weights corresponding to discount factors) and moving averages tend to smooth the series averaged. Moreover, while real dividends did vary over this sample period, they did not vary long enough or far enough to cause major movements in p^*. For example, while one normally thinks of the Great Depression as a time when business was bad, real dividends were substantially below their long-run exponential growth path (i.e., 10–25 percent below the

---

[*]Associate professor, University of Pennsylvania, and research associate, National Bureau of Economic Research. I am grateful to Christine Amsler for research assistance, and to her as well as Benjamin Friedman, Irwin Friend, Sanford Grossman, Stephen LeRoy, Stephen Ross, and Jeremy Siegel for helpful comments. This research was supported by the National Bureau of Economic Research as part of the Research Project on the Changing Roles of Debt and Equity in Financing U.S. Capital Formation sponsored by the American Council of Life Insurance and by the National Science Foundation under grant SOC-7907561. The views expressed here are solely my own and do not necessarily represent the views of the supporting agencies.

[1]The stock price index may look unfamiliar because it is deflated by a price index, expressed as a proportion of the long-run growth path and only January figures are shown. One might note, for example, that the stock market decline of 1929–32 looks smaller than the recent decline. In real terms, it was. The January figures also miss both the 1929 peak and 1932 trough.

[2]The price and dividend series as a proportion of the long-run growth path are defined below at the beginning of Section I. Assumptions about public knowledge or lack of knowledge of the long-run growth path are important, as shall be discussed below. The series p^* is computed subject to an assumption about dividends after 1978. See text and Figure 3 below.

FIGURE 1

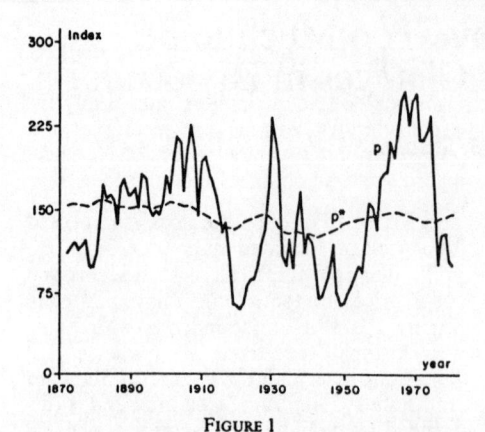

Note: Real Standard and Poor's Composite Stock Price Index (solid line p) and *ex post* rational price (dotted line p^*), 1871–1979, both detrended by dividing a long-run exponential growth factor. The variable p^* is the present value of actual subsequent real detrended dividends, subject to an assumption about the present value in 1979 of dividends thereafter. Data are from Data Set 1, Appendix.

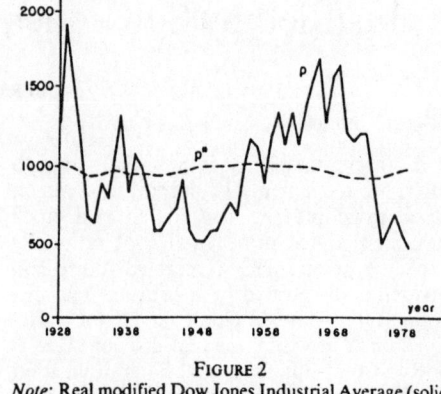

FIGURE 2

Note: Real modified Dow Jones Industrial Average (solid line p) and *ex post* rational price (dotted line p^*), 1928-1979, both detrended by dividing by a long-run exponential growth factor. The variable p^* is the present value of actual subsequent real detrended dividends, subject to an assumption about the present value in 1979 of dividends thereafter. Data are from Data Set 2, Appendix.

growth path for the Standard and Poor's series, 16–38 percent below the growth path for the Dow Series) only for a few depression years: 1933, 1934, 1935, and 1938. The moving average which determines p^* will smooth out such short-run fluctuations. Clearly the stock market decline beginning in 1929 and ending in 1932 could not be rationalized in terms of subsequent dividends! Nor could it be rationalized in terms of subsequent earnings, since earnings are relevant in this model only as indicators of later dividends. Of course, the efficient markets model does not say $p=p^*$. Might one still suppose that this kind of stock market crash was a rational mistake, a forecast error that rational people might make? This paper will explore here the notion that the very volatility of p (i.e., the tendency of big movements in p to occur again and again) implies that the answer is no.

To give an idea of the kind of volatility, comparisons that will be made here, let us consider at this point the simplest inequality which puts limits on one measure of volatility: the standard deviation of p. The efficient markets model can be described as asserting that $p_t = E(p_t^*)$, i.e., p_t is the mathematical expectation conditional on all information available at time t of p_t^*. In other words, p_t is the optimal forecast of p_t^*. One can define the forecast error as $u_t = p_t^* - p_t$. A fundamental principle of optimal forecasts is that the forecast error u_t must be uncorrelated with the forecast; that is, the covariance between p_t and u_t must be zero. If a forecast error showed a consistent correlation with the forecast itself, then that would in itself imply that the forecast could be improved. Mathematically, it can be shown from the theory of conditional expectations that u_t must be uncorrelated with p_t.

If one uses the principle from elementary statistics that the variance of the sum of two uncorrelated variables is the sum of their variances, one then has $var(p^*) = var(u) + var(p)$. Since variances cannot be negative, this means $var(p) \leq var(p^*)$ or, converting to more easily interpreted standard deviations,

(1) $\qquad \sigma(p) \leq \sigma(p^*)$

This inequality (employed before in the

papers by LeRoy and Porter and myself) is violated dramatically by the data in Figures 1 and 2 as is immediately obvious in looking at the figures.[3]

This paper will develop the efficient markets model in Section I to clarify some theoretical questions that may arise in connection with the inequality (1) and some similar inequalities will be derived that put limits on the standard deviation of the innovation in price and the standard deviation of the change in price. The model is restated in innovation form which allows better understanding of the limits on stock price volatility imposed by the model. In particular, this will enable us to see (Section II) that the standard deviation of Δp is highest when information about dividends is revealed smoothly and that if information is revealed in big lumps occasionally the price series may have higher kurtosis (fatter tails) but will have *lower* variance. The notion expressed by some that earnings rather than dividend data should be used is discussed in Section III, and a way of assessing the importance of time variation in real discount rates is shown in Section IV. The inequalities are compared with the data in Section V.

This paper takes as its starting point the approach I used earlier (1979) which showed evidence suggesting that long-term bond yields are too volatile to accord with simple expectations models of the term structure of interest rates.[4] In that paper, it was shown how restrictions implied by efficient markets on the cross-covariance function of short-term and long-term interest rates imply inequality restrictions on the spectra of the long-term interest rate series which characterize the smoothness that the long rate should display. In this paper, analogous implications are derived for the volatility of stock prices, although here a simpler and more intuitively appealing discussion of the model in terms of its innovation representation is used. This paper also has benefited from the earlier discussion by LeRoy and Porter which independently derived some restrictions on security price volatility implied by the efficient markets model and concluded that common stock prices are too volatile to accord with the model. They applied a methodology in some ways similar to that used here to study a stock price index and individual stocks in a sample period starting after World War II.

It is somewhat inaccurate to say that this paper attempts to contradict the extensive literature of efficient markets (as, for example, Paul Cootner's volume on the random character of stock prices, or Eugene Fama's survey).[5] Most of this literature really examines different properties of security prices. Very little of the efficient markets literature bears directly on the characteristic feature of the model considered here: that expected *real* returns for the aggregate stock market are constant through time (or approximately so). Much of the literature on efficient markets concerns the investigation of nominal "profit opportunities" (variously defined) and whether transactions costs prohibit their exploitation. Of course, if real stock prices are "too volatile" as it is defined here, then there may well be a sort of real profit opportunity. Time variation in expected real interest rates does not itself imply that any

---

[3]Some people will object to this derivation of (1) and say that one might as well have said that $E_t(p_t) = p_t^*$, i.e., that forecasts are correct "on average," which would lead to a reversal of the inequality (1). This objection stems, however, from a misinterpretation of conditional expectations. The subscript t on the expectations operator E means "taking as given (i.e., nonrandom) all variables known at time t." Clearly, p_t is known at time t and p_t^* is not. In practical terms, if a forecaster gives as his forecast anything other than $E_t(p_t^*)$, then high forecast is not optimal in the sense of expected squared forecast error. If he gives a forecast which equals $E_t(p_t^*)$ only on average, then he is adding random noise to the optimal forecast. The amount of noise apparent in Figures 1 or 2 is extraordinary. Imagine what we would think of our local weather forecaster if, say, actual local temperatures followed the dotted line and his forecasts followed the solid line!

[4]This analysis was extended to yields on preferred stocks by Christine Amsler.

[5]It should not be inferred that the literature on efficient markets uniformly supports the notion of efficiency put forth there, for example, that no assets are dominated or that no trading rule dominates a buy and hold strategy, (for recent papers see S. Basu; Franco Modigliani and Richard Cohn; William Brainard, John Shoven and Lawrence Weiss; and the papers in the symposium on market efficiency edited by Michael Jensen).

trading rule dominates a buy and hold strategy, but really large variations in expected returns might seem to suggest that such a trading rule exists. This paper does not investigate this, or whether transactions costs prohibit its exploitation. This paper is concerned, however, instead with a more interesting (from an economic standpoint) question: what accounts for movements in real stock prices and can they be explained by new information about subsequent real dividends? If the model fails due to excessive volatility, then we will have seen a new characterization of how the simple model fails. The characterization is not equivalent to other characterizations of its failure, such as that one-period holding returns are forecastable, or that stocks have not been good inflation hedges recently.

The volatility comparisons that will be made here have the advantage that they are insensitive to misalignment of price and dividend series, as may happen with earlier data when collection procedures were not ideal. The tests are also not affected by the practice, in the construction of stock price and dividend indexes, of dropping certain stocks from the sample occasionally and replacing them with other stocks, so long as the volatility of the series is not misstated. These comparisons are thus well suited to existing long-term data in stock price averages. The robustness that the volatility comparisons have, coupled with their simplicity, may account for their popularity in casual discourse.

I. The Simple Efficient Markets Model

According to the simple efficient markets model, the real price P_t of a share at the beginning of the time period t is given by

$$(2) \quad P_t = \sum_{k=0}^{\infty} \gamma^{k+1} E_t D_{t+k} \qquad 0 < \gamma < 1$$

where D_t is the real dividend paid at (let us say, the end of) time t, E_t denotes mathematical expectation conditional on information available at time t, and γ is the constant real discount factor. I define the constant real interest rate r so that $\gamma = 1/(1+r)$. Information at time t includes P_t and D_t and their lagged values, and will generally include other variables as well.

The one-period holding return $H_t \equiv (\Delta P_{t+1} + D_t)/P_t$ is the return from buying the stock at time t and selling it at time $t+1$. The first term in the numerator is the capital gain, the second term is the dividend received at the end of time t. They are divided by P_t to provide a rate of return. The model (2) has the property that $E_t(H_t) = r$.

The model (2) can be restated in terms of series as a proportion of the long-run growth factor: $p_t = P_t/\lambda^{t-T}$, $d_t = D_t/\lambda^{t+1-T}$ where the growth factor is $\lambda^{t-T} = (1+g)^{t-T}$, g is the rate of growth, and T is the base year. Dividing (2) by λ^{t-T} and substituting one finds[6]

$$(3) \quad p_t = \sum_{k=0}^{\infty} (\lambda\gamma)^{k+1} E_t d_{t+k}$$

$$= \sum_{k=0}^{\infty} \bar{\gamma}^{k+1} E_t d_{t+k}$$

The growth rate g must be less than the discount rate r if (2) is to give a finite price, and hence $\bar{\gamma} \equiv \lambda\gamma < 1$, and defining $\bar{r}$ by $\bar{\gamma} \equiv 1/(1+\bar{r})$, the discount rate appropriate for the p_t and d_t series is $\bar{r} > 0$. This discount rate $\bar{r}$ is, it turns out, just the mean dividend divided by the mean price, i.e, $\bar{r} = E(d)/E(p)$.[7]

---

[6] No assumptions are introduced in going from (2) to (3), since (3) is just an algebraic transformation of (2). I shall, however, introduce the assumption that d_t is jointly stationary with information, which means that the (unconditional) covariance between d_t and z_{t-k}, where z_t is any information variable (which might be d_t itself or p_t), depends only on k, not t. It follows that we can write expressions like $var(p)$ without a time subscript. In contrast, a realization of the random variable the conditional expectation $E_t(d_{t+k})$ is a function of time since it depends on information at time t. Some stationarity assumption is necessary if we are to proceed with any statistical analysis.

[7] Taking unconditional expectations of both sides of (3) we find

$$E(p) = \frac{\bar{\gamma}}{1-\bar{\gamma}} E(d)$$

using $\bar{\gamma} = 1/1 + \bar{r}$ and solving we find $\bar{r} = E(d)/E(p)$.

Index

FIGURE 3

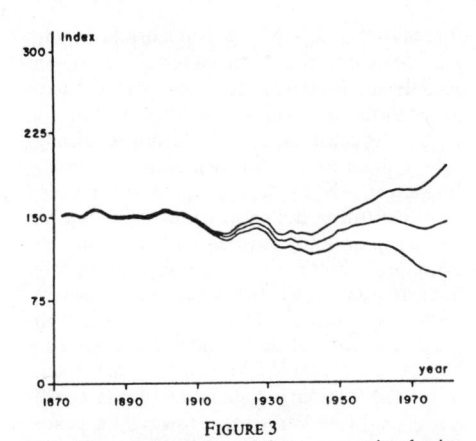

Note: Alternative measures of the *ex post* rational price p^*, obtained by alternative assumptions about the present value in 1979 of dividends thereafter. The middle curve is the p^* series plotted in Figure 1. The series are computed recursively from terminal conditions using dividend series d of Data Set 1.

We may also write the model as noted above in terms of the *ex post* rational price series p_t^* (analogous to the *ex post* rational interest rate series that Jeremy Siegel and I used to study the Fisher effect, or that I used to study the expectations theory of the term structure). That is, p_t^* is the present value of actual subsequent dividends:

(4) $$p_t = E_t(p_t^*)$$

where $$p_t^* = \sum_{k=0}^{\infty} \bar{\gamma}^{k+1} d_{t+k}$$

Since the summation extends to infinity, we never observe p_t^* without some error. However, with a long enough dividend series we may observe an approximate p_t^*. If we choose an arbitrary value for the terminal value of p_t^* (in Figures 1 and 2, p^* for 1979 was set at the average detrended real price over the sample) then we may determine p_t^* recursively by $p_t^* = \bar{\gamma}(p_{t+1}^* + d_t)$ working backward from the terminal date. As we move back from the terminal date, the importance of the terminal value chosen declines. In data set (1) as shown in Figure 1, $\bar{\gamma}$ is .954 and $\bar{\gamma}^{108} = .0063$ so that at the beginning of the sample the terminal value chosen has a negligible weight in the determination of p_t^*. If we had chosen a different terminal condi-

TABLE 1—DEFINITIONS OF PRINCIPAL SYMBOLS

γ = real discount factor for series before detrending; $\gamma = 1/(1+r)$
$\bar{\gamma}$ = real discount factor for detrended series; $\bar{\gamma} \equiv \lambda\gamma$
D_t = real dividend accruing to stock index (before detrending)
d_t = real detrended dividend; $d_t \equiv D_t/\lambda^{t+1-T}$
Δ = first difference operator $\Delta x_t \equiv x_t - x_{t-1}$
δ_t = innovation operator; $\delta_t x_{t+k} \equiv E_t x_{t+k} - E_{t-1} x_{t+k}$; $\delta x \equiv \delta_t x_t$
E = unconditional mathematical expectations operator. $E(x)$ is the true (population) mean of x.
E_t = mathematical expectations operator conditional on information at time t; $E_t x_t \equiv E(x_t | I_t)$ where I_t is the vector of information variables known at time t.
λ = trend factor for price and dividend series; $\lambda \equiv 1 + g$ where g is the long-run growth rate of price and dividends.
P_t = real stock price index (before detrending)
p_t = real detrended stock price index; $p_t = P_t/\lambda^{t-T}$
p_t^* = *ex post* rational stock price index (expression 4)
r = one-period real discount rate for series before detrending
$\bar{r}$ = real discount rate for detrended series; $\bar{r} = (1-\bar{\gamma})/\bar{\gamma}$
$\bar{r}_2$ = two-period real discount rate for detrended series; $\bar{r}_2 = (1+\bar{r})^2 - 1$
t = time (year)
T = base year for detrending and for wholesale price index; $p_T = P_T$ = nominal stock price index at time T

tion, the result would be to add or subtract an exponential trend from the p^* shown in Figure 1. This is shown graphically in Figure 3, in which p^* is shown computed from alternative terminal values. Since the only thing we need know to compute p^* about dividends after 1978 is p^* for 1979, it does not matter whether dividends are "smooth" or not after 1978. Thus, Figure 3 represents our uncertainty about p^*.

There is yet another way to write the model, which will be useful in the analysis which follows. For this purpose, it is convenient to adopt notation for the innovation in a variable. Let us define the innovation operator $\delta_t \equiv E_t - E_{t-1}$ where E_t is the conditional expectations operator. Then for any variable X_t the term $\delta_t X_{t+k}$ equals $E_t X_{t+k} - E_{t-1} X_{t+k}$ which is the change in the conditional expectation of X_{t+k} that is made in response to new information arriving between $t-1$ and t. The time subscript t may be dropped so that δX_k denotes $\delta_t X_{t+k}$ and

δX denotes δX_0 or $\delta_t X_t$. Since conditional expectations operators satisfy $E_j E_k = E_{min(j,k)}$ it follows that $E_{t-m} \delta_t X_{t+k} = E_{t-m} (E_t X_{t+k} - E_{t-1} X_{t+k}) = E_{t-m} X_{t+k} - E_{t-m} X_{t+k} = 0$, $m \geq 0$. This means that $\delta_t X_{t+k}$ must be uncorrelated for all k with all information known at time $t-1$ and must, since lagged innovations are information at time t, be uncorrelated with $\delta_{t'} X_{t+j}$, $t' < t$, all j, i.e., innovations in variables are serially uncorrelated.

The model implies that the innovation in price $\delta_t p_t$ is observable. Since (3) can be written $p_t = \bar{\gamma}(d_t + E_t p_{t+1})$, we know, solving, that $E_t p_{t+1} = p_t / \bar{\gamma} - d_t$. Hence $\delta_t p_t \equiv E_t p_t - E_{t-1} p_t = p_t + d_{t-1} - p_{t-1}/\bar{\gamma} = \Delta p_t + d_{t-1} - \bar{r} p_{t-1}$. The variable which we call $\delta_t p_t$ (or just δp) is the variable which Clive Granger and Paul Samuelson emphasized should, in contrast to $\Delta p_t \equiv p_t - p_{t-1}$, by efficient markets, be unforecastable. In practice, with our data, $\delta_t p_t$ so measured will approximately equal Δp_t.

The model also implies that the innovation in price is related to the innovations in dividends by

$$(5) \qquad \delta_t p_t = \sum_{k=0}^{\infty} \bar{\gamma}^{k+1} \delta_t d_{t+k}$$

This expression is identical to (3) except that δ_t replaces E_t. Unfortunately, while $\delta_t p_t$ is observable in this model, the $\delta_t d_{t+k}$ terms are not directly observable, that is, we do not know when the public gets information about a particular dividend. Thus, in deriving inequalities below, one is obliged to assume the "worst possible" pattern of information accrual.

Expressions (2)–(5) constitute four different representations of the same efficient markets model. Expressions (4) and (5) are particularly useful for deriving our inequalities on measures of volatility. We have already used (4) to derive the limit (1) on the standard deviation of p given the standard deviation of p^*, and we will use (5) to derive a limit on the standard deviation of δp given the standard deviation of d.

One issue that relates to the derivation of (1) can now be clarified. The inequality (1) was derived using the assumption that the forecast error $u_t = p_t^* - p_t$ is uncorrelated with p_t. However, the forecast error u_t is not serially uncorrelated. It is uncorrelated with all information known at time t, but the lagged forecast error u_{t-1} is not known at time t since p_{t-1}^* is not discovered at time t. In fact, $u_t = \sum_{k=1}^{\infty} \bar{\gamma}^k \delta_{t+k} p_{t+k}$, as can be seen by substituting the expressions for p_t and p_t^* from (3) and (4) into $u_t = p_t^* - p_t$, and rearranging. Since the series $\delta_t p_t$ is serially uncorrelated, u_t has first-order autoregressive serial correlation.[8] For this reason, it is inappropriate to test the model by regressing $p_t^* - p_t$ on variables known at time t and using the ordinary t-statistics of the coefficients of these variables. However, a generalized least squares transformation of the variables would yield an appropriate regression test. We might thus regress the transformed variable $u_t - \bar{\gamma} u_{t+1}$ on variables known at time t. Since $u_t - \bar{\gamma} u_{t+1} = \bar{\gamma} \delta_{t+1} p_{t+1}$, this amounts to testing whether the innovation in price can be forecasted. I will perform and discuss such regression tests in Section V below.

To find a limit on the standard deviation of δp for a given standard deviation of d_t, first note that d_t equals its unconditional expectation plus the sum of its innovations:

$$(6) \qquad d_t = E(d) + \sum_{k=0}^{\infty} \delta_{t-k} d_t$$

If we regard $E(d)$ as $E_{-\infty}(d_t)$, then this expression is just a tautology. It tells us, though, that d_t, $t = 0, 1, 2, \ldots$ are just different linear combinations of the same innovations in dividends that enter into the linear combination in (5) which determine $\delta_t p_t$, $t = 0, 1, 2, \ldots$. We can thus ask how large $var(\delta p)$ might be for given $var(d)$. Since innovations are serially uncorrelated, we know from (6) that the variance of the sum is

---

[8]It follows that $var(u) = var(\delta p)/(1 - \bar{\gamma}^2)$ as LeRoy and Porter noted. They base their volatility tests on our inequality (1) (which they call theorem 2) and an equality restriction $\sigma^2(p) + \sigma^2(\delta p)/(1 - \bar{\gamma}^2) = \sigma^2(p^*)$ (their theorem 3). They found that, with postwar Standard and Poor earnings data, both relations were violated by sample statistics.

the sum of the variances:

(7) $$var(d) = \sum_{k=0}^{\infty} var(\delta d_k) = \sum_{k=0}^{\infty} \sigma_k^2$$

Our assumption of stationarity for d_t implies that $var(\delta_{t-k}d_t) \equiv var(\delta d_k) \equiv \sigma_k^2$ is independent of t.

In expression (5) we have no information that the variance of the sum is the sum of the variances since all the innovations are time t innovations, which may be correlated. In fact, for given $\sigma_0^2, \sigma_1^2, \ldots$, the maximum variance of the sum in (5) occurs when the elements in the sum are perfectly positively correlated. This means then that so long as $var(\delta d) \neq 0$, $\delta_t d_{t+k} = a_k \delta_t d_t$, where $a_k = \sigma_k/\sigma_0$. Substituting this into (6) implies

(8) $$\hat{d}_t = \sum_{k=0}^{\infty} a_k \varepsilon_{t-k}$$

where a hat denotes a variable minus its mean: $\hat{d}_t \equiv d_t - E(d)$ and $\varepsilon_t \equiv \delta_t d_t$. Thus, if $var(\delta p)$ is to be maximized for given $\sigma_0^2, \sigma_1^2, \ldots$, the dividend process must be a moving average process in terms of its own innovations.[9] I have thus shown, rather than assumed, that if the variance of δp is to be maximized, the forecast of d_{t+k} will have the usual ARIMA form as in the forecast popularized by Box and Jenkins.

We can now find the maximum possible variance for δp for given variance of d. Since the innovations in (5) are perfectly positively correlated, $var(\delta p) = (\sum_{k=0}^{\infty} \bar{\gamma}^{k+1} \sigma_k)^2$. To maximize this subject to the constraint $var(d) = \sum_{k=0}^{\infty} \sigma_k^2$ with respect to $\sigma_0, \sigma_1, \ldots$, one may set up the Lagrangean:

(9) $$L = \left(\sum_{k=0}^{\infty} \bar{\gamma}^{k+1} \sigma_k \right)^2 + \nu \left(var(d) - \sum_{k=0}^{\infty} \sigma_k^2 \right)$$

[9] Of course, all indeterministic stationary processes can be given linear moving average representations, as Hermann Wold showed. However, it does not follow that the process can be given a moving average representation in terms of its own innovations. The true process may be generated nonlinearly or other information besides its own lagged values may be used in forecasting. These will generally result in a less than perfect correlation of the terms in (5).

where ν is the Lagrangean multiplier. The first-order conditions for $\sigma_j, j = 0, \ldots \infty$ are

(10) $$\frac{\partial L}{\partial \sigma_j} = 2 \left(\sum_{k=0}^{\infty} \bar{\gamma}^{k+1} \sigma_k \right) \bar{\gamma}^{j+1} - 2\nu \sigma_j = 0$$

which in turn means that σ_j is proportional to $\bar{\gamma}^j$. The second-order conditions for a maximum are satisfied, and the maximum can be viewed as a tangency of an isoquant for $var(\delta p)$, which is a hyperplane in $\sigma_0, \sigma_1, \sigma_2, \ldots$ space, with the hypersphere represented by the constraint. At the maximum $\sigma_k^2 = (1 - \bar{\gamma}^2) var(d) \bar{\gamma}^{2k}$ and $var(\delta p) = \bar{\gamma}^2 var(d)/(1 - \bar{\gamma}^2)$ and so, converting to standard deviations for ease of interpretation, we have

(11) $$\sigma(\delta p) \leq \sigma(d)/\sqrt{\bar{r}_2}$$

where $\bar{r}_2 = (1 + \bar{r})^2 - 1$

Here, $\bar{r}_2$ is the two-period interest rate, which is roughly twice the one-period rate. The maximum occurs, then, when d_t is a first-order autoregressive process, $\hat{d}_t = \bar{\gamma} \hat{d}_{t-1} + \varepsilon_t$, and $E_t \hat{d}_{t+k} = \bar{\gamma}^k \hat{d}_t$, where $\hat{d} \equiv d - E(d)$ as before.

The variance of the innovation in price is thus maximized when information about dividends is revealed in a smooth fashion so that the standard deviation of the new information at time t about a future dividend d_{t+k} is proportional to its weight in the present value formula in the model (5). In contrast, suppose all dividends somehow became known years before they were paid. Then the innovations in dividends would be so heavily discounted in (5) that they would contribute little to the standard deviation of the innovation in price. Alternatively, suppose nothing were known about dividends until the year they are paid. Here, although the innovation would not be heavily discounted in (5), the impact of the innovation would be confined to only one term in (5), and the standard deviation in the innovation in price would be limited to the standard deviation in the single dividend.

Other inequalities analogous to (11) can also be derived in the same way. For example, we can put an upper bound to the standard deviation of the change in price (rather than the innovation in price) for given standard deviation in dividend. The only difference induced in the above procedure is that Δp_t is a different linear combination of innovations in dividends. Using the fact that $\Delta p_t = \delta_t p_t + \bar{r} p_{t-1} - d_{t-1}$ we find

$$(12) \quad \Delta p_t = \sum_{k=0}^{\infty} \bar{\gamma}^{k+1} \delta_t d_{t+k}$$

$$+ \bar{r} \sum_{j=1}^{\infty} \delta_{t-j} \sum_{k=0}^{\infty} \bar{\gamma}^{k+1} d_{t+k-1} - \sum_{j=1}^{\infty} \delta_{t-j} d_{t-1}$$

As above, the maximization of the variance of δp for given variance of d requires that the time t innovations in d be perfectly correlated (innovations at different times are necessarily uncorrelated) so that again the dividend process must be forecasted as an ARIMA process. However, the parameters of the ARIMA process for d which maximize the variance of Δp will be different. One finds, after maximizing the Lagrangean expression (analogous to (9)) an inequality slightly different from (11),

$$(13) \quad \sigma(\Delta p) \leq \sigma(d)/\sqrt{2\bar{r}}$$

The upper bound is attained if the optimal dividend forecast is first-order autoregressive, but with an autoregressive coefficient slightly different from that which induced the upper bound to (11). The upper bound to (13) is attained if $\hat{d}_t = (1-\bar{r})\hat{d}_{t-1} + \varepsilon_t$ and $E_t d_{t+k} = (1-\bar{r})^k \hat{d}_t$, where, as before, $\hat{d}_t \equiv d_t - E(d)$.

II. High Kurtosis and Infrequent Important Breaks in Information

It has been repeatedly noted that stock price change distributions show high kurtosis or "fat tails." This means that, if one looks at a time-series of observations on δp or Δp, one sees long stretches of time when their (absolute) values are all rather small and then an occasional extremely large (absolute) value. This phenomenon is commonly attributed to a tendency for new information to come in big lumps infrequently. There seems to be a common presumption that this information lumping might cause stock price changes to have high or infinite variance, which would seem to contradict the conclusion in the preceding section that the variance of price is limited and is maximized if forecasts have a simple autoregressive structure.

High sample kurtosis does not indicate infinite variance if we do not assume, as did Fama (1965) and others, that price changes are drawn from the stable Paretian class of distributions.[10] The model does not suggest that price changes have a distribution in this class. The model instead suggests that the existence of moments for the price series is implied by the existence of moments for the dividends series.

As long as d is jointly stationary with information and has a finite variance, then p, p^*, δp, and Δp will be stationary and have a finite variance.[11] If d is normally distributed, however, it does not follow that the price variables will be normally distributed. In fact, they may yet show high kurtosis.

To see this possibility, suppose the dividends are serially independent and identically normally distributed. The kurtosis of the price series is defined by $K = E(\hat{p})^4 / (E(\hat{p})^2)^2$, where $p \equiv \hat{p} - E(p)$. Suppose, as an example, that with a probability of $1/n$

---

[10] The empirical fact about the unconditional distribution of stock price changes in not that they have infinite variance (which can never be demonstrated with any finite sample), but that they have high kurtosis in the sample.

[11] With any stationary process X_t, the existence of a finite $var(X_t)$ implies, by Schwartz's inequality, a finite value of $cov(X_t, X_{t+k})$ for any k, and hence the entire autocovariance function of X_t, and the spectrum, exists. Moreover, the variance of $E_t(X_t)$ must also be finite, since the variance of X equals the variance of $E_t(X_t)$ plus the variance of the forecast error. While we may regard real dividends as having finite variance, innovations in dividends may show high kurtosis. The residuals in a second-order autoregression for d_t have a studentized range of 6.29 for the Standard and Poor series and 5.37 for the Dow series. According to the David-Hartley-Pearson test, normality can be rejected at the 5 percent level (but not at the 1 percent level) with a one-tailed test for both data sets.

the public is told d_t at the beginning of time t, but with probability $(n-1)/n$ has no information about current or future dividends.[12] In time periods when they are told d_t, $\hat{p}_t$ equals $\bar{\gamma}d_t$, otherwise $\hat{p}_t = 0$. Then $E(\hat{p}_t^4) = E((\bar{\gamma}d_t)^4)/n$ and $E(\hat{p}_t^2) = E((\bar{\gamma}d_t)^2)/n$ so that kurtosis equals $nE(\bar{\gamma}d_t)^4)/E((\bar{\gamma}d_t)^2)$ which equals n times the kurtosis of the normal distribution. Hence, by choosing n high enough one can achieve an arbitrarily high kurtosis, and yet the variance of price will always exist. Moreover, the distribution of $\hat{p}_t$ conditional on the information that the dividend has been revealed is also normal, in spite of high kurtosis of the unconditional distribution.

If information is revealed in big lumps occasionally (so as to induce high kurtosis as suggested in the above example) $var(\delta p)$ or $var(\Delta p)$ are not especially large. The variance loses more from the long interval of time when information is not revealed than it gains from the infrequent events when it is. The highest possible variance for given variance of d indeed comes when information is revealed smoothly as noted in the previous section. In the above example, where information about dividends is revealed one time in n, $\sigma(\delta p) = \bar{\gamma}n^{1/2}\sigma(d)$ and $\sigma(\Delta p) = \bar{\gamma}(2/n)^{1/2}\sigma(d)$. The values of $\sigma(\delta p)$ and $\sigma(\Delta p)$ implied by this example are for all n strictly below the upper bounds of the inequalities (11) and (13).[13]

III. Dividends or Earnings?

It has been argued that the model (2) does not capture what is generally meant by efficient markets, and that the model should be replaced by a model which makes price the present value of expected earnings rather than dividends. In the model (2) earnings

[12] For simplicity, in this example, the assumption elsewhere in this article that d_t is always known at time t has been dropped. It follows that in this example $\delta_t p_t \neq \Delta p_t + d_{t-1} - rp_{t-1}$ but instead $\delta_t p_t = p_t$.

[13] For another illustrative example, consider $\hat{d}_t = \bar{\gamma}\hat{d}_{t-1} + \epsilon_t$ as with the upper bound for the inequality (11) but where the dividends are announced for the next n years every $1/n$ years. Here, even though $\hat{d}_t$ has the autoregressive structure, ϵ_t is not the innovation in d_t. As n goes to infinity, $\sigma(\delta p)$ approaches zero.

may be relevant to the pricing of shares but only insofar as earnings are indicators of future dividends. Earnings are thus no different from any other economic variable which may indicate future dividends. The model (2) is consistent with the usual notion in finance that individuals are concerned with returns, that is, capital gains plus dividends. The model implies that expected total returns are constant and that the capital gains component of returns is just a reflection of information about future dividends. Earnings, in contrast, are statistics conceived by accountants which are supposed to provide an indicator of how well a company is doing, and there is a great deal of latitude for the definition of earnings, as the recent literature on inflation accounting will attest.

There is no reason why price per share ought to be the present value of expected earnings per share if some earnings are retained. In fact, as Merton Miller and Franco Modigliani argued, such a present value formula would entail a fundamental sort of double counting. It is incorrect to include in the present value formula both earnings at time t and the later earnings that accrue when time t earnings are reinvested.[14] Miller and Modigliani showed a formula by which price might be regarded as the present value of earnings corrected for investments, but that formula can be shown, using an accounting identity to be identical to (2).

Some people seem to feel that one cannot claim price as present value of expected dividends since firms routinely pay out only a fraction of earnings and also attempt somewhat to stabilize dividends. They are right in the case where firms paid out no dividends, for then the price p_t would have to grow at the discount rate $\bar{r}$, and the model (2) would not be the solution to the difference equation implied by the condition $E_t(H_t) = r$. On the other hand, if firms pay out a fraction of dividends or smooth short-run fluctuations in dividends, then the price of the firm will grow at a rate less than the

[14] LeRoy and Porter do assume price as present value of earnings but employ a correction to the price and earnings series which is, under additional theoretical assumptions not employed by Miller and Modigliani, a correction for the double counting.

discount rate and (2) is the solution to the difference equation.[15] With our Standard and Poor data, the growth rate of real price is only about 1.5 percent, while the discount rate is about $4.8\% + 1.5\% = 6.3\%$. At these rates, the value of the firm a few decades hence is so heavily discounted relative to its size that it contributes very little to the value of the stock today; by far the most of the value comes from the intervening dividends. Hence (2) and the implied p^* ought to be useful characterizations of the value of the firm.

The crucial thing to recognize in this context is that once we know the terminal price and intervening dividends, we have specified all that investors care about. It would not make sense to define an *ex post* rational price from a terminal condition on price, using the same formula with earnings in place of dividends.

IV. Time-Varying Real Discount Rates

If we modify the model (2) to allow real discount rates to vary without restriction through time, then the model becomes untestable. We do not observe real discount rates directly. Regardless of the behavior of P_t and D_t, there will always be a discount rate series which makes (2) hold identically. We might ask, though, whether the movements in the real discount rate that would be required aren't larger than we might have expected. Or is it possible that small movements in the current one-period discount rate coupled with new information about such movements in future discount rates could account for high stock price volatility?[16]

---

[15]To understand this point, it helps to consider a traditional continuous time growth model, so instead of (2) we have $P_0 = \int_0^\infty D_t e^{-rt} dt$. In such a model, a firm has a constant earnings stream I. If it pays out all earnings, then $D = I$ and $P_0 = \int_0^\infty I e^{-rt} dt = I/r$. If it pays out only s of its earnings, then the firm grows at rate $(1-s)r$, $D_t = sIe^{(1-s)rt}$ which is less than I at $t=0$, but higher than I later on. Then $P_0 = \int_0^\infty sIe^{(1-s)rt} e^{-rt} dt = \int_0^\infty sI e^{-srt} dt = sI/(rs)$. If $s \neq 0$ (so that we're not dividing by zero) $P_0 = I/r$.

[16]James Pesando has discussed the analogous question: how large must the variance in liquidity premia be in order to justify the volatility of long-term interest rates?

The natural extension of (2) to the case of time varying real discount rates is

$$(14) \quad P_t = E_t \left(\sum_{k=0}^{\infty} D_{t+k} \prod_{j=0}^{k} \frac{1}{1+r_{t+j}} \right)$$

which has the property that $E_t((1+H_t)/(1+r_t)) = 1$. If we set $1 + r_t = (\partial U/\partial C_t)/(\partial U/\partial C_{t+1})$, i.e., to the marginal rate of substitution between present and future consumption where U is the additively separable utility of consumption, then this property is the first-order condition for a maximum of expected utility subject to a stock market budget constraint, and equation (14) is consistent with such expected utility maximization at all times. Note that while r_t is a sort of *ex post* real interest rate not necessarily known until time $t+1$, only the conditional distribution at time t or earlier influences price in the formula (14).

As before, we can rewrite the model in terms of detrended series:

$$(15) \quad p_t = E_t(p_t^*)$$

where
$$p_t^* \equiv \sum_{k=0}^{\infty} d_{t+k} \prod_{j=0}^{k} \frac{1}{1+\bar{r}_{t+j}}$$

$$1 + \bar{r}_{t+j} \equiv (1+r_t)/\lambda$$

This model then implies that $\sigma(p_t) \leq \sigma(p_t^*)$ as before. Since the model is nonlinear, however, it does not allow us to derive inequalities like (11) or (13). On the other hand, if movements in real interest rates are not too large, then we can use the linearization of p_t^* (i.e., Taylor expansion truncated after the linear term) around $d = E(d)$ and $\bar{r} = E(\bar{r})$; i.e.,

$$(16) \quad \hat{p}_t^* \approx \sum_{k=0}^{\infty} \bar{\gamma}^{k+1} \hat{d}_{t+k} - \frac{E(d)}{E(\bar{r})} \sum_{k=0}^{\infty} \bar{\gamma}^{k+1} \hat{\bar{r}}_{t+k}$$

where $\bar{\gamma} = 1/(1 + E(\bar{r}))$, and a hat over a variable denotes the variable minus its mean. The first term in the above expression is just the expression for p_t^* in (4) (demeaned). The second term represents the effect on p_t^* of movements in real discount rates. This second term is identical to the expression for p^* in (4) except that d_{t+k} is replaced by $\bar{r}_{t+k}$ and the expression is premultiplied by $-E(d)/E(\bar{r})$.

It is possible to offer a simple intuitive interpretation for this linearization. First note that the derivative of $1/(1+\bar{r}_{t+k})$, with respect to $\bar{r}$ evaluated at $E(\bar{r})$ is $-\bar{\gamma}^2$. Thus, a one percentage point increase in $\bar{r}_{t+k}$ causes $1/(1+\bar{r}_{t+k})$ to drop by $\bar{\gamma}^2$ times 1 percent, or slightly less than 1 percent. Note that all terms in (15) dated $t+k$ or higher are premultiplied by $1/(1+\bar{r}_{t+k})$. Thus, if $\bar{r}_{t+k}$ is increased by one percentage point, all else constant, then all of these terms will be reduced by about $\bar{\gamma}^2$ times 1 percent. We can approximate the sum of all these terms as $\bar{\gamma}^{k-1}E(d)/E(\bar{r})$, where $E(d)/E(\bar{r})$ is the value at the beginning of time $t+k$ of a constant dividend stream $E(d)$ discounted by $E(\bar{r})$, and $\bar{\gamma}^{k-1}$ discounts it to the present. So, we see that a one percentage point increase in $\bar{r}_{t+k}$, all else constant, decreases p_t^* by about $\bar{\gamma}^{k+1}E(d)/E(\bar{r})$, which corresponds to the kth term in expression (16). There are two sources of inaccuracy with this linearization. First, the present value of all future dividends starting with time $t+k$ is not exactly $\bar{\gamma}^{k-1}E(d)/E(\bar{r})$. Second, increasing $\bar{r}_{t+k}$ by one percentage point does not cause $1/(1+\bar{r}_{t+k})$ to fall by exactly $\bar{\gamma}^2$ times 1 percent. To some extent, however, these errors in the effects on p_t^* of $\bar{r}_t, \bar{r}_{t+1}, \bar{r}_{t+2}, \ldots$ should average out, and one can use (16) to get an idea of the effects of changes in discount rates.

To give an impression as to the accuracy of the linearization (16), I computed p_t^* for data set 2 in two ways: first using (15) and then using (16), with the same terminal condition p_{1979}^*. In place of the unobserved $\bar{r}_t$ series, I used the actual four–six-month prime commercial paper rate plus a constant to give it the mean $\bar{r}$ of Table 2. The commercial paper rate is a *nominal* interest rate, and thus one would expect its fluctuations represent changes in inflationary expectations as well as real interest rate movements. I chose it nonetheless, rather arbitrarily, as a series which shows much more fluctuation than one would normally expect to see in an expected *real* rate. The commercial paper rate ranges, in this sample, from 0.53 to 9.87 percent. It stayed below 1 percent for over a decade (1935–46) and, at the end of the sample, stayed generally well above 5 percent for over a decade. In spite of this erratic behavior, the correlation coefficient between p^* computed from (15) and p^* computed from (16) was .996, and $\sigma(p_t^*)$ was 250.5 and 268.0 by (15) and (16), respectively. Thus the linearization (16) can be quite accurate. Note also that while these large movements in $\bar{r}_t$ cause p_t^* to move much more than was observed in Figure 2, $\sigma(p^*)$ is still less than half of $\sigma(p)$. This suggests that the variability $\bar{r}_t$ that is needed to save the efficient

TABLE 2—SAMPLE STATISTICS FOR PRICE AND DIVIDEND SERIES

		Data Set 1: Standard and Poor's	Data Set 2: Modified Dow Industrial
	Sample Period:	1871–1979	1928–1979
1)	$E(p)$	145.5	982.6
	$E(d)$	6.989	44.76
2)	$\bar{r}$	.0480	0.456
	$\bar{r}_2$	.0984	.0932
3)	$b = \ln\lambda$	.0148	.0188
	$\hat{\sigma}(b)$	(.0011)	(1.0035)
4)	$cor(p, p^*)$	.3918	.1626
	$\sigma(d)$	1.481	9.828
Elements of Inequalities:			
Inequality (1)			
5)	$\sigma(p)$	50.12	355.9
6)	$\sigma(p^*)$	8.968	26.80
Inequality (11)			
7)	$\sigma(\Delta p + d_{-1} - \bar{r}p_{-1})$	25.57	242.1
	$min(\sigma)$	23.01	209.0
8)	$\sigma(d)/\sqrt{\bar{r}_2}$	4.721	32.20
Inequality (13)			
9)	$\sigma(\Delta p)$	25.24	239.5
	$min(\sigma)$	22.71	206.4
10)	$\sigma(d)/\sqrt{2\bar{r}}$	4.777	32.56

Note: In this table, E denotes sample mean, σ denotes standard deviation and $\hat{\sigma}$ denotes standard error. $Min(\sigma)$ is the lower bound on σ computed as a one-sided χ^2 95 percent confidence interval. The symbols p, d, $\bar{r}$, $\bar{r}_2$, b, and p^* are defined in the text. Data sets are described in the Appendix. Inequality (1) in the text asserts that the standard deviation in row 5 should be less than or equal to that in row 6, inequality (11) that σ in row 7 should be less than or equal to that in row 8, and inequality (13) that σ in row 9 should be less than that in row 10.

markets model is much larger yet, as we shall see.

To put a formal lower bound on $\sigma(\bar{r})$ given the variability of Δp, note that (16) makes $\hat{p}_t^*$ the present value of $z_t, z_{t+1}, \ldots$ where $z_t \equiv \hat{d}_t - \hat{r}_t E(d)/E(\bar{r})$. We thus know from (13) that $2E(\bar{r})var(\Delta p) \le var(z)$. Moreover, from the definition of z we know that $var(z) \le var(d) + 2\sigma(d)\sigma(\bar{r})E(d)/E(\bar{r}) + var(\bar{r})E(d)^2/E(\bar{r})^2$ where the equality holds if d_t and $\bar{r}_t$ are perfectly negatively correlated. Combining these two inequalities and solving for $\sigma(\bar{r})$ one finds

(17)
$$\sigma(\bar{r}) \ge \left(\sqrt{2E(\bar{r})}\,\sigma(\Delta p) - \sigma(d)\right)E(\bar{r})/E(d)$$

This inequality puts a lower bound on $\sigma(\bar{r})$ proportional to the discrepancy between the left-hand side and right-hand side of the inequality (13).[17] It will be used to examine the data in the next section.

V. Empirical Evidence

The elements of the inequalities (1), (11), and (13) are displayed for the two data sets (described in the Appendix) in Table 2. In both data sets, the long-run exponential growth path was estimated by regressing $ln(P_t)$ on a constant and time. Then λ in (3) was set equal to e^b where b is the coefficient of time (Table 2). The discount rate $\bar{r}$ used to compute p^* from (4) is estimated as the average d divided by the average p.[18] The terminal value of p^* is taken as average p.

With data set 1, the nominal price and dividend series are the real Standard and Poor's Composite Stock Price Index and the associated dividend series. The earlier observations for this series are due to Alfred Cowles who said that the index is

> intended to represent, ignoring the elements of brokerage charges and taxes, what would have happened to an investor's funds if he had bought, at the beginning of 1871, all stocks quoted on the New York Stock Exchange, allocating his purchases among the individual stocks in proportion to their total monetary value and each month up to 1937 had by the same criterion redistributed his holdings among all quoted stocks. [p. 2]

In updating his series, Standard and Poor later restricted the sample to 500 stocks, but the series continues to be value weighted. The advantage to this series is its comprehensiveness. The disadvantage is that the dividends accruing to the portfolio at one point of time may not correspond to the dividends forecasted by holders of the Standard and Poor's portfolio at an earlier time, due to the change in weighting of the stocks. There is no way to correct this disadvantage without losing comprehensiveness. The original portfolio of 1871 is bound to become a relatively smaller and smaller sample of U.S. common stocks as time goes on.

With data set 2, the nominal series are a modified Dow Jones Industrial Average and associated dividend series. With this data set, the advantages and disadvantages of data set 1 are reversed. My modifications in the Dow Jones Industrial Average assure that this series reflects the performance of a single unchanging portfolio. The disadvantage is that the performance of only 30 stocks is recorded.

Table 2 reveals that all inequalities are dramatically violated by the sample statistics for both data sets. The left-hand side of the inequality is always at least five times as great as the right-hand side, and as much as thirteen times as great.

The violation of the inequalities implies that "innovations" in price as we measure them can be forecasted. In fact, if we regress $\delta_{t+1}p_{t+1}$ onto (a constant and) p_t, we get significant results: a coefficient of p_t of $-.1521$ ($t=-3.218$, $R^2=.0890$) for data set 1 and a coefficient of $-.2421$ ($t=-2.631$, $R^2=.1238$) for data set 2. These results are

---

[17] In deriving the inequality (13) it was assumed that d_t was known at time t, so by analogy this inequality would be based on the assumption that r_t is known at time t. However, without this assumption the same inequality could be derived anyway. The maximum contribution of $\bar{r}_t$ to the variance of ΔP occurs when $\bar{r}_t$ is known at time t.

[18] This is not equivalent to the average dividend price ratio, which was slightly higher (.0514 for data set 1, .0484 for data set 2).

not due to the representation of the data as a proportion of the long-run growth path. In fact, if the holding period return H_t is regressed on a constant and the dividend price ratio D_t/P_t, we get results that are only slightly less significant: a coefficient of 3.533 ($t=2.672$, $R^2=.0631$) for data set 1 and a coefficient of 4.491 ($t=1.795$, $R^2=.0617$) for data set 2.

These regression tests, while technically valid, may not be as generally useful for appraising the validity of the model as are the simple volatility comparisons. First, as noted above, the regression tests are not insensitive to data misalignment. Such low R^2 might be the result of dividend or commodity price index data errors. Second, although the model is rejected in these very long samples, the tests may not be powerful if we confined ourselves to shorter samples, for which the data are more accurate, as do most researchers in finance, while volatility comparisons may be much more revealing. To see this, consider a stylized world in which (for the sake of argument) the dividend series d_t is absolutely constant while the price series behaves as in our data set. Since the actual dividend series is fairly smooth, our stylized world is not too remote from our own. If dividends d_t are absolutely constant, however, it should be obvious to the most casual and unsophisticated observer by volatility arguments like those made here that the efficient markets model must be wrong. Price movements cannot reflect new information about dividends if dividends never change. Yet regressions like those run above will have limited power to reject the model. If the alternative hypothesis is, say, that $\hat{p}_t = \rho \hat{p}_{t-1} + \varepsilon_t$, where ρ is close to but less than one, then the power of the test in short samples will be very low. In this stylized world we are testing for the stationarity of the p_t series, for which, as we know, power is low in short samples.[19] For example, if post-war data from, say, 1950–65 were chosen (a period often used in recent financial markets studies) when the stock market was drifting up, then clearly the regression tests will not reject. Even in periods showing a reversal of upward drift the rejection may not be significant.

Using inequality (17), we can compute how big the standard deviation of real discount rates would have to be to possibly account for the discrepancy $\sigma(\Delta p) - \sigma(d)/(2\bar{r})^{1/2}$ between Table 2 results (rows 9 and 10) and the inequality (13). Assuming Table 2 $\bar{r}$ (row 2) equals $E(\bar{r})$ and that sample variances equal population variances, we find that the standard deviation of $\bar{r}_t$ would have to be at least 4.36 percentage points for data set 1 and 7.36 percentage points for data set 2. These are very large numbers. If we take, as a normal range for $\bar{r}_t$ implied by these figures, a ±2 standard deviation range around the real interest rate $\bar{r}$ given in Table 2, then the real interest rate $\bar{r}_t$ would have to range from −3.91 to 13.52 percent for data set 1 and −8.16 to 17.27 percent for data set 2! And these ranges reflect lowest possible standard deviations which are consistent with the model only if the real rate has the first-order autoregressive structure and perfect negative correlation with dividends!

These estimated standard deviations of *ex ante* real interest rates are roughly consistent with the results of the simple regressions noted above. In a regression of H_t on D_t/P_t and a constant, the standard deviation of the fitted value of H_t is 4.42 and 5.71 percent for data sets 1 and 2, respectively. These large standard deviations are consistent with the low R^2 because the standard deviation of H_t is so much higher (17.60 and 23.00 percent, respectively). The regressions of $\delta_t p_t$ on p_t suggest higher standard deviations of expected real interest rates. The standard deviation of the fitted value divided by the average detrended price is 5.24 and 8.67 percent for data sets 1 and 2, respectively.

VI. Summary and Conclusions

We have seen that measures of stock price volatility over the past century appear to be far too high—five to thirteen times too

---

[19]If dividends are constant (let us say $d_t=0$) then a test of the model by a regression of $\delta_{t+1} p_{t+1}$ on p_t amounts to a regression of p_{t+1} on p_t with the null hypothesis that the coefficient of p_t is $(1+\bar{r})$. This appears to be an explosive model for which *t*-statistics are not valid yet our true model, which in effect assumes $\sigma(d) \neq 0$, is nonexplosive.

high—to be attributed to new information about future real dividends if uncertainty about future dividends is measured by the sample standard deviations of real dividends around their long-run exponential growth path. The lower bound of a 95 percent one-sided χ^2 confidence interval for the standard deviation of annual changes in real stock prices is over five times higher than the upper bound allowed by our measure of the observed variability of real dividends. The failure of the efficient markets model is thus so dramatic that it would seem impossible to attribute the failure to such things as data errors, price index problems, or changes in tax laws.

One way of saving the general notion of efficient markets would be to attribute the movements in stock prices to changes in expected real interest rates. Since expected real interest rates are not directly observed, such a theory can not be evaluated statistically unless some other indicator of real rates is found. I have shown, however, that the movements in expected real interest rates that would justify the variability in stock prices are very large—much larger than the movements in nominal interest rates over the sample period.

Another way of saving the general notion of efficient markets is to say that our measure of the uncertainty regarding future dividends—the sample standard deviation of the movements of real dividends around their long-run exponential growth path—understates the true uncertainty about future dividends. Perhaps the market was rightfully fearful of much larger movements than actually materialized. One is led to doubt this, if after a century of observations nothing happened which could remotely justify the stock price movements. The movements in real dividends the market feared must have been many times larger than those observed in the Great Depression of the 1930's, as was noted above. Since the market did not know in advance with certainty the growth path and distribution of dividends that was ultimately observed, however, one cannot be sure that they were wrong to consider possible major events which did not occur. Such an explanation of the volatility of stock prices, however, is "academic," in that it relies fundamentally on unobservables and cannot be evaluated statistically.

APPENDIX

A. *Data Set 1: Standard and Poor Series*

Annual 1871–1979. The price series P_t is Standard and Poor's Monthly Composite Stock Price index for January divided by the Bureau of Labor Statistics wholesale price index (January *WPI* starting in 1900, annual average *WPI* before 1900 scaled to 1.00 in the base year 1979). Standard and Poor's Monthly Composite Stock Price index is a continuation of the Cowles Commission Common Stock index developed by Alfred Cowles and Associates and currently is based on 500 stocks.

The Dividend Series D_t is total dividends for the calendar year accruing to the portfolio represented by the stocks in the index divided by the average wholesale price index for the year (annual average *WPI* scaled to 1.00 in the base year 1979). Starting in 1926 these total dividends are the series "Dividends per share...12 months moving total adjusted to index" from Standard and Poor's statistical service. For 1871 to 1925, total dividends are Cowles series Da-1 multiplied by .1264 to correct for change in base year.

B. *Data Set 2: Modified Dow Jones Industrial Average*

Annual 1928–1979. Here P_t and D_t refer to real price and dividends of the portfolio of 30 stocks comprising the sample for the Dow Jones Industrial Average when it was created in 1928. Dow Jones averages before 1928 exist, but the 30 industrials series was begun in that year. The published Dow Jones Industrial Average, however, is not ideal in that stocks are dropped and replaced and in that the weighting given an individual stock is affected by splits. Of the original 30 stocks, only 17 were still included in the Dow Jones Industrial Average at the end of our sample. The published Dow Jones Industrial Average is the simple sum of the price per share of the 30 companies divided by a divisor which changes through time. Thus, if a stock splits two for one, then Dow Jones continues to include only one share but changes the divisor to prevent a sudden drop in the Dow Jones average.

To produce the series used in this paper, the *Capital Changes Reporter* was used to trace changes in the companies from 1928 to 1979. Of the original 30 companies of the Dow Jones Industrial Average, at the end of our sample (1979), 9 had the identical names, 12 had changed only their names, and 9 had been acquired, merged or consolidated. For these latter 9, the price and dividend series are continued as the price and dividend of the shares exchanged by the acquiring corporation. In only one case was a cash payment, along with shares of the acquiring corporation, exchanged for the shares of the acquired corporation. In this case, the price and dividend series were continued as the price and dividend of the shares exchanged by the acquiring corporation. In four cases, preferred shares of the acquiring corporation were among shares exchanged. Common shares of equal value were substituted for these in our series. The number of shares of each firm included in the total is determined by the splits, and effective splits effected by stock dividends and merger. The price series is the value of all these shares on the last trading day of the preceding year, as shown on the Wharton School's Rodney White Center Common Stock tape. The dividend series is the total for the year of dividends and the cash value of other distributions for all these shares. The price and dividend series were deflated using the same wholesale price indexes as in data set 1.

REFERENCES

C. Amsler, "An American Consol: A Reexamination of the Expectations Theory of the Term Structure of Interest Rates," unpublished manuscript, Michigan State Univ. 1980.

S. Basu, "The Investment Performance of Common Stocks in Relation to their Price-Earnings Ratios: A Test of the Efficient Markets Hypothesis," *J. Finance*, June 1977, *32*, 663–82.

G. E. P. Box and G. M. Jenkins, *Time Series Analysis for Forecasting and Control*, San Francisco: Holden-Day 1970.

W. C. Brainard, J. B. Shoven, and L. Weiss, "The Financial Valuation of the Return to Capital," *Brookings Papers*, Washington 1980, *2*, 453–502.

Paul H. Cootner, *The Random Character of Stock Market Prices*, Cambridge: MIT Press 1964.

Alfred Cowles and Associates, *Common Stock Indexes, 1871–1937*, Cowles Commission for Research in Economics, Monograph No. 3, Bloomington: Principia Press 1938.

E. F. Fama, "Efficient Capital Markets: A Review of Theory and Empirical Work," *J. Finance*, May 1970, *25*, 383–420.

_____, "The Behavior of Stock Market Prices," *J. Bus., Univ. Chicago*, Jan. 1965, *38*, 34–105.

C. W. J. Granger, "Some Consequences of the Valuation Model when Expectations are Taken to be Optimum Forecasts," *J. Finance*, Mar. 1975, *30*, 135–45.

M. C. Jensen et al., "Symposium on Some Anomalous Evidence Regarding Market Efficiency," *J. Financ. Econ.*, June/Sept. 1978, *6*, 93–330.

S. LeRoy and R. Porter, "The Present Value Relation: Tests Based on Implied Variance Bounds," *Econometrica*, forthcoming.

M. H. Miller and F. Modigliani, "Dividend Policy, Growth and the Valuation of Shares," *J. Bus., Univ. Chicago*, Oct. 1961, *34*, 411–33.

F. Modigliani and R. Cohn, "Inflation, Rational Valuation and the Market," *Financ. Anal. J.*, Mar./Apr. 1979, *35*, 24–44.

J. Pesando, "Time Varying Term Premiums and the Volatility of Long-Term Interest Rates," unpublished paper, Univ. Toronto, July 1979.

P. A. Samuelson, "Proof that Properly Discounted Present Values of Assets Vibrate Randomly," in Hiroaki Nagatani and Kate Crowley, eds., *Collected Scientific Papers of Paul A. Samuelson*, Vol. IV, Cambridge: MIT Press 1977.

R. J. Shiller, "The Volatility of Long-Term Interest Rates and Expectations Models of the Term Structure," *J. Polit. Econ.*, Dec. 1979, *87*, 1190–219.

_____ and J. J. Siegel, "The Gibson Paradox and Historical Movements in Real Interest Rates," *J. Polit. Econ.*, Oct. 1979, *85*, 891–907.

H. Wold, "On Prediction in Stationary Time Series," *Annals Math. Statist.* 1948, *19*, 558–67.

Commerce Clearing House, *Capital Changes Reporter*, New Jersey 1977.

Dow Jones & Co., *The Dow Jones Averages 1855–1970*, New York: Dow Jones Books 1972.

Standard and Poor's *Security Price Index Record*, New York 1978.

[11]

Econometrica, Vol. 56, No. 1 (January, 1988), 37-61

DIVIDEND INNOVATIONS AND STOCK PRICE VOLATILITY

By Kenneth D. West[1]

A standard efficient markets model states that a stock price equals the expected present discounted value of its dividends, with a constant discount rate. This is shown to imply that the variance of the innovation in the stock price is smaller than that of a stock price forecast made from a subset of the market's information set. The implication follows even if prices and dividends require differencing to induce stationarity. The relation between the variances appears not to hold for some annual U.S. stock market data. The rejection of the model is both quantitatively and statistically significant.

KEYWORDS: Volatility test, efficient markets, stock price, nonstationary, random walk.

1. INTRODUCTION

THE SOURCES OF FLUCTUATIONS in stock prices have long been argued. Some observers have suggested that a major part of the fluctuations results from self fulfilling rumors about potential price fluctuations. In a famous passage, Keynes, for example, described the stock market as a certain type of beauty contest in which judges try to guess the winner of the contest: speculators devote their "intelligence to anticipating what average opinion expects average opinion to be" (1964, p. 136). An examination of practically any modern finance text (e.g., Brealey and Myers (1981)) indicates that the economics profession tends to hold the opposite view. Stock price fluctuations are argued to result solely from changes in the expected present discounted value of dividends.

The subject has received increased attention in recent years because of the volatility tests of Leroy and Porter (1981) and, especially, Shiller (1981a). These tests seem to indicate that stock price fluctuations are too large to result solely from changes in the expected present discounted value (PDV) of dividends. There is, however, some question as to the validity of this conclusion. Marsh and Merton (1986) have objected to the tests' assumption that dividends are stationary around a time trend; Flavin (1983) and Kleidon (1985, 1986) have argued that in small samples the tests are biased toward finding excess volatility.

This paper develops and applies a stock market volatility test that is not subject to these criticisms. The test is based on an inequality on the variance of the innovation in the expected PDV of a given stock's dividend stream, and was first suggested by Blanchard and Watson (1982).[2] The inequality states that if discount rates are constant this variance is smaller when expectations are conditional on

---

[1] I thank A. Blinder, J. Campbell, G. Chow, S. Fischer, R. Flood, L. P. Hansen, W. Newey, J. Rotemberg, R. Trevor, J. Taylor, the referees, and an editor of this journal for helpful comments, and the National Science Foundation for financial support. Responsibility for remaining errors is my own. This paper was revised while I was a National Fellow at the Hoover Institution. An earlier version of this paper was circulated under the title "Speculative Bubbles and Stock Price Volatility."

[2] While Blanchard and Watson (1982) do suggest examining the inequality that is the focus of this paper, they do not formally establish the validity of the inequality, consider possible nonstationarity of dividends or prices, or test the inequality rigorously. Subsequent to the initial circulation of this paper, however, M. Watson sent me a proof of this inequality that is valid when prices and dividends are stationary.

the market's information set than when expectations are conditional on a smaller information set. It may be shown that this implies that the variance of the innovation in a stock price is bounded above by a certain function of the variance of the innovation in the corresponding dividend.

The paper checks whether the bound is satisfied by some long term annual data on the Standard and Poor 500 and the Dow Jones indices. It is not. The estimated variance of the stock price innovation is about four to twenty times its theoretical upper bound. The violation of the inequality is in all cases highly statistically significant.

It is to be emphasized that the inequality is valid even when prices and dividends are an integrated ARIMA process with infinite variances, and that the empirical work allows for such nonstationarity. In addition, the test procedure does not require calculation of a perfect foresight price; this price appears to be central to the small sample biases that are argued by Flavin (1983), Kleidon (1985, 1986), and Marsh and Merton (1986) to plague the Shiller (1981a) volatility test. The paper nonetheless performs some small Monte Carlo experiments to check whether under certain simple circumstances small sample bias in this paper's test procedure is likely to explain the results of the test. The answer is no.

While one of the purposes of this paper is to apply a volatility test with a relatively weak set of maintained statistical assumptions, that is not its only aim. It also considers the consistency of some of the test's maintained economic assumptions with the data, to help determine which among these should be relaxed, so that the excess price volatility might be explained. To that end, the paper uses a battery of formal diagnostic tests on the regressions that must be estimated to calculate the inequality. The test results are in general quite consistent with the test's maintained hypotheses of rational expectations and, perhaps surprisingly, of a constant rate for discounting future dividends. Some additional, less formal analysis, which considers further the constant discount rate hypothesis, does not suggest that the excessive price variability results solely from variation in discount rates.

The evidence, then, does not suggest that the excess volatility is caused by a simple failure of the rational expectations or constant discount rate assumptions. This suggests the possibility that the volatility is due either to rational bubbles (e.g., Blanchard and Watson (1982)) or nearly rational "fads" (e.g., Summers (1986)), whose profit opportunities (if any) are difficult to detect. The paper does not, however, attempt to make a case for bubbles, fads or, for that matter, any other factor, as the explanation of the excess volatility. Instead what is emphasized are two empirical regularities that seem to characterize the data studied here. The first is that prices appear to be too variable to be set as the expected PDV of dividends, with a constant discount rate; this holds even if prices and dividends are nonstationary. The second is that it is difficult to attribute the excess variability to variations in discount rates. Reconciliation of these two points is a task left for future research.

Before turning to the details of the subject at hand, two final introductory remarks seem worth making. The first is that the inequality established here may be of general interest in that it could be used to test other infinite horizon present value models. Possible examples include testing whether consumption is too variable to be consistent with the permanent income hypothesis (see Deaton (1985), West (1988)) or whether exchange rates are too variable to be consistent with a standard monetary model (West (1986a)). That the inequality is valid even in a nonstationary environment makes it particularly appealing in these and perhaps other contexts. The second remark concerns the estimation technique. This is in part an application of West's (1986b) result that it is not always necessary to difference regressions on nonstationary variables, to obtain asymptotically normal parameter estimates. The key requirement is that the nonstationary variables have a drift. Since this is plausible for not only stock prices but for many other macroeconomic variables as well, the estimation technique applied in this paper may be of general interest.

The plan of the paper is as follows. Section 2 establishes the basic inequality. Section 3 explains how the inequality may be used to test a rational expectations, constant discount rate stock price model. Section 4 presents formal econometric results. Section 5 considers informally whether small sample bias or discount rate variation are likely to explain the Section 4 results. Section 6 has conclusions. The Appendix has some econometric and algebraic details.

2. THE BASIC INEQUALITY

The following proposition is the basis of this paper.

PROPOSITION 1. *Let I_t be the linear space spanned by the current and past values of a finite number of random variables, with I_t a subset of I_{t+1} for all t. It is assumed that after s differences, all random variables in I_t jointly follow a covariance stationary ARMA (q, r) process, for some finite s, q, $r \geq 0$. This s'th difference is assumed without loss of generality to have zero mean. All variables are assumed to be identically zero for $t \leq q$.*

Let d_t be one of these variables. Let H_t be a subset of I_t consisting of the space spanned by current and past values of some subset of the variables in I_t, including at a minimum current and past values of d_t. Let b be a positive constant, $0 \leq b < 1$. Let $P(\cdot|\cdot)$ denote linear projections, calculated for $s > 0$ as in Hansen and Sargent (1980). Let

$$x_{tI} = \lim_{k \to \infty} P\left(\sum_0^k b^j d_{t+j} \bigg| I_t \right), \qquad x_{tH} = \lim_{k \to \infty} P\left(\sum_0^k b^j d_{t+j} \bigg| H_t \right).$$

(All summations in this section run over j.) Let E denote mathematical expectations. Then

(1) $\qquad E[x_{tH} - P(x_{tH}|H_{t-1})]^2 \geq E[x_{tI} - P(x_{tI}|I_{t-1})]^2.$

PROOF:[3] Since d_t is in I_t,

(2) $\quad x_{tI} = d_t + bP\left(\sum_0^\infty b^j d_{t+j+1} \big| I_t\right)$

$\qquad = d_t + bx_{t+1,I} - be_{t+1},$

$\quad e_{t+1} = x_{t+1,I} - P\left(\sum_0^\infty b^j d_{t+j+1} \big| I_t\right) = x_{t+1,I} - P(x_{t+1,I} | I_t).$

Equation (2) may be rewritten as

$\qquad x_{tI} - d_t = bx_{t+1,I} - be_{t+1}.$

Recursive substitution for $x_{t+1,I}$, then for $x_{t+2,I}$, etc., yields

(3) $\quad x_{tI} - \sum_0^{k-1} b^j d_{t+j} = b^k x_{t+k,I} - \sum_1^k b^j e_{t+j}.$

The assumptions of the proposition insure that as $k \to \infty$, $b^k x_{t+k,I} \to 0$ in mean square. Consider first the ARIMA $(q, s, 0)$ case. The formulas in Hansen and Sargent (1980) state that x_{tI} is a finite distributed lag on the variables in I_t. Since these variables started up at a finite date in the past, and some arithmetic difference of each variable has a finite variance, the rate of growth of the variance of each variable, and therefore of the variance of x_{tI} as well, is some power of t. Since $\lim_{k\to\infty} b^{2k}(t+k)^n = 0$ for any fixed $n \geq 0$, $\lim_{k\to\infty} \mathrm{var}(b^k x_{t+k,I}) = 0$. The argument for the ARIMA (q, s, r) case is implied by Hansen and Sargent (1980) since for $j > r$, $P(d_{t+j} | I_t)$ is determined by a difference equation that depends only on s and the autoregressive parameters.

The assumptions of the proposition also guarantee that e_t has constant, finite variance and is serially uncorrelated. For the ARIMA $(q, s, 0)$ case, this follows directly from inspection of the formula for x_{tI} in Hansen and Sargent (1980). Once again, this argument immediately extends to the ARIMA (q, s, r) case. Therefore, $\sum_1^\infty b^j e_{t+j}$ exists, in the sense that $\lim_{k\to\infty} E(\sum_1^k b^j e_{t+j} - \sum_1^\infty b^j e_{t+j})^2 = 0$, $\mathrm{var}(\sum_1^\infty b^j e_{t+j}) = b^2(1-b^2)^{-1} Ee_t^2$ (Fuller (1976, p. 36)). Equation (3) therefore implies

(4) $\quad x_{tI} - \sum_0^\infty b^j d_{t+j} = -\sum_1^\infty b^j e_{t+j}.$

By a similar argument, involving projections onto H_t,

(5) $\quad x_{tH} - \sum_0^\infty b^j d_{t+j} = -\sum_1^\infty b^j f_{t+j},$

$\quad f_{t+j} = x_{t+j,H} - P(x_{t+j,H} | H_{t+j-1}), \quad \mathrm{var}\left(-\sum_1^\infty b^j f_{t+j}\right) = b^2(1-b^2)^{-1} Ef_t^2.$

---

[3] J. Campbell suggested the basic idea of this proof. L. P. Hansen and M. Watson have provided alternative proofs. S. Leroy has pointed out to me that a similar proposition is implied in the stationary case in Leroy and Porter (1981, p. 568). My own, rather tedious, proof may be found in an earlier version of this paper (West (1984)).

DIVIDEND INNOVATIONS

Now,

(6) $\quad \operatorname{var}\left(-\sum_1^\infty b^j f_{t+j}\right) = \operatorname{var}\left(x_{tH} - \sum_0^\infty b^j d_{t+j}\right)$

$\qquad = \operatorname{var}\left(x_{tH} - x_{tI} + x_{tI} - \sum_0^\infty b^j d_{t+j}\right)$

$\qquad = \operatorname{var}\left(x_{tH} - x_{tI} - \sum_1^\infty b^j e_{t+j}\right)$

$\qquad = \operatorname{var}\left(x_{tH} - x_{tI}\right) + \operatorname{var}\left(-\sum_1^\infty b^j e_{t+j}\right)$

$\qquad \geq \operatorname{var}\left(-\sum_1^\infty b^j e_{t+j}\right).$

The last equality follows since for $j \geq 1$, e_{t+j} is uncorrelated with anything in I_t, including, in particular, $x_{tH} - x_{tI}$. It follows from (6) that $b^2(1-b^2)^{-1} E f_t^2 \geq b^2(1-b^2)^{-1} E e_t^2 \Rightarrow E e_t^2 \geq E f_t^2$, i.e., $E[x_{tH} - P(x_{tH}|H_{t-1})]^2 \geq E[x_{tI} - P(x_{tI}|I_{t-1})]^2$.

Q.E.D.

A verbal restatement of Proposition 1 is as follows. Suppose we are forecasting the present discounted value of d_t, by calculating x_{tI} and x_{tH}. Each period as new data become available we revise our forecast. $E(x_{tI} - P(x_{tI}|I_{t-1}))^2$ and $E(x_{tH} - P(x_{tH}|H_{t-1}))^2$ are measures of the average size of this period to period revision. Proposition 1 says that with less information the size of the revision tends to be larger. That is, when less information is used, the variance of the innovation in the expected present discounted value of d_t is larger.

It is worth making four comments on the conditions under which (1) is valid. First, if the random variables in I_t are stationary without differencing, Proposition (1) does not require that the variables follow a finite parameter ARMA (q, r) process. The ARIMA assumption is maintained because to my knowledge infinite horizon prediction for nonstationary variables has been developed only for ARIMA processes. Second, (1) may not extend immediately if logarithms or logarithmic differences are required to induce stationarity in d_t, even if linear projections are replaced with mathematical expectations. If, for example, $\log(d_t) = \log(d_{t-1}) + \varepsilon_t$, $\varepsilon_t \sim N(0, \sigma^2)$, and H_t is the information set generated by past d_t, it may be shown that $[x_{tH} - E(x_{tH}|H_{t-1})]^2$ is proportional to d_{t-1}^2. Third, the inequality need not hold for a finite horizon. That is, it need not hold if we consider the variance of the innovation in the expected PDV of $\sum_0^n b^j d_{t+j}$ instead of $\sum_0^\infty b^j d_{t+j}$. An example is given in footnote 4 of West (1986c). The reason is that terms of the form $b^{n+1} x_{t+n+1,I}$ and $b^{n+1} x_{t+n+i,H}$ are present. See equation (3). Fourth, (1) does not hold for arbitrary subsets of I_t. If, for example, H_t were the empty set, x_{tI} would also be the empty set, and the left-hand side of (1) would be identically zero.

Before developing the implications of (1) for stock price volatility, it may be helpful to work through a simple example. Suppose I_t consists of lags of d_t and of one other variable, z_t. Let H_t consist simply of lags of d_t. Let the bivariate (d_t, z_t) representation be

(7) $\begin{bmatrix} d_t \\ z_t \end{bmatrix} = \begin{bmatrix} \phi & 1 \\ 0 & 0 \end{bmatrix} \begin{bmatrix} d_{t-1} \\ z_{t-1} \end{bmatrix} + \begin{bmatrix} \varepsilon_{1t} \\ \varepsilon_{2t} \end{bmatrix}$

with $|\phi| \leq 1$, ε_{1t} and ε_{2t} i.i.d., $E\varepsilon_{1t}\varepsilon_{2s} = 0$ for all t, s. Let $E\varepsilon_{1t}^2 = \sigma_1^2$, $E\varepsilon_{2t}^2 = \sigma_2^2$. The univariate representation of d_t clearly is $d_t = \phi d_{t-1} + v_t$, $v_t = \varepsilon_{1t} + z_{t-1} = \varepsilon_{1t} + \varepsilon_{2t-1}$, $Ev_t^2 = \sigma_1^2 + \sigma_2^2$. Let us calculate both sides of (1).

(8) $P(d_{t+j}|H_t) = \phi^j d_t$

$\Rightarrow x_{tH} = P\left(\sum_0^\infty b^j d_{t+j} \bigg| H_t\right) = (1-b\phi)^{-1} d_t$

$\Rightarrow E[x_{tH} - P(x_{tH}|H_{t-1})]^2 = E[(1-b\phi)^{-1}v_t]^2 = (1-b\phi)^{-2}(\sigma_1^2 + \sigma_2^2)$.

$P(d_t|I_t) = d_t$.

$P(d_{t+j}|I_t) = \phi^j d_t + \phi^{j-1} z_t, \quad j > 0,$

$\Rightarrow x_{tI} = P\left(\sum_0^\infty b^j d_{t+j}\bigg|I_t\right) = (1-b\phi)^{-1}(d_t + bz_t)$

$\Rightarrow E[x_{tI} - P(x_{tI}|I_{t-1})]^2 = E[(1-b\phi)^{-1}(\varepsilon_{1t} + bz_t)]^2$

$\qquad = (1-b\phi)^{-2}(\sigma_1^2 + b^2\sigma_2^2)$.

Since $b^2 < 1$, $\sigma_1^2 + \sigma_2^2 > \sigma_1^2 + b^2\sigma_2^2$, so (1) holds. Observe that (1) holds even when $\phi = 1$ so that d_t is nonstationary.

3. THE MODEL

According to a standard efficient markets model, a stock price is determined by the relationship (9) (Brealey and Myers (1981, pp. 42–45)):

(9) $p_t = bE[(p_{t+1} + d_{t+1})|I_t]$,

where p_t is the real stock price at the end of period t, b the constant ex-ante real discount rate, $0 < b = 1/(1+r) < 1$, r the constant expected return, E denotes mathematical expectations, d_{t+1} the real dividend paid to the owner of the stock in period $t+1$, and I_t the information set common to traders in period t. I_t is assumed to contain, at a minimum, current and past dividends, and, in general, other variables that are useful in forecasting dividends.

Equation (9) may be solved recursively forward to get

(10) $p_t = \sum_1^n b^j E(d_{t+j}|I_t) + b^n E(p_{t+n}|I_t)$.

DIVIDEND INNOVATIONS

If the transversality condition

(11) $\lim_{n\to\infty} b^n E(p_{t+n}|I_t) = 0$

holds, then

(12) $p_t = \sum_{1}^{\infty} b^j E(d_{t+j}|I_t).$

It will be assumed that in forecasts of $\sum_{1}^{\infty} b^j d_{t+j}$ from I_{t-k}, for any $k \geq 0$, mathematical expectations conditional on the market's information set are the same as linear projections. So x_{tI}, defined in Proposition 1 as the linear projection of $\sum_{0}^{\infty} b^j d_{t+j}$ onto a period t set of random variables equals $E(\sum_{0}^{\infty} b^j d_{t+j}|I_t)$. Similarly, the linear projection of x_{tI} onto the market's period $t-1$ set of random variables equals $E(x_{tI}|I_{t-1})$.

Proposition 1 is used to test the model (12) as follows. Since $x_{tI} = E(\sum_{0}^{\infty} b^j d_{t+j}|I_t)$, (12) implies that $x_{tI} = p_t + d_t$. So $E[x_{tI} - E(x_{tI}|I_{t-1})]^2 = E[p_t + d_t - E(p_t + d_t|I_{t-1})]^2$, and, therefore,

(13) $E[x_{tH} - P(x_{tH}|H_{t-1})]^2 \geq E[p_t + d_t - E(p_t + d_t|I_{t-1})]^2.$

The intuitive reason that the model (12) implies (13) is as follows. $E(x_{tH} - P(x_{tH}|H_{t-1}))^2$ is by definition a measure of the average size of the innovation in the expected present discounted value (PDV) of dividends, when expectations are conditional on H_t. According to (12), price adjusts unexpectedly only in response to news about dividends. $E[p_t + d_t - E(p_t + d_t|I_{t-1})]^2$ is a measure of the average size of the innovation in the expected PDV of dividends, with expectations conditional on the market's information set I_t. Since the market is presumed to use the variables in I_t to forecast optimally, the market's forecasts tend to be more precise, i.e., (13) holds.[4]

To make (13) operational, both sides of it must be calculated. Consider first $E[p_t + d_t - E(p_t + d_t|I_{t-1})]^2$. A consistent estimate of this is easily obtained by estimating (9) with the instrumental variables method of McCallum (1976) and Hansen and Singleton (1982). Rewrite (9) as

(14) $p_t = b(p_{t+1} + d_{t+1}) - b[p_{t+1} + d_{t+1} - E(p_{t+1} + d_{t+1}|I_t)]$

$= b(p_{t+1} + d_{t+1}) + u_{t+1},$

$\sigma_u^2 = b^2 E[p_t + d_t - E(p_t + d_t|I_{t-1})]^2.$

Equation (14) can be estimated by instrumental variables, using as instruments variables known at time t. An estimate of $E[p_t + d_t - E(p_t + d_t|I_{t-1})]^2$ is then obtainable as $\hat{b}^{-2}\hat{\sigma}_u^2$.

---

[4] Note that inequality (13) holds even for the class of dividend and price processes studied by Marsh and Merton (1986), as long as arithmetic differences suffice to induce stationarity. This is because the March and Merton (1984) model implies that $H_t = I_t$. When $H_t = I_t$, inequality (13) holds trivially, as a strict equality. See the discussion in West (1984).

Estimation of $E[x_{tH} - P(x_{tH}|H_{t-1})]^2$ is slightly more involved. It requires first of all specification of H_t. The simplest possible one is $H_t = \{1, d_{t-j}|j \geq 0\}$, and H_t defined this way is what is used in this paper's empirical work.[5] Choices of H_t that include lags of additional variables might produce sharper results, but would also entail more complex calculations. With $H_t = \{1, d_{t-j}|j \geq 0\}$, $E[x_{tH} - P(x_{tH}|H_{t-1})]^2$ can be calculated as a function of d_t's univariate ARIMA parameters. Suppose $d_t \sim \text{ARIMA}(q, s, 0)$,

$$(15) \quad \Delta^s d_{t+1} = \mu + \phi_1 \Delta^s d_t + \cdots + \phi_q \Delta^s d_{t-q+1} + v_{t+1},$$

where $\Delta^s = (1-L)^s$, L the lag operator. (A moving average component to d_t is assumed absent for notational and computational simplicity.) Then $x_{tH} = P(\sum b^j d_{t+j}|H_t) = m + \sum_1^{q+s} \delta_i d_{t-i+1}$. The δ_i are complicated functions of b and the ϕ_i. Hansen and Sargent (1980) provide explicit formulas for the δ_i. In particular, given b and the ARIMA parameters of d_t, one can use the Hansen and Sargent (1980) formula for δ_1 to calculate $\delta_1^2 \sigma_v^2 = E[x_{tH} - E(x_{tH}|H_{t-1})]^2$. To test the null hypothesis that prices are determined according to (12), then we calculate

$$(16) \quad \delta_1^2 \sigma_v^2 - b^{-2} \sigma_u^2$$

and test $H_0: \delta_1^2 \sigma_v^2 - b^{-2} \sigma_u^2 \geq 0$. If the estimate of (16) is negative (that is, the implications of (12) for the innovation variances are not borne out by the data), a convenient way to quantify the extent of the failure of the model (12) is to calculate

$$(17) \quad -100(\delta_1^2 \sigma_v^2 - b^{-2} \sigma_u^2)/(b^{-2} \sigma_u^2).$$

When (16) is negative, (17) yields a number between 0 and 100. I will refer to this somewhat loosely as the percentage of the variance of the innovation in p_t that is excessive. This is of course somewhat imprecise in that $b^{-2} \sigma_u^2$ is the variance of the innovation in the *sum* of dividends and prices. But given that price innovations are much larger than dividend innovations (see the empirical results below), this terminology does not seem misleading.[6]

What alternatives might explain a rejection of the null hypothesis that (16) is positive? Three have figured prominently in discussions of related work: gross expectational irrationality, of the sort that systematically leads to profit opportunities (e.g., Ackley (1983)); variation in discount rates (e.g., Leroy (1984)); and rational or nearly rational bubbles or fads (e.g., Blanchard and Watson (1982), Summers (1986)), whose profit opportunities (if any) are very difficult to detect. In light of some empirical evidence yet to be presented, it is of interest to note that diagnostic tests on the estimates of (14) and (15) can help to distinguish between bubbles and fads on the one hand, and gross expectational irrationality

---

[5] Proposition 1 assumed that variables had zero mean. If not, H_t and I_t must be expanded to include suitable deterministic terms. In the annual data used here, a constant is the only relevant such term.

[6] In fact, in some empirical work the variable that is here called d_{t+1} is assumed known at time t and thus has an innovation of zero when forecast at time t (Shiller (1981a), Leroy and Porter (1981)).

DIVIDEND INNOVATIONS

and time varying discount rates on the other, as possible explanations of any excess price volatility. Technically, when rational bubbles are absent (i.e., the transversality condition (11) holds), equation (14) and the dividend equation (15) together imply that (16) is positive. But when rational bubbles are present, (14) and (15) need not imply that (16) is positive (West (1986c)). So bubbles provide a logical explanation of any excess price volatility if (14) and (15) appear to be well specified. More generally, since it may be difficult to detect small departures from the rational bubble alternative in a given finite sample, evidence that (14) and (15) appear legitimate, despite excess price volatility, is consistent as well with nearly rational bubbles or fads of the sort considered in Summers (1986). So an essential part of the strategy used here to distinguish between rational or nearly rational bubbles or fads versus other alternatives as explanations of excess price variability is to perform diagnostic tests on equations (14) and (15). The greater the extent to which these two equations appear to be well specified, the more persuasive is the inference that bubbles or fads explain the excess volatility.[7]

4. EMPIRICAL EVIDENCE

A. *Data and Estimation Technique*

The data used were those used by Shiller (1981a) in his study of stock price volatility, and were supplied by him. There were two data sets, both containing annual aggregate price and dividend data. One had the Standard and Poor 500 for 1871-1980 (p_t is price in January divided by producer price index (1979 = 100), d_{t+1} is the sum of dividends from that same January to the following December, deflated by the average of that year's producer price index). The other data set was a modified Dow Jones index, 1928-1978 (p_t, d_{t+1} as above). See Shiller (1981a) for a discussion of the data.

The following aspects of estimation will be discussed in turn: (i) selection of the lag length q of the dividend process, (ii) estimation of (14), (15), and (16), (iii) calculation of the variance-covariance matrix of the parameters estimated, and (iv) diagnostic tests performed.

(i) It was assumed that the univariate d_t process required at most one difference to induce stationarity. That is, in equation (15), $s = 0$ (the original series was used) or $s = 1$ (first difference of original series used). No other values of s were tried.

For both the differenced and undifferenced versions of each data set's dividend process, two values of the lag length q were used. One was arbitrarily selected

---

[7] Unless, of course, one has a theoretical presumption that bubbles are not present: a consensus view on how general are the equilibria that admit bubbles is far from established. For a general equilibrium model that allows bubbles, see Tirole (1985). For an argument that bubbles are inconsistent with rationality, see Diba and Grossman (1985). For discussions on the use of volatility tests versus other techniques in studying present value models, see Hamilton and Whiteman (1984), Hansen and Sargent (1981), and Shiller (1981b). See West (1987) on the interpretation of the Summers (1986) alternative as a nearly rational bubble.

as $q=4$. The other was the q selected by the information criterion of Hannan and Quinn (1979). This criterion chooses the value of q that minimizes a certain function of the estimated parameters. Conditional on q being no greater than some fixed upper bound, which I set to 4, the correct q will be chosen asymptotically if the process truly has a finite order autoregressive representation.[8]

Thus, for each data set up to four sets of parameter estimates were calculated: $q=4$, where $q=$ lag length selected by the information criterion, for differenced and undifferenced data. In one case (Dow Jones, differenced), the Hannan and Quinn (1979) criterion chose $q=4$. So only three sets of parameters were calculated for the Dow Jones.

(ii) Calculation of (16) required estimation of the bivariate system consisting of equations (14) and (15). Equation (14) was estimated by Hansen's (1982) and Hansen and Singleton's (1982) two-step, two-stage least squares. The first step obtained the optimal instrumental variables estimator. The $q+1$ instruments used were the variables on the right hand side of (15), i.e., a constant term and q lags of $\Delta^s d_t$ ($s=0$ or $s=1$). Equation (15) was estimated by OLS, with the covariance matrix of the parameter estimates adjusted for conditional heteroskedasticity as described in (iii).

With $\Delta^s d_t \sim AR(q)$, the δ_1 parameter in the formula (16) is $[(1-b)^s \Phi(b)]^{-1}$, $\Phi(b) = 1 - \sum_1^q b^j \phi_j$ (Hansen and Sargent (1980)). Thus, formula (16) was calculated as $[(1-\hat{b})^s(1-\sum_1^q \hat{b}^j \hat{\phi}_j)]^{-1} \hat{\sigma}_v^2 - \hat{b}^{-2} \hat{\sigma}_u^2$.

The innovation variances $\hat{\sigma}_v^2$ and $\hat{\sigma}_u^2$ were calculated from the moments of the residuals of the regressions, with a degree of freedom correction used for $\hat{\sigma}_v^2$:

$$(18) \quad \hat{\sigma}_u^2 = (T-s)^{-1} \sum_{t=1}^{T-s} \hat{u}_{t+1}^2,$$

$$\hat{\sigma}_v^2 = (T-s-q-1)^{-1} \sum_{t=1}^{T-s} \hat{v}_{t+1}^2.$$

T is the number of observations; $T=110$ for the Standard and Poor's index, $T=51$ for the Dow Jones index.

The parameter vector estimated was thus $\hat{\theta} = (\hat{b}, \hat{\mu}, \hat{\phi}_1, \ldots, \hat{\phi}_q, \hat{\sigma}_v^2, \hat{\sigma}_u^2)$. $\hat{\theta}$ is asymptotically normal with an asymptotic covariance matrix V (see the Appendix and (iii) below).[9] Let $f(\theta)$ be formula (16) above. The standard error on the

---

[8] The Hannan-Quinn procedure selects the q that minimizes

$\ln \hat{\sigma}_v^2 + T^{-1} 2qk \ln \ln T,$

for $q < Q$ for some fixed Q, with $k > 1$. I set $Q=4$, $k=1.001$. The choice of $k=1.001$ was made because Hannan and Quinn (1979, p. 194) seem to suggest a value very close to one is appropriate for sample sizes such as those used in this paper.

[9] A referee has suggested that I emphasize that West (1986b), the references for the asymptotic distribution of parameter estimates for differenced specifications, requires $E(\Delta d_t + \Delta p_t) \neq 0$. While this certainly seems reasonable a priori given that the data are from a stock market in a growing economy, the upward drift in the data is not particularly well reflected in formal statistical tests. See, for example, the insignificant constant terms in all the differenced specifications in Table 1B. It is reassuring, then, that the Monte Carlo simulations in West (1986b), which assume data as noisy as those used here, suggest that the asymptotic normal approximation can be useful even with the sample sizes used here.

DIVIDEND INNOVATIONS

estimate of (16) was calculated as $[(\partial f/\partial\theta) V(\partial f/\partial\theta)']$. The derivatives of f were calculated analytically.

(iii) The estimate of V, the variance covariance matrix of $\hat{\theta}$, was calculated by the methods of Hansen (1982), Newey and West (1987), and West (1986c), so that the estimate would be consistent for an *arbitrary* ARMA process for u_t and v_t. This is necessary because, for example, the correlation between u_t and v_{t+j} may in principle be nonzero for all $j \geq 0$. The Newey and West (1987) procedure was used to insure that V was positive semidefinite. Details may be found in the Appendix. It suffices to note here that the procedure for calculating the standard error on (16) properly accounts for the uncertainty in the estimates of both the regression parameters and the variances of the residuals.

(iv) The final item discussed before results are presented is diagnostic tests on equations (14) and (15). Four diagnostic checks were performed.

The first checked for serial correlation in the residuals to the equations, using a pair of tests. As noted above, u_{t+1}, the disturbance to equation (14), is an expectational error. If expectations are rational, then u_{t+1} will be serially uncorrelated. Equation (15)'s disturbance v_{t+1} should also be serially uncorrelated, since v_{t+1} is the innovation in the dividend process.

The first of the pair of serial correlation tests checked for first order serial correlation in u_{t+1} and v_{t+1}. The calculation of the standard errors for this is described in the Appendix. The second of the pair of serial correlation tests, performed only for (15), calculated the Box–Pierce Q statistic for the residuals. This statistic of course simultaneously tests for first and higher order serial correlation. See Granger and Newbold (1977, p. 93).

The second of the four diagnostic checks was performed only on equation (14). This was a test of instrument-residual orthogonality, basically checking whether the residual to (14) is uncorrelated with lagged dividends (Hansen and Singleton (1982)). Let Z_t be the $(q+1) \times 1$ vector of instruments and $\hat{b}$ the estimate of b. The orthogonality test is computed as:

$$(19) \quad \left\{ \sum_{t=1}^{T-s} Z_t'[p_t - \hat{b}(p_{t+1} + d_{t+1})] \right\} (T\hat{S}_z) \left\{ \sum_{t=1}^{T-s} Z_t[p_t - \hat{b}(p_{t+1} + d_{t+1})] \right\}.$$

$\hat{S}_z$ is an estimate of $E(Z_t u_{t+1})(Z_t u_{t+1})'$ and was calculated as $T^{-1}(\sum Z_t Z_t' \bar{u}_{t+1}^2)$, where $\bar{u}_t$ is the 2SLS residual to (14). The statistic (19) is asymptotically distributed as a chi-squared random variable with q degrees of freedom. This test has the power to detect irrational expectational errors and variations in discount rates that are correlated with dividends.

The third of the four diagnostic checks tested for the stability of the regression coefficients in (14) and (15). Each sample was split in half, a pair of regression estimates was obtained, and equality of the pair was tested. The resulting statistic is asymptotically chi-squared, with one degree of freedom for (14) and $(q+1)$ degrees of freedom for (15). This test clearly has the power to detect shifts in the discount rate, as well as in the dividend process.

The fourth and final diagnostic check performed is implicit in the estimation procedure described above. A variety of specifications for the dividend process were used—differenced and undifferenced, with a variety of lag lengths. Since the results did not prove sensitive to the specification of the dividend process, the likelihood is relatively small that changes in the specification of the dividend process will affect the results.

B. *Empirical Results*

Regression results for (14) and (15) are reported in Tables I-A and I-B. The results in Table I-A suggest that the basic arbitrage equation (1) is a sensible one. The entries in column (4) do not reject the null hypothesis of no serial correlation in u_{t+1}, the disturbance to equation (14). The test statistic in all cases is far from significant at the .05 level. The equation (19) test for instrument-residual orthogonality also does not reject the null hypothesis of no correlation between the instruments and the residuals at the .05 level, for any specification. See column (5).[10]

TABLE 1-A: EQUATION 14
REGRESSION RESULTS

Data Set	(1) Differenced	(2)[c] q	(3)[c] b	(4)[c] ρ	(5)[c] H/sig	(6)[c] Stability/sig
S and P						
1873–1980	no	2[a]	.9311 (.0186)[b]	.0695 (.0766)	5.50/.064	4.55/.033
1874–1980	yes	2[a]	.9413 (.0170)	.0670 (.0974)	2.87/.238	.33/.566
1875–1980	no	4	.9315 (.0158)	.0661 (.0754)	6.96/.138	3.69/.055
1876–1980	yes	4	.9449 (.0136)	.0671 (.0984)	3.15/.533	.28/.594
Modified Dow Jones						
1931–1978	no	3[a]	.9402 (.0301)	−.1040 (.0806)	5.42/.144	1.56/.211
1933–1978	yes	4[a]	.9379 (.0188)	−.1182 (.0752)	5.20/.267	2.02/.154
1932–1978	no	4	.9271 (.0253)	−.1112 (.1493)	6.08/.108	.49/.483

See notes to Table I-B.

[10] Some results of Flood, Hodrick, and Kaplan (1986) should, however, be noted. They apply the test of instrument-residual orthogonality to these data using three lags of d_t/p_t as instruments, and estimating (14) in the form $1 = b(p_{t+1} + d_{t+1})/p_t +$ error. They report $\chi^2(3)$ test statistics with significance levels of .03 for the S and P and .08 for the Dow Jones. This suggests some mild evidence against the model. They also report stronger rejections using some indirect tests of the constant expected return model. See Section 5B for further discussion.

DIVIDEND INNOVATIONS

TABLE I-B: EQUATION 15 REGRESSION RESULTS

Data Set	(1) Differenced	(2)[c] q	(3)[c] μ	(4)[c] ϕ_1	(5)[c] ϕ_2	(6)[c] ϕ_3	(7)[c] ϕ_4	(8)[c] ρ	(9)[c] Q/sig	(10)[c] Stability/sig
S and P										
1873–1930	no	2[a]	.168 (.084)[b]	1.196 (.114)	−.238 (.103)			.045 (.025)	36.87/.181	12.93/.005
1874–1930	yes	2[a]	.034 (.029)	.262 (.118)	−.214 (.071)			.002 (.023)	22.79/.824	2.71/.438
1875–1930	no	4	.150 (.080)	1.247 (.116)	−.480 (.093)	.227 (.113)	−.029 (.066)	.001 (.010)	21.39/.875	33.49/.000
1876–1930	yes	4	.036 (.031)	.264 (.115)	−.230 (.094)	.026 (.080)	−.006 (.153)	.001 (.011)	23.98/.773	4.34/.501
Modified Dow Jones										
1931–1978	no	3[a]	1.945 (1.037)	1.265 (.112)	−.664 (.108)	.333 (.098)		.002 (.054)	4.05/1.000	7.53/.111
1933–1978	yes	4[a]	.275 (.405)	.302 (.119)	−.351 (.133)	.051 (.093)	.050 (.176)	−.024 (.067)	9.77/.939	8.06/.153
1932–1978	no	4	1.925 (1.900)	1.263 (.111)	−.662 (.208)	.330 (.209)	.004 (.134)	.005 (.022)	4.06/1.000	10.22/0.69

[a] Lag length q chosen by Hannan and Quinn (1979) procedure.
[b] Asymptotic standard errors in parentheses.
[c] Symbols: q is lag length of dividend autoregression (15); parameters b, μ, ϕ_i are defined in equations (9) and (15); ρ is the first order serial correlation coefficient of disturbance; H is the statistic in equation (19), $H \sim \chi^2(q)$; "stability" is test for stability of coefficients, as described in text, distributed $\chi^2(1)$ in Table I-A and $\chi^2(q+1)$ in Table I-B; Q is Box-Pierce Q statistic, $Q \sim \chi^2(30)$ for S and P, $Q \sim \chi^2(18)$ for Dow Jones. For the "H", "stability", and "Q" columns, "sig" refers to the probability of seeing the statistic under the null hypothesis.

Most important, the discount rate b is estimated plausibly and extremely precisely in all regressions. See column (3). The implied annual real interest rates are about six to seven per cent. These rates are quite near the arithmetic means for ex post returns: 8.1 per cent for the S and P index (1872–1981) and 7.4 per cent for the Dow Jones index (1929–1979). The estimates of the discount rate therefore are reasonable. Moreover, there is little evidence that the rate was different in the two halves of either sample. As indicated in column (6), the null hypothesis of equality cannot be rejected at the five per cent level for any specification except the S and P, undifferenced, $q = 2$. In addition, no evidence against the constancy of the discount rate may be found in a comparison of the two halves' mean ex post returns. For the S and P index, these were (in per cent) 8.09 (1872–1926) versus 8.12 (1927–1981); for the Dow Jones the figures are 7.87 (1929–1954) versus 6.92 (1955–1979).

In general, then, the specification of the arbitrage equation (14) seems acceptable, with the possible exception of the S and P data set with dividends undifferenced. Let us now turn to the estimates for the dividend process, reported in Table I-B. Once again, the entries in columns (8) and (9) allow comfortable acceptance of the null hypothesis of no serial correlation in the disturbance to equation (15). With one exception, both test statistics in all regressions are far from significant. The only possible exception was the estimate of the first order serial correlation coefficient $\hat{\rho}$ for the S and P index, undifferenced, lag length = 2. Note, however, that this regression's Q statistic in column (9) comfortably accepts the null hypothesis of no serial correlation. Overall, then, no serial correlation to the residual to (15) is apparent. Also, the estimates of most regression coefficients are fairly precise, at least when the lag length q was chosen by the Hannan and Quinn (1979) procedure. Finally, the null hypothesis that the parameters of the dividend process are the same in the two halves of each sample cannot be rejected for any specification except the Standard and Poor's, undifferenced. See column (10). Overall, then, the specification of the dividend process seems quite acceptable, again with the possible exception of the S and P data set, undifferenced.

The null hypothesis that price is the expected present discounted value of dividends, with a constant discount rate, does not, however, appear acceptable, for any specification. As may be seen from column (7) in Table II, formula (16) is always negative, and significantly so. The asymptotic z-stat (ratio of parameter to asymptotic standard error) was always larger than 2.5. This means that the column (7) entries are always significant at the one-half per cent level, using a one-tailed test. The null hypothesis may therefore be rejected at traditional significance levels. Furthermore, the fraction of the variance of the price innovation that is excessive is substantial, about 80 to 95 per cent (column (8) of Table II).

The residual price fluctuation might reflect grossly irrational reaction to news about dividends, variation in discount rates, or some combination of these and other factors. For the S and P undifferenced specifications, the econometric evidence perhaps is not particularly helpful in discriminating among the various possibilities. It is worth noting, however, that for the other specifications, the

TABLE II
Test Stastics

Data Set	(1) Differenced	(2) q	(3)[c] b	(4)[c] δ_1	(5)[d] σ_u^2	(6)[d] $\hat{\sigma}_v^2$	(7)[d] Eqn. (16)	(8) Eqn. (17)
S and P	No	2[a]	.9311 (.0186)[b]	10.82 (3.47)	215.2 (79.0)	.1501 (.0543)	−230.66 (87.10)	92.92
	Yes	2[a]	.9413 (.0170)	18.06 (6.22)	214.1 (80.2)	.1485 (.0523)	−193.22 (71.07)	79.95
	No	4	.9315 (.0158)	10.76 (3.10)	219.4 (73.4)	.1502 (.0510)	−235.51 (90.12)	93.12
	Yes	4	.9449 (.0136)	18.45 (5.64)	218.2 (81.1)	.1538 (.0511)	−192.05 (73.63)	78.58
Modified Dow-Jones	No	3[a]	.9402 (.0301)	8.28 (2.85)	19,653 (5,836)	9.980 (3.383)	−21,545 (5,978)	96.92
	Yes	4[a]	.9379 (.0188)	15.78 (8.13)	19,342 (5,871)	9.014 (2.655)	−19,740 (5,852)	89.79
	No	4	.9271 (.0253)	7.55 (3.12)	19,228 (3,912)	10.453 (2.427)	−21,777 (4,309)	97.34

[a] Lag length q chosen by Hannan-Quinn (1979) criterion.
[b] Asymptotic standard errors in parentheses.
[c] Symbols: q = lag length in dividend regression; b defined in equation (9); δ_1 defined above equation (18); σ_u^2 and σ_v^2 defined in equation (18).
[d] Units for columns (5)–(7) are 1979 dollars squared. For the S and P, $P_{1979} = 99.71$, $d_{1979} = 5.65$; for the Dow-Jones, $P_{1979} = 468.94$, $d_{1978} = 30.91$.

results of the diagnostic tests were more consistent with the residual volatility being due to bubbles or fads whose profit opportunities are difficult to detect, than to a misspecification of the arbitrage or dividend equations.[11]

5. SOME ADDITIONAL ANALYSIS

This section considers the possibilities that the previous section's results are due to (A) small sample bias, or (B) variation in discount rates. It is to be emphasized that the analysis is informal, and the conclusions are far from definitive. The goal here is simply to gather some evidence on whether either possibility explains the results; a complete, rigorous econometric examination of either possibility would require a separate paper.

A. *Small Sample Bias*

This section uses two small Monte Carlo experiments to get a feel for the importance of two types of bias. Part (a) below considers whether under certain simple circumstances small sample bias is likely to account for the finding of excess variability. Part (b) studies whether under equally simple circumstances low small sample power of the equation (19) test of instrument residual volatility is likely to explain the generally favorable results of the diagnostic tests.

a. *Bias in Estimate of Excess Volatility*

It is important to consider whether small sample bias explains the finding of excess variability, in light of the evidence in Kleidon (1985, 1986) and Marsh and Merton (1986) suggesting that if prices and dividends are nonstationary, the Shiller (1981a) variance bounds test is strongly biased towards finding excess variability. To see whether there is a similar bias in the present paper's test, an environment similar to that in Kleidon (1985, 1986) and Marsh and Merton (1986) was assumed. Two Monte Carlo experiments were performed. The first assumed that dividends follow a random walk, $\Delta d_t = \mu + v_t$, the second that dividends follow a lognormal random walk, $\Delta(\log d_t) = f + w_t$. In both experiments, it was assumed that only lagged dividends were used to forecast future dividends, so that $H_t = I_t$.

---

[11] This seems an appropriate place to give the results of another test of this model, suggested to me by a referee. Equation (6) states that $\text{var}(x_{tH} - \sum_0^\infty b^j d_{t+j}) - \text{var}(x_{tI} - \sum_0^\infty b^j d_{t+j}) - \text{var}(x_{tH} - x_{tI}) = 0$. So, under the null hypothesis that $x_{tI} = p_t + d_t$,

$$\delta_1^2 \sigma_v^2 - b^{-2}\sigma_u^2 - b^{-2}(1-b^2)\text{var}[p_t + d_t - (m + \sum_1^{q+s} \delta_i d_{t-i+1})] = 0.$$

The formulas for $m, \delta_1, \ldots, \delta_{q+s}$, which are needed to calculate x_{tH} under the null, may be found in West (1987).

I tested this equality constraint for all seven specifications, with the number of lags used in the calculation of the matrix $\hat{S}$ (defined in the Appendix) set to 11. The z-statistics for the seven specifications, presented in the same order as in Table II, were: 1.88, 2.07, 1.71, 2.23, 1.85, 2.17, 1.71. Thus this suggests some mild evidence against the null hypothesis.

The basic reason for the relatively low statistics was a very noisy estimate of $\text{var}[p_t + d_t - (m + \sum_1^{q+s} \delta_i d_{t-i+1})]$. This was insignificantly different from zero at the five per cent level, for all seven specifications.

DIVIDEND INNOVATIONS

In the first experiment, μ and σ_v^2 were matched to the S and P sample values of the mean and variance of Δd_t, $\mu = .0373$, $\sigma_v^2 = .1574$. b was set to .9413, the value estimated in line 2 of Table I-A. For each of 1000 samples, the following was done: A vector of 100 independent normal shocks was drawn, $(v_1, \ldots, v_{100})$, using the IMSL routine GGNPM. Dividends and prices were calculated as $\Delta d_t = .0373 + v_t$; $d_t = d_0 + \sum \Delta d_s$ $(d_0 = 1.3)$; $p_t = \sum (.9413)^j E d_{t+j} | I_t = m + \delta_1 d_t$, $m = (.0373)*(.9413)/(1-.9413)$, $\delta_1 = .9413/(1-.9413)$. $\hat{\mu}$ and $\hat{\sigma}_v^2$ were then estimated by an OLS regression of Δd_t on a constant, $\hat{b}$ and $\hat{\sigma}_u^2$ by an instrumental variables regression of equation (14), with a constant as the only instrument. Finally, formula (17), the percentage of price variability that is excessive, was calculated from the estimated parameters. Since $H_t = I_t$, the population value of (17) is zero.

Table III-A presents the empirical distribution of the estimates of formula (17). Ideally, the median value of this distribution would be zero, with half the samples yielding a positive value to (17). Instead, there appears to be a very slight bias towards finding excess variability, with 53 per cent of the estimates being positive. The bias is not, however, particularly marked, and fewer than 5 per cent of the simulated regressions produced the extreme values of the sort found in all of the Table II specifications.

The second experiment assumed that log differences are required to induce stationarity, as in the Monte Carlo evidence in Kleidon (1986). It was noted earlier that the proof of Proposition 1 assumes that arithmetic differences suffice to induce stationarity. Since this is not true in the present Monte Carlo experiment, it is not clear what value (if any) formula (17) will converge to as the sample size grows.[12] The aim of the experiment, then, is not to evaluate the small sample divergence of estimates of (17) from a population value, but to see if this form of nonstationarity is likely to account for the large values found in column (8) of Table II.

The experiment assumed that $\Delta (\log d_t) = f + w_t$, with f and σ_w^2 matched to the S and P sample values for the mean and variance of $\Delta(\log d_t)$, $f = .013$, $\sigma_w^2 = .016$. b was again set to .9413. The log d_t data were generated by the obvious analogue to the procedure described above for the first experiment, with $d_t = \exp[\log(d_t)]$ and $p_t = \delta d_t$, $\delta = \exp(f + \sigma_w^2/2)/[b^{-1} - \exp(f + \sigma_w^2/2)] = 24.82$. This experiment used a different seed than did the first to initiate the generation of the random w_t. The parameters needed to calculate (17) were estimated exactly as in the first

TABLE III-A
Monte Carlo Distribution of Formula (17) for Arithmetic Random Walk

Percentile	1	5	50	53
Formula (17)	100.0	31.1	1.7	0.0

---

[12] In this model one can, however, place a theoretical lower bound on the variance of the innovation in the first difference of log dividends. I tested this in West (1987) and, once again, found that this variance is so small that it is unlikely that a lognormal random walk model generates the data.

experiment. So, for example, arithmetic first differences of d_t were regressed on a constant, even though logarithmic first differences were in fact required to induce stationarity.

Table III-B presents the results of the experiment. This time, over four fifths of the estimates of (17) were positive, suggesting a tendency to find excess volatility. Once again, however, fewer than 5 per cent of the simulated regressions produced the extreme values found in all the Table II specifications. This indicates that it is unlikely that the basic results of the empirical work are attributable to the small sample effects of the misspecification considered in this experiment. More generally, in conjunction with the other Monte Carlo experiment and the empirical results in the previous section, this indicates that the apparent inconsistency of the simple efficient markets model with the S and P and Dow Jones data is unlikely to result from the nonstationarity that is central to Kleidon's (1986) critique of Shiller (1981a).

That the estimates for the artificial data rarely display the extreme Table II excess variability suggests more strongly than might be immediately apparent that small sample bias does not explain the Table II results. This is because Table III-A, and possibly Table III-B as well, contain worst case figures, since they are based on simulations in which $H_t = I_t$. Proposition 1 implies that for any given b and univariate Δd_t process, σ_u^2 will be smaller when I_t contains additional variables useful in forecasting d_t than when $I_t = H_t$. This suggests that when I_t contains these variables estimates of σ_u^2 and of formula (17) will be smaller as well. But a simulation with such variables in I_t does not seem worth undertaking, because even under worst case circumstances assumed here, there is little to suggest that small sample bias explains the extreme excess variability reported in Table II.

b. *Bias in Test of Instrument-Residual Orthogonality*

It is possible that the diagnostic tests reported basically favorable results because the tests have low power against some interesting alternatives; see Summers (1986), for example, on tests for serial correlation. It is particularly difficult to consider this comprehensively, even if only one of the diagnostic tests is analyzed. This is because Monte Carlo experiments here are potentially quite burdensome computationally. This will be true if p_t or d_t are generated nonlinearly under the alternative, as will be the case, for example, in most formulations of the Lucas (1978) asset pricing model.

TABLE III-B
MONTE CARLO DISTRIBUTION OF FORMULA (17) FOR LOGNORMAL RANDOM WALK

Percentile	1	5	50	83
Formula (17)	81.0	73.9	41.1	0.0

DIVIDEND INNOVATIONS

So this section has a relatively modest aim, of using a single diagnostic test and a single, simple form of misspecification, to suggest whether the data and sample size are such that the diagnostic tests are unlikely to detect plausible misspecifications. The test that is used is the equation (19) test of instrument residual orthogonality. The misspecification that is assumed is that expectations are static rather than rational, $Ed_{t+j}|I_t = d_t$. In such a case, the disturbance to the arbitrage equation (14) is $-b(\Delta p_{t+1} + \Delta d_{t+1})$. So the test must pick up a correlation between $\Delta p_{t+1} + \Delta d_{t+1}$ on the one hand and lagged Δd_t (the instruments, assuming a differenced specification) on the other. Note that there are variations in (mathematically) expected returns.

Under this alternative, $p_t = [b/(1-b)]d_t$; $b = .9413$ was again assumed. Dividends were assumed to be generated by an ARIMA (2, 1, 0) process, with the parameters given by line (2) of Table I-B. The following was done 1000 times. A vector of 100 independent normal disturbances was generated, with the variance of the disturbances equal to that reported in line (2), column (6) of Table II, and with a different random number seed than those used in the other experiments. One hundred Δd_t's, and then one hundred d_t's and p_t's, were computed, with initial conditions matching the initial values of the S and P ($\Delta d_{-1} = .16$, $\Delta d_0 = .11$, $d_0 = 1.61$). $\hat{b}$ was then estimated by two-step, 2SLS, with a constant, Δd_t, and Δd_{t-1} as instruments. Finally, the equation (19) statistic was calculated.

The distribution of this statistic, which is a $\chi^2(2)$ random variable under the null, is reported in Table III-C. In over three fourths of the samples, the statistic was above 5.99, the ninety-five per cent level for a $\chi^2(2)$ random variable. In over nine tenths of the samples, the statistic was over 2.87, the value reported in line (2), column (5), in Table I-A.

Against this alternative, then, the test of instrument residual orthogonality appears to have reasonable power. Whether this applies to other alternatives or to the other diagnostic tests performed is uncertain. But the limited amount of evidence presented here at any rate does not suggest that the favorable results of the diagnostic tests result solely from low power of the tests.

B. Variation in Discount Rates

One possible explanation for the excess variability found in Section 4 is that discount rates are time varying, so that the error in equation (14) reflects not only news about dividends but also about discount rates (or, equivalently, expected returns). Special consideration of the plausibility of this variation as an explanation seems warranted, given theoretical work such as Lucas (1978) and

TABLE III-C
MONTE CARLO DISTRIBUTION OF EQUATION (19)

Percentile	5	10	50	77	95
Equation (19)	∞6.57	14.83	8.86	5.99	2.89

empirical evidence such as in Shiller (1984) and Flood, Hodrick, and Kaplan (1986).

This will be done in two separate exercises. The first (part (a) below) assumes as in, e.g., Hansen and Singleton (1982) that a consumption based asset pricing model determines expected returns, with the representative consumer's utility function displaying constant relative risk aversion. For small values of the coefficient of relative risk aversion, this permits exact calculation of formula (17), the percentage excess variability. The second (part (b) below) does not model expected returns parametrically but instead uses Shiller's (1981a) linearized version of a completely general model. This permits calculation of a lower bound to how large a standard deviation in expected returns is required to explain the excess variability reported in Table II.

a. *Consumption Based Asset Pricing Model*

Consider the class of models (e.g., Hansen and Singleton (1982)) in which the first order condition for the return on a stock is $E\{\{\beta C_{t+1}/C_t\}^{-\alpha}[(p_{t+1}+d_{t+1})/p_t]\}|I_t\} = 1$, where β, $0 < \beta < 1$, is the representative consumer's subjective discount rate, C_t is his real consumption, α his coefficient of relative risk aversion, with E, d_t, p_t, and I_t defined as above. This may be rearranged as

(20) $\quad \tilde{p}_t = \beta E[(\tilde{p}_{t+1} + \tilde{d}_{t+1})|I_t],$

$\tilde{p}_t = p_t C_t^{-\alpha}, \quad \tilde{d}_t = d_t C_t^{-\alpha}.$

Equation (20) is of the same form as equation (9). R. Flood has pointed out to me that if $\tilde{d}_t$ is stationary, perhaps after one or more differences are taken, the statistics computed in the constant discount rate case can be computed in this model as well. Repetition of the entire procedure is beyond the scope of this paper (and, in light of the results about to be presented, seems pointless). Instead, I will focus on obtaining a point estimate of formula (17), the percentage excess variability, for various imposed values of β and α.

The C_t variable used in these calculations was the Grossman and Shiller (1981) annual figure on real, per Capita consumption of nondurables and services, 1889–1978. $\tilde{d}_t$ and $\tilde{p}_t$ were calculated using the S and P data for various values of α. A simple plot of $\tilde{d}_t$ suggested that $\tilde{d}_t$ in neither levels nor first nor higher differences is stationary for α much bigger than one. The problem is that for big α, $\tilde{d}_t$ displays a marked secular decline, because annual C_t growth was slightly higher than annual d_t growth.

I nonetheless calculated (17), the percentage excess variability, for a wide range of α, just in case $\tilde{d}_t$ really is stationary for large α. This was done for $\beta = .95$ and $\beta = .98$, with very similar results. In all cases the lag length of the $\tilde{d}_t$ autoregression was set to four. Table IV-A contains the figures that resulted for some of the α, with $\beta = .98$. Since (17) was not only positive but large, the price and dividend data are as inconsistent with the model implied by (20) as they are with the constant expected return model assumed in Sections 3 and 4. There is

TABLE IV-A
Percentage Excess Price Variability

α	.5	1	2	3	10	25	50
Formula (17)	96.5	97.5	80.9	88.4	99.6	100.0	100.0

therefore no evidence supporting the hypothesis that the excess variability displayed in Table II is explained solely by the sort of variation in expected returns predicted by this asset pricing model.[13]

Since $\tilde{d}_t$ does not appear stationary for α much bigger than unity, it is equally true that Table IV-A contains no evidence against the hypothesis that the Table II excess variability is explained by variation in expected returns associated with a coefficient of risk aversion greater than, say, one. Table IV-A does, however, suggest if the model of expected returns assumed here is correct, that the Table II excess variability is unlikely to be due to variation in expected returns associated with a coefficient of relative risk aversion of less than, say, one.

b. *Linearized Model*

Let us now consider a general model that does not parameterize expected returns, linearized as in Shiller (1981a) to make the analysis tractable. Let r_{t+j} be the one period return expected by the market at period $t+j$, assumed covariance stationary. Suppose $p_t = E\{\{\sum_{j=1}^{\infty} [\prod_{i=1}^{j} (1+r_{t+i-1})^{-1}] d_{t+j}\} | I_t\}$. Let us linearize the quantity in braces around $\bar{r}$ and $\bar{d}$. $\bar{r}$ is the mean of r_t; selection of $\bar{d}$ is discussed below. Define $b = (1+\bar{r})^{-1}$, $a = -\bar{d}/\bar{r}$. Then (Shiller (1981a)) $p_t \approx E\{\{\sum_{j=1}^{\infty} b^j [a(r_{t+j-1}-\bar{r}) + d_{t+j}]\} | I_t\}$. Let $u_{t+1} = p_t - b(p_{t+1} + d_{t+1})$. Proposition 1 may be used to show that in this linearized model

$$(21) \quad \delta_1^2 \sigma_v^2 - b^{-2}\sigma_u^2 \geq -[a^2 + (1-b^2)^{-1}a^2]\sigma_r^2 - [2(1-b^2)^{-1/2} a\delta_1 \sigma_v]\sigma_r,$$

where σ_r is the standard deviation of r_t, and δ_1 and σ_v are as defined in formula (16). The algebra to derive (21) is in the Appendix.

The left-hand side of (21) is precisely the quantity studied in Sections 3 and 4. If this is positive, as it will be in the model (12), $\sigma_r = 0$ would of course satisfy the inequality. The empirical estimates of (16), in Table II, column (7), however, were negative; the minimum return variability needed to explain the Table II results is given by the positive σ_r that makes (21) hold with equality.

This lower bound σ_r was calculated for all seven of the specifications. σ_u^2, σ_v^2, δ_1, and b were set equal to the estimated values reported in Table II. When dividends were assumed stationary, $\bar{d}$ was set equal to mean dividends, $\bar{d} = T^{-1}\sum d_t$. When dividends were assumed nonstationary, $\bar{d}$ was set equal to average

---
[13] Note that the entries in the table are not a monotonic function of α. To make sure that the entries were representative, I calculated the percentage excess variability for α in steps of 0.1 from 0 to 3.0, in steps of 1.0 from 3.0 to 10.0, and in steps of 5.0 from 10.0 to 50.0. The results were quite similar to those reported in the table. The lowest percentage happened to occur at $\alpha = 2.0$.

TABLE IV-B
MINIMUM σ_r NEEDED TO EXPLAIN EXCESS VARIABILITY

Data Set	S&P	S&P	S&P	S&P	DJ	DJ	DJ
Differenced	no	yes	no	yes	no	yes	no
Lags	2	2	4	4	3	4	4
σ_r	.146	.222	.146	.201	.127	.176	.169

expected discounted dividends, $\bar{d} = (1-b) \sum_{t=1}^{\infty} b^{t-1} E_0 d_t$, where: $E_0 d_t = E_0 d_0 + t E \Delta d_t$, $E_0 d_0 = d_0$, d_0 the level of dividends at the beginning of the sample, and $E \Delta d_t$ calculated as $T^{-1} \sum \Delta d_t$. The parameter a was in all cases set to $-\bar{d}/\bar{r}$, with $\bar{r}$ defined implicitly by $(1+\bar{r})^{-1} = b$.

The resulting lower bound values may be found in Table IV-B. They are rather large. None of the estimates are less than .12. With $\sigma_r = .12$ and $\bar{r} = .07$, a two standard deviation confidence interval for the (real) expected return is about -17 per cent to $+31$ per cent. This would seem to be an implausibly large range.

In the linearized model considered here, then, Table IV-B suggests that variations in ex ante discount rates do not plausibly explain the excess variability of stock prices. How well this conclusion applied to any given nonlinear model of course depends on how well the linear model approximates the nonlinear one. An example in Shiller (1981a) suggests that if dividends are stationary the approximation can be quite good, even when changes in expected returns are larger than are typically considered reasonable. It is of course debatable that the approximation makes any sense, let alone is very accurate, if dividends are nonstationary. But the results here can in any case be said not to lend support to the hypothesis that the excess price variability reported in Table II is solely due to variation in expected returns.

6. CONCLUSIONS

This paper has derived and applied a stock price volatility test. The test required neither of two strong assumptions required by the Shiller (1981a) volatility test: that prices and dividends have finite variance, and that a satisfactory approximation to a perfect foresight price can be calculated from a finite data series.

The test indicated that stock prices are too volatile to be the expected present discounted value of dividends, with a constant discount rate. Among the explanations for the test results are that discount rates vary and that there are rational or nearly rational bubbles or fads. The possibility that the excess volatility is caused by discount rate fluctuations has been considered in detail, with largely negative results. The possibility that the excess volatility is due to bubbles has received little direct attention. But since this alternative is consistent with the econometric diagnostics, it seems worthy of further investigation.

A detailed case for bubbles, or, for that matter, any other factor as the explanation of the excess volatility is, however, beyond the scope of this paper.

A challenging task for future research is to make such a case, explaining the apparently excessive price volatility.

Woodrow Wilson School, Princeton University, Princeton, NJ 08544, U.S.A.

Manuscript received December, 1984; final revision received March, 1987.

APPENDIX

A. CALCULATION OF THE VARIANCE-COVARIANCE MATRIX

This describes the calculation of the variance-covariance matrix of the parameter vector $\theta = (b, \phi, \sigma_u^2, \sigma_v^2) = (b, \mu, \phi_1, \ldots, \phi_q, \sigma_u^2, \sigma_v^2)$.

Let $Z_t = (1, \Delta'd_t, \ldots, \Delta'd_{t-q+1})'$ be the $(q+1) \times 1$ vector of instruments, $s = 0$ or $s = 1$, $n_{t+1} = (d_{t+1} + p_{t+1})$ be the right-hand side variable in (14). One way of describing the estimation technique is to note that $\hat\theta$ was chosen to satisfy the orthogonality condition

$$0 = T^{-1} \sum h_t(\hat\theta) = \begin{bmatrix} T^{-1}(T^{-2s} \sum n_{t+1} Z_t')(\hat S_z)^{-1} \sum Z_t(p_t - n_{t+1} \hat b) \\ T^{-1} \sum Z_t(\Delta' d_{t+1} - Z_t' \hat\phi) \\ \hat\sigma_u^2 - T^{-1} \sum (p_t - n_{t+1} \hat b)^2 \\ \hat\sigma_v^2 - T^{-1} \sum (\Delta' d_{t+1} - Z_t' \hat\phi)^2 \end{bmatrix}.$$

(The degrees of freedom corrections in $\hat\sigma_u^2$ and $\hat\sigma_v^2$ are suppressed for notational simplicity.) The summations in the orthogonality condition run over t, from 1 to $T - s$. $\hat S_z$ is an estimate of $EZ_t Z_t' u_{t+1}^2$, calculated as described below equation (19). Thus $\hat b$ is estimated by two-step, 2SLS, $\hat\phi$ by OLS, $\hat\sigma_u^2$ and $\hat\sigma_v^2$ from moments of the residuals.

Since $Eh_t(\theta) = 0$, where θ is the true but unknown parameter vector, it may be shown that under fairly general conditions, $C_T(\hat\theta - \theta)$ is asymptotically normal with a covariance matrix $V = (\text{plim } F_T^{-1} \sum h_{t\theta} F_T^{-1})^{-1} S (\text{plim } F_T^{-1} \sum h_{t\theta}' F_T^{-1})^{-1}$ (Hansen (1982), West (1986c)). C_T and F_T are $(q+4) \times (q+4)$ diagonal normalizing matrices, $C_T = F_T = \text{diag}(T^{1/2}, \ldots, T^{1/2})$ for undifferenced specifications, $C_T = \text{diag}(T^{3/2}, T^{1/2}, \ldots, T^{1/2})$ and $F_T = \text{diag}(T, T^{1/2}, \ldots, T^{1/2})$ for differenced specifications. $h_{t\theta}$ is the $(q+4) \times (q+4)$ matrix of derivatives of h_t with respect to θ and $S = Eh_t h_t' + \sum_{j=1}^{\infty} [Eh_t h_{t-j}' + (Eh_t h_{t-j}')']$. $h_{t\theta}$ is straightforward to calculate. Calculation of S is slightly more involved. Newey and West (1986) and West (1986c) show that in general S and thus V are consistently estimated if $\hat S = \hat\Omega_0 + \sum_{i=1}^{m} w(i, m)(\hat\Omega_i + \hat\Omega_i')$, where $m \to \infty$ as $T \to \infty$ and m is $o(T^{1/2})$; $w(i, m) = i/(m+1)$; $\hat\Omega_i = T^{-1} \sum_{t=i+1}^{T} \tilde h_t \tilde h_{t-i}'$, $\tilde h_t = h_t(\tilde\theta)$, $\tilde\theta$ an initial consistent estimate (2SLS and OLS). The weights $w(i, m)$ insure that $\hat S$ is positive semidefinite. In the absence of any theoretical or Monte Carlo evidence on the small sample properties of various choices of m, I tried various values: $m = 3, 7$, or 11. The value of m that led to the *largest* standard error in column (7) of Table II is what is reported in Table II. For all specifications, this turned out to be $m = 11$.

It is easy to show that the $T^{3/2}$ rate for $\hat b$ when $s = 1$ implies that uncertainty about b can be ignored when calculating the standard error for $\hat\rho$ in column (5) of Table I-A. I therefore did so, and used the OLS standard error of the regression of the 2SLS residual on a lagged residual. The standard errors for the undifferenced specifications in Table I-A were calculated according to equation (50) in Pagan and Hall (1983). All standard errors in column (8) of Table I-B were calculated according to Theorem 3 in Pagan and Hall (1983).

B. DERIVATION OF EQUATION (21)

In the linearized model the analogue to equation (9) is $p_t = bE[a(r_t - \bar r) + d_{t+1} + p_{t+1}|I_t]$. Let $y_{t+j} = a(r_{t+j-1} - \bar r) + d_{t+j}$ and redefine $x_{tt} = E(\sum b^j y_{t+j}|I_t)$. (Of course, if expected returns are constant, $r_t = \bar r$ for all t, x_{tt} as defined here reduces to its Proposition 1 counterparts.) To simplify the argument, it will be assumed throughout this section that linear projections and mathematical expectations are equivalent. The efficient markets model considered in Section 3 implies $x_{tt} = d_t + p_t$;

the one currently under consideration implies $x_{tt} = y_t + p_t = a(r_{t-1} - \bar{r}) + d_t + p_t$. So with r_{t-1} an element of I_{t-1}, $x_{tt} - E(x_{tt}|I_{t-1}) = d_t + p_t - E(d_t + p_t|I_{t-1})$. Now,

(A.1) $\quad u_{t+1} = p_t - b(d_{t+1} + p_{t+1}) = [ba(r_t - \bar{r}) + bE(p_{t+1} + d_{t+1}|I_t) - b(d_{t+1} + p_{t+1})]$

$= b\{a(r_t - \bar{r}) - [x_{t+1,t} - E(x_{t+1,t}|I_t)]\}$

$\Rightarrow b^{-2}\sigma_u^2 = a^2\sigma_r^2 + E[x_{t+1,t} - E(x_{t+1,t}|I_t)]^2$

$\Rightarrow E[x_{t+1,t} - E(x_{t+1,t}|I_t)]^2 = b^{-2}\sigma_u^2 - a^2\sigma_r^2.$

Now define J_t as the information set determined by a constant and all current and lagged dividends and expected returns, $x_{tJ} = E(\sum b^j y_{t+j}|J_t)$. Let $x_{tJ} - E(x_{tJ}|J_{t-1}) = aw_{1t} + w_{2t}$, where w_{1t} and w_{2t} are the innovations in the expected present discounted values of r_t and d_t. Shiller (1981a) shows that $\sigma_{w_1}^2 \le \sigma_r^2/(1 - b^2)$. Assume that d_t or Δd_t follows the autoregression (15). Then since H_t is a subset of J_t, Proposition 1 tells us that $\sigma_{w_2}^2 \le \delta_1^2 \sigma_v^2$, where, as previously, σ_v^2 is the variance of the univariate dividend innovation and δ_1 is defined above formula (16). So

(A.2) $\quad E[x_{tJ} - E(x_{tJ}|J_{t-1})]^2 = a^2\sigma_{w_1}^2 + 2a\sigma_{w_1 w_2} + \sigma_{w_2}^2$

$\le a^2\sigma_{w_1}^2 + 2a\sigma_{w_1}\sigma_{w_2} + \sigma_{w_2}^2$

$\le (1 - b^2)^{-1}a^2\sigma_r^2 + 2a(1 - b^2)^{-1/2}\delta_1\sigma_v\sigma_r + \delta_1^2\sigma_v^2.$

Since J_t is a subset of I_t, Proposition 1 tells us that $E[x_{tt} - E(x_{tt}|I_{t-1})]^2 \le E[x_{tJ} - E(x_{tJ}|J_{t-1})]^2$. With a little rearrangement, (A.1) and (A.2) together imply equation (21) in the text.

REFERENCES

ACKLEY, G. (1983): "Commodities and Capital: Prices and Quantities," *American Economic Review*, 73, 1–16.
BLANCHARD, O., AND M. WATSON (1982): "Bubbles, Rational Expectations and Financial Markets," NBER Working Paper No. 945.
BREALEY, R., AND S. MYERS (1981): *Principles of Corporate Finance*. New York, NY: McGraw Hill.
DIBA, B. T., AND H. I. GROSSMAN (1985): "The Impossibility of Rational Bubbles," NBER Working Paper No. 1615.
DEATON, A. (1985): "Life Cycle Models of Consumption: Is the Evidence Consistent with the Theory?" manuscript, Princeton University.
FLAVIN, M. (1983): "Excess Volatility in the Financial Markets: A Reassessment of the Empirical Evidence," *Journal of Political Economy*, 91, 929–956.
FLOOD, R., R. HODRICK, AND P. KAPLAN (1986): "An Evaluation of Recent Evidence on Stock Market Bubbles," manuscript, Northwestern University.
FULLER, W. A. (1976): *Introduction to Statistical Time Series*. New York: John Wiley and Sons.
GRANGER, C. W. J., AND P. NEWBOLD (1977): *Forecasting Economic Time Series*. New York, NY: Academic Press.
GROSSMAN, S., AND R. SHILLER (1981). "The Determinants of the Variability of Stock Prices," *American Economic Review*, 71, 222–227.
HAMILTON, J., AND C. WHITEMAN (1984): "The Observable Implications of Self Fulfilling Prophecies," manuscript, University of Virginia.
HANNAN, E. J., AND B. G. QUINN (1979): "The Determination of the Order of an Autoregression," *Journal of the Royal Statistical Society Series B*, 41, 190–195.
HANSEN, L. P. (1982): "Large Sample Properties of Generalized Method of Moments Estimators," *Econometrica*, 50, 1029–1054.
HANSEN, L. P., AND T. J. SARGENT (1980): "Formulating and Estimating Dynamic Linear Rational Expectations Models," *Journal of Economic Dynamics and Control*, 2, 7–46.
——— (1981): "Exact Linear Rational Expectations Models: Specification and Estimation," Federal Reserve Bank of Minneapolis Staff Report 71.
HANSEN, L. P., AND K. J. SINGLETON (1982): "Generalized Instrumental Variables Estimation of Nonlinar Rational Expectations Models," *Econometrica*, 50, 1269–1286.
KEYNES, J. M. (1964): *The General Theory of Employment, Interest and Money*. New York, NY: Harcourt, Brace, and World.
KLEIDON, A. W. (1985): "Bias in Small Sample Tests of Stock Price Rationality," Stanford University Graduate School of Business Research Paper 819R.

—— (1986): "Variance Bounds Tests and Stock Price Valuation Models," *Journal of Political Economy*, 94, 953-1001.
LEROY, S. (1984): "Efficiency and Variability of Asset Prices," *American Economic Review*, 74, 183-187.
LEROY, S. AND R. PORTER (1981): "The Present Value Relation: Tests Based on Implied Variance Bounds," *Econometrica*, 64, 555-574.
LUCAS, R. E., JR. (1978): "Asset Prices in an Exchange Economy," *Econometrica*, 46, 1429-1445.
MARSH, T. A., AND R. C. MERTON (1986): "Dividend Variability and Variance Bounds Tests for the Rationality of Stock Market Prices," *American Economic Review*, 76, 483-498.
MCCALLUM, B. (1976): "Rational Expectations and the Natural Rate Hypothesis: Some Consistent Estimates," *Econometrica*, 44, 43-52.
NEWEY, W. K., AND K. D. WEST (1987): "A Simple, Positive, Semidefinite, Heteroskedasticity and Autocorrelation Consistent Covariance Matrix," *Econometrica*, 55, 703-708.
PAGAN, A. R., AND A. D. HALL (1983): "Diagnostic Tests as Residual Analysis," *Econometric Reviews*, 2, 159-218.
SHILLER, R. J. (1981a): "Do Stock Prices Move Too Much to be Justified by Subsequent Changes in Dividends?" *American Economic Review*, 71, 421-436.
—— (1981b): The Use of Volatility Measures in Assessing Market Efficiency," *Journal of Finance*, 35, 291-304.
—— (1984): "Stock Prices and Social Dynamics," *Brookings Papers on Economic Activity*, 457-498.
SUMMERS, L. H. (1986): "Does the Stock Market Rationally Reflect Fundamental Values?" *Journal of Finance*, 41, 591-600.
TIROLE, J. (1985): "Asset Bubbles and Overlapping Generations," *Econometrica*, 53, 1071-1100.
WEST, K. D. (1984): "Speculative Bubbles and Stock Price Volatility," Princeton University Financial Research Memorandum No. 54.
—— (1987): "A Specification Test for Speculative Bubbles," *Quarterly Journal of Economics*, 102, 553-580.
—— (1986a): "A Standard Monetary Model and the Variability of the Deutschemark-Dollar Exchange Rate," forthcoming, *Journal of International Economics*.
—— (1986b): "Asymptotic Normality, When Regressors Have a Unit Root," Princeton University Woodrow Wilson School Discussion Paper No. 110.
—— (1986c): "Dividend Innovations and Stock Price Volatility," NBER Working Paper No. 1833.
—— (1988): "The Insensitivity of Consumption to News About Income," forthcoming, *Journal of Monetary Economics*.

Part II
Overreaction and Underreaction

[12]

An Empirical Evaluation of Accounting Income Numbers

RAY BALL* and PHILIP BROWN†

Accounting theorists have generally evaluated the usefulness of accounting practices by the extent of their agreement with a particular analytic model. The model may consist of only a few assertions or it may be a rigorously developed argument. In each case, the method of evaluation has been to compare existing practices with the more preferable practices implied by the model or with some standard which the model implies all practices should possess. The shortcoming of this method is that it ignores a significant source of knowledge of the world, namely, the extent to which the predictions of the model conform to observed behavior.

It is not enough to defend an analytical inquiry on the basis that its assumptions are empirically supportable, for how is one to know that a theory embraces all of the relevant supportable assumptions? And how does one explain the predictive powers of propositions which are based on unverifiable assumptions such as the maximization of utility functions? Further, how is one to resolve differences between propositions which arise from considering different aspects of the world?

The limitations of a completely analytical approach to usefulness are illustrated by the argument that income numbers cannot be defined substantively, that they lack "meaning" and are therefore of doubtful utility.[1] The argument stems in part from the patchwork development of account-

---

* University of Chicago.   † University of Western Australia. The authors are indebted to the participants in the Workshop in Accounting Research at the University of Chicago, Professor Myron Scholes, and Messrs. Owen Hewett and Ian Watts.

[1] Versions of this particular argument appear in Canning (1929); Gilman (1939); Paton and Littleton (1940); Vatter (1947), Ch. 2; Edwards and Bell (1961), Ch. 1; Chambers (1964), pp. 267–68; Chambers (1966), pp. 4 and 102; Lim (1966), esp. pp. 645 and 649; Chambers (1967), pp. 745–55; Ijiri (1967), Ch. 6, esp. pp. 120–31; and Sterling (1967), p. 65.

ing practices to meet new situations as they arise. Accountants have had to deal with consolidations, leases, mergers, research and development, price-level changes, and taxation charges, to name just a few problem areas. Because accounting lacks an all-embracing theoretical framework, dissimilarities in practices have evolved. As a consequence, net income is an aggregate of components which are not homogeneous. It is thus alleged to be a "meaningless" figure, not unlike the difference between twenty-seven tables and eight chairs. Under this view, net income can be defined only as the result of the application of a set of procedures $\{X_1, X_2, \cdots\}$ to a set of events $\{Y_1, Y_2, \cdots\}$ with no other definitive substantive meaning at all. Canning observes:

> What is set out as a measure of net income can never be supposed to be a fact in any sense at all except that it is the figure that results when the accountant has finished applying the procedures which he adopts.[2]

The value of analytical attempts to develop measurements capable of definitive interpretation is not at issue. What is at issue is the fact that an analytical model does not itself assess the significance of departures from its implied measurements. Hence it is dangerous to conclude, in the absence of further empirical testing, that a lack of substantive meaning implies a lack of utility.

An empirical evaluation of accounting income numbers requires agreement as to what real-world outcome constitutes an appropriate test of usefulness. Because net income is a number of particular interest to investors, the outcome we use as a predictive criterion is the investment decision as it is reflected in security prices.[3] Both the content and the timing of existing annual net income numbers will be evaluated since usefulness could be impaired by deficiencies in either.

An Empirical Test

Recent developments in capital theory provide justification for selecting the behavior of security prices as an operational test of usefulness. An impressive body of theory supports the proposition that capital markets are both efficient and unbiased in that if information is useful in forming capital asset prices, then the market will adjust asset prices to that information quickly and without leaving any opportunity for further abnormal gain.[4] If, as the evidence indicates, security prices do in fact adjust rapidly to new information as it becomes available, then changes in security prices will re-

---

[2] Canning (1929), p. 98.
[3] Another approach pursued by Beaver (1968) is to use the investment decision, as it is reflected in transactions volume, for a predictive criterion.
[4] For example, Samuelson (1965) demonstrated that a market without bias in its evaluation of information will give rise to randomly fluctuating time series of prices. See also Cootner (ed.) (1964); Fama (1965); Fama and Blume (1966); Fama, et al. (1967); and Jensen (1968).

flect the flow of information to the market.[5] An observed revision of stock prices associated with the release of the income report would thus provide evidence that the information reflected in income numbers is useful.

Our method of relating accounting income to stock prices builds on this theory and evidence by focusing on the information which is unique to a particular firm.[6] Specifically, we construct two alternative models of what the market expects income to be and then investigate the market's reactions when its expectations prove false.

EXPECTED AND UNEXPECTED INCOME CHANGES

Historically, the incomes of firms have tended to move together. One study found that about half of the variability in the level of an average firm's earnings per share (EPS) could be associated with economy-wide effects.[7] In light of this evidence, at least part of the change in a firm's income from one year to the next is to be expected. If, in prior years, the income of a firm has been related to the incomes of other firms in a particular way, then knowledge of that past relation, together with a knowledge of the incomes of those other firms for the present year, yields a conditional expectation for the present income of the firm. Thus, apart from confirmation effects, the amount of new information conveyed by the present income number can be approximated by the difference between the actual change in income and its conditional expectation.

But not all of this difference is necessarily new information. Some changes in income result from financing and other policy decisions made by the firm. We assume that, to a first approximation, such changes are reflected in the average change in income through time.

Since the impacts of these two components of change—economy-wide and policy effects—are felt simultaneously, the relationship must be estimated jointly. The statistical specification we adopt is first to estimate, by Ordinary Least Squares (OLS), the coefficients (a_{1jt}, a_{2jt}) from the linear regression of the change in firm j's income ($\Delta I_{j,t-\tau}$) on the change in the average income of all firms (other than firm j) in the market ($\Delta M_{j,t-\tau}$)[8] using data up to the end of the previous year ($\tau = 1, 2, \cdots, t-1$):

$$\Delta I_{j,t-\tau} = \hat{a}_{1jt} + \hat{a}_{2jt}\Delta M_{j,t-\tau} + \hat{u}_{j,t-\tau} \qquad \tau = 1, 2, \cdots, t-1, \qquad (1)$$

[5] One well documented characteristic of the security market is that useful sources of information are acted upon and useless sources are ignored. This is hardly surprising since the market consists of a large number of competing actors who can gain from acting upon better interpretations of the future than those of their rivals. See, for example, Scholes (1967); and footnote 4 above. This evaluation of the security market differs sharply from that of Chambers (1966, pp. 272-73).

[6] More precisely, we focus on information not common to all firms, since some industry effects are not considered in this paper.

[7] Alternatively, 35 to 40 per cent could be associated with effects common to all firms when income was defined as tax-adjusted Return on Capital Employed. [Source: Ball and Brown (1967), Table 4.]

[8] We call M a "market index" of income because it is constructed only from firms traded on the New York Stock Exchange.

where the hats denote estimates. The expected income change for firm j in year t is then given by the regression prediction using the change in the average income for the market in year t:

$$\Delta \hat{I}_{jt} = \hat{a}_{1jt} + \hat{a}_{2jt}\Delta M_{jt}.$$

The unexpected income change, or forecast error $(\hat{u}_{jt})$, is the actual income change minus expected:

$$\hat{u}_{jt} = \Delta I_{jt} - \Delta \hat{I}_{jt}. \tag{2}$$

It is this forecast error which we assume to be the new information conveyed by the present income number.

THE MARKET'S REACTION

It has also been demonstrated that stock prices, and therefore rates of return from holding stocks, tend to move together. In one study,[9] it was estimated that about 30 to 40 per cent of the variability in a stock's monthly rate of return over the period March, 1944 through December, 1960 could be associated with market-wide effects. Market-wide variations in stock returns are triggered by the release of information which concerns all firms. Since we are evaluating the income report as it relates to the individual firm, its contents and timing should be assessed relative to changes in the rate of return on the firm's stocks net of market-wide effects.

The impact of market-wide information on the monthly rate of return from investing one dollar in the stock of firm j may be estimated by its predicted value from the linear regression of the monthly price relatives of firm j's common stock[10] on a market index of returns:[11]

---

[9] King (1966).

[10] The monthly price relative of security j for month m is defined as dividends (d_{jm}) + closing price $(p_{j,m+1})$, divided by opening price (p_{jm}):

$$PR_{jm} = (p_{j,m+1} + d_{jm})/p_{jm}.$$

A monthly price relative is thus equal to the discrete monthly rate of return plus unity; its natural logarithm is the monthly rate of return compounded continuously. In this paper, we assume discrete compounding since the results are easier to interpret in that form.

[11] Fama, et al. (1967) conclude that "regressions of security on market returns over time are a satisfactory method for abstracting from the effects of general market conditions on the monthly rates of return on individual securities." In arriving at their conclusion, they found that "scatter diagrams for the [returns on] individual securities [vis-à-vis the market return] support very well the regression assumptions of linearity, homoscedasticity, and serial independence." Fama, et al. studied the natural logarithmic transforms of the price relatives, as did King (1966). However, Blume (1968) worked with equation (3). We also performed tests on the alternative specification:

$$\ln_e (PR_{jm}) = b'_{1j} + b'_{2j}\ln_e (L_m) + v'_{jm}, \tag{3a}$$

where $\ln_e$ denotes the natural logarithmic function. The results correspond closely with those reported below.

EMPIRICAL EVALUATION OF ACCOUNTING INCOME NUMBERS   163

$$[PR_{jm} - 1] = \hat{b}_{1j} + \hat{b}_{2j}[L_m - 1] + \hat{v}_{jm}, \tag{3}$$

where PR_{jm} is the monthly price relative for firm j and month m, L is the link relative of Fisher's "Combination Investment Performance Index" [Fisher (1966)], and v_{jm} is the stock return residual for firm j in month m. The value of $[L_m - 1]$ is an estimate of the market's monthly rate of return. The m-subscript in our sample assumes values for all months since January, 1946 for which data are available.

The residual from the OLS regression represented in equation (3) measures the extent to which the realized return differs from the expected return conditional upon the estimated regression parameters (b_{1j}, b_{2j}) and the market index $[L_m - 1]$. Thus, since the market has been found to adjust quickly and efficiently to new information, the residual must represent the impact of new information, about firm j alone, on the return from holding common stock in firm j.

SOME ECONOMETRIC ISSUES

One assumption of the OLS income regression model[12] is that M_j and u_j are uncorrelated. Correlation between them can take at least two forms, namely the inclusion of firm j in the market index of income (M_j), and the presence of industry effects. The first has been eliminated by construction (denoted by the j-subscript on M), but no adjustment has been made for the presence of industry effects. It has been estimated that industry effects probably account for only about 10 per cent of the variability in the level of a firm's income.[13] For this reason equation (1) has been adopted as the appropriate specification in the belief that any bias in the estimates a_{1jt} and a_{2jt} will not be significant. However, as a check on the statistical efficiency of the model, we also present results for an alternative, naive model which predicts that income will be the same for this year as for last. Its forecast error is simply the change in income since the previous year.

As is the case with the income regression model, the stock return model, as presented, contains several obvious violations of the assumptions of the OLS regression model. First, the market index of returns is correlated with the residual because the market index contains the return on firm j, and because of industry effects. Neither violation is serious, because Fisher's index is calculated over all stocks listed on the New York Stock Exchange (hence the return on security j is only a small part of the index), and because industry effects account for at most 10 per cent of the variability in the rate

---

[12] That is, an assumption necessary for OLS to be the minimum-variance, linear, unbiased estimator.

[13] The magnitude assigned to industry effects depends upon how broadly an industry is defined, which in turn depends upon the particular empirical application being considered. The estimate of 10 per cent is based on a two-digit classification scheme. There is some evidence that industry effects might account for more than 10 per cent when the association is estimated in first differences [Brealey (1968)].

of return on the average stock.[14] A second violation results from our prediction that, for certain months around the report dates, the expected values of the v_j's are nonzero. Again, any bias should have little effect on the results, inasmuch as there is a low, observed autocorrelation in the $\hat{v}_j$'s,[15] and in no case was the stock return regression fitted over less than 100 observations.[16]

SUMMARY

We assume that in the unlikely absence of useful information about a particular firm over a period, its rate of return over that period would reflect only the presence of market-wide information which pertains to all firms. By abstracting from market effects [equation (3)] we identify the effect of information pertaining to individual firms. Then, to determine if part of this effect can be associated with information contained in the firm's accounting income number, we segregate the expected and unexpected elements of income change. If the income forecast error is negative (that is, if the actual change in income is less than its conditional expectation), we define it as bad news and predict that if there is some association between accounting income numbers and stock prices, then release of the income number would result in the return on that firm's securities being less than

---

[14] The estimate of 10 per cent is due to King (1966). Blume (1968) has recently questioned the magnitude of industry effects, suggesting that they could be somewhat less than 10 per cent. His contention is based on the observation that the significance attached to industry effects depends on the assumptions made about the parameters of the distributions underlying stock rates of return.

[15] See Table 4, below.

[16] Fama, et al. (1967) faced a similar situation. The expected values of the stock return residuals were nonzero for some of the months in their study. Stock return regressions were calculated separately for both exclusion and inclusion of the months for which the stock return residuals were thought to be nonzero. They report that both sets of results support the same conclusions.

An alternative to constraining the mean v_j to be zero is to employ the Sharpe Capital Asset Pricing Model [Sharpe (1964)] to estimate (3b):

$$PR_{jm} - RF_m - 1 = b'_{1j} + b'_{2j} [L_m - RF_m - 1] + v'_{jm}, \qquad (3b)$$

where RF is the risk-free ex ante rate of return for holding period m. Results from estimating (3b) (using U.S. Government Bills to measure RF and defining the abnormal return for firm j in month m now as $b'_{1j} + v'_{jm}$) are essentially the same as the results from (3).

Equation (3b) is still not entirely satisfactory, however, since the mean impact of new information is estimated over the whole history of the stock, which covers at least 100 months. If (3b) were fitted using monthly data, a vector of dummy variables could be introduced to identify the fiscal year covered by the annual report, thus permitting the mean residual to vary between fiscal years. The impact of unusual information received in month m of year t would then be estimated by the sum of the constant, the dummy for year t, and the calculated residual for month m and year t. Unfortunately, the efficiency of estimating the stock return equation in this particular form has not been investigated satisfactorily, hence our report will be confined to the results from estimating (3).

TABLE 1
Deciles of the Distributions of Squared Coefficients of Correlation, Changes in Firm and Market Income*

Variable	Decile								
	.1	.2	.3	.4	.5	.6	.7	.8	.9
(1) Net income	.03	.07	.10	.15	.23	.30	.35	.43	.52
(2) EPS	.02	.05	.11	.16	.23	.28	.35	.42	.52

* Estimated over the 21 years, 1946–1966.

would otherwise have been expected.[17] Such a result ($\hat{u} < 0$) would be evidenced by negative behavior in the stock return residuals ($\hat{v} < 0$) around the annual report announcement date. The converse should hold for a positive forecast error.

Two basic income expectations models have been defined, a regression model and a naive model. We report in detail on two measures of income [net income and EPS, variables (1) and (2)] for the regression model, and one measure [EPS, variable (3)] for the naive model.

Data

Three classes of data are of interest: the contents of income reports; the dates of the report announcements; and the movements of security prices around the announcement dates.

INCOME NUMBERS

Income numbers for 1946 through 1966 were obtained from Standard and Poor's *Compustat* tapes.[18] The distributions of the squared coefficients of correlation[19] between the changes in the incomes of the individual firms and the changes in the market's income index[20] are summarized in Table 1. For the present sample, about one-fourth of the variability in the changes

---

[17] We later divide the total return into two parts: a "normal return," defined by the return which would have been expected given the normal relationship between a stock and the market index; and an "abnormal return," the difference between the actual return and the normal return. Formally, the two parts are given by: $b_{1j} + b_{2j}[L_m - 1]$; and v_{jm}.

[18] Tapes used are dated 9/28/1965 and 7/07/1967.

[19] All correlation coefficients in this paper are product-moment correlation coefficients.

[20] The market net income index was computed as the sample mean for each year. The market EPS index was computed as a weighted average over the sample members, the number of stocks outstanding (adjusted for stock splits and stock dividends) providing the weights. Note that when estimating the association between the income of a particular firm and the market, the income of that firm was excluded from the market index.

TABLE 2
Deciles of the Distributions of the Coefficients of First-Order Autocorrelation in the Income Regression Residuals*

Variable	Decile								
	.1	.2	.3	.4	.5	.6	.7	.8	.9
(1) Net income...	−.35	−.28	−.20	−.12	−.05	.02	.12	.20	.33
(2) EPS..........	−.39	−.29	−.21	−.15	−.08	−.03	.07	.17	.35

* Estimated over the 21 years, 1946–1966.

in the median firm's income can be associated with changes in the market index.

The association between the levels of the earnings of firms was examined in the forerunner article [Ball and Brown (1967)]. At that time, we referred to the existence of autocorrelation in the disturbances when the levels of net income and EPS were regressed on the appropriate indexes. In this paper, the specification has been changed from levels to first differences because our method of analyzing the stock market's reaction to income numbers presupposes the income forecast errors to be unpredictable at a minimum of 12 months prior to the announcement dates. This supposition is inappropriate when the errors are autocorrelated.

We tested the extent of autocorrelation in the residuals from the income regression model after the variables had been changed from levels to first differences. The results are presented in Table 2. They indicate that the supposition is not now unwarranted.

ANNUAL REPORT ANNOUNCEMENT DATES

The *Wall Street Journal* publishes three kinds of annual report announcements: forecasts of the year's income, as made, for example, by corporation executives shortly after the year end; preliminary reports; and the complete annual report. While forecasts are often imprecise, the preliminary report is typically a condensed preview of the annual report. Because the preliminary report usually contains the same numbers for net income and EPS as are given later with the final report, the announcement date (or, effectively, the date on which the annual income number became generally available) was assumed to be the date on which the preliminary report appeared in the *Wall Street Journal*. Table 3 reveals that the time lag between the end of the fiscal year and the release of the annual report has been declining steadily throughout the sample period.

STOCK PRICES

Stock price relatives were obtained from the tapes constructed by the Center for Research in Security Prices (CRSP) at the University of Chi-

EMPIRICAL EVALUATION OF ACCOUNTING INCOME NUMBERS

TABLE 3
Time Distribution of Announcement Dates

Per cent of firms	Fiscal year								
	1957	1958	1959	1960	1961	1962	1963	1964	1965
25	2/07[a]	2/04	2/04	2/03	2/02	2/05	2/03	2/01	1/31
50	2/25	2/20	2/18	2/17	2/15	2/15	2/13	2/09	2/08
75	3/10	3/06	3/04	3/03	3/05	3/04	2/28	2/25	2/21

[a] Indicates that 25 per cent of the income reports for the fiscal year ended 12/31/1957 had been announced by 2/07/1958.

TABLE 4
Deciles of the Distributions of the Squared Coefficient of Correlation for the Stock Return Regression, and of the Coefficient of First-Order Autocorrelation in the Stock Return Residuals*

Coefficient name	Decile								
	.1	.2	.3	.4	.5	.6	.7	.8	.9
Return regression r^2...	.18	.22	.25	.28	.31	.34	.37	.40	.46
Residual autocorrelation..	−.17	−.14	−.11	−.10	−.08	−.05	−.03	−.01	.03

* Estimated over the 246 months, January, 1946 through June, 1966.

cago.[21] The data used are monthly closing prices on the New York Stock Exchange, adjusted for dividends and capital changes, for the period January, 1946 through June, 1966. Table 4 presents the deciles of the distributions of the squared coefficient of correlation for the stock return regression [equation (3)], and of the coefficient of first-order autocorrelation in the stock residuals.

INCLUSION CRITERIA

Firms included in the study met the following criteria:
1. earnings data available on the *Compustat* tapes for each of the years 1946–1966;
2. fiscal year ending December 31;
3. price data available on the CRSP tapes for at least 100 months; and
4. *Wall Street Journal* announcement dates available.[22]

Our analysis was limited to the nine fiscal years 1957–1965. By beginning the analysis with 1957, we were assured of at least 10 observations when

[21] The Center for Research in Security Prices at the University of Chicago is sponsored by Merrill Lynch, Pierce, Fenner and Smith Incorporated.

[22] Announcement dates were taken initially from the *Wall Street Journal Index*, then verified against the *Wall Street Journal*.

estimating the income regression equations. The upper limit (the fiscal year 1965, the results of which are announced in 1966) is imposed because the CRSP file terminated in June, 1966.

Our selection criteria may reduce the generality of the results. The subpopulation does not include young firms, those which have failed, those which do not report on December 31, and those which are not represented on *Compustat*, the CRSP tapes, and the *Wall Street Journal*. As a result, it may not be representative of all firms. However, note that (1) the 261 remaining firms[23] are significant in their own right, and (2) a replication of our study on a different sample produced results which conform closely to those reported below.[24]

Results

Define month 0 as the month of the annual report announcement, and API_M, the Abnormal Performance Index at month M, as:

$$API_M = \frac{1}{N} \sum_{n}^{N} \prod_{m=-11}^{M} (1 + v_{nm}).$$

Then API traces out the value of one dollar invested (in equal amounts) in all securities n ($n = 1, 2, \ldots, N$) at the end of month -12 (that is, 12 months prior to the month of the annual report) and held to the end of some arbitrary holding period ($M = -11, -10, \ldots, T$) after abstracting from market affects. An equivalent interpretation is as follows. Suppose two individuals A and B agree on the following proposition. B is to construct a portfolio consisting of one dollar invested in equal amounts in N securities. The securities are to be purchased at the end of month -12 and held until the end of month T. For some price, B contracts with A to take (or make up), at the end of each month M, only the normal gains (or losses) and to return to A, at the end of month T, one dollar plus or minus any abnormal gains or losses. Then API_M is the value of A's equity in the mutual portfolio at the end of each month M.[25]

Numerical results are presented in two forms. Figure 1 plots API_M first for three portfolios constructed from all firms and years in which the income forecast errors, according to each of the three variables, were positive (the top half); second, for three portfolios of firms and years in which the income forecast errors were negative (the bottom half); and third, for a single portfolio consisting of all firms and years in the sample (the line which wanders just below the line dividing the two halves). Table 5 includes the numbers on which Figure 1 is based.

---

[23] Due to known errors in the data, not all firms could be included in all years. The fiscal year most affected was 1964, when three firms were excluded.

[24] The replication investigated 75 firms with fiscal years ending on dates other than December 31, using the naive income-forecasting model, over the longer period 1947–65.

[25] That is, the value expected at the end of month T in the absence of further abnormal gains and losses.

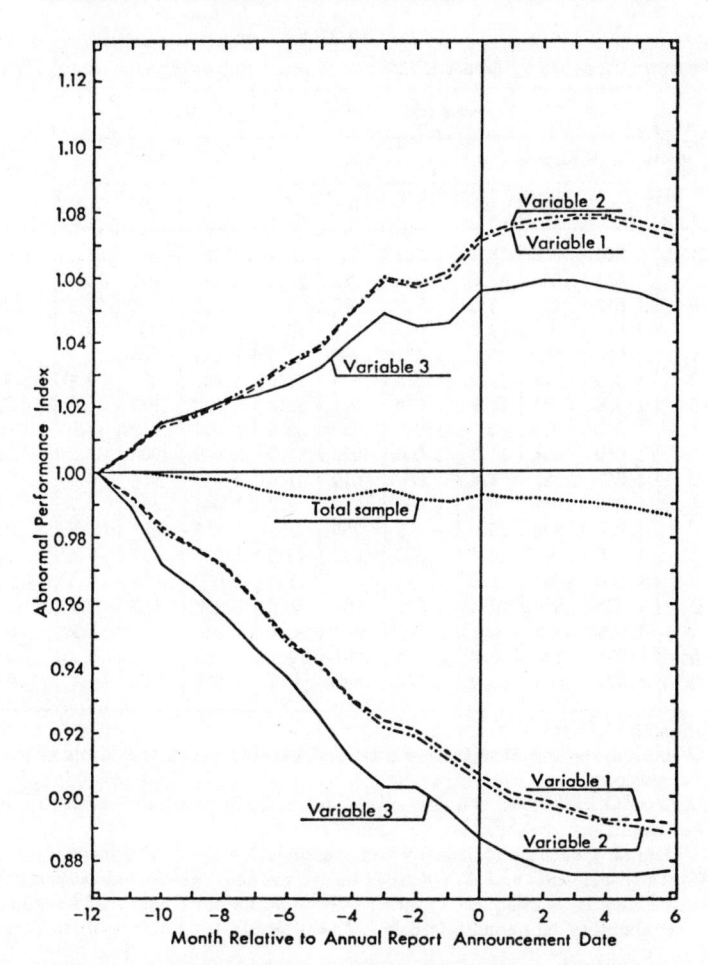

FIG. 1 Abnormal Performance Indexes for Various Portfolios

Since the first set of results may be sensitive to the distributions of the stock return disturbances,[26] a second set of results is presented. The third column under each variable heading in Table 5 gives the chi-square statistic for a two-by-two classification of firms by the sign of the income forecast error, and the sign of the stock return residual for that month.

OVERVIEW

As one would expect from a large sample, both sets of results convey essentially the same picture. They demonstrate that the information contained in the annual income number is useful in that if actual income differs

[26] The empirical distributions of the stock return residuals appear to be described well by symmetric, stable distributions that are characterized by tails longer than those of the normal distribution [Fama (1965); Fama, et al. (1967)].

TABLE 5
Summary Statistics by Month Relative to Annual Report Announcement Date

Month relative to annual report announcement date	Regression model							Naive model			Total sample
	Net income			EPS			EPS			
	(1)[a]	(2)	(3)	(1)	(2)	(3)	(1)	(2)	(3)	
−11	1.006	.992	16.5	1.007	.992	20.4	1.006	.989	24.1	1.000
−10	1.014	.983	17.3	1.015	.982	20.2	1.015	.972	73.4	.999
−9	1.017	.977	7.9	1.017	.977	3.7	1.018	.965	20.4	.998
−8	1.021	.971	9.5	1.022	.971	12.0	1.022	.956	9.1	.998
−7	1.026	.960	21.8	1.027	.960	27.1	1.024	.946	9.0	.995
−6	1.033	.949	42.9	1.034	.948	37.6	1.027	.937	19.4	.993
−5	1.038	.941	17.9	1.039	.941	21.3	1.032	.925	21.0	.992
−4	1.050	.930	40.0	1.050	.930	39.5	1.041	.912	41.5	.993
−3	1.059	.924	35.3	1.060	.922	33.9	1.049	.903	37.2	.995
−2	1.057	.921	1.4	1.058	.919	1.8	1.045	.903	0.1	.992
−1	1.060	.914	8.2	1.062	.912	8.2	1.046	.896	5.7	.991
0	1.071	.907	28.0	1.073	.905	28.9	1.056	.887	35.8	.993
1	1.075	.901	6.4	1.076	.899	5.5	1.057	.882	9.4	.992
2	1.076	.899	2.7	1.078	.897	1.9	1.059	.878	8.1	.992
3	1.078	.896	0.6	1.079	.895	1.2	1.059	.876	0.1	.991
4	1.078	.893	0.1	1.079	.892	0.1	1.057	.876	1.2	.990
5	1.075	.893	0.7	1.077	.891	0.1	1.055	.876	0.6	.989
6	1.072	.892	0.0	1.074	.889	0.2	1.051	.877	0.1	.987

[a] Column headings:
(1) Abnormal Performance Index—firms and years in which the income forecast error was positive.
(2) Abnormal Performance Index—firms and years in which the income forecast error was negative.
(3) Chi-square statistic for two-by-two classification by sign of income forecast error (for the fiscal year) and sign of stock return residual (for the indicated month).
Note: Probability (chi-square $\geq$ 3.84 | $\chi^2 = 0$) = .05, for 1 degree of freedom.
Probability (chi-square $\geq$ 6.64 | $\chi^2 = 0$) = .01, for 1 degree of freedom.

from expected income, the market typically has reacted in the same direction. This contention is supported both by Figure 1 which reveals a marked, positive association between the sign of the error in forecasting income and the Abnormal Performance Index, and by the chi-square statistic (Table 5). The latter shows it is most unlikely that there is no relationship between the sign of the income forecast error and the sign of the rate of return residual in most of the months up to that of the annual report announcement.

However, most of the information contained in reported income is anticipated by the market before the annual report is released. In fact, anticipation is so accurate that the actual income number does not appear to cause any unusual jumps in the Abnormal Performance Index in the announcement month. To illustrate, the drifts upward and downward begin at least 12 months before the report is released (when the portfolios are first

EMPIRICAL EVALUATION OF ACCOUNTING INCOME NUMBERS

TABLE 6
Contingency Table of the Signs of the Income Forecast Errors—by Variable

	Sign of income forecast error						
Sign of income forecast error	Variable (1)		Variable (2)		Variable (3)	
	+	−	+	−	+	−
Variable (1)						
+	1231	—	1148	83	1074	157
−	—	1109	83	1026	399	710
Variable (2)						
+	1148	83	1231	—	1074	157
−	83	1026	—	1109	399	710
Variable (3)						
+	1074	399	1074	399	1473	—
−	157	710	157	710	—	867

constructed) and continue for approximately one month after. The persistence of the drifts, as indicated by the constant signs of the indexes and by their almost monotonic increases in absolute value (Figure 1), suggests not only that the market begins to anticipate forecast errors early in the 12 months preceding the report, but also that it continues to do so with increasing success throughout the year.[27]

SPECIFIC RESULTS

1. There appears to be little difference between the results for the two regression model variables. Table 6, which classifies the sign of one variable's forecast error contingent upon the signs of the errors of the other two variables, reveals the reason. For example, on the 1231 occasions on which the income forecast error was positive for variable (1), it was also positive on 1148 occasions (out of a possible 1231) for variable (2). Similarly, on the 1109 occasions on which the income forecast error was negative for variable (1), it was also negative on 1026 occasions for variable (2). The fact that the results for variable (2) strictly dominate those for variable (1) suggests, however, that when the two variables disagreed on the sign of an income forecast error, variable (2) was more often correct.

While there is little to choose between variables (1) and (2), variable (3) (the naive model) is clearly best for the portfolio made up of firms with negative forecast errors. A contributing factor is the following. The naive model gives the same forecast error as the regression model would give if

---
[27] Note that Figure 1 contains averages over many firms and years and is not indicative of the behavior of the securities of any particular firm in any one year. While there may be, on average, a persistent and gradual anticipation of the contents of the report throughout the year, evidence on the extent of autocorrelation in the stock return residuals would suggest that the market's reaction to information about a particular firm tends to occur rapidly.

(a) the change in market income were zero, and (b) there were no drift in the income of the firm. But historically there has been an increase in the market's income, particularly during the latter part of the sample period, due to general increase in prices and the strong influence of the protracted expansion since 1961. Thus, the naive model [variable (3)] typically identifies as firms with negative forecast errors those relatively few firms which showed a decrease in EPS when most firms showed an increase. Of the three variables, one would be most confident that the incomes of those which showed negative forecast errors for variable (3) have in fact lost ground relative to the market.

This observation has interesting implications. For example, it points to a relationship between the magnitudes of the income forecast errors and the magnitudes of the abnormal stock price adjustments. This conclusion is reinforced by Figure 1 which shows that the results for positive forecast errors are weaker for variable (3) than for the other two.

2. The drift downward in the Abnormal Performance Index computed over all firms and years in the sample reflects a computational bias.[28] The bias arises because

$$E[\prod_m (1 + v_m)] \neq \prod_m [1 + E(v_m)],$$

where E denotes the expected value. It can readily be seen that the bias over K months is at least of order $(K - 1)$ times the covariance between v_m and v_{m-1}.[29] Since this covariance is typically negative,[30] the bias is also negative.

While the bias does not affect the tenor of our results in any way, it should be kept in mind when interpreting the values of the various API's. It helps explain, for example, why the absolute changes in the indexes in the bottom panel of Figure 1 tend to be greater than those in the top panel; why the indexes in the top panel tend to turn down shortly after month 0; and finally, why the drifts in the indexes in the bottom panel tend to persist beyond the month of the report announcement.

3. We also computed results for the regression model using the additional definitions of income:

(a) cash flow, as approximated by operating income,[31] and

(b) net income before nonrecurring items.

Neither variable was as successful in predicting the signs of the stock return

---

[28] The expected value of the bias is of order minus one-half to minus one-quarter of one per cent per annum. The difference between the observed value of the API computed over the total sample and its expectation is a property of the particular sample (see footnote 26).

[29] In particular, the approximation neglects all permutations of the product $v_s \cdot v_t$, $s = 1, 2, \cdots, K-2, t = s+2, \cdots, K$, as being of a second order of smallness.

[30] See Table 4.

[31] All variable definitions are specified in Standard and Poor's *Compustat Manual* [see also Ball and Brown (1967), Appendix A].

EMPIRICAL EVALUATION OF ACCOUNTING INCOME NUMBERS 173

residuals as net income and EPS. For example, by month 0, the Abnormal Performance Indexes for forecast errors which were positive were 1.068 (net income, including nonrecurring items) and 1.070 (operating income). These numbers compare with 1.071 for net income [Table 5, variable (1)]. The respective numbers for firms and years with negative forecast errors were 0.911, 0.917, and 0.907.

4. Both the API's and the chi-square test in Table 5 suggest that, at least for variable (3), the relationship between the sign of the income forecast error and that of the stock return residual may have persisted for as long as two months beyond the month of the announcement of the annual report. One explanation might be that the market's index of income was not known for sure until after several firms had announced their income numbers. The elimination of uncertainty about the market's income subsequent to some firms' announcements might tend, when averaged over all firms in the sample, to be reflected in a persistence in the drifts in the API's beyond the announcement month. This explanation can probably be ruled out, however, since when those firms which made their announcements in January of any one year were excluded from the sample for that year, there were no changes in the patterns of the overall API's as presented in Figure 1, although generally there were reductions in the χ^2 statistics.[32]

A second explanation could be random errors in the announcement dates. Drifts in the API's would persist beyond the announcement month if errors resulted in our treating some firms as if they had announced their income numbers earlier than in fact was the case. But this explanation can also probably be ruled out, since all announcement dates taken from the *Wall Street Journal Index* were verified against the *Wall Street Journal*.

A third explanation could be that preliminary reports are not perceived by the market as being final. Unfortunately this issue cannot be resolved independently of an alternative hypothesis, namely that the market does take more time to adjust to information if the value of that information is less than the transactions costs that would be incurred by an investor who wished to take advantage of the opportunity for abnormal gain. That is, even if the relationship tended to persist beyond the announcement month, it is clear that unless transactions costs were within about one per cent,[33]

[32] The general reduction in the χ^2 statistic is due largely to the reduction in sample size.

[33] This result is obtained as follows. The ratio API_m/API_{m-1} is equal to the marginal return in month m plus unity:

$$\frac{API_m}{API_{m-1}} = (1 + r_m).$$

Similarly,

$$\frac{API_m}{API_{m-2}} = \frac{API_m}{API_{m-1}} \cdot \frac{API_{m-1}}{API_{m-2}} = (1 + r_m) \cdot (1 + r_{m-1}),$$

there was no opportunity for abnormal profit once the income information had become generally available. Our results are thus consistent with other evidence that the market tends to react to data without bias, at least to within transactions costs.

THE VALUE OF ANNUAL NET INCOME RELATIVE TO OTHER SOURCES OF INFORMATION[34]

The results demonstrate that the information contained in the annual income number is useful in that it is related to stock prices. But annual accounting reports are only one of the many sources of information available to investors. The aim of this section is to assess the relative importance of information contained in net income, and at the same time to provide some insight into the timeliness of the income report.

It was suggested earlier that the impact of new information about an individual stock could be measured by the stock's return residual. For example, a negative residual would indicate that the actual return is less than what would have been expected had there been no bad information. Equivalently, if an investor is able to take advantage of the information either by selling or by taking a short position in advance of the market adjustment, then the residual will represent, ignoring transactions costs, the extent to which his return is greater than would normally be expected.

If the difference between the realized and expected return is accepted as also indicating the value of new information, then it is clear that the value of new, monthly information, good or bad, about an individual stock is given by the absolute value of that stock's return residual for the given month. It follows that the value of all monthly information concerning the average firm, received in the 12 months preceding the report, is given by:

$$TI_0 = \frac{1}{N} \sum_j^N \left[\prod_{m=-11}^{0} (1 + |v_{jm}|) \right] - 1.00,$$

and, in general,

$$\frac{API_m}{API_s} = (1 + r_{s+1}) \cdots (1 + r_m).$$

Thus, the marginal return for the two months after the announcement date on the portfolio consisting of firms for which EPS decrease would have been $0.878/0.887 - 1 \cong -.010$; similarly, the marginal return on the portfolio of firms for which EPS increased would have been $1.059/1.056 - 1 \cong .003$. After allowing for the computational bias, it would appear that transactions costs must have been within one per cent for opportunities to have existed for abnormal profit from applying some mechanical trading rule.

[34] This analysis does not consider the *marginal* contribution of information contained in the annual income number. It would be interesting to analyze dividends in a way similar to that we have used for income announcements. We expect there would be some overlap. To the extent that there is an overlap, we attribute the information to the income number and consider the dividend announcement to be the medium by which the market learns about income. This assumption is highly artificial in that historical income numbers and dividend payments might both simply be reflections of the same, more fundamental informational determinants of stock prices.

where TI denotes total information.[35] For our sample, averaged over all firms and years, this sum was 0.731.

For any one particular stock, some of the information between months will be offsetting.[36] The value of net information (received in the 12 months preceding the report) about the average stock is given by:

$$NI_0 = \frac{1}{N} \sum_{j}^{N} \left| \prod_{m=-11}^{0} (1 + v_{jm}) - 1.00 \right|,$$

where NI denotes net information. This sum was 0.165.

The impact of the annual income number is also a net number in that net income is the result of both income-increasing and income-decreasing events. If one accepts the forecast error model,[37] then the value of information contained in the annual income number may be estimated by the average of the value increments from month -11 to month 0, where the increments are averaged over the two portfolios constructed from (buying or selling short) all firms and years as classified by the signs of the income forecast errors. That is,

$$II_0 = \frac{N1(API_0^{N1} - 1.00) - N2(API_0^{N2} - 1.00)}{(N1 + N2)},$$

where II denotes income information, and $N1$ and $N2$ the number of occasions on which the income forecast error was positive and negative respectively. This number was 0.081 for variable (1), 0.083 for variable (2), and 0.077 for variable (3).

From the above numbers we conclude:

(1) about 75 per cent [(.731 − .165)/.731] of the value of all information appears to be offsetting, which in turn implies that about 25 per cent persists; and

(2) of the 25 per cent which persists, about half [49%, 50%, and 47%—calculated as .081/.165, .083/.165, and .077/.165—for variables (1)-(3)] can be associated with the information contained in reported income.

Two further conclusions, not directly evident, are:

(3) of the value of information contained in reported income, no more than about 10 to 15 per cent (12%, 11%, and 13%) has not been anticipated by the month of the report;[38] and

---

[35] Note that the information is reflected in a value increment; thus, the original $1.00 is deducted from the terminal value.

[36] This assertion is supported by the observed low autocorrelation in the stock return residuals.

[37] Note that since we are interested in the "average firm," an investment strategy must be adopted on every sample member. Because there are only two relevant strategies involved, it is sufficient to know whether one is better off to buy or to sell short. Note also that the analysis assumes the strategy is first adopted 12 months prior to the announcement date.

[38] The average monthly yield from a policy of buying a portfolio consisting of all firms with positive forecast errors and adopting a short position on the rest would have resulted in an average monthly abnormal rate of return, from −11 to −1, of

(4) the value of information conveyed by the income number at the time of its release constitutes, on average, only 20 per cent (19%, 18%, and 19%) of the value of all information coming to the market in that month.[39]

The second conclusion indicates that accounting income numbers capture about half of the net effect of all information available throughout the 12 months preceding their release; yet the fourth conclusion suggests that net income contributes only about 20 per cent of the value of all information in the month of its release. The apparent paradox is presumably due to the fact that: (a) many other bits of information are usually released in the same month as reported income (for example, via dividend announcements, or perhaps other items in the financial reports); (b) 85 to 90 per cent of the net effect of information about annual income is already reflected in security prices by the month of its announcement; and (c) the period of the annual report is already one-and-one-half months into history.

Ours is perhaps the first attempt to assess empirically the relative importance of the annual income number, but it does have limitations. For example, our results are systematically biased against findings in favor of accounting reports due to:

1. the assumption that stock prices are from transactions which have taken place simultaneously at the end of the month;
2. the assumption that there are no errors in the data;
3. the discrete nature of stock price quotations;
4. the presumed validity of the "errors in forecast" model; and
5. the regression estimates of the income forecast errors being random variables, which implies that some misclassifications of the "true" earnings forecast errors are inevitable.

Concluding Remarks

The initial objective was to assess the usefulness of existing accounting income numbers by examining their information content and timeliness. The mode of analysis permitted some definite conclusions which we shall briefly restate. Of all the information about an individual firm which becomes available during a year, one-half or more is captured in that year's income number. Its content is therefore considerable. However, the annual income report does not rate highly as a timely medium, since most of its content (about 85 to 90 per cent) is captured by more prompt media which perhaps include interim reports. Since the efficiency of the capital market

---

0.63%, 0.66%, and 0.60% for variables (1), (2), and (3) respectively. The marginal rate of return in month 0 for that same strategy would have been 0.92%, 0.89%, and 0.94% respectively. However, relatively much more information is conveyed in the month of the report announcement than in either of the two months immediately preceding the announcement month or in the two months immediately following it. This result is consistent with those obtained by Beaver (1968).

[39] An optimum policy (that is, one which takes advantage of all information) would have yielded an abnormal rate of return of 4.9% in month 0.

is largely determined by the adequacy of its data sources, we do not find it disconcerting that the market has turned to other sources which can be acted upon more promptly than annual net income.

This study raises several issues for further investigation. For example, there remains the task of identifying the media by which the market is able to anticipate net income: of what help are interim reports and dividend announcements? For accountants, there is the problem of assessing the cost of preparing annual income reports relative to that of the more timely interim reports.

The relationship between the magnitude (and not merely the sign) of the unexpected income change and the associated stock price adjustment could also be investigated.[40] This would offer a different way of measuring the value of information about income changes, and might, in addition, furnish insight into the statistical nature of the income process, a process little understood but of considerable interest to accounting researchers.

Finally, a mechanism has been provided for an empirical approach to a restricted class of the controversial choices in external reporting.

REFERENCES

BALL, RAY AND PHILIP BROWN (1967). "Some Preliminary Findings on the Association between the Earnings of a Firm, Its Industry and the Economy," *Empirical Research in Accounting: Selected Studies, 1967*, Supplement to Volume 5 of the *Journal of Accounting Research*, pp. 55–77.

BEAVER, WILLIAM H. (1968). "The Information Content of Annual Earnings Announcements," forthcoming in *Empirical Research in Accounting: Selected Studies 1968*, Supplement to Volume 6 of the *Journal of Accounting Research*.

BLUME, MARSHALL E. (1968). "The Assessment of Portfolio Performance" (unpublished Ph.D. dissertation, University of Chicago).

BREALEY, RICHARD A. (1968). "The Influence of the Economy on the Earnings of the Firm" (unpublished paper presented at the Sloane School of Finance Seminar, Massachusetts Institute of Technology, May, 1968).

BROWN, PHILIP AND VICTOR NIEDERHOFFER (1968). "The Predictive Content of Quarterly Earnings," *Journal of Business*.

CANNING, JOHN B. (1929). *The Economics of Accountancy* (New York: The Ronald Press Co.).

CHAMBERS, RAYMOND J. (1964). "Measurement and Objectivity in Accounting," *The Accounting Review*, XXXIX (April, 1964), 264–74.

—— (1966). *Accounting, Evaluation, and Economic Behavior* (Englewood Cliffs, N.J.: Prentice-Hall).

—— (1967). "Continuously Contemporary Accounting—Additivity and Action," *The Accounting Review*, XLII (October, 1967), 751–57.

COOTNER, PAUL H., ed. (1964). *The Random Character of Stock Market Prices* (Cambridge, Mass.: The M.I.T. Press).

---

[40] There are some difficult econometric problems associated with this relationship, including specifying the appropriate functional form, the expected statistical distributions of the underlying parameters, the expected behavior of the regression residuals, and the extent and effects of measurement errors in both dependent and independent variables. (The functional form need not necessarily be linear, if only because income numbers convey information about the covariability of the income process.)

EDWARDS, EDGAR O. AND PHILIP W. BELL (1961). *The Theory and Measurement of Business Income* (Berkeley, Cal.: The University of California Press).

FAMA, EUGENE F. (1965). "The Behavior of Stock Market Prices," *Journal of Business*, XXXVIII (January, 1965), 34–105.

—— AND MARSHALL E. BLUME (1966). "Filter Rules and Stock Market Trading," *Journal of Business*, XXXIX (Supplement, January, 1966), 226–41.

——, LAWRENCE FISHER, MICHAEL C. JENSEN, AND RICHARD ROLL (1967). "The Adjustment of Stock Prices to New Information," Report No. 6715 (University of Chicago: Center for Mathematical Studies in Business and Economics; forthcoming in the *International Economic Review*).

FISHER, LAWRENCE (1966). "Some New Stock Market Indices," *Journal of Business*, XXXIX (Supplement, January, 1966), 191–225.

GILMAN, STEPHAN (1939). *Accounting Concepts of Profit* (New York: The Ronald Press Co.).

IJIRI, YUJI (1967). *The Foundations of Accounting Measurement* (Englewood Cliffs, N.J.: Prentice-Hall).

JENSEN, MICHAEL C. (1968). "Risk, the Pricing of Capital Assets, and the Evaluation of Investment Portfolios" (unpublished Ph.D. dissertation, University of Chicago).

KING, BENJAMIN F. (1966). "Market and Industry Factors in Stock Price Behavior," *Journal of Business*, XXXIX (Supplement, January, 1966), 139-90.

LIM, RONALD S. (1966). "The Mathematical Propriety of Accounting Measurements and Calculations," *The Accounting Review*, XLI (October, 1966), 642–51.

PATON, W. A. AND A. C. LITTLETON (1940). *An Introduction to Corporate Accounting Standards* (American Accounting Association Monograph No. 3).

SAMUELSON, PAUL A. (1965). "Proof That Properly Anticipated Prices Fluctuate Randomly," *Industrial Management Review*, 7 (Spring, 1965), 41–49.

SCHOLES, MYRON J. (1967). "The Effect of Secondary Distributions on Price" (unpublished paper presented at the Seminar on the Analysis of Security Prices, University of Chicago).

SHARPE, WILLIAM F. (1964). "Capital Asset Prices: A Theory of Market Equilibrium under Conditions of Risk," *Journal of Finance*, XIX (September, 1964), 425–42.

STERLING, ROBERT R. (1967). "Elements of Pure Accounting Theory," *The Accounting Review*, XLII (January, 1967), 62–73.

VATTER, WILLIAM J. (1947). *The Fund Theory of Accounting* (Chicago: The University of Chicago Press).

EVIDENCE THAT STOCK PRICES DO NOT FULLY REFLECT THE IMPLICATIONS OF CURRENT EARNINGS FOR FUTURE EARNINGS*

Victor L. BERNARD

Harvard Business School, Boston, MA 02163, USA
University of Michigan, Ann Arbor, MI 48109, USA

Jacob K. THOMAS

Columbia University, New York, NY 10027, USA

Received May 1990, final version received December 1990

Evidence presented here is consistent with a failure of stock prices to reflect fully the implications of current earnings for future earnings. Specifically, the three-day price reactions to announcements of earnings for quarters $t+1$ through $t+4$ are predictable, based on earnings of quarter t. Even more surprisingly, the signs and magnitudes of the three-day reactions are related to the autocorrelation structure of earnings, as if stock prices fail to reflect the extent to which each firm's earnings series differs from a seasonal random walk.

1. Introduction

Several studies have documented that estimated abnormal returns are predictable, based on previously-announced earnings [e.g., Ball and Brown (1968), Joy, Litzenberger, and McEnally (1977), Watts (1978), Rendleman, Jones, and Latane (1982), and Foster, Olsen, and Shevlin (1984)]. Repeated attempts to explain this 'post-earnings-announcement drift' as a product of research design flaws, including failure to adjust abnormal returns fully for

---

*We would like to acknowledge Thomas Lys, the referee, whose suggestions led to substantive improvements in the paper. We are grateful to Jim Wahlen for his research assistance and suggestions, and to Harry DeAngelo, Charles Jones, and members of Prudential Bache's Quantitative Research department, who helped plant the seeds that led to this research. We also appreciate comments received from Ray Ball, Robert Bowen, Michael Brennan, Larry Brown, Susan Chaplinsky, Gene Fama, Mark Grinblatt, Gautam Kaul, Han Kim, S.P. Kothari, Gene Imhoff, Maurice Joy, Robert Freeman, Robert Lipe, Jim McKeown, Pat O'Brien, Gordon Richardson, Jay Ritter, Michael Salinger, Nejat Seyhun, Doug Skinner, Ross Watts (the editor), and other participants in workshops at Baruch College, Columbia University, Florida State University, Harvard Business School, M.I.T., Notre Dame, Penn State University, and the Universities of Colorado, Illinois, Kansas, Michigan, Rochester, Southern California, and South Carolina. Victor Bernard is grateful for the support of the Price Waterhouse Foundation.

risk, have failed to resolve the anomaly.[1] Bernard and Thomas (1989) describe an implementable strategy, based upon the anomaly, that produces an estimated annualized abnormal return of 18 percent (before transactions costs) during the first quarter subsequent to the earnings announcement. Smaller abnormal returns appear to persist for at least two additional quarters.

It is difficult to understand why stock prices would appear not to respond completely and immediately to information as visible and freely available as publicly announced earnings. Although they do not purport to identify the reason for post-announcement drift, Bernard and Thomas (1989) and Freeman and Tse (1989) do provide one clue that could aid in the pursuit for an explanation. Specifically, they find that a disproportionately large fraction of the post-announcement drift is 'delayed' until the subsequent quarter's earnings announcement. In other words, given that a firm announces positive (negative) unexpected earnings for quarter t, the market tends to be positively (negatively) surprised in the days surrounding the announcement for quarter $t + 1$. As Bernard and Thomas note, the evidence is consistent with a market that 'fails to adequately revise its expectations for quarter $t + 1$ earnings upon receipt of the news for quarter t' (p. 27).

This paper investigates the possibility that stock prices fail to reflect fully the implications of current earnings for future earnings. Specifically, we entertain the hypothesis that prices fail to reflect the extent to which the time-series behavior of earnings deviates from a naive expectation: a seasonal random walk, where expected earnings are simply earnings for the corresponding quarter from the previous year.[2] It is well known that earnings

---

[1] A battery of tests in Bernard and Thomas (1989, p. 34) produces evidence that 'cannot plausibly be reconciled with arguments built on risk mismeasurement'. Specifically, Bernard and Thomas show that (1) contrary to the prediction of Ball, Kothari, and Watts (1988) shifts in beta are far too small to explain the drift; (2) five other measures of risk identified in the arbitrage pricing literature fail to explain the drift; (3) there is no evidence of any other (unidentified) risk surfacing in the form of a loss – that is, returns to a zero-investment trading strategy are consistently positive over time; and (4) in violation of plausible predictions of capital asset pricing theory as they would apply to a broad cross-section of stocks, the mean *raw* (total) post-announcement returns on 'bad news' stocks are significantly less than Treasury bill rates. Both Bernard and Thomas (1989) and Foster, Olsen, and Shevlin (1984) also cast doubt on the viability of other explanations based on potential research design flaws, such as various forms of hindsight bias, survivorship bias, and biases in return calculations.

[2] We are not the first to consider this possibility. That credit goes to Rendleman, Jones, and Latane (1987), who showed that when one controls for quarter $t + 1$ earnings, much of the drift associated with quarter t earnings is eliminated. They conclude that post-announcement drift can be explained in part as a predictable response to the subsequent earnings announcement. However, since that study focuses on abnormal returns measured over long windows, it is difficult to rule out alternative explanations for the results (e.g., certain risk-based arguments). Freeman and Tse (1989) document (1) the predictability of the short-window response to quarter $t + 1$ earnings that is also documented in Bernard and Thomas (1989) and (2) that when one controls for the effect of quarter $t + 1$ earnings at least half of the drift associated with quarter t earnings is eliminated. On that basis, they conclude that 'the time-series behavior of earnings

forecast errors based on such a naive model are correlated through time [see, for example, Freeman and Tse (1989)]. In contrast, in a market that fully impounds all prior earnings information, forecast errors should not be autocorrelated (by definition). What we study here is the possibility that market prices can be modeled partially as reflections of naive expectations, and that as a result, the reactions of prices to future earnings are predictable, just as the forecast errors of a naive expectation model are predictable.

Our results are surprisingly consistent with this depiction of stock-price behavior. By assuming that stock prices are at least partially influenced by the above naive earnings expectation, we are able to predict with a significant degree of accuracy the three-day reaction to *future* earnings announcements (up to four quarters ahead), given only *current* earnings and information about the (historical) time-series behavior of earnings. Moreover, we can relate not only the *signs* but the relative *magnitudes* of the future reactions to the autocorrelation structure of forecast errors based on the naive seasonal random-walk earnings expectation.

One of the most surprising aspects of our evidence pertains to our predictions of market reactions four quarters ahead. In contrast to the well-documented *positive* relation between unexpected earnings for quarter t and post-announcement drift for quarter $t + 1$, we find a *negative* relation between unexpected earnings of quarter t and the abnormal returns around the announcement of earnings for quarter $t + 4$. This finding would not be predicted by any existing explanations for post-announcement drift based on concerns about potential research design flaws. However, this pattern in the data is precisely what would be expected if the prices failed to reflect fully that, while seasonally-differenced earnings are *positively* correlated for adjacent quarters, they are *negatively* correlated four quarters apart. That is, the data behave as if the market is consistently surprised that a portion of an earnings change tends to be reversed four quarters later.

A stock market in which prices are influenced by traders who anchor on a comparison of year-to-year changes in quarterly earnings, much like the financial press does in its coverage of earnings announcements (e.g., the Wall Street Journal's Digest of Earnings Reports), represents a disturbing departure from what would be predicted by existing models of efficient markets. For zero-investment portfolios constructed on the basis of the historical time-series behavior of earnings, the indicated abnormal returns from the day after the earnings announcement through the subsequent earnings announcement are approximately 8 to 9 percent, or 35 percent on an annualized basis, before transactions costs. Even higher abnormal returns per unit time (67

---

provides a partial explanation of the drift phenomenon'. However, that possibility was not the main focus of the Freeman and Tse paper, and thus they did not draw the links between post-announcement drift and the time-series properties of earnings that are documented here.

percent on an annualized basis) are available for portfolios constructed 15 days prior to the expected date for the upcoming announcement and held through the announcement.

The evidence in this paper offers two main contributions beyond the previous literature on post-announcement drift. First, the paper relates the signs and magnitudes of reactions to subsequent earnings announcements to the historical autocorrelation structure of earnings; this linkage may help identify the cause of post-announcement drift. Second, the evidence as a whole creates several added obstacles to contentions that the drift might ultimately be explained by errors in the methodology used to estimate expected returns. For example, an explanation based on failure to control for risk would now have to argue that 'good-news' firms experience 'delayed' increases in risk over three-day intervals that coincide with each of the next three earnings announcements, and then a decrease in risk over the three-day interval coinciding with the fourth subsequent announcement. The converse would have to hold for 'bad-news' firms. At a minimum, any rationale for such behavior must have a more complex structure than explanations suggested to date.

The nature of the evidence in this paper is also distinct in an important way from that in the growing body of other studies that question semi-strong or weak-form market efficiency [e.g., Ou and Penman (1989a, b), Poterba and Summers (1988)]. While such studies conclude that discrepancies appear to exist between stock prices and underlying fundamentals, they make only vague predictions about *when* the discrepancies will be eliminated and associated abnormal returns realized. In contrast, our assumption about earnings expectations allows us to successfully predict within days the timing of subsequent abnormal returns. By linking what appears to be the elimination of a discrepancy between prices and fundamentals to prespecified information events, the study presents perhaps the most direct evidence to date that a market-efficiency anomaly is rooted in a failure of information to flow completely into price. The evidence also emphasizes that even in a market where prices fail to reflect all available information, one can still observe unusual stock-price activity concentrated around news releases. The puzzling question is, if a portion of the 'news' became predictable months earlier, why did the associated price movements not occur then?

The rest of the paper is organized as follows. In section 2, we review the time-series behavior of earnings and develop hypotheses about how stock prices would behave if the earnings expectations embedded in such prices failed to reflect fully those time-series properties. Section 3 includes tests of those hypotheses. Questions raised by the evidence and potential alternative explanations for the results are discussed in section 4. We discuss the links between this and other research in section 5, and offer concluding remarks in section 6.

2. Hypothesis development

2.1. Time-series properties of quarterly earnings

Several studies have documented the time-series behavior of quarterly earnings [e.g., Watts (1975), Foster (1977), Griffin (1977), Brown and Rozeff (1979), Bathke and Lorek (1984), Brown, Hagerman, Griffin, and Zmijewski (1987)]. The cumulative evidence indicates that seasonal differences in quarterly earnings are correlated, and that the pattern of correlations can be viewed as including two components. First, there is a positive correlation between seasonal differences that is strongest for adjacent quarters, but that remains positive over the first three lags. Thus, a change in earnings of quarter t (relative to the comparable quarter of the prior year) tends to be followed by progressively smaller changes of the same sign in quarters $t + 1$, $t + 2$, and $t + 3$. Second, there is a negative correlation between seasonal differences that are four quarters apart. That is, a portion of the change for quarter t is 'reversed' in quarter $t + 4$.

To offer a more specific description of the time-series behavior of earnings, table 1 presents summary statistics for the sample to be studied here, which is based on the sample used in Bernard and Thomas (1989).[3] The earnings number used is net income before extraordinary items and discontinued items (item 8 from the quarterly Compustat tape). Panel A confirms that, consistent with prior research, the autocorrelations at the first three lags are positive but declining; the sample means of autocorrelations estimated separately for each firm are 0.34, 0.19, and 0.06 for lags 1, 2, and 3, respectively. Also consistent with prior research, there is a negative autocorrelation at the fourth lag (mean = -0.24). Beyond the fourth lag, the mean autocorrelations remain negative, but much smaller: -0.08, -0.07, -0.07, -0.06 for lags 5 through 8, respectively.

To obtain an intuitive sense for the implications of these autocorrelations, consider the following example. A firm reports quarterly earnings in year 0 of $10, $10, $10, and $20. Actual earnings for the first quarter of year 1 rise $1, to $11. Assuming no linear trend in earnings and that the autocorrelation structure of the firm's earnings is as depicted for the mean firm in table 1, the

---

[3]The sample is obtained from firms listed on the 1987 edition of the daily CRSP file and also listed on any edition of the Compustat quarterly files from 1982 to 1987. Based on earnings data beginning in 1970, we obtained estimates of unexpected earnings for 96,087 announcements over the period 1974–1986 for 2,649 firms. Abnormal returns data were available for up to 85,753 announcements, depending upon the return interval used. The number of observations reported in the tables varies across tests, depending upon factors such as the availability of measures of unexpected earnings at the specified lags and the interval over which abnormal returns are cumulated.

Table 1
Time-series behavior of quarterly earnings, 2,626 firms, 1974–1986.

Panel A: Autocorrelations in seasonally differenced quarterly earnings							
Lag	1	2	3	4	5	6	7	8

Distribution of firm-specific autocorrelations in seasonally-differenced earnings

	1	2	3	4	5	6	7	8
Mean	0.34	0.19	0.06	−0.24	−0.08	−0.07	−0.07	−0.06
25th percentile	0.14	0.05	−0.10	−0.46	−0.26	−0.24	−0.24	−0.25
Median	0.36	0.18	0.06	−0.29	−0.09	−0.08	−0.06	−0.06
75th percentile	0.57	0.35	0.21	−0.07	0.08	0.08	0.09	0.11

Distribution of mean autocorrelations for 37 industries[a]

	1	2	3	4	5	6	7	8
Number of positive mean autocorrelations (out of 37)	37	37	35	0	5	8	6	7
25th percentile (of 37 means)	0.29	0.14	0.00	−0.29	−0.13	−0.12	−0.12	−0.10
Median (of 37 means)	0.35	0.19	0.07	−0.24	−0.09	−0.08	−0.08	−0.08
75th percentile (of 37 means)	0.38	0.22	0.09	−0.18	−0.04	−0.01	−0.04	−0.03

Mean firm-specific autocorrelations within size categories[b]

	1	2	3	4	5	6	7	8
Small (bottom 4 deciles)	0.28	0.14	0.03	−0.29	−0.09	−0.08	−0.08	−0.08
Medium	0.31	0.19	0.07	−0.23	−0.07	−0.08	−0.06	−0.04
Large (top 3 deciles)	0.36	0.20	0.06	−0.20	−0.09	−0.05	−0.06	−0.06

Panel B: Autocorrelations in seasonally-differenced earnings and standardized unexpected earnings (SUE)[c]

Lag	1	2	3	4	5	6	7	8

Mean of firm-specific autocorrelations

	1	2	3	4	5	6	7	8
Seasonally differenced earnings (as in panel A)	0.34	0.19	0.06	−0.24	−0.08	−0.07	−0.07	−0.06
SUEs	0.40	0.22	0.06	−0.21	−0.10	−0.09	−0.09	−0.08
SUE deciles	0.41	0.23	0.07	−0.18	−0.09	−0.09	−0.09	−0.08

[a] Mean of firm-specific autocorrelations is calculated for each industry to obtain distribution of 37 autocorrelations at each lag. Only the 37 two-digit SIC industries that contain at least 20 members are represented here.

[b] Small, medium, and large firms are in size deciles 1 to 4, 5 to 7, and 8 to 10, respectively, based on January 1 market values of equity for NYSE–AMEX firms.

[c] SUEs are forecast errors from a seasonal random walk with trend, scaled by their standard deviation within the trend estimation period (up to 36 observations). SUE deciles are based on rankings within calender quarters.

expected earnings for the next four quarters would be as indicated in italics below.

	Year 0	Year 1	Year 2
Quarter I	$10.00	$11.00	*$10.76*
Quarter II	10.00	*10.34*	
Quarter III	10.00	*10.19*	
Quarter IV	20.00	*20.06*	

For the next three quarters, one would expect additional increases over the prior year level, but the amounts of the expected increases decline over the three quarters. Looking four quarters ahead to the first quarter of year 2, we expect earnings will decline relative to this year; that is, a portion of the initial earnings change is not expected to persist.

Panel A also shows that this kind of autocorrelation pattern is quite consistent across firms. First, the pattern persists generally across the 37 two-digit SIC industries for which our sample includes 20 or more firms. For example, the signs of the within-industry means of the firm-specific autocorrelations calculated are in agreement for all 37 industries at lags 1, 2, and 4, and for 35 of 37 industries at lag 3. Second, the pattern of mean autocorrelations calculated within size categories is similar across small, medium, and large firms (those in the bottom four, middle three, and top three deciles of the NYSE/AMEX population). However, the autocorrelations over the first four lags tend to be somewhat more positive for large firms.

Panel B compares the autocorrelations in seasonally differenced earnings with those for *standardized unexpected earnings* (*SUE*), which will be a key variable in our empirical tests. The numerator of *SUE* is equal to actual earnings minus an expectation based on a seasonal random walk with trend (where the trend is estimated using up to 36 quarters of history, if available); that is, it is simply the detrended seasonal difference in earnings. The denominator is equal to the standard deviation of this measure of unexpected earnings over the trend estimation period. To reduce the influence of outliers, *SUE* values greater (less) than 5 (-5) are winsorized to 5 (-5). The autocorrelations in *SUE* are calculated for each firm in the sample, and a mean across firms is obtained for the autocorrelation at each lag.

The first two rows of panel B confirm that the pattern of autocorrelations in the *SUE*s is similar to the pattern already discussed for seasonally differenced earnings (although the magnitudes are slightly higher when *SUE* is the unit of analysis). The similarity indicates that the process of scaling the seasonal differences does not have a large influence on the degree of autocorrelation.

The last row of panel B presents autocorrelations in the *decile assignments* of *SUE*s (based on the distribution of all *SUE*s for a given calendar quarter), as opposed to *SUE*s *per se*. These statistics are of interest because much of our subsequent analysis is based on *SUE* deciles. As expected, the results indicate that *SUE* deciles have time-series properties very similar to those of the *SUE*s.

2.2. Hypothesis development

We now consider the behavior of stock prices in a market where earnings expectations fail to reflect the autocorrelation pattern described above. That is, we entertain the possibility that the earnings expectations reflected in stock prices follow a seasonal random walk with trend.[4] Even though market prices may reflect less naive expectations, our goal is to develop predictions for this extreme case and then test the extent to which such predictions are supported by the data. That is, we assume that the expectation of earnings for quarter t that is embedded in the market price, denoted by $E^M(Q_t)$, is as follows:

$$E^M[Q_t] = \delta + Q_{t-4}. \tag{1}$$

When earnings Q_t are announced, the market perceives the unexpected component of earnings to be $Q_t - E^M[Q_t]$. Given an 'earnings response coefficient' λ, the resulting abnormal return is

$$AR_t = \lambda(Q_t - E^M[Q_t]) = \lambda(Q_t - Q_{t-4} - \delta). \tag{2}$$

Note that the abnormal return reflects a component equal to the current detrended seasonal difference in earnings. Thus, the abnormal return should be correlated with past detrended seasonal differences in earnings, in the same way that the current detrended seasonal difference is correlated with past detrended seasonal differences. Specifically, we hypothesize the following:

Hypothesis 1. If prices reflect an earnings expectation described by a seasonal random walk with trend, there should be positive but declining associations between the abnormal return at the announcement of quarter t earnings and the detrended seasonal differences in earnings for quarters $t-1$, $t-2$, and $t-3$. There should be a negative association between the abnormal return at the announcement of quarter t earnings and the detrended seasonal difference in earnings for quarter $t-4$.

A useful feature of Hypothesis 1 is that it links the relation between abnormal returns and prior-period earnings data to the autocorrelation patterns presented in prior research and in table 1, and does so without the need to specify explicitly a particular model of the actual earnings process. However, the hypothesis represents a statement about the *simple* relation between abnormal returns and earnings changes of each prior period *taken individually*. If we are more precise about the actual time-series process of earnings, we can conveniently relate abnormal returns to earnings data from

---

[4] If we assume instead that the expectation is a seasonal random walk with *no* trend, then Hypothesis 1 below would be stated in terms of seasonal differences, *before detrending*. Empirical tests based on this alternative approach yield results similar to those reported here.

multiple prior periods simultaneously. This, in turn, will prove useful in assessing the economic importance of the predictable component of the abnormal returns.

Based on prior research, we assume that the most accurate univariate description of the time-series process of earnings is provided by the Brown and Rozeff (1979) model, modified to include a trend term:[5]

$$Q_t = \delta + Q_{t-4} + \phi(Q_{t-1} - Q_{t-5}) + \theta \varepsilon_{t-4} + \varepsilon_t, \qquad (3)$$

where ε_t is the white-noise earnings shock of period t, $\phi > 0$, and θ is sufficiently negative to ensure that the fourth-order autocorrelation in seasonally-differenced earnings is negative.

The Brown–Rozeff model includes a first-order autoregressive term $[\phi(Q_{t-1} - Q_{t-5})]$, which is designed to account for the positive but decaying autocorrelations in seasonally differenced earnings at lags 1 through 3. The model also includes a seasonal moving-average term $(\theta \varepsilon_{t-4})$ to account for the negative autocorrelation noted at the fourth lag. The earnings expectation implied by the Brown–Rozeff model is

$$E[Q_t] = \delta + Q_{t-4} + \phi(Q_{t-1} - Q_{t-5}) + \theta \varepsilon_{t-4}. \qquad (4)$$

Several studies [e.g., Brown and Rozeff (1979) and Bathke and Lorek (1984)] have documented that the Brown–Rozeff model fits earnings data well and generates more accurate out-of-sample earnings forecasts than other time-series models. However, the margin of superiority is not 'large'; Bathke and Lorek (1984) find a 9 percent reduction in mean absolute percentage forecast errors when moving from a seasonal random walk with trend to the Brown–Rozeff model. Thus, even if market expectations are characterized by a seasonal random walk with trend, the resulting predictable errors in those expectations might not be substantial. Any ability to predict stock-price reactions to future earnings announcements based on past earnings and the autocorrelation structure of earnings therefore becomes that much more surprising.

---

[5]Allowing for a trend in earnings was less of a concern for Brown and Rozeff, who dealt with per-share data. We assume that the trend term equals that embedded in stock prices [eq. (1)]. This assumption simplifies the development of Hypothesis 2, without altering the thrust of our conclusions. If a difference between the trend terms does exist and it varies across firms, then the observed association (in pooled cross-section) between abnormal returns and each past seasonal difference would be more positive; the negative association at the fourth lag would arise only if θ is sufficiently negative to overcome this effect. It turns out, however, that the observed association at the fourth lag is not only negative, but consistent in terms of magnitude with predictions based on the development of Hypothesis 2. Thus the benefits of a more complex treatment of the trend term appear minimal.

If the time-series process of earnings is best described by a Brown–Rozeff model, but earnings expectations embedded in prices are nevertheless based on a seasonal random walk with trend, then the abnormal return around earnings announcements presented in eq. (2) can be rewritten as shown below. We begin by decomposing the abnormal return in eq. (2) into an unpredictable component, $Q_t - E[Q_t]$, and its complement, $E[Q_t] - E^M[Q_t]$, that is predictable based on knowledge about the time-series behavior of earnings:[6]

$$AR_t = \lambda(Q_t - E^M[Q_t])$$
$$= \lambda(Q_t - E[Q_t]) + \lambda(E[Q_t] - E^M[Q_t]). \quad (5)$$

Relying on the Brown–Rozeff model, we can replace $(Q_t - E[Q_t])$ with the difference between eqs. (3) and (4), and replace $(E[Q_t] - E^M[Q_t])$ with the difference between eqs. (4) and (1):

$$AR_t = \lambda \varepsilon_t + \lambda \phi (Q_{t-1} - Q_{t-5}) + \lambda \theta \varepsilon_{t-4}. \quad (6)$$

Since $(Q_{t-1} - Q_{t-5})$ can be written in terms of prior period shocks, eq. (6) can also be written as

$$AR_t = \lambda \varepsilon_t + \lambda \phi \varepsilon_{t-1} + \lambda \phi^2 \varepsilon_{t-2} + \lambda \phi^3 \varepsilon_{t-3}$$
$$+ \lambda(\theta + \phi^4)\varepsilon_{t-4} + \lambda \nu, \quad (7)$$

where ν is a linear combination of earnings shocks from periods prior to $t-4$, that are uncorrelated with the shocks of periods t through $t-4$, and which have coefficients of order $\theta \phi$ or smaller.

Eqs. (6) and (7) provide the basis for our second hypothesis:

Hypothesis 2. If prices reflect an earnings expectation described by a seasonal random walk with trend, while the univariate times-series process of earnings is best described by the Brown–Rozeff (1979) model as written in eq. (3), then the abnormal return at the announcement of quarter t earnings should have a positive partial correlation with the seasonal difference in earnings for quarter $t-1$, and a negative partial correlation with the earnings shock of period $t-4$.

---

[6]The earnings response coefficient, λ, is assumed constant across the two components of the earnings change, because the market would have no way of distinguishing between the two components given that its expectations are based on a seasonal random walk with trend. The empirical tests, however, do not rely on this assumption as we estimate unrestricted coefficients for the regression models derived from eq. (5).

as specified in eq. (6). Alternatively, the abnormal return at the announcement of quarter *t* earnings should have positive but declining partial correlations with the earnings shocks of quarters $t-1$, $t-2$, and $t-3$, and a negative partial correlation with the earnings shock of period $t-4$ as specified in eq. (7).

Note that Hypothesis 1 and Hypothesis 2 lead to tests of the same fundamental notion that prices are based on an earnings expectation that fails to reflect fully the extent to which the earnings series departs from a seasonal random walk. Hypothesis 2 is distinct from Hypothesis 1 only in that it makes a more specific assumption about the actual time-series properties of earnings. This additional assumption can potentially increase the power of our tests, as well as facilitate the construction of portfolios based on multiple prior-period earnings signals.

3. Empirical tests

3.1. Portfolio tests of Hypothesis 1

Tests of Hypothesis 1 are conducted by forming ten portfolios for each calendar quarter, based on the *SUE* deciles of firms announcing earnings within that quarter. We then observe the relation between the *SUE* assignments and three-day market reactions to earnings announcements for subsequent quarters. (The three-day window includes the two days prior to and the disclosure date as reported on Compustat – from the Wall Street Journal or Dow Jones News Service.) If Hypothesis 1 is correct, then we should observe a positive relation for each of the next three announcements (but with the magnitude of the association declining over the three quarters) and a negative relation for the fourth subsequent announcement.

The measure of abnormal returns used is the same size-adjusted return described in Bernard and Thomas (1989). Daily abnormal returns for a given firm are obtained by subtracting from the total return the return on a portfolio of the NYSE/AMEX firms in the same size decile, based on January 1 market value of equity. Daily size-adjusted returns are summed across firms and cumulated over time to obtain portfolio cumulative abnormal returns.

Prior to reviewing the results, we offer one final comment on an econometric issue. Even though the primary tests focus on short (three-day) return intervals, there is some overlapping of event windows in calendar time. Thus, standard *t*-tests applied to mean abnormal returns would potentially be subject to bias due to cross-correlation in the data [see Bernard (1987)]. Therefore, for each of the major *t*-tests presented here, we also present an 'alternative *t*-test' designed by Jaffe (1974) and Fama and MacBeth (1973) to

Table 2

Predictions of market reactions to future earnings announcements based on current earnings information, 2,463 firms, 1974–1986 (72,076 to 85,482 observations).[a]

Panel A: Three-day percentage abnormal return in quarter $t+k$, for portfolios based on earnings information from quarter t (t-statistics in parentheses)

Portfolio held (based on SUE decile of quarter t)	Holding period (relative to announcement for quarter $t+k$)	$t+1$	$t+2$	$t+3$	$t+4$	$t+5$	$t+6$	$t+7$	$t+8$
10 (good news)	Three-day [−2, 0]	0.76 (13.21)	0.44 (8.05)	0.13 (2.21)	−0.22 (−4.11)	−0.05 (−0.85)	−0.04 (−0.76)	0.01 (0.21)	−0.04 (−0.66)
1 (bad news)	Three-day [−2, 0]	−0.56 (−8.04)	−0.26 (−4.16)	0.09 (0.13)	0.43 (6.82)	0.26 (4.10)	0.19 (2.99)	0.16 (2.43)	0.34 (5.22)
Long in 10/short in 1	Three-day [−2, 0]	1.32 (14.63)	0.70 (8.46)	0.04 (0.45)	−0.66 (−7.86)	−0.31 (−3.68)	−0.23 (−2.73)	−0.15 (−1.70)	−0.38 (−4.44)
Alternative t-test[b]		(7.40)	(5.56)	(1.63)	(−3.38)	(−2.53)	(−2.01)	(−0.89)	(−1.73)

Panel B: Comparison of three-day percentage abnormal returns with percentage abnormal returns since quarter t announcement

Portfolio held	Holding period	$t+1$	$t+2$	$t+3$	$t+4$	$t+5$	$t+6$	$t+7$	$t+8$
Long in 10/short in 1 (reversed after quarter $t+3$)	Sum of three-day abnormal returns for quarters $t+1,\ldots,t+k$	1.32	2.02	2.06	2.72	3.02	3.25	3.40	3.78
Long in 10/short in 1 (reversed after quarter $t+3$)	From day after announcement for quarter t through announcement for quarter $t+k$	5.69	7.48	8.10	8.61	8.72	8.39	8.03	8.63

| Ratio of three-day sum through $t+k$ to CAR since quarter t announcement, long in 10/short in 1 (reversed after quarter $t+3$) | 0.23 | 0.27 | 0.25 | 0.31 | 0.35 | 0.39 | 0.42 | 0.44 |

Panel C: Correlation between SUE for quarter t and three-day $[-2, 0]$ percentage abnormal returns around subsequent earnings announcements[c]

Correlation between	Type	$t+1$	$t+2$	$t+3$	$t+4$	$t+5$	$t+6$	$t+7$	$t+8$
SUE deciles and abnormal return (for decile portfolio)	Spearman	1.00[d]	0.95[d]	0.36	−0.99[d]	−0.76[d]	−0.68[d]	−0.64[d]	−0.47
	Pearson	0.97[d]	0.94[d]	0.32	−0.96[d]	−0.79[d]	−0.77[d]	−0.65[d]	−0.45
SUE deciles and abnormal return (for firm-quarters)	Spearman	0.09[d]	0.05[d]	0.01[d]	−0.04[d]	−0.02[d]	−0.02[d]	−0.01[d]	−0.00
	Pearson	0.07[d]	0.03[d]	−0.00	−0.04[d]	−0.02[d]	−0.02[d]	−0.01[d]	−0.01[d]

[a] Standardized unexpected earnings (SUE) represent forecast errors from a seasonal random walk with drift, scaled by their estimation-period standard deviation. Earnings announcements are grouped into deciles, based on the distribution of SUE each calendar quarter, to generate the SUE deciles used to form portfolios. Abnormal returns are the difference between daily returns for individual firms in the portfolio and returns for NYSE–AMEX firms of the same size decile.
[b] Alternative t-test is conducted by calculating mean abnormal returns for each of 13 years, and dividing by the time-series standard error of that mean.
[c] In the top half of panel C, correlations are computed between the mean abnormal returns over the three-day holding periods for each SUE decile and the decile numbers (1 = lowest SUE, 10 = highest SUE). In the bottom half, the correlations are computed between the three-day abnormal returns and SUE deciles for individual announcements.
[d] Statistically significant at 0.05 level, two-tailed test.

eliminate bias from cross-sectional dependence. Specifically, we calculate the value of any given portfolio return (or in the regression tests of Hypothesis 2, any given coefficient) for each of the 13 years in the database. We then compare the mean of the resulting 13 values to its time-series standard error to construct the alternative t-test. In most cases, this alternative calculation generates a smaller t-statistic, probably reflecting both a loss of power and an elimination of some bias. (The loss of power arises because equal weight is placed on data from each year, which is generally suboptimal.)

The first test of Hypothesis 1 is presented in table 2, panel A. We form portfolios that are long in extreme 'good-news' ($SUE = 10$) firms and short in 'bad-news' ($SUE = 1$) firms based on quarter t earnings information, and then measure the mean abnormal returns for these portfolios around subsequent quarters' earnings announcements. We focus here on extreme deciles to enhance the power of our tests and provide results directly comparable to prior research. However, we later examine the behavior of all deciles.

The evidence shows that the three-day abnormal returns around earnings announcements are predictable, at least four quarters in advance. Moreover, the signs and magnitudes of the abnormal returns reflect the pattern of autocorrelations hypothesized in the previous section. The zero-investment portfolio created on the basis of quarter t earnings information generates a significant positive mean abnormal return (1.32 percent) upon the announcement of quarter $t + 1$ earnings, as if market prices fail to reflect fully that a given SUE in quarter t tends to be followed by an SUE of the same sign in quarter $t + 1$. As predicted, we also observe positive but smaller mean abnormal returns around the announcement of earnings for quarters $t + 2$ and $t + 3$. Finally, again consistent with our predictions, we observe significant negative mean abnormal returns around the announcement of earnings for quarter $t + 4$, as if prices fail to reflect fully that a given earnings change in quarter t is likely to be partially reversed in quarter $t + 4$.

We did not offer predictions about the behavior of market reactions around earnings announcements beyond quarter $t + 4$. However, based on the autocorrelations observed in table 1, we would expect small but negative market reactions to the announcements of quarters $t + 5$ through $t + 8$, for long (short) positions in quarter t's good-news (bad-news) firms. In fact, that is what we observe: the abnormal returns are -0.31 percent, -0.23 percent, -0.15 percent, and -0.38 percent for quarter $t + 5$ through $t + 8$, respectively. (The statistical significance of the last two amounts depends on the t-test used.) We hesitate to emphasize these particular results, however, because unlike the signs of the autocorrelations at the first four lags, the signs for lags 5 through 8 have not been robust across samples and time periods examined in prior studies [compare Foster (1977) with our evidence], and therefore might not have been predictable at the beginning of the test period.

Table 3

Correspondence between relative magnitude of *autocorrelations* in earnings data and relative magnitude of *abnormal returns* predicted on the basis of the past earnings.

Lag	1	2	3	4	5	6	7	8
Magnitudes of *autocorrelations* in SUE deciles at lag k, relative to autocorrelation at lag 1[a]	1.00	0.56	0.17	−0.44	−0.22	−0.22	−0.22	−0.20
Magnitudes of predictable *abnormal returns* at announcement for quarter $t + k$, relative to predictable abnormal return at announcement for quarter $t + 1$[b]	1.00	0.53	0.03	−0.50	−0.23	−0.17	−0.11	−0.28

[a]Autocorrelations are taken from table 1, panel B, which reports means of firm-specific autocorrelations in *SUE* deciles. Thus, the amount 0.56 shown above for lag 2 is the ratio of the mean autocorrelation in *SUE* deciles at lag 2 (0.23), divided by the mean autocorrelation in *SUE* deciles at lag 1 (0.41).

*SUE*s are forecast errors from a seasonal random walk with trend, scaled by their standard deviation within the trend-estimation period (up to 36 observations). *SUE* deciles are based on rankings within calendar quarters.

[b]Abnormal returns are taken from table 2, panel A, third section, which reports the return for the three-day window surrounding the announcement of earnings for quarter $t + k$, for a long position in firms with quarter t *SUE* in decile 10, combined with a short position in firms with quarter t *SUE* in decile 1. Thus, the amount 0.53 shown above for lag 2 is the ratio of the abnormal return around the announcement of earnings for quarter $t + 2$ (0.70 percent), divided by the corresponding amount for quarter $t + 1$ (1.32 percent).

Hypothesis 1 is borne out in the data not only in terms of the signs of future abnormal returns, but also in terms of magnitudes. That is, the relative magnitudes of the abnormal returns around subsequent earnings announcements are in general accordance with the relative magnitudes of the autocorrelations in *SUE*s documented earlier. The mean autocorrelations in *SUE* deciles at lag k (from the last row of table 1, panel B), relative to the autocorrelation at lag 1, are shown in the first row of table 3. They are compared with the mean abnormal returns around announcements for quarter $t + k$ (from the third section of table 2, panel A) relative to that for quarter $t + 1$. The strength of the correspondence between the two series is striking.

Returning to table 2, panel A, we note that the predictably positive abnormal returns around the first *three* subsequent announcements could simply reflect evidence already documented in prior research based on longer return intervals, if the three-day abnormal returns represented a proportionate allocation of the post-announcement drift already shown to exist over six to nine months [e.g., Watts (1978), Bernard and Thomas (1989)]. To check that possibility, table 2, panel B compares the three-day abnormal returns around subsequent earnings announcements to the abnormal return cumulated over periods from the day after the announcement for quarter t, through the announcements for subsequent quarters.[7] We assume a long (short) position in the good-news (bad-news) firms over the first three quarters after the earnings announcement, and then reverse that position at the beginning of the fourth subsequent quarter. The cumulative abnormal return is 5.7 percent through the announcement for quarter $t + 1$ and 8.6 percent through the announcement for quarter $t + 4$. The last row of panel B shows that the three-day abnormal returns (summed over announcements to date) account for 23 to 31 percent of the cumulative post-announcement drift through quarter $t + 4$. Given that the three-day announcement periods account for only about 5 percent of the total trading days, the announcement period reactions clearly represent a disproportionate share of the drift. This constitutes an extension of similar evidence provided by Bernard and Thomas (1989) and Freeman and Tse (1989) for the first subsequent announcement.

The evidence in table 2, panel B suggests that some portion of the post-announcement adjustment to earnings is rapid even though it is delayed. The rapid adjustments went undetected in research prior to Bernard and Thomas (1989), because subsequent earnings-announcement dates were scattered in event time. By not realigning the data at each subsequent announcement date, researchers smoothed the sharp adjustments that occur at those dates.

Table 2, panel C shows that the phenomenon documented above is not driven by extreme deciles; it persists throughout the sample. Panel C presents the simple correlations between *SUE*s of quarter t and the three-day abnormal return surrounding each of the eight subsequent earnings announcements, at both the level of *SUE* decile portfolios and individual firm quarters. The Spearman and Pearson correlations indicate that the relation between *SUE* deciles for quarter t and the ten corresponding mean abnormal returns around the next four earnings announcements is not only close to monotonic, but is almost perfectly linear. The sole exception is the relation for quarter $t + 3$, which was not expected to be strong. Movement from analysis at the portfolio level to the level of individual firm-quarters causes the correlations to decline considerably, as expected, but the predicted pattern remains.

---

[7]While the firm's *SUE* is known on the day prior to the commencement of this return interval, the firm's *SUE* decile assignment is not known until all firms have announced earnings for the quarter. Assuming the ability to calculate decile assignments prior to that time introduces a form of hindsight bias studied by Holthausen (1983). To overcome this potential bias, Foster, Olsen, and Shevlin (1984) and Bernard and Thomas (1989) assign *SUE*s to deciles by comparing them to the distribution of *SUE*s for the *prior* quarter. However, in this sample, the magnitude of post-announcement drift is insensitive to this adjustment.

Note that this form of hindsight bias is not an issue in the primary tests based on three-day return intervals, because by the time of the subsequent earnings announcement, the firm's *SUE* decile assignment would be known.

A final note on table 2 concerns an apparent asymmetry in the returns for 'good-news' and 'bad-news' firms in panel A. If one simply *adds* announcement-period abnormal returns across the two groups, rather than offsetting long and short positions, the result is a positive abnormal return of approximately 0.20 percent, regardless of the subsequent quarter examined. That announcement-period abnormal returns are on average positive has been documented previously by Chari et al. (1988) and Ball and Kothari (1990). Why this occurs is unclear. However, note that this effect would tend to 'work against' our prediction for bad-news firms for the first three lags and good-news firms for the fourth lag, and should cancel out in our combined long and short positions. Thus, while the effect is evident in our data, it cannot explain the results of our tests.

Table 4 presents evidence like that in table 2 for firms classified as small, medium, and large (those in size deciles 1 to 4, 5 to 7, and 8 to 10, respectively, based on January 1 market value of equity for all NYSE and AMEX firms). Fig. 1 summarizes the information from table 4 in the form of a *CAR* plot.[8] We are motivated to partition the data by firm size because it may be more plausible that published earnings information would fail to be impounded fully in the prices of small firms relative to large firms. For example, Foster, Olsen, and Shevlin (1984) suggest that the market for information might be less well developed for small firms, thus motivating their examination of post-announcement drift as a function of firm size.

The patterns noted above are present for each size group – in every case, positive but declining abnormal returns around the announcement of earnings for quarter $t+1$, $t+2$, and $t+3$, and negative abnormal returns around the announcement of earnings for quarter $t+4$. However, the effects are more pronounced for small firms. Note that this cannot be attributed to differences in the time-series behavior of earnings, since there is *less* autocorrelation in earnings changes for small firms (table 1) and *SUE*s actually vary *less* for small firms than large firms. Thus, the data are consistent with stock prices failing to reflect fully the implications of current earnings for future earnings for all firms, but the failure is more apparent for small stocks. Interestingly, however, the *fraction* of post-announcement drift that is delayed until subsequent earnings announcements is similar across the three size groups.

In addition to partitioning the data by firm size, we also checked the robustness of the results across fiscal quarters by partitioning on both the quarter of portfolio formation and the quarter to which the subsequent announcements pertain. The results (not reported here) are consistent across

---

[8]While Freeman and Tse (1989) present a similar plot for their overall sample (fig. 2), they offer no discussion of the reactions to announcements beyond quarter $t+1$.

Table 4

Predictions of market reactions to future earnings announcements for portfolios based on current quarter's SUE; results by firm-size group.

	Subsequent quarter for which earnings are announced			
	$t+1$	$t+2$	$t+3$	$t+4$

Small firms (28,877 to 30,904 observations)

Abnormal return three days [−2, 0] around announcement, long (short) in quarter t SUE decile 10 (1)	1.92	0.82	0.10	−1.15
t-statistic	(8.26)	(4.09)	(0.48)	(−5.51)
Alternative t-test[b]	(4.76)	(2.80)	(0.97)	(−2.45)
Sum of above returns (position reversed in quarter $t+4$)	1.92	2.74	2.84	3.99
Ratio of sum of three-day abnormal returns through $t+k$ to CAR since quarter t announcement (with reversal of long and short positions in quarter $t+4$)	0.24	0.28	0.27	0.35

Medium firms (23,541 to 30,904 observations)

Abnormal return three days [−2, 0] around announcement, long (short) in quarter t SUE decile 10 (1)	1.46	0.98	0.21	−0.44
t-statistic	(10.43)	(7.01)	(1.46)	(−3.05)
Alternative t-test	(4.86)	(4.26)	(1.83)	(−1.62)
Sum of above returns (position reversed in quarter $t+4$)	1.46	2.44	2.65	3.09
Ratio of sum of three-day abnormal returns through $t+k$ to CAR since quarter t announcement (with reversal of long and short positions in quarter $t+4$)	0.22	0.27	0.27	0.31

Large firms (27,342 to 29,088 observations)

Abnormal return three days [−2, 0] around announcement, long (short) in quarter t SUE decile 10 (1)	0.84	0.48	0.04	−0.31
t-statistic	(8.84)	(5.10)	(0.40)	(−3.24)
Alternative t-test	(6.76)	(3.87)	(−0.30)	(−1.74)
Sum of above returns (position reversed in quarter $t+4$)	0.84	1.32	1.36	1.67
Ratio of sum of three-day abnormal returns through $t+k$ to CAR since quarter t announcement (with reversal of long and short positions in quarter $t+4$)	0.26	0.31	0.32	0.34

[a] Abnormal returns are the sum of daily returns for individual firms in the portfolio, less returns for NYSE-AMEX firms of the same size decile, based on January 1 market values of equity. Small, medium, and large firms are in size deciles 1 to 4, 5 to 7, and 8 to 10, respectively. CAR is the sum of abnormal returns over all days since the announcement for quarter t.

SUE represents the forecast error from a seasonal random-walk (with trend) earnings-expectation model, scaled by its estimation-period standard deviation. SUE decile portfolios are based on ranking of SUEs within the calendar quarter of the announcement of quarter t earnings.

[b] Alternative t-test is conducted by calculating mean abnormal return for each of 13 years, and dividing by the time-series standard error of that mean.

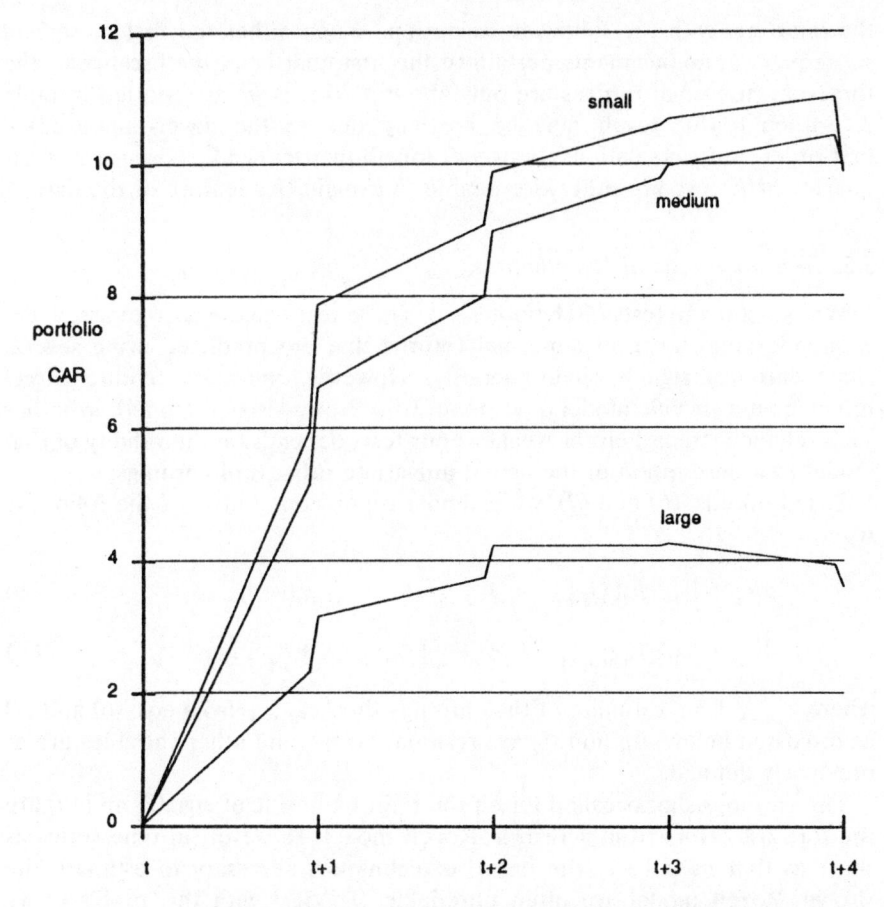

Fig. 1. Percentage cumulative abnormal returns for *SUE* portfolios: Returns aligned by subsequent earnings announcements.

Portfolio *CAR* is the percentage cumulative abnormal return over holding periods beginning after the earnings-announcement day for quarter t, for a portfolio invested long (short) in the highest (lowest) decile of standardized unexpected earnings (*SUE*) at quarter t. *SUE* represents forecast error from the seasonal random-walk (with trend) earnings-expectation model scaled by its estimation-period standard deviation. Abnormal returns are the differences between daily returns for individual firms in an *SUE* decile portfolio and returns for NYSE–AMEX firms of the same size decile, based on January 1 market values of equity. Small, medium, and large firms are in size deciles 1 to 4, 5 to 7, and 8 to 10, respectively. Holding periods are obtained by splitting the period between adjacent earnings-announcement dates into a three-day pre-announcement window (day −2 to day 0) and an inter-announcement window. While the actual inter-announcement windows vary in length, the mean value of 60 days is used to illustrate the differential price responses occurring in the two windows.

the quarters, with the following exception. When either the first or second subsequent announcements pertain to the first quarter of the fiscal year, the three-day abnormal returns are only about half as large as reported in table 2. Although this result may be partially due to the lower-than-average first-order autocorrelations between fourth-quarter and subsequent first-quarter SUEs, we are otherwise unable to explain this feature of the data.

3.2. Regression tests of Hypothesis 2

We now turn to tests of Hypothesis 2. These tests can be used to assess the economic importance of abnormal returns that are predicted using several prior earnings signals simultaneously. However, the tests require direct reliance on a specific model of earnings (the Brown–Rozeff model). Whether such reliance strengthens or weakens our tests depends on the validity of that model as a description of the actual univariate process of earnings.

Based on eqs. (6) and (7), we estimate regression models of the following form:

$$AR_{jt} = b_0 + b_1(Q_{j,t-1} - Q_{j,t-5}) + b_4 e_{j,t-4} + u_{jt}, \qquad (8)$$

$$AR_{jt} = b_0 + b_1 e_{j,t-1} + b_2 e_{j,t-2} + b_3 e_{j,t-3} + b_4 e_{j,t-4} + v_{jt}, \qquad (9)$$

where $e_{j,t-k}$ is an estimate of the earnings shock $\varepsilon_{j,t-k}$ from eqs. (6) and (7) as discussed below, u_{jt} and v_{jt} are residual errors, and other variables are as previously defined.

The earnings shocks called for on the right-hand side of eqs. (8) and (9) are the forecast errors from a Brown–Rozeff model. However, in time series as short as that used here, the iterative techniques necessary to estimate the Brown–Rozeff model are often unreliable. To deal with this problem, we produced two sets of estimates of (8) and (9). One is based on a subset (36 percent) of the sample for which 36 historical observations are available to estimate the Brown–Rozeff earnings forecasts; forecast errors for this sample are available only beginning in 1980. The second approach uses the full sample, extending from 1974 through 1986, but substitutes forecast errors from an alternative model developed by Foster (1977).[9] Such errors are highly correlated with Brown–Rozeff forecast errors, even though the Foster model differs by excluding the fourth-order moving-average term.[10] While

---

[9]The Foster model was estimated from the most recent 36 quarters of earnings data (after seasonal differencing), where available. Where fewer than 16 quarterly observations were available, we relied on a seasonal random walk to generate earnings expectations. This was necessary in about 6 percent of the cases.

[10]The correlation between the two forecast errors is 0.86, when each is converted to a winsorized SUE as was done previously with the seasonal differences; the correlation is 0.80, when each is converted to SUE deciles.

the substitution of Foster forecast errors weakens our tests by introducing some measurement error in the regressors, the impact should be small.[11] In fact, for the subsample where both Brown–Rozeff and Foster forecast errors are available, the results are essentially the same; those results are, in turn, similar to those based on the full sample and Foster model forecasts errors.

Given that the alternative approaches yield similar results, we choose to report only one in detail. The approach selected is that based on the full sample (using the Foster model), because the results of that approach are readily comparable to those in the previous tables. Moreover, by emphasizing that the predicted results hold when Foster model forecast errors are used, we can remove any doubt that the implied abnormal returns could only have been obtained through application of the computer-intensive statistical estimation required by the Brown–Rozeff model. The Foster model, in contrast, could easily have been estimated throughout our sample period, using a simple regression.

Another measurement issue concerns scaling of the regressors. Both the seasonal difference $Q_{t-1} - Q_{t-5}$ and the earnings shocks e_{t-1} through e_{t-4} are scaled by their historical standard deviations (using up to 36 observations, where available), just as the SUEs were in the previous section. [Thus, the regressors could themselves be viewed as SUEs based on forecasts from a seasonal random walk (for $Q_{t-1} - Q_{t-5}$) and a Foster model (for e_{t-1} through e_{t-4}).] The resulting scaled variables are then placed in deciles within quarters (to guard against the potential for difficulties with outliers) and the decile rankings (1 to 10) are reduced by one and then divided by nine so as to range between 0 and 1.

Given the way we have constructed the regressions, the coefficients can be interpreted as abnormal returns on portfolios with certain useful properties. [See Fama and MacBeth (1973) and Bernard (1984) for similar interpretations.] First, denoting the dependent variable as R and the matrix of regressors as X, note that the ordinary-least-squares (OLS) regression coefficients [written as $(X'X)^{-1}X'R$] represent abnormal returns on portfolios, where the portfolio weights are given by the rows of the matrix $(X'X)^{-1}X'$. Second, note that since the regression includes an intercept, the portfolio weights for the slope coefficients must sum to zero, and thus the slope coefficients can be viewed as abnormal returns to *zero-investment* portfolios. Third, to help interpret the economic meaning of the coefficient, note that a coefficient from a regression of abnormal returns can always be interpreted

---

[11]If the Brown–Rozeff and Foster model parameters could be estimated precisely, then movement from the former to the latter to estimate eq. (8) should introduce a bias toward zero in b_1 that is trivial and in b_4 that is on the order of 6 percent. (Details are available upon request.) For the subsample where both Brown–Rozeff and Foster forecast errors are available, the coefficient estimates based on the Foster model are indeed closer to zero, in the amount of 1 percent and 2 percent, respectively.

as the abnormal return on a portfolio with a value of 1 for the associated regressor, and a value of 0 for the remaining regressors. Thus, the amount $b_1 - b_4$ in eq. (8) represents the abnormal return on a zero-investment portfolio with a value of 1 for $Q_{t-1} - Q_{t-5}$ and -1 for e_{t-4}; the amount $b_1 + b_2 + b_3 - b_4$ in eq. (9) represents the abnormal return on a zero-investment portfolio with value of 1 for e_{t-1}, e_{t-2}, and e_{t-3} and -1 for e_{t-4}. (Of course, regressors for individual observations range from 0 to 1, spanning the ten deciles of the distribution, but the observations are weighted so that these statements hold for the *portfolio*.)

The above interpretations imply that, given how the regressors are scaled [with a value of 1 (0) representing the highest (lowest) decile of a regressor distribution], the portfolio underlying $b_1 - b_4$ in eq. (8) is comparable to a zero-investment portfolio with long (short) positions in firms within the highest (lowest) decile of $Q_{t-1} - Q_{t-5}$ and short (long) positions in firms within the highest (lowest) decile of e_{t-4}. Specifically, the two portfolios are comparable in the sense that both have values of 1 for $Q_{t-1} - Q_{t-5}$ and -1 for e_{t-4}.[12] Similarly, the portfolio underlying $b_1 + b_2 + b_3 - b_4$ in (9) is comparable to a zero-investment portfolio with long (short) positions in firms within the highest (lowest) deciles of e_{t-1}, e_{t-2}, and e_{t-3} and short (long) positions in firms within the highest (lowest) decile of e_{t-4}.

The essential point is that the linear combination of coefficients in regression (8) or (9) can be interpreted as abnormal returns on zero-investments portfolios that, unlike the portfolios in table 2 and prior research, are based on information about *multiple* earnings signals. Nevertheless, the portfolios implicit in the regression are scaled so as to permit comparisons with portfolios based on single earnings signals. In addition, the weights underlying them are determinable on the basis of information (the regressors) available prior to the beginning of the return interval.

Estimates of eqs. (8) and (9) are presented in table 5, panel A. The primary estimates based on three-day return intervals appear at the top of that panel. The abnormal returns implied by using the combination of prior period earnings signals [that is, $b_1 - b_4$ for eq. (8) and $b_1 + b_2 + b_3 - b_4$ for eq. (9)] appear in the rightmost column of panel A.

Coefficient estimates for both eqs. (8) and (9) at the top of panel A all have the predicted signs (b_1, b_2, and b_3 are all positive and b_4 is negative) and are always statistically significant. The relative magnitudes of the coefficients are also in accord with our expectations; that is, $b_1 > b_2 > b_3 > 0 > b_4$. The adjusted R^2 is low in regressions (8) and (9) – less than 1 percent – indicating that only a small fraction of the variance in stock returns is predictable

---

[12] The portfolio underlying $b_1 - b_4$ differs from the other portfolio in that, under the assumptions of OLS, the former is minimum variance. However, since the assumptions of OLS are unlikely to hold perfectly, the portfolio will not literally be minimum variance, thus weakening our tests.

Table 5
Regression tests of relation between market reactions to quarterly earnings announcements and earnings information.

Panel A: Predicting market reaction using lagged earnings information[a]

$$(8) \quad AR_{jt} = b_0 + b_1(Q_{j,t-1} - Q_{j,t-5}) + b_4 e_{j,t-4} + u_{jt}$$

$$(9) \quad AR_{jt} = b_0 + b_1 e_{j,t-1} + b_2 e_{j,t-2} + b_3 e_{j,t-3} + b_4 e_{j,t-4} + v_{jt}$$

Regression model	Holding period for abnormal returns	b_1	b_2	b_3	b_4	Adj. R^2	Implied portfolio abnormal return
		(t-statistic and alternative t-test)					
Equation 8 (N = 75,653)	Three-day [−2, 0] announcement period for quarter t	1.30 (20.59) (12.22)			−0.84 (−13.29) (−6.06)	0.7%	2.14%
Equation 9 (N = 75,045)	Three-day [−2, 0] announcement period for quarter t	0.98 (15.66) (9.14)	0.62 (9.89) (14.43)	0.28 (4.44) (2.83)	−0.71 (−11.41) (−9.04)	0.7%	2.59%
Equation 8 (N = 75,443)	From day after prior announcement, to quarter t announcement (avg. 63 days)	6.24 (34.40) (9.41)			−2.44 (−13.41) (−9.64)	1.6%	8.68%
Equation 9 (N = 74,837)	From day after prior announcement, to quarter t announcement (avg. 63 days)	5.38 (29.99) (6.56)	1.46 (8.10) (3.22)	0.53 (2.94) (0.18)	−1.56 (−8.68) (−5.32)	1.4%	8.93%

Panel B: Contemporaneous association: market reaction and earnings information[a]

$$(A) \quad AR_{jt} = b_0 + b_1 e_{jt} + w_{jt}$$

$$(B) \quad AR_{jt} = b_0 + b_1(Q_{j,t} - Q_{j,t-4}) + z_{jt}$$

Regression model	Holding period for abnormal returns	Regression coefficient, b_1 (t-statistic and alternative t-test)	Adj. R^2	Implied portfolio abnormal return
Equation A (N = 82,734)	Three-day [−2, 0] announcement period for quarter t	4.18 (71.61) (26.34)	5.8%	4.18%
Equation B (N = 85,493)	Three-day [−2, 0] announcement period for quarter t	4.43 (76.27) (19.27)	6.4%	4.43%

[a] Abnormal returns, AR_{jt}, represent the sum over the indicated holding periods of the differences between daily returns for firm j and returns for NYSE–AMEX firms of the same size decile, based on January 1 market values of equity. $Q_t - Q_{t-4}$ is seasonally differenced quarterly earnings and e_t is the forecast error from the Foster (1977) first-order autoregressive earnings-expectation model (in seasonal differences); both are scaled by their historical standard deviation. All regressors are assigned to deciles, based on the current quarter distribution, and then scaled so that they range from 0 (for the lowest decile) to 1 (for the highest decile). Implied portfolio abnormal returns are equal to $(b_1 - b_4)$ and $(b_1 + b_2 + b_3 - b_4)$ in panel A, and b_1 in panel B. Alternative t-test is conducted by estimating regressions for each of 13 years, and comparing each coefficient's mean to its time-series standard error.

based on previously announced earnings information. However, we will show later (table 7) that the remaining variance is largely diversifiable within annual cross-sections, yielding abnormal returns with the predicted signs consistently from year to year.

Turning to the implied portfolio abnormal return on the right-hand side of panel A, we see that a combination of prior period earnings signals improves our ability to predict future reactions to earnings announcements. Note that the implied abnormal returns are larger than any of the coefficients on individual regressors, and larger than any of the portfolio returns in table 2, each of which is based on a single earnings signal. Results based on eqs. (8) and (9) imply that, on average, historical earnings information could have been used to construct a portfolio with an abnormal return of 2.1 percent and 2.6 percent, respectively, over the three-day announcement-period interval.

Table 5 also provides two ways to assess the economic importance of the predictions. The first moves away from emphasis on three-day intervals surrounding subsequent earnings announcements, and focuses instead on portfolios formed immediately after the current announcement.[13] The portfolios are held until the next announcement (a period of approximately 63 trading days, on average). If an investor believes that post-announcement drift represents a delayed price response, there would be no good reason to wait until just prior to subsequent announcements to take a position. Moreover, the timing of the subsequent announcement cannot be predicted perfectly in advance. Thus, transacting just after the current announcement may represent a better depiction of the strategy an investor might pursue. However, the movement to longer windows increases the concerns about measurement error in abnormal returns.

Regressions using the longer return intervals are presented at the bottom of table 5, panel A. The implied abnormal return over one quarter for the portfolio constructed using information about two earnings signals – $(Q_{t-1} - Q_{t-5})$ and e_{t-4} – is 8.7 percent. When signals about each of the prior four earnings announcements are used – e_{t-1}, e_{t-2}, e_{t-3}, and e_{t-4} – the implied abnormal return is 8.9 percent. The magnitudes of these abnormal returns, corresponding to implied annualized abnormal returns on the order of 35 percent, are significant in economic as well as statistical terms.

There is a second approach to evaluating the economic importance of the effects documented here, that has more direct implications for methodology. We compare the implied three-day abnormal return from panel A, which is predicted solely on the basis of historical information, to the three-day abnormal return that could be generated if earnings were known with

[13] The values of two regressors, the decile assignments of $(Q_{t-1} - Q_{t-5})$ and e_{t-1}, depend on a firm's earnings *relative* to other firms, and thus cannot be calculated until all firms have announced earnings. However, as explained in footnote 7, the potential hindsight bias this introduces appears trivial in this sample.

certainty three days before the announcement. The latter abnormal return is presented in panel B, where we regress abnormal returns around the announcement of earnings for quarter t against measures of unexpected earnings (either $Q_t - Q_{t-4}$ or e_t) for that same quarter. (Consistent with our approach in panel A, the regressor ranges from 0 to 1, depending on the decile to which estimated unexpected earnings belongs.) The regression indicates that the zero-investment portfolio comparable to one with a long (short) position in stocks in the highest (lowest) decile of current unexpected earnings generates an abnormal return of 4.2 or 4.4 percent, depending on how unexpected earnings is defined. These amounts can then be compared to the three-day abnormal returns of 2.1 or 2.6 percent in panel A.

The above comparison indicates that, using only historical, publicly available earnings data, we are able to generate an abnormal return about half as large as that based on perfect foresight of earnings. *Thus, the abnormal return that can be predicted in advance is approximately half as large as the stock-price reaction to what is labeled 'unexpected earnings' in many accounting research studies.* This result calls into question the reliability of studies that rely heavily on the assumption that prices reflect all publicly available earnings information quickly. Of some consolation, however, is the observation that the fraction of variance in announcement-period abnormal returns explained by prior-period earnings information is small (0.7 percent), in both absolute terms and relative to the R-squared based on current earnings, which is 5.8 percent.

Eq. (8) is re-estimated within firm-size categories in table 6, panel A. Using the combination of indicators from prior earnings numbers, the mean three-day abnormal return on the implied zero-investment portfolio is 3.4 percent, 2.2 percent, and 1.2 percent for small, medium, and large firms, respectively. The regression results in panel B indicate that if one could forecast the *SUE* perfectly, the resulting mean three-day abnormal return would be 6.8 percent, 3.7 percent, and 2.3 percent, for small, medium, and large firms, respectively. In each case, the return based solely on historical information is about half as large as that based on perfect foresight.

A final note concerns the potential for further improvement in the ability to predict abnormal returns around future earnings announcements by considering cross-sectional differences in the parameters of individual firms' time-series processes. We examined this issue in two ways. First, in regressions not reported here, we used historical estimates of ϕ and θ in eq. (8), as called for by eq. (6). Predictive ability was not improved; the implied abnormal returns were similar to those reported in table 5. Second, we stratified the sample into four quartiles, first based on historical estimates of ϕ and then (separately) based on historical estimates of θ, and repeated the portfolio tests of table 2 within each group. As expected, the abnormal return at the announcement of quarter $t + 1$ earnings was most (least) positive for

Table 6

Regression tests of relation between market reactions to quarterly earnings announcements and earnings information; results by firm-size group.

Panel A: Predicting market reaction using lagged earnings information[a]

(8) $AR_{jt} = b_0 + b_1(Q_{j,t-1} - Q_{j,t-5}) + b_4 e_{j,t-4} + u_{jt}$

Firm-size category	b_1 (t-statistic and alternative t-test)	b_4	Adj. R^2	Implied portfolio abnormal return
Small firms (N = 26,841)	1.98 (13.37) (9.88)	−1.37 (−9.32) (−7.30)	0.8%	3.35%
Medium firms (N = 22,204)	1.49 (14.76) (5.40)	−0.71 (−7.00) (−4.66)	1.0%	2.20%
Large firms (N = 26,438)	0.80 (11.69) (1.88)	−0.43 (−6.52) (−1.30)	0.6%	1.23%

Panel B: Contemporaneous association: market reaction and earnings information[a]

$AR_{jt} = b_0 + b_1 e_{jt} + w_{jt}$

Firm-size category	Regression coefficient, b_1 (t-statistic and alternative t-test)	Adj. R^2	Implied portfolio abnormal return
Small firms (N = 29,694)	6.77 (50.58) (19.97)	7.9%	6.77%
Medium firms (N = 24,163)	3.74 (40.32) (24.57)	6.3%	3.74%
Large firms (N = 28,482)	2.28 (36.45) (15.92)	4.5%	2.28%

[a] Abnormal returns, AR_{jt}, represent the sum over the three-day [−2,0] holding period (relative to the announcement date for quarter t) of the differences between daily returns for firm j and returns for NYSE–AMEX firms of the same size decile, based on January 1 market values of equity. Small, medium, and large firms are in size deciles 1 to 4, 5 to 7, and 8 to 10, respectively. $Q_t - Q_{t-4}$ is seasonally differenced quarterly earnings and e_t is the forecast error from the Foster (1977) first-order autoregressive earnings-expectation model (in seasonal differences); both are scaled by their historical standard deviation. All regressors are assigned to deciles, based on the current-quarter distribution, and then scaled so that they range from 0 (for the lowest decile) to 1 (for the highest decile). Implied portfolio abnormal returns are equal to $(b_1 - b_4)$ in panel A and b_1 in panel B. Alternative t-test is conducted by estimating regressions for each of 13 years, and comparing each coefficient's mean to its time-series standard error.

the portfolio with the largest (smallest) historical value for ϕ (1.54 percent versus 1.21 percent), and the abnormal return at quarter $t + 4$ was most (least) negative for the portfolio with the largest (smallest) historical value for θ (-1.09 percent versus -0.74 percent). However, the differences were not statistically significant. One possible explanation is that cross-sectional differences in time-series parameters are too small to provide much predictive power. (Recall the similarity in time-series behavior across industries in table 1.) Another possibility is that while cross-sectional differences exist, they are unstable or estimated with considerable error. Much of the time-series literature [e.g., Albrecht, Lookabill, and McKeown (1977), Foster (1977), Watts and Leftwich (1977)] is consistent with such cross-sectional differences not being predictable out of sample.

4. Alternative explanations and additional evidence

It is difficult to understand how stock prices could fail to reflect the implications of current earnings for future earnings in such a systematic way. The evidence naturally raises several questions, which we discuss below.

(1) *Can this evidence be explained in terms of rational investors' desire to await 'confirmation' that a previous earnings change is not transitory?*
An immediate problem with this explanation is that, at best, it fits only the patterns observed around the announcements of earnings for quarters $t + 1$, $t + 2$, and $t + 3$; the reactions for quarter $t + 4$ are consistent with investors treating previous earnings as if they were more permanent than they turned out to be.

There is a more fundamental problem with this explanation, however. No matter how much uncertainty surrounds the implications of earnings already announced for quarter t, prices in an efficient market would immediately reflect an unbiased expectation of future earnings, and future abnormal returns would be uncorrelated with past earnings changes. Even if increased uncertainty caused by extreme earnings changes is relevant for pricing, it could not explain the evidence. While it is true in that case that a postannouncement drift (actually, a risk premium) would be observed, *it would be positive for both extreme-bad-news and extreme-good-news firms.* [See Brown, Harlow, and Tinic (1988).] Both the existing literature on post-announcement drift and this study (see table 2) document a negative drift for bad-news firms.

(2) *Does the evidence reflect autocorrelations in earnings that were observable ex post, but not predictable ex ante?*
Two pieces of evidence contradict this explanation. First, the autocorrelation patterns we observed in our sample period were also observed by Foster for

Table 7

Consistency (over time) of relation between market reactions to future earnings announcements and current-quarter earnings information.

Mean abnormal return during three-day [−2,0] window around earnings announcement for quarter $t + k$, for portfolio including long (short) position in firms in highest (lowest) decile of SUE in quarter t[a] (predicted sign of abnormal return in parentheses)

Year	$t+1$ (+)	$t+2$ (+)	$t+3$ (+)	$t+4$ (−)
1974	3.74[c]	3.05[c]	0.89	NA[b]
1975	2.28[c]	0.80[c]	−0.43	−1.32[c]
1976	1.30[c]	0.41	−0.15	−0.98[c]
1977	1.69[c]	0.87[c]	−0.01	−0.41
1978	1.06[c]	0.78[c]	0.69[c]	−0.15
1979	1.08[c]	0.76[c]	−0.10	−0.39
1980	1.48[c]	0.87[c]	0.21	−0.98[c]
1981	1.10[c]	0.78[c]	0.20	−0.57[c]
1982	1.08[c]	0.26	−0.19	−1.05[c]
1983	1.11[c]	0.73[c]	0.12	−0.75[c]
1984	0.70[c]	0.50[c]	0.27	−0.06
1985	1.12[c]	0.19	−0.70	−0.91[c]
1986	0.84[c]	0.81[c]	0.54	−0.19

[a]SUE represents forecast error from the seasonal random-walk (with trend) earnings-expectation model, scaled by its estimation-period standard deviation. Abnormal returns are the differences between daily returns for individual firms in the SUE decile portfolio and returns for NYSE–AMEX firms of the same size decile, based on January 1 market values of equity.

[b]Since SUEs are calculated beginning in the first quarter of 1974, four-quarter-ahead predictions are not possible for any quarter in that year.

[c]Statistically significant at 0.05 level, one-tailed test.

1946–1974. In fact, the positive autocorrelations in earnings changes at lags 1, 2, and 3 are *weaker* during our sample period than in Foster's earlier period, making it difficult to argue that the market was justified in being surprised at the degree of autocorrelation in earnings observed in our sample. [Our own expectations were based largely on the evidence in Foster (1977), and the evidence in tables 2 through 5 was generated *before* we produced the autocorrelations reported in table 1.]

The second piece of evidence is presented in table 7. Although the market might err in its expectations about the degree of autocorrelation in earnings, it is difficult to explain how it could justifiably err in the same direction year after year. Table 7 shows that the mean three-day abnormal returns around the announcement for quarter $t + 1$ and $t + 2$ (for portfolios formed based on earnings of quarter t, as they were for table 2) is positive for *13 consecutive years*. The mean abnormal return around the announcement of quarter $t + 4$ earnings is negative for each of the 12 years for which we have data. (Results for quarter $t + 3$ are weak, but that is not unexpected, given the weak third-order autocorrelation in seasonally differenced earnings.) Of course, the consistency in the results also makes it that much harder to understand how competitive market forces could fail to eliminate the anomaly.

Incidentally, there is a suggestion in table 7 that the predictable component of the reaction to earnings announcements is larger in the first two to four years of our sample period (that is, 1974, 1975, and perhaps 1976 and 1977) than in subsequent years. This may raise questions about whether the effect has for some reason dissipated over time. However, when we conduct similar tests for the years 1971–1973, the results are quite similar to those for years after 1977.[14]

(3) *Is the evidence explainable in terms of transactions costs?*

One immediate response to this question is that, when the entire period from one earnings announcement to the next is considered, the abnormal returns appear to be in excess of transactions costs, perhaps even for small investors. (Recall the implied abnormal returns between the announcements for quarters t and $t+1$ of about 9 percent for the combined long and short positions underlying the last two regressions in table 5, panel A; the more simple strategy of going long (short) in extreme-good-news (extreme-bad-news) firms yields an abnormal return over 180 days of 4.5 percent, 8.9 percent, and 9.9 percent for large, medium, and small firms [Bernard and Thomas (1989, table 1)]. Moreover, Freeman and Tse (1989, table 7) document that when *SUE*s are measured using analysts' forecasts, the indicated drift is even larger – by 50 percent – than when *SUE*s are based on the statistical forecasts used by Bernard and Thomas.

Even if the abnormal returns *are* within transactions costs for small investors, a transactions-cost argument can at best provide only a partial explanation. First, and most important, *even if transactions costs cause 'sluggishness' in prices, it is hard to understand why the resulting 'mispricing' would last for months, or why it would be related to the historical time-series behavior of earnings. It is particularly difficult to reconcile 'price sluggishness' with the 'return reversal' we detect upon the announcement of earnings for quarter $t+4$.* Second, any transactions-cost-based explanation raises questions about why information can't be impounded in prices by traders for whom transactions costs are low, or other traders for whom the transactions costs are irrelevant (because they have already committed to buy or sell for reasons unrelated to earnings information). Third, while transactions costs may prevent trades and therefore prevent the impounding of new information, they cannot explain why information is not completely impounded, *given that trades have occurred.*

---

[14]Since our earnings data begin only in 1970, we have insufficient data to calculate the denominator of the *SUE* for years prior to 1974. Thus, for this supplemental analysis, we scaled unexpected earnings by the beginning-of-quarter stock-market value of equity. For the years for which both scale factors were available (1974–1986), the choice of scale factor does not alter the general nature of the results.

(4) *Could a research design flaw, such as a failure to control for risk, explain the evidence?*

While these possibilities can never be completely dismissed, we believe the evidence is more difficult to explain as a research design flaw than any previous evidence on post-announcement drift. Consider, for example, what would be necessary to explain the results in terms of a failure to control for risk shifts. Firms announcing good (bad) news at quarter t would need to experience a temporary upward (downward) shift in risk that occurs three months later, six months later, and nine months later, and then a downward (upward) shift in risk twelve months later. In addition to requiring risk changes in *opposite* directions for the same portfolios, this explanation also requires that the changes occur over short periods that coincide with an earnings-announcement date. Moreover, one would have to explain why the risk shifts are large, relative to those that generate 'normal' risk premia. Note that the three-day abnormal return around the announcement for quarter $t+1$ in table 2, panel A represents an annualized amount on the order of 200 percent (with no compounding).

Even if an explanation based on risk shifts could accommodate each of the above-mentioned features of the data, one important feature would remain to be explained. If the positive mean abnormal returns to zero-investment portfolios represent only a compensation for risk-bearing, then that risk should surface from time to time in the form of a loss. However, the consistent behavior of the abnormal returns through time (see table 7) indicates that the zero-investment strategy suggested by the anomaly would have earned positive abnormal returns for 13 consecutive years.

Potential bias related to imbalances in bids and asks. Even though risk shifts seem unlikely to explain the evidence, other research design flaws remain to be considered. Marais (1989), in discussing the post-announcement drift documented by Bernard and Thomas, notes that one 'cannot rule out consideration' of measurement errors in CRSP returns caused by an imbalance of bids and asks at the end of earnings-announcement days. Note that since CRSP prices are not 'true' prices, but may equal either the closing bid or closing ask, CRSP returns may be biased for any portfolio where there are more end-of-day transactions recorded at the bid than the ask, or vice versa [Keim (1989)]. Although such a bias could possibly play a role in our results, there is no compelling reason to expect it *ex ante*. It is not obvious why earnings for quarter t would have any bearing on whether closing prices are recorded at the bid or the ask after announcements that occur three to twelve months later. Further, it is not obvious why the bias from the imbalance would be a function of quarter t *SUE*s, or why it would switch signs from quarter $t+3$ to quarter $t+4$. One possibility is that institutional arrangements might lead some investors to prefer to buy (sell) after a year-to-year earnings increase (decrease) in earnings, even though the increase (decrease) was predictable and already reflected in prices. If so, their actions could cause stocks with good (bad) earnings news for quarter t to tend to close at the ask (bid) after the earnings announcement for quarter $t+1$, $t+2$, and $t+3$, and at the bid (ask) for quarter $t+4$. The resulting measurement error in CRSP returns would then give the appearance of abnormal returns in the directions we hypothesize.

To investigate this explanation, we conducted a test for bias due to imbalances in bid–ask spreads. If there is an imbalance between bids and asks on a given earnings announcement day, the bias should be reversed in subsequent days as the proportion of bids and asks returns to normal. Therefore, the positive (negative) estimated abnormal returns in the announcement period would be offset by negative (positive) estimated abnormal returns over the subsequent days. However, we find no compelling evidence of such a reversal in the two-day returns subsequent to the earnings-announcement day. Recall from table 2 that the abnormal returns for the three days prior to and including announcements for quarters $t+1$, $t+2$, $t+3$, and $t+4$ are 1.32 percent, 0.70 percent, 0.04 percent, and -0.66 percent for portfolios based on extreme SUE deciles. The corresponding abnormal returns for the two days after the announcement are -0.04 percent, -0.07 percent, -0.03 percent, and 0.05 percent. The *signs* of these abnormal returns are all consistent with a reversal of a bid–ask bias, but the *magnitudes* are statistically insignificant and fall far short of the amounts necessary to offset the announcement period returns. (Upon detecting evidence at least weakly consistent with a partial reversal over the first *two* post-announcement days, we then examined the *ten*-day post-announcement period, but again there was little or no evidence of a reversal.)

Potential hindsight bias arising from restatements of Compustat data. Another possibility is that our results are biased by the use of earnings data that represent Compustat restatements, rather than the earnings information actually made available on the announcement day. Compustat restates prior quarter earnings when firms undergo major acquisitions, make accounting changes, or separately report income from discontinued operations. Evidence in at least two prior studies [Watts (1978) and Foster, Olsen, and Shevlin (1984)] suggests that these restatements are not responsible for inducing post-announcement drift.[15] Furthermore, we can conceive of no reason why such restatements would induce a bias related to the autocorrelation structure of earnings.

---

[15] In his study of post-announcement drift, Watts (1978) used earnings data as originally reported. Foster, Olsen, and Shevlin (1984) collected earnings data as it was originally reported for a subsample of firms and detected post-announcement drift for that sample. [Foster, Olsen, and Shevlin (1984, p. 580) report that they hand-collected earnings-announcement dates. However, conversation with Olsen revealed that the earnings information itself was also hand-collected for this subsample.]

Despite the indications that Compustat restatements are unlikely to explain our results, we conducted an additional test for this form of hindsight bias. Our approach was to identify the 275 sample firms for which Compustat's annual earnings amount (which is *not* restated) matched (within one thousand dollars) the sum of quarterly earnings per Compustat for each of the 13 years in the dataset. When Compustat restatements occur in the first three quarters of the year, prior-year quarterly numbers are affected, thus destroying the articulation between Compustat's quarterly and annual amounts. Thus, our subsample includes firms for which over a 13-year period there was either never a restatement or only restatements that occurred in the fourth quarter (affecting only the first three interim reports of the current year). Thus, this subsample includes firms for which restatements (1) were probably less frequent than for the sample as a whole and (2) should not have affected the reported fourth-quarter earnings. Therefore, if restatements of Compustat data explain our results, then within this subsample we would expect (1) a weakening of the results across all quarters and (2) no ability to predict reactions to future earnings announcements based on fourth-quarter earnings information. In contrast, however, whether we use earnings information from all quarters or the fourth quarter only, we obtain results that are similar to (and actually somewhat stronger than) those for the full sample.

(5) *Do the three-day abnormal returns documented here represent the return on an implementable trading strategy, particularly since earnings-announcement dates cannot be predicted perfectly in advance?*

The evidence based on three-day abnormal returns is not intended as a study of an implementable strategy; rather, it is intended to help us better understand a previously documented, more readily implementable trading strategy that involves holding stocks over much longer intervals beginning the day after an earnings announcement [see table 2, panel B, the bottom half of table 5, panel A, and Bernard and Thomas (1989, especially section 3.2.5)]. Nevertheless, since post-announcement drift is concentrated around subsequent earnings announcements and since the timing of those announcements is rather predictable [Chambers and Penman (1984)], an interesting question arises. How large an abnormal return per unit time could be generated by taking positions just prior to the *expected* dates of earnings announcements?

To examine the issue, we assume investors construct portfolios in the same way implicit in regression eq. (8), and that the positions are taken 15 trading days prior to the expected announcement date, where the expected date is the actual announcement date for the comparable quarter of the prior year. We hold the position until the day earnings are announced, or for 30 days, whichever occurs first. The actual holding period is, on average, 15 days. The implied abnormal return to this strategy is 4.2 percent. On an annualized basis (before compounding), this is equivalent to 67 percent.

5. Relation to other research

Aside from Bernard and Thomas (1989) and Freeman and Tse (1989), the evidence presented here is most closely related to that of Wiggins (1990) and Mendenhall (forthcoming). Wiggins documents abnormal returns around subsequent earnings announcements that are consistent with those reported in our table 2; the most important distinction between this paper and Wiggins is that we develop the detailed relations between the signs and magnitudes of the abnormal returns and the autocorrelation structure of earnings.[16]

Mendenhall tests the validity of the Bernard and Thomas (1989) conjecture that market prices 'fail to reflect the full implications of current earnings for future earnings.' Mendenhall first documents that Value Line earnings forecasts are not efficient with respect to information in the latest earnings announcement – which is consistent with at least one set of market participants failing to respond completely to recent earnings information. Mendenhall then documents that reactions to earnings announcements can be partially predicted in advance, based on the most recent Value Line earnings-forecast revision. Thus, in forming earnings expectations, stock prices appear to ignore not only the full implications of prior earnings information, as documented here, but also previously announced analyst forecasts.

The evidence summarized here is also related to several other streams of research that are not focused directly on the issue of post-announcement drift.

Alternative earnings forecasts as proxies for market expectations. Several studies have compared earnings-forecast errors from alternative sources (analysts, statistical models, etc.) in terms of their ability to explain contemporaneous stock returns. Surprisingly, Foster (1977) finds that forecast errors from a seasonal random-walk model yield marginally greater explanatory power than errors from more accurate statistical models. Bathke and Lorek (1984) and O'Brien (1988) provide evidence that is inconsistent with Foster's anomalous result, but O'Brien offers another anomaly that is at least as surprising. Specifically, she finds that forecast errors from the Foster model provide better explanations of contemporaneous stock returns than forecast errors of analysts who report to IBES, even though the analysts' forecasts are more accurate. [However, Brown, Griffin, Hagerman, and Zmijewski (1987) find that forecast errors based on Value Line are more highly associated with contemporaneous returns.]

The evidence presented here suggests that the 'anomalies' uncovered in prior research may in fact reflect predictable errors in the earnings expecta-

---

[16]Although the first draft of this paper predates the first draft of the Wiggins (1990) paper, the two papers were developed independently.

tions underlying stock prices, as opposed to a research design flaw or some other explanation. If prices fail to reflect the implications of all publicly available information for future earnings, then it is possible that contemporaneous movements in stock prices are better explained by forecast errors based on an inferior forecasting source.

Rationality' of the contemporaneous stock-price response to earnings. Kormendi and Lipe (1987) and Easton and Zmijewski (1989) find evidence consistent with stock prices reflecting cross-sectional differences in the timeseries behavior of earnings, in terms of differences in the response to current earnings. Freeman and Tse (1989) find evidence consistent with stock prices reflecting at least some of the implications of current earnings for future earnings. The evidence presented here suggests that, while stock prices may *partially* reflect such information, they evidently do not reflect *all* available information. In fact, given that post-announcement drift per unit time is not much smaller than pre-announcement drift [see Bernard and Thomas (1989, figs. 1 and 2)], the evidence suggests that the market's impounding of available information may be far from complete.

Other evidence on market efficiency. Several recent studies offer evidence interpreted as inconsistent with semi-strong market efficiency. At least two of these [Hand (1990) and Ou and Penman (1989)] could be viewed as indications that stock prices reflect a naive earnings expectation. In that sense, the studies are consistent with the evidence presented here. However, Hand focuses on an unusual sample (firms that reported gains from debt–equity swaps), and thus it is not clear that the phenomenon underlying his results is linked with that studied here. Ou and Penman (1989, p. 327) conclude that their ability to predict future abnormal returns based on fundamental analysis is distinct from the phenomenon of post-announcement drift. Perhaps no single theme could explain each of these anomalies.

6. Concluding remarks

The evidence summarized here is consistent with the hypothesis that stock prices partially reflect a naive earnings expectation: that future earnings will be equal to earnings for the comparable quarter of the prior year. We considered a variety of alternative explanations for the evidence, including problems with risk adjustment and the impact of transactions costs, but were unable to support the viability of any of them.

In some ways, evidence like that presented here raises more questions than it answers. Why markets as competitive as the NYSE or AMEX would behave as if they are influenced by naive earnings expectations is difficult to understand.

Another question concerns the economic importance of the effects documented here. In one sense, the degree of 'mispricing' that might be indicated by post-announcement drift is 'small' – less than 5 percent of price per position, even for cases of extreme earnings realizations [see Bernard and Thomas (1989) and the long-interval results in tables 2 and 4 of this paper]. However, in some other ways, the potential effect is large. First, previous studies [e.g., Bernard and Thomas (1989, table 1)] have found that what appears to be a delayed reaction to earnings is more than one-third as large as the anticipatory and contemporaneous reaction. Second, we find here that the three-day announcement-period returns on portfolios constructed with only *prior*-quarter earnings information are approximately half as large as the return to portfolios constructed using the *contemporaneous* earnings information. Such evidence may be cause for concern in interpreting the results of the many studies that assume that earnings information is fully impounded by the end of the earnings-announcement day. Moreover, if market prices fail to reflect fully the implications of information as freely available as earnings, how well do they reflect information that is not as well-publicized?

References

Albrecht, S., L. Lookabill, and J. McKeown, 1977, The time series properties of annual earnings, Journal of Accounting Research 15, 226–244.
Ball, R. and S.P. Kothari, 1990, Security returns around earnings announcements, Working paper (University of Rochester, Rochester, NY).
Ball, R., S.P. Kothari, and R. Watts, 1988, The economics of the relation between earnings changes and stock returns, Working paper (University of Rochester, Rochester, NY).
Bathke, A. and K. Lorek, 1984, The relationship between time-series models and the security market's expectation of quarterly earnings, The Accounting Review 59, 163–176.
Bernard, V., 1984, The use of market data and accounting data in hedging against consumer price inflation, Journal of Accounting Research 22, 445–466.
Bernard, V., 1987, Cross-sectional dependence and problems in inference in market-based accounting research, Journal of Accounting Research 25, 1–48.
Bernard, V. and J. Thomas, 1989, Post-earnings-announcement drift: Delayed price response or risk premium? Journal of Accounting Research, Suppl. 27, 1–36.
Brown, L., P. Griffin, R. Hagerman, and M. Zmijewski, 1987, An evaluation of alternative proxies for the market's assessment of unexpected earnings, Journal of Accounting and Economics 9, 159–194.
Brown, L.P. and M. Rozeff, 1979, Univariate time-series models of quarterly accounting earnings per share: A proposed model, Journal of Accounting Research 17, 179–189.
Brown, K., W. Harlow, and S. Tinic, 1988, Risk aversion, uncertain information, and market efficiency, Journal of Financial Economics 21, 355–386.
Chambers, A. and S. Penman, 1984, Timeliness of reporting and the stock price reaction to earnings announcements, Journal of Accounting Research 21, 21–47.
Chari, V., R. Jagannathan, and A. Ofer, 1988, Seasonalities in security returns: The case of earnings announcements, Journal of Financial Economics 21, 101–121.
Easton, P. and M. Zmijewski, 1989, Cross-sectional variation in the stock market response to the announcement of accounting earnings, Journal of Accounting and Economics 11, 117–142.
Fama, E. and J. MacBeth, 1973, Risk, return, and equilibrium: Empirical tests, Journal of Political Economy 38, 607–636.

Foster, G., 1977, Quarterly accounting data: Time series properties and predictive-ability results, The Accounting Review 52, 1–21.
Foster, G., C. Olsen, and T. Shevlin, 1984, Earnings releases, anomalies, and the behavior of security returns, The Accounting Review 59, 574–603.
Freeman, R. and S. Tse, 1989, The multi-period information content of earnings announcements: Rational delayed reactions to earnings news, Journal of Accounting Research, Suppl. 27, 49–79.
Hand, J.R., 1990, A test of the extended functional fixation hypothesis, The Accounting Review 65, 740–763.
Holthausen, R., 1983, Abnormal returns following quarterly earnings announcements, in: Proceedings of the CRSP seminar on the analysis of security prices (University of Chicago, Chicago, IL) 37–59.
Jaffe, J.F., 1974, Special information and insider trading, Journal of Business 47, 410–428.
Joy, O.M., R. Litzenberger, and R. McEnally, 1977, The adjustment of stock prices to announcements of unanticipated changes in quarterly earnings, Journal of Accounting Research 15, 207–225.
Keim, D.B., 1989, Trading patterns, bid–ask spreads and estimated security returns: The case of common stocks at calendar turning points, Journal of Financial Economics 25, 75–98.
Kormendi, R. and R. Lipe, 1987, Earnings innovations, earnings persistence, and stock returns, Journal of Business 60, 323–346.
Marais, M.L., 1989, Discussion of post-earnings-announcement drift: Delayed price response or risk premium?, Journal of Accounting Research, Suppl. 27, 37–48.
Mendenhall, R., forthcoming, Evidence of possible underweighting of earnings-related information, Journal of Accounting Research.
O'Brien, P., 1988, Analysts' forecasts as earnings expectations, Journal of Accounting and Economics 10, 53–83.
Ou, J. and S. Penman, 1989a, Financial statement analysis and the prediction of stock returns, Journal of Accounting and Economics 11, 295–330.
Ou, J. and S. Penman, 1989b, Accounting measurement, price–earnings ratios, and the information content of security prices, Journal of Accounting Research, Suppl. 27, 111–144.
Poterba, J.M. and L.H. Summers, 1988, Mean reversion in stock prices: Evidence and implications, Journal of Financial Economics 21, 27–59.
Rendleman, R.J., Jr., C.P. Jones, and H.A. Latane, 1982, Empirical anomalies based on unexpected earnings and the importance of risk adjustments, Journal of Financial Economics 10, 269–287.
Rendleman, R.J., Jr., C.P. Jones, and H.A. Latane, 1987, Further insight into the standardized unexpected earnings anomaly: Size and serial correlation effects, The Financial Review 22, 131–144.
Watts, R.L., 1975, The time series behavior of quarterly earnings, Working paper (University of Newcastle, Newcastle, NSW).
Watts, R.L., 1978, Systematic 'abnormal' returns after quarterly earnings announcements, Journal of Financial Economics 6, 127–150.
Wiggins, J.B., 1990, Do misperceptions about the earnings process contribute to post-announcement drift, Working paper (Cornell University, Ithaca, NY).

[14]

K. C. Chan
Ohio State University

On the Contrarian Investment Strategy*

I. Introduction

A contrarian stock selection strategy consists of buying stocks that have been losers and selling short stocks that have been winners. Preached by market practitioners for years, it is still in vogue on Wall Street and La Salle Street. The strategy is formulated on the premise that the stock market overreacts to news, so winners tend to be overvalued and losers undervalued; an investor who exploits this inefficiency gains when stock prices revert to fundamental values. Many investment strategies, such as those based on the price/earnings ratio, or the book/market ratio, can be regarded as variants of this strategy.[1]

The contrarian strategy has many critics in academe, for any trading rule based on past prices violates the weakest form of market efficiency hypothesized by finance theorists. However, the recent resurgence of the academic debate on market efficiency and the theory of

Recent research found an abnormal return on the strategy of buying losers and selling winners in the stock market, a finding sometimes interpreted as support for the market overreaction hypothesis. This article explores an alternative interpretation of this evidence. We find that the risks of losers and winners are not constant. The estimation of the return of this strategy is, therefore, sensitive to the methods used. When risk changes are controlled for, we find only small abnormal returns. The model of risk and return used in the paper is the standard Capital Asset Pricing Model.

---

* Some results in this paper appeared earlier in ch. 1 of my University of Chicago Ph.D. dissertation, "Market Value Changes and Time-varying Risk" (1985). I thank Nai-fu Chen, my committee chairman, for guidance, Merton Miller for discussion, and Werner De Bondt for comments on an earlier draft. I also thank my discussant, Don Panton, and participants at the 1987 Western Finance Association annual meeting in San Diego for comments. All errors are my own. This research has been supported by an Ohio State University seed grant.

1. The price/earnings ratio and the book/market ratio are correlated with cumulative past returns. See De Bondt and Thaler (1987).

(*Journal of Business*, 1988, vol. 61, no. 2)
© 1988 by The University of Chicago. All rights reserved.
0021-9398/88/6102-0001$01.50

nonrational behavior has given the contrarian investment strategy a new respectability.[2]

A study in experimental psychology by Kahneman and Tversky (1982) finds that people tend to overreact to unexpected and dramatic events. Applying this result to the stock market, De Bondt and Thaler (1985) report that, on the basis of the past half century of data, large abnormal returns can be earned by the contrarian investment strategy. The two authors interpret this as support for the market-overreaction hypothesis. In his review of the current debate on market efficiency, Merton (1985) considers the work of De Bondt and Thaler to be "particularly noteworthy because it represents a first attempt at a formal test of cognitive misperceptions theories as applied to the general stock market."[3]

This article offers an alternative interpretation of the evidence on the performance of the contrarian strategy. We propose that the risks of winner and loser stocks are not constant over time. The risk of the strategy appears to correlate with the level of expected market-risk premium. The estimation of abnormal returns may, therefore, be sensitive to how the risks are estimated. Second, there are measurement errors in the betas estimated from the period during which losers and winners are sorted. The model of risk and return we adopt is the standard Sharpe-Lintner Capital Asset Pricing Model (CAPM). Our approach differs from Fama and French (1986) in that they explain the reversal effect by means of the size effect.

The rest of the article is organized as follows: in Section II, the samples are discussed. One sample is constructed using the procedure reported by De Bondt and Thaler (1985), while the other contains more stocks. In Section III, we present the test for abnormal returns and discuss the nonstationarity nature of the betas. We find no evidence of excess returns from the contrarian strategy. Section IV explores the correlation between the betas and the market-risk premium. We propose that the time variations of the betas and the risk premium are related to changes in the real activity. The last section is the conclusion.

II. Description of the Samples

Portfolios Construction

De Bondt and Thaler (1985) conduct their test on different samples of winning and losing stocks. Maximum annual performance is found when winners and losers are measured by performance in the previous 3 years. The 3-year samples are described in detail in that article, so

---

2. See Merton (1985) for a review of the literature.
3. Ibid., p. 23.

similar portfolios are constructed for this study. Returns over the recent 3 years are used to identify winners and losers.[4] The samples are constructed every 3 years, at the end of each year, 1932, 1935, 1938, and so on, to 1983. In addition, De Bondt and Thaler require their sampled stocks to be listed in the 7-year period preceding the rank date—4 years more than needed—to ensure that the sample consists of established firms. When a stock is no longer available after portfolio formation, however, we drop it from the sample and rebalance the portfolio after the last return is incorporated. For instance, in the first sample, formed at the end of 1932, all stocks listed in the New York Stock Exchange in the previous 7 years (1926–32) are ranked according to their recent 3-year (1930–32) market-adjusted returns. The top 35 performers are put into the winner portfolio, and the bottom 35 stocks are put into the loser portfolio. We call the period 1930–32 the *rank period*. The performance of the winner and loser portfolios are tracked for the following 3 years, labeled here as the *test period*. As the Center for Research in Security Prices (CRSP) data end in 1985, the sample formed at the end of 1983 is only 2 years long. All together, 53 years or 636 months of nonoverlapping returns for the winner and loser portfolios are obtained.

We also collect another sample for this study.[5] The second sample differs from the first in the following respects: winners and losers are identified as the top and bottom deciles of stocks instead of the extreme 35. A decile contains about 70 stocks in 1933 and about 140 stocks in 1985. These samples will help us determine whether the De Bondt and Thaler finding holds for broader-based investment strategies. In addition, stocks are not required to be listed before their returns are needed to determine winners and losers. Stocks in the second sample are, therefore, less established than those in the first.

Size Characteristics

Both winner and loser portfolios experience large changes in market value (number of shares × share price) during the rank period. In the De Bondt and Thaler sample, the average value change of loser stocks is −45%, and that of winner stocks is 365%. The changes in capitalization are so large that, although the median loser stock is bigger than the median winner at the beginning of most rank periods, it becomes smaller than the median winner at the end. This is documented in table 1.

If market value is a good proxy for risk, as suggested by the size-effect literature, the losers are safer in the beginning but become riskier

---

4. De Bondt and Thaler (1985) define their performance measures as the arithmetic sum of the market adjusted returns. I follow their procedure.
5. Other samples are also investigated but not reported by De Bondt and Thaler (1985).

TABLE 1   Changes in Capitalization during the Rank Periods (1930–83)
(De Bondt and Thaler Sample)

	Losers			Winners		
Portfolio Formation Month	Median Capitalization Beginning	End	Average Change (%)	Median Capitalization Beginning	End	Average Change (%)
12/32	22.95*	2.73*	−92	14.82	1.74	−48
12/35	22.25*	12.88*	−23	.33	2.91	138
12/38	5.29*	1.53	−69	3.50	8.02	180
12/41	3.49*	.51	−84	1.43	2.14	150
12/44	58.50*	55.30*	−1	.63	4.69	686
12/47	18.04*	11.49	11	6.61	23.26	224
12/50	11.44*	8.35	−36	6.38	18.93	160
12/53	5.70	2.25	−25	17.58	34.24	95
12/56	27.64*	15.29	−28	23.52	107.54	528
12/59	37.16*	15.89	−44	14.99	51.07	417
12/62	38.35*	19.79	−52	26.45	49.60	125
12/65	56.32*	36.68	−35	23.09	118.00	423
12/78	563.94*	427.56*	−24	26.71	174.68	589
12/71	95.40	23.24	−74	157.44	373.16	148
12/74	133.38*	13.39	−90	111.98	240.00	87
12/77	316.17*	211.69*	−32	15.63	69.61	335
12/80	120.87*	50.52	−47	41.89	383.38	642
12/83	636.22*	253.92	−53	56.19	352.55	446
Mean over rank periods			−45			365

NOTE.—Median capitalization is in millions of dollars.
* The median loser stock value is bigger than the median winner stock value.

than winners by the end of the formation period. Stocks whose values diminish become more risky for many reasons. From option pricing theory, a change in the firm value has a bigger effect on the market value of equity than on the market value of debt and other debtlike liabilities of the firm. Thus, barring any offsetting actions taken by the firm, the financial leverage (on and off balance sheet) of the loser firm becomes bigger as the stock price falls, increasing the risk of the stock. The risk of the firm may also increase as the firm value falls because of the loss of economies of scale and increase in the operating leverage. This leverage effect reduces the risk of the winner stocks as their values increase during the rank period.

If we estimate a beta in the rank period, failing to model the changes in risk, the estimated beta will be a biased estimate of the beta in the test period. Since the risk of the loser portfolio increases during the rank period, the rank-period beta underestimates the test-period beta. For the winners, the bias is in the opposite direction.

The combination of the initial size characteristics and subsequent size changes explain why De Bondt and Thaler find that winners' betas computed with rank-period returns are larger than losers'. The two authors argue that, since winners have larger betas than losers, their estimate of the reversal effect, with the assumption that winners and losers have equal beta, in effect underestimates the true reversal effect. But since the rank-period betas are misestimated, this claim may be incorrect. One must estimate the test-period betas directly to make the risk adjustment.

Since loser stocks are smaller than winners at the beginning of the test periods, the reversal effect may be related to the size effect, the well-known relation between average returns and market values.[6] Fama and French (1986) compare the returns of the De Bondt and Thaler winners and losers with returns of size-matched portfolios. Their results suggest that the size effect explains part, but only part, of the reversal effect.

III. A Time-Series Test for Abnormal Returns

Model

Our test for abnormal returns is identical to the time-series test of the CAPM run by Black, Jensen, and Scholes (1972). We assume that expected returns are generated by the Sharpe-Lintner CAPM. With appropriate distributional assumptions, the following ordinary least squares (OLS) regression equation for asset i is well specified:

$$r_{it} - r_{ft} = \alpha_i + \beta_i(r_{mt} - r_{ft}) + \epsilon_{it}, \quad t = 1, \ldots, T. \quad (1)$$

The equally weighted CRSP market index serves as our market portfolio r_m. Equation (1) is tested over the test period, in which the beta is assumed to be constant. We interpret the null hypothesis that asset i earns no abnormal return to mean that $\alpha_i = 0$.[7] This implies that we ignore any bias introduced by the size effect. If the size effect is significant in our sample, it will, however, bias against our null hypothesis of no abnormal returns, as the loser stocks are smaller than winners at the beginning of the test periods.

The OLS estimate of α_i is centered around the true parameter, and its variance is given by

$$\hat{\sigma}^2(\hat{\alpha}_i) = (1/T)(1 + \overline{r_m^T}^2/s_{m'}^2)\hat{\sigma}_\epsilon^2,$$

where $\overline{r_m^T}$ is the sample mean of the market return less the risk-free rate; $s_{m'}^2$ is the sample variance of $(r_{mt} - r_{ft})$ without an adjustment for degrees of freedom; and $\hat{\sigma}_\epsilon^2$ is the sample variance of ϵ_{it}. Assuming that ϵ_{it} is normally distributed, under the null hypothesis the ratio of $\hat{\alpha}_i$ to its

---

6. See, e.g., Banz (1981).
7. The performance evaluation is ambiguous if we do not know if the market index we use is ex ante efficient. See Roll (1977).

standard error, $\hat{\sigma}(\hat{\alpha}_i)$, is distributed as a student-t with $(T - 1)$ degrees of freedom.

Betas and abnormal returns are thus simultaneously estimated in the test periods. There are no errors in variables because we presume to know what market index to use, and the test is conditioned on that choice. The estimated intercept in equation (1) is consistent, and its standard error reflects the uncertainty of the estimated beta. This time-series test is well suited to our problem because there is no need to have a separate period for estimating the beta. We could go back to the rank period to estimate the beta, but to do it correctly, we would have to model the beta's time variation, a formidable task. However, going forward to use future data after the test period might violate the stationarity assumption and, worse, introduce survivorship bias.

The estimates of the regression parameters for the 1933–85 period are weighted averages of the parameters in individual test periods. The weights are proportional to the length of the test periods—the last period has 2 years while all others have 3. To aggregate the t-statistics, we make use of the fact that the test periods (each with T_i observations) are nonoverlapping. Under the null hypothesis, by the independence assumption and the central limit theorem, the following statistic based on t values from the test periods approaches a standard normal distribution,

$$U = \frac{1}{\sqrt{N}} \sum_{i=1}^{N} t_i \sqrt{(T_i - 3)/(T_i - 1)} \sim N(0, 1),$$

as the number of test periods, N, gets large. This will be our test statistic for the entire period.

Performance and Risk in the Rank Period and the Test Period

The basis of the contrarian strategy is that the rank-period abnormal return is followed by a reversal in the test period. By modifying the regression equation (1) slightly, we can examine the risk and performance in the rank period and the test period in a single equation. We are particularly interested in finding out whether the betas change from the rank period to the test period.

We run the following regression:

$$r_{it} - r_{ft} = \alpha_{1i}(1 - D_t) + \alpha_{2i}D_t \\ + \beta_i(r_{mt} - r_{ft}) + \beta_{iD}(r_{mt} - r_{ft})D_t + \epsilon_{it}, \tag{2}$$

where $t = 1$ to 72 (or 60, as in the 1983 sample), r_{mt} is the equally weighted CRSP index, r_{ft} is the risk-free rate; the dummy variable D_t is equal to zero in the preranking period ($t \leq 36$) and to one in the test period ($t > 36$), letting us estimate different intercepts and betas for the 2 periods. The mean abnormal return in the rank period is estimated by

$\hat{\alpha}_{1i}$ and that of the test period is estimated by $\hat{\alpha}_{2i}$. The rank-period beta is estimated by $\hat{\beta}_i$ and the test-period beta is $(\hat{\beta}_i + \hat{\beta}_{iD})$. The rank-period beta may not be constant, but under certain independence assumptions the OLS estimate of β_i is the mean estimate for the moving beta. However, if the beta is constant throughout the rank and test periods, $\hat{\beta}_{iD}$ should be indistinguishable from zero. We assume that ϵ_{it} is normally distributed with a variance of σ_{i1}^2 in the rank period and σ_{i2}^2 in the test period, the two variances being not necessarily different. Due to our variance assumption, the estimated coefficients and standard errors of the α's are no different from what are obtained by running regression equation (1) in the rank period and the test period separately.

We run the regression equation (2) using as dependent variables the excess returns of the loser and winner portfolios and the return of a self-financed arbitrage portfolio (loser − winner), which consists of a long position on the losers and a short position on the winners. Regression estimates for the De Bondt and Thaler sample and the decile sample are reported separately in tables 2 and 3. The tables show that losers have large negative abnormal returns and that winners have large positive abnormal returns in the rank periods, ranging from 2.2% to 3.1% monthly in absolute magnitude, and that the arbitrage portfolio (losers − winners) loses 4.56% per month in the 3-year rank period in one sample and 5.87% in another.

Small abnormal returns between losers and winners. We observe only small abnormal returns to the contrarian strategy during the test period. Controlling for transaction costs, that is probably not economically significant. In table 2, the mean monthly abnormal returns are −.095%, −.228%, and .133% per month for the loser, winner, and arbitrage portfolios. The aggregate test statistic for the arbitrage portfolio excess return is .88, far below the standard normal value normally taken to suggest significant difference from zero. Only the winner portfolio's abnormal return may be interpreted to be reliably different from zero, using the usual probability value.

In the broader-based decile sample, in table 3, the mean is .032% for the losers, −.236% for the winners, and .269% for the arbitrage portfolio per month. The arbitrage portfolio return is higher in this sample than the other sample. But in any case, the abnormal return of the arbitrage portfolio in either sample is neither large nor reliably different from zero.

Risk changes from the rank to the test periods. The estimated rank-period betas are smaller for losers and bigger for winners. This is not surprising as losers have larger capitalization than winners at the beginning of the rank period. Since the OLS rank-period beta is only some

TABLE 2 Testing for Abnormal Returns under the Assumption that the Rank-Period and Test-Period Betas Are Not Equal—the De Bondt and Thaler Sample

	Loser				Winner				Loser − Winner			
	$\hat{\alpha}_{1i}$	$\hat{\alpha}_{2i}$	$\hat{\beta}_i$	$\hat{\beta}_{iD}$	$\hat{\alpha}_{1i}$	$\hat{\alpha}_{2i}$	$\hat{\beta}_i$	$\hat{\beta}_{iD}$	$\hat{\alpha}_{1i}$	$\hat{\alpha}_{2i}$	$\hat{\beta}_i$	$\hat{\beta}_{iD}$
1930–35	−.0343 (−6.44)	.0013 (.14)	.97 (32.50)	.27 (4.34)	.0566 (3.99)	.0025 (.22)	1.32 (16.62)	−.17 (−1.62)	−.0909 (−6.40)	−.0011 (−.07)	−.35 (−4.42)	.44 (3.54)
1933–38	−.0259 (−3.54)	−.0077 (−1.72)	.55 (12.59)	.43 (7.16)	.0254 (2.66)	−.0018 (−.43)	1.71 (29.97)	−.40 (−5.83)	−.0513 (−3.45)	−.0059 (−.86)	−1.16 (−13.05)	.83 (7.65)
1936–41	−.0316 (−7.85)	.0054 (.43)	.99 (27.09)	.64 (4.92)	.0387 (4.18)	−.0034 (−.55)	1.64 (19.65)	−.08 (−.80)	−.0704 (−7.22)	.0089 (.81)	−.66 (−7.48)	.73 (5.17)
1939–44	−.0390 (−4.15)	−.0008 (−.07)	1.07 (11.40)	1.26 (6.02)	.0471 (2.54)	−.0027 (−.51)	2.09 (11.36)	−.93 (−4.60)	−.0861 (−3.44)	.0019 (.15)	−1.03 (−4.12)	2.19 (6.97)
1942–47	−.0122 (−2.90)	.0019 (1.13)	.50 (7.85)	.22 (3.09)	.0094 (.57)	−.0059 (−.91)	2.76 (11.12)	−1.31 (−4.79)	−.0216 (−1.11)	.0078 (1.11)	−2.26 (−7.67)	1.52 (4.78)
1945–50	−.0229 (−6.06)	.0002 (.04)	1.07 (16.16)	.32 (2.94)	.0250 (4.64)	.0021 (.91)	1.26 (13.40)	−.09 (−.90)	−.0480 (−7.42)	−.0019 (−.33)	−.19 (−1.72)	.42 (2.57)
1948–53	−.0213 (−6.55)	−.0048 (−1.65)	.96 (14.63)	.07 (.64)	.0233 (5.17)	−.0040 (−1.83)	1.17 (12.91)	.07 (.58)	−.0446 (−6.75)	−.0008 (−.21)	−.21 (−1.58)	.01 (.03)
1951–56	−.0305 (−7.81)	−.0073 (−1.02)	1.08 (8.68)	.28 (1.21)	.0195 (9.06)	.0031 (1.10)	1.15 (16.68)	−.11 (−1.09)	−.0501 (−9.89)	−.0104 (−1.29)	−.07 (−.40)	.39 (1.43)
1954–59	−.0257 (−7.38)	.0039 (.92)	.94 (9.90)	.52 (3.44)	.0225 (5.33)	−.0085 (−2.43)	1.53 (13.21)	−.25 (−1.66)	−.0483 (−7.70)	.0124 (1.96)	−.58 (−3.41)	.77 (3.16)

Period											
1957–62	−.0302 (−9.04)	−.0044 (−.92)	1.40 (15.40)	−.17 (−1.30)	.0329 (5.83)	−.0068 (−1.78)	1.34 (8.71)	.12 (.68)	−.0631 (−8.30)	.0024 (.32)	.06 (.31)	−.29 (−1.12)
1960–65	−.0259 (−7.92)	.0002 (.05)	1.23 (18.11)	.40 (2.52)	.0238 (8.36)	−.0001 (−.03)	1.17 (19.71)	−.22 (−2.40)	−.0498 (−10.81)	.0003 (.05)	.07 (.68)	.61 (3.22)
1963–68	−.0222 (−8.11)	.0018 (.46)	.91 (10.23)	.22 (1.82)	.0258 (4.89)	−.0093 (−1.57)	1.94 (11.34)	−.48 (−2.29)	−.0479 (−8.94)	.0111 (1.58)	−1.03 (−5.94)	.70 (3.09)
1966–71	−.0176 (−6.51)	.0012 (.40)	.73 (13.12)	.08 (1.07)	.0296 (4.65)	−.0038 (−.85)	1.61 (12.27)	−.18 (−1.23)	−.0472 (−5.72)	.0050 (.77)	−.88 (−5.17)	.26 (1.32)
1969–74	−.0307 (−6.21)	.0083 (.93)	1.39 (17.37)	−.11 (−.67)	.0291 (8.20)	.0031 (.55)	.96 (16.71)	.11 (.98)	−.0598 (−8.35)	.0052 (.39)	.43 (3.68)	−.21 (−.90)
1972–77	−.0334 (−4.69)	−.0139 (−1.91)	1.30 (11.63)	.60 (3.93)	.0437 (4.63)	.0012 (.17)	.99 (6.67)	−.66 (−3.68)	−.0772 (−5.13)	−.0150 (−1.35)	.31 (1.33)	1.26 (4.41)
1975–80	−.0223 (−4.25)	.0049 (.99)	.53 (7.06)	.54 (4.93)	.0320 (4.61)	.0038 (.99)	1.61 (16.23)	−.42 (−3.60)	−.0543 (−5.60)	.0011 (.16)	−1.08 (−7.78)	.97 (5.41)
1978–83	−.0340 (−7.85)	.0095 (1.42)	1.04 (14.92)	.09 (.57)	.0400 (5.82)	−.0131 (−2.47)	1.54 (13.92)	−.19 (−1.22)	−.0740 (−8.28)	.0225 (2.60)	−.50 (−3.48)	.28 (1.21)
1981–85	−.0377 (−4.73)	−.0250 (−2.17)	1.11 (6.62)	.19 (.59)	.0349 (7.00)	.0048 (.89)	1.34 (12.81)	−.14 (−.85)	−.0726 (−6.51)	−.0298 (−1.91)	−.23 (−1.00)	.33 (.75)
Aggregate	−.0277 (−25.6)	−.00095 (−.58)	.99 (58.4)	.33 (10.8)	.0311 (21.1)	−.00228 (−1.95)	1.51 (60.3)	−.30 (−7.86)	−.0587 (−27.7)	.00133 (.88)	−.52 (−14.0)	.63 (12.1)

NOTE.—t-statistics are in parentheses. The aggregate test statistic is constructed from test-period t-statistics, and it follows a standard normal distribution. Model:

$$r_{it} - r_{ft} = \alpha_{1t}(1 - D_t) + \alpha_{2t}D_t + \beta_t(r_{mt} - r_{ft}) + \beta_{tD}(r_{mt} - r_{ft})D_t + \epsilon_{it},$$

where r_{mt} is the market index, r_{ft} is the risk-free rate; $D_t = 0$, and $\epsilon_{it} \sim N(0, \sigma_{1}^2) \sim N(0, \sigma_{1}^2)$ in the rank period; $D_t = 1$ and $\epsilon_{it} \sim N(0, \sigma_{2}^2)$ in the test period. Thus α_{1t} = rank-period abnormal return; α_{2t} = test-period abnormal return; β_t = rank period beta; β_{tD} = change in beta from the rank period to the test period.

TABLE 3 Testing for Abnormal Returns under the Assumption that the Rank-Period and Test-Period Betas Are Not Equal—the Decile Sample

	Loser			Winner				Loser − Winner		
	$\hat{\alpha}_{1i}$	$\hat{\alpha}_{2i}$	$\hat{\beta}_i$	$\hat{\beta}_{i,D}$	$\hat{\alpha}_{1i}$	$\hat{\alpha}_{2i}$	$\hat{\beta}_i$	$\hat{\beta}_{i,D}$	$\hat{\alpha}_{1i}$	$\hat{\alpha}_{2i}$	$\hat{\beta}_i$	$\hat{\beta}_{i,D}$
1930–35	−.0332 (−7.45)	−.0023 (−.29)	.940 (37.64)	.391 (7.15)	.0528 (4.53)	−.0016 (−.19)	1.367 (20.93)	−.167 (−2.01)	−.0861 (−7.11)	−.0007 (−.06)	−.427 (−6.30)	.558 (5.76)
1933–38	−.0204 (−3.29)	−.0080 (−2.47)	.544 (14.67)	.295 (6.25)	.0187 (1.35)	−.0010 (−.28)	1.724 (20.86)	−.379 (−4.28)	−.0391 (−2.10)	−.0070 (−1.34)	−1.180 (−10.59)	.675 (5.58)
1936–41	−.0263 (−9.35)	.0053 (.76)	.929 (36.56)	.405 (5.48)	.0297 (6.13)	−.0038 (−1.27)	1.456 (33.30)	−.131 (−2.48)	−.0560 (−9.94)	.0091 (1.16)	−.526 (−10.34)	.536 (5.77)
1939–44	−.0306 (−4.50)	.0029 (.36)	1.027 (15.19)	.918 (6.49)	.0348 (3.00)	−.0020 (−.57)	1.691 (14.66)	−.708 (−5.59)	−.0654 (−3.78)	.0049 (.51)	−.664 (−3.85)	1.625 (7.22)
1942–47	−.0096 (−2.34)	.0017 (1.26)	.504 (8.07)	.241 (3.60)	.0056 (.55)	−.0051 (−1.05)	2.292 (14.90)	−.876 (−4.99)	−.0152 (−1.12)	.0068 (1.24)	−1.789 (−8.63)	1.117 (4.89)
1945–50	−.0195 (−5.95)	.0002 (.05)	1.014 (17.80)	.255 (2.48)	.0201 (7.12)	.0002 (−.11)	1.188 (24.19)	−.053 (−.88)	−.0396 (−8.33)	.0004 (.08)	−.174 (−2.11)	.308 (2.34)
1948–53	−.0173 (−7.22)	−.0052 (−2.57)	.980 (20.40)	.006 (.07)	.0183 (6.49)	−.0030 (−2.26)	1.214 (21.41)	−.038 (−.54)	−.0356 (−7.77)	−.0021 (−.81)	−.234 (−2.54)	.044 (.35)
1951–56	−.0232 (−9.88)	−.0037 (−.86)	1.181 (15.82)	.139 (1.01)	.0160 (9.49)	.0029 (1.33)	1.084 (20.25)	−.088 (−1.10)	−.0392 (−10.81)	−.0066 (−1.12)	.097 (.84)	.228 (1.16)
1954–59	−.0165 (−7.86)	.0034 (1.46)	.803 (14.04)	.256 (2.99)	.0188 (7.76)	−.0067 (−2.82)	1.329 (20.10)	−.099 (−1.07)	−.0353 (−9.36)	.0101 (2.42)	−.526 (−5.12)	.355 (2.32)
1957–62	−.0240 (−10.62)	−.0028 (−.80)	1.291 (21.00)	−.190 (−1.99)	.0240 (7.99)	−.0018 (−.72)	1.146 (13.99)	.134 (1.38)	−.0480 (−10.26)	−.0010 (−.19)	.145 (1.14)	−.324 (−1.90)

Contrarian Investment Strategy

1966–65	−.0217 (−7.56)	.0014 (.52)	1.213 (20.35)	.312 (2.93)	.0195 (7.32)	−.0014 (−1.08)	1.120 (20.17)	−.232 (−3.31)	−.0412 (−8.22)	.0028 (.80)	.093 (.89)	.543 (3.50)
1965–68	−.0179 (−13.00)	.0028 (.84)	.885 (19.79)	.193 (2.32)	.0187 (7.47)	−.0061 (−1.64)	1.645 (20.21)	−.366 (−3.27)	−.0366 (−11.94)	.0089 (1.62)	−.760 (−7.63)	.558 (3.69)
1966–71	−.0143 (−5.18)	.0014 (.49)	.691 (12.11)	.048 (.65)	.0220 (5.92)	−.0033 (−1.25)	1.378 (17.91)	−.112 (−1.27)	−.0363 (−6.02)	.0047 (.98)	−.687 (−5.51)	.160 (1.09)
1969–74	−.0236 (−6.05)	.0092 (1.43)	1.377 (21.84)	−.067 (−.56)	.0228 (8.24)	.0016 (.34)	.944 (21.01)	.085 (1.00)	−.0464 (−7.85)	.0077 (.74)	.434 (4.53)	−.152 (−.81)
1972–77	−.0292 (−5.56)	−.0027 (−.52)	1.265 (15.33)	.473 (4.27)	.0303 (5.02)	.0001 (.02)	.922 (9.72)	−.435 (−3.71)	−.0595 (−5.52)	−.0028 (−.33)	.343 (2.03)	.908 (4.35)
1975–80	−.0186 (−5.68)	.0023 (.97)	.640 (13.66)	.334 (5.53)	.0174 (4.28)	.0021 (.85)	1.609 (27.61)	−.319 (−4.50)	−.0360 (−5.53)	.0002 (.04)	−.969 (−10.39)	.653 (5.80)
1978–83	−.0224 (−7.21)	.0077 (2.86)	.743 (14.86)	.053 (.70)	.0290 (6.40)	−.0134 (−3.55)	1.382 (18.95)	−.084 (−.78)	−.0514 (−7.13)	.0211 (3.56)	−.639 (−5.51)	.137 (.81)
1981–85	−.0301 (−5.68)	−.0122 (−1.79)	1.128 (10.13)	.040 (.21)	.0251 (6.01)	.0012 (.35)	1.280 (14.56)	−.085 (−.71)	−.0552 (−6.67)	−.0134 (−1.41)	−.152 (−.87)	.126 (.44)
Aggregate	−.0221 (−28.47)	.00032 (.39)	.953 (75.4)	.231 (11.4)	.0235 (24.1)	−.00236 (−3.18)	1.376 (81.2)	−.222 (−8.72)	−.0456 (−29.65)	.00269 (1.80)	−.423 (−16.0)	.453 (12.0)

NOTE.—*t*-statistics are in parentheses. The aggregate test statistic is constructed from test-period *t*-statistics, and it follows a standard normal distribution. Model:

$$r_{it} - r_{ft} = \alpha_{1t}(1 - D_t) + \alpha_{2t}D_t + \beta_i(r_{mt} - r_{ft}) + \beta_{iD}(r_{mt} - r_{ft})D_t + \epsilon_{it},$$

where r_{mt} is the market index, r_{ft} is the risk-free rate; $D_t = 0$ and $\epsilon_{it} \sim N(0, \sigma_{i1}^2)$ in the rank period; $D_t = 1$ and $\epsilon_{it} \sim N(0, \sigma_{i2}^2)$ in the test period. Thus α_{1i} = rank-period abnormal return; α_{2i} = test-period abnormal return; β_i = rank-period beta; β_{iD} = change in beta from the rank period to the test period.

average of the true changing beta, the losers are probably even safer in the beginning than the regression estimates suggest. Consistent with the risk explanation of the contrarian strategy, we observe large changes of betas from the rank period to the test period, such that losers are riskier than winners after portfolio formation.

The direction of change of the beta is consistent with the option-leverage effect. In table 3 (the decile sample), for example, losers' betas increase in 16 out of 18 cases, with an average gain of .231. In 11 cases, the change in the beta appears to be reliably different from zero, if we use the 95% level of the t-distribution as the critical level. Winners' betas decrease also in the same 16 periods as the losers' betas increase, with an average drop of .222. Out of these 16 are 9 cases where the decrease in beta appears to be reliably different from zero. The beta of the arbitrage portfolio (losers − winners) is on average negative in the rank period but increases in the test period with an average gain of .453. A similar summary can be made for the De Bondt and Thaler sample. In fact, in that sample, the beta of the arbitrage portfolio increases even more, by .604, from the rank period to the test period.[8]

A comparison of different adjustment methods. The difference between our conclusion and that drawn by De Bondt and Thaler is due to the different empirical methods used. A comparison of our methods illustrates the sensitivity of abnormal return estimation to different empirical assumptions.

In table 4, we show the market-adjusted returns (raw returns − equally weighted CRSP returns) similar to those De Bondt and Thaler report in their paper. In addition, we also report the CAPM adjusted returns with betas estimated from the rank period and the abnormal returns estimated with test period betas (from tables 2 and 3) for comparison. We report the mean monthly returns and the mean of cumulative returns compounded over individual test periods.[9] The cumulative return on the arbitrage portfolio is calculated as the difference between

---

8. It has been suggested to me that the estimated changes in betas might be caused partly by measurement errors of another kind such that the true magnitude of changes is overstated. It is argued that, since the loser (winner) stocks are chosen because they have had large negative (positive) returns, we introduce a negative (positive) correlation between the stocks' returns and the market return because the average market return is positive. Thus we underestimate the rank-period betas of losers and overestimate those of winners. This reasoning is incorrect because we select stocks by their mean returns, and the mean returns in excess of the market will be captured by the rank-period intercept in the regression eq. (2). There are, of course, still the measurement errors caused by the true changes in betas. But, as argued before, our OLS estimates probably understate the true changes that occur from the beginning of the rank period to the test period.

9. The last test period consisting of only 2 years is weighted as 2/3.

TABLE 4 Returns of the Winner and Loser Portfolios after Different Methods of Risk Adjustment, 1933–85

	Monthly*			Cumulative (3-year)†		
	Market-adjusted Returns	Past Beta-adjusted Returns	Test-Period Beta-adjusted Returns	Market-adjusted Returns	Past Beta-adjusted Returns	Test-Period Beta-adjusted Returns
De Bondt and Thaler sample (1933–85):						
Loser	.00491	.00547	−.00095	.294	.349	−.022
	(2.45)	(2.72)	(−.58)	(1.69)	(1.75)	(.45)
Winner	−.00095	−.00792	−.00228	−.046	−.091	−.081
	(−.62)	(−4.74)	(−1.95)	(−.91)	(−5.04)	(−2.18)
Loser − Winner	.00586	.01397	.00133	.340	.439	.058
	(2.34)	(4.33)	(.88)	(1.99)	(2.20)	(.82)
Decile sample (1933–85):						
Loser	.00460	.00548	.00032	.251	.334	.019
	(3.13)	(3.71)	(.39)	(1.94)	(2.08)	(.47)
Winner	−.00122	−.00664	−.00236	−.047	−.119	−.080
	(−1.07)	(−5.42)	(−3.18)	(−1.10)	(−2.88)	(−2.84)
Loser − Winner	.00582	.01212	.00269	.298	.453	.098
	(2.93)	(5.07)	(1.80)	(2.10)	(2.71)	(1.72)

NOTE.—t-statistics for market-adjusted returns and past beta-adjusted returns are in parentheses. In the case of the test-period beta-adjusted returns, the statistic is an aggregate of test-period t-statistics and follows a standard normal distribution.

* Market-adjusted return = raw return minus the return on the equally weighted index. Past beta-adjusted return is the prediction error of the Sharpe-Lintner Capital Asset Pricing Model with beta estimated from the rank period. Test period beta-adjusted returns are those reported in tables 2 and 3.

† Cumulative (3-year) return is compounded return over the 3 years after portfolio formation. The 1984–85 period is weighted by 2/3.

the cumulative sums rather than as the cumulative sum of the monthly difference.[10]

The mean monthly market-adjusted return on the arbitrage portfolio (loser − winner) of the De Bondt and Thaler sample is .586% with a t-statistic of 2.34, and the mean cumulative compounded return over the 3-year test period is 33.9% with a t-statistic of 1.99, similar to the results reported by De Bondt and Thaler. In comparison, our estimate for the mean difference in cumulative excess returns between losers and winners is 5.84% for 3 years in the De Bondt and Thaler sample and 9.86% for 3 years in the decile sample.

As expected from the rank-period betas, the arbitrage portfolio earns

---

10. Although the cumulative return reported is not strictly a buy-and-hold return, taking the difference of two cumulative returns implicitly requires less rebalancing than does computing the cumulative sum of the difference.

an even larger abnormal gain when we adjust returns with rank-period betas. The return between losers and winners in the De Bondt and Thaler sample is 1.126%, and the return in the broader sample is 1.211% per month, or 44% and 45% in 3 years. It should be noted that De Bondt and Thaler do not report returns estimated by means of this procedure in their paper, but this example serves to illustrate one property of the contrarian strategy—its risk can be badly misestimated when securities are experiencing large value changes.

In sum, if our risk adjustment is appropriate and adequate, we find only weak evidence of price reversals, even though the stocks in our sample have experienced very large abnormal gains or losses prior to the test periods.[11] It is worth emphasizing that our conclusion is reached on the basis of the size of abnormal return as well as the reliability of the effect. The magnitude of the price reversals we find is small and probably conveys little economic information.

IV. Correlation between Beta and the Market-Risk Premium

Although the return to the strategy of buying losers and selling winners can be explained by beta, the average beta of this strategy is in fact very small when compared to the average return to be explained. Thus the ability of the CAPM to explain the reversal effect is owing not to the long-term difference between the betas of the loser and winner portfolios but to the short-term differences measured over 3-year test periods. From table 2, the average test-period betas ($\hat{\beta}_i + \hat{\beta}_{iD}$) of the loser and winner portfolios in the De Bondt and Thaler sample are 1.315 and 1.208, respectively, with a difference of .107. The average market-risk premium in 1933–85 is 1.218% per month, thus the average beta only explains .13% per month (.107 × 1.218%) of the .586% difference in average monthly returns. In the decile sample, we find a similar disparity. The average beta of the arbitrage portfolio is .030 and the average return to be explained is .582%.

The insignificance of the difference in long-term betas between losers and winners suggests that our risk-adjustment procedure is successful in explaining most of the return difference because it is able to capture the correlation between the (time-varying) betas and the market-risk premium. In our empirical model, the portfolio beta changes at resampling every 3 years. In other words, for the CAPM to explain the raw returns we observe, losers' betas need not be bigger than winners' betas all the time or even on average; they just need to be bigger in the

---

11. When the test-period beta is allowed to vary from year to year, the mean estimated abnormal returns of the arbitrage portfolio is even smaller than previously estimated. It drops by .1% to .03% (t = .12) and by .068% to .201% (t = 1.10) per month in the De Bondt and Thaler and decile samples, respectively. We have no statistical evidence that the test-period beta is nonstationary.

test period when the expected market premium is high. To illustrate this argument, we stack the different test periods together and write down a return-generating model for portfolio i in the 1933–85 period as

$$r_{it} = \alpha_{it} + \beta_{it} r_{mt} + \epsilon_{it}, \qquad (3)$$

where returns are excess returns. The α_{it} and β_{it} are assumed to be constant within a test period, but they change as we move to a different test period. Making use of the definition of sample covariance, the sample average return is given by

$$\bar{r}_i = \bar{\alpha}_i + \widehat{\text{cov}}(\beta_{it}, r_{mt}) + \bar{\beta}_i \cdot \bar{r}_m. \qquad (4)$$

If we simply perform risk adjustment with the long-term beta $\bar{\beta}_i$, the mean risk-adjusted return $(\bar{r}_i - \bar{\beta}_i \cdot \bar{r}_m)$ will contain the true excess return $\bar{\alpha}_i$ and the covariance term. One way to make this mistake is to run equation (3) as a regression over all testing periods. Since the OLS beta is somewhat like the average of the time-varying betas, the intercept will contain the covariance term.

Table 5 provides a breakdown of the explained average returns into two components, the covariance component and the average beta component. The $\bar{\alpha}_i$ is the average abnormal return estimated by test-period betas in tables 2 and 3, the average beta component is computed as the average test-period beta (from tables 2 and 3) multiplied by the average market-risk premium, and the covariance component is then inferred from equation (4). The covariance component is nontrivial. For in-

TABLE 5   Components in the Explained Average Return

	Average Beta $\bar{\beta}_i$	Average Excess Return $\bar{r}_i'$	Average Beta $\bar{\beta}_i \cdot \bar{r}_m'$	Covariance Effect $\text{cov}(\beta_{it}, r_{mt}')$	Unexplained Return $\bar{\alpha}_i$
De Bondt and Thaler' sample (1933–85):					
Loser	1.315	.01709	.01602	.00202	−.00095
Winner	1.208	.01123	.01471	−.00121	−.00228
Loser − Winner	.107	.00586	.00130	.00323	.00133
Decile sample (1933–85):					
Loser	1.184	.01678	.01442	.00204	.00032
Winner	1.154	.01096	.01406	−.00073	−.00236
Loser − Winner	.030	.00582	.00037	.00277	.00268

NOTE.—Average betas and average unexplained returns are estimated under the assumption the beta in the test period is constant. See tables 2 and 3. Model:

$$\bar{r}_i' = \bar{\alpha}_i + \text{cov}(\beta_{it}, r_{mt}') + \bar{\beta}_i \cdot \bar{r}_m',$$

where $r_{it}' = (r_{it} - r_{ft})$ and $r_{mt}' = r_{mt} - r_{ft}$, r_{mt} and r_{it} being the market return and the bill rate.

stance, the Sharpe-Lintner CAPM explains .453% of the arbitrage portfolio return in the De Bondt and Thaler sample. Of that, .130% is explained by the average beta, and .323% by the covariance between the beta and the market premium. The covariance component explains .277% of the arbitrage return in the decile sample. The table also suggests that the loser portfolio's beta is positively, and the winner portfolio's beta negatively, correlated with the market-risk premium.

This correlation is unlikely to be due to estimation errors of the betas because the estimation errors are uncorrelated with the expected risk premium. An interpretation of the correlation is that our portfolio selection procedure picks very risky losers when the expected market-risk premium is high and less risky losers when the expected market-risk premium is low, so that the difference in risk between losers and winners is positively correlated to the market-risk premium. We will suggest how this correlation is possible.

While many economic variables might explain the variation of the market-risk premium, we expect that the real output of the economy is one of the more important determinants. An explanation of the correlation between betas and the market-risk premium, therefore, is that the betas are correlated with real activity. A way to get this correlation, and one that we have demonstrated, is that betas increase as the stock values fall. If the stocks that go into the loser portfolio suffer larger losses in recession than in economic expansion, the portfolio beta will be negatively related to the level of economic activity. Similar effects in the opposite direction may affect the winner portfolios. In any case, since cross-sectional betas of all securities must sum to one, the winner portfolio beta decreases when the loser portfolio beta increases, other things being equal. Because the expected market-risk premium is probably also negatively correlated with the level of the economic activity, it will be positively correlated with the loser portfolio's beta and negatively correlated with the winner portfolio's beta. The discussion above is drawn on Chan and Chen (1986, 1987), who find some evidence that the market-risk premium and betas of portfolios sorted by size are correlated with the predetermined industrial production index. We find similar correlation between the industrial production and the betas of the loser and winner portfolios, but the industrial production index alone appears to account for a part of the variations in betas and the risk premium.[12]

V. Conclusion

The estimation of the abnormal return to the contrarian investment strategy is sensitive to the model and estimation methods. Using a

12. Detailed results are available upon request.

simple asset-pricing model, the CAPM, and an empirical method that is free of the problems caused by risk changes, we find that the contrarian strategy earns a very small abnormal return, which is probably economically insignificant. If the experiment is interpreted as a test of market overreaction, we find no strong evidence in support of the hypothesis.

Two features about winners and losers in the stock market make the estimation of abnormal returns sensitive to the procedures used. First, the losers' betas increase after a period of abnormal loss, and the winners' betas decrease after a period of abnormal gain. Betas estimated from the past should not be used. Second, when we evaluate the risk-return relation over an extended period of time that involves updating of portfolios, it is incorrect to base the analysis on the relation between the average return and average beta because both the betas and expected market-risk premium might respond to some common state variables and are thus correlated. The contrarian strategy appears to have an ability to pick riskier losers when the expected market-risk premium is high, probably because losers suffer larger losses at economic downturns than at upturns. An investor who follows the contrarian strategy is likely to find that his or her risk exposure varies inversely with the level of economic activity (and consumption). On average, the investor realizes above-market returns, but that excess return is likely to be a normal compensation for the risk in the investment strategy.

References

Banz, Rolf. 1981. The relationship between return and market value of common stock. *Journal of Financial Economics* 9:3–18.
Black, F.; Jensen, M.; and Scholes, M. 1972. The capital asset pricing model: Some empirical tests. In M. Jensen (ed.), *Studies in the Theory of Capital Markets*. New York: Praeger.
Chan, K. C., and Chen, Nai-fu. 1986. Unconditional test of asset pricing and the role of firm size as an instrumental variable for risk. Working paper. Columbus: Ohio State University.
Chan, K. C., and Chen, Nai-fu. 1987. Business cycles and the returns of small and large firms. Working paper. Chicago: University of Chicago.
De Bondt, Werner, and Thaler, Richard. 1985. Does the stock market overreact? *Journal of Finance* 40, no. 3 (July): 793–805.
De Bondt, Werner, and Thaler, Richard. 1987. Further evidence on investor overreaction and stock market seasonality. *Journal of Finance* 42, no. 3 (July): 557–82.
Fama, Eugene, and French, Kenneth R. 1986. Common factors in the serial correlation of stock returns. Working paper. Chicago: University of Chicago.
Kahneman, D., and Tversky, A. 1982. Intuitive prediction: Biases and corrective procedures. In D. Kahneman, P. Slovic, and A. Tversky (eds.), *Judgement under Uncertainty: Heuristics and Biases*. New York: Cambridge University Press.
Merton, Robert C. 1985. On the current state of the stock market rationality hypothesis. Working Paper no. 1717-85. Cambridge, Mass.: Massachusetts Institute of Technology, Sloan School of Management, October.
Roll, Richard. 1977. A critique of the asset pricing theory's tests: Part I: On past and potential testability of the theory. *Journal of Financial Economics* 4 (March): 129–76.

Measuring abnormal performance

Do stocks overreact?

Navin Chopra
Temple University, Philadelphia, PA 19122, USA

Josef Lakonishok and Jay R. Ritter
University of Illinois, Champaign, IL 61820, USA

Received June 1991, final version received November 1991

A highly controversial issue in financial economics is whether stocks overreact. In this paper we find an economically-important overreaction effect even after adjusting for size and beta. In portfolios formed on the basis of prior five-year returns, extreme prior losers outperform extreme prior winners by 5–10% per year during the subsequent five years. Although we find a pronounced January seasonal, our evidence suggests that the overreaction effect is distinct from tax-loss selling effects. Interestingly, the overreaction effect is substantially stronger for smaller firms than for larger firms. Returns consistent with the overreaction hypothesis are also observed for short windows around quarterly earnings announcements.

1. Introduction

The predictability of stock returns is one of the most controversial topics in financial research. Various researchers have documented predictable returns

---

*We gratefully acknowledge comments from seminar participants at Georgetown, Loyola of Chicago, Northwestern, Southern Methodist, and Temple Universities; the Universities of Chicago, Colorado, Florida, Illinois, Rochester, and Virginia; the Amsterdam Institute of Finance, the University of Wisconsin Johnson Symposium, the 1991 Tokyo Conference on Capital Markets, and the NBER/Behavioral Finance working group; and from Christopher Barry, Victor Bernard, William Bryan, Louis Chan, Eugene Fama, Kenneth French, Robert Harris, Thomas Lys, Prafulla Nabar, George Pennacchi, Gita Rao, Marc Reinganum (the referee), Andrei Shleifer, Thomas Stober, Seha Tinic, Paul Zarowin, Richard Zeckhauser, and G. William Schwert (the editor). We wish to thank Tim Loughran and especially Brian Bielinski for extensive research assistance.

over long and short horizons for both individual securities and indices.[1] While there is now a consensus that returns are predictable, there is widespread disagreement about the underlying reasons for this predictability. Fama (1991) observes that the interpretation of the evidence on return predictability runs 'head-on into the joint-hypothesis problem; that is, does return predictability reflect rational variation through time in expected returns, irrational deviations of price from fundamental value, or some combination of the two?'

One of the most influential, and controversial, papers in this line of research is by De Bondt and Thaler (1985), who present evidence of economically-important return reversals over long intervals. In particular, stocks that experience poor performance over the past three-to-five years (losers) tend to substantially outperform prior-period winners during the subsequent three-to-five years. De Bondt and Thaler interpret their evidence as a manifestation of irrational behavior by investors, which they term 'overreaction'.

Various authors [e.g., Chan (1988) and Ball and Kothari (1989)], however, have argued that these return reversals are due primarily to systematic changes in equilibrium-required returns that are not captured by De Bondt and Thaler. One of the main arguments for why required returns on extreme winners and losers vary substantially follows from pronounced changes in leverage. Since the equity beta of a firm is a function of both asset risk and leverage, a series of negative abnormal returns will increase the equity beta of a firm, thus increasing the expected return on the stock (assuming that the asset beta is positive and does not decrease substantially, and that the firm does not change its debt to fully offset the decline in the value of its equity). Following the same logic, a decrease in the equity beta is expected for winners. Consistent with the prediction of the leverage hypothesis, Ball and Kothari report that the betas of extreme losers exceed the betas of extreme winners by a full 0.76 following the portfolio formation period. Such a large difference in betas, coupled with historical risk premiums, can account for substantial differences in realized returns.

Another reason that has been advanced for why losers outperform winners relates to the size effect. Zarowin (1990) and others have argued that the superior performance of losers relative to winners is not due to investor overreaction, but instead is a manifestation of the size and/or January effects, in that by the end of the ranking period, losers tend to be smaller-sized firms than winners.

In general, attempts to discriminate between market inefficiency and changing equilibrium-required returns are most difficult when long return

---

[1]Among the many recent studies documenting time-series return predictability for long and short horizons are Rosenberg, Reid, and Lanstein (1985), Keim and Stambaugh (1986), Fama and French (1988), Lo and MacKinlay (1988), Poterba and Summers (1988), Conrad and Kaul (1989), Jegadeesh (1990), Lehmann (1990), Jegadeesh and Titman (1991), and Brock, Lakonishok, and LeBaron (1992).

intervals are used. This is because the measurement of abnormal performance over long horizons is very sensitive to the performance benchmark used, as emphasized by Dimson and Marsh (1986). In this paper, in addition to allowing time variation in betas, as recently applied in this context by Ball and Kothari (1989), we use three methodological innovations that enable us to perform a comprehensive evaluation of the overreaction hypothesis. Our methodology is applicable to any study measuring abnormal performance over long horizons.

First, we use the empirically-determined price of beta risk, rather than that assumed by a specific highly-structured model such as the Sharpe–Lintner capital asset pricing model (CAPM). Since the betas of extreme prior-period winners and losers differ dramatically, large differences in returns between winners and losers can be accounted for by the Sharpe–Lintner CAPM, in which the compensation per unit of beta risk is $r_m - r_f$, where r_m is the return on the market and r_f is the risk-free rate. In the 1931–82 period, $r_m - r_f$ averages almost 15% per year using an equally-weighted index of NYSE stocks for r_m and Treasury bills for r_f. The Sharpe–Lintner CAPM assumption is innocuous in many other studies, where the portfolio betas typically do not differ much from 1.0. But in this study, the betas of winners are markedly different from the betas of losers. Numerous empirical studies, starting with Black, Jensen, and Scholes (1972), find a much flatter slope than that assumed by the Sharpe–Lintner CAPM.[2] Indeed, Fama and French (1992) question whether there is any relation at all between beta and realized returns.

Second, we calculate abnormal returns using a comprehensive adjustment for size. Numerous studies have found a relation between size and future returns. Portfolios of losers are typically comprised of smaller stocks than portfolios of winners. Thus, in order to ascertain whether there is an independent overreaction effect, a size adjustment is appropriate. However, because small-firm portfolios contain proportionately more losers, the common procedure of adjusting for size might overadjust and thus create a bias against finding an independent overreaction effect. To address this possibility, we purge stocks with extreme performance from our size-control portfolios.[3] Our methodology enables us to disentangle the effects of size and prior performance in calculating abnormal returns on winner and loser portfolios.

---

[2] Black, Jensen, and Scholes (1972), Miller and Scholes (1972), Fama and MacBeth (1973), Tinic and West (1984), Lakonishok and Shapiro (1986), Amihud and Mendelson (1989), and Ritter and Chopra (1989), among others, find flatter slopes than predicted by the Sharpe–Lintner CAPM.

[3] Fama and French (1986) use a nearly identical procedure for controlling for size effects. For size deciles, they compare the average return on prior winners and losers with stocks in the same size decile that were in the middle 50% of returns during the portfolio formation period. They use continuously-compounded returns over three-year periods rather than the annual arithmetic returns over five-year periods that we use, but obtain somewhat similar results to those reported here.

In addition, we explore the generality of the effect in both January and non-January months.

Third, we examine abnormal returns over short periods of time. Abnormal returns calculated over long intervals are inherently sensitive to the benchmark used. Currently, there is no consensus on the 'best' benchmark, and research documenting abnormal returns calculated over long intervals is frequently treated with suspicion. Therefore, in one of our tests, we focus on short windows in which a relatively large amount of new information is disseminated, an approach analogous to that employed by Bernard and Thomas (1989, 1990) in their investigation of abnormal returns following earnings announcements. We compute abnormal returns for winners and losers for the three-day period in which quarterly earnings announcements occur. Positive abnormal returns at subsequent earnings announcements for prior losers, and negative abnormal returns for prior winners, are consistent with the overreaction hypothesis. In drawing our inferences, we are careful in adjusting for size effects and the higher volatility that other researchers [e.g., Chari, Jagannathan, and Ofer (1988)] have documented at earnings announcement dates.

Our results indicate that there is an economically-significant overreaction effect present in the stock market. Moreover, it is unlikely that this effect can be attributed to risk measurement problems, since returns consistent with the overreaction hypothesis are also observed for short windows around quarterly earnings announcements. Depending upon the procedure employed, extreme losers outperform extreme winners by 5–10% per year in the years following the portfolio formation period. Interestingly, the overreaction effect is much stronger among smaller firms, which are predominantly held by individuals; there is at most only weak evidence of an overreaction effect among the largest firms, which are predominantly held by institutions. One interpretation of our findings might be that individuals overreact, but institutions do not.

There is a strong January seasonal in the return patterns, but long-term overreaction is not merely a manifestation of tax-loss selling effects, as captured by the prior year's performance. To examine this issue, we form portfolios based upon prior one-year returns, and examine the performance of these portfolios over the subsequent five years. One-year and five-year formation periods produce dramatically different patterns in returns during the subsequent five years. We find much smaller differences in returns between extreme portfolios when portfolios are formed based upon one-year returns rather than five-year returns. Much of this difference in behavior occurs in the first of the five post-ranking years: portfolios of winners and losers formed on the basis of one-year returns display momentum, rather than immediate return reversals.

The structure of the remainder of this paper is as follows. In section 2, we measure the extent of abnormal performance for portfolios formed on the basis of prior returns while alternately controlling for beta and size effects. In section 3, we present evidence on the abnormal returns for winners and losers while simultaneously controlling for beta and size effects. We also explore seasonal and cross-sectional patterns in the extent of overreaction. In section 4, we present evidence from the market's reaction to earnings announcements. Section 5 concludes the paper.

2. Beta and size-adjusted abnormal returns

2.1. Methodology

For comparability with prior studies [e.g., Ball and Kothari (1989)] we use the CRSP monthly tape of New York Stock Exchange issues from 1926 to 1986. All stocks that are continuously listed for the prior five calendar years are ranked each year on the basis of their five-year buy-and-hold returns and assigned to one of twenty portfolios. Thus, the first ranking period ends in December 1930, and the last one ends in December 1981, a total of 52 ranking periods. The post-ranking periods are overlapping five-year intervals starting with 1931–35 and ending with 1982–86. For each of the twenty portfolios, this procedure results in a time series of 52 portfolio returns for each of the ten event years -4 to $+5$, with the last year of the ranking period designated as year 0. These 52 observations are used to estimate betas and abnormal returns for the ten event years.

Annual portfolio returns for each firm are constructed from the monthly CRSP returns by compounding the monthly returns in a calendar year to create an annual buy-and-hold return. The annual returns of the firms assigned to a portfolio are then averaged to get the portfolio's annual return. If a firm is delisted within a calendar year, its annual return for that year is calculated by using the CRSP equally-weighted index return for the remainder of that year. In subsequent years, the firm is deleted from the portfolio.

To estimate the market model coefficients, we use Ibbotson's (1975) returns across time and securities (RATS) procedure. For each event year $\tau = -4, \ldots, 0, +1, \ldots, +5$ and portfolio p, we run the following regression using 52 observations:

$$r_{pt}(\tau) - r_{ft}(\tau) = \alpha_p(\tau) + \beta_p(\tau)[r_{mt} - r_{ft}] + e_{pt}(\tau), \tag{1}$$

where $r_{pt}(\tau)$ is the annual return on portfolio p in calendar year t and event year τ, r_{mt} is the equally-weighted market return on NYSE stocks meeting our sample selection criteria in calendar year t, and r_{ft} is the annual return on T-bills [from Ibbotson Associates (1988)]. The intercept in eq. (1) is known as Jensen's (1969) alpha, and is a measure of abnormal performance.

2.2. Beta-adjusted excess returns

In columns (1)–(3) of table 1, we have formed portfolios by ranking firms according to their prior five-year returns. We report the annual returns, alphas, and betas averaged over the five years following the portfolio formation (ranking) period.[4] Our numbers are slightly different from those reported in Ball and Kothari's (1989) table 1 because of the different sample selection criteria employed. Ball and Kothari require that their firms remain listed on the NYSE for the entire five-year post-ranking period, whereas we do not impose such a requirement. Their sample selection criteria imposes a survivorship bias. In our sample, approximately 22% of the extreme loser portfolio's firms are delisted by the end of the post-ranking period, but only 8% of the extreme winner portfolio's firms are delisted. (In the 1930s, many of the delistings occurred due to bankruptcies, whereas by the 1970s, takeovers are the main reason for delistings. As might be expected, bankruptcies are rare among the extreme winners.)

The most striking result in table 1 is the inverse relation between the past and subsequent returns. Portfolio 1 (the prior-period losers) has a post-ranking-period average annual return of 27.3%, while portfolio 20 (the prior-period winners) has a post-ranking-period average annual return of 13.3%, a difference of 14.0% per year.[5] Over the five-year post-ranking period, even before compounding, this difference cumulates to 70%! The debate revolves around how much of this difference is attributable to equilibrium compensation for risk differences, and how much is an abnormal return. In fact, as demonstrated by Ball and Kothari, much of this difference can be explained by the Sharpe–Lintner CAPM. According to column (3) of table 1, the

---

[4]Two issues (at least) are raised by the procedure of averaging the returns, alphas, and betas over the five post-ranking years. First, since the last price of the ranking period is the first price of the post-ranking period, negative serial correlation might be induced by bid–ask spread effects. To examine the sensitivity of our results to this issue, in work not reported here, we have also calculated average returns, alphas, and betas using only event years +2 to +5. Our results are nearly identical to those found using event years +1 to +5. This raises the second issue: if the return reversals are due to overreaction, with firms whose market price has deviated from fundamental value eventually reverting, how long does this reversion take? One might expect a stronger reversion in event years +1 and +2 than in years +4 and +5. This is in fact the case: the per-year abnormal returns are slightly greater when a three-year post-ranking period is used rather than a five-year post-ranking period.

[5]De Bondt and Thaler (1985) find a smaller difference in post-ranking-period returns between winners and losers than we (and Ball and Kothari) do. In their fig. 3, they find a difference of about 8% per year for their five-year post-ranking period, compared to our 14% per year. There are a number of reasons for this difference, most notably because the definition of extreme winners and losers is not the same. In most of their work, De Bondt and Thaler define their portfolios as the most extreme 35 firms in each year, whereas the number of firms in each of our portfolios increases from about 20 in the 1930s to about 50 in the 1970s, averaging about 43 firms. Further differences are that our last ranking period ends in 1981, whereas their last ranking period ends in 1978, and they use monthly return intervals versus our annual return intervals.

Table 1

Average annual post-ranking-period percentage returns, alphas, and betas for twenty portfolios formed on the basis of either ranking-period returns or ranking-period betas. Average monthly post-ranking-period percentage returns, alphas, and betas are also reported for portfolios formed on the basis of five-year ranking-period returns.

Alphas and betas are estimated from time-series regressions with 52 observations, for ranking periods ending in 1930–81, for each of the five post-ranking years. The alphas and betas reported are the averages of these five post-ranking-period numbers. In columns (1)–(5) and (9)–(11), portfolio 1 is comprised of stocks with the lowest ranking-period returns, and portfolio 20 is comprised of the stocks with the highest ranking-period returns. In columns (6)–(8), portfolio 1 is comprised of stocks having the highest ranking-period betas, and portfolio 20 is comprised of stocks having the lowest ranking-period betas. EW and VW are, respectively, equally-weighted and value-weighted market indices of NYSE stocks. Columns (1)–(8) are based upon annual returns, whereas columns (9)–(11) are based upon monthly returns.

| Port-folio | Average annual return (%) (1) | Portfolios formed on the basis of ranking-period returns ||||| Portfolios formed on the basis of ranking-period betas ||| Portfolios formed on the basis of ranking-period returns |||
| | | Computed using EW index || Computed using VW index || Average annual return (%) (6) | Computed using EW index || Average monthly return (%) (9) | Computed using EW index ||
		Alpha (2)	Beta (3)	Alpha (4)	Beta (5)		Alpha (7)	Beta (8)		Alpha (10)	Beta (11)
1	27.3	−0.2	1.65	2.7	1.95	21.0	−3.0	1.42	2.36	0.26	1.52
2	23.0	0.5	1.31	2.5	1.62	19.4	−3.5	1.34	1.90	0.07	1.30
3	21.0	0.1	1.20	1.9	1.51	20.3	−1.2	1.25	1.80	0.05	1.23
4	21.2	0.9	1.16	2.9	1.45	20.4	−0.8	1.22	1.73	0.09	1.14
5	20.5	1.2	1.09	2.8	1.39	21.0	−0.6	1.24	1.65	0.09	1.07
6	19.9	0.7	1.08	2.2	1.40	20.2	0.0	1.15	1.59	0.06	1.05
7	19.4	0.0	1.09	1.6	1.40	20.2	0.1	1.14	1.52	0.01	1.03
8	18.5	1.5	0.94	2.9	1.24	19.8	0.1	1.12	1.48	0.06	0.95
9	17.6	0.2	0.95	1.7	1.26	18.5	−0.2	1.04	1.41	−0.03	0.98
10	17.8	0.7	0.94	2.1	1.24	18.3	−0.5	1.06	1.43	0.03	0.94
11	16.9	0.2	0.91	1.4	1.22	19.3	0.5	1.05	1.35	−0.04	0.93
12	16.6	0.1	0.89	1.2	1.22	17.3	0.0	0.95	1.34	−0.03	0.92
13	16.7	0.2	0.90	1.4	1.22	17.2	0.4	0.91	1.33	−0.00	0.88
14	16.1	−0.2	0.88	0.8	1.21	17.2	0.8	0.89	1.29	−0.06	0.90
15	15.5	−0.2	0.84	0.9	1.16	16.2	0.9	0.82	1.25	−0.07	0.87
16	15.3	−0.6	0.85	0.3	1.18	15.4	0.6	0.78	1.20	−0.07	0.83
17	14.6	0.1	0.76	1.0	1.08	15.2	1.4	0.72	1.16	−0.05	0.78
18	14.5	−1.3	0.85	−0.5	1.18	14.2	1.7	0.62	1.10	−0.12	0.79
19	14.3	−1.3	0.84	−0.7	1.19	14.4	1.1	0.67	1.11	−0.12	0.79
20	13.3	−2.7	0.86	−2.0	1.21	13.7	2.1	0.56	1.01	−0.24	0.81
Mean	18.0	0.0	1.00	1.35	1.32	18.0	0.0	1.00	1.45	−0.06	0.98
$r_1 - r_{20}$	14.0	2.5	0.79	4.7	0.74	7.3	−5.1	0.86	1.35	0.50	0.71

difference in post-ranking betas between the extreme winner and loser portfolios is 0.79. Given a market risk premium $(r_m - r_f)$ in the 14–15% range using an equally-weighted portfolio of NYSE stocks, the CAPM predicts a difference in returns of approximately 11%, leaving only about 3% of the 14.0% difference unaccounted for. Indeed, using this approach, Ball and Kothari report a difference in alphas between extreme winner and loser portfolios of 3.9% per year, which they view as economically insignificant. Using our sample, we find an even smaller difference in alphas between extreme portfolios: only 2.5% per year.

Although not apparent from the numbers reported in table 1, the beta estimates for winners and losers are very different depending on whether the realized market risk premium $(r_m - r_f)$ is positive or negative. This raises a question, discussed in the appendix, about what beta really is measuring. Table 7 reports the beta estimates for up and down markets separately.

The conclusion that most of the difference in post-ranking returns between winners and losers can be accounted for as compensation for risk bearing is heavily dependent upon the Sharpe–Lintner CAPM's assumption that the return per unit of beta risk provided by the market is $r_m - r_f$. However, numerous empirical studies (see footnote 2) have invariably found a much flatter slope.

In order to estimate the empirical relation between risk and return, we form portfolios on the basis of ranking-period betas, using the same sample and the same methodology as in columns (1)–(3). The ranking-period beta of each firm has been calculated on the basis of a 60-observation regression using monthly returns during the ranking period. For each of the 52 ranking periods, firms are then ranked on the basis of these betas, and assigned to one of twenty portfolios. The post-ranking-period portfolio betas are then estimated using the RATS procedure during each of the five post-ranking years with annual returns. In columns (6)–(8), we report the average annual returns and the average alphas and betas computed using the RATS methodology for the five post-ranking years for portfolios formed on the basis of ranking-period betas. The dispersion in betas between the extreme portfolios reported in column (8) is 0.86, slightly greater than the 0.79 reported in column (3). This large difference in betas in column (8), however, is associated with a difference in returns between the two extreme portfolios of only 7.3%, dramatically less than the 14.0% reported when portfolios are formed on the basis of ranked prior returns. It should be noted that the only difference between columns (1)–(3) and (6)–(8) is in how the portfolios are formed: the universe of firms and the estimation methodology are identical.

Using the twenty post-ranking-period portfolio returns and betas reported in columns (6) and (8), respectively, we estimate the market compensation per unit of beta risk. The resulting regression has an intercept of 8.5% and a slope of 9.5%. These coefficients are consistent with those reported by other

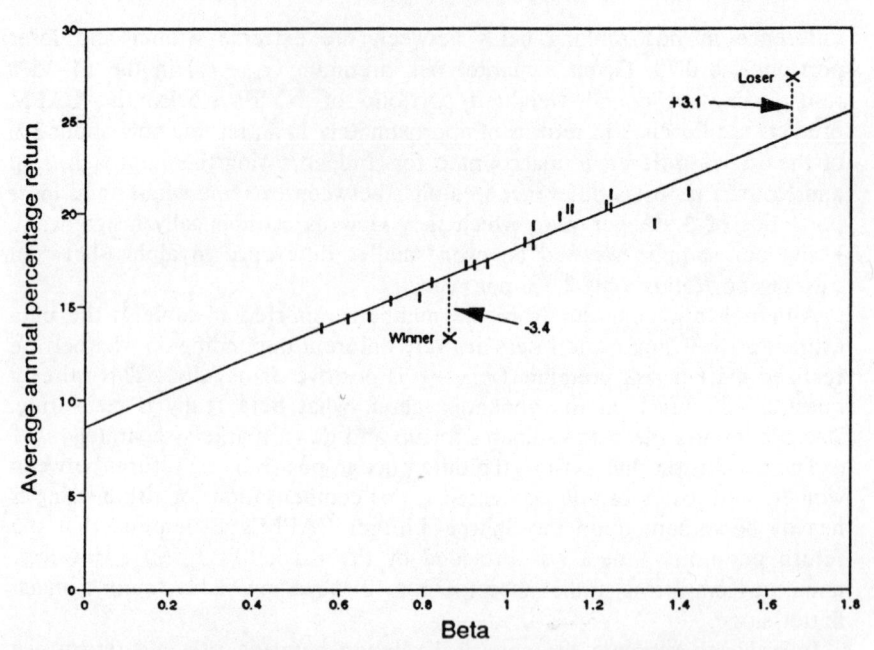

Fig. 1a. Plot of the empirical security market line (SML) calculated using annual data from the realized post-ranking-period returns and betas for twenty portfolios formed on the basis of ranking-period betas, and the realized post-ranking-period return on extreme winner and loser portfolios.

The empirical SML is estimated from the twenty portfolio returns and betas reported in columns (6) and (8) of table 1. The empirical SML has an intercept of 8.5% and a slope of 9.5%. Alphas are calculated as deviations from the empirical SML.

researchers (see footnote 2). Note that the 8.5% intercept is considerably higher than the average risk-free rate during the sample period of about 3.5%, and the slope coefficient of 9.5% is considerably lower than the 14–15% market risk premium. (In fact, the RATS procedure may overestimate the relation between realized returns and beta, because the betas are estimated contemporaneously with the post-ranking-period returns.) In other words, differences in betas do not generate differences in returns during the sample period as great as assumed by the Sharpe–Lintner CAPM.

In figs. 1a and 1b, we have plotted the regression equation estimated from the twenty portfolios formed on the basis of prior betas. The two extreme winner and loser portfolios are also plotted. In fig. 1a, we use annual data from columns (6) and (8) of table 1. In fig. 1b, we use monthly data (not reported in table 1). Using annual data, the extreme winner portfolio underperforms a portfolio with the same beta by 3.4%, while the extreme loser

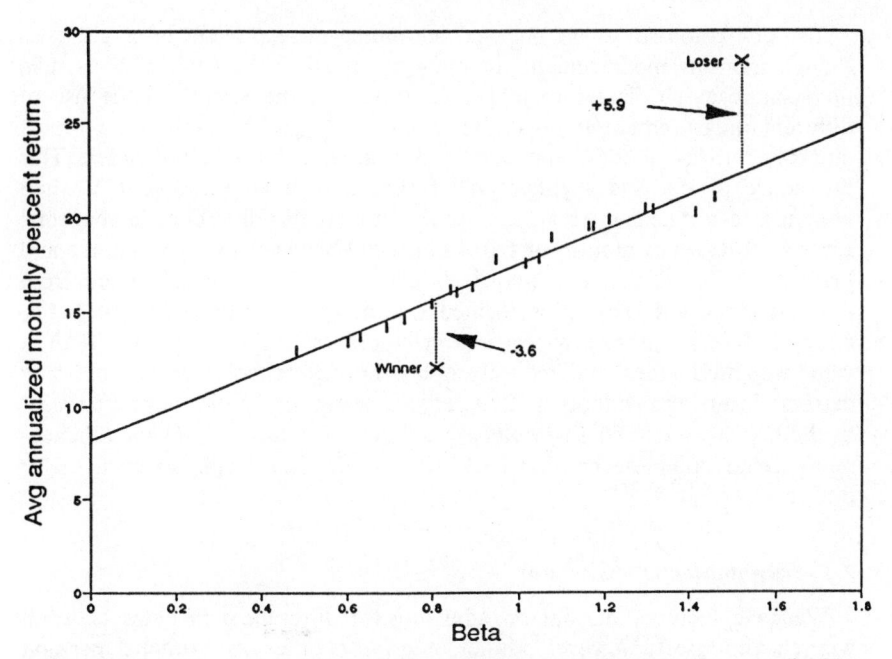

Fig. 1b. Similar to fig. 1a, except that monthly returns are used, which are then annualized by multiplying by 12 before plotting.

The empirical SML has an intercept of 8.2% and a slope of 9.3%. Alphas are calculated as deviations from the empirical SML. The mean annualized return is 17.5% rather than the 18.0% in fig. 1a due to our procedure of multiplying the average monthly returns by 12, rather than compounding them.

portfolio outperforms a portfolio with the same beta by 3.1%. Thus, the difference in abnormal returns is 6.5%, substantially higher than the 2.5% reported in column (2). The difference between these two numbers is attributable to different assumptions about the slope of the security market line (SML). Using the Sharpe–Lintner model's theoretical risk premium results in a lower estimate of the overreaction effect than when the empirical risk premium is used.

To examine the sensitivity of the results to the choice of a market index, columns (4) and (5) present results for annual measurement intervals using a value-weighted market index. The betas are all above 1.0, reflecting the fact that the equally-weighted index itself has a beta of 1.3 with respect to the value-weighted index. The difference in alphas between the extreme winners and losers widens from the 2.5% reported using an equally-weighted market index to 4.7% using a value-weighted index. Using the empirical security market line increases these spreads.

The discussion so far has focused on annual measurement intervals, even though monthly measurement intervals are much more commonly used in financial research. To examine the sensitivity of the results to the use of different measurement intervals, in columns (9)–(11) of table 1 we report monthly returns, alphas, and betas using an equally-weighted index. This procedure produces a slightly smaller spread in betas (0.71 vs 0.79 when annual measurement intervals are used) and a greater difference in abnormal returns (0.50% per month, or 6.0% per year) between extreme winner and loser portfolios. Using the empirical security market line calculated from monthly data with portfolios formed on the basis of ranked prior betas, extreme losers outperform extreme winners by 9.5% per year. With a value-weighted index and monthly data, the difference in alphas between extreme losers and winners is 12% per year using the Sharpe–Lintner model as the benchmark.[6] (These results are not reported here.) Applying a benchmark based upon the empirical security market line yields an even larger difference.

2.3. Size-adjusted excess returns

We have focused thus far on adjusting for differences in betas between winners and losers. However, winners and losers differ on another dimension as well. Prior research [e.g., Zarowin (1990)] has found that losers have lower market capitalizations than winners, on average, indicating that measurement of excess returns must be careful to control for size effects. The correlation of size and prior returns is apparent in fig. 2, which plots the percentage of each size quintile that falls into each prior return quintile. (We plot quintile results, rather than the twenty portfolios that we use in the empirical work, to minimize the clutter that would otherwise obscure the figure.) For example, fig. 2 shows that in the smallest size quintile, 40% of the firms are in the extreme loser quintile, while only 10% are in the extreme winner quintile. Because of this correlation between size and prior returns, a simple size adjustment may cause the extent of any overreaction effect to be underestimated.

In fig. 3, we plot the joint distribution of annual raw percentage returns for the same quintile portfolios used in fig. 2. Inspection of this figure shows that, holding size constant, returns are higher the lower are prior returns, and holding prior returns constant, returns are higher the smaller is size. On average, holding size constant, the extreme loser quintile has a 5.4% higher

---

[6]A caveat is in order, however, in regard to the use of monthly returns. As Conrad and Kaul (1991) discuss, monthly arithmetic returns on low-priced stocks are biased upwards in a manner that overestimates the magnitude of size and prior return effects. This is because small firms and losers are more frequently low-priced stocks. Our annual return measures, however, suffer from minimal bias.

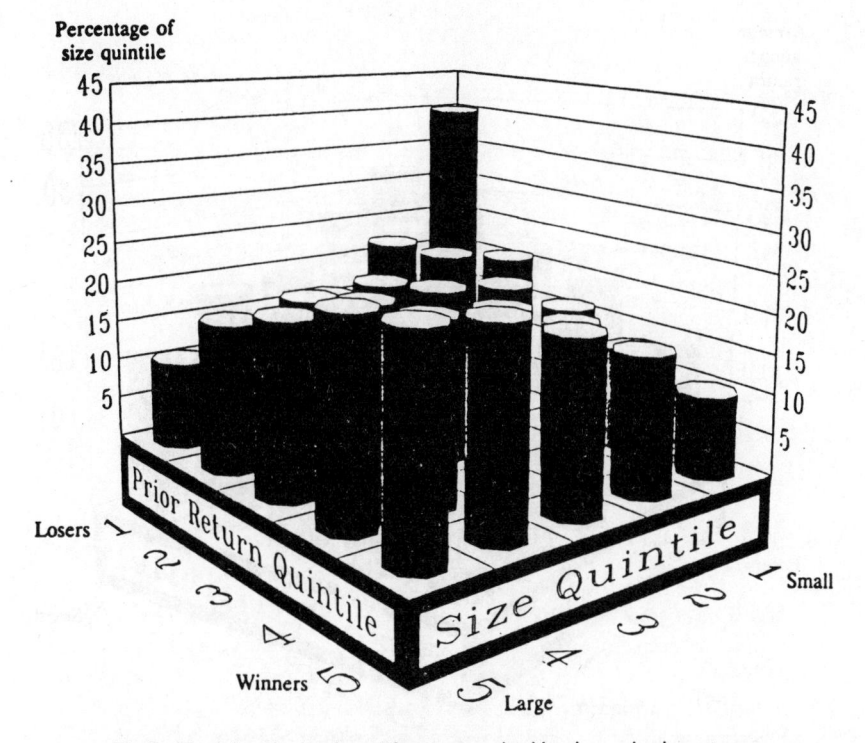

Fig. 2. The joint distribution of firms categorized by size and prior returns.

For each size quintile, the percentage of firms falling in each prior return quintile is plotted. Quintile portfolios are plotted rather than the twenty portfolios used in the empirical work because 400 portfolios (20 × 20) produces too cluttered a figure compared with the 25 portfolios plotted.

average annual return than the extreme winner quintile. On average, holding prior returns constant, the smallest size quintile has an 8.2% higher average annual return than the largest size quintile.

In column (1) of table 2, we report the average annual returns on twenty portfolios [these numbers are the same as in column (1) of table 1]. In column (2), we report the returns on control portfolios formed by matching on size, which we refer to as size-control portfolios. To construct the size-control portfolios, we rank the population of firms at the end of each of the 52 portfolio formation periods on the basis of market capitalization, and then assign the firms to twenty portfolios formed on the basis of size. In computing the average annual returns on the twenty size portfolios, we follow the same procedure used in table 1 with the twenty prior-return portfolios. For each of the twenty prior-return portfolios, we form a size-control portfolio. This

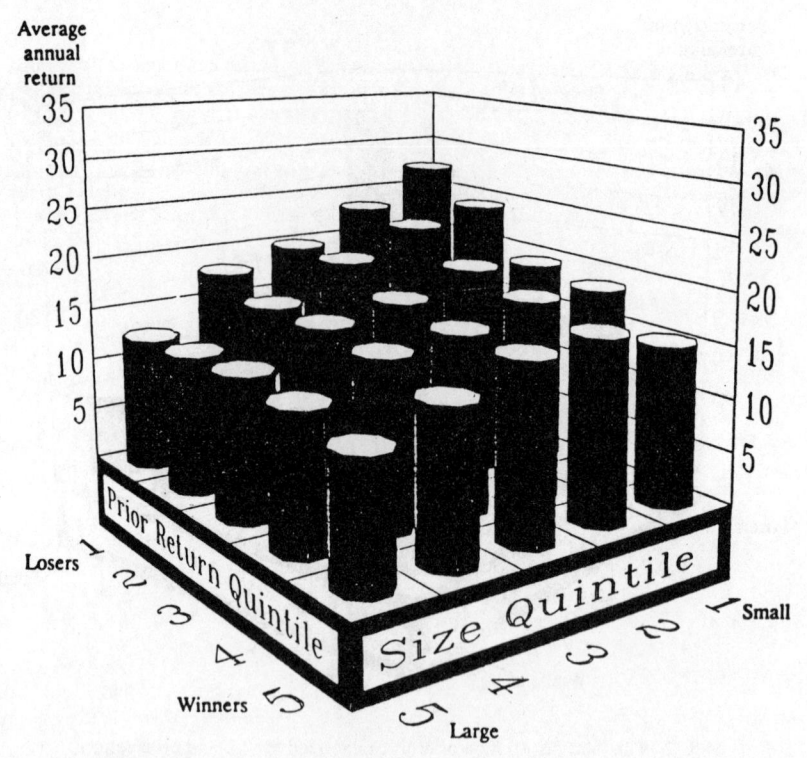

Fig. 3. The joint distribution of average annual returns in the post-ranking period categorized by size and prior returns.

The average annual return on the smallest quintile of losers is 27.37%, while the average annual return on the largest quintile of winners is 11.59%.

size-control portfolio is constructed to have the same size composition as its corresponding prior return portfolio, with the weights being determined by the proportion of the prior-return portfolio that falls in each size classification.

In column (3) of table 2, we report the average annual returns on size-control portfolios formed in a manner identical to that employed in column (2), with the exception that the population of firms from which the size portfolios are drawn has been purged of firms in prior return portfolios 1–5 (losers) and 16–20 (winners). Because of the correlation of size and prior returns, more than 50% of the smallest (and largest) firms are purged, and slightly less than 50% of moderate-size firms are purged. The purpose of this purging is to minimize the confounding of any overreaction effects with size effects.

Table 2

Average annual post-ranking-period percentage returns for twenty portfolios of firms ranked by their five-year ranking-period returns, size-control portfolios with and without losers and winners purged, and the associated size-adjusted returns.

The twenty size-control portfolios are constructed to have approximately the same market values as the twenty ranked portfolios. Excess returns are computed two different ways: (i) size-adjusted returns using all firms (unpurged) and (ii) size-adjusted returns after the portfolios have been purged of all firms in the top five and the bottom five portfolios of prior returns (purged).

Portfolio	Ranked firms (r_p) (1)	Unpurged (r_s) (2)	Purged (r_s) (3)	Difference (2)−(3) (4)	Unpurged (1)−(2) (5)	Purged (1)−(3) (6)
1	27.3	23.4	20.4	3.0	3.9	6.9
2	23.0	21.3	19.3	2.0	1.7	3.7
3	21.0	20.6	19.0	1.6	0.4	2.0
4	21.2	20.0	18.8	1.2	1.2	2.4
5	20.5	19.4	18.0	1.4	1.1	2.5
6	19.9	18.8	18.0	0.8	1.1	1.9
7	19.4	18.9	18.1	0.8	0.5	1.3
8	18.5	18.1	17.6	0.5	0.4	0.9
9	17.6	17.9	17.4	0.5	−0.3	0.2
10	17.8	17.5	17.2	0.3	0.3	0.6
11	16.9	17.3	16.9	0.4	−0.4	0.0
12	16.6	17.0	16.7	0.3	−0.4	−0.1
13	16.7	16.9	16.8	0.1	−0.2	−0.1
14	16.1	16.6	16.3	0.3	−0.5	−0.2
15	15.5	16.6	16.4	0.2	−1.1	−0.9
16	15.3	16.6	16.4	0.2	−1.3	−1.1
17	14.6	16.2	16.1	0.1	−1.6	−1.5
18	14.5	16.0	16.1	−0.1	−1.5	−1.6
19	14.3	16.0	15.9	0.1	−1.7	−1.6
20	13.3	16.0	16.1	−0.1	−2.7	−2.8
Mean	18.0	18.0	17.4	0.6	0.0	0.6
$r_1 - r_{20}$	14.0	7.4	4.3	3.1	6.6	9.7

Average annual return (%) in years +1 to +5. Size-adj. returns (%) $e = r_p - r_s$.

In column (5) of table 2, we report excess returns computed by subtracting the unpurged size-control returns. There is a nearly monotonic decrease in the excess returns as one goes from portfolio 1 (the losers) to portfolio 20 (the winners). The difference in excess returns between the extreme portfolios is 6.6% per year during the five post-ranking years.

In column (6), we report the excess returns computed using the purged size-control portfolios. The pattern in column (5) is accentuated, confirming our conjecture that controlling for size without taking the correlation of size and prior returns into account understates the overreaction effect. The difference between the extreme portfolio excess returns is 9.7% per year during the five post-ranking years. From these numbers, it appears that there is an economically-significant overreaction effect above and beyond any size effect.

2.4. Seasonal patterns in returns, tax-loss selling, and momentum

In table 3, we report the average post-ranking-period raw and size-adjusted (using purged size controls) returns using annual, January, and February–December returns. The February–December returns are 11-month returns, computed by compounding the monthly returns. In columns (1)–(6), the portfolios are formed on the basis of five-year prior returns; the annual numbers are identical to those reported in columns (1) and (6) of table 2. In columns (7)–(12), the portfolios are formed on the basis of one-year prior returns, although the post-ranking period remains five years. The population of returns used in columns (1)–(6) and (7)–(12) are identical; what is different is the ranking criteria to form the twenty portfolios.

Inspection of columns (1)–(6) discloses that the overreaction effect is disproportionately concentrated in January, consistent with the graphical evidence presented in De Bondt and Thaler's (1985) fig. 3. While the differences in average annual and January returns between portfolios 1 and 20 are reliably different from zero, the February–December difference is not significantly different from zero at conventional levels for either raw returns or size-adjusted returns. The January seasonal raises the question of whether there is an independent overreaction effect, above and beyond tax-loss selling effects.

To distinguish between these two effects, in columns (7)–(12) we report returns on portfolios formed on ranked one-year returns, which should produce a cleaner measure of the influence of tax-loss selling effects. The choice of one-year formation periods to examine tax-loss selling effects is consistent with prior work in this area. [Reinganum (1983), Chan (1986), and others form portfolios based upon return intervals that correspond to the short-term capital gains holding period, which has varied from six to twelve months at various times during our sample period, and Roll (1983) uses one-year returns.] In columns (7)–(12), there are much smaller return reversals than in columns (1)–(6), and they are much more concentrated in January. Using annual size-adjusted returns, the difference in returns between the extreme winners and losers is 9.7% per year using five-year ranking periods, but only 3.5% per year using one-year ranking periods. As in columns (1)–(6), only the annual and January return differences are reliably different from zero. Although the return differences $(r_1 - r_{20})$ are generally lower in columns (7)–(12) than in columns (1)–(6), the p-values tend to be similar because there is less time-series variability and less autocorrelation in the portfolio return series when one-year ranking periods are used than when five-year ranking periods are used.

Table 3

Seasonal patterns in raw returns and size-adjusted returns for ranking periods of five years and one year.[a]

Portfolio	Five-year ranking periods							One-year ranking periods				
	Avg. raw returns (%)			Avg. size-adj. returns[b] (%)			Avg. raw returns (%)			Avg. size-adj. returns[b] (%)		
	Annual (1)	Jan. (2)	Feb.–Dec. (3)	Annual (4)	Jan. (5)	Feb.–Dec. (6)	Annual (7)	Jan. (8)	Feb.–Dec. (9)	Annual (10)	Jan. (11)	Feb.–Dec. (12)
1	27.3	13.1	12.9	6.9	7.2	−0.8	23.5	11.2	11.3	2.6	4.7	−2.2
2	23.0	8.8	13.3	3.7	3.5	0.1	20.5	7.4	12.0	1.3	1.9	−1.0
3	21.0	7.4	12.9	2.0	2.5	−0.4	19.8	6.6	12.4	0.9	1.4	−0.5
4	21.2	6.6	13.8	2.4	1.7	0.7	18.4	5.9	11.9	0.1	0.8	−0.6
5	20.5	5.7	14.0	2.5	1.2	1.2	18.7	5.5	12.6	1.0	0.8	0.4
6	19.9	5.6	13.5	1.9	1.2	0.5	18.1	5.3	12.1	0.3	0.7	−0.4
7	19.4	5.1	13.6	1.3	0.9	0.5	17.5	5.0	12.0	−0.3	0.4	−0.4
8	18.5	4.7	13.2	0.9	0.5	0.5	18.2	4.6	12.8	0.7	0.2	−0.5
9	17.6	4.5	12.4	0.2	0.4	−0.2	16.8	4.4	11.8	−0.4	0.1	−0.5
10	17.8	4.2	13.0	0.6	0.2	0.5	17.5	4.0	12.8	0.2	−0.2	0.4
11	16.9	4.1	12.3	0.0	0.1	0.1	16.9	4.3	12.3	−0.6	0.0	−0.2
12	16.6	3.9	12.2	−0.1	0.0	−0.1	17.6	4.0	12.8	0.3	−0.1	0.3
13	16.7	3.6	12.6	−0.1	−0.1	0.2	17.0	3.9	12.5	0.0	−0.3	0.3
14	16.1	3.3	12.3	−0.2	−0.3	0.3	16.6	3.8	12.3	−0.5	−0.4	0.0
15	15.5	3.3	11.8	−0.9	−0.3	−0.4	16.8	3.6	12.7	0.0	−0.4	0.5
16	15.3	3.2	11.4	−1.1	−0.4	−0.8	16.9	3.7	12.6	−0.1	−0.3	0.3
17	14.6	3.1	11.0	−1.5	−0.5	−0.9	16.9	3.5	12.7	0.1	−0.6	0.7
18	14.5	3.0	10.8	−1.6	−0.4	−1.2	16.3	3.6	12.2	−1.2	−0.7	−0.3
19	14.3	2.7	10.9	−1.6	−0.7	−1.0	17.5	3.7	13.1	−0.4	−0.8	0.5
20	13.3	2.6	10.0	−2.8	−0.7	−2.1	17.7	4.3	12.8	−0.9	−0.6	−0.1
$r_1 - r_{20}$	14.0	10.5	2.9	9.7	7.9	1.3	5.8	6.9	−1.5	3.5	5.3	−2.1
p-values[c]	0.001	0.001	0.105	0.005	0.004	0.273	0.001	0.001	0.072	0.004	0.001	0.024

	Five-year ranking periods						One-year ranking periods					
	Avg. raw returns (%)			Avg. size-adj. returns[b] (%)			Avg. raw returns (%)			Avg. size-adj. returns[b] (%)		
Portfolio	Annual (1)	Jan. (2)	Feb.–Dec. (3)	Annual (4)	Jan. (5)	Feb.–Dec. (6)	Annual (7)	Jan. (8)	Feb.–Dec. (9)	Annual (10)	Jan. (11)	Feb.–Dec. (12)
$r_1 - r_{20}$ in year + 1[d]	15.3	15.1	−0.7	11.0	12.6	−2.6	−7.2	8.6	−15.1	−8.6	7.2	−15.2
p-values[e]	0.011	0.000	0.425	0.028	0.000	0.176	0.013	0.000	0.000	0.004	0.000	0.000
Tests of the hypothesis that $r_1 - r_{20}$ with five-year ranking periods = $r_1 - r_{20}$ with one-year ranking periods:												
p-values[f]	0.002	0.003	0.007	0.009	0.035	0.037						

[a] All numbers, except for the row labeled '$r_1 - r_{20}$ in year + 1', are the equally-weighted averages of the five post-ranking years, for all 52 post-ranking periods beginning in 1931–1982. The January returns are monthly averages. The February–December returns are averages of eleven-month compounded returns.

[b] The size-control portfolios have been purged of extreme winners and losers, using the procedures described in table 2. The purged firms for the one-year ranking periods are those in the bottom 25% and the top 25% of one-year returns.

[c] The p-values test the hypothesis that the mean value of $r_1 - r_{20}$ is zero; p-values are computed adjusting for fourth-order autocorrelation as follows, and the standard deviation of the mean value of $r_1 - r_{20}$ is computed as

$$\text{s.d.} = \frac{\sigma}{T}\sqrt{T + 2(T-1)\rho_1 + 2(T-2)\rho_2 + 2(T-3)\rho_3 + 2(T-4)\rho_4},$$

with $T = 52$, where σ is the standard deviation of the portfolio returns and ρ_n is the estimated nth-order simple autocorrelation coefficient. (Four lags are used because of the five-year overlapping post-ranking periods.) The T observations are the time series of five-year average portfolio returns, expressed as annual numbers.

[d] The numbers in this row represent the average value of $r_1 - r_{20}$ in the first year of the five post-ranking years.

[e] The p-values test the hypothesis that the mean value of $r_1 - r_{20}$ is zero. A time series of 52 nonoverlapping year + 1 observations are used to calculate the standard deviation of the mean, adjusting for first-order autocorrelation. The autocorrelation coefficients are as high as 0.406 for the size-adjusted January returns in column (5). For February–December returns, the autocorrelations are insignificantly different from zero.

[f] The p-values are calculated from a time-series of 52 values of $(r_1 - r_{20})_{5,t} - (r_1 - r_{20})_{1,t}$, adjusted for fourth-order autocorrelation, where $(r_1 - r_{20})_{i,t}$ is the average return difference over the five-year post-ranking period starting in year t with ranking period of length i.

In the last row of the table, we report the results of a test of the hypothesis that the return differences ($r_1 - r_{20}$) using five-year ranking periods are the same as those using one-year ranking periods. The p-values of 0.002 to 0.037 indicate that the higher return differences using five-year ranking periods are generally reliably so, even in February–December.

While the portfolios formed on the basis of five-year returns display greater return reversals during the subsequent five years than those formed on the basis of one-year returns, an interesting pattern is obscured. Specifically, the portfolios formed on the basis of one-year returns display return *momentum*, as shown in the row '$r_1 - r_{20}$ in year $+1$'. In this row, we report the average difference in returns on extreme portfolios during the first post-ranking year. Focusing on size-adjusted returns, in the first post-ranking year, prior five-year losers outperform winners by 11.0% in column (4), whereas prior one-year losers *underperform* winners by 8.6% in column (10). This underperformance is entirely in the February–December period, where column (12) reports that one-year losers underperform winners by 15.2%. In plain English, when winners and losers are chosen on the basis of one-year returns, losers continue to lose and winners continue to win during the next year. Similar momentum patterns are also reported by De Bondt and Thaler (1985, table 1), Ball and Kothari (1989, table 5), and Jegadeesh and Titman (1991). These momentum patterns may explain the Value Line anomaly [see Huberman and Kandel (1987)] and the post-earnings announcement drift anomaly [see Bernard and Thomas (1989, 1990)].

3. Multiple regression tests

In the previous section, we controlled for, respectively, beta and size in computing abnormal portfolio returns. In this section, we present multiple regression evidence that simultaneously incorporates the effects of beta, size, and prior returns on post-ranking period returns. This analysis uses 400 portfolios, each containing an unequal number of firms, formed on the basis of independent rankings of firm size and prior returns. For each of these portfolios, a beta is calculated from a pooled (across both post-ranking years and firms) regression, using $r_{it} - r_{ft}$ as the dependent variable and $r_{mt} - r_{ft}$ as the explanatory variable, where r_{it} is the return on firm i in year t. The portfolio excess return is also calculated as the pooled (across both firms and post-ranking years) average excess return.[7]

---

[7]When annual returns are used, if a given portfolio, e.g., the largest extreme losers (size portfolio 20, return portfolio 1) has a total of 83 firms in it over the entire 52 formation periods (an average of 1.6 firms per formation period), there are up to 83×5 annual returns (if each of the 83 firms lasts for all five post-ranking years).

In table 8 of the appendix, we report results using two alternative procedures for calculating betas and returns for each of the 400 portfolios. In general, the results are qualitatively similar.

In panels A and B of table 4, we report the results of estimating eq. (2) using 400 portfolios constructed on the basis of independent rankings of prior returns and size:

$$r_p - r_f = a_0 + a_1 SIZE_p + a_2 RETURN_p + a_3 beta_p + e_p. \qquad (2)$$

The explanatory variables in panels A and B are relative market capitalization (*SIZE*), measured as the portfolio rank (1 small, 20 large), prior five-year returns (*RETURN*), measured as the portfolio rank (1 losers, 20 winners), and the portfolio beta.[8] In panel A, using annual returns, we find that all three explanatory variables are reliably different from zero and the coefficients have the predicted signs. Furthermore, a large fraction of the variation in portfolio returns is explained (the R^2 is 0.68). The *RETURN* coefficient of -0.254 implies that after controlling for size and beta, extreme losers outperform extreme winners by 4.8% per year on average for the five post-ranking years. [Since *RETURN* (and *SIZE*) is measured as the portfolio rank, -0.254 multiplied by (1 minus 20) results in the 4.8% difference.] Also noteworthy is that in panel A, the coefficient on beta of 5.438% is lower than the 9.5% slope reported in fig. 1a. Apparently, estimates of the SML slope from single-variable regressions suffer from an omitted variable bias. Another aspect worth noting is that the magnitude of the overreaction effect is nearly as great as that of the size effect, as can be seen by comparing the two coefficients.

A straightforward approach to estimating the *t*-statistics for table 4 would be to use the standard errors from the pooled regressions with 400 observations. The resulting *t*-statistics, however, would be vastly overstated, because the pooled regression standard errors do not account for the time-series variability of the empirical relations. Consequently, the *t*-statistics that we report in panel A are based upon the time-series variability of the coefficients from 52 annual cross-sectional regressions. In general, these coefficients would be intertemporally dependent. Furthermore, our procedure of using overlapping post-ranking periods will induce strong autocorrelation in the parameter estimates. Thus, in computing the standard errors for the point

---

[8]We have explored some alternatives to our use of portfolio rankings as measures of prior returns and size. For example, using the actual prior return rather than the portfolio rank produces a slightly better fit and a stronger measured overreaction effect. One reason for our preference for the use of portfolio rankings to measure size is that market capitalizations changed substantially over time during our 52-year sample period. This poses a problem for pooling observations over time. For a detailed discussion of some of the issues involved, see Chan, Hamao, and Lakonishok (1991). We have not attempted to conduct a comprehensive examination of alternative specifications, for this would then introduce data-snooping biases.

Table 4
OLS regressions of average percentage excess returns for the first five post-ranking years for portfolios of NYSE firms formed on the basis of size and prior returns.

For each of the 52 ranking periods ending on December 31 of 1930 to 1981, firms are independently ranked on the basis of their December 31 market value and their five-year prior return, and assigned to one of 400 portfolios. Each portfolio beta is the pooled (over firms and post-ranking years) beta for the firms in the cell, calculated using annual returns and equally-weighted market returns. SIZE is measured as the portfolio ranking (1 to 20, with 1 being smallest), and RETURN is measured as the portfolio ranking (1 to 20, with 1 being the most extreme prior losers). In panels C and D, DS is a dummy variable equal to one if a portfolio is among the bottom 40% of SIZE vitiles, DM is a dummy variable equal to one if a portfolio is among SIZE portfolios 9 to 16 (the middle 40%), and DL is a dummy variable equal to one if a portfolio is among the largest 20% of SIZE portfolios. T-statistics are in parentheses. These are computed using a Fama–MacBeth (1973) procedure adjusted for fourth-order autocorrelation as follows: the t-statistic for coefficient a_i is computed as $a_i/$s.e., where

$$\text{s.e.} = \frac{\sigma}{T}\sqrt{T + 2(T-1)\rho_1 + 2(T-2)\rho_2 + 2(T-3)\rho_3 + 2(T-4)\rho_4},$$

with $T = 52$, where σ is the time-series standard deviation of the coefficient estimates and ρ_i is the estimated nth-order simple autocorrelation coefficient. (Four lags are used because of the five-year overlapping post-ranking periods.) The T observations are the time series of cross-sectional regression coefficients. The first-order autocorrelations in panel A vary from 0.142 for the intercept to 0.649 for the coefficient on RETURN. The R^2 values are based upon the pooled regressions, and do not reflect the year-to-year variability in the regressions.

$$r_p - r_f = a_0 + a_1 SIZE_p + a_2 RETURN_p + a_3 Beta_p + e_p$$

Coefficient estimates

Intercept	SIZE	RETURN	Beta	R^2_{adjusted}
Panel A: Annual percentage returns					
14.443	−0.364	−0.254	5.438	0.68
(10.517)	(−3.779)	(−2.996)	(1.707)	
Panel B: Monthly percentage returns, all months					
1.236	−0.031	−0.023	0.369	0.68
(4.671)	(−2.926)	(−3.039)	(1.393)	

$$r_p - r_f = a_0 + a_1 SIZE_p + a_2 DS \cdot RETURN_p + a_3 DM \cdot RETURN_p + a_4 DL \cdot RETURN_p + a_5 Beta_p + e_p$$

Coefficient estimates

Intercept	SIZE	DS · RETURN	DM · RETURN	DL · RETURN	Beta	R^2_{adjusted}
Panel C: Annual percentage returns						
18.113	−0.597	−0.417	−0.182	−0.136	4.364	0.72
(9.915)	(−5.440)	(−4.257)	(−2.009)	(−1.433)	(1.298)	
Panel D: Monthly percentage returns, all months						
1.631	−0.055	−0.039	−0.018	−0.010	0.238	0.73
(6.431)	(−5.675)	(−4.733)	(−2.235)	(−1.326)	(0.898)	

estimates reported in panel A, we have adjusted for fourth-order autocorrelation using the formula reported in table 4. Without these adjustments, the t-statistics from the pooled cross-sectional regressions are approximately three times as large.

To examine the sensitivity of our conclusions to the use of annual returns rather than monthly returns (which are more commonly used in empirical studies), panel B reports results from monthly regressions. (In panels B and D, we use monthly returns to calculate betas, and we use the same procedure to calculate t-statistics as used in panel A.) These results, after multiplying the monthly coefficients by 12, are qualitatively similar to those in panel A. The overreaction effect is slightly stronger using monthly returns, with panel B reporting that extreme losers outperform extreme winners by 5.2% per year, ceteris paribus. The compensation per unit of beta is 4.4% per year using monthly data, a decrease from the 5.4% per year reported in panel A using annual returns.

In panels C and D, we permit the overreaction effect to vary by firm size by estimating three different slope coefficients, depending upon whether a portfolio is comprised of small, middle-size, or large firms. Panel C reveals that the overreaction effect is strongest among smaller firms. The $DS \cdot RETURN$ coefficient of -0.417 implies a 7.9% per year abnormal return difference between portfolios 1 and 20 for the smallest (bottom 40%) firms. For middle-size firms, this difference is 3.5%, while for the larger (upper 20%) firms, the difference is 2.6%. This relation between firm size and the extent of overreaction has not previously been emphasized.

To examine the robustness of our table 4 results, we have also run the regressions for the 1931-56 and 1957-82 subperiods. Our results (not reported here) indicate that there is a significant overreaction effect in both subperiods, although the effects are stronger in the second subperiod, in contrast to the evidence on index autocorrelations over three-to-five year periods reported by Fama and French (1988), who find weaker results for subperiods excluding the 1930s.

The evidence in panels C and D of table 4 demonstrates that the overreaction effect is stronger for smaller firms. This finding deserves further analysis. In table 5, we examine the extent of overreaction within each of ten size deciles by reporting regression results with $RETURN$ and beta as explanatory variables. Each of the ten regressions uses the 40 portfolios out of the 400 formed for our table 4 analysis that correspond to the appropriate size grouping. In table 5, the coefficient on $RETURN$ is generally closer to zero the larger is the size decile. The last column in the table reports the implied annual difference in returns between the extreme winner and loser portfolios, holding size and beta constant. These differences in returns are plotted in fig. 4. The numbers demonstrate that for the smaller firms an overreaction effect on the order of 10% per year (50% per five years, even before compounding)

Table 5

OLS regressions of annual average percentage excess returns on ranking-period returns and beta by size decile.

RETURN is measured 1 to 20 (1 = losers, 20 = winners), where prior returns are measured over the five years prior to the portfolio formation date. Firms are assigned to size deciles (1 = small, 10 = large) on the basis of their market capitalization at the end of the ranking period. The beta of each portfolio is calculated as the pooled (over firms and post-ranking years) beta. Each of the ten regressions uses forty observations (two ranks of size with twenty prior-return portfolios in each size rank). T-statistics, computed using the fourth-order autoregressive process described in table 4, are in parentheses.

$$r_p - r_f = a_0 + a_1 RETURN_p + a_2 Beta_p + e_p$$

Size decile	Intercept	RETURN	Beta	$R^2_{adjusted}$	$-19 \times RETURN$ coefficient[a]
1	9.888 (2.463)	−0.578 (−2.119)	9.980 (2.670)	0.76	10.98%
2	27.658 (4.379)	−0.729 (−6.436)	−2.784 (−0.426)	0.74	13.85%
3	21.218 (4.723)	−0.510 (−3.382)	0.402 (0.078)	0.65	9.69%
4	18.942 (6.730)	−0.350 (−3.811)	0.739 (0.242)	0.51	6.65%
5	16.356 (3.715)	−0.140 (−2.629)	−0.641 (−0.101)	0.10	2.66%
6	14.226 (1.982)	−0.293 (−2.242)	2.489 (0.288)	0.52	5.57%
7	9.149 (4.691)	−0.153 (−1.755)	4.838 (2.463)	0.51	2.91%
8	8.018 (3.012)	−0.113 (−0.764)	5.171 (1.000)	0.37	2.15%
9	6.101 (1.634)	−0.016 (−0.149)	4.524 (0.572)	0.01	0.30%
10	5.080 (1.932)	0.040 (0.327)	2.471 (0.466)	0.01	−0.76%

[a] Multiplying the coefficients on RETURN by −19 gives the expected difference in annual returns for the five post-ranking years between prior-return portfolios 1 and 20, controlling for beta, for firms categorized by their size decile.

is present, while for the largest 20% of NYSE firms (roughly the S&P 500) no overreaction effect is apparent. Since individuals are the primary holders of the smaller firms, while institutions are the dominant holders of the larger firms, the results are consistent with the hypothesis that individuals overreact, while institutional investors do not.

Our finding that overreaction is concentrated among smaller firms is consistent with results reported in Fama and French (1988), where small-firm

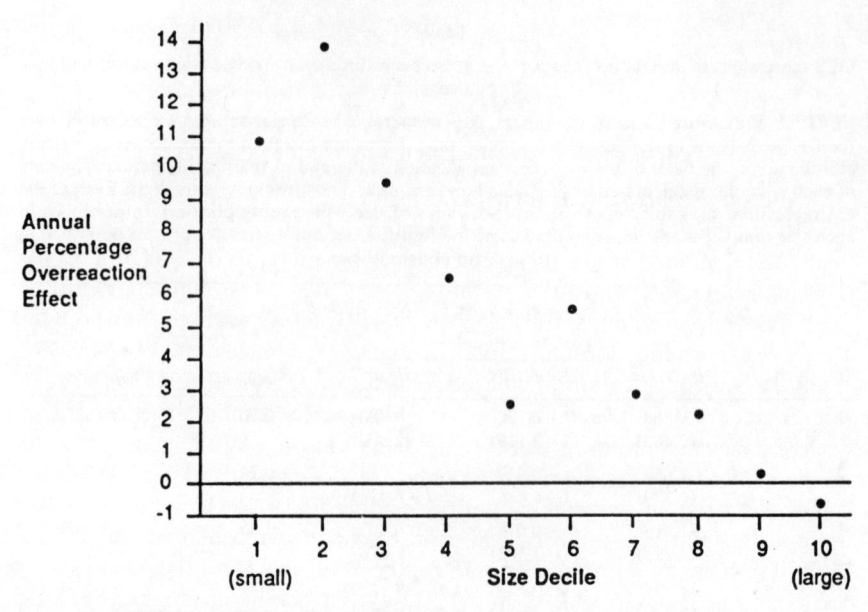

Fig. 4. The difference in annual abnormal returns between extreme loser and winner portfolios by size decile.

The numbers plotted are the coefficients on RETURN in table 5 multiplied by −19. This represents the expected difference in annual returns for the five post-ranking years between prior return portfolios 1 and 20, controlling for beta, for firms categorized by their size decile.

portfolios are found to have greater negative serial correlation than large-firm portfolios. Furthermore, Poterba and Summers (1988) provide evidence that there is greater long-term negative serial correlation in countries with less-developed capital markets than in countries such as the U.S. or Britain. Together, this evidence is consistent with the hypothesis that the further one moves away from large-capitalization stocks in well-developed capital markets, the more likely it is that stocks take prolonged swings away from their fundamental value.

Another noteworthy aspect of the table 5 regressions is that in contrast to the importance of the *RETURN* variable, which is statistically significant at the 0.05 level for the six smallest size deciles, the coefficient on beta is highly variable and statistically significant in only two of the ten regressions. For the largest two size deciles, which account for the majority of market capitalization, beta is far from statistically significant. For these two deciles, the compensation per unit of beta risk is substantially below the 5.4% reported in panel A of table 4 and the 9.4% reported in fig. 1a. Also noteworthy is that for these largest two deciles, the R^2s are essentially zero: neither prior returns nor beta are related to realized returns. In other words, a stock is a stock.

4. Evidence from earnings announcements

The evidence presented so far indicates that even after controlling for size and beta effects, there is an overreaction effect. However, because the magnitude of any effect measured over long intervals is sensitive to the benchmark employed, we also present evidence of overreaction around earnings announcements. Focusing on short windows such as the three-day period surrounding earnings announcements minimizes the sensitivity of results to misspecification of controls, which can provide further evidence on the existence of an overreaction effect. However, it cannot shed much light on the exact magnitude because there is no reason why the return towards fundamental value should occur on only a few discrete dates.

For the firms in the ranking periods ending in 1970–81, we searched the Compustat quarterly industrial, historical, and research files for their quarterly earnings announcements during the five years of the post-ranking periods.[9] Our search resulted in 227,522 earnings announcements. For each of the twenty portfolios formed by ranking firms on prior returns, we computed the average raw return for earnings announcements for a three-day window of $[-2, 0]$ relative to the Compustat-listed announcement date. This three-day window is commonly used in the earnings announcement literature [e.g., Bernard and Thomas (1990)].

In fig. 5, we plot the raw three-day earnings-announcement-period returns using the same size and prior-return quintiles as in figs. 2 and 3. The small losers have average returns of 0.958% per three days, while the large winners have average returns of 0.001% per three days.

Returning to the twenty portfolios, the average earnings-announcement-period return for firms in portfolio 1 (losers) is 0.63%. For firms in prior-return portfolio 20, the average earnings-announcement-period return is zero. Thus, the evidence from earnings announcements indicates that the market is systematically surprised at subsequent earnings announcements in a manner consistent with the overreaction hypothesis.

Recent research, however, finds anomalous returns at earnings announcement dates. [Much of the literature on earnings announcements is surveyed

---

[9]The quarterly industrial file contains only companies that are currently publicly-traded. The research file contains companies that were delisted. Combining these data files gives us a sample that covers almost all of the NYSE firms in our sample, but only for the most recent 48 quarters. Adding the historical data extends the sample back into the 1970s. Compustat's data on quarterly earnings announcement dates becomes progressively less comprehensive for earlier years, which is why we restrict our analysis to the 1970s and 1980s, rather than the full 52 years of data.

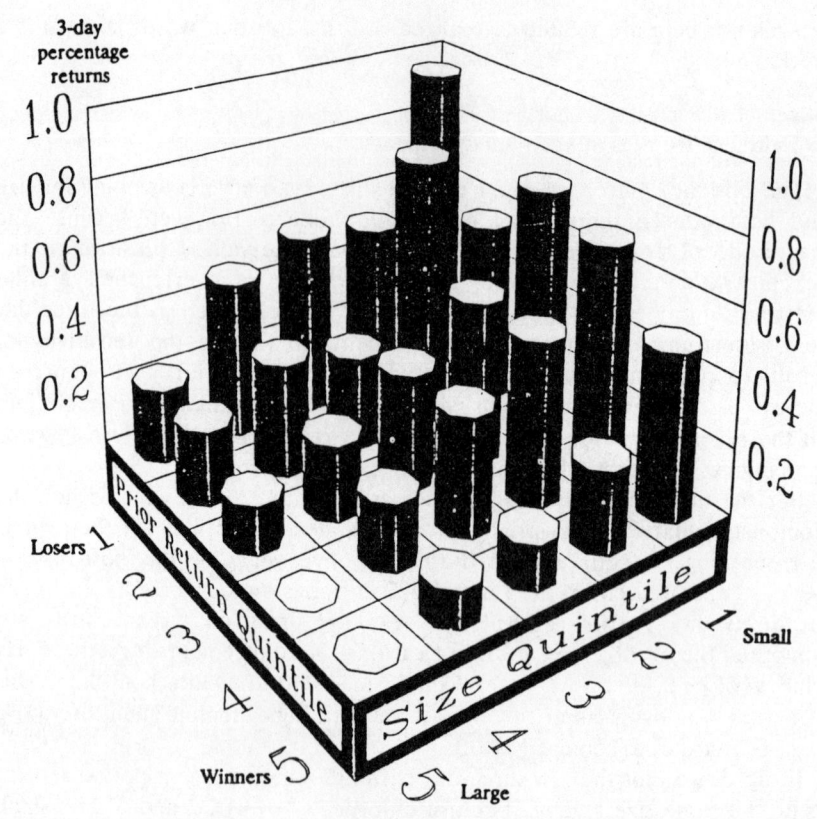

Fig. 5. The joint distribution of three-day earnings announcement returns categorized by market capitalization and prior returns.

Firms are assigned to portfolios based upon independent rankings of size and prior returns. The average three-day raw return at subsequent earnings announcements is computed for Compustat-listed quarterly earnings announcement dates during the five-year post-ranking period. The average three-day raw return is 0.001% for the largest extreme winners and 0.958% for the smallest extreme losers.

in Ball and Kothari (1991).] In particular, Chari, Jagannathan, and Ofer (1988) document that small firms tend to have higher earnings-announcement-period returns than large firms, and in our case, a disproportionate fraction of losers are small. Chari, Jagannathan, and Ofer hypothesize that because of the increased flow of information around earnings announcements, these periods are riskier than nonannouncement periods. Therefore, to examine whether past price changes affect returns around earnings an-

Table 6
Regression of three-day earnings announcement portfolio returns on size, prior returns, and beta.

394 portfolios are used (400 portfolios based on independently ranking firms by size and prior return, with six portfolios deleted which had fewer than 100 earnings announcements). Size is measured with the smallest firms in portfolio 1, and the largest in portfolio 20. Prior returns (measured over the five prior years) are also ranked from 1 to 20, with 1 being the losers. Betas are calculated for each portfolio using all earnings announcement returns for all firms in the portfolio. The dependent variable is measured as the percentage return per three-day announcement period $[-2,0]$, for earnings announcements made during the first five post-ranking years. Earnings announcement days are from Compustat's industrial, historical, and research tapes, for announcements during the five post-ranking years following the ranking periods ending in 1970–81. There are 227,522 earnings announcements. T-statistics, computed using the time-series variance of the cross-sectional regression coefficients, adjusted for first-order autocorrelation, are in parentheses.

$$R_p = a_0 + a_1 SIZE_p + a_2 RETURN_p + a_3 Beta_p + e_i$$

Coefficient estimates

Intercept	SIZE	RETURN	Beta	$R^2_{adjusted}$
0.641	−0.027	−0.014	0.111	0.32
(3.230)	(−7.701)	(−2.548)	(2.018)	

nouncements, we have to control for both size and risk, which we accomplish by using an approach similar to that employed in eq. (2). The analysis uses 400 portfolios formed on the basis of independent rankings of firm size and prior returns. For each of these 400 portfolios, we compute an average raw three-day holding period return. We also calculate a portfolio beta by running a pooled market model regression (over both firms and earnings announcements) using three-day announcement-period returns and three-day market returns.

In table 6 we report the results of a regression based on 394 observations (six portfolios with less than 100 earnings announcements are deleted) where the portfolio three-day return is the dependent variable. Explanatory variables are SIZE (as measured by the size portfolio number), RETURNS (as measured by the prior returns portfolio number), and beta. The coefficients indicate that, holding beta and firm size constant, the earnings announcement returns are more positive for prior losers than winners. In particular, multiplying the coefficient of −0.0142 by (1 minus 20) is 0.27% per announcement. Since there are four quarterly earnings announcements per year, this is a difference of 1.08% during each calendar year for these 12 trading days alone, reinforcing our earlier results on the existence of an overreaction effect. Corroborating evidence is also found in Hand (1990), where differential earnings announcement effects are found depending upon the proportion of shares held by individuals.

5. Summary and conclusions

One of the most controversial issues in financial economics in recent years is the question of whether stocks overreact. De Bondt and Thaler (1985) present evidence that stocks with poor performance (losers) over the past three-to-five years outperform prior-period winners during the subsequent three-to-five years. This work has received considerable attention because the authors find a very large difference in returns between winners and losers during the five-year post-ranking period (about 8% per year), and they interpret their findings as evidence that there are systematic valuation errors in the stock market caused by investor overreaction.

Subsequent papers suggest that De Bondt and Thaler's findings are subject to various methodological problems. In particular, Ball and Kothari (1989) show that when betas are estimated using annual returns, nearly all of the estimated abnormal returns disappear in the context of the Sharpe–Lintner CAPM. In another paper, Zarowin (1990) argues that the overreaction effect is merely a manifestation of the size effect. It is apparent that the quantitative magnitude of the overreaction effect is highly sensitive to the procedures used in computing abnormal returns, particularly in any study in which abnormal returns are being computed over multiple-year periods.

In this paper, we estimate event time-varying betas but do not use the restrictive assumptions of the Sharpe–Lintner CAPM in computing abnormal returns for winners and losers. The Sharpe–Lintner model assumes that the compensation per unit of beta risk is about 14–15% per year when an equally-weighted market portfolio is used. Given that the betas of extreme winners and losers differ by about 0.8 when annual returns are used, an adjustment for beta risk explains a large portion of the overreaction effect. We rely instead on the estimated market compensation per unit of beta risk, which is substantially smaller than that assumed by the Sharpe–Lintner model. We obtain results that are consistent with a substantial overreaction effect. Using annual return intervals, extreme losers outperform extreme winners by 6.5% per year. Using monthly return intervals, this spread increases to 9.5% per year. Furthermore, we show that the overreaction effect is not just a manifestation of the size effect. We demonstrate that the common procedure of adjusting for size underestimates the spread in abnormal returns between winners and losers, because part of the size effect is attributable to return reversals. After adjusting for size, but before adjusting for beta effects, we find that extreme losers outperform extreme winners by 9.7% per year after purging size-control portfolios of winners and losers.

In general, because size, prior returns, and betas are correlated, any study that relates realized returns to just one or two of these variables suffers from an omitted variable bias. In the context of a multiple regression using all three of these variables, we find an economically-significant overreaction effect of about 5% per year. This overreaction effect, however, has a pronounced January seasonal, consistent with the findings of other authors, which raises the question of whether there is an overreaction effect that is distinct from previously-documented tax-loss selling effects. To address this issue, we construct portfolios based upon prior one-year returns, a common measure of tax-loss selling intensity, and measure their performance over the subsequent five years. We find much smaller differences in returns between extreme portfolios than when portfolios are formed based upon five-year returns.

The overreaction effect, however, is not homogeneous across size groups. Instead, it is much stronger for smaller companies than for larger companies, with extreme losers outperforming extreme winners by about 10% per year among small firms. These smaller firms are held predominantly by individuals. In contrast, there is virtually no evidence of overreaction among the largest firms, where institutional investors are the dominant holders. This suggests that overreaction by individuals is more prevalent than overreaction by institutions.

In common with other studies that examine returns over long intervals, there is always the possibility that what we attribute to overreaction is instead equilibrium compensation for some omitted risk factor (or factors). However, we feel that our results cannot be explained by risk mismeasurement since returns consistent with overreaction are observed for the short windows surrounding quarterly earnings announcement days. We find that even after adjusting for the size effect and the higher risk that is present at earnings announcements, losers have significantly higher returns than winners.

If the return reversals documented here and elsewhere are not merely compensation for risk bearing, then why is it that the patterns do not disappear due to the actions of arbitrageurs? Shleifer and Vishny (1991) argue that 'smart money' investors are exposed to opportunity costs if there is no certainty that mispricing will be corrected in a timely manner. The periodic evaluation of money managers by their clients contributes to their unwillingness to undertake long-term arbitrage positions. For these reasons, 'smart money' will flock to short-term rather than long-term arbitrage opportunities, and resources devoted to long-term arbitrage will be quite limited. The trading strategies discussed in this paper require capital commitments over extended horizons in smaller firms, which may be why these opportunities can persist for so long.

In summary, we have documented an economically-important overreaction effect in the stock market, concentrated among smaller firms. While the underlying reasons for the valuation errors have not been uncovered, the fact that the effect is strongest for smaller stocks may indicate that a productive area for future research is understanding the difference in the investment patterns between individuals and institutions.

Table 7

RATS betas on winner and loser portfolios for each event year from −6 to +5 for ranking periods in all markets, down markets ($r_{mt} - r_{ft} < 0$), and up markets ($r_{mt} - r_{ft} > 0$). Years −6 to −5 are the pre-ranking period, years −4 to 0 are the ranking period, and years +1 to +5 are the post-ranking period.[a]

$$r_{pt} - r_{ft} = \alpha_p + \beta_p(r_{mt} - r_{ft}) + \varepsilon_{pt}$$

Beta coefficient estimates

Year relative to ranking year 0	All 52 years		Years when $r_m - r_f < 0$ only		Years when $r_m - r_f > 0$ only	
	Winners	Losers	Winners	Losers	Winners	Losers
−6	1.15	1.19	1.20	1.03	1.01	1.10
−5	1.21	1.12	1.12	1.07	1.17	1.06
−4	1.58	0.78	1.11	0.96	2.02	0.52
−3	1.52	0.83	0.99	0.87	1.86	0.58
−2	1.47	0.95	0.99	0.75	1.78	0.83
−1	1.48	1.02	0.98	0.86	1.72	0.99
0	1.21	1.06	0.94	0.83	1.13	1.03
+1	0.85	1.54	0.94	0.97	0.63	1.73
+2	0.79	1.63	0.93	1.26	0.56	1.89
+3	0.86	1.54	0.80	1.22	0.74	1.71
+4	0.94	1.55	0.72	1.08	0.95	1.78
+5	0.88	1.61	0.77	0.95	0.88	1.88
Average, −6 to −5	1.18	1.15	1.16	1.05	1.09	1.08
Average, −4 to 0	1.45	0.93	1.00	0.85	1.70	0.79
Average, +1 to +5	0.86	1.57	0.83	1.10	0.75	1.80

[a] Winner and loser portfolios consist of the stocks with the most extreme total returns over the five years −4 to 0. The 50 best and the 50 worst stocks in each ranking are assigned to the winner and loser portfolios. In the first two columns, α_p and β_p coefficients are estimated using a time series of 52 annual portfolio returns, using Ibbotson's (1975) RATS methodology. For years −6 and −5, respectively, 50 and 51 annual returns are used because of the lack of CRSP data for 1924 and 1925. There are between 15 and 21 down-market years and 31 to 37 up-market years, for the years −6 to +5. Riskless annual returns are from Ibbotson Associates (1988). The market return is defined to be the equally-weighted market return on NYSE stocks with at least five years of returns.

Appendix

A.1. Asymmetries in beta changes

Ibbotson's (1975) RATS procedure is ideally suited for estimating event time-varying betas in a situation where the sample firms are experiencing dramatic changes in their market capitalization over relatively short intervals. In the context of this study, substantial differences in betas between winners and losers are observed using this procedure.

One of the attractive features of the RATS procedure is that one can observe on a period-by-period basis how the betas are changing within the ranking or post-ranking periods. Ball and Kothari (1989) present evidence, in their tables 4 and 5 and fig. 1, that the betas of winner and loser portfolios change over time in the direction that would be predicted due to leverage changes. We replicate these patterns in columns (1) and (2) of our table 7. In this table, following De Bondt and Thaler (1985) and Ball and Kothari (1989), we have defined winners and losers to be the 50 stocks with the most extreme ranking-period returns. We have calculated betas for each year of a two-year pre-ranking period (years -6 to -5), for the ranking period (years -4 to 0), and for the post-ranking period (years $+1$ to $+5$). The changes in the betas from the pre-ranking period to the ranking period, and from the ranking period to the post-ranking period, are striking. The ranking-period betas appear to suffer from severe biases. Apparently, the timing of the extreme returns on winners (and losers) is correlated with the market excess return. What is particularly noteworthy is that in the pre-ranking period, the firms that subsequently become the extreme winners and losers have betas that are practically indistinguishable from each other.[10] From year -5 to -4, the beta of the winner portfolio jumps from 1.21 to 1.58, whereas the beta of the loser portfolio falls from 1.12 to 0.78. These dramatic shifts are in the opposite direction to the changes predicted by the leverage hypothesis.

The leverage hypothesis predicts that, since year -4 is part of the ranking period, the beta of winners should fall and the beta of losers should rise. (In the ranking period, the winners have an average annual raw return of 55% for five years, while the losers have an average annual raw return of -9% for five years.) Throughout the ranking period, the betas of the winners remain high and the betas of the losers remain low. As soon as the ranking period ends, there is another huge change in betas. Between years 0 and $+1$, the winners' betas decrease by 0.36 and the losers' betas increase by 0.48, a combined swing of 0.84. One would expect a much smaller change, given that the market capitalizations change by a smaller amount between years 0 and $+1$ than between any two adjacent years during the ranking period. In contrast, the swing in betas during the entire five-year ranking period in which the relative market capitalizations changed dramatically is only 0.65 (0.27 for winners and 0.38 for losers).

These abrupt changes in betas cast doubt on the hypothesis that the changes are primarily due to movements in leverage. Thus, a fundamental question is raised about just what phenomenon is being captured by the betas of the winners and losers. The puzzle deepens when the patterns in betas for

---

[10]The betas of both the subsequent winners and losers are above 1.0 during the pre-ranking period. Small firms tend to have high betas, and firms with a lot of unique risk are overrepresented among both extreme winners and extreme losers. Large firms are generally more diversified, and are thus less likely to become extreme winners or losers.

Table 8

OLS regressions of average annual percentage excess returns for the first five post-ranking years for portfolios of NYSE firms formed on the basis of size and prior returns.

For each of the 52 ranking periods ending on December 31 of 1930 to 1981, firms are independently ranked on the basis of their December 31 market value and their five-year prior return, and assigned to one of 400 portfolios. *SIZE* is measured as the size portfolio ranking (1 to 20, with 1 being smallest), and *RETURN* is measured as the prior-return portfolio ranking (1 to 20, with 1 being the most extreme prior losers). Annual returns and an equally-weighted market index are used in all three panels. *T*-statistics, computed using the autocorrelation-adjusted Fama–MacBeth procedure described in table 4, are in parentheses.

Panel A reports results using betas that are calculated by pooling observations across both firms and post-ranking event years. This is identical to panel A in table 4. Panels B and C report results using the two alternative procedures. In all three panels, *t*-statistics are based upon variation in the coefficients from a 52-observation time series of cross-sectional regressions, adjusted for fourth-order autocorrelation.

In panel B, the procedure is analogous to that used in table 1: for each of the 400 portfolios we run a time-series regression using (up to) 52 portfolio returns in each of the five post-ranking years, and then compute the portfolio beta as the average of these five numbers. A disadvantage of this procedure is that there are many portfolios that have missing observations in some of the 52 years.

In panel C, the procedure calculates separate betas for each of the five post-ranking years and then averages these five numbers to calculate the portfolio beta.

$$r_p - r_f = a_0 + a_1 SIZE_p + a_2 RETURN_p + a_3 Beta_p + e_p$$

Coefficient estimates

Intercept	SIZE	RETURN	Beta	$R^2_{adjusted}$
Panel A: Betas computed with pooling over both firms and event years				
14.443	−0.364	−0.254	5.438	0.68
(10.517)	(−3.779)	(−2.996)	(1.707)	
Panel B: Betas computed using the RATS procedure				
15.637	−0.290	−0.204	7.210	0.70
(4.949)	(−2.007)	(−2.259)	(2.062)	
Panel C: Betas computed with pooling over firms				
17.838	−0.314	−0.266	5.817	0.67
(6.381)	(−2.194)	(−3.022)	(1.646)	

up and down markets are observed. [De Bondt and Thaler (1987) first documented these differences in betas between up and down markets.] During down markets, defined as years for which $r_m - r_f < 0$, the betas of winner and loser portfolios show little variation between the ranking and post-ranking periods. Furthermore, in the post-ranking period the down-market betas differ by only 0.27 (0.83 for winners, 1.10 for losers). In contrast, during up markets, defined as years for which $r_m - r_f > 0$, the betas of winners fall by roughly half from the ranking period to the post-ranking period, while the betas of losers approximately double. Furthermore, during the post-ranking period, the up-market betas of winners and losers differ by a full 1.05 (0.75 for winners, 1.80 for losers). Thus, the large difference in betas between winners and losers in the post-ranking period emphasized by Ball and Kothari is driven primarily by the extraordinarily high betas on losers during up markets. Thus, while the difference in betas during the post-ranking period between portfolios comprised of the 50 most extreme winners and losers is 0.70 (0.79 using extreme vitile portfolios in table 1), we have serious reservations whether the difference in risk that investors face is actually of this magnitude.

What is beta capturing? This is an open issue that requires further study. Work by Bhandari (1988) and Braun, Nelson, and Sunier (1990) finds only a weak association between changes in leverage and equity betas. Stroyny (1991) finds that heteroskedasticity in the returns distribution induces some of the biases, since percentage variances tend to be asymmetric between up and down markets.

A.2. Sensitivities to alternative measures of beta computation

In table 8, we report the results of alternative beta computation procedures for the table 4 regression using annual returns. As can be seen, the qualitative conclusions are not highly dependent on the procedure employed.

References

Amihud, Yakov and Haim Mendelson, 1989, The effects of beta, bid–ask spread, residual risk, and size on stock returns, Journal of Finance 44, 479–486.

Ball, Ray and S.P. Kothari, 1989, Nonstationary expected returns: Implications for tests of market efficiency and serial correlation in returns, Journal of Financial Economics 25, 51–74.

Ball, Ray and S.P. Kothari, 1991, Security returns around earnings announcements, The Accounting Review 66, 718–738.

Bernard, Victor L. and Jacob K. Thomas, 1989, Post-earnings-announcement drift: Delayed price response or risk premium?, Journal of Accounting Research 27, 1–36.

Bernard, Victor L. and Jacob K. Thomas, 1990, Evidence that stock prices do not fully reflect the implications of current earnings for future earnings, Journal of Accounting and Economics 13, 305–340.

Bhandari, Laxmi, 1988, Debt/equity ratio and expected common stock returns: Empirical evidence, Journal of Finance 43, 507–528.

Black, Fischer, Michael C. Jensen, and Myron Scholes, 1972, The capital asset pricing model: Some empirical tests, in: Michael C. Jensen, ed., Studies in the theory of capital markets (Praeger Publishers, New York, NY).

Braun, Philip A., Daniel B. Nelson, and Alain M. Sunier, 1990, Good news, bad news, volatility, and betas, Working paper (University of Chicago, Chicago, IL).

Brock, William, Josef Lakonishok, and Blake LeBaron, 1992, Simple technical trading rules and the stochastic properties of stock returns, Journal of Finance, forthcoming.

Chan, Louis, Yasushi Hamao, and Josef Lakonishok, 1991, Fundamentals and stock returns in Japan, Journal of Finance 46, 1739–1764.

Chan, K.C., 1986, Can tax-loss selling explain the January seasonal in stock returns?, Journal of Finance 41, 1115–1128.

Chan. K.C., 1988, On the contrarian investment strategy, Journal of Business 61, 147–163.

Chari, V.V., Ravi Jagannathan, and Aharon R. Ofer, 1988, Seasonalities in security returns: The case of earnings announcements, Journal of Financial Economics 21, 101–121.

Conrad, Jennifer and Gautum Kaul, 1989, Mean reversion in short-horizon expected returns, Review of Financial Studies 2, 225–240.

Conrad, Jennifer and Gautum Kaul, 1991, Long-term market overreaction or biases in computed returns?, Working paper (University of North Carolina, Chapel Hill, NC).

De Bondt, Werner F.M. and Richard M. Thaler, 1985, Does the stock market overreact?, Journal of Finance 40, 793–805.

De Bondt, Werner F.M. and Richard M. Thaler, 1987, Further evidence on investor overreaction and stock market seasonality, Journal of Finance 42, 557–581.

Dimson, Elroy and Paul Marsh, 1986, Event study methodologies and the size effect: The case of UK press recommendations, Journal of Financial Economics 17, 113–142.

Fama, Eugene F., 1991, Efficient capital markets: II, Journal of Finance 46, 1575–1617.

Fama, Eugene F. and Kenneth R. French, 1986, Common factors in the serial correlation of stock returns, Working paper (University of Chicago, Chicago, IL).

Fama, Eugene F. and Kenneth R. French, 1988, Permanent and temporary components of stock market prices, Journal of Political Economy 96, 246–273.

Fama, Eugene F. and Kenneth R. French, 1992, Cross-sectional variation in expected stock returns, Journal of Finance 47.

Fama, Eugene F. and James D. MacBeth, 1973, Risk, return, and equilibrium: Empirical tests, Journal of Political Economy 71, 607–636.

Hand, John R., 1990, A test of the extended functional fixation hypothesis, The Accounting Review 65, 740–763.

Huberman, Gur and Shmuel Kandel, 1987, Value Line rank and firm size, Journal of Business 60, 577–589.

Ibbotson Associates, 1988, Stocks, bonds, bills and inflation 1988 yearbook (Ibbotson Associates, Inc., Chicago, IL).

Ibbotson, Roger G., 1975, Price performance of common stock new issues, Journal of Financial Economics 2, 235–272.

Jegadeesh, Narasimhan, 1990, Evidence of predictable behavior of security returns, Journal of Finance 45, 881–898.

Jegadeesh, Narasimhan and Sheridan Titman, 1991, Returns to buying winners and selling losers: Implications for stock market efficiency, Working paper (University of California, Los Angeles, CA).

Jensen, Michael C., 1969, Risk, the pricing of capital assets, and the evaluation of investment portfolios, Journal of Business 42, 167–247.

Keim, Donald B. and Robert F. Stambaugh, 1986, Predicting returns in the stock and bond markets, Journal of Financial Economics 17, 357–390.

Lakonishok, Josef and Alan C. Shapiro, 1986, Systematic risk, total risk and size as determinants of stock market returns, Journal of Banking and Finance 10, 115–132.

Lehmann, Bruce N., 1990, Fads, martingales, and market efficiency, Quarterly Journal of Economics 105, 1–28.

Lo, Andrew W. and A. Craig MacKinlay, 1988, Stock market prices do not follow random walks: Evidence from a simple specification test, Review of Financial Studies 1, 41–66.

Miller, Merton H. and Myron Scholes, 1972, Rates of return in relation to risk: A re-examination of some recent findings, in: Michael C. Jensen, editor., Studies in the theory of capital markets (Praeger Publishers, New York, NY).

Poterba, James M. and Lawrence H. Summers, 1988, Mean reversion in stock prices: Evidence and implications, Journal of Financial Economics 22, 27–59.

Reinganum, Marc R., 1983, The anomalous stock market behavior of small firms in January: Empirical tests for tax-loss selling effects, Journal of Financial Economics 12, 89–104.

Ritter, Jay R. and Navin Chopra, 1989, Portfolio rebalancing and the turn-of-the-year effect, Journal of Finance 44, 149–166.

Roll, Richard, 1983, Vas ist das? The turn-of-the-year effect and the return premia of small firms, Journal of Portfolio Management 9, 18–28.

Rosenberg, Barr, K. Reid, and R. Lanstein, 1985, Persuasive evidence of market inefficiency, Journal of Portfolio Management 11, 9–16.

Shleifer, Andrei and Robert W. Vishny, 1991, Equilibrium short horizons of investors and firms, American Economic Review Papers and Proceedings 80, 148–153.

Stroyny, Alvin L., 1991, Heteroscedasticity and estimation of systematic risk, Ph.D. dissertation (University of Wisconsin, Madison, WI).

Tinic, Seha M. and Richard R. West, 1984, Risk and return: January vs. the rest of the year, Journal of Financial Economics 13, 561–574.

Zarowin, Paul, 1990, Size, seasonality, and stock market overreaction, Journal of Financial and Quantitative Analysis 25, 113–125.

Does the Stock Market Overreact?

WERNER F. M. De BONDT and RICHARD THALER*

ABSTRACT

Research in experimental psychology suggests that, in violation of Bayes' rule, most people tend to "overreact" to unexpected and dramatic news events. This study of market efficiency investigates whether such behavior affects stock prices. The empirical evidence, based on CRSP monthly return data, is consistent with the overreaction hypothesis. Substantial weak form market inefficiencies are discovered. The results also shed new light on the January returns earned by prior "winners" and "losers." Portfolios of losers experience exceptionally large January returns as late as five years after portfolio formation.

AS ECONOMISTS INTERESTED IN both market behavior and the psychology of individual decision making, we have been struck by the similarity of two sets of empirical findings. Both classes of behavior can be characterized as displaying *overreaction*. This study was undertaken to investigate the possibility that these phenomena are related by more than just appearance. We begin by describing briefly the individual and market behavior that piqued our interest.

The term overreaction carries with it an implicit comparison to some degree of reaction that is considered to be appropriate. What is an appropriate reaction? One class of tasks which have a well-established norm are probability revision problems for which Bayes' rule prescribes the correct reaction to new information. It has now been well-established that Bayes' rule is not an apt characterization of how individuals actually respond to new data (Kahneman et al. [14]). In revising their beliefs, individuals tend to overweight recent information and underweight prior (or base rate) data. People seem to make predictions according to a simple matching rule: "The predicted value is selected so that the standing of the case in the distribution of outcomes matches its standing in the distribution of impressions" (Kahneman and Tversky [14, p. 416]). This rule-of-thumb, an instance of what Kahneman and Tversky call the representativeness heuristic, violates the basic statistical principal that the extremeness of predictions must be moderated by considerations of predictability. Grether [12] has replicated this finding under incentive compatible conditions. There is also considerable evidence that the actual expectations of professional security analysts and economic forecasters display the same overreaction bias (for a review, see De Bondt [7]).

One of the earliest observations about overreaction in markets was made by J. M. Keynes:"... day-to-day fluctuations in the profits of existing investments,

---

* University of Wisconsin at Madison and Cornell University, respectively. The financial support of the C.I.M. Doctoral Fellowship Program (Brussels, Belgium) and the Cornell Graduate School of Management is gratefully acknowledged. We received helpful comments from Seymour Smidt, Dale Morse, Peter Bernstein, Fischer Black, Robert Jarrow, Edwin Elton, and Ross Watts.

which are obviously of an ephemeral and nonsignificant character, tend to have an altogether excessive, and even an absurd, influence on the market" [17, pp. 153–154]. About the same time, Williams noted in this *Theory of Investment Value* that "prices have been based too much on current earning power and too little on long-term dividend paying power" [28, p. 19]. More recently, Arrow has concluded that the work of Kahneman and Tversky "typifies very precisely the exessive reaction to current information which seems to characterize all the securities and futures markets" [1, p. 5]. Two specific examples of the research to which Arrow was referring are the excess volatility of security prices and the so-called price earnings ratio anomaly.

The excess volatility issue has been investigated most thoroughly by Shiller [27]. Shiller interprets the Miller-Modigliani view of stock prices as a constraint on the likelihood function of a price-dividend sample. Shiller concludes that, at least over the last century, dividends simply do not vary enough to rationally justify observed aggregate price movements. Combining the results with Kleidon's [18] findings that stock price movements are strongly correlated with the following year's earnings changes suggests a clear pattern of overreaction. In spite of the observed trendiness of dividends, investors seem to attach disproportionate importance to short-run economic developments.[1]

The price earnings ratio (P/E) anomaly refers to the observation that stocks with extremely low P/E ratios (i.e., lowest decile) earn larger risk-adjusted returns than high P/E stocks (Basu [3]). Most financial economists seem to regard the anomaly as a statistical artifact. Explanations are usually based on alleged misspecification of the capital asset pricing model (CAPM). Ball [2] emphasizes the effects of omitted risk factors. The P/E ratio is presumed to be a proxy for some omitted factor which, if included in the "correct" equilibrium valuation model, would eliminate the anomaly. Of course, unless these omitted factors can be identified, the hypothesis is untestable. Reinganum [21] has claimed that the small firm effect subsumes the P/E effect and that both are related to the same set of missing (and again unknown) factors. However, Basu [4] found a significant P/E effect after controlling for firm size, and earlier Graham [11] even found an effect within the thirty Dow Jones Industrials, hardly a group of small firms!

An alternative behavioral explanation for the anomaly based on investor overreaction is what Basu called the "price-ratio" hypothesis (e.g., Dreman [8]). Companies with very low P/E's are thought to be temporarily "undervalued" because investors become excessively pessimistic after a series of bad earnings reports or other bad news. Once future earnings turn out to be better than the unreasonably gloomy forecasts, the price adjusts. Similarly, the equity of companies with very high P/E's is thought to be "overvalued," before (predictably) falling in price.

While the overreaction hypothesis has considerable a priori appeal, the obvious question to ask is: How does the anomaly survive the process of arbitrage? There

---

[1] Of course, the variability of stock prices may also reflect changes in real interest rates. If so, the price movements of other assets—such as land or housing—should match those of stocks. However, this is not actually observed. A third hypothesis, advocated by Marsh and Merton [19], is that Shiller's findings are a result of his misspecification of the dividend process.

is really a more general question here. What are the equilibria conditions for markets in which some agents are not rational in the sense that they fail to revise their expectations according to Bayes' rule? Russell and Thaler [24] address this issue. They conclude that the existence of some rational agents is not sufficient to guarantee a rational expectations equilibrium in an economy with some of what they call quasi-rational agents. (The related question of market equilibria with agents having heterogeneous expectations is investigated by Jarrow [13].) While we are highly sensitive to these issues, we do not have the space to address them here. Instead, we will concentrate on an empirical test of the overreaction hypothesis.

If stock prices systematically overshoot, then their reversal should be predictable from past return data alone, with no use of any accounting data such as earnings. Specifically, two hypotheses are suggested: (1) Extreme movements in stock prices will be followed by subsequent price movements in the opposite direction. (2) The more extreme the initial price movement, the greater will be the subsequent adjustment. Both hypotheses imply a violation of weak-form market efficiency.

To repeat, our goal is to test whether the overreaction hypothesis is *predictive*. In other words, whether it does more for us than merely to explain, ex post, the P/E effect or Shiller's results on asset price dispersion. The overreaction effect deserves attention because it represents a behavioral principle that may apply in many other contexts. For example, investor overreaction possibly explains Shiller's earlier [26] findings that when long-term interest rates are high relative to short rates, they tend to move down later on. Ohlson and Penman [20] have further suggested that the increased volatility of security returns following stock splits may also be linked to overreaction. The present empirical tests are to our knowledge the first attempt to use a behavioral principle to predict a new market anomaly.

The remainder of the paper is organized as follows. The next section describes the actual empirical tests we have performed. Section II describes the results. Consistent with the overreaction hypothesis, evidence of weak-form market inefficiency is found. We discuss the implications for other empirical work on asset pricing anomalies. The paper ends with a brief summary of conclusions.

I. The Overreaction Hypothesis: Empirical Tests

The empirical testing procedures are a variant on a design originally proposed by Beaver and Landsman [5] in a different context. Typically, tests of semistrong form market efficiency start, at time $t = 0$, with the formation of portfolios on the basis of some event that affects all stocks in the portfolio, say, an earnings announcement. One then goes on to investigate whether later on ($t > 0$) the estimated residual portfolio return $\hat{u}_{pt}$—measured relative to the single-period CAPM—equals zero. Statistically significant departures from zero are interpreted as evidence consistent with semistrong form market inefficiency, even though the results may also be due to misspecification of the CAPM, misestimation of the relevant alphas and/or betas, or simply market inefficiency of the weak form.

In contrast, the tests in this study assess the extent to which systematic nonzero residual return behavior in the period after portfolio formation ($t > 0$) is associated with systematic residual returns in the preformation months ($t < 0$). We will focus on stocks that have experienced either extreme capital gains or extreme losses over periods up to five years. In other words, "winner" (W) and "loser" portfolios (L) are formed *conditional upon past excess returns*, rather than some firm-generated informational variable such as earnings.

Following Fama [9], the previous arguments can be formalized by writing the efficient market's condition,

$$E(\tilde{R}_{jt} - E_m(\tilde{R}_{jt} | F_{t-1}^m) | F_{t-1}) = E(\tilde{u}_{jt} | F_{t-1}) = 0$$

where F_{t-1} represents the complete set of information at time $t-1$, $\tilde{R}_{jt}$ is the return on security j at t, and $E_m(\tilde{R}_{jt} | F_{t-1}^m)$ is the expectation of $\tilde{R}_{jt}$, assessed by the market on the basis of the information set F_{t-1}^m. The efficient market hypothesis implies that $E(\tilde{u}_{Wt} | F_{t-1}) = E(\tilde{u}_{Lt} | F_{t-1}) = 0$. As explained in the introduction, the overreaction hypothesis, on the other hand, suggests that $E(\tilde{u}_{Wt} | F_{t-1}) < 0$ and $E(\tilde{u}_{Lt} | F_{t-1}) > 0$.

In order to estimate the relevant residuals, an equilibrium model must be specified. A common procedure is to estimate the parameters of the market model (see e.g., Beaver and Landsman [5]). What will happen if the equilibrium model is misspecified? As long as the variation in $E_m(\tilde{R}_{jt} | F_{t-1}^m)$ is small relative to the movements in $\tilde{u}_{jt}$, the exact specification of the equilibrium model makes little difference to tests of the efficient market hypothesis. For, even if we knew the "correct" model of $E_m(\tilde{R}_{jt} | F_{t-1}^m)$, it would explain only small part of the variation in $\tilde{R}_{jt}$.[2]

Since this study investigates the return behavior of specific portfolios over extended periods of time (indeed, as long as a decade), it cannot be merely *assumed* that model misspecification leaves the conclusions about market efficiency unchanged. Therefore, the empirical analysis is based on three types of return residuals: market-adjusted excess returns; market model residuals; and excess returns that are measured relative to the Sharpe-Lintner version of the CAPM. However, since all three methods are single-index models that follow from the CAPM, misspecification problems may still confound the results. De Bondt [7] formally derives the econometric biases in the estimated market-adjusted and market model residuals if the "true" model is multifactor, e.g., $\tilde{R}_{jt} = A_j + B_j \tilde{R}_{mt} + C_j \tilde{X}_t + \tilde{e}_{jt}$. As a final precaution, he also characterizes the securities in the extreme portfolios in terms of a number of financial variables. If there were a persistent tendency for the portfolios to differ on dimensions that may proxy for "risk," then, again, we cannot be sure whether the empirical results support market efficiency or market overreaction.

It turns out that, whichever of the three types of residuals are used, the results

---

[2] Presumably, this same reasoning underlies the common practice of measuring abnormal security price performance by way of easily calculable mean-adjusted excess returns [where, by assumption, $E(\tilde{R}_j)$ equals a constant K_j], market-adjusted excess returns (where, by assumption, $\alpha_j = 0$ and $\beta_j = 1$ for all j), rather than more complicated market model residuals, let along residuals relative to some multifactor model.

of the empirical analysis are similar and that the choice does not affect our main conclusions. Therefore, we will only report the results based on market-adjusted excess returns. The residuals are estimated as $\hat{u}_{jt} = R_{jt} - R_{mt}$. There is no risk adjustment except for movements of the market as a whole and the adjustment is identical for all stocks. Since, for any period t, the same (constant) market return R_{mt} is subtracted from all R_{jt}'s, the results are interpretable in terms of raw (dollar) returns. As shown in De Bondt [7], the use of market-adjusted excess returns has the further advantage that it is likely to bias the research design *against* the overreaction hypothesis.[3] Finally, De Bondt shows that winner and loser portfolios, formed on the basis of market-adjusted excess returns, do not systematically differ with respect to either market value of equity, dividend yield or financial leverage.

We will now describe the basic research design used to form the winner and loser portfolios and the statistical test procedures that determine which of the two competing hypotheses receives more support from the data.

A. Test Procedures: Details

Monthly return data for New York Stock Exchange (NYSE) common stocks, as compiled by the Center for Research in Security Prices (CRSP) of the University of Chicago, are used for the period between January 1926 and December 1982. An equally weighted arithmetic average rate of return on all CRSP listed securities serves as the market index.

1. For every stock j on the tape with at least 85 months of return data (months 1 through 85), without any missing values in between, and starting in January 1930 (month 49), the next 72 monthly residual returns u_{jt} (months 49 through 120) are estimated. If some or all of the raw return data beyond month 85 are missing, the residual returns are calculated up to that point. The procedure is repeated 16 times starting in January 1930, January 1933, ..., up to January 1975. As time goes on and new securities appear on the tape, more and more stocks qualify for this step.

2. For every stock j, starting in December 1932 (month 84; the "portfolio formation date") ($t = 0$), we compute the cumulative excess returns $CU_j = \sum_{t=-35}^{t=0} u_{jt}$ for the prior 36 months (the "portfolio formation" period, months 49 through 84). The step is repeated 16 times for all nonoverlapping three-year periods between January 1930 and December 1977. On each of the 16 relevant portfolio formation dates (December 1932, December 1935, ..., December 1977), the CU_j's are ranked from low to high and portfolios are formed. Firms in the top 35 stocks (or the top 50 stocks, or the top decile) are assigned to the winner portfolio W; firms in the bottom 35 stocks (or the bottom 50 stocks, or the bottom decile) to the loser portfolio L. Thus, the portfolios are formed conditional upon excess return behavior prior to $t = 0$, the portfolio formation date.

3. For both portfolios in each of 16 nonoverlapping three-year periods ($n =$

---

[3] We will come back to this bias in Section II.

1, ..., N; $N = 16$), starting in January 1933 (month 85, the "starting month") and up to December 1980, we now compute the cumulative average residual returns of all securities in the portfolio, for the next 36 months (the "test period," months 85 through 120), i.e., from $t = 1$ through $t = 36$. We find $CAR_{W,n,t}$ and $CAR_{L,n,t}$. If a security's return is missing in a month subsequent to portfolio formation, then, from that moment on, the stock is permanently dropped from the portfolio and the CAR is an average of the available residual returns. Thus, whenever a stock drops out, the calculations involve an implicit rebalancing.[4]

4. Using the CAR's from all 16 test periods, *average* CAR's are calculated for both portfolios and each month between $t = 1$ and $t = 36$. They are denoted $ACAR_{W,t}$ and $ACAR_{L,t}$. The overreaction hypothesis predicts that, for $t > 0$, $ACAR_{W,t} < 0$ and $ACAR_{L,t} > 0$, so that, by implication, $[ACAR_{L,t} - ACAR_{W,t}] > 0$. In order to assess whether, at any time t, there is indeed a statistically significant difference in investment performance, we need a pooled estimate of the population variance in CAR_t,

$$S_t^2 = [\sum_{n=1}^{N}(CAR_{W,n,t} - ACAR_{W,t})^2 + \sum_{n=1}^{N}(CAR_{L,n,t} - ACAR_{L,t})^2]/2(N-1).$$

With two samples of equal size N, the variance of the difference of sample means equals $2S_t^2/N$ and the t-statistic is therefore

$$T_t = [ACAR_{L,t} - ACAR_{W,t}]/\sqrt{2S_t^2/N}.$$

Relevant t-statistics can be found for each of the 36 postformation months but they do not represent independent evidence.

5. In order to judge whether, for any month t, the average residual return makes a contribution to either $ACAR_{W,t}$ or $ACAR_{L,t}$, we can test whether it is significantly different from zero. The sample standard deviation of the winner portfolio is equal to

$$s_t = \sqrt{\sum_{n=1}^{N}(AR_{W,n,t} - AR_{W,t})^2/N - 1}.$$

Since $s_t/\sqrt{N}$ represents the sample estimate of the standard error of $AR_{W,t}$, the t-statistic equals

$$T_t = AR_{W,t}/(s_t/\sqrt{N}).$$

Similar procedures apply for the residuals of the loser portfolio.

B. Discussion

Several aspects of the research design deserve some further comment. The choice of the data base, the CRSP Monthly Return File, is in part justified by

---

[4] Since this study concentrates on companies that experience extraordinary returns, either positive or negative, there may be some concern that their attrition rate sufficiently deviates from the "normal" rate so as to cause a survivorship bias. However, this concern is unjustified. When a security is delisted, suspended or halted, CRSP determines whether or not it is possible to trade at the last listed price. If no trade is possible, CRSP tries to find a subsequent quote and uses it to compute a return for the last period. If no such quote is available because the stockholders receive nothing for their shares, the return is entered as minus one. If trading continues, the last return ends with the last listed price.

our concern to avoid certain measurement problems that have received much attention in the literature. Most of the problems arise with the use of daily data, both with respect to the risk and return variables. They include, among others, the "bid-ask" effect and the consequences of infrequent trading.

The requirement that 85 subsequent returns are available before any firm is allowed in the sample biases the selection towards large, established firms. But, if the effect under study can be shown to apply to them, the results are, if anything, more interesting. In particular, it counters the predictable critique that the overreaction effect may be mostly a small-firm phenomenon. For the experiment described in Section A, between 347 and 1,089 NYSE stocks participate in the various replications.

The decision to study the CAR's for a period of 36 months after the portfolio formation date reflects a compromise between statistical and economic considerations, namely, an adequate number of independent replications versus a time period long enough to study issues relevant to asset pricing theory. In addition, the three-year period is also of interest in light of Benjamin Graham's contention that "the interval required for a substantial underevaluation to correct itself averages approximately 1½ to 2½ years" [10, p. 37]. However, for selected experiments, the portfolio formation (and testing) periods are one, two, and five years long. Clearly, the number of independent replications varies inversely with the length of the formation period.

Finally, the choice of December as the "portfolio formation month" (and, therefore, of January as the "starting month") is essentially arbitrary. In order to check whether the choice affects the results, some of the empirical tests use May as the portfolio formation month.

II. The Overreaction Hypothesis: Empirical Results

A. Main Findings

The results of the tests developed in Section I are found in Figure 1. They are consistent with the overreaction hypothesis. Over the last half-century, loser portfolios of 35 stocks outperform the market by, on average, 19.6%, thirty-six months after portfolio formation. Winner portfolios, on the other hand, earn about 5.0% less than the market, so that the difference in cumulative average residual between the extreme portfolios, $[ACAR_{L,36} - ACAR_{W,36}]$ equals 24.6% (t-statistic: 2.20). Figure 1 shows the movement of the ACAR's as we progress through the test period.

The findings have other notable aspects. First, the overreaction effect is asymmetric; it is much larger for losers than for winners. Secondly, consistent with previous work on the turn-of-the-year effect and seasonality, most of the excess returns are realized in January. In months $t = 1$, $t = 13$, and $t = 25$, the loser portfolio earns excess returns of, respectively, 8.1% (t-statistic: 3.21), 5.6% (3.07), and 4.0% (2.76). Finally, in surprising agreement with Benjamin Graham's claim, the overreaction phenomenon mostly occurs during the second and third year of the test period. Twelve months into the test period, the difference in performance between the extreme portfolios is a mere 5.4% (t-statistic: 0.77).

Average of 16 Three-Year Test Periods
Between January 1933 and December 1980
Length of Formation Period: Three Years

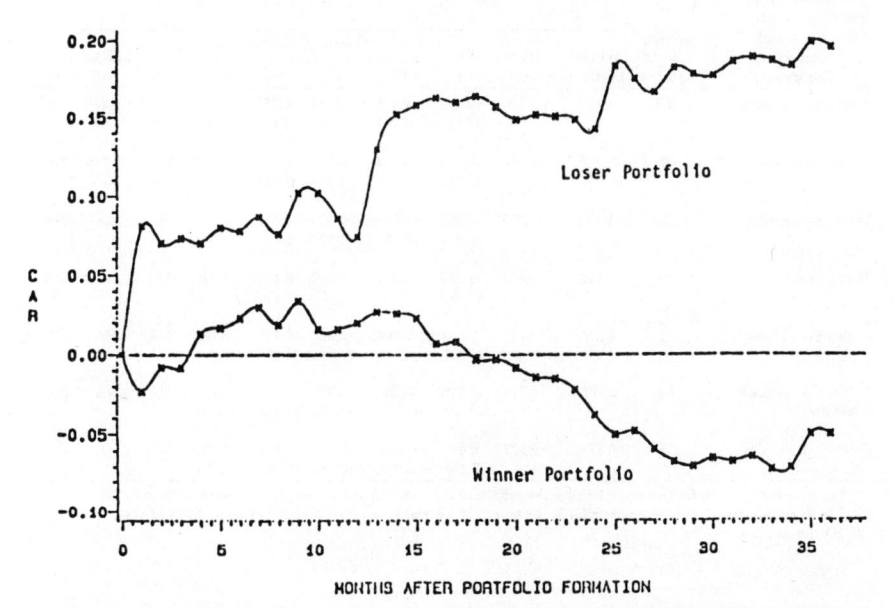

Figure 1. Cumulative Average Residuals for Winner and Loser Portfolios of 35 Stocks (1-36 months into the test period)

While not reported here, the results using market model and Sharpe-Lintner residuals are similar. They are also insensitive to the choice of December as the month of portfolio formation (see De Bondt [7]).

The overreaction hypothesis predicts that, as we focus on stocks that go through more (or less) extreme return experiences (during the formation period), the subsequent price reversals will be more (or less) pronounced. An easy way to generate more (less) extreme observations is to lengthen (shorten) the portfolio formation period; alternatively, for any given formation period (say, two years), we may compare the test period performance of less versus more extreme portfolios, e.g., decile portfolios (which contain an average 82 stocks) versus portfolios of 35 stocks. Table I confirms the prediction of the overreaction hypothesis. As the cumulative average residuals (during the formation period) for various sets of winner and loser portfolios grow larger, so do the subsequent price reversals, measured by $[ACAR_{L,t} - ACAR_{W,t}]$ and the accompanying t-statistics. For a formation period as short as one year, no reversal is observed at all.

Table I and Figure 2 further indicate that the overreaction phenomenon is qualitatively different from the January effect and, more generally, from season-

Table I
Differences in Cumulative Average (Market-Adjusted) Residual Returns Between the Winner and Loser Portfolios at the End of the Formation Period, and 1, 12, 13, 18, 24, 25, 36, and 60 Months into the Test Period

Portfolio Selection Procedures: Length of the Formation Period and No. of Independent Replications	Average No. of Stocks	CAR at the End of the Formation Period — Winner Portfolio	CAR at the End of the Formation Period — Loser Portfolio	Difference in CAR (t-Statistics) Months After Portfolio Formation: 1	12	13	18	24	25	36	60
10 five-year periods	50	1.463	−1.194	0.070 (3.13)	0.156 (2.04)	0.248 (3.14)	0.256 (3.17)	0.196 (2.15)	0.228 (2.40)	0.230 (2.07)	0.319 (3.28)
16 three-year periods	35	1.375	−1.064	0.105 (3.29)	0.054 (0.77)	0.103 (1.18)	0.167 (1.51)	0.181 (1.71)	0.234 (2.19)	0.246 (2.20)	NA[c]
24 two-year periods[a]	35	1.130	−0.857	0.062 (2.91)	−0.006 (−0.16)	0.074 (1.53)	0.136 (2.02)	0.101 (1.41)	NA	NA	NA
25 two-year periods[b]	35	1.119	−0.866	0.089 (3.98)	0.011 (0.19)	0.092 (1.48)	0.107 (1.47)	0.115 (1.55)	NA	NA	NA
24 two-year periods[a] (deciles)	82	0.875	−0.711	0.051 (3.13)	0.006 (0.19)	0.066 (1.71)	0.105 (1.99)	0.083 (1.49)	NA	NA	NA
25 two-year periods[b] (deciles)	82	0.868	−0.714	0.068 (3.86)	0.008 (0.19)	0.071 (1.46)	0.078 (1.41)	0.072 (1.29)	NA	NA	NA
49 one-year periods	35	0.774	−0.585	0.042 (2.45)	−0.076 (−2.32)	−0.006 (−0.15)	0.007 (0.14)	−0.005 (−0.09)	NA	NA	NA

[a] The formation month for these portfolios is the month of December in all uneven years between 1933 and 1979.
[b] The formation month for these portfolios is the month of December in all even years between 1932 and 1980.
[c] NA, not applicable.

ality in stock prices. Throughout the test period, the difference in ACAR for the experiment with a three-year formation period (the upper curve) exceeds the same statistic for the experiments based on two- and one-year formation periods (middle and lower curves). But all three experiments are clearly affected by the same underlying seasonal pattern.

In Section I, it was mentioned that the use of market-adjusted excess returns is likely to bias the research design against the overreaction hypothesis. The bias can be seen by comparing the CAPM-betas of the extreme portfolios. For all the experiments listed in Table I, the average betas of the securities in the winner portfolios are significantly larger than the betas of the loser portfolios.[5] For example, for the three-year experiment illustrated in Figure 1, the relevant numbers are respectively, 1.369 and 1.026 (t-statistic on the difference: 3.09). Thus, the loser portfolios not only outperform the winner portfolios; if the CAPM is correct, they are also significantly less risky. From a different viewpoint, therefore, the results in Table I are likely to *underestimate* both the true magnitude and statistical significance of the overreaction effect. The problem is particularly severe with respect to the winner portfolio. Rather than 1.369, the residual return calculations assume the CAPM-beta of that portfolio to equal

---

[5] The CAPM-betas are found by estimating the market model over a period of 60 months prior to portfolio formation.

Average of 49 One-Year Periods,
24 Two-Year Periods, 16 Three-year Periods
Between January 1931 and December 1982

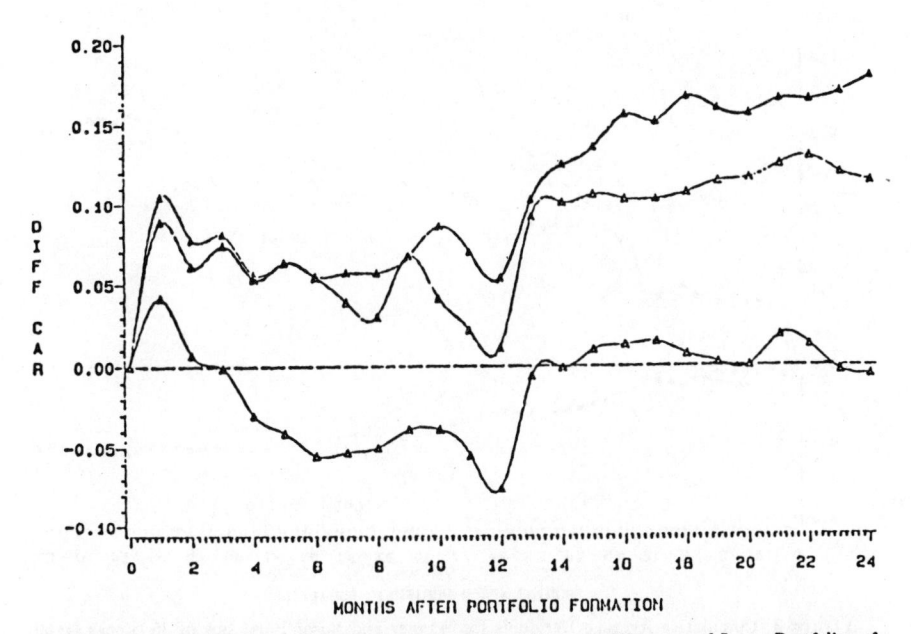

Figure 2. Differences in Cumulative Average Residual Between Winner and Loser Portfolios of 35 Stocks (formed over the previous one, two, or three years; 1-24 months into the test period)

1.00 only. This systematic bias may be responsible for the earlier observed asymmetry in the return behavior of the extreme portfolios.

To reiterate, the previous findings are broadly consistent with the predictions of the overreaction hypothesis. However, several aspects of the results remain without adequate explanation. Most importantly, the extraordinarily large positive excess returns earned by the loser portfolio in January.

One method that allows us to further accentuate the strength of the January effect is to increase the number of replications. Figure 3 shows the ACAR's for an experiment with a five-year-long test period. Every December between 1932 and 1977, winner and loser portfolios are formed on the basis of residual return behavior over the previous five years. Clearly, the successive 46 yearly selections are not independent. Therefore, no statistical tests are performed. The results in Figure 3 have some of the properties of a "trading rule." They represent the average (cumulative) excess return (before transaction costs) that an investor, aware of the overreaction phenomenon, could expect to earn following any

Average of 46 Yearly Replications
Starting Every January Between 1933 and 1978
Length of Formation Period: Five Years

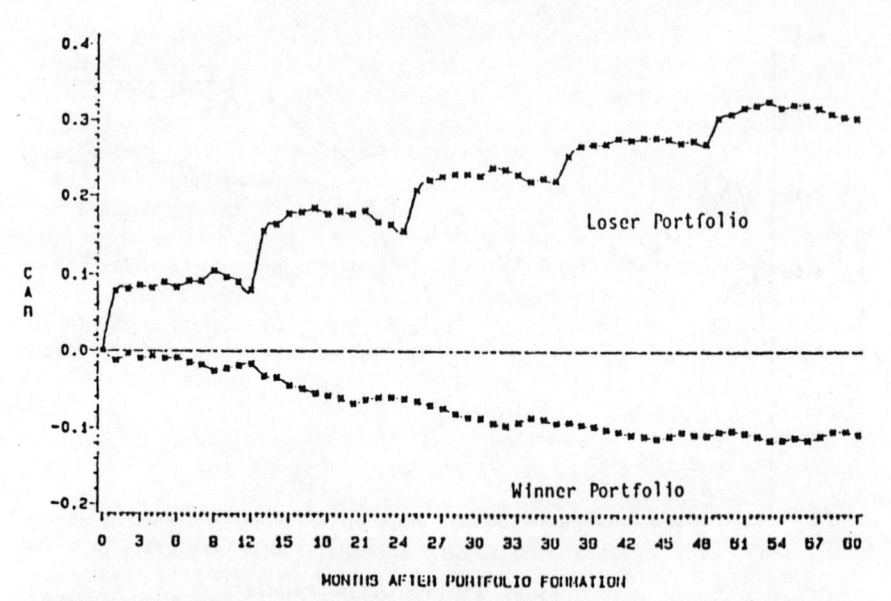

Figure 3. Cumulative Average Residuals for Winner and Loser Portfolios of 35 Stocks (1–60 months into the test period)

December in which he chose to try the strategy. The effect of multiplying the number of replications is to remove part of the random noise.

The outstanding feature of Figure 3 is, once again, the January returns on the loser portfolio. The effect is observed as late as five Januaries after portfolio formation! Careful examination of Figure 3 also reveals a tendency, on the part of the loser portfolio, to decline in value (relative to the market) between October and December. This observation is in agreement with the naive version of the tax-loss selling hypothesis as explained by, e.g., Schwert [25]. The winner portfolio, on the other hand, gains value at the end of the year and loses some in January (for more details, see De Bondt [7]).

B. Implications for Other Empirical Work

The results of this study have interesting implications for previous work on the small firm effect, the January effect and the dividend yield and *P/E* effects. Blume and Stambaugh [6], Keim [16], and Reinganum [21] have studied the interaction between the small firm and January effects. Their findings largely redefine the small firm effect as a "losing firm" effect around the turn-of-the-year.[6] Our own results lend further credence to this view. Persistently, losers earn exceptionally large January returns while winners do not. However, the companies in the extreme portfolios do not systematically differ with respect to market capitalization.

The January phenomenon is usually explained by tax-loss selling (see, e.g., Roll [23]). Our own findings raise new questions with respect to this hypothesis. First, if in early January selling pressure disappears and prices "rebound" to equilibrium levels, why does the loser portfolio—even while it outperforms the market—"rebound" once again in the second January of the test period? And again, in the third and fourth Januaries? Secondly, if prices "rebound" in January, why is that effect so much larger in magnitude than the selling pressure that "caused" it during the final months of the previous year? Possible answers to these questions include the argument that investors may wait for years before realizing losses, and the observed seasonality of the market as a whole.

With respect to the P/E effect, our results support the price-ratio hypothesis discussed in the introduction, i.e., high P/E stocks are "overvalued" whereas low P/E stocks are "undervalued." However, this argument implies that the P/E effect is also, for the most part, a January phenomenon. At present, there is no evidence to support that claim, except for the persistent positive relationship between dividend yield (a variable that is correlated with the P/E ratio) and January excess returns (Keim [15]).

III. Conclusions

Research in experimental psychology has suggested that, in violation of Bayes' rule, most people "overreact" to unexpected and dramatic news events. The question then arises whether such behavior matters at the market level.

Consistent with the predictions of the overreaction hypothesis, portfolios of prior "losers" are found to outperform prior "winners." Thirty-six months after portfolio formation, the losing stocks have earned about 25% more than the winners, even though the latter are significantly more risky.

Several aspects of the results remain without adequate explanation; most importantly, the large positive excess returns earned by the loser portfolio every January. Much to our surprise, the effect is observed as late as five years after portfolio formation.

---

[6] Even after purging the data of tax-loss selling effects, Reinganum [22] finds a (considerably smaller) January seasonal effect related to company size. This result may be due to his particular definition of the tax-loss selling measure. The measure is related to the securities' relative price movements over the last *six months* prior to portfolio formation only. Thus, if many investors choose to wait longer than six months before realizing losses, the portfolio of small firms may still contain many "losers."

REFERENCES

1. K. J. Arrow. "Risk Perception in Psychology and Economics." *Economic Inquiry* 20 (January 1982), 1–9.

2. R. Ball. "Anomalies in Relationships Between Securities' Yields and Yield-Surrogates." *Journal of Financial Economics* 6 (June–September 1978), 103–26.
3. S. Basu. "Investment Performance of Common Stocks in Relation to Their Price-Earnings Ratios: A Test of the Efficient Market Hypothesis." *Journal of Finance* 3 (June 1977), 663–82.
4. ———. "The Relationship Between Earnings' Yield, Market Value and Return for NYSE Common Stocks: Further Evidence." *Journal of Financial Economics* 12 (June 1983), 129–56.
5. W. Beaver and W. R. Landsman. "Note on the Behavior of Residual Security Returns for Winner and Loser Portfolios." *Journal of Accounting and Economics* 3 (December 1981), 233–41.
6. M. Blume and R. Stambaugh. "Biases in Computed Returns: An Application to the Size Effect." *Journal of Financial Economics* 12 (November 1983), 387–404.
7. W. F. M. De Bondt. "Does the Stock Market Overreact to New Information?" Unpublished Ph.D. dissertation, Cornell University, 1985.
8. D. N. Dreman. *The New Contrarian Investment Strategy*. New York: Random House, 1982.
9. E. F. Fama. *Foundations of Finance*. New York: Basic Books, Inc., 1976.
10. B. Graham. *The Intelligent Investor, A Book of Practical Counsel*, 3rd ed. New York: Harper & Brothers Publishers, 1959.
11. ———. *The Intelligent Investor, A Book of Practical Counsel*, 4th rev. ed. New York: Harper & Brothers Publishers, 1973.
12. D. M. Grether. "Bayes Rule as a Descriptive Model: The Representativeness Heuristic." *Quarterly Journal of Economics* 95 (November 1980), 537–57.
13. R. Jarrow. "Beliefs, Information, Martingales, and Arbitrage Pricing." Working Paper, Johnson Graduate School of Management, Cornell University, November 1983.
14. D. Kahneman and A. Tversky. "Intuitive Prediction: Biases and Corrective Procedures." In D. Kahneman, P. Slovic, and A. Tversky, (eds.), *Judgment Under Uncertainty: Heuristics and Biases*. London: Cambridge University Press, 1982.
15. D. Keim. "Further Evidence on Size Effects and Yield Effects: The Implications of Stock Return Seasonality." Working Paper, Graduate School of Business, University of Chicago, April 1982.
16. ———. "Size-Related Anomalies and Stock Return Seasonality: Further Empirical Evidence." *Journal of Financial Economics* 12 (June 1983), 13–32.
17. J. M. Keynes. *The General Theory of Employment, Interest and Money*. London: Harcourt Brace Jovanovich, 1964 (reprint of the 1936 edition).
18. A. W. Kleidon. "Stock Prices as Rational Forecasters of Future Cash Flows." Working Paper, Graduate School of Business, University of Chicago, November 1981.
19. T. A. Marsh and R. C. Merton. "Aggregate Dividend Behavior and Its Implications for Tests of Stock Market Rationality." Working Paper No. 1475-83, Sloan School of Management, MIT, September 1983.
20. J. A. Ohlson and S. H. Penman. "Variance Increases Subsequent to Stock Splits: An Empirical Aberration." Working Paper, Graduate School of Business, Columbia University, September 1983.
21. M. R. Reinganum. "Misspecification of Capital Asset Pricing: Empirical Anomalies Based on Earnings' Yields and Market Values." *Journal of Financial Economics* 9 (March 1981), 19–46.
22. ———. "The Anomalous Stock Market Behavior of Small Firms in January." *Journal of Financial Economics* 12 (June 1983), 89–104.
23. R. Roll. "Vas ist das?". *Journal of Portfolio Management* 10 (Winter 1983), 18–28.
24. T. Russell and R. Thaler. "The Relevance of Quasi-Rationality in Competitive Markets." *American Economic Review* 75 (1985), forthcoming.
25. G. W. Schwert. "Size and Stock Returns, and Other Empirical Regularities." *Journal of Financial Economics* 12 (June 1983), 3–12.
26. R. J. Shiller. "The Volatility of Long-Term Interest Rates and Expectations Models of the Term Structure." *Journal of Political Economy* 87 (December 1979), 1190–1219.
27. ———. "Do Stock Prices Move Too Much to be Justified by Subsequent Changes in Dividends?" *American Economic Review* 71 (June 1981), 421–36.
28. J. B. Williams. *The Theory of Investment Value*. Amsterdam: North-Holland, 1956 (reprint of 1938 edition).

THE QUARTERLY JOURNAL OF ECONOMICS

Vol. CV   February 1990   Issue 1

FADS, MARTINGALES, AND MARKET EFFICIENCY*

Bruce N. Lehmann

> Predictable variation in equity returns might reflect either (1) predictable changes in expected returns or (2) market inefficiency and stock price "overreaction." These explanations can be distinguished by examining returns over short time intervals since systematic changes in fundamental valuation over intervals like a week should not occur in efficient markets. The evidence suggests that the "winners" and "losers" one week experience sizeable return reversals the next week in a way that reflects apparent arbitrage profits which persist after corrections for bid-ask spreads and plausible transactions costs. This probably reflects inefficiency in the market for liquidity around large price changes.

I. Introduction

Much of the theoretical basis for current monetary and financial theory rests on the efficiency of financial markets. Considerable effort has been expended testing the efficient markets hypothesis, usually in the form of the random walk model for stock prices. Most early studies supported the random walk model, finding that the predictable variation in equity returns was both economically and

---

*Thanks are due to Joanna W. Woos for efficient and remarkably joyful research assistance. This paper was completed while I was a National Fellow at the Hoover Institution and an Olin Fellow at the National Bureau of Economic Research. I am extremely grateful to both organizations for their support, hospitality, and excellent research environments. I thank David Cutler, Sandy Grossman, Ravi Jagannathan, Greg Kipnis, Peter Kyle, Dean LeBaron, Dick Michaud, Jay Ritter, Andrei Shleifer, Seymour Smidt, Larry Summers, Steve Zeldes, and seminar participants at the Berkeley Program in Finance, Brown University, Carnegie Mellon University, Columbia University, Cornell University. Harvard University, Massachusetts Institute of Technology, the NBER Summer Institute and Universities Research Conference on Financial Markets and Macroeconomic Stability, Stanford University, the University of Alberta, the Universities of California at Berkeley, Davis, San Diego, and Santa Cruz, the University of Illinois, the University of Iowa, the University of Michigan, the University of Minnesota, and the University of Pennsylvania for helpful comments. They share no responsibility for any remaining errors.

© 1990 by the President and Fellows of Harvard College and the Massachusetts Institute of Technology.
The Quarterly Journal of Economics, February 1990

statistically small. However, much recent research has found evidence that equity returns can be predicted with some reliability.[1]

These are two competing explanations of this phenomenon. The first is that required returns vary through time, resulting in predictable, but efficient, mean reversion in stock prices. Alternatively, the predictability of equity returns may reflect the overreaction of stock prices, "fads," or the cognitive misperceptions of investors in an inefficient market as suggested by Shiller [1984], Black [1986], Poterba and Summers [1987], DeBondt and Thaler [1985, 1987], and Shefrin and Statman [1985].

These two explanations can be distinguished by examining asset returns over short time intervals. As Sims [1984] and others have emphasized, asset prices should follow a martingale process over very short time intervals even if there are predictable variations in expected security returns over longer horizons—systematic short-run changes in fundamental values should be negligible in an efficient market with unpredictable information arrival. Fads models, in contrast, predict serial correlation over all time intervals, although most versions emphasize predictability over long time intervals.

While rejection of martingale behavior over short horizons is evidence against market efficiency, such evidence probably reflects inefficiency in the market for liquidity in common stocks. In other words, short-run price movements probably provide little information about the long-term differences between prices and fundamental values typically emphasized in fads models. Pricing fads may be more economically interesting, but potential short-run inefficiencies in financial markets are probably more easily and precisely measured.[2]

Nevertheless, there remain severe econometric problems associated with the construction of powerful tests of this short-run martingale hypothesis. Shiller [1981], Shiller and Perron [1985], and Summers [1986] have emphasized the low power of standard tests for serial correlation when applied to security returns. This problem is particularly severe over short differencing intervals.

---

1. See Fama [1970] and Singleton [1987] for surveys of the evidence on predictable variation.
2. There is considerable evidence of systematic reversals in stock returns over longer intervals. DeBondt and Thaler [1985], Fama and French [1987], and Poterba and Summers [1987] found evidence for such variation over three-to-ten-year intervals. Rosenberg, Reid, and Lanstein [1985] and Jegadeesh [1987] provided sharp evidence at the monthly frequency. Chan [1988] argued that the evidence in DeBondt and Thaler [1985] is attributable in part to changes in the riskiness of winners and losers, an interpretation contested in DeBondt and Thaler [1987].

FADS, MARTINGALES, AND MARKET EFFICIENCY

Many assets are traded on organized securities markets. It is reasonable to suppose that any stock price overreaction infects many security returns for both security or industry-specific and market-wide reasons. Hence, well-diversified portfolios composed of either "winners" or "losers" might be expected to experience return reversals in these circumstances, suggesting a simple heuristic strategy for testing market efficiency: study the profits of costless (i.e., zero net investment) portfolios which give negative weight to recent winners and positive weight to recent losers. The short-run martingale model predicts that these costless portfolios should tend to earn zero profits. In contrast, these costless portfolios will typically profit from return reversals over some horizon if stock prices "overreact."[3]

The remainder of the paper quantifies this intuition and tests its empirical implications. The next section analyzes the testing procedure and contrasts it with more conventional approaches. The subsequent section discusses implementation issues and addresses some potential problems. The fourth section provides empirical evidence, and the final section contains concluding remarks.

II. THE PROFITS ON RETURN REVERSAL PORTFOLIO STRATEGIES

Portfolios that involve short positions in securities that experienced recent price increases and long positions in those that suffered recent price declines might earn abnormal profits if asset prices partially reflect overreaction to speculative fads. The employment of this intuition to test the market efficiency hypothesis requires the development of measures of abnormal profits. This section discusses the comparative merits of two such strategies.

To make matters concrete, consider the following portfolio strategies involving a given set of N securities over T time periods. At the beginning of period t, buy w_{it-k} dollars of each security i. This involves going long security i when w_{it-k} is positive and short selling it when this quantity is negative. Each position is closed out at the end of time t. Choose the weights w_{it-k} so that they are negative when security i is a winner and positive when security i is a loser.

In particular, set the number of dollars invested in each security proportional to the previous period's return (R_{it-k}) less the

---

3. This strategy avoids the power difficulties associated with *time series* autocorrelation tests by the *cross-sectional* aggregation of autocorrelation information, an intuition exploited by Jegadeesh [1987] to develop powerful cross-sectional tests of linear asset pricing relations.

return of an equally weighted portfolio of these N assets in that period ($\bar{R}_{t-k}$). Ignoring the factor of proportionality, the weights are given by

(1) $$w_{it-k} = -[R_{it-k} - \bar{R}_{t-k}]; \qquad \bar{R}_{t-k} = \frac{1}{N} \sum_{i=1}^{N} R_{it-k}.$$

Accounting profits in period t ($\pi_{t,k}$) are[4]

(2) $$\pi_{t,k} = \sum_{i=1}^{N} w_{it-k} R_{it} = -\sum_{i=1}^{N} [R_{it-k} - \bar{R}_{t-k}][R_{it} - \bar{R}_t],$$

so that the average profit ($\bar{\pi}_k$) on this k period ahead portfolio strategy over T periods is

(3) $$\bar{\pi}_k = \frac{1}{T} \sum_{t=1}^{T} \pi_{t,k} = -\frac{1}{T} \sum_{t=1}^{T} \sum_{i=1}^{N} [R_{it-k} - \bar{R}_{t-k}][R_{it} - \bar{R}_t].$$

Algebraic manipulation of this expression yields

(4) $$\bar{\pi}_k = \frac{N}{T} \sum_{t=1}^{T} [\bar{R}_{t-k} - \bar{\bar{R}}][\bar{R}_t - \bar{\bar{R}}]$$
$$- \frac{1}{T} \sum_{t=1}^{T} \sum_{i=1}^{N} [R_{it-k} - \bar{R}_i][R_{it} - \bar{R}_i] - \sum_{i=1}^{N} [\bar{R}_i - \bar{\bar{R}}]^2,$$

where

(5) $$\bar{\bar{R}} = \frac{1}{T} \sum_{t=1}^{T} \bar{R}_t; \qquad \bar{R}_i = \frac{1}{T} \sum_{t=1}^{T} R_{it}$$

are the average returns of the equally weighted portfolio and of security i over time, respectively.[5] Thus, average portfolio profits depend on the autocovariances of the returns of an equally weighted portfolio, the autocovariances of the returns of the individual securities, and the cross-sectional variation in the unconditional mean returns of the individual securities.

Does the hypothesis of market efficiency place restrictions on either $\bar{\pi}_k$ or $\pi_{t,k}$? The traditional answer to this question reflects Fama's [1970, pp. 413–14] suggestion that the efficient markets hypothesis "only has empirical content, however, within a context of a more specific model of market equilibrium, that is, a model that specifies the nature of market equilibrium when prices 'fully reflect' available information." For example, it is common to assume that security returns are independently distributed (and often identically distributed as well) with constant expected returns in both the filter rule and the monthly return reversal literatures.

---

4. These are profits because this is a zero net investment strategy, and hence, returns are not defined.
5. Relation (4) holds for population moments as well and is studied in Lo and MacKinlay [1988].

If security returns are independently distributed over time, the population autocovariances of both individual securities and the equally weighted portfolio are zero. Hence, expected average profits on the return reversal portfolio strategies are

$$(6) \qquad E\{\overline{\pi}_k\} = -E\left\{\sum_{i=1}^{N} [\overline{R}_i - \overline{\overline{R}}]^2\right\}$$

with two testable implications: expected average profits should be negative and identical for each value of k.[6] This makes intuitive sense—on average, return reversal strategies are long securities with below average expected returns and short those with above average expected returns and thus systematically lose the cross-sectional variation in expected returns in these circumstances.

As with most market efficiency tests, rejection of the hypothesis that average portfolio profits are identical for each value of k might simply indicate that returns are not independently distributed, perhaps because of time-varying expected returns in an efficient market. Put differently, the probability of rejecting the null hypothesis of market efficiency when it is true (i.e., a Type I error) involves both the usual sampling errors and the probability that security returns are not independently distributed. In other words, the conventional approach to testing the hypothesis of market efficiency with return reversal portfolios is not likely to yield a useful test in the absence of a plausible a priori model of temporal variation in expected returns.

An alternative strategy is suggested by the local martingale literature: the variation in short-run expected returns cannot be too pronounced, or else intertemporally well-diversified portfolio strategies will be too profitable. That is, strategies that bet on expected return changes without concentrating investment in any short period will earn arbitrage profits if very short-run security price changes are predictable.[7] If securities experience predictable price reversals, a simple market efficiency test can be based on time-

---

6. This is a version of a result derived in Jegadeesh [1987] for linear asset pricing relations.

7. The following example illustrates the intertemporal diversification argument. The typical annualized standard deviation of daily returns is 20 percent per year. Let E_t be the conditional expected return of a security in day t. Consider the strategy of buying E_t dollars of the security (which is a short sale when this quantity is negative) at the beginning of day t and closing out the position at the end of the day. If both the variance of squared daily expected returns and the covariance between squared daily expected returns and security volatility make a negligible contribution to portfolio profit variance, the expected annual profit on this strategy is more than 6,000 times its variance. This strategy is virtually riskless, unless daily expected returns and their variance are both very small (i.e., if there are no "near" arbitrage opportunities).

aggregated return reversal portfolio profits, which reflect the payoff to an intertemporally well-diversified strategy.

In particular, consider the J period profits:

$$\pi^J_{t,k} = \sum_{j=t+1}^{t+J} \pi_{j,k}. \tag{7}$$

The return reversal strategies reflect a *measured* arbitrage opportunity if these J period profits are consistently of one sign over the T/J periods covered by the data. This is evidence against the market efficiency hypothesis since these costless portfolios are riskless ex post in these circumstances. Failure to find a measured arbitrage opportunity involves failure to reject the joint hypothesis that the market is efficient and that the J period profits reflect the payoff of an intertemporally well-diversified portfolio strategy.

There is a major difference between the test based on measured arbitrage opportunities and that predicted on a model of market equilibrium. This test has a small Type I error rate, although it can easily result in failure to reject the market efficiency hypothesis when it is false (i.e., a Type II error).[8] This stands in sharp contrast to the conventional approach where Type I errors result from both the usual sampling problems and failure of the underlying model of market equilibrium.[9]

This test avoids the problems associated with specifying a model for expected return variation at the cost of requiring measured arbitrage opportunities to reject the hypothesis of market efficiency, a very stringent test that makes false rejection of the market efficiency hypothesis difficult. In addition, these portfolio strategies can, at best, only detect sources of market inefficiency that give rise to particular short-term arbitrage opportunities. For example, it is possible to construct models in which prices deviate from fundamental values because of fads or noise trading without giving rise to riskless arbitrage opportunities as in Campbell and

---

8. A Type I error occurs when an investigator concludes that an ex ante costless portfolio that was self-financing (i.e., earned strictly positive profits) ex post by chance was riskless ex ante.

9. There is another way to see this distinction. Average return reversal profits converge to zero in the limit of continuous trading. The assumption that J period profits reflect the payoff of an intertemporally well-diversified strategy involves the assumption that trading over discrete time intervals closely approximates continuous trading. A test of the null hypothesis that average return reversal portfolio profits are zero encounters the same conceptual difficulty as that based on the independence of security returns. The probability of rejecting this null hypothesis when it is true depends on the sampling errors in average return reversal portfolio profits as well as the probability that discrete trading well approximates continuous trading.

Kyle [1987] and De Long, Shleifer, Summers, and Waldmann [1987]. Alternatively, speculative fads may be market-wide, giving rise to long-term swings in stock prices such as bull and bear markets. In other words, speculative fads may have an important influence on asset prices but need not be reflected in short-run return reversal portfolio profits.

III. EMPIRICAL METHODS, POTENTIAL PROBLEMS, AND SAFEGUARDS

While the discussion of the previous section pointed to a general strategy for testing market efficiency, it left several choices open: (1) the appropriate set of securities; (2) the lag length k; (3) the horizon over which to aggregate portfolio profits (i.e., J); and (4) the time interval t over which the local martingale model applies under the efficient markets hypothesis. Moreover, the discussion neglected taxes, transactions costs, and other impediments to trade and presumed that prices could be measured without error.

Each of these issues requires careful a priori consideration. While this is a truism about empirical work in general, it has special force here since the strategy involves the search for unexploited arbitrage opportunities. It is obviously trivial to generate portfolio strategies that were profitable ex post but that need not have been profitable ex ante.

The empirical work that follows reflects one plausible set of a priori choices.[10] The asset menu was restricted to equity securities listed on the New York and American Stock Exchanges because the Center for Research in Security Prices (**CRSP**) returns file contains daily observations on all such securities from 1962 to present. Portfolio weights were taken to be proportional to the difference between the return of security i and the return on an equally weighted portfolio at different lags. Finally, a week was taken to be a sufficiently short period for the local martingale model to apply

---

10. This is also the only strategy that I have studied, and hence, the results reflect no obvious retrospective biases with one major exception: the fact that I read papers in the monthly and longer horizon return reversal literature prior to embarking on this study (particularly Jegadeesh [1987]). However, note that there is one ex ante forecast implicit here: the 1986 results were obtained after the first draft of this paper was circulated. Note also that most reasonable alterations of the analysis would probably increase measured portfolio profits. For example, all securities listed on the **NYSE** and the **AMEX** were included, even though a reasonable ex ante expectation is that small winners and losers contribute primarily to transactions costs and not to portfolio profitability.

while the horizon of the portfolio strategy was set to twenty-six weeks.[11]

The empirical work proceeded as follows. Every week, all securities that were listed on the New York and American Stock Exchanges in that week and k weeks previously were selected for inclusion in the portfolio strategy.[12] The number of dollars invested in each security was proportional to the return in week k less the return of the equally weighted portfolio of the included securities.[13] The factor of proportionality was the inverse of the sum of the positive deviations of individual security returns from this mean, making the portfolios long and short one dollar of equity securities. Hence, the number of dollars invested in security i in week t was

$$(8) \qquad w_{it-k} = -[R_{it-k} - \overline{R}_{t-k}] \bigg/ \sum_{\{R_{it-k} - \overline{R}_{t-k} > 0\}} R_{it-k} - \overline{R}_{t-k}.$$

These portfolio weights yield profits that are the difference in the returns on two dollar portfolios and, hence, are measured in units of percent per week.[14] The weights were then multiplied by the return on the corresponding security k weeks hence, and these returns were summed to arrive at portfolio profits for the week as in (2). Finally, this process was repeated for J weeks to generate the total profits on the strategy for the portfolio horizon J as in (7).[15]

---

11. Shorter intervals such as days were deemed inappropriate for reasons discussed below and other strategy horizons are reported below. A week was taken to begin on Wednesday and end on Tuesday to mimimize the number of days that exchanges were closed over the sample.

12. There is some room for selection bias since an investor would not know now that a firm would still exist in k weeks. Fortunately, the amount of delisting on the CRSP tapes is sufficiently small (especially over a few weeks) that this bias probably has little impact on the results. In addition, delisting alone overstates any upward bias in portfolio profits since firms typically leave the CRSP tapes for many reasons including name changes and takeovers.

13. Investors do not have full use of the proceeds of short sales in equity markets and, hence, cannot finance long positions with short sales. This is probably not cause for concern for three reasons. First, costless portfolios can be thought of as either an arbitrage strategy or as a marginal change in an existing portfolio that is long all of the securities that meet the criterion for inclusion. The restriction on the use of the proceeds from short sales has no force under the latter interpretation. Second, existing margin requirements require putting up margin for half of the market value of the long position, and large investors (such as broker-dealers) can costlessly use available marginable securities as collateral. Finally, borrowing costs are very small (less than 0.2 percent per week).

14. This is not necessarily innocuous since the scaling factor changes from week to week. The results change little when this scaling factor is omitted. The scaling factor can be thought of as a measure of the cross-sectional variation in returns in a given week.

15. Note that the profits for horizon J are the unweighted sum of the profits for each of the J weeks. This ignores the interest that could be earned (or the interest expense that could be incurred) on these profits within the J weeks. This is analogous to the treatment of dividends and coupon payments in the computation of bond and stock returns.

FADS, MARTINGALES, AND MARKET EFFICIENCY

There is a major empirical problem with using weekly security returns to detect market inefficiency in this fashion: there are predictable fluctuations in *measured* security returns that have nothing to do with market inefficiency. Eighty percent of the price movements over successive transactions are between the bid and asked prices, giving the appearance of pronounced negative serial correlation even in daily returns. The **CRSP** data files list only closing prices without regard for whether the last transaction was executed at the bid price, the offer price, or within the bid-ask spread. Stocks will tend to look like winners (losers) if the last transaction on Tuesday was at the bid (offer) price. This will make the one-week strategy look more profitable than it is—stocks that appeared to be winners (losers) because the last transaction on Tuesday was at the bid (ask) price will move to the offer (bid) price next Tuesday roughly half of the time, yielding an apparent profit on the short (long) position in that stock.

This problem is mitigated by a few simple precautions. First, these biases are only a serious issue for portfolio strategies linking this week's return to that of next week (i.e., when $k = 1$). In addition, the use of weekly data reduces the severity of bid-ask spread bias. As an added precaution, the portfolio weights (but not the profits) for this strategy were also computed using four-day returns (i.e., from Wednesday through Monday). The absence of the security returns for the intervening Tuesday substantially reduces this bias by reducing the correlation between the portfolio weights and the measurement error in subsequent returns. Note that this is a conservative procedure—it eliminates the useful Tuesday returns (i.e., those that moved from bid to bid or ask to ask) as well as the corrupted ones (i.e., those that moved from bid to ask or ask to bid) and, hence, is likely to overstate the contribution of bid-ask spread bias to portfolio profits.

Most investigators think the fact that a security traded at the bid or the ask price on Monday is typically unrelated to the state at the close of trade on Tuesday. This presumption is false if the market is not sufficiently liquid to accommodate the needs of traders in the day or two after large price movements. Suppose that a random price increase occurs which is not expected to persist. Investors might be expected to sell some of their stock to rebalance their portfolios and market makers might be expected to buy to replenish their inventories to the extent that they were selling during the initial price increase. If investor portfolio adjustment and market maker inventory adjustment took several days following a large price movement, the price at the close of trade on

Monday could systematically be at the bid (ask), while that at the close of trade on Tuesday could systematically be at the ask (bid). My interpretation of the four-day return calculation requires that the market be sufficiently liquid to accommodate such trading needs in a day or two.

Another important issue is transactions costs. These portfolio strategies involve extreme portfolio turnover, typically requiring more than 2,000 transactions each week. Of course, the strategy could be modified to reduce the frequency of trading. Furthermore, it is not clear what transactions costs are relevant since costs are smaller for an investor treating this as a marginal change in an existing active trading strategy. Instead of searching for low transactions costs versions of these strategies (and risking the potentially serious retrospective bias that could then arise), portfolio profits were computed under different transactions cost assumptions.

Transactions cost per security per week was computed as $tc^*|w_{it} - w_{it-1}|$, where tc is the assumed one-way transactions cost per dollar transaction and w_{it} is the number of dollars invested in security i in week t. The profits are reported for several values of tc: 0.05 percent, 0.10 percent, 0.20 percent, 0.30 percent, 0.40 percent, and 1.0 percent. These numbers treat this portfolio strategy as if it generates *typical* trades in *typical* stocks. For large traders using market orders, one-way transactions costs are the clearing house costs of 0.05 percent plus one half the bid-ask spread (which ranges from 0.5 to 4.5 percent) times the fraction of trades in which specialists participate (approximately 10 to 15 percent of trades on the **NYSE**), suggesting one-way transactions costs of less than 0.20 percent for such investors.[16]

These numbers might be too low. The trades generated by this portfolio strategy are not in *typical* stocks. They are tilted toward smaller market capitalization firms that have larger bid-ask spreads and a greater proportion of trades taking place at the bid or offer price. If the strategy requires typical trades in these stocks, one-way transactions costs are probably closer to 1 percent.

These numbers might be too high because the strategy does not

---

16. Any price pressure generated by this trading strategy is ignored in these computations. For a given value of *tc*, transactions costs are probably overstated because the strategies, especially those based on four-day returns and on the returns in previous weeks, would afford investors the time to shop around for the best execution prices. The computations also ignore strategies for reducing transactions costs—trading at the open (at which time there is no bid-ask spread) and employing limit orders. Neither strategy can be simulated on **CRSP** data, which contain only closing prices.

FADS, MARTINGALES, AND MARKET EFFICIENCY

generate *typical* trades. If a security is a big winner (loser), the market maker is typically a net seller to (buyer from) the public. Market makers want to rebalance their inventories in these circumstances so that patient traders like portfolio rebalancers and investors following reversal strategies can typically trade on favorable terms since they are providing needed liquidity. Hence, this strategy will typically be trading when bid-ask spreads are relatively low and when trades are executed within the bid-ask spread more frequently than usual. Baesel, Shows, and Thorp [1983] argued that Beebower and Priest [1979] found approximately zero net transactions costs in a sample of actual trades for this reason.[17]

There are several minor empirical problems which are not accounted for here but which are probably unimportant. The analysis presumes that it is possible to buy at the close of trade on one Tuesday and sell at the close of trade on the subsequent Tuesday. Although it may not have been possible to execute these transactions at these prices, the four-day return computation largely eliminates any bias that might arise.[18] In addition, SEC regulations require that short sales take place only on upticks. This probably has a small impact on the results since most of the profits come from the long and not the short positions. Finally, the portfolio profit computations ignore any price pressure generated by this trading strategy—a serious problem only if large positions are taken in illiquid securities. Typical position sizes will be reported below.

---

17. See Sweeney [1986] for a detailed discussion of these issues. This view is also supported by the experience of price-sensitive value-based portfolio managers, like Batterymarch Financial Management, and proprietary trading operations, such as those at Morgan, Stanley, & Co. and Bear, Stearns, & Co. They typically confront out-of-pocket costs of less than 0.10 percent and total transactions costs inclusive of price pressure of less than 0.20 percent one-way on similar trading strategies. I am grateful to Dean LeBaron of Batterymarch Financial Management and Greg Kipnis of Morgan, Stanley, & Co. for helpful discussions.

18. The direct effect of the bid-ask spread is accounted for in the transactions cost calculation. The bias arises because the closing price on the **CRSP** tapes is either at the bid or the offer, so that half the time the profit calculation assumes that one is buying (selling) at too low (high) a price since one buys (sells) at the asked (bid) price. Of course, this also means that the profit calculation assumes that one subsequently closes out the position at too low (high) a price for exactly the same reasons, leaving only a Jensen's inequality bias. From Blume and Stambaugh [1983], the bias (relative to true returns) is approximately

$$E\{\pi_{t,k}\} = \pi_{t,k}^{true} + \sum_{i=1}^{N} w_{it}\delta_i^2,$$

where δ_i is the percentage bid-ask spread. The bias is trivial even if the bid-ask spread is 2 or 3 percent and is made even smaller by the observation that the portfolio weights sum to zero.

IV. Empirical Results

This section evaluates the profitability of the costless portfolio strategies described in the previous section. The strategies were applied to virtually all securities listed on the New York and American Stock Exchanges between July 1962 and December 1986.[19] The portfolio weights were based on the following: the previous full week's returns, previous four-day returns (to mitigate bid-ask spread bias), and on the returns two, three, four, thirteen, twenty-six, and fifty-two weeks ago.

Table I presents the main results of the paper. The table reports the profits for five horizons (i.e., values of J): one, four, thirteen, twenty-six, and fifty-two weeks. Six summary statistics are provided: the mean profit and its t statistic, the standard deviation of profits, the maximum and minimum profit, and fraction of periods for which profits were positive. All of these computations ignore transactions costs, which will be dealt with below.

The results in Table I sharply reject the efficient markets hypothesis ignoring market frictions. The two one-week portfolio strategies earned positive profits for each of the 49 twenty-six-week periods (and for all 98 quarterly and 24 annual observations as well).[20] Table I also reveals little persistence in the return reversal effect. The portfolio strategy based on returns two weeks previously did earn positive profits in each of the six-month periods, but this observation does not survive the inclusion of transactions costs (in Table V). None of the other strategies earned strictly positive profits for any portfolio horizon.

Table II provides a more detailed description of the anatomy of the return reversal effect. It reports the same summary statistics for the dollar portfolios of winners and losers as Table I, including the sample correlation between the winner and loser portfolio returns as well.[21] The weekly mean returns of the two one-week portfolio

---

19. I calculated all of the results presented in the tables for 1987 except those found in Tables III and IV. The results for 1962–1986 persist in 1987. In particular, the two one-week strategies proved as profitable net and gross of transactions costs in 1987 as they were in the sample described here.

20. It is interesting to consider why such return reversals were not found in the early market efficiency tests. As summarized in Fama [1970], these investigations found evidence of slight negative serial correlation in individual security return autocorrelations and of slight positive autocorrelation in individual security return runs tests with weekly data. The values were so small that it seemed implausible that they reflected anything like an unexploited arbitrage opportunity. This analysis differs by using information on many securities (i.e., winners and losers) as opposed to the "weak form" tests based on only lagged individual security prices.

21. Since these are portfolio returns, the statistics for the winners portfolio are the opposite of those implicit in the profits reported in Table I (i.e., winners are sold short in the costless portfolios).

strategies were of opposite sign, and the mean return of the winners portfolio was on the order of one half the magnitude of the mean return of the losers portfolio. The sample variances of the weekly returns of the two one-week portfolio strategies were comparable. The sample correlations of the weekly returns of the two one-week portfolio strategies were large and positive—0.851 for the full-week strategy and 0.873 for the four-day strategy. A short position in the winners portfolio had a large negative correlation with a long position in the losers portfolio, greatly reducing the variance of the resulting costless portfolio (by approximately 60 percent of the standard deviation of the losers portfolio) and increasing its average profit (by approximately 40 percent over the mean of the losers portfolio).

Put differently, the winners and losers portfolios had weekly mean returns within an order of magnitude of their standard deviations. This implies that the weekly mean returns were much larger than the corresponding sample variances—by a factor of six to nine for the winners portfolio and of nine to fourteen for the losers portfolio. The resulting costless portfolios had mean profits approximately equal to their standard deviations (and between 50 and 75 times their variances) because of the large negative correlations between the long and short positions in the losers and winners portfolios. As a consequence, the mean profits on these strategies over twenty-six-week periods were more than three times their standard deviations, and the profits were positive in each six-month period.[22]

It is worth emphasizing the role of the short position in the winners portfolio in these profits. It is not the case that the returns on the losers portfolio were nearly always positive; they were positive in 65 to 70 percent of the weeks. Similarly, the short position in the winners portfolio typically had positive returns in more than half of the weeks. The short position in the winners portfolio had a large negative correlation with the losers portfolio, rendering the costless portfolio profits positive in between 85 and 94 percent of the weeks. The integral nature of the short position in the winners portfolio in the costless portfolios' profits stands in sharp contrast to the role of short positions in the filter rule

---

22. Recall that the instantaneous mean and variance of individual asset and portfolio returns must be of the same order of magnitude to prevent the occurrence of riskless arbitrage opportunities in the continuous time asset pricing literature. While the relevance of this observation for weekly returns is open to question, the semiannual time aggregation of weekly return reversal portfolio profits has the same kind of effect as intertemporal portfolio diversification in continuous time.

TABLE I
PROFITS ON COSTLESS RETURN REVERSAL PORTFOLIO STRATEGIES BY PORTFOLIO HORIZON, 1962–1986

Portfolio horizon (weeks)	Mean	Standard deviation	t statistic	Maximum	Minimum	Fraction positive	Number of observations
Panel A: Portfolio weights based on previous week's return							
One	0.0179	0.0156	41.07	0.2294	−0.0539	0.934	1276
Four	0.0717	0.0355	36.06	0.2709	−0.0219	0.991	319
Thirteen	0.2329	0.0803	28.71	0.5029	0.0845	1.000	98
Twenty-six	0.4657	0.1449	22.50	0.9446	0.2555	1.000	49
Fifty-two	0.9289	0.2709	16.80	1.7277	0.5850	1.000	24
Panel B: Portfolio weights based on first four days of previous week's return							
One	0.0121	0.0144	30.02	0.2132	−0.0629	0.867	1276
Four	0.0484	0.0298	28.98	0.2380	−0.0301	0.972	319
Thirteen	0.1573	0.0571	27.27	0.4032	0.0526	1.000	98
Twenty-six	0.3146	0.0923	23.87	0.5947	0.1515	1.000	49
Fifty-two	0.6281	0.1699	18.11	1.1281	0.4115	1.000	24
Panel C: Portfolio weights based on one-week return two weeks ago							
One	0.0050	0.0118	15.15	0.1064	−0.0497	0.695	1275
Four	0.0200	0.0257	13.87	0.1241	−0.0599	0.802	318
Thirteen	0.0651	0.0460	14.02	0.2727	−0.0451	0.929	98
Twenty-six	0.1302	0.0658	13.86	0.3936	−0.0242	1.000	49
Fifty-two	0.2590	0.1129	11.24	0.5830	0.0719	1.000	24
Panel D: Portfolio weights based on one-week return three weeks ago							
One	0.0018	0.0112	5.77	0.1085	−0.0556	0.575	1274
Four	0.0073	0.0246	5.31	0.1242	−0.0909	0.638	318
Thirteen	0.0236	0.0442	5.28	0.1708	−0.1104	0.694	98
Twenty-six	0.0472	0.0702	4.71	0.2812	−0.1186	0.776	49
Fifty-two	0.0993	0.1075	4.53	0.3682	−0.1115	0.833	24

	Panel E: Portfolio weights based on one-week return four weeks ago
One	0.0011	0.0111	3.56	0.1273	−0.0515	0.521	1273
Four	0.0043	0.0235	3.31	0.1324	−0.0638	0.569	318
Thirteen	0.0136	0.0379	3.53	0.1370	−0.0655	0.649	97
Twenty-six	0.0279	0.0581	3.32	0.1887	−0.0880	0.646	48
Fifty-two	0.0557	0.0921	2.96	0.3106	−0.0900	0.750	24
	Panel F: Portfolio weights based on one-week return thirteen weeks ago
One	−0.0009	0.0088	−3.47	0.0400	−0.0465	0.438	1264
Four	−0.0034	0.0182	−3.35	0.0617	−0.0599	0.415	316
Thirteen	−0.0112	0.0351	−3.15	0.0770	−0.1494	0.371	97
Twenty-six	−0.0210	0.0432	−3.37	0.0546	−0.1179	0.354	48
Fifty-two	−0.0421	0.0566	−3.64	0.0584	−0.1540	0.167	24
	Panel G: Portfolio weights based on one-week return twenty-six weeks ago
One	−0.0004	0.0086	−1.71	0.0511	−0.0415	0.473	1251
Four	−0.0017	0.0177	−1.70	0.0759	−0.0530	0.455	312
Thirteen	−0.0055	0.0335	−1.62	0.0944	−0.0969	0.458	96
Twenty-six	−0.0111	0.0359	−2.14	0.0773	−0.1204	0.396	48
Fifty-two	−0.0222	0.0478	−2.27	0.0459	−0.1588	0.375	24
	Panel H: Portfolio weights based on one-week return fifty-two weeks ago
One	−0.0016	0.0092	−6.18	0.0284	−0.1170	0.424	1225
Four	−0.0065	0.0220	−5.14	0.0490	−0.1555	0.366	306
Thirteen	−0.0210	0.0417	−4.87	0.0807	−0.1762	0.298	94
Twenty-six	−0.0419	0.0589	−4.91	0.0740	−0.2009	0.234	47
Fifty-two	−0.0831	0.0976	−4.09	0.0873	−0.3801	0.130	23

TABLE II
WEEKLY RETURNS ON DOLLAR PORTFOLIOS OF WINNERS AND LOSERS, 1962–1986

Portfolio	Mean	Standard deviation	t statistic	Maximum	Minimum	Fraction positive	Pairwise correlation
\multicolumn{8}{l}{Panel A: Portfolio weights based on previous week's return}
Winners	−0.0055	0.0248	−7.96	0.1296	−0.1264	0.413	0.851
Losers	0.0124	0.0297	14.92	0.3321	−0.1338	0.714	0.851
\multicolumn{8}{l}{Panel B: Portfolio weights based on first four days of previous week's return}
Winners	−0.0035	0.0247	−5.05	0.1171	−0.1311	0.460	0.873
Losers	0.0086	0.0295	10.43	0.3211	−0.1354	0.665	0.873
\multicolumn{8}{l}{Panel C: Portfolio weights based on one-week return two weeks ago}
Winners	0.0003	0.0253	0.41	0.1638	−0.1458	0.579	0.911
Losers	0.0053	0.0286	6.63	0.2702	−0.1344	0.620	0.911
\multicolumn{8}{l}{Panel D: Portfolio weights based on one-week return three weeks ago}
Winners	0.0022	0.0261	3.07	0.2154	−0.1406	0.711	0.917
Losers	0.0041	0.0282	5.14	0.2254	−0.1340	0.598	0.917

		Panel E: Portfolio weights based on one-week return four weeks ago				
Winners	0.0025	0.0262	3.42	0.2041	−0.1129	0.736	0.920
Losers	0.0036	0.0283	4.56	0.2320	−0.1569	0.590	0.920
		Panel F: Portfolio weights based on one-week return thirteen weeks ago				
Winners	0.0039	0.0268	5.17	0.2006	−0.1286	0.816	0.947
Losers	0.0030	0.0271	3.97	0.2174	−0.1376	0.578	0.947
		Panel G: Portfolio weights based on one-week return twenty-six weeks ago				
Winners	0.0038	0.0268	4.98	0.2191	−0.1288	0.821	0.949
Losers	0.0034	0.0268	4.43	0.2140	−0.1499	0.592	0.949
		Panel H: Portfolio weights based on one-week return fifty-two weeks ago				
Winners	0.0045	0.0280	5.59	0.2326	−0.1410	0.842	0.944
Losers	0.0028	0.0261	3.82	0.2124	−0.1355	0.585	0.944

literature—as Sweeney [1986] has emphasized, short positions contribute primarily transactions costs (and not profits) to filter rule profits.

It is difficult to interpret the behavior of these portfolios as reflecting time-varying expected returns even if one rejects the market inefficiency interpretation of this evidence. Suppose that market prices were determined by the consumption-based capital asset pricing model with time-varying consumption betas and risk premiums. If firms with consumption betas above the market average one week typically had consumption betas above the market average next week as well, the consumption risk premium would have to be highly negatively serially correlated from week to week to explain these results. It is certainly difficult to rationalize such a short-run relation.[23]

Table II also accounts for the failure to find pronounced persistence in the return reversal effect. On averge, the winners portfolio only had negative mean returns in the subsequent week and had positive and increasing mean returns over the next month. Similarly, the losers portfolio had large positive mean returns in the subsequent week which diminished over the next month. This measured mean reversion in stock returns is studied further in Lehmann [1988].

Tables III and IV provide a detailed description of the characteristics of the winners and losers portfolios, respectively, for the two one-week strategies and those based on one-week returns two and three weeks ago. Eight statistics are given for each of the five quintiles of the winners and losers portfolios (running from largest to smallest). As before, the tables report the mean return and its t statistic, the standard deviation of returns, and the maximum and minimum return for each quintile (i.e., for each 20 cents of the dollar invested in the winners or losers portfolio). In addition, the tables provide three summary measures of quintile characteristics:

23. To make matters concrete, let the excess return of security i be given by

$$R_{it} - R_{ft} = \beta_{ict}[R_{ct} - R_{ft}] + \epsilon_{ict},$$

where β_{ict} is the consumption beta of security i at time t, R_{ct} is the return on the portfolio of these N assets that has the largest correlation with aggregate consumption, R_{ft} is the return on the riskless asset, and ϵ_{ict} is the portion of the return on security i conditionally uncorrelated with aggregate consumption. If the unconditional covariances cov $\{\beta_{ict}\beta_{ict+1}, [R_{ct} - R_{ft}][R_{ct+1} - R_{ft+1}]\}$ and cov $\{\epsilon_{ict}\beta_{ict+1}[R_{ct+1} - R_{ft+1}]\}$ are both zero (ignoring, for example, the small effect of weekly leverage changes on consumption betas), then $E\{[R_{ct} - R_{ft}][R_{ct+1} - R_{ft+1}]\} < 0$ if cov $\{\beta_{ict}, \beta_{ict+1}\} > 0$ to account for the observed positive average portfolio profits. It is hard to rationalize pronounced negative serial correlation in either $[R_{ct} - R_{ft}]$ or β_{ict}, especially in weekly data.

FADS, MARTINGALES, AND MARKET EFFICIENCY

average turnover, average investment per firm, and weighted average market capitalization. The portfolio turnover calculation is the average sum across securities within each quintile of the transactions cost base $|w_{it} - w_{it-1}|$. Average investment per firm in each quintile is the average value of 20 cents divided by the number of firms in each quintile in each week. The market value calculation is the sample average of the portfolio weighted market capitalization of the firms in each quintile of those firms for which price and share data existed at the beginning of the week.

The measured arbitrage profits on the two one-week strategies reflect returns on reasonably well-diversified portfolios (with weights typically ranging from 0.03 to 0.53 percent), not the reward to investing in a few big winners and losers. To be sure, the largest winners and losers experienced the largest subsequent reversals. However, the top three quintiles of winners and all five quintiles of losers typically experienced large reversals in the next week. Moreover, the average market capitalizations of the quintile portfolios were in size deciles six through nine, mitigating concern about price pressure and liquidity. Note also the extraordinary volume of transactions generated by the strategies: approximately three dollars a week per dollar long in the return reversal portfolio strategy. In other words, the two one-week strategies profited from the exploitation of many relatively small predictable price reversals each week and, hence, probably would not have required large positions in illiquid stocks.

Of course, there are legitimate concerns about the economic relevance of the profits documented in Table I. In particular, the costless portfolio strategies typically generate more than 2,000 round-trip transactions per week, and hence, the resulting transactions costs might be expected to wipe out the profits reported in Table I. Table V reports the semiannual profits for the two one-week strategies and those based on one-week returns two and three weeks ago under assumed one-way transactions costs ranging from 0.05 to 1.0 percent.

The results in Table V differ somewhat from those in Table I without altering the main conclusions, as long as the one-way transactions costs confronting large traders are less than 0.20 percent. The two one-week portfolio strategies still yielded measured arbitrage profits at this level of transactions costs. The strategy based on returns two weeks ago did not yield positive profits in each of the 49 six-month periods at any level of transactions costs, and hence, its profits do not constitute a true arbitrage

TABLE III
WEEKLY RETURNS AND CHARACTERISTICS OF SELECTED DOLLAR PORTFOLIOS OF WINNERS BY QUINTILE, 1962–1986

Portfolio quintile	Mean	Standard deviation	t statistic	Maximum	Minimum	Portfolio turnover (cents)	Investment per firm (cents)	Market value in millions of dollars
Panel A: Portfolio weights based on previous week's return								
One	−0.0041	0.0076	−19.02	0.0396	−0.0529	22.57	0.49	77.7
Two	−0.0014	0.0055	−9.10	0.0424	−0.0255	23.09	0.25	171.8
Three	−0.0005	0.0050	−3.35	0.0259	−0.0213	24.23	0.16	284.3
Four	0.0001	0.0046	0.46	0.0219	−0.0226	27.07	0.10	393.5
Five	0.0003	0.0044	2.78	0.0269	−0.0237	52.07	0.03	497.8
Panel B: Portfolio weights based on first four days of previous week's return								
One	−0.0030	0.0075	−14.32	0.0415	−0.0810	22.00	0.53	71.9
Two	−0.0008	0.0054	−5.11	0.0284	−0.0277	22.52	0.26	165.8
Three	−0.0003	0.0049	−2.04	0.0237	−0.0275	23.84	0.16	274.0
Four	0.0002	0.0047	1.15	0.0213	−0.0223	26.88	0.10	380.8
Five	0.0004	0.0044	3.60	0.0296	−0.0237	52.39	0.03	493.8
Panel C: Portfolio weights based on one-week return two weeks ago								
One	−0.0007	0.0070	−3.42	0.0430	−0.0320	21.21	0.49	77.3
Two	−0.0000	0.0056	−0.16	0.0378	−0.0313	21.85	0.25	171.7
Three	0.0002	0.0051	1.44	0.0277	−0.0283	23.41	0.16	285.1
Four	0.0003	0.0047	2.35	0.0292	−0.0285	26.60	0.10	393.7
Five	0.0005	0.0044	3.81	0.0300	−0.0257	52.16	0.03	497.8
Panel D: Portfolio weights based on one-week return three weeks ago								
One	0.0002	0.0070	0.94	0.0461	−0.0314	20.89	0.49	77.8
Two	0.0004	0.0058	2.41	0.0463	−0.0313	21.53	0.25	172.1
Three	0.0005	0.0053	3.27	0.0458	−0.0289	23.00	0.16	284.2
Four	0.0006	0.0049	4.15	0.0407	−0.0259	26.23	0.10	394.2
Five	0.0006	0.0045	4.81	0.0365	−0.0230	52.14	0.03	497.3

TABLE IV
WEEKLY RETURNS AND CHARACTERISTICS OF SELECTED DOLLAR PORTFOLIOS OF LOSERS BY QUINTILE, 1962–1986

Portfolio quintile	Mean	Standard deviation	t statistic	Maximum	Minimum	Portfolio turnover (cents)	Investment per firm (cents)	Market value in millions of dollars
Panel A: Portfolio weights based on previous week's return
One	0.0065	0.0084	27.71	0.0918	−0.0274	24.34	0.29	110.9
Two	0.0027	0.0066	14.47	0.0747	−0.0260	23.60	0.17	198.6
Three	0.0016	0.0059	9.70	0.0668	−0.0282	24.14	0.12	294.7
Four	0.0010	0.0053	6.51	0.0537	−0.0295	26.54	0.08	385.9
Five	0.0007	0.0049	4.92	0.0451	−0.0271	52.37	0.03	480.9
Panel B: Portfolio weights based on first four days of previous week's return
One	0.0036	0.0080	16.14	0.0854	−0.0307	22.50	0.30	113.4
Two	0.0019	0.0065	10.61	0.0726	−0.0286	22.79	0.17	198.9
Three	0.0013	0.0059	8.01	0.0638	−0.0277	23.72	0.12	297.0
Four	0.0010	0.0054	6.43	0.0566	−0.0281	26.72	0.08	397.6
Five	0.0008	0.0048	5.82	0.0457	−0.0256	53.49	0.03	489.8
Panel C: Portfolio weights based on one-week return two weeks ago
One	0.0014	0.0076	6.44	0.0766	−0.0304	21.99	0.29	111.6
Two	0.0011	0.0063	6.36	0.0516	−0.0292	21.85	0.17	199.9
Three	0.0011	0.0057	6.77	0.0508	−0.0252	23.56	0.12	295.8
Four	0.0009	0.0052	6.39	0.0501	−0.0274	26.90	0.08	387.0
Five	0.0008	0.0047	6.12	0.0412	−0.0226	53.90	0.03	481.6
Panel D: Portfolio weights based on one-week return three weeks ago
One	0.0009	0.0075	4.39	0.0607	−0.0312	21.70	0.29	111.5
Two	0.0009	0.0063	5.00	0.0656	−0.0273	21.53	0.17	199.9
Three	0.0008	0.0056	4.95	0.0438	−0.0269	23.17	0.12	295.0
Four	0.0008	0.0051	5.27	0.0419	−0.0242	26.57	0.08	386.2
Five	0.0007	0.0046	5.59	0.0323	−0.0244	54.01	0.03	480.1

TABLE V
PROFITS ON SELECTED TWENTY-SIX WEEK COSTLESS RETURN REVERSAL PORTFOLIO STRATEGIES BY ONE-WAY TRANSACTIONS COST, 1962–1986

Transactions cost (percent)	Mean	Standard deviation	t statistic	Maximum	Minimum	Fraction positive	Number of observations
Panel A: Portfolio weights based on previous week's return							
0.05	0.4267	0.1445	20.67	0.9099	0.2171	1.000	49
0.10	0.3877	0.1442	18.82	0.8702	0.1786	1.000	49
0.20	0.3097	0.1436	15.10	0.7909	0.1018	1.000	49
0.30	0.2317	0.1429	11.35	0.7114	0.0249	1.000	49
0.40	0.1537	0.1423	7.56	0.6321	−0.0520	0.898	49
1.00	−0.3143	0.1374	−16.01	0.1561	−0.5133	0.041	49
Panel B: Portfolio weights based on first four days of previous week's return							
0.05	0.2760	0.0921	20.98	0.5558	0.1131	1.000	49
0.10	0.2374	0.0920	18.07	0.5168	0.0747	1.000	49
0.20	0.1602	0.0917	12.24	0.4389	−0.0021	0.979	49
0.30	0.0830	0.0914	6.36	0.3610	−0.0789	0.898	49
0.40	0.0059	0.0911	0.45	0.2830	−0.1558	0.449	49
1.00	−0.4573	0.0893	−35.85	−0.1846	−0.6168	0.000	49
Panel C: Portfolio weights based on one-week return two weeks ago							
0.05	0.0922	0.0656	9.84	0.3551	−0.0136	0.939	49
0.10	0.0541	0.0654	5.79	0.3165	−0.0513	0.837	49
0.20	−0.0220	0.0651	−2.36	0.2394	−0.1269	0.306	49
0.30	−0.0981	0.0647	−10.61	0.1622	−0.2024	0.041	49
0.40	−0.1742	0.0644	−18.94	0.0851	−0.2780	0.020	49
1.00	−0.6308	0.0613	−72.03	−0.4377	−0.7314	0.000	49
Panel D: Portfolio weights based on one-week return three weeks ago							
0.05	0.0095	0.0700	0.95	0.2431	−0.1550	0.551	49
0.10	−0.0282	0.0698	−2.83	0.2050	−0.1913	0.306	49
0.20	−0.1036	0.0693	−10.46	0.1288	−0.2639	0.041	49
0.30	−0.1790	0.0689	−18.18	0.0525	−0.3365	0.020	49
0.40	−0.2544	0.0685	−26.00	−0.0237	−0.4092	0.000	49
1.00	−0.7068	0.0660	−74.96	−0.4811	−0.8451	0.000	49

FADS, MARTINGALES, AND MARKET EFFICIENCY

opportunity. Note that the plausibility of my transactions cost assumptions is crucial here: neither one-week strategy yields a measured arbitrage opportunity if one-way transactions costs exceed 0.20 percent; and mean profits are zero if they are 0.40 percent.

Figure I provides two additional summary measures of the behavior of the two one-week portfolio strategies: time series plots and histograms of their weekly profits gross of transactions costs.[24] The series are dominated by white noise with positive mean. There is no noticeable pattern in the portfolio profits processes and, in particular, no tendency for profits or their mean to decline over time. Large (i.e., 1 to 4 percent per week) profits are the rule rather than the exception, and the profitability of these strategies is pervasive throughout the sample period.[25]

It is interesting to summarize these results by considering the profits for strategies that are long $100 million of losers and short $100 million of winners. The average semiannual profits net of the 0.10 percent one-way transactions costs that might be relevant for floor traders and large broker-dealers were $38.77 million for the conventional one-week strategy and $23.74 million for that based on four-day returns. The minimum semiannual profits were $17.86 million and $7.47 million, respectively, while the largest semiannual profits were $87.02 million and $51.68 million, respectively. Moreover, market liquidity is typically sufficient to accommodate transactions of this scale—typically $300,000 in the extreme losers and $500,000 in the extreme winners. These costless portfolio strategies earned measured arbitrage profits despite generating $300 million of transactions a week (the theoretical maximum is $400 million), more than one third of which was generated by the unprofitable transactions in the fifth quintile of smallest winners and losers. It is hard to believe that these numbers are either trivial or were

---

24. The cells of the histograms are ±0.5 percent of the integer displayed (i.e., 1 percent denotes the cell with observations ranging from 0.5 to 1.5 percent). The histograms exclude cells with fewer than 12 (out of 1,276) observations. There are 9 negative observations and 38 positive observations not reflected in the histograms.

25. Fama and French [1987], Chan [1988], and Jegadeesh [1987] provide evidence that the return reversal effects measured at longer differencing intervals are, in part, attributable to the now well-known turn-of-the-year effect—the pronounced tendency for the returns on stocks with small market capitalizations to exceed those of stocks with large market capitalizations in the month of January. Results not reported here suggest that return reversal strategies are, if anything, more profitable outside of the month of January. This is primarily a consequence of the returns on the winners portfolio outside of the month of January. The average return on each version of the winners portfolio was more negative, and negative returns occurred in a slightly larger fraction of twenty-six-week periods than the corresponding observations including January returns.

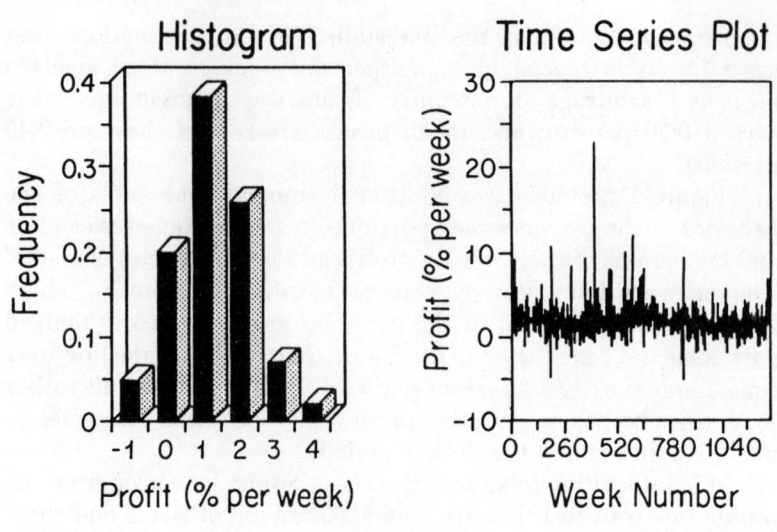

FIGURE Ia
Weekly Portfolio Profits—Full Week Strategy

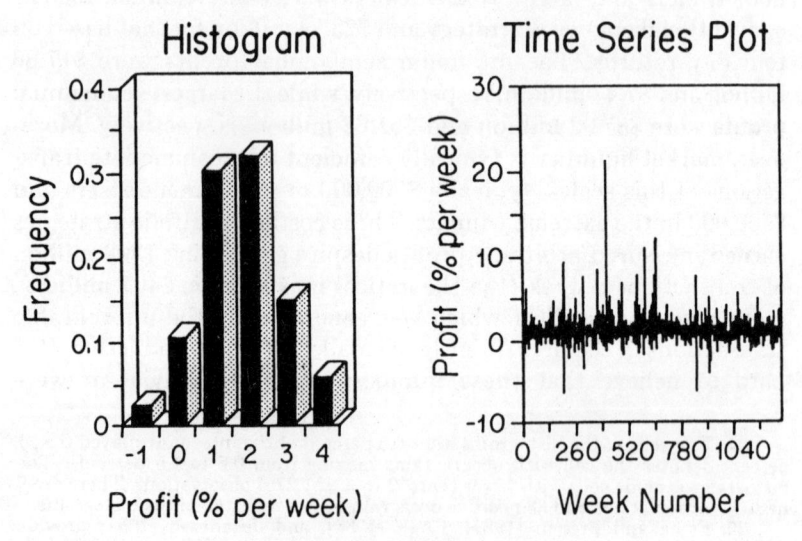

FIGURE Ib
Weekly Portfolio Profits—Four Day Strategy

unattainable for investors unless stocks are typically illiquid following large price movements.[26]

V. Conclusion

Financial economics has enjoyed considerable success in interpreting stock price movements as reflections of the arrival of new information in an efficient capital market. Early empirical studies found little evidence against the hypothesis that equity prices were set in an efficient market with constant expected returns. Theoretical developments since then have suggested that expected returns typically vary in our equilibrium asset pricing models, and not surprisingly, recent empirical research has found evidence of predictable variation in security returns. While it is conventional practice to refer to this evidence as a reflection of time-varying expected returns, the suggestion that predictable variation in security returns arises instead from security price overreaction to speculative fads or the cognitive misperceptions of investors in an inefficient market is currently enjoying a resurgence not seen in two decades.

This paper has tested the market efficiency hypothesis by examining security prices for evidence of unexploited arbitrage opportunities. It did so by examining the profits on feasible ex ante costless portfolios that should not earn riskless profits in an efficient market but could earn such profits if stock price overreaction affects many equity returns. This practice avoids the problems associated with specifying a model for variation in expected returns at the cost of requiring the presence of measured arbitrage opportunities to reject the hypothesis of market efficiency—a very stringent test.

The results strongly suggest rejection of the efficient markets hypothesis. Portfolios of securities that had positive returns in one week typically had negative returns in the next week (−0.35 to −0.55 percent per week on average), while those with negative

---

26. It is difficult to provide a quantitative measure of the inefficiency in the market for liquidity represented by these results. The following calculation may provide an order of magnitude estimate of the typical pricing error. If a week is sufficiently short for the local martingale model to apply, the costless return reversal portfolios should have mean zero profits net of transactions costs. The mean profits of the two one-week strategies are approximately zero at 0.40 percent one-way transactions costs. This suggests a typical pricing error estimate of 0.80 percent if it is reasonable to label this measured inefficiency as unmeasured transactions costs. This calculation probably understates true "total" transactions costs because the two one-week strategies are probably much less profitable than optimal return reversal strategies.

returns in one week typically had positive returns in the next week (0.86 to 1.24 percent per week on average). The costless portfolio that is the difference between the winners and losers portfolios had positive profits in roughly 90 percent of the weeks and, if the strategy is viewed as having a twenty-six-week horizon, the profits were positive in each of the 49 six-month periods covered by the data.

It is difficult to account for these results within the efficient markets framework. These measured arbitrage profits persist after corrections for the mismeasurement of security returns due to bid-ask spreads and for plausible levels of transactions costs. In addition, the strategies involved only modest positions in liquid securities, suggesting that they could have been implemented without generating substantial price pressure unless markets are illiquid following large price changes. Finally, it is hard to rationalize short-run return reversals of this magnitude within an intertemporal asset pricing framework even ignoring the evidence of market inefficiency suggested by the measured arbitrage opportunities.[27]

In fact, the return reversals associated with winners and losers probably reflect imbalances in the market for short-run liquidity. This is consistent with the notion that market makers are only intermediaries between patient and impatient traders and, hence, supply only very short-term (i.e., intraday) liquidity as in Treynor [1981]. By contrast, market-wide proprietary trading by large broker-dealers (who are patient traders) is probably the natural source of supply of liquidity over intervals like days or weeks in response to transitory changes in the demand for liquidity by impatient traders. Such trading is only a recent phenomenon, however, and so the results probably reflect an inefficiency in the market for short-term liquidity.

Since there is little persistence in the return reversal effects, there are two potential responses to these results. First, one could emphasize the short-run nature of the arbitrage opportunity and presume that equity markets are (on average) efficient over longer

---

27. After completing this research, I learned that Rosenberg Institutional Equity Management successfully markets a version of the portfolio strategy described in Rosenberg, Reid, and Lanstein [1985]. In addition, this firm does index arbitrage with a long position in a version of the losers portfolio and a short position in S&P 500 futures contracts. We academicians apparently benefit from similar strategies—the College Retirement Equity Fund has successfully pursued such a return reversal strategy as part of its actively managed portfolio. Similarly, computerized proprietary trading operations seeking to exploit reversals are now commonplace. Presumably their activities, especially the systematic computer-generated versions, will eliminate any such arbitrage opportunities in the future, yielding the opportunity to write a paper entitled "Return Reversals Revisited" at a future date!

horizons, such as a month. On this view, these results provide an interesting puzzle for students of security market microstructure and of the market for short-run liquidity.[28] Alternatively, one could emphasize the low power of these tests for detecting longer term market inefficiencies and continue to seek additional evidence (and reinterpret existing evidence) of market inefficiency. Both responses will presumably increase our understanding of the determination of security prices.

DEPARTMENT OF ECONOMICS AND GRADUATE SCHOOL OF BUSINESS, COLUMBIA UNIVERSITY, AND THE NATIONAL BUREAU OF ECONOMIC RESEARCH

REFERENCES

Baesel, J. B., G. Shows, and Edward Thorp, "The Cost of Liquidity Services in Listed Options: A Note," *Journal of Finance*, XXXVIII (1983), 989–95.
Beebower, Gilbert, and W. Priest, "The Tricks of the Trade," *Journal of Portfolio Management*, VI (1979), 36–42.
Black, Fischer, "Noise," *Journal of Finance*, XLI (1986), 529–43.
Blume, Marshall E., and Robert F. Stambaugh, "Biases in Computed Returns: An Application to the Size Effect," *Journal of Financial Economics*, XII (1983), 387–404.
Campbell, John Y., and Albert S. Kyle, "Smart Money, Noise Trading, and Stock Price Behavior," unpublished manuscript, Department of Economics, Princeton University, 1987.
Chan, K. C., "On the Contrarian Investment Strategy," *Journal of Business*, LXI (1988), 147–163.
De Bondt, Werner F. M., and Richard Thaler, "Does the Stock Market Overreact?" *Journal of Finance*, XL (1985), 793–805.
———, and ———, "Further Evidence on Investor Overreaction and Stock Market Seasonality," *Journal of Finance*, XLII (1987), 557–81.
DeLong, J. Bradford, Andrei Shleifer, Lawrence H. Summers, and Robert J. Waldmann, "The Economic Consequences of Noise Traders," National Bureau of Economic Research Working Paper No. 2395, 1987.
Fama, Eugene F., "Efficient Capital Markets: A Review of Theory and Empirical Work," *Journal of Finance*, XXV (1970), 383–417.
———, and Marshal E. Blume, "Filter Rules and Stock Market Trading," *Journal of Business*, XXXIX (1966), 226–41.
———, and Kenneth R. French, "Permanent and Temporary Components of Stock Prices," *Journal of Political Economy*, XCVI (1987), 246–73.
CRSP Working Paper No. 178, University of Chicago, 1986.
Hall, Peter E., and C. C. Heyde, *Martingale Limit Theory and Its Applications* (New York: Academic Press, 1980).
Jegadeesh, Narasimhan, "Evidence of the Predictability of Equity Returns," unpublished manuscript, Graduate School of Business, Columbia University, 1987.
Lehmann, Bruce N., "Winners, Losers, and Mean Reversion in Weekly Equity Returns," unpublished manuscript, Graduate School of Business, Columbia University, 1988.
Lo, Andrew W., and A. Craig MacKinlay, "Stock Prices Do Not Follow Random Walks: Evidence from a Simple Specification Test," *Review of Financial Studies*, I (1988), 41–66.

28. Equity desks and research groups have traditionally been organized by industry with comparatively little internecine contact concerning individual securities. Since winners and losers freely cross industry bounds, this institutional observation suggests a possible reason why this apparent inefficiency has been overlooked and why it may have been costly to exploit.

Merton, Robert C., "On the Mathematics and Economic Assumptions of Continuous Time Models," in *Financial Economics: Essays in Honor of Paul Cootner,* William F. Sharpe and C. M. Cootner, eds. (Englewood Cliffs, NJ: Prentice-Hall, 1982).

Poterba, James M., and Lawrence H. Summers, "Mean Reversion in Stock Prices: Evidence and Implications," *Journal of Financial Economics,* XXII (1987), 27–59.

Roll, Richard W., "On Computing Mean Returns and the Small Firm Premium," *Journal of Financial Economics,* XII (1983), 371–86.

Rosenberg, Barr, Kenneth Reid, and Ronald Lanstein, "Persuasive Evidence of Market Inefficiency," *Journal of Portfolio Management,* XII (1985), 9–16.

Shefrin, Hersh M., and Meir Statman, "The Disposition to Ride Winners too Long and Sell Losers too Soon: Theory and Evidence," *Journal of Finance,* XLI (1985), 774–90.

Shiller, Robert J., "The Use of Volatility Measures in Assessing Market Efficiency," *Journal of Finance,* XXXVI (1981), 291–304.

——, "Stock Prices and Social Dynamics," *Brookings Papers on Economic Activity,* XII (1984), 457–98.

——, and Pierre Perron, "Testing the Random Walk Hypothesis: Power versus Frequency of Observation," *Economics Letters,* XVIII (1985), 381–86.

Sims, Christopher A., "Martingale-like Behavior of Prices and Interest Rates," Discussion Paper No. 205, Center for Economic Research, University of Minnesota, 1984.

Singleton, Kenneth J., "Specification and Estimation of Intertemporal Asset Pricing Models," in *Handbook of Monetary Economics,* Benjamin Friedman and Frank Hahn, eds. (New York: North-Holland, 1987).

Summers, Lawrence H., "Does the Stock Market Rationally Reflect Fundamental Values?" *Journal of Finance,* XLI (1986), 591–600.

Sweeney, Richard J., "Some New Filter Rule Tests: Methodology and Results," unpublished manuscript, Claremont McKenna College and Claremont Graduate School, 1986.

Treynor, Jack, "What It Takes to Win the Trading Game," *Financial Analysts Journal,* XXXVII (1981), 55–60.

When Are Contrarian Profits Due to Stock Market Overreaction?

Andrew W. Lo
Sloan School of Management
Massachusetts Institute of Technology

A. Craig MacKinlay
Wharton School
University of Pennsylvania

If returns on some stocks systematically lead or lag those of others, a portfolio strategy that sells "winners" and buys "losers" can produce positive expected returns, even if no stock's returns are negatively autocorrelated as virtually all models of overreaction imply. Using a particular contrarian strategy we show that, despite negative autocorrelation in individual stock returns, weekly portfolio returns are strongly positively autocorrelated and are the result of important cross-autocorrelations. We find that the returns of large stocks lead those of smaller stocks, and we present evidence against overreaction as the only source of contrarian profits.

Since the publication of Louis Bachelier's thesis *Theory of Speculation* in 1900, the theoretical and empir-

---

Research support from the Batterymarch Fellowship (Lo), the Geewax-Terker Research Fund (MacKinlay), the National Science Foundation (Grant No. SES-8821583), the John M. Olin Fellowship at the NBER (Lo), and the Q Group is gratefully acknowledged. The authors thank Andy Abel, Michael Brennan, Werner DeBondt, Mike Gibbons, Don Keim, Bruce Lehmann, Jay Ritter, Rob Stambaugh, a referee, and seminar participants at Harvard University, Princeton University, the University of Alberta, the University of Maryland, the University of Minnesota, the University of Western Ontario, and the Wharton School for useful suggestions and discussion. Address reprint requests to Andrew Lo, Sloan School of Management, M.I.T., 50 Memorial Drive, Cambridge, MA 02139.

ical implications of the random walk hypothesis as a model for speculative prices have been subjects of considerable interest to financial economists. First developed by Bachelier from rudimentary economic considerations of "fair games," the random walk has received broader support from the many early empirical studies confirming the unpredictability of stock-price changes.[1] Of course, as Leroy (1973) and Lucas (1978) have shown, the unforecastability of asset returns is neither a necessary nor a sufficient condition of economic equilibrium. And, in view of the empirical evidence in Lo and MacKinlay (1988), it is also apparent that historical stock market prices do not follow random walks.

This fact surprises many economists because the defining property of the random walk is the uncorrelatedness of its increments, and deviations from this hypothesis necessarily imply price changes that are forecastable to some degree. But our surprise must be tempered by the observation that forecasts of stock returns are still imperfect and may be subject to considerable forecast errors, so that "excess" profit opportunities and market inefficiencies are not necessarily consequences of forecastability. Nevertheless, several recent studies maintain the possibility of significant profits and market inefficiencies, even after controlling for risk in one way or another.

Some of these studies have attributed this forecastability to what has come to be known as the "stock market overreaction" hypothesis, the notion that investors are subject to waves of optimism and pessimism and therefore create a kind of "momentum" that causes prices to temporarily swing away from their fundamental values [see, e.g., DeBondt and Thaler (1985, 1987), DeLong, Shleifer, Summers, and Waldmann (1989), Lehmann (1988), Poterba and Summers (1988), and Shefrin and Statman (1985)]. Although such a hypothesis does imply predictability, since what goes down must come up and vice versa, a well-articulated equilibrium theory of overreaction with sharp empirical implications has yet to be developed.

But common to virtually all existing theories of overreaction is one very specific empirical implication: Price changes must be *negatively* autocorrelated for some holding period. For example, DeBondt and Thaler (1985) write: "If stock prices systematically overshoot, then their reversal should be predictable from past return data alone." Therefore, the extent to which the data are consistent with stock market overreaction, broadly defined, may be distilled into an empir-

---

[1] See, for example, the papers in Cootner (1964), and Fama (1965, 1970). Our usage of the term "random walk" differs slightly from the classical definition of a process with independently and identically distributed increments. Since historically the property of primary economic interest has been the uncorrelatedness of increments, we also consider processes with uncorrelated but heterogeneously distributed dependent increments to be random walks.

ically decidable question: Are return reversals responsible for the predictability in stock returns?

A more specific consequence of overreaction is the profitability of a contrarian portfolio strategy, a strategy that exploits negative serial dependence in asset returns in particular. The defining characteristic of a contrarian strategy is the purchase of securities that have performed poorly in the past and the sale of securities that have performed well.[2] Selling the "winners" and buying the "losers" will earn positive expected profits in the presence of negative serial correlation because current losers are likely to become future winners and current winners are likely to become future losers. Therefore, one implication of stock market overreaction is positive expected profits from a contrarian investment rule. It is the apparent profitability of several contrarian strategies that has led many to conclude that stock markets do indeed overreact.

In this article, we question this reverse implication, namely, that the profitability of contrarian investment strategies necessarily implies stock market overreaction. As an illustrative example, we construct a simple return-generating process in which each security's return is serially independent and yet will still yield positive expected profits for a portfolio strategy that buys losers and sells winners.

This counterintuitive result is a consequence of positive *cross-autocovariances* across securities, from which contrarian portfolio strategies benefit. If, for example, a high return for security A today implies that security B's return will probably be high tomorrow, then a contrarian investment strategy will be profitable even if each security's returns are unforecastable using past returns of that security alone. To see how, suppose the market consists of only the two stocks, A and B; if A's return is higher than the market today, a contrarian sells it and buys B. But if A and B are positively cross-autocorrelated, a higher return for A today implies a higher return for B tomorrow on average, thus the contrarian will have profited from his long position in B on average. Nowhere is it required that the stock market overreacts, that is, that individual returns are negatively autocorrelated. Therefore, the fact that some contrarian strategies have positive expected profits need not imply stock market overreaction. In fact, for the particular contrarian strategy we examine, over half of the expected profits are due to cross effects and not to negative autocorrelation in individual security returns.

Perhaps the most striking aspect of our empirical findings is that these cross effects are generally positive in sign and have a pro-

---

[2] Decisions about how performance is defined and for what length of time generate as many different kinds of contrarian strategies as there are theories of overreaction.

nounced lead–lag structure: The returns of large-capitalization stocks almost always lead those of smaller stocks. This result, coupled with the observation that individual security returns are generally weakly negatively autocorrelated, indicates that the recently documented positive autocorrelation in weekly returns indexes is *completely* attributable to cross effects. This provides important guidance for theoretical models of equilibrium asset prices attempting to explain positive index autocorrelation via time-varying conditional expected returns. Such theories must be capable of generating lead–lag patterns, since it is the cross-autocorrelations that are the source of positive dependence in stock returns.

Of course, positive index autocorrelation and lead–lag effects are also a symptom of the so-called "nonsynchronous trading" or "thin trading" problem, in which the prices of distinct securities are mistakenly assumed to be sampled simultaneously. Perhaps the first to show that nonsynchronous sampling of prices induces autocorrelated portfolio returns was Fisher (1966); hence the nonsynchronous trading problem is also known as the "Fisher effect."[3] Lead–lag effects are also a natural consequence of thin trading, as the models of Cohen et al. (1986) and Lo and MacKinlay (1989) show. To resolve this issue, we examine the magnitudes of index autocorrelation and cross-autocorrelations generated by a simple but general model of thin trading. We find that, although some of the correlation observed in the data may be due to this problem, to attribute all of it to thin trading would require unrealistically thin markets.

Because we focus only on the expected profits of the contrarian investment rule and not on its risk, our results have implications for stock market efficiency only insofar as they provide restrictions on economic models that might be consistent with the empirical results. In particular, we do not assert or deny the existence of "excessive" contrarian profits. Such an issue cannot be addressed without specifying an economic paradigm within which asset prices are rationally determined in equilibrium. Nevertheless, we show that the contrarian investment strategy is still a convenient tool for exploring the autocorrelation properties of stock returns.

In Section 1 we provide a summary of the autocorrelation properties of weekly returns, documenting the positive autocorrelation in portfolio returns and the negative autocorrelations of individual returns. Section 2 presents a formal analysis of the expected profits from a specific contrarian investment strategy under several different return-generating mechanisms and shows that positive expected profits need

---

[3] We refrain from this usage since the more common usage of the Fisher effect (that of Irving Fisher) is the one-for-one change in nominal interest rates with changes in expected inflation.

not be related to overreaction. We also develop our model of nonsynchronous trading and calculate the effect on the time-series properties of the observed data, to be used later in our empirical analysis. In Section 3, we attempt to quantify empirically the proportion of contrarian profits that can be attributed to overreaction, and find that a substantial portion cannot be. We show that a systematic lead-lag relationship among returns of size-sorted portfolios is an important source of contrarian profits, and is the *sole* source of positive index autocorrelation. Using the nontrading model of Section 2, we also conclude that the lead-lag patterns cannot be completely attributed to nonsynchronous prices. In Section 4 we provide some discussion of our use of weekly returns in contrast to the much longer-horizon returns used in previous studies of stock market overreaction, and we conclude in Section 5.

1. A Summary of Recent Findings

In Table 1 we report the first four autocorrelations of weekly equal-weighted and value-weighted returns indexes for the sample period from July 6, 1962, to December 31, 1987, where the indexes are constructed from the Center for Research in Security Prices (CRSP) daily returns files.[4] During this period, the equal-weighted index has a first-order autocorrelation $\hat{\rho}_1$ of approximately 30 percent. Since its heteroskedasticity-consistent standard error is .046, this autocorrelation is statistically different from zero at all conventional significance levels. The subperiod autocorrelations show that this significance is not an artifact of any particularly influential subsample; equal-weighted returns are strongly positively autocorrelated throughout the sample. Higher-order autocorrelations are also positive although generally smaller in magnitude, and decay at a somewhat slower rate than the geometric rate of an autoregressive process of order 1 [AR(1)] (for example, $\hat{\rho}_1^2$ is 8.8 percent whereas $\hat{\rho}_2$ is 11.6 percent).

To develop a sense of the economic importance of the autocorrelations, observe that the R^2 of a regression of returns on a constant and its first lag is the square of the slope coefficient, which is simply the first-order autocorrelation. Therefore, an autocorrelation of 30 percent implies that 9 percent of weekly return variation is predictable using only the preceding week's returns. In fact, the autocorrelation coefficients implicit in Lo and MacKinlay's (1988) variance ratios are as high as 49 percent for a subsample of the portfolio of stocks in the smallest-size quintile, implying an R^2 of about 25 percent.

---

[4] Unless stated otherwise, we take returns to be simple returns and not continuously compounded.

Table 1
Sample statistics for the weekly equal-weighted and value-weighted CRSP NYSE-AMEX stock-return indexes, for the period from July 6, 1962, to December 31, 1987, and subperiods

Time period	Sample size	Mean return, % × 100	Std. dev. of return, % × 100	$\hat{\rho}_1$ (SE)	$\hat{\rho}_2$ (SE)	$\hat{\rho}_3$ (SE)	$\hat{\rho}_4$ (SE)
Equal-weighted							
620706–871231	1330	.359	2.277	.296 (.046)	.116 (.037)	.081 (.034)	.045 (.035)
620706–750403	665	.264	2.326	.338 (.053)	.157 (.048)	.082 (.052)	.044 (.053)
750404–871231	665	.455	2.225	.248 (.076)	.071 (.058)	.078 (.042)	.040 (.045)
Value-weighted							
620706–871231	1330	.210	2.058	.074 (.040)	.007 (.037)	.021 (.036)	−.005 (.037)
620706–750403	665	.135	1.972	.055 (.058)	.020 (.055)	.058 (.060)	−.021 (.058)
750404–871231	665	.285	2.139	.091 (.055)	−.003 (.049)	−.014 (.042)	.007 (.046)

Heteroskedasticity-consistent standard errors for autocorrelation coefficients are given in parentheses.

It may, therefore, come as some surprise that individual returns are generally weakly negatively autocorrelated. Table 2 shows the cross-sectional average of autocorrelation coefficients across all stocks that have at least 52 nonmissing weekly returns during the sample period. For the entire cross section of the 4786 such stocks, the average first-order autocorrelation coefficient, denoted by $\overline{\hat{\rho}}_1$, is −3.4 percent with a cross-sectional standard deviation of 8.4 percent. Therefore, most of the individual first-order autocorrelations fall between −20 percent and 13 percent. This implies that most R^2's of regressions of individual security returns on their return last week fall between 0 and 4 percent, considerably less than the predictability of equal-weighted index returns. Average higher-order autocorrelations are also negative, though smaller in magnitude. The negativity of autocorrelations may be an indication of stock market overreaction for individual stocks, but it is also consistent with the existence of a bid–ask spread. We discuss this further in Section 2.

Table 2 also shows average autocorrelations within size-sorted quintiles.[5] The negative autocorrelations are stronger in the smallest quintile, but even the largest quintile has a negative average auto-

---

[5] Securities are allocated to quintiles by sorting only once (using market values of equity at the end of their sample periods); hence, the composition of quintiles does not change over time.

Contrarian Profits and Stock Market Overreaction

Table 2
Averages of autocorrelation coefficients for weekly returns on individual securities, for the period July 6, 1962, to December 31, 1987

Sample	Number of securities	$\bar{\rho}_1$ (SD)	$\bar{\rho}_2$ (SD)	$\bar{\rho}_3$ (SD)	$\bar{\rho}_4$ (SD)
All stocks	4786	−.034 (.084)	−.015 (.065)	−.003 (.062)	−.003 (.061)
Smallest quintile	957	−.079 (.095)	−.017 (.077)	−.007 (.068)	−.004 (.071)
Central quintile	958	−.027 (.082)	−.015 (.068)	−.003 (.067)	−.000 (.065)
Largest quintile	957	−.013 (.054)	−.014 (.050)	−.002 (.050)	−.005 (.047)

The statistic $\bar{\rho}_j$ is the average of jth-order autocorrelation coefficients of returns on individual stocks that have at least 52 nonmissing returns. The population standard deviation (SD) is given in parentheses. Since the autocorrelation coefficients are not cross-sectionally independent, the reported standard deviations cannot be used to draw the usual inferences; they are presented merely as a measure of cross-sectional variation in the autocorrelation coefficients.

correlation. Compared to the 30 percent autocorrelation of the equal-weighted index, the magnitudes of the individual autocorrelations indicated by the means (and standard deviations) in Table 2 are generally much smaller.

To conserve space, we omit corresponding tables for daily and monthly returns, in which similar patterns are observed. Autocorrelations are strongly positive for index returns (35.5 and 14.8 percent $\hat{\rho}_1$'s for the equal-weighted daily and monthly indexes, respectively), and weakly negative for individual securities (−1.4 and −2.9 percent $\bar{\rho}_1$'s for daily and monthly returns, respectively).

The importance of cross-autocorrelations is foreshadowed by the general tendency for individual security returns to be negatively autocorrelated and for portfolio returns, such as those of the equal- and value-weighted market index, to be positively autocorrelated. To see this, observe that the first-order autocovariance of an equal-weighted index may be written as the sum of the first-order own-autocovariances and *cross-autocovariances* of the component securities. If the own-autocovariances are generally negative, and the index autocovariance is positive, then the cross-autocovariances must be positive. Moreover, the cross-autocovariances must be large, so large as to exceed the sum of the negative own-autocovariances. Whereas virtually all contrarian strategies have focused on exploiting the negative own-autocorrelations of individual securities [see, e.g., DeBondt and Thaler (1985, 1987) and Lehmann (1988)], primarily attributed to overreaction, we show below that forecastability *across* securities is at least as important a source of contrarian profits both in principle and in fact.

181

2. Analysis of Contrarian Profitability

To show the relationship between contrarian profits and the cross effects that are apparent in the data, we examine the expected profits of one such strategy under various return-generating processes. Consider a collection of N securities and denote by R_t the $N \times 1$ vector of their period t returns $[R_{1t} \cdots R_{Nt}]'$. For convenience, we maintain the following assumption throughout this section:

Assumption 1. R_t *is a jointly covariance-stationary stochastic process with expectation* $E[R_t] = \mu \equiv [\mu_1\, \mu_2 \cdots \mu_N]'$ *and autocovariance matrices* $E[(R_{t-k} - \mu)(R_t - \mu)'] = \Gamma_k$ *where, with no loss of generality, we take* $k \geq 0$ *since* $\Gamma_k = \Gamma'_{-k}$.[6]

In the spirit of virtually all contrarian investment strategies, consider buying stocks at time t that were losers at time $t - k$ and selling stocks at time t that were winners at time $t - k$, where winning and losing is determined with respect to the equal-weighted return on the market. More formally, if $\omega_{it}(k)$ denotes the fraction of the portfolio devoted to security i at time t, let

$$\omega_{it}(k) = -(1/N)(R_{it-k} - R_{mt-k}) \qquad i = 1, \ldots, N \qquad (1)$$

where $R_{mt-k} \equiv \sum_{i=1}^{N} R_{it-k}/N$ is the equal-weighted market index.[7] If, for example, $k = 1$, then the portfolio strategy in period t is to short the winners and buy the losers of the previous period, $t - 1$. By construction, $\omega_t(k) \equiv [\omega_{1t}(k)\, \omega_{2t}(k) \cdots \omega_{Nt}(k)]'$ is an arbitrage portfolio since the weights sum to zero. Therefore, the total investment long (or short) at time t is given by $I_t(k)$ where

$$I_t(k) \equiv \frac{1}{2} \sum_{i=1}^{N} |\omega_{it}(k)| \qquad (2)$$

Since the portfolio weights are proportional to the differences between the market index and the returns, securities that deviate more positively from the market at time $t - k$ will have greater negative weight

---

[6] Assumption 1 is made for notational simplicity, since joint covariance-stationarity allows us to eliminate time indexes from population moments such as μ and Γ_k; the qualitative features of our results will not change under the weaker assumptions of weakly dependent heterogeneously distributed vectors R_t. This would merely require replacing expectations with corresponding probability limits of suitably defined time averages. The empirical results of Section 3 are based on these weaker assumptions; interested readers may refer to Assumptions A1–A3 in Appendix B.

[7] This is perhaps the simplest portfolio strategy that captures the essence of the contrarian principle. Lehmann (1988) also considers this strategy, although he employs a more complicated strategy in his empirical analysis in which the portfolio weights [Equation (1)] are renormalized each period by a random factor of proportionality, so that the investment is always $1 long and short. This portfolio strategy is also similar to that of DeBondt and Thaler (1985, 1987), although in contrast to our use of weekly returns, they consider holding periods of three years. See Section 4 for further discussion.

182

in the time t portfolio, and vice versa. Such a strategy is designed to take advantage of stock market overreactions as characterized, for example, by DeBondt and Thaler (1985): "(1) Extreme movements in stock prices will be followed by extreme movements in the opposite direction. (2) The more extreme the initial price movement, the greater will be the subsequent adjustment." The profit $\pi_t(k)$ from such a strategy is simply

$$\pi_t(k) = \sum_{i=1}^{N} \omega_{it}(k) R_{it} \tag{3}$$

Rearranging Equation (3) and taking expectations yields the following:

$$E[\pi_t(k)] = \frac{\iota' T_k \iota}{N^2} - \frac{1}{N} \text{tr}(\Gamma_k) - \frac{1}{N} \sum_{i=1}^{N} (\mu_i - \mu_m)^2 \tag{4}$$

where $\mu_m \equiv E[R_{mt}] = \mu' \iota/N$ and $\text{tr}(\cdot)$ denotes the trace operator.[8] The first term of Equation (4) is simply the kth-order autocovariance of the equal-weighted market index. The second term is the cross-sectional average of the kth-order autocovariances of the individual securities, and the third term is the cross-sectional variance of the mean returns. Since this last term is independent of the autocovariances Γ_k and does not vary with k, we define the *profitability index* $L_k \equiv L(\Gamma_k)$ and the constant $\sigma^2(\mu)$ as

$$L_k \equiv \frac{\iota' T_k \iota}{N^2} - \frac{1}{N} \text{tr}(\Gamma_k) \qquad \sigma^2(\mu) \equiv \frac{1}{N} \sum_{i=1}^{N} (\mu_i - \mu_m)^2 \tag{5}$$

Thus,

$$E[\pi_t(k)] = L_k - \sigma^2(\mu) \tag{6}$$

For purposes that will become evident below, we rewrite L_k as

$$L_k = C_k + O_k \tag{7}$$

where

$$C_k \equiv \frac{1}{N^2} [\iota' T_k \iota - \text{tr}(\Gamma_k)] \qquad O_k \equiv -\left(\frac{N-1}{N^2}\right) \text{tr}(\Gamma_k) \tag{8}$$

Hence,

$$E[\pi_t(k)] = C_k + O_k - \sigma^2(\mu) \tag{9}$$

---

[8] The derivation of Equation (4) is included in Appendix 1 for completeness. This is the population counterpart of Lehmann's (1988) sample moment equation (5) divided by N.

Written this way, it is apparent that expected profits may be decomposed into three terms: one (C_k) depending on only the off-diagonals of the autocovariance matrix Γ_k, the second (O_k) depending on only the diagonals, and a third $[\sigma^2(\mu)]$ that is independent of the autocovariances. This allows us to separate the fraction of expected profits due to the cross-autocovariances C_k versus the own-autocovariances O_k of returns.

Equation (9) shows that the profitability of the contrarian strategy (1) may be perfectly consistent with a positively autocorrelated market index and negatively autocorrelated individual security returns. Positive cross-autocovariances imply that the term C_k is positive, and negative autocovariances for individual securities imply that O_k is also positive. Conversely, the empirical finding that equal-weighted indexes are strongly positively autocorrelated while individual security returns are weakly negatively autocorrelated implies that there must be significant positive cross-autocorrelations across securities. To see this, observe that the first-order autocorrelation of the equal-weighted index R_{mt} is simply

$$\frac{\text{Cov}[R_{mt-1}, R_{mt}]}{\text{Var}[R_{mt}]} = \frac{\iota'\Gamma_1\iota}{\iota'\Gamma_0\iota} = \frac{\iota'\Gamma_1\iota - \text{tr}(\Gamma_1)}{\iota'\Gamma_0\iota} + \frac{\text{tr}(\Gamma_1)}{\iota'\Gamma_0\iota} \qquad (10)$$

The numerator of the second term on the right-hand side of Equation (10) is simply the sum of the first-order autocovariances of individual securities; if this is negative, then the first term must be positive in order for the sum to be positive. Therefore, the positive autocorrelation in weekly returns may be attributed solely to the positive cross-autocorrelations across securities.

The expression for L_k also suggests that stock market overreaction need not be the reason that contrarian investment strategies are profitable. To anticipate the examples below, if returns are positively cross-autocorrelated, then a return-reversal strategy will yield positive profits on average, even if individual security returns are *serially independent*! The presence of stock market overreaction, that is, negatively autocorrelated individual returns, enhances the profitability of the return-reversal strategy, but it is not required for such a strategy to earn positive expected returns.

To organize our understanding of the sources and nature of contrarian profits, we provide five illustrative examples below. Although simplistic, they provide a useful taxonomy of conditions necessary for the profitability of the portfolio strategy (1).

2.1 The independently and identically distributed benchmark

Let returns R_t be both cross-sectionally and serially independent. In this case $\Gamma_k = 0$ for all nonzero k; hence,

$$L_k = C_k = O_k = 0 \qquad E[\pi_t(k)] = -\sigma^2(\mu) \le 0 \qquad (11)$$

Although returns are both serially and cross-sectionally unforecastable, the expected profits are negative as long as there is some cross-sectional variation in expected returns. In this case, our strategy reduces to shorting the higher and buying the lower mean return securities, respectively, a losing proposition even when stock market prices do follow random walks. Since $\sigma^2(\mu)$ is generally of small magnitude and does not depend on the autocovariance structure of R_t, we will focus on L_k and ignore $\sigma^2(\mu)$ for the remainder of Section 2.

2.2 Stock market overreaction and fads

Almost any operational definition of stock market overreaction implies that individual security returns are negatively autocorrelated over some holding period, so that "what goes up must come down," and vice versa. If we denote by $\gamma_{ij}(k)$ the (i, j)th element of the autocovariance matrix Γ_k, the overreaction hypothesis implies that the diagonal elements of Γ_k are negative, that is, $\gamma_{ii}(k) < 0$, at least for $k = 1$ when the span of one period corresponds to a complete cycle of overreaction.[9] Since the overreaction hypothesis generally does not restrict the cross-autocovariances, for simplicity we set them to zero, that is, $\gamma_{ij}(k) = 0$, $i \ne j$. Hence, we have

$$\Gamma_k = \begin{bmatrix} \gamma_{11}(k) & 0 & \cdots & 0 \\ 0 & \gamma_{22}(k) & \cdots & 0 \\ \vdots & \vdots & \ddots & \vdots \\ 0 & 0 & \cdots & \gamma_{NN}(k) \end{bmatrix} \qquad (12)$$

The profitability index under these assumptions for R_t is then

$$L_k = O_k = -\left(\frac{N-1}{N^2}\right)\text{tr}(\Gamma_k)$$

$$= -\left(\frac{N-1}{N^2}\right)\sum_{i=1}^{N}\gamma_{ii}(k) > 0 \qquad (13)$$

where the cross-autocovariance term C_k is zero. The positivity of L_k follows from the negativity of the own-autocovariances, assuming $N > 1$. Not surprisingly, if stock markets do overreact, the contrarian investment strategy is profitable on average.

Another price process for which the return-reversal strategy will

---

[9] See Section 4 for further discussion of the importance of the return horizon.

yield positive expected profits is the sum of a random walk and an AR(1), which has been recently proposed, by Summers (1986), for example, as a model of "fads" or "animal spirits." Specifically, let the dynamics for the log-price X_{it} of each security i be given by

$$X_{it} = Y_{it} + Z_{it} \tag{14}$$

where

$$Y_{it} = \mu_i + Y_{it-1} + \epsilon_{it} \qquad Z_{it} = \rho_i Z_{it-1} + \nu_{it} \qquad 0 < \rho < 1 \tag{15}$$

and the disturbances $\{\epsilon_{it}\}$ and $\{\nu_{it}\}$ are serially, mutually, and cross-sectionally independent at all *nonzero* leads and lags.[10] The kth-order autocovariance for the return vector R_t is then given by the following diagonal matrix:

$$\Gamma_k = \text{diag}\left[-\rho_1^{k-1}\left(\frac{1-\rho_1}{1+\rho_1}\right)\sigma_{\nu_1}^2, \ldots, -\rho_N^{k-1}\left(\frac{1-\rho_N}{1+\rho_N}\right)\sigma_{\nu_N}^2\right] \tag{16}$$

and the profitability index follows immediately as

$$L_k = O_k = -\left(\frac{N-1}{N^2}\right)\text{tr}(\Gamma_k)$$

$$= \frac{N-1}{N^2} \sum_{i=1}^{N} \rho_i^{k-1}\left(\frac{1-\rho_i}{1+\rho_i}\right)\sigma_{\nu_i}^2 > 0 \tag{17}$$

Since the own-autocovariances in Equation (16) are all negative, this is a special case of Equation (12) and therefore may be interpreted as an example of stock market overreaction. However, the fact that returns are negatively autocorrelated at all lags is an artifact of the first-order autoregressive process and need not be true for the sum of a random walk and a general stationary process, a model that has been proposed for both stock market fads and time-varying expected returns [e.g., see Fama and French (1988) and Summers (1986)]. For example, let the "temporary" component of Equation (14) be given by the following stationary AR(2) process:

$$Z_{it} = \frac{9}{7} Z_{it-1} - \frac{5}{7} Z_{it-2} + \nu_{it} \tag{18}$$

It is easily verified that the first difference of Z_{it} is positively autocorrelated at lag 1 implying that $L_1 < 0$. Therefore, stock market overreaction necessarily implies the profitability of the portfolio strategy

---

[10] This last assumption requires only that ϵ_{it-k} be independent of ϵ_{it} for $k \neq 0$; hence, the disturbances may be contemporaneously cross-sectionally dependent without loss of generality.

Contrarian Profits and Stock Market Overreaction

(1) (in the absence of cross-autocorrelation), but stock market fads do not.

2.3 Trading on white noise and lead-lag relations

Let the return-generating process for R_t be given by

$$R_{it} = \mu_i + \beta_i \Lambda_{t-i} + \epsilon_{it} \quad \beta_i > 0 \quad i = 1, \ldots, N \quad (19)$$

where Λ_t is a serially independent common factor with zero mean and variance σ_λ^2, and the ϵ_{it}'s are assumed to be both cross-sectionally and serially independent. These assumptions imply that for each security i, its returns are white noise (with drift) so that future returns to i are not forecastable from its past returns. This serial independence is *not* consistent with either the spirit or form of the stock market overreaction hypothesis. And yet it *is* possible to predict i's returns using past returns of security j, where $j < i$. This is an artifact of the dependence of the ith security's return on a lagged common factor, where the lag is determined by the security's index. Consequently, the return to security 1 leads that of securities 2, 3, etc.; the return to security 2 leads that of securities 3, 4, etc.; and so on. However, the current return to security 2 provides no information for future returns to security 1, and so on. To see that such a lead-lag relation will induce positive expected profits for the contrarian strategy (1), observe that when $k < N$, the autocovariance matrix Γ_k has zeros in all entries except along the kth superdiagonal, for which $\gamma_{ii+k} = \sigma_\lambda^2 \beta_i \beta_{i+k}$. Also, observe that this lead-lag model yields an *asymmetric* autocovariance matrix Γ_k. The profitability index is then

$$L_k = C_k = \frac{\sigma_\lambda^2}{N^2} \sum_{i=1}^{N-k} \beta_i \beta_{i+k} > 0 \quad (20)$$

This example highlights the importance of the cross effects—although each security is individually unpredictable, a contrarian strategy may still profit if securities are positively cross-correlated at various leads and lags. Less contrived return-generating processes will also yield positive expected profits to contrarian strategies, as long as the cross-autocovariances are sufficiently large.

2.4 Lead-lag effects and nonsynchronous trading

One possible source of such cross effects is what has come to be known as the "nonsynchronous trading" or "nontrading" problem, in which the prices of distinct securities are mistakenly assumed to be sampled simultaneously. Treating nonsynchronous prices as if they were observed at the same time can create spurious autocorrelation and cross-autocorrelation, as Fisher (1966), Scholes and Williams

(1977), and Cohen et al. (1986) have demonstrated. To gauge the importance of nonsynchronous trading for contrarian profits, we derive the magnitude of the spurious cross-autocorrelations using the nontrading model of Lo and MacKinlay (1989).[11]

Consider a collection of N securities with *unobservable* "virtual" continuously compounded returns R_{it} at time t, where $i = 1, \ldots, N$, and assume that they are generated by the following stochastic model:

$$R_{it} = \mu_i + \beta_i \Lambda_t + \epsilon_{it} \qquad i = 1, \ldots, N \qquad (21)$$

where Λ_t is some zero-mean common factor and ϵ_{it} is zero-mean idiosyncratic noise that is temporally and cross-sectionally independent at all leads and lags. Since we wish to focus on nontrading as the *sole* source of autocorrelation, we also assume that the common factor Λ_t is independently and identically distributed and is independent of ϵ_{it-k} for all i, t, and k.

In each period t there is some chance that security i does not trade, say with probability p_i. If it does not trade, its observed return for period t is simply 0, although its true or virtual return R_{it} is still given by Equation (21). In the next period $t + 1$ there is again some chance that security i does not trade, also with probability p_i. We assume that whether or not the security traded in period t does not influence the likelihood of its trading in period $t + 1$ or any other future period; hence, our nontrading mechanism is independent and identically distributed for each security i.[12] If security i does trade in period $t + 1$ and did not trade in period t, we assume that its observed return R^o_{it+1} at $t + 1$ is the sum of its virtual returns R_{it+1}, R_{it}, and virtual returns for all past *consecutive* periods in which i has not traded. In fact, the observed return in any period is simply the sum of its virtual returns for all past consecutive periods in which it did not trade. This captures the essential feature of nontrading as a source of spurious autocorrelation: News affects those stocks that trade more frequently first and influences the returns of thinly traded securities with a lag. In this framework, the effect of news is captured by the virtual returns process (21), and the lag induced by nonsynchronous trading is therefore built into the observed returns process R^o_{it}.

More formally, the observed returns process may be written as the following weighted average of past virtual returns:

$$R^o_{it} = \sum_{k=0}^{\infty} X_{it}(k) R_{it-k} \qquad i = 1, \ldots, N \qquad (22)$$

---

[11] The empirical relevance of other nontrading effects, such as the negative autocorrelation of individual returns, is beyond the scope of this study and is explored in depth by Atkinson et al. (1987) and Lo and MacKinlay (1989).

[12] This assumption may be relaxed to allow for state-dependent probabilities, that is, autocorrelated nontrading [see Lo and MacKinlay (1989) for further details].

Contrarian Profits and Stock Market Overreaction

Here the (random) weights $X_{it}(k)$ are defined as products of no-trade indicators:

$$X_{it}(k) \equiv (1 - \delta_{it})\delta_{it-1}\delta_{it-2} \cdots \delta_{it-k}$$

$$= \begin{cases} 1 & \text{with probability } (1 - p_i)p_i^k \\ 0 & \text{with probability } 1 - (1 - p_i)p_i^k \end{cases} \quad (23)$$

for $k > 0$, $X_{it}(0) \equiv 1 - \delta_{it}$, and where the δ_{it}'s are independently and identically distributed Bernoulli random variables that take on the value 1 when security i does not trade at time t, and 0 otherwise. The variable $X_{it}(k)$ is also an indicator variable, and takes on the value 1 if security i trades at time t but not in any of the k previous periods, and takes on the value 0 otherwise. If security i does not trade at time t, then $\delta_{it} = 1$, which implies that $X_{it}(k) = 0$ for all k; thus, $R_{it}^o = 0$. If i does trade at time t, then its observed return is equal to the sum of today's virtual return R_{it} and its past $\tilde{k}_{it}$ virtual returns, where the random variable $\tilde{k}_{it}$ is the number of past *consecutive* periods that i has not traded. We call this the *duration* of nontrading, and it may be expressed as

$$\tilde{k}_{it} \equiv \sum_{k=1}^{\infty} \left(\prod_{j=1}^{k} \delta_{it-j} \right) \quad (24)$$

To develop some intuition for the nontrading probabilities p_i, observe that

$$E[\tilde{k}_{it}] = p_i/(1 - p_i) \quad (25)$$

If $p_i = \frac{1}{2}$, then the average duration of nontrading for security i is one period. However, if $p_i = \frac{3}{4}$, then the average duration of nontrading increases to three periods. As expected if the security trades every period so that $p_i = 0$, the mean (and variance) of $\tilde{k}_{it}$ is zero.

Further simplification results from grouping securities with common nontrading probabilities into portfolios. If, for example, an equal-weighted portfolio contains securities with common nontrading probability p_κ, then the observed return to portfolio κ may be approximated as

$$R_{\kappa t}^o \stackrel{a}{=} \mu_\kappa + (1 - p_\kappa)\beta_\kappa \sum_{k=0}^{\infty} p_\kappa^k \Lambda_{t-k} \quad (26)$$

where the approximation becomes exact as the number of securities in the portfolio approaches infinity, and where β_κ is the average beta of the securities in the portfolio.

Now define $R_{\kappa\tau}^o(q)$ as the observed return of portfolio κ over q periods, that is, $R_{\kappa\tau}^o(q) \equiv \sum_{i=(\tau-1)q+1}^{\tau q} R_{\kappa\tau}^o$. We wish to work with time-aggregated returns $R_{\kappa\tau}^o(q)$ to allow nontrading to take place at intervals finer than the sampling interval.[13] Using Equation (26), we have the following moments and co-moments of observed portfolio returns:[14]

$$E[R_{\kappa\tau}^o](q) \stackrel{a}{=} q\mu_\kappa = E[R_{\kappa\tau}(q)] \tag{27}$$

$$\text{Var}[R_{\kappa\tau}^o(q)] \stackrel{a}{=} \left[q - 2p_\kappa \frac{1-p_\kappa^q}{1-p_\kappa^2}\right]\beta_\kappa^2 \sigma_\lambda^2 \tag{28}$$

$$\text{Cov}[R_{\kappa\tau-k}^o(q), R_{\kappa\tau}^o(q)] \stackrel{a}{=} \left[\frac{1-p_\kappa}{1+p_\kappa}\right]\left[\frac{1-p_\kappa^q}{1-p_\kappa}\right]^2 p_\kappa^{kq-q+1}\beta_\kappa^2 \sigma_\lambda^2 \quad k>0 \tag{29}$$

$$\text{Corr}[R_{a\tau-k}^o(q), R_{b\tau}^o(q)] \stackrel{a}{=} \frac{(1-p_\kappa^q)^2 \, p_\kappa^{kq-q+1}}{q(1-p_\kappa^2) - 2p_\kappa(1-p_\kappa^q)} \quad k>0 \tag{30}$$

$$\text{Cov}[R_{a\tau-k}^o(q), R_{b\tau}^o(q)] \stackrel{a}{=} \frac{(1-p_a)(1-p_b)}{1-p_a p_b}\left[\frac{1-p_b^q}{1-p_b}\right]^2 p_b^{kq-q+1}\beta_a\beta_b\sigma_\lambda^2 \tag{31}$$

$$\text{Corr}[R_{a\tau-k}^o(q), R_{b\tau}^o(q)] \equiv \rho_{ab}^q(k)$$

$$\stackrel{a}{=} \left[\frac{(1-p_a)(1-p_b)}{1-p_a p_b}\left(\frac{1-p_b^q}{1-p_b}\right)^2 p_b^{kq-q+1}\right] \tag{32}$$

$$\times \left(\sqrt{q - 2p_a\frac{1-p_a^q}{1-p_a^2}} \sqrt{q - 2p_b\frac{1-p_b^q}{1-p_b^2}}\right)^{-1}$$

where $R_{a\tau}^o(q)$ and $R_{b\tau}^o(q)$ are the time-aggregated observed returns of two arbitrary portfolios a and b. Using (29) and (31), the effects of nontrading on contrarian profits may be quantified explicitly. A lead-lag structure may also be deduced from Equation (32). To see this, consider the ratio of the cross-autocorrelation coefficients:

$$\frac{\rho_{ab}^q(k)}{\rho_{ba}^q(k)} = \left[\left(\frac{1-p_b^q}{1-p_a^q}\right)\left(\frac{1-p_b}{1-p_a}\right)\right]^2 \left(\frac{p_b}{p_a}\right)^{kq-q+1}$$

$$\gtreqless 1 \quad \text{as} \quad p_b \gtreqless p_a \tag{33}$$

which shows that portfolios with higher nontrading probabilities tend to lag those with lower nontrading probabilities. For example, if $p_b > p_a$ so that securities in portfolio b trade less frequently than those in portfolio a, then the correlation between today's return on a and

---

[13] So, for example, although we use weekly returns in our empirical analysis below, the implications of nontrading that we are about to derive still obtain for securities that may not trade on some days within the week.

[14] See Lo and MacKinlay (1989) for the derivations.

tomorrow's return on *b* exceeds the correlation between today's return on *b* and tomorrow's return on *a*.

To check the magnitude of the cross-correlations that can result from nonsynchronous prices, consider two portfolios *a* and *b* with daily nontrading probabilities $p_a = .10$ and $p_b = .25$. Using Equation (32), with $q = 5$ for weekly returns and $k = 1$ for the first-order cross-autocorrelation, yields $\text{Corr}[R_{at-1}, R_{bt}] = .066$ and $\text{Corr}[R_{bt-1}, R_{at}] = .019$. Although there is a pronounced lead-lag effect, the cross-autocorrelations are small. We shall return to these cross-autocorrelations in our empirical analysis below, where we show that values of .10 and .25 for nontrading probabilities are considerably larger than the data suggest. Even if we eliminate nontrading in portfolio *a* so that $p_a = 0$, this yields $\text{Corr}[R_{at-1}, R_{bt}] = .070$ and $\text{Corr}[R_{bt-1}, R_{at}] = .000$. Therefore, as we shall see below, the magnitude of weekly cross-autocorrelations cannot be completely attributed to the effects of nonsynchronous trading.

2.5 A positively dependent common factor and the bid-ask spread

A plausible return-generating mechanism consistent with positive index autocorrelation and negative serial dependence in individual returns is to let each R_{it} be the sum of three components: a positively autocorrelated common factor, idiosyncratic white noise, and a bid-ask spread process.[15] More formally, let

$$R_{it} = \mu_i + \beta_i \Lambda_t + \eta_{it} + \epsilon_{it} \qquad (34)$$

where

$$E[\Lambda_t] = 0 \qquad E[\Lambda_{t-k}\Lambda_t] \equiv \gamma_\lambda(k) > 0 \qquad (35)$$

$$E[\epsilon_{it}] = E[\eta_{it}] = 0 \qquad \forall i, t \qquad (36)$$

$$E[\epsilon_{it-k}\epsilon_{jt}] = \begin{cases} \sigma_i^2 & \text{if } k = 0 \text{ and } i = j \\ 0 & \text{otherwise} \end{cases} \qquad (37)$$

$$E[\eta_{it-k}\eta_{jt}] = \begin{cases} -\dfrac{s_i^2}{4} & \text{if } k = 1 \text{ and } i = j \\ 0 & \text{otherwise} \end{cases} \qquad (38)$$

Implicit in Equation (38) is Roll's (1984) model of the bid-ask spread, in which the first-order autocorrelation of η_{it} is the negative of one-fourth the square of the percentage bid-ask spread s_i, and all higher-order autocorrelations and all cross-correlations are zero. Such a return-

---

[15] This is suggested in Lo and MacKinlay (1988). Conrad, Kaul, and Nimalendran (1988) investigate a similar specification.

generating process will yield a positively autocorrelated market index since averaging the white-noise and bid–ask components will trivialize them, leaving the common factor Λ_t. Yet if the bid–ask spread is large enough, it may dominate the common factor for each security, yielding negatively autocorrelated individual security returns.

The autocovariance matrices for Equation (34) are given by

$$\Gamma_1 = \gamma_\lambda(1)\beta\beta' - \tfrac{1}{4}\mathrm{diag}[s_1^2, s_2^2, \ldots, s_N^2] \qquad (39)$$

$$\Gamma_k = \gamma_\lambda(k)\beta\beta' \qquad k > 1 \qquad (40)$$

where $\beta \equiv [\beta_1, \beta_2 \cdots \beta_N]'$. In contrast to the lead–lag model of Section 2.4, the autocovariance matrices for this return-generating process are all symmetric. This is an important empirical implication that distinguishes the common factor model from the lead–lag process, and will be exploited in our empirical appraisal of overreaction.

Denote by β_m the cross-sectional average $\Sigma_{i=1}^N \beta_i/N$. Then the profitability index is given by

$$L_1 = -\frac{\gamma_\lambda(1)}{N}\sum_{i=1}^N (\beta_i - \beta_m)^2 + \frac{N-1}{N^2}\sum_{i=1}^N \frac{s_i^2}{4} \qquad (41)$$

$$L_k = -\frac{\gamma_\lambda(k)}{N}\sum_{i=1}^N (\beta_i - \beta_m)^2 \qquad k > 1 \qquad (42)$$

Equation (41) shows that if the bid–ask spreads are large enough and the cross-sectional variation of the β_k's is small enough, the contrarian strategy (1) may yield positive expected profits when using only one lag ($k = 1$) in computing portfolio weights. However, the positivity of the profitability index is due solely to the negative autocorrelations of individual security returns induced by the bid–ask spread. Once this effect is removed, for example, when portfolio weights are computed using lags 2 or higher, relation (42) shows that the profitability index is of the opposite sign of the index autocorrelation coefficient $\gamma_\lambda(k)$. Since $\gamma_\lambda(k) > 0$ by assumption, expected profits are negative for lags higher than 1. In view of the empirical results to be reported in Section 3, in which L_k is shown to be positive for $k > 1$, it seems unlikely that the return-generating process (34) can account for the weekly autocorrelation patterns in the data.

3. An Empirical Appraisal of Overreaction

To see how much of contrarian profits is due to stock market overreaction, we estimate the expected profits from the return-reversal strategy of Section 2 for a sample of CRSP NYSE-AMEX securities.

Contrarian Profits and Stock Market Overreaction

Recall that $E[\pi_t(k)] = C_k + O_k - \sigma^2(\mu)$ where C_k depends only on the cross-autocovariances of returns and O_k depends only on the own-autocovariances. Table 3 shows estimates of $E[\pi_t(k)]$, C_k, O_k, and $\sigma^2(\mu)$ for the 551 stocks that have no missing weekly returns during the entire sample period from July 6, 1962, to December 31, 1987. Estimates are computed for the sample of all stocks and for three size-sorted quintiles. All size-sorted portfolios are constructed by sorting only once (using market values of equity at the middle of the sample period); hence, their composition does not change over time. We develop the appropriate sampling theory in Appendix 2, in which the covariance-stationarity assumption 1 is replaced with weaker assumptions allowing for serial dependence and heterogeneity.

Consider the last three columns in Table 3, which show the magnitudes of the three terms $\hat{C}_k$, $\hat{O}_k$, and $\sigma^2(\hat{\mu})$ as percentages of expected profits. At lag 1, half the expected profits from the contrarian strategy are due to positive cross-autocovariances. In the central quintile, about 67 percent of the expected profits is attributable to these cross effects. The results at lag 2 are similar: Positive cross-autocovariances account for about 50 percent of the expected profits, 66 percent for the smallest quintile.

The positive expected profits at lags 2 and higher provide direct evidence against the common component/bid-ask spread model of Section 2.5. If returns contained a positively autocorrelated common factor and exhibited negative autocorrelation due to "bid-ask bounce," expected profits can be positive only at lag 1; higher lags must exhibit negative expected profits as Equation (42) shows. Table 3 shows that estimated expected profits are significantly positive for lags 2 through 4 in all portfolios except one.

The z-statistics for $\hat{C}_k$, $\hat{O}_k$, and $\hat{E}[\pi_t(k)]$ are asymptotically standard normal under the null hypothesis that the population values corresponding to the three estimators are zero. At lag 1, they are almost all significantly different from zero at the 1 percent level. At higher lags, the own- and cross-autocovariance terms are generally insignificant. However, estimated expected profits retains its significance even at lag 4, largely as a result of the behavior of small stocks. The curious fact that $\hat{E}[\pi_t(k)]$ is statistically different from zero whereas $\hat{C}_k$ and $\hat{O}_k$ are not suggests that there is important negative correlation between the two estimators $\hat{C}_k$ and $\hat{O}_k$.[16] That is, although they are both noisy estimates, the variance of their sum is less than each of their variances because they co-vary negatively. Since $\hat{C}_k$ and $\hat{O}_k$ are both functions of second moments and co-moments, significant correlation of the two estimators implies the importance of fourth co-

---

[16] We have investigated the unlikely possibility that $\sigma^2(\hat{\mu})$ is responsible for this anomaly; it is not.

Table 3
Analysis of the profitability of the return-reversal strategy applied to weekly returns, for the sample of 551 CRSP NYSE-AMEX stocks with nonmissing weekly returns from July 6, 1962, to December 31, 1987 (1330 weeks)

Portfolio	Lag k	$\hat{C}_k$[1] (z-stat.)	$\hat{O}_k$[1] (z-stat.)	$\sigma^2(\hat{\mu})$[1]	$\hat{E}[\pi_t(k)]$[1] (z-stat.)	$\bar{I}_t(k)$[1] (SD[1])	%·$\hat{C}_k$	%·$\hat{O}_k$	%·$\sigma^2(\hat{\mu})$
All stocks	1	0.841 (4.95)	0.862 (4.54)	.009	1.694 (20.81)	151.9 (31.0)	49.6	50.9	−0.5
Smallest	1	2.048 (6.36)	2.493 (7.12)	.009	4.532 (18.81)	208.8 (47.3)	45.2	55.0	−0.2
Central	1	0.703 (4.67)	0.366 (2.03)	.011	1.058 (13.84)	138.4 (32.2)	66.5	34.6	−1.0
Largest	1	0.188 (1.18)	0.433 (2.61)	.005	0.617 (11.22)	117.0 (28.1)	30.5	70.3	−0.8
All stocks	2	0.253 (1.64)	0.298 (1.67)	.009	0.542 (10.63)	151.8 (31.0)	46.7	54.9	−1.6
Smallest	2	0.803 (3.29)	0.421 (1.49)	.009	1.216 (8.86)	208.8 (47.3)	66.1	34.7	−0.7
Central	2	0.184 (1.20)	0.308 (1.64)	.011	0.481 (7.70)	138.3 (32.2)	38.3	64.0	−2.3
Largest	2	−0.053 (−0.39)	0.366 (2.28)	.005	0.308 (5.89)	116.9 (28.1)	−17.3	118.9	−1.6
All stocks	3	0.223 (1.60)	−0.066 (−0.39)	.009	0.149 (3.01)	151.7 (30.9)	149.9	−44.0	−5.9
Smallest	3	0.552 (2.73)	0.038 (0.14)	.009	0.582 (3.96)	208.7 (47.3)	94.9	6.6	−1.5
Central	3	0.237 (1.66)	−0.192 (−1.07)	.011	0.035 (0.50)	138.2 (32.1)	677.6	−546.7	−30.9
Largest	3	0.064 (0.39)	−0.003 (−0.02)	.005	0.056 (1.23)	116.9 (28.1)	114.0	−5.3	−8.8
All stocks	4	0.056 (0.43)	0.083 (0.51)	.009	0.130 (2.40)	151.7 (30.9)	43.3	63.5	−6.7
Smallest	4	0.305 (1.53)	0.159 (0.59)	.009	0.455 (3.27)	208.7 (47.3)	67.0	34.9	−1.9
Central	4	0.023 (0.18)	−0.045 (−0.26)	.011	−0.033 (−0.44)	138.2 (32.0)	—[2]	—[2]	—[2]
Largest	4	−0.097 (−0.65)	0.128 (0.77)	.005	0.026 (0.52)	116.8 (28.0)	−374.6	493.4	−18.8

Expected profits are given by $E[\pi_t(k)] = C_k + O_k - \sigma^2(\mu)$, where C_k depends only on cross-autocovariances and O_k depends only on own-autocovariances. All z-statistics are asymptotically $N(0, 1)$ under the null hypothesis that the relevant population value is zero, and are robust to heteroskedasticity and autocorrelation. The average long position $\bar{I}_t(k)$ is also reported, with its sample standard deviation in parentheses underneath. The analysis is conducted for all stocks as well as for the five size-sorted quintiles; to conserve space, results for the second and fourth quintiles have been omitted.

[1] Multiplied by 10,000.
[2] Not computed when expected profits are negative.

moments, perhaps as a result of co-skewness or kurtosis. This is beyond the scope of our article, but bears further investigation.

Table 3 also shows the average long (and hence short) positions generated by the return-reversal strategy over the 1330-week sample period. For all stocks, the average weekly long-short position is $152 and the average weekly profit is $1.69. In contrast, applying the same strategy to a portfolio of small stocks yields an expected profit of $4.53 per week, but requires only $209 long and short each week on average.

Contrarian Profits and Stock Market Overreaction

The ratio of expected profits to average long investment is 1.1 percent for all stocks, and 2.2 percent for stocks in the smallest quintile. Of course, in the absence of market frictions such comparisons are irrelevant, since an arbitrage portfolio strategy may be scaled arbitrarily. However, if the size of one's long–short position is constrained, as is sometimes the case in practice, then the average investment figures shown in Table 3 suggest that applying the contrarian strategy to small firms would be more profitable on average.

Using stocks with continuous listing for over 20 years obviously induces a survivorship bias that is difficult to evaluate. To reduce this bias we have performed similar analyses for two subsamples: stocks with continuous listing for the first and second halves of the 1330-week sample, respectively. In both subperiods positive cross effects account for at least 50 percent of expected profits at lag 1, and generally more at higher lags. Since the patterns are virtually identical to those in Table 3, to conserve space we omit these additional tables.

To develop further intuition for the pattern of these cross effects, we report in Table 4 cross-autocorrelation matrices $\hat{\Upsilon}_k$ for the vector of returns on the five size-sorted quintiles and the equal-weighted index using the sample of 551 stocks. Let Z_t denote the vector $[R_{1t}\ R_{2t}\ R_{3t}\ R_{4t}\ R_{5t}\ R_{mt}]'$, where R_{it} is the return on the equal-weighted portfolio of stocks in the ith quintile, and R_{mt} is the return on the equal-weighted portfolio of all stocks. Then the kth-order autocorrelation *matrix* of Z_t is given by $\Upsilon_k \equiv D^{-1/2} E[(Z_{t-k} - \mu)(Z_t - \mu)'] \times D^{-1/2}$, where $D \equiv \text{diag}[\sigma_1^2, \ldots, \sigma_5^2, \sigma_m^2]$ and $\mu \equiv E[Z_t]$. By this convention, the (i, j)th element of Υ_k is the correlation of R_{it-k} with R_{jt}. The estimator $\hat{\Upsilon}_k$ is the usual sample autocorrelation matrix. Note that it is only the upper left 5 × 5 submatrix of Υ_k that is related to Γ_k, since the full matrix Υ_k also contains autocorrelations between portfolio returns and the equal-weighted market index R_{mt}.[17]

An interesting pattern emerges from Table 4: The entries below the diagonals of $\hat{\Upsilon}_k$ are, almost always larger than those above the diagonals (excluding the last row and column, which are the autocovariances between portfolio returns and the market). This implies that current returns of smaller stocks are correlated with past returns of larger stocks, but not vice versa, a distinct lead–lag relation based on size. For example, the first-order autocorrelation between last week's return on large stocks $(R_{5,t-1})$ with this week's return on small stocks $(R_{1,t})$ is 27.6 percent, whereas the first-order autocorrelation between last week's return on small stocks $(R_{1,t-1})$ with this week's return on large stocks $(R_{5,t})$ is only 2.0 percent! Similar patterns may

---

[17] We include the market return in our autocovariance matrices so that those who wish to may compute portfolio betas and market volatilities from our tables.

Table 4
Autocorrelation matrices of the vector $Z_t \equiv [R_{1t}, R_{2t}, R_{3t}, R_{4t}, R_{5t}, R_{mt}]'$ where R_{it} is the return on the portfolio of stocks in the ith quintile, $i = 1, \ldots, 5$ (quintile 1 contains the smallest stocks) and R_{mt} is the return on the equal-weighted index, for the sample of 551 stocks with nonmissing weekly returns from July 6, 1962, to December 31, 1987 (1330 observations)

		R_{1t}	R_{2t}	R_{3t}	R_{4t}	R_{5t}	R_{mt}
$\hat{\Upsilon}_0 =$	R_{1t}	1.000	0.919	0.857	0.830	0.747	0.918
	R_{2t}	0.919	1.000	0.943	0.929	0.865	0.976
	R_{3t}	0.857	0.943	1.000	0.964	0.925	0.979
	R_{4t}	0.830	0.929	0.964	1.000	0.946	0.974
	R_{5t}	0.747	0.865	0.925	0.946	1.000	0.933
	R_{mt}	0.918	0.976	0.979	0.974	0.933	1.000
$\hat{\Upsilon}_1 =$	R_{1t-1}	0.333	0.244	0.143	0.101	0.020	0.184
	R_{2t-1}	0.334	0.252	0.157	0.122	0.033	0.195
	R_{3t-1}	0.325	0.265	0.175	0.140	0.051	0.207
	R_{4t-1}	0.316	0.262	0.177	0.139	0.050	0.204
	R_{5t-1}	0.276	0.230	0.154	0.122	0.044	0.178
	R_{mt-1}	0.333	0.262	0.168	0.130	0.041	0.202
$\hat{\Upsilon}_2 =$	R_{1t-2}	0.130	0.087	0.044	0.022	0.005	0.064
	R_{2t-2}	0.133	0.101	0.058	0.039	0.017	0.076
	R_{3t-2}	0.114	0.088	0.046	0.027	0.002	0.061
	R_{4t-2}	0.101	0.085	0.048	0.029	0.008	0.059
	R_{5t-2}	0.067	0.055	0.020	0.008	−0.012	0.031
	R_{mt-2}	0.115	0.087	0.045	0.026	0.004	0.061
$\hat{\Upsilon}_3 =$	R_{1t-3}	0.089	0.047	0.015	0.013	−0.005	0.036
	R_{2t-3}	0.094	0.066	0.038	0.041	0.018	0.056
	R_{3t-3}	0.096	0.079	0.059	0.061	0.041	0.072
	R_{4t-3}	0.084	0.067	0.047	0.049	0.031	0.059
	R_{5t-3}	0.053	0.044	0.031	0.034	0.015	0.038
	R_{mt-3}	0.087	0.063	0.038	0.040	0.020	0.054
$\hat{\Upsilon}_4 =$	R_{1t-4}	0.050	0.001	−0.014	−0.029	−0.030	−0.002
	R_{2t-4}	0.064	0.023	−0.002	−0.012	−0.020	0.014
	R_{3t-4}	0.065	0.029	0.006	−0.002	−0.017	0.019
	R_{4t-4}	0.072	0.042	0.017	0.005	−0.008	0.029
	R_{5t-4}	0.048	0.023	0.002	−0.007	−0.022	0.011
	R_{mt-4}	0.062	0.024	0.001	−0.010	−0.021	0.014

Note that $\Upsilon_k \equiv D^{-1/2} E[(Z_{t-k} - \mu)(Z_t - \mu)']D^{-1/2}$ where $D \equiv \text{diag}[\sigma_1^2, \ldots, \sigma_5^2, \sigma_m^2]$, thus the i, jth element is the correlation between R_{it-k} and R_{jt}. Asymptotic standard errors for the autocorrelations under an i.i.d. null hyphothesis are given by $1/\sqrt{T} = 0.027$.

be seen in the higher-order autocorrelation matrices, although the magnitudes are smaller since the higher-order cross-autocorrelations decay. The asymmetry of the $\hat{\Upsilon}_k$ matrices implies that the autocovariance matrix estimators $\hat{\Gamma}_k$ are also asymmetric. This provides further evidence against the sum of the positively autocorrelated factor and the bid-ask spread as the true return-generating process, since Equation (34) implies symmetric autocovariance (and hence autocorrelation) matrices.

196

Of course, the nontrading model of Section 2.4 also yields an asymmetric autocorrelation matrix. However, it is easy to see that unrealistically high probabilities of nontrading are required to generate cross-autocorrelations of the magnitude reported in Table 4. For example, consider the first-order cross-autocorrelation between R_{2t-1} (the return of the second-smallest quintile portfolio) and R_{1t} (the return of the smallest quintile portfolio), which is 33.4 percent. Using Equation (32) with $k = 1$ and $q = 5$ days, we may compute the set of daily nontrading probabilities (p_1, p_2) of portfolios 1 and 2, respectively, that yield such a weekly cross-autocorrelation. For example, the combinations (.010, .616), (.100, .622), (.500, .659), (.750, .700), and (.990, .887) all yield a cross-autocorrelation of 33.4 percent. But none of these combinations are empirically plausible nontrading probabilities—the first pair implies an average duration of nontrading of 1.6 days for securities in the second smallest quintile, and the implications of the other pairs are even more extreme! Figure 1 plots the iso-autocorrelation loci for various levels of cross-autocorrelations, from which it is apparent that nontrading cannot be the sole source of cross-autocorrelation in stock market returns.[18]

Further evidence against nontrading comes from the pattern of cross-autocorrelations within each column of the first-order autocorrelation matrix $\hat{T}_1$.[19] For example, consider the first column of $\hat{T}_1$ whose first element is .333 and fifth element is .276. These values show that the correlation between the returns of portfolio a this week and those of portfolio b next week do not change significantly as portfolio a varies from the smallest firms to the largest. However, if cross-autocorrelations on the order of 30 percent are truly due to nontrading effects, Equation (32) implies an inverted U-shaped pattern for the cross-autocorrelation as portfolio a is varied. This is most easily seen in Figure 2a and b, in which an inverted U-shape is obtained by considering the intersection of the cross-autocorrelation surface with a vertical plane parallel to the p_a axis and perpendicular to the p_b axis, where the intersection occurs in the region where the surface rises to a level around 30 percent. The resulting curve is the nontrading-induced cross-autocorrelation for various values of p_a, holding p_b fixed at some value. These figures show that the empirical cross-autocorrelations are simply not consistent with nontrading, either in pattern or in the implied nontrading probabilities.

---

[18] Moreover, the implications for nontrading probabilities are even more extreme if we consider *hourly* instead of daily nontrading, that is, if we set $q = 35$ hours (roughly the number of trading hours in a week). Also, relaxing the restrictive assumptions of the nontrading model of Section 2.4 does not affect the order of magnitude of the above calculations. See Lo and MacKinlay (1989) for further details.

[19] We are grateful to Michael Brennan for suggesting this analysis.

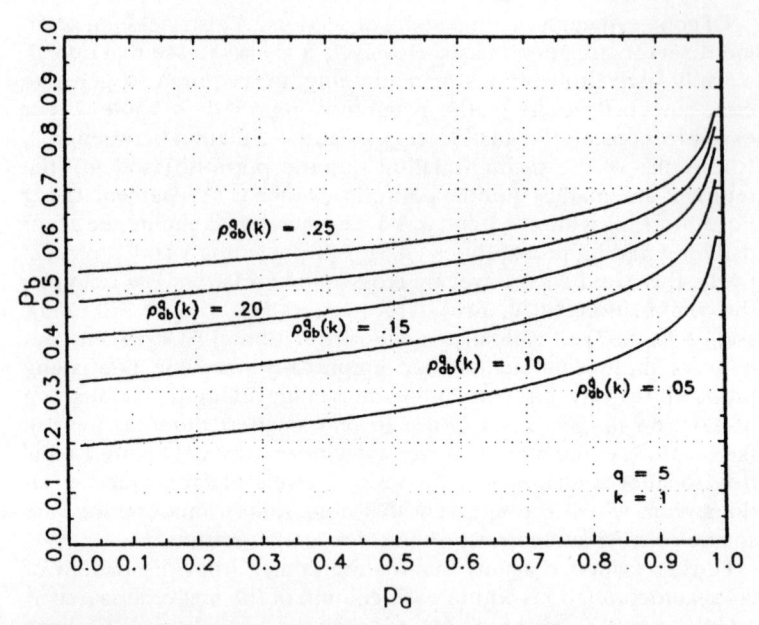

Figure 1
Loci of nontrading probability pairs (p_a, p_b) that imply a constant cross-autocorrelation $\rho_{ab}^q(k)$, for $\rho_{ab}^q(k)$ = .05, .10, .15, .20, .25, k = 1, q = 5
If the probabilities are interpreted as *daily* probabilities of nontrading, then $\rho_{ab}^q(k)$ represents the first-order weekly cross-autocorrelation between this week's return to portfolio a and next week's return to portfolio b when q = 5 and k = 1.

The results in Tables 3 and 4 point to the complex patterns of cross effects among securities as significant sources of positive index autocorrelation, as well as expected profits for contrarian investment rules. The presence of these cross effects has important implications, irrespective of the nature of contrarian profits. For example, if such profits are genuine, the fact that at least half may be attributed to cross-autocovariances suggests further investigation of mechanisms by which aggregate shocks to the economy are transmitted from large capitalization companies to small ones.

4. Long Horizons Versus Short Horizons

Since several recent studies have employed longer-horizon returns in examining contrarian strategies and the predictability of stock returns, we provide some discussion here of our decision to focus on weekly returns. Distinguishing between short- and long-return horizons is important, as it is now well known that weekly fluctuations

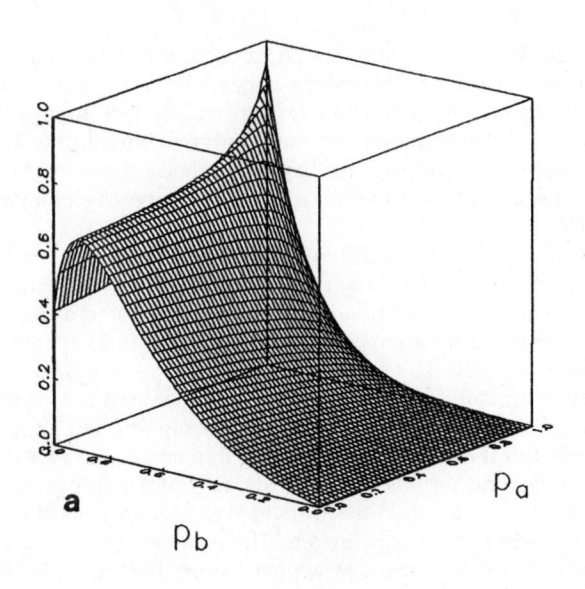

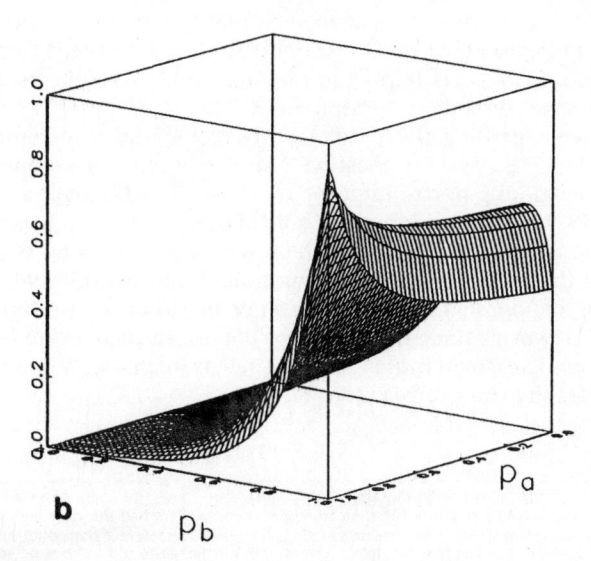

Contrarian Profits and Stock Market Overreaction

Figure 2
Cross-autocorrelation $\rho_{ab}^*(k)$ as a function of p_a and p_b, for q = 5, k = 1
a: Front view; *b*: rear view.

in stock returns differ in many ways from movements in three- to five-year returns. Therefore, inferences concerning the performance of the long-horizon strategies cannot be drawn directly from results such as ours. Because our analysis of the contrarian investment strategy (1) uses only weekly returns, we have little to say about the behavior of long-horizon returns. Nevertheless, some suggestive comparisons are possible.

Statistically, the predictability of short-horizon returns, especially weekly and monthly, is stronger and more consistent through time. For example, Blume and Friend (1978) have estimated a time series of cross-sectional correlation coefficients of returns in adjacent months using monthly NYSE data from 1926 to 1975, and found that in 422 of the 598 months the sample correlation was negative. This proportion of negative correlations is considerably higher than expected if returns are unforecastable. But in their framework, a negative correlation coefficient implies positive expected profits in our Equation (4) with $k = 1$. Jegadeesh (1988) provides further analysis of monthly data and reaches similar conclusions. The results are even more striking for weekly stock returns, as we have seen. For example, Lo and MacKinlay (1988) show evidence of strong predictability for portfolio returns using New York and American Stock Exchange data from 1962 to 1985. Using the same data, Lehmann (1988) shows that a contrarian strategy similar to Equation (1) is almost always profitable.[20] Together these two observations imply the importance of cross effects, a fact we established directly in Section 3.

Evidence regarding the predictability of long-horizon returns is more mixed. Perhaps the most well-known studies of a contrarian strategy using long-horizon returns are those of DeBondt and Thaler (1985, 1987) in which winners are sold and losers are purchased, but where the holding period over which winning and losing is determined is three years. Based on data from 1926 through 1981 they conclude that the market overreacts since the losers outperform the winners. However, since the difference in performance is due largely to the January seasonal in small firms, it seems inappropriate to attribute this to long-run overreaction.[21]

---

[20] Since such profits are sensitive to the size of the transactions costs (for some cases a one-way transactions cost of 0.40 percent is sufficient to render them positive half the time and negative the other half), the importance of Lehmann's findings hinges on the relevant costs of turning over securities frequently. The fact that our Table 3 shows the smallest firms to be the most profitable on average (as measured by the ratio of expected profits to the dollar amount long) may indicate that a round-trip transaction cost of 0.80 percent is low. In addition to the bid-ask spread, which is generally $0.125 or larger and will be a larger percentage of price for smaller stocks, the price effect of trades on these relatively thinly traded securities may become significant.

[21] See Zarowin (1988) for further discussion.

Fama and French (1988) and Poterba and Summers (1988) have also examined the predictability of long-horizon portfolio returns and find negative serial correlation, a result consistent with those of DeBondt and Thaler. However, this negative serial dependence is quite sensitive to the sample period employed and may be largely due to the first 10 years of the 1926 to 1987 sample [see Kim, Nelson, and Startz (1988)]. Furthermore, the statistical inference on which the long-horizon predictability is based has been questioned by Richardson (1988), who shows that properly adjusting for the fact that multiple time horizons (and test statistics) are considered simultaneously yields serial correlation estimates that are statistically indistinguishable from zero.

These considerations point to short-horizon returns as the more immediate source from which evidence of predictability and stock market overreaction might be culled. This is not to say that a careful investigation of returns over longer time spans will be uninformative. Indeed, it may be only at these lower frequencies that the effect of economic factors, such as the business cycle, is detectable. Moreover, to the extent that transaction costs are greater for strategies exploiting short-horizon predictability, long-horizon predictability may be a more genuine form of unexploited profit opportunity.

5. Conclusion

Traditional tests of the random walk hypothesis for stock market prices have generally focused on the returns either to individual securities or to portfolios of securities. In this article, we show that the cross-sectional interaction of security returns over time is an important aspect of stock-price dynamics. We document the fact that stock returns are often positively cross-autocorrelated, which reconciles the negative serial dependence in individual security returns with the positive autocorrelation in market indexes. This also implies that stock market overreaction need not be the sole explanation for the profitability in contrarian portfolio strategies. Indeed, the empirical evidence suggests that less than 50 percent of the expected profits from a contrarian investment rule may be attributed to overreaction; the majority of such profits are due to the cross effects among the securities. We have also shown that these cross effects have a very specific pattern for size-sorted portfolios: They display a lead-lag relation, with the returns of larger stocks generally leading those of smaller ones. But a tantalizing question remains to be investigated: What are the economic sources of positive cross-autocorrelations across securities?

Appendix 1: Derivation of Equation (4)

$$\pi_t(k) = \sum_{i=1}^{N} \omega_{it}(k) R_{it} = -\frac{1}{N} \sum_{i=1}^{N} (R_{it-k} - R_{mt-k}) R_{it} \quad \text{(A1)}$$

$$= -\frac{1}{N} \sum_{i=1}^{N} R_{it-k} R_{it} + \frac{1}{N} \sum_{i=1}^{N} R_{mt-k} R_{it} \quad \text{(A2)}$$

$$= -\frac{1}{N} \sum_{i=1}^{N} R_{it-k} R_{it} + R_{mt-k} R_{mt} \quad \text{(A3)}$$

$$E[\pi_t(k)] = -\frac{1}{N} \sum_{i=1}^{N} E[R_{it-k} R_{it}] + E[R_{mt-k} R_{mt}] \quad \text{(A4)}$$

$$= -\frac{1}{N} \sum_{i=1}^{N} (\text{Cov}[R_{it-k}, R_{it}] + \mu_i^2) \quad \text{(A5)}$$

$$+ (\text{Cov}[R_{mt-k}, R_{mt}] + \mu_m^2) \quad \text{(A6)}$$

$$= -\frac{1}{N} \text{tr}(\Gamma_k) - \frac{1}{N} \sum_{i=1}^{N} \mu_i^2 + \frac{\iota' \Gamma_k \iota}{N^2} + \mu_m^2 \quad \text{(A7)}$$

$$E[\pi_t(k)] = \frac{\iota' \Gamma_k \iota}{N^2} - \frac{1}{N} \text{tr}(\Gamma_k) - \frac{1}{N} \sum_{i=1}^{N} (\mu_i - \mu_m)^2$$

Appendix 2: Sampling Theory for $\hat{C}_k$, $\hat{O}_k$, and $\hat{E}[\pi_t(k)]$

To derive the sampling theory for the estimators $\hat{C}_k$, $\hat{O}_k$, and $\hat{E}[\pi_t(k)]$, we reexpress them as averages of artificial time series and then apply standard asymptotic theory to those averages. We require the following assumptions:

Assumption A1. *For all t, i, j, and k the following condition is satisfied for finite constants $K > 0$, $\delta > 0$, and $r \geq 0$:*

$$E[|R_{it-k} R_{jt}|^{4(r+\delta)}] < K < \infty \quad \text{(A8)}$$

Assumption A2. *The vector of returns R_t is either α-mixing with coefficients of size $2r/(r-1)$ or ϕ-mixing with coefficients of size $2r/(2r-1)$.*

These assumptions specify the trade-off between dependence and heterogeneity in R_t that is admissible while still permitting some form of the central limit theorem to obtain. The weaker is the moment condition (Assumption A2), the quicker the dependence in R_t must decay, and vice versa.[22] Observe that the covariance-stationarity of R_t is *not* required. Denote by C_{kt} and O_{kt} the following two time series:

$$C_{kt} \equiv R_{mt-k}R_{mt} - \hat{\mu}_m^2 - \frac{1}{N^2}\sum_{i=1}^{N}(R_{it-k}R_{it} - \hat{\mu}_i^2) \tag{A9}$$

$$O_{kt} \equiv -\frac{N-1}{N^2}\sum_{i=1}^{N}(R_{it-k}R_{it} - \hat{\mu}_i^2) \tag{A10}$$

where $\hat{\mu}_i$ and $\hat{\mu}_m$ are the usual sample means of the returns to security i and the equal-weighted market index, respectively. Then the estimators $\hat{C}_k$, $\hat{O}_k$, and $\sigma^2(\hat{\mu})$ are given by

$$\hat{C}_k = \frac{1}{T-k}\sum_{t=k+1}^{T} C_{kt} \tag{A11}$$

$$\hat{O}_k = \frac{1}{T-k}\sum_{t=k+1}^{T} O_{kt} \tag{A12}$$

$$\sigma^2(\hat{\mu}) = \frac{1}{N}\sum_{i=1}^{N}(\hat{\mu}_i - \hat{\mu}_m)^2 \tag{A13}$$

Because we have not assumed covariance-stationarity, the population quantities C_k and O_k obviously need not be interpretable according to Equation (8) since the autocovariance matrix of R_t may now be time dependent. However, we do wish to interpret C_k and O_k as some fixed quantities that are time independent; thus, we require:

Assumption A3. *The following limits exist and are finite:*

$$\lim_{T\to\infty}\frac{1}{T-k}\sum_{t=k+1}^{T} E[C_{kt}] = C_k \tag{A14}$$

$$\lim_{T\to\infty}\frac{1}{T-k}\sum_{t=k+1}^{T} E[O_{kt}] = O_k. \tag{A15}$$

Although the expectations $E(C_{kt})$ and $E(O_{kt})$ may be time dependent, Assumption A3 asserts that their averages converge to well-defined limits; hence, the quantities C_k and O_k may be viewed as "average" cross- and own-autocovariance contributions to expected profits. Consistent estimators of the asymptotic variance of the estimators $\hat{C}_k$ and $\hat{O}_k$ may then be obtained along the lines of Newey and West (1987), and are given by $\hat{\sigma}_c^2$ and $\hat{\sigma}_o^2$, respectively, where

$$\hat{\sigma}_c^2 = \frac{1}{T-k}\left[\hat{\gamma}_{c_k}(0) + 2\sum_{j=1}^{q}\alpha_j(q)\hat{\gamma}_{c_k}(j)\right] \tag{A16}$$

---

[22] See Phillips (1987) and White (1984) for further discussion of this trade-off.

$$\hat{\sigma}_o^2 = \frac{1}{T-k}\left[\hat{\gamma}_{o_k}(0) + 2\sum_{j=1}^{q}\alpha_j(q)\hat{\gamma}_{o_k}(j)\right]$$

$$\alpha_j(q) \equiv 1 - \frac{j}{q+1} \qquad q < T \qquad \text{(A17)}$$

and $\hat{\gamma}_{c_k}(j)$ and $\hat{\gamma}_{o_k}(j)$ are the sample jth order autocovariances of the time series C_{kt} and O_{kt}, respectively, that is,

$$\hat{\gamma}_{c_k}(j) = \frac{1}{T-k}\sum_{t=k+j+1}^{T}(C_{kt-j} - \hat{C}_k)(C_{kt} - \hat{C}_k) \qquad \text{(A18)}$$

$$\hat{\gamma}_{o_k}(j) = \frac{1}{T-k}\sum_{t=k+j+1}^{T}(O_{kt-j} - \hat{O}_k)(O_{kt} - \hat{O}_k) \qquad \text{(A19)}$$

Assuming that $q \sim o(T^{\frac{1}{4}})$, Newey and West (1987) show the consistency of $\hat{\sigma}_c^2$ and $\hat{\sigma}_o^2$ under our Assumptions A1–A3.[23] Observe that these asymptotic variance estimators are robust to general forms of heteroskedasticity and autocorrelation in the C_{kt} and O_{kt} time series. Since the derivation of heteroskedasticity- and autocorrelation-consistent standard errors for the estimated expected profits $\hat{E}[\pi_t(k)]$ is virtually identical, we leave this to the reader.

References

Atkinson, M., K. Butler, and R. Simonds, 1987, "Nonsynchronous Security Trading and Market Index Autocorrelation," *Journal of Finance*, 42, 111–118.

Bachelier, L., 1900, *Theory of Speculation*, reprinted in P. Cootner (ed.), *The Random Character of Stock Market Prices*, M.I.T. Press, Cambridge, 1964.

Blume, M., and I. Friend, 1978, *The Changing Role of the Individual Investor*, Wiley, New York.

Cohen, K., S. Maier, R. Schwartz, and D. Whitcomb, 1986, *The Microstructure of Securities Markets*, Prentice-Hall, Englewood Cliffs, N.J.

Conrad, J., G. Kaul, and M. Nimalendran, 1988, "Components of Short-Horizon Security Returns," working paper, University of Michigan.

Cootner, P. (ed.), 1964, *The Random Character of Stock Market Prices*, M.I.T. Press, Cambridge.

DeBondt, W., and R. Thaler, 1985, "Does the Stock Market Overreact?" *Journal of Finance*, 40, 793–805.

DeBondt, W., and R. Thaler, 1987, "Further Evidence on Investor Overreaction and Stock Market Seasonality," *Journal of Finance*, 42, 557–582.

DeLong, B., A. Shleifer, L. Summers, and R. Waldmann, 1989, "Positive Feedback Investment Strategies and Destabilizing Rational Speculation," NBER Working Paper 2880.

Fama, E., 1965, "The Behavior of Stock Market Prices," *Journal of Business*, 38, 34–105.

---

[23] In our empirical work we choose $q = 8$.

Contrarian Profits and Stock Market Overreaction

Fama, E., 1970, "Efficient Capital Markets: A Review of Theory and Empirical Work," *Journal of Finance*, 25, 383–417.

Fama, E., and K. French, 1988, "Permanent and Temporary Components of Stock Prices," *Journal of Political Economy*, 96, 246–273.

Fisher, L., 1966, "Some New Stock Market Indexes," *Journal of Business*, 39, 191–225.

Jegadeesh, N., 1988, "Evidence of Predictable Behavior of Security Returns," Working Paper 6-88, Anderson Graduate School of Management, U.C.L.A.

Kim, M., C. Nelson, and R. Startz, 1988, "Mean Reversion in Stock Prices? A Reappraisal of the Empirical Evidence," NBER Working Paper 2795.

Lehmann, B., 1988, "Fads, Martingales, and Market Efficiency," Working Paper 2533, National Bureau of Economic Research; forthcoming in *Quarterly Journal of Economics*.

Leroy, S. F., 1973, "Risk Aversion and the Martingale Property of Stock Returns," *International Economic Review*, 14, 436–446.

Lo, A. W., and A. C. MacKinlay, 1988, "Stock Market Prices Do Not Follow Random Walks: Evidence from a Simple Specification Test," *Review of Financial Studies*, 1, 41–66.

Lo, A. W., and A. C. MacKinlay, 1989, "An Econometric Analysis of Nonsynchronous-Trading," Working Paper 3003-89-EFA, Sloan School of Management, Massachusetts Institute of Technology; forthcoming in *Journal of Econometrics*.

Lucas, R. E., 1978, "Asset Prices in an Exchange Economy," *Econometrica*, 46, 1429–1446.

Newey, W. K., and K. D. West, 1987, "A Simple Positive Definite, Heteroscedasticity and Autocorrelation Consistent Covariance Matrix," *Econometrica*, 55, 703–705.

Phillips, P. C. B., 1987, "Time Series Regression with a Unit Root," *Econometrica*, 55, 277–302.

Poterba, J., and L. Summers, 1988, "Mean Reversion in Stock Returns: Evidence and Implications," *Journal of Financial Economics*, 22, 27–60.

Richardson, M., 1988, "Temporary Components of Stock Prices: A Skeptic's View," unpublished working paper, Wharton School, University of Pennsylvania.

Roll, R., 1984, "A Simple Implicit Measure of the Effective Bid-Ask Spread in an Efficient Market," *Journal of Finance*, 39, 1127–1140.

Scholes, M., and J. Williams, 1977, "Estimating Beta from Non-synchronous Data," *Journal of Financial Economics*, 5, 309–327.

Shefrin, H., and M. Statman, 1985, "The Disposition to Ride Winners Too Long and Sell Losers Too Soon: Theory and Evidence," *Journal of Finance*, 41, 774–790.

Summers, L., 1986, "Does the Stock Market Rationally Reflect Fundamental Values?," *Journal of Finance*, 41, 591–600.

White, H., 1984, *Asymptotic Theory for Econometricians*, Academic Press, New York.

Zarowin, P., 1988, "Size, Seasonality and Stock Market Overreaction," working paper, Graduate School of Business, New York University.

Part III
Anomalies

THE RELATIONSHIP BETWEEN RETURN AND MARKET VALUE OF COMMON STOCKS*

Rolf W. BANZ

Northwestern University, Evanston, IL 60201, USA

Received June 1979, final version received September 1980

This study examines the empirical relationship between the return and the total market value of NYSE common stocks. It is found that smaller firms have had higher risk adjusted returns, on average, than larger firms. This 'size effect' has been in existence for at least forty years and is evidence that the capital asset pricing model is misspecified. The size effect is not linear in the market value; the main effect occurs for very small firms while there is little difference in return between average sized and large firms. It is not known whether size *per se* is responsible for the effect or whether size is just a proxy for one or more true unknown factors correlated with size.

1. Introduction

The single-period capital asset pricing model (henceforth CAPM) postulates a simple linear relationship between the expected return and the market risk of a security. While the results of direct tests have been inconclusive, recent evidence suggests the existence of additional factors which are relevant for asset pricing. Litzenberger and Ramaswamy (1979) show a significant positive relationship between dividend yield and return of common stocks for the 1936–1977 period. Basu (1977) finds that price–earnings ratios and risk adjusted returns are related. He chooses to interpret his findings as evidence of market inefficiency but as Ball (1978) points out, market efficiency tests are often joint tests of the efficient market hypothesis and a particular equilibrium relationship. Thus, some of the anomalies that have been attributed to a lack of market efficiency might well be the result of a misspecification of the pricing model.

This study contributes another piece to the emerging puzzle. It examines the relationship between the total market value of the common stock of a firm and its return. The results show that, in the 1936–1975 period, the common stock of small firms had, on average, higher risk-adjusted returns

*This study is based on part of my dissertation and was completed while I was at the University of Chicago. I am grateful to my committee, Myron Scholes (chairman), John Gould, Roger Ibbotson, Jonathan Ingersoll, and especially Eugene Fama and and Merton Miller, for their advice and comments. I wish to acknowledge the valuable comments of Bill Schwert on earlier drafts of this paper.

than the common stock of large firms. This result will henceforth be referred to as the 'size effect'. Since the results of the study are not based on a particular theoretical equilibrium model, it is not possible to determine conclusively whether market value *per se* matters or whether it is only a proxy for unknown true additional factors correlated with market value. The last section of this paper will address this question in greater detail.

The various methods currently available for the type of empirical research presented in this study are discussed in section 2. Since there is a considerable amount of confusion about their relative merit, more than one technique is used. Section 3 discusses the data. The empirical results are presented in section 4. A discussion of the relationship between the size effect and other factors, as well as some speculative comments on possible explanations of the results, constitute section 5.

2. Methodologies

The empirical tests are based on a generalized asset pricing model which allows the expected return of a common stock to be a function of risk β and an additional factor ϕ, the market value of the equity.[1] A simple linear relationship of the form

$$E(R_i) = \gamma_0 + \gamma_1 \beta_i + \gamma_2 [(\phi_i - \phi_m)/\phi_m], \qquad (1)$$

is assumed, where

$E(R_i)$ = expected return on security i,
γ_0 = expected return on a zero-beta portfolio,
γ_1 = expected market risk premium,
ϕ_i = market value of security i,
ϕ_m = average market value, and
γ_2 = constant measuring the contribution of ϕ_i to the expected return of a security.

If there is no relationship between ϕ_i and the expected return, i.e., $\gamma_2 = 0$, (1) reduces to the Black (1972) version of the CAPM.

Since expectations are not observable, the parameters in (1) must be estimated from historical data. Several methods are available for this purpose. They all involve the use of pooled cross-sectional and time series regressions to estimate γ_0, γ_1, and γ_2. They differ primarily in (a) the assumption concerning the residual variance of the stock returns (homoscedastic or heteroscedastic in the cross-sectional), and (b) the treatment of the

---

[1]In the empirical tests, Φ_i and Φ_m are defined as the market proportion of security i and average market proportion, respectively. The two specifications are, of course, equivalent.

errors-in-variables problem introduced by the use of estimated betas in (1). All methods use a constrained optimization procedure, described in Fama (1976, ch. 9), to generate minimum variance (m.v.) portfolios with mean returns $\hat{\gamma}_i$, $i=0,\ldots,2$. This imposes certain constraints on the portfolio weights, since from (1)

$$E(R_p) \equiv \gamma_i = \gamma_0 \sum_j w_j + \gamma_1 \sum_j w_j \beta_j$$
$$+ \gamma_2 \left[\left(\sum_j w_j \phi_j - \phi_m \sum_j w_j \right) \Big/ \phi_m \right], \quad i=0,\ldots,2, \qquad (2)$$

where the w_j are the portfolio proportions of each asset j, $j=1,\ldots,N$. An examination of (2) shows that $\hat{\gamma}_0$ is the mean return of a standard m.v. portfolio ($\sum_j w_j = 1$) with zero beta and $\phi_p \equiv \sum_j w_j \phi_j = \phi_m$ [to make the second and third terms of the right-hand side of (2) vanish]. Similarly, $\hat{\gamma}_1$ is the mean return on a zero-investment m.v. portfolio with beta of one and $\phi_p = 0$, and $\hat{\gamma}_2$ is the mean return on a m.v. zero-investment, zero-beta portfolio with $\phi_p = \phi_m$. As shown by Fama (1976, ch. 9), this constrained optimization can be performed by running a cross-sectional regression of the form

$$R_{it} = \gamma_{0t} + \gamma_{1t}\beta_{it} + \gamma_{2t}[(\phi_{it} - \phi_{mt})/\phi_{mt}] + \varepsilon_{it}, \quad i=1,\ldots,N, \qquad (3)$$

on a period-by-period basis, using estimated betas $\hat{\beta}_{it}$ and allowing for either homoscedastic or heteroscedastic error terms. Invoking the usual stationarity arguments the final estimates of the gammas are calculated as the averages of the T estimates.

One basic approach involves grouping individual securities into portfolios on the basis of market value and security beta, reestimating the relevant parameters (beta, residual variance) of the portfolios in a subsequent period, and finally performing either an ordinary least squares (OLS) regression [Fama and MacBeth (1973)] which assumes homoscedastic errors, or a generalized least squares (GLS) regression [Black and Scholes (1974)] which allows for heteroscedastic errors, on the portfolios in each time period.[2] Grouping reduces the errors-in-variables problem, but is not very efficient because it does not make use of all information. The errors-in-variables problem should not be a factor as long as the portfolios contain a reasonable number of securities.[3]

Litzenberger and Ramaswamy (1979) have suggested an alternative method which avoids grouping. They allow for heteroscedastic errors in the cross-section and use the estimates of the standard errors of the security

---
[2]Black and Scholes (1974) do not take account of heteroscedasticity, even though their method was designed to do so.
[3]Black, Jensen and Scholes (1972, p. 116).

betas as estimates of the measurement errors. As Theil (1971, p. 610) has pointed out, this method leads to unbiased maximum likelihood estimators for the gammas as long as the error in the standard error of beta is small and the standard assumptions of the simple errors-in-variables model are met. Thus, it is very important that the diagonal model is the correct specification of the return-generating process, since the residual variance assumes a critical position in this procedure. The Litzenberger–Ramaswamy method is superior from a theoretical viewpoint; however, preliminary work has shown that it leads to serious problems when applied to the model of this study and is not pursued any further.[4]

Instead of estimating equation (3) with data for all securities, it is also possible to construct arbitrage portfolios containing stocks of very large and very small firms, by combining long positions in small firms with short positions in large firms. A simple time series regression is run to determine the difference in risk-adjusted returns between small and large firms. This approach, long familiar in the efficient markets and option pricing literature, has the advantage that no assumptions about the exact functional relationships between market value and expected return need to be made, and it will therefore be used in this study.

3. Data

The sample includes all common stocks quoted on the NYSE for at least five years between 1926 and 1975. Monthly price and return data and the number of shares outstanding at the end of each month are available in the monthly returns file of the Center for Research in Security Prices (CRSP) of the University of Chicago. Three different market indices are used; this is in response to Roll's (1977) critique of empirical tests of the CAPM. Two of the three are pure common stock indices — the CRSP equally- and value-weighted indices. The third is more comprehensive: a value-weighted combination of the CRSP value-weighted index and return data on corporate and government bonds from Ibbotson and Sinquefield (1977) (henceforth 'market index').[5] The weights of the components of this index are derived from information on the total market value of corporate and government bonds in various issues of the *Survey of Current Business* (updated annually) and from the market value of common stocks in the CRSP monthly index file. The stock indices, made up of riskier assets, have both higher returns

[4]If the diagonal model (or market model) is an incomplete specification of the return generating process, the estimate of the standard error of beta is likely to have an upward bias, since the residual variance estimate is too large. The error in the residual variance estimate appears to be related to the second factor. Therefore, the resulting gamma estimates are biased.

[5]No pretense is made that this index is complete; thus, the use of quotation marks. It ignores real estate, foreign assets, etc.; it should be considered a first step toward a comprehensive index. See Ibbotson and Fall (1979).

and higher risk than the bond indices and the 'market index'.[6] A time series of commercial paper returns is used as the risk-free rate.[7] While not actually constant through time, its variation is very small when compared to that of the other series, and it is not significantly correlated with any of the three indices used as market proxies.

4. Empirical results

4.1. Results for methods based on grouped data

The portfolio selection procedure used in this study is identical to the one described at length in Black and Scholes (1974). The securities are assigned to one of twenty-five portfolios containing similar numbers of securities, first to one of five on the basis of the market value of the stock, then the securities in each of those five are in turn assigned to one of five portfolios on the basis of their beta. Five years of data are used for the estimation of the security beta; the next five years' data are used for the reestimation of the portfolio betas. Stock price and number of shares outstanding at the end of the five year periods are used for the calculation of the market proportions. The portfolios are updated every year. The cross-sectional regression (3) is then performed in each month and the means of the resulting time series of the gammas could be (and have been in the past) interpreted as the final estimators. However, having used estimated parameters, it is not certain that the series have the theoretical properties, in particular, the hypothesized beta. Black and Scholes (1974, p. 17) suggest that the time series of the gammas be regressed once more on the excess return of the market index. This correction involves running the time series regression (for $\hat{\gamma}_2$)

$$\hat{\gamma}_{2t} - R_{Ft} = \hat{\alpha}_2 + \hat{\beta}_2(R_{mt} - R_{Ft}) + \hat{\varepsilon}_{2t}. \tag{4}$$

It has been shows earlier that the theoretical β_2 is zero. (4) removes the effects of a non-zero $\hat{\beta}_2$ on the return estimate $\hat{\gamma}_2$ and $\hat{\alpha}_2$ is used as the final estimator for $\hat{\gamma}_2 - R_F$. Similar corrections are performed for γ_0 and γ_1. The

[6] Mean monthly returns and standard deviations for the 1926–1975 period are:

	Mean return	Standard deviation
'Market index'	0.0046	0.0178
CRSP value-weighted index	0.0085	0.0588
CRSP equally-weighted index	0.0120	0.0830
Government bond index	0.0027	0.0157
Corporate bond index	0.0032	0.0142

[7] I am grateful to Myron Scholes for making this series available. The mean monthly return for the 1926–1975 period is 0.0026 and the standard deviation is 0.0021.

derivations of the $\hat{\beta}_i$, $i=0,\ldots,2$, in (4) from their theoretical values also allow us to check whether the grouping procedure is an effective means to eliminate the errors-in-beta problem.

The results are essentially identical for both OLS and GLS and for all three indices. Thus, only one set of results, those for the 'market index' with GLS, is presented in table 1. For each of the gammas, three numbers are reported: the mean of that time series of returns which is relevant for the test of the hypothesis of interest (i.e., whether or not $\hat{\gamma}_0$ and $\hat{\gamma}_1$ are different from the risk-free rate and the risk premium, respectively), the associated t-statistic, and finally, the estimated beta of the time series of the gamma from (4). Note that the means are corrected for the deviation from the theoretical beta as discussed above.

The table shows a significantly negative estimate for γ_2 for the overall time period. Thus, shares of firms with large market values have had smaller returns, on average, than similar small firms. The CAPM appears to be misspecified. The table also shows that γ_0 is different from the risk-free rate. As both Fama (1976, ch. 9) and Roll (1977) have pointed out, if a test does not use the true market portfolio, the Sharpe–Lintner model might be wrongly rejected. The estimates for γ_0 are of the same magnitude as those reported by Fama and MacBeth (1973) and others. The choice of a market index and the econometric method does not affect the results. Thus, at least within the context of this study, the choice of a proxy for the market portfolio does not seem to affect the results and allowing for heteroscedastic disturbances does not lead to significantly more efficient estimators.

Before looking at the results in more detail, some comments on econometric problems are in order. The results in table 1 are based on the 'market index' which is likely to be superior to pure stock indices from a theoretical viewpoint since it includes more assets [Roll (1977)]. This superiority has its price. The actual betas of the time series of the gammas are reported in table 1 in the columns labeled $\hat{\beta}_i$. Recall that the theoretical values of β_0 and β_1 are zero and one, respectively. The standard zero-beta portfolio with return $\hat{\gamma}_0$ contains high beta stocks in short positions and low beta stocks in long positions, while the opposite is the case for the zero-investment portfolio with return $\hat{\gamma}_1$. The actual betas are all significantly different from the theoretical values. This suggests a regression effect, i.e., the past betas of high beta securities are overestimated and the betas of low beta securities are underestimated.[8] Past beta is not completely uncorrelated with the error of the current beta and the instrumental variable approach to the error-in-variables problem is not entirely successful.[9]

---

[8]There is no such effect for β_2 because that portfolio has both zero beta and zero investment; i.e., net holdings of both high and low beta securities are, on average, zero.

[9]This result is first documented in Brenner (1976) who examines the original Fama–McBeth (1973) time series of $\hat{\gamma}_{0t}$.

Table 1

Portfolio estimators for $\hat{\gamma}_0$, $\hat{\gamma}_1$ and $\hat{\gamma}_2$ based on the 'market index' with generalized least squares estimation.[a]

$$R_{it} = \hat{\gamma}_{0t} + \hat{\gamma}_{1t}\beta_{it} + \hat{\gamma}_{2t}[(\phi_{it} - \phi_{mt})/\phi_{mt}]$$

Period	$\hat{\gamma}_0 - R_F$	$t(\hat{\gamma}_0 - R_F)$	β_0	$\hat{\gamma}_1 - (R_M - R_F)$	$t(\hat{\gamma}_1 - (R_M - R_F))$	β_1	$\hat{\gamma}_2$	$t(\hat{\gamma}_2)$	β_2
1936–1975	0.00450	2.76	0.45	−0.00092	−1.00	0.75	−0.00052	−2.92	0.01
1936–1955	0.00377	1.66	0.43	−0.00060	−0.80	0.80	−0.00043	−2.12	0.01
1956–1975	0.00531	2.22	0.46	−0.00138	−0.82	0.73	−0.00062	−2.09	0.01
1936–1945	0.00121	0.30	0.63	−0.00098	−0.77	0.82	−0.00075	−2.32	−0.01
1946–1955	0.00650	2.89	0.03	−0.00021	−0.26	0.75	−0.00015	−0.65	0.06
1956–1965	0.00494	2.02	0.34	−0.00098	−0.56	0.96	−0.00039	−1.27	−0.01
1966–1975	0.00596	1.43	0.49	−0.00232	−0.80	0.69	−0.00080	−1.55	0.01

[a] $\hat{\gamma}_0 - R_F$ = mean difference between return on zero beta portfolio and risk-free rate, $\hat{\gamma}_1 - (R_M - R_F)$ = mean difference between actual risk premium ($\hat{\gamma}_1$) and risk premium stipulated by Sharpe–Lintner model ($R_M - R_F$). $\hat{\gamma}_2$ = size premium. β_i = actual estimated market risk of $\hat{\gamma}_i$ (theoretical values: $\beta_0 = 0$, $\beta_1 = 1$, $\beta_2 = 0$); all β_0, β_1 are significantly different from the theoretical values. $t(\cdot)$ = t-statistic.

The deviations from the theoretical betas are largest for the 'market index', smaller for the CRSP value-weighted index, and smallest for the CRSP equally-weighted index. This is due to two factors: first, even if the true covariance structure is stationary, betas with respect to a value-weighted index change whenever the weights change, since the weighted average of the betas is constrained to be equal to one. Second, the betas and their standard errors with respect to the 'market index' are much larger than for the stock indices (a typical stock beta is between two and three), which leads to larger deviations — a kind of 'leverage' effect. Thus, the results in table 1 show that the final correction for the deviation of $\hat{\beta}_0$ and $\hat{\beta}_1$ from their theoretical values is of crucial importance for maket proxies with changing weights.

Estimated portfolio betas and portfolio market proportions are (negatively) correlated. It is therefore possible that the errors in beta induce an error in the coefficient of the market proportion. According to Levi (1973), the probability limit of $\hat{\gamma}_1$ in the standard errors-in-the-variables model is

$$\text{plim } \hat{\gamma}_1 = \gamma_1/(1 + (\sigma_u^2 \cdot \sigma_2^2)/D) < \gamma_1,$$

with

$$D = (\sigma_1^2 + \sigma_u^2) \cdot \sigma_2^2 - \sigma_{12}^2 > 0,$$

where σ_1^2, σ_2^2 are the variances of the true factors β and ϕ, respectively, σ_u^2 is the variance of the error in beta and σ_{12} is the covariance of β and ϕ. Thus, the bias in $\hat{\gamma}_1$ is unambiguously towards zero for positive γ_1. The probability limit of $\hat{\gamma}_2 - \gamma_2$ is [Levi (1973)]

$$\text{plim } (\hat{\gamma}_2 - \gamma_2) = (\sigma_u^2 \cdot \sigma_{12} \cdot \gamma_1)/D.$$

We find that the bias in $\hat{\gamma}_2$ depends on the covariance between β and ϕ and the sign of γ_1. If σ_{12} has the same sign as the covariance between $\hat{\beta}$ and ϕ, i.e., $\sigma_{12} < 0$, and if $\gamma_1 > 0$, then $\text{plim}(\hat{\gamma}_2 - \gamma_2) < 0$, i.e., $\text{plim} \hat{\gamma}_2 < \gamma_2$. If the grouping procedure is not successful in removing the error in beta, then it is likely that the reported $\hat{\gamma}_2$ overstates the true magnitude of the size effect. If this was a serious problem in this study, the results for the different market indices should reflect the problem. In particular, using the equally-weighted stock index should then lead to the smallest size effect since, as was pointed out earlier, the error in beta problem is apparently less serious for that kind of index. In fact, we find that there is little difference between the estimates.[10]

[10] For the overall time period, $\hat{\gamma}_2$ with the equally-weighted CRSP index is -0.00044, with the value weighted CRSP index -0.00044 as well as opposed to the -0.00052 for the 'market index' reported in table 1. The estimated betas of $\hat{\gamma}_0$ and $\hat{\gamma}_1$ which reflect the degree of the error in beta problems are 0.07 and 0.91, respectively, for the equally-weighted CRSP index and 0.13 and 0.87 for the value-weighted CRSP index.

Thus, it does not appear that the size effect is just a proxy for the unobservable true beta even though the market proportion and the beta of securities are negatively correlated.

The correlation coefficient between the mean market values of the twenty-five portfolios and their betas is significantly negative, which might have introduced a multicollinearity problem. One of its possible consequences is coefficients that are very sensitive to addition or deletion of data. This effect does not appear to occur in this case: the results do not change significantly when five portfolios are dropped from the sample. Revising the grouping procedure — ranking on the basis of beta first, then ranking on the basis of market proportion — also does not lead to substantially different results.

4.2. A closer look at the results

An additional factor relevant for asset pricing — the market value of the equity of a firm — has been found. The results are based on a linear model. Linearity was assumed only for convenience and there is no theoretical reason (since there is no model) why the relationship should be linear. If it is nonlinear, the particular form of the relationship might give us a starting point for the discussion of possible causes of the size effect in the next section. An analysis of the residuals of the twenty-five portfolios is the easiest way to look at the linearity question. For each month t, the estimated residual return

$$\hat{\varepsilon}_{it} = R_{it} - \hat{\gamma}_{0t} - \hat{\gamma}_{1t}\hat{\beta}_{it} - \hat{\gamma}_{2t}[(\phi_{it} - \phi_{mt})/\phi_{mt}], \qquad i = 1,\ldots,25, \qquad (5)$$

is calculated for all portfolios. The mean residuals over the forty-five year sample period are plotted as a function of the mean market proportion in fig. 1. Since the distribution of the market proportions is very skewed, a logarithmic scale is used. The solid line connects the mean residual returns of each size group. The numbers identify the individual portfolios within each group according to beta, '1' being the one with the largest beta, '5' being the one with the smallest beta.

The figure shows clearly that the linear model is misspecified.[11] The residuals are not randomly distributed around zero. The residuals of the portfolios containing the smallest firms are all positive; the remaining ones are close to zero. As a consequence, it is impossible to use $\hat{\gamma}_2$ as a simple size premium in the cross-section. The plot also shows, however, that the misspecification is not responsible for the significance of $\hat{\gamma}_2$ since the linear model underestimates the true size effect present for very small firms. To illustrate this point, the five portfolios containing the smaller firms are

---

[11]The nonlinearity cannot be eliminated by defining ϕ_i as the log of the market proportion.

deleted from the sample and the parameters reestimated. The results, summarized in table 2, show that the $\hat{\gamma}_2$ remain essentially the same. The relationship is still not linear; the new $\hat{\gamma}_2$ still cannot be used as a size premium.

Fig. 1 suggests that the main effect occurs for very small firms. Further support for this conclusion can be obtained from a simple test. We can regress the returns of the twenty-five portfolios in each result on beta alone and examine the residuals. The regression is misspecified and the residuals contain information about the size effect. Fig. 2 shows the plot of those residuals in the same format as fig. 1. The smallest firms have, on average, very large unexplained mean returns. There is no significant difference between the residuals of the remaining portfolios.

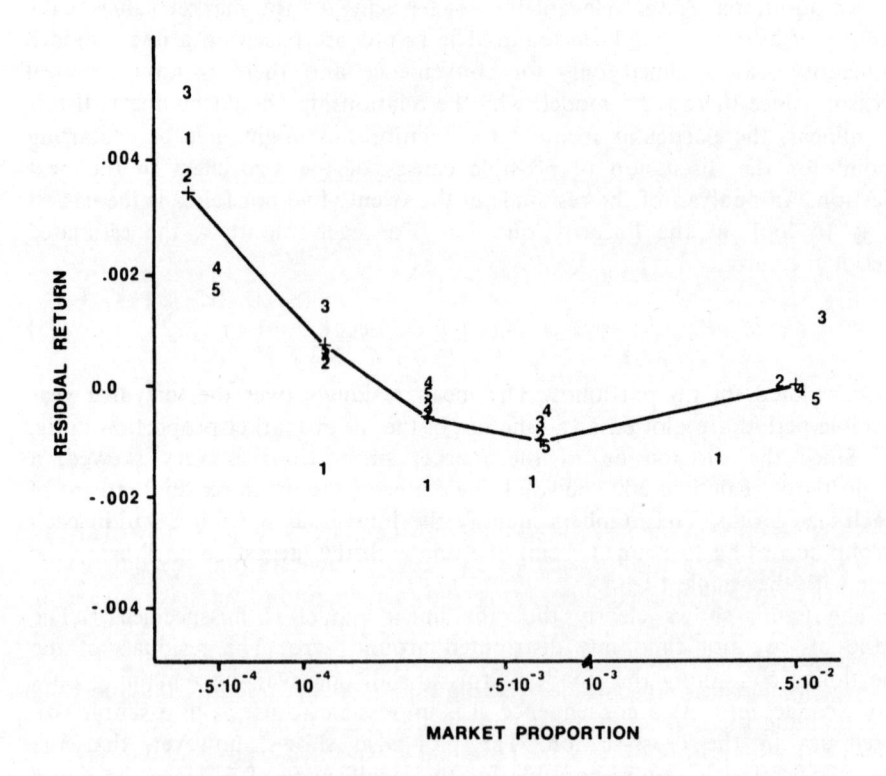

Fig. 1. Mean residual returns of portfolios (1936–1975) with equally-weighted CRSP index as market proxy. The residual is calculated with the three-factor model [eq. (3)]. The numbers 1,...,5 represent the mean residual return for the five portfolios within each size group (1: portfolio with largest beta,..., 5: portfolio with smallest beta). +. represents the mean of the mean residuals of the five portfolios with similar market values.

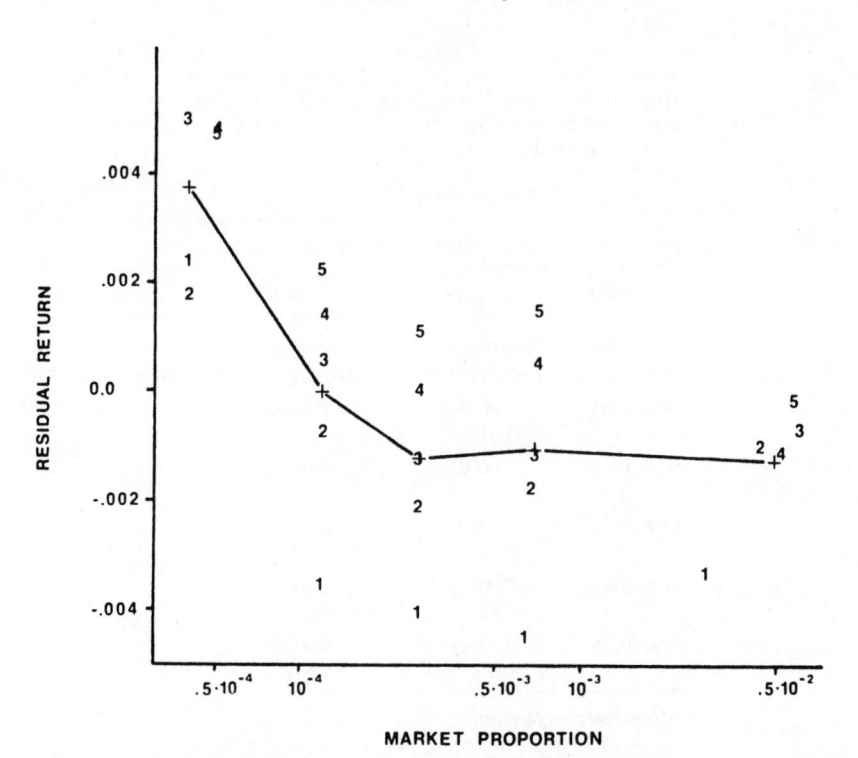

Fig. 2. Mean residual returns of portfolios (1936–1975) with equally-weighted CRSP index as market proxy. The residual is calculated with the two-factor model ($\hat{\varepsilon}_{it} = R_{it} - \hat{\gamma}_{0t} - \hat{\gamma}_{1t}\hat{\beta}_{it}$). The symbols are as defined for fig. 1.

4.3. 'Arbitrage' portfolio returns

One important empirical question still remains: How important is the size effect from a practical point of view? Fig. 2 suggests that the difference in returns between the smallest firms and the remaining ones is, on average, about 0.4 percent per month. A more dramatic result can be obtained when the securities are chosen solely on the basis of their market value.

As an illustration, consider putting equal dollar amounts into portfolios containing the smallest, largest and median-sized firms at the beginning of a year. These portfolios are to be equally weighted and contain, say, ten, twenty or fifty securities. They are to be held for five years and are rebalanced every month. They are levered or unlevered to have the same beta. We are then interested in the differences in their returns,

$$R_{1t} = R_{st} - R_{lt}, \qquad R_{2t} = R_{st} - R_{at}, \qquad R_{3t} = R_{at} - R_{lt}, \qquad (6)$$

Table 2
Portfolio estimators for γ_2 for all 25 portfolios and for 20 portfolios (portfolios containing smallest firms deleted) based on CRSP equally weighted index with generalized least-squares estimation.[a]

Period	Size premium $\hat{\gamma}_2$ with 25 portfolios	20 portfolios
1936–1975	−0.00044 (−2.42)	−0.00043 (−2.54)
1936–1955	−0.00037 (−1.72)	−0.00041 (−1.88)
1956–1975	−0.00056 (−1.91)	−0.00050 (−1.91)
1936–1945	−0.00085 (−2.81)	−0.00083 (−2.48)
1946–1955	0.00003 (0.12)	−0.00003 (−0.13)
1956–1965	−0.00023) (−0.81)	−0.00017 (−0.65)
1966–1975	−0.00091 (−1.78)	−0.00085 (−1.84)

[a]t-statistic in parentheses.

where R_{st}, R_{at} and R_{lt} are the returns on the portfolios containing the smallest, median-sized and largest firms at portfolio formation time (and $R_{1t} = R_{2t} + R_{3t}$). The procedure involves (a) the calculation of the three differences in raw returns in each month and (b) running time series regressions of the differences on the excess returns of the market proxy. The intercept terms of these regressions are then interpreted as the $\bar{R}_i$, $i = 1, \ldots, 3$. Thus, the differences can be interpreted as 'arbitrage' returns, since, e.g., R_{1t} is the return obtained from holding the smallest firms long and the largest firms short, representing zero net investment in a zero-beta portfolio.[12] Simple equally weighted portfolios are used rather than more sophisticated minimum variance portfolios to demonstrate that the size effect is not due to some quirk in the covariance matrix.

Table 3 shows that the results of the earlier tests are fully confirmed. $\bar{R}_2$, the difference in returns between very small firms and median-size firms, is typically considerably larger than $\bar{R}_3$, the difference in returns between median-sized and very large firms. The average excess return from holding very small firms long and very large firms short is, on average, 1.52 percent

[12]No *ex post* sample bias is introduced, since monthly rebalancing includes stocks delisted during the five years. Thus, the portfolio size is generally accurate only for the first month of each period.

Table 3

Mean monthly returns on 'arbitrage' portfolios.[a]

$$R_j - R_k = \hat{\alpha}_i + \hat{\beta}_i(R_m - R_F)$$

	$\tilde{\alpha}_1$[b]			$\tilde{\alpha}_2$[c]			$\tilde{\alpha}_3$[d]		
	n=10	n=20	n=50	n=10	n=20	n=50	n=10	n=20	n=50
Overall period									
1931–1975	0.0152 (2.99)	0.0148 (3.53)	0.0101 (3.07)	0.0130 (2.90)	0.0124 (3.56)	0.0089 (3.64)	0.0021 (1.06)	0.0024 (1.41)	0.0012 (0.85)
Five-year subperiods									
1931–1935	0.0589 (2.25)	0.0597 (2.81)	0.0427 (2.35)	0.0462 (1.92)	0.0462 (2.55)	0.0326 (2.46)	0.0127 (1.09)	0.0134 (1.49)	0.0101 (1.42)
1936–1940	0.0201 (0.82)	0.0182 (0.97)	0.0089 (0.67)	0.0118 (0.55)	0.0145 (0.90)	0.0064 (0.65)	0.0084 (1.20)	0.0037 (0.62)	0.0025 (0.49)
1941–1945	0.0430 (2.29)	0.0408 (2.46)	0.0269 (2.17)	0.0381 (2.29)	0.0367 (2.54)	0.0228 (2.02)	0.0049 (1.25)	0.0038 (1.09)	0.0041 (1.68)
1946–1950	−0.0060 (−1.17)	−0.0046 (−0.97)	−0.0036 (−0.97)	−0.0058 (−1.03)	−0.0059 (−1.29)	−0.0029 (−0.83)	−0.0002 (−0.07)	−0.0104 (−0.50)	−0.0007 (−0.38)
1951–1955	−0.0067 (−0.89)	−0.0011 (−0.21)	0.0013 (0.32)	−0.0004 (−0.07)	0.0026 (0.72)	0.0010 (0.39)	−0.0062 (−1.29)	−0.0037 (−0.99)	0.0003 (0.11)
1956–1960	0.0039 (0.67)	0.0008 (0.15)	0.0037 (0.89)	0.0007 (0.14)	−0.0027 (−0.64)	0.0011 (0.45)	0.0031 (0.88)	0.0035 (1.16)	0.0026 (0.97)
1961–1965	0.0131 (1.38)	0.0060 (0.67)	0.0024 (0.31)	0.0096 (1.11)	0.0046 (0.72)	0.0036 (0.77)	0.0035 (0.59)	0.0014 (0.24)	−0.0012 (−0.24)
1966–1970	0.0121 (1.64)	0.0117 (2.26)	0.0077 (1.91)	0.0129 (1.93)	0.0110 (2.71)	0.0071 (2.43)	0.0008 (0.23)	0.0007 (0.22)	0.0006 (0.27)
1971–1975	0.0063 (0.60)	0.0108 (1.23)	0.0098 (1.45)	0.0033 (0.39)	0.0077 (1.18)	0.0083 (1.79)	0.0030 (0.64)	0.0031 (0.72)	0.0015 (0.43)

[a]Equally-weighted portfolios with n securities, adjusted for differences in market risk with respect to CRSP value-weighted index, t-statistics in parentheses.
[b]Small firms held long, large firms held short.
[c]Small firms held long, median-size firms held short.
[d]Median-size firms held long, large firms held short.

per month or 19.8 percent on an annualized basis. This strategy, which suggests very large 'profit opportunities', leaves the investor with a poorly diversified portfolio. A portfolio of small firms has typically much larger residual risk with respect to a value-weighted index than a portfolio of very large firms with the same number of securities [Banz (1978, ch. 3)]. Since the fifty largest firms make up more than 25 percent of the total market value of NYSE stocks, it is not surprising that a larger part of the variation of the return of a portfolio of those large firms can be explained by its relation with the value-weighted market index. Table 3 also shows that the strategy would not have been successful in every five year subperiod. Nevertheless, the magnitude of the size effect during the past forty-five years is such that it is of more than just academic interest.

5. Conclusions

The evidence presented in this study suggests that the CAPM is misspecified. On average, small NYSE firms have had significantly larger risk adjusted returns than large NYSE firms over a forty year period. This size effect is not linear in the market proportion (or the log of the market proportion) but is most pronounced for the smallest firms in the sample. The effect is also not very stable through time. An analysis of the ten year subperiods show substantial differences in the magnitude of the coefficient of the size factor (table 1).

There is no theoretical foundation for such an effect. We do not even know whether the factor is size itself or whether size is just a proxy for one or more true but unknown factors correlated with size. It is possible, however, to offer some conjectures and even discuss some factors for which size is suspected to proxy. Recent work by Reinganum (1980) has eliminated one obvious candidate: the price–earnings (P/E) ratio.[13] He finds that the P/E-effect, as reported by Basu (1977), disappears for both NYSE and AMEX stocks when he controls for size but that there is a significant size effect even when he controls for the P/E-ratio, i.e., the P/E-ratio effect is a proxy for the size effect and not vice versa. Stattman (1980), who found a significant negative relationship between the ratio of book value and market value of equity and its return, also reports that this relationship is just a proxy for the size effect. Naturally, a large number of possible factors remain to be tested.[14] But the Reinganum results point out a potential problem with some of the existing negative evidence of the efficient market hypothesis. Basu believed to have identified a market inefficiency but his P/E-effect is

---

[13]The average correlation coefficient between P/E-ratio and market value is only 0.16 for individual stocks for thirty-eight quarters ending in 1978. But for the portfolios formed on the basis of P/E-ratio, it rises to 0.82. Recall that Basu (1977) used ten portfolios in his study.

[14]E.g., debt–equity ratios, skewness of the return distribution [Kraus and Litzenberger (1976)].

just a proxy for the size effect. Given its longevity, it is not likely that it is due to a market inefficiency but it is rather evidence of a pricing model misspecification. To the extent that tests of market efficiency use data of firms of different sizes and are based on the CAPM, their results might be at least contaminated by the size effect.

One possible explanation involving the size of the firm directly is based on a model by Klein and Bawa (1977). They find that if insufficient information is available about a subset of securities, investors will not hold these securities because of estimation risk, i.e., uncertainty about the true parameters of the return distribution. If investors differ in the amount of information available, they will limit their diversification to different subsets of all securities in the market.[15] It is likely that the amount of information generated is related to the size of the firm. Therefore, many investors would not desire to hold the common stock of very small firms. I have shown elsewhere [Banz (1978, ch. 2)] that securities sought by only a subset of the investors have higher risk-adjusted returns than those considered by all investors. Thus, lack of information about small firms leads to limited diversification and therefore to higher returns for the 'undesirable' stocks of small firms.[16] While this informal model is consistent with the empirical results, it is, nevertheless, just conjecture.

To summarize, the size effect exists but it is not at all clear why it exists. Until we find an answer, it should be interpreted with caution. It might be tempting to use the size effect, e.g., as the basis for a theory of mergers — large firms are able to pay a premium for the stock of small firms since they will be able to discount the same cash flows at a smaller discount rate. Naturally, this might turn out to be complete nonsense if size were to be shown to be just a proxy.

The preceding discussion suggests that the results of this study leave many questions unanswered. Further research should consider the relationship between size and other factors such as the dividend yield effect, and the tests should be expanded to include OTC stocks as well.

[15] Klein and Bawa (1977, p. 102).
[16] A similar result can be obtained with the introduction of fixed holding costs which lead to limited diversification as well. See Brennan (1975), Banz (1978, ch. 2) and Mayshar (1979).

References

Ball, Ray, 1978, Anomalies in relationships between securities' yields and yield surrogates, Journal of Financial Economics 6, 103–126.
Banz, Rolf W., 1978, Limited diversification and market equilibrium: An empirical analysis, Ph.D. dissertation (University of Chicago, Chicago, IL).
Basu, S., 1977, Investment performance of common stocks in relation to their price-earnings ratios: A test of market efficiency, Journal of Finance 32, June, 663–682.

Black, Fischer, 1972, Capital market equilibrium with restricted borrowing, Journal of Business 45, July, 444–454.
Black, Fischer, and Myron Scholes, 1974, The effects of dividend yield and dividend policy on common stock prices and returns, Journal of Financial Economics 1, May, 1–22.
Black, Fischer, Michael C. Jensen and Myron Scholes, 1972, The capital asset pricing model: Some empirical tests, in: M.C. Jensen, ed., Studies in the theory of capital markets (Praeger, New York) 79–121.
Brennan, Michael J., 1975, The optimal number of securities in a risky asset portfolio when there are fixed costs of transacting: Theory and some empirical evidence, Journal of Financial and Quantitative Analysis 10, Sept., 483–496.
Brenner, Menachem, 1976, A note on risk, return and equilibrium: Empirical tests, Journal of Political Economy 84, 407–409.
Fama, Eugene F., 1976, Foundations of finance (Basic Books, New York).
Fama, Eugene F. and James D. MacBeth, 1973, Risk return and equilibrium: Some empirical tests, Journal of Political Economy 71, May–June, 607–636.
Ibbotson, Roger G. and Carol L. Fall, 1979, The United States market wealth portfolio, Journal of Portfolio Management 6, 82–92.
Ibbotson, Roger G. and Rex A. Sinquefield, 1977, Stocks, bonds, bills and inflation: The past (1926–1976) and the future (1977–2000) (Financial Analysis Research Foundation).
Klein, Roger W. and Vijay S. Bawa, 1977, The effect of limited information and estimation risk on optimal portfolio diversification, Journal of Financial Economics 5, Aug., 89–111.
Kraus, Alan and Robert H. Litzenberger, 1976, Skewness preference and the valuation of risk assets, Journal of Finance 31, 1085–1100.
Levi, Maurice D., 1973, Errors in the variables bias in the presence of correctly measured variables, Econometrica 41, Sept., 985–986.
Litzenberger, Robert H. and Krishna Ramaswamy, 1979, The effect of personal taxes and dividends on capital asset prices: Theory and empirical evidence, Journal of Financial Economics 7, June, 163–195.
Mayshar, Joram, 1979, Transaction costs in a model of capital market equilibrium, Journal of Political Economy 87, 673–700.
Reinganum, Marc R., 1980, Misspecification of capital asset pricing: Empirical anomalies based on earnings yields and market values, Journal of Financial Economics, this issue.
Roll, Richard, 1977, A critique of the asset pricing theory's tests: Part I, Journal of Financial Economics 4, Jan., 120–176.
Stattman, Dennis, 1980, Book values and expected stock returns, Unpublished M.B.A. honors paper (University of Chicago, Chicago, IL).
Theil, Henri, 1971, Principles of econometrics (Wiley, New York).
U.S. Department of Commerce, Office of Business Economics, 1969, 1970, Survey of current business 49, May, 11–12; 50, May, 14.

INVESTMENT PERFORMANCE OF COMMON STOCKS IN RELATION TO THEIR PRICE-EARNINGS RATIOS: A TEST OF THE EFFICIENT MARKET HYPOTHESIS

S. BASU*

I. INTRODUCTION

IN AN EFFICIENT CAPITAL MARKET, security prices fully reflect available information in a rapid and unbiased fashion and thus provide unbiased estimates of the underlying values. While there is substantial empirical evidence supporting the efficient market hypothesis,[1] many still question its validity. One such group believes that price-earnings (P/E) ratios are indicators of the future investment performance of a security. Proponents of this price-ratio hypothesis claim that low P/E securities will tend to outperform high P/E stocks.[2] In short, prices of securities are biased, and the P/E ratio is an indicator of this bias.[3] A finding that returns on stocks with low P/E ratios tends to be larger than warranted by the underlying risks, even after adjusting for any additional search and transactions costs, and differential taxes, would be inconsistent with the efficient market hypothesis.[4]

The purpose of this paper is to determine empirically whether the investment performance of common stocks is related to their P/E ratios. In Section II data, sample, and estimation procedures are outlined. Empirical results are discussed in Section III, and conclusions and implications are given in Section IV.

---

* Faculty of Business, McMaster University. The author is indebted to Professors Harold Bierman, Jr., Thomas R. Dyckman, Roland E. Dukes, Seymour Smidt, Bernell K. Stone, all of Cornell University, and particularly to this *Journal's* referees, Nancy L. Jacob and Marshall E. Blume, for their very helpful comments and suggestions. Of course, any remaining errors are the author's responsibility. Research support from the Graduate School of Business and Public Administration, Cornell University is gratefully acknowledged.

1. See Fama [8] for an extensive discussion of the efficient market hypothesis and a synthesis of much of the empirical evidence on this issue.

2. See Williamson [28; p. 162].

3. Smidt [27] argues that one potential source of market inefficiency is inappropriate market responses to information. Inappropriate responses to information implicit in P/E ratios are believed to be caused by exaggerated investor expectations regarding growth in earnings and dividends; i.e., exaggerated optimism leads, on average, to high P/E securities and exaggerated pessimism leads, on average, to stocks with low P/E ratios. For an elaboration on this point see [19; p. 28], [20], [21] and [28; p. 161–162]. A contrary position is discussed in [22].

4. In general, results of previous empirical research by Breen [5], Breen & Savage [6], McWilliams [18], Miller & Widmann [19] and Nicholson [20] seem to support the price-ratio hypothesis. While this may suggest a violation of the semi-strong form of the efficient market hypothesis, all of these studies have one or more of the following limitations: (i) retroactive selection bias, (ii) no adjustment for risk, marginal information processing and transactions costs, and differential tax effects pertaining to capital gains and dividends, and (iii) earnings information is assumed to be available on or before the reporting date.

II. Data and Methodology

The following general research design was employed to examine the relationship between P/E ratios and investment performance of equity securities. For any given period under consideration, two or more portfolios consisting of securities with similar P/E ratios are formed. The risk-return relationships of these portfolios are compared and their performance is then evaluated in terms of pre-specified measures. Finally, as a test of the efficient market hypothesis, the returns of the low P/E portfolio are compared to those of a portfolio composed of randomly selected securities with the same overall level of risk. The data base and methodological details are now discussed.

Data Base & Sample Selection Criteria

The primary data for this study is drawn from a merged magnetic tape at Cornell University that includes the COMPUSTAT file of NYSE Industrial firms, the Investment Return file from the CRSP tape and a delisted file containing selected accounting data and investment returns for securities delisted from the NYSE.[5] With the inclusion of the delisted file (375–400 firms), the data base represents over 1400 industrial firms, which actually traded on the NYSE between September 1956–August 1971.

For any given year under consideration, three criteria were used in selecting sample firms:[6] (i) the fiscal year-end of the firm is December 31 (fiscal years being considered are 1956–1969); (ii) the firm actually traded on the NYSE as of the beginning of the portfolio holding period and is included in the merged tape described above; and (iii) the relevant investment return and financial statement data are not missing. A total of 753 firms satisfied the above requirements for at least one year, with about 500, on average, qualifying for inclusion in each of the 14 years.

Method of Analysis

Beginning with 1956, the P/E ratio of every sample security was computed. The numerator of the ratio was defined as the market value of common stock (market price times number of shares outstanding) as of December 31 and the denominator as reported annual earnings (before extraordinary items) available for common

---

5. To the extent data for the delisted file was not available from the COMPUSTAT-CRSP tapes, it was collected by this author. The principal sources for financial statement data were *Moody's Industrial Manual* (1956–71) and corporate annual reports. For the investment return segment, data was collected from: (i) *Bank and Quotation Record & National Association of Security Dealers, Monthly Stock Summary* (1956–71), (ii) *Moody's Dividend Record* (1956–71), (iii) *Capital Changes Reporter* (1972), and (iv) *Directory of Obsolete Securities* (1972). The following assumptions were made in computing the monthly returns on firms that were acquired or liquidated: (i) all proceeds received on a merger were reinvested in the security of the acquiring firm, and (ii) all liquidating dividends were reinvested in Fisher's Arithmetic Investment Performance (Return) Index (see Fisher [12]).

6. The fiscal year requirement was imposed since P/E portfolios are formed by ranking P/E ratios as of the fiscal year-end, and it isn't clear that these ratios computed at different points in time are comparable. Further, for reasons indicated in Section III, all firms having less than 60 months of investment return data preceding the start of the portfolio holding period in any given year were excluded.

Investment Performance of Common Stocks in Relation to Price-Earnings 665

stockholders. These ratios were ranked and five[7] portfolios were formed.[8] Although the P/E ratio was computed as of December 31, it is unlikely that investors would have access to the firm's financial statements, and exact earnings figures at that time, even though Ball & Brown [1] among others indicates that the market reacts as though it possesses such information. Since over 90% of firms release their financial reports within three months of the fiscal year-end (see [1]), the P/E portfolios were assumed to be purchased on the following April 1. The monthly returns on each of these portfolios were then computed for the next twelve months assuming an equal initial investment in each of their respective securities and then a buy-and-hold policy.[9]

The above procedure was repeated annually on each April 1 giving 14 years (April 1957–March 1971) of return data for each of the P/E portfolios. Each of these portfolios may be viewed as a mutual fund with a policy of acquiring securities in a given P/E class on April 1, holding them for a year, and then reinvesting the proceeds from disposition in the same class on the following April 1.[10]

If capital markets are dominated by risk-averse investors and portfolio (security) returns incorporate a risk premium, then the appropriate measures of portfolio (security) performance are those that take into consideration both risk and return. Three such evaluative measures have been developed by Jensen, Sharpe and Treynor, and are employed here.[11] While these measures were originally based upon the Sharpe-Lintner version of the capital asset pricing model (see [26], [17], and [9] for example), recent empirical and theoretical developments in the area (see [2], [3], [11]) suggest an alternate specification might be more appropriate. Accordingly, performance measures underlying both specifications of the asset pricing equation are estimated:

$$r_{pt} - r_{ft} = \hat{\delta}_{pf} + \hat{\beta}_{pf}[r_{mt} - r_{ft}] \tag{1}$$

$$r_{pt} - r_{zt} = \hat{\delta}_{pz} + \hat{\beta}_{pz}[r_{mt} - r_{zt}] \tag{2}$$

where r_{pt} = continuously compounded return on P/E portfolio p in month t;

---

7. Although the construction of five portfolios is arbitrary, that number represents a balance between obtaining as large a spread in P/E's as possible and a reasonable number of securities (about 100) in each portfolio.

8. Actually, the reciprocal of the P/E ratio was employed in ranking the securities. Consequently, firms with negative earnings (losses) were included in the highest P/E portfolio (see [18]). Since it is somewhat questionable whether such firms should be included in the highest P/E group, a sixth portfolio was constructed by excluding these firms from the highest P/E portfolio.

9. See [16] for computational details. The entire analysis was repeated assuming monthly reallocation with substantially identical results.

10. A survey of the industry distributions (20 SIC groups) of the five P/E portfolios reveals that although firms in high technology industries, such as chemicals and electronics, are disproportionately concentrated in the high P/E classes, the various portfolios consist of securities drawn from the entire spectrum of industries. The results of a chi-square test, however, reject the hypothesis that the proportion of firms in the 20 industry groups is the same in all P/E portfolios.

11. See Friend & Blume [13] for an excellent discussion comparing these three measures.

computed as the natural logarithm of one plus the realized monthly return (wealth relative).

r_{mt} = continuously compounded return on "market portfolio" in month t; measured by the natural logarithm of the link relative of Fisher's "Arithmetic Investment Performance (Return) Index" (see [12]).

r_{ft} = continuously compounded "risk-free" return in month t; measured by the natural logarithm of one plus the monthly return on 30-day U.S. treasury bills.

r_{zt} = continuously compounded return on "zero-beta" portfolio; measured by the natural logarithm of one plus the ex post estimate, $\hat{\gamma}_{0t}$.[12]

$\hat{\delta}_{pf}, \hat{\delta}_{pz}$ = estimated intercepts (differential return – Jensen's measure).

$\hat{\beta}_{pf}, \hat{\beta}_{pz}$ = estimated slopes (systematic risk).

III. EMPIRICAL RESULTS

Relative Performance of the P/E Portfolios

Equations (1) and (2) were estimated by ordinary least squares (OLS) using 168 months of return data (April 1957–March 1971). Table 1 shows the scores of the three performance measures and selected summary statistics for the (i) five P/E portfolios (A = highest P/E, B, C, D and E = lowest P/E); (ii) highest P/E portfolio (A) excluding firms with negative earnings, A^*; (iii) sample, S and (iv) Fisher's Index, F.

The following observations on the results in Table 1 seem pertinent.[13] First, consider the median price-earnings ratio and inter-quartile range for each of the P/E portfolios over the 14-year period ending March 31, 1971. The differences in P/E ratios for the various portfolios are, of course, significant. Since these statistics are based on 1957–71 pooled data, the inter-quartile ranges reflect the dispersion of P/E ratios over the 14-year period.

Second, the two low P/E portfolios, D and E, earned on average 13.5% and 16.3% per annum respectively over the 14-year period; whereas the two high P/E portfolios, A (or A^*) and B, earned 9.3–9.5% per year. In fact, Table 1 indicates that the average annual rates of return decline (to some extent monotonically) as one moves from the low P/E to high P/E portfolios.[14] However, contrary to capital market theory, the higher returns on the low P/E portfolios were not associated with higher levels of systematic risk; the systematic risks of portfolios D and E are lower than those for portfolios A, A^* and B. Accordingly, Jensen's

---

12. Ex post estimates of $r_{zt}, \hat{\gamma}_{0t}$, for the period 1935–1968 (June) were generously provided by Professors Fama and MacBeth (see [11]). Using their methodology, estimates for the period July 1968–71 were computed. As in the case of r_{ft} and r_{mt}, $\hat{\gamma}_{0t}$ is assumed to be exogenously determined.

13. It should be noted that the results in Table 1 are based on continuous compounding and that although monthly return data were employed in estimating equations (1) and (2), $\bar{r}_p$, $\bar{r}'_p$, $\hat{\delta}_p$ and $\sigma(\bar{r}'_p)$ in that table have been stated on an annual basis by multiplying their mean monthly values by 12. This is always possible under continuous compounding due to the additive property of logarithms, i.e. if $\bar{r}_p^*$ and $\bar{r}_p$ are the continuously compounded mean monthly and annual returns respectively, then it can be easily shown that $\bar{r}_p = 12\bar{r}_p^*$.

Furthermore, the entire analysis was repeated assuming monthly compounding with substantially similar results.

14. A year-by-year comparison reveals that this pattern is not discernible for certain periods, e.g. for the years ended March 31, 1958 and 1970.

Investment Performance of Common Stocks in Relation to Price-Earnings

TABLE 1
PERFORMANCE MEASURES & RELATED SUMMARY STATISTICS
(April 1957–March 1971)

Performance Measure/ Summary Statistic	CAPM defined with	A	A*	B	C	D	E	S	F
				P/E Portfolios[1]				Market Portfolios[1]	
Median P/E ratio and inter-quartile range[2]	—	35.8 (41.8)	30.5 (21.0)	19.1 (6.7)	15.0 (3.2)	12.8 (2.6)	9.8 (2.9)	15.1 (9.6)	
Average annual rate of return ($\bar{r}_p$)[3]	—	0.0934	0.0955	0.0928	0.1165	0.1355	0.1630	0.1211	0.1174
Average annual excess return ($\bar{r}'_p$)[4]	r_f	0.0565	0.0585	0.0558	0.0796	0.0985	0.1260	0.0841	0.0804
	r_z	0.0194	0.0214	0.0187	0.0425	0.0613	0.0889	0.0470	0.0433
Systematic risk ($\hat{\beta}_p$)	r_f	1.1121	1.0579	1.0387	0.9678	0.9401	0.9866	1.0085	1.0000
	r_z	1.1463	1.0919	1.0224	0.9485	0.9575	1.0413	1.0225	1.0000
Jensen's differential return ($\hat{\delta}_p$) and t-value in parenthesis	r_f	−0.0330 (−2.62)	−0.0265 (−2.01)	−0.0277 (−2.85)	0.0017 (0.18)	0.0228 (2.73)	0.0467 (3.98)	0.0030 (0.62)	
	r_z	−0.0303 (−2.59)	−0.0258 (−2.04)	−0.0256 (−2.63)	0.0014 (0.15)	0.0198 (2.34)	0.0438 (3.80)	0.0027 (0.57)	
Treynor's reward-to-volatility measure:[5] $r'_p / \hat{\beta}_p$	r_f	0.0508	0.0553	0.0537	0.0822	0.1047	0.1237	0.0834	0.0804
	r_z	0.0169	0.0196	0.0183	0.0448	0.0640	0.0854	0.0460	0.0433
Sharpe's reward-to-variability measure:[6] $r'_p / \sigma(\bar{r}'_p)$	r_f	0.0903	0.0978	0.0967	0.1475	0.1886	0.2264	0.1526	0.1481
	r_z	0.0287	0.0331	0.0312	0.0762	0.1095	0.1444	0.0797	0.0755
Coefficient of correlation: $\rho(\bar{r}'_p, \bar{r}'_m)$	r_f	0.9662	0.9594	0.9767	0.9742	0.9788	0.9630	0.9936	
	r_z	0.9748	0.9676	0.9780	0.9767	0.9809	0.9705	0.9946	
Coefficient of serial correlation: $\rho(\tilde{e}_{t+1}, \tilde{e}_t)$	r_f	0.0455	0.0845	0.0285	−0.1234	0.0065	0.1623	0.1050	
	r_z	0.0048	0.0681	0.0163	−0.1447	0.0408	0.1485	0.0763	
F-Statistics for Test on Homogeneity of Asset-Pricing Relationships (Chow-test)[7]	r_f	2.3988	2.2527	0.4497	1.2249	1.1988	0.2892	0.0496	
	r_z	0.8918	0.2490	0.9767	0.3575	0.6987	0.4761	0.2826	

1. A = highest P/E quintile, E = lowest P/E quintile, A^* = highest P/E quintile excluding firms with negative earnings, S = sample and F = Fisher Index.

2. Based on 1957–71 pooled data; inter-quartile range is shown in parenthesis.

3. $\bar{r}_p = (\sum_{t=1}^{168} r_{pt})/14$, where r_{pt} is the continuously compounded return of portfolio p in month t (April 1957–March 1971).

4. $\bar{r}'_p = (\sum_{t=1}^{168} r'_{pt})/14$, where r'_{pt} is the continuously compounded excess return (r_{pt} minus r_{ft} or r_{zt}) of portfolio p in month t (April 1957–March 1971).

5. Mean excess return on portfolio p, $\bar{r}'_p$, divided by its systematic risk, $\hat{\beta}_p$.

6. Mean excess return on portfolio p, $\bar{r}'_p$, divided by its standard deviation, $\sigma(\bar{r}'_p)$.

7. None of the computed figures are significant at the 0.05 level: $Pr(F(2,120) > 3.07) = 0.01$; $Pr(F(2, \infty) > 3.0) = 0.05$ and degrees of freedom in denominator = 164.

measure (differential return) indicates that, if we ignore differential tax effects regarding dividends and capital gains, the low P/E portfolios, E and D, earned about $4\frac{1}{2}\%$ and 2% per annum respectively *more* than that implied by their levels of risk, while the high P/E portfolios earned $2\frac{1}{2}$–3% per annum *less* than that implied by their levels of risk. Furthermore, assuming normality,[15] these differential returns are statistically significant at the 0.05 level or higher.[16] Since the relative systematic risks of the P/E portfolios are not substantially different, relative performance as indicated by Treynor's measure (reward-to-volatility) is consistent with that indicated by $\hat{\delta}_p$. As would be expected, all of the P/E portfolios are well diversified[17]— the correlation coefficients for the return of the various portfolios and the market (Fisher Index) are all greater than 0.95. Consequently, the Sharpe measure (reward-to-variability) also shows that the performance of the low P/E portfolios is superior to that of their high ratio counterparts.

Third, with the exception of portfolios E and C, the serial correlation in the regression residuals is fairly small for both versions of the asset pricing model. The residuals from the regressions for portfolios E and C were tested for positive and negative first order serial correlation respectively. Results of the Von Neumann test (see [15]) indicate that (i) the null hypothesis of zero positive first order autocorrelation could be rejected at the 0.05 level for portfolio E, and (ii) for portfolio C, the null hypothesis (zero negative first order autocorrelation) could be rejected for the "zero-beta" version at the 0.05 level. Consequently, while the estimated differential returns and systematic risks for portfolios E and C are unbiased, the conventional methods for determining statistical significance, strictly speaking, are not applicable.[18]

A fundamental assumption underlying the results in Table 1 is stationarity of the regression relationships—differential return (intercept) and systematic risk (slope) —over the entire 14-year period. To determine the validity of this assumption, the 14 years were divided into two non-overlapping sub-periods of seven years each (April 1957–March 1964 and April 1964–March 1971). Equations (1) and (2) were then estimated by OLS for each of the various P/E portfolios and the sample in each of these two sub-periods. The homogeneity of the estimated regression coefficients in the two time-periods was tested statistically,[19] and the results of this

---

15. The reader should use some caution in accepting the significance levels since the normality assumption can be questioned. For example, see Fama [10].

16. The results in Table 1 assume that the P/E portfolios are formed and traded annually. To investigate the impact of frequency of trading, the analysis was repeated for intervals of up to five years. For the bi-annual trading situation, the differential returns are largely similar to those shown in Table 1. For longer periods, in particular the five-year case (i.e., trading occurs in April 1962 and April 1967), the differential returns for all of the P/E portfolios, as might be expected, are not statistically different from zero.

17. Recall that, on average, each of the P/E portfolios (except A^*) is composed of about 100 securities. Portfolio A^*, which includes the securities in A other than those with negative earnings, has on average about 80 securities in each of the annual trading periods.

18. Scheffé [24] shows that by using the (estimated) autocorrelation coefficient and the asymptotic property of the t-distribution, one can estimate the effect of serial correlation on confidence intervals. Computations, however, show that after adjusting for serial correlation in portfolio E's residuals, the nominal significance levels are not altered significantly.

19. The statistical test employed is often referred to as the "Chow test." See Johnston [15].

Investment Performance of Common Stocks in Relation to Price-Earnings

test appear in the last panel in Table 1. It will be noted that none of the F-statistics are significant at the 0.05 level. This finding, of couse, is consistent with the hypothesis that systematic risk, differential returns, and related measures of performance for each of the seven portfolios were not different in the two time-periods.

Differential Tax Effects

The results in Table 1 ignore the effect of the differential treatment given to the taxation of dividends and capital gains. Empirical evidence on whether capital asset prices incorporate this differential tax effect is conflicting. Brennan [7] concluded that differential tax effects are important in the determination of security yields. Black & Scholes [4], on the other hand, question Brennan's analysis. On the basis of their empirical results, they argue that there are virtually no differential returns earned by investors who buy high dividend-yielding securities or low dividend-yielding ones. However, to verify the sensitivity of the results in Table 1 to these tax effects, the following approach was employed. Assuming the tax rate on capital gains and dividends to be 0.25 and 0.50 respectively, the monthly returns, net of tax, for each of the P/E portfolios, the sample, the risk-free asset[20] and the market portfolio (Fisher Index) were computed. Equation (1) was then re-estimated by OLS employing the 168 months of after-tax return data. Selected summary statistics from these regressions appear in Table 2.

TABLE 2

PERFORMANCE MEASURES, NET OF TAX, AND RELATED SUMMARY STATISTICS
(CAPM: $r_m - r_f$; April 1957–March 1971)

Performance Measure/Statistic[1,2]

Portfolio	$\bar{r}_p$	$\hat{\beta}_p$	$\hat{\delta}_p$	$t(\hat{\delta}_p)$	$\bar{r}'_p/\hat{\beta}_p$	$\bar{r}'_p/\sigma(\bar{r}'_p)$	$\rho(\bar{r}'_p,\bar{r}'_m)$	$\rho(\hat{e}_t,\hat{e}_{t+1})$	Chow Test:[3] F-Statistic
A	0.0699	1.1161	−0.0198	−2.10	0.0460	0.1094	0.9667	0.0404	2.4093
A*	0.0703	1.0611	−0.0158	−1.61	0.0488	0.1153	0.9603	0.0827	2.1886
B	0.0647	1.0428	−0.0203	−2.86	0.0443	0.1064	0.9779	0.0360	0.4766
C	0.0810	0.9711	0.0006	0.09	0.0644	0.1543	0.9753	−0.1271	1.1642
D	0.0941	0.9451	0.0153	2.43	0.0800	0.1924	0.9788	0.0104	1.1574
E	0.1145	0.9913	0.0328	3.73	0.0969	0.2293	0.9632	0.1541	0.3168
S	0.0852	1.0126	0.0022	0.63	0.0659	0.1611	0.9941	0.1172	0.0289
F	0.0822	1.0000	—	—	0.0637	0.1566	—	—	—

1. Continuously compounded annual rates, net of 25% and 50% tax on capital gains and dividends respectively.

2. $\bar{r}_p$ = average annual return; $\bar{r}'_p$ = average annual excess return; $\hat{\beta}_p$ = estimated systematic risk; $\hat{\delta}_p$ = estimated differential return; $t(\hat{\delta}_p)$ = t-value for $\hat{\delta}_p$; $\bar{r}'_p/\hat{\beta}_p$ = reward-to-volatility ratio; $\bar{r}'_p/\sigma(\bar{r}'_p)$ = reward-to-variability ratio; $\rho(\bar{r}'_p,\bar{r}'_m)$ = correlation coefficient for $\bar{r}'_p$ and $\bar{r}'_m$; $\rho(\hat{e}_t,\hat{e}_{t+1})$ = serial correlation coefficient.

3. Test on homogeneity of asset pricing relationships; none of the values are significant at the 0.05 level.

---

20. The returns on the risk-free asset (30-day treasury bills) were treated as ordinary income for tax purposes. No attempt was made to estimate equation (2) on an after-tax basis due to the inherent difficulty in specifying the return on the zero-beta portfolio, $\bar{r}_z$, on an after-tax basis.

Although the adjustment for tax effects result in $\hat{\delta}_p$ being closer to zero,[21] the general relationships discussed in connection with the before-tax case also seem to hold here. Therefore, assuming the tax rate estimates are reasonably realistic, differential tax rates on dividends and capital gains cannot entirely explain the relative before-tax performance of the various portfolios.

The Effect of Risk on Performance Measures

The propriety of the one-parameter performance measures employed in this paper is conditional upon the validity of the asset pricing models underlying equations (1) and (2). To the extent these models do not reflect the equilibrium risk-return relationships in capital markets, the related evaluative measures also do not appropriately measure the performance of the various P/E portfolios. Previous empirical work by Friend & Blume [13], and Black, Jensen & Scholes [3] among others, indicate that, contrary to theory, the differential returns, δ's are on average non-zero and are inversely related to the level of systematic risk;[22] low risk (low β) portfolios, on average, earn significantly more than that predicted by the model ($\delta > 0$) and, on average, high risk portfolios earn significantly less than that predicted by the model ($\delta < 0$).

A review of the data presented in Table 1 shows that those results seem to display this property. If this is the case, conclusions regarding the relative performance of the P/E portfolios would have to be qualified. The following test was conducted to determine the bias, if any, caused by β. For each of the P/E portfolios (A, A^*, B, C, D and E) and the sample, (S), five sub-portfolios were constructed so as to maximize the dispersion of their systematic risks.[23] Equations (1) and (2) were then estimated by OLS for each of these sub-portfolios using 14 years of monthly data. Table 3 includes selected summary statistics for these regressions.

Consistent with the results of Friend & Blume and Black, Jensen & Scholes, Table 3 shows that the $\hat{\delta}$ of a portfolio does seem to depend on its $\hat{\beta}$; the higher the $\hat{\beta}$ the lower the $\hat{\delta}$. This observation holds for each of the P/E classes and the sample. When $\hat{\beta}$ is held constant, $\hat{\delta}$ seems to depend on its P/E class. To see this more clearly, a scatter diagram of $\hat{\delta}$ and $\hat{\beta}$ for the P/E classes and the sample

---

21. Note that $\hat{\delta}_p$ for A^* is not significantly different from zero at the 0.05 level or higher.

22. Friend & Blume [13] also show empirically that, in addition to the Jensen measure, the Treynor and Sharpe measures are also related to β and state that the three one-parameter measures based on capital market theory "seem to yield seriously biased estimates of performance, with the magnitude of the bias related to portfolio risk" (p. 574). Since the bias seems to be shared by the three measures, only Jensen's differential return is investigated in this sub-section.

23. The methodology employed in the construction of these sub-portfolios is similar to that described in Black, Jensen & Scholes [3]. Consider the formation of sub-portfolios for P/E class E. Starting with April 1957 β for each of the securities included in portfolio E was estimated by regressing that security's excess return ($r_{jt} - r_{ft}$ or $r_{jt} - r_{zt}$ as the case may be) on the excess return on the market using 60 months of *historical* data. Continuously compounded data was employed for this purpose. These securities were then ranked on estimated β from maximum to minimum, and 5 groups (sub-portfolios) were formed. The monthly returns on each of these 5 sub-portfolios were computed for the next 12 months assuming an equal initial investment and then a buy-and-hold policy. This procedure was repeated annually on each April 1 giving 14 years of return data for each of the 5 sub-portfolios for P/E class E. The sub-portfolios for the other P/E classes and the sample were computed in an analogous fashion.

TABLE 3

MEAN EXCESS & DIFFERENTIAL RETURNS BY P/E AND SYSTEMATIC RISK CLASSES[1]
(April 1957–March 1971)

Portfolio P/E Class	β Class	\multicolumn{5}{c}{$r_m - r_f$}	\multicolumn{5}{c}{$r_m - r_z$}
		$\hat{\beta}_p$	$\bar{r}'_p$	$\hat{\delta}_p$	$t(\hat{\delta}_p)$	$\hat{\rho}$	$\hat{\beta}_p$	$\bar{r}'_p$	$\hat{\delta}_p$	$t(\hat{\delta}_p)$	$\hat{\rho}$
A	1	0.724	0.059	0.001	0.06	0.84	0.753	0.021	−0.012	−0.54	0.85
	2	0.936	0.089	0.014	0.72	0.90	0.971	0.013	−0.029	−1.44	0.91
	3	1.121	0.058	−0.032	−1.50	0.91	1.132	0.023	−0.026	−1.28	0.93
	4	1.282	0.041	−0.063	−2.50	0.91	1.370	0.020	−0.039	−1.67	0.93
	5	1.554	0.019	−0.106	−3.76	0.92	1.552	0.002	−0.065	−2.34	0.93
A*	1	0.683	0.064	0.009	0.42	0.81	0.723	0.021	−0.010	−0.46	0.82
	2	0.938	0.074	−0.001	−0.06	0.88	0.912	0.020	−0.020	−0.97	0.89
	3	1.017	0.063	−0.018	−0.76	0.87	1.073	0.027	−0.020	−0.94	0.92
	4	1.222	0.042	−0.056	−2.39	0.91	1.261	0.006	−0.049	−2.02	0.92
	5	1.498	0.034	−0.087	−2.93	0.91	1.547	0.016	−0.051	−1.84	0.93
B	1	0.753	0.044	−0.016	−0.95	0.88	0.691	0.017	−0.013	−0.79	0.88
	2	0.903	0.073	0.001	0.04	0.91	0.897	0.009	−0.030	−1.81	0.93
	3	1.039	0.037	−0.046	−2.84	0.94	1.015	0.018	−0.026	−1.68	0.95
	4	1.196	0.065	−0.031	−1.54	0.93	1.160	0.037	−0.013	−0.64	0.93
	5	1.337	0.043	−0.064	−2.96	0.93	1.373	−0.002	−0.061	−3.12	0.95
C	1	0.658	0.102	0.049	2.79	0.85	0.588	0.070	0.044	2.94	0.87
	2	0.840	0.095	0.027	1.62	0.90	0.811	0.045	0.009	0.65	0.93
	3	0.952	0.070	−0.007	−0.45	0.93	0.922	0.032	−0.008	−0.56	0.94
	4	1.039	0.058	−0.025	−1.44	0.93	1.108	0.049	0.001	0.04	0.94
	5	1.381	0.061	−0.051	−2.35	0.94	1.347	0.005	−0.054	−2.58	0.94
D	1	0.649	0.127	0.075	5.02	0.88	0.706	0.094	0.063	4.16	0.90
	2	0.898	0.116	0.044	2.66	0.92	0.838	0.074	0.038	2.38	0.92
	3	0.961	0.095	0.017	1.22	0.94	0.945	0.051	0.010	0.62	0.94
	4	1.022	0.097	0.014	0.85	0.93	1.065	0.047	0.000	0.03	0.95
	5	1.203	0.047	−0.050	−2.59	0.94	1.264	0.030	−0.025	−1.48	0.96
E	1	0.742	0.130	0.070	3.60	0.85	0.784	0.108	0.074	3.57	0.86
	2	0.911	0.125	0.052	3.00	0.91	0.917	0.084	0.044	2.34	0.91
	3	0.913	0.122	0.049	2.82	0.91	1.038	0.075	0.030	1.76	0.94
	4	1.101	0.106	0.018	0.88	0.92	1.171	0.078	0.027	1.33	0.93
	5	1.281	0.134	0.031	1.31	0.92	1.310	0.085	0.028	1.31	0.94
Sample (S)	1	0.701	0.093	0.037	3.46	0.94	0.677	0.053	0.023	2.55	0.96
	2	0.886	0.095	0.024	2.89	0.98	0.891	0.051	0.012	1.39	0.98
	3	0.969	0.091	0.013	1.57	0.98	1.002	0.052	0.009	1.07	0.98
	4	1.134	0.070	−0.021	−2.21	0.98	1.147	0.040	−0.101	−1.18	0.99
	5	1.383	0.064	−0.047	−3.16	0.97	1.422	0.032	−0.030	−2.67	0.98

1. Continuously compounded annual rates; details are described in footnote 13.

2. $\hat{\beta}_p$ = estimated systematic risk; $\bar{r}'_p$ = mean excess return; $\hat{\delta}_p$ = estimated differential return; $t(\hat{\delta}_p)$ = t-value for $\hat{\delta}_p$ and $\hat{\rho}$ = coefficient of correlation between $\bar{r}'_p$ and the excess return on the market $\bar{r}'_m$.

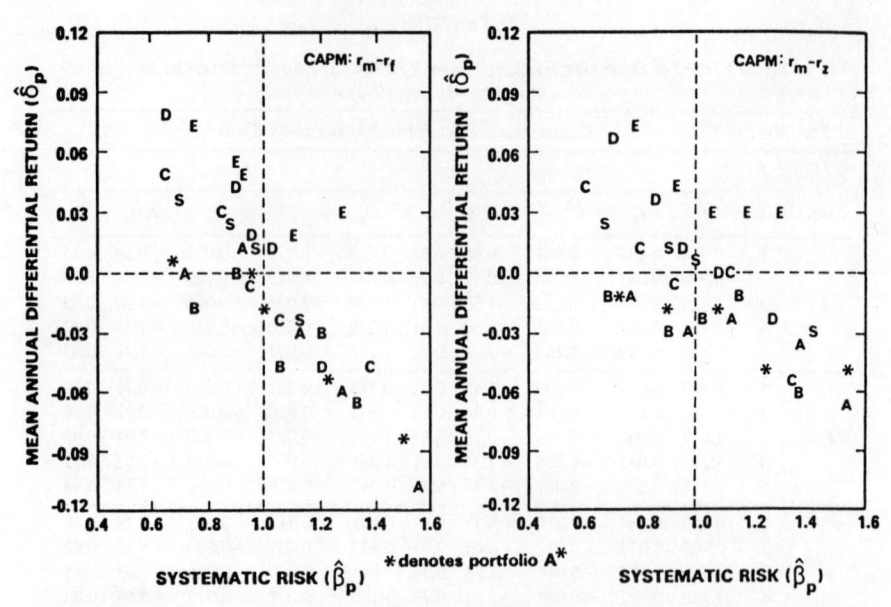

FIGURE 1. Scatter Diagram of Mean Annual Differential Return vs. Systematic Risk by P/E Classes (April 1957–March 1971)

appears in Figure 1. It will be observed that $\hat{\delta}$ for the low P/E classes is larger than that for the high P/E's. This is generally true for most levels of $\hat{\beta}$.

These results are consistent with one of the following two propositions. First, it seems that the asset pricing models do not completely characterize the equilibrium risk-return relationships during the period studied and that, perhaps, these models are mis-specified because of the omission of other relevant factors.[24] However, this line of reasoning, when combined with our results, suggests that P/E ratios seem to be a proxy for some omitted risk variable. On the other hand, if the asset pricing models are assumed to be valid, the results included in Table 3 and Figure 1 confirm the earlier remarks on the relative performance of the P/E portfolios. Nevertheless, the bias caused by β is sufficiently severe that it would be inappropriate to rely exclusively on CAPM performance measures.

Comparisons with Randomly Selected Portfolios of Equivalent Risk

Pettit & Westerfield [23] argue that empirical studies employing asset pricing models should present performance measures for portfolios composed of randomly selected securities of the same overall level of risk. Their approach attempts to neutralize the bias described above by holding the level of β constant in performance comparisons and allows a direct comparison to be made between the realized return on a P/E portfolio with that on the related random portfolio of equivalent risk. In order to make these comparisons, the following procedures were employed.

For *each* of the six P/E portfolios (A, A*, B, C, D & E) ten portfolios consisting

---

24. See Friend & Blume [13] for an elaboration.

Investment Performance of Common Stocks in Relation to Price-Earnings 673

of randomly selected securities with β's comparable to the P/E portfolio were formed.[25] Equations (1) and (2) were then estimated by OLS for each of these 60 random portfolios using 168 months of before-tax return data.[26] From the ten random portfolios associated with each P/E portfolio, the one whose estimated systematic risk, $\hat{\beta}$, was closest to that of the P/E portfolio was selected for analysis.[27]

Panel A in Table 4 shows on a before- and after-tax basis for the Sharpe-Lintner version of CAPM:[28] (i) the estimated systematic risk, $\hat{\beta}_R$, for six random portfolios (*RA*, *RA**, *RB*, *RC*, *RD* & *RE*) related to the six P/E portfolios (*A*, *A**, *B*, *C*, *D* & *E*) respectively, (ii) the deviation of the random portfolio's systematic risk from the associated P/E portfolio beta ($\hat{\beta}_p$), $\hat{\beta}_d$ (e.g. for portfolio *RA*, $\hat{\beta}_d = \hat{\beta}_A - \hat{\beta}_{RA}$) and (iii) the computed standard normal variates for Hollander's distribution-free test (see [14]) of the hypothesis $\hat{\beta}_d = 0$, $Z(\hat{\beta}_d)$. While the estimated systematic risks for portfolios *RA**, *RB*, *RC* and *RE* are extremely close to that of *A**, *B*, *C* and *E* respectively, the deviations are slightly higher for *RA* and *RD*. Hollander's test for the parallelism of two regression lines, however, indicates that none of the $\hat{\beta}_d$ are significantly different from zero. Therefore, from a statistical viewpoint, the estimated systematic risk for all of the random portfolios is not significantly different from the $\hat{\beta}$ of their associated P/E portfolios.

Consequently, a direct comparison between the returns on the random portfolios and those on the related P/E portfolio is possible. The mean annual return on each of the six random portfolios, $\bar{r}_R$, and the mean deviation from the return on associated P/E portfolio ($\bar{r}_p$), $\bar{r}_d$ (e.g. for portfolio *RA*, $\bar{r}_d = \bar{r}_A - \bar{r}_{RA}$) are shown in Panel B of Table 4. Consistent with the previous discussion, the low P/E portfolios

---

25. The basic technique employed in constructing random portfolios of equivalent risk is stratified random sampling. Beginning with April 1957 β for all n_s securities in the sample was estimated using 60 months of historical data. The n_p securities included in P/E portfolio p were then ranked on estimated β from minimum to maximum and the first 9 deciles from the distribution of β's in P/E portfolio p, $d_p(k)$, $k = 1,...,9$, were identified. Fourth, all n_s securities included in the sample were then ranked on estimated β from minimum to maximum and 10 groups were formed using $d_p(k)$ as end points. If we let β_j be the beta for security j in the sample s, then sample group k for P/E portfolio p, $g_p(k)$ $k = 1,...,10$, was formed as follows:

$$g_p(k) = \begin{cases} \{[j \in s | \beta_j < d_p(k)], j = 1,...,n_s\} & k = 1 \\ \{[j \in s | d_p(k-1) < \beta_j < d_p(k)], j = 1,...,n_s\} & k = 2,...,9 \\ \{[j \in s | d_p(k-1) < \beta_j], j = 1,...,n_s\} & k = 10 \end{cases}$$

Fifth, from each of these 10 sample groups for P/E portfolio p, $n_p/10$ securities were randomly selected by using a uniformly distributed random number generator. The n_p randomly selected securities then constituted one random portfolio associated with P/E class p, and this procedure was repeated to generate 10 random portfolios for each P/E class p. The monthly returns on each of these random portfolios were then computed for the next 12 months assuming an equal initial investment in each security and then a buy-and-hold policy. The above procedure was repeated annually on each April 1 to yield 14 years of return data for each of the random portfolios associated with P/E portfolio p.

26. Equation (1) was also estimated using after-tax return data. For the reason mentioned earlier, equation (2) was not estimated on an after-tax basis.

27. Results for all 10 random portfolios selected are not shown due to space limitations.

28. The before-tax results for the zero-beta version of CAPM are omitted since they generally parallel those reported in Table 4.

TABLE 4
SUMMARY STATISTICS FOR RANDOM PORTFOLIOS WITH SYSTEMATIC RISKS EQUIVALENT TO P/E PORTFOLIOS
(CAPM: $r_m - r_f$; April 1957–March 1971)

Random Portfolio[1,2]

	Summary Statistic[3]	Before Tax						Net of Tax					
		RA	RA*	RB	RC	RD	RE	RA	RA*	RB	RC	RD	RE
PANEL A	$\hat{\beta}_R$	1.0789	1.0576	1.0321	0.9653	0.9603	0.9891	1.0844	1.0613	1.0385	0.9695	0.9650	0.9947
	$\hat{\delta}_d = \hat{\beta}_p - \hat{\beta}_R$	0.0332	0.0003	0.0066	0.0025	−0.0202	−0.0025	0.0317	−0.0002	0.0043	0.0016	−0.0199	0.0034
	$Z(\hat{\beta}_d)$	0.92	0.80	0.06	−0.29	−0.00	0.16	1.08	0.14	−0.06	0.28	−0.22	−0.14
PANEL B	r_R	0.1177	0.1102	0.1345	0.1136	0.1253	0.1310	0.0835	0.0777	0.0952	0.0796	0.0881	0.0925
	$r_d = r_p - r_R$	−0.0243	−0.0147	−0.0417	0.0029	0.0101	0.0320	−0.0136	−0.0074	−0.0305	0.0014	0.0060	0.0220
	$t(r_d)$	−1.95	−1.07	−4.00	0.34	1.12	2.74	−1.44	−0.72	−3.94	0.21	0.87	2.49
	$Z(r_d)$	−2.17	−1.08	−3.45	0.36	1.39	2.62	−1.71	−0.83	−3.35	0.21	1.16	2.43
PANEL C	$\hat{\delta}_R$	−0.0060	−0.0118	0.0146	−0.0010	0.0111	0.0145	−0.0041	−0.0084	0.0106	−0.0006	0.0081	0.0106
	$t/\hat{\delta}_R$	−0.71	−1.23	1.73	−0.13	1.30	1.55	−0.66	−1.19	1.71	−0.11	1.27	1.54
	$\hat{\delta}_d = \hat{\delta}_p - \hat{\delta}_R$	−0.0270	−0.0147	−0.0423	0.0027	0.0117	0.0322	−0.0157	−0.0074	−0.0309	0.0012	0.0072	0.0222
	$r'_R/\hat{\beta}_R$	0.0748	0.0692	0.0945	0.0920	0.0752	0.0950	0.0599	0.0558	0.0739	0.0631	0.0722	0.0744
	$(r'/\beta)_d$	−0.0240	−0.0139	−0.0408	0.0029	0.0127	0.0287	−0.0139	−0.0070	−0.0296	0.0013	0.0078	0.0225
	$r'_R/\sigma(\tilde{r}'_R)$	0.1354	0.1247	0.1709	0.1658	0.1362	0.1709	0.1448	0.1343	0.1785	0.1525	0.1737	0.1787
	$(\tilde{r}'/\sigma(\tilde{r}'))_d$	−0.0451	−0.0269	−0.0742	0.0039	0.0228	0.0555	−0.0354	−0.0190	−0.0721	0.0018	0.0187	0.0506

1. Continuously compounded annual rates; details are described in footnote 13.
2. Portfolios RA through RE refer to random portfolios with systematic risks equivalent to P/E portfolio A through E respectively.
3. $\hat{\beta}_p, \hat{\beta}_R$ = estimated systematic risk of P/E portfolio p and related random portfolio R respectively; $Z(\hat{\beta}_d) = N(0,1)$ variates for Hollander's distribution-free test for the parallelism of two regression lines (P/E portfolio and its associated random portfolio); $\bar{r}_p, \bar{r}_R$ = average annual return on P/E portfolio p and related random portfolio R; $t(\bar{r}_d) = \bar{r}_d/(\sigma(\bar{r}_d)/\sqrt{n}) = t$-value for $\bar{r}_d = \bar{r}_p - \bar{r}_R$ and $n = 168$; $Z(\bar{r}_d) = N(0,1)$ variates for Wilcoxon's distribution-free test of the hypothesis $\bar{r}_d = 0$; $\hat{\delta}_p, \hat{\delta}_R$ = estimated differential return for P/E portfolio p and related random portfolio R; $t(\hat{\delta}_R) = t$-value for $\hat{\delta}_R$; $\bar{r}'_R/\hat{\beta}_R$ = reward-to-volatility ratio for R; $(\bar{r}'/\beta)_d$ = reward-to-volatility ratio for P/E portfolio minus that for related random portfolio; $\bar{r}'_R/\sigma(\tilde{r}'_R)$ = reward-to-variability ratio for R; $(\bar{r}'/\sigma(\tilde{r}'))_d$ = reward-to-variability ratio for P/E portfolio minus that for related random portfolio.

(E and D) have generally earned returns higher than random portfolios of equivalent risk ($\bar{r}_d > 0$), while the high P/E's (A, A^* and B) have generally earned returns lower than their related random portfolios ($\bar{r}_d < 0$). Results of the parametric t-test, $t(\bar{r}_d)$, and Wilcoxon's distribution-free test (see [14]), $Z(\bar{r}_d)$, however, indicate that $\bar{r}_d$ is significantly different from zero at the 0.05 level or higher for portfolios A, B and E only.

Panel C in Table 4 includes Jensen's differential return, Treynor's reward-to-volatility and Sharpe's reward-to-variability performance scores for the various random portfolios, as well as the mean differences in the scores between the P/E portfolios and their randomly selected counterparts. As might be expected, these results bear out the same general relationship just discussed.

An analysis of the distributions of the wealth relatives[29] for the various P/E and randomly selected portfolios provides additional insight into the differential performance of the P/E classes. Table 5 shows selected fractiles (deciles) from those distributions. In substantially all of the nine deciles shown, the low P/E portfolios, E and D, have earned a higher return (wealth relative) than their randomly selected equivalents. This, however, does not seem to be the case for the high P/E's. Furthermore, in all of the nine deciles, the highest wealth relative is obtained on the low P/E portfolios.[30]

Three additional comments may be made. The percentage of securities in each of the P/E portfolios with one-year wealth relatives greater than the median of their associated randomly selected portfolio, and the standard normal variates for the binomial test of the hypothesis that these percentages differ from 0.50 are shown in the last two columns. These results are consistent with the analysis at the portfolio level (Panel B in Table 4). Second, Table 5 shows that *all* of the portfolios consist of securities that may be considered to be "winners" and "losers". Investors who held relatively small undiversified portfolios of securities in a particular P/E class (or for that matter across such classes) during the period 1957–71 could have earned returns that were considerably higher or lower than the averages previously reported. Finally, an analysis of the tails of the distributions of wealth relatives revealed that none of the portfolios had significantly more outliers. In short, the performance of the various P/E portfolios is not dominated by the related performance of a few securities.

P/E Ratios & Trading Profits

One final issue remains outstanding: Was the performance of the lowest P/E portfolio (E), after adjustments for portfolio-related costs (e.g., transactions, search and information processing costs) and tax effects, superior to that of portfolios composed of randomly selected securities with the same overall level of risk? Could alternative classes of investors have capitalized on the market's reaction to P/E information during 1957–71?

Ten randomly selected portfolios with betas similar to that of E are considered.

---

29. $1 was assumed to be invested in each security every April 1 and dividends received during the year were reinvested in their respective securities; the natural logarithm of the one-year wealth relative of a security is the continuously compounded annual return on that specific security.

30. Strictly speaking, the wealth relatives of low P/E portfolios are not comparable with those of the high P/E's since the portfolios do not have the same overall level of risk.

TABLE 5

SELECTED FRACTILES FROM THE DISTRIBUTIONS OF ONE-YEAR WEALTH RELATIVES
(April 1957–March 1971 Data Pooled)

	Portfolio	0.10	0.20	0.30	Fractile[1] 0.40	0.50	0.60	0.70	0.80	0.90	% Above Random Portfolio Median	$N(1,0)$ Variates[2]
Before Tax	A (RA)	0.7110 (0.7579)	0.8354 (0.8702)	0.9167 (0.9518)	0.9845 (1.0229)	1.0556 (1.1019)	1.1311 (1.1684)	1.2171 (1.2484)	1.3412 (1.3440)	1.5445 (1.5318)	44.14	−4.33
	A* (RA*)	0.7355 (0.7651)	0.8504 (0.8663)	0.9376 (0.9375)	1.0065 (1.0055)	1.0670 (1.0755)	1.1364 (1.1412)	1.2198 (1.2313)	1.3401 (1.3437)	1.5187 (1.5308)	48.73	−0.80
	B (RB)	0.7644 (0.7800)	0.8694 (0.8899)	0.9356 (0.9639)	1.0009 (1.0386)	1.0634 (1.1085)	1.1406 (1.1756)	1.2093 (1.2658)	1.3129 (1.3744)	1.4848 (1.5774)	43.98	−4.47
	C (RC)	0.7925 (0.7946)	0.8974 (0.9006)	0.9686 (0.9556)	1.0358 (1.0174)	1.1078 (1.0909)	1.1729 (1.1556)	1.2437 (1.2334)	1.3376 (1.3284)	1.4897 (1.5038)	52.44	1.80
	D (RD)	0.8209* (0.7889)	0.9185* (0.8916)	0.9880 (0.9746)	1.0542* (1.0344)	1.1150 (1.1018)	1.1870 (1.1590)	1.2599 (1.2450)	1.3539 (1.3559)	1.5268 (1.5201)	52.09	1.53
	E (RE)	0.8209* (0.7769)	0.9149 (0.8901)	0.9892* (0.9667)	1.0509 (1.0325)	1.1233* (1.0951)	1.1997* (1.1715)	1.2844* (1.2592)	1.4106* (1.3584)	1.6066* (1.5587)	54.49	3.34
	S	0.7784	0.8858	0.9612	1.0247	1.0959	1.1649	1.2468	1.3504	1.5316		

Investment Performance of Common Stocks in Relation to Price-Earnings 677

<table>
<tr><td rowspan="14">Net of Tax</td><td>A
(RA)</td><td>0.7795
(0.8157)</td><td>0.8790
(0.9012)</td><td>0.9428
(0.9622)</td><td>0.9945
(1.0194)</td><td>1.0433
(1.0713)</td><td>1.1002
(1.1212)</td><td>1.614
(1.1801)</td><td>1.2553
(1.2464)</td><td>1.3934
(1.3793)</td><td>45.37</td><td>−3.42</td></tr>
<tr><td>A*
(RA*)</td><td>0.7971
(0.8182)</td><td>0.8912
(0.8968)</td><td>0.9590
(0.9530)</td><td>1.0067
(1.0005)</td><td>1.0546
(1.0534)</td><td>1.1031
(1.1063)</td><td>1.1630
(1.1653)</td><td>1.2530
(1.2461)</td><td>1.3711
(1.3814)</td><td>50.24</td><td>0.12</td></tr>
<tr><td>B
(RB)</td><td>0.8203
(0.8309)</td><td>0.8989
(0.9140)</td><td>0.9476
(0.9729)</td><td>1.0003
(1.0250)</td><td>1.0456
(1.0756)</td><td>1.0996
(1.1284)</td><td>1.1534
(1.1911)</td><td>1.2258
(1.2703)</td><td>1.3419
(1.4100)</td><td>44.48</td><td>−4.09</td></tr>
<tr><td>(C)
(RC)</td><td>0.8375
(0.8411)</td><td>0.9187
(0.9198)</td><td>0.9727
(0.9676)</td><td>1.0222
(1.0097)</td><td>1.0759
(1.0638)</td><td>1.1238
(1.1099)</td><td>1.1724
(1.1662)</td><td>1.2405
(1.2369)</td><td>1.3493
(1.3556)</td><td>52.59</td><td>1.90</td></tr>
<tr><td>D
(RD)</td><td>0.8571
(0.8371)</td><td>0.9358*
(0.9169)</td><td>0.9877*
(0.9779)</td><td>1.0350*
(1.0211)</td><td>1.0794
(1.0712)</td><td>1.1320
(1.1166)</td><td>1.1847
(1.1764)</td><td>1.2516
(1.2531)</td><td>1.3668
(1.3740)</td><td>51.80</td><td>1.31</td></tr>
<tr><td>E
(RE)</td><td>0.8617*
(0.8326)</td><td>0.9289
(0.9147)</td><td>0.9848
(0.9766)</td><td>1.0335
(1.0215)</td><td>1.0864*
(1.0674)</td><td>1.1447*
(1.1244)</td><td>1.2021*
(1.1869)</td><td>1.2890*
(1.2572)</td><td>1.4317*
(1.3981)</td><td>53.85</td><td>2.86</td></tr>
<tr><td>S</td><td>0.8306</td><td>0.9127</td><td>0.9687</td><td>1.0162</td><td>1.0675</td><td>1.1189</td><td>1.1784</td><td>1.2510</td><td>1.3806</td><td></td><td></td></tr>
</table>

1. (i) Underscored items indicate that the P/E portfolio under consideration has a higher wealth relative than its random counterpart in a given decile; and (ii) * denotes the portfolio yielding the highest wealth relative in a given decile.

2. Computed standard normal variates for the binomial test of the hypothesis that the observed fraction above random portfolio median (previous column) is significantly different from 0.50.

Panel A in Table 6 shows for each of these random portfolios the (i) estimated systematic risk (Sharpe-Lintner model) on a before- and after-tax basis, $\hat{\beta}_R$ and $\hat{\beta}'_R$ respectively; (ii) deviation of $\hat{\beta}_R$ and $\hat{\beta}'_R$ from portfolio E's systematic risk, $\hat{\beta}_d$ and $\hat{\beta}'_d$; and (iii) standard normal variates for Hollander's distribution-free test of the hypothesis that $\hat{\beta}_d$, $\hat{\beta}'_d = 0$, $Z(\hat{\beta}_d)$ and $Z(\hat{\beta}'_d)$. With the exception of random portfolio 7, the beta's of the various portfolios are not significantly different from that of E.[31] This finding makes it possible to directly compare the returns on E, after adjusting for portfolio-related costs and tax effects, with those of the randomly selected portfolios. The adjustments for transactions costs,[32] search and information processing costs and taxes, however, are related to the type of investor.

Four classes of investors, who are assumed to trade or rebalance their portfolios annually, are considered. They are: (I) tax-exempt reallocator, (II) tax-paying reallocator, (III) tax-exempt trader and (IV) tax-paying trader. The first two groups include investors who enter the securities market for some pre-specified portfolio readjustment reason other than speculation (e.g. adjustment of portfolio β and diversification). On the other hand, the next two categories are composed of "traders" or "speculators" who wish to capitalize on the market's reaction to P/E information per se. The distinction between "reallocator" and "trader" is important for evaluating the performance of E versus a randomly selected portfolio of equivalent risk, R, because of the different effective costs of transacting.[33] In addition to transactions costs, three further types of adjustments were made. First, marginal costs of search and information processing for portfolio E were assumed to be $\frac{1}{4}$th of 1% per annum. Second, the returns on E and R accruing to tax-paying investors were stated on an after-tax basis by assuming that capital gains (net of commissions, if any) and dividends (net of search costs, if any) were taxable annually at the 25% and 50% rates respectively.[34] Finally, in evaluating the profitability of a tax-paying trader investing in E as opposed to R, the effect of tax deferral by trading R at the end of the 14-year period rather than annually was deducted from E.[35]

---

31. Since random portfolio 7 and E do not have similar betas, due caution should be exercised in comparing the performance of the two portfolios. Incidentally, random portfolio 8 was employed in our earlier analysis and was designated as RE.

32. The data on round-lot commissions were obtained primarily from the 1956–71 issues of the *New York Stock Exchange Fact Book*. In the month of purchase, the security price plus commission is assumed to be invested and commission is deducted from the selling price in the month of sale. Commissions for reinvestment of dividends were ignored.

33. The effective transactions costs of acquiring E for a reallocator are the incremental commissions associated with acquiring E rather than R. However, a trader could have avoided incurring annual commissions on R by holding that portfolio over the 14-year period. Accordingly, a trader's effective transactions costs of acquiring E annually are equal to the actual commissions on E. The April 1, 1957 and March 31, 1971 commissions on R are ignored.

Computations of transactions costs also reflect the fact that a rational trader would not have incurred unnecessary charges by selling at the end of one year and then purchasing at the beginning of the next, those securities included in portfolio E in both years. On average, only 51% of the securities in E are traded annually.

34. Tax savings on capital losses are assumed to accrue to investors.

35. The capital gain earned on R over the 14-year period was assumed to be realized on March 31, 1971 and taxable at the 25% rate.

TABLE 6
AN ANALYSIS OF THE PROFITABILITY OF INVESTING IN PORTFOLIO E FOR ALTERNATIVE INVESTOR CLASSES

Summary Statistic[2]					Random Portfolio[1]					
	1	2	3	4	5	6	7	8	9	10

PANEL A

$\hat{\beta}_R$	1.0029	1.0103	0.9919	0.9832	1.0159	1.0099	1.0355	0.9891	1.0088	1.0050
$\hat{\beta}_E - \hat{\beta}_R$	−0.0163	−0.0237	−0.0043	0.0034	−0.0293	−0.0233	−0.0489	−0.0025	−0.0222	−0.0184
$Z(\hat{\beta}_d)$	−0.18	−0.21	−0.47	−0.15	−0.71	−1.30	−1.84	0.16	−0.81	−0.68
$\hat{\beta}_R^*$	1.0087	1.0143	0.9971	0.9859	1.0211	1.0147	1.0384	0.9947	1.0121	1.0082
$\hat{\beta}_E^* - \hat{\beta}_R^*$	−0.0174	−0.0230	−0.0058	−0.0054	−0.0298	−0.0234	−0.0471	0.0034	−0.0208	−0.0169
$Z(\hat{\beta}_d^*)$	−0.31	−0.42	−1.02	−0.64	−1.14	−1.41	−2.08	−0.14	−0.58	−0.73

PANEL B

I. TAX-EXEMPT PORTFOLIO REALLOCATOR

$\bar{r}_d = \overline{((r_E - C_E) - S)} - \overline{(r_R - C_R)}$	0.0332	0.0372	0.0277	0.0254	0.0307	0.0247	0.0360	0.0280	0.0381	0.0284
$t(\bar{r}_d)$	3.832	3.375	2.558	2.172	3.955	2.051	2.531	2.179	3.041	2.478
Wilcoxon: $Pr(\bar{r}_d = 0)$	0.000	0.003	0.021	0.045	0.000	0.029	0.021	0.025	0.008	0.015

II. TAX-PAYING PORTFOLIO REALLOCATOR

$\bar{r}_d = \overline{((r_E^* - C_E^*) - S^*)} - \overline{(r_R^* - C_R^*)}$	0.0247	0.0278	0.0203	0.0187	0.0229	0.0184	0.0269	0.0208	0.0285	0.0212
$t(\bar{r}_d)$	3.490	3.205	2.364	2.004	3.611	1.962	2.414	2.071	2.898	2.308
Wilcoxon: $Pr(\bar{r}_d = 0)$	0.002	0.003	0.029	0.052	0.001	0.034	0.021	0.034	0.008	0.025

III. TAX-EXEMPT TRADER

$\bar{r}_d = \overline{((r_E - C_E) - S)} - \bar{r}_R$	0.0229	0.0269	0.0178	0.0149	0.0204	0.0145	0.0257	0.0182	0.0281	0.0180
$t(\bar{r}_d)$	2.579	2.341	1.619	1.264	2.555	1.197	1.805	1.399	2.282	1.548
Wilcoxon: $Pr(\bar{r}_d = 0)$	0.021	0.025	0.077	0.196	0.029	0.163	0.059	0.134	0.012	0.121

IV. TAX-PAYING TRADER

$\bar{r}_d = \overline{((r_E^* - C_E^*) - S^*)} - (\bar{r}_R^* + d_R^*)$	0.0111	0.0147	0.0060	0.0038	0.0088	0.0036	0.0135	0.0066	0.0158	0.0062
$t(\bar{r}_d)$	1.533	1.626	0.689	0.402	1.361	0.378	1.212	0.648	1.634	0.670
Wilcoxon: $Pr(\bar{r}_d = 0)$	0.086	0.086	0.232	0.476	0.213	0.207	0.232	0.313	0.045	0.359

1. Continuously compounded annual rates; portfolio construction is described in footnote 25.
2. $\hat{\beta}_R, \hat{\beta}_R^*$ = estimated systematic risk (Sharpe-Lintner model) for random portfolio R on a before and after tax basis respectively; $\hat{\beta}_d$ = estimated systematic risk of E (0.9866) minus $\hat{\beta}_R$; $\hat{\beta}_d^*$ = estimated net of tax systematic risk of E (0.9913) minus $\hat{\beta}_R^*$; $Z(\hat{\beta}_d), Z(\hat{\beta}_d^*) = N(0,1)$ variates for Hollander's distribution-free test of parallelism of two regression lines; r_E, r_R = before-tax annual return on E and R; r_E^*, r_R^* = after-tax annual return on E and R; C_E, C_R = transactions costs on E and R, assuming all securities traded annually; C_E^*, C_R^* = transactions costs, net of tax savings, on E and R, assuming all securities traded annually; $C_E^{\ddagger}, C_R^{\ddagger}$ = before-tax and after-tax effective (actual) transactions costs on E; S, S' = before-tax and after-tax search and information processing costs; d_R^* = tax-savings from deferring payments by trading R once over 14 years, rather than annually; $t(\bar{r}_d) = \bar{r}_d / (\sigma(\bar{r}_d)/\sqrt{n})$ = t-value for $\bar{r}_d$, the mean return on E minus that on R, net of applicable portfolio-related costs, and $n = 14$; and Wilcoxon: $Pr(\bar{r}_d = 0)$ = significance levels for Wilcoxon's one sample distribution-free test of the hypothesis $\bar{r}_d = 0$.

Panel B in Table 6 shows, for each of these four categories of investors, the mean incremental returns ($\bar{r}_d$) that could have been earned by acquiring E rather than R, after adjusting for portfolio-related costs and taxes. Also shown are the t-values and the computed significance levels for Wilcoxon's one sample distribution-free test of the hypothesis $\bar{r}_d = 0$. By investing in E the portfolio reallocators could have earned returns, after cost and after tax, amounting to 2%–3½% per annum *more* than the associated random portfolios of equivalent risk. These incremental returns are statistically significant at the 0.05 level or higher. On the other hand, although the traders could also have earned ½%–2½% per annum *more* by investing in E rather than in the randomly selected portfolios, the differences in returns are generally not significantly different from zero.

IV. Summary and Conclusions

In this paper an attempt was made to determine empirically the relationship between investment performance of equity securities and their P/E ratios. While the efficient market hypothesis denies the possibility of earning excess returns, the price-ratio hypothesis asserts that P/E ratios, due to exaggerated investor expectations, may be indicators of future investment performance.

During the period April 1957–March 1971, the low P/E portfolios seem to have, on average, earned higher absolute and risk-adjusted rates of return than the high P/E securities. This is also *generally* true when bias on the performance measures resulting from the effect of risk is taken into account. These results suggest a violation in the joint hypothesis that (i) the asset pricing models employed in this paper have descriptive validity and (ii) security price behavior is consistent with the efficient market hypothesis. If (i) above is assumed to be true, conclusions pertaining to the second part of the joint hypothesis may be stated more definitively. We therefore assume that the asset pricing models are valid.

The results reported in this paper are consistent with the view that P/E ratio information was not "fully reflected" in security prices in as rapid a manner as postulated by the semi-strong form of the efficient market hypothesis. Instead, it seems that disequilibria persisted in capital markets during the period studied. Securities trading at different multiples of earnings, on average, seem to have been inappropriately priced vis-a-vis one another, and opportunities for earning "abnormal" returns were afforded to investors. Tax-exempt and tax-paying investors who entered the securities market with the aim of rebalancing their portfolios annually could have taken advantage of the market disequilibria by acquiring low P/E stocks. From the point of view of these investors a "market inefficiency" seems to have existed. On the other hand, transactions and search costs and tax effects hindered traders or speculators from exploiting the market's reaction and earning net "abnormal" returns which are significantly greater than zero. Accordingly, the hypothesis that capital markets are efficient in the sense that security price behavior is consistent with the semi-strong version of the "fair game" model cannot be rejected unequivocally.

In conclusion, the behavior of security prices over the 14-year period studied is, perhaps, not completely described by the efficient market hypothesis. To the extent low P/E portfolios did earn superior returns on a risk-adjusted basis, the propositions of the price-ratio hypothesis on the relationship between investment performance of equity securities and their P/E ratios seem to be valid. Contrary to the growing belief that publicly available information is instantaneously impounded in security prices, there seem to be lags and frictions in the adjustment process. As a result, publicly available P/E ratios seem to possess "information content" and may warrant an investor's attention at the time of portfolio formation or revision.

REFERENCES

1. Ray Ball and Philip Brown. "An Empirical Evaluation of Accounting Income Numbers", *Journal of Accounting Research* (Autumn 1968), pp. 159–178.
2. Fischer Black. "Capital Market Equilibrium with Restricted Borrowing", *Journal of Business* (July 1972), pp. 444–455.
3. Fischer Black, Michael C. Jensen and Myron Scholes. "The Capital Asset Pricing Model: Some Empirical Tests", in *Studies in the Theory of Capital Markets*, Michael C. Jensen, ed. (New York: Praeger, 1972), pp. 79–121.
4. Fischer Black and Myron Scholes. "The Effects of Dividend Yield and Dividend Policy on Common Stock Prices and Returns", *Journal of Financial Economics*, I (1974), pp. 1–22.
5. William Breen. "Low Price-Earnings Ratios and Industry Relatives", *Financial Analysts Journal* (July–August 1968), pp. 125–127.
6. William Breen and James Savage. "Portfolio Distributions and Tests of Security Selection Models", *Journal of Finance* (December 1968), pp. 805–819.
7. Michael J. Brennan. "Investor Taxes, Market Equilibrium and Corporate Finance" (Unpublished Ph.D. thesis, Massachusetts Institute of Technology, June 1970).
8. Eugene F. Fama. "Efficient Capital Markets: A Review of Theory and Empirical Work", *Journal of Finance* (May 1970), pp. 383–417.
9. ———. "Risk, Return and Equilibrium: Some Clarifying Comments", *Journal of Finance* (March 1968), pp. 29–40.
10. ———. "The Behavior of Stock-Market Prices", *Journal of Business* (January 1965), pp. 34–105.
11. Eugene F. Fama and James D. MacBeth. "Risk, Return and Equilibrium: Some Empirical Tests", *Journal of Political Economy* (May–June 1973), pp. 607–636.
12. Lawrence Fisher. "Some New Stock Market Indices", *Journal of Business* (January 1966), pp. 191–225.
13. Irwin Friend and Marshall Blume. "Measurement of Portfolio Performance Under Uncertainty", *The American Economic Review* (September 1970), pp. 561–575.
14. Myles Hollander and Douglas A. Wolfe. *Nonparametric Statistical Methods* (New York: John Wiley, 1973).
15. J. Johnston. *Econometric Methods*, 2nd Edition (New York: McGraw Hill, 1972).
16. Henry A. Latane and William E. Young. "Test of Portfolio Building Rules", *Journal of Finance* (September 1969), pp. 595–612.
17. John Lintner. "The Valuation of Risky Assets and the Selection of Risky Investments in Stock Portfolios and Capital Budgets", *Review of Economics and Statistics* (February 1965), pp. 13–37.
18. James D. McWilliams. "Prices, Earnings and P. E. Ratios", *Financial Analysts Journal* (May–June 1966), pp. 137–142.
19. Paul F. Miller and Ernest R. Widmann. "Price Performance Outlook for High & Low P/E Stocks", *1966 Stock and Bond Issue, Commercial & Financial Chronicle* (September 29, 1966), pp. 26–28.
20. Francis Nicholson. "Price Ratios in Relation to Investment Results", *Financial Analysts Journal* (January–February 1968), pp. 105–109.
21. ———. "Price-Earnings Ratios", *Financial Analysts Journal* (July–August 1960, pp. 43–45).
22. Aharon R. Ofer. "Investors' Expectations of Earnings Growth, Their Accuracy and Effects on the Structure of Realized Rates of Return", *Journal of Finance* (May 1975), pp. 509–523.

23. R. Richardson Pettit and Randolph Westerfield. "Using the Capital Asset Pricing Model and the Market Model to Predict Security Returns", *Journal of Financial and Quantitative Analysis* (September 1974), pp. 579–605.
24. H. A. Scheffé. *The Analysis of Variance* (New York: Wiley, 1960).
25. W. F. Sharpe. *Portfolio Theory and Capital Markets* (New York: McGraw Hill, 1970).
26. ———. "Capital Asset Prices: A Theory of Market Equilibrium Under Conditions of Risk", *Journal of Finance* (September 1964), pp. 425–442.
27. Seymour Smidt. "A New Look at the Random Walk Hypothesis", *Journal of Financial and Quantitative Analysis* (September 1968), pp. 235–262.
28. J. P. Williamson. *Investments—New Analytic Techniques* (New York: Praeger, 1970).

Survivorship Bias in Performance Studies

Stephen J. Brown
New York University

William Goetzmann
Columbia University

Roger G. Ibbotson
Stephen A. Ross
Yale University

Recent evidence suggests that past mutual fund performance predicts future performance. We analyze the relationship between volatility and returns in a sample that is truncated by survivorship and show that this relationship gives rise to the appearance of predictability. We present some numerical examples to show that this effect can be strong enough to account for the strength of the evidence favoring return predictability.

Past performance does not guarantee future performance. Empirical work from the classic study by Cowles (1933) to work by Jensen (1968) suggests that there is only very limited evidence that professional money managers can outperform the market averages

---

The first-named author acknowledges support of a Yamaichi Faculty Fellowship. We thank, for their unusually constructive comments and support, Campbell Harvey, Thomas Philips, Richard Roll, the editor (Chester Spatt), the referee (Peter Bossaerts), participants in presentations at Berkeley, Columbia, Cornell, New York University, Stanford, University of Massachusetts at Amherst, Vanderbilt University, Washington University at St. Louis, the 1991 Johnson Symposium at the University of Wisconsin, the Second Conference on Finance and Accounting at the University of Buffalo, 1991, and the 1992 Western Finance Association meetings. Remaining errors are our own. Address correspondence to Stephen J. Brown, Department of Finance, Stern School of Business, New York University, 44 West 4th St., New York, NY 10012-1126.

on a risk-adjusted basis. While more recent evidence[1] qualifies this negative conclusion somewhat [Grinblatt and Titman (1989), Ippolito (1988)], there is still no strong evidence that manager performance over and above the market indices can justify the fees managers charge and the commission costs they incur.

The fact that managers as a group perform poorly does not preclude the possibility that particular managers have special skills. Given the high turnover of managers, it is conceivable that the market selects out those managers with skills. Skillful managers are those who succeed and survive. It is this view, fostered by annual mutual fund performance reviews of the type published by *Barrons, Business Week, Consumer Reports,* and other publications, that leads to the popular investment strategy of selling shares in mutual funds that underperform the average manager in any given year, and buying shares in those funds with superior performance. Despite the popular impression that "hot hands" exist among mutual funds, there has been very limited empirical evidence to address this issue.

Past performance is usually a highly significant input into the decision to hire or fire pension fund money managers. However, Kritzman (1983) reports that for fixed-income pension fund money managers retained for at least 10 years, there is no relationship either in returns or in relative rankings between the performance in the first five years and the second five years. In an unpublished portion of the same study, this finding also extended to equity managers. Similar results are found for institutional funds by Dunn and Theisen (1983) and for commodity funds by Elton, Gruber, and Rentzler (1990).[2] In contrast to these findings, Elton and Gruber (1989, p. 602) conclude on the basis of a Securities and Exchange Commission (1971) study that mutual funds which outperform other funds in one period will tend to outperform them in a second. Grinblatt and Titman (1988) suggest that five-year risk-adjusted mutual fund returns do contain some predictive power for subsequent returns. Lehmann and Modest report similar results for the period 1968–1982, but suggest that this finding is sensitive to the method used to compute risk-adjusted performance measures.

On the basis of data for the period 1974–1988 both Hendricks, Patel, and Zeckhauser (1991) and Goetzmann and Ibbotson (1991) obtain far stronger results. The first study is limited to 165 equity

---

Some of this evidence is controversial in nature. See Elton et al. (1993) for a discussion of the Ippolito findings.

The commodity fund result applies to returns on funds. However, Elton, Gruber, and Rentzler (1990) find evidence of persistence in performance of different funds managed by the same general partner. It would be interesting to discover whether dispersion in risk across surviving managers would suffice to explain this result.

Survivorship Bias in Performance Studies

funds for the period 1974–1988, while the latter study considers a much larger sample of 728 mutual funds for the period 1976–1988, 258 of which survived for the entire period. The major conclusions of the two studies are similar. Performance persists.[3]

While the experimental designs and data of these studies differ considerably, the generic results may be illustrated on Tables 1 and 2. The relationship between successive three-year growth equity fund risk-adjusted total returns for the period 1976–1987 is documented in Table 1. The 2 × 2 contingency tables show the frequency with which managers who performed in the top half of all managers [on a Jensen (1968) α risk-adjusted basis] for a given three-year interval also performed in the top half in the subsequent three-year interval. For every period studied, the results are similar. If a manager wins in the first three years, the probability is greater than 50 percent that the manager will win in the second three years. These results are also statistically significant in at least two of the three successive three-year intervals.[4]

Goetzmann and Ibbotson (1991) report contingency tables similar to those given in Table 1 for a variety of time periods and performance horizon intervals. The data on which Table 1 is based are similar to those of the Hendricks, Patel, and Zeckhauser (1991) study. An alternative approach is to regress second-period Jensen's α's against first-period Jensen's α's. A significantly positive slope coefficient is evidence of persistence. The result of this exercise is presented in Table 2. The results correspond with those reported in Table 1. The evidence of persistence is strongest in the first and third subperiod of the data. Hendricks, Patel, and Zeckhauser (1991) suggest computing the returns on a self-financing portfolio strategy, a methodology they

---

[3] Note that the Kritzman (1983) and Dunn and Theisen (1983) results apply to pension fund money managers, while the other studies that indicate persistence all refer to mutual funds. Representatives from Frank Russell Company and other pension fund consulting companies indicate that efforts to replicate the mutual fund persistence results using pension fund data have to this date been unsuccessful. Part of the reason for this difference might be that mutual fund returns are measured after fees, while pension fund returns typically are measured before commissions (see note 6).

[4] One has to be a little careful interpreting the statistical significance of the χ^2 values. The identification of managers as winners or losers is actually ex post. For this reason, we expect to find the winners-following-winners result at least 50 percent of the time. This ex post conditioning also implies that the standard χ^2 tests (with or without the Yates 2 × 2 continuity correction) will be misspecified. Fortunately, an alternative statistic, the cross-product ratio (given as the ratio of the product of the principal diagonal cell counts to the product of the off-diagonal counts in the 2 × 2 table), has well-known statistical properties. Statisticians prefer the cross-product ratio (or measures closely related to it) because it simultaneously provides a test of the hypothesis that the two classifications are independent, as well as giving a measure of the dependence [Bishop et al. (1975, p. 373ff.)] In the present case, row and column sums of each 2 × 2 contingency table are fixed because of ex post conditioning. Thus, the winner-winner cell count determines all other cell counts, and is distributed as the hypergeometric distribution conditional on row and column counts. Thus, the p-value of the cross-product ratio statistic is given by the sum of hypergeometric probabilities of cell counts at least as great as the observed winner–winner count [Agresti (1990, p. 60)]. This is known as Fisher's *exact test*.

Table 1
Two-way table of growth managers classified by risk-adjusted returns over successive intervals 1976–1987

Winners and losers defined relative to performance of median manager

	1979–1981 winners	1979–1981 losers	
1976–1978 winners	44	19	63
1976–1978 losers	19	44	63
	63	63	126

$\chi^2 = 19.84$ ($p = .0$)
χ^2 (Yates correction) $= 20.40$ ($p = .0$)
Cross-product ratio $= 5.36$ ($p = .0$)

	1982–1984 winners	1982–1984 losers	
1979–1981 winners	35	33	68
1979–1981 losers	33	35	68
	68	68	136

$\chi^2 = 0.12$ ($p = .732$)
χ^2 (Yates correction) $= 0.12$ ($p = .732$)
Cross-product ratio $= 1.12$ ($p = .432$)

	1985–1987 winners	1985–1987 losers	
1982–1984 winners	52	25	77
1982–1984 losers	25	52	76
	77	76	153

$\chi^2 = 18.35$ ($p = .0$)
χ^2 (Yates correction) $= 18.74$ ($p = .0$)
Cross-product ratio $= 4.24$ ($p = .0$)

This table is derived from total returns on growth equity mutual funds made available by Ibbotson Associates and Morningstar, Inc. Risk-adjustment is the Jensen (1968) α measure relative to total returns on the S&P 500 Index. Each cell represents the number of funds in the sample that share the characteristic defined by the row and the column. For example, the number of funds that were in the top half of mutual funds over the 1976–1978 period and were subsequently also in the top half of mutual funds over the 1979–1981 period may be found in the first row and first column of the upper 2 × 2 table. The χ^2 and χ^2 (Yates correction) refer to standard χ^2 test statistics for independence, where Yates refers to Yates 2 × 2 continuity correction. The cross-product ratio is the ratio of the product of principal diagonal cell counts to the product of the off-diagonal counts. Where (as in this case) the row and column sums are determined ex post the p-value can be inferred from the hypergeometric distribution of the upper left-hand cell count in the 2 × 2 table (Fisher's *exact test*).

attribute to Grinblatt and Titman (1989). The portfolio weights are proportional to the deviation of prior performance measures from the mean performance measure across managers. The performance measure of such a portfolio is a measure of persistence. This measure is computed in Table 2. The results are qualitatively similar to ones reported by Hendricks, Patel, and Zeckhauser (1991).

These results of course require careful interpretation. It is tempting to conclude from the type of results reported in Tables 1 and 2 that "hot hands" exist among mutual fund managers. Actually, the methodologies are silent on whether the persistence relates to positive or

Survivorship Bias in Performance Studies

Table 2
Regression-based measures of persistence in performance, 1976–1987

Cross-section regression approach[1]
  Period January 1976–December 1981:
  $\hat{\alpha}_2 = .0885 + .4134\hat{\alpha}_1$
  (5.38)   (6.47)
  $R^2 = 2.53; n = 126$

  Period January 1979–December 1984:
  $\hat{\alpha}_2 = -.0831 + .0070\hat{\alpha}_1$
  (−3.69)   (0.07)
  $R^2 = .000; n = 134$

  Period January 1982–December 1987:
  $\hat{\alpha}_2 = -.0753 + .3052\hat{\alpha}_1$
  (−6.53)   (5.28)
  $R^2 = .156; n = 153$

Time-series self-financing portfolio approach[2]
  Period January 1977–December 1987:
  $r_{pt} = .0018 - .0078 r_{mt}$
  (2.88)   (−.61)
  $R^2 = .003; n = 132$

(t-values in parentheses)

[1] Jensen's α is computed for the sample of funds described in Table 1 for each of four three-year subperiods of data starting in 1976–1978. Each panel reports results from the cross-section regression of performance measures on prior performance measures. The first panel gives results from the regression of Jensen's α measures estimated on the basis of data for the period January 1979–December 1981 on similar measures estimated for the period January 1976–December 1978.

[2] This corresponds to the measure employed by Hendricks, Patel, and Zeckhauser (1991) with four quarter evaluation and holding periods. For each year starting in 1976, Jensen's α measures are computed. The deviation of these measures from their mean corresponds to a self-financing portfolio, which is then applied to excess returns on funds measured for the subsequent year. The portfolio is updated at the end of each year. The regression reports results from the time-series regression of the resulting monthly excess returns on market excess returns. The intercept corresponds to a performance measure for this portfolio strategy.

negative performance. This is most readily apparent in Table 1 when we observe that the row and column sums are specified ex post given the sample of money managers. In other words, given the row and column sums and the "winner–winner" cell count, the "loser–loser" count is simply the residual. Given the "loser–loser" count, the "winner–winner" is the residual. When we measure risk-adjusted performance relative to zero (Table 3), we find that persistence can just as easily relate to negative performance as it does to positive performance. Sometimes (1976–1981) good performance is rewarded by subsequent good performance. "Hot hands" are evident. Sometimes (1982–1987) it is the case that bad performance is punished by further bad news. This result is also apparent examining the intercepts of the cross-section regressions reported in Table 2. Results reported in Table 4 indicate that the persistence of poor performance serves to explain some but not all of the results reported in the previous tables. This table gives regression-based measures of persistence excluding those managers who experienced negative average Jensen's α for the

Table 3
Two-way table of growth managers classified by risk-adjusted returns over successive intervals 1976–1987

Winners and losers defined relative to zero risk-adjusted performance measure

	1979–1981 winners	1979–1981 losers	
1976–1978 winners	88	11	99
1976–1978 losers	16	11	27
	104	22	126

$$\chi^2 = 12.92 \ (p = .0)$$
$$\chi^2 \text{ (Yates correction)} = 11.14 \ (p = .001)$$
Cross-product ratio = 5.50

	1982–1984 winners	1982–1984 losers	
1979–1981 winners	42	72	114
1979–1981 losers	4	18	22
	46	90	136

$$\chi^2 = 2.87 \ (p = .09)$$
$$\chi^2 \text{ (Yates correction)} = 3.13 \ (p = .08)$$
Cross-product ratio = 2.62

	1985–1987 winners	1985–1987 losers	
1982–1984 winners	20	34	54
1982–1984 losers	15	84	99
	35	118	153

$$\chi^2 = 9.49 \ (p = .002)$$
$$\chi^2 \text{ (Yates correction)} = 9.15 \ (p = .002)$$
Cross-product ratio = 3.29

This table is derived using the same data as that reported in Table 2. Risk-adjustment is the Jensen's α measured relative to total returns on the S&P Index. Winners and losers are defined relative to Jensen's α measure of zero. For example, the number of funds that experienced a positive α over the 1976–1978 period and subsequently experienced a positive α over the 1979–1981 period may be found in the first row and first column of the upper 2 × 2 table. The χ^2 and χ^2 (Yates correction) refer to standard χ^2 test statistics for independence, where Yates refers to Yates 2 × 2 continuity correction. The cross-product ratio is the ratio of the product of principal diagonal cell counts to the product of the off-diagonal counts.

entire period 1976–1987. The results are similar to those reported in Table 3. The significance of apparent persistence has fallen. However, both the cross-section and the self-financing portfolio results indicate that there is still statistically significant evidence that performance persists for at least part of the period.

The persistence of negative performance is not surprising. Negative performance can persist where a subset of managers are immune from periodic performance review and where it is difficult to short sell shares of mutual funds.[5] It can be only institutional reasons such as

---

[5] In fact, Hendricks, Patel, and Zeckhauser provide little reliable evidence of "hot hands." Using either the value-weighted or the equal-weighted CRSP index benchmark, there is no significant

Survivorship Bias in Performance Studies

Table 4
Regression-based measures of persistence in performance, 1976–1987 (excluding poor performers)

Cross-section regression approach[1]

Period January 1976–December 1981:
$$\hat{\alpha}_2 = .1463 + .2736\hat{\alpha}_1$$
$$(5.48) \quad (3.13)$$
$$R^2 = .113; n = 79$$

Period January 1979–December 1984:
$$\hat{\alpha}_2 = .0317 - .1815\hat{\alpha}_1$$
$$(1.04) \quad (-1.55)$$
$$R^2 = .029; n = 82$$

Period January 1982–December 1987:
$$\hat{\alpha}_2 = -.0334 + .0521\hat{\alpha}_1$$
$$(-3.09) \quad (.81)$$
$$R^2 = .008; n = 88$$

Time-series self-financing portfolio approach[2]
Period January 1977–December 1987:
$$r_{pt} = .0008 - .0015 r_{mt}$$
$$(2.15) \quad (-.20)$$
$$R^2 = .000; n = 132$$

(*t*-values in parentheses)

This table is intended to show the effect that different standards of performance review might have on measures of persistence in returns. The procedures and data are the same as those presented in Table 2, with the exception that managers are excluded whose average value of Jensen's α is negative over the entire period for which data is available.

[1] Jensen's α is computed for the sample of funds described in Table 1 for each of four three-year subperiods, of data starting in 1976–1978, excluding those funds that performed poorly over the entire period. Each panel reports results from the cross-section regression of performance measures on prior performance measures.

[2] This corresponds to the measure employed by Hendricks, Patel, and Zeckhauser (1991) with four quarter evaluation and holding periods, excluding poor performing funds.

---

these that allow a fund with sustained poor performance to survive.[6] It is the persistence of positive returns that would be remarkable, if true. The problems of interpretation caused by the ex post definition of winners and losers suggests that the results may also be sensitive to the most obvious source of ex post conditioning: survival.

It is clear that all managers depicted in the 2 × 2 tables have passed the market test, at least for the successive three-year periods. We have no data for the managers who did not survive. If the probability of

---

persistence of positive performance. The only benchmark for which they find any statistically significant evidence of persistence in positive performance is a self-created benchmark consisting of an equal-weighted average of returns on the mutual funds in their sample.

Hendricks, Patel, and Zeckhauser (1991) give the example of the 44 Wall Street funds that survived the period 1975–1988 with a negative annual α of −1.90 (relative to the value-weighted CRSP index) and −4.27 (relative to the equal-weighted CRSP index). One potential explanation for the persistence of negative performance might be that mutual fund data compute returns after fees but before sales and load charges. The negative performance may simply reflect the persistence of high fees.

survival depends on past performance to date, we might expect that the set of managers who survive will have a higher ex post return than those who did not survive. Managers who take on significant risk and lose may also have a low probability of survival. This observation suggests that past performance numbers are biased by survivorship; we only see the track record of those managers who have survived. This does not suggest, however, that performance persists. If anything, it suggests the reverse. If survival depends on cumulative performance, a manager who does well in one period does not have to do so well in the next period in order to survive. Certainly, this survivorship argument cannot explain results suggested by Table 1. Moreover, there is a general perception that the survivorship bias effect cannot be very substantial. In a recent study, Grinblatt and Titman (1989) report that the survivorship effect accounts for only about 0.1 to 0.4 percent return per year measured on a risk-adjusted basis before transaction costs and fees. We shall see that the survivorship bias in mean excess returns is small in magnitude relative to a more subtle, yet surprisingly powerful, survival bias that implies persistence in performance.

A manager who takes on a great deal of risk will have a high probability of failure. However, *if* he or she survives, the probability is that this manager took a large bet and won. High returns persist. If they do not persist, we would not see this high-risk manager in our sample.[7] Note that this is a total risk effect; risk-adjustment using β or other measure of nonidiosyncratic risk may not fully correct for it. To illustrate this effect, observe in Table 3 that the additional 10 firms that come into the database in 1979–1981 are all ex post successful. The average value of residual risk (0.0323) for the new entrants is significantly greater than that of the population of managers (0.0242), with a *t*-value of 2.02. The new entrants who survived took on more risk and were successful.

The magnitude of the persistence will depend on the precise way in which survivorship depends on past performance and whether there is any strategic risk management response on the part of surviving money managers.[8] The intent is to show that the apparent

---

[7] Hendricks, Patel, and Zeckhauser (1991) argue that because fund data is eliminated from their database as the fund ceases to exist or is merged into other funds, their sample is free of survivorship bias effects. However, all funds considered at each evaluation point survived at least until the end of an evaluation period that could extend from one quarter to two years. They are excluded from the analysis *subsequent to* the evaluation period. The numerical example given in Section 2 of this article matches this experimental design, and provides a counterexample to a presumption of freedom from survivorship bias effects. The results of such a study would be free of survival bias only if it can be established that the probability of termination or elimination from the sample is unrelated to performance. However, Hendricks, Patel, and Zeckhauser indicate (note 5) that, in fact, funds that go under do quite poorly in the quarter of demise.

[8] We show in the Appendix that the effect is mitigated somewhat where cumulative performance

persistence of performance documented in Tables 1 and 2 is not necessarily any indication of skill among surviving managers.

To the extent that survivorship depends on past returns, ranking managers who survive by realized returns may induce an apparent persistence in performance. Survivorship implies that managers will be selected according to total risk. One way of explaining the Table 1 results is to observe that the set of managers studied represent a heterogeneous mix of management styles. Each management style is characterized by a certain vector of risk attributes. By examining the survivors, we are really only looking at those styles that were ex post successful. It may appear that one resolution of this problem is to concentrate on only one defined management style. There are two problems with this approach. In the first instance, we have to be careful to define the style sufficiently broadly that there are more than a few managers represented. In the second instance, we may exacerbate the effect if our definition of manager style is synonymous with taking high total risk positions.

We only observe the performance of managers who survive performance evaluations. The purpose of this article is to examine the extent to which this fact is sufficient to explain the magnitude of persistence we seem to see in the data. In Section 1, we examine the relationship between total risk differentials and survivorship-induced persistence in performance. In Section 2, we present some numerical results that show that a very small survivorship effect is sufficient to generate a strong and significant appearance of dependence in serial returns. We conclude in Section 3.

1. Relationship between Volatility and Returns Induced by Survivorship

There are many possible quite complex sample selection rules. We will look at the implications of one class of these rules. Our purpose in this section is to demonstrate that sample survivorship bias is a force that can lead to persistence in performance rankings. For simplicity, assume all distributions are atomless. Our tool is the following lemma.

---

rather than one-period performance is used as a survival criterion. The analysis of a strategic response is beyond the scope of this article. A possible strategic response is for surviving managers who are subject to the same survival criterion to converge in residual risk characteristics. The results in the next section require only that the ranking of managers by residual risk be constant. This kind of strategic response would also tend to mitigate the effect. This analysis is complicated by the fact that survival criteria are not necessarily the same for all managers.

561

Lemma. Assume

(i) x, y independent random variables,
(ii) $\Pr(x \geq 0) = \Pr(y \geq 0) > 0$,
(iii) $\Pr(x > a) \geq \Pr(y > a)$, $\quad \forall\, a \geq 0$, with strict inequality for some a.

It follows that

$$\Pr[x > y \mid x,y > 0] > \tfrac{1}{2}.$$

Before proving the lemma, note that its conditions are satisfied by x and y if they are both normal with mean zero, and if x has a higher variance than y. More generally, for both x and y with mean zero, it is sufficient if x is distributed as λy, where $\lambda > 1$.

Proof. Let F_x and F_y be the respective cumulative distributions of x and y, and let G_x and G_y be the reverse cumulants

$$G_x \equiv 1 - F_x, \qquad G_y \equiv 1 - F_y.$$

Now,

$$\Pr(x > y \mid x,y > 0)$$
$$= [\Pr(x,y > 0)]^{-1} \Pr(x > y,\, x > 0,\, y > 0)$$
$$= [G_x(0)G_y(0)]^{-1} \int_0^\infty \int_u^\infty dF_x(z)\, dF_y(u)$$
$$= [G_x(0)G_y(0)]^{-1} \int_0^\infty G_x(u)\, dF_y(u)$$
$$\geq [G_x(0)G_y(0)]^{-1} \int_0^\infty G_y(u)\, dF_y(u)$$
$$= [G_x(0)G_y(0)]^{-1} \{-\tfrac{1}{2} G_y^2(u)|_0^\infty\}$$
$$= \frac{1}{2}\left\{\frac{G_y(0)}{G_x(0)}\right\} = \frac{1}{2},$$

with strict inequality if $G_x > G_y$ on some set of positive measure. ∎

The following corollary establishes that the result generalizes to cases where x and y represent nonzero mean random variates.

Corollary 1. *Let ϵ_x and ϵ_y satisfy the conditions of the lemma and let*

$$x = f + \epsilon_x \quad \text{and} \quad y = f + \epsilon_y;$$

Survivorship Bias in Performance Studies

then
$$\Pr[x > y \mid \epsilon_x, \epsilon_y > 0] > \tfrac{1}{2}.$$

Proof. Immediate. ∎

For the following set of results, let x and y be two random variables drawn from a family of distributions indexed by a spread parameter $\sigma \in [0, \infty)$. The family has the property that
$$G(0 \mid \sigma) = G(0)$$
and ($\forall\ a \geq 0$) $\sigma' > \sigma$ implies that
$$G[a \mid \sigma'] \geq G[a \mid \sigma].$$

Corollary 2. *It follows that*
$$\Pr[\sigma_x > \sigma_y \mid x > y;\ x,y > 0] > \tfrac{1}{2}.$$

Proof. From the lemma
$$\Pr[x > y \mid \sigma_x > \sigma_y;\ x,y > 0] > \tfrac{1}{2},$$
and, therefore, by initial symmetry and Bayes' theorem,

$$\Pr[\sigma_x > \sigma_y \mid x > y;\ x,y > 0]$$
$$= \frac{\Pr[x > y \mid \sigma_x > \sigma_y;\ x,y > 0]\Pr[\sigma_x > \sigma_y \mid x,y > 0]}{\Pr[x > y \mid x,y > 0]}$$
$$> \frac{1}{2}\left(\frac{1/2}{1/2}\right) = \frac{1}{2}. \qquad \blacksquare$$

The next two corollaries verify that if one random variable exceeds another in one observation period, it is likely to do so in other periods.

Corollary 3. *Let x and y be independent and (unconditionally) identically distributed with unknown spreads drawn from the family described above. It follows that*
$$\Pr[x_2 > y_2 \mid x_1 > y_1;\ x_1, y_1, x_2, y_2 > 0] > \tfrac{1}{2}.$$

Proof. For notational ease we will omit the ubiquitous conditioning on $x_i, y_i > 0$. From Bayes' theorem,

$$\Pr[x_2 > y_2 \mid x_1 > y_1]$$
$$= \Pr[x_2 > y_2 \mid \sigma_x > \sigma_y,\ x_1 > y_1]\ \Pr[\sigma_x > \sigma_y \mid x_1 > y_1]$$
$$+ \Pr[x_2 > y_2 \mid \sigma_x \leq \sigma_y,\ x_1 > y_1]\ \Pr[\sigma_x \leq \sigma_y \mid x_1 > y_1]$$

563

$$= \Pr[x_2 > y_2 \mid \sigma_x > \sigma_y] \Pr[\sigma_x > \sigma_y \mid x_1 > y_1]$$
$$+ \Pr[x_2 > y_2 \mid \sigma_x \leq \sigma_y] \Pr[\sigma_x \leq \sigma_y \mid x_1 > y_1],$$

since σ is sufficient statistic.

By the a priori symmetry of x and y,

$$1 = \Pr[x_2 > y_2 \mid \sigma_x \leq \sigma_y] + \Pr[x_2 \leq y_2 \mid \sigma_x \leq \sigma_y]$$
$$= \Pr[x_2 > y_2 \mid \sigma_x \leq \sigma_y] + \Pr[x_2 \geq y_2 \mid \sigma_x \geq \sigma_y].$$

From the lemma we know that

$$\Pr[x_2 > y_2 \mid \sigma_x > \sigma_y] \equiv \tfrac{1}{2} + p, \qquad p > 0,$$

and from Corollary 2 we know that

$$\Pr[\sigma_x > \sigma_y \mid x_1 > y_1] \equiv \tfrac{1}{2} + q, \qquad q > 0.$$

Hence,

$$\Pr[x_2 > y_2 \mid x_1 > y_1]$$
$$= (\tfrac{1}{2} + p)(\tfrac{1}{2} + q) + (1 - (\tfrac{1}{2} + p))(1 - (\tfrac{1}{2} + q))$$
$$= \tfrac{1}{2} + 2pq > \tfrac{1}{2}. \qquad\blacksquare$$

Corollary 4. *The conditions are the same as for Corollary 3 except that the unknown spread parameter is not constant, although ranking by volatility is preserved, that is,*

$$\sigma_{x_1} > \sigma_{y_1} \Rightarrow \sigma_{x_2} > \sigma_{y_2}.$$

Proof. Immediate, given

$$\Pr[x_2 > y_2 \mid \sigma_{x_2} > \sigma_{y_2}] = \Pr[x_2 > y_2 \mid \sigma_{x_1} > \sigma_{y_1}] \equiv \tfrac{1}{2} + p, \quad p > 0. \qquad\blacksquare$$

This concludes our analytic verification of the relation between volatility and returns in a sample that is truncated by survivorship bias. To say whether this effect is larger or smaller than the natural tendency for regression to the mean depends on the exact sample selection rules.

If the selection rule in a two-period model is $x_1 + x_2 > 0$ (and/or $x_1 > 0$), then we have verified the tendency for one fund to persist in outperforming the other if its volatility is higher. However, with the rule $x_1 + x_2 > 0$, there is another opposing force. In particular, if $x_1 > y_1 > 0$, then x does not have to pass so extreme a hurdle in the next period, and we are likely to have $x_2 < y_2$ if there is no dispersion in volatility across managers (see the Appendix). We avoided this problem in Corollary 3 by only conditioning on $x_1, y_1 >$

Survivorship Bias in Performance Studies

0 and not on $x_1 + x_2 > 0$ and $y_1 + y_2 > 0$. This two-period selection effect would tend to counterbalance the variance-induced apparent persistence of returns. The net effect will depend on assumptions made about the distribution of returns absent the selection effects.

Another mitigating factor would arise if we allow managers to adjust their portfolio policies to adjust risk levels on survival. While the above results require only that the ranking by risk be constant from one period to the next, the extent of the persistence will depend on the way in which survival affects the differences in risk across managers.

It is clear that the magnitude of the persistence in returns will depend on assumptions that are made about the precise nature of survivorship, the distribution of returns across managers, and the way in which portfolio policies of managers evolve through time. In the next section, we shall examine a simple numerical example that demonstrates that very mild survivorship criteria are sufficient to induce strong persistence in performance for a reasonable specification of the distribution of returns across managers.

2. A Numerical Illustration of the Magnitude of Induced Persistence in Returns

To examine the numerical magnitude of the persistence in performance induced by survivorship, annual returns were generated for a cross section of managers. The moments of the distribution of returns are chosen to match those observed in the data, although it is assumed that manager returns are serially uncorrelated. There is a natural presumption that persistence in observed returns implies that manager returns are predictable. The purpose of this experiment is to provide a reasonable counterexample to this presumption. While there may be many factors that are in fact responsible for the persistence in performance, a simple survivorship argument suffices to explain the magnitude of persistence we observe in the data.

Conditional on systematic risk measure β_i and nonsystematic risk σ_i, annual returns are generated from

$$R_{it} = r_f + \beta_i(R_{mt} - r_f) + \epsilon_{it},$$

where the annual Treasury bill rate r_f is taken to be 0.07 and the annual equity risk premium is assumed to be normal with mean 0.086 and standard deviation (SD) 0.208 corresponding to the Ibbotson and Sinquefeld (1990) numbers for the period 1926–1989. The idiosyncratic term ϵ_{it} is assumed to be distributed as normal with mean zero and SD σ_i.

The managers are defined by their risk measures β_i and σ_i. It is difficult to know what are reasonable values for these parameters. If observed mutual fund data is truncated in possibly complex ways by survivorship, then that data may yield biased measures of the parameters. If, on the other hand, it is held that this truncation is of a second order of importance, then, given this maintained hypothesis, the cross-sectional distribution of the parameters will give some measure of the underlying dispersion of risk. For the purpose of this experiment, it is assumed that β_i is distributed in the cross section of managers as normal with mean 0.95, and SD 0.25 corresponding to the cross-sectional distribution of β observed in the Goetzmann and Ibbotson sample of money managers.[9]

The distribution of nonsystematic risk across managers is functionally dependent on β. Closet index funds with β's close to unity typically have very low values of nonsystematic risk, whereas managers whose β's deviate from the market tend to be less well diversified. This suggests a relationship between nonsystematic risk and β approximated by[10]

$$\sigma_i^2 = k(1 - \beta_i)^2.$$

---

[9] As seen from Table 5, a 5 percent performance cut will lead to an increase in the average β of about 5 percent. The increase is due solely to the truncation in the cross-sectional distribution of β. This is an important caveat in interpreting Table 5 to imply a calibration of survival measures. There is a more subtle issue here. If there is a performance cut, ordinary least squares will not be appropriate. Beta should be estimated taking account of the fact that the distribution of residuals is truncated by survival. Assuming that the truncation by survival occurs on a quarterly basis, and that the minimum observed return among survivors (relative to the market) defines the point at which the residuals are truncated, it is possible to estimate a truncated regression model for the data described in Table 1. The measure of β was not sensitive to truncation; however, the measure of residual risk rose, on average, 2.5 percent. To the extent that our results depend on the distribution of the residual risk across managers, this represents another caveat to the results reported in Table 5.

[10] This proportional relationship does not only capture the apparent segmentation of mutual funds into closet index funds characterized by a β of unity and a low residual risk, and less well-diversified funds with β's less than or greater than unity. It also matches the empirical regularity that suggests that residual risk is an increasing function of the absolute difference of portfolio β from unity [e.g., Black, Jensen, and Scholes (1972)]. This relationship also follows for size-ranked portfolios and managed funds [Connor and Korajczyk (1991), Elton et al. (1993, Table 6)]. The constant of proportionality, k, was chosen so that the cross-sectional average R^2 matches the average value of .90 for the Goetzmann and Ibbotson sample. This value also corresponds to the available data. For the 438 money managers for whom Goetzmann and Ibbotson have data for the period 1984–1988, a regression of residual risk on the deviation of β from unity yields the following:

$$\hat{\sigma}_i^2 = .000374 + .00012\ (1 - \hat{\beta}_i) + .005294\ (1 - \hat{\beta}_i)^2,$$
$$(4.928)\quad (-3.827)\quad\quad (13.014)$$
$$R^2 = .360,\quad N = 438$$

(t-values in parentheses). To account for the possibility that this relationship may be an artifact of leptokurtosis in fund manager returns, β and residual risk are estimated on the basis of alternate-month returns [for a discussion of the related issue of skewness-induced correlation of sample mean returns and volatility, see Roll and Ross (1980)]. Assuming that the cross-sectional distribution of returns is truncated by the lowest observed return in that month (the survivor), a truncated regression approach applied to the same data yields a coefficient on the squared term of .003552 (t-value 15.325) with intercept and linear terms statistically insignificant. These values expressed on an annualized basis correspond closely to the value for k, 0.05349, used in the simulation experiments.

Survivorship Bias in Performance Studies

The value of k chosen in the simulation experiment is 0.05349, which is the value that ensures that the average R^2 across managers is 0.90, given the distribution of β and the assumed variance of the equity risk premium.

The experiment proceeds as follows. For each of 600 managers, a value of β_i is chosen. This defines a measure of nonsystematic risk σ_i given the assumed relationship between the two parameters. Four annual returns are drawn for each manager according to the assumed return generating process. For each of four years, the worst performing managers are eliminated from the group.[11] Four-year returns are computed for each of the managers that survive this sequential cut, and contingency tables corresponding to those of Table 1 and regression-based measures of persistence corresponding to Tables 2 and 4 are calculated.

The results of this experiment will obviously depend on the severity of the cut. In a base case analysis, no managers are cut. In a second scenario, only the bottom 5 percent of managers are cut in each year. In the third and fourth scenarios, the bottom 10 percent and 20 percent of managers are eliminated each year. The entire experiment is then repeated 20,000 times. In this way, we examine not only the expected frequency of persistence as a function of the selection criterion, but also the sampling properties of this persistence.

In our first exercise, we generate results corresponding to Table 1. Risk-adjusted performance measures are evaluated for each manager using Jensen's α, and the cumulated risk-adjusted returns are computed for the first two years and second two years. "Winners" and "losers" are defined relative to the risk-adjusted performance of the median manager in each two-year period. This experimental design follows closely the approach adopted by Hendricks, Patel, and Zeckhauser (1991) and Goetzmann and Ibbotson (1991), with the important exception that in constructing risk-adjusted returns, β is assumed known. Thus, we do not consider the possible complications that arise from the necessity to estimate this quantity.

The average values of the frequency of persistence in risk-adjusted return across the replications of this experiment, for different assumed cutoff points, are given in Table 5. When there is no truncation by survivorship, there is no apparent persistence of performance. However, when managers are excluded from the sample for performance reasons, there is evidence of apparent persistence in performance. The probability is greater than 50 percent that a manager who wins

---

[11] Consistent with Corollary 3, managers are truncated in the final year. Failure to truncate in the final year leads to a small decrease in the apparent persistence of performance in Table 5. However, the qualitative conclusions are not affected by this change.

Table 5
Two-way table of managers classified by risk-adjusted returns over successive intervals, a summary of 20,000 simulations assuming 0, 5, 10, and 20 percent cutoffs

	Second-period winners	Second-period losers
	No cutoff ($n = 600$)	
First-period winners	150.09	149.51
First-period losers	149.51	150.09

Average $\chi^2 = 1.04$
Average cross-product ratio = 1.014
Average cross-section t-value = −.004
Average annual excess return = 0.0%
Average β = 0.950

	5% cutoff ($n = 494$)	
First-period winners	127.49	119.51
First-period losers	119.51	127.49

Average $\chi^2 = 1.64$
Average cross-product ratio = 1.159
Average cross-section t-value = 2.046
Average annual excess return = 0.44%
Average β = 0.977

	10% cutoff ($n = 398$)	
First-period winners	106.58	92.42
First-period losers	92.42	106.58

Average $\chi^2 = 3.28$
Average cross-product ratio = 1.366
Average cross-section t-value = 3.356
Average annual excess return = 0.61%
Average β = 0.994

	20% cutoff ($n = 249$)	
First-period winners	71.69	53.31
First-period losers	53.31	70.69

Average $\chi^2 = 7.13$
Average cross-product ratio = 1.919
Average cross-section t-value = 4.679
Average annual excess return = 0.80%
Average β = 1.018

For each simulation, manager annual returns are drawn from the market model described in the text, allowing for a dispersion in β and nonsystematic risk in the cross section of managers. In each of the four years, managers who experience returns in the lowest percentile indicated by the cutoff value are excluded from the sample, and this experiment is repeated 20,000 times. Thus, the numbers in the first 2 × 2 table give the average frequency with which the 600 managers fall into the respective classifications. The second panel shows the average frequencies for the 494 managers who survive the performance cut, while the third and fourth panels give corresponding results for 398 and 249 managers. For each simulation, the winners are defined as those managers whose average two-year Jensen's α measure was greater than or equal to that of the median manager in that sample. The average χ^2 refers to the average value of the standard χ^2 test statistic for independence (without Yates' correction) across the simulations, while the average cross-product ratio refers to the average value of the ratio of the product of principal diagonal cell counts to the product of the off-diagonal counts.

Survivorship Bias in Performance Studies

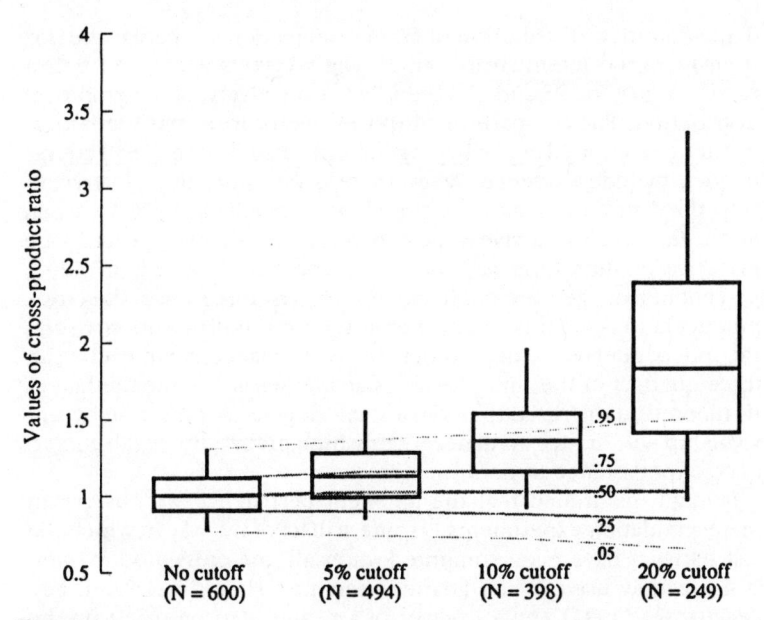

Figure 1
Boxplots of 20,000 simulated values of the cross-product ratio for different performance cutoff levels
The solid line within each box represents the median of the empirical distribution of cross-product ratios, whereas the box itself gives the interquartile range. The whiskers above and below each box give the 95th and 5th percentiles, respectively, of the empirical distribution. The gray lines give the stated fractiles of the theoretical distribution implied by the hypergeometric distribution of cell counts assuming independence.

in the first period will also win in the second. This probability increases with the extent to which the sample is truncated by survivorship. The effect of truncation is also evident in the increase in the average value of χ^2 and cross-product ratio statistics with the degree to which managers are excluded from the sample for performance reasons. The effect is particularly marked when we regress performance measures in the second two-year period on similar measures computed for the first two-year period. With no cutoff, the mean t-value for the slope coefficient of this regression is zero. However, both the mean and the median t-values are in excess of 2 with just a 5 percent performance cut. This means that on the basis of a cross-section regression of successive α's, we would reject the hypothesis of no persistence at least 50 percent of the time!

The effect of truncation on the distribution of test statistics for dependence is quite marked. In Figure 1, we display the boxplots of simulated values of the cross-product ratio for different performance cutoff levels. This solid line within each box represents the median

569

of the empirical distribution of cross-product ratios, whereas the box itself gives the interquartile range. The whiskers above and below each box give the 95 and 5 percentiles, respectively, of the empirical distribution. For comparison purposes, we provide the theoretical distribution implied by the hypergeometric distribution of cell counts implied by independence. When there is no truncation by survivorship, the distribution of this statistic is well specified. However, when managers have to survive a performance cut, there appears to be evidence of short-term dependence in performance. When only 5 percent of managers are cut in each of the first three years, the cross-product ratio is too high relative to its theoretical distribution assuming independence. With a 10 percent performance cutoff each year, three quarters of the time the test statistic lies above the median of its theoretical distribution. Even a small degree of truncation by survivorship will induce an unacceptably high probability of false inference of persistence in performance.

It might be argued that the apparent persistence we observe in these simulation experiments is some artifact of the way in which the test statistics have been computed. After all, the cross-product ratio is not widely used in the finance literature. Hendricks, Patel, and Zeckhauser (1991) argue in favor of a t-value statistic based on the returns computed on the basis of a self-financing portfolio strategy where the portfolio weights are proportional to the deviation of performance measures from the average performance measure across managers. The results of this kind of approach are given in Table 2, and the simulation results are presented in Figure 2. Note that this test statistic is, if anything, more misspecified under a performance cut than is the cross-product ratio. Given that this is true even in the special case where we know precisely the β of the self-financing portfolio, and can compute the theoretical variance of the performance measure, we would expect the performance of the statistic under realistic experimental conditions to be much worse.

It is important to note that truncation by survivorship may imply an apparent persistence in performance without significantly affecting average risk-adjusted returns. As we observed before, Grinblatt and Titman (1989) find that survivorship bias can account for only about 0.1 to 0.4 percent return per year. Table 5 shows the average risk-adjusted returns for managers who survive the various performance cuts. While there are substantial differences in average risk-adjusted return between managers who did well and poorly in the successive two-year periods, the net effect of survivorship bias on average risk-adjusted returns for all managers in the sample is very small and corresponds to about 0.4 to 0.6 percent per year on a risk-adjusted basis for the 5 to 10 percent cutoff examples. The corresponding

Survivorship Bias in Performance Studies

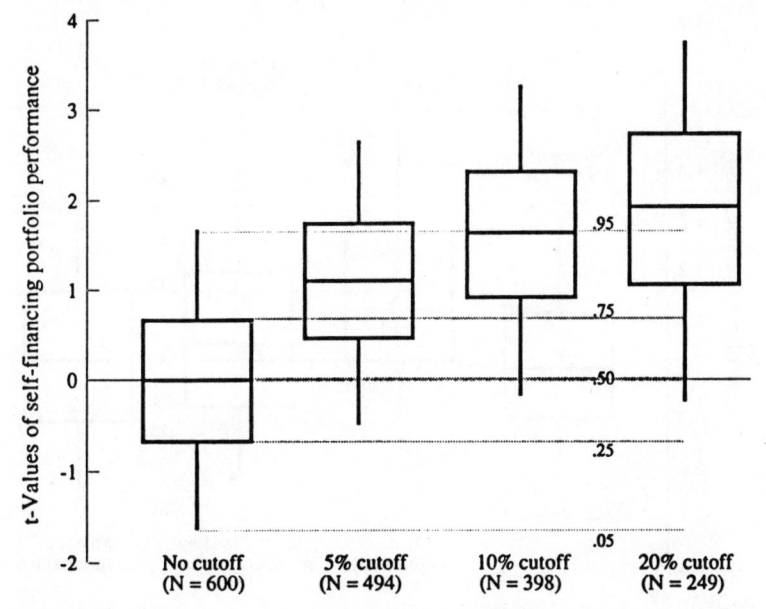

Figure 2
Boxplots of *t*-values associated with 20,000 simulated values of the self-financing portfolio performance measure
The solid line within each box represents the median of the empirical distribution of *t*-values associated with the Jensen's α of the self-financing portfolio strategy described in the text (assuming β known), whereas the box itself gives the interquartile range. The whiskers above and below each box give the 95th and 5th percentiles, respectively, of the empirical distribution. The gray lines give the stated fractiles of the theoretical distribution implied by the null hypothesis of a zero performance measure.

number is 0.8 percent for the 20 percent cutoff. These numbers do not differ significantly from those reported by Grinblatt and Titman. It would appear from the results reported in Table 5 that truncation of raw returns is compensated for by a corresponding truncation in the cross-sectional distribution of β, leading to no net effect on average risk-adjusted returns.

Of course, it might be said that these results are something of a straw man. After all, the example assumes that manager performance is evaluated on a total return basis. Actually, the apparent persistence in performance is even stronger than that reported in Table 5 if managers are terminated for low α, representing risk-adjusted returns. This result is implied by Corollary 1 above. In this example, what is important is not the dispersion across managers of total risk, but rather the dispersion of residual risk. This suggests that it may be possible to mitigate some of the survival effect by simply standardizing per-

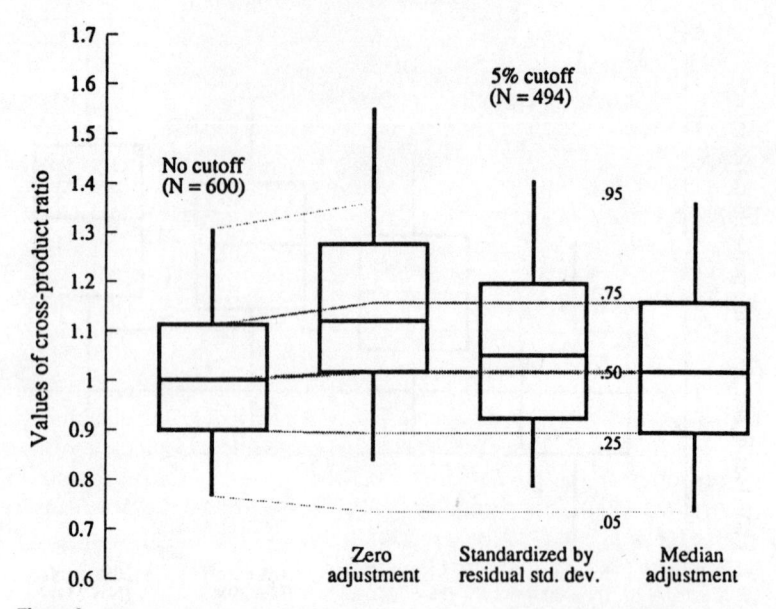

Figure 3
Boxplots of 20,000 simulated values of the cross-product ratio showing the effect of different adjustments for survivorship bias with a 5 percent performance cutoff
Zero adjustment refers to the boxplot given in Figure 1, where there is a 5 percent performance cutoff. Standardized by the residual standard deviation refers to the cross-product ratio calculated on the basis of defining "winners" and "losers" relative to the median appraisal ratio. Median adjustment corrects the median for the fact that the distribution of appraisal ratios is truncated by survivorship. This correction is described in the text.

formance measures by the residual standard deviation.[12] In fact, classifying managers into winner and loser categories by α measured in units of residual risk does reduce the apparent persistence in Table 5. This reduces the dispersion of measures of persistence but does not eliminate the survivor-induced bias. To eliminate the bias we need to adjust excess returns to account for the fact that the median excess return will be greater than zero by virtue of survivorship.[13] The

---

[12] This application of the *appraisal ratio*, originally due to Treynor and Black (1972), was suggested to us by William Sharpe. A recent study to examine the properties of this ratio is Lehmann and Modest (1987).

[13] If the performance cut occurs at the 10th percentile of the unconditional distribution of manager returns, the median of the truncated distribution will occur at the 55th percentile of the unconditional distribution. To correct for survivorship bias, we first compute the fractile p of the distribution of excess returns for the particular manager that corresponds to the minimum observed return. The quantity q given as the $(1 - (1 - p)/2)$th quantile of the distribution of excess returns is the median excess return induced by survivorship. The median adjustment given in Figure 2 is obtained by subtracting q computed for each manager from that manager's annual excess returns. Obviously, this adjustment is highly sensitive to the assumptions made about the distribution of excess returns for each manager, and about the effect of past performance on survival.

Survivorship Bias in Performance Studies

effect of these separate adjustments on the apparent survivorship effect is illustrated in Figure 3.

The numerical example is unrealistic in at least one important respect. In common with the results reported in Table 1, it assumes that the excess of returns of managers are cross-sectionally uncorrelated. Of course, there are patterns of performance related to styles of management, and we would expect excess returns to be correlated. In fact, in the sample period covered by Table 1, the intra-manager correlation of excess returns can reach as high as .98. This will exacerbate the effect if the pattern of intercorrelation depends on measures of risk. One high-risk manager surviving will increase the chance that other high-risk managers will also survive.

The degree of intercorrelation among managers does indeed appear to be functionally dependent upon β and residual risk.[14] Results of an experiment where the cross-sectional correlation of excess returns corresponds to the Goetzmann and Ibbotson study[15] are presented in Figure 4. The cross-correlation effect is sufficiently strong to cause a false inference of persistence even in the absence of a performance cut. Where there are performance cuts, this effect is considerably exacerbated.

Figure 4 indicates that the cross-product ratio test statistic is seriously misspecified. To obtain some idea of the order of magnitude, recall that a cross-product ratio of 4 corresponds to a contingency table where the cell counts on the diagonal are twice the off-diagonal terms. With a 5 percent performance cut, apparent dependence of this magnitude will be observed at least five percent of the time. It is important to note that the simple cross-section regression approach is also misspecified. The upper 95 percentile of the resulting test statistic, 1.65, is exceeded 32.9 percent of the time with no performance cut. With a 5 percent performance cut, this percentile is

---

[14] Two hundred fifty money managers in the Goetzmann and Ibbotson database were ranked according to β. The average β and intracorrelation of performance measures was computed for each of 20 groupings by β. As a purely descriptive measure, the average intracorrelations were related to β as follows:

$$\hat{\rho}_{ij} = \underset{(2.04)}{.558} - \underset{(-2.66)}{.732(\hat{\beta}_i + \hat{\beta}_j)} + \underset{(4.29)}{1.216(\hat{\beta}_i \times \hat{\beta}_j)},$$

$$R^2 = .3580, \quad N = 190$$

(*t*-values in parentheses). If the true correlation matrix corresponds to this regression equation, it is a simple exercise in matrix algebra to show that the distribution of residual returns is a two-factor structure, with factor loadings and idiosyncratic variances given as analytic functions of the β and β-product terms. This two-factor structure is used to generate Figures 3 and 4 in the text. As an aside, the same exercise in linear algebra shows that principal components will be an ineffective control for cross-sectional dependence, since the idiosyncratic variances of residual returns will be a quadratic function of β. Using principal components assumes the idiosyncratic variances are constant in the cross section.

As discussed earlier, this result is subject to the important caveat that the residual covariance matrix and β are estimated without regard to the possible effects of survival on the cross sectional distribution of these parameters and on the distribution of residuals.

[15] This uses the two-factor structure described in note 14.

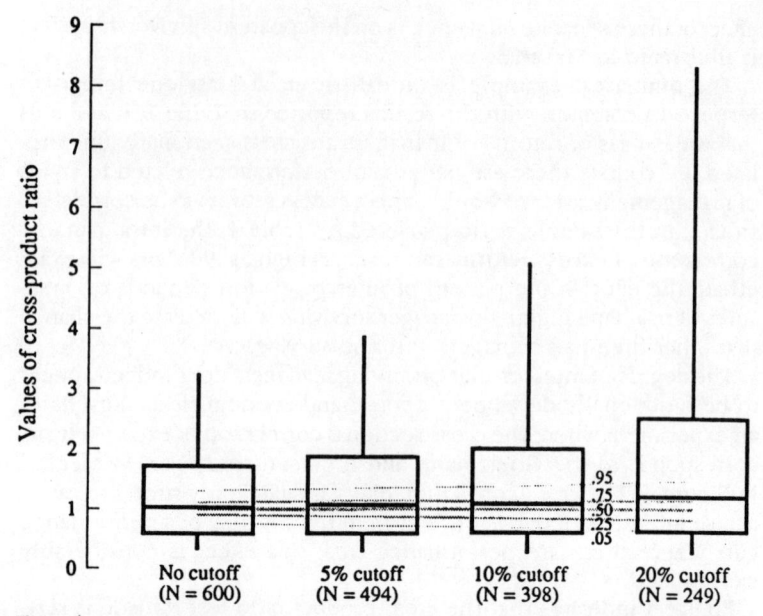

Figure 4
Boxplots of 20,000 simulated values of the cross-product ratio showing the effect of cross-correlation in performance measures
This figure corresponds to Figure 1, where the cross-correlation of performance measures matches that of the Goetzmann and Ibbotson (1991) sample. The procedure used to induce this level of cross-correlation is described in the text.

exceeded 54.39 percent of the time. The median value of the distribution of t-value statistics is 2.09.

The theoretical distribution assumes the performance measures are uncorrelated in the cross section of managers. Where we induce cross-sectional correlation into the performance measures, with no performance cut the cross-product ratio is unbiased but the variance is far greater than the theoretical distribution would imply. The cross-section regression approach, which imposes far more restrictive assumptions on the process generating sequential returns, is even more seriously affected. One concludes that the combination of dependence in the cross-section distribution of returns with truncation by performance might be sufficient to explain the results reported in Table 1.

Where there is cross-sectional dependence, the median adjustment is not well specified, although it does represent an improvement over the unadjusted statistics, as indicated in Figure 5. This adjustment assumes the excess returns are independent in the cross section. It is sensitive to violations of this assumption. While it is possible to

Survivorship Bias in Performance Studies

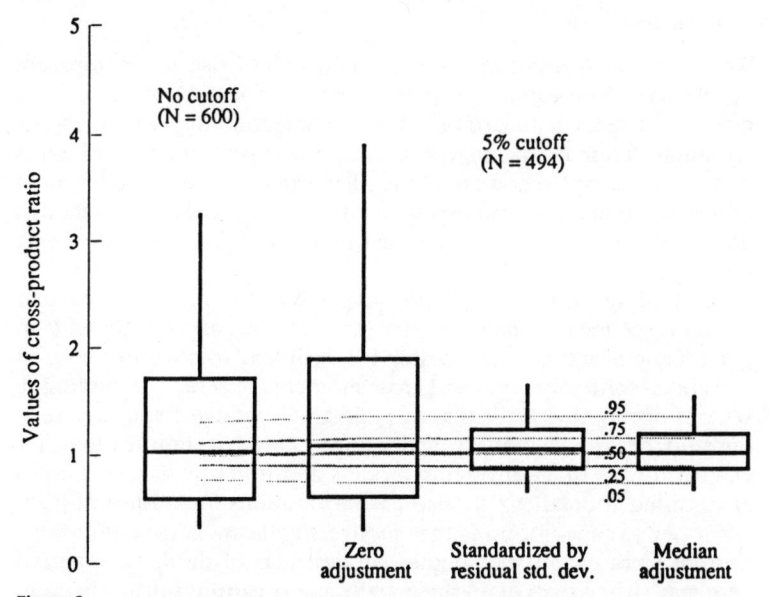

Figure 5
Boxplots of 20,000 simulated values of the cross-product ratio showing the effect of cross-correlation on alternative adjustments for survivorship bias
This figure corresponds to Figure 3, where the cross-correlation of performance measures matches that of the Goetzmann and Ibbotson (1991) sample. The procedure used to induce this level of cross-correlation is described in the text.

conceive of an exact adjustment based on the order statistics assuming dependence in manager excess returns, it is interesting to note that the simple residual standard deviation adjustment does at least as well as the median adjustment. This simple measure requires no information about the magnitude of the performance cut. The result suggests the conjecture that the simple prescription of normalizing performance numbers by residual standard deviations may represent a reasonably robust performance statistic.[16]

To illustrate the likely effects of normalizing performance measures by residual standard deviation, results reported in Table 4 were recomputed using this approach. The α and standard deviation measures are estimated using a truncated regression approach, where each month's return is assumed truncated from below by the return of the lowest manager in the group (the survivor). All measures of persistence are now statistically insignificant. The cross-section t-value for 1976–1981 falls from 3.13 to 1.77. The t-value for the self-financing portfolio approach performance now measures 1.76, whereas before it was 2.16. Two important caveats are in order. The result is sensitive to assumptions made about the way in which past performance influences survival. One could use information on firms that leave the sample to derive an explicit model for survival to construct a more powerful test. This would appear to be a standard application of the censored regression methodology were it not for the model-specific heteroskedasticity implied [see, e.g., Hurd (1979)]. Among other things, such a model would also need to account for cross-sectional correlation of manager performance. The second caveat is that these tests assume manager returns are independent through time. We would not expect such tests to be powerful against an alternative that allows manager returns to be autocorrelated absent the survival effect.

3. Conclusion

We show that truncation by survivorship gives rise to an apparent persistence in performance where there is dispersion of risk among money managers. Standard risk-adjustment technology, which adjusts for single-factor β risk, may not suffice to correct for this effect. A numerical example shows that this effect can give rise to a substantial probability that statistical tests based on risk-adjusted return data will give rise to the false inference that there is in fact dependence in security returns.

Our findings in this article are suggestive of implications beyond performance measurement. Where inclusion in a sample depends in part on rate of return, survivorship bias will lead to obvious biases in first and second moments and cross moments of return, including β. What is not so obvious is that this effect will induce a spurious relationship between volatility and return. This has implications for empirical tests of asset pricing models and in particular for studies of so-called anomalies.[17] It also has implications for studies of post-event performance of firms that survive significant corporate events. Current work examines whether survival bias of the kind reported here may suffice to explain the puzzling post-earnings-drift phenomenon first noted by Ball and Brown (1968) if there is dispersion of residual risk among those firms that survive into the post-earnings sample.[18]

Whether these results suffice to explain the strength of results reported by Goetzmann and Ibbotson (among others) is at this point an open question. We have shown that truncation by survival has a measurable impact on the observed returns of those managers who survive the performance cut. Clearly, the magnitude of the effect will depend on the fraction of managers who in fact survive the performance cut.[19] Furthermore, the numerical example was based on the dispersion of risk measures for managers *who survived.* In addition

---

[17] Since small firms are less diverse in their activities, we do not find it surprising that the residual risk for such firms is greater than for larger firms. The results of this article would suggest a survival-induced correlation between size and average (risk-adjusted) return.

[18] For more discussion on the post-earnings drift phenomenon, see Foster, Olson, and Shevlin (1984) and Bernard and Thomas (1989, 1990). For a discussion of survival bias effects as they relate to measures of accounting earnings, see Salamon and Smith (1977) and Ball and Watts (1979).

[19] Inspecting various annual issues of the Wiesenberger Investment Companies Service *Investment Companies* periodical, we find that for the period 1977–1987 the apparent attrition rate given as the fraction of equity fund managers who simply disappear from coverage, merge, or change their names ranges from 2.6 percent in 1985 to 8.5 percent in 1977, an average attrition rate of 4.8 percent. This average attrition is very close to the 5 percent attrition found by Grinblatt and Titman (1989). However, this number is very much a lower bound on the true attrition rate. To the extent that the number of equity funds increases through time, we should expect that the attrition rate will also increase.

Survivorship Bias in Performance Studies

it is assumed that survival depends on four annual reviews based solely on returns measured over the previous year.

To calibrate the magnitude of the possible bias, we need to know how the characteristics of managers who survive differ from other managers, and the role of past performance in determining which managers survive. Clearly, cumulative performance must have a role in this process. The strength of the apparent persistence evident in Table 1 seems to broadly correlate with periods of high volatility in the markets; market conditions may also play a role. As Hendricks, Patel, and Zeckhauser (1991) indicate, in the period 1974–1988, a subset of poorly performing managers appears to be immune from performance review. This factor alone seems to explain most of the apparent persistence in their study. These represent important issues for future research. Until they are resolved, it is difficult to devise a simple adjustment to standard performance measures that will correct for this survivorship bias.

Finally, the simulation results lead to the conjecture that the simple prescription of normalizing performance measures by the residual standard deviation might provide a performance measure that is relatively robust to this source of misspecification. However, there is an important caveat. These experiments assume that the true parameters of the process are known to the investigator. The task of estimating the risk measures in the presence of a potential performance cut and of designing a performance measure that corrects for the resulting apparent persistence in performance is the subject of ongoing research.

Appendix

In the text, we demonstrate that with the selection rule conditioning on early performance, there is a tendency for performance to persist. In this section, we show that if the selection rule conditions on overall (two-period) performance, then there is a tendency for performance reversal. The net effect of these two forces must be resolved empirically.

The basic problem we want to consider is

$$\Pr[x_2 > y_2 \mid x_1 > y_1, c],$$

where

$$c = \{x_1 + x_2 > 0, y_1 + y_2 > 0\}.$$

From Bayes' theorem

$$\Pr[x_2 > y_2 \mid x_1 > y_1, c] = \frac{\Pr[x_2 > y_2, x_1 > y_1, c]}{\Pr[x_1 > y_1, c]},$$

and again, by Bayes' theorem,

$$\Pr[x_1 > y_1, c] = \Pr[x_1 > y_1, c] = \Pr[x_1 > y_1 \mid c]\Pr[c].$$

For the purposes of this section we will ignore the possibility of dispersion in the spread parameter and assume x and y have independent and identical distributions. It follows that

$$\Pr[x_1 > y_1 \mid c] = \tfrac{1}{2}.$$

If we further assume that the distributions are symmetric about the origin, then

$$\Pr[c] = \tfrac{1}{4}, \qquad \Pr[x_1 > y_1, c] = (\tfrac{1}{2})(\tfrac{1}{4}) = \tfrac{1}{8}.$$

We now have the following result.

Lemma. *Under the above conditions*

$$\Pr[x_2 > y_2 \mid x_1 > y_1, x_1 + x_2 > 0, y_1 + y_2 > 0] < \tfrac{1}{2}.$$

Proof.

$$\Pr[x_2 > y_2, x_1 > y_1, c]$$
$$\equiv \Pr[x_2 > y_2, x_1 > y_1, x_1 + x_2 > 0, y_1 + y_2 > 0]$$
$$= \Pr[x_2 > y_2, x_1 > y_1, y_1 + y_2 > 0]$$
$$= \int_{-\infty}^{\infty} \int_{y_1}^{\infty} dF \left\{ \int_{-y_1}^{\infty} \int_{y_2}^{\infty} dF \, dF_{y_2} \right\} dF_{y_1}$$
$$= \int_{-\infty}^{\infty} G(y_1) \int_{-y_1}^{\infty} G(y_2) \, dF_{y_2} \, dF_{y_1}$$
$$= \int_{-\infty}^{\infty} G(y_1) \left\{ -\tfrac{1}{2} G^2(y_2) \Big|_{-y_1}^{\infty} \right\} dF_{y_1}$$
$$= \tfrac{1}{2} \int_{-\infty}^{\infty} G(y_1) G^2(-y_1) \, dF_{y_1}$$
$$= \tfrac{1}{2} \int_{-\infty}^{\infty} G(y_1)[1 - G(y_1)]^2 \, dF_{y_1} \quad \text{(by symmetry)}$$
$$= \tfrac{1}{2}(-\tfrac{1}{2}G^2 + \tfrac{2}{3}G^3 - \tfrac{1}{4}G^4)\big|_{-\infty}^{\infty}$$
$$= \tfrac{1}{2}\{\tfrac{1}{2} - \tfrac{2}{3} + \tfrac{1}{4}\} = \tfrac{1}{24}.$$

Hence,

$$\Pr[x_2 > y_2 \mid x_1 > y_1, c] = \frac{1/24}{1/8} = \frac{1}{3} < \frac{1}{2}.$$ ∎

This is the tendency for reversal in the absence of any inferences about volatility from returns. It is clear, by continuity, that if we permitted a small disparity in ex post spreads for x and y, this effect would still dominate. However, as the possibility of spreads is increased, the persistence described in the text also increases. In theory and in practice, which effect is dominant depends on both the exact form of the selection rules and the potential dispersion of the spread parameter.

References

Agresti, A., 1990, *Analysis of Ordinal Categorical Data*, Wiley, New York.

Ball, R., and P. Brown, 1968, "An Empirical Examination of Accounting Income Numbers," *Journal of Accounting Research*, 6, 159-178.

Ball, R., and R. Watts, 1979, "Some Additional Evidence on Survival Biases," *Journal of Finance*, 34, 1802-1808.

Bernard, V., and J. Thomas, 1989, "Post-earnings-announcement Drift: Delayed Price Response or Risk Premium," *Journal of Accounting Research*, 27, 1-36.

Bernard, V., and J. Thomas, 1990, "Evidence that Stock Prices Do Not Fully Reflect the Implications of Current Earnings for Future Earnings," *Journal of Accounting and Economics*, 13, 305-340.

Bishop, Y., S. Fienberg, and P. Holland, 1975, *Discrete Multivariate Analysis: Theory and Practice*, MIT Press, Cambridge, Mass.

Black, F., M. Jensen, and M. Scholes, 1972, in M. Jensen (ed.), *Studies in the Theory of Capital Markets*, Praeger, New York.

Connor, G., and R. Korajczyk, 1991, "The Attributes, Behavior and Performance of U.S. Mutual Funds," *Review of Quantitative Finance and Accounting*, 1, 5-26.

Cowles, A., 1933, "Can Stock Market Forecasters Forecast?" *Econometrica*, 1, 309-325.

Dunn, P., and R. Theisen, 1983, "How Consistently Do Active Managers Win?" *Journal of Portfolio Management*, 9, 47-50.

Elton, E., and M. Gruber, 1989, *Modern Portfolio Theory and Investment Analysis*, Wiley, New York.

Elton, E., M. Gruber, and J. Rentzler, 1990, "The Performance of Publicly Offered Commodity Funds," *Financial Analysts Journal*, 46, 23-30.

Elton, E., M. Gruber, S. Das, and M. Hlavka, 1993, "Efficiency with Costly Information: A Reinterpretation of Evidence for Managed Portfolios," forthcoming in *Review of Financial Studies*.

Foster, G., C. Olsen, and T. Shevlin, 1984, "Earnings Releases, Anomalies, and the Behavior of Security Returns," *Accounting Review*, 59, 574-603.

Goetzmann, W., and R. Ibbotson, 1991, "Do Winners Repeat? Patterns in Mutual Fund Behavior," working paper, Yale School of Organization and Management.

Grinblatt, M., and S. Titman, 1988, "The Evaluation of Mutual Fund Performance: An Analysis of Monthly Returns," Working Paper 13-86, John E. Anderson Graduate School of Management, University of California at Los Angeles.

Grinblatt, M., and S. Titman, 1989, "Mutual Fund Performance: An Analysis of Quarterly Portfolio Holdings," *Journal of Business*, 62, 393-416.

Hendricks, D., J. Patel, and R. Zeckhauser, 1991, "Hot Hands in Mutual Funds: The Persistence of Performance, 1974-88," working paper, John F. Kennedy School of Government, Harvard University.

Hurd, M., 1979, "Estimation in Truncated Samples When There Is Heteroscedasticity," *Journal of Econometrics*, 11, 247-258.

Ibbotson, R., and R. Sinquefeld, 1990, *Stocks Bonds Bills and Inflation: 1990 Yearbook*, Ibbotson Associates, Chicago.

Ippolito, R., 1989, "Efficiency with Costly Information: A Study of Mutual Fund Performance 1965-1984," *Quarterly Journal of Economics*, 104, 1-23.

Jensen, M., 1968, "The Performance of Mutual Funds in the Period 1945-1964," *Journal of Finance*, 23, 389-416.

Kritzman, M., 1983, "Can Bond Managers Perform Consistently?" *Journal of Portfolio Management*, 9, 54-56.

Lehmann, B., and D. Modest, 1987, "Mutual Fund Performance Evaluation: A Comparison of Benchmarks and Benchmark Comparisons," *Journal of Finance*, 21, 233-265.

Roll, R., and S. Ross, 1980, "An Empirical Investigation of the Arbitrage Pricing Theory," *Journal of Finance*, 35, 1073-1103.

Salamon, G., and E. D. Smith, 1977, "Additional Evidence on the Time Series Properties of Reported Earnings Per Share," *Journal of Finance*, 32, 1795-1801.

Treynor, J., and F. Black, 1972, "Portfolio Selection Using Special Information under the Assumptions of the Diagonal Model with Mean Variance Portfolio Objectives and without Constraints," in G. P. Szego and K. Shell (eds.), *Mathematical Models in Investment and Finance*, North-Holland, Amsterdam.

THE VALUE LINE ENIGMA (1965–1978)
A Case Study of Performance Evaluation Issues

Thomas E. COPELAND and David MAYERS*
University of California, Los Angeles, CA 90024, USA

Received November 1981, final version received July 1982

The performance of *Value Line Investment Survey* recommendations made between 1965 and 1978 is evaluated by applying a future benchmark technique. The future benchmark technique avoids selection bias problems associated with using historic benchmarks as well as known difficulties of using Capital Asset Pricing Model benchmarks. Potential problems (implicit in the technique) are discussed and resolved within the conduct of the experiment. Results indicate statistically significant abnormal performance when future benchmarks are computed using a market model.

1. Introduction

Value Line is the world's largest (based on number of subscriptions) published advisory service, employing over 200 people and providing a range of investment information on approximately 1700 stocks. The information they provide includes performance predictions by assigning rankings from 1 to 5 to the stocks in their universe.[1] The ranking of 1 indicates that most favorable performance is expected and 5 indicates the worst. Rankings are updated weekly and based entirely (at least currently) on publicly available information.[2]

Black (1971) is the most frequently cited academic study of the performance of Value Line's rankings.[3] Black used Jensen's (1969) Capital

---

*Aid from the Cantor–Fitzgerald Fund for Financial Research is gratefully acknowledged. We thank L. Dann, K. French, M. Jensen, R. Masulis, R. Roll, M. Rozeff and the members of the UCLA Finance Workshop for helpful discussion and comments.

[1] Value Line started their current ranking system in April 1965. Security rankings result from a complex filter rule which utilizes four criteria: (1) the earnings and price rank of each security relative to all others; (2) a price momentum factor; (3) year-to-year relative changes in quarterly earnings; and (4) an earnings 'surprise' factor. Roughly 53% of the stocks are ranked 3rd, 18% are ranked 2nd or 4th, and 6% are ranked 1st or 5th.

[2] See Eisenstadt (1980).

[3] Other studies about Value Line have been done by Shelton (1967), Hausman (1969), Kaplan–Weil (1973), and more recently by Holloway (1981). The Holloway piece came to our attention when this work was well in progress. Although our results are consistent with Holloway's, our study is more extensive and more directly comparable to Black's work. Also, the Holloway study has a potential benchmark problem (as does Black's) that we directly control for. The Shelton, Hausman and Kaplan–Weil studies are not direct tests of Value Line performance.

Asset Pricing Model based performance evaluation technique. His results indicate statistically significant abnormal performance for stocks ranked 1, 2, 4 and 5, and economic significance for stocks ranked 1 and 5.[4] Black's results are startling and provide motivation for further study because significant abnormal performance associated with the Value Line rankings is in conflict with the semi-strong form of the efficient markets hypothesis.[5]

Performance evaluation is a current issue in the theory of finance and the technology used by Black (although the best at the time) has potential problems. For example, the theoretical basis of Jensen's (1969) methodology was criticized by Roll (1977, 1978) and subsequently defended by Mayers–Rice (1979). But, even assuming the theoretical basis were salvageable, other difficulties remain; the efforts of Banz (1981), Basu (1977), Litzenberger–Ramaswamy (1979), Long (1978), Reinganum (1981) and others point to empirical regularities that provide potential sources of error in performance measurement that uses the Jensen (1969) methodology.[6]

Cornell (1979) has outlined a plausible solution to these problems:[7]

(1) Using a sample from prior to the test period, calculate the sample mean return of the portfolio being evaluated.
(2) Use this estimated mean return as a benchmark and compute the portfolio's unexpected return over the test period.[8]
(3) Repeat the experiment and test to determine whether the mean unexpected return is significantly different from zero.

In other words, rather than using a particular (perhaps suspect) model of asset pricing as a benchmark, estimate the appropriate expected returns directly from the data.[9]

---

[4]Black evaluated equally weighted portfolios that were rebalanced monthly. Portfolios 1 and 5 (that contained stocks of rank 1 and 5, respectively) had risk-adjusted rates of return before transaction costs of +10% and −10%, respectively. Portfolio 1, for example, had an annual turnover rate of 130%. Yet even with round-trip transaction costs of 2%, the net rate of return for a long position in portfolio 1 would have still been positive.

[5]See Fama (1970) for an excellent discussion of the efficient markets theory. The designation of semi-strong form indicates that the 'information set' used in the trading rule is publicly available.

[6]Jensen's (1969) methodology assumes the correctness of the Capital Asset Pricing Model (CAPM). Thus misspecification of the CAPM can lead to performance measurement error. See Roll (1980) for a discussion in this context. The empirical regularities are those that relate to firm size [Banz (1981) and Reinganum (1981)], earnings price ratios [Basu (1977) and Reinganum (1981)] and dividend yields [Litzenberger–Ramaswamy (1979) and Long (1978)]. Note also that other CAPM-related performance measurement methodologies such as the two-factor market model [Fama–MacBeth (1973)] and paired sample designs based on the CAPM risk measure are also potentially problematic.

[7]This is our wording of Cornell's outline.

[8]The procedure assumes stationarity of the underlying generating process. This assumption is usual in econometric modelling.

[9]As noted by Cornell (1979), this solution has been in the literature for some time; e.g. Fama (1970, 1976) and Masulis (1978). Lloyd-Davies–Canes (1978) use a variation of the procedure for

As plausible and as simple as this procedure may appear to be, thorny issues arise when it is used to evaluate the performance of a managed portfolio. Our paper documents these issues and the difficulties involved in attempting to resolve them while evaluating the performance rankings supplied by *The Value Line Investment Survey*.

We observe significant abnormal performance. It is considerably less than that reported by Black (1971), but the possibility of economic significance for some investors remains. However, (as with other studies) our results must be interpreted in light of the problems we encounter in conducting the experiment. For example, our methodology requires the selection of a benchmark estimation period that is separate from the test period. This separation leads to the most worrisome of the problems we encounter because it forces us to assume that the mean of the return generating process is stationary across the two periods. Subtle but persistent non-stationarities can yield anomalous results if the benchmark returns are systematically biased. We present evidence which leads to the conclusion that non-stationarity is not of major importance in our results. Moreover, our experiment controls for sources of error in past studies of Value Line that use CAPM-based methodologies (like Black's). We conclude that the Value Line rankings do exhibit abnormal performance.

Overview of the paper

Section 2 is a description of the data. Section 3 presents the details of the experimental design. We employ the mean return and the familiar market model as benchmarks.[10] The selection of the benchmark estimation period is an important problem which is discussed in some detail. We also discuss a serial correlation problem caused by the structure of our experimental design.

Section 4 contains direct tests of the Value Line rankings. The results of these tests are consistent with abnormal performance. This conclusion is corroborated by the evidence in section 5, where we focus our tests on

---

evaluating what is essentially a managed portfolio and, of course, most event studies use some variation of the procedure.

[10] The market model posits a linear relationship between a security or portfolio rate of return, R_p, and the return on an index portfolio, R_m, i.e.,

$$R_{pt} = \alpha_p + \beta_p R_{mt} + \varepsilon_{pt}.$$

See Fama (1976, pp. 63-132) for a discussion of this model. See also Brown-Warner (1980) for empirical justification of the market model in performance evaluation and Roll (1979) for theoretical justification. Tests using the market model are potentially more powerful than those using the simple mean return benchmark. This does not have to be the case, however. See for example, the discussion in Brown-Warner (1980, pp. 209-210) and their results. Our results contrast with theirs. In our application, tests using the market model, appear to be more powerful. Consequently, we present only initial mean return benchmark results.

changes in rankings (i.e., either up or down). In section 6, we address the problem of nonstationarity. Section 7 contains a discussion of transactions costs and presents our conclusions.

2. Data description and sources

The primary data were obtained from *The Value Line Investment Survey* and from the daily rate of return file obtained from the Center for Research in Securities Prices (CRSP) at the University of Chicago.[11]

The Value Line Investment Survey (Weekly Summary of Advices and Index) lists the Value Line rankings for the set of securities contained in their universe. These rankings range from 1 to 5; stocks in group 1 are expected to have the best price performance over the next 12 months and stocks in group 5 the worst performance over the next 12 months.[12] Value Line also indicates whether a performance assignment is a change from the previous week and the direction of change.

Two Value Line data sets were obtained. Beginning with the November 26, 1965 *Survey*, Value Line Performance rankings were obtained at 26-week intervals for a total of 24 periods for all firms that are also contained on the CRSP daily rate of return file. Thus our study uses rankings from November 26, 1965 through February 3, 1978.[13] Ranking changes were collected in a separate file indicating whether a particular firm has just been moved up or down in the ranking.[14] These data were obtained at 13-week intervals for a total of 48 periods commencing at the same date as the 'rankings' file.

The daily CRSP rate of return file was converted to a weekly file. Each week begins with a Friday closing price and ends with the following Friday closing price.[15] The rates of return are adjusted, by CRSP, for dividends, splits, etc. A weekly equally weighted arithmetic average rate of return index of all CRSP listed securities was also constructed as a market index.[16]

[11]The CRSP file contains daily returns for all New York and American Stock Exchange listed securities, since the middle of 1962.
[12]Value Line details their criteria for ranking in a pamphlet entitled *Investing in Common Stocks*.
[13] Exact ranking dates are in the appendix. The intervals are occasionally slightly irregularly spaced because the early data was originally collected for a different experiment. The intervals always contain at least 26 weeks, for example, there are 3 occasions when the intervals are greater than 26 weeks.
[14]The rankings file contains an average of 1,270 securities each period. The change file contains an average of 39 upgraded and 41 downgraded securities in each period.
[15]Of some concern is the timing of Value Line activities and when the clients actually have the Value Line recommendation. The construction of our weekly rate of return file assumes investors buy or sell at the closing price on the date of the recommendation, which is always a Friday. Value Line staggers mailings so they will arrive on the recommendation date. The recommendations are actually printed over the weekend preceding the ranking date. Thus Value Line analysis is completed the week prior to the week that the recommendation arrives and recommendations are one week old when received.
[16]See Brown–Warner (1980) for justification of this index in performance evaluation.

3. Specifics and tests

Test periods are defined as the 26-week period following Value Line recommendations for the rankings file and the 13-week period following recommendations for the change file. Thus our test periods are (essentially) consecutive and adjacent. Weekly excess (unexpected) rates of return and standardized rates of return are calculated for weeks within the test periods. The excess rates of return are used to test for the significance of cumulative performance while the standardized rates of return are used for testing the significance of individual weekly performance, e.g., week one excess rate of return performance.

As an example, consider one of the change portfolios (up or down) and the mean return benchmark.[17] The portfolio rate of return is defined as

$$R_{pt} = \ln\left(1 + \sum_{j=1}^{N_t} R_{jt}/N_t\right). \tag{1}$$

Here R_{jt} is the weekly rate of return for security j in the portfolio of interest during week t of period p.[18] R_{pt} is calculated for each week in both the benchmark and test periods.[19] The number of firms, N, is subscripted by t to note the possibility of delisting or listing.[20] The mean return benchmark is calculated as

$$\bar{R}_p = \sum_{t=1}^{T} R_{pt}/T. \tag{2}$$

Thus $\bar{R}_p$ is the average weekly portfolio rate of return from the benchmark period, where T is the number of weeks in the benchmark period. The estimated standard deviation of the portfolio rate of return over the benchmark period,

$$SD_p = \left[\sum_{t=1}^{T} (R_{pt} - \bar{R}_p)^2 \Big/ (T-1)\right]^{\frac{1}{2}}, \tag{3}$$

is used along with the mean return benchmark to calculate the standardized

---

[17] We use the mean return benchmark here because the notation is simpler than for the market model benchmark.

[18] For tests of performance using the rankings file we repeated the experiment in non-log form. The results were practically identical to the log form. The log form results slightly favor Value Line. Thus we report the log results with appropriate contrasts.

[19] Thus we are explicitly using a weekly rebalanced equally weighted portfolio. The implications of this procedure and why it was chosen are discussed in footnote 21.

[20] The amount of listing and delisting is minor. Some numbers are presented in section 6.

portfolio rate of return for week w ($w=1,\ldots,13$) of the test period,

$$SR_{pw} = (R_{pw} - \bar{R}_p)/SD_p. \tag{4}$$

Each standardized rate of return is an individual t-statistic for the portfolio excess rate of return in its respective week. The standardized portfolio rates of return for week w of the test periods are then averaged,

$$\overline{SR}_{pw} = \sum_{p=1}^{48} SR_{pw}/48, \tag{5}$$

and the following t-statistic is calculated for each week in the test period:

$$t_w = \overline{SR}_{pw}/(1/\sqrt{48}). \tag{6}$$

The degrees of freedom are $48 \times (T-1)$ in this example. The t-statistic tests for the significance of excess rate of return performance for individual weeks within the test period.

We also estimate the average cumulative excess rate of return,

$$ACR = \frac{1}{48} \sum_{p=1}^{48} \sum_{w=1}^{13} (R_{pw} - \bar{R}_p), \tag{7}$$

and test for whether the true cumulative excess rate of return performance is different from zero.[21] We estimate the standard deviation for this test using

---

[21]The fact that we explicitly use a weekly rebalanced equally weighted portfolio for performance measurement can be cause for concern because we don't really have in mind an investor that rebalances weekly to an equally weighted portfolio. Our performance measure should have a more general interpretation. Our ACR calculation is approximately equivalent to calculating the Cumulative Average Residual of Fama, Fisher, Jensen and Roll (1969) for each test period and then taking the average. It would be equivalent, for example, if there were no missing data. An alternative performance measure is the Abnormal Performance Index (API),

$$API = N^{-1} \sum_{j=1}^{N} \prod_{t=1}^{T} (1 + e_{jt}).$$

The API of a portfolio of N securities is the value of one dollar invested equally in the abnormal performance of all N securities and held through T compounding intervals with no rebalancing. The average API, on the surface is a more intuitively appealing performance measure. The problem is that the API calculation requires a benchmark estimate for each security. As will become clear shortly, our benchmark periods postdate the test periods. Consequently, we would be unable to estimate benchmarks for securities that are delisted, have trading suspensions or for whatever reason lack sufficient data in the benchmark periods for estimation of an individual security benchmark. These are likely to be important securities and eliminating them from the experiment could greatly influence our findings. Because of concern for the generality of the results, we estimated the average API. The average API and the ACR results were very close. The evidence was consistent with some ex post selection bias associated with the average API.

the usual unbiased estimator (e.g., (3) above) calculated with the period-by-period cumulative test period excess returns.[22]

3.1. Benchmark period selection

The choice of a benchmark period is important because it can affect the outcome of the experiment. The obvious selection, the period immediately preceding the test period, is contaminated because Value Line uses a variant of the relative strength criterion in its performance grouping assignment rule.[23] Using data immediately prior to the Value Line ranking date biases the benchmarks against finding abnormal performance (in the right direction) because the portfolio 1 benchmark returns are overstated and vice versa for portfolio 5.[24] Using past data may also be hazardous if Value Line includes as part of its selection criterion changes in those factors (for example, dividend yield) that are associated with the empirical regularities noted in the introduction. In this case the past price data would not reflect the return effects of such changes. For these reasons we use benchmark periods from the future. We skip the test period (26 weeks following Value Line's announcements) and use the subsequent 52 or 26 weeks as our benchmark periods.[25] One concern was that the benchmark period should be long enough to ensure that our parameter estimates are reasonably accurate; thus, our choice of 52 weeks. Another concern was the potential for non-stationarities; thus, our choice of 26 weeks.[26]

---

[22]These tests and calculations are the same using the market model benchmark except that $\dot{\alpha}_p + \beta_p R_{mw}$ is used in the place of $\bar{R}_p$ and the square root of the estimated forecast variance is used in the place of SD_p. The forecast variance formula is

$$\sigma_{pw}^2 = \sigma_p^2 \left[1 + T^{-1} + (R_{mw} - \bar{R}_m)^2 \Big/ \sum_{t=1}^{T} (R_{mt} - \bar{R}_m)^2 \right],$$

where σ_p^2 is the portfolio residual variance over T weeks in the benchmark period. The degrees of freedom of the t-statistic (6) are $48 \times (T-2)$ in the example using the market model benchmark.

[23]In other words, Value Line attaches a favorable weighting to stocks that have had recent good price performance and an unfavorable weighting to stocks that have had recent bad price performance. 'Good' and 'bad' are defined relative to earlier performance and relative to all stocks in the Value Line universe. The selection strategy appears very clearly in the data. See Levy (1967), one of the original proponents of this criterion, and Jensen–Bennington (1970) for a thorough critique.

[24]Replication of our experiment for the rankings file using the 26 weeks before the Value Line ranking date showed significant negative performance for Group 1 stocks and significant positive performance for Group 5 stocks.

[25]Because the 20th week of the last benchmark period is the last data week on our rate of return file we use 46 weeks and 20 weeks for the last two 52-week benchmark calculations and 20 weeks for the last 26-week benchmark calculation.

[26]Our experimental design, including our choices of test and benchmark periods, was also influenced by our concern for the data seasonality problem. See, for example, the work of Rozeff–Kinney (1976) or more recently that of Keim (1981), Reinganum (1982) and Roll (1982). As long as the seasonality is stationary from year to year the problem should be controlled for ACR's computed for the full test period. ACR's computed for less than the full test period and weekly performance measures can be influenced by data seasonality.

Of course, there is still the possibility that Value Line's predictive ability could bias our benchmarks. We believe there is little such bias and this can be judged from the evidence. For example, suppose Value Line *is* able to predict future information events better than the market. There are two extreme scenarios. In the first, the market correctly believes Value Line and market prices adjust immediately. In this case benchmarks estimated from future data are unbiased.[27] In the second scenario the market ignores Value Line and all price adjustments occur naturally. In this case benchmarks calculated from future data can be biased.[28] The question is: What behavior should we expect of the average excess (unexpected) rates of return during weeks subsequent to Value Line recommendations if the estimated benchmarks are unbiased?

The behavior of the average excess rates of return will depend on the time pattern of information events subsequent to the Value Line announcements. A reasonable assumption about the time pattern is that Value Line is better able to predict near events than far events.[29] With this assumption, the estimated benchmarks would be biased against Value Line only if predictive ability extends into the benchmark period. In this event, abnormal performance would be detected, but it would be understated. The average of the cumulative excess rates of return (for a good information portfolio, e.g. portfolio 1) would rise continuously across the test period.[30] If Value Line's predictive ability does not extend into the benchmark period, the benchmarks are unbiased and the average of the cumulative excess rates of return would initially rise and then be flat from the point where Value Line predictive ability disappears.

Thus, if the average of the cumulative excess rates of return are either flat across the test period (no excess rate of return performance indicated) or become flat during the test period (consistent with excess rate of return performance) we will conclude our benchmark period choice has yielded unbiased benchmarks.

3.2. Dependencies in the experimental design

There are two sources of serial correlation that can pose problems for our

[27]This discussion assumes that the underlying generating processes are stationary. In other words, data drawn from beyond the point where prices reflect Value Line's predictive ability are assumed to provide unbiased estimates of the appropriate ex ante assessments for the test period. Non-stationarity is, of course, a potential source of bias. We discuss this source and present evidence starting in section 6.

[28]There is also a third possibility that Value Line has a temporary effect because the market incorrectly believes Value Line. We ignore this self-fulfilling prophesy hypothesis.

[29]Essentially, the mean of the frequency distribution of events, assumed to be zero and uniform in time without Value Line information, is positive (a good information portfolio) and declines monotonically as a function of time from the announcement date.

[30]For a bad information portfolio (e.g., portfolio 5 of the rankings portfolios), the average of the cumulative excess rates of return would fall continuously across the test period.

significance tests. These sources are potentially important because of the overlapping experimental design.[31] First, the portfolios for the rankings file (and perhaps the change file as well) are not independent drawings from the Value Line universe from period to period.[32] The second source arises because security rates of return are cross-sectionally correlated.

We estimate auto-correlation coefficients for weekly standardized returns, weekly excess returns and test period cumulative excess returns for lags of one to six periods. For the rankings portfolios, enough of the auto-correlation coefficients are significant and of the appropriate sign to suggest negative auto-correlation of lag 1.[33] The change portfolio evidence was weaker.

The evidence of serial correlation is consistent with our a priori suspicions. For the rankings portfolios there is reason to suspect an understatement of levels of significance for our tests. For the tests of cumulative excess rate of return performance we attempt to incorporate the dependencies by repeating the tests, using

$$\sigma_A^2 = (\sigma^2/P^2)[P + 2(P-1)r_1 + \cdots + 2(P-6)r_6]$$

as the variance estimator,[34] where r_j are the auto-correlation coefficients for a lag of j periods, σ^2 is the variance of the periodic cumulative excess rates of return and P is the number of periods.

4. Inferences: Five Value Line rankings portfolios

The discussion of the Value Line rankings evidence follows in two parts.

---

[31] Note that benchmark periods and the following test periods coincide identically for the 26-week benchmarks. If the mean return benchmark, for example, estimated for a particular test period and portfolio, is positively related to the portfolio gross return of the following test period, the time series of portfolio excess returns can have first-order negative auto-correlation even if security rates of return are serially independent. An alternating structure of test and benchmark periods would avoid the problem. It would also increase the data requirements of the experiment.

[32] The independence of Value Line portfolio composition was examined by computing transition probability matrices. There is evidence of persistence in the five rankings portfolios. For example, the probability that a rank 1 stock, will be ranked 1 six months hence is estimated to be 0.30. Were the drawings independent (with replacement) this probability would be approximately 0.06. Persistence appears even as far out as a year. Thus skipping an entire year before estimating the benchmarks would not solve the problem. We find little evidence of change portfolio persistence. For example, the probability that a particular stock in the up portfolio will again be in the up portfolio 13 weeks hence is estimated to be only 0.04. Thus, with an average of 39 securities in the up portfolio we expect only 1.56 of them to be in the up portfolio in any following period.

[33] Tables are omitted to save space.

[34] This formula is easily derived by taking the variance of a sample mean without the assumption of independence for lags up to six. Assuming independence the variance of a sample mean is simply σ^2/P. Also, the statistics that assume independence are referred to as t-stat$_1$. Those that do not are t-stat$_2$. The distribution of t-stat$_2$ is standard normal in large samples.

The first describes unadjusted Value Line performance and presents some summary benchmark period information. The second presents the excess rate of return evidence.

4.1. Raw return performance and benchmark characteristics

Table 1 contains average cumulative raw rates of return from weeks 1 to 26 for the five portfolios. On an unadjusted basis, Value Line shows considerable discriminating ability. Cumulative performance is ordered perfectly with the rankings: portfolio 1 achieved an average (across 24 six-

Table 1

Value Line average cumulative raw returns for 24 ranking dates from November 26, 1965 to February 3, 1978.[a]

Week relative to Value Line ranking date	Portfolio number				
	1	2	3	4	5
1	0.0000	−0.0009	−0.0029	−0.0051	−0.0074
2	−0.0037	−0.0051	−0.0093	−0.0144	−0.0167
3	0.0095	0.0061	−0.0007	−0.0069	−0.0116
4	0.0170	0.0135	0.0068	−0.0001	−0.0068
5	0.0120	0.0090	0.0017	−0.0057	−0.0105
6	0.0200	0.0153	0.0074	−0.0019	−0.0099
7	0.0235	0.0182	0.0073	−0.0028	−0.0099
8	0.0246	0.0179	0.0066	−0.0030	−0.0107
9	0.0302	0.0224	0.0103	0.0008	−0.0111
10	0.0369	0.0292	0.0160	0.0035	−0.0097
11	0.0378	0.0301	0.0130	−0.0010	−0.0161
12	0.0404	0.0333	0.0144	0.0009	−0.0183
13	0.0428	0.0359	0.0168	0.0020	−0.0189
14	0.0481	0.0359	0.0162	−0.0020	−0.0222
15	0.0425	0.0375	0.0172	0.0010	−0.0214
16	0.0477	0.0417	0.0212	0.0063	−0.0188
17	0.0494	0.0432	0.0218	0.0073	−0.0167
18	0.0445	0.0392	0.0180	0.0026	−0.0250
19	0.0420	0.0370	0.0149	−0.0005	−0.0313
20	0.0509	0.0449	0.0220	0.0049	−0.0253
21	0.0621	0.0560	0.0337	0.0203	−0.0041
22	0.0576	0.0609	0.0389	0.0285	0.0060
23	0.0711	0.0640	0.0419	0.0314	0.0085
24	0.0723	0.0645	0.0419	0.0298	0.0082
25	0.0712	0.0623	0.0385	0.0266	0.0037
26	0.0738	0.0651	0.0410	0.0270	0.0037

[a] Portfolio numbers correspond to the Value Line rankings of the securities in the portfolios. On average, portfolios 1 to 5 contain 91, 273, 521, 270 and 91 securities. The rates of return are the average (across the 24 periods) of the weekly rates of return cumulated to the designated week relative to the ranking date. All 24 ranking dates are available in the appendix.

Table 2
Average benchmark period portfolio characteristics for the five Value Line rankings portfolios.[a]

Statistic	Portfolio number				
	1	2	3	4	5
26-week benchmark period averages					
Market model intercept, $\hat{\alpha}_p$	0.0000	0.0002	−0.0000	−0.0003	−0.0007
Market model slope, $\hat{\beta}_p$	1.0426	0.9552	0.8870	0.8815	1.0032
Correlation coefficient, $\hat{\rho}(R_p, R_m)$	0.9409	0.9625	0.9700	0.9672	0.9378
Mean return benchmark, $\hat{\mu}_p$	0.0020	0.0020	0.0016	0.0013	0.0011
52-week benchmark period averages					
Market model intercept, $\hat{\alpha}_p$	−0.0003	−0.0001	−0.0001	−0.0002	−0.0007
Market model slope, $\hat{\beta}_p$	1.0209	0.9472	0.8779	0.8778	1.0039
Correlation coefficient, $\hat{\rho}(R_p, R_m)$	0.9549	0.9647	0.9714	0.9680	0.8470
Mean return benchmark, $\hat{\mu}_p$	0.0019	0.0020	0.0018	0.0014	0.0011

[a]Portfolio numbers correspond to the Value Line rankings of the securities in the portfolios. Each statistic is an arithmetic average of the estimates obtained from the 24 benchmark periods of a given length (26 or 52 weeks).

month test periods) six-month rate of return of 7.38% whereas portfolio 5 achieved only 0.37%.[35]

Table 2 contains summary information from the benchmark periods for the five portfolios. Averages of the estimates of the intercepts ($\hat{\alpha}_p$) and slope coefficients ($\hat{\beta}_p$) from the market model along with correlation coefficient estimates ($\hat{\rho}(R_{pt}, R_{mt})$) and mean return benchmark estimates ($\hat{\mu}_p$) are presented for each of the five portfolios and both benchmark estimation periods.

The mean return benchmark estimates are consistent with a portfolio selection strategy that assigns high risk securities to portfolio 1 and low risk securities to portfolio 5; the returns are lower for portfolio 5. It appears that this risk is not adequately captured by our beta estimates. The market model slope coefficients are estimates of the CAPM beta during the benchmark periods. For portfolios 1 and 5, the averages of these estimates are very close, albeit higher for portfolio 1 (1.0209 vs. 1.0039 or 1.0426 vs. 1.0032). Moreover, unlike the cumulative raw performance, the average slope coefficients are not ordered with the rankings. It appears that the CAPM benchmark is unable to explain the differential raw performance of the five Value Line portfolios.[36]

[35]As mentioned earlier these are all log calculations. The non-log calculations indicate higher raw performance for both portfolio 1 and 5, but the differential performance is almost identical. The average of the cumulative (six-month) rates of return (non-log) is 8.86% for portfolio 1 and 1.79% for portfolio 5. The difference is 7.07% as compared with 7.01% above.

[36]Looking just at the averages can be deceptive. For example, period-by-period there appears to be an inverse relation between the slope coefficients of portfolios 1 and 5; when $\hat{\beta}_p$ is greater than one for portfolio 1 it is generally less than one for portfolio 5 and *vice versa*. Also, whereas the simple averages of the $\hat{\beta}_p$ are very close, the mean absolute difference is a significant 0.25 for the 52-week benchmark periods. It seems unlikely, however, that even this magnitude of difference could explain portfolio 1 and 5 differential raw performance.

JFE—C

4.2. The Value Line record: Excess returns

The primary evidence on Value Line excess rate of return performance for the rankings portfolios is in table 3. This table contains the average cumulative 26-week excess rates of return and t-statistics for each of the five portfolios, for both benchmarks and for both benchmark periods for the entire 24-period history. Fig. 1 contains plots of cumulative performance for weeks relative to the ranking using the market model benchmark estimated over 52 and 26 weeks.[37]

The numbers in table 3 indicate statistically significant abnormal performance (using t-stat$_1$ as a guide) for the lowest ranked portfolio (portfolio 5).[38] Significance is indicated only for the market model benchmark. This reflects the greater power of this benchmark relative to the mean return benchmark.[39] Both benchmarks, however, yield similar estimates of excess rate of return performance.[40] Note also that, for all cases, the performance of the five portfolios is in almost perfect order with the Value Line rankings. This lends additional support to Value Line's claim that their rankings have discriminating ability.[41]

The plots of the average cumulation weekly excess rates of return are also interesting. We have indicated the existence of significant abnormal performance for portfolio 5. Note that it appears to be spread over the first 13 weeks (approximately) after the Value Line rankings are published. The

---

[37]Similar plots using the mean return benchmark are much noisier and the portfolio ACR's, although separated, indicate considerable contemporaneous positive correlation.

[38]The statistic, t-stat$_2$, incorporates the lag 1 to 6 estimated auto-correlation coefficients in the estimated variance as outlined in section 3.2. This statistic corroborates the existence of predominantly negative serial correlation in the cumulative excess returns. t-stat$_2$ is not reported for the mean return benchmarks. Note from the equation in section 3.2. that the estimated variance has the potential to be negative. This could be caused, for example, by measurement error. This occurred in mean return benchmark cases even though all the auto-correlation coefficients were insignificant.

[39]The Brown–Warner (1980) simulations indicate similar power for the mean return and market model benchmarks, but they were dealing with individual securities. We are dealing with portfolios of (on average) a minimum of 91 securities. Thus it's reasonable to expect that measurement error problems that could potentially negate a market model advantage would be less.

[40]Similar in the sense that the differences between portfolios 1 and 5 were quite close. For example, the difference between 1 and 5 for the market model benchmark (52 weeks) is 4.49% and for the mean return benchmark 4.88%. The abnormal performance for the mean return benchmark appears more symmetric, however, using the mean return benchmark on the market index itself indicates positive performance. This calculation was only made for the non-log runs where, for example, for the 52 week benchmarks the market index indicated a positive average cumulative 26 week excess rate of return of 0.0185. For this same run, portfolios 1 and 5 (using the mean return benchmark) indicated 0.0359 and −0.0105 respectively. Crudely adjusting the yields for the market index performance gives 0.0174 and −0.029 for portfolios 1 and 5.

[41]The probability of drawing numbered events 1 through 5 in exact sequence is only 0.83% in a random sample.

T.E. Copeland and D. Mayers, A study of value line performance

Table 3

Excess rate of return performance for five Value Line rankings portfolios for 24 ranking dates from November 26, 1965 to February 3, 1978; market model and mean return benchmarks (52- and 26-week benchmark periods).[a]

Benchmark and estimation period		Portfolio number				
		1	2	3	4	5
Market model 52 weeks	ACR	0.0152	0.0112	−0.0021	−0.0107	−0.0297
	AR	0.0006	0.0004	−0.0001	−0.0004	−0.0011
	t-stat$_1$	1.3342	1.3440	−0.2588	−1.1875	−2.7372[b]
	t-stat$_2$	3.6571	3.2011	−0.3269	−1.6327	−4.1210
Market model 26 weeks	ACR	0.0033	0.0035	−0.0057	−0.0112	−0.0305
	AR	0.0001	0.0001	−0.0002	−0.0004	−0.0012
	t-stat$_1$	0.2545	0.3801	−0.5935	−1.0074	−2.1258[b]
	t-stat$_2$	1.0106	0.5161	−0.7320	−1.4633	−2.7384
Mean return 52 weeks	ACR	0.0238	0.0123	−0.0046	−0.0105	−0.0250
	AR	0.0009	0.0005	−0.0002	−0.0004	−0.0010
	t-stat$_1$	0.5604	0.2964	−0.1171	−0.2547	−0.5387
Mean return 26 weeks	ACR	0.0217	0.0128	−0.0011	−0.0073	−0.0237
	AR	0.0008	0.0005	−0.0000	−0.0003	−0.0009
	t-stat$_1$	0.4327	0.2802	−0.0242	−0.1558	−0.4376

[a]Portfolio numbers correspond to the Value Line rankings of the securities in the portfolios. ACR is the average cumulative 26-week test period excess rate of return, AR the average weekly excess rate of return, t-stat$_1$ the t-statistic under the null hypothesis that $ACR=0$, and t-stat$_2$ incorporates the lag 1 to 6 estimated auto-correlation coefficients in the estimated variance as outlined in section 3.2. Degrees of freedom for t-stat$_1$ are 23. Thus, any t-stat$_1$ greater than 2.069 is significant at the 0.05 level.
[b]Significant at the 0.05 level or better.

portfolio appears fully adjusted by then with no further significant drift.[42] Table 4 contains weekly performance measures and t-statistics based on the market model benchmark estimated over 52 weeks.[43] The t-statistics support these findings, especially for portfolio 5, where there is a preponderance of large negative t-statistics in the first 13 weeks immediately following the Value Line announcements.[44]

[42]Note also that either panel A of fig. 1 (52 weeks) or panel B (26 weeks) appears consistent with benchmarks that are essentially unbiased. The earlier leveling off for portfolios 1 and 2 in panel B is consistent with benchmark bias caused by Value Line predictive ability beyond the test period or by some non-stationarity for these portfolios. It's difficult to conceive why (based on their published methodology) Value Line predictive ability should be asymmetric. I.e., we don't observe the same behavior for portfolio 5 between the two benchmark periods. In section 6 we present suggestive evidence on the non-stationarity hypothesis.
[43]Similar tables using the mean return benchmark show a general lack of significance. The results using the market model benchmark estimated over 26 weeks are similar to those presented in table 4. In addition, the non-log calculations were all very similar to the log calculations, both for the mean return and market model benchmarks.
[44]Evidence for the two 12-period subhistories (with recommendation dates November 1965 to February 1972 and August 1972 to May 1978) is qualitatively the same as for the overall history. The evidence from the subhistories is of course noisier and thus more difficult to

Panel A: Market Model 52 Week Benchmarks

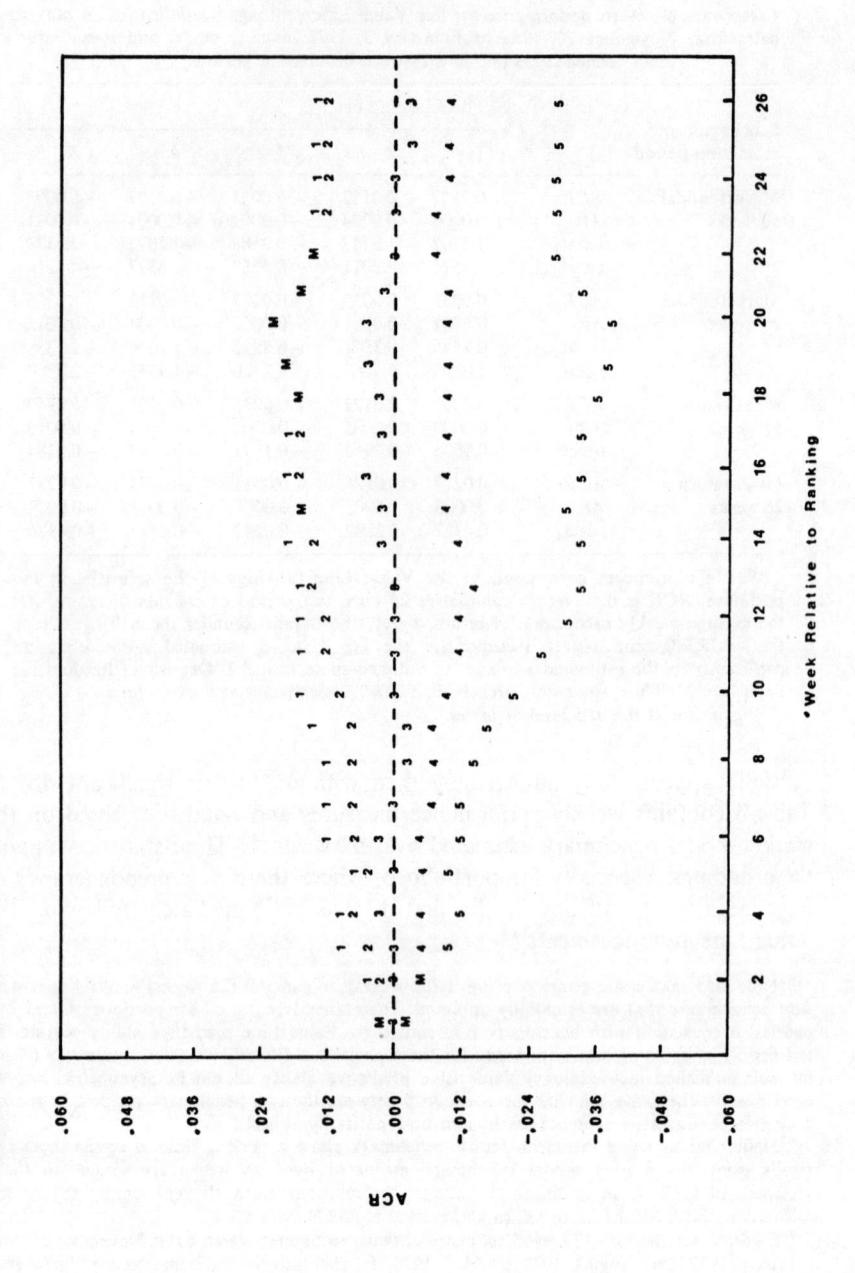

Panel B: Market Model 26 Week Benchmarks

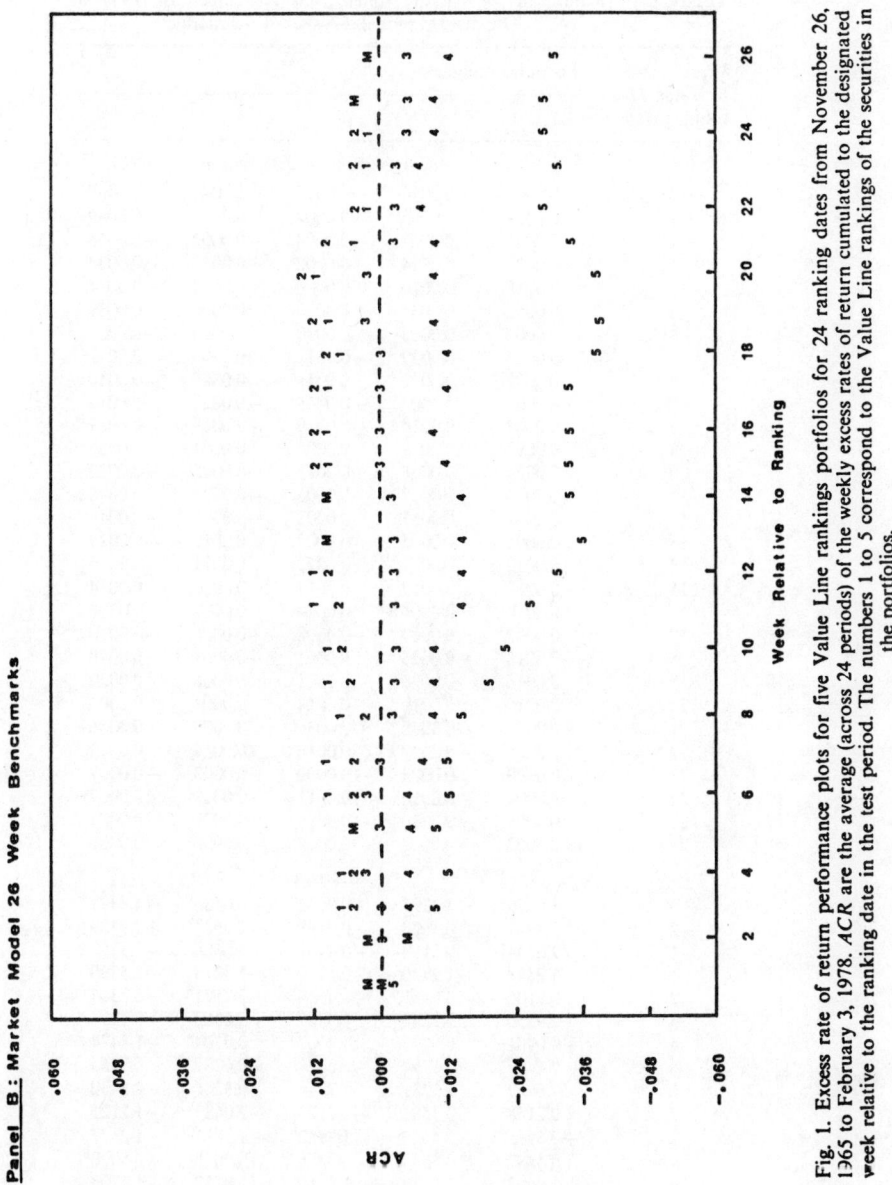

Fig. 1. Excess rate of return performance plots for five Value Line rankings portfolios for 24 ranking dates from November 26, 1965 to February 3, 1978. *ACR* are the average (across 24 periods) of the weekly excess rates of return cumulated to the designated week relative to the ranking date in the test period. The numbers 1 to 5 correspond to the Value Line rankings of the securities in the portfolios.

Table 4

Average weekly Value Line portfolio excess returns and t-statistics for weekly performance for 24 ranking dates from November 26, 1965 to February 3, 1978; market model, 52-week benchmarks.[a]

Week relative to Value Line ranking date	Portfolio numbers				
	1	2	3	4	5

Average weekly excess returns

−3	0.0060	0.0014	−0.0012	−0.0043	−0.0068
−2	0.0039	0.0005	−0.0007	−0.0029	−0.0049
−1	0.0031	0.0007	−0.0004	−0.0002	−0.0018
1	0.0023	0.0014	0.0002	−0.0013	−0.0032
2	0.0018	0.0010	−0.0006	−0.0024	−0.0014
3	0.0052	0.0034	0.0010	−0.0006	−0.0039
4	0.0002	0.0005	0.0010	0.0003	−0.0026
5	−0.0013	−0.0012	−0.0012	−0.0009	0.0012
6	0.0032	0.0016	0.0016	0.0007	−0.0010
7	0.0008	0.0007	−0.0018	−0.0020	−0.0014
8	−0.0005	−0.0014	−0.0019	−0.0019	−0.0019
9	0.0023	0.0011	0.0004	0.0001	−0.0036
10	0.0024	0.0028	0.0011	−0.0015	−0.0032
11	0.0013	0.0018	−0.0005	−0.0028	−0.0048
12	0.0001	0.0011	−0.0005	−0.0004	−0.0048
13	−0.0005	0.0005	0.0007	−0.0010	−0.0029
14	0.0010	0.0017	0.0022	0.0011	0.0005
15	−0.0012	0.0017	0.0017	0.0022	0.0014
16	0.0010	0.0004	0.0004	0.0012	−0.0010
17	0.0002	0.0001	−0.0008	−0.0006	−0.0010
18	−0.0016	−0.0005	0.0001	−0.0001	−0.0028
19	0.0016	0.0020	0.0011	0.0008	−0.0020
20	0.0010	0.0019	0.0014	0.0001	0.0003
21	−0.0052	−0.0048	−0.0036	0.0004	0.0056
22	−0.0024	−0.0027	−0.0016	0.0017	0.0037
23	0.0009	−0.0003	−0.0002	−0.0003	−0.0007
24	−0.0001	−0.0010	−0.0011	−0.0019	0.0009
25	0.0009	−0.0006	−0.0016	−0.0009	−0.0004
26	−0.0002	−0.0002	0.0004	−0.0008	−0.0006

t-statistics

−3	3.8270[b]	1.3227	−0.9232	−4.0886[b]	−4.6391[b]
−2	2.4267[b]	0.5628	−0.9149	−2.9684[b]	−2.9339[b]
−1	2.0144[b]	0.5180	−0.4181	−0.0686	−1.3362
1	1.2238	1.2230	0.1110	−1.3215	−1.5880
2	0.9105	0.9451	−0.4654	−2.3171[b]	−0.7304
3	2.9256[b]	2.7862[b]	0.9867	−0.0863	−2.4236[b]
4	−0.0901	0.1297	1.2007	0.0204	−1.8474
5	−0.4165	−1.1794	−0.8824	−0.6277	0.7953
6	1.6052	1.3281	1.7864	0.8246	−0.5432
7	0.2148	0.3581	−1.7123	−2.0683[b]	−1.2125
8	−0.5973	−1.4470	−1.9982[b]	−1.7831	−1.2877
9	0.5882	0.4683	−0.0386	0.0048	−2.5000[b]
10	1.0693	1.8620	1.3110	−1.0137	−1.4703
11	1.0419	1.4472	−0.4461	−2.4008[b]	−3.3827[b]
12	−0.4245	0.7693	−0.7145	−0.1416	−3.0623[b]
13	−0.2723	0.5056	0.5436	−1.0022	−2.1761[b]

Table 4 (continued)

Week relative to Value Line ranking date	Portfolio numbers				
	1	2	3	4	5
14	0.6545	1.3443	2.3425[b]	1.1713	0.7419
15	−0.2400	1.5287	1.3496	1.7215	1.1350
16	0.2388	0.4002	0.4054	0.9359	−0.6006
17	−0.3768	0.0367	−1.1073	−0.4076	−0.7213
18	−1.3153	−0.5281	−0.1799	0.1970	−1.6130
19	0.8070	1.6530	0.9033	1.0225	−1.0647
20	1.4765	1.2939	1.0097	0.0777	0.2059
21	−2.7254[b]	−3.6131[b]	−3.0509[b]	0.1131	2.7761[b]
22	−1.5061	−2.4499[b]	−1.6782	0.8953	2.0761[b]
23	0.2057	−0.5000	0.0822	−0.3366	0.0516
24	−0.1383	−0.6885	−0.9936	−1.5899	0.6366
25	0.6051	−0.4500	−1.4759	−0.9871	−0.3421
26	0.1267	−0.1226	0.7258	−0.6097	−0.8828

[a]Portfolio numbers correspond to the Value Line rankings of the securities in the portfolios. The average excess returns are averages (across the 24 periods) of the designated weekly excess rates of return. The t-statistics are based on the average standardized portfolio returns for weeks relative to the rankings. The degrees of freedom are $24 \times (T-2)$ or 1,200 where $T=52$. Thus the critical value for the t-statistics is 1.96 at the 0.05 level.

[b]Significant at the 0.05 level.

We believe, because of the greater apparent estimation precision as indicated by t-stat$_1$, that our best quantitative estimates of abnormal performance are based on the market model benchmark. For this reason we omit the mean return benchmark results from further discussion. Over the twelve-year history portfolio 1 earned an abnormal (but insignificant) six-month rate of return of 1.52% and portfolio 5 earned a significant −2.97% based on the 52-week benchmark. For the 26-week benchmark the numbers are 0.33% and −3.05% for portfolios 1 and 5, respectively. Portfolio 5 abnormal performance appears to persist throughout the first 13 weeks

---

interpret. Large t-statistics (in table 4) for portfolios 1, 4 and 5 in weeks −3 and −2 reflect the relative price movement criterion used by Value Line in their selection process. Weeks 21 and 22 are more peculiar; i.e., the signs are in the opposite direction predicted by the rankings and the t-statistics are large. This phenomenon is explained by recent research on the turn-of-the-year effect. See, for example, Keim (1981), Reinganum (1982), or Roll (1982). Roll has discovered a negative relationship between the turn-of-the-year return and the returns over the preceding 12 months for New York and American Stock Exchange listed securities. The turn-of-the-year includes the last trading day of December and the first four trading days of January. Half of our 24 test periods contain the turn-of-the-year. In 6 test periods the turn-of-the-year occurs during weeks 21 and 22. The other turn-of-the-year weeks were 5 and 6 (one test period), 7 and 8 (one test period), 8 and 9 (three test periods) and 14 and 15 (one test period).

following Value Line announcements. Thus there seems to have been some ability to select stocks which were subsequently underperformers.

5. Inferences: Change portfolios

The change portfolios are interesting because they represent Value Line's new information and because the larger number of test periods offers more precise performance estimation. The larger number of observations allows us to investigate the chronological performance of Value Line's recommendations. Unfortunately, the change portfolios do not allow us to focus on those securities Value Line ranks highest and lowest.[45]

Table 5 contains excess rate of return performance for the up and down portfolios and for a combined strategy of buying the up portfolio and selling the down portfolio short. Thus the combined portfolio demonstrates the average performance of both portfolios. Performance is estimated for all 48 periods and for three chronological subhistories of 16 periods each.[46] The ACR's are 13-week excess rates of return computed using both the 52- and 26-week benchmark periods.[47] Fig 2 presents plots of cumulative performance (all 48 periods) for both benchmark periods that start at week -3 and go to week 13. We start the plots at -3 to demonstrate the prior-to-recommendation ACR behavior.

Looking at table 5 and the two plots, the down portfolio exhibits very similar behavior for the over-all history using either benchmark period. The behavior is similar to that of portfolio 5; the ACR's continue to fall across the 13 weeks subsequent to the ranking date. The ACR's for the down portfolio are statistically significant for all 48 periods and the first two subhistories using the 52-week benchmarks. The 26-week benchmark periods indicate significance only for the over-all history.[48] The down portfolio ACR's

---

[45]The up portfolio contains securities moved up in ranking by Value Line. Thus these securities rank 1 through 4. Similarly the down portfolio securities rank 2 through 5. Assuming the changes are drawn independently each period from the Value Line universe and the up or down probabilities are the same for all stocks, the expected up and down portfolio weights by ranking would be approximately:

Rank	1	2	3	4	5
Up	0.23	0.46	0.23	0.08	
Down		0.08	0.23	0.46	0.23

[46]The three subhistories were based on the following inclusive recommendation dates: November 26, 1965 to February 6, 1970; May 8, 1970 to May 10, 1974; and August 9, 1974 to May 5, 1978.

[47]The non-overlapping test periods are 13 weeks long in this part of the experiment. Moreover, the evidence from section 5 indicates 13 weeks can be sufficient to adequately measure Value Line performance.

[48]The lack of power in the subhistories should be noted. Also note that t-stat$_2$ is reported for all 48 periods performance. The deviations between t-stat$_2$ and t-stat$_1$ are consistent with some negative dependence in our experimental design.

Table 5

Excess rate of return performance for Value Line change portfolios; market model, 52- and 26-week benchmarks.[a]

	52-week benchmarks			26-week benchmarks		
	Change portfolio designation			Change portfolio designation		
	up	down	combined	up	down	combined
All 48 periods (Value Line ranking dates: November 26, 1965 to May 5, 1978)						
ACR	0.0115	−0.0161	0.0138	0.0077	−0.0142	0.0110
t-stat$_1$	2.2417[b]	−4.2661[b]	5.9155[b]	1.2376	−2.7136[b]	3.8786[b]
t-stat$_2$	2.8403	−6.0704	7.3671	3.0858	−3.0226	63.3445
First 16 periods (Value Line ranking dates: November 26, 1965 to February 6, 1970)						
ACR	0.0079	−0.0167	0.0123	0.0132	−0.0140	0.0136
t-stat$_1$	0.8482	−2.3865[b]	2.5599[b]	0.2929	−1.4546	2.5580[b]
Second 16 periods (Value Line ranking dates: May 8, 1970 to May 10, 1974)						
ACR	0.0143	−0.0199	0.0171	0.0032	−0.0179	0.0105
t-stat$_1$	1.4272	−3.0047[b]	4.1531[b]	0.2605	−1.9209	2.0734
Third 16 periods (Value Line ranking dates: August 9, 1974 to May 5, 1978)						
ACR	0.0124	−0.0118	0.0121	0.0067	−0.0108	0.0088
t-stat$_1$	1.6009	−1.8804	3.7789[b]	0.6567	−1.2284	1.9469

[a]ACR is the average cumulative 13-week test period excess rate of return, t-stat$_1$ the t-statistic under the null hypothesis that $ACR=0$, and t-stat$_2$ incorporates the lag 1 to 6 estimated auto-correlation coefficients in the estimated variance as outlined in section 3.2. Degrees of freedom for t-stat$_1$ are 47 (48 periods) and 15 (16 periods). Thus critical values for t-stat$_1$ are 1.96 and 2.131 (for 48 and 16 periods, respectively) at the 0.05 level.

[b]Significant at the 0.05 level or better.

are only slightly smaller using the 26-week benchmark periods. Thus the down portfolio evidence is also similar to the portfolio 5 evidence in that it is reasonably robust with respect to choice of benchmark period.

The up portfolio, however, does not appear to be as robust. For the over-all history, the 52-week benchmark periods yield approximately 50% higher excess returns than do the 26-week periods. Moreover, up portfolio performance is significant only with the 52-week benchmarks and only for the over-all history. Thus the up portfolio evidence is similar to portfolio 1 evidence; cumulative performance is less when the benchmark period is restricted to be closer to the test period.[49]

Table 6 contains weekly average excess returns and weekly performance t-statistics for both benchmark periods using all 48 test periods. Of importance is that, for both benchmark periods, weeks 1 and 2 for the combined

---

[49]Thus the comment of footnote 42 applies here as well. In the next section we attempt to rationalize a choice between the 52- and 26-week benchmark periods.

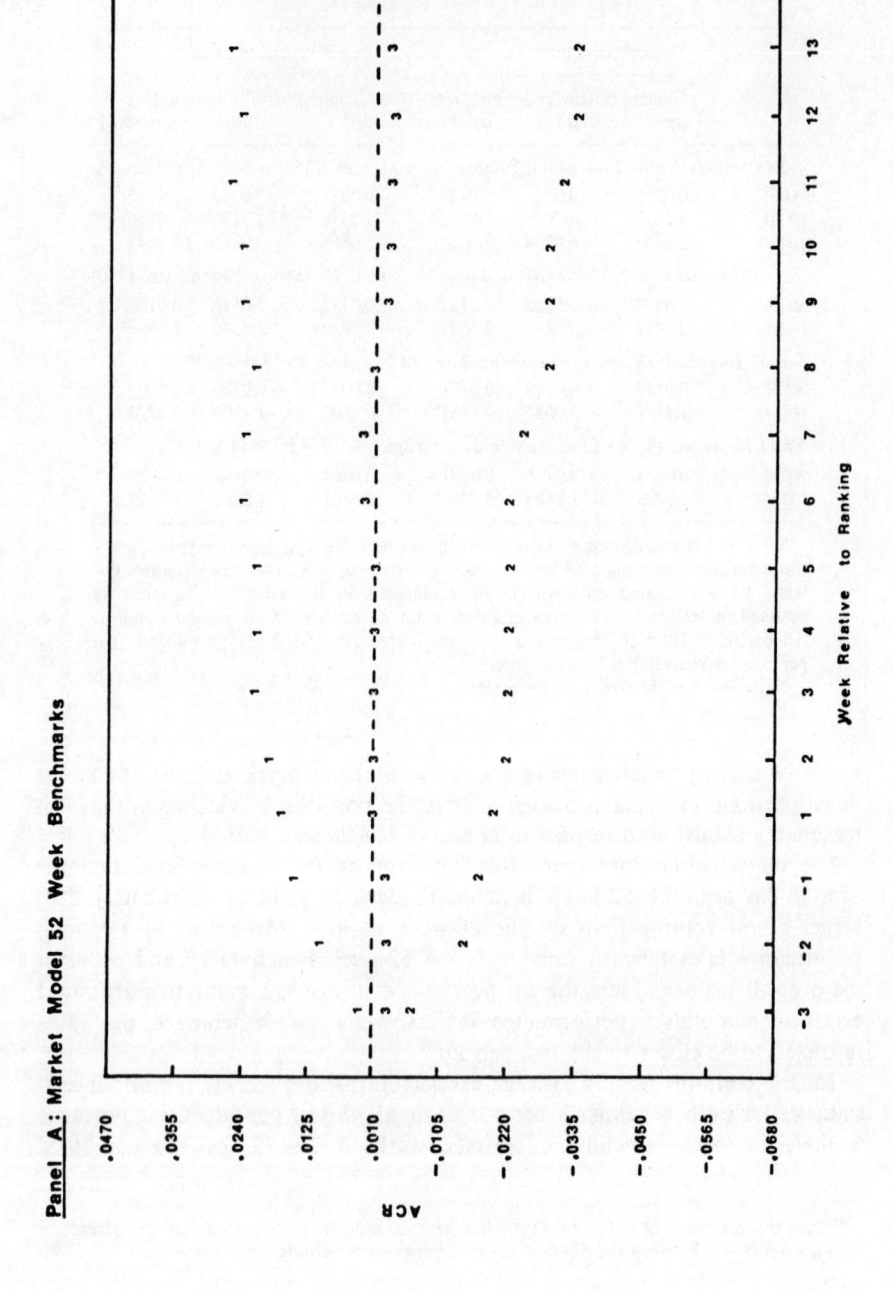

Panel A: Market Model 52 Week Benchmarks

Panel B: Market Model 26 Week Benchmarks

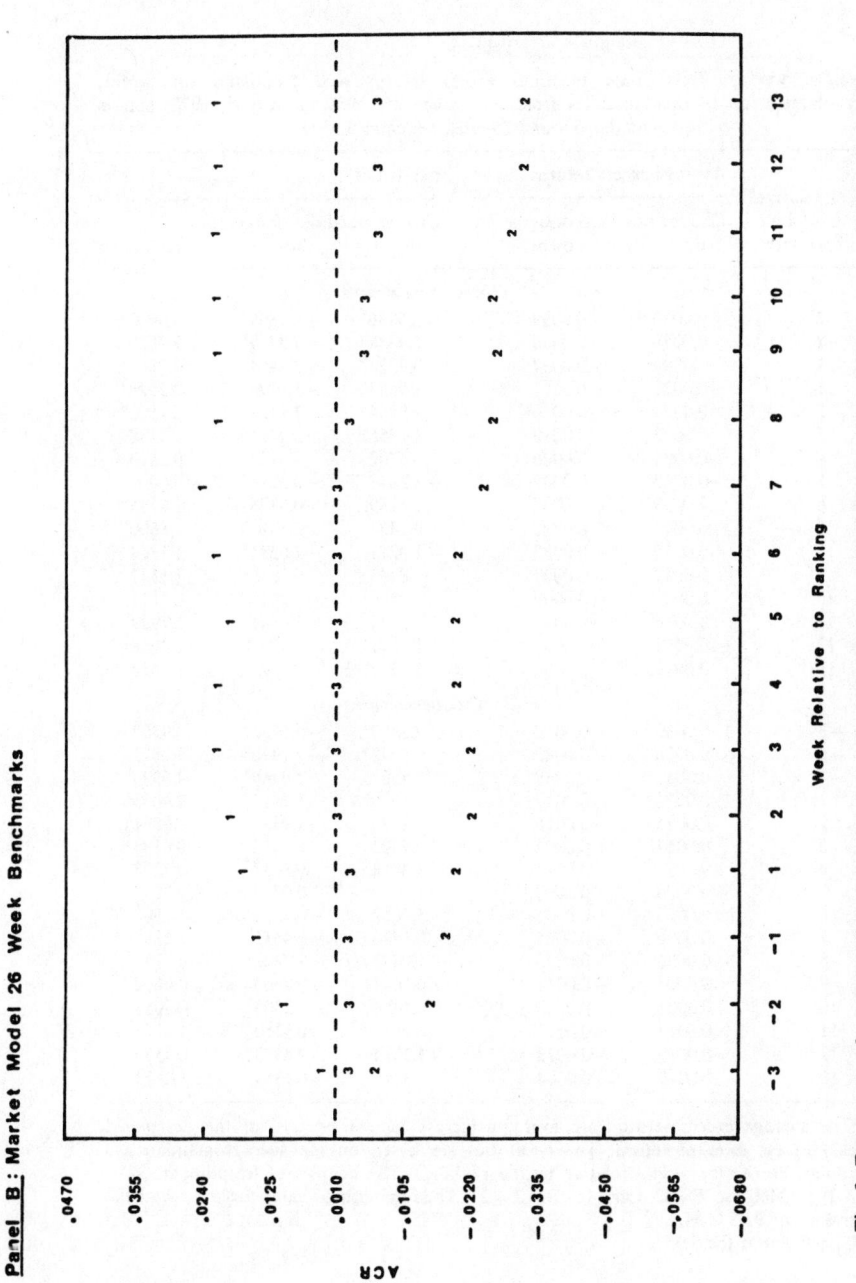

Fig. 2. Excess rate of return performance plots for Value Line change portfolios for 48 ranking dates from November 26, 1965 to May 5, 1978. The numbers 1, 2 and 3 designate the up, down and no change portfolios, respectively. The no change portfolio consists of all securities in the change file which had no rating change on a given ranking date. On average it has 1,190 securities. ACR are the average (across 48 periods) of the weekly excess rates of return cumulated from week −3 to the designated week relative to the ranking date.

Table 6
Average weekly Value Line portfolio excess returns and t-statistics for weekly performance for 48 ranking dates from November 26, 1965 to May 5, 1978; market model, 52- and 26-week benchmarks.[a]

Week relative to Value Line ranking date	Average excess returns — Change portfolio designation up	Average excess returns — Change portfolio designation down	t-statistics — Change portfolio designation up	t-statistics — Change portfolio designation down	combined
			52-week benchmarks		
−3	0.0030	−0.0059	2.5836[b]	−4.5809[b]	5.0660[b]
−2	0.0076	−0.0083	6.4338[b]	−7.3717[b]	9.7620[b]
−1	0.0044	−0.0037	3.7225[b]	−3.0464[b]	4.7864[b]
1	0.0021	−0.0017	1.9553	−1.2306	2.2528[b]
2	0.0025	−0.0016	1.9254	−1.1151	2.1500[b]
3	0.0022	−0.0010	1.1755	−0.5411	1.2138
4	0.0008	0.0006	0.9702	0.5725	0.2813
5	−0.0019	−0.0002	−1.1843	−0.3275	−0.6059
6	0.0029	−0.0007	1.8289	−0.5378	1.6735
7	0.0008	−0.0025	0.1491	−2.4813[b]	1.8600
8	−0.0015	−0.0032	−1.0211	−2.6281[b]	1.1364
9	0.0012	−0.0009	0.8443	−0.7879	1.1542
10	0.0003	−0.0000	0.2289	−0.2195	0.3171
11	0.0016	−0.0013	1.3705	−1.1641	1.7922
12	−0.0014	−0.0033	−1.1691	−3.0201[b]	1.3088
13	0.0019	−0.0004	1.3262	−0.2893	1.1423
			26-week benchmarks		
−3	0.0030	−0.0059	2.3892[b]	−4.5952[b]	4.9387[b]
−2	0.0076	−0.0082	6.5992[b]	−7.1996[b]	9.7572[b]
−1	0.0041	−0.0039	3.4589[b]	−3.0386[b]	4.5944[b]
1	0.0021	−0.0017	2.1576[b]	−1.2415	2.4035[b]
2	0.0025	−0.0015	1.8770	−1.9360	1.9894[b]
3	0.0017	−0.0004	0.9203	−0.0452	0.6188
4	0.0010	0.0011	1.3418	0.8753	0.3298
5	−0.0020	0.0002	−1.2090	−0.0712	−0.8045
6	0.0026	−0.0004	1.3662	−0.2612	1.1507
7	0.0006	−0.0025	−0.1426	−2.4615[b]	1.6397
8	−0.0026	−0.0033	−1.9043	−2.7232[b]	−0.5791
9	0.0004	−0.0011	0.1044	−0.8363	0.6652
10	0.0001	0.0002	0.1484	−0.2803	0.3031
11	0.0013	−0.0012	0.9893	−0.8860	1.3261
12	−0.0017	−0.0033	−1.3834	−2.4483[b]	0.7530
13	0.0017	−0.0004	1.3385	−0.1355	1.0423

[a] The average excess returns are averages (across the 48 periods) of the designated weekly excess rates of return. The t-statistics are based on the average standardized portfolio returns for weeks relative to the rankings. The degrees of freedom are 48 × $(T-2)$ or 2400 for $T=52$ and 1152 for $T=26$. Thus the critical value for the t-statistics is 1.96 at the 0.05 level.

[b] Significant at the 0.05 level.

portfolio indicate significant performance.[50] Significant performance immediately following the Value Line recommendations is strong evidence supporting the abnormal performance hypothesis.

Thus, we are left, as at the end of section 4, with a two-part puzzle. One part has to do with Value Line's apparent superior forecasting ability based on presumably publicly available information. The other has to do with the lag in the market's adjustment to Value Line recommendations; the table 6 t-statistics for weeks 1 and 2 are relatively large for the up and the combined portfolios.

6. The non-stationarity problem

Non-stationarity of the mean of the return generating process can yield anomalous results. In this section we discuss the non-stationarity problem in two parts. In the first, we present some suggestive evidence on non-stationarity relating to the benchmark period choices. The evidence is consistent with the 26-week benchmarks being a better choice. Based on this observation, we offer additional interpretation of the Value Line change portfolio evidence. In the second part we discuss some attempts to identify specific sources of non-stationarity that could explain our portfolio 5 results.

6.1. Benchmark period choice, non-stationarity and a conjecture

When benchmarks are estimated closer to the test period (26-week benchmark) rather than farther (52-week benchmark), estimated abnormal performance declines for portfolios 1 and 2 and remains unchanged for portfolios 4 and 5.[51] This behavior is consistent with the hypothesis that the benchmark returns for portfolios 1 and 2 are too large because Value Line predictive ability extends into the benchmark periods for these portfolios. It is also consistent with the proposition that the benchmark returns are too low when estimated over 52 weeks because of non-stationarities in the underlying generating processes.

It is difficult to understand why Value Line's predictive ability should be more farsighted for securities in portfolio 1 than in portfolio 5, especially when the value of their predictive ability appears far superior for portfolio 5. Yet portfolio 5 performance appears essentially unchanged as we vary the length of the benchmark period. Thus the portfolio 5 evidence appears

[50]Weeks 7 and 8, also significant for the down portfolio, are likely to be contaminated by the turn-of-the-year effect discussed in footnote 44. The turn-of-the-year weeks for the change portfolios were 8 and 9 (seven test periods), 7 and 8 (three test periods), 5 and 6 (one test period) and 1 and 2 (one test period). Week minus one, which is supposed to follow Value Line's analysis, also indicates significant performance. See footnote 15 for a discussion of the timing of Value Line activities.

[51]The results for the up and down portfolios were similar.

consistent with the stationarity assumption and the assumption that the benchmark period is unbiased by Value Line predictive ability.

Table 7 contains average estimated slope coefficients from the market model for portfolios 1 and 5 estimated over different intervals relative to the ranking dates. These average estimated slope coefficients exhibit different behavior for portfolios 1 and 5. The mean estimate for portfolio 5 is close to 1.0 for all estimation intervals, i.e., consistent with stationarity. The mean for portfolio 1 on the other hand is significantly different during the test period (1 to 26) than during the 52-week benchmark period (27 to 78).[52] The mean difference between the test period and the 26-week benchmark period (27 to 52) is not significant. Thus there is evidence of non-stationarity in the portfolio 1 return generating process.[53] The identified non-stationarity appears smaller with the 26-week benchmark periods. Moreover, although the evidence is subtle, the ACR plots of fig. 2 appear consistent with biased 52-week benchmarks and unbiased 26-week benchmarks. For example, from about week 3, the ACR (up portfolio) using the 52-week benchmark periods appears to rise linearly for the remaining 10 weeks. It appears to be flat for the remaining 10 weeks in the 26-week case. The subhistories exhibit similar behavior. A linearly rising ACR is consistent with a non-stationarity problem where the return generating process is stationary through the test period. The table 7 evidence is consistent with the return generating process being stationary through the 26-week benchmark period. Additionally, if the

Table 7

Average market model slope coefficients for Value Line rankings portfolios 1 and 5 estimated over different intervals.[a]

Estimation interval (weeks relative to Value Line ranking dates)	Portfolio 1 $\bar{\beta}$	Portfolio 5 $\bar{\beta}$
−55 to −4	1.0564	0.9808
−29 to −4	1.0762	0.9782
1 to 26	1.0764	0.9853
27 to 52	1.0426	1.0032
27 to 78	1.0209	1.0039

[a]The average estimated market model slope coefficients, $\bar{\beta}$, are the arithmetic average of the estimates obtained during the designated weeks relative to the 24 Value Line ranking dates.

---

[52]The t-statistic calculated on the average difference is 2.10, significant at the 0.05 level with 23 degrees of freedom.

[53]The same experiment on the up and down portfolios gave the same results; the down portfolio slope coefficients were consistent with stationarity while the up portfolio evidenced significant non-stationarity between the test and 52-week benchmark periods.

problem was caused by Value Line's forecasting ability, the ACR's should rise at a decreasing rate across the test period for both benchmark periods.[54] For these reasons we conclude that the 26-week benchmark periods are best in the sense of being unbiased.

In the last section the Value Line puzzle was divided into two parts; the second part concerning the lag in the market's adjustment to Value Line recommendations. One potential rationalization for this part of the puzzle lies in the 26-week benchmark subhistory evidence. There is pre-selection bias in our study. Value Line is a surviving advisory service and presumably has survived because of the value of its services. The opening period of our study coincides closely with the beginning of Value Line's current system.[55] Thus the market's adjustment to Value Line recommendations could have been unbiased vis-à-vis the usual value of information contained in recommendations made by similar services. Investors, of course, had to conduct their own performance evaluation just as we have done. The ratio of noise in the data to excess rate of return performance is high. Consequently investors required a lengthy history for evaluation purposes. That is, the market was unable to instantaneously assess the value of the information. The 26-week benchmark subhistory evidence is consistent with this conjecture.

Looking at the combined portfolio ACR (table 5, 26-week benchmark), we see that excess rate of return performance is less with each succeeding subhistory. There is also evidence that the mass of the performance occurs earlier in the more recent subhistories. Table 8 contains average excess returns and weekly performance t-statistics for the three subhistories. Note that week 1 and 2 performance for the combined portfolio is significant in only the third subhistory.[56] This evidence appears strongly consistent with the above conjecture and thus with the abnormal performance hypothesis.[57]

Although pre-selection bias may help explain the second part of the puzzle, it would appear to offer less help with the first part. That is if Value Line

---

[54]As mentioned in section 3, our intuition suggests that Value Line's forecasting ability should be a declining function of the horizon length. This intuition is consistent with the evidence presented in Brown and Rozeff (1978) where Value Line's earnings forecasts are compared with those of alternative models such as Box and Jenkins.

[55]Black (1971) states the current system began in April, 1965. The first period of our study commences with the November 26, 1965 performance rankings.

[56]The ACR's from week −3 to 13 (combined) are of similar magnitude for each subhistory: 0.0249, 0.0312 and 0.0260, respectively. Thus there is more adjustment prior to week 1 with each succeeding subhistory. Additionally for the third subhistory the week 2 ACR (combined) is 0.0067. Thus in the third subhistory, over 75% of the excess rate of return performance occurs in the first two weeks.

[57]Evidence from the two 12-period subhistories of the rankings portfolios (see footnote 44 for the dates) is also consistent with the conjecture. Portfolio 5 performance was significant only for the first 12-period subhistory with $ACR = -0.0450$ and $t\text{-stat}_1 = -2.22$. For the second subhistory the $ACR = -0.0161$ and $t\text{-stat}_1 = -0.7894$. Portfolio 1 was not significant for either subhistory.

Table 8
Average weekly Value Line change portfolio excess returns and t-statistics for three 16-period subhistories; market model, 26-week benchmarks.[a]

Week relative to Value Line ranking date	Average excess returns Change portfolio designation up	down	t-statistics Change portfolio designation up	down	combined
First 16 periods (Value Line ranking dates: November 26, 1965 to February 6, 1970)					
−3	0.0024	−0.0056	1.0511	−2.1782[b]	2.2834[b]
−2	0.0008	−0.0029	0.6982	−1.5571	1.5947
−1	0.0058	−0.0052	2.4639[b]	−2.1606[b]	3.2700[b]
1	0.0011	−0.0027	0.6753	−0.6661	0.9485
2	0.0039	−0.0014	1.5673	−0.6996	1.6029
3	0.0033	−0.0008	1.2242	−0.3839	1.1371
4	−0.0008	−0.0004	0.0434	−0.3530	0.2803
5	−0.0021	0.0022	−0.9187	0.6612	−1.1172
6	0.0029	−0.0016	0.9478	−0.8044	1.2390
7	0.0016	−0.0042	0.1907	−2.2143[b]	1.7007
8	−0.0020	−0.0035	−0.6397	−1.4548	0.5764
9	−0.0001	−0.0027	−0.1292	−0.9620	0.5889
10	0.0022	0.0034	0.6482	0.7921	−0.1017
11	0.0031	−0.0007	0.6194	−0.2113	0.5874
12	−0.0055	−0.0002	−1.7303	0.3754	−1.4890
13	0.0055	−0.0015	2.2579[b]	−0.6395	2.0488[b]
Second 16 periods (Value Line ranking dates: May 8, 1970 to May 10, 1974)					
−3	0.0056	−0.0083	2.1750[b]	−3.7692[b]	4.2032[b]
−2	0.0117	−0.0104	4.7880[b]	−4.8441[b]	6.8109[b]
−1	0.0012	−0.0040	0.4444	−1.9774[b]	1.7125
1	0.0023	0.0006	1.1496	0.3945	0.5339
2	0.0015	0.0022	0.6343	1.0877	−0.3206
3	0.0035	−0.0031	1.3868	−1.2417	1.8586
4	−0.0007	−0.0001	−0.1760	−0.1282	−0.0338
5	−0.0032	−0.0013	−1.4389	−0.7502	−0.4860
6	0.0040	−0.0007	1.6294	−0.5768	1.5600
7	0.0012	−0.0000	0.2625	−0.3733	0.4496
8	−0.0050	−0.0041	−2.3047[b]	−1.9688[b]	−0.2375
9	0.0012	0.0005	0.4678	0.2534	0.1516
10	0.0001	−0.0032	0.1271	−1.4937	1.1461
11	−0.0001	−0.0032	0.0158	−1.2529	0.8971
12	0.0015	−0.0051	−0.0471	−2.3745[b]	1.6457
13	−0.0030	−0.0005	−1.2530	−0.2267	−0.7257
Third 16 periods (Value Line ranking dates: August 9, 1974 to May 5, 1978)					
−3	0.0011	−0.0039	0.9121	−2.0118[b]	2.0675[b]
−2	0.0103	−0.0112	5.9439[b]	−6.0689[b]	8.4944[b]
−1	0.0054	−0.0025	3.0828[b]	−1.1250	2.9753[b]
1	0.0030	−0.0032	1.9122	−1.8787	2.6806[b]
2	0.0020	−0.0052	1.0495	−2.0093[b]	2.1629[b]
3	−0.0016	0.0025	−1.0170	1.7038	−1.9239
4	0.0044	0.0038	2.4567[b]	1.9973[b]	0.3248
5	−0.0008	−0.0003	0.2636	−0.0344	0.2109
6	0.0010	0.0012	−0.2108	0.9289	−0.8059
7	−0.0010	−0.0032	−0.7002	−1.6758	0.6899
8	−0.0008	−0.0022	−0.3540	−1.2932	0.6641

T.E. Copeland and D. Mayers, A study of value line performance

Table 8 (continued)

Week relative to Value Line ranking date	Average excess returns		t-statistics		
	Change portfolio designation		Change portfolio designation		
	up	down	up	down	combined
9	0.0001	−0.0011	−0.1578	−0.7400	0.4117
10	−0.0019	0.0004	−0.5183	−0.2161	−0.5193
11	0.0009	0.0002	1.0784	−0.0705	0.8124
12	−0.0012	−0.0045	−0.6187	−2.2414[b]	1.1474
13	0.0026	0.0008	1.3134	0.6314	0.4822

[a]The average excess returns are averages (across the 16 periods) of the designated weekly excess rates of return. The t-statistics are based on the average standardized portfolio returns for weeks relative to the rankings. The degrees of freedom are 16 × (T−2) or 384 for all three panels. Thus the critical value for the t-statistics is 1.96 at the 0.05 level.
[b]Significant at the 0.05 level.

were just a lucky survivor we would not expect to find the abnormal performance concentrated systematically in the early weeks after their recommendations are made. There is, of course, a positive probability of this occurring by chance as well.

6.2. Non-stationarity sources

We have focused on the potential problem of Value Line predictive ability extending into the benchmark period and believe our results are free of this bias. However, the portfolio 5 results are consistent with the absence of predictive ability by Value Line[58] if there is non-stationarity in the return generating process which is resolved by approximately week 13 (one quarter of a year). We have investigated several potential non-stationarity sources attempting to 'explain' our results. At the outset we should warn that we have no good explanation — there is no surprise.

CRSP handling of delistings. If there were some peculiarity in the way CRSP handles delistings and the frequency of delistings were different between the test and benchmark periods anomalous results could occur. We find nothing peculiar to report. The number of delistings for portfolio 5 was approximately the same during the test periods as in each of the two subsequent six-month periods. In addition the average last week return was approximately the same for the delisted firms in the three periods.[59] We did

[58]Portfolio 1 through 4 abnormal performance is not significant with the 26-week benchmarks. Hence, our main interest is in portfolio 5.
[59]The actual number delisted in the test periods (portfolio 5) was 31 (for all 24 periods). In the two succeeding 6-month periods there were 39 and 30 delistings. The average last week rates of return were −0.01, −0.03 and −0.01, respectively.

find fewer firms delisted and more firms listed for portfolio 1 than 5 during the test periods. The number of delistings during the subsequent two six-month periods were about the same for both portfolios.[60] Value Line's use of the relative strength criteria would predict more listings and fewer delistings for portfolio 1 during the test periods.

Leverage changes. If portfolio 5 firms have higher leverage during the benchmark period than during the test period the benchmarks could be too large.[61] Book value leverage is available on the Compustat tapes. We computed the average leverage for a sample of firms in portfolios 1 and 5 around the time of the rankings and one year later.[62] We found no significant difference and the actual leverage changes were in the wrong direction. Portfolio 1 firms slightly increased and portfolio 5 firms slightly decreased their leverage following the ranking dates.

Dividend policy. It is possible that significant systematic changes in dividend policy between the test and benchmark periods could also have an impact. We estimated the average portfolio dividend yields for portfolios 1 and 5 as of the end of the month of the Value Line rankings and one year later. Relatively low dividend yield stocks are assigned to portfolio 1 whereas relatively high dividend yield stocks are assigned to portfolio 5.[63] This is consistent with Value Line's stated concern for price performance.

For portfolios 1 and 5 the following regression was run, using dividend yields as of the end of the ranking month,

$$D_{ip} = a + bD_{mp} + cp + \varepsilon_{ip}, \qquad i = 1 \text{ and } 5.$$

Here, D_{ip} is the portfolio average dividend yield for period, $p = 1, \ldots, 24$, and D_{mp} is the associated market dividend yield.[64] The estimated coefficients and the 'market' dividend yield from one year later were used to predict the one year later actual dividend yield. Portfolio 1 was actually 0.44% above its predicted value (t-stat = 3.93) and portfolio 5 was 0.73% below (t-stat = -2.32).

---

[60]The portfolio 1 delisting numbers were 18, 31 and 28 for the three periods. There were eleven portfolio 1 listings during the test periods and only one portfolio 5 listing.

[61]For portfolio 1, of course, the converse could be a possibility. Also, our portfolio 5 results would imply that the leverage changes would have been essentially accomplished by week 13.

[62]For each of the 24 periods we selected those firms ranked by Value Line and listed by Compustat that had fiscal year ends within plus or minus one month of the ranking month. This procedure left 20% of the firms ranked by Value Line in the sample.

[63]Over all periods the average portfolio dividend yields were 0.0238, 0.0287, 0.0345, 0.0408 and 0.0409 for portfolios 1 through 5 computed as of the end of the month of the Value Line rankings. The average difference between portfolio 1 and 5 is significant.

[64]The market dividend yield is the equally weighted dividend yield of all the Value Line securities in our sample.

Thus we have discovered a source of potential non-stationarity in the return distributions. Assuming the evidence of Long (1978) is correct, the non-stationarity would tend to bias portfolio 1 benchmarks down and portfolio 5 benchmarks up. But this rather subtle change in dividend yield could at best account for a small fraction of the abnormal performance we detected for portfolio 5. More likely the decrease in the dividend yield of portfolio 5 results from the relatively poor earnings performance of the portfolio 5 firms. A similar test for nonstationarity in dividend yields was performed on the change portfolios and no significant non-stationarities were found. This was to be expected because the change portfolios are weighted averages of the ranking portfolios (see footnote 45) and we would expect that regression toward the mean would be less strong than for portfolios 1 and 5. Note, however, that the patterns of residuals for the ranking portfolios and the change portfolios are similar. For example, portfolio 5 and the down portfolio both show *ACR*'s which fall during the first thirteen weeks, then level off. If non-stationarities in dividend yield were causing the pattern, the pattern of residuals should differ for the change portfolios.

Thin-trading effect. It would be possible for our market model benchmark coefficients to be biased by a thin-trading effect, but we doubt this is the case. Portfolio 1 and 5 firms were indistinguishable based on the aggregate equity values of the firms in the two portfolios.[65] In addition, the mean return benchmarks do not suffer from thin trading biases and those results are quantitatively similar to the market model benchmark results.

Tender offers. If the frequency of successful tender offer expirations for shares in portfolio 5 during the test periods was greater than during the benchmark periods, some of the portfolio 5 anomaly could be explained. We know from Dann (1981), Vermaelen (1981) and Bradley (1980) that on the expiration of a successful tender offer there is a price decline of, on average, about 3%. An actual holder of shares who tenders optimally suffers no wealth loss at the tender expiration. One could probably argue that firms that have had recent stock price declines (e.g. portfolio 5 firms) would be more likely to either tender for their own shares or be takeover targets. We have no evidence to present here. But even if the argument were true it would be highly unlikely that it could explain our results. The abnormal performance is too large.

Non-stationarity sources summary. It is, of course, possible that some combination of rather subtle non-stationarities could have contributed to our

---

[65] Aggregate equity values were calculated by multiplying the price of the end of the ranking month by the most recent record of the number of shares outstanding. This data was obtained from the CRSP monthly file. Also thin-trading effects have been empirically associated with firm size. See, for example Roll (1981).

findings.[66] The fact that Value Line bases its recommendations (in part) on recent price performance points to this. Transitory changes in the underlying generating process may be signalled by price changes.

Points that go against the non-stationarity argument arise from the subhistory evidence. The fact that abnormal performance is diminished in the more recent periods is consistent with the non-stationarity argument if the environment changed or if Value Line changed their evaluation procedures during the time period of our study. It is also consistent with superior ability and the learning argument. Additionally from the subhistory evidence we noted significant weekly performance localized to the two weeks following Value Line announcements in the final subhistory. This seems more consistent with the abnormal performance hypothesis than with the non-stationarity hypothesis.

7. Conclusions

This paper demonstrates that care must be exercised when evaluating the performance of managed portfolios using data derived benchmarks. Most portfolio managers or investment advisors probably rely, to some degree, either directly on past prices or on variables that are related to past prices in formulating their portfolio composition decisions or recommendations. Thus prior benchmark periods are suspect. The alternative of a future benchmark period runs the risk of the evaluation being biased by the manager's predictive ability and limits the set of acceptable performance measures because of the potential problem of ex post selection bias.

The potential for non-stationarities is perhaps the most worrisome of the problems we encountered. This problem makes it difficult to interpret the results of performance measurement studies that use data derived benchmarks and, especially, cumulative performance measures. We attempted to search out major sources of potential non-stationarity to explain our results, but none seemed material.

Thus our paper documents the existence of abnormal performance for Value Line predictions over the period 1965–1978. We interpret the results obtained with the market model and the 26-week benchmark periods as providing the best estimates of abnormal performance. Abnormal performance was indicated in three subhistories as well and appeared smaller in the later subhistories than in the earlier ones. This indicates Value Line may not be as valuable now as it had been. More important, however, is the interpretation offered: the simultaneous lessening of performance and shifting of the remaining performance to earlier weeks relative to the ranking dates appears strongly consistent with the abnormal performance hypothesis.

---

[66]Subtle in the sense that each by itself would be statistically inconsequential.

The reader should note that the gross abnormal performance measured via the future benchmark technique appears lower than that found by Black (1971) using the Jensen methodology. Where Black reported (roughly) 20 percent per year (revising on a monthly basis between April 1965 and 1970) for an investor who was long in portfolio 1 and short in portfolio 5, we find an annual rate of return of about 6.8% (revising semiannually between 1965 and 1978) for a similar although not strictly comparable strategy. Moreover where Black's measured performance appears symmetrical, ours does not. Virtually all the abnormal performance appears in portfolio 5.

Transactions costs. The size of the abnormal performance we find does not indicate a gross market inefficiency. If one allows for a brokerage commission of one percent each way, the abnormal performance would have been insufficient for profitable operation of a pure trading rule based on Value Line recommendations.[67] Some strategies, however, could have been profitable. Consider an investor who follows a modified buy and hold policy. He assesses his portfolio at the end of every six months and sells those stocks ranked 5 and uses the proceeds to purchase rank 1 stocks. Portfolio 5 indicated an average excess rate of return of −3.05% and portfolio 1 an average excess rate of return of 0.33% (market model, 26-week benchmarks). A sale of stock just ranked 5 and simultaneous purchase of an equivalent rank 1 stock would have netted the investor an average 0.76%.[68] If Value Line costs $300 per year, the investor would have paid for his subscription with $39,474 worth of transactions in that year. An investor following this rebalancing policy would have traded approximately 5% of his securities every six months. This implies he would have broken even on his Value Line investment if his total common stock portfolio value was about $394,740.[69]

For other categories of traders the benefits of the Value Line performance rankings are difficult to assess. They obviously depend on the frequency and value of transactions. For example, an investor that would have been transacting anyway could have gained the entire 3.38% abnormal performance. The brokerage commissions and bid-ask spread costs are not

---

[67]One obvious strategy would be to sell short portfolio 5 and simultaneously buy portfolio 1. Before transactions costs the excess rate of return performance would be 3.38% (0.33+3.05%, market model, 26-week benchmarks, assuming equal dollars long and short). These portfolios turn over 70% every 6 months. Thus, assuming one percent each way, the brokerage commissions would amount to 2.8% (0.7 × 4.0%). Assuming an average NYSE bid–ask spread [at least 0.62%, see Phillips and Smith (1980)] on each round trip adds an additional 0.87% (0.7 × 2 × 0.62%) for a total 3.67%. This assumes the proceeds from the short position can be used for the long.

[68]This assumes one percent each way in brokerage commissions plus 0.62% for the bid–ask spread (see footnote 67).

[69]Value Line provides more than its rankings. Thus this is an overstatement. Many investors undoubtedly attach value to the corporate summary information provided, for example. Moreover, we are implicitly assuming the rankings are used in isolation from other data, but this assumption is usual.

marginal for his decision. Assuming he could find suitable portfolio 1 for 5 swaps (or the equivalent), he need generate only $8,876 worth of transactions in any year to pay for the service. Thus for some market participants the excess rate of return performance we report may have been economically worthwhile.

Appendix

Dates of selected Value Line rankings: 1965–1978 (*YYMMDD*); odd numbers = dates for both rankings and change portfolios; even numbers = dates for change portfolios.

1	651126	9	680322	17	700508	25	720811	33	740809	41	760806
2	660225	10	680621	18	700807	26	721110	34	741108	42	761105
3	660527	11	681108	19	701106	27	730209	35	750207	43	770204
4	660826	12	690207	20	710205	28	730511	36	750509	44	770506
5	670324	13	690509	21	710514	29	730810	37	750808	45	770805
6	670623	14	690808	22	710813	30	731109	38	751107	46	771104
7	670922	15	691107	23	711112	31	740208	39	760206	47	780203
8	671222	16	700206	24	720211	32	740510	40	760507	48	780505

References

Banz, R., 1981, The relationship between return and market value of common stocks, Journal of Financial Economics 9, March, 3–18.

Basu, S., 1977, Investment performance of common stocks in relation to their price earnings ratios: A test of market efficiency, Journal of Finance 32, June, 663–682.

Bernhard, A., 1979, Value line methods of evaluating common stocks (Arnold Bernhard, New York).

Black, F., 1971, Yes Virginia, there is hope: Test of the value line ranking system, May (Graduate School of Business, University of Chicago, Chicago, IL).

Bradley,M., 1980, Interfirm tender offers and the market for corporate control, Journal of Business 53, Oct., 345–376.

Brown, S. and M. Rozeff, 1978, The superiority of analysts forecasts as measures of expectations: Evidence from earnings, Journal of Finance 33, March, 1–16.

Brown, S. and J. Warner, 1980, Measuring security price performance, Journal of Financial Economics 8, Sept., 205–258.

Cornell, B., 1979, Asymmetric information and portfolio performance measurement, Journal of Financial Economics 4, Dec., 381–390.

Dann, L., 1981, The effects of common stock repurchase on securityholder's returns, Journal of Financial Economics 9, June, 112–138.

Eisenstadt, S., 1980, An update on the value line performance rankings, Unpublished mimeo.

Fama, E., 1970, Efficient capital markets: A Review of theory and empirical work, Journal of Finance 25, May, 383–417.

Fama, E., 1976, Foundations of finance (Basic Books, New York).

Fama, E. and J. MacBeth, 1973, Risk, return and equilibrium: Empirical tests, Journal of Political Economy 81, May/June, 607–636.

Hausman, W., 1969, A note on the value line contest: A test of the predictability of stock price changes, Journal of Business 42, July, 317–320.

Holloway, C., 1981, A note on testing an aggressive investment strategy using value line ranks, Journal of Finance 36, June 711–719.

Jensen, M., 1969, Risk, the pricing of capital assets, and the evaluation of investment portfolios, Journal of Business 42, April, 167–247.

Jensen, M. and G. Bennington, 1970, Random walks and technical theories: Some additional evidence, Journal of Finance 25, May, 469–482.

Kaplan, R.S. and R.L. Weil, 1973, Risk, and the value line contest, Financial Analysts Journal 29, July/Aug., 56–60.

Keim, D., 1981, Size related anomalies and stock return seasonality: Further empirical evidence, Working paper (Graduate School of Business, University of Chicago, Chicago, IL).

King, B., 1966, Market and industry factors in stock price behavior, Journal of Business 39, supp., Jan., 139–190.

Levy, R., 1967, Random walks: Reality or Myth, Financial Analysts Journal 23, Nov., 69–76.

Litzenberger, R. and K. Ramaswamy, 1979, The effect of personal taxes and dividends on capital assets prices: Theory and empirical evidence, Journal of Financial Economics 7, June, 163–195.

Lloyd-Davies, P. and Canes, 1978, Stock prices at the publication of second hand information, Journal of Business 51, Jan., 43–56.

Long, J., 1978, The market valuation of cash dividends: A case to consider, Journal of Financial Economics 6, June/Sept., 235–264.

Masulis, R., 1978, The effects of capital structure change on security prices, Ph. D. dissertation (Graduate School of Business, University of Chicago, Chicago, IL).

Masulis, R., 1980, The effects of capital structure change on security prices: A study of exchange offers, Journal of Financial Economics 8, June, 139–178.

Masulis, R., 1980, Stock repurchase by tender offer: An analysis of the causes of common stock price changes, Journal of Finance 35, May, 305–318.

Mayers, D. and E. Rice, 1979, Measuring portfolio performance and the empirical content of asset pricing models, Journal of Financial Economics 7, March, 3–28.

Phillips S. and C. Smith, 1980, Trading Costs for listed options: The implications for market efficiency, Journal of Financial Economics 8, June, 179–201.

Reinganum, M., 1981, Misspecification of capital asset pricing: Empirical anomalies based on earnings' yields and market value, Journal of Financial Economics 9, March, 19–46.

Reinganum, M., 1982, The anomalous stock market behavior of small firms in January: Empirical tests for year end tax effects, Working paper (Graduate School of Business, University of Southern California, Los Angeles, CA).

Roll, R., 1977, A critique of the asset pricing theory's tests, Journal of Financial Economics 4, March, 129–176.

Roll, R. 1978, Ambiguity when performance is measured by the securities market line, Journal of Finance 33, Sept., 1051–1069.

Roll, R., 1981, A possible explanation for the small firm effect, Journal of Finance 36, Sept., 879–888.

Roll, R., 1982, The turn-of-the-year effect and the return premia of small firms, Working paper (Graduate School of Management, University of California, Los Angeles, CA).

Rozeff, M. and W. Kinney, Jr., 1976, Capital market seasonality: The case of stock returns, Journal of Financial Economics 3, Oct., 379–402.

Sharpe, W., 1966 Mutual fund performance, Journal of Business 39, Jan., 119–138.

Shelton, J., 1967, The value line contest: A test of the predictability of stock price changes, Journal of Business 40, July, 251–269.

Vermaelen, T., 1981, An analysis of common stock repurchases, Journal of Financial Economics 9, June, 139–184.

… no commentary required …

SIZE-RELATED ANOMALIES AND STOCK RETURN SEASONALITY

Further Empirical Evidence

Donald B. KEIM*

University of Pennsylvania, Philadelphia, PA 19104, USA

Received June 1981, final version received June 1982

This study examines, month-by-month, the empirical relation between abnormal returns and market value of NYSE and AMEX common stocks. Evidence is provided that daily abnormal return distributions in January have large means relative to the remaining eleven months, and that the relation between abnormal returns and size is *always* negative and more pronounced in January than in any other month — even in years when, on average, large firms earn larger risk-adjusted returns than small firms. In particular, nearly fifty percent of the average magnitude of the 'size effect' over the period 1963–1979 is due to January abnormal returns. Further, more than fifty percent of the January premium is attributable to large abnormal returns during the first week of trading in the year, particularly on the first trading day.

1. Introduction

Recent empirical research in financial economics has revealed abnormal returns inconsistent with equilibrium in a market where the CAPM holds. Banz (1981) and Reinganum (1981) report a significant negative relation between abnormal returns and market value of common equity for samples of NYSE and NYSE–AMEX firms, respectively.[1] Whereas Banz and Reinganum implicitly assume that the negative relation between abnormal returns and size is stable over the periods examined, Brown, Kleidon and Marsh (1983) report a reversal of the size anomaly for certain years and reject the hypothesis of stationary year-to-year abnormal returns attributable to size.

---

*I would like to thank Susan Chaplinsky, Eugene Fama, Robert Holthausen, Michael Jensen, Allan Kleidon, Richard Leftwich, Merton Miller, Myron Scholes, and the referee Marc Reinganum for helpful comments. Financial assistance was provided by the Center for Research in Security Prices at the University of Chicago.

[1]Although it is not clear that the anomalous returns derive explicitly from failure of the CAPM to account for firm size, several studies have shown that anomalous return behavior associated with firm-specific variables is largely subsumed under the 'size effect'. For example, Reinganum (1981) finds that the relation between abnormal returns and P/E ratios reported by Basu (1977) appears to vanish after controlling for size. Keim (1980) and Stattman (1980) find a significant negative relation between abnormal returns and the degree to which market value of equity exceeds book value of equity, and also interpret this relation as a proxy for the size effect.

This study examines the month-to-month stability of the size anomaly over the period from 1963–1979. The evidence indicates that nearly fifty percent of the average magnitude of the risk-adjusted premium of small firms relative to large firms over this period is due to anomalous January abnormal returns. Further, more than twenty-six percent of the size premium is attributable to large abnormal returns during the first week of trading in the year and almost eleven percent is attributable to the first trading day. The data do not reveal significant seasonal behavior in any other month.

Hypotheses advanced by others to explain the size effect appear unable to explain the January effect. For example, Brown, Kleidon and Marsh argue that at least part of the size effect may be explained by an omitted risk factor in the pricing model. Even if part of the average size effect is due to an unspecified risk variable, however, the behavior observed in January cannot be due solely to this cause because risk alone cannot explain a return premium observed in the same month each year.[2] Stoll and Whaley (1983) contend that transaction costs can explain the size effect because such costs prevent arbitrageurs from eliminating the average return differential. However, only if transaction costs are seasonal in nature, implying some degree of market power for market makers, can such costs explain the January effect.

The results in this paper shed further light on the magnitude and nature of the size anomaly and also carry implications for empirical work using daily data. In particular, market efficiency studies relying on a model that does not account for non-stationary returns across months may be biased when investigating events concentrated in January if the event is unrelated to the true cause of the anomalous January abnormal returns.

1.1. Outline of the paper

The previously observed negative relation between abnormal returns and size is reproduced across a sample of NYSE and AMEX firms in section 2, and the relation is judged to be insensitive to misassessment of risk caused by infrequent trading of securities. In section 3 the effects of month-to-month stock return seasonality on the size effect are investigated, and evidence is presented that implies almost fifty percent of the average size anomaly is due to large January abnormal returns. Several possible explanations of the January effect are considered in section 4, and a brief summary is presented in section 5.

---

[2]Thus, it appears that we can separate the 'size effect' into two distinct components: a large premium *every* January and a much smaller and, on average, positive differential between risk-adjusted returns of small and large firms in every other month. A complete explanation of the 'size effect' requires two separate explanations for these very different phenomena.

2. Evidence on anomalous excess returns

In this section I investigate the anomalous negative relation between firm size, measured by total market value of common equity, and abnormal risk-adjusted returns for the sample of NYSE and AMEX firms used in this study. Careful attention is paid to Roll's (1981) conjecture that the apparent return premia of smaller firms may be at least partially attributable to an observed downward bias in the OLS betas for these portfolios. To avoid this bias, I employ beta estimates that adjust for non-synchronous trading and trading infrequency in the computation of abnormal returns. Although the adjustments result in a near monotone declining relation between beta and size, the portfolio abnormal returns computed with adjusted betas still exhibit a pronounced negative relation to firm size.

2.1. Data and portfolio selection

The data for this study are drawn from the CRSP daily stock files for the seventeen-year period from 1963 to 1979. The sample consists of firms which were listed on the NYSE or AMEX and had returns on the CRSP files during the entire calendar year under consideration. Thus, every year firms enter or leave the sample due to mergers, bankruptcies, delistings and new listings. The number of sample firms in a given year ranges from approximately 1,500 in the mid-1960's to 2,400 in the late 1970's.

Each year I rank all sample firms on the market value of their common equity. The market values, derived from the CRSP daily master file, are computed by multiplying the number of shares of common stock outstanding at year-end by the year-end price of the firm's common shares. I then divide the yearly distributions of market values equally into ten portfolios on the basis of size, portfolio one containing the smallest firms and portfolio ten containing the largest firms. Thus, each portfolio is updated annually and, on average, contains approximately two hundred firms.

2.2. Sensitivity of the size anomaly to trading infrequency

Roll (1981) conjectures that the size effect may be a statistical artifact of improperly measured risk. Scholes and Williams (1977) point out that non-synchronous trading of securities imparts a downward bias to the estimated beta when the underlying security trades infrequently. Dimson (1979) also argues that trading infrequency biases beta estimates and predicts a downward bias for infrequently traded shares and an upward bias for frequently traded shares. Roll maintains that since the shares of small firms are generally the most infrequently traded and the shares of large firms are the most frequently traded, the betas for small firms are downward biased while the betas of large firms are upward biased. Thus, estimation of abnormal returns using risk estimates that are not adjusted for trading infrequency may yield the observed size effect. In a recent paper, however, Reinganum (1982) reports that, while the direction of the bias in beta estimation is consistent with Roll's conjecture, portfolio excess returns computed with these adjusted betas will still exhibit a pronounced negative relation to firm size.

I have independently investigated the effects of improperly estimated betas on the size effect and the results corroborate Reinganum's (1982) findings. Estimates of OLS betas, Scholes–Williams betas and Dimson betas are presented, along with other statistics discussed below, in table 1 and three interesting results emerge. First, there is no distinguishable relation between the OLS estimates of beta and firm size measured by market value of equity. Of particular interest are the low levels of beta for the two smallest firm portfolios. Second, although the Scholes–Williams beta estimates for smaller firms are generally higher than the corresponding OLS estimates, there still is no distinct ordering of the betas according to firm size. Third, the Dimson beta estimate for the portfolio of smallest firms is significantly larger than the largest firm portfolio beta, and there is a near monotone declining relation between firm size and Dimson beta. However, not even the Dimson estimator results in the upward revision of small firm betas necessary to eliminate the excess returns for the small firm portfolios. Given the levels of average annual return for portfolio one (35.0%) and for the value-weighted market (7.0%) over the 1963–1979 period, extremely large average betas would have been necessary to ensure zero average excess returns.[3] Thus, the magnitude of the size anomaly does not appear to be sensitive to different estimators of beta.

2.3. The size anomaly: Some empirical results based on Scholes–Williams beta estimates

To test the relation between anomalous returns and size, I use security abnormal returns obtained from the CRSP daily excess return file. The CRSP daily excess return file contains control portfolios constructed by annually ranking the stocks in its file into ten portfolios of descending order of risk as measured by estimated Scholes–Williams betas. Security excess returns are computed as the security daily return less the equal-weighted daily return of the control portfolio into which the security is ranked.[4] I

---

[3]The Dimson estimator used in this study is defined in footnote e to table 1. The choice of ten lagged terms conforms with the findings of Schultz (1982) that even the smallest AMEX firms rarely go untraded for more than ten days. Nevertheless, Dimson estimates were also computed with twenty-one lagged, five leading, and contemporaneous value-weighted market returns and yielded small and large firm portfolio betas of 1.69 and 0.97, respectively. This larger beta for the small firm portfolio reflects positive but insignificant coefficients on the eleventh through twenty-first lagged market returns.

[4]See Center for Research in Security Prices (1980) for more details.

compute the average daily excess returns for the size deciles by weighting the CRSP excess returns for the securities in each decile equally.

Average daily portfolio excess returns are presented in table 1. The results are based on seventeen years of daily excess returns for each portfolio, beginning on the first trading day in January 1963.[5] That is, the daily excess returns for the twelve-month period following each portfolio update are stacked into one time series vector. Table 1 also contains the average median market value of equity for each portfolio and the first-order autocorrelation coefficient of the portfolio excess returns. The average excess returns are plotted in fig. 1 as a function of the decile of equity value. The plot suggests that, even after the Scholes–Williams adjustment of beta for non-synchronous trading, excess returns are a monotone decreasing function of firm size as measured by total market value of equity. The average return of the portfolio of smallest firms is about 20.7 percent per year (0.082 percent per day × 252 trading days per year) greater than the return implied by its beta risk. On the other hand, the portfolio of largest firms earned a return 9.6 percent per year

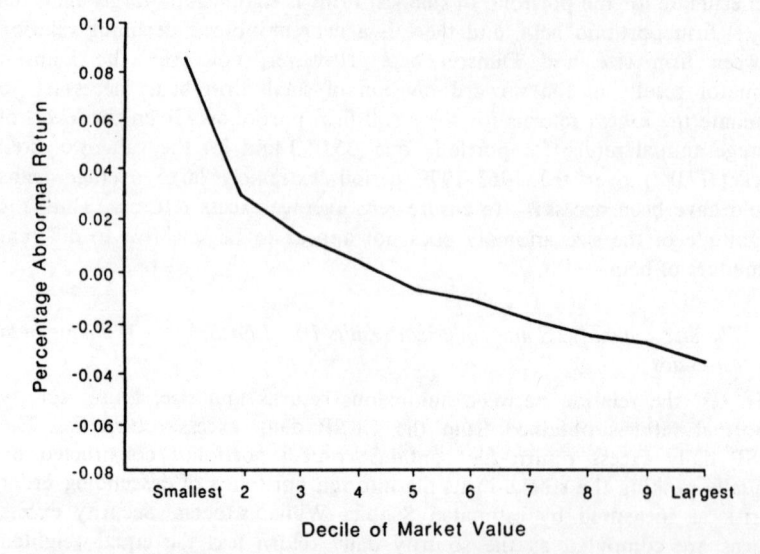

Fig. 1. Average daily abnormal returns (in percent) for ten market value portfolios constructed from firms on the NYSE and AMEX over the period 1963–1979. Abnormal returns are provided by CRSP.

[5]Think of the excess returns as being generated by the following strategy: Compute firm equity values on the last trading day of 1962. Construct portfolios on the first trading day in 1963 by ranking on the estimates of firm size and track the excess returns over the next twelve months. Update the firm equity values at the end of 1963, restructure the portfolios at the beginning of 1964 based on the updated information and again track the excess returns for one year. Repeat the process through December 1979.

Table 1

Average daily excess returns (in percent), size measured by market value of equity, beta estimates and autocorrelations of excess returns for ten portfolios constructed from firms on the NYSE and AMEX over the period 1963–1979.

Portfolio	Average excess return[a]	Market value of equity[b]	OLS beta[c]	Scholes–Williams beta[d]	Dimson beta[e]	1st order autocorrelation of excess return[a]
Smallest	0.082 (10.38)	$ 4.4	0.76	0.92	1.47	0.222
2	0.030 (5.83)	10.5	0.87	1.01	1.47	0.131
3	0.015 (3.88)	18.9	0.91	1.03	1.43	0.065
4	0.003 (0.97)	30.3	0.93	1.08	1.42	0.028
5	−0.007 (−2.24)	46.7	0.99	1.08	1.42	0.029
6	−0.014 (−4.82)	73.4	0.98	1.08	1.30	0.097
7	−0.020 (−6.40)	118.1	0.95	1.03	1.27	0.180
8	−0.024 (−6.74)	210.2	0.97	1.04	1.22	0.278
9	−0.029 (−7.20)	433.0	0.96	1.02	1.12	0.345
Largest	−0.038 (−7.19)	1092.1	0.96	0.97	0.98	0.351

[a]Excess returns are provided by CRSP; the excess return statistics and autorrelations are based on 4262 daily observations for each portfolio; t-statistics are in parentheses.

[b]Market value of equity is measured by the average, across all sample years, of the median market value of the particular size decile in each year; Market values are in millions of dollars.

[c]The OLS beta is obtained by regressing daily portfolio returns against the daily returns of the CRSP value-weighted index for the entire 1963–1979 period.

[d]The Scholes–Williams beta estimates are defined as

$$b_i = \sum_{k=-1}^{+1} B_{ik}/(1+2r), \quad i=1,10,$$

where r is the autocorrelation of the CRSP value-weighted daily market return and the B_{ik} are the slope coefficients from three separate OLS regressions,

$$R_{it} = a_{ik} + B_{ik} R_{m,t+k} + v_t, \quad k=-1,0,1, \quad i=1,10.$$

[e]The Dimson beta estimates are obtained by summing the slope coefficients on the ten lagged, five leading and the contemporaneous CRSP value-weighted daily market returns in the following OLS regression:

$$R_{it} = a_i + \sum_{k=-10}^{+5} b_{ik} R_{m,t+k} + u_{it}, \quad i=1,10.$$

(-0.032 percent $\times$ 252) less than that implied by its beta risk. The annual difference of 30.3 percent between the risk-adjusted returns of these two portfolios is comparable to the twenty-five percent annual difference reported by Reinganum (1981).[6]

Also of interest in table 1 is the pattern of autocorrelations across the various size portfolios. In particular, the average excess returns of the smallest *and* largest firms (e.g., portfolio one and portfolio ten) are highly autocorrelated while the intermediate portfolios exhibit little autorrelation. This appears counterintuitive given the evidence of Scholes and Williams (1977) and Dimson (1979) that only returns of infrequently traded shares (i.e., smaller firms) should display positive autocorrelation. Roll (1981) argues, however, that excessive autocorrelation in the extreme portfolios is consistent with the definition of excess returns as $r_t = R_{pt} - R_{ct}$, where p indicates the portfolio under study and c indicates an equal-weighted control portfolio. As Roll (1981, p. 882) points out:

> The serial covariance in excess returns, $\text{cov}(r_t, r_{t-1})$, e.g., is composed of $\text{cov}(R_{pt}, R_{p,t-1}) + \text{cov}(R_{ct}, R_{c,t-1}) - \text{cov}(R_{ct}, R_{p,t-1}) - \text{cov}(R_{pt}, R_{c,t-1})$.
> When trading frequency is different for p and c, one of the first two dominates [implying positive autocorrelation]. Otherwise, the four mutually cancel.

Since the large firm portfolio excess returns are relative to an equal-weighted control portfolio (which is more heavily represented by smaller component firms) autocorrelation is induced into the large firm portfolio excess returns by the equal-weighted control portfolio.[7]

3. Size-related anomalies and stock return seasonality

In this section I investigate the month-to-month stability of the size anomaly. The evidence indicates that the magnitude of the anomaly depends on the month of the year and that nearly fifty percent of the anomaly is concentrated in the month of January. Further, more than twenty-seven percent of the size effect in an average year can be attributed to the first week of trading in January. I turn first, though, to the seasonality in stock returns.

---

[6]Reinganum (1981) finds the betas of the market value portfolios used in his study close to one and computes excess returns by subtracting the daily return of the equal-weighted NYSE–AMEX index from the daily portfolio return. I replicated Reinganum's risk-adjustment procedure using both equal- and value-weighted NYSE–AMEX control portfolios for the ten market value portfolios in this study with similar results.

[7]Small firm portfolio returns generally exhibit higher autocorrelation than large firm portfolio returns. As evidence, for the period 1963–1979, the daily equal-weighted NYSE–AMEX index has first-order autocorrelation of 0.408, while the daily value-weighted NYSE–AMEX index has first-order autocorrelation of 0.205.

3.1. Stock return seasonality

Much evidence has accumulated [see Fama (1965, 1970)] indicating that common stock prices follow a multiplicative random walk. Thus, the return on an equal-weighted portfolio of stocks conforms to the following process:

$$\tilde{R}_t = \mu + \tilde{e}_t, \qquad (1)$$

where $\tilde{R}_t$ is the random portfolio return, $\mu = E(\tilde{R}_t | I_{t-1})$, I_{t-1} is the information set available at $t-1$, and $\tilde{e}_t$ is an i.i.d. random variable with zero mean.

While the random walk model implies portfolio return distributions are time-invariant, recent empirical evidence [French (1980), Gibbons and Hess (1981), Officer (1975), and Rozeff and Kinney (1976)] indicates that portfolio return distributions do indeed differ temporally. For example, Rozeff and Kinney test the seasonal model

$$\tilde{R}_{tm} = \mu + \lambda_m + \tilde{e}_t, \qquad (2)$$

where m denotes the month of the year and $\tilde{e}_t$ is i.i.d. with zero mean. They examine monthly returns on an equal-weighted NYSE index over the period 1904–1974 and report large average monthly returns in January relative to the remaining eleven months. Rozeff and Kinney conclude that expected portfolio returns depend on the month of the year.

Keim (1982) presents evidence that the January seasonal in stock returns is more pronounced for portfolios of small firms than for portfolios of large firms. Employing the ten market value portfolios of NYSE–AMEX stocks used in this study, Keim tests the hypothesis of stable month-to-month average returns for each portfolio and finds that ability to reject the hypothesis declines as average firm size increases. In fact, the results indicate that one cannot reject the hypothesis for the portfolio of largest firms.

3.2. Seasonality and the size anomaly: A January effect

The finding that the magnitude of the January return seasonal is related to firm size provides some basis for suspecting month-to-month instability in the size effect. To address this suspicion, I plot in fig. 2 the negative relation between abnormal return and firm size separately for each month of the year during the period 1963–1979. The plots in fig. 2 dramatically display a difference in the size effect between January and the other eleven months. The January relation between abnormal returns and market value is steep and negative while the plots for the other months have, relative to January, only a slight negative slope and are tightly clustered around zero abnormal

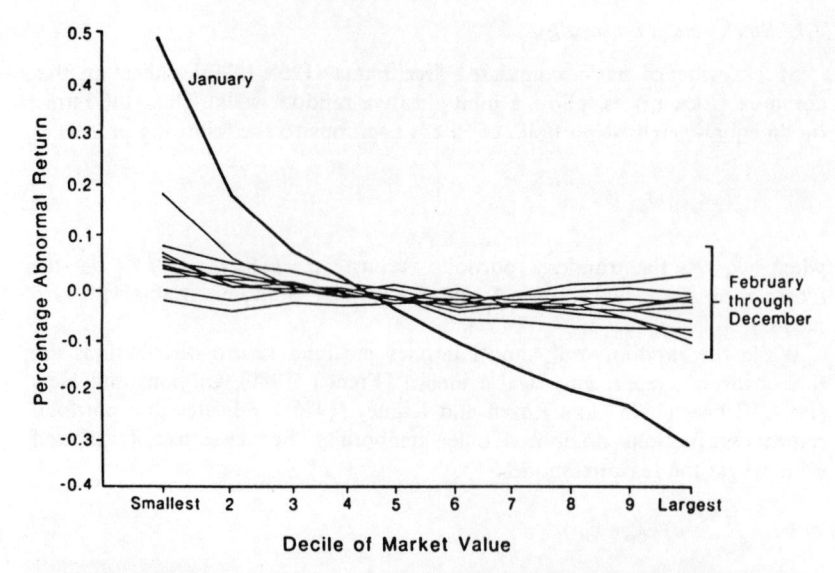

Fig. 2. The relation between average daily abnormal returns (in percent) and decile of market value *for each month* over the period 1963–1979. The ten market value portfolios (deciles) are constructed from firms on the NYSE and AMEX. Abnormal returns are provided by CRSP.

return. The figure shows clearly that the size effect is more pronounced in January than in the other months, and also that the anomaly has similar characteristics from February through December. (The non-January observation that stands apart from the cluster in the decile of smallest market value is the February observation.)

While fig. 2 suggests that the size effect is more pronounced in January than in any other month, further support for this conclusion can be obtained from examination of the month-to-month magnitude of the size effect measured by the difference in risk-adjusted returns between the smallest market value portfolio and the largest market value portfolio. Table 2 contains the differences in average daily CRSP excess returns between the smallest and largest market value portfolios for every month of every year during the period 1963–1979. Differences averaged across all months for each year (rightmost column) and averaged across all years for each month (bottom row) are also provided. The most striking feature of the data is the persistence, magnitude and statistical significance of the excess returns in January: a monthly size effect of 15.0% (average daily percentage return of 0.714 multiplied by twenty-one trading days per month) is implied in January in contrast to the implied monthly excess of return of 2.5% (0.121 × 21) averaged over all months and all years. No consistent pattern is apparent

Table 2

Average differences (t-statistics) between daily (CRSP) excess returns (in percent) of portfolios constructed from firms in the top and bottom decile of size (measured by market value of equity) on the NYSE and AMEX over the period 1963–1979.

	Jan.	Feb.	March	April	May	June	July	Aug.	Sept.	Oct.	Nov.	Dec.	Mean daily return over all months
1963	0.309 (2.26)	0.093 (1.23)	−0.085 (−0.81)	−0.045 (−0.55)	0.172 (2.56)	0.056 (0.73)	−0.026 (−0.39)	0.000 (0.00)	0.040 (0.51)	−0.021 (−0.26)	0.011 (0.08)	−0.123 (−1.38)	0.032 (1.16)
1964	0.170 (1.52)	0.105 (1.30)	0.097 (1.37)	0.007 (0.12)	−0.084 (−1.34)	−0.037 (−0.56)	0.121 (1.66)	0.104 (1.42)	0.077 (1.08)	0.136 (2.03)	−0.019 (−0.23)	−0.111 (−1.64)	0.048 (2.14)
1965	0.288 (2.34)	0.228 (2.68)	0.204 (2.63)	0.133 (2.25)	0.025 (0.38)	−0.212 (−2.41)	0.070 (1.05)	0.104 (1.34)	−0.023 (−0.44)	0.314 (4.16)	0.343 (3.74)	0.202 (1.79)	0.137 (5.29)
1966	0.388 (4.63)	0.448 (4.44)	0.183 (1.52)	0.192 (2.11)	−0.278 (−1.82)	0.017 (0.24)	−0.009 (−0.08)	−0.177 (−1.78)	−0.025 (−0.23)	−0.423 (−2.31)	0.138 (1.47)	0.001 (0.01)	0.033 (0.92)
1967	0.765 (4.59)	0.413 (5.04)	0.142 (2.35)	0.149 (1.54)	0.240 (2.56)	0.599 (3.87)	0.403 (4.15)	0.235 (3.09)	0.512 (5.59)	0.268 (2.70)	−0.120 (−0.64)	0.427 (4.40)	0.336 (9.34)
1968	0.834 (6.20)	−0.197 (−1.25)	−0.079 (−0.52)	0.427 (2.70)	0.727 (6.52)	0.096 (1.11)	0.222 (1.30)	0.348 (3.37)	0.345 (4.15)	−0.002 (−0.03)	0.091 (0.88)	0.434 (4.12)	0.285 (6.78)
1969	0.128 (1.00)	−0.253 (−2.49)	−0.059 (−0.62)	−0.139 (−1.94)	0.082 (1.19)	−0.265 (−2.47)	−0.241 (−1.88)	−0.073 (−0.61)	−0.006 (−0.07)	0.247 (2.48)	−0.148 (−2.16)	−0.349 (−4.06)	−0.085 (−2.76)
1970	0.612 (2.49)	−0.257 (−1.58)	0.033 (0.31)	−0.213 (−1.39)	−0.016 (−0.07)	−0.082 (−0.47)	−0.164 (−0.80)	−0.074 (−0.48)	0.315 (2.91)	−0.019 (−0.16)	−0.434 (−4.44)	0.136 (1.08)	−0.011 (−0.22)

1971	0.886 (7.44)	0.432 (2.59)	0.159 (2.05)	−0.156 (−2.09)	−0.066 (−1.05)	−0.246 (−3.57)	−0.053 (−0.75)	0.004 (0.03)	0.095 (1.19)	−0.052 (−0.63)	−0.175 (−1.78)	0.130 (0.98)	0.074 (2.12)
1972	0.760 (5.32)	0.197 (2.44)	0.005 (0.06)	−0.054 (−0.68)	−0.181 (−2.87)	−0.061 (−0.69)	−0.022 (−0.26)	−0.204 (−2.63)	−0.098 (−1.03)	−0.200 (−2.19)	−0.065 (−0.68)	−0.154 (−1.19)	−0.008 (−0.26)
1973	0.368 (1.78)	−0.137 (−1.47)	−0.060 (−0.48)	−0.109 (−0.79)	−0.406 (−1.86)	−0.011 (−0.07)	0.367 (2.61)	−0.144 (−1.60)	−0.080 (−0.60)	0.169 (1.61)	−0.298 (−1.76)	−0.494 (−2.07)	−0.067 (−1.39)
1974	1.464 (3.67)	0.047 (0.25)	0.313 (2.12)	0.127 (0.86)	0.017 (0.12)	0.063 (0.31)	0.331 (1.57)	0.313 (1.09)	0.224 (0.65)	−0.380 (−1.20)	0.015 (0.06)	−0.187 (−0.48)	0.199 (2.39)
1975	2.068 (3.95)	0.278 (1.15)	0.929 (3.76)	−0.126 (−0.66)	0.293 (1.83)	0.426 (1.53)	0.489 (2.48)	−0.274 (−1.69)	−0.083 (−0.54)	−0.210 (−1.29)	0.123 (0.74)	0.220 (0.63)	0.345 (4.06)
1976	1.109 (4.02)	1.638 (4.55)	−0.062 (−0.50)	0.022 (0.18)	−0.089 (−0.75)	−0.158 (−1.17)	0.106 (1.04)	−0.125 (−0.93)	0.007 (−0.08)	−0.010 (−0.07)	0.225 (1.47)	0.534 (3.35)	0.250 (4.23)
1977	0.954 (4.60)	0.241 (2.29)	0.098 (0.98)	0.082 (0.64)	0.129 (1.11)	0.040 (0.41)	0.328 (2.44)	0.066 (0.74)	0.085 (0.78)	0.093 (1.16)	0.249 (1.73)	0.007 (0.06)	0.194 (5.05)
1978	0.444 (3.47)	0.343 (2.81)	0.350 (3.15)	0.268 (2.63)	0.414 (3.75)	0.213 (1.45)	−0.065 (−0.67)	0.755 (5.48)	0.328 (1.91)	−0.988 (−2.88)	0.230 (0.85)	−0.097 (−0.71)	0.186 (3.26)
1979	0.548 (4.13)	0.157 (1.30)	0.183 (1.34)	0.202 (2.07)	0.200 (1.57)	0.059 (0.61)	−0.039 (−0.32)	0.205 (2.80)	−0.104 (−0.85)	−0.092 (−0.44)	−0.049 (−0.32)	0.153 (1.20)	0.121 (3.05)
Mean daily return over all years	0.714 (11.81)	0.223 (5.07)	0.136 (4.34)	0.042 (1.42)	0.072 (2.13)	0.028 (0.80)	0.105 (3.11)	0.063 (1.88)	0.092 (2.74)	−0.070 (−1.65)	0.006 (0.16)	0.42 (0.93)	0.121 (10.31)

across the remaining eleven months; although a few display significant positive size premia (e.g., February, March and July) that are much lower than January, the month of October displays a size discount.

The studies by Banz (1981) and Reinganum (1981) implicitly assume that anomalous size-related excess returns are obtained continuously; i.e., month-by-month, year-by-year small firms earn larger returns than large firms after controlling for risk. The evidence in table 2 casts doubt on the month-to-month constancy of the anomalous size effect. In fact, a significant proportion of the size effect, averaged over 1963–1979, is due to return premia observed during January in *every* year. Exclusion of the large January abnormal returns reduces the overall magnitude of the anomaly by almost fifty percent: the average annual size premium of 30.3 percent declines to 15.4 percent when the January observations are removed.[8]

To test the null hypothesis of equal expected abnormal returns for each month of the year, I use the regression

$$R_t = a_1 + a_2 D_{2t} + a_3 D_{3t} + \ldots + a_{12} D_{12t} + e_t. \tag{3}$$

In the regression, R_t is the average daily CRSP excess return for day t for the size portfolio under consideration, and the dummy variables indicate the month of the year in which the excess return is observed (D_{2t} = February, D_{3t} = March, etc.). The excess return for January is measured by a_1, while a_2 through a_{12} represent the differences between the excess return for January and the excess returns for the other months. If the expected excess return is the same for each month of the year, the estimates of a_2 through a_{12} should be close to zero and the F-statistic measuring the joint significance of the dummy variables should be insignificant.

Due to heteroskedastic residuals in the OLS estimate of (3), I estimate eq. (3) as weighted least squares (WLS) where the weight applied to an observation in month t is the normalized value of the inverse of the standard error for month t of the residuals from the OLS estimate of (3).[9] WLS

---

[8]These abnormal returns are derived from table 2. The estimate of the average annual size premium equals the overall average daily difference in abnormal returns between the smallest and largest market value portfolios (0.121) multiplied by the number of trading days per year (252). The component of the size effect occurring in January equals the average daily difference between the smallest and largest market value portfolios (0.714) multiplied by the average number of trading days in January (21). The average January effect of 15% is 49.3% of the average magnitude of the size effect.

[9]Heteroskedasticity is induced into the residuals by way of the heteroskedasticity in the excess returns. The value of a generalized likelihood ratio test for equality of excess return variances across months [see Mood, Graybill and Boes (1974, p. 439)] ranges from 319.4 for portfolio 1 (smallest firms) to 27.2 for portfolio 5. These values are significant at the 1% level and one can therefore reject the hypothesis of equal excess return variance across months for any particular portfolio.

Although autocorrelated disturbances are present in the OLS estimates of (3), I do not adjust for the autocorrelation in the test of the month-to-month stability hypothesis. Vinod (1975)

estimates of (3) are presented in table 3. In addition to tests of the hypothesis that the mean abnormal returns of the ten size portfolios are temporally constant, I also test for the month-to-month stationarity of the differences in mean abnormal returns between the smallest and largest market value portfolios. Three interesting results emerge. First, average excess returns for smaller firms appear disproportionately large in January relative to the remaining eleven months. For example, the F-statistic of 14.59 for the smallest firm portfolio is significant at any level and allows rejection of the null hypothesis. Second, and somewhat surprisingly, January abnormal returns for the larger firm portfolios are *negative* and lower than the mean excess returns in any other month. The large F-statistic of 17.63 for the largest firm portfolio also allows rejection of the hypothesis of temporal constancy of excess returns for large firms. Third, the estimates of (3) for differences in average excess returns between the smallest and largest market value portfolios indicates the observed size premium in January is positive and significantly larger than the average premium in any other month. The F-statistic of 18.9 permits rejection of the hypothesis of a stable month-to-month size effect.

3.3. A closer look at the January effect: The first five trading days

A major implication of the previous section is that a significant portion of the size effect, averaged over 1963–1979, is due to return premia observed in the month of January in every year. Closer examination of the abnormal returns within the month of January reveals a large portion of the size effect occurs during the first five trading days of the year. The magnitude of the size effect during the first week of trading in the year is shown in table 4 which contains the difference in average abnormal return between the smallest and largest market value portfolios for these five days. The first trading day's difference in abnormal returns between the smallest and largest market value portfolios averages 3.2 percent with a standard deviation of 2.0 percent for the 1963–1979 period. The first day's difference is positive in *every* year and the average difference is significant at any level. Further, the difference in abnormal return between the smallest and largest market value portfolios averaged 8.0 percent over the first five trading days in January.[10] Thus, 10.5 percent (3.2 ÷ 30.4) of the annual size effect for an average year

---

estimates bounds for the F-statistic from an OLS equation estimated in the presence of AR(1) errors. These bounds are used to assess the likelihood of making an incorrect test decision given that the residuals from the OLS estimate of (3) are approximately AR(1). The relevant bounds for the test here indicate that the F-statistic remains significant if (3) is estimated while directly accounting for the autocorrelation.

[10]The second through fifth trading days in January display 17, 16, 16 and 15 positive differences, respectively, out of a possible 17 over the 1963–1979 period.

Table 3

Test of the month-to-month stability of the size effect using CRSP daily excess returns (in percent) of portfolios constructed from firms in each decile of size (measured by market value of equity) on the NSYE–AMEX over the period 1963–1979.[a]

$R_t = a_1 + a_2 D_{2t} + a_3 D_{3t} + a_4 D_{4t} + a_5 D_{5t} + a_6 D_{6t} + a_7 D_{7t} + a_8 D_{8t} + a_9 D_{9t} + a_{10} D_{10t} + a_{11} D_{11t} + a_{12} D_{12t} + e_t$

Decile	a_1	a_2	a_3	a_4	a_5	a_6	a_7	a_8	a_9	a_{10}	a_{11}	a_{12}	R^2	F-statistic	Degrees of freedom
Smallest	0.43 (13.28)	−0.27 (−6.04)	−0.35 (−8.62)	−0.40 (−9.80)	−0.36 (−8.78)	−0.40 (−9.73)	−0.37 (−9.04)	−0.37 (−9.08)	−0.40 (−9.68)	−0.44 (−10.75)	−0.43 (−10.33)	−0.41 (−9.44)	0.036	14.59	11;4250
2	0.19 (9.30)	−0.13 (−4.76)	−0.15 (−5.76)	−0.17 (−6.65)	−0.17 (−6.69)	−0.18 (−6.69)	−0.14 (−5.31)	−0.18 (−7.10)	−0.17 (−6.49)	−0.21 (−8.05)	−0.20 (−7.49)	−0.16 (−5.85)	0.020	8.03	11;4250
3	0.09 (5.92)	−0.07 (−3.38)	−0.05 (−2.80)	−0.08 (−4.10)	−0.08 (−4.30)	−0.08 (−3.92)	−0.07 (−3.41)	−0.08 (−4.41)	−0.09 (−4.57)	−0.10 (−4.73)	−0.07 (−3.73)	−0.07 (−3.62)	0.008	3.06	11;4250
4	0.02 (1.71)	−0.01 (−0.53)	−0.00 (−0.06)	−0.03 (−1.73)	−0.03 (−2.01)	−0.03 (−1.62)	−0.01 (−0.45)	−0.01 (−0.83)	−0.02 (−1.39)	−0.04 (−2.56)	−0.00 (−0.18)	−0.01 (−0.75)	0.004	1.39	11;4250
5	−0.03 (−3.13)	0.02 (1.25)	0.03 (2.10)	0.04 (2.64)	0.02 (1.24)	0.03 (2.16)	0.03 (2.21)	0.02 (1.55)	0.02 (1.64)	0.02 (1.35)	0.05 (3.03)	0.04 (2.61)	0.004	1.38	11;4250
6	−0.09 (−7.84)	0.06 (3.90)	0.07 (4.61)	0.07 (5.02)	0.07 (4.80)	0.07 (4.47)	0.09 (6.01)	0.09 (6.46)	0.09 (5.98)	0.07 (4.98)	0.09 (6.16)	0.07 (4.89)	0.014	5.54	11;4250
7	−0.13 (−11.57)	0.10 (6.54)	0.11 (7.31)	0.12 (7.66)	0.12 (7.75)	0.12 (7.83)	0.12 (7.83)	0.14 (9.56)	0.11 (7.44)	0.13 (8.60)	0.16 (9.91)	0.14 (8.48)	0.030	11.92	11;4250
8	−0.19 (−14.00)	0.15 (7.96)	0.17 (9.72)	0.18 (10.36)	0.17 (9.72)	0.19 (10.61)	0.17 (9.52)	0.19 (11.30)	0.16 (9.40)	0.21 (11.89)	0.21 (11.44)	0.19 (10.17)	0.044	17.85	11;4250
9	−0.22 (−14.00)	0.16 (7.73)	0.18 (9.23)	0.22 (10.72)	0.20 (9.54)	0.21 (10.32)	0.20 (9.64)	0.22 (10.94)	0.19 (9.35)	0.25 (11.59)	0.24 (11.41)	0.20 (9.52)	0.044	17.70	11;4250
Largest	−0.28 (−13.83)	0.22 (8.20)	0.23 (8.86)	0.28 (10.79)	0.28 (10.60)	0.29 (10.86)	0.24 (8.94)	0.28 (10.67)	0.23 (8.54)	0.34 (11.81)	0.28 (9.97)	0.26 (9.67)	0.044	17.63	11;4250
Smallest − largest	0.71 (14.88)	−0.49 (−7.68)	0.58 (−9.80)	−0.67 (−11.47)	−0.64 (−10.68)	−0.69 (−11.39)	−0.61 (−10.12)	−0.65 (−10.90)	−0.62 (−10.36)	−0.78 (−12.55)	−0.71 (−11.44)	−0.67 (−10.58)	0.047	18.90	11;4250

[a]The dummy variables indicate in which month of the year each excess return is observed (D_{2t} = February, D_{3t} = March, etc.), and the estimated t-values are in parentheses. The F-statistic tests the hypothesis that a_2 through a_{12} are zero. Fractiles of the F-distribution: $F_{10,\infty}(95\%_0) = 1.83$, $F_{10,\infty}(99.9\%_0) = 2.96$.

Table 4
Differences in average daily (CRSP) excess returns (in percent) between portfolios constructed from firms in the top and bottom decile of size (measured by market value of equity) on the NYSE and AMEX for the first five trading days in each of the years 1963–1979.

Trading day	1963	1964	1965	1966	1967	1968
1	2.30	1.99	2.09	1.34	3.39	2.18
2	0.00	0.26	0.85	0.69	0.58	1.47
3	0.72	0.19	0.60	0.52	0.96	0.17
4	0.48	0.02	0.75	0.25	0.27	1.43
5	−0.69	0.38	0.36	0.43	1.08	1.55
Avg.	0.56	0.57	0.93	0.65	1.26	1.36

Trading day	1969	1970	1971	1972	1973	1974
1	1.25	3.98	1.66	2.36	3.68	6.46
2	0.65	3.68	0.88	1.56	1.59	5.72
3	−0.36	1.44	1.92	1.40	0.46	3.84
4	−1.63	1.19	1.59	1.63	0.84	3.19
5	−0.23	0.43	1.12	1.12	0.62	2.72
Avg.	−0.06	2.14	1.43	1.61	1.44	4.38

Trading day	1975	1976	1977	1978	1979	Avg. for 1963–1979
1	8.47	5.26	3.84	2.28	1.82	3.20
2	4.54	2.36	2.14	0.27	1.36	1.68
3	3.17	2.27	1.74	0.94	1.26	1.25
4	6.00	0.81	0.77	0.63	1.13	1.14
5	4.64	0.47	0.13	0.09	0.90	0.89
Avg.	5.36	2.23	1.72	0.84	1.29	1.63

can be attributed to the *first* trading day of the year and 26.3 percent (8.0÷30.4) can be attributed to the *first five* trading days. In contrast, if the small firm premium were spread uniformly throughout the year, then approximately 0.4 percent of the annual premium is expected on each day.

3.4. The January effect and the year-to-year stationarity of the size effect

Brown, Kleidon and Marsh (1983) report that the size effect is not stable from year to year during the 1967–1979 period, but identify two distinct subperiods when the relation between size and abnormal return is relatively stable. There is a stable positive relation from 1969 to 1973 and a stable negative relation from 1974 to 1979. The reversal of the size anomaly during the 1969–1973 period is apparent in the rightmost column of table 2. With the exception of 1971, large firms consistently outperform small firms over this period.[11]

The year-to-year instability of the size effect implies that estimation of (3) across all three subperiods, and without regard to important differences in the size effect within each subperiod, may be inappropriate. I therefore estimate eq. (3) within each subperiod identified above, and the results permit us to conclude that the January effect is insensitive to the year-to-year instability of the overall size effect. The average January differences in *monthly* percentage abnormal returns between the smallest and largest market value portfolios, and corresponding t-statistics in parentheses, for the three subperiods are: 1963–1968, 9.7(10.2); 1969–1973, 11.3(9.1); 1974–1979, 23.1(13.0). Two interesting observations are obtained from the subperiod evidence. First, the magnitude of the January effect increases through time in the 1963–1979 period. Second, and more importantly, even during the 1969–1973 subperiod when large firms have higher risk-adjusted returns than small firms, the size premium is significantly positive in January. An interesting implication is that after accounting for the (always) positive January effect, the year-to-year instability of the size anomaly remains.

3.5. The January anomaly and abnormal return autocorrelation

Roll (1981), following Scholes and Williams (1977) and Dimson (1979), argues that observed autocorrelations of abnormal returns for small firms may be due to infrequent trading. The evidence in the previous sections suggests an alternative explanation for the observed autocorrelations. In particular, non-stationary mean abnormal returns may induce autocorrelation in the time series calculations. If average daily abnormal returns in January are large relative to average daily abnormal returns during the remaining eleven months, then most daily abnormal returns will be less than the grand mean based on all days. This may result in positive computed autocorrelations, suggesting that autocorrelations be computed while controlling for a varying mean daily abnormal return. If the positive autocorrelations vanish, the test results imply that the source of the autocorrelation is a misspecified stochastic process and not infrequent trading.

To test the hypothesis that non-stationary mean abnormal returns may cause autocorrelation, I estimate eq. (3) with OLS. The residuals from (3) are mean-adjusted abnormal returns and, therefore, are used to compute autocorrelations that are free of the changing mean problem. The computed first-order autocorrelation of the residuals for the smallest market value

---

[11]The average differences in annualized percentage excess returns between the smallest and largest market value portfolios, and corresponding t-statistics in parentheses, for three subperiods are: 196–1968, 35.3(10.4); 1969–1973, −5.0(−1.1); and 1974–1979, 55.4(8.5).

portfolio is 0.189 and for the largest market value portfolio is 0.320. These autocorrelations are not significantly different from those reported for the unadjusted excess return series in table 1.

Autocorrelations were also computed for another adjusted time series of abnormal returns, adjusted so that all January observations are excluded. Elimination of the January abnormal returns reduces the first-order autocorrelation to 0.187 for the smallest market value portfolio and 0.274 for the largest market value portfolio. These adjusted autocorrelations are still significantly different from zero for the extreme portfolios. It does not appear that the non-stationary mean of excess returns is the cause of the observed autocorrelation in excess returns.

4. Hypotheses regarding the January effect

Several hypotheses have been suggested to explain the January seasonal in stock returns. Most prominent are a tax loss selling hypothesis and an information hypothesis, although neither has been theoretically nor empirically linked to the return seasonal. The testable implications of these potential explanations may, nevertheless, yield insights into the nature of the January premia for small firms. It appears, however, that the ability of either hypothesis to explain the January effect is diminished either on grounds of plausibility or as a result of some preliminary testing.

4.1. Tax loss selling hypothesis

Wachtel (1942) and Branch (1977) formulate an explanation for disproportionately large January returns based on year-end tax loss selling of shares that have declined in value over the previous year.[12] Since size is measured here as total market value of equity, the smallest firm portfolios are biased toward inclusion of shares that have experienced large price declines and, therefore, are likely candidates for tax loss selling.[13] The possible association between tax loss selling and the January effect merits consideration.

The theoretical value of the tax loss selling hypothesis diminishes, however, with the existence of arbitrage possibilities in non-segmented markets with non-taxable investors.[14] In addition, the hypothesis is not clearly supported

---

[12]Dyl (1977) reports abnormally heavy trading volume at year-end for shares with previous twelve-month price declines and interprets the results as evidence of tax loss selling.

[13]Evidence presented in Keim (1982) indicates that the largest abnormal returns recorded in the first five trading days of January are associated with low-priced shares that have gravitated to the smallest market value portfolio. Most of these shares sell for less than two dollars.

[14]Roll (1982) argues that the annual pattern in small firm returns is strongly associated with tax loss selling, and conjectures that large transactions costs for smaller firm shares prevent arbitragers from eliminating the large abnormal returns in the first few days in January.

empirically. If the January effect is the result of year-end tax loss selling, then the magnitude and significance of the measured January effect should, *ceteris paribus*, vary with the level of personal income tax rates. For example, the January effect should be less significant in pre-World War II years when personal tax rates were relatively low. Keim (1982) reports, however, that the January effect is, on average, larger in the 1930's than in any subsequent subperiod.[15]

Of course, other things are not always equal. The methods available today for shielding income from taxes did not exist in the earlier years in this century. Thus, the marginal benefit of the capital loss offset may have been much greater in the 1930's than in later years, even though the tax rates in the former period were significantly lower. A more direct test of the tax loss selling hypothesis is possible though. The month-to-month behavior of abnormal returns across countries with tax codes similar to the United States' code but with differing tax year-ends (e.g., Great Britain has a May tax year-end) can be examined. If, in the month immediately following the tax year-end, abnormal returns of small firms in other countries are large relative to both other months and larger firms in that country, then the evidence is consistent with the tax loss selling hypothesis.[16]

4.2. Information hypothesis

Rozeff and Kinney (1976) note that 'January marks the beginning and ending of several potentially important financial and informational events... January is the start of the tax year for investors, and the beginning of the tax and accounting years for most firms, and preliminary announcements of the previous calendar year's accounting earnings are made'. Thus, at least for those firms with year-end fiscal closings, the month of January marks a period of increased uncertainty and anticipation due to the impending release of important information. In addition, the gradual dissemination of this information during January may have a greater impact on the prices of small firms relative to large firms for which the gathering and processing of information by investors is a less costly process. The recurrence of significant small firm premia at the same time each year due to inadequate adjustment of prices to information is, however, inconsistent with a rational expectations equilibrium in the market. Nonetheless, the information hypothesis is testable. One test involves aligning all firm excess returns in event time rather

---

[15]Branch (1977), Dyl (1977) and Roll (1982) examine tax loss selling in the post-1960 period only.

[16]Korajczyk (1982), using value-weighted stock market indices from eighteen countries with widely varying tax regimes and tax year-ends, finds evidence of a January seasonal in stock returns for each country (except Spain) over the period January 1973 to January 1982.

than in calendar time, where the event is the firm's fiscal year-end.[17] If the magnitude of the average excess returns immediately following the fiscal year-end in event time is greater than the measured excess returns in the month of January in calendar time, then the evidence would support the information hypothesis.

4.3. Other possible explanations

There remains the possibility that the measured January effect may not have an economic cause. That is, the effect may be due to spurious causes such as outliers, concentration of listings and delistings at year-end, or data base errors. Keim (1982) reports that the cross-sectional distribution of excess returns for the decile of smallest NYSE–AMEX firms is positively skewed for the first trading day in January. However, elimination of extreme observations (greater than three standard errors from the sample mean) does not significantly reduce the mean of the distribution. Roll (1982) investigates the other two 'non-exploitable' causes and dismisses them for lack of evidence.[18]

5. Summary and conclusions

Recent empirical investigations of the traditional CAPM report the existence of anomalous abnormal returns that appear to be negatively related to size. Evidence in section 3 indicates that daily abnormal return distributions in January have large means relative to the remaining eleven months, and that the relation between abnormal returns and size is always negative and more pronounced in January than in any other month — even in years when, on average, large firms earn larger risk-adjusted returns than small firms. Nearly fifty percent of the average magnitude of the size anomaly over the period 1963–1979 is due to January abnormal returns. Further, more than fifty percent of the January premium is attributable to large abnormal returns during the first week of trading in the year, particularly on the first trading day. Hypotheses advanced to explain the size effect appear unable to explain the January effect. Several alternative explanations with testable implications are discussed, but the tests are deferred for future research.

[17]Approximately sixty percent of the firms listed on the NYSE and AMEX have December 31 fiscal year-ends.

[18]The method used in this study for computing portfolio abnormal returns (1) requires restructuring portfolio composition at each year-end and (2) may induce a survival bias because of the requirement of one year of trading for all sample firms. Investigation of the January effect may be sensitive to these strict requirements. The results in section 3 were duplicated, however, with differences in returns between daily equal- and value-weighted NYSE–AMEX indices. Biases due to survival and year-end portfolio restructuring are eliminated when using those indices.

References

Banz, R.W., 1981, The relationship between return and market value of common stocks, Journal of Financial Economics 9, 3–18.
Basu, S., 1977, The investment performance of common stocks in relation to their price-earnings ratios: A test of the efficient market hypothesis, Journal of Finance 32, 663–682.
Branch, B., 1977, A tax loss trading rule, Journal of Business 50, 198–207.
Brown, P., A. Kleidon and T. Marsh, 1983, New evidence on the nature of size-related anomalies in stock prices, Journal of Financial Economics, this issue.
Center for Research in Security Prices, 1980, CRSP daily excess return file, Unpublished manuscript (Graduate School of Business, University of Chicago, Chicago, IL).
Dimson, E., 1979, Risk measurement when shares are subject to infrequent trading, Journal of Financial Economics 7, 197–216.
Dyl, E.A., 1977, Capital gains taxation and year-end stock market behavior, Journal of Finance 32, 165–175.
Fama, E.F., 1965, The behavior of stock market prices, Journal of Business 38, 34–105.
Fama, E.F., 1970, Efficient capital markets: A review of the theory and empirical work, Journal of Finance 25, 383–420.
Fama, E.F., 1976, Foundations of finance (Basic Books, New York).
French, K.R., 1980, Stock returns and the weekend effect, Journal of Financial Economics 8, 55–70.
Gibbons, M.R. and P.J. Hess, 1981, Day of the week effects and asset returns, Journal of Business 54, 579–596.
Keim, D.B., 1980, Asset pricing anomalies and capital market seasonality: Empirical evidence, Unpublished manuscript (University of Chicago, Chicago, IL).
Keim, D.B., 1982, Further evidence on size effects and yield effects: The implications of stock return seasonally, Unpublished manuscript (University of Chicago, Chicago, IL).
Korajczyk, R., 1982, Stock market seasonality: Some international evidence, Unpublished manuscript (University of Chicago, Chicago, IL).
Mood, A.M., F.A. Graybill and D.C. Boes, 1974, Introduction to the theory of statistics (McGraw-Hill, New York).
Officer, R.R., 1975, Seasonality in Australian capital markets: Market efficiency and empirical issues, Journal of Financial Economics 2, 29–52.
Reinganum, M.R., 1981, Misspecification of capital asset pricing: Empirical anomalies based on earnings yields and market values, Journal of Financial Economics 9, 19–46.
Reinganum, M.R., 1982, A direct test of Roll's conjecture on the firm size effect, Journal of Finance 37, 27–36.
Roll, R., 1981, A possible explanation of the small firm effect, Journal of Finance 36, 879–888.
Roll, R., 1982, The turn of the year effect and the return premia of small firms, Working paper (Graduate School of Management, University of California, Los Angeles, CA).
Rozeff, M.S. and W.R. Kinney, Jr., 1976, Capital market seasonality: The case of stock returns, Journal of Financial Economics 3, 379–402.
Scholes, M. and J. Williams, 1977, Estimating betas from nonsynchronous data, Journal of Financial Economics 5, 309–327.
Schultz, P., 1982, Some additional evidence on the small firm effect, Unpublished manuscript (University of Chicago, Chicago, IL).
Stattman, D., 1980, Book values and expected stock returns, Unpublished MBA honors paper (University of Chicago, Chicago, IL).
Stoll, H.R. and R.E. Whaley, 1983, Transaction costs and the small firm effect, Journal of Financial Economics, this issue.
Vinod, H.D., 1976, Effects of ARMA errors on the significance tests for regression coefficients, Journal of the American Statistical Association 71, 929–933.
Wachtel, S.B., 1942, Certain observations on seasonal movements in stock prices, Journal of Business 15, 184–193.

[24]

Are Seasonal Anomalies Real? A Ninety-Year Perspective

Josef Lakonishok
University of Illinois

Seymour Smidt
Cornell University

This study uses 90 years of daily data on the Dow Jones Industrial Average to test for the existence of persistent seasonal patterns in the rates of return. Methodological issues regarding seasonality tests are considered. We find evidence of persistently anomalous returns around the turn of the week, around the turn of the month, around the turn of the year, and around holidays.

In recent years there has been a proliferation of empirical studies documenting unexpected or anomalous regularities in security rates of return. In addition to the widely studied relation between firm size and rate of return,[1] these include seasonal regularities related to the time of the day [Harris (1986)], the day of the week [see Ball and Bowers (1986), Cross (1973), French (1980), Gibbons and Hess (1981), Jaffe and Westerfield (1985), Keim and Stambaugh (1984), and Lakonishok and Levi (1982)], the time of the month [Ariel (1987)], and the turn of the year [see Haugen and Lakonishok (1988), Jones, Pearce, and Wilson (1987), Lakonishok

---

This article has been presented at Cornell University, the University of Illinois at Urbana-Champaign, Indiana University, the University of Texas at Austin, the University of Toronto, the University of Waterloo, the University of Wisconsin at Madison, the Western Finance Association meetings, the TIMS/ORSA meetings, and the European Finance Association meetings in Istanbul. The authors appreciate helpful comments from Robin Brenner, William Brock, William Carleton, Robert Haugen, Robert Jarrow, Paul Halpern, Maureen O'Hara, Marc Reinganum, Richard Thaler, and especially Michael Brennan and Stephen J. Brown. Robin Brenner and Romeo D. Uyan assisted in the data collection and programming. Address reprint requests to Dr. Smidt, Johnson Graduate School of Management, Malott Hall, Cornell University, Ithaca, NY 14853.

[1] Early work on the size effect was done by Banz (1981) and Reinganum (1981). Schwert (1983) provides a survey.

The Review of Financial Studies 1988, Volume 1, number 4, pp. 403–425
© 1989 The Review of Financial Studies 0893-9454/88/$1.50

and Smidt (1984), and Schultz (1985)]. The findings present a potentially serious challenge to classical models of market equilibrium and have stimulated the development of new theories that can account for them [see Rock (1989), Admati and Pfleiderer (1988a, 1988b), and Foster and Viswanathan (1987)].

However, it is at least possible that these new facts are really chimeras, the product of sampling error and data mining. For this reason it is important to test for the existence of these regularities in data samples that are different from those in which they were originally discovered. In this article we provide evidence on several seasonal return anomalies over a long period of time using a uniform data base and methodology. The study is based on the daily closing prices of the Dow Jones Industrial Average from 1897 to 1986, practically the whole time that a U.S. security market index has existed.

We examine monthly, semimonthly, weekend, holiday, end-of-December, and turn-of-the-month seasonalities. In several cases our sample period is considerably longer than that used in earlier studies. The holiday and the semimonthly effects were recently investigated using post-1962 data [see Ariel (1985, 1987)]; we add 65 years of new data. Studies of the weekend effect have used data going back to 1928 [see Ball and Bowers (1986), Cross (1973), French (1980), Gibbons and Hess (1981), Jaffe and Westerfield (1985), Keim and Stambaugh (1984), and Lakonishok and Levi (1982)]; we add 30 years of additional data. The end-of-December effect and the turn-of-the-month effect have not been thoroughly explored previously. We add little new data for the monthly seasonals and present results mainly for completeness.

The remainder of this article is organized as follows. The first section discusses the quality of the existing evidence of anomalies. The second section describes the Dow Jones Industrial Average, which is the basis for our analyses. Sections 3 through 7 consider particular anomalies. Section 8 discusses the sensitivity of the results to the pattern of dividend payments. The final section presents our conclusions.

1. Quality of the Evidence

Anomalies in securities returns have been reported by many investigators using a variety of research procedures, so that skepticism about their existence must be based on characteristics that are common to essentially all the studies or to our interpretations of them. Three generic considerations provide support for a skeptical attitude. We call them boredom, noise, and data snooping.

Merton (1985) emphasized the danger of attaching undue importance to studies that report anomalies because of a selection bias, which we call the boredom factor. Even if studies that fail to reject established doctrines are more numerous, they are less likely to be published because they support beliefs that are already widely held and hence do not add much new knowledge. A reader who noted that many published studies report anomalous findings might overestimate the evidence supporting their existence. A similar form of selection bias was studied by Ross (1986).

Fischer Black's (1986) presidential address stressed the importance of noise in security returns. Anomalous changes in average rates of return are difficult to detect if there is a high level of nonstationarity in the return-generating process. On the other hand, if we underestimate the noise level, which Black believes is common, we are likely to report anomalies when we have actually encountered only noise.

A third consideration, the attempt to both discover and test hypotheses using the same data, is called data snooping. The statistical tests routinely used in financial economics are usually interpreted as if they were being applied to new data. But the data available in finance are seldom new. Low-cost computing and reliable data bases such as the Center for Research in Security Prices (CRSP) and COMPUSTAT have led to a huge supply of empirical research on stock prices. Most of this research is based on relatively few data bases. In this situation, the dangers of data snooping are substantial.

As a defense against data snooping, the finance profession has developed a strong preference for empirical studies based on hypotheses derived from theory. This may provide temporary protection, but the degree of security provided is quite subtle when theories are refined and revised based on past studies and the revised theories are then tested using essentially the same data. Moreover, the empirical studies that reported seasonality in rates of return were not based on previously defined theories.

Data snooping is sometimes thought of as an individual sin. One researcher tests many different hypotheses on the same data (perhaps reporting only the most exciting results). However, it is also a collective sin. A hundred researchers using the same data test a hundred different hypotheses. The 101st derives a theory after studying the previous results and tests and theory using more or less the same data.

The best remedy for data snooping is new data. When new data are not available, significance levels on tests of individual hypotheses must be adjusted if multiple tests are performed on the same data. Conventional significance levels may be grossly inadequate in the presence of data snooping. But if significance levels are corrected, it is not necessarily inappro-

---

[2] In studying seasonal patterns for a five-day trading week, there are 30 ($2^5 - 2$) possible hypotheses. If the 30 hypotheses are tested on the same data (by one or more researchers), each using a conventional 5 percent significance level for each hypothesis, and if the tests are statistically independent, the significance level of the so-called induced test implied by the search for the largest possible t values would not be 5 percent, but only 0.79 [$1 - (1 - 0.05)^{30}$]. This result, based on the Bonferroni inequality [see, e.g., Feller (1968, p. 110)], is described in detail in Savin (1984, pp. 834–835). There is a 0.21 probability that one or more of the tests will be significant, even if none of the patterns truly exists. To achieve a joint significance level of 0.05, the significance levels of the individual hypotheses must be reduced to 0.17 percent (0.0017) because $0.05 = 1 - (1 - 0.0017)^{30}$. This requires at least 10 observations ($0.5^9 > 0.0017 > 0.5^{10}$). In the case of monthly seasonals, there are 4094 ($2^{12} - 2$) possible hypotheses. If we want a joint test to be significant at the 0.05 level, the individual tests must be significant at the 0.00001253 level, which requires at least 17 years of data ($0.5^{16} > 0.0000125 > 0.5^{17}$).

priate to test many hypotheses with the same data.[2] Our study can be thought of as an effort to test many hypotheses about seasonal patterns on the same data, not all of which are new. In interpreting our results, we assign considerable importance to evidence that a particular seasonal pattern persists through most or all of the several nonoverlapping subperiods. We report the standard test statistics and their conventional significance but do not interpret the significance levels literally, in part because of the issues raised above.[3]

2. The Dow Jones Industrial Average

On October 7, 1896, the *Wall Street Journal* published two sets of daily stock price averages for the previous 30 days: an average of 20 railroad stock prices and an average of 12 industrial stock prices. Stock price averages for both classes of securities have been published regularly ever since. Thus, a Dow Jones Industrial Average (DJIA) is available on a daily basis back to September 8, 1896. Before this date, Charles H. Dow, editor of the *Wall Street Journal,* had occasionally published stock averages of various kinds, but not on a regular basis. No other American stock average has been available continuously for so long. Our study includes data from the first trading day in 1897 (January 4) through June 11, 1986, approximately 90 years.

The industrial averages were based on 12 stocks until October 3, 1916, when the list was expanded to 20 stocks. On October 1, 1928, the list was expanded to 30 stocks. Since then, the number of stocks has not changed.

The particular stocks included in the DJIA have changed from time to time. Changes were more frequent in the early days than they have been recently. The stated objective is to choose companies that are "representative of the broad market and of American industry . . . major factors in their industries . . . and widely held by individuals and institutional investors" [Dow Jones (1986)]. From the beginning, the list was composed of large, well-known, actively traded industrial stocks.

The DJIA is available for every day the market has been open. The stock market closed from August 1, 1914, until December 12, 1914, because of World War I. Beginning on June 1, 1952, Saturday trading sessions were eliminated. For a few years before that, Saturday trading was suspended at certain times, mainly during the summer months. During the last six months of 1968, the exchange closed on Wednesdays so that brokers' back-office operations could catch up with the volume of trading.

The permanent elimination of Saturday trading sessions in 1952 provides a convenient point for partitioning the data. The pre-1952 period was

---

[3] The "percent of positive returns" statistic is reported in most tables as a measure of central tendency. Conventional significance levels are reported as an additional descriptive statistic. But Brown and Warner (1980) showed that this test is not correctly specified when the distribution of returns is asymmetric, so that these significance levels cannot be taken literally.

Are Seasonal Anomalies Real?

partitioned into four subperiods, each approximately 14 years long; the second major period was similarly partitioned into three subperiods, each approximately 12 years long. To facilitate making judgments about the persistence of characteristics of the data, we report in most cases the findings for each of 10 separate periods: the entire 90 years, two major periods, and seven nonoverlapping subperiods.

The DJIA is a reasonable proxy for the large capitalization industrial company component of the market portfolio. The 30 stocks in the index represent about 25 percent of the market value of all NYSE stocks. Concentrating on large, actively traded firms minimizes problems associated with nonsynchronous trading and makes the DJIA an extremely useful index for representing short-term market movements [see Rudd (1979)]. Therefore, the DJIA is particularly suited for our study. The DJIA does not include dividends. Our results do not seem to be affected by the omission of dividends. Evidence on the effect of dividends is provided in Section 8. Our data cannot be used to evaluate seasonal anomalies, such as the January effect, that are characteristic of small companies.

3. Monthly Regularities

The evidence relating to monthly seasonals is presented in the Appendix. From prior research we know that there is a very high January return for small companies but no such pattern for large U.S. companies.[4] Our results are consistent with the previous findings for large companies.

Turning to within-month regularities, Ariel (1987) reported an intriguing result based on 19 years of data from 1963 through 1981—positive rates of return occur in the stock market only during the first half of each month. For example, he reports an average rate of return of 0.826 percent for the value-weighted CRSP Index during the first part of the month and a negative average rate of return, −0.182 percent, during the second part of the month. There have been some recent attempts to explain the higher rates of returns of small firms in January by considering the possibility that risk is not constant across the year [see, e.g., Rogalski and Tinic (1986)]. It is very unlikely that changes in risk within a month would produce such a pattern of rates of return for a value-weighted index.

Ariel's definition of the first part of the month includes the last trading day of the previous month. His justification for this is that the average rate of return on the last trading day of a month is high. Such a justification is

---

[4] Previous researchers utilized long time series in exploring monthly returns. Rozeff and Kinney (1976) used data for 1909 to 1974. Schultz (1985) utilized data from 1900 to 1929 and Jones, Pearce, and Wilson (1987) used monthly data from as early as 1871 (their period was 1871 to 1929). In the Rozeff and Kinney study, the high January return was obtained for equally weighted portfolios of NYSE or NYSE and AMEX stocks. They obtained their long time series by splicing together several indices. Some of these were value-weighted and others were equal-weighted. At the time they did their study, the importance of the difference between these types of series was not well understood.

[5] In Section 7 we examine rates of return for days around the turn of the month.

Table 1
Differences in rates of return of the Dow Jones Industrial Average between first and last half of the month by periods, in percent

Period	Mean[1]	Standard deviation	Median	Percent[2] positive differences	No. of months
1897-5/86	0.237	5.438	0.546	55.4**	1068
1897-5/52	0.153	6.235	0.486	54.2**	660
6/52-5/86	0.313	3.815	0.562	57.3**	408
1897-1910	−0.517	5.906	0.079	50.2	167
1911-1924	−0.455	5.631	0.202	52.9	164
1925-1938	1.143	8.508	0.832	56.5	168
1939-5/52	0.229	3.764	0.706	57.5	161
6/52-1963	0.299	3.160	0.278	56.7	139
1964-1975	0.582	3.925	1.023	61.8**	144
1976-5/86	0.029	4.327	0.336	52.8	125

[1] The significance levels are based on a *t*-test of the null hypothesis that the mean is zero.
[2] The significance levels are based on a sign test of the null hypothesis that the probability of a positive return is 50 percent and will not be correct if the return distribution is asymmetric.
* Significant at 5 percent level.
** Significant at 1 percent level.

questionable because it relies on an examination of the data.[5] We define the first half of the month as the first through the fifteenth calendar day of the month, if it is a trading day, or if not, through the next trading day. The last half of the month consists of the remaining days.

Table 1 shows differences in the average rates of return between the first and last half of the month for each of the 10 periods. The average difference for the entire period is 0.237 percent, which is much less than the 1 percent difference reported by Ariel. Furthermore, the average rate of return is positive for both halves of the month. The average difference between the two halves is positive for the two major periods. It is negative in two of the seven subperiods and practically zero in the last subperiod. The second largest difference in any of the seven nonoverlapping subperiods, 0.582 percent, occurs during the 12-year period from 1964 through 1975, which is wholly contained in Ariel's 19-year observation period. Based on a *t*-test (5 percent significance level), we could not reject the null hypothesis that the two halves of the month have the same rate of return for any of the 10 periods.[6]

We used the parametric test to examine the difference between the first and last halves of months on a month-by-month basis. For the total period and the two major subperiods, significant differences between the first and

---
[6] Table 1 also shows the percentage of months in which returns are higher in the first half than in the second half. For the whole sample, 55.4 percent of the months have higher returns in the first half than in the second half. The null hypothesis that the two halves of the month are the same can be rejected at the 1 percent level. The results are similar for both the pre- and post-1952 periods and for the one subperiod, 1964-1975, that was wholly included in Ariel's observation period. To summarize, the parametric test does not detect significant differences between the two halves of the month, whereas the nonparametric test finds a superior performance during the first half of the month. The difference between the results of the parametric and nonparametric tests may be attributable to skewness in the distribution of returns, in which case the nonparametric test is not correctly specified.

Are Seasonal Anomalies Real?

second halves of the month are observed, in general, only for April and December. In April, the first half of the month performs exceptionally well, and in December the second half has an exceptional performance. For the seven nonoverlapping subperiods, we find only two differences significant at the 5 percent level of 84 (12 × 7) possible, which is less than would be expected by chance. Looking at the signs of the differences we find 49 positive differences (58 percent) and 35 negative differences. This result is in the direction of Ariel's findings. But a two-tailed sign test does not reject the null hypothesis that positive and negative changes are equally likely, even at the 10 percent level.[7]

The evidence described so far provides only mild support for the idea that rates of return are larger in the first half of the month than in the last half. Ariel's evidence of a higher average rate of return during the first half of the month appears to be partly the result of idiosyncratic characteristics of the period he studied and partly the result of including the last trading day of the previous month as part of the first half of a month.[8]

For the total period of 90 years the average rate of return during the second half of December is 1.54 percent. This is the highest rate of return of any of the 24 half-months. In each of the seven subperiods the average rate of return of the DJIA during the last half of December exceeded 1 percent. In 75 percent of the years the rate of return in the second half of December was positive, compared with 56 percent positive for a typical half-month. Such a relatively consistent high rate of return for the largest companies over such a short period of time deserves further investigation. It is consistent with the widely held opinions on Wall Street about window dressing.[9]

If the importance of an anomalous rate of return is evaluated in terms of its impact on a dollar-weighted portfolio, then the high average end-of-December rate of return for large companies is far more important than the high average rate of return for small companies in January. This very high rate of return in the second half of December may reflect high returns before holidays. Lakonishok and Smidt (1984, pp. 446–447) report high rates of return for large companies on the last trading day of the year (0.61 percent) and around Christmas. The end-of-December period is investigated further in Section 6.

---

[7] To conserve space, detailed results on rates of return for the first and second halves of the month by calendar month are not reported but are summarized in the text. Detailed data are available from the authors.

[8] Of course, some differences may exist that are not detected because of the large semimonthly standard deviation. In fact, even for the total period which includes 1068 months, a difference of 0.33 percent would be necessary to make the results significant at the 5 percent level.

[9] For example: "Before retailers take down their Christmas window displays, big investors are likely to do some window dressing of their own this week. That should keep blue chip stocks dancing along, while smaller stocks lag behind," *U.S.A. Today*, December 29, 1986. See also, "Heard on the Street," *Wall Street Journal*, May 18, 1988; "Abreast of the Market," *Wall Street Journal*, June 27, 1988, which discusses quarterly window dressing; and Solveig Jansson, "The Fine Art of Window Dressing," *Institutional Investor*, December 1983. The topic of window dressing also has been considered by academic writers as a partial explanation for some seasonal patterns. See Ritter and Chopra (1989) and Haugen and Lakonishok (1989).

4. The Weekend Effect

One of the most puzzling empirical findings is that mean stock rates of return vary according to the day of the week. Rates of return on Monday tend to be significantly negative, and rates of return on the last trading day of the week tend to be high. The weekend effect is documented in many papers.[10]

The customary trading days have changed during the period of our study. Before June 1, 1952, the New York Stock Exchange was usually open for trading six days a week. On Saturdays, however, the exchange was open only until noon. From 1945 until 1952, when Saturday trading was permanently eliminated, there were times, usually during the summer months, in which the exchange was closed on Saturday.

Therefore, in presenting our results for periods before June 1, 1952, we report rates of return for two groups of Fridays: those followed by Saturday trading and those followed by a long weekend. To test for differences in mean rates of return across the days of the week, we use an F-test for the joint significance of the coefficients in the regression

$$r_t = \alpha_1 D_{1t} + \alpha_2 D_{2t} + \alpha_3 D_{3t} + \alpha_4 D_{4t} + \alpha_5^1 D_{5t}^1 + \alpha_5^2 D_{5t}^2 + \alpha_6 D_{6t} + \epsilon_t$$
$$t = 1, 2, \ldots, T$$

where r_t is the rate of return of the DJIA on day t and $D_{1t}, D_{2t}, D_{3t}, D_{4t},$ and D_{6t} are dummy variables that equal 1 if trading day t is a Monday, Tuesday, Wednesday, Thursday, or Saturday, respectively, and 0 otherwise; D_{5t}^1 equals 1 if day t is a Friday followed by Saturday trading, and D_{5t}^2 equals 1 if day t is a Friday followed by a nontrading Saturday; otherwise, D_{5t}^1 and D_{5t}^2 equal 0.

The results are presented in Table 2.[11] The null hypothesis that all days of the week have the same rate of return is rejected for all 10 periods at the 1 percent significance level. The most noticeable pattern is the negative rate of return on Mondays for each of the 10 periods. The negative Monday rates of return are significantly different from zero at the 1 percent level for the total sample, the pre- and post-1952 periods, and in three of the subperiods.[12] In two additional subperiods, Monday rates of return are significantly different from zero at the 5 percent level.

We have two subperiods, 1897–1910 and 1911–1924, that were not con-

---

[10] See Cross (1973), French (1980), Gibbons and Hess (1981), Lakonishok and Levi (1982), Keim and Stambaugh (1984), Jaffe and Westerfield (1985), Harris (1986), and Ball and Bowers (1986). Many of the previous studies use the CRSP Daily Returns File, which began in 1962. The study by Keim and Stambaugh (1984) analyzed 55 years of data on the Standard and Poors Composite Index, 1928–1982. The data before 1928 have not been examined in any recent study but were considered by Fields (1931, 1934).

[11] There is some evidence that returns before holidays tend to be high. It is also possible that the average rate of return on the day after a holiday could tend to be different from that on a regular day. In examining the day of the week, the last trading day before a holiday and the first trading day after a holiday were excluded to avoid confounding day-of-the-week and holiday effects.

[12] The magnitude of the negative Monday return is worthy of note. The total period rate of return of −0.144 percent per day would result in an annual compounded decrease of more than 30 percent per year on a 250-trading-day basis, or a cumulative decrease on Mondays of around 7.5 percent per year.

Are Seasonal Anomalies Real?

sidered in any recent study. In these periods the regulatory environment, the institutional setting, the mechanics of trading, the availability of information, and many other details were different from the setting more recently, but the negative Monday return has a remarkable tendency to persist. Combining these two subperiods, the average Monday return is −0.076 percent, and it is significantly different from zero at the 1 percent level.

In general, there are somewhat larger and statistically significant positive rates of return on the last trading day of the week. In most studies, Friday was the last trading day.[13] We find that there is a tendency for a higher rate of return on the last trading day of the week, whether the last day is Friday or Saturday. Even when Friday is not the last trading day of the week, it still has a relatively high rate of return (see the period 1897–1952), possibly because Saturday was a short trading day. (The exchange was, in general, open for two hours—until noon.)

The nonparametric results shown in Table 2 support the daily seasonal. The only negative median rates of return for the total period or the two major subperiods are on Monday. In general, the percentage of positive rates of return is significantly below 50 percent for Monday and significantly above 50 percent for Friday and Saturday.[14]

5. Holiday Returns

The consistency of the pattern around the weekend closing suggests that it may apply to any gap in trading. High rates of return before holidays have been documented in previous studies.[15] Table 3 shows average rates of return around holidays. Days are classified as preholiday, postholiday, or regular (neither) without regard to the day of the week.[16] The average preholiday rate of return is 0.220 percent for the total sample, compared with the regular daily rate of return of 0.0094 percent per day. Therefore, the preholiday rate of return is 23 times larger than the regular daily rate of return, and holidays account for about 50 percent of the price increase in the DJIA. The percentage of positive rates of return before holidays is 63.9. The results for the subperiods are, in general, consistent with the total-period results.

Although it is possible that the preholiday and preweekend returns have

---

[13] Keim and Stambaugh's (1984) paper is an exception.

[14] Something like a weekend effect has also been detected in an experimental market [Coursey and Dyl (1986)].

[15] For example, Roll (1983) observed high rates of return on the last trading day of December and Lakonishok and Smidt (1984) reported high rates of return around Christmas. Ariel (1985) found preholiday daily rates of return of 0.53 percent and 0.36 percent for the CRSP equal-weighted index and value-weighted index, respectively, for the period 1963 to 1982. He reported that for the value-weighted index, the eight holidays per year account for 38 percent of the total annual rate of return.

[16] For this purpose a holiday was defined as a day when trading would normally have occurred but did not. For the post-1952 period, a Friday was counted as a day before a holiday if there was no trading on the following Monday. The special Wednesday closings in 1968 were not counted as holidays.

411

The Review of Financial Studies / Winter, 1988

Table 2
Daily rates of return of the Dow Jones Industrial Average by day of the week, in percent

Period	Monday	Tuesday	Wednesday
1897–1986			
Mean[1]	−0.144**	0.029	0.045**
Standard deviation	1.139	1.040	1.083
Median	−0.079	0.035	0.056
Percent of positive days[2]	45.4**	51.9*	52.6**
Number of days	3700	3962	3977
1897–5/30/52			
Mean[1]	−0.145**	0.035	0.032
Standard deviation	1.269	1.155	1.222
Median	−0.050	0.056	0.050
Percent of positive days[2]	47.0**	50.3	52.2*
Number of days	2205	2440	2394
6/1/52–1988			
Mean[1]	−0.142**	0.020	0.064**
Standard deviation	0.915	0.822	0.829
Median	−0.113	0.009	0.064
Percent of positive days[2]	43.0**	50.5	53.2*
Number of days	1495	1522	1583
1897–1910			
Mean[1]	−0.045	0.023	0.007
Standard deviation	1.234	1.062	1.025
Percent of positive days[2]	49.6	49.6	52.9
Number of days	599	629	630
1911–1924			
Mean[1]	−0.110*	0.048	0.001
Standard deviation	1.020	0.918	0.985
Percent of positive days[2]	47.3	53.9	49.2
Number of days	558	586	571
1925–1938			
Mean[1]	−0.331**	0.073	0.047
Standard deviation	1.744	1.583	1.822
Percent of positive days[2]	43.2**	55.5**	52.3
Number of days	578	623	608
1939–5/30/52			
Mean[1]	−0.084*	−0.004	0.072*
Standard deviation	0.771	0.904	0.766
Percent of positive days[2]	47.9	52.2	54.2*
Number of days	470	602	585
6/1/52–1963			
Mean[1]	−0.194**	0.015	0.084
Standard deviation	0.802	0.678	0.691
Percent of positive days[2]	41.3**	52.9	55.0*
Number of days	509	522	533
1964–1975			
Mean[1]	−0.164**	−0.011	0.081*
Standard deviation	0.897	0.803	0.891
Percent of positive days[2]	40.6**	49.0	54.3*
Number of days	527	526	547
1976–1985			
Mean[1]	−0.060	0.060	0.025
Standard deviation	1.040	0.974	0.891
Percent of positive days[2]	47.7	49.6	50.3
Number of days	459	474	503

Excludes days preceded or followed by holidays.

[1] The significance levels are based on a *t*-test of the null hypothesis that the mean is zero.

[2] The significance levels are based on a sign test of the null hypothesis that the probability of a positive return is 50 percent and will not be correct if the return distribution is asymmetric.

Are Seasonal Anomalies Real?

**Table 2
Extended**

Thursday	Trading Saturday	Friday before no-trading Saturday	Saturday
0.024	0.050*	0.070**	0.052**
1.042	1.227	0.721	0.837
0.021	0.094	0.079	0.074
51.0	54.4**	54.6**	56.5**
4111	2316	1645	2308
0.012	0.050*	0.115	0.052**
1.173	1.227	0.626	0.837
0.012	0.094	0.052	0.074
50.3	54.4**	53.6	56.5**
2507	2316	110	2308
0.040*	—	0.067**	
0.795	—	0.727	
0.037	—	0.090	
51.9	—	54.7**	
1604	—	1535	
−0.031	0.082*	—	−0.013
1.084	1.032	—	0.845
50.3	55.6**	—	51.8
648	620	—	623
−0.013	0.075	—	0.090**
1.083	0.931	—	0.668
47.8	53.9	—	56.3**
603	586	—	588
0.082	0.044	—	0.032
1.582	1.804	—	1.161
53.5	56.0**	—	56.0**
637	612	—	600
0.011	0.012	0.067**	0.112**
0.789	0.810	0.727	0.441
49.6	51.2	54.7	63.4**
619	498	1535	497
0.039	—	0.119**	
0.620	—	0.579	
54.0	—	60.7**	
550	—	527	
0.048	—	0.028	
0.835	—	0.786	
49.5	—	53.0	
549	—	540	
0.033	—	0.054	
0.911	—	0.800	
52.3	—	50.1	
505	—	468	

* Significant at 5 percent level for two-tailed test.
** Significant at 1 percent level for two-tailed test.

Table 3
Daily rates of return of the Dow Jones Industrial Average before and after holidays and on regular days, in percent

Period	Before-holiday days	After-holiday days	Regular days
1897–1986 (No. of holidays = 915/22,019)[1]			
Mean[2]	0.220**	−0.017	0.009
Standard deviation	1.061	1.314	1.050
Median	0.196	0.054	0.035
Percent of positive days[3]	63.9**	50.1	51.7
1897–1951 (No. of holidays = 543/14,280)[1]			
Mean[2]	0.241**	−0.101	0.008
Standard deviation	1.143	1.490	1.154
Median	0.196	0.000	0.045
Percent of positive days[3]	64.3**	50.0	52.2
1952–1986 (No. of holidays = 372/7739)[1]			
Mean[2]	0.181**	0.106*	0.011
Standard deviation	0.897	0.987	0.822
Median	0.196	0.103	0.017
Percent of positive days[3]	63.2**	55.9*	50.8
1897–1910 (No. of holidays = 123/3749)[1]			
Mean[2]	0.285**	−0.020	0.004
Standard deviation	1.011	1.320	1.052
Percent of positive days[3]	70.1**	48.3	51.6
1911–1924 (No. of holidays = 139/3492)[1]			
Mean[2]	0.083	0.001	0.016
Standard deviation	1.040	1.206	0.945
Percent of positive days[3]	55.7	51.3	51.4
1925–1938 (No. of holidays = 138/3658)[1]			
Mean[2]	0.449**	−0.268	0.000
Standard deviation	1.601	2.089	1.636
Percent of positive days[3]	66.3**	47.6	52.9
1939–5/1952 (No. of holidays = 143/3381)[1]			
Mean[2]	0.130**	−0.097	0.021
Standard deviation	0.593	1.138	0.764
Percent of positive days[3]	65.4**	48.9	53.0
6/1952–1963 (No. of holidays = 123/2641)[1]			
Mean[2]	0.323**	0.216**	0.014
Standard deviation	0.717	0.799	0.685
Percent of positive days[3]	72.2**	65.8**	52.9
1964–1975 (No. of holidays = 146/2689)[1]			
Mean[2]	0.178*	−0.045	−0.001
Standard deviation	0.868	0.836	0.847
Percent of positive days[3]	61.3*	50.7	49.3
1976–6/1986 (No. of holidays = 103/2409)[1]			
Mean[2]	0.011	0.189	0.023
Standard deviation	1.089	1.317	0.926
Percent of positive days[3]	54.4	51.5	50.0

[1] The numbers shown are the number of holidays and the total number of trading days. The number of days before and after holidays equals the number of holidays. All other trading days are regular days.
[2] The significance levels are based on a *t*-test of the null hypothesis that the mean is zero.
[3] The significance levels are based on a sign test of the null hypothesis that the probability of a positive return is 50 percent and will not be correct if the return distribution is asymmetric.
* Significant at 5 percent level for two-tailed test.
** Significant at 1 percent level for two-tailed test.

a common origin in the closing of the exchange the following day, the preholiday rates of return are generally two to five times larger than preweekend rates of return. Therefore, there appears to be an additional factor at work.

The average rate of return after holidays is negative for the total period, −0.017 percent. However, this rate of return is not significantly different from zero or from the average rate of return on regular days and is much less negative than the rate of return on Mondays.

6. End-of-December Returns

We have already mentioned that the last half of December has exceptionally high returns. Possibly, this is because the period includes the trading days before two major holidays, Christmas and New Year's Day. The results in the previous section document high preholiday rates of return. Table 4 focuses on the last half of December. This period was partitioned into three intervals as follows: (1) from mid-December up to, but not including, the last trading day before Christmas (the pre-Christmas period); (2) from the first trading day after Christmas up to, but not including, the last trading day before New Year's Day (the interholiday period); and (3) the last trading day before Christmas and the last trading day before New Year's Day (the preholiday days). The average number of trading days per year in each of the three intervals is 3.5, 3.3, and 2 for the pre-Christmas period, interholiday period, and preholiday days, respectively.

The average daily rate of return for the pre-Christmas period is slightly negative but not significantly different from the typical daily rate of return. The increase in the DJIA index during the last half of December is concentrated in the period beginning on the last pre-Christmas trading day. The average rates of increase during this brief time are very large: 0.248 percent per day during the interholiday period and 0.386 percent per day on the two preholiday days. Overall, the average rate of increase in the DJIA index during this week is on the order of 1.6 percent (3.3 × 0.248 + 2 × 0.386). These high rates of increase are persistent across all the subperiods; for the pre-1952 period the average rate of increase is 1.8 percent, and for the post-1952 period it is 1.2 percent.[17]

7. The Turn-of-the-Month Returns

Ariel (1987) analyzed the 1963–1981 period and provided some evidence that days around the turn of the month exhibit high rates of return. We examine this issue in depth.

---

[17] The nonparametric statistics confirm the previous results with respect to the total period and the subperiods. The frequency of positive rates of return is high during the interholiday period and especially on the preholiday days. On the two preholiday days the rate of return is positive on 71 percent of the days compared with 51 percent on a typical day.

Table 4
Daily rates of return of Dow Jones Industrial Average during last half of December by period, in percent

Period	Pre-Christmas period[1]	Interholiday period[2]	Preholiday days[3]
1897–1986			
Mean[4]	−0.039	0.248**	0.386**
Standard deviation	1.100	1.011	0.714
Median	0.003	0.134	0.256
Percent of positive days[5]	49.7	57.3*	70.9**
Number of days	314	293	172
1897–1951			
Mean[4]	−0.042	0.288**	0.423**
Standard deviation	1.266	1.156	0.811
Median	0.023	1.644	0.299
Percent of positive days[5]	52.1	57.4*	72.1**
Number of days	209	190	104
1952–1985			
Mean[4]	−0.034	0.175**	0.329**
Standard deviation	0.661	0.663	0.532
Median	−0.105	0.083	0.184
Percent of positive days[5]	44.8	57.3	69.1**
Number of days	105	103	68
1897–1910			
Mean[4]	0.055	0.504**	0.359*
Standard deviation	1.109	1.139	0.901
Percent of positive days[5]	53.8	61.7	65.4
Number of days	52	47	26
1911–1924			
Mean[4]	0.033	0.185	0.685**
Standard deviation	1.523	0.992	0.959
Percent of positive days[5]	52.9	53.1	84.6**
Number of days	51	49	26
1925–1938			
Mean[4]	−0.218	0.217	0.508**
Standard deviation	1.569	1.548	0.826
Percent of positive days[5]	52.5	51.0	71.4*
Number of days	59	49	28
1939–1951			
Mean[4]	−0.009	0.252*	0.111*
Standard deviation	0.447	0.790	0.259
Percent of positive days[5]	48.9	64.4	66.7
Number of days	47	45	24
1952–1963			
Mean[4]	−0.104	0.216*	0.295**
Standard deviation	0.508	0.509	0.344
Percent of positive days[5]	37.8	64.7	79.2**
Number of days	37	34	24
1964–1975			
Mean[4]	−0.151	0.190	0.392**
Standard deviation	0.651	0.753	0.673
Percent of positive days[5]	45.9	56.8	62.5
Number of days	37	37	24
1976–1985			
Mean[4]	0.189	0.115	0.293*
Standard deviation	0.790	0.713	0.549
Percent of positive days[5]	51.6	50.0	65.0
Number of days	31	32	20

[1] From mid-December up to, but not including, the last trading day before Christmas.

[2] From the first trading day after Christmas up to, but not including, the last trading day before New Year's Day. (Table notes continued, p. 417.)

Are Seasonal Anomalies Real?

Table 5 shows statistics on rates of return for eight days around the turn of the month. Days −1 and 1 are the last and the first trading days of a month, respectively. The results reveal a strong turn-of-the-month effect. Focusing on the total sample, the average rates of return are especially high for days −1 to 3. The cumulative rate of increase over the four days around the turn of the month is 0.473 percent, whereas for an average four-day period the rate of increase is 0.0612 percent. This difference is statistically significant at the 0.1 percent level. The frequency of positive rates of return around the turn of the month is more than 56 percent compared to less than 52 percent for a regular day.

The average price increase during the four-day period around the turn of the month exceeds the average monthly price increase, which is 0.349 percent. Therefore, the DJIA goes down during the non-turn-of-the-month period. We found an average daily rate of return of −0.001 percent for days 5 to 9 and −0.032 percent per day for the interval −5 to −9.

The results are, in general, consistent across the major subperiods. For example, the four-day rate of return is 0.492 percent and 0.443 percent for the first and second major subperiods, respectively. The results remained essentially the same when the last trading day of December and the first three trading days of January were excluded.[18]

8. Dividend Effects

The DJIA is not adjusted for dividends. Seasonalities in dividend payments could induce seasonal patterns in the reported rates of return on the DJIA even though there was no seasonal pattern in the dividend-adjusted rates of return. To investigate this issue we collected dividend data for the stocks in the DJIA during five calendar years—1941, 1951, 1961, 1971 and 1981—and computed the dividend return to the DJIA on each day that any Dow stock went ex dividend. The total dividend return (a simple sum of the daily dividend returns) for these years was 6.2, 5.8, 3.0, 3.5, and 6.0 percent, respectively.[19] Data on the seasonal pattern for the first and last of these years and the average of the five years are shown in Table 6.

---

[18] This turn-of-the-month pattern may partly be due to pension fund managers concentrating their buying at the end of the month to avoid a downward bias in estimated rates of return (Stewart, 1987).

[19] We acknowledge the help of Mr. Steven Wheeler, assistant archivist of the New York Stock Exchange, who provided information on New York Stock Exchange ex-dividend period regulations for the 1875–1933 period, and of Professor Michael Barclay of the University of Rochester, who kindly shared with us some data on ex-dividend days around the turn of the century that were collected for his article (1987).

←

[3] The last trading day before Christmas and the last trading day before New Year's Day.
[4] The significance levels are based on a *t*-test of the null hypothesis that the mean is zero.
[5] The significance levels are based on a sign test of the null hypothesis that the probability of a positive return is 50 percent and will not be correct if the return distribution is asymmetric.
* Significant at 5 percent level for two-tailed test.
** Significant at 1 percent level for two-tailed test.

Table 5
Daily rates of return of the Dow Jones Industrial Average around the turn of the month, in percent

	−4	−3	−2
1897–1986			
Mean[1] (1052 obs.)	0.002	−0.023	0.061
Standard deviation	1.093	1.104	1.049
Median	0.051	0.000	0.087
Percent of positive days[2]	52.3	49.8	54.1**
1897–1952			
Mean[1] (643 obs.)	−0.001	−0.061	0.090*
Standard deviation	1.256	1.217	1.100
Median	0.028	0.000	0.107
Percent of positive days[2]	51.5	49.1	56.0**
1952–1986			
Mean[1] (409 obs.)	0.017	0.035	0.014
Standard deviation	0.772	0.897	0.847
Median	0.082	0.018	0.032
Percent of positive days[2]	53.5	50.9	51.1
1897–1910			
Mean[1] (163 obs.)	0.173*	−0.026	0.133
Standard deviation	1.126	1.046	0.987
Percent of positive days[2]	60.1*	51.5	52.1
1911–1924			
Mean[1] (156 obs.)	−0.001	−0.037	0.045
Standard deviation	0.962	0.928	0.900
Percent of positive days[2]	48.1	42.3	56.4
1925–1938			
Mean[1] (164 obs.)	−0.237	−0.209	0.090
Standard deviation	1.853	1.853	1.546
Percent of positive days[2]	43.9	53.1	57.3
1939–5/1952			
Mean[1] (160 obs.)	0.043	0.032	0.092
Standard deviation	0.750	0.690	0.805
Percent of positive days[2]	53.8	49.4	58.1*
6/1952–1963			
Mean[1] (139 obs.)	0.029	0.082	0.149*
Standard deviation	0.682	0.909	0.802
Percent of positive days[2]	54.7	56.1	58.3
1964–1975			
Mean[1] (144 obs.)	−0.063	0.028	−0.033
Standard deviation	0.828	0.949	0.829
Percent of positive days[2]	51.4	47.2	43.8
1976–5/1986			
Mean[1] (126 obs.)	0.094	0.000	−0.082
Standard deviation	0.796	0.825	0.900
Percent of positive days[2]	54.8	49.2	51.6

[1] The significance levels are based on a *t*-test of the null hypothesis that the mean is zero.
[2] The significance levels are based on a sign test of the null hypothesis that the probability of a positive return is 50 percent and will not be correct if the return distribution is asymmetric.

The top panel in Table 6 shows the monthly dividend returns for 1941 and 1981. Most companies pay their regular dividends on a quarterly basis. Two seasonal patterns are noteworthy. The first is a tendency for the dividend return during the middle month of each calendar quarter to be higher

Are Seasonal Anomalies Real?

**Table 5
Extended**

−1	1	2	3	4
0.122**	0.084*	0.127**	0.140**	0.016
0.980	1.119	1.014	1.068	1.071
0.123	0.137	0.147	0.132	0.079
56.5**	56.9**	57.8**	56.8**	53.1*
0.123**	0.114*	0.113**	0.142**	0.019
1.100	1.181	1.103	1.195	1.221
0.123	0.170	0.123	0.133	0.071
56.3**	59.3**	56.6**	56.5**	52.6
0.120**	0.036	0.149**	0.138**	0.013
0.754	1.015	0.857	0.833	0.782
0.123	0.079	0.188	0.129	0.083
56.7**	53.3	59.7**	57.2**	54.0
0.103	0.181*	0.060	0.024	−0.062
1.035	1.113	0.870	0.990	1.007
55.9	60.7**	51.5	52.8	49.7
0.072	0.077	0.110	0.069	0.016
1.072	1.109	1.084	0.928	0.998
51.3	59.0*	57.7	55.1	51.9
0.215	0.086	0.074	0.273*	0.161
1.471	1.594	1.557	1.744	1.840
59.8*	56.1	54.3	59.8*	57.9*
0.098	0.111	0.212**	0.198**	−0.043
0.669	0.747	0.703	0.876	0.721
58.1*	61.3**	63.1**	58.1*	50.6
0.188**	0.122*	0.277**	0.141*	0.010
0.670	0.668	0.639	0.673	0.640
66.2**	63.3**	69.1**	59.7*	50.4
0.142*	0.000	0.045	0.186*	0.074
0.822	0.924	0.851	0.875	0.732
53.5	49.7	56.9	60.4*	58.3*
0.018	0.000	0.128	0.078	−0.054
0.755	1.371	1.042	0.938	0.960
50.0	48.4	52.4	50.8	53.1

* Significant at 5 percent level for two-tailed test.
** Significant at 1 percent level for two-tailed test.

than the dividend return during either the first or last month of the quarter. This tendency has intensified over time. In 1941, 48 percent of the dividend return for the year occurred in the middle months of the quarter; by 1981 this had risen to 68 percent. The second pattern is a tendency for firms to

Table 6
Dividend yields for the Dow Jones Industrial Average

	1941	1981	Average[1]
By month (percent per month)			
January	0.17	0.31	0.18
February	0.64	0.99	0.71
March	0.50	0.10	0.24
April	0.24	0.22	0.16
May	0.72	1.04	0.78
June	0.54	0.11	0.22
July	0.17	0.31	0.16
August	0.65	1.10	0.79
September	0.47	0.07	0.19
October	0.18	0.63	0.28
November	0.95	0.93	0.86
December	1.00	0.15	0.33
By day of the week (percent per day)			
Monday	0.0126	0.0480	0.0240
Tuesday	0.0082	0.0226	0.0225
Wednesday	0.0134	0.0129	0.0117
Thursday	0.0453	0.0131	0.0134
Friday	0.0404	0.0179	0.0229
Around the turn of the month (percent per day)			
−4	0.0016	0.0469	0.0133
−3	0.0071	0.0103	0.0144
−2	0.0149	0.0062	0.0120
−1	0.0037	0.0381	0.0148
1	0.0053	0.0809	0.0342
2	0.0090	0.0210	0.0215
3	0.0355	0.0237	0.0185
4	0.0375	0.0348	0.0257

[1] Average across the years 1941, 1951, 1961, 1971, and 1981.

pay an extra dividend during December. This tendency has weakened. Four Dow companies paid an extra dividend in December 1941. None did during December 1981.

The monthly pattern of dividend returns does not change any of our conclusions regarding monthly returns on the Dow. The dividend rate of return in January is below average, but, as we have seen, without dividends there is not a statistically significant difference between the January DJIA rate of return and the rate of return of the other months. The dividend pattern indicates that adjusting for dividends would not lead to any changes in our conclusions about monthly rate-of-return seasonality.

The middle panel in Table 6 shows dividend returns by day of the week. The high dividend return on Mondays is a recent phenomenon. In 1981, 42 percent of the dividends were paid on Mondays. However, the daily dividend returns are much too small to explain the weekly seasonal. The largest daily dividend return in the table is 0.048 percent, whereas the average rate of return on Mondays is −0.144 percent.

The bottom panel in Table 6 shows dividend returns around the end of the month. Again, there does not seem to be any pattern, certainly not any that is large enough to explain the turn-of-the-month effect.

9. Conclusions

In summary, DJIA returns are persistently anomalous over a 90-year period around the turn of the week, around the turn of the month, around the turn of the year, and around holidays. Specifically, the rate of return on Monday is substantially negative (−0.14 percent), the price increase around the turn of the month exceeds the total monthly price increase, the price increase from the last trading day before Christmas to the end of the year is over 1.5 percent, and the rate of return before holidays is more than 20 times the normal rate of return. The possibility that these particular anomalies could have occurred by chance cannot be excluded, but this is very unlikely. We do not find either a consistent monthly pattern in the returns or any consistent tendency for returns in the first part of the month to be higher.

It is useful to relate the magnitude of the anomalies with the size of a tick (the smallest price change), which is 12.5 cents. Because the average price per share on the NYSE is about $40, a movement of one tick corresponds to a price change of 0.313 percent or more, which is much larger than most seasonal anomalies discussed in this paper. For example, the average Monday price decrease of −0.144 percent is well within one tick.

Notwithstanding the small magnitude of these regularities, their persistence demands explanation and focuses attention on the processes by which prices in securities markets are set. It is unlikely that there is a single explanation of the various seasonalities. Possible explanations that have been suggested include inventory adjustments of different traders [Rock (1989) and Ritter (1988)], the timing of trades by informed and uninformed traders [Admati and Pfleiderer (1988a)], and specialists' strategies in response to informed traders [Admati and Pfleiderer (1988b)], as well as the timing of corporate news releases [Penman (1987)], seasonal patterns in cash flows to individuals and institutional investors, tax-induced trading [Lakonishok and Smidt (1986)], and the window dressing induced by periodic evaluation of portfolio managers [Haugen and Lakonishok (1988) and Ritter and Chopra (1989)].

Appendix

Descriptive statistics for average rates of return by month for the total sample and the pre- and post-1952 periods are shown in Table A1. The results reveal that none of the months is consistently different than average.[20] August, which had the highest rate of return in the first subperiod, had a relatively low rate of return in the second subperiod. January is

---

[20] Table A1 also shows the percentage of months with positive rates of return and the results of a sign test in which the null hypothesis is that the percentage of positive rates of return in the given month is equal for all months. The results of this nonparametric test are consistent with the findings presented above.

Table A1
Monthly rates of return of the Dow Jones Industrial Average by period, 1897–1986, in percent

	January	February	March	April	May
1897–5/86					
Mean[1]	0.818	−0.456	0.483	0.647	−0.554
Standard deviation	4.463	4.188	5.597	6.569	6.085
Median	0.952	−0.245	1.035	0.479	−0.113
Number of months	90	90	89	90	90
Percent of positive months	62	48	60	54	49
Sign test (z-statistic)[2]	1.085	−1.680	0.570	−0.404	−1.467
1897–5/52					
Mean[1]	0.776	−0.622	0.307	0.050	−0.306
Standard deviation	4.016	4.701	6.743	7.770	7.236
Median	0.841	−0.518	0.996	−0.461	0.221
Number of months	55	56	56	56	56
Percent of positive months	64	45	55	48	54
Sign test (z-statistic)[2]	0.999	−1.863	−0.244	−1.323	−0.514
6/52–1986					
Mean[1]	0.883	−0.182	0.979	1.631*	−0.961
Standard deviation	5.149	3.214	2.993	3.762	3.513
Median	1.336	0.323	1.444	1.190	−0.753
Number of months	35	34	34	34	34
Percent of positive months	60	53	62	65	41
Sign test (z-statistic)[2]	0.536	−0.300	0.735	1.080	−1.681

[1] The significance levels are based on a t-test of the null hypothesis that the mean is zero.
[2] The significance levels are based on a sign test of the null hypothesis that the probability of a positive return is 50 percent and will not be correct if the return distribution is asymmetric.

definitely not an above-average month. There are quite a number of months with higher rates of return.[21]

Tests of the null hypothesis that all months are the same are reported in Table A2. An F-test of the equality of mean rates of return across months is significant at the 1 percent level for the total period and one short subperiod and at the 5 percent level for one of the main subperiods (not reported). However, months that performed well in one subperiod are not, in general, months that performed well in other subperiods. Therefore, it seems that there is no consistent monthly pattern in the stock market. A chi-square test of the equality of the fraction of positive returns in each month yields similar results.

Monthly data provides a good illustration of Black's (1986) point about the difficulty of testing hypotheses with noisy data. It is quite possible that some month is indeed unique, but even with 90 years of data the standard

---

[21] Based on the total sample, the strongest candidates for months having exceptional rates of return are the late-summer months July and August, with high positive rates of return (1.29 percent and 1.58 percent, respectively) and September, with high negative rates of return (−1.47 percent). One can see in the pre-1952 period the basis for the widespread belief in the summer market rally among practitioners. If any persistent tendency for prices to rise in the summer once existed, which may be doubted, there is no evidence in recent data for its continued existence; July and August in the post-1952 period have rates of return similar to a typical month.

Are Seasonal Anomalies Real?

Table A1
Extended

June	July	August	September	October	November	December	Entire period average
0.430	1.290*	1.578*	−1.470*	−0.092	0.603	0.895	0.349
5.562	5.588	5.676	6.580	5.774	5.948	5.279	
0.030	2.115	1.476	−0.537	0.344	0.819	1.886	
89	89	88	88	88	88	89	
51	62	67	41	55	60	71	
−1.141	0.998	1.985*	−2.961**	−0.380	0.695	2.709**	
0.700	1.603	2.539**	−1.855	−0.414	−0.018	0.566	0.265
6.603	6.439	6.143	7.798	6.635	6.537	6.360	
0.108	2.958	2.294	−0.222	0.755	0.464	2.353	
55	55	54	54	54	54	55	
51	65	76	46	52	56	73	
−0.908	1.271	2.813**	−1.584	−0.760	−0.210	2.360*	
−0.006	0.783	0.052	−0.859	0.420	1.589	1.426**	0.484
3.290	3.872	4.519	3.981	4.094	4.797	2.769	
0.000	0.964	0.479	−1.058	0.269	1.989	1.186	
34	34	34	34	34	34	34	
50	56	53	32	59	68	68	
−0.645	0.045	−0.300	−2.716**	0.390	1.425	1.425	

* Significant at 5 percent level for two-tailed test.
** Significant at 1 percent level for two-tailed test.

deviation of the mean monthly return is very high (around 0.5 percent). Therefore, unless the unique month outperforms other months by more than 1 percent, it would not be identified as a special month.

Another interesting observation is that January had the lowest standard deviation in the first major subperiod and the highest standard deviation

Table A2
Significance tests for monthly rates of return of the Dow Jones Industrial Average

Period	Equality of months F-value (DF)	Chi-square (DF)	January vs. average of other months, t-statistic
1897–1986	2.204** (12, 1055)	29.61** (11)	1.0642
1897–5/30/52	1.560 (12, 647)	25.60** (11)	0.890
6/1/52–1986	2.148* (12, 396)	17.01 (11)	0.593

[1] The significance levels are based on a t-test of the null hypothesis that the mean is zero.
[2] The significance levels are based on a sign test of the null hypothesis that the probability of a positive return is 50 percent and will not be correct if the return distribution is asymmetric.
* Significant at 5 percent level for two-tailed test.
** Significant at 1 percent level for two-tailed test.

in the second major subperiod. Perhaps changes in the timing of information releases can account for this change.

References

Admati, A. R., and P. Pfleiderer, 1988a, "A Theory of Intraday Patterns: Volume and Price Variability," *Review of Financial Studies,* 1, 3–40.

Admati, A. R., and P. Pfleiderer, 1988b, "Divide and Conquer: A Theory of Intra-Day and Day of the Week Mean Effects," Working Paper 1002, Graduate School of Business, Stanford University.

Ariel, R. A., 1985, "High Stock Returns Before Holidays," Unpublished Working Paper, Department of Finance, Massachusetts Institute of Technology.

Ariel, R. A., 1987, "A Monthly Effect in Stock Returns," *Journal of Financial Economics,* 17, 161–174.

Ball, R., and J. Bowers, 1986, "Daily Seasonals in Equity and Fixed-Interest Returns: Australian Evidence and Tests of Plausible Hypotheses," Unpublished Working Paper, Australian Graduate School of Management.

Banz, R. W., 1981, "The Relationship Between Return and Market Value of Common Stock," *Journal of Financial Economics,* 9, 3–18.

Barclay, M., 1987, "Dividends, Taxes and Common Stock Prices: The Ex-Dividend Day Behavior of Common Stock Prices Before the Income Tax," *Journal of Financial Economics,* 19, 31–44.

Black, F., 1986, "Noise," *Journal of Finance,* 41, 529–543.

Brown, S. J., and J. B. Warner, 1980, "Measuring Security Price Performance," *Journal of Financial Economics,* 8, 205–258.

Coursey, D. L., and E. A. Dyl, 1986, "Price Effects of Trading Interruptions in an Experimental Market," Unpublished Working Paper, University of Wyoming.

Cross, F., 1973, "The Behavior of Stock Prices on Fridays and Mondays," *Financial Analysts Journal,* November–December, 67–69.

Dow Jones and Company, Inc. Educational Service Bureau, 1986, *The Dow Jones Averages: A Non-Professional's Guide* (rev. ed.), McGraw-Hill, New York.

Feller, W., 1968, *An Introduction to Probability Theory and Its Applications* (3d ed.), Wiley, New York.

Fields, M. J., 1931, "Stock Prices: A Problem in Verification," *Journal of Business,* 4, 415–418.

Fields, M. J., 1934, "Security Prices and Stock Exchange Holidays in Relation to Short Selling," *Journal of Business,* 7, 328–338.

Foster, D. F., and S. Viswanathan, 1987, "Interday Variations in Volumes and Spreads," Working Paper 87-101, Fuqua School of Business, Duke University.

French, K. R., 1980, "Stock Returns and the Weekend Effect," *Journal of Financial Economics,* 8, 55–70.

Gibbons, M. R., and P. Hess, 1981, "Day of the Week Effects and Asset Returns," *Journal of Business,* 54, 579–596.

Harris, L., 1986, "A Transaction Data Study of Weekly and Intradaily Patterns in Stock Returns," *Journal of Financial Economics,* 16, 99–117.

Haugen, R. A., and J. Lakonishok, 1988, *The Incredible January Effect,* Dow Jones–Irwin, Homewood, Ill.

Jaffe, J., and R. Westerfield, 1985, "The Week-End Effect in Common Stock Returns: The International Evidence," *Journal of Finance,* 40, 433–454.

Jones, C. P., D. K. Pearce, and J. W. Wilson, 1987, "Can Tax-Loss Selling Explain the January Effect? A Note," *Journal of Finance,* 42, 453–461.

Keim, D. B., and R. F. Stambaugh, 1984, "A Further Investigation of the Weekend Effect in Stock Returns," *Journal of Finance,* 39, 819–835.

Are Seasonal Anomalies Real?

Lakonishok, J., and M. Levi, 1982, "Weekend Effects on Stock Returns," *Journal of Finance*, 37, 883–889.

Lakonishok, J., and S. Smidt, 1984, "Volume and Turn-of-the-Year Behavior," *Journal of Financial Economics*, 13, 435–456.

Lakonishok, J., and S. Smidt, 1986, "Volume for Winners and Losers: Taxation and Other Motives for Stock Trading," *Journal of Finance*, 41, 951–974.

Merton, R. C., 1985, "On the Current State of the Stock Market Rationality Hypothesis," in R. Dornbusch and S. Fischer (eds.), *Macroeconomics and Finance*, MIT Press, Cambridge, Mass.

Penman, S. H., 1987, "The Distribution of Earnings News Over Time and Seasonalities in Aggregate Stock Returns," *Journal of Financial Economics*, 18, 199–228.

Reinganum, M. R., 1981, "Misspecification of Capital Asset Pricing: Empirical Anomalies Based on Earnings Yields and Market Values," *Journal of Financial Economics*, 9, 19–46.

Ritter, J. R., 1988, "The Buying and Selling Behavior of Individual Investors at the Turn of the Year," *Journal of Finance*, 43, 701–717.

Ritter, J. R., and N. Chopra, 1989, "Portfolio Rebalancing and the Turn of the Year Effect," *Journal of Finance*, 44, 149–166.

Rock, K., 1989, "The Specialist's Order Book: A Possible Explanation for the Year-End Anomaly," forthcoming in *The Review of Financial Studies*.

Rogalski, R., and S. Tinic, 1986, "The January Size Effect: Anomaly or Risk Mismeasurement," *Financial Analysts Journal*, November–December, 63–70.

Roll, R., 1983, "Vas is das? The Turn-of-the-Year Effect and the Return Premia of Small Firms," *Journal of Portfolio Management*, 9, 18–28.

Ross, S. A., 1986, "Regression to the Max," unpublished manuscript, Yale School of Management.

Rozeff, M. S., and W. R. Kinney, Jr., 1976, "Capital Market Seasonality: The Case of Stock Returns," *Journal of Financial Economics*, 3, 379–402.

Rudd, A. T., 1979, "The Revised Dow Jones Industrial Average: New Wine in Old Bottles?" *Financial Analysts Journal*, November–December, 57–63.

Savin, N. E., 1984, "Multiple Hypothesis Testing," in Z. Griliches and M. D. Intriligator (eds.), *Handbook of Econometrics*, vol. 2, North Holland, Amsterdam, chap. 14.

Schultz, P., 1985, "Personal Income Taxes and the January Effect: Small Firm Stock Returns Before the War Revenue Act of 1917: A Note," *Journal of Finance*, 40, 333–343.

Schwert, D. G., 1983, "Size and Stock Returns and Other Empirical Regularities," *Journal of Financial Economics*, 12, 3–12.

Stewart, S. D., 1987, "Bias in Performance Measurement During Contributions: A Note," *The Financial Review*, 22, 339–343.

[25]

Data-Snooping Biases in Tests of Financial Asset Pricing Models

Andrew W. Lo
Sloan School of Management
Massachusetts Institute of Technology

A. Craig MacKinlay
Wharton School
University of Pennsylvania

Tests of financial asset pricing models may yield misleading inferences when properties of the data are used to construct the test statistics. In particular, such tests are often based on returns to portfolios of common stock, where portfolios are constructed by sorting on some empirically motivated characteristic of the securities such as market value of equity. Analytical calculations, Monte Carlo simulations, and two empirical examples show that the effects of this type of data snooping can be substantial.

The reliance of economic science upon nonexperimental inference is, at once, one of the most challenging and most nettlesome aspects of the discipline. Because of the virtual impossibility of controlled experimentation in economics, the importance of sta-

---

Research support from the Batterymarch Fellowship (Lo), the Geewax-Terker Research Fund (MacKinlay), the John M. Olin Fellowship at the National Bureau of Economic Research (Lo), and the National Science Foundation (SES-8821583) is gratefully acknowledged. We thank David Aldous, Cliff Ball, Michael Brennan, Herbert David, Mike Gibbons, Jay Shanken, a referee, and seminar participants at the Board of Governors of the Federal Reserve, Boston College, Columbia, Dartmouth, Harvard, M.I.T., Northwestern, Princeton, Stanford, University of Chicago, University of Michigan, University of Wisconsin at Madison, Washington University, and Wharton for useful comments and suggestions. Address reprint requests to Andrew Lo, Sloan School of Management, M.I.T., 50 Memorial Drive, Cambridge, MA 02139.

The Review of Financial Studies 1990 Volume 3, number 3, pp. 431–467
© 1990 The Review of Financial Studies 0893-9454/90/$1.50

tistical data analysis is now well-established. However, there is a growing concern that the procedures under which formal statistical inference have been developed may not correspond to those followed in practice.[1] For example, the classical statistical approach to selecting a method of estimation generally involves minimizing an expected loss function, irrespective of the actual data. Yet in practice the properties of the realized data almost always influence the choice of estimator.

Of course, ignoring obvious features of the data can lead to nonsensical inferences even when the estimation procedures are optimal in some metric. But the way we incorporate those features into our estimation and testing procedures can affect subsequent inferences considerably. Indeed, by the very nature of empirical innovation in economics, the axioms of classical statistical analysis are violated routinely: future research is often motivated by the successes and failures of past investigations. Consequently, few empirical studies are free of the kind of data-instigated pretest biases discussed in Leamer (1978). Moreover, we can expect the degree of such biases to increase with the number of published studies performed on any single data set—the more scrutiny a collection of data is subjected to, the more likely will interesting (spurious) patterns emerge. Since stock market prices are perhaps the most studied economic quantities to date, tests of financial asset pricing models seem especially susceptible.

In this paper, we attempt to quantify the inferential biases associated with one particular method of testing financial asset pricing models such as the capital asset pricing model (CAPM) and the arbitrage pricing theory (APT). Because there are often many more securities than there are time series observations of stock returns, asset pricing tests are generally performed on the returns of *portfolios* of securities. Besides reducing the cross-sectional dimension of the joint distribution of returns, grouping into portfolios has also been advanced as a method of reducing the impact of measurement error. However, the selection of securities to be included in a given portfolio is almost never at random, but is often based on some of the stocks' empirical characteristics. The formation of size-sorted portfolios, portfolios based on the market value of the companies' equity, is but one example. Conducting classical statistical tests on portfolios formed this way creates potentially significant biases in the test statistics. These are

---

[1] Perhaps the most complete analysis of such issues in economic applications is by Leamer (1978). Recent papers by Lakonishok and Smidt (1988), Merton (1987), and Ross (1987) address data snooping in financial economics. Of course, data snooping has been a concern among probabilists and statisticians for quite some time, and is at least as old as the controversy between Bayesian and classical statisticians. Interested readers should consult Berger and Wolpert (1984, chapter 4.2) and Leamer (1978, chapter 9) for further discussion.

Data-Snooping Biases

examples of "data-snooping statistics," a term used by Aldous (1989, p. 252) to describe the situation "where you have a family of test statistics $T(a)$ whose null distribution is known for fixed a, but where you use the test statistic $T = T(a)$ for some a chosen using the data." In our application the quantity a may be viewed as a vector of zeros and ones that indicates which securities are to be included in or omitted from a given portfolio. If the choice of a is based on the data, then the sampling distribution of the resulting test statistic is generally not the same as the null distribution with a fixed a; hence, the actual size of the test may differ substantially from its nominal value under the null. Under plausible assumptions our calculations show that this kind of data snooping can lead to rejections of the null hypothesis with probability 1 even when the null hypothesis is true!

Although the term "data snooping" may have an unsavory connotation, our usage neither implies nor infers any sort of intentional misrepresentation or dishonesty. That prior empirical research may influence the way current investigations are conducted is often unavoidable, and this very fact results in what we have called data snooping. Moreover, it is not at all apparent that this phenomenon necessarily imparts a "bias" in the sense that it affects inferences in an undesirable way. After all, the primary reason for publishing scientific discoveries is to add to a store of common knowledge on which future research may build.

But when scientific discovery is statistical in nature, we must weigh the significance of newly discovered relations in view of past inferences. This is recognized implicitly in many formal statistical circumstances, as in the theory of sequential hypothesis testing. But it is considerably more difficult to correct for the effects of specification searches in practice since such searches often consist of *sequences* of empirical studies undertaken by many individuals over many years.[2] For example, as a consequence of the many investigations relating the behavior of stock returns to size, Chen, Roll, and Ross (1986, p. 394) write: "It has been facetiously noted that size may be the best theory we now have of expected returns. Unfortunately, this is less of a theory than an empirical observation." Then, as Merton (1987, p. 107) asks in a related context: "Is it reasonable to use the standard t-statistic as a valid measure of significance when the test is conducted on the same data used by many earlier studies whose results influenced the choice of theory to be tested?" We rephrase this question

---

[2] Statisticians have considered a closely related problem, known as the "file drawer problem," in which the overall significance of several published studies must be assessed while accounting for the possibility of unreported insignificant studies languishing in various investigators' file drawers. An excellent review of the file drawer problem and its remedies, which has come to be known as "meta-analysis," is provided by Iyengar and Greenhouse (1988).

in the following way: Are standard tests of significance valid when the construction of the test statistics is influenced by empirical relations derived from the very same data to be used in the test? Our results show that using prior information only marginally correlated with statistics of interest can distort inferences dramatically.

In Section 1, we quantify the data-snooping biases associated with testing financial asset pricing models with portfolios formed by sorting on some empirically motivated characteristic. Using the theory of induced order statistics, we derive in closed form the asymptotic distribution of a commonly used test statistic before and after sorting. This not only yields a measure of the effect of data snooping, but also provides the appropriate sampling theory when snooping is unavoidable. In Section 2, we report the results of Monte Carlo experiments designed to gauge the accuracy of the asymptotic approximations used in Section 1. In Section 3, two empirical examples are provided that illustrate the potential importance of data-snooping biases in existing tests of asset pricing models, and, in Section 4, we show how these biases can arise naturally from our tendency to focus on the unusual. We conclude in Section 5.

1. Quantifying Data-Snooping Biases With Induced Order Statistics

Many tests of the CAPM and APT have been conducted on returns of groups of securities rather than on individual security returns, where the grouping is often according to some empirical characteristic of the securities. Perhaps the most common attribute by which securities are grouped is market value of equity or "size." The prevalence of size-sorted portfolios in recent tests of asset pricing models has not been precipitated by any economic theory linking size to asset prices. It is a consequence of a series of empirical studies demonstrating the statistical relation between size and the stochastic behavior of stock returns.[3] Therefore, we must allow for our foreknowledge of size-related phenomena in evaluating the actual significance of tests performed on size-sorted portfolios. More generally, grouping securities by some characteristic that is empirically motivated may affect the size of the usual significance tests,[4] particularly when the empirical motivation is derived from the very data set on which the test is based.

---

[3] See Banz (1978, 1981), Brown, Kleidon, and Marsh (1983), and Chan, Chen, and Hsieh (1985), for example. Although Banz's (1978) original investigation may have been motivated by theoretical considerations, virtually all subsequent empirical studies exploiting the size effect do so because of Banz's empirical findings, and not his theory.

[4] Unfortunately the use of "size" to mean both market value of equity and type I error is unavoidable. Readers beware.

Data-Snooping Biases

We quantify these effects in the following sections by appealing to asymptotic results for induced order statistics, and show that even mild forms of data snooping can change inferences substantially. In Section 1.1, a brief summary of the asymptotic properties of induced order statistics is provided. In Section 1.2, results for tests based on individual securities are presented, and in Section 1.3, corresponding results for portfolios are reported. We provide a more positive interpretation of data-snooping biases as power against deviations from the null hypothesis in Section 1.4.

1.1. Asymptotic properties of induced order statistics

Since the particular form of data snooping we are investigating is most common in empirical tests of financial asset pricing models, our exposition will lie in that context. Suppose for each of N securities we have some consistent estimator $\hat{\alpha}_i$ of a parameter α_i which is to be used in the construction of an aggregate test statistic. For example, in the Sharpe–Lintner CAPM, $\hat{\alpha}_i$ would be the estimated intercept from the following regression:

$$R_{it} - R_{ft} = \hat{\alpha}_i + (R_{mt} - R_{ft})\beta_i + \epsilon_{it} \qquad (1)$$

where R_{it}, R_{mt}, and R_{ft} are the period-t returns on security i, the market portfolio, and a risk-free asset, respectively. A test of the null hypothesis that $\alpha_i = 0$ would then be a proper test of the Sharpe–Lintner version of the CAPM; thus, $\hat{\alpha}_i$ may serve as a test statistic itself. However, more powerful tests may be obtained by combining the $\hat{\alpha}_i$'s for many securities. But how should we combine them?

Suppose for each security i we observe some characteristic X_i, such as its out-of-sample market value of equity or average annual earnings, and we learn that X_i is correlated empirically with $\hat{\alpha}_i$. By this we mean that the relation between X_i and $\hat{\alpha}_i$ is an empirical fact uncovered by "searching" through the data, and not motivated by any a priori theoretical considerations. This search need not be a systematic sifting of the data, but may be interpreted as any one of Leamer's (1978) six specification searches, which even the most meticulous of classical statisticians has conducted at some point. The key feature is that our interest in characteristic X_i is derived from a look at the data, the same data to be used in performing our test. Common intuition suggests that using information contained in the X_i's can yield a more powerful test of economic restrictions on the $\hat{\alpha}_i$'s. But if this characteristic is not a part of the original null hypothesis, and only catches our attention after a look at the data (or after a look at another's look at the data), using it to form our test statistics may lead us to reject those economic restrictions even when they obtain. More formally,

435

if we write $\hat{\alpha}_i$ as

$$\hat{\alpha}_i = \alpha_i + \zeta_i, \qquad (2)$$

then it is evident that under the null hypothesis where $\alpha_i = 0$, any correlation between X_i and $\hat{\alpha}_i$ must be due to correlation between the characteristic and estimation or measurement error ζ_i. Although measurement error is usually assumed to be independent of all other relevant economic variables, the very process by which the characteristic comes to our attention may induce spurious correlation between X_i and ζ_i. We formalize this intuition in Section 4 and proceed now to show that such spurious correlation has important implications for testing the null hypothesis.

This is most evident in the extreme case where the null hypothesis $\alpha_i = 0$ is tested by performing a standard t-test on the largest of the $\hat{\alpha}_i$'s. Clearly such a test is biased toward rejection unless we account for the fact that the largest $\hat{\alpha}_i$ has been drawn from the set $\{\hat{\alpha}_j\}$. Otherwise, extreme realizations of estimation error will be confused with a violation of the null hypothesis. If, instead of choosing $\hat{\alpha}_i$ by its value relative to other $\hat{\alpha}_j$'s, our choice is based on some characteristic X_i correlated with the estimation errors of $\hat{\alpha}_i$, a similar bias might arise, albeit to a lesser degree.

To formalize the preceding intuition, suppose that only a subset of n securities is used to form the test statistic and these n are chosen by sorting the X_i's. That is, let us reorder the bivariate vectors $[X_i, \hat{\alpha}_i]'$ according to their first components, yielding the sequence

$$\begin{pmatrix} X_{1:N} \\ \hat{\alpha}_{[1:N]} \end{pmatrix}, \begin{pmatrix} X_{2:N} \\ \hat{\alpha}_{[2:N]} \end{pmatrix}, \ldots, \begin{pmatrix} X_{N:N} \\ \hat{\alpha}_{[N:N]} \end{pmatrix}, \qquad (3)$$

where $X_{1:N} < X_{2:N} < \cdots < X_{N:N}$ and the notation $X_{i:N}$ follows that of the statistics literature in denoting the ith order statistic from the sample of N observations $\{X_i\}$.[5] The notation $\hat{\alpha}_{[i:N]}$ denotes the ith *induced order statistic* corresponding to $X_{i:N}$, or the ith *concomitant* of the order statistic $X_{i:N}$.[6] That is, if the bivariate vectors $[X_i, \hat{\alpha}_i]'$ are ordered according to the X_i entries, $\hat{\alpha}_{[i:N]}$ is defined to be the second component of the ith ordered vector. The $\hat{\alpha}_{[i:N]}$'s are not themselves

---

[5] It is implicitly assumed throughout that both $\hat{\alpha}_i$ and X_i have continuous joint and marginal cumulative distribution functions; hence, strict inequalities suffice.

[6] The term *concomitant* of an order statistic was introduced by David (1973), who was perhaps the first to systematically investigate its properties and applications. The term *induced* order statistic was coined by Bhattacharya (1974) at about the same time. Although the former term seems to be more common usage, we use the latter in the interest of brevity. See Bhattacharya (1984) for an excellent review.

Data-Snooping Biases

ordered but correspond to the ordering of the $X_{i:N}$'s.[7] For example, if X_i is firm size and $\hat{\alpha}_i$ is the intercept from a market-model regression of firm i's excess return on the excess market return, then $\hat{\alpha}_{[j:N]}$ is the $\hat{\alpha}$ of the jth smallest of the N firms. We call this procedure *induced ordering* of the $\hat{\alpha}_i$'s.

It is apparent that if we construct a test statistic by choosing n securities according to the ordering (3), the sampling theory cannot be the same as that of n securities selected independently of the data. From the following remarkably simple result by Yang (1977), an asymptotic sampling theory for test statistics based on induced order statistics may be derived analytically:[8]

Theorem 1.1. *Let the vectors $[X_i \hat{\alpha}_i]'$, $i = 1, \ldots, N$, be independently and identically distributed and let $1 < i_1 < i_2 < \cdots < i_n < N$ be sequences of integers such that, as $N \to \infty$, $i_k/N \to \xi_k \in (0, 1)$ ($k = 1, 2, \ldots, n$). Then*

$$\lim_{N \to \infty} \Pr(\hat{\alpha}_{[i_1:N]} < a_1, \ldots, \hat{\alpha}_{[i_n:N]} < a_n)$$
$$= \prod_{k=1}^{n} \Pr(\hat{\alpha}_k < a_k \mid F_x(X_k) = \xi_k), \qquad (4)$$

where $F_x(\cdot)$ is the marginal cumulative distribution function of X_i.

Proof. See Yang (1977). ∎

This result gives the large-sample joint distribution of a finite subset of induced order statistics whose identities are determined solely by their relative rankings ξ_k (as ranked according to the order statistics $X_{k:N}$). From (4) it is evident that the $\hat{\alpha}_{[i_k:N]}$'s are mutually independent in large samples. If X_i were the market value of equity of the ith company, Theorem 1.1 shows that the $\hat{\alpha}_i$ of the security with size at, for example, the 27th percentile is asymptotically independent of the $\hat{\alpha}_j$ of the security with size at the 45th percentile.[9] If the characteristics $\{X_i\}$ and $\{\hat{\alpha}_i\}$ are statistically independent, the joint distribution of

---

[7] If the vectors are independently and identically distributed and X_i is perfectly correlated with $\hat{\alpha}_i$, then $\hat{\alpha}_{[i:N]}$ are also order statistics. But as long as the correlation coefficient ρ is strictly between -1 and 1, then, for example, $\hat{\alpha}_{[N:N]}$ will generally not be the largest $\hat{\alpha}_i$.

[8] See also David and Galambos (1974) and Watterson (1959). In fact, Yang (1977) provides the exact finite-sample distribution of any finite collection of induced order statistics, but even assuming bivariate normality does not yield a tractable form of this distribution.

[9] This is a limiting result and implies that the identities of the stocks with 27th and 45th percentile sizes will generally change as N increases.

the latter clearly cannot be influenced by ordering according to the former. It is tempting to conclude that as long as the correlation between X_i and $\hat{\alpha}_i$ is economically small, induced ordering cannot greatly affect inferences. Using Yang's result we show the fallacy of this argument in Sections 1.2 and 1.3.

1.2 Biases of tests based on individual securities
We evaluate the bias of induced ordering under the following assumption:

(A) The vectors $[X_i \; \hat{\alpha}_i]'$ ($i = 1, 2, \ldots, N$) are independently and identically distributed bivariate normal random vectors with mean $[\mu_x \; \alpha]'$, variance $[\sigma_x^2 \; \sigma_\alpha^2]'$, and correlation $\rho \in (-1, 1)$.

The null hypothesis H is then

$$H: \alpha = 0.$$

Examples of asset pricing models that yield restrictions of this form are the Sharpe–Lintner CAPM and the exact factor pricing version of Ross's APT.[10] Under this null hypothesis, the $\hat{\alpha}_i$'s deviate from zero solely through estimation error.

Since the sampling theory provided by Theorem 1.1 is asymptotic, we construct our test statistics using a finite subset of n securities where it is assumed that $n \ll N$. If these securities are selected without the prior use of data, then we have the following well-known result:

$$\theta \equiv \frac{1}{\hat{\sigma}_\alpha^2} \sum_{i=1}^{n} \hat{\alpha}_i^2 \stackrel{a}{\sim} \chi_n^2, \tag{5}$$

where $\hat{\sigma}_\alpha^2$ is any consistent estimator of σ_α^2.[11] Therefore, a 5 percent test of H may be performed by checking whether θ is greater or less than $C_{.05}^n$, where $C_{.05}^n$ is defined by

$$F_{\chi_n^2}(C_{.05}^n) = .95 \tag{6}$$

and $F_{\chi_n^2}(\cdot)$ is the cumulative distribution function of a χ_n^2 variate.

Now suppose we construct θ from the induced order statistics

---

[10] See Chamberlain (1983), Huberman and Kandel (1987), Lehmann and Modest (1988), and Wang (1988) for further discussion of exact factor pricing models. Examples of tests that fit into the framework of H are those in Campbell (1987), Connor and Korajczyk (1988), Gibbons, Ross, and Shanken (1989), Huberman and Kandel (1987), Lehmann and Modest (1988), and MacKinlay (1987).

[11] In most contexts the consistency of $\hat{\sigma}_\alpha^2$ is with respect to the number of time series observations T. In that case something must be said of the relative rates at which T and N increase without bound so as to guarantee convergence of θ. However, under H the parameter σ_α^2 may be estimated cross-sectionally; hence, the relation $\stackrel{a}{\sim}$ in (5) need only represent N-asymptotics.

438

Data-Snooping Biases

$\hat{\alpha}_{[i_k:N]}$, $k = 1, \ldots, n$, instead of the $\hat{\alpha}_i$'s. Specifically, define the following test statistic:

$$\tilde{\theta} \equiv \frac{1}{\hat{\sigma}_\alpha^2} \sum_{k=1}^n \hat{\alpha}_{[i_k:N]}^2. \tag{7}$$

Using Theorem 1.1, the following proposition is easily established:

Proposition 1.1. *Under the null hypothesis H and assumption (A), as N increases without bound the induced order statistics $\hat{\alpha}_{[i_k:N]}$ ($k = 1, \ldots, n$) converge in distribution to independent gaussian random variables with mean μ_k and variance σ_k^2, where*

$$\mu_k \equiv \rho(\sigma_\alpha/\sigma_x)[F_x^{-1}(\xi_k) - \mu_x] = \rho\sigma_\alpha \Phi^{-1}(\xi_k), \tag{8}$$

$$\sigma_k^2 \equiv \sigma_\alpha^2(1 - \rho^2), \tag{9}$$

which implies

$$\tilde{\theta} \stackrel{a}{\sim} (1 - \rho^2) \cdot \chi_n^2(\lambda), \tag{10}$$

with noncentrality parameter

$$\lambda = \sum_{k=1}^n \left(\frac{\mu_k}{\sigma_k}\right)^2 = \frac{\rho^2}{1 - \rho^2} \sum_{k=1}^n [\Phi^{-1}(\xi_k)]^2, \tag{11}$$

where $\Phi(\cdot)$ is the standard normal cumulative distribution function.

Proof. This follows directly from the definition of a noncentral chi-squared variate. The second equality in (8) follows from the fact that $\Phi(\xi_k) = F_x(\xi_k \sigma_x + \mu_x)$. ∎

Proposition 1.1 shows that the null hypothesis H is violated by induced ordering since the means of the ordered $\hat{\alpha}_i$'s are no longer zero. Indeed, the mean of $\hat{\alpha}_{[i_k:N]}$ may be positive or negative depending on ρ and the (limiting) relative rank ξ_k. For example, if $\rho = .10$ and $\sigma_\alpha = 1$, the mean of the induced order statistic in the 95th percentile is 0.164.

The simplicity of $\tilde{\theta}$'s asymptotic distribution follows from the fact that the $\hat{\alpha}_{[i_k:N]}$'s become independent as N increases without bound. It follows from the fact that induced order statistics are conditionally independent when conditioned on the order statistics that determine the induced ordering. This seemingly counterintuitive result is easy to see when $[X_i, \hat{\alpha}_i]$ is bivariate normal, since, in this case

$$\hat{\alpha}_i = \alpha + \rho(\sigma_\alpha/\sigma_x)[X_i - \mu_x] + Z_i,$$

$$Z_i \text{ i.i.d. } N(0, \sigma_\alpha^2(1 - \rho^2)), \tag{12}$$

where X_t and Z_t are independent. Therefore, the induced order statistics may be represented as

$$\hat{\alpha}_{[i_k:N]} = \alpha + \rho(\sigma_\alpha/\sigma_x)[X_{i_k:N} - \mu_x] + Z_{[i_k]},$$
$$Z_{[i_k]} \quad \text{i.i.d.} \quad N(0, \sigma_\alpha^2(1 - \rho^2)), \tag{13}$$

where the $Z_{[i_k]}$ are independent of the (order) statistics $X_{i_k:N}$. But since $X_{i_k:N}$ is an order statistic, and since the sequence i_k/N converges to ξ_k, $X_{i_k:N}$ converges to the ξ_kth quantile, $F^{-1}(\xi_k)$. Using (13) then shows that $\hat{\alpha}_{[i_k:N]}$ is gaussian, with mean and variance given by (8) and (9), and independent of the other induced order statistics.[12]

To evaluate the size of a 5 percent test based on the statistic $\tilde{\theta}$, we need only evaluate the cumulative distribution function of the noncentral $\chi_n^2(\lambda)$ at the point $C_{.05}^n/(1 - \rho^2)$, where $C_{.05}^n$ is given in (6). Observe that the noncentrality parameter λ is an increasing function of ρ^2. If $\rho^2 = 0$ then the distribution of $\tilde{\theta}$ reduces to a central χ_n^2 which is identical to the distribution of θ in (5)—sorting on a characteristic that is statistically independent of the $\hat{\alpha}_t$'s cannot affect the null distribution of θ. As $\hat{\alpha}_t$ and X_t become more highly correlated, the noncentral χ^2 distribution shifts to the right. However, this does not imply that the actual size of a 5 percent test necessarily increases since the relevant critical value for $\tilde{\theta}$, $C_{.05}^n/(1 - \rho^2)$, also grows with ρ^2.[13]

Numerical values for the size of a 5 percent test based on $\tilde{\theta}$ may be obtained by first specifying choices for the relative ranks $\{\xi_k\}$ of the n securities. We choose three sets of $\{\xi_k\}$, yielding three distinct test statistics $\tilde{\theta}_1$, $\tilde{\theta}_2$, and $\tilde{\theta}_3$:

$$\tilde{\theta}_1 \leftrightarrow \xi_k = \frac{k}{n+1}, \quad k = 1, 2, \ldots, n; \tag{14}$$

---

[12] In fact, this shows how our parametric specification may be relaxed. If we replace normality by the assumption that $\hat{\alpha}_t$ and X_t satisfy the linear regression equation,

$$\hat{\alpha}_t = \mu_\alpha + \beta_t(X_t - \mu_x) + Z_t,$$

where Z_t is independent of X_t, then our results remain unchanged. Moreover, this specification may allow us to relax the rather strong i.i.d. assumption since David (1981, chapters 2.8 and 5.6) does present some results for order statistics in the nonidentically distributed and the dependent cases separately. However, combining and applying them to the above linear regression relation is a formidable task which we leave to the more industrious.

[13] In fact, if $\rho^2 = 1$, the limiting distribution of $\tilde{\theta}$ is degenerate since the test statistic converges in probability to the following limit:

$$\sum_{k=1}^{n} [\Phi^{-1}(\xi_k)]^2.$$

This limit may be greater or less than $C_{.05}^n$ depending on the values of ξ_k; hence, the size of the test in this case may be either zero or unity.

Data-Snooping Biases

$$\tilde{\theta}_2 \leftrightarrow \xi_k = \begin{cases} \dfrac{k}{(m+1)(n_o+1)}, & \text{for } k=1,2,\ldots,n_o, \\ \dfrac{k+m(n_o+1)-n_o}{(m+1)(n_o+1)}, & \text{for } k=n_o+1,\ldots,2n_o; \end{cases} \quad (15)$$

$$\tilde{\theta}_3 \leftrightarrow \xi_k = \begin{cases} \dfrac{k+n_o+1}{(m+1)(n_o+1)}, & \text{for } k=1,2,\ldots,n_o, \\ \dfrac{k+(m-1)(n_o+1)-n_o}{(m+1)(n_o+1)}, & \text{for } k=n_o+1,\ldots,2n_o; \end{cases} \quad (16)$$

where $n \equiv 2n_o$ and n_o is an arbitrary positive integer. The first method (14) simply sets the ξ_k's so that they divide the unit interval into n equally spaced increments. The second procedure (15) first divides the unit interval into $m + 1$ equally spaced increments, sets the first half of the ξ_k's to divide the *first* such increment into equally spaced intervals each of width $1/(m + 1)(n_o + 1)$, and then sets the remaining half so as to divide the *last* increment into equally spaced intervals also of width $1/(m + 1)(n_o + 1)$ each. The third procedure is similar to the second, except that the ξ_k's are chosen to divide the second smallest and second largest $m + 1$ increments into equally spaced intervals of width $1/(m + 1)(n_o + 1)$.

These three ways of choosing n securities allow us to see how an attempt to create (or remove) dispersion—as measured by the characteristic X_i—affects the null distribution of the statistics. The first choice for the relative ranks is the most disperse, being evenly distributed on $(0, 1)$. The second yields the opposite extreme: the $\hat{\alpha}_{(i_k:N)}$'s selected are those with characteristics in the lowest and highest $100/(m + 1)$-percentiles. As the parameter m is increased, more extreme outliers are used to compute $\tilde{\theta}_2$. This is also true for $\tilde{\theta}_3$, but to a lesser extent since the statistic is based on $\hat{\alpha}_{(i_k:N)}$'s in the second lowest and second highest $100/(m + 1)$-percentiles.

Table 1 shows the size of the 5 percent test using $\tilde{\theta}_1$, $\tilde{\theta}_2$, and $\tilde{\theta}_3$ for various values of n, ρ^2, and m. For concreteness, observe that ρ^2 is simply the R^2 of the cross-sectional regression of $\hat{\alpha}_i$ on X_i, so that $\rho = \pm.10$ implies that only 1 percent of the variation in $\hat{\alpha}_i$ is explained by X_i. For this value of R^2, the entries in the second panel of Table 1 show that the size of a 5 percent test using $\tilde{\theta}_1$ is 4.9 percent for samples of 10 to 100 securities. However, using securities with extreme characteristics does affect the size, as the entries in the "$\tilde{\theta}_2$-test" and "$\tilde{\theta}_3$-test" columns indicate. Nevertheless the largest deviation is only 8.1 percent. As expected, the size is larger for the test based on $\tilde{\theta}_2$ than for that of $\tilde{\theta}_3$ since the former statistic is based on more extreme induced order statistics than the latter.

441

Table 1
Theoretical sizes of nominal 5 percent χ_n^2-tests of $H: \alpha_i = 0$ ($i = 1, \ldots, n$) using the test statistics $\hat{\theta}_j$

n	$\hat{\theta}_1$-test	$\hat{\theta}_2$-test ($m = 4$)	$\hat{\theta}_3$-test ($m = 4$)	$\hat{\theta}_2$-test ($m = 9$)	$\hat{\theta}_3$-test ($m = 9$)	$\hat{\theta}_2$-test ($m = 19$)	$\hat{\theta}_3$-test ($m = 19$)
$R^2 = .005$							
10	0.049	0.051	0.049	0.053	0.050	0.054	0.052
20	0.050	0.052	0.049	0.054	0.050	0.056	0.052
50	0.050	0.053	0.048	0.056	0.050	0.060	0.053
100	0.050	0.054	0.047	0.059	0.050	0.064	0.054
$R^2 = .01$							
10	0.049	0.053	0.048	0.056	0.050	0.059	0.053
20	0.049	0.054	0.047	0.058	0.050	0.063	0.054
50	0.049	0.056	0.046	0.063	0.051	0.071	0.057
100	0.049	0.059	0.045	0.069	0.051	0.081	0.059
$R^2 = .05$							
10	0.045	0.063	0.041	0.080	0.051	0.101	0.066
20	0.045	0.070	0.038	0.096	0.052	0.130	0.073
50	0.046	0.086	0.033	0.135	0.053	0.201	0.087
100	0.047	0.107	0.028	0.190	0.054	0.304	0.106
$R^2 = .10$							
10	0.040	0.076	0.032	0.116	0.052	0.166	0.083
20	0.041	0.093	0.028	0.158	0.053	0.244	0.099
50	0.042	0.133	0.020	0.267	0.055	0.442	0.137
100	0.043	0.192	0.014	0.423	0.058	0.680	0.191
$R^2 = .20$							
10	0.030	0.104	0.019	0.202	0.052	0.330	0.121
20	0.032	0.146	0.013	0.318	0.054	0.528	0.163
50	0.034	0.262	0.006	0.599	0.059	0.862	0.272
100	0.036	0.432	0.002	0.857	0.064	0.987	0.429

$\hat{\theta}_j \equiv \Sigma_{i=1}^{n} \hat{\alpha}_{(i_h(j):N)}^2 / \hat{\sigma}_\alpha^2$, $j = 1, 2, 3$, for various sample sizes n. The statistic $\hat{\theta}_1$ is based on induced order statistics with relative ranks evenly spaced in (0,1); $\hat{\theta}_2$ is constructed from induced order statistics ranked in the lowest and highest $100/(m + 1)$-percent fractiles; and $\hat{\theta}_3$ is constructed from those ranked in the second lowest and second highest $100/(m + 1)$-percent fractiles. The R^2 is the square of the correlation between $\hat{\alpha}_i$ and the sorting characteristics.

When the R^2 increases to 10 percent the bias becomes more important. Although tests based on a set of securities with evenly spaced characteristics still have sizes approximately equal to their nominal 5 percent value, the size deviates more substantially when securities with extreme characteristics are used. For example, the size of the $\hat{\theta}_2$ test that uses the 100 securities in the lowest and highest characteristic decile is 42.3 percent! In comparison, the 5 percent test based on the second lowest and second highest deciles exhibits only a 5.8 percent rejection rate. These patterns become even more pronounced for R^2's higher than 10 percent.

The intuition for these results may be found in (8)—the more extreme induced order statistics have means farther away from zero; hence, a statistic based on evenly distributed $\hat{\alpha}_{(i_h:N)}$'s will not provide evidence against the null hypothesis $\alpha = 0$. If the relative ranks are

442

Data-Snooping Biases

extreme, as is the case for $\tilde{\theta}_2$ and $\tilde{\theta}_3$, the resulting $\hat{\alpha}_{\{i_k:N\}}$'s may appear to be statistically incompatible with the null.

1.3 Biases of tests based on portfolios of securities

The entries in Table 1 show that as long as the n securities chosen have characteristics evenly distributed in relative rankings, test statistics based on individual securities yield little inferential bias. However, in practice the ordering by characteristics such as market value of equity is used to group securities into *portfolios,* and the portfolio returns are used to construct test statistics. For example, let $n \equiv n_o q$, where n_o and q are arbitrary positive integers, and consider forming q portfolios with n_o securities in each portfolio, where the portfolios are formed randomly. Under the null hypothesis H we have the following:

$$\phi_k \equiv \frac{1}{n_o} \sum_{j=(k-1)n_o+1}^{kn_o} \hat{\alpha}_j \sim N\left(0, \frac{\sigma_\alpha^2}{n_o}\right), \quad k = 1, 2, \ldots, q, \quad (17)$$

$$\theta_p \equiv \frac{n_o}{\hat{\sigma}_\alpha^2} \sum_{k=1}^{q} \phi_k^2 \stackrel{a}{\sim} \chi_q^2, \quad (18)$$

where ϕ_k is the estimated alpha of portfolio k and θ_p is the aggregate test statistic for the q portfolios. To perform a 5 percent test of H using θ_p, we simply compare it with the critical value C_{95}^q defined by

$$F_{\chi_q^2}(C_{95}^q) = .95. \quad (19)$$

Suppose, however, we compute this test statistic using the induced order statistics $\{\hat{\alpha}_{\{i_k:N\}}\}$ instead of randomly chosen $\{\hat{\alpha}_i\}$. From Theorem 1.1 we have:

Proposition 1.2. *Under the null hypothesis H and assumption (A), as N increases without bound, the statistics $\tilde{\phi}_k$ ($k = 1, 2, \ldots, q$) and $\tilde{\theta}_p$ converge in distribution to the following:*

$$\tilde{\phi}_k \equiv \frac{1}{n_o} \sum_{j=(k-1)n_o+1}^{kn_o} \hat{\alpha}_{\{i_j:N\}} \stackrel{a}{\sim} N\left(\sum_{j=(k-1)n_o+1}^{kn_o} \frac{\mu_j}{n_o}, \frac{\sigma_\alpha^2(1-\rho^2)}{n_o}\right), \quad (20)$$

$$\tilde{\theta}_p \equiv \frac{n_o}{\hat{\sigma}_\alpha^2} \sum_{k=1}^{q} \tilde{\phi}_k^2 \stackrel{a}{\sim} (1-\rho^2) \cdot \chi_q^2(\lambda), \quad (21)$$

with noncentrality parameter

$$\lambda = \frac{n_o \rho^2}{1-\rho^2} \sum_{k=1}^{q} \left(\frac{1}{n_o} \sum_{j=(k-1)n_o+1}^{kn_o} [\Phi^{-1}(\xi_j)]\right)^2. \quad (22)$$

Proof. Again, this follows directly from the definition of a noncentral chi-squared variate and the asymptotic independence of the induced order statistics. ∎

The noncentrality parameter (22) is similar to that of the statistic based on individual securities—it is increasing in ρ^2 and equals zero when $\rho = 0$. However, it differs in one respect: because of portfolio aggregation, each term of the outer sum (the sum with respect to k) is the average of $\Phi^{-1}(\xi_j)$ over all securities in the kth portfolio. To see the importance of this, consider the case where the relative ranks ξ_j are chosen to be evenly spaced in $(0, 1)$, that is,

$$\xi_j = j/(n_o q + 1). \tag{23}$$

Recall from Table 1 that for individual securities the size of 5 percent tests based on *evenly spaced* ξ_j's was not significantly biased. Table 2 reports the size of 5 percent tests based on the portfolio statistic $\tilde{\theta}_p$, also using evenly spaced relative rankings. The contrast is striking—even for as low an R^2 as 1 percent, which implies a correlation of only ± 10 percent between $\hat{\alpha}_i$ and X_i, a 5 percent test based on 50 portfolios with 50 securities in each rejects 67 percent of the time! We can also see how portfolio grouping affects the size of the test for a fixed number of securities by comparing the $(q = i, n_o = j)$ entry with the $(q = j, n_o = i)$ entry. For example, in a sample of 250 securities a test based on 5 portfolios of 50 securities has size 16.5 percent, whereas a test based on 50 portfolios of 5 securities has only a 7.5 percent rejection rate. Grouping securities into portfolios increases the size considerably. The entries in Table 2 are also monotonically increasing across rows and across columns, implying that the test size increases with the number of securities, regardless of whether the number of portfolios or the number of securities per portfolio is held fixed.

To understand why forming portfolios yields much higher rejection rates than using individual securities, recall from (8) and (9) that the mean of $\hat{\alpha}_{[i_k:N]}$ is a function of its relative rank i_k/N (in the limit), whereas its variance $\sigma_\alpha^2(1 - \rho^2)$ is fixed. Forming a portfolio of the induced order statistics within a characteristic-fractile amounts to averaging a collection of n_o approximately independent random variables with similar means and identical variances. The result is a statistic $\tilde{\phi}_k$ with a comparable mean but with a variance n_o times smaller than each of the $\hat{\alpha}_{[i_k:N]}$'s. This variance reduction amplifies the importance of the deviation of the $\tilde{\phi}_k$ mean from zero, and is ultimately reflected in the entries of Table 2. A more dramatic illustration is provided in Table 3, which reports the appropriate 5 percent critical values for the tests in Table 2—when $R^2 = .05$, the 5 percent critical

Data-Snooping Biases

Table 2
Theoretical sizes of nominal 5 percent χ_q^2-tests of H: $\alpha_i = 0$ ($i = 1, \ldots, n$) using the test statistic $\hat{\theta}_p$

q	$n_o = 5$	$n_o = 10$	$n_o = 20$	$n_o = 25$	$n_o = 50$
$R^2 = .005$					
5	0.053	0.058	0.068	0.073	0.102
10	0.055	0.062	0.077	0.086	0.134
20	0.057	0.067	0.091	0.105	0.185
25	0.058	0.070	0.097	0.113	0.208
50	0.062	0.079	0.123	0.148	0.311
$R^2 = .01$					
5	0.056	0.066	0.087	0.099	0.165
10	0.060	0.075	0.110	0.130	0.247
20	0.065	0.088	0.146	0.179	0.382
25	0.067	0.093	0.161	0.202	0.440
50	0.075	0.117	0.232	0.302	0.669
$R^2 = .05$					
5	0.080	0.140	0.288	0.368	0.716
10	0.104	0.212	0.477	0.602	0.941
20	0.142	0.333	0.728	0.854	0.998
25	0.159	0.387	0.808	0.914	1.000
50	0.235	0.607	0.971	0.995	1.000
$R^2 = .10$					
5	0.114	0.255	0.568	0.697	0.971
10	0.174	0.434	0.847	0.935	1.000
20	0.276	0.688	0.985	0.998	1.000
25	0.323	0.773	0.996	1.000	1.000
50	0.523	0.960	1.000	1.000	1.000
$R^2 = .20$					
5	0.193	0.514	0.913	0.971	1.000
10	0.348	0.816	0.997	1.000	1.000
20	0.596	0.980	1.000	1.000	1.000
25	0.688	0.994	1.000	1.000	1.000
50	0.926	1.000	1.000	1.000	1.000

$\hat{\theta}_p = n_o \Sigma_{i=1}^{q} \hat{\phi}_k^2/\sigma_o^2$, and $\hat{\phi}_k = (1/n_o)\Sigma_{j=(k-1)q+1}^{kq} \hat{\alpha}_{(j; N)}$ is constructed from portfolio k, with portfolios formed by sorting on some characteristic correlated with estimates $\hat{\alpha}_i$. This induced ordering alters the null distribution of $\hat{\theta}_p$ from χ_q^2 to $(1 - R^2)/\chi_q^2(\lambda)$, where the noncentrality parameter λ is a function of the number q of portfolios, the number n_o of securities in each portfolio, and the squared correlation coefficient R^2 between $\hat{\alpha}_i$ and the sorting characteristic.

value for the χ^2 test with 50 securities in each of 50 portfolios is 211.67. If induced ordering is unavoidable, these critical values may serve as a method for bounding the effects of data snooping on inferences.

When the R^2 increases to 10 percent, implying a cross-sectional correlation of about ±32 percent between $\hat{\alpha}_i$ and X_i, the size approaches unity for tests based on 20 or more portfolios with 20 or more securities in each portfolio. These results are especially surprising in view of the sizes reported in Table 1, since the portfolio test statistic is based on evenly spaced induced order statistics

445

Table 3
Critical values $C_{.05}$ for 5 percent χ^2-tests of $H: \alpha_i = 0$ ($i = 1, \ldots, n$) using the test statistic $\tilde{\theta}_p$

q	$C_{.05}\cdot\chi_q^2$	$C_{.05}\cdot\chi_q^2(\lambda)$ ($n_o = 5$)	$C_{.05}\cdot\chi_q^2(\lambda)$ ($n_o = 10$)	$C_{.05}\cdot\chi_q^2(\lambda)$ ($n_o = 20$)	$C_{.05}\cdot\chi_q^2(\lambda)$ ($n_o = 25$)	$C_{.05}\cdot\chi_q^2(\lambda)$ ($n_o = 50$)
$R^2 = .005$						
5	11.07	11.22	11.45	11.93	12.16	13.29
10	18.31	18.60	19.03	19.87	20.28	22.31
20	31.41	31.97	32.72	34.22	34.96	38.58
25	37.65	38.33	39.24	41.05	41.94	46.33
50	67.50	68.78	70.44	73.72	75.35	83.39
$R^2 = .01$						
5	11.07	11.36	11.83	12.74	13.19	15.31
10	18.31	18.89	19.73	21.36	22.16	26.00
20	31.41	32.52	34.01	36.93	38.36	45.31
25	37.65	39.01	40.81	44.34	46.08	54.52
50	67.50	70.05	73.33	79.79	82.98	98.60
$R^2 = .05$						
5	11.07	12.45	14.53	18.39	20.21	28.68
10	18.31	21.09	24.88	32.00	35.41	51.54
20	31.41	36.72	43.62	56.75	63.09	93.59
25	37.65	44.18	52.56	68.59	76.35	113.82
50	67.50	79.85	95.41	125.47	140.16	211.67
$R^2 = .10$						
5	11.07	13.65	17.45	24.37	27.63	42.96
10	18.31	23.58	30.62	43.74	50.02	79.98
20	31.41	41.60	54.63	79.32	91.27	148.98
25	37.65	50.21	66.13	96.44	111.15	182.43
50	67.50	91.49	121.42	179.11	207.33	345.24
$R^2 = .20$						
5	11.07	15.70	22.44	34.82	40.71	68.73
10	18.31	27.98	40.86	65.01	76.65	132.76
20	31.41	50.51	74.89	121.32	143.91	253.93
25	37.65	61.32	91.29	148.61	176.58	313.10
50	67.50	113.43	170.67	281.43	335.83	603.10

$\tilde{\theta}_p = n_o\Sigma_{k=1}^{q}\tilde{\phi}_k^2/\sigma_a^2$, and $\tilde{\phi}_k = (1/n_o)\Sigma_{j=n_o(k-1)+1}^{n_o k}\hat{\alpha}_{(j:N)}$ is constructed from portfolio k, with portfolios formed by sorting on some characteristic correlated with estimates $\hat{\alpha}_i$. This induced ordering alters the null distribution of $\tilde{\theta}_p$ from χ_q^2 to $(1 - R^2)/\chi_q^2(\lambda)$, where the noncentrality parameter λ is a function of the number q of portfolios, the number n_o of securities in each portfolio, and the squared correlation coefficient R^2 between $\hat{\alpha}_i$ and the sorting characteristic. $C_{.05}$ is defined implicitly by the relation $\Pr(\tilde{\theta}_p > C_{.05}) = 1 - F_{\chi_q^2(\lambda)}(C_{.05}/(1 - R^2)) = .05$. For comparison, we also report the 5 percent critical value of the central χ_q^2 distribution in the second column.

$\hat{\alpha}_{(i_k:N)}$. Using 100 securities, Table 1 shows a size of 4.3 percent with evenly spaced $\hat{\alpha}_{(i_k:N)}$'s; Table 2 shows that placing those 100 securities into 5 portfolios with 20 securities in each increases the size to 56.8 percent. Computing $\tilde{\theta}_p$ with extreme $\hat{\alpha}_{(i_k:N)}$ would presumably yield even higher rejection rates. The biases reported in Tables 2 and 3 are even more surprising in view of the limited use we have made of the data. The only data-related information impounded in the induced order statistics is the rankings of the characteristics $\{X_i\}$. Nowhere

Data-Snooping Biases

have we exploited the actual values of the X_i's, which contain considerably more precise information about the $\hat{\alpha}_i$'s.

1.4 Interpreting data-snooping bias as power

We have so far examined the effects of data snooping under the null hypothesis that $\alpha_i = 0$, for all i. Therefore, the degree to which induced ordering increases the probability of rejecting this null is implicitly assumed to be a bias, an increase in type I error. However, the results of the previous sections may be reinterpreted as describing the power of tests based on induced ordering against certain alternative hypotheses.

Recall from (2) that $\hat{\alpha}_i$ is the sum of α_i and estimation error ζ_i. Since all α_i's are zero under H, the induced ordering of the estimates $\hat{\alpha}_i$ creates a spurious incompatibility with the null arising solely from the sorting of the estimation errors ζ_i. But if the α_i's are nonzero and vary across i, then sorting by some characteristic X_i related to α_i and forming portfolios does yield a more powerful test. Forming portfolios reduces the estimation error through diversification (or the law of large numbers), and grouping by X_i maintains the dispersion of the α_i's across portfolios. Therefore what were called biases in Sections 1.1–1.3 may also be viewed as measures of the power of induced ordering against alternatives in which the α_i's differ from zero and vary cross-sectionally with X_i. The values in Table 2 show that grouping on a marginally correlated characteristic can increase the power substantially.[14]

To formalize the above intuition within our framework, suppose that the α_i's were i.i.d. random variables independent of ζ_i and have mean μ_α and variance σ_α^2. Then the $\hat{\alpha}_i$'s are still independently and identically distributed, but the null hypothesis that $\alpha_i = 0$ is now violated. Suppose the estimation error ζ_i were identically zero, so that all variation in $\hat{\alpha}_i$ was due to variations in α_i. Then the values in Table 2 would represent the *power* of our test against this alternative, where the squared correlation is now given by

$$\rho_p^2 = \frac{\text{Cov}^2[X_i, \alpha_i]}{\text{Var}[X_i] \cdot \text{Var}[\alpha_i]}. \tag{24}$$

If, as under our null hypothesis, all α_i's were identically zero, then

---

[14] However, implicit in Table 2 is the assumption that the $\hat{\alpha}_i$'s are cross-sectionally independent, which may be too restrictive a requirement for interesting alternative hypotheses. For example, if the null hypothesis $\alpha_i = 0$ corresponds to the Sharpe–Lintner CAPM, then one natural alternative might be a two-factor APT. In that case, the $\hat{\alpha}_i$'s of assets with similar factor loadings would tend to be positively cross-sectionally correlated as a result of the omitted factor. This positive correlation reduces the benefits of grouping. Grouping by induced ordering does tend to cluster $\hat{\alpha}_i$'s with similar (nonzero) means together, but correlation works against the variance reduction that gives portfolio-based tests their power. The importance of cross-sectional dependence is evident in MacKinlay's (1987) power calculations. We provide further discussion in Section 2.3.

the values in Table 2 must be interpreted as the *size* of our test, where the squared correlation reduces to

$$\rho_s^2 = \frac{\text{Cov}^2[X_i, \zeta_i]}{\text{Var}[X_i] \cdot \text{Var}[\zeta_i]}. \qquad (25)$$

More generally, the squared correlation ρ^2 is related to ρ_s^2 and ρ_p^2 in the following way:

$$\rho^2 = \frac{\text{Cov}^2[X_i, \hat{\alpha}_i]}{\text{Var}[X_i] \cdot \text{Var}[\hat{\alpha}_i]} = \frac{(\text{Cov}[X_i, \alpha_i] + \text{Cov}[X_i, \zeta_i])^2}{\text{Var}[X_i] \cdot (\text{Var}[\alpha_i] + \text{Var}[\zeta_i])} \qquad (26)$$

$$= \left(\rho_s \sqrt{\pi} + \rho_p \sqrt{1 - \pi}\right)^2, \quad \pi \equiv \frac{\text{Var}[\zeta_i]}{\text{Var}[\hat{\alpha}_i]}. \qquad (27)$$

Holding the correlations ρ_s and ρ_p fixed, the importance of the spurious portion of ρ^2, given by ρ_s, increases with π, the fraction of variability in $\hat{\alpha}_i$ due to estimation error. Conversely, if the variability of $\hat{\alpha}_i$ is largely due to fluctuations in α_i, then ρ^2 will reflect mostly ρ_p^2.

Of course, the essence of the problem lies in our inability to identify π except in very special cases. We observe an empirical relation between X_i and $\hat{\alpha}_i$, but we do not know whether the characteristic varies with α_i or with estimation error ζ_i. It is a type of identification problem that is unlikely to be settled by data analysis alone, but must be resolved by providing theoretical motivation for a relation, or no relation, between X_i and α_i. That is, economic considerations must play a dominant role in determining π. We shall return to this issue in the empirical examples of Section 3.

2. Monte Carlo Results

Although the values in Tables 1–3 quantify the magnitude of the biases associated with induced ordering, their practical relevance may be limited in at least three respects. First, the test statistics we have considered are similar in spirit to those used in empirical tests of asset pricing models, but implicitly use the assumption of cross-sectional independence. The more common practice is to estimate the covariance matrix of the N asset returns using a finite number T of time series observations, from which an F-distributed quadratic form may be constructed. Both sampling error from the covariance matrix estimator and cross-sectional dependence will affect the null distribution of $\hat{\theta}$ in finite samples.

Second, the sampling theory of Section 1 is based on asymptotic approximations, and few results on rates of convergence for Theorem

Data-Snooping Biases

1.1 are available.[15] How accurate are such approximations for empirically realistic sample sizes?

Finally, the form of the asymptotics does not correspond exactly to procedures followed in practice. Recall that the limiting result involves a finite number n of securities with relative ranks that converge to fixed constants ξ_i as the number of securities N increases without bound. This implies that as N increases, the number of securities in between any two of our chosen n must also grow without bound. However, in practice characteristic-sorted portfolios are constructed from *all* securities within a fractile, not just from those with particular relative ranks. Although intuition suggests that this may be less problematic when n is large (so that within any given fractile there will be many securities), it is surprisingly difficult to verify.[16]

In this section we report results from Monte Carlo experiments that show the asymptotic approximations of Section 1 to be quite accurate in practice despite these three reservations. In Section 2.1, we evaluate the quality of the asymptotic approximations for the $\tilde{\theta}_p$ test used in calculating Tables 2 and 3. In Section 2.2, we consider the effects of induced ordering on F-tests with fixed N and T when the covariance matrix is estimated and the data-generating process is cross-sectionally independent. In Section 2.3, we consider the effects of relaxing the independence assumption.

2.1 Simulation results for $\tilde{\theta}_p$

The $\chi_q^2(\lambda)$ limiting distribution of $\tilde{\theta}_p$ obtains because any finite collection of induced order statistics, each with a fixed distinct limiting relative rank ξ_i in $(0, 1)$, becomes mutually independent as the total number N of securities increases without bound. This asymptotic approximation implies that between any two of the n chosen securities there will be an increasing number of securities omitted from all portfolios as N increases. In practice, all securities within a particular characteristic fractile are included in the sorted portfolios; hence, the theoretical sizes of Table 2 may not be an adequate approximation to this more empirically relevant situation. To explore this possibility we simulate bivariate normal vectors $(\hat{\alpha}_i, X_i)$ with squared correlation R^2, form portfolios using the induced ordering by the X_i's, compute $\tilde{\theta}_p$ using *all* the $\hat{\alpha}_{[i:N]}$'s (in contrast to the asymptotic

---

[15] However, see Bhattacharya (1984) and Sen (1981).

[16] When n is large relative to a finite N, the asymptotic approximation breaks down. In particular, the dependence between adjacent induced order statistics becomes important for nontrivial n/N. A few elegant asymptotic approximations for sums of induced order statistics are available using functional central limit theory and may allow us to generalize our results to the more empirically relevant case. See, for example, Bhattacharya (1974), Nagaraja (1982a, 1982b, 1984), Sandström (1987), Sen (1976, 1981), and Yang (1981a, 1981b). However, our Monte Carlo results suggest that this generalization may be unnecessary.

449

Table 4
Empirical sizes of nominal 5 percent χ^2_r-tests of $H: \alpha_i = 0$ $(i = 1, \ldots, n)$ using the test statistic $\tilde{\theta}_p$

q	$n_o = 5$	$n_o = 10$	$n_o = 20$	$n_o = 25$	$n_o = 50$
$R^2 = .005$					
5	0.055	0.057	0.067	0.075	0.108
10	0.054	0.063	0.080	0.084	0.139
20	0.056	0.068	0.086	0.106	0.182
25	0.062	0.070	0.104	0.112	0.209
50	0.059	0.077	0.119	0.146	0.314
$R^2 = .01$					
5	0.058	0.064	0.093	0.105	0.174
10	0.059	0.076	0.119	0.130	0.257
20	0.057	0.083	0.140	0.188	0.385
25	0.069	0.100	0.170	0.206	0.445
50	0.083	0.118	0.244	0.300	0.679
$R^2 = .05$					
5	0.091	0.149	0.310	0.392	0.723
10	0.117	0.227	0.493	0.611	0.943
20	0.156	0.351	0.744	0.854	0.999
25	0.163	0.401	0.818	0.916	1.000
50	0.249	0.616	0.971	0.997	1.000
$R^2 = .10$					
5	0.141	0.285	0.601	0.721	0.973
10	0.197	0.473	0.854	0.937	1.000
20	0.308	0.709	0.985	0.998	1.000
25	0.338	0.789	0.995	1.000	1.000
50	0.545	0.961	1.000	1.000	1.000
$R^2 = .20$					
5	0.267	0.577	0.922	0.974	1.000
10	0.405	0.833	0.997	1.000	1.000
20	0.635	0.982	1.000	1.000	1.000
25	0.728	0.996	1.000	1.000	1.000
50	0.933	1.000	1.000	1.000	1.000

$\tilde{\theta}_p = n_o \Sigma_{k=1}^{q} \tilde{\phi}_k^2 / \sigma_a^2$, and $\tilde{\phi}_k = (1/n_o) \Sigma_{j=n_o(k-1)+1}^{n_o k} \hat{\alpha}_{(j:N)}$ is constructed from portfolio k, with portfolios formed by sorting on some characteristic correlated with estimates $\hat{\alpha}_i$. This induced ordering alters the null distribution of $\tilde{\theta}_p$ from χ_q^2 to $(1 - R^2) \cdot \chi_q^2(\lambda)$, where the noncentrality parameter λ is a function of the number q of portfolios, the number n_o of securities in each portfolio, and the squared correlation coefficient R^2 between $\hat{\alpha}_i$ and the sorting characteristic. Each simulation is based on 5000 replications; asymptotic standard errors for the size estimates may be obtained from the usual binomial approximation, and is 3.08×10^{-3} for the 5 percent test.

experiment where only those induced order statistics of given relative ranks are used), and then repeat this procedure 5,000 times to obtain the finite sample distribution.

Table 3 reports the results of these simulations for the same values of R^2, n_o, and q as in Table 2. Except when both n_o and q are small, the empirical sizes of Table 4 match their asymptotic counterparts in Table 2 closely. Consider, for example, the $R^2 = .05$ panel; with five portfolios each with five securities, the difference between the theoretical and empirical size is 1.1 percentage points, whereas this difference is only 0.2 percentage points for 25 portfolios each with 25 securities. When n_o and q are both small, the theoretical and empirical sizes differ more for larger R^2, by as much as 7.4 percent when $R^2 = .20$. However, for the more relevant values of R^2, the empirical and theoretical sizes of the $\tilde{\theta}_p$ test are virtually identical.

2.2 Effects of induced ordering on F-tests

Although the results of Section 2.1 support the accuracy of our asymptotic approximation to the sampling distribution of $\tilde{\theta}_p$, the closely related F-statistic is used more frequently in practice. In this section we consider the finite-sample distribution of the F-statistic after induced ordering. We perform Monte Carlo experiments under the now standard multivariate data-generating process common to virtually all static financial asset pricing models. Let r_{it} denote the return of asset i between dates $t - 1$ and t, where $i = 1, 2, \ldots, N$ and $t = 1, 2, \ldots, T$. We assume that for all assets i and dates t the following obtains:

$$r_{it} = \alpha_i + \sum_{j=1}^{k} \beta_{ij} r_t^j + \epsilon_{it}, \qquad (28)$$

where α_i and β_{ij} are fixed parameters, r_t^j is the return on some portfolio j (systematic risk), and ϵ_{it} is mean-zero (idiosyncratic) noise. Depending on the particular application, r_{it} may be taken to be nominal, real, or excess asset returns. The process (28) may be viewed as a factor model where the factors correspond to particular portfolios of traded assets, often called the "mimicking portfolios" of an exact factor pricing model. In matrix notation, we have

$$r_t = \alpha + Br_t^p + \epsilon_t, \quad E[\epsilon_t \mid r_t^p] = 0, \quad E[r_t^p] = \mu_p; \qquad (29)$$

$$E[\epsilon_s \epsilon_t'] = \begin{cases} \Sigma, & \text{for } s = t, \\ 0, & \text{otherwise;} \end{cases} \qquad (30)$$

$$E[(r_s^p - \mu_p)(r_t^p - \mu_p)'] = \begin{cases} \Omega, & \text{for } s = t, \\ 0, & \text{otherwise.} \end{cases} \qquad (31)$$

Here, r_t is the $N \times 1$ vector of asset returns at a time t, B is the $N \times k$ matrix of factor loadings, r_t^p is the $k \times 1$ vector of time-t spanning portfolio returns, and α and ϵ_t are $N \times 1$ vectors of asset return intercepts and disturbances, respectively.

This data-generating process is the starting point of the two most popular static models of asset pricing, the CAPM and the APT. Further restrictions are usually imposed by the specific model under consideration, often reducing to the following null hypothesis:

$$H: g(\alpha, B) = 0,$$

where the function g is model dependent.[17] Many tests simply set $g(\alpha, B) = \alpha$ and define r_t as excess returns, such as those of the Sharpe–Lintner CAPM and the exact factor-pricing APT. With the added assumption that r_t and r_t^p are jointly normally distributed, the finite-sample distribution of the following test statistic is well known:

$$\psi = \kappa \cdot \frac{\hat{\alpha}'\hat{\Sigma}^{-1}\hat{\alpha}}{1 + \bar{r}^p \hat{\Omega}^{-1} \bar{r}^p} \sim F_{N,T-k-N}, \quad \kappa \equiv \frac{T - k - N}{N}, \quad (32)$$

where $\hat{\Sigma}$ and $\hat{\Omega}$ are the maximum likelihood estimators of the covariance matrices of the disturbances $\hat{\epsilon}_t$ and the spanning portfolio returns r_t^p, respectively, and $\bar{r}^p$ is the vector of sample means of r_t^p. If the number of available securities N is greater than the number of time series observations T less $k + 1$, the estimator $\hat{\Sigma}$ is singular and the test statistic (32) cannot be computed without additional structure. This problem is most often circumvented in practice by forming portfolios. That is, let r_t be a $q \times 1$ vector of returns of q portfolios of securities where $q \ll N$. Since the return-generating process is linear for each security i, a linear relation also obtains for portfolio returns. However, as the analysis of Section 1 foreshadows, if the portfolios are constructed by sorting on some characteristic correlated with $\hat{\alpha}$ then the null distribution of ψ is altered.

To evaluate the null distribution of ψ under characteristic-sorting data snooping, we design our simulation experiments in the following way. The number of time series observations T is set to 60 for all simulations. With little loss in generality, we set the number of spanning portfolios k to zero so that $\hat{\alpha}_i = \Sigma_{t=1}^{T} r_{it}/T$. To separate the effects of *estimating* the covariance matrix from the effects of cross-sectional dependence, we first assume that the covariance matrix Σ of ϵ_t is equal to the identity matrix I—this assumption is relaxed in Section 2.3. We simulate T observations of the $N \times 1$ gaussian vector r_t (where N takes the values 200, 500, and 1000), and compute $\hat{\alpha}$. We then form q portfolios (where q takes the values 10 and 20) by constructing a characteristic X_i that has correlation ρ with $\hat{\alpha}_i$ (where ρ^2 takes the

---

[17] Examples of tests that fit into this framework are those in Campbell (1987), Connor and Korajczyk (1988), Gibbons (1982), Gibbons and Ferson (1985), Gibbons, Ross, and Shanken (1989), Huberman and Kandel (1987), MacKinlay (1987), Lehmann and Modest (1988), Stambaugh (1982), and Shanken (1985).

Data-Snooping Biases

values .005, .01, .05, .10, and .20), and then sorting the $\hat{\alpha}_i$'s by this characteristic. To do this, we define

$$X_i \equiv \hat{\alpha}_i + \eta_i, \quad \eta_i \text{ i.i.d. } N(0, \sigma_\eta^2), \quad \sigma_\eta^2 = \frac{1-\rho^2}{T\rho^2}. \quad (33)$$

Having constructed the X_i's, we order $\{\hat{\alpha}_i\}$ to obtain $\{\hat{\alpha}_{[i:N]}\}$, construct portfolio intercept estimates that we call $\hat{\phi}_k$, $k = 1, \ldots, n$,

$$\hat{\phi}_k = \frac{1}{n_o} \sum_{i=(k-1)n_o+1}^{kn_o} \hat{\alpha}_{[i:N]}, \quad N \equiv n_o q, \quad (34)$$

from which we form the F-statistic

$$\psi = \kappa \cdot \hat{\phi}' \hat{\Sigma}^{-1} \hat{\phi} \sim F_{q,T-q}, \quad \kappa \equiv (T-q)/q, \quad (35)$$

where $\hat{\phi}$ denotes the $q \times 1$ vector of $\hat{\phi}_k$'s, and $\hat{\Sigma}$ is the maximum likelihood estimator of the $q \times q$ covariance matrix of the q portfolio returns. This procedure is repeated 5000 times, and the mean and standard deviation of the resulting distribution for the statistic ψ are reported in Table 5, as well as the size of 1, 5, and 10 percent F-tests.

Even for as small an R^2 as 1 percent, the empirical size of the 5 percent F-test differs significantly from its nominal value for all values of q and n_o. For the sample of 1000 securities grouped into ten portfolios, the empirical rejection rate of 36.7 percent deviates substantially from 5 percent. When the 1000 securities are grouped into 20 portfolios, the size is somewhat lower—26.8 percent—matching the pattern in Table 2. Also similar is the monotonicity of the size with respect to the number of securities. For 200 securities the empirical size is only 7.1 percent with 10 portfolios, but it is more than quintupled with 1000 securities. When the squared correlation between $\hat{\alpha}_i$ and X_i increases to 10 percent, the size of the F-test is essentially unity for sample sizes of 500 or more. Thus even for finite sample sizes of practical relevance, the importance of data snooping via induced ordering cannot be overemphasized.

2.3 F-tests with cross-sectional dependence

The substantial bias that induced ordering imparts on the size of portfolio-based F-tests comes from the fact that the induced order statistics $\{\hat{\alpha}_{[i:N]}\}$ generally have nonzero means;[18] hence, the averages of these statistics within sorted portfolios also have nonzero means but reduced variances about those means. Alternatively, the bias from portfolio formation is a result of the fact that the $\hat{\alpha}_i$'s of the extreme portfolios do not approach zero as more securities are combined,

---

[18] Only those $\hat{\alpha}_{[i:N]}$ for which $i/N \to \frac{1}{2}$ will have zero expectation under the null hypothesis H.

Table 5
Empirical size of $F_{q,T-q}$ tests based on q portfolios sorted by a random characteristic whose squared correlation with $\hat{\alpha}_i$ is R^2

q	n_o	n	Mean	Std. Dev.	Size 10%	Size 5%	Size 1%
$R^2 = .005$							
10	20	200	1.111	0.542	0.124	0.041	0.014
20	10	200	1.081	0.424	0.107	0.054	0.009
10	50	500	1.238	0.611	0.177	0.070	0.026
20	25	500	1.147	0.462	0.152	0.079	0.018
10	100	1000	1.406	0.679	0.270	0.118	0.046
20	50	1000	1.240	0.500	0.194	0.114	0.033
$R^2 = .01$							
10	20	200	1.225	0.619	0.181	0.071	0.026
20	10	200	1.148	0.460	0.148	0.079	0.018
10	50	500	1.512	0.728	0.318	0.152	0.070
20	25	500	1.301	0.514	0.240	0.143	0.036
10	100	1000	2.030	0.908	0.576	0.367	0.203
20	50	1000	1.554	0.596	0.405	0.268	0.098
$R^2 = .05$							
10	20	200	1.980	0.883	0.549	0.342	0.189
20	10	200	1.505	0.582	0.369	0.241	0.082
10	50	500	3.501	1.335	0.945	0.846	0.700
20	25	500	2.264	0.801	0.798	0.670	0.382
10	100	1000	5.991	1.976	0.999	0.997	0.986
20	50	1000	3.587	1.169	0.992	0.972	0.879
$R^2 = .10$							
10	20	200	2.961	1.196	0.868	0.713	0.538
20	10	200	1.977	0.727	0.658	0.510	0.257
10	50	500	5.939	1.931	0.999	0.997	0.987
20	25	500	3.526	1.128	0.988	0.968	0.868
10	100	1000	10.888	3.050	1.000	1.000	1.000
20	50	1000	6.123	1.811	1.000	1.000	0.999
$R^2 = .20$							
10	20	200	4.831	1.657	0.997	0.982	0.937
20	10	200	2.895	0.992	0.948	0.882	0.667
10	50	500	10.796	3.022	1.000	1.000	1.000
20	25	500	6.005	1.758	1.000	1.000	0.998
10	100	1000	20.695	5.112	1.000	1.000	1.000
20	50	1000	11.194	2.988	1.000	1.000	1.000

n_o is the number of securities in each portfolio and $n = n_o q$ is the total number of securities. The number of time series observations T is set to 60. The mean and standard deviation of the test statistic over the 5000 replications are reported. The population mean and standard deviation of $F_{10,50}$ are 1.042 and 0.523, respectively; those of the $F_{20,40}$ are 1.053 and 0.423, respectively. Asymptotic standard errors for the size estimates may be obtained from the usual binomial approximation; they are 4.24×10^{-3}, 3.08×10^{-3}, and 1.41×10^{-3} for the 10, 5, and 1 percent tests, respectively.

whereas the residual variances of the portfolios (and consequently the variances of the portfolio $\hat{\alpha}_i$'s) do tend to zero. Of course, our assumption that the disturbances ϵ_t of (29) are cross-sectionally independent implies that the portfolio residual variance approaches zero rather quickly (at rate $1/n_o$). But in many applications (such as the CAPM), cross-sectional independence is counterfactual. Firm size and industry membership are but two factors that might induce cross-sectional correlation in return residuals. In particular, when the resid-

Data-Snooping Biases

uals are positively cross-sectionally correlated, the bias is likely to be smaller since there is less variance reduction in forming portfolios than in the cross-sectionally independent case.

To see how restrictive the independence assumption is, we simulate a data-generating process in which disturbances are cross-sectionally correlated. The design is identical to that of Section 2.2 except that the residual covariance matrix Σ is no longer diagonal. Instead, we set

$$\Sigma = \delta\delta' + I, \qquad (36)$$

where δ is an $N \times 1$ vector of parameters and I is the identity matrix. Such a covariance matrix would arise, for example, from a single common factor model for the $N \times 1$ vector of disturbances ϵ_t:

$$\epsilon_t = \delta\Lambda_t + \nu_t, \qquad (37)$$

where Λ_t is some i.i.d. zero-mean unit-variance common factor independent of ν_t, and ν_t is N-dimensional vector white noise with covariance matrix I. For our simulations, the parameters δ are chosen to be equally spaced in the interval $[-1, 1]$. With this design the cross-correlation of the disturbances will range from -0.5 to 0.5. The X_i's are constructed as in (33) with

$$\sigma_\eta^2 = \frac{(1 - \rho^2)\sigma^2(\alpha)}{\rho^2}, \qquad \sigma^2(\alpha) \equiv \frac{1}{NT}\sum_{i=1}^{N}(\delta_i^2 + 1), \qquad (38)$$

where ρ^2 is fixed at .05.

Under this design, the results of the simulation experiments may be compared to the third panel of Table 5, and are reported in Table 6.[19] Despite the presence of cross-sectional dependence, the impact of induced ordering on the size of the F-test is still significant. For example, with 20 portfolios each containing 25 securities the empirical size of the 5 percent test is 32.3 percent; with 10 portfolios of 50 securities each the empirical size increases to 82.0 percent. As in the cross-sectionally independent case, the bias increases with the number of securities given a fixed number of portfolios, and the bias decreases as the number of portfolios is increased given a fixed number of securities. Not surprisingly, for fixed n_o and q, cross-sectional dependence of the $\hat{\alpha}_i$'s lessens the bias. However, the entries in Table 6 demonstrate that the effects of data snooping may still be substantial even in the presence of cross-sectional dependence.

---

[19] The correspondence between the two tables is not exact because the dependency induced in (36) induces cross-sectional heteroskedasticity in the $\hat{\alpha}_i$'s; hence, $\rho^2 = .05$ yields an R^2 of .05 only approximately.

Table 6
Empirical size of $F_{a,\tau-q}$ tests based on q portfolios sorted by a random characteristic whose squared correlation with $\hat{a}_i$ is approximately .05

q	n_o	n	Mean	Std. Dev.	Size 10%	Size 5%	Size 1%
$R^2 \approx .05$							
10	20	200	1.700	0.763	0.422	0.216	0.100
20	10	200	1.372	0.528	0.270	0.167	0.047
10	50	500	2.520	1.041	0.765	0.565	0.367
20	25	500	1.867	0.693	0.593	0.322	0.205
10	100	1000	3.624	1.605	0.925	0.820	0.682
20	50	1000	2.516	0.966	0.844	0.743	0.501

n_o is the number of securities in each portfolio and $n = n_o q$ is the total number of securities. The $\hat{a}_i$'s of the portfolios are cross-sectionally correlated, where the source of correlation is an i.i.d. zero-mean common factor in the returns. The number of time series observations T is set to 60. The mean and standard deviation of the test statistic over the 5000 replications are reported. The population mean and standard deviation of $F_{10,50}$ are 1.042 and 0.523, respectively; those of the $F_{20,40}$ are 1.053 and 0.423, respectively. Asymptotic standard errors for the size estimates may be obtained from the usual binomial approximation; they are 4.24×10^{-3}, 3.08×10^{-3}, and 1.41×10^{-3} for the 10, 5, and 1 percent tests, respectively.

3. Two Empirical Examples

To illustrate the potential relevance of data-snooping biases associated with induced ordering, we provide two examples drawn from the empirical literature. The first example is taken from the early tests of the Sharpe–Lintner CAPM, where portfolios were formed by sorting on out-of-sample betas. We show that such tests can be biased towards falsely rejecting the CAPM if in-sample betas are used instead, underscoring the importance of the elaborate sorting procedures used by Black, Jensen, and Scholes (1972) and Fama and MacBeth (1973). Our second example concerns tests of the APT that reject the zero-intercept null hypothesis when applied to portfolio returns sorted by market value of equity. We show that data-snooping biases can account for much the same results, and that only additional economic restrictions will determine the ultimate source of the rejections.

3.1 Sorting by beta

Although tests of the Sharpe–Lintner CAPM may be conducted on individual securities, the potential benefits of using multiple securities are well known. One common approach for allocating securities to portfolios has been to rank them by their betas and then group the sorted securities. Beta-sorted portfolios will exhibit more risk dispersion than portfolios of randomly chosen securities, and may therefore yield more information about the CAPM's risk–return relation. Ideally, portfolios would be formed according to their true betas. However, since the population betas are unobservable, in practice

Data-Snooping Biases

portfolios have grouped securities by their estimated betas. For example, both Black, Jensen, and Scholes (1972) and Fama and MacBeth (1973) use portfolios formed by sorting on estimated betas, where the betas are estimated with a *prior* sample of stock returns. Their motivation for this more complicated procedure was to avoid grouping common estimation or measurement error since, within the sample, securities with high estimated betas will tend to have positive realizations of estimation error, and vice versa for securities with low estimated betas.

Suppose, instead, that securities are grouped by betas estimated *in sample*. Can grouping common estimation error change inferences substantially? To answer this question within our framework, suppose the Sharpe–Lintner CAPM obtains so that

$$r_{it} = \beta_i r_{mt} + \epsilon_{it}, \qquad \mathrm{E}[\epsilon_t \mid r_{mt}] = 0, \qquad \mathrm{E}[\epsilon_t \epsilon_t'] = \sigma_\epsilon^2 I, \qquad (39)$$

where r_{it} denotes the excess return of security i, r_{mt} is the excess market return, and ϵ_t is the $N \times 1$ vector of disturbances. To assess the impact of sorting on in-sample betas, we require the squared correlation of $\hat{\alpha}_i$ and $\hat{\beta}_i$. However, since our framework requires that both $\hat{\alpha}_i$ and $\hat{\beta}_i$ be independently and identically distributed, and since $\hat{\beta}_i$ is the sum of β_i and estimation error ζ_i, we assume β_i to be random to allow for cross-sectional variation in the betas. Therefore, let

$$\beta_i \text{ i.i.d. } N(\mu_\beta, \sigma_\beta^2), \qquad i = 1, 2, \ldots, N,$$

where each β_i is independent of all ϵ_{jt} in (39). The squared correlation between $\hat{\alpha}_i$ and $\hat{\beta}_i$ may then be explicitly calculated as

$$\rho^2(\hat{\alpha}_i, \hat{\beta}_i) = \frac{\mathrm{Cov}^2[\hat{\alpha}_i, \hat{\beta}_i]}{\mathrm{Var}[\hat{\alpha}_i]\,\mathrm{Var}[\hat{\beta}_i]} = \frac{\hat{S}_m^2}{1 + \hat{S}_m^2} \cdot \frac{1}{1 + (\sigma_\beta^2 \hat{\sigma}_m^2/\sigma_\epsilon^2)T}, \qquad (40)$$

where $\hat{\mu}_m$ and $\hat{\sigma}_m$ are the sample mean and standard deviation of the excess market return, respectively, $S_m \equiv \hat{\mu}_m/\hat{\sigma}_m$ is the ex post Sharpe measure, and T is the number of time series observations used to estimate the α_i's and β_i's.

The term $\sigma_\beta^2 \hat{\sigma}_m^2 T/\sigma_\epsilon^2$ in (40) captures the essence of the errors-in-variables problem for in-sample beta sorting. This is simply the ratio of the cross-sectional variance in betas, σ_β^2, to the variance of the beta estimation error, $\sigma_\epsilon^2/(\hat{\sigma}_m^2 T)$. When the cross-sectional dispersion of the betas is much larger than the variance of the estimation errors, this ratio is large, implying a small value for ρ^2 and little data-snooping bias. In fact, since the estimation error of the betas declines with the number of observations T, as the time period lengthens, in-sample beta sorting becomes less problematic. However, when the variance of the estimation error is large relative to the cross-sectional variance

Table 7
Theoretical sizes of nominal 5 percent χ_q^2-tests under the null hypothesis of the Sharpe-Lintner CAPM using q in-sample beta-sorted portfolios with n_o securities per portfolio

Sample period	$\hat{R}^2$	$q = 10$ $n_o = 250$	$q = 20$ $n_o = 125$	$q = 50$ $n_o = 50$
January 1954–December 1958	.044	1.000	1.000	1.000
January 1959–December 1963	.007	0.790	0.656	0.435
January 1964–December 1968	.048	1.000	1.000	1.000
January 1969–December 1973	.008	0.869	0.756	0.529
January 1974–December 1978	.001	0.183	0.139	0.100
January 1979–December 1983	.023	1.000	1.000	0.991
January 1984–December 1988	.002	0.248	0.183	0.123

$\hat{R}^2$ is the estimated squared correlation between $\hat{\beta}_i$ and $\hat{\alpha}_i$ under the null hypothesis that $\alpha_i = 0$ and that the β_i's are i.i.d. normal random variables with mean and variance μ_β and σ_β^2, respectively. Within each subsample, the estimate $\hat{R}^2$ is based on the first 200 stocks in the CRSP monthly returns files with complete return histories over the five-year subperiod, and the CRSP equal-weighted index. For illustrative purposes, the theoretical size is computed under the assumption that the total number of securities $n = n_o q$ is fixed at 2500.

of the betas, then ρ^2 is large and grouping common estimation errors becomes a more serious problem.

To show just how serious this might be in practice, we report in Table 7 the estimated ρ^2 between $\hat{\alpha}_i$ and $\hat{\beta}_i$ for five-year subperiods from January 1954 to December 1988, where each estimate is based on the first 200 securities listed in the CRSP monthly returns files with complete return histories within the particular five-year subsample, and the CRSP equal-weighted index. Also reported is the probability of rejecting the null hypothesis $\alpha_i = 0$ when it is true using a 5 percent test, assuming a sample of 2500 securities, where the number of portfolios q is 10, 20, or 50 and the number of securities per portfolio n_o is defined accordingly.[20]

The entries in Table 7 show that the null hypothesis is quite likely to be rejected even when it is true. For many of the subperiods, the probability of rejecting the null is unity, and when only 10 beta-sorted portfolios are used, the smallest size of a nominal 5 percent test is still 18.3 percent. We conclude, somewhat belatedly, that the elaborate out-of-sampling sorting procedures used by Black, Jensen, and Scholes (1972) and Fama and MacBeth (1973) were indispensable to the original tests of the Sharpe–Lintner CAPM.

3.2 Sorting by size

As a second example of the practical relevance of data-snooping biases, we consider Lehmann and Modest's (1988) multivariate test of a 15-

---

[20] Our analysis is limited by the counterfactual assumption that the market model disturbances are cross-sectionally uncorrelated. But the simulation results presented in Section 2.3 indicate that biases are still substantial even in the presence of cross-sectional dependence. A more involved application would require a deeper analysis of cross-sectional dependence in the ϵ_n's.

Data-Snooping Biases

factor APT model, in which they reject the zero-intercept null hypothesis using five portfolios formed by grouping securities ordered by market value of equity.[21] We focus on this particular study because of the large number of factors employed—our framework requires the disturbances ϵ_i of (29) to be cross-sectionally independent, and since 15 factors are included in Lehmann and Modest's cross-sectional regressions, a diagonal covariance matrix for ϵ_i is not implausible.

It is well-known that the estimated intercept $\hat{\alpha}_i$ from the single-period CAPM regression (excess individual security returns regressed on an intercept and the market risk premium) is negatively cross-sectionally correlated with log size.[22] Since this $\hat{\alpha}_i$ will in general be correlated with the estimated intercept from a 15-factor APT regression, it is likely that the estimated APT intercept and log size will also be empirically correlated.[23] Unfortunately, we do not have a direct measure of the correlation of the APT intercept and log size which is necessary to derive the appropriate null distribution after induced ordering.[24] As an alternative, we estimate the cross-sectional R^2 of the estimated CAPM alpha with the logarithm of size, and we use this R^2 as well as $\frac{1}{2}R^2$ and $\frac{1}{4}R^2$ to estimate the bias attributable to induced ordering.

Following Lehmann and Modest (1988), we consider four five-year time periods from January 1963 to December 1982. X_i is defined to be the logarithm of beginning-of-period market values of equity. The $\hat{\alpha}_i$'s are the intercepts from regressions of excess returns on the market risk premium as measured by the difference between an equal-weighted NYSE index and monthly Treasury bill returns, where the NYSE index is obtained from the Center for Research in Security Prices (CRSP) database. The R^2's of these regressions are reported in the second column of Table 8. One cross-sectional regression of $\hat{\alpha}_i$ on log size X_i is run for each five-year time period using monthly NYSE-AMEX data from CRSP. We run regressions only for those stocks having complete return histories within the relevant five-year period.

Table 8 contains the test statistics for a 15-factor APT framework using five size-sorted portfolios. The first four rows contain results

---

[21] See Lehmann and Modest (1988, table 1, last row). Connor and Korajczyk (1988) report similar findings.

[22] See, for example, Banz (1981) and Brown, Kleidon, and Marsh (1983).

[23] We recognize that correlation is not transitive, so if X is correlated with Y and Y with Z, X need not be correlated with Z. However, since the intercepts from the two regressions will be functions of some common random variables, situations in which they are independent are the exception rather than the rule.

[24] Nor did Lehmann and Modest prior to their extensive investigations. If they are subject to any data-snooping biases it is only from their awareness of size-related empirical results for the single-period CAPM, and of corresponding results for the APT as in Chan, Chen, and Hsieh (1985).

Table 8
Comparison of p-values for Lehmann and Modest's (1988) tests of the APT with and without correcting for the effects of induced ordering

Sample	N	$\hat{R}^2$	$\tilde{\theta}_p$	χ^2 p-value	$\chi^2(\lambda_1)$ p-value	$\chi^2(\lambda_2)$ p-value	$\chi^2(\lambda_3)$ p-value
6301–6712	1001	0.015	13.70	0.018	0.687	0.315	0.131
6801–7212	1359	0.040	15.50	0.008	1.000	0.919	0.520
7301–7712	1346	0.033	10.20	0.070	1.000	0.963	0.720
7801–8212	1281	0.004	12.05	0.034	0.272	0.134	0.078
Aggregate	—	—	51.45	0.00014	1.000	0.917	0.298

In the absence of data snooping, the appropriate test statistics and their p-values (using the central χ^2 distribution) are given in Lehmann and Modest (1988, table 1) and reported below in columns 4 and 5 (we transform their F-statistics into χ^2 variates for purposes of comparison). Corresponding p-values that account for induced ordering are calculated in columns labeled "$\chi^2(\lambda_i)$ p-value" ($i = 1, 2, 3$) (using the noncentral χ^2 distribution), where λ_1, λ_2, and λ_3 are noncentrality parameters computed with $\hat{R}^2$, $\frac{1}{2}\hat{R}^2$, and $\frac{1}{3}\hat{R}^2$, respectively. In all cases, five portfolios are formed from the total number of securities; this yields five degrees of freedom for the χ^2 statistics in the first four rows, and 20 degrees of freedom for the aggregate χ^2 statistics.

for each of the four subperiods and the last row contains aggregate test statistics. To apply the results of Sections 1 and 2 we transform Lehmann and Modest's (1988) F-statistics into (asymptotic) χ^2 variates.[25] The total number of available securities ranges from a minimum of 1001 for the first five-year subperiod to a maximum of 1359 for the second subperiod. For each test statistic in Table 8 we report four different p-values: the first is with respect to the null distribution that ignores data snooping, and the next three are with respect to null distributions that account for induced ordering to various degrees.

The entries in Table 8 show that the potential biases from sorting by characteristics that have been empirically selected can be immense. The p-values range from 0.008 to 0.070 in the four subperiods according to the standard theoretical null distribution, yielding an aggregate p-value of 0.00014, considerable evidence against the null. When we adjust for the fact that the sorting characteristic is selected empirically (using the $\hat{R}^2$ from the cross-sectional regression of $\hat{\alpha}_i$ on X_i), the p-values for these same four subperiods range from 0.272 to 1.000, yielding an aggregate p-value of 1.000! Therefore, whether or not induced ordering is allowed for can change inferences dramatically.

The appropriate R^2 in the preceding analysis is the squared correlation between log size and the intercept from a 15-factor APT regression, and not the one used in Table 8. To see how this may affect our conclusions, recall from (2) that the cross-sectional correlation between $\hat{\alpha}_i$ and log size can arise from two sources: the

---

[25] Since Lehmann and Modest (1988) use weekly data, the null distribution of their test statistics is $F_{5,240}$. In practice the inferences are virtually identical using the χ^2_5 distribution after multiplying the test statistic by 5.

estimation error ζ_i in $\hat{\alpha}_i$, and the cross-sectional dispersion in the "true" CAPM α_i (which is zero under the null hypothesis). Correlation between X_i and ζ_i will be partially reflected in correlation between the estimated APT intercept and log size. The second source of correlation will not be relevant *under the APT null hypothesis* since under that scenario we assume that the 15-factor APT obtains and therefore the intercept vanishes for all securities. As a conservative estimate for the appropriate R^2 to be used in Table 8, we set the squared correlation equal to $\frac{1}{2}\hat{R}^2$ and $\frac{1}{4}\hat{R}^2$, yielding the p-values reported in the last two columns of Table 8. Even when the squared correlation is only $\frac{1}{4}\hat{R}^2$, the inferences change markedly after induced ordering, with p-values ranging from 0.078 to 0.720 in the four subperiods and 0.298 in the aggregate. This simple example illustrates the severity with which even a mild form of data snooping can bias our inferences in practice.

Nevertheless, it should not be inferred from Table 8 that all size-related phenomena are spurious. After all, the correlation between X_i and $\hat{\alpha}_i$ may be the result of cross-sectional variations in the population α_i's, and not estimation error. Even so, tests using size-sorted portfolios are still biased if based on the same data from which the size effect was previously observed. A procedure that is free from such biases is to decide today that size is an interesting characteristic, collect ten years of new data, and then perform tests on size-sorted portfolios from this fresh sample. Provided that the old and new samples are statistically independent, this will yield a perfectly valid test of the null hypothesis H, since the only possible source of correlation between the X_i's and the $\hat{\alpha}_i$'s in the new sample is from the α_i's (presumably the result of some underlying economic relation between the two), and not from the estimation errors. In such cases, induced ordering cannot affect the distribution of the test statistics under the null hypothesis, and will yield a considerably more powerful test against many alternatives.

4. How the Data Get Snooped

Whether the probabilities of rejection in Table 2 are to be interpreted as size or power depends, of course, on the particular null and alternative hypotheses at hand, the key distinction being the source of correlation between $\hat{\alpha}_i$ and the characteristic X_i. Since our starting point in Section 1 was the assertion that this correlation is "spurious," we view the values of Table 2 as probabilities of falsely rejecting the null hypothesis. We suggested in Section 1 that the source of this spurious correlation is correlation between the characteristic and the estimation errors in $\hat{\alpha}_i$, since such errors are the only source of vari-

461

ation in $\hat{\alpha}_i$ under the null. But how does this correlation arise? One possibility is the very mechanism by which characteristics are selected. Without any economic theories for motivation, a plausible behavioral model of how we determine characteristics to be particularly "interesting" is that we tend to focus on those that have unusually large squared sample correlations or R^2's with the $\hat{\alpha}_i$'s. In the spirit of Ross (1987), economists study "interesting" events, as well as events that are interesting from a theoretical perspective. If so, then even in a collection of K characteristics all of which are independent of the $\hat{\alpha}_i$'s, correlation between the $\hat{\alpha}_i$'s and the most "interesting" characteristic is artificially induced.

More formally, suppose for each of N securities we have a collection of K distinct and mutually independent characteristics Y_{ik}, $k = 1, 2, \ldots, K$, where Y_{ik} is the kth characteristic of the ith security. Let the null hypothesis obtain so that $\alpha_i = 0$, for all i, and assume that all characteristics are independent of $\{\hat{\alpha}_i\}$. This last assumption implies that the distribution of a test statistic based on grouped $\hat{\alpha}_i$'s is unaffected by sorting on any of the characteristics. For simplicity let each of the characteristics and the $\hat{\alpha}_i$'s be normally distributed with zero mean and unit variance, and consider the sample correlation coefficients:

$$\hat{\rho}_k = \frac{\sum_{i=1}^{N}(Y_{ik} - \bar{Y}_k)(\hat{\alpha}_i - \bar{\hat{\alpha}})}{\sqrt{\sum_{i=1}^{N}(Y_{ik} - \bar{Y}_k)^2} \cdot \sqrt{\sum_{i=1}^{N}(\hat{\alpha}_i - \bar{\hat{\alpha}})^2}}, \quad k = 1, 2, \ldots, K, \quad (41)$$

where $\bar{Y}_k$ and $\bar{\hat{\alpha}}$ are the sample means of characteristic k and the $\hat{\alpha}_i$'s, respectively. Suppose we choose as our sorting characteristic the one that has the largest squared correlation with the $\hat{\alpha}_i$'s, and call this characteristic X_i. That is, $X_i \equiv Y_{ik^*}$, where the index k^* is defined by

$$\hat{\rho}_{k^*}^2 = \underset{1 \le k \le K}{\operatorname{Max}} \hat{\rho}_k^2. \quad (42)$$

This X_i is a new characteristic in the statistical sense, in that its distribution is no longer the same as that of the Y_{ik}'s.[26] It is apparent that X_i and $\hat{\alpha}_i$ are not mutually independent since the $\hat{\alpha}_i$'s were used in selecting this characteristic. By construction, extreme realizations of the random variables $\{X_i\}$ tend to occur when extreme realizations of $\{\hat{\alpha}_i\}$ occur.

To estimate the magnitude of correlation spuriously induced between X_i and $\hat{\alpha}_i$, first observe that although the correlation between Y_{ik} and $\hat{\alpha}_i$ is zero for all k, $E[\hat{\rho}_k^2] = 1/(N - 1)$ under our normality assumption. Therefore, $1/(N - 1)$ should be our benchmark in assessing the degree of spurious correlation between X_i and $\hat{\alpha}_i$. Since the $\hat{\rho}_k^2$'s are well-known to be independently and identically distributed

Data-Snooping Biases

Beta$(\frac{1}{2}, \frac{1}{2}(N-2))$ variates, the distribution and density functions of $\hat{\rho}_{k^*}^2$, denoted by $F_*(v)$ and $f_*(v)$, respectively, may be readily derived as[27]

$$F_*(v) = [F_\beta(v)]^K, \quad v \in (0, 1), \tag{43}$$

$$f_*(v) = K[F_\beta(v)]^{K-1} f_\beta(v), \quad v \in (0, 1), \tag{44}$$

where F_β and f_β are the cumulative distribution function and probability density function of the Beta distribution with parameters $\frac{1}{2}$ and $\frac{1}{2}(N-2)$. A measure of that portion of squared correlation between X_i with $\hat{\alpha}_i$ due to sorting on $\hat{\rho}_k^2$ is then given by

$$\gamma \equiv E[\hat{\rho}_{k^*}^2] - E[\hat{\rho}_k^2] = \int_0^1 v f_*(v) \, dv - \frac{1}{N-1}. \tag{45}$$

For 25 securities and 50 characteristics, γ is 20.5 percent![28] With 100 securities, γ is still 5.4 percent and only declines to 1.1 percent for 500 securities. With only 25 characteristics, the values of γ for 25, 100, and 500 securities fall to 16.4, 4.2, and 0.8 percent, respectively. However, these smaller values of γ can still yield misleading inferences for tests based on few portfolios, each containing many securities. This is seen in Table 9, in which the theoretical sizes of 5 percent tests with R^2's equal to the appropriate γ for each cell are displayed. For example, the first entry in the first row of Table 9, 0.163, is the size of the 5 percent portfolio-based test with five portfolios and five securities in each, where the R^2 used to perform the calculation is the γ corresponding to 25 securities and 25 characteristics, or 16.4 percent. As the number of securities per portfolio grows, γ declines but the bias worsens—with 50 securities in each of 5 portfolios, γ is only 1.7 percent but the actual size of a 5 percent test is 26.4 percent. Although there is in fact no statistical relation between

---

[26] In fact, if we denote by Y_k the $N \times 1$ vector containing values of characteristic k for each of the N securities, then the vector most highly correlated with $\hat{\alpha}$ (which we have called X) may be viewed as the concomitant $Y_{[K:K]}$ of the Kth order statistic $\hat{\rho}_{[K:K]}^2 = \hat{\rho}_{k^*}^2$. As in the scalar case, induced ordering does change the distribution of the vector concomitants.

[27] That the squared correlation coefficients are i.i.d. Beta random variables follows from our assumptions of normality and the mutual independence of the characteristics and the $\hat{\alpha}_i$'s [see Stuart and Ord (1987, chapter 16.28) for example]. The distribution and density functions of the maximum follow directly from this.

[28] Note that γ is only an approximation to the squared population correlation:

$$\left[\frac{E(X_i - E[X_i])(\hat{\alpha}_i - E[\hat{\alpha}_i])}{\sqrt{E(X_i - E[X_i])^2} \cdot \sqrt{E(\hat{\alpha}_i - E[\hat{\alpha}_i])^2}} \right]^2.$$

However, Monte Carlo simulations with 10,000 replications show that this approximation is excellent even for small sample sizes. For example, fixing K at 50, the correlation from the simulations is 22.82 percent for $N = 25$, whereas (45) yields $\gamma = 20.47$ percent; for $N = 100$ the simulations yield a correlation of 6.25 percent, compared to a γ of 5.39 percent.

463

Table 9
Theoretical sizes of nominal 5 percent χ_q^2-tests of $H: \alpha_i = 0$ ($i = 1, \ldots, n$) using the test statistic $\bar{\theta}_p$

q	$n_o = 5$	$n_o = 10$	$n_o = 20$	$n_o = 25$	$n_o = 50$
K = 25					
5	0.163	0.216	0.246	0.253	0.264
10	0.150	0.182	0.200	0.202	0.210
20	0.125	0.144	0.153	0.155	0.159
25	0.117	0.132	0.140	0.142	0.145
50	0.096	0.104	0.109	0.110	0.112
K = 50					
5	0.197	0.270	0.311	0.319	0.337
10	0.183	0.228	0.254	0.259	0.270
20	0.151	0.178	0.192	0.195	0.201
25	0.141	0.163	0.175	0.177	0.182
50	0.112	0.125	0.131	0.133	0.136

$\bar{\theta}_p = n_o \Sigma_{k=1}^q \bar{\phi}_k^2/\sigma_a^2$, and $\bar{\phi}_k = (1/n_o)\Sigma_{j=1}^{n_o} \hat{\alpha}_{[(k-1)q+j, N]}$ is constructed from portfolio k, with portfolios formed by sorting on some characteristic correlated with estimates $\hat{\alpha}_i$. This induced ordering alters the null distribution of $\bar{\theta}_p$ from χ_q^2 to $(1 - R^2) \cdot \chi_q^2(\lambda)$, where the noncentrality parameter λ is a function of the number q of portfolios, the number n_o of securities in each portfolio, and the squared correlation coefficient R^2 between $\hat{\alpha}_i$ and the sorting characteristic. The values of R^2 used for the size calculations vary with the total number of securities $n_o q$ and with K, the total number of independent characteristics from which the most "interesting" is selected.

any of the characteristics and the $\hat{\alpha}_i$'s, a procedure that focuses on the most striking characteristic can *create* spurious statistical dependence.

As the number of securities N increases, this particular source of dependence becomes less important since all the sample correlation coefficients $\hat{\rho}_k$ converge almost surely to zero, as does γ. However, recall from Table 2 that as the sample size grows the bias increases if the number of portfolios is held fixed; hence, as Table 9 illustrates, a larger N and thus a smaller γ need not imply a smaller bias. Moreover, since γ is increasing in the number of characteristics K, we cannot find refuge in the law of large numbers without weighing the number of securities against the number of characteristics and portfolios in some fashion. Table 9 provides one informal measure of this trade-off.

Perhaps even the most unscrupulous investigator might hesitate at the kind of data snooping we have just considered. However, the very review process that published research undergoes can have much the same effect, since competition for limited journal space tilts the balance in favor of the most striking and dissonant of empirical results. Indeed, the "Anomalies" section of the *Journal of Economic Perspectives* is the most obvious example of our deliberate search for the unusual in economics. As a consequence, interest may be created in otherwise theoretically irrelevant characteristics. In the absence of an economic paradigm, such data-snooping biases are not easily

Data-Snooping Biases

distinguishable from violations of the null hypothesis. This inability to separate pretest bias from alternative hypotheses is the most compelling criticism of "measurement without theory."

5. Conclusion

Although the size effect may signal important differences between the economic structure of small and large corporations, how these differences are manifested in the stochastic properties of their equity returns cannot be reliably determined through data analysis alone. Much more convincing would be the empirical significance of size, or any other quantity, that is based on a model of economic equilibrium in which the characteristic is related to the behavior of asset returns endogenously. Our findings show that tests using securities grouped according to theoretically motivated correlations between X_i and $\hat{\alpha}_i$ can be powerful indeed—interestingly, tests of the APT with portfolios sorted by such characteristics (own-variance and dividend yield) no longer reject the null hypothesis [see Lehmann and Modest (1988)]. Sorting on size yields rejections whereas sorting on theoretically relevant characteristics such as own-variance and dividend yield does not. This suggests that data-instigated grouping procedures should be employed cautiously.

It is widely acknowledged that incorrect conclusions may be drawn from procedures violating the assumptions of classical statistical inference, but the nature of these violations is often as subtle as it is profound. In observing that economists (as well as those in the natural sciences) tend to seek out anomalies, Merton (1987, p. 104) writes: "All this fits well with what the cognitive psychologists tell us is our natural individual predilection to focus, often disproportionately so, on the unusual. . . . This focus, both individually and institutionally, together with little control over the number of tests performed, creates a fertile environment for both unintended selection bias and for attaching greater significance to otherwise unbiased estimates than is justified." The recognition of this possibility is a first step in guarding against it. The results of our paper provide a more concrete remedy for such biases in the particular case of portfolio formation via induced ordering on data-instigated characteristics. However, nonexperimental inference may never be completely free from data-snooping biases since the attention given to empirical anomalies, incongruities, and unusual correlations is also the modus operandi for genuine discovery and progress in the social sciences. Formal statistical analyses such as ours may serve as primitive guides to a better understanding of economic phenomena, but the ability to distinguish between the spurious and the substantive is likely to remain a cherished art.

References

Aldous, D., 1989, *Probability Approximations via the Poisson Clumping Heuristic*, Springer, New York.

Banz, R. W., 1978, "Limited Diversification and Market Equilibrium: An Empirical Analysis," Ph.D. dissertation, University of Chicago.

Banz, R. W., 1981, "The Relationship Between Return and Market Value of Common Stocks," *Journal of Financial Economics*, 9, 3–18.

Berger, J., and R. Wolpert, 1984, *The Likelihood Principle*, Lecture Notes—Monograph Series Volume 6, Institute of Mathematical Statistics, Hayward, Cal.

Bhattacharya, P. K., 1974, "Convergence of Sample Paths of Normalized Sums of Induced Order Statistics," *Annals of Statistics*, 2, 1034–1039.

Bhattacharya, P. K., 1984, "Induced Order Statistics: Theory and Applications," in P. R. Krishnaiah and P. K. Sen (eds.), *Handbook of Statistics 4: Nonparametric Methods*, North-Holland, Amsterdam.

Black, F., M. Jensen, and M. Scholes, 1972, "The Capital Asset Pricing Model: Some Empirical Tests," in M. Jensen (ed.), *Studies in the Theory of Capital Markets*, Praeger, New York.

Brown, P., A. Kleidon, and T. Marsh, 1983, "New Evidence on the Nature of Size Related Anomalies in Stock Prices," *Journal of Financial Economics*, 12, 33–56.

Campbell, J. Y., 1987, "Stock Returns and the Term Structure," *Journal of Financial Economics*, 18, 373–400.

Chamberlain, G., 1983, "Funds, Factors, and Diversification in Arbitrage Pricing Models," *Econometrica*, 51, 1305–1323.

Chan, K., N. Chen, and D. Hsieh, 1985, "An Exploratory Investigation of the Firm Size Effect," *Journal of Financial Economics*, 14, 451–471.

Chen, N., R. Roll, and S. Ross, 1986, "Economic Forces and the Stock Market," *Journal of Business*, 59, 383–403.

Connor, G., and R. Korajczyk, 1988, "Risk and Return in an Equilibrium APT: Application of a New Test Methodology," *Journal of Financial Economics*, 21, 255–290.

David, H. A., 1973, "Concomitants of Order Statistics," *Bulletin of the International Statistical Institute*, 45, 295–300.

David, H. A., 1981, *Order Statistics* (2nd ed.), Wiley, New York.

David, H. A., and J. Galambos, 1974, "The Asymptotic Theory of Concomitants of Order Statistics," *Journal of Applied Probability*, 11, 762–770.

Fama, E., and J. MacBeth, 1973, "Risk, Return, and Equilibrium: Empirical Tests," *Journal of Political Economy*, 71, 607–636.

Gibbons, M. R., 1982, "Multivariate Tests of Financial Models: A New Approach," *Journal of Financial Economics*, 10, 3–27.

Gibbons, M. R., and W. Ferson, 1985, "Testing Asset Pricing Models with Changing Expectations and an Unobservable Market Portfolio," *Journal of Financial Economics*, 14, 217–236.

Gibbons, M. R., S. A. Ross, and J. Shanken, 1989, "A Test of the Efficiency of a Given Portfolio," *Econometrica*, 57, 1121–1152.

Huberman, G., and S. Kandel, 1987, "Mean Variance Spanning," *Journal of Finance*, 42, 873–888.

Iyengar, S., and J. Greenhouse, 1988, "Selection Models and the File Drawer Problem," *Statistical Science*, 3, 109–135.

Data-Snooping Biases

Lakonishok, J., and S. Smidt, 1988, "Are Seasonal Anomalies Real? A Ninety-Year Perspective," *Review of Financial Studies,* 1, 403–426.

Leamer, E., 1978, *Specification Searches,* Wiley, New York.

Lehmann, B. N., and D. Modest, 1988, "The Empirical Foundations of the Arbitrage Pricing Theory," *Journal of Financial Economics,* 21, 213–254.

MacKinlay, A. C., 1987, "On Multivariate Tests of the CAPM," *Journal of Financial Economics,* 18, 341–372.

Merton, R., 1987, "On the Current State of the Stock Market Rationality Hypothesis," in R. Dornbusch, S. Fischer, and J. Bossons (eds.), *Macroeconomics and Finance: Essays in Honor of Franco Modigliani,* M.I.T. Press, Cambridge, Mass.

Nagaraja, H. N., 1982a, "Some Asymptotic Results for the Induced Selection Differential," *Journal of Applied Probability,* 19, 233–239.

Nagaraja, H. N., 1982b, "Some Nondegenerate Limit Laws for the Selection Differential," *Annals of Statistics,* 10, 1306–1310.

Nagaraja, H. N., 1984, "Some Nondegenerate Limit Laws for Sample Selection Differential and Selection Differential," *Sankhyā,* 46, Series A, 355–369.

Ross, S., 1987, "Regression to the Max," Working Paper, Yale School of Organization and Management.

Sandström, A., 1987, "Asymptotic Normality of Linear Functions of Concomitants of Order Statistics," *Metrika,* 34, 129–142.

Sen, P. K., 1976, "A Note on Invariance Principles for Induced Order Statistics," *Annals of Probability,* 4, 474–479.

Sen, P. K., 1981, "Some Invariance Principles for Mixed Rank Statistics and Induced Order Statistics and Some Applications," *Communications in Statistics,* A10, 1691–1718.

Shanken, J., 1985, "Multivariate Tests of the Zero-Beta CAPM," *Journal of Financial Economics,* 14, 327–348.

Stambaugh, R. F., 1982, "On the Exclusion of Assets from Tests of the Two Parameter Model," *Journal of Financial Economics,* 10, 235–268.

Stuart, A., and J. Ord, 1987, *Kendall's Advanced Theory of Statistics,* Oxford U.P., New York.

Wang, T., 1988, *Essays on the Theory of Arbitrage Pricing,* unpublished doctoral dissertation, Wharton School, University of Pennsylvania.

Watterson, G. A., 1959, "Linear Estimation in Censored Samples from Multivariate Normal Populations," *Annals of Mathematical Statistics,* 30, 814–824.

Yang, S. S., 1977, "General Distribution Theory of the Concomitants of Order Statistics," *Annals of Statistics,* 5, 996–1002.

Yang, S. S., 1981a, "Linear Functions of Concomitants of Order Statistics with Application to Nonparametric Estimation of a Regression Function," *Journal of the American Statistical Association,* 76, 658–662.

Yang, S. S., 1981b, "Linear Combinations of Concomitants of Order Statistics with Application to Testing and Estimation," *Annals of the Institute of Statistical Mathematics,* 33 (Part A), 463–470.

Vas ist das?*

The turn-of-the-year effect and the return premia of small firms.

Richard Roll

For eighteen consecutive years, from 1963 through 1980, average returns of small firms have been larger than average returns of large firms on the first trading day of the calendar year. That day's difference in returns between equally-weighted indices of AMEX-listed and NYSE-listed stocks has averaged 1.16% over the 18 years. The t-statistic of the difference was 8.18. For the 18 calendar years available on the current CRSP tape, the equally-weighted index return exceeded the value-weighted return on the first trading day of every year. The mean difference in returns was 1.19% and the t-statistic of the difference was 8.39. Although data on equally-weighted returns are not yet available for the first days of January in 1981 and 1982, the same results seem to have obtained; the advance/decline ratio on these dates was $NYSE_{1981}$ = 2.143, $AMEX_{1981}$ = 2.388, $NYSE_{1982}$ = 1.671, $AMEX_{1982}$ = 1.791.

This phenomenon was discovered by Donald Keim [1981], who reported that small firm returns during the month of January were significantly larger than large firm returns and that the difference was not as large during other months. Keim noted that January's returns were concentrated in the first few days of the month. Related results were reported by earlier scholars and by market professionals. A January abnormal return phenomenon was examined in a provocative paper by Branch [1977]. The market professional's viewpoint is illustrated by a study of the "year-end rally" in the annual *Stock Trader's Almanac*, Hirsch [1970, p. 105].[1] Although neither of these latter authors relate the turn-of-the-year effect to small firms, we shall see below that the two are closely connected.

The first thought of anyone brought up in the tradition of efficient markets is to ascribe such phenomena to a non-exploitable cause. Previously, I argued [1981] that the large average return difference between small and large firms found by Banz [1981] and Reinganum [1981] might be due to differences in risk; but risk alone is not likely to explain a return premium that is observed on the same date in *every* year. Even if part of the average return differential is a result of the greater riskiness of small firms, we cannot ascribe the behavior observed around the first of the year solely to this cause.

What then is responsible? In the sections below, I investigate a number of possible non-exploitable causes — and dismiss them for lack of supporting empirical evidence. A disturbing phenomenon for efficient markets theory will be reported: It may persist because of trading costs.

THE TURN-OF-THE-YEAR EFFECT

In the hope of discovering a seasonal effect on other dates that might suggest a cause of the January 1st effect, I calculated the mean difference in returns between an equally-weighted index and a value-weighted index for the first 20 trading days and the last 20 trading days of every calendar month between July 1962 and December 1980, inclusive (the CRSP availability period). The t-statistics for differences in return indicated that no period except the period around early January displayed an exceptional premium for small firms. There were occasional significant t-values scattered throughout the year, but that is to be anticipated even when there are no differences in expected returns between small and large firms.

The 5 largest daily mean return differences and the only daily differences in excess of 100% (annualized) occurred on 5 consecutive days: the last trading day of December and the first 4 trading days of

---

* Discussions with my UCLA colleagues, especially David Mayers, have been most helpful in developing the ideas tested herein. I am also grateful for the comments of Gordon Alexander, George Constantinides, Thomas Copeland, Eugene Fama, George Foster, David Fowler, Donald Keim, and Myron Scholes.
The paper was partly supported by the Cantor-Fitzgerald Research Program in Finance.

1. Footnotes appear at the end of the article.

January. Mean return differences and their t-statistics are reported in Table 1 for these dates.[2]

TABLE 1

Mean Return Difference, Equally-Weighted (EW) Less Value-Weighted (VW) Index by Trading Day Around the First of the Year, 1963-1979

Last Trading Day of December	January Trading Day			
	First	Second	Third	Fourth

MEAN RETURN DIFFERENCE EW - VW, percent per day
(t-statistic)

.5647	1.186	.6067	.6107	.4527
(4.72)	(8.39)	(3.86)	(3.96)	(3.05)

The t-statistic is calculated from the standard deviation (across years) of the return difference on the trading day indicated. There were 19 December observations and 18 January observations. (The CRSP tape begins in July 1962 and ends in December 1980.)

Later days in January also display significant small firm premia; during the next 10 trading days, t-statistics exceed 2.0 on 8 days. Nevertheless, no mean return difference on a later trading day in January is as large as the mean return differences on the first 4 days. As Table 1 shows, the very first day displays the largest difference of all.

The positive small firm return difference on the last day of December is unique. No other day in December displayed a large mean return difference. To my knowledge, this is the first time that a last-day-of-December small firm excess return has been documented.[3]

To put the turn-of-the-year effect into perspective, the average annual return differential between equally-weighted and value-weighted indices of NYSE and AMEX stocks was 9.31% for calendar years 1963-1980 inclusive. During those same years, the average return for the 5 days of the turn-of-the-year (last day of December and first 5 days of January) was 3.45%. Thus, about 37% of the entire yearly differential appears to occur during just 5 trading days; 67% of the annual differential occurs during the first 20 trading days of January (which is almost the whole month), plus the last day of December.

DISMISSAL OF SOME POSSIBLE SPURIOUS CAUSES OF THE TURN-OF-THE-YEAR EFFECT.

In searching for a non-exploitable cause of this unusual pattern, one might posit some peculiarity associated with year-end exchange trading or with data base construction around the calendar year end. Reasonable possibilities seemed to include:
a. Data base errors in CRSP might be associated with annual tape updating;
b. New listings might be concentrated at the first of the year and contain multi-day returns or an exceptional number of erroneous returns (because the pre-listing price was hard to find or could only be found on a distant date);
c. De-listings might be concentrated around the first of the year and be associated with multi-day returns (because distressed stocks trade infrequently), or
d. The mean returns might be polluted by a few securities which had "phony" transactions. For example, a closely-held firm might have a first-of-year price recorded for valuation or tax purposes. (Admittedly, there would seem to be little *a priori* reason for such events to display abnormally high returns).

In checking out the listing and de-listing possibilities, I had the number of such firms printed out by calendar date for every day covered in the CRSP data base. There was no discernible pattern for new listings. They occur uniformly over the calendar year, although there are more new listings during years with market upswings.

De-listings, however, occur more frequently near January 1. During several calendar years, there were 8 to 13 de-listings during the first week in January. This promised to be a solution to the puzzle, since the last return included by CRSP could be a post-de-listing return. CRSP explains that,

> when a security was de-listed, suspended, or halted, CRSP determined whether or not it would have been possible to trade at the last listed price. If no trade was possible, CRSP tried to find a subsequent quote for the security. If such a quote was available, CRSP used this quote to compute a return for the last period.... For a 'merger' event, ... the last ... return ... includes the distributed property ... For a total liquidation event ... the last ... return includes the liquidation distributions and the 'final price.' CRSP [1979, p. 10].

To ascertain whether the CRSP treatment of de-listing (or of listing) is responsible for the turn-of-the-year effect, an equally-weighted index was constructed excluding such events. The index excluded the 5 daily returns prior to de-listing and the 5 returns just after listing of any stock. For good measure, I also excluded all multi-day returns.

The results were indistinguishable from those already reported. The small firm average premium actually increased slightly on the last day of December and on the first 4 days of January.

In checking for CRSP errors and for the possibility that a few outliers might be responsible for the results, the first step was to compute the percentage of firms with positive returns on the AMEX and NYSE during the turn-of-the-year, the last trading day of December through the fourth trading day of January. The results appear in Table 2. In most years, 12 out of 18, the frequency of positive returns was larger on the AMEX. The principal feature to notice about both NYSE and AMEX stocks, however, is that high average returns are closely associated with high frequencies of positive returns. That is, more than just a few stocks are causing high mean returns. These results

TABLE 2

Mean Returns and Frequency of Positive Returns During Turn-of-the-Year[a]

Year[b]	NYSE NUMBER OF SECURITIES	AMEX	NYSE PERCENT POSITIVE	AMEX	NYSE MEAN ± S[c] RETURN	AMEX
1962	1142	842	86.5	82.9	4.46	6.54
1963	1140	787	74.8	74.7	2.78	5.75
1964	1174	815	72.7	74.6	2.20	4.76
1965	1192	825	64.0	66.2	1.63	3.40
1966	1225	851	81.1	77.8	3.91	6.52
1967	1207	843	56.8	60.6	1.50	3.72
1968	1190	945	20.1	26.4	-2.61	-2.64
1969	1228	866	73.6	83.0	3.78	9.34
1970	1286	949	68.0	74.8	2.46	6.08
1971	1336	1018	76.2	83.1	3.68	9.29
1972	1422	1052	75.4	79.4	3.05	6.39
1973	1480	1116	85.1	90.2	9.68	16.8
1974	1522	1074	93.0	90.5	16.9	19.1
1975	1515	1057	95.2	89.1	8.51	11.7
1976	1530	995	52.3	69.8	1.09	4.69
1977	1516	944	21.1	43.0	-2.63	.0665
1978	1526	865	90.1	85.9	5.96	8.11
1979	1504	812	43.3	55.8	.173	2.05

[a] The turn-of-the-year is defined as the last trading day of December and the first four trading days of January.
[b] Indicates the year for last trading day of December.
[c] Returns are for equally-weighted averages over the 5 trading days constituting the turn-of-the-year. They are not annualized. (Annualized returns would be approximately 52 times the numbers reported.)
To be included in the average, a stock must have had at least one recorded return during the just prior year — beginning with the sixth trading day of that year and ending with the sixth from last trading day of that year.

refute the outlier theory and suggest also that CRSP errors are probably not responsible for the results.

Just to check further on possible CRSP errors, I printed out the 25 largest returns on each January first and checked them in the financial press. No errors were found in CRSP. On the other hand, this checking did disclose an interesting fact: Most of the large turn-of-the-year returns were on extremely low-priced stocks, many of which were selling for less than $2 a share. A typical price pattern was: $1 per share on every day during the last 2 weeks of December, then an increase to 1⅛ on the last day of December (a daily return of 12½%), then another increase to 1⅜ on January 1 (a daily return of 22.2%). The price then stayed at 1⅜ for the rest of January. There was usually some trading volume every day. The low-priced stock effect corroborates the earlier results of Blume and Husic [1973], who seem to have been early observers of the phenomenon now known as the "small-firm effect."

The upshot of this checking was that *if* such low prices contain errors, the errors were not induced by CRSP's transcription from the financial press. Furthermore, the number of such events and the significant volume of trading make it unlikely that "phony" transaction prices are responsible.

AN INEFFICIENT MARKET PHENOMENON?

Perhaps there is some other non-exploitable explanation of these results. Since I could not think of one, it seemed worthwhile to consider the unthinkable — that the market was not removing an obvious seasonal regularity.

There is some suggestive supporting evidence in the form of market folklore about the "end-of-the-year rally." The *Los Angeles Times*, in commenting on the market's behavior on December 31, 1981, noted,

The year-end rally many traders had been hoping for came late, and when it did appear, starting in Wednesday's [December 31] session, it was unimpressive (section IV, page 1, January 1, 1982).

It may have been "unimpressive" to the *Times* but the AMEX index return for the day was still 1.07% while the NYSE index return was .296%.

The year-end rally is supposedly a reaction to "tax selling" (see Branch [1977] and Keim [1981]). The argument goes as follows. There is downward price pressure on stocks that have already declined during the year, because investors sell them to realize capital losses. After the year's end, this price pressure is relieved and the returns during the next few days are large as those same stocks jump back up to their equilibrium values.

This argument is ridiculous, of course. If investors realized that such a pattern were persistent, they would bid up prices before the end of the year and there would be no significant positive returns after January first. But, the argument might counter, "There is indeed evidence of such speculative activity. Prices start rising on the last day of December!"

Although we might want to rebut with "Why not the next-to-last-day of December?", we are obliged to test every theory, even one so patently absurd as this, by the empirical strength of its predictions and not by its assumptions or even by its external logic. Accordingly, for each stock present on the last day of December in each calendar year, I computed the return during that year, excluding the first 5 and last 5 trading days (in order to excise the "year-end rally.") Then a second return was calculated for the stock over the 5 trading days from the last day of December through the first 4 trading days of January in the next calendar year. I then computed a cross-sectional regression between the two returns. Effectively, this tests a trading rule for selecting stocks at the end of December based upon their returns over the preceding year (there is no survivorship bias since the rule is not triggered until the last day of December).

If the tax selling pressure hypothesis is correct, there should be a negative relationship between the two returns; the results given in Table 3 are consistent with the hypothesis. For AMEX stocks, the regression coefficient is negative in every year and highly significant in all but 1 year of the 19.

For NYSE stocks, the negative coefficient is actually more significant in more years, 11 of 19, than the coefficient for AMEX listed stocks. This is not attributable entirely to the greater number of NYSE stocks in the cross-section; the correlation coefficient was also larger for NYSE issues in 7 of those 11 years.

Each year's regression was cross-sectional, so the observations are not independently distributed. To ascertain whether this may have resulted in an overstatement of the regression's significance, the cross-sectional coefficients were averaged over the 19 years and a standard error was computed from the 19 observations. Based on the assumption that the 19 observations constitute a random sample, a t-statistic to test for the significance of the mean coefficient was thereby obtained.

Here are the results. For the NYSE, I found $\hat{b}$ = −.0325 and $t_{\hat{b}}$ = −5.28; for the AMEX, I found $\hat{b}$ = −.0640 and $t_{\hat{b}}$ = −4.41. If there was any doubt from Table 3, this demonstrates that there is indeed a significant negative relationship between the turn-of-the-year return and the return over the preceding year.[4]

Eugene Fama pointed out that the slope coefficient in Table 3 could be interpreted as the fraction of the negative return during the previous year that is attributable solely to tax loss selling. A stock with losses has declined because of unfavorable information, but it might then decline even further due to tax selling. On average, there would be no rebound from the information, but there would be a full recovery from tax selling after the new year.

In addition to the cross-sectional negative relationship between the turn-of-the-year return and the previous year's return for individual stocks, there is a negative intertemporal correlation between mean returns. When the preceding year's average return has been lower, there is a greater reaction in the average during the turn-of-the-year. For NYSE issues, the simple correlation is −.588 between the mean return (equally-weighted) during the preceding year and the mean return during the subsequent turn-of-the-year. For AMEX issues the correlation is −.169. The simple linear intertemporal regression between mean returns is reported in Table 4.

Table 4 also reports the results when we limit the sample to stocks that had negative returns over the preceding year. If the tax selling hypothesis is correct, such stocks should have greater returns during the subsequent turn-of-the-year, because they represent securities with larger tax losses. Of course, tax loss selling would not be limited to such stocks. Others with positive returns over the entire year might still have had losses over holding periods shorter than a year or over longer holding periods.

Despite this caveat, the results in Table 4 show indeed that stocks with negative returns over the entire preceding year had higher returns around January 1. They display a stronger intertemporal correlation between mean returns. Again, AMEX stocks declined more than NYSE stocks within this group, and they rebounded more as well.

The year-by-year individual stock cross-sectional regressions analagous to those reported in Table 3, but limited to issues with negative returns over the preceding year, had negative and significant

TABLE 3
Cross-Sectional Regressions Predicting Turn-of-the-Year Return[a] by the Return Over the Preceding Year[b]

Preceding Year	NYSE	AMEX	NYSE	AMEX
	Regression [c] slope coefficient		t-statistic for Regression slope	coefficient
1962	−.0774	−.127	−8.32	−9.35
1963	−.0142	−.0450	−2.75	−6.16
1964	−.0221	−.0423	−5.02	−7.73
1965	−.0150	−.0142	−4.93	−3.90
1966	−.0731	−.0664	−12.5	−8.24
1967	−.0186	−.00766	−7.46	−3.55
1968	−.0236	−.0139	−8.53	−6.46
1969	−.0962	−.127	−15.7	−14.5
1970	−.0482	−.0776	−9.38	−8.64
1971	−.0418	−.0969	−9.41	−13.5
1972	−.0317	−.0568	−6.86	−9.35
1973	−.104	−.160	−10.6	−9.66
1974	−.356	−.246	−19.4	−14.3
1975	−.0519	−.0355	−12.2	−6.08
1976	−.00252	−.0227	−.651	−3.99
1977	−.0341	−.0491	−8.51	−9.17
1978	−.0171	−.00735	−3.92	−1.26
1979	−.00171	−.0150	.561	−2.91
1980	−.00472	−.00611	−3.25	−2.53

[a] For every year except 1980, the turn-of-the-year return, R_y, includes the last trading day in December and the first 4 trading days in the January immediately following. For 1980, only the last day in December is included, since the CRSP tape ends on that date.

[b] For every year except 1962, the preceding year's return, R_p, covers the entire year excluding the first 5 and last 5 trading days. For 1962, only the last half-year is on the CRSP tape, so R_p includes that half year excluding the last 5 trading days.

[c] The regression equation is $R_{yj} = \hat{a} + \hat{b}R_{pj}$, j = 1,...N where N is the number of stocks with available R_p's.

TABLE 4

The Intertemporal Relation Between Preceding-Year Mean Return[a] and Subsequent Turn-of-the-Year Return.[b] (N = 19 years, 1962-1980 inclusive)

SAMPLE	NYSE Preceding Year MEAN RETURN [c] (%)	AMEX Preceding Year MEAN RETURN [c] (%)	NYSE Turn-of-the-Year MEAN RETURN [c] (%)	AMEX Turn-of-the-Year MEAN RETURN [c] (%)	NYSE REGRESSION SLOPE [d]	AMEX REGRESSION SLOPE [d]	NYSE t-statistic for Regression Slope	AMEX t-statistic for Regression Slope
All Observations	10.7	14.3	3.55	6.46	-.118	-.0896	-3.00	-3.25
Stocks with Negative Returns During Preceding Year	-17.9	-25.1	4.92	8.58	-.335	-.310	-3.27	-3.28

[a] The preceding year's mean return, $\bar{R}_p$, is an equally-weighted average of all stocks listed during the year, excluding the first 5 and last 5 trading days. For 1962, only the last half-year was available.
[b] The turn-of-the-year mean return, $\bar{R}_y$, is an equally-weighted average of all stocks during the last day of December and the first 4 days of January. For 1980, only the last day in December was available.
[c] These are the grand means (over 19 years and over individual stocks).
[d] The regression was $\bar{R}_y = \hat{a} + \hat{b} R_p$.

coefficients in every year for both exchanges. The cross-sectional correlation coefficients were more negative in 11 of 19 years for the NYSE and in 10 of 19 years for the AMEX than the corresponding coefficients using all stocks (regardless of the preceding year's return). In contrast, when the cross-sectional regression was limited to issues with positive returns during the preceding year, the correlation was not as negative in any year as the correlation using all observations. Also, in 9 years (out of 19) for the NYSE and in 5 years for the AMEX, the intertemporal correlation was positive between mean returns.

A dissertation by Dyl [1973] (summarized in Dyl [1977]) examined the year-end pattern of prices and trading volume for a subset of NYSE issues. Dyl found that trading volume was abnormally high during December for stocks that had experienced large losses over the previous year. He found also that volume was abnormally low for stocks that had experienced large gains. This latter pattern was attributed to investors "locked in" by previous price appreciation and motivated to retain their shares until after the New Year in order to postpone taxes on realized gains. Some further evidence about investor timing of tax loss selling is presented in the appendix.

Dyl [1973] reports significant abnormal January returns for stocks that had experienced losses over the previous year (cf. Table 4.3, p. 74, where an abnormal return t-statistic of 5.58 is reported for the decile of lowest previous-year's-return stocks).

The apparent strength of the NYSE results found by Branch [1977] and Dyl and confirmed here raises a doubt that the year-end rally is really the source of the turn-of-the-year premium of small stocks. It might appear plausible that the year-end rally and the small-firm premium are distinct phenomena that just happen to manifest themselves during the same season. The next section examines this important question.

WHY DO SMALL FIRMS HAVE BIGGER YEAR-END RALLIES AND HIGHER AVERAGE RETURNS?

Two questions arise in connection with tax selling and the year-end rally as explanations of the small-firm effect. First, why do small firms have bigger year-end rallies? Second, why is the small-firm year-end rally not offset by price declines during the remainder of the year, thereby eliminating the long-term average return premium of small firms?

There may be a simple answer to the first question: small firms are more volatile than large firms. The cross-sectional distribution of observed returns has a larger variance. Since the average long-run (expected) return is positive, the greater variance implies that a small firm has a higher probability of achieving a negative return over a given period; i.e., it is a more likely candidate for tax loss selling.[5]

Small firms may have larger sales and earnings volatilities because they have fewer product lines and are less diversified. But whatever the source, the empirical evidence supports the observation that their returns *are* more volatile. During the 19 years on the CRSP tape, the cross-sectional standard deviation, $\hat{\sigma}$, of annual individual returns (excluding the first 5 and the last 5 trading days) was larger for AMEX than for NYSE issue in every year. The mean value of the ratio $\hat{\sigma}_{AMEX}/\hat{\sigma}_{NYSE}$ was 1.60, and the t-statistic of the difference between this ratio and unity was 6.70. In 14 of 19 years, the percentage of negative returns was also larger for the AMEX issues. The mean value of the difference in negative percentages (NYSE-AMEX) was −7.82, and its t-ratio was −3.31.

This evidence links tax loss selling to the small firm effect. Larger returns during the turn-of-the-year period accrue to small firms on average because they are more likely to have registered losses during the preceding year.

It is important to ascertain whether the entire turn-of-the-year return is caused by tax selling or whether smallness per se has an additional effect. If two different-sized stocks had declined by the same percentage amount over the preceding year, would their turn-of-the-year returns be equal or would the smaller firm have a higher return? I examined this possibility using a time series of pooled cross-sectional regressions. Both AMEX and NYSE issues were included in the same model. For each year, individual stock turn-of-the-year returns were regressed on their preceding year's returns plus an AMEX dummy. In all 19 years, the preceding year's return had a negative and significant coefficient. The least significant t-statistic was −2.47, and the average was −11.1. The time-averaged mean coefficient was −.0600 with a t-statistic of −3.68.

The AMEX dummy was included to measure the marginal effect of smallness in addition to the effect of tax selling induced by negative returns over the preceding year. The AMEX dummy had a positive coefficient every year and a very significant t-statistic in 17 of 19 years. The mean t-statistic was 8.14. The time-averaged mean coefficient was 2.66% with a t-statistic of 7.94.

The results suggest that smallness has an effect beyond that induced by higher volatility and concommitant tax selling, but there are reasons to hesitate before reaching a definite conclusion. First, since the preceding year's return is not a perfect indicator of tax selling, the regression is subject to an errors-in-variables problem that could have allowed the AMEX dummy to become spuriously important because it is a proxy for larger variance of returns. Second, the long-term mean returns of small firms may be higher because they are more risky. Third, higher transaction costs for small firms may allow a greater price effect from tax selling and a higher turn-of-the-year rebound. In the next section, I shall examine this last possibility in more detail.

Let us now turn to the second and more puzzling question asked above: Why are the large returns on small firms during the turn-of-the-year period not offset by lower returns during the rest of the year? In fact, they are not. Mean returns during periods *excluding* the turn-of-the-year are also higher for small firms. The average difference between AMEX and NYSE equally-weighted returns was 3.66% over the 19 CRSP sample years, excluding turn-of-the-year. Unlike the AMEX/NYSE return difference during the turns-of-the-year themselves, however, the t-statistic of the difference during the remainder of the year is only .614. Also, in 10 years of the 19, the NYSE actually had a higher return.

Perhaps posing the question above reflects my biases and training more than anything else. The question seemed to arise naturally because (one would think that) a high return in one calendar period must be offset by a low return in another *because mean returns are determined by risk* and an invariably positive excess return for a particular 5-day period certainly cannot be explained by risk.[6] Thus, there should be *some* period offsetting the turn-of-the-year returns. But if we are contemplating the possibility that markets are not efficient, we might as well contemplate the possibility that returns are not determined by risk. Bias, training, and even logic seem weak in the face of such a puzzling phenomenon.

It is still possible, of course, that the *long-term* average return premium of small firms *is* due to some type of risk, as yet unmeasured. The long-term premium accrues during two distinct calendar periods, a modest-sized and statistically insignificant premium over 50 weeks or so and a large premium around every New Year. Long-term investors would expect to receive both components. But why their total compensation should be divided into these two parts is a puzzle. The dichotomy seems to be evidence against the weak form of the efficient market hypothesis since the seasonal could be exploited to bring a risk-adjusted excess return.

CAN TRANSACTION COSTS EXPLAIN WHY THE TURN-OF-THE-YEAR PREMIUM IS NOT ELIMINATED?

Small firms are often firms with low prices and firms with low prices have large transaction costs. The normal bid/ask spread on small firms could conceivably preclude arbitrageurs from exploiting the turn-of-the-year pattern induced by tax selling. If the bid/ask spread on a low-priced stock were, say, 20% of the average transaction price, most of the tax sales near the year's end would be purchased by the specialist; the majority of transactions would occur near the low side of the bid/ask spread.

After the new year, the trading would revert to the normal pattern of a roughly equal number of buyers and sellers and an average transaction price close to the center of the bid/ask spread. Although the registered return across the turn-of-the-year would be positive, the arbitrageur could not exploit it, because he would have to buy at or near the specialist's ask price. The size of the average return over the turn-of-the-year is in a range that transaction costs could conceivably explain.

Trading costs cannot explain why the long-term average returns of small firms are so large: We still need risk for that. Nevertheless, they could explain why the small firm premium arrives in two distinct calendar periods and why that pattern has no tendency to disappear. Whether or not actual bid/ask spreads are sufficient to impede arbitrage requires (and merits) further study.

The transaction cost explanation may seem merely to push market inefficiency back one step. If the bid/ask spread is large, what is to prevent an arbitrageur from entering a limit order at or just an eighth above the specialist's bid? Then the next seller would sell to the arbitrageur, and the latter would eventually realize almost the full return that the specialist would have realized. The key point is that the usual bid/ask spread, which is determined by volatility and volume of trading during normal periods, does not apply when tax sellers are the predominant traders. Under these conditions, the spread should narrow as arbitrageurs compete for what they know confidently will be subsequent price increases. Of course, for low-priced securities, such a narrowing is limited to ⅛, the minimum possible spread.

There is also an information hindrance to such arbitrage. It may not be possible to tell for sure which issues are going to have the most tax sellers. Unless the stock is at its all-time low near the year's end, some holders will have unrealized gains. Of course, a stock that has had recent negative returns is more likely to have tax sellers — but their number would be uncertain and perhaps this risk, along with commissions, is sufficient to preclude full arbitrage.

In an attempt to investigate this question more fully, I tried a simple trading rule. The rule specified that purchases would be made of the first 10 (alphabetical) stocks on each exchange that achieved their annual low on the sixth from the last trading day.[7] The stock would then be purchased on the second from last trading day and sold at the close of the fourth trading day of the new year. Before transaction costs, this rule seemed to work very well indeed. For NYSE issues, the mean return over 18 years was 6.89% for 5 days (t-statistic =4.04), while for AMEX issues the mean return was 14.2% (t-statistic = 5.74). Note that the level of mean returns on both exchanges and the excess mean return of AMEX over NYSE are larger for this selected group of stocks than for all stocks.

It is difficult to obtain data on total trading costs. Phillips and Smith [1980, p. 185] report percentage spreads for NYSE issues that have options listed on the Chicago Board Options Exchange. The percentage spreads have a median of .56%, which is too small to explain the returns of 7% and 14% for the trading rule. On the other hand, stocks with listed options are the largest firms, and one would expect them to have very low transaction costs. Phillips and Smith report a mean percentage spread of 15% for listed puts; perhaps a listed put is an asset more similar in volume and in volatility to a small stock.

More comprehensive data on trading costs are reported in a recent paper by Stoll and Whaley [1982]. Dividing firms into 10 portfolios ranked by size, they found that the smallest-firm portfolio had an average bid/ask spread of 2.93% for 1960-79 and an average commission rate of 1.92%. The round-trip trading costs would thus amount to 2.93 + 2 × 1.92 = 6.77%. The comparable figure for the largest firm portfolio was 2.57%.[8]

As a detailed example of the actual experience likely under a trading rule, Table 5 presents daily data for the 10 stocks chosen by the above rule at the end of 1978. This was a representative, recent, and slightly below median year for the trading rule, the average return being 3.94% for the NYSE and 10.3% for the AMEX. As Table 5 shows, the turn-of-the-year return for NYSE issues was positive for 9 of the 10 firms and zero for the other firm. One AMEX firm had a negative return. (See the next-to-last column, labelled "CRSP Turn-of-the-Year Five Day Return.")

Although bid/ask spreads are not available on days with transactions, information of a similar nature is impounded in the trading spread, the difference between the day's high and low transaction prices. If new information about a stock is equally likely to be favorable and unfavorable, the trading spread should be no larger than the specialist's spread.[9]

The last column of Table 5 reports the turn-of-the-year return if a speculator, following the trading rule, purchased at the high side of the spread on the next-to-last day of the year and sold at the low side of the spread on the fourth trading day of January. For NYSE issues, this reduced the mean return from 3.94% to 1.27%. If the trader were not an exchange member, commissions would still have to be deducted from the 1.27%. Although 1978 was a slightly below-average year, it would appear that no profit remains, at least for NYSE issues.

For AMEX issues, however, it might appear that the trading rule would still turn a profit. The mean return drops from 10.3% to 7.25% when the purchase and sale are at the high and low sides of the spread, respectively. A gross profit of 7.25% would still be larger than commissions. Yet, the data on volume of transactions, also given in Table 5, make it seem doubtful that the trading rule could actually be implemented. Notice that the volume is very low after the first of January for all 10 AMEX stocks. For 5 stocks out of 10, there is *zero* volume on the closing day of the rule. (When such an event occurs, CRSP reports a return equal to the average of the bid/ask spread). Even if a transaction had been initiated, there is no guarantee that it would have occurred at the specialist's quote. A small amount of speculation in such thinly-traded securities would probably affect the quoted prices. Nevertheless, an astute trader with a good floor broker might make a small profit in AMEX issues.

The pattern of trading volume on both exchanges is of some interest in its own right. Notice the dramatic fall in volume on January 2 for most issues. (Burlington Industries is an exception.) For low volume NYSE stocks and for all of the AMEX stocks, year-end tax selling is clearly revealed in the volume of trading.

RISK AND RETURN WITH SEASONAL DATA

If there is an annual seasonal in stock prices induced by tax selling and if transactions costs prevent artibrageurs from eliminating the seasonal, could sys-

TABLE 5
Trading Rule Results Using Stocks Which Achieved Year's Low on December 21, 1978

COMPANY	Dec. '78 28	29	Jan. '79 2	3	4	5	Dec. '78 28	29	Jan. '79 2	3	4	5	Dec. '78 28	29	Jan. '79 2	3	4	5	CRSP Turn-of-the-Year Five-Day Return (%)	Trading
	VOLUME (100 shares)						BID/ASK OR TRADING SPREAD (1/8's) a/						CLOSING PRICE ($.1/8's)					Mean →		
									N Y S E										3.94	1.27
Allegheny Power Sys.	283	325	213	183	185	214	1	2	2	3	3	3	15.4	15.4	15.5	15.7	16.1	16.4	6.45	6.45
Armada Corp.	5	24	0	4	1	4	1	1	-	0	0	1	6 5.7	5.6	5.7	5.7	5.7	6 6.1	4.26	0.0
Asso.Dry Goods	180	154	155	207	374	227	4	3	5	2	5	3	16.5	16.3	16.7	16.7	17.4	17	2.26	2.26
Atlantic City Elec.	72	70	37	51	41	53	2	2	4	4	4	2	18.1 18	18	18.2	18.4	19	18.6 19	5.56	3.49
Becton Dickinson	317	387	64	67	29	191	5	7	5	6	4	6	31.7 31.4	31.2	31.6	32.1	32.4	32 32.4	3.18	.392
Bethlehem Steel	1821	1026	290	944	1249	1391	3	2	3	3	6	8	20.1 19.7	19.5	19.7	20	20.4	20.5 21.2	6.92	2.48
Brockway Glass	46	123	21	71	47	40	4	3	5	7	5	6	16.6 16.3	16.2	16.6	17.2	17.1	16.4 17	3.82	-1.49
Burlington Inds.	225	211	732	747	489	158	3	2	3	8	3	4	17.2 17	17	17.2	18	17.6	17.5 17.6	4.41	2.17
CP Natl.	20	26	6	11	12	16	3	2	1	1	1	1	14.7 14.6	14.5	14.7	15.1	15.2	15 15.1	2.54	.840
Certainteed	507	126	55	483	63	156	3	1	2	1	2	2	16.3 16	16	16	16	16	15.6 16	0.0	-3.82
									A M E X									Mean →	10.3	7.25
AAV COS	23	40	0	8	0	9	2	3	3	2	1	1	4 3.6	3.7	4.0^d	4.2	4.1^d	4.2	13.3	6.25
Automatic Radio Mfg.	42	61	17	2	10	5	1	1	2	0	0	0	2	2	2.3	2.3	2.2	2.3	18.75	18.75
Baker Michael	24	21	3	3	3	3	2	1	0	0	0	2	3.2	3.1	3.2	3.3	3.2	3.3	3.84	3.84
Baldwin Secs	5	0	0	0	2	7	0	2	2	2	0	1	6	6.2	6.1^d	6.1^d	6.2	6.4	8.33	8.33
Bethlehem	12	65	0	13	3	0	0	2	1	2	0	2	2	2	2.0^d	2.3	2.3	8.2 2.3^d	18.75^c	12.5
Bro Dart	18	33	2	0	11	8	1	2	0	1	0	0	3.2	3.4	3.3	3.2½^d	3.2	3.2	0.0	-3.70
C.W. Trans	10	21	10	54	3	0	4	10	0	10	2	2	13	14.4	15.2	17.2	16.6	16.6 16.7^d	29.8^c	28.8
Chicago Rivet & Mach	15	19	2	0	0	0	3	4	1	3	3	3	21.4 20.6	21.4	21.5	21.5½^d	21.5½	21.4 21.5½^d	4.52^c	2.38
Connelly Containers	13	16	0	0	0	0	1	1	2	2	2	2	3.2	3	3.1^d	3.1^d	3.1^d	3 3.1^d	-3.85^c	-7.69
Continental Matls	21	87	1	4	6	0	1	3	0	1	0	2	4.2 4.1	4.3	4.2	4.3	4.4	4.3 4.4^d	9.09^c	2.94

a The spread reported in 1/8$ is the difference between the High and Low transaction price on days with trading volume and the difference between ask and bid on days with no trading volume.
b The "CRSP" return is the return that would be computed with CRSP return tape data. The "Trading" return assumes that a purchase was made at the higher price of the spread and a sale made at the lower price. These latter prices are given above the reported closing price when they are different.
c Return is affected by the CRSP practice of using the bid/ask average.
d Average of bid/ask price.

tematic risk models still offer an explanation of the long-term mean return, i.e., could the capital asset pricing model's beta or the arbitrage pricing model's beta vector still be the only numbers necessary to explain expected return?

It might at first seem unlikely that these models would retain their exclusive explanatory power; we have already noted, for instance, that the total variance, systematic *and* non-systematic risk, is more closely associated with the probability of tax selling pressure and thus with the turn-of-the-year positive return than is systematic risk alone. Non-systematic variability helps explain the tax selling induced seasonality, but the question now is whether it helps explain long-term average returns.

From a long-term perspective, systematic risk could still be the only thing that matters. Of course, systematic risk *estimates* would be very biased with data more frequent than yearly, and measuring systematic risk would be difficult with annual data because of the paucity of observations. Nevertheless, if a good annual-based estimate were obtained, it might be sufficient to explain mean returns.

To see why this could be true, note that the annual seasonal is of no concern to any investor who measures his results over exactly a one-year period. The beginning and ending points of his year are irrelevant. His measurement period need not coincide with the peaks of the seasonal. He will not attempt to trade on the seasonal because of high transaction costs. He will not attempt to measure systematic risk with frequent data, because the seasonality will cause a downward bias in smaller or more volatile firms. He will, nevertheless, demand compensation for the contribution of each asset to the annual volatility of his diversified portfolio's return. The same argument is true for an investor whose holding period is random. Further investigation is required to determine whether an investor with, say, a monthly horizon would also be indifferent to the seasonality because of transaction costs.

In attempting to estimate long-term systematic risk, we should keep in mind that techniques such as Scholes/Williams' [1977] and Dimson's [1979] were not designed for coping with seasonality. Applied to daily or to monthly data, such techniques will not correct for the turn-of-the-year effect and will not produce betas that are unbiased estimates of true long-term betas. It would appear that the only technique currently available is the use of annual data. This will yield error-ridden estimates of systematic risk for individual securities but at least these errors can be diversified away in portfolios. Admittedly, estimates from annual data will provide poor ability to assess the effect of adding a particular asset to a portfolio.

SUMMARY AND CONCLUSION.

There is a striking annual pattern in stock returns. Around the turn of the year, average returns are high in general and the average returns of small firms are invariably greater than the average returns of large firms. The pattern cannot be explained by data errors, listings, de-listings, or outliers. Instead, it is closely associated with tax loss selling induced by negative returns over the previous year. Transaction costs and low liquidity probably prevent arbitrageurs from eliminating the return seasonality. The presence of the seasonality creates a substantial econometric problem in measuring systematic risk and in testing risk/return relationships.

APPENDIX

THE TIMING OF TAX LOSS SELLING AND ITS EFFECT ON RETURNS

There is one final topic to consider in connection with the tax loss selling hypothesis: If the turn-of-the-year return is really a rebound from tax selling, we should observe negative returns during late December when that selling is taking place. The Dyl [1973] evidence on trading volume seems to suggest that December selling *does* occur. Yet, December displays no significant return, either positive or negative, for any day other than the last day, and *its* return is significantly *positive*.

The absence of a significant December price decline might be explained as follows. When a particular stock declines during any earlier period (such a decline being caused initially by unfavorable news), a tax loss situation is created immediately for investors who have purchased at a higher price. The new lower price incorporates all information, including the information that some investors now expect a tax loss credit during the current year. This implies that December tax selling will be anticipated. In the absence of effective arbitrage, the price should decline immediately and remain depressed until the turn-of-the-year. No significant negative returns should be observed in December.

There is something of a puzzle in the large December volume of stocks with embedded losses. Investors have an incentive to realize losses immediately and not wait until December. The expected return is positive, so an embedded loss may be offset by the normal price rise before the year's end. Furthermore, a sale and repurchase initiates a new qualification period for favorable capital gains treatment.[10] This suggests that the earlier a price decline, the less tax selling will occur near the year's end. Both the normal positive return and exogenous purchases by non-arbitrageurs will dampen the effect of tax selling over time.

To test for such a pattern, a time series of individual stock cross-sectional *multiple* regressions was employed. In each of the 18 years, 1963-80, the turn-of-the-year return was regressed cross-sectionally on returns from all twelve of the preceding months. The multiple regression coefficients formed twelve different time series, one corresponding to each calendar month. The mean values and standard errors from these time series were used to construct Figure 1.

FIGURE 1

Turn-of-the-Year Return as a Function of Returns in each of the Twelve Preceding Months. Estimates of the Marginal Effect of Each Month as a Percentage of the Total Turn-of-the-Year Return: From a Time Series of Cross-Sectional Multiple Regressions 1963 - 1980

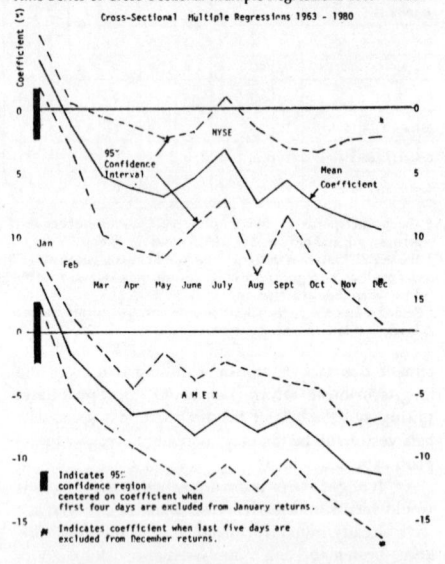

As the figure shows, there is a clear downward pattern; the largest negative effect on the turn-of-the-year return comes from the just-preceding December and the effect diminishes with more distant months. (Although the pattern is not strictly monotonic, the blips for July and September are not significant.)

Each month from March through December has a statistically significant negative impact. The t-statistics are all in the 3.0 to 6.0 range. February's effect, though still negative, would not be regarded as significant except at a low significance level.

Perhaps the most surprising effect is that of the preceding January. It is *positive* and highly significant, with t-statistics of 4.09 for the NYSE and 4.37 for the AMEX. This would seem to be evidence against tax loss selling and in favor of a simple annual (unexplained) seasonal. Consider, however, the following possibility: Since all stocks are volatile, every year every stock will bring a loss to some investors. Tax loss selling will therefore invariably occur to some extent. More volatile stocks should have more investors with tax losses because of larger and more frequent price declines, which are offset on average by larger and more frequent price increases. The most volatile stocks should experience greater tax loss selling every year. They should have larger turn-of-the-year rebounds every year as well. Thus, the turn-of-the-year return will be positively related cross-sectionally to the previous turn-of-the-year return. Since much of the January return occurs during the first few trading days, a positive impact will be observed for the January return on the following year's turn-of-the-year return.

Support for this argument shows up in Figure 1. The shaded bar at January is the 95% confidence region centered on the multiple regression coefficient obtained for January when the first four days of the year are excluded. The remaining days of January do not have a significant impact on the subsequent turn-of-the-year return.

The results of Figure 1 and the absence of statistically significant negative returns in December both suggest that investors do not wait until December for tax selling. The Dyl volume data, to the contrary, imply that at least some investors wait. This is also suggested by the volume data in Table 5. Perhaps transaction costs inhibit selling immediately after a loss and also make it difficult to detect the December price impact of those who wait.

In an attempt to detect late December selling with a test more powerful than simply averaging returns by trading day, I regressed the December returns (excluding the last day) cross-sectionally every year on the returns from each of the preceding 11 months. The multiple regression coefficients formed 11 time series that were tested for significant differences from zero. For both NYSE and AMEX, the averaged coefficients were positive for every month from January through October. Most of the AMEX t-statistics were above 2.0 and less than 3.0. For the NYSE, only 2 months had t-statistics above 1.6. (See Table 6.)

Significant positive coefficients are to be expected if the loss experienced in an earlier month induces tax selling in December. Thus, the results support the view that some investors wait before realizing losses and that their actions have an impact on December prices, probably resulting in more trades at the bid. There is, unfortunately, another reason why these coefficients could be positive. Since expected returns differ across stocks, cross-sectional rankings of returns will tend to persist. The results using November's rather than December's return as dependent variable (see Table 6) favor the expected return explanation.[11]

The regressions just described produced yet another anomaly. Although returns from January through October displayed the anticipated positive coefficients, the return from November had a *negative* and significant effect on December's return. The t-statistic for its mean coefficient was −2.76 for the NYSE and −2.38 for the AMEX. This result cannot be attributed to tax selling, since it would imply that

TABLE 6

T-Statistics of Mean Regression Coefficients From Time Series of Cross-Sectional Multiple Regressions, December and November Returns On Returns in Preceding Months, 1963-80.

Month of Independent Variable's Return	NYSE Month of Dependent Variable's Return December	NYSE November	AMEX December	AMEX November
January	.987	1.38	1.96	1.39
February	1.65	2.44	1.84	2.54
March	1.63	1.76	2.69	2.33
April	1.07	2.97	3.42	6.01
May	1.26	.948	2.33	1.87
June	.650	2.50	2.85	3.44
July	1.49	1.39	2.25	4.52
August	1.30	1.43	2.73	3.13
September	1.08	1.35	2.35	.956
October	.233	-2.54	2.05	-3.18
November	-2.76		-2.38	

November losses induce December purchases. David Mayers suggested that the anomaly might be due to some stocks selling at the bid price and others at the asked price on the last trade of November. Since the ending November price is in the numerator of November's return and the denominator of December's return, an "error-in-the-variable" is included in both returns but with an opposite sign. I tested this in two ways. First I computed the correlation between November's and October's return, where it was negative and significant; next I excluded the last day of November from November's return. This reduced drastically the AMEX' negative November effect; its t-statistic was brought down to −1.07. However, the NYSE data still produced a t-statistic of −2.03.

In a small supplemental experiment using data from 1980, the first 200 stocks present on the CRSP tape were used to calculate cross-sectional correlation coefficients for various lags. For example, returns on the first trading day of the year were correlated cross-sectionally with the returns on the second day. The second day's returns were correlated cross-sectionally with day three, and so on for each successive pair of days. The resulting coefficients were averaged intertemporally. Based on the null hypothesis of zero intertemporal dependence, a t-statistic was computed for the time series mean of the cross-sectional coefficients. A similar operation was performed for longer lags between successive cross-sections.

Mean correlation coefficients for the first five lags were all negative and had t-statistics of −8.42, −2.76, −4.34, −1.82, −1.19, respectively. Further lags were mixed in sign and were insignificant.

---

[1] In Hirsch's 1982 edition of the *Stock Trader's Almanac*, the "year-end rally" has been dropped as a topic. The 1970 edition alleged, incorrectly it would seem, that the "year-end rally is dead" because "the market always tends to discount the obvious" (p. 105). The 1982 edition still notes that January has the highest returns of any month. See "The Best Months of the Year" (p. 121). Hirsch's *Almanac* is a treasury of testable trading patterns. For instance, the weekly seasonal, high returns on Friday and negative returns on Monday, investigated by French [1980], was reported in the 1970 edition (p. 119) and updated with little apparent change in the 1982 edition (p. 118).

[2] It was noted above that the return difference between equally-weighted and value-weighted indices is positive on the first trading day of January in all 18 years on the CRSP tapes. The other trading dates were nearly as strong. The last December trading day displayed 17 of 19 positive return differences. The second through fourth trading days in January displayed 17, 17, and 15 positive differences, respectively, out of 18.

[3] In a private communication, Donald Keim reported finding this December anomaly too.

[4] The regression specification was checked also by sorting the independent variable, the preceding year's return and computing the Durbin-Watson statistic. It was near 2.0 in every year. Normal probability plots of the residuals indicated the usual thick tails but nothing else exceptional.

[5] For this argument to be correct, the variability of returns has to more than offset the higher mean return of small firms. That is, if μ_L and μ_S are the expected returns of large and small firms, σ_L and σ_S are their standard deviations, and z is a standardized random variate, we require

$$P(\mu_L + \sigma_L \hat{z} < 0) > P(\mu_L + \sigma_L \hat{z} < 0).$$

Given the extremely large volatilities of individuals stocks, it seems likely that this condition is satisfied.

[6] Notice that "risk" was used here without specification. Regardless of whether the risk is systematic or idiosyncratic or whether the capital asset pricing model, arbitrage model, or some other model is supposed to portray risk, no risk parameter can explain the turn-of-the-year phenomenon.

[7] The sixth from the last trading day was selected to be consistent with previous results reported in this paper, which generally excluded the first and last 5 trading days of each "previous" year. The number of securities was limited to 10 on the grounds that an actual speculator could easily handle 10 issues. Not every year had 10 securities that achieved their yearly low on the sixth from last trading day. On the AMEX, the minimum number was 5 over the 18 years. On the NYSE, the minimum number was 7 for the years included but there were 2 years in which no stock qualified. No other trading rule was tried.

[8] There is a possible problem with the Stoll/Whaley data in the context of the turn-of-the-year phenomenon. Stoll and Whaley collected bid/ask spreads only on the last trading day of the year. If the spread is narrowed during that period by arbitrageurs attempting to exploit the turn-of-the-year effect, the actual trading costs on the selling date, after the New Year, will be higher than the Stoll/Whaley figure.

[9] The bid/ask spreads in Table 5 for days with no trading volume are often larger than the trading spreads. This may be due to the well-known phenomenon of trading within the quoted spread.

[10] For example, suppose on July 1 that a long-term investor expects a 20% annual return but owns a stock that has declined by 10% since it was purchased 6 months ago. If the investor sells now, realizes the loss, and repurchases a similar stock (he has to wait 30 days to repurchase the identical stock, according to law, or else he forfeits the tax loss credit), he will have an expected tax liability of $20(\tau/2) - 10\tau = 0$, as of next July 1, ignoring the timing difference between the loss and capital gain and assuming a capital gains tax rate one-half the ordinary rate τ. If he waits, intending to sell at the year's end, the current embedded tax loss will be wiped out by December due to the expected price rise; his tax liability next July will be $(20 - 10) (\tau/2) = 5\tau > 0$.

A recent paper by Constantinides [1982] analyses this issue much more rigorously. Constantinides derives the optimal strategy for realizing capital gains and losses without transaction costs; it is to realize losses immediately and to defer the realization of gains until liquidation is "forced," (by, say, the necessity to consume). Transaction costs would undoubtedly delay the optimal realization of losses and result in a policy wherein the probability of loss realization increases as the tax year nears its end.

[11] In what turned out to be a naive attempt to expunge the expected returns from the data, all the individual security returns were "de-meaned" by subtracting the sample mean computed from the available observations. This left the basic pattern in Table 6 virtually unchanged, although the specific numbers shifted somewhat among months. Since the November dependent variable still had a positive relation to previous months (except October), apparently the subtraction of the expected return was offset by the addition of the error in the sample mean. (Note that the latter addition will, *ceteris paribus*, increase the cross-sectional correlation.)

REFERENCES

Banz, Rolf. "The Relationship Between Return and Market Value of Common Stocks." *Journal of Financial Economics*, March 1981, pp. 3-18.

Blume, Marshall and Frank Husic. "Price, Beta, and Exchange Listing." *Journal of Finance*, May 1973, pp. 283-299.

Branch, Ben. "A Tax Loss Trading Rule." *Journal of Business*, April 1977, pp. 198-207.

Constantinides, George M. "Capital Market Equilibrium with Personal Tax." WP 33, Graduate School of Business, University of Chicago, July 1981.

CRSP, Center for Research in Securities Prices. "CRSP Stock Files Monthly and Daily User's Guide." Graduate School of Business, University of Chicago, September 1979.

Dimson, Elroy. "Risk Measurement When Shares are Subject to Infrequent Trading." *Journal of Financial Economics*, June 1979, pp. 197-226.

Dyl, Edward A. "The Effect of Capital Gains Taxation on the Stock Market." Unpublished dissertation, Graduate School of Business, Stanford University, August 1973.

Dyl, Edward A. "Capital Gains Taxation and Year-End Stock Market Behavior." *Journal of Finance*, 32, March 1977, pp. 165-175.

French, Kenneth R. "Stock Returns and the Weekend Effect." *Journal of Financial Economics*, March 1980, pp. 55-69.

Hirsch, Yale. *The Stock Trader's Almanac*. Old Tappan, N. J.: The Hirsch Organization, 1970 and 1982.

Keim, Donald. "Size-Related Anomalies and Stock Return Seasonality: Further Empirical Evidence." Graduate School of Business, University of Chicago, October 1980.

Phillips, Susan M., and Clifford W. Smith, Jr. "Trading Costs for Listed Options: The Implications for Market Efficiency." *Journal of Financial Economics*, June 1980, pp. 179-201.

Reinganum, Marc R. "Misspecification of Capital Asset Pricing: Empirical Anomalies Based on Earnings' Yields and Market Values." *Journal of Financial Economics*, March 1981, pp. 19-46.

Roll, Richard. "A Possible Explanation of the Small Firm Effect." *Journal of Finance*, September 1981, pp. 879-888.

Scholes, Myron and Joseph Williams. "Estimating Betas from Non-Synchronous Data." *Journal of Financial Economics*, December 1977, pp. 309-327.

Stoll, Hans R. and Robert E. Whaley. "Transaction Costs and the Small Firm Effect." Working Paper 81-116, Owen Graduate School of Management, Vanderbilt University, January 1982.

[27]

Orange Juice and Weather

By Richard Roll*

Frozen concentrated orange juice is an unusual commodity. It is concentrated not only hydrologically, but also geographically; more than 98 percent of U.S. production takes place in the central Florida region around Orlando.[1] Weather is a major influence on orange juice production and unlike commodities such as corn and oats, which are produced over wide geographical areas, orange juice output is influenced primarily by the weather at a single location. This suggests that frozen concentrated orange juice is a relatively good candidate for a study of the interaction between prices and a truly exogenous determinant of value, the weather.

The relevant weather for OJ production is easy to measure. It is reported accurately and consistently by a well-organized federal agency, the National Weather Service of the Department of Commerce. Forecasts of weather are provided by the same agency and this makes it possible to assess the predictive ability of OJ futures prices against a rather exacting standard.

Geographic concentration is the most important attribute of orange juice for our empirical purposes, but the commodity also possesses other convenient features. It seems unlikely to be sensitive to *non*weather influences on supply and demand. For example, although the commodity is frozen and not very perishable, only a small amount is carried over in inventory from one year to the next. During 1978, for example, inventory declined to about 20 percent of the year's "pack" of new juice.[2]

Data on short-term variability in demand are nonexistent, but there is little reason to suspect much. Orange juice demand might very well respond to price variation in substitutes such as, say, apple juice; but national income and tastes probably do not fluctuate enough to explain a significant part of the *daily* OJ juice movement[3] (which is substantial, as we shall see).

Short-term variations in supply induced by planting decision must also be quite low because of the nature of the product. Oranges grow on trees that require five to fifteen years

---

*Graduate School of Management, University of California, Los Angeles, CA 90024. I am grateful for discussions with Eugene Fama and Stephen Ross, for comments on an earlier draft by Gordon Alexander, Thomas Copeland, Michael Darby, David Mayers, Huston McCulloch, and Sheridan Titman, for the cooperation of Paul Polger of the National Oceanographic and Atmospheric Administration, and for comments in seminars from the finance faculties of the universities of British Columbia, Alberta, and Illinois. Kathy Gillies provided excellent research assistance. Financial assistance was provided by Allstate, the Center for Research in Financial Markets and Institutions at UCLA and by the Center for the Study of Futures Markets at Columbia.

[1] The proportion produced in Florida is now close to 100 percent. Indeed, the annual publication, *Agricultural Statistics*, by the U.S. Department of Agriculture, no longer gives a breakdown by area, reporting the production only for Florida (presumably because production elsewhere is so small). The last breakdown by area was for 1961 (see *Agricultural Statistics*, 1972, Table 324). In 1961, Florida produced 115,866,000 gallons while California and Arizona combined produced 2,369,000 gallons. It may surprise the reader to know that OJ production for frozen concentrate is mainly a Florida industry; many *table* oranges do come from California. This difference between Florida and California oranges is attributable to differences in their sugar and juice content and in their exteriors. Florida oranges are sweeter and make better-tasting juice. California oranges, being less sweet, have a longer shelf life and they also tend to have less juice but more appealing skins. Apparently, there is not as much substitutability as might have been imagined. Actually, Florida produces the bulk of all oranges for both table and juice. In 1972–73, for example, Florida orange production by weight was about 80 percent of the U.S. total. (See *Florida Agricultural Statistics*, Table 3, p. 4.)

[2] See Tables 380 and 382 of *Agricultural Statistics* (1979, pp. 252 and 254).

[3] A rough indication of exogenous shifts in demand due to income and tastes can be obtained from U.S. consumption of all citrus fruit which has hovered closely around 27 pounds per capita for a number of years (see Table 384, p. 255, *Agricultural Statistics*, 1979).

to mature.[4] Thus, any vagaries in farmers' planting decisions are felt much later and do not impact the current year's crop. There might, however, be short-term effects from farming decisions concerning fertilizer use or harvesting methods. These could be influenced by the prices of fertilizer and energy.

It should be emphasized that even unstable conditions of demand and supply would not eliminate the influence of weather, they would simply make that influence harder to measure empirically. The main argument in favor of studying orange juice instead of other commodities is the geographical concentration of OJ production. The fact that nonweather influences seem unlikely to generate much empirical noise is simply an added benefit.

I. Data

A. *Orange Juice Futures*

Futures contracts in frozen concentrated orange juice are traded by the Citrus Associates of the New York Cotton Exchange. There are usually nine contracts outstanding with deliveries (expirations) scheduled every second month, January, March, etc., the most distant delivery being 17 to 18 months from the present. A contract is for 15,000 pounds of orange solids standardized by concentration (termed "degrees Brix") and with minimum "scores" for color, flavor, and defects.[5]

Price data[6] are available for each day since the exchange began OJ trading in the early

---

[4] See John McPhee (1967) for a fascinating and entertaining description of orange tree propagation and of the citrus business in general.

[5] The contract quality is specified as follows: "U.S. Grade A with a Brix value of not less than 51° having a Brix value to acid ratio of not less than 13 to 1 nor more than 19.0 to 1 and a minimum score of 94, with the factor of color and flavor each scoring 37 points or higher, and defects at 19 or better..., provided that [OJ] with a Brix value of more than 66° shall be calculated as having 7.278 pounds of solids per gallon" (*Citrus Futures*, undated). "Degrees Brix" is a term used in honor of a nineteenth-century German scientist, Adolf F. W. Brix (McPhee, p. 129).

[6] The price used here is the "settlement" price. This price (which may or may not reflect an actual transac-

1970's. However, the weather data are available only for October 1975 through December 1981, so this constitutes the sample period. There were 1,564 trading days during this period.

As is typical of many commodities, trading volume in OJ futures tends to be concentrated in the near-maturity contracts. The open interest of distant contracts, say 8 to 18 months maturity, is often only 10 percent or less of the open interest in nearer contracts, say from 2 to 6 months maturity. Because of well-known problems in price data from thin markets,[7] the fourth and longer maturities were discarded in the following empirical work.

The nearest-maturity contract was also discarded after a close examination of its price behavior around the maturity date. Volume of trading is quite high in the nearest contract until just a few days before expiration. But in the last several days of the contract's life, open interest declines and price volatility increases substantially. A good example of the ensuing econometric problem involved the contract which matured on November 16, 1977. During the last fifteen minutes before expiration, its price rose from $1.30 to $2.20 per pound, an annualized rate of return of about 1.8 *million* percent. Such events would seem to have little to do with the weather.

This leaves us with two contracts having, respectively, between 2 and 4 months and between 4 and 6 months to maturity; an equally weighted average of the daily returns on these two contracts was chosen as the basic OJ return for use in all subsequent analysis. (Using either contract separately gives virtually identical results. This is to be expected because the correlation between their returns is .97.)

On a contract expiration day, the shorter of these two contracts is dropped and a new contract, previously the fourth-from-

---

tion) is determined by members of the exchange at the close of each day's trading. It is the price reported in the financial press.

[7] See Myron Scholes and Joseph Williams (1977), Elroy Dimson (1979), Marshall Blume and Robert Stambaugh (1983).

TABLE 1—OJ FUTURES DAILY RETURNS BY DAY OF WEEK AND BY SEASON
OCTOBER 1975–DECEMBER 1981

Day of Week	Mean Returns[a]				
	Winter[b]	Spring	Summer	Autumn	All Seasons
Monday[c]	−.256	−.321	−.107	.0309	−.158
	(2.58)	(1.84)	(1.52)	(1.84)	(1.96)
Tuesday	.224	.269	.199	−.107	.146
	(2.11)	(1.37)	(.147)	(1.48)	(1.62)
Wednesday	.301	.188	−.102	−.169	.0540
	(1.72)	(1.54)	(1.40)	(1.36)	(1.52)
Thursday	.167	−.219	.113	.153	.0518
	(2.14)	(1.16)	(1.21)	(1.35)	(1.51)
Friday	.290	.0227	−.125	.242	.108
	(1.98)	(1.55)	(1.63)	(1.53)	(1.68)
Post-Holiday	−.0554	.311	.278	−.0817	.0102
	(1.78)	(1.72)	(1.25)	(1.37)	(1.52)
All Days	.141	−.00741	−.00079	.0253	.0392
	(2.09)	(1.51)	(1.51)	(1.52)	(1.66)

Notes: Levene's test (see Morton Brown and Alan Forsythe, 1974) for equal variances: $F = 3.59$; tail probability ≈ 0. Dummy variable regression:

$$R_t = \underset{(1.86)}{.0886} - \underset{(-2.30)}{.247} d_m - \underset{(.328)}{.0784} d_h \quad R^2 = .00211$$

where d_m is 1 on Monday, 0 otherwise, and d_h is 1 on post-holiday day, zero otherwise.

[a] Average of the second- and third-nearest maturity contracts' returns. The mean returns (standard deviations) of the two contracts separately were .0388(1.70) and .0397(1.65), respectively; their correlation was .969. The returns are shown in percent; standard deviations are shown below in parentheses.

[b] Winter is defined as December, January, February, inclusive. Spring, Summer, and Autumn include, respectively, each subsequent three months.

[c] Monday returns are from settlement price Friday to settlement price Monday. Other days are from settlement on previous day. Post-Holiday returns are from settlement on day before holiday to close on day after holiday.

the-shortest maturity, starts to be used in construction of the return series. The return on the new contract over the expiration date replaces the return on what has become the shortest maturity contract.[8]

[8] Specifically, let $R_{T,t}$ be the continuously compounded return on day t of a contract which matures on calendar date T. Say that contracts mature on days $T = 60, 120, 180, 240, 360$. The return series ($R_t^*$) used here is calculated as follows

$$R_t^* = (R_{120,t} + R_{180,t})/2 \quad t \le 60$$

$$R_t^* = (R_{180,t} + R_{240,t})/2 \quad 120 \ge t > 60$$

$$R_t^* = (R_{240,t} + R_{360,t})/2 \quad 180 \ge t > 120,$$

and similarly as times goes on and contracts mature.

Table 1 gives information about OJ returns over the sample period. The grand mean return is .0392 percent per day, about 10.3 percent per annum. The rather large volatility of these returns is shown by the fact that the standard error of the mean daily return is $1.66/(1563)^{1/2} = .0420$. The standard error is larger than the mean despite the large sample size.

In the body of the table, means and standard deviations are broken down by season and by day of the week. The seasonal pattern shows a larger mean and larger variability during winter. This might have been anticipated on the grounds that colder temperatures and the risk of freezing make investments in orange juice more hazardous during the winter months. A finer breakdown indicates, however, that the larger winter mean OJ return is due to January alone, perhaps for the same reason that equities of small firms have larger January returns.[9] (Compare Donald Keim, 1983.)

The day-of-the-week results can be compared to recent work on equity returns (Kenneth French, 1980; Michael Gibbons and Patrick Hess, 1981) which found a significantly negative Monday effect. A similar pattern is observed here in the means.[10] Thus, insofar as mean returns are concerned, OJ futures seem to display annual and weekly seasonals similar to equities.

The intraweek pattern of standard deviations is interesting for what it does *not* display. Since Monday's return covers a three-day period, while other days of the week cover only 24 hours, one might have thought that Monday's variance of returns would be approximately three times as large as the other days. Yet the ratio of Monday's to the average of the other days' variances is only about $(1.96/1.58)^2 = 1.54$. Monday's return has too low a variance. (Note that post-holiday returns, which are always for at least two calendar days, also have too low a variance.) Because of this pattern of variances across days, it must be admitted that weather may not be the only relevant factor for OJ returns after all. If weather alone were moving OJ prices, Monday's return volatility should be larger because weather surprises must occur just as readily on a weekend as on any other day. Nevertheless, since no one has yet discovered just what factors *are* causing day-of-the-week patterns, I shall proceed with an examination of weather, which is at least a known factor.

The OJ futures exchange imposes limits on price movements. These limit rules (see Table 2) prevent the price from moving by

---

[9] January's average daily OJ return was .701 percent (standard error = .238) while all other months combined had an average daily return of −.0193 percent (standard error = .0402).

[10] When compared against other days of the week in an analysis of variance, Monday's return is found to be significantly lower (*F*-statistic of 5.20 and tail probability of .0228). Monday's mean return is, however, only marginally significantly negative; the standard error of the mean (of −.158) is .114 percent. The dummy variable regression reported at the bottom of the table shows that the Monday effect is significant but that the explained variance is low.

TABLE 2—LIMIT RULES OF THE CITRUS ASSOCIATES OF THE NEW YORK COTTON EXCHANGE AFTER (BEFORE) JANUARY 1, 1979

General Rule: Prices may move no more than 5 (3) cents per pound, $750 ($450) per contract, above or below the settlement price of the previous market session.

Increased Limit Rule: When three or more contract months have closed at the limit in the same direction for three successive business days, the limit is raised to 8 (5) cents per pound for those contract months. The limit remains at 8 (5) cents until fewer than three contract months close at the limit in the same direction, then the limit reverts to 5 (3) cents on the next business day.

Current Rule for Near Contract: On the last three days before the near contract's expiration, its limit is 10 cents per pound. If that limit is reached during the market session, trading is suspended on *all* contracts for fifteen minutes. Then another 10 cents is added to or deducted from the near contract's limit and trading recommences. Limit moves and fifteen-minute suspensions can be repeated until the market's close. If this happens on the last day before expiration, trading hours are extended.

---

more than a certain amount from the previous day's settlement price. When a significant event, such as a freeze in Florida, causes the price to move the limit, the settlement price on that day cannot fully reflect all available information. In other words, limit rules cause a type of market information inefficiency (but not a profit opportunity). This might be inconsequential if limit moves occurred rarely; unfortunately, they are rather common. During the October 1975–December 1981 period, one or both of the two contracts being used here moved the price limit on 160 different trading days, slightly over 10 percent of the trading days in the sample. This implies that about 10 percent of the recorded prices in the sample are known in advance not to reflect all relevant available information.

Limit rules might be suspected as the reason why Monday's variance is too low since these rules would be more frequently applied to limit the three-day weekend/Monday return. It turns out, however, that only 40 of the 160 limit moves in the sample occurred on Monday. This frequency is slightly higher than the frequency of 20 percent which would be expected if all five weekday returns

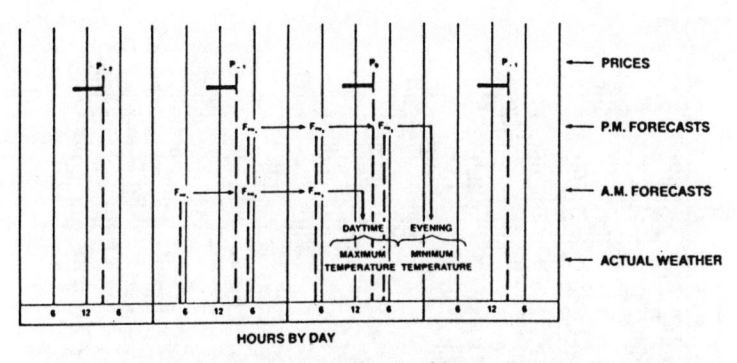

FIGURE 1. TIMING SCHEMATIC OF OJ FUTURES MARKET, WEATHER FORECASTS, AND ACTUAL PERIOD OF WEATHER AT ORLANDO

Note: — indicates market trading hours

covered the same number of hours. The ratio of Monday's return variance to the average variance on the other days is only 1.75 even when all limit move observations are excluded.

B. Central Florida Weather

The U.S. Weather Service reporting station in Orlando issues a variety of different weather bulletins. The most relevant information for oranges involve temperature and rainfall; the data[11] used here consist of daily information on these two variables.

Each 24-hour interval is divided into 12-hour daytime and evening periods. The daytime period begins at 7:00 A.M., eastern standard time, and ends at 7:00 P.M. on the same day. The evening period begins at 7:00 P.M. and ends at 7:00 A.M. the following day. For the daytime period, the weather service reports actual rainfall and the *maximum* temperature, while for the evening period, the rainfall and *minimum* temperature are reported.

Three different forecasts of both rainfall and temperature are also provided. They correspond to periods 36 hours, 24 hours, and 12 hours in advance of the 12-hour period to which the forecast applies. For example, say that the forecast is of the maximum temperature on January 5 (which could occur anytime from 7:00 A.M. until 7:00 P.M.). The first forecast is issued about 5:00 A.M. on January 4. (I call this the 36-hour-ahead forecast because it is developed and issued during the third 12-hour period prior to the 12-hour observation period of the actual maximum temperature.) A second forecast applying to the maximum January 5 temperature is issued at 5:00 P.M. on January 4; then, the third forecast is issued at 5:00 A.M. on January 5. This same cycle, but delayed by 12 hours, is used to issue forecasts of the minimum temperature on January 5 (from 7:00 P.M. January 5 until 7:00 A.M. January 6). Rainfall forecasts for the daytime and evening periods are issued along with the temperature forecasts.

Figure 1 gives a timing schematic of the actual weather, the forecasts of weather, and the trading times of orange juice futures. The symbol p_0 indicates the OJ settlement price on a particular calendar date. Note that p_0 is observed during the 12-hour daytime period, well before the evening period begins, and even before the last forecast of evening weather issued by the weather service. For this reason, we might anticipate that surprises in daytime weather would be

---

[11] The cooperation of Paul Polger of the National Oceanographic and Atmospheric Administration, who provided these data and provided a detailed explanation, is gratefully acknowledged.

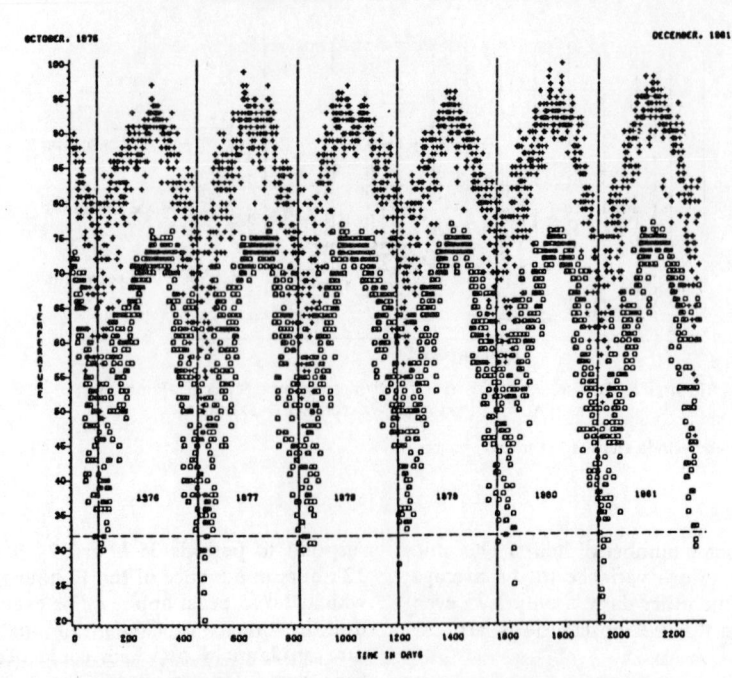

FIGURE 2. MAXIMUM AND MINIMUM DAILY TEMPERATURES AT ORLANDO

associated with price movements of p_{-1} to p_0 while evening weather surprises would influence price changes p_0 to p_{+1}.

The actual daily temperatures are plotted for the sample period in Figure 2 (+ indicates daily maximum and □ indicates minimum). The figure shows that temperatures in central Florida are not only lower during the winter season, they are also more variable. Damage to orange trees occurs if the temperature drops below freezing and stays there for a period of several hours. Thus, the minimum (P.M.) temperature during the winter months would seem to be an important factor influencing the size of the crop and the price of futures.

Table 3 shows that the Weather Service's short-term forecasts of temperature are quite accurate on average and that the forecast improves as its period approaches.[12] The OJ futures market has access to both the 36-hour-ahead and the 24-hour-ahead forecast of that day's P.M. minimum temperature (compare Figure 1). These two forecasts are issued prior to the market's opening. Thus, even aside from whatever private weather forecasts are made by OJ futures traders, two reasonably accurate forecasts of the day's

---

[12] However, there is a curiosity in these forecasts. Note that the A.M. level regressions tend to have slopes

($\hat{b}$) below 1.0. This could be due to errors in the data (rather than in the forecasts). The data were filtered and obvious transcription errors were corrected as detected. Of course, there may still be errors remaining. Errors-in-variables-induced attenuation bias cannot, however, explain why the P.M. forecast intercept is significantly negative. The Theil inequality proportions indicate significant bias in the P.M. forecasts. Note that the low Durbin-Watson statistics on the 36-hour-ahead forecasts are to be expected since there is an intervening actual between this forecast and the actual to which the forecast applies. (See Figure 1.) In other words, the 36-hour-ahead forecast on day t is issued before the forecast error is known for the 36-hour-ahead forecast from day $t-1$. This induces positive dependence in adjacent forecast errors.

TABLE 3—TEMPERATURE FORECAST ACCURACY FOR ORLANDO
OCTOBER 1975–DECEMBER 1981

Hours Forecast is Ahead[a]	Temperature Level				Temperature Change			
	$\hat{a}$ (1)	$\hat{b}$ (2)	R^2 (3)	U^m (4)	$\hat{a}$ (1)	$\hat{b}$ (2)	R^2 (3)	U^m (4)
Maximum (A.M.) Temperature Forecast								
36	4.23	.953	.872	1.15	.357	.832	.604	.777
(2,040)	(6.34)	(118.)	(1.53)	(1.60, 97.3)	(3.34)	(55.7)	(1.81)	(5.82, 93.4)
24	4.60	.951	.896	3.24	.667	.912	.663	2.57
(2,049)	(7.79)	(133.)	(1.81)	(2.16, 94.6)	(6.73)	(63.4)	(1.97)	(1.75, 95.7)
12	4.32	.952	.911	1.90	.511	.984	.708	1.55
(2,048)	(7.96)	(145.)	(1.91)	(2.46, 95.6)	(5.56)	(70.3)	(1.90)	(.061, 98.4)
Minimum (P.M.) Temperature Forecast								
36	−1.48	1.01	.884	6.14	−1.62	.771	.495	6.28
(2,048)	(−2.93)	(125.)	(1.42)	(.035, 93.8)	(−9.24)	(44.8)	(1.64)	(7.49, 86.2)
24	−2.71	1.03	.907	8.88	−1.89	.823	.575	8.86
(2,038)	(−5.92)	(141.)	(1.58)	(.532, 90.6)	(−11.7)	(52.5)	(1.64)	(5.35, 85.8)
12	−.852	1.00	.922	6.23	−1.49	.902	.648	5.92
(2,048)	(−2.11)	(155.)	(1.76)	(0.0, 93.8)	(−10.2)	(61.3)	(1.82)	(2.01, 92.1)

Notes: Regression: Actual = $\hat{a} + \hat{b}$ (forecast). The "actual" is the minimum or maximum temperature observed during a 12-hour period. In the "changes" regression, the dependent variable is the actual percentage change from the previous day's corresponding 12-hour period and the explanatory variable is the predicted percentage change.

Cols. (1),(2): *t*-statistics are shown in parentheses.

Cols. (3): Durbin-Watson statistics are shown in parentheses.

Cols. (4): U^r, U^d are shown in parentheses. The inequality proportions are shown in percent. See Henri Theil (1966, pp. 32–34). U^m = bias, U^r = regression, U^d = disturbance, proportions of mean squared prediction error due to, respectively, bias, deviation of regression slope from 1.0, and residuals.

[a] Sample size is shown in parentheses. There were 2,284 calendar days in the sample. However, the data contain numerous missing observations.

crucial minimum temperature are publicly available during trading hours.

Rainfall is also predicted by the Weather Service, but the form of the forecast is less useful for our purposes than in the case of temperature. The forecast "probability" of rain is always an even decile such as 30 percent and it rarely exceeds 60 percent. Weather service officials have told me that this forecast is intended to convey the chance of *any* measurable precipitation.

Table 4 reports the complete sample distribution of rainfall forecasts and actuals (the latter are provided in categories only). As shown, high forecast probabilities of rain are unusual even though there is measurable rainfall during about 28 percent of the reporting periods. The last column shows that the actual frequency of the rain is not far from the forecast probability. There is not a strong connection between the forecast probability and the *amount* of rain, but the Weather Service forecast is not intended to predict the amount, simply the chance of rain in *any* amount.

As shall be shown in the next section, there is an obvious relation between temperature and the price of OJ futures. The relation between rainfall and price is much more difficult to detect, if it is there at all. Perhaps this is due to temperature being a more important variable for the crop. Perhaps it is due to less useful weather data regarding rainfall.

TABLE 4—FORECAST PROBABILITY OF RAIN VS. ACTUAL RAINFALL BY CATEGORY IN ORLANDO
OCTOBER 1975–DECEMBER 1981

Forecast Probability of Rain[a]	\multicolumn{10}{c}{Actual Rainfall (inches)}	Frequency of Measurable Precipitation[a]
	0	.001–.009	.01–.120	.121–.25	.251–.50	.501–1.0	1.01–2.0	2.01–3.0	3.01–4.0	Total	
	\multicolumn{10}{c}{Frequency (All Forecasts)}	
0	3157	79	28	12	3	1	1	0	0	3281	3.78
10	2439	216	100	39	29	14	9	1	0	2847	16.7
20	1401	266	153	51	34	17	11	2	0	1935	27.6
30	904	260	180	83	39	34	17	2	0	1519	40.5
40	420	178	156	68	58	56	35	7	1	979	57.1
50	279	133	177	80	72	59	40	6	5	851	67.2
60	116	70	120	63	48	37	30	0	3	487	76.2
70	18	22	29	22	16	23	7	1	0	138	87.0
80	8	4	6	2	5	12	3	1	0	41	80.5
90	1	1	7	3	0	5	1	0	0	18	94.4
100	0	0	1	0	0	1	1	0	0	3	100.
Total	8743	1229	957	423	304	259	155	20	9	12099	

Note: χ^2 Test of Dependence:

	χ^2	Tail Probability	Forecasts	χ^2	Tail Probability
All Forecasts	4151	$p = 0.0$	36-Hours-Ahead	1185	$p = 0.0$
All A.M. Forecasts	2277	$p = 0.0$	24-Hours-Ahead	1421	$p = 0.0$
All P.M. Forecasts	1559	$p = 0.0$	12-Hours-Ahead	1744	$p = 0.0$

[a]Shown in percent.

II. Empirical Results

A. Temperature

Cold weather is bad for orange production. Orange trees cannot withstand freezing temperatures that last for more than a few hours. Florida occasionally has freezing weather and the history of citrus production in the state has been marked by famous freezes. In 1895, almost every orange tree in Florida was killed to the ground on February 8, production declined by 97 percent, and 16 years passed before it recovered to its previous level.[13] Farmers have since learned how to counter freezes with hardier trees, smudge pots, water spraying,[14] and air circulation by large fans; but although the trees are now more likely to survive a freeze, the crop can be severely damaged. Even a mild freeze will prompt the trees to drop significant amounts of fruit.

Figure 3 illustrates the impact of freezing weather on OJ futures prices during the sample period. The actual minimum temperature at Orlando is plotted along with the OJ price level.[15] Freezing level is indicated by the horizontal dashed line.

During this 6¼-year period, there were 27 recorded freezing temperatures (below 32°) at Orlando out of 2284 calendar days. However, only four periods registered temperatures below 30°. These occurred on January 17–21, 1977, January 2, 1979, March 2, 1980, January 11–13 and 18, 1981. (See Figure 2 also.) Figure 3 shows that these episodes were accompanied by significant price increases. The January freezes in 1977 and 1981 were particularly harsh in that six successive days and three successive nights,

---

[13]McPhee (p. 101).
[14]Spraying trees with water during a freeze can protect them under certain conditions. The water, freezing on the trees' leaves and buds, gives off heat in the process of changing from a liquid to a solid.

[15]Thirty cents has been added to the OJ price in order to keep the plots apart. The price is an average of the second and third shortest-maturity contracts. (See Section I.)

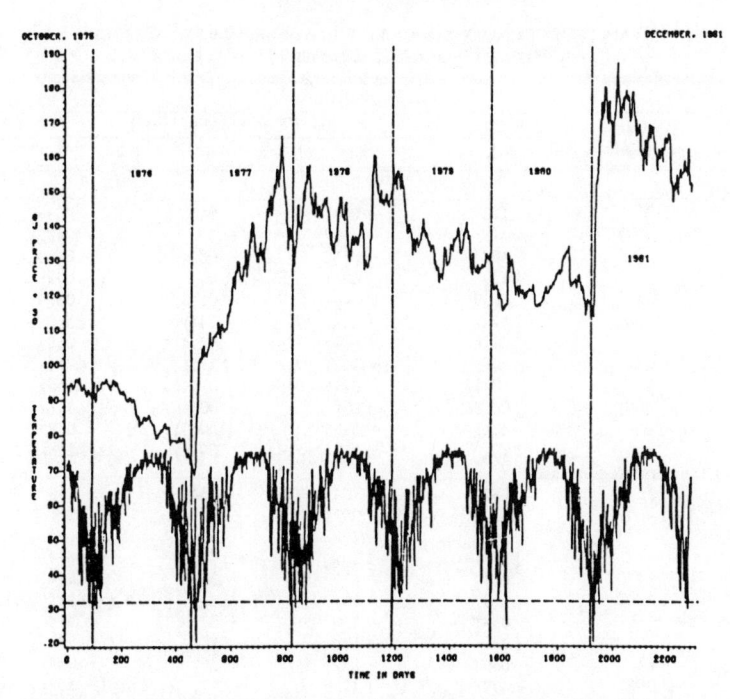

FIGURE 3. OJ FUTURES PRICES AND MINIMUM TEMPERATURES AT ORLANDO

respectively, had freezing temperatures. The most severe freeze during this sample, and the largest accompanying price increase, occurred during the latter period, on January 11, 12, and 13, 1981, when successive daily minimum temperatures were 24°, 23°, and 20°. During the week of January 12–16, OJ futures prices were up the limit on all five trading days.

Market participants realize, of course, that severe freezes are more likely during winter, so the price of OJ futures in the autumn should be high enough to reflect the probability of a freeze during the coming season. Each day thereafter that passes without a freeze should be accompanied by a slight price decline, a relief that winter is one day closer to being over. Also, harvesting of oranges begins in the fall and lasts until early summer, and inventories typically increase over the winter months.

For both of these reasons: freezes that do not occur and inventory build-up; there is a downtrend in futures prices during a typical nonfreeze winter. This pattern can be seen in every year of the sample (Figure 3), except 1977. A general downward movement with small fluctuations is interrupted by occasional sharp price increases sufficient to bring positive returns, on average, to those with long positions.[16] The distribution of returns is very skewed to the right.

If the OJ futures market is an efficient information processor, it should incorporate all publicly available long-term and short-term weather forecasts. Any private forecasts should be incorporated to the extent that traders who are aware of those forecasts are also in command of significant resources. The futures price should, therefore, incorporate the predictable part of weather in advance. Unpredicted weather alone should be

[16] An extensive theoretical discussion of this phenomenon is given by Benoit Mandelbrot (1966).

TABLE 5—OJ FUTURES RETURNS AND TEMPERATURE FORECAST ERRORS
WITH AND WITHOUT WEIGHTING, OCTOBER 1975–DECEMBER 1981

Seasons	Hours Forecast is Ahead[a]	b_{-2}	b_{-1}	b_0	b_{+1}	b_{+2}
Maximum (A.M.) Temperature Forecast						
Unweighted	36	.105	−.00414	−.0463	−.00397	−.322
	(1,391)	(1.31)	(−.0507)	(−.567)	(−.0487)	(−3.91)
Weighted		.102	−.0558	−.0894	−.0600	−.490
		(1.15)	(−.624)	(−1.00)	(−.673)	(−5.37)
Unweighted	24	.0639	−.0497	−.0113	.0379	−.247
	(1,408)	(.872)	(−.673)	(−.154)	(.510)	(−3.36)
Weighted		.0374	−.0615	.0224	.0585	−.379
		(.461)	(−.750)	(.275)	(.714)	(−4.71)
Unweighted	12	.000123	−.0715	−.000467	.0565	−.123
	(1,400)	(.00186)	(−1.07)	(−.00699)	(.838)	(−1.84)
Weighted		−.0851	−.0905	.00691	.0295	−.191
		(−1.17)	(−1.23)	(.0936)	(.398)	(−2.62)
Minimum (P.M.) Temperature Forecast						
Unweighted	36	.0822	−.104	−.154	.136	.0570
	(1,407)	(.632)	(−.791)	(−1.17)	(1.03)	.436
Weighted		.101	−.198	−.379	.133	.0561
		(.664)	(−1.30)	(−2.49)	(.874)	(.374)
Unweighted	24	.0412	−.139	−.352	−.238	−.0404
	(1,399)	(.357)	(−1.20)	(−3.03)	(−2.03)	(−.348)
Weighted		.0593	−.220	−.673	−.544	−.139
		(.442)	(−1.62)	(−4.96)	(−3.99)	(−1.09)
Unweighted	12	−.0698	−.152	−.263	−.0849	.104
	(1,398)	(−.677)	(−1.47)	(−2.52)	(−.807)	(.991)
Weighted		−.0796	−.231	−.549	−.217	.133
		(−.678)	(−1.97)	(−4.62)	(−1.83)	(1.13)

Notes: The regression equation is $\log(A/F)_t = a + b_{-2}R_{t-2} + b_{-1}R_{t-1} + b_0R_t + b_1R_{t+1} + b_2R_{t+2}$, where A is actual temperature, F is forecast temperature and R_t is the return on day t of an equally weighted sum of two futures contracts.

T-statistics are shown in parentheses. All Durbin-Watson statistics were in the range 1.6–1.9. Adjusted R^2s were between 1 and 3 percent.

The weighting scheme is January = 7, February = 6, March = 5, April = 4, May = 3, June = 2, July = 1, August = 2, September = 3, October = 4, November = 5, December = 6.

[a] Sample size is shown in parentheses.

contemporaneously correlated with price movements.

To examine the market's information processing ability, a series of empirical tests were carried out relating surprises in temperature to OJ futures price changes. The temperature forecast error, the percentage difference between the actual temperature and the forecast temperature provided by the National Weather Service, was taken as a measure of surprise. Price change was measured by the average of the daily returns on the second- and the third-shortest maturity contracts (see Section I).

Table 5 presents the first results. The regressions there use the temperature forecast error as the dependent variable. The independent variables are the same day's OJ return plus the returns on two leading and two lagged days. (There is no causality implied or intended by choosing the "dependent" and "independent" variables in this way. Causality actually runs from weather to prices.) Results are given separately in Table 5 for the daily maximum and minimum temperatures, for each of the three available forecasts, and for observations weighted and unweighted by season.

TABLE 6—OJ FUTURES RETURNS AND TEMPERATURE FORECAST ERRORS WITH AGGREGATION OF LIMIT MOVES, OCTOBER 1975–DECEMBER 1981, OBSERVATIONS WEIGHTED BY SEASON

Hours Forecast is Ahead	b_{-2}	b_{-1}	b_0	b_{+1}	b_{+2}
Maximum (A.M.) Temperature Forecast					
36	.0692	.0671	−.102	.0449	−.0341
	(1.257)	(1.46)	(1.25)	(−2.31)	(1.01)	(−.686)
24	.0654	−.00721	−.111	.0234	−.0545
	(1.272)	(1.48)	(−.165)	(−2.74)	(.570)	(−1.33)
12	.0518	.0196	−.0121	.0482	−.0368
	(1.263)	(1.30)	(.495)	(−.327)	(1.30)	(−.987)
Minimum (P.M.) Temperature Forecast					
36	.0542	−.101	−.236	.167	.0291
	(1.272)	(.652)	(−1.23)	(−3.08)	(2.16)	(.377)
24	−.0955	−.00879	−.622	−.0395	−.00346
	(1.263)	(−1.32)	(−.122)	(−9.25)	(−.584)	(−.0510)
12	−.00910	.0641	−.143	.0226	.106
	(1.262)	(−.138)	(.981)	(−2.37)	(.375)	(1.74)

Notes: For regression and weights, see Table 5. All Durbin-Watson statistics were in the range 1.50–1.95. Adjusted R^2s were between 1 and 4 percent.

Given the preceding discussion, it might seem that the only relevant temperature observations would be for winter evenings (since freezes do not occur at other times); but the futures market deals in anticipations, so forecast errors during the morning hours or even errors during the summer months could conceivably contain meaningful information about the *probability* of a freeze later. The unweighted regressions with A.M. temperature errors do indeed contain some statistical significance. But the P.M. regressions weighted[17] by season are more significant. In the P.M. weighted cases, the contemporaneous OJ return is always statistically significant with the anticipated negative sign.

The P.M. temperature results indicate that the OJ futures price on a given day at the close of trading (2:45 P.M.) is a statistically significant predictor of the forecast *error* of the minimum temperature later that evening (from 7:00 P.M. until 7:00 A.M. the following morning). The price appears to be a slightly better predictor of the error in the forecast issued by the National Weather Service at 5:00 A.M. that same morning than of the errors made by the two other forecasts (5:00 P.M. the previous evening and 5:00 P.M. later the same day).

The futures price is not informationally efficient, however, because several later returns are statistically significant in some regressions. The significant negative coefficient b_{+1} in the P.M. 24-hour ahead case might be consistent with efficiency since trading ceases on day zero before the evening period begins and recommences on day +1 after the evening period ends (see Figure 1). However, the significant two-day later negative coefficients (b_{+2}) for the A.M. temperatures cannot be so easily dismissed.

There is ample a priori reason to suspect some effective informational inefficiency induced by limit move rules. There were 160 limit moves during the sample and prices on these days cannot reflect all information (see Section I). In a first attempt to eliminate this source of inefficiency, limit moves were "aggregated." The results are given in Table 6. For data used in this table, if a particular day registered a limit price move, the "eco-

---

[17] The weighting scheme is rather arbitrary but is was the only one I tried. January observations, in the middle of winter, receive the highest weight; July observations, in the middle of summer, receive the lowest. January observations are weighted seven times more heavily than July observations, intervening months are weighted linearly between January and July; i.e., February = 6, March = 5, ... June = 2, ... December = 6.

nomic" closing price for that day was assumed to be the price on the next subsequent day which did not have a limit move.

On Tuesday, January 6, 1976, for example, the March contract closed at 59.75 cents per pound. The next day registered a limit move of 3 cents; the reported closing price was 62.75 cents. On Thursday (January 8), which was not a limit move day, the settlement price was 64.4 cents. This was taken as an estimate of what the price would have been the preceding day (January 7) if the exchange had imposed no limits. Thus, the daily return for January 7 used in the regression was $\log_e(64.4/59.75) = 7.5$ percent. There was no observation used for January 8.

Limit moves often occur one after another. In such cases, the price on the first day with no limit move was brought back to the day of the first limit move and all intervening days were discarded.[18]

This procedure obviously overestimates the ability of the market to predict temperatures. Hindsight was used in that no one could know for sure on the first limit move day how many additional days with limit moves would follow. Thus, the results in Table 6 are biased in favor of finding market efficiency, as opposed to those in Table 5 that are biased against finding efficiency because of the exchange's own rules.

In Table 6, there is no longer a significant negative relation of temperature forecast error and later OJ returns. This indicates that the statistical significance of the lagging coefficients found in Table 5 was indeed due to the exchange's limit rules and not to some other possible source of informational inefficiency.[19] Notice that five of the six contemporaneous coefficients are significant and negative.[20]

To estimate the predictive content of OJ prices without resorting to hindsight, while at the same time including the extra information known to market participants that particular days had limit moves, the regressions in Table 7 were computed. A contemporaneous return and a lagged daily return were included as predictors along with slope dummies for limit move days.

Slope dummies are more appropriate than intercept dummies because the size of a limit move changed during the sample period (see Table 2).[21] Before January 1, 1979, the limit was 3 cents while it was 5 cents thereafter. As a consequence, only 39 out of 160 limit move days occurred during 1979–81 even though almost one-half of the sample observations were in those years. Thus, during 1979–81, the settlement price was more informationally efficient and the news that a particular day displayed a limit move constituted more material information. Slope dummies may not perfectly capture the greater importance of limit moves in the last three years of the sample, but at least they do weight these observations more heavily (by approximately 67 percent).

The F-statistics for these regressions indicate that the A.M. forecast errors cannot be

---

[18] If an up limit was followed by a down limit (or vice versa), day 1 was treated as if the return were zero and day 2 was discarded. The next included observation was then for day 3 (if it was not a limit move). In other words, for any sequence of limit moves followed immediately by another sequence in the opposite direction, the first closing price after reversal was brought back to the first day of the initial sequence. Then the price on the first day with no limit move is brought back to the first day of the second sequence.

[19] The one anomalous coefficient, b_{+1} in the 36-hour P.M. regression, has a positive sign. A single "significant" coefficient such as this is to be expected by chance among so many possibilities.

[20] The reader may notice that the number of observations differs by only one, 1263 to 1262, between the P.M. 24- and 12-hour regressions; yet the t-statistics on the contemporaneous returns are -9.25 and -2.37. Could this be caused by a single observation out of more than 1200? The answer is no. There are actually 138 observations that differed in these two regressions (due to missing data), but almost exactly one-half were missing from each regression. (There were other *common* missing observations.)

[21] Also, a slope dummy preserves the sign of the price change. This could be done, too, with intercept dummies, for example, using $+1$, 0, and -1 for up limit, normal, and down limit, but the slope dummy accomplishes this feat automatically while allowing for the nonstationarity in the size of a limit move.

TABLE 7—PREDICTIVE MODEL OF TEMPERATURE FORECAST ERRORS USING SLOPE DUMMY VARIABLES
FOR LIMIT MOVE DAYS OCTOBER 1975–DECEMBER 1981, WEIGHTING BY SEASONS

Hours Forecast is Ahead	Contemporaneous b_0	d_0	Lagged One Day b_{-1}	d_{-1}	F^a
Maximum (A.M.) Temperature Forecast					
36	−.0636	−.0839	.0750	−.348	2.80
(1,391)	(−.495)	(−.475)	(.580)	(−1.91)	
24	.0992	−.213	−.0989	.0422	.897
(1,408)	(.835)	(−1.34)	(−.845)	(.254)	
12	.0198	−.0581	−.0807	−.0859	1.16
(1,400)	(.186)	(−.386)	(−.766)	(−.576)	
Minimum (P.M.) Temperature Forecast					
36	−.672	−.418	.0282	−.276	2.71
(1,407)	(−.329)	(−1.39)	(.131)	(−.898)	
24	.119	−1.55	.184	−.588	23.9
(1,399)	(.616)	(−5.82)	(.961)	(−2.17)	
12	−.119	−.643	.217	−.781	14.7
(1,398)	(−.697)	(−2.78)	(1.30)	(−3.32)	

Notes: The regression equation is $\log(A/F)_t = a + b_0 R_t + d_0 \delta_t R_t + b_{-1} R_{t-1} + d_{-1} \delta_{t-1} R_{t-1}$, where A is actual temperature, F is forecast temperature, R_t is return on day t, $\delta_t = 1$ if there was a limit move on day t and zero otherwise.
See weighting scheme in Table 5.
T-statistics are shown in parentheses. Durbin-Watsons were in the range 1.59 to 1.99. Adjusted R^2s were in the range .0018 to .038.
[a] F-statistics for the regressors having no effect. The 95 percent fractile is approximately 5.6.

predicted by the current and lagged OJ returns plus a limit move slope dummy. This is also true for the P.M. 36-hour ahead forecasts. However, both the 24- and 12-hour ahead forecast errors can be improved by prior OJ returns.

The lack of predictive content of A.M. temperatures is, perhaps, not all that surprising because A.M. temperatures are relevant only to the extent that they predict freezes that evening. Apparently, this link is too weak to be picked up with statistical reliability by OJ returns.

The low predictive content for P.M. temperatures may be a disappointment until one reflects upon the scope of *possible* predictive ability. As shown in Table 3, about 90 percent of the variability in temperature is removed by the National Weather Service's forecast. The OJ prices predict a very small but still significant part of the remaining 10 percent.[22]

[22] It should be noted that all of the contemporaneous slope dummies (d_0) have negative signs. Also, the differences between the last two regressions in the table are intriguing but puzzling. The lagged slope dummy (d_{-1}) is more important for the 12-hour forecast error than for the 24-hour forecast error. Could this be related to the fact that the 12-hour forecast is not issued until after the market closes, while the 24-hour forecast is issued before it opens?

B. Rainfall

Orange juice prices are replotted in Figure 4 along with the day's total rainfall[23] (in tenths of inches) at Orlando. Unlike the earlier plot of price and temperature (Figure 3), no relation between the two series in Figure 4 is apparent to the naked eye.

The effect of rainfall on the crop is much less obvious than the effect of temperature. Most of the groves in Florida are not irrigated, so a long dry spell might be damag-

[23] Rainfall data are available only in the categories shown in Table 4. To construct Figure 4, the midpoint of each category was used as an estimate of the actual rainfall in inches. The A.M. and P.M. figures were added to obtain the total precipitation for the day.

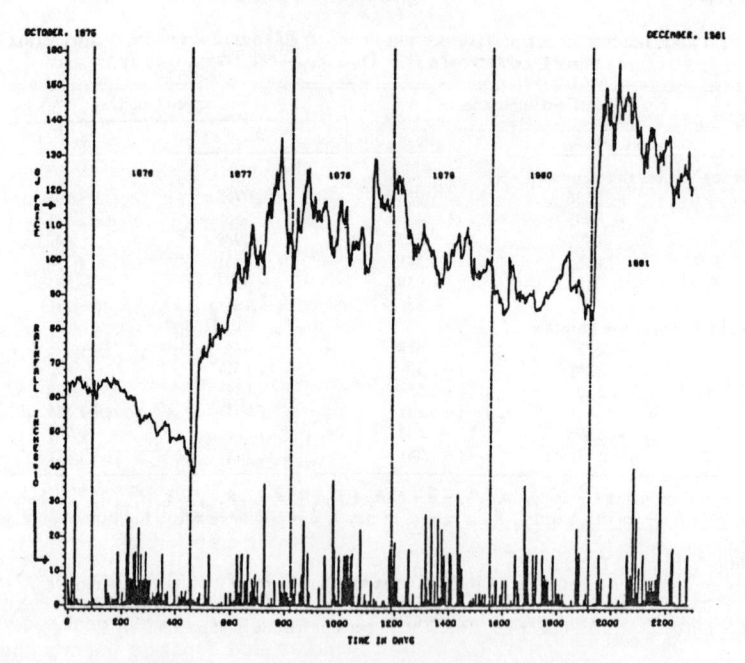

FIGURE 4. OJ FUTURES PRICES AND DAILY RAINFALL AT ORLANDO

ing. On the other hand, the crop could be reduced by extremely heavy rain or by wind damage from tropical storms (that appear in the rainfall time series because they also drop a lot of water).

For example, on November 6, 1981, the *Wall Street Journal* reported higher orange juice prices "...on news of a hurricane off the Florida coast," and on February 18, 1983, prices were purportedly higher due to "...talk of heavy rain." Some confusion about the effect of rainfall is disclosed in the latter story; it included a statement from the Florida Citrus Commission that the orange crop was "unscathed" by the rain. " 'Our oranges are enjoying the weather,' said a department spokesman, 'oranges need a lot of moisture.' " A commodities "analyst" stated that OJ traders drove up prices because they were confused by reports of rain damage to strawberries and tomatoes!

Whether or not the futures market understands the effect of rainfall is rather moot if the empiricist does not understand it well enough to develop a measure of rainfall surprise. With this admission in mind, let us plunge ahead into this turbid subject.

As shown previously in Section II (Table 4), National Weather Service rainfall forecasts are statistically significant but imperfect predictors of actual precipitation. I experimented with several different models of rainfall forecasts (including "probit" and logarithmic models), in order to find the most reliable predictor. It turned out that the largest reduction in variance was obtained with the simplest of regression models,

$$A_t = a + bF_t,$$

where $A_t = 1,...,9$ is the actual rainfall by category on day t and F_t is the forecast "probability of rain." The adjusted R^2 of this regression ranged between .118 and .332 (see Table 8). It is interesting to note that predictive ability for rainfall rises more rapidly as the prediction period approaches than it does in the case of temperature (compare Table 3).

Table 8 contains F-statistics from regressions relating the rainfall forecast error to

TABLE 8—PREDICTIVE MODEL OF RAINFALL FORECAST ERRORS USING SLOPE DUMMY VARIABLES FOR LIMIT MOVE DAYS OCTOBER 1975–DECEMBER 1981, NO WEIGHTING

Hours Forecast is Ahead	Adjusted R^2 of Weather Service Forecast[a]	F-Statistic of OJ Return Predictive Power[b,c]
A.M. Rainfall		
36	.239	.362
(1,371)		
24	.265	.410
(1,393)		
12	.332	.417
(1,372)		
P.M. Rainfall		
36	.118	.388
(1,393)		
24	.165	.230
(1,374)		
12	.225	.629
(1,384)		

[a] Actual rainfall A_t by category, ($A_t = 1, 2, \ldots 9$), was predicted by the Weather Service's "probability of rain," F_t, in the simple regression model $A_t = \hat{a} + \hat{b}F_t + \epsilon_t$; the forecast error ϵ_t was then used as the dependent variable in another regression model with OJ returns as predictors (see fn. c below).
[b] The 95 percent fractile of the F-statistic is approximately 5.6.
[c] The regression model was $\epsilon_t = a + b_0 R_t + d_0 \delta_t R_t + b_{-1} R_{t-1} + d_{-1} \delta_{t-1} R_{t-1}$, where ϵ_t is the Weather Service's rainfall prediction error, R_t is the OJ return on day t and δ_t is +1 if day t had a limit move, otherwise zero. No coefficient was significant and coefficients are not reported for reasons of space.

the contemporaneous and lagged OJ return plus a slope dummy for limit moves, that is, the same purely predictive model as the one for temperature in Table 7. As might have been anticipated in light of the preceding discussion, OJ returns appear to have no significant predictive power for rainfall.[24] There was not a single significant coefficient

[24] A similar model was computed with a dependent variable defined as the *absolute value* of the rainfall forecast's prediction error. Of course, this would not be a legitimate model from an efficient markets perspective since it would not imply predictive ability of the direction of error (even if it had worked). It is, however, suggested by the possibility that either too much or too little rain is bad for the orange crop. As it turned out, the model had even lower explained variance than the model in Table 8 which preserved the sign of the rainfall prediction error.

out of the 24 possible and no F-statistic is significant in any of the six regressions.

C. Nonweather Influences on OJ Prices

The small predictive power for temperature and rainfall seems to imply that influences other than weather are affecting OJ returns. What might they be? In an attempt to find out, news stories in the financial press were systematically examined.

From October 1, 1975 through December 31, 1981 (the sample period of the paper), a total of 91 articles related to oranges appeared in the *Wall Street Journal*; 26 articles reported either results of weather (17) or forecasts of weather (9). Of the 26 weather articles, 25 concerned temperature and 1 concerned rainfall. There were 22 articles disclosing crop forecasts by the U.S. Department of Agriculture, 15 articles reporting price movements with no explanation, 7 articles about international conditions (Canadian and Japanese imports and Brazilian exports), 6 articles about supermarket supplies, and 15 miscellaneous articles. In this last category, the subjects ranged from product quality (4) and new products (1) through antitrust action against the Sunkist cooperative in California (3), to such truly unclassifiable stories as orange rustlers in Florida and advertising contracts with Anita Bryant.

The number and content of weather stories shows that weather is considered important and that rainfall is a relatively minor factor compared to temperature. Among the other topics, *ex post* stories about futures price movements per se and most of the miscellaneous stories could not possibly have been about true influences on earlier OJ price variation. Agricultural crop forecasts, though, would seem likely to have moved prices in some direction. Perhaps international news, reports of supermarket supplies, and antitrust actions are also relevant. The variability of returns was computed for periods ending on the *Wall Street Journal* publication date of such articles and including two prior trading days (to allow for news leakage). This variability is compared in Table 9 to the variability of returns on dates with no orange juice news.

TABLE 9—VARIABILITY OF OJ FUTURES RETURNS ON DAYS WITH NEWS ABOUT
ORANGE JUICE IN THE *WALL STREET JOURNAL*, OCTOBER 1975–DECEMBER 1981

	No News (1)	Weather (2)	Crop Forecast (3)	Supplies, Antitrust, International (4)	Miscellaneous (5)
Standard Deviation of Returns	1.53 (1361)	2.86 (64)	2.01 (60)	1.97 (34)	1.37 (34)

	Comparisons Among	F-Statistic	Tail Probability
Levene's Test for Equal Variances[a]	Cols. (1)–(5)	22.5	0.0000
	Cols. (1), (3), (4), (5)	9.83	.0018
	Cols. (2), (3), (4).	8.99	.0033

Notes: Standard deviation of returns are shown in percent per day, with sample size shown in parentheses; returns on an equally weighted index of the second and third from the shortest maturity contracts on the day of the news story and on the two preceding trading days.

Sample sizes are smaller than the number of possible days because of overlapping dates among articles. For overlapping dates, returns were assigned hierarchically to category (2) (Weather) first, then to categories (3), (4), and (5), respectively.

[a] See Brown and Forsythe.

The miscellaneous category has a low volatility. It is even lower than the variability of returns on days with no news stories. Volatility of returns is highest during periods when stories about weather were published. During periods associated with stories about crop forecasts, retail supplies, antitrust actions, and international events, volatility is higher than during "no news" periods. However, it is significantly *lower* than during periods with weather-related news stories.

From this evidence, weather remains as the most important identifiable factor influencing OJ returns. Crop forecasts and other newsworthy events have an influence, but their frequency is too small and their impact too slight to explain a material part of the variability in returns left unexplained by weather. As Table 9 shows, there is substantial volatility (a daily standard deviation of returns of 1.53 percent per day), on days that are not associated with *any* story about oranges in the *Wall Street Journal*; and these days constitute about 87 percent of the sample observations.

In addition to events important enough to appear in special orange juice stories in the financial press, other influences on supply and demand might be directly measurable. For instance, stock market returns could measure general economic activity and thus provide a proxy for consumer demand. Canada is the largest customer for U.S. orange juice, so the Canadian dollar/U.S. dollar exchange rate might have a measurable impact on orange juice because it would proxy for Canadian demand. Energy prices could affect short-term supply because they influence the cost of operating farm equipment and the costs of processing and distributing the product. Petroleum is also a direct ingredient of fertilizer and a major component of fertilizer production costs.

Table 10 offers evidence about the influence of these and other variables on OJ price movements. Two regressions were computed. The first involves the OJ return as dependent variable. It shows that cold temperatures indeed cause OJ price movements, but general stock market returns, changes in the Canadian dollar exchange rate, and oil stock returns (a measure of energy prices), have no significant influence.

The second regression in Table 10 uses the squared OJ return as dependent variable. This was done because the objective here is merely to identify sources of price movements in either direction, as opposed to test-

TABLE 10—T-STATISTICS OF EXPLANATORY FACTORS FOR OJ RETURNS, NO CONSIDERATION OF LIMIT MOVES, DAILY DATA, OCTOBER 1975–DECEMBER 1981

Explanatory Variable	Dependent Variable	
	OJ Return	Squared OJ Return
Max $(32 - T_{-1}, 0)$[a]	5.40	7.99
Max $(32 - T_{-0}, 0)$	3.69	8.09
(Oil Stock Return)$_{-1}$[b]	−.618	.385[g]
(Oil Stock Return)$_0$	.624	2.11[g]
(VW Market Return)$_{-1}$[c]	.525	−1.05[g]
(VW Market Return)$_0$	−.120	−1.53[g]
(Δ CDN exch. Rate)$_{-1}$[d]	−.417	−.759[g]
(Δ CDN exch. Rate)$_0$	.577	.938[g]
Monday[e]	−2.18	4.23
Weather-Related News Story[f]	–	9.36
Crop Forecast News Story[f]	–	3.35
Supplies or Int'l News Story[f]	–	−.563
Miscellaneous News Story[f]	–	−1.47
Multiple Adjusted R^2	.0668	.268
F-Statistic for Regression	13.4	45.0
Durbin-Watson	1.81	1.39
Number of Observations	1,559	1,559

[a] T_t is the minimum temperature at Orlando on day t.
[b] Return on an equally weighted portfolio of oil stocks listed on the NYSE and the AMEX, consisting of up to 45 firms. The sample consisted of all listed oil firms covered in the 1982 *Value Line* service.
[c] Value-weighted index of all NYSE and AMEX stocks.
[d] Percentage change in the Canadian/U.S. dollar exchange rate.
[e] Dummy variable; 1 if Monday, 0 otherwise.
[f] Dummy variable; 1 if news story in this category in the *Wall Street Journal* on day t or $t+1$, zero otherwise.
[g] T-statistic for the squared explanatory variable.

ing the direction of influence of particular variables. Using the squared return permits the inclusion of dummy variables on news story dates without having to decide whether the story should be associated with a positive or negative price change. To illustrate the problem, take the case of crop forecast stories. It would be very hard to know whether a particular forecast by the Department of Agriculture is above or below the previously expected production level without looking at the OJ price movement itself.

In this second regression, cold weather remains very significant and stories related to weather and to crop forecasts are significant as well (the latter result confirms the implications drawn from Table 9). The contemporaneous squared oil stock return is also significant, though its t-statistic indicates a much lower level of influence. (This is something of a curiosity in that oil stock returns are unrelated in direction to OJ returns in the first regression.) Finally, notice that only 27 percent of the variability in squared OJ returns is explained by all of these variables combined. Most of the variability remains unexplained.[25]

D. *Supply Shocks vs. Demand Shocks*

Variability in OJ prices could be caused by shifts in demand induced by changes in the prices of substitute products. The prices of apple juice, tomato juice, and soft drinks, inter alia, should influence the demand for orange juice. We have seen already in Table 10 that general consumer demand and the demand of the largest foreign customer (Canada) are not important relative to the supply shocks of weather, energy prices, and crop forecasts. Table 11 provides information about the relative importance of more micro demand shocks.

For firms in the orange juice business and for certain firms producing substitutes, daily stock returns were related, firm by firm, to OJ returns. In each case, the firm's return was regressed on the contemporaneous OJ return, plus two leading and two lagged OJ returns, plus slope dummies for limit move days on the OJ exchange. The F-statistics of the regression were examined for significance. In cases where significance was indicated, the coefficients were examined for direction of comovement between equity and OJ returns.

Two basic types of firms were examined. The first type consists of firms whose SIC (standard industrial classification) code on the CRSP tape indicated that it was in some aspect of the orange juice or a related food-processing business. (It had the same SIC

---

[25] These regressions are obviously misspecified (for example, notice the Durbin-Watson statistics in the second regression). However, they are intended merely to characterize the data, not to test any particular theory, so it seems doubtful that much can be learned by using more sophisticated econometric methods.

TABLE 11—RETURNS ON AGRICULTURE RELATED EQUITIES AND RETURNS ON ORANGE JUICE FUTURES[a]

Company[b]	Line of Business	Relation to OJ Returns[c]
American Agronomics	Owns 9200 acres of Fl. citrus; Produces and markets OJ	None (+)
CHB Foods	Produces and markets pet food, fish, vegetables and fruit	None
Castle & Cooke	Produces and markets pineapples, bananas, fish, broccoli, sugar; Owns Hawaii land	Positive
Consolidated Foods	Manufactures and distributes coffee, candy, sugar, soft drinks	Positive
Curtice-Burns	Processes and packs fruits and vegetables, soft drinks, Mexican food, frozen vegetables	None
Del Monte[d]	Produces fresh bananas and pineapples; processes seafood	None
Di Giorgio	Diversified food processor including citrus, Italian food, sells OJ in Europe; Has some Fl. land	None
Green Giant[d]	Produces canned and frozen vegetables	None
Norton Simon	Produces tomato-based food products, popcorn, cooking oil, liquor	None (−)
Orange-Co. Inc.	Owns 8100 acres of Fl. citrus; Produces and markets OJ	None
J. M. Smucker	Produces jellies, condiments, syrups, and canned fruit drinks	None (−)
Stokeley Van Camp	Produces Gatorade and canned and frozen vegetables	None
Tropicana[d]	Processes citrus juice; Owns a few Fl. groves which are experimental plantings	Negative
United Foods	Produces frozen vegetables	None

[a] Equities with the standard industrial classification of food manufacturers and processors with the same four-digit SIC codes as Di Giorgio, Orange-Co. or Tropicana, and with at least 100 daily return observations in the period October 1975–December 1981.

[b] In addition to these companies, regressions were also run with soft drink equities, Coca-Cola, Dr. Pepper, MEI, Pepsi Cola, and Royal Crown. None of these regressions were significant.

[c] "Positive" or "Negative" indicates that the regression's F-statistic was significant at the 5 percent level. The regression's dependent variable is the equity's return and independent variables are two leading, contemporaneous, and two lagged orange juice futures returns plus corresponding slope dummies for limit moves. A symbol in parentheses indicates a marginally significant regression (at the 10 percent level).

[d] Companies no longer listed on the New York or American Exchange.

code as Di Giorgio, Tropicana, or Orange-Co., three companies known in advance to be in the orange juice business.) All such companies are listed by name in Table 11.

The second type of company produced soft drinks (see Table 11, fn. b). No soft drink producer had a significant relation to orange juice. So changes in OJ demand due to changes in soft drink prices are not revealed in the data.[26]

Turning back to the first type of firm, Table 11 indicates that many were not related to OJ prices. This was true even for such companies as Orange-Co., whose principal business is growing oranges and producing juice. There are several possible explanations for the lack of significant comovement in such a firm. First, consider the impact of supply shocks: an increase in OJ prices due to, say, cold weather, would not affect the firm if the gain in the value of its Florida land were offset by a reduction in the value of its processing and distribution divisions, or if the firm had hedged its own supply by selling OJ futures.

A demand shock, however, should affect the firm unequivocally unless it overhedged in the futures market. For example, an exogenous increase in OJ demand raises the value of its land and, if there are fixed costs, also raises the value of its production and distribution facilities. Thus, the lack of significant comovement between OJ prices and firms such as Orange-Co., Di Giorgio, and Amer-

---

[26] One of these companies, Coca-Cola, also produces orange juice, so a lack of comovement due to shifts in prices of orange juice substitutes might be expected for this particular firm; roughly, what it gains in the soft drink business might be lost in the orange juice business, or vice versa.

ican Agronomics, who grow *and* process juice, suggests that most of the OJ price volatility is due to supply shocks instead of demand shocks.

This is reinforced by the case of Tropicana, a processor owning virtually no land. It is the only such firm and also the only firm whose equity comoves negatively and significantly with OJ prices. It is conceivable, of course, that this negative relation is induced by a combination of demand shocks and Tropicana purchasing too many futures contracts (more than its own anticipated requirements), but it seems more plausible that the relation is induced directly by supply shocks that squeeze Tropicana's profit margin.

Two companies, Castle & Cooke and Consolidated Foods, produce OJ substitutes and have positive comovement with OJ prices (as is expected if OJ prices move because of supply shocks). One firm, Smucker, buys oranges for jam and has a marginally negative comovement (also explainable by OJ supply shocks). The only anomalous firm is Norton Simon, a producer of substitutes such as tomato juice and liquor (but its negative comovement is of only marginal significance). Some wits have suggested that Norton-Simon actually produces a complement, not a substitute, product. Vodka, one of its biggest sellers, is often consumed with orange juice.

Overall, the evidence in Table 11 supports the view that supply shocks are the principal cause of OJ price movements. Unfortunately, the identity of such shocks remains at least a partial mystery. Weather is important, but measured weather explains only a small fraction of the volatility in OJ prices.

III. Summary and Conclusion

The market price of frozen concentrated orange juice is affected by the weather, particularly by cold temperatures. A statistically significant relation was found between OJ returns and subsequent errors in temperature forecasts issued by the National Weather Service for the central Florida region where most juice oranges are grown. Orange juice prices are much less related to errors in rainfall prediction. Indeed, no significant statistical association was found between these variables.

The OJ futures price is rendered informationally inefficient by the existence of exchange-imposed limits on price movements. This inefficiency manifests itself in the data by allowing temperature surprises to have apparent predictive power for *later* price changes. When limit moves are taken into account, however, temperature has no remaining predictive content.

There is, nevertheless, a puzzle in the OJ futures market. Even though weather is the most obvious and significant influence on the orange crop, weather surprises explain only a small fraction of the observed variability in futures prices. The importance of weather is confirmed by the fact that it is the most frequent topic of stories concerning oranges in the financial press and by the ancillary fact that other topics are associated with even less price variability than is weather.

Possible sources of orange juice demand and supply movements such as substitute product prices, general demand, export demand, and production costs were also examined here. Yet *no* factor was identified that can explain more than a small part of the daily price movement in orange juice futures. There is a large amount of inexplicable price volatility.

REFERENCES

Blume, Marshall, E., and Stambaugh, Robert F., "Biases in Computed Returns: An Application to the Size Effect," *Journal of Financial Economics*, November 1983, *12*, 387–404.

Brown, Morton B. and Forsythe, Alan B., "Robust Tests for the Equality of Variances," *Journal of the American Statistical Association*, June 1974, *69*, 364–67.

Dimson, Elroy, "Risk Measurement When Shares are Subject to Infrequent Trading," *Journal of Financial Economics*, June 1979, *7*, 197–226.

French, Kenneth R., "Stock Returns and the Weekend Effect," *Journal of Financial Economics*, March 1980, *8*, 55–69.

Gibbons, Michael R. and Hess, Patrick, "Day of the Week Effects and Asset Returns,"

Journal of Business, October 1981, *54*, 579-96.

Hopkins, James T., *Fifty Years of Citrus: The Florida Citrus Exchange: 1909-1959*, Gainesville: University of Florida Press, 1960.

Keim, Donald B., "Size Related Anomalies and Stock Return Seasonality: Further Empirical Evidence," *Journal of Financial Economics*, June 1983, *12*, 13-32.

Mandelbrot, Benoit, "Forecasts of Future Prices, Unbiased Markets, and 'Martingale' Models," *Journal of Business*, January 1966, *39*, 242-55.

McPhee, John, *Oranges*, New York: Farrar, Straus, and Giroux, 1967.

Scholes, Myron and Williams, Joseph, "Estimating Betas from Nonsynchronous Data," *Journal of Financial Economics*, December 1977, *5*, 309-27.

Theil, Henri, *Applied Economic Forecasting*, Amsterdam: North-Holland, 1966.

Citrus Associates of the New York Cotton Exchange, *Citrus Futures*, Four World Trade Center, NY 10048, undated.

Florida Department of Agriculture, *Florida Agricultural Statistics Summary*, Tallahassee: Florida Department of Agriculture, various years.

U.S. Department of Agriculture, *Agricultural Statistics*, Washington: USGPO, various years.

[28]
Persuasive evidence of market inefficiency

A book/price strategy and a "specific-return-reversal" strategy, subject to careful tests, lead to the "inescapable conclusion" that prices on the NYSE are inefficient.

Barr Rosenberg, Kenneth Reid, and Ronald Lanstein

This article reports the statistically significant abnormal performance of two strategies. One strategy is a "book/price" strategy. The strategy buys stocks with a high ratio of book value of common equity per share to market price per share and sells stocks with a low book/price ratio, where "book value" is common equity per share, including intangibles. The second strategy is a "specific-return-reversal" strategy. This strategy calculates the difference between the investment return for the previous month on the stock and a fitted value for that return based upon common factors in the stock market in the previous month. This differential return is the "specific return" that is unique to the stock. This strategy expects the specific return to reverse in the subsequent month. It therefore buys stocks having negative specific returns in the prior month.

We selected both strategies as interesting candidates for tests of market inefficiency based on data through 1980. We evaluated the prior performance of the strategies in 1980 and described them in speeches and articles in 1982 [6, 7, 10, 11]. Based on monthly returns since the completion of the prior study, both strategies have shown persuasive evidence of market inefficiency.

Despite the relatively short time span, the strategies have separately achieved t-statistics of 3.7 and 11.54, respectively, each implying that the null hypothesis of market efficiency can be rejected at a very high level of confidence. Further, both strategies produced performance in this evaluation period that was closely consistent with their prior performance. We obtained still higher t-statistics when the prior data and the evaluation-period data were combined.

The two strategies are also expected to be statistically independent a priori, because the results have shown a negative and statistically insignificant correlation during the evaluation period. Thus, each study is an independent test of market inefficiency, which means that the confluence of the two results suggests still stronger evidence for market inefficiency.

We defined the strategies and singled them out for prospective study because we felt that they arose naturally as straightforward tests of market efficiency. Each strategy can be viewed as the result of using an "instrumental variable" for pricing error. To the extent that pricing errors, for whatever cause, are present in the U.S. stock market, we anticipated that these tests might show up that inefficiency by means of the instrumental variables (the book/price ratio and the prior month's specific return, respectively) that are used. We believe that this study leads to the inescapable conclusion that prices on the New York Stock Exchange are inefficient.

PROPERTIES OF THE STRATEGIES

We define each strategy by a set of weights, w_n, for each of the approximately 1400 stocks in a prospectively defined universe of large companies, called the HICAP universe. The set of weights is calculated as of the end of the previous month, based upon data available on or before that date. The outcome of the strategy, called the "return to the strategy" and denoted by "f," is the weighted average of the monthly returns for the stocks:

$$f = \Sigma w_n r_n,$$

where r_n is the rate of return on stock n.

The set of weights for each strategy has the following characteristics:

(1) The weights are both positive and negative, and the sum of the weights is zero. Consequently, the return to the strategy can be viewed as the return on a "pure hedge portfolio" with a zero investment value.

(2) The weights are constructed so that the sum of the weights is zero within each of 55 industry groups. Each strategy therefore takes both long and short positions in each industry, which average out to zero, and so is immunized against industry factors of return.

(3) The strategy is also constructed to be orthogonal to a set of "risk indexes," with which common factors of return are also associated. The weighted sum of each of the following risk indexes, weighted by the strategy weights, is zero:

1. *Variability in Markets.* Beta prediction based upon stock price behavior, option price, etc.
2. *Success.* Past success of the company, as measured by stock's performance and earnings growth.
3. *Size.* A size index based on assets and capitalization.
4. *Trading Activity.* Indicators of share turnover.
5. *Growth.* A predictive index for subsequent earnings per share growth.
6. *Earnings/Price.* Ratio of estimated current normal earnings per share to stock price.
7. *Earnings Variation.* Variability of earnings and cash flow.
8. *Financial Leverage.* Balance sheet and operating leverage of industrial companies.
9. *Foreign Income.* Proportion of income identified as foreign.
10. *Labor Intensity.* Ratio of labor cost to capital cost.
11. *Yield.* Predicted common stock dividend yield.

Consequently, the return to the strategy is immunized against any common factor returns associated with these stock characteristics.

(4) The book/price and specific-return-reversal strategies are orthogonal to one another. The two sets of weights have zero cross-product. Consequently, the return on each strategy is expected to be independent of the other one.

(5) Each strategy is standardized, so as to imply an exposure to the variable that is constant over time. For the book/price strategy, the weighted sum of book/price ratios differs from the market average by one cross-sectional standard deviation of that ratio. In other words, the strategy is persistently located one standard deviation away from the capitalization-weighted mean value for all stocks. For the specific-return-reversal strategy, the sum of the positive weights is 1.0, and the sum of the negative weights is -1.0, so the return on the strategy corresponds to the difference between returns on a "buy portfolio" of stocks with negative prior specific returns and a "sell portfolio" of stocks with positive prior specific returns. (With respect to an "indicator variable" for the sign of the previous month's specific return, this strategy is positioned at two cross-sectional standard deviations away from the mean, so that it is, in a precise sense, twice as aggressive with respect to its instrumental variable as the book/price ratio strategy is with respect to its instrumental variable.)

(6) The set of weights for each strategy is calculated so as to minimize the variance of the strategy's return arising from the specific returns of the individual companies, subject to meeting the above five restrictions. In other words, the noise resulting from the random specific returns of the individual stocks is made as small as possible.

Because each strategy is a "pure hedge portfolio," we can view the return to the strategy as a potential incremental return that an investor can earn by adjusting an existing portfolio in the direction of the strategy.

Let h_n denote the investment proportions in an ordinary portfolio of common stocks. Let r_0 denote the investment rate of return on that portfolio. Then if the initial portfolio is adjusted in the direction of the hedged portfolio, so that the resulting investment weights are each ($h_n + w_n$), then the rate of return on the adjusted portfolio will be $r_0 + f$. For this reason, statistically significant performance of the strategy — to the extent that that performance is uncorrelated with the return on the initial portfolio — implies that it is necessarily possible to improve the mean/variance characteristics of the initial portfolio by making the adjustment, and so suggests that the investor holding portfolio weights h_n would prefer to hold portfolio weights $h_n + w_n$; thus, good performance suggests an inefficiency in the marketplace.

THE TWO STRATEGIES AS INSTRUMENTS FOR MARKET INEFFICIENCY

Suppose that the market is in fact inefficient, in the sense that if v_n is the "fair value" of stock n, then the stock price p_n differs from the fair value by a pricing error e_n, i.e., $p_n = v_n + e_n$. The usual presumption is that the market price is unfair in the sense that the pricing error e will be reversed in the future. Consequently, the rate of return in the subsequent month, r_n, is negatively correlated with e_n. A variable, x_n, will serve as an "instrumental variable" for subsequent performance, r_n, if it is correlated with the initial pricing error, e_n. Therefore, to search for market inefficiency, we should search for a variable, x, which we expect to be negatively correlated with e, and therefore positively correlated with subsequent return, r. This variable will define the strategy that tests for the existence of the pricing error, by means of the test of subsequent returns.

One way to obtain an instrument for e is to find a variable that is correlated with the difference v − p, since −e = v − p. For a variable x to be positively correlated with v − p, x must increase when the value of the firm increases relative to the price of the firm.

Traditionally, ratios of the firm's activity to the stock price have been used for this purpose. In principle, any ratio, such as book/price, earnings/price, or dividend/price = yield, can be used. Nevertheless, the value of these financial ratios as instruments may be destroyed if they are used in the process of security analysis or as a quantitative screen by investors using quantitative techniques.

If an investor uses the variable x as an indication of the desirable stock quality, so that stock price is bid up in proportion to x, then x may acquire a positive correlation with p, over and above the indirect relationship with p, which x obtains through its link to underlying value, v. As the correlation with p increases (as the stocks with high x values are bid up in price and stocks with low x values are bid down in price), the result is to reduce the correlation of x with v − p and eventually to destroy its usefulness entirely. Since substantial work had previously been done with yield as a criterion for investment, and since the earnings/price ratio was much emphasized in security analysis and had previously been studied in the finance literature by S. Basu, we felt that the book/price ratio was an intriguing candidate for study. Since it had not been heavily described in the quantitative literature, it might possibly serve as an as-yet unspoiled instrument.

Another approach to obtaining an instrumental variable is to attempt to find a variable x that is directly correlated with the pricing error e. The previous month's specific return, $u_{n,t-1}$, is a natural instrument for this purpose.

The explanation of this relationship is straightforward. Suppose that a common-factor model is used to fit the most probable return for this stock in the previous month, by analogy with the returns with similar stocks. In other words, the common-factor model explains the returns on all stocks as a result of their characteristics, and so estimates factors of return associated with industry groups and with risk indexes. Then, to the extent that the stock's previous month's return differed from this fitted return, the difference was unique to that stock. If there is a pricing error for the stock, that error would probably show up as a component of this unique return.

In fact, we can consider the difference between the pricing error for the stock at the end of the prior month and the pricing error at the inception of that month as one of the components of the previous month's specific return. Therefore, in the absence of some adjustment to remove this relationship, we would expect that the previous month's specific return would be positively correlated with every one of its components and, particularly, with the component that was the change in the pricing error.

The final step in the argument is to notice that the pricing error at the end of the previous month is the starting point for the current month's return: A larger change in pricing error over the previous month implies, ceteris paribus, a likelihood of a larger pricing error at the end of the previous month.

The complete linkage is as follows: The previous month's specific return is positively correlated with its component, which is the change in the pricing error over the previous month, which is positively correlated with the magnitude of the pricing error at the end of the previous month. Therefore, the previous month's specific return is intrinsically positively correlated with the pricing error at the end of the previous month. Consequently, we can expect the negative of the specific return to be positively correlated with this month's investment return.

As in the case of the book/price variable, we must ask whether this correlation would be vitiated by use of the previous month's specific return by technicians as a transaction strategy. In other words, if market participants were actively seeking to profit from anticipated specific return reversals, the results would be to reduce, and even eliminate, the use of the instrumental variable.

There are two reasons, however, to think that the instrument might remain valid. First of all, because the strategy requires a high rate of turnover, the inhibition provided by transaction costs could leave a significant correlation even if the investment value of the strategy had been fully removed. Second, because of the strong bias toward market efficiency that has been present in academic circles, there might be skepticism about the use of such a simple, technical, quantitative rule for trading strategies.

For these reasons, we felt that the book/price (B/P) strategy and the specific-return-reversal (SRR) strategy were natural instruments to use in the search for market inefficiencies.

IMPLEMENTATION OF THE STRATEGIES AND CALCULATION OF THE RESULTS

We based the initial retrospective test of these strategies on a data base of monthly stock data from January 1973 through March 1980 for the B/P strategy, and on through December 1980 for the SRR strategy. For the retrospective study, we strove to assure that all data used in calculation of the weights in the strategies would have been available prior to the month for which the return was calculated. We also carefully screened the data base to remove as many errors as possible, so that the investment returns would be valid.

We based this analysis primarily upon the Standard & Poor's Compustat data base and the IBES Analytics data base. There was no retrospective bias in the latter, and retrospective bias in the former could be avoided by use of the Compustat Research Tape. As a result, we were able to avoid survivorship bias and retrospective inclusion bias.

For present purposes, the key concern is with the prospective tests, beginning with the endpoints of the retrospective studies. Strategy weights for every month were calculated, based upon data through to the prior month's close, and calculation of the strategy weights was usually completed by the second or third business day of the month. The sample was defined prospectively as the HICAP universe. The strategic returns calculated here are therefore a true test of the outcome of a predefined investment strategy.

PERFORMANCE OF THE BOOK/PRICE STRATEGY

The monthly strategy returns f_t can be analyzed for their relationships with the market returns by means of the time-series regression:

$$f_t = \alpha + \beta r_{Mt} + \epsilon_t, \quad t = 1, \ldots, T \quad (1)$$

where r_{Mt} is the excess return on the market (the monthly S&P 500 return minus the monthly 30-day Treasury Bill return), and ϵ_t is the unexplained return. The coefficient β gives the responsiveness of the strategy return to the market portfolio, and α is the average residual factor return. Let ω denote the standard deviation of the residual return, $\omega = $ std. dev. (ϵ).

Table 1 summarizes the results of this regres-

TABLE 1
Monthly Performance of the Book/Price Strategy

	1973.1-1980.3	1980.4-1984.9	1973.1-1984.9
α (basis points)	41	32	36
t-statistic	4.5	3.7	5.7
ω (basis points)	83	62	76
Number of months positive	64	38	102
Number of months negative	23	16	39
Number of months total	87	54	141

sion for the 87 months of the retrospective study, for the 54 months of the prospective study, and for the total sample of 141 months. Each panel provides the average residual return (α) for this strategy and the standard deviation of the residual return (ω), in basis points per month. For example, the average residual return for the entire period was $\alpha = 36$ basis points, or 0.36 percent per month, and the standard deviation of the monthly residual return was 76 basis points. The systematic risk coefficient, β, was indistinguishable from zero, so it is not reported in the table. The foot of Table 1 shows the number of monthly returns that were positive, negative, and the total for each subperiod and for the entire history.

The return to the B/P strategy was positive in 38 of the 54 months of the prospective evaluation. The mean residual return was 32 basis points and the standard deviation of monthly residual return was 62 basis points. This led to a t-statistic of 3.7, which permits us to reject the hypothesis that the mean residual return is zero at the 99.95% level of confidence. The performance of the B/P strategy in the evaluation period was consistent with the prior experience. Therefore, we are justified in combining the entire sample history into a single test of market efficiency.

Table 2 shows an intriguing aspect of the B/P returns for the 12 calendar months. The left-hand

TABLE 2
Seasonality of Book Price Returns (Basis Points)

	1973.1-1980.3			1980.4-1984.9			1973.1-1984.9		
	μ	σ	t-stat	μ	σ	t-stat	μ	σ	t-stat
January	193	125	(4.39)	133	62	(4.29)	173	109	(5.58)
February	37	45	(2.31)	77	42	(3.67)	50	47	(3.70)
March	50	87	(1.63)	47	67	(1.39)	49	78	(2.18)
April	18	30	(1.63)	47	40	(2.64)	30	36	(2.88)
May	21	40	(1.40)	23	34	(0.85)	22	36	(2.15)
June	36	40	(2.43)	-17	53	(-0.72)	14	51	(0.97)
July	47	61	(2.05)	39	39	(2.22)	44	51	(2.97)
August	20	68	(0.78)	-13	86	(-0.33)	6	74	(0.25)
September	43	55	(2.07)	10	75	(0.30)	29	63	(1.61)
October	-28	69	(-1.08)	-16	23	(-1.39)	-24	55	(-1.45)
November	33	75	(1.16)	38	44	(1.75)	35	63	(1.85)
December	-13	42	(-0.81)	25	29	(1.71)	1	41	(0.05)

panel shows the mean and standard deviation of the returns over the historical sample. Both the mean (μ) and the standard deviation (σ) of the book/price return were much higher in January than in any other month. There appears to be a downward trend in μ over the course of the year. As the monthly t-statistics in the left-hand panel show, the mean return was highly significant in January (t-statistic = 4.39), and the t-statistic exceeded 2 in February, June, July, and September. We emphasized this seasonal pattern in our discussions of the strategy in 1982 [11].

The central panel of Table 2 displays the monthly means and standard deviations during the prospective evaluations. Again, the January mean stands out sharply and, again, there is an appearance of a downtrend in the mean values from January through December. Despite the brevity of the sample, the January and February means achieve high statistical significance, and the April and July means have t-statistics greater than 2.0.

The right-hand panel shows the seasonality for the entire eleven- and-three-quarter year sample. Here the downward trend from January through to the end of the year is pronounced, and the t-statistics for January, February, March, April, May, and July are each separately greater than 2.0.

PERFORMANCE OF THE SPECIFIC-RETURN-REVERSAL STRATEGY

The SRR strategy defined in the earlier paper [10] (Rosenberg and Rudd (1982)) used the negative of the previous month's specific return as the instrumental variable. Table 3 reports the strategy reported in the earlier paper, together with the subsequent performance of the strategy.

TABLE 3
Monthly Performance of Specific-Return-Reversal Strategy

	1973.5-1980.12	1981.1-1984.10	1973.5-1984.10
μ (basis points)	112	104	109
t-statistic	10.4	10.34	13.83
σ (basis points)	103	68	93
Number of months positive	83	43	126
Number of months negative	9	3	12
Number of months total	92	46	138

The performance in the prospective evaluation is similar to the historical study. The mean monthly return is smaller, but the time-series variability of the return is reduced even more, so that the strategy achieves even higher significance per unit time after the prospective evaluation. In fact, the results are positive 43 months out of 46. The result is a t-statistic of 10.3, which permits an essentially conclusive rejection of the null hypothesis that the actual mean return of the strategy is 0.0.

To provide a still clearer strategy, and to insulate the results from the effects of misrecorded prices, we considered an alternative strategy in which the instrumental variable is the sign of the previous month's specific return. In other words, the strategy is simplified to purchasing an equal-weighted "buy portfolio" of stocks whose previous month's specific returns were negative and selling short an equal-weighted portfolio whose previous month's specific returns were positive. The monthly return on that strategy is simply the difference between the monthly returns for the buy and sell portfolios, which coincides with the difference between the average return for the month on the stocks whose previous month's specific returns were negative and the average return in the month for the stocks whose previous month's specific returns were positive. The results of that strategy appear in Table 4. As the beta was significantly different from zero, we carried out the time-series regression on the market return (Equation 1) and report the alpha, beta, and residual standard deviation, omega, in the table. This strategy achieves an even higher level of statistical significance, with a t-statistic of 11.5 for the 46-month sample. The results are positive 45 months out of 46. Average January abnormal profits were 202 basis points, versus 129 basis points on average for the other eleven months of the year. This difference is intriguing, but it was not statistically significant.

TABLE 4
SRR Monthly Return (Basis Points)

α	β	ω
136	0.10	80
(11.54)	(3.65)	

t-statistics in parentheses.

TRADING THE STRATEGIES

Trading costs are an important aspect to be considered in applying these strategies. Trading costs include the direct expenses of commissions and taxes, plus the price effect of trading. Trading costs for an institutional investor utilizing the B/P strategy would almost certainly have had a negligible effect upon performance. Urgent trading of the B/P strategy is not necessary, because the B/P criterion variable is not timely; a round-trip trading cost of 100 basis points is probably an ample allowance. Portfolio turnover is less than 5% per month, so that the drain from trading costs would be less than 5 basis points per month, as against an average abnormal performance of 36 basis points per month for the entire history.

The performance of the SRR strategy, on the other hand, would be greatly reduced for an investor experiencing trading costs. The strategy relies on timely data, so that urgent trading is important. Since the SRR strategy reported in Table 4 involves holding one portfolio long and another portfolio short, and since approximately 50% of the stocks in each portfolio are switched each month, there is a trading cost drain equal to 100% of the round-trip trading cost each month. Therefore, a drain of 100 basis points or more against a monthly performance of 136 basis points is not unlikely.

Some investors would not be faced with these trading costs. Brokers and dealers, for example, might face trading costs that were a fraction of this. Also, the investor who had determined to trade for other reasons, and who was using the SRR strategy as a timing device, would face no incremental trading costs from exploiting it.

The abnormal return of 136 basis points per month reported in Table 4 for the SSR strategy may be unobtainable if an investor is unable to sell short the "sell portfolio" at the month-end closing prices.[1] We evaluated an alternate strategy where the investor takes a long position in the "buy portfolio" and sells short the S&P500 index.[2] The average residual return declines from 136 to 96 basis points per month. The long side of the SRR strategy, taken alone, provides most of the abnormal return.

MULTICOLLINEARITY OF MULTIPLE STRATEGIES

Multicollinearity of the strategy variables is another potential problem in studies of factors in market returns. When a variable is used in raw form to construct a strategy, without any attempt to immunize the strategy against other factors, the strategy weights are directly related to that variable. The mode of analysis corresponds to a simple regression on that variable, and we can define the results as a "simple factor" of return. When that approach is taken, the major potential criticism of our study is that that variable may have served as a surrogate for other variables more closely related to the subsequent abnormal returns.

In the present case, we have made each strategy orthogonal to the other strategy, to 55 industry groupings, and to 11 other "risk indexes," which are continuous variables characterizing the stocks. This approach is subject to the criticism that this orthogonalization of the strategy weights may create wildly variable weightings because of multicollinearity of these strategy variables with the other dimensions.

Fortunately, this is not a problem. We deliberately constructed the risk indexes so that multicollinearity would not be severe. As a matter of fact, the time-series standard deviation of the B/P strategy return discussed here is only 76 basis points, whereas the time-series variation of the simple B/P strategy return is 139 basis points. Both strategies have the same standardized exposure to the B/P ratio, so a reduction in the time-series variability can occur only if the risk reduction from immunizing the effects of other common factors has exceeded the risk increase due to higher specific variance from the wider variable weightings. In other words, the multiple-factor strategy has substantially lower time-series risk, which confirms the benefits from orthogonalizing the weights.

Another important question related to the two tests is the extent to which they are independent of each other. Since the weightings are orthogonal a priori, we should expect the strategies to show independent returns. The realized outcome was consistent with this: The correlation between the monthly residual returns on the B/P and SRR strategies was −.19 for the 45 overlapping months, which was insignificantly different from zero. A "super strategy" that exploited a portfolio of the two strategies would therefore have achieved an even higher t-statistic than either strategy separately.

The B/P and SRR strategies are independent in another important sense. The B/P strategy corresponds to a "slow idea," and the SRR strategy to a "fast idea." Specifically, the B/P strategy exploits a decision criterion having data that are one to four months out of date (depending upon the month in the calendar quarter), and stocks purchased based on that criterion tend to be held for more than a year, on average. The SRR strategy exploits timely data, with 50% of the stocks in the portfolio traded at the end of the month. The success of two such diverse strategies tends to confirm, in our minds, the existence of underlying pricing errors in the market, which can be imperfectly detected by either alternative instrument.

POSSIBLE BIAS

One potential problem in the study is a positive bias in the results due to errors in the recorded prices. The B/P and SRR strategies use instrumental variables for pricing error, and these will single out undervalued securities, whether the low price is a true market

---
1. Footnotes appear at the end of the article.

price or a problem in recording the price itself. There is a real potential that a pricing error will cause the stock to appear desirable by B/P or SRR criteria and that the correction of the pricing problem in a subsequent month will induce a spurious, favorable return. We have taken much care to eliminate this source of bias.

First, we screened the data base for errors in prices and adjustment factors. Second, we calculated the B/P variable only once at the inception of each quarter, and the market price used as the denominator is lagged one month prior to the beginning of the quarter. For example, the B/P strategy for the months of January, February, and March is based upon a value of B obtained from the Compustat tapes in mid-December and upon the closing market price P at the end of November. Since the vast majority of pricing errors in the U.S. common stock data bases are reversed within the following month, the one-month lag almost assures that there will be no spurious upward bias in returns due to errors in the denominator of the B/P ratio.

For the SRR strategy, timing is of the essence: It is detrimental to lag the month in which the specific return is calculated. Accordingly, we cannot use lagging to eliminate the potential upward bias from the reversal of the prior month's error during the current month.

We applied two modifications to the original strategy to minimize this bias, relying on the tendency of pricing errors in these data bases to be rare but large. Usual errors arise from mistyping or reversing the digits of the price or from mistiming a stock adjustment; in either instance, the error is likely to be more than 10%. Further, it is the large errors whose reversals have the potential to significantly bias the results in an upward direction. The SRR strategy reported in the previous paper [10] used the prior month's specific return itself as the instrument, and so undertook positions in stocks that were proportional to the prior month's specific return. This resulted in large weights on the few stocks with large errors, and so in substantial potential profit.

The SRR strategy reported here, in which the weight on the stock depends only on the sign of the prior month's specific return and not on the magnitude, is a natural adjustment to minimize the impact. Even if there is a 50% downward pricing error in the previous month, the weight on the stock in this month's buy portfolio will be only 1/700, so that the spurious positive return when the stock returns to the correct price in the current month will be only 1/700 of 100%, or 14 basis points. The results in Table 4 reflect this SRR strategy.

As a second check, we applied the SRR strategy only to those stocks with specific returns between −10% and +10% in the prior month. We deleted all stocks with specific returns beyond these boundaries. This caused more than 15% of the stocks to be ignored, and these were the stocks that would be most desirable according to the logic of the SRR instrument.

Evidently, this strategy is expected to perform less well than the strategy based on all stocks, but the key question is the extent of sacrificed return. If the original return were somehow due to undetected data errors, then we could expect that discarding the stocks with extreme prior specific returns to wipe out the effect. As Table 5 shows, exclusion of the prior returns does reduce the monthly productivity of this strategy from 136 basis points to 105 basis points, which is probably no more than would be expected in the absence of data error. The results for the truncated sample remain excellent, with a time-series t-statistic of 10.94 for the abnormal return.

TABLE 5
SRR Return Excluding Outlying Prior Returns
(Basis Points)

α	β	ω
105	0.08	66
(10.94)	(3.43)	

t-statistics in parentheses.

In short, we have been able to satisfy ourselves that the results reported here are not due to pricing error. Rather they reflect opportunities available when trading at the month-end market prices of U.S. common stocks.

Sample bias in favor of survivors is another potential problem in this sort of study. Both strategies single out stocks that have done poorly in the marketplace lately; they may not be as likely to survive as other companies. Any retrospective bias toward survivors would tend to reduce the losses of the strategies and so bias their performance upward. For the study through 1980, we took care to avoid retrospective sample biases, but it is possible that some crept in. For the evaluation since 1980, on the other hand, the sample was routinely defined in advance, and so no retrospective bias was possible.[3]

CONCLUSION

This study has evaluated two prospectively defined strategies for obtaining abnormal performance. Both strategies independently achieved highly significant results, which were consistent with their prior performance in the retrospective study. Therefore, we conclude that — for this universe of stocks during this time period — the actual market prices were inefficient. The universe of stocks consists of 1400 of the largest companies in the Computstat data base. The time period is from 1980 to 1984. The stocks are priced largely on the NYSE, and a few are priced on the ASE, other regional exchanges, or NASDAQ.

The success of two such diverse instrumental variables in detecting market inefficiency suggests that there are still larger potential profits to be made, provided that the security analyst can identify the valuation errors that correlate with these instruments.

---

[1] Investors can sell short only on up-ticks. It follows that in a declining market, the sell side of the SRR strategy would be difficult to implement in a timely fashion.

[2] This strategy could be implemented by selling S&P500 futures contracts.

[3] In an earlier version of the paper presented at the American Finance Association meeting (December 1984), we included only those stocks with a valid price within the last week of the month. We have since verified that the results also apply when all stocks which trade at any time within the month are included, with investment return calculated through to the last price.

REFERENCES

1. Fischer Black and Myron Scholes. "The Effects of Dividend Yield Policy on Common Stock Prices and Returns." *Journal of Financial Economics*, May 1974, pp. 1-22.
2. Sanjoy Basu. "Investment Performance of Common Stocks in Relation to Their Price-earnings Ratios: A Test of the Efficient Market Hypothesis." *Journal of Finance*, June 1977, pp. 663-682.
3. Eugene Fama. "Efficient Capital Markets: A Review of Theory and Empirical Work." *Journal of Finance*, May 1970, pp. 383-417.
4. Lawrence Fisher. "Some New Stock Market Indices." *Journal of Business*, January 1966, pp. 202-207.
5. Robert Litzenberger and Krishna Ramaswamy. "The Effect of Personal Taxes and Dividends on Capital Asset Prices." *Journal of Financial Economics*, June 1979, pp. 163-195.
6. Kenneth Reid. "Average Returns to Equity Characteristics." A paper presented at the Berkeley Program in Finance Seminar on *Recent Evidence Concerning Securities Market Efficiency*, March 1982.
7. ———. "Factors in the Pricing of Common Equity." Unpublished doctoral dissertation, Graduate School of Business, University of California, Berkeley, June 1982.
8. Marc Reinganum. "Misspecification of Capital Asset Pricing: Empirical Anomalies Based on Earnings' Yields and Market Values." *Journal of Financial Economics*, March 1981, pp. 19-46.
9. Barr Rosenberg and Vinay Marathe. "Common Factors in Security Returns: Microeconomic Determinants and Macroeconomic Correlates." *Proceedings of the Seminar on the Analysis of Security Prices*, May 1976, pp. 61-115.
10. Barr Rosenberg and Andrew Rudd. "Factor-related and Specific Returns of Common Stocks: Serial Correlation and Market Inefficiency." *Journal of Finance*, May 1982, pp. 543-554.
11. Barr Rosenberg, Kenneth Reid, and Ronald Lanstein. "Factor Portfolios and Studies of Reward to Equity Characteristics." A paper presented at the Quantitative Discussion Group, May 1982.
12. Michael Solt and Meir Statman. "A Stock Return Regularity Based on Tobin's Q-Ratio." Unpublished manuscript, Leavey School of Business, University of Santa Clara, Santa Clara, California, November 1984.
13. Timothy Sullivan. "A Note on Market Power and Returns to Stockholders." *Review of Economics and Statistics*, February 1977, pp. 108-113.

CAPITAL MARKET SEASONALITY: THE CASE OF STOCK RETURNS

Michael S. ROZEFF and William R. KINNEY, Jr.

The University of Iowa, Iowa City, IA 52242, U.S.A.

Received January 1976, revised version received March 1976

In this paper we present evidence on the existence of seasonality in monthly rates of return on the New York Stock Exchange from 1904–1974. With the exception of the 1929–1940 period, there are statistically significant differences in mean returns among months due primarily to large January returns. Dispersion measures reveal no consistent seasonal patterns and the characteristic exponent seems invariant among months. We also explore possible implications of the observed seasonality for the capital asset pricing model and other research.

1. Introduction

Although the existence of seasonality in stock returns has important implications for capital market theory, capital market efficiency and the nature of the distribution of stock returns, the subject has only recently received much attention in the literature [see Bonin and Moses (1974) and Officer (1975)]. These studies, which find seasonality, conflict with earlier studies which do not [see Granger and Morgenstern (1963, 1970)]. Due to the relative lack of evidence and the use of various techniques to measure seasonality, there is no consensus of opinion as to even the existence of seasonality. The result has been little or no testing of hypotheses about possible causes of seasonality and no consideration of the implications of seasonality for the finance models which ignore its presence.

In this paper we present evidence on the existence of seasonality and its implications for other research. We concentrate on the question of existence. Possible explanations for the presence of seasonality are left for future research.

After the development of models in section 2 and a review of previous studies in section 3, section 4 presents evidence for the existence of seasonality in monthly stock returns on the New York Stock Exchange for various periods since 1904. The autocorrelation functions of the time series indicate *no* consistent seasonal pattern. However, using parametric and non-parametric tests, we do generally find statistically significant differences in measures of central tendency by month of the year due primarily to consistently high rates of return in January. Differences in dispersion measures among months are significant for some periods but not others, giving no consistent pattern over the various time periods. The characteristic exponents of the monthly returns seem relatively invariant among months.

Section 5 examines some implications of stock market seasonality for finance models. Of particular concern are the efficient market model and the possible effects of seasonality on the computation of disequilibrium rates of return and betas. We find, for example, that seasonality in stock returns seems to have had a major impact on Fama and Macbeth's (1973) estimates of slope and intercept in the two-parameter capital asset pricing model, since time series of these estimates (like stock returns) have pronounced distributional differences when examined by month.

2. Statistical models of stock returns

A wealth of evidence [see Cootner (1964) and Fama (1970)] indicates that stock price behavior is well-described by a multiplicative random walk model (tildes indicate random variables),

$$(\tilde{P}_{jt} + \tilde{D}_{jt}) = P_{j,t-1} \exp(\tilde{e}_{jt} + \mu_{jt}), \tag{1}$$

where $\tilde{P}_{jt}$ is the price of stock j at time t, $\tilde{D}_{jt}$ is the dividend from $t-1$ to t, $\tilde{e}_{jt}$ is a random variable with zero mean, independently and identically distributed through time, and μ_{jt} is the stock's expected rate of return, conditional on the information set available at $t-1$, (I_{t-1}). With the additional assumption that $\mu_{jt} = \mu_j$, a time-invariant constant, and rearranging, we obtain

$$\ln\left(\frac{\tilde{P}_{jt} + \tilde{D}_{jt}}{P_{j,t-1}}\right) \equiv \ln(1 + \tilde{r}_{jt}) = \mu_j + \tilde{e}_{jt}. \tag{2}$$

For $\tilde{r}_{jt} \leq 0.15$, $\ln(1+\tilde{r}_{jt}) \approx \tilde{r}_{jt}$, so that approximately,

$$\tilde{r}_{jt} \approx \mu_j + \tilde{e}_{jt}, \tag{3}$$

and $\mu_j = E(\tilde{r}_{jt}|I_{t-1})$. The assumed time-invariant mean and the assumptions of (1) on $\tilde{e}_{jt}$ imply that autocovariances of $\tilde{e}_{jt}$ and $\tilde{r}_{jt}$ are zero, a property displayed by stock returns [see Cootner (1964)].[1]

If N individual stocks are aggregated into an arithmetic index in which each stock has an equal weight, $X_{jt} = 1/N$, we obtain

$$\sum_{j=1}^{N} X_{jt}\tilde{r}_{jt} = \sum_{j=1}^{N} X_{jt}\mu_{jt} + \sum_{j=1}^{N} X_{jt}\tilde{e}_{jt}, \tag{4}$$

or

$$\tilde{R}_t = \mu + \tilde{e}_t, \tag{5}$$

[1] If $E(\tilde{r}_{jt}|I_{t-1})$ is not time stationary, then the variable $\tilde{z}_{jt} = \tilde{r}_{jt} - E(\tilde{r}_{jt}|I_{t-1}) = \tilde{e}_{jt}$ will have an unconditional expectation of zero *so long as* the assumptions of (1) hold with respect to $\tilde{e}_{jt}$. In this case, the variable $\tilde{z}_{jt}$ will display zero autocovariances, but $\tilde{r}_{jt}$ will not necessarily have zero autocovariances. See Fama (1970) for a discussion of this point.

where each weighted sum is denoted by its market equivalent. The multiplicative random walk is therefore applicable in principle to stock indexes as well as individual stocks.[2] Officer's (1975, p. 35) analysis shows that seasonality is more likely to be detected in an index of shares than in individual shares. For this reason, we restrict the tests in this paper to a market index.

In models (3) and (5), the random variables $\tilde{e}$ and $\tilde{r}$ seem well-described by a symmetric distribution lacking finite second and higher moments and belonging to the Stable Paretian family of distributions with characteristic exponent less than two.[3] Due to controversy over the exact nature of the distribution, we employ both non-parametric tests which assume only that the distributions are continuous and parametric tests which assume normal distributions with finite moments. For the most part, we use terms applicable to Stable distributions and refer to *location* and *scale* parameters rather than the more common terms, mean and variance.

Departures from model (5) can occur in many ways. A simple seasonal alternative to (5) of some interest assumes that $\tilde{e}_t$'s are independently distributed random variables whose distributions differ only in location parameter by season or month. Letting subscript m denote the month of the year this model is

$$\tilde{R}_{tm} = \mu + \tilde{e}_{tm}. \tag{6}$$

Letting $E(\tilde{e}_{tm}) = \lambda_m$, this can be written

$$\tilde{R}_{tm} = \mu + \lambda_m + \tilde{e}_t, \tag{7}$$

where $\tilde{e}_t$ is again independent and identically distributed with mean zero. In the modified model, expected rates of return depend upon the month or season of the year and autocovariances of rates of return are non-zero.[4] Assuming that model (5) is the true model we test the null hypothesis that expected rates of return conditional on month of the year are equal, that is,

$$H_0 : E(\tilde{R}_1) = E(\tilde{R}_2) = \ldots = E(\tilde{R}_{12}) = \mu. \tag{8}$$

We also examine the autocorrelation function of stock returns to verify the implication of (5) that serial covariances are zero.

---

[2]Due, however, to the fact that rates of return on many securities may not be measured simultaneously at time t, it is usually observed that indexes show larger first-order autocorrelations than do the individual securities which compose them. This spurious effect causes no difficulty in the tests undertaken below.

[3]For evidence that stock return distributions are Stable Paretian, see, for example, Mandelbrot (1963, 1967), Fama (1965), Fama and Roll (1968, 1971). Some other viewpoints may be found in Press (1967), Teichmoller (1971), Officer (1972), Barnea and Downes (1973), Blattberg and Gonedes (1974), Hsu, Miller and Wichern (1974).

[4]Officer (1975, p. 31) presents model (6) and discusses it.

The error terms, $\tilde{e}_{tm}$, in (6) may differ in scale as well as location and differences in characteristic exponent by month are also possible. We therefore test the following hypothesis:

$$H_0 : d_1 = d_2 = \ldots = d_{12} = d, \tag{9}$$

that dispersion parameters, d_i, of stock return distributions do not differ by month. We also examine the characteristic exponent, α, of each return distribution by month.

3. Previous studies

Although statistical tests of location (central tendency) and scale (dispersion) parameters of stock return distributions by month are absent from the literature, previous studies do provide evidence on seasonality by applying (I) spectral analysis [Granger and Morgenstern (1963, 1970)], (II) Bureau of the Census X-11 procedures [Shiskin (1967) and Bonin and Moses (1974)], and (III) the time series methods of Box and Jenkins [Officer (1975)].[5] Other studies provide further evidence but lack statistical tests [Wachtel (1942) and Zinbarg (1964)].

Using aggregate monthly price data from 1875–1956, Granger and Morgenstern (1970, p. 130) concluded that spectral analysis 'gave no evidence of a seasonal (12-month) peak in the spectra although small peaks corresponding to seasonal harmonics (4, 3, 2.4 months) were quite frequently observed'. This conclusion is in basic agreement with the evidence from the autocorrelation function of returns presented below especially in view of (i) the fact that Granger and Morgenstern first removed a trend in price with moving averages, a procedure which makes implicit assumptions about the stochastic process and can lead to non-comparability with the autocorrelation function obtained from data on returns; and (ii) the difficulties in estimating a spectrum and establishing significance tests for individual peaks.[6]

Bonin and Moses look for seasonality in the 30 individual Dow–Jones Industrial stocks using monthly price data adjusted for capital changes over the period 1962–1971. Using the Census X-11 program, they remove price trends via moving average procedures and adjustment of extreme values. Due to these initial procedures, the analysis of variance tests performed on the residual variation must be interpreted with caution. Aware of this, the authors apply several other criteria – comparisons with other time series and tests on a

---

[5]See Box and Jenkins (1970). Note that spectral analysis and Box–Jenkins methods should reach the same conclusions since both employ the autocorrelation function as a basic descriptive device. The Census X-11 procedures might reach different conclusions since (unlike Box–Jenkins procedures) they impose strong a priori assumptions about the stochastic process generating the time series.

[6]Their time period also includes, as we see below, a sub-period during which the dispersion of the generating process noticeably increased, 1929–1940.

holdout period – before accepting seasonality. They conclude that 7 of the stocks display significant and persistent seasonal patterns.

Officer studies aggregate Australian stock returns over 1958–1970 and develops a mixed autoregressive and moving average linear stochastic model which includes seasonal elements. He then shows that forecast errors using the seasonal model are lower in a holdout period than forecast errors using a simple random walk model. The predictive test is a helpful complement to tests of significance for individual autocorrelations since these are based on the assumption of normal distributions, not strictly true for stock returns. The correspondence of the prediction test and the correlation tests may indicate that it is useful to examine sample statistics on the usual normal distribution assumptions.

In contrast with Granger and Morgenstern, Officer finds a 9-month, 6-month and lesser 12-month seasonal in the autocorrelation function. Below we briefly compare the autocorrelation function for the United States with Officer's Australian and Granger and Morgenstern's U.S. results; however, our main concern is the direct examination of stock return distributions by month.

In other less rigorous studies of seasonality, Zinbarg notes the tendency of advances to outnumber declines in the months of January and July from 1918–1962 and, similarly, Wachtel finds a marked tendency for January price advances in the overlapping period, 1927–1942. In addition, Wachtel formulates an explanation based on year-end tax selling.

4. Statistical tests

4.1. The data

We examine aggregate rates of return on the New York Stock Exchange for the period January, 1904 through December, 1974. Rates of return from 1904–1909 are computed from the aggregate Cowles Commission (1938) price indexes. From 1910–1925 they are derived from price relatives of Standard & Poor's aggregate index, omitting 1914 during which the Exchange was closed for four months. From 1926–1974 the data are equally-weighted arithmetic rates of return inclusive of dividends and adjusted for capital changes for all common stocks on the New York Stock Exchange, computed from Standard & Poor's 1975 version of the CRSP file.[7] For all statistical tests reported below, we use the natural logarithm of 1 plus the rate of return $[\ln(1 + R_{tm})]$.

Visual inspection of the monthly rates of return since 1904 shows that returns seem to have been generated by a stochastic process that is mean stationary (see fig. 1). The mean rate of return of the (unlogged) time series is 0.009 per month. However, the dispersion increases noticeably during the Great Depression,

---

[7]All tests were also carried out on Fisher's (1966) Investment Performance Index substituted for the years 1926–70 with essentially the same results.

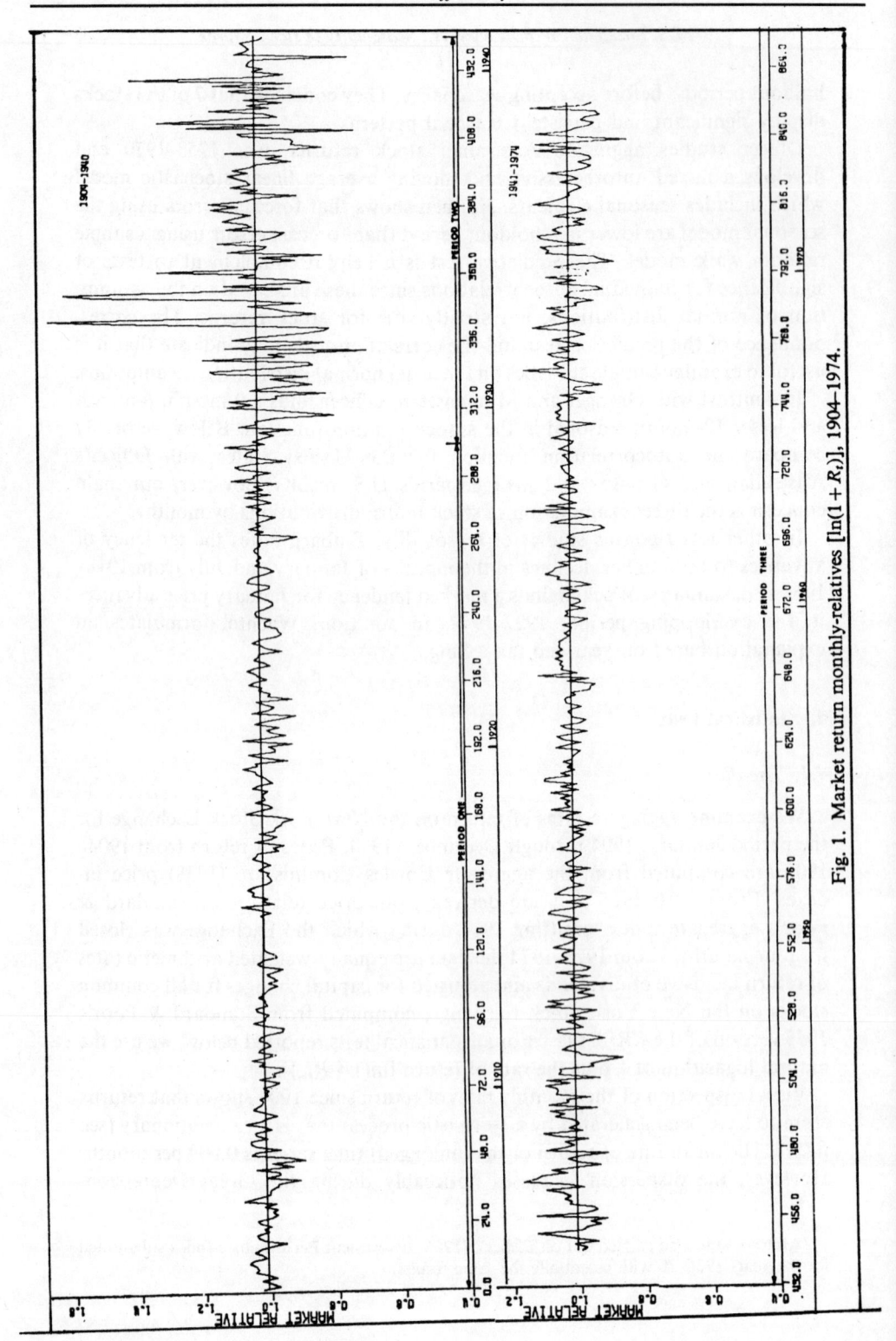

Fig. 1. Market return monthly-relatives [$\ln(1+R_t)$], 1904–1974.

implying drawings from a different distribution. The period of high variability is neatly bracketed by two months October, 1929 and May, 1940 which lie more than 3 standard deviations from the mean. Outside this time period, no observations lie more than 3 standard deviations from the mean. Since all the statistical tests could be influenced by observations during this period, we analyze the time series over 4 time periods: 1904–1928 (months 1–288); 1929–1940 (months 289–432); 1941–1974 (months 433–840); and 1904–1928 *combined* with 1941–1974 (months 1–288 and months 433–840). We denote these periods 1 through 4 respectively. For completeness, statistics are also computed for the entire time period, 1904–1974, denoted period 5.

4.2. Autocorrelation function

The autocorrelation function, which consists of serial correlations at various lags, provides a starting point to compare the U.S. data to that of the Australian market and to the spectral analysis of Granger and Morgenstern of U.S. data. For this comparison, use of raw rates of return or natural logarithms of 1 plus the rate of return give essentially identical results. The autocorrelation functions in the natural logarithm form for all 5 periods and Officer's time period are presented in fig. 2. Two standard errors of the estimated autocorrelation coefficients [see Box and Jenkins (1970, p. 34)] are shown by the horizontal lines on either side of each function.

The significance levels of individual lags in the autocorrelation function must be interpreted with some caution due to the lack of strict normality. Given this warning, we see that sample autocorrelations are significant at lag 1 for all periods, an artifact (as noted in footnote 2) of index measurement which, of course, has nothing to do with seasonality. Generally, the sample autocorrelations are quite small with very few greater than two standard deviations from zero. The position of significant lags depends to some extent on the time period studied. In period 1, the first homogeneous subperiod (1904–1928), lags 1 and 6 are significant. Over period 3 (1941–1974), *no* autocorrelations (other than at lag 1) are more than two standard deviations from zero, indicating a random walk model with no (multiplicative) seasonal effects. Autocorrelations at lags 3, 9 and 12 are unimportant in both periods. In combined period 4, (1904–1928 and 1941–1974), the data have significant autocorrelations at lags 4 and 6 but lags 3, 9 and 12 remain unimportant.[8] These results are in broad agreement with those of Granger and Morgenstern, namely, a flat function with a tendency to peaks at lags of 4 months and less. However we also find signs of a 6 month seasonal. Certaintly, longer seasonals of 9 or 12 months seem absent.

Comparing the U.S. and Australian sample autocorrelations over the identical

---

[8]The autocorrelation function of the time series over the entire period is not emphasized due to the nonhomogeneity of the series inclusive of 1929–40. For those who are curious, lags 1, 3, and 9 are significant with logged data; in addition, lag 10 is significant with unlogged data.

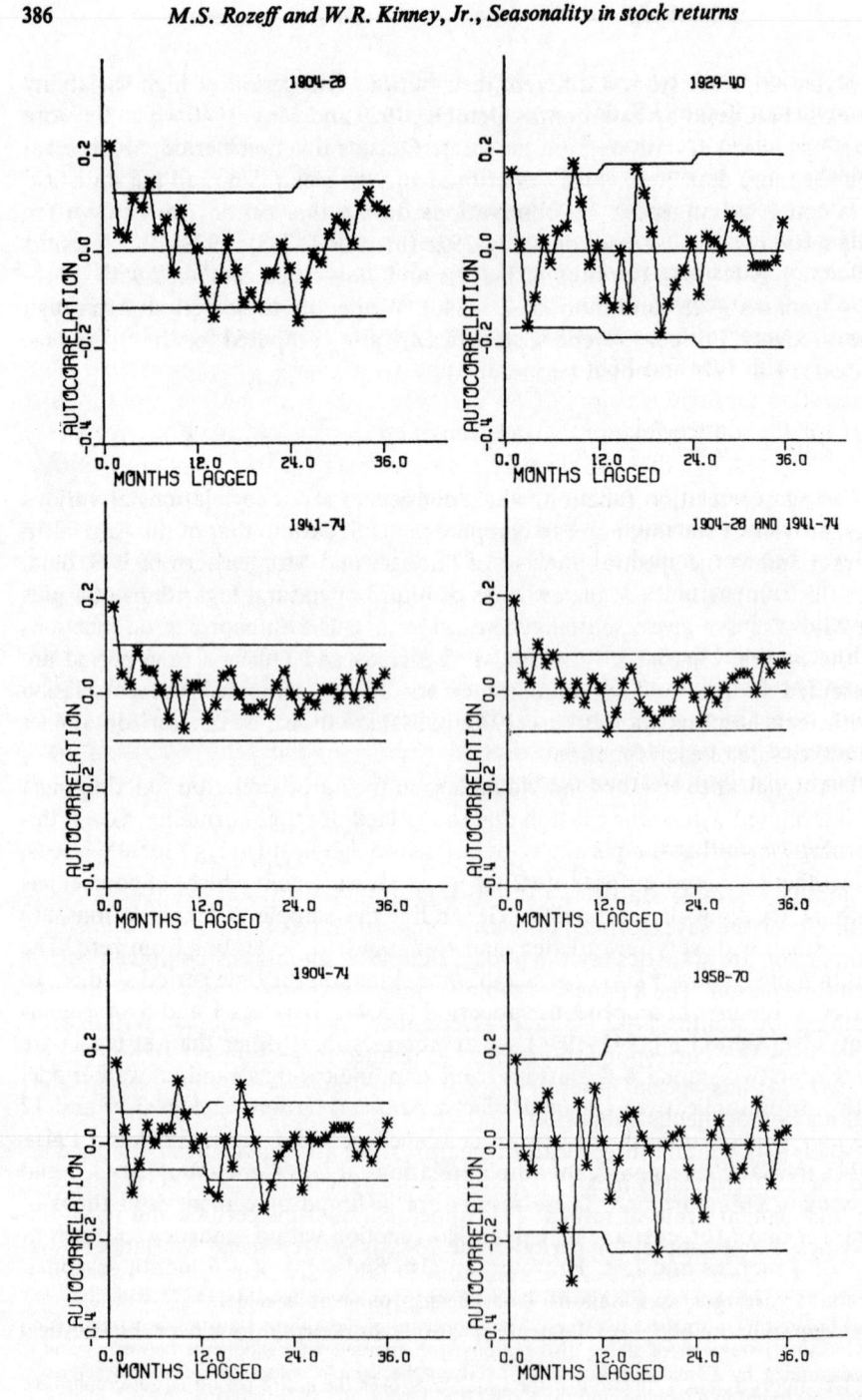

Fig. 2. Autocorrelation function for monthly market return relative for various periods. Solid horizontal lines indicate two standard errors of the estimated autocorrelation coefficients.

time period used by Officer (2/1958–6/1970), we find that lags 6 and 9 are unimportant in the U.S. data in contrast to the Australian data, while lag 8 with a sample autocorrelation of -0.28 shows up significant in the U.S. data. Such a finding may be due to sampling error.

The concept of seasonality implied by significant lagged autocorrelations differs from that expressed by our hypotheses presented in (8) and (9). To see the difference, consider, for example, a six-month seasonal which appears as a significant autocorrelation at lag 6. This seasonal means that on average each month's observation is linked or related to that of the sixth preceding month, January with July and February with August and so on. Since the sample autocorrelation for lag 6 is computed or averaged over all six pairs of months, note that for the autocorrelation between observations six months apart to appear significant requires that the effect be strong enough for those pairs for which it occurs so as not to be hidden by its possible absence in other pairs. The sample autocorrelation function is best at uncovering systematic homogeneous cyclicalities between months but might fail to reveal peculiarities of individual months (or even pairs, triples, etc. of months) if the remaining months display no relationship.

Furthermore, the sample autocorrelation function provides no direct evidence about the distributions of stock returns by month. In the next several subsections, we examine stock return distributions by month directly, The tests can be interpreted as tests for seasonality in the sense that some month(s) have different distributions than other months.

4.3. Sample statistics

Summary sample statistics of the stock return distributions calculated *by month*, over the several time periods are presented in Table 1. Also included for comparison are statistics for the pooled sample of all months combined within each time period. The 8 panels of table 1 contain 8 sample statistics of interest, arranged by months 1–12 (January–December) and 'all' months. Within each panel, lines 1–5 correspond to periods 1–5 defined in section 4.1 above. Period 3 (1941–74) has special interest since it is the longest and most recent contiguous homogeneous subperiod.

Panels a – c contain three location measures: the arithmetic mean, the median and the 75% truncated mean.[9] The most consistent feature of these statistics is the high January rate of return. This appears in all time periods and in all the statistics. For example, for period 3 the 75% truncated mean for January was

[9]The 75% truncated sample mean is the arithmetic average of the middle 75% of the observations ordered from smallest to largest. The properties of these three statistics as estimators of the location parameter of stable distributions with characteristic exponents between 1 and 2 are examined by Fama and Roll (1968). Given the sample values of α (the characteristic exponent) found in 4.6 below and the Fama–Roll results, the 75% truncated mean is probably the most efficient location estimator.

Table 1
Summary descriptive statistics for returns by month.

Period		1	2	3	4	5	6	7	8	9	10	11	12	all
Location measures														
a. Mean	1	0.0130	−0.0097	0.0017	0.0122	0.0033	−0.0058	0.0090	0.0102	0.0101	0.0042	0.0127	0.0010	0.0052
	2	0.0663	0.0191	−0.0528	0.0080	−0.0331	0.0403	0.0497	0.0487	−0.0510	−0.0510	−0.0123	−0.0314	0.0019
	3	0.0391	0.0056	0.0142	0.0016	0.0017	−0.0063	0.0153	0.0056	0.0002	0.0085	0.0100	0.0201	0.0096
	4	0.0283	−0.0008	0.0090	0.0060	0.0024	−0.0061	0.0127	0.0075	0.0043	0.0067	0.0111	0.0122	0.0078
	5	0.0348	0.0026	−0.0016	0.0063	−0.0037	0.0018	0.0190	0.0146	0.0052	0.0007	0.0071	0.0047	0.0068
b. Median	1	0.0136	−0.0135	0.0010	−0.0011	−0.0031	0.0021	0.0071	0.0227	0.0068	0.0058	0.0228	0.0021	0.0062
	2	0.0421	0.0250	−0.0328	0.0014	−0.0729	0.0399	0.0383	0.0220	−0.0436	−0.0212	0.0369	−0.0175	0.0074
	3	0.0393	0.0115	0.0127	0.0106	0.0080	−0.0068	0.0115	0.0057	−0.0112	0.0014	0.0147	0.0210	0.0138
	4	0.0224	0.0038	0.0127	0.0078	0.0076	0.0013	0.0115	0.0209	0.0051	0.0058	0.0207	0.0151	0.0107
	5	0.0247	0.0085	0.0048	0.0054	0.0036	0.0035	0.0135	0.0220	0.0010	0.0039	0.0107	0.0149	0.0107
c. Trunc. mean	1	0.0133	−0.0099	0.0051	0.0090	0.0035	−0.0016	0.0101	0.0150	0.0125	0.0081	0.0131	0.0033	0.0070
	2	0.0598	0.0212	−0.0395	−0.0114	−0.0558	−0.0424	0.0442	0.0194	−0.0569	−0.0235	−0.0153	−0.0227	−0.0014
	3	0.0379	0.0055	0.0133	0.0046	0.0046	−0.0054	0.0158	0.0111	0.0021	0.0069	0.0153	0.0217	0.0107
	4	0.0247	−0.0008	0.0097	0.0081	0.0045	−0.0039	0.0131	0.0126	0.0068	0.0073	0.0145	0.0124	0.0091
	5	0.0297	0.0030	0.0063	0.0053	−0.0012	−0.0011	0.0169	0.0117	0.0021	0.0058	0.0099	0.0092	0.0082
Scale measures														
d. Std. dev.	1	0.0238	0.0347	0.0423	0.0321	0.0374	0.0332	0.0272	0.0387	0.0267	0.0397	0.0486	0.0338	0.0355
	2	0.0931	0.0654	0.1191	0.1696	0.1955	0.1316	0.1398	0.1577	0.1719	0.1192	0.0930	0.0816	0.1348
	3	0.0523	0.0427	0.0379	0.0516	0.0484	0.0467	0.0498	0.0431	0.0518	0.0418	0.0602	0.0452	0.0486
	4	0.0445	0.0400	0.0399	0.0445	0.0438	0.0413	0.0418	0.0410	0.0432	0.0406	0.0552	0.0416	0.0473
	5	0.0568	0.0454	0.0643	0.0789	0.0887	0.0669	0.0690	0.0748	0.0818	0.0617	0.0631	0.0526	0.0685
e. M.A.D.	1	0.0201	0.0272	0.0326	0.0268	0.0322	0.0267	0.0214	0.0296	0.0207	0.0289	0.0391	0.0261	0.0280
	2	0.0686	0.0409	0.0884	0.1160	0.1288	0.0956	0.0968	0.0978	0.1188	0.0997	0.0778	0.0624	0.0960
	3	0.0419	0.0320	0.0304	0.0411	0.0391	0.0372	0.0414	0.0337	0.0417	0.0324	0.0421	0.0339	0.0380
	4	0.0343	0.0315	0.0314	0.0342	0.0362	0.0329	0.0332	0.0323	0.0334	0.0309	0.0409	0.0316	0.0339
	5	0.0414	0.0343	0.0413	0.0482	0.0541	0.0443	0.0459	0.0419	0.0491	0.0430	0.0485	0.0373	0.0444
f. Statistic č	1	0.0201	0.0246	0.0295	0.0250	0.0357	0.0296	0.0191	0.0279	0.0193	0.0222	0.0364	0.0307	0.0246
	2	0.0635	0.0152	0.0784	0.0849	0.0768	0.0873	0.1010	0.0476	0.0917	0.0979	0.0510	0.0734	0.0731
	3	0.0437	0.0279	0.0251	0.0411	0.0338	0.0338	0.0438	0.0266	0.0403	0.0247	0.0310	0.0277	0.0308
	4	0.0273	0.0244	0.0297	0.0289	0.0346	0.0305	0.0294	0.0234	0.0293	0.0217	0.0294	0.0234	0.0277
	5	0.0290	0.0291	0.0298	0.0338	0.0419	0.0319	0.0345	0.0296	0.0328	0.0321	0.0394	0.0274	0.0305
Higher moments														
g. Skewness	1	−0.0000	−0.0000	−0.0015	0.0007	−0.0001	−0.0009	−0.0002	−0.0012	−0.0006	−0.0017	−0.0002	−0.0009	−0.0006
	2	0.0052	−0.0021	−0.0152	0.0297	−0.0472	−0.0008	0.0060	0.0503	0.0089	−0.0039	0.0032	−0.0068	0.0113
	3	0.0005	0.0005	0.0004	−0.0014	−0.0010	−0.0002	−0.0001	−0.0016	−0.0011	0.0007	−0.0038	−0.0004	−0.0006
	4	0.0013	0.0004	−0.0005	−0.0010	−0.0007	−0.0002	−0.0001	−0.0006	−0.0007	0.0006	−0.0025	−0.0003	−0.0005
	5	0.0040	0.0003	−0.0098	0.0100	0.0105	0.0039	0.0058	0.0213	−0.0051	−0.0042	−0.0019	−0.0036	0.0029
h. Kurtosis	1	−1.1180	−0.4543	0.5994	−0.6433	−1.2009	−0.2389	−0.5552	−0.1418	0.2650	1.3774	−0.5364	0.5534	0.5299
	2	0.0958	0.8796	0.4122	0.4984	1.6019	−0.6185	0.3889	3.4558	0.4786	1.2582	−1.4327	−0.3025	2.3956
	3	−0.6002	0.5485	−0.2128	0.2144	−0.6171	−0.4674	−0.8126	0.0651	0.1870	−0.0344	2.0174	−0.2251	0.6269
	4	0.2616	0.5611	0.6525	0.9156	−0.5401	−0.1462	−0.2309	0.1211	1.1822	0.6865	1.7488	−0.1783	0.8904
	5	3.2340	1.3334	9.5048	9.3797	12.1698	4.1685	7.9625	23.9807	8.4130	2.8396	3.3562	3.3301	11.1597

0.0379 (panel c, line 3), which is nearly 3/4 again as large as the next highest return, December, at 0.0217. Panels d–f contain three scale measures: standard deviation, mean absolute deviation and the statistic $\hat{c}$, defined as (72nd fractile − 28th fractile)/2(0.827), the Fama–Roll (1971) dispersion measure.[10] For these scale measures, the differences among months do not seem to be as pronounced or consistent as for the location measures; nevertheless they are substantial. Note, for example, that for statistic $\hat{c}$, regarded as the most stable dispersion measure (panel f), for period 3 the statistics span 0.0247 to 0.0438. Also note that the sample standard deviations by month are not wildly erratic in comparison with the order statistic $\hat{c}$. Again referring to period 3, the *orderings* of months from high dispersion to low which are achieved by $\hat{c}$ and by standard deviation are highly correlated: the Spearman's rho is 0.75. This feature of the data is particularly important if we are to have confidence in the parametric analysis of variance tests which rely on the standard deviation as a dispersion measure.

Finally, panels g and h measure sample skewness and kurtosis.[11] No departures from symmetry are evident as indicated by the skewness measures close to zero. In panel h positive entries imply positive kurtosis (usually due to a peaked center and fat tails). Note that for the pooled samples in the last column, where sample size is at least 144, kurtosis is always positive as others have found by inspecting the density function. For individual months, a fair number of negative statistics appear, usually when the sample size is 50 or less. This behavior of sample kurtosis drawn from non-normal distributions parallels Mandelbrot's (1967) finding for samples of size fifty drawn from daily spot prices of cotton, 1900–1905.[12]

In the next two subsections the location and scale hypotheses [eqs.(8) and (9)], are tested using both non-parametric and parametric tests. We begin with the non-parametric tests since they require less restrictive distributional assumptions. Parametric tests follow for completeness and to allow testing of some relevant subhypotheses.

4.4. Non-parametric tests

The Kruskal–Wallis test statistic, fully described in Conover (1971, p. 157), is a test which uses 'ranks' and requires no distributional assumptions other than that the random variables are continuous and measurable on an ordinal scale. The Kruskal–Wallis test statistic is used to test the hypothesis that all 12 of the populations from which the 12 samples are drawn have identical popula-

---

[10] For the α values of the samples, $\hat{c}$ is probably the most efficient scale estimator.

[11] Let x_i denote the ith sample value, $\bar{x}$ the sample mean of n observations and $M_k = \Sigma_{i=1}^{n}(x_i - \bar{x})^k/n$. Then sample skewness is $M_3/(M_2\sqrt{M_2})$, and sample kurtosis is $(M_4/M_2^2) - 3$.

[12] Geary's kurtosis measure, the ratio of the mean absolute deviation to the standard deviation is very poorly behaved and usually indicates negative kurtosis even in large samples.

tion distributions.[13] The test statistic is approximately distributed as chi-square with 11 degrees of freedom and a one-tailed rejection region is appropriate.[14]

The results are shown in table 2 in panel a. For period 3 the null hypothesis can be rejected at the 10% level; in period 4, the combined period, the hypothesis can be rejected at the 5% level. Given the conservative nature of the test,

Table 2
Summary non-parametric test statistics for returns by month.

a. *All months combined*

Period	Kruskal–Wallis statistic	Siegel–Tukey statistic
1. 1904–28	11.46	20.69[b]
2. 1929–40	17.51[a]	16.72
3. 1941–74	18.04[a]	17.30[a]
4. 1904–28 and 1941–70	21.30[b]	13.71
5. 1904–74	23.19[b]	13.73

b. *Pairwise comparisons*

Probability level	Period	Location	Dispersion
0.99	3. 1941–74	None	None
	4. 1904–28 and 1941–74	Jan. > June	None
0.95	3. 1941–74	Jan. > June	None
	4. 1904–28 and 1941–74	Jan. > June, Feb.	None
0.90	3. 1941–74	Jan. > all except Dec. Dec. > June	Feb. < Jan., July, Sept., Nov., Dec.
	4. 1904–28 and 1941–74	Jan. > all except July, Nov., Dec. July > Feb., June Nov. > Feb., June Dec. > Feb., June	None

[a]Significant at the 0.90 level.
[b]Significant at the 0.95 level.

this is rather convincing evidence for seasonality in stock rates of return, in that at least one of the population distributions from which the samples are drawn

[13]Since the Kruskal–Wallis statistic is designed to be sensitive to differences in population means, the test may more loosely be regarded as testing the hypothesis that all the distributions have identical means.

[14]Kruskal and Wallis found that for 10% significance levels or less, the *true* significance level is *smaller* than that given with the chi-square distribution [see Conover (1971)]. In other words, the chi-square gives a conservative hypothesis test. This feature of the test is consistent with the higher significance levels generally found in the parametric tests.

differs from some of the rest in location. In contrast, the autocorrelation function gave no signs of seasonality in period 3.

In order to find the months that are responsible for the result, we conduct multiple sequential pairwise comparisons among months using the rank sums for each month and investigating the differences in rank sums. The sequential procedure is due to Hartley (1955); Wilcoxon and Wilcox (1964) provide the standard deviation of rank sum totals required in the test. Note that the sequential nature of the test protects against logical contradictions that arise in less powerful methods of making pairwise comparisons when many treatments are being considered.

Restricting attention to the longer homogeneous periods 3 and 4, we find that January has a significantly greater mean rank than June at the 1% level in period 4 and at the 5% level in period 3. At the 10% level, other differences are detectable. For example, in period 4 January has a greater mean rank than all other months except November, July and December which are the months with the highest rank totals (and 75% truncated means) after January. The sequential procedure then tests these months against the remaining months. November, July and December all have significantly greater mean ranks (at the 10% level) than February and June.

Referring back to the statistics in table 1, we see that the rank tests mirror the differences in location statistics. For example, in panel c, line 4, January has the highest truncated mean of 0.0247 while June and February have the lowest means of -0.0039 and -0.0008, respectively. By the usual interpretation of significance levels differences at the 10% level would be considered as 'weak', but in numerical terms they are quite large. December's mean monthly rate of return in period 4 of 0.0124 (about 15% on an annual basis) compares for example to February's 0% annual return. Since the 75% truncated mean eliminates extreme observations and the non-parametric tests do not give extra weight to extreme observations, it is difficult to accept the view that these differences are merely the result of sampling error and not the result of factors giving rise to seasonal differences.

For a distribution-free test of differences in scale, we use the Siegel–Tukey statistic [see Conover (1971, p. 229)], a rank test designed to detect differences in dispersion. The test requires that the populations be aligned according to location; lacking knowledge of the true population location, the usual procedure is to adjust the samples by a sample measure of location such as mean or median, adjusting to the sample in the middle. The location measure we use to make the adjustment is the 75% truncated mean. The chi-square table is again appropriate. Referring to column 3 of table 2, we see that over 1941–1974, the statistic is just significant at the 10% level; it is also significant in period 1. In combined period 4, however, it is not significant, being smaller in contrast with the larger Kruskal–Wallis statistic. This result is consistent with the relatively lower heterogeneity in scale measures compared to location measures noted above.

Taking the larger sample size as the more reliable, it appears that differences in scale among months are at best rather weak. These results are consistent with Bartlett's (parametric) Homogeneity of Variances tests reported in the next section.

As a possible explanation for seasonality in the Australian stock index, Officer suggests (1975, p. 47) that months with high returns may also have a higher market factor risk and vice versa, but finds no evidence for this hypothesis. To examine this hypothesis we make sequential pairwise comparisons of dispersion differences despite the weak significance of such differences when all months are considered together. For period 4 there are no differences that are statistically significant even at the 10% level. For period 3 which has a Siegel–Tukey statistic that is significant at the 10% level, we find that dispersion in February is significantly less than in January, July, September, November and December. This may be partial verification of Officer's hypothesis since February is a low return month and January, July, November and December are high return months. On the other hand, September (a high dispersion month) is also a *low* return month and June (a low return month) does not have low dispersion.

Consider now the non-parametric statistics for Officer's Australian data. Using his Dex126 over 1959–1970, the Kruskal–Wallis statistic is 33.67 and the Siegel–Tukey statistic is 40.10, indicating that at least one monthly population distribution likely differs from the rest in location and similarly for scale. The highly significant scale difference is in contrast to the U.S. data. The strength of seasonal effects also is much more clearly evident in the Australian index.

The pairwise comparisons of means show that July exceeds March and September (5% level) and January exceeds March. The pairwise scale comparisons show that December has greater dispersion than all other months in the year excepting October and November. It is of considerable interest that in the U.S. data, January and July are also relatively high return months. Over 1941–1974 for example, January is highest and July third highest, measured by the truncated mean. On the other hand, the extraordinary variability of December returns in the Australian data finds no parallel in the U.S. data

In summary, seasonality in the U.S. aggregate market data is a statistically significant phenomenon that is clearly observable when the data are examined by month. At least one distribution is different from the rest as shown by the Kruskal–Wallis test. The pairwise tests allow the inference that January has this distribution and examination of the data indicates that January's relatively high mean rate of return is likely the source of the distributional difference.

4.5. Parametric tests

Initially the distribution test results of Fama (1965) and Fama and Roll (1968, 1971) led to skepticism concerning the usefulness of parametric statistics such as mean and standard deviation in the context of distributions with characteristic exponent less than two. Evidence which has since accumulated has shown among other things that the standard deviation as a scale measure seems well-behaved and that a representation by a normal distribution with finite variance may be adequate in many instances [see Officer (1971) and Hsu, Miller and Wichern (1974)]. In addition, we have seen that Officer's inferences (1975) from the autocorrelation function which are based on the assumption of normality are correct inferences in a holdout time period. Finally we have pointed out in examining the raw data that the various scale and location measures do seem to correspond closely with each other. For all these reasons, and the generally recognized robustness of the analysis of variance model, it seems appropriate to consider hypothesis tests based on parametric statistics.

To test the hypothesis of equal means, analysis of variance techniques in conjunction with Bartlett's test for homogeneity of variances are applied. Each month is considered as a separate 'treatment' level and tests are conducted for each of the five time periods. Using Bartlett's (1937) test, we find that homogeneity of variances can be rejected for periods 1, 2 and 5 (see table 3, panel a). We therefore report the analysis of variance tests only for the remaining periods 3 and 4. The linear model assumed is [see eq. (7)]

$$\ln(1+\tilde{R}_{tm}) = \mu + \lambda_m + \tilde{e}_{tm}. \tag{10}$$

The analysis of variance results are given in panel b of table 3. The hypothesis that the mean monthly rates of return are equal over all months can be rejected at above the 0.975 level for each period, confirming the results of the non-parametric tests. We again consider which month(s) seem to be significantly different from the rest. Such a determination may allow further understanding of the phenomenon for the eventual construction and testing of theories which explain the seasonality as well as the incorporation of such knowledge in decision models.

Two comparisons or linear contrasts are considered in panel c. These are

$$C_1: 11\lambda_1 - (\lambda_2 + \lambda_3 + \ldots + \lambda_{12}), \tag{11}$$

$$C_2: (\lambda_4 + \lambda_5 + \lambda_6) - (\lambda_{10} + \lambda_{11} + \lambda_{12}). \tag{12}$$

There are strong a priori reasons to consider C_1: (1) the high return for January (month 1), is a phenomenon which others have noted [see Wachtel (1942) and Zinbarg (1964)]; (2) January marks the beginning and ending of several potentially important financial and informational events. As examples of the latter, January is the start of the tax year for investors, the beginning of the tax and accounting years for most firms[15] and the period during which

[15]For example 59.8% of the COMPUSTAT firms had accounting year closings in December for 1974.

preliminary (and in many cases final) announcements of the previous calendar (fiscal) year's accounting earnings are made. It is possible that seasonality is in some way associated with these accounting events.

Contrast C_2, on the other hand, is derived from observation of the data. The contiguous months of April, May and June seem to have below average returns while six months later the contiguous months of October, November and

Table 3
Summary parametric test statistics for returns by month.

a. *Bartlett's test for homogeneity of variances*

	1904–28	1929–40	1941–74	1904–28 & 1941–74	1904–74
Corrected χ^2	20.67[a]	20.48[b]	11.46	10.92	53.49[b]

b. *Analysis of variance*

Source of variation	df	Sum of squares	Mean square	F
1941–74				
Month	11	0.052210	0.004746	2.06330
Residual	396	0.910956	0.002300	
Corrected total	407	0.963166	0.002366	
1904–28 & 1941–74				
Month	11	0.045733	0.004157	2.21604
Residual	684	1.283271	0.001876	
Corrected total	695	1.329004	0.001912	

c. *Contrasts*

C_1: 1904–28 & 1941–74: $F = 14.18$[b]
 1941–74: $F = 13.99$[b]
C_2: 1904–28 & 1941–74: $F = 3.99$[a]
 1941–74: $F = 4.27$[a]

[a]Significant at the 0.95 level.
[b]Significant at the 0.99 level.

December have above average returns. In addition, each of these groups of months is followed by a month that has above average returns, July and January respectively.

To test whether a contrast is equal to zero, the appropriate test statistic [Winer (1962, p. 69)] is

$$F = \left(\sum_{i=1}^{12} c_i T_i \right)^2 \bigg/ \left(n \left(\sum_{i=1}^{12} c_i \right) MS \right),$$

where c_i is the contrast coefficient for level i, n is the number of observations per month ($n = 34$ for period 3), $T_i = n\lambda_i$ and MS is the within-treatments mean square. The statistic is compared to a theoretical $F_{\alpha,1,11n}$ value. In panel c the returns for January are shown to be significantly greater than those for the rest of the year on average and the low Spring returns are significantly smaller than the high Fall returns.

These parametric analysis of variance tests are consistent with the non-parametric tests in indicating that monthly distributional differences may be attributed to location rather than scale parameters. Again it appears that January is the responsible month. In addition, contrast C_2 gives statistical evidence of a systematic difference between second-quarter and fourth-quarter months, a difference also clearly observable in the descriptive sample statistics.

4.6. Characteristic exponents

Symmetric stable distributions are described by three parameters and two have been examined: the scale and location parameters. The third parameter, denoted by α, is the characteristic exponent. Individual stock return distributions usually have α's less than 2. In line with interest in seasonality, we will examine, to the extent possible, the hypothesis that the stock return index distributions by month have the same α's. Lacking firm knowledge of the sampling distribution of α, our conclusions are tentative.

Estimates for α are computed using the order statistic technique described by Fama and Roll (1971, p. 333) in combination with table 2 of their earlier (1968) paper. As they did, we use the 96th fractile in estimating α. When the order statistic required by the fractile is not integral, the next lower integer is consistently used, that is we truncate rather than round or interpolate. The results for the three homogeneous periods 1, 3 and 4 are shown in table 4. Fama and Roll also present Monte Carlo sampling distributions of α for sample sizes of 24, 49, and 74. We use these for indications of significant differences.

Our period 1 with sample size 24 by coincidence is represented in their choice of sample size. Under the null hypothesis that α is 1.5, the standard error is 0.367. It is 0.309 for $\alpha = 1.9$, and 0.25 for $\alpha = 2.0$. With the population parameter unknown, the α value for all months combined within a subperiod is used as a benchmark. For period 1 this value is 1.96. The α values estimated for individual months are quite close to 1.96 with the exception of October's 1.42 which is approximately two standard deviations away. Thus for period 1 there is no strong indication that the monthly stock return distributions have different α's.

In period 3 the sample size is 34, and in period 4 it is 58. For these sample sizes the Fama–Roll results show that a standard error of 0.30 is conservative, that is, an upper bound. Under the hypothesis that the pooled population values of α are 1.62 and 1.7 respectively in periods 3 and 4, all values of α

estimated for individual monthly samples lie well within two standard deviations or 0.60. We conclude that the evidence is consistent with the hypothesis that stock return distributions (in aggregate form) by month have the same characteristic exponents.

5. Implications of seasonality

5.1. Capital market efficiency

The fact that expected returns vary by month is not necessarily inconsistent with market efficiency. We have demonstrated in this paper that the simple

Table 4
Characteristic exponents by month.

Month	Period 1 1904–28	Period 3 1941–74	Period 4 1904–28 and 1941–74
Jan.	2.0	2.0	1.75
Feb.	1.8	2.0	1.86
March	1.7	2.0	1.75
April	2.0	2.0	1.86
May	2.0	2.0	2.0
June	2.0	2.0	2.0
July	1.93	2.0	2.0
Aug.	2.0	1.75	2.0
Sept.	1.86	1.91	2.0
Oct.	1.42	1.71	1.64
Nov.	2.0	1.31	1.49
Dec.	2.0	1.76	1.46
All	1.96	1.62	1.7

random walk model does not hold, not that the market is inefficient with respect to information regarding seasonality. Trading rule tests will have to be carried out to test for market efficiency. It is our expectation that the seasonal patterns we have found will not allow the investor to earn abnormal rates of return which are incommensurate with the degree of risk that is accepted. We hold this view for several reasons: (1) the large amount of evidence consistent with market efficiency; (2) the tendency of high return months over 1941–1974 to be also high dispersion months; and (3) the anecdotal and other evidence which indicates that seasonal effects have not gone unnoticed by Wall Street's technical analysts. It is unlikely that seasonality in stock returns will raise any serious problem for the efficient market model. Since, however, market efficiency is usually stated in terms of equilibrium expected returns, models of market equilibrium may require seasonal effects in expected returns.

5.2. Nature of the distribution of stock returns

Recent tests describing the distribution of stock returns have concentrated on the stability of the characteristic exponent, alpha, under addition. Good estimates of alpha are crucial. We have found some evidence that differences in alpha by month are explainable by sampling error, but the estimates by month do vary widely. Our findings should serve as a warning for those engaged in empirical research on stock return distributions, especially if monthly data are used. Use of daily data may perhaps bypass any possible problems although here too very little is known about distributional differences by day. Fama (1965) documents a difference between dispersion in Friday and Monday returns. Phenomena of this type which may well affect investigations of the stability of alpha should not be ignored.[16]

5.3. Expected return models

Many applications which require the computation of abnormal or disequilibrium rates of return have used as models for expected rates of return the market model and the two-parameter capital asset pricing model. Both compute expected returns conditional on market returns and the security's risk, measured by the beta coefficient of the security. Since market returns seem to depend on month of the year, the calculation of abnormal returns may be affected. The next two subsections examine the effects of seasonality on the market model and two-parameter model.

5.3.1. Market model

The market model assumes the existence of a linear regression of the jth security's rate of return, $\tilde{r}_{jt}$, with the market rate of return, $\tilde{R}_t$,

$$E(\tilde{r}_{jt}|R_t) = \alpha_j + \beta_j R_t. \tag{13}$$

The minimum variance linear estimator of $E(\tilde{r}_{jt}|\cdot)$ is

$$\hat{r}_{jt} = \widehat{E(\tilde{r}_{jt}|\cdot)} = \hat{\alpha}_j + \hat{\beta}_j R_t, \tag{14}$$

where $\hat{\alpha}_j$, $\hat{\beta}_j$ are least squares estimates of α_j and β_j.

---

[16] Teichmoeller (1971) was careful to use only calendar-day changes and also avoided changes over mid-week holidays. Barnea and Downes (1973) do not specify their selection procedure.

Now assume the existence of h linear regressions in h strata corresponding to distinct 'seasons' (e.g., January may form one stratum and the remaining months of the year another stratum),

$$E(\tilde{r}_{jth}|R_{th}) = \alpha_{jh} + \beta_{jh}R_{th}. \tag{15}$$

For the special case in which β_j is common to all strata, sampling theory [see Cochran (1963, pp. 200–203)] suggests the pooled least squares estimate

$$\hat{\beta}_j = \sum_h \sum_{t\in h} (r_{jth} - \bar{r}_{jh})(R_{th} - \bar{R}_h) \bigg/ \sum_h \sum_{t\in h} (R_{th} - \bar{R}_h)^2. \tag{16}$$

This estimate assumes proportional sampling in strata which will be the case for months of the year. The pooled estimate should result in a more efficient estimate of β_j than the usual least squares estimate. If the regression coefficients vary by stratum, then a separate regression estimate of β_{jh} can be computed for each stratum. A weighted average of the $\hat{\beta}_{jh}$ may, in many cases be an efficient estimate [Cochran (1963, p. 203)].

5.3.2. Two-parameter model

Black, Jensen and Scholes (1972) and Fama and Macbeth (1973) propose a model of expected returns of the form.

$$E(\tilde{r}_j) = E(\tilde{R}_0) + [E(\tilde{R}) - E(\tilde{R}_0)]\beta_j, \tag{17}$$

where $E(\tilde{R}_0)$ is the expected return on the minimum variance portfolio which has zero covariance with market returns. The second component of the right-hand side represents a risk premium for security j.

A stochastic version of (17) is

$$\tilde{r}_{jt} = \tilde{\gamma}_{0t} + \tilde{\gamma}_{1t}\beta_j + \tilde{e}_{jt}. \tag{18}$$

To overcome error measurement in β_j, (18) has been estimated using portfolio returns. Since $E(\tilde{\gamma}_{1t}) = E(\tilde{R}_t) - E(\tilde{R}_{0t})$ and since $E(\tilde{R}_t)$ has been shown above to be conditional on the month of the year, one is led to consider possible seasonality in estimates of γ_{1t}. For generality we also at the same time examine $\tilde{\gamma}_{0t}$.

We apply the same nonparametric and parametric tests to Fama and Macbeth's monthly estimates of γ_{0t} and γ_{1t} as have been applied to R_t.[17] Selected sample descriptive statistics for each month and all months combined

---
[17]We thank Professor Fama for making this data available.

Table 5

Statistics for γ_1 and γ_0, estimated intercept and slope of the two-parameter model (eq. (18)).

						Month							
	1	2	3	4	5	6	7	8	9	10	11	12	all

a. *Summary descriptive statistics*

1. 75% truncated mean

γ_0: 1935–67	0.0006	0.0068	0.0092	0.0080	0.0107	0.0055	0.0184	0.0076	−0.0033	0.0023	0.0168	0.0142	0.0081
1941–67	−0.0033	0.0017	0.0124	0.0068	0.0061	0.0012	0.0191	0.0124	0.0019	0.0050	0.0183	0.0107	0.0078
γ_1: 1935–67	−0.0430	0.0054	0.0017	−0.0003	0.0013	−0.0007	0.0168	−0.0080	−0.0008	0.0046	−0.0036	0.0068	0.0049
1941–67	0.0450	0.0045	0.0065	−0.0011	0.0098	−0.0014	0.0054	−0.0087	−0.0065	−0.0001	−0.0020	0.0140	0.0056

2. Standard deviation

γ_0: 1935–67	0.0283	0.0306	0.0452	0.0356	0.0520	0.0311	0.0312	0.0278	0.0479	0.0353	0.0414	0.0335	0.0376
1941–67	0.0267	0.0302	0.0296	0.0273	0.0303	0.0294	0.0296	0.0256	0.0290	0.0281	0.0282	0.0301	0.0289
γ_1: 1935–67	0.0682	0.0567	0.0554	0.0558	0.0517	0.0654	0.0590	0.0398	0.1208	0.0596	0.0607	0.0565	0.0660
1941–67	0.0595	0.0580	0.0364	0.0424	0.0432	0.0439	0.0496	0.0348	0.0457	0.0410	0.0489	0.0527	0.0486

3. Statistic c

γ_0: 1935–67	0.0206	0.0178	0.0112	0.0227	0.0151	0.0218	0.0134	0.0146	0.0251	0.0164	0.0175	0.0226	0.0194
1941–67	0.0148	0.0194	0.0119	0.0258	0.0160	0.0189	0.0122	0.0174	0.0222	0.0118	0.0175	0.0297	0.0178
γ_1: 1935–67	0.0293	0.0133	0.0232	0.0286	0.0371	0.0272	0.0318	0.0200	0.0349	0.0232	0.0239	0.0354	0.0300
1941–67	0.0267	0.0142	0.0245	0.0286	0.0317	0.0318	0.0318	0.0177	0.0351	0.0187	0.0199	0.0286	0.0252

b. *Summary test statistics*

	Non-parametric tests		Parametric tests			
	Kruskal–Wallis	Siegel–Tukey	F	d.f.	Bartlett's test	
1. γ_0: 1935–67	15.5	34.10[c]	1.25	11,384	32.58[c]	
1941–67	18.51[a]	31.20[c]	1.47	11,312	1.61	
2. γ_1: 1935–67	21.10[b]	12.16	1.84[b]	11,384	59.58[c]	
1941–67	27.81[c]	8.71	3.16[c]	11,312	15.81[a]	

[a]Significant at the 0.90 level.
[b]Significant at the 0.95 level.
[c]Significant at the 0.99 level.

are shown in table 5, panel a, for $\hat{\gamma}_{0t}$ and $\hat{\gamma}_{1t}$ for two time periods covering (1) 1935–1967, Fama and MacBeth's entire time period, and (2) 1941–1967, which we have seen is a period of more homogeneous stock returns. Panel b of table 5 contains the statistical tests.

Examining the statistical tests of location in table 5, the nonparametric and parametric tests show a close correspondence. Both tests reject the hypothesis of equal means for γ_1 at the 1% level for 1941–67. The χ^2 of 15.8 which is significant at a 10% level and indicates a lack of homogeneity of variances, disagrees slightly with the low Siegel–Tukey statistic. However, given the large difference in means which is evident in the sample values of the 75% truncated mean, we are quite confident of highly significant differences in mean γ_1 by month. In particular the January mean of 0.0450 compared to the average of 0.0056 for all months is truly extraordinary. $\hat{\gamma}_1$, it will be recalled, estimates the risk premium inherent in the security market line and has expected value $[E(\tilde{R}) - E(\tilde{R}_0)]$. It appears then that possible seasonal effects in $E(\tilde{R}_0)$ do not negate those we have found earlier for $E(\tilde{R})$. To the extent that realizations from our somewhat small sample size of 27 monthly observations adequately measure expectations, it seems that the tradeoff of return for risk demanded and received by the market in January is much greater than in other months of the year. This conclusion should perhaps be somewhat tempered by observing that fully five months of the year – April, June, August, September, and October – show realized *negative* risk premiums; however, the largest of these, -0.0087 for August, is dwarfed in absolute terms by January's $+0.0450$.

Seasonal effects in $\hat{\gamma}_0$ which estimates $E(\tilde{R}_0)$ seem also to be present, approximately to the extent shown by stock returns themselves. The Kruskal–Wallis statistic is of the same order of magnitude while the analysis of variance indicates a lower level of significance (10.8%) as compared with stock returns (1% level). Seasonality in $E(\tilde{R}_0)$ therefore seems to be weaker, if anything, than that in $E(\tilde{R})$.

Concerning possible differences in scale among distribution of γ_0 and γ_1 by month, we have noted that such differences for γ_1 seem to be weak, if not absent. For γ_0 the χ^2 and Siegel–Tukey statistics shown in table 5 give conflicting results. The very low χ^2 statistic of 1.614 reflects the homogeneity of standard deviations observable in table 5, panel a, with standard deviations ranging only from 0.0256 to 0.0303. On the other hand, $\hat{c}$ ranges from 0.0118 to 0.0297 and the rank statistic seems to be reflecting the variability in this order statistic. We therefore are unable to reach a definite conclusion concerning variability in γ_0.

The two-parameter model seems to impound seasonality in the coefficient estimates. One would expect, therefore, that the abnormal returns computed from this model will be free from seasonal effects, or at least much more free than the market model residuals. While this is a plus, seasonality in the risk premium has no obvious explanation while seasonality in expected market returns may be somewhat easier to rationalize. Seasonality in the risk premium may simply be induced by that in market returns. Also possible is a capital asset pricing model which incorporates seasonal effects and gives rise to the fluctuating market risk premium observed here. Chen, Kim and Kon (1975) present a model in which the market price of risk depends upon cash demands and liquidity risk. If the latter, in turn display seasonal characteristics, perhaps such a model can explain the seasonal in the risk premium.

6. Conclusions

Seasonality on the New York Stock Exchange, undetectable with any clarity in the autocorrelation function of returns, becomes clearly evident once rates of return are tested by month. The most outstanding feature of this seasonality is the higher mean of return of the January distribution of returns compared with most other months. Other seasonal peculiarities include relatively high mean returns in July, November and December and low mean returns in February and June. Differences among months in the dispersion parameters of the probability distributions are present to a much lesser extent and can probably be disregarded for most purposes. Seasonal effects on the New York Stock Exchange seem to be weaker than those Officer found in Australian stocks. Interestingly, July and January (in that order) are the highest return months in the Australian stock market.

Seasonality is also a prominent feature of 'risk premiums' estimated from the two-parameter capital asset pricing model. Again it is January with a relatively large risk premium which differs noticeably from the other months.

Hypotheses which seek to explain seasonality are not tested in this paper, our main purpose having been to demonstrate its existence and point out a few of its possible ramifications. Promising avenues of exploration that we have noted in passing are as follows: (1) tax-selling hypothesis, (2) accounting information hypothesis, (3) stochastic cash demand hypothesis. All three we believe deserve elaboration and testing.

References

Barnea, A. and D. H. Downes, 1973, A reexamination of the empirical distribution of stock price changes, Journal of the American Statistical Association 68, 348–350.

Bartlett, M.S., 1937, Some examples of statistical methods of research in agriculture and applied biology, Journal of the Royal Statistical Society Supplement 4, 137.

Black, F., M.C. Jensen and M. Scholes, 1972, The capital asset pricing model: Some empirical tests, in: M.C. Jensen, ed., Studies in the theory of capital markets (Praeger, New York).

Blattberg, R.C. and N.J. Gonedes, 1974, A comparison of the stable and student distributions as statistical models for stock prices, Journal of Business 47, 244–280.

Bonin, J.M. and E.A. Moses, 1974, Seasonal variations in prices of individual Dow–Jones industrial stocks, Journal of Financial and Quantitative Analysis 9, 963–991.

Box, G.E.P. and G. Jenkins, 1970, Time series analysis, forecasting and control (Holden-Day, San Francisco, CA).

Chen, A.H., E.H. Kim and S.J. Kon, 1975, Cash demand, liquidation costs and capital market equilibrium under uncertainty, Journal of Financial Economics 2, 293–308.

Cochran, W.G., 1963, Sampling techniques (Wiley, New York).

Conover, W.J., 1971, Practical nonparametric statistics (Wiley, New York).

Cootner, P.H., 1964, The random character of stock market prices (M.I.T. Press, Cambridge, MA).

Cowles, A., 1938, Common-stock indexes 1871–1937 (Principia Press, Bloomington, IL).

Fama, E.F., 1965, The behavior of stock market prices, Journal of Business 37, 34–105.

Fama, E.F., 1970, Efficient capital markets: A review of theory and empirical work, Journal of Finance 25, 383–417.

Fama, E.F. and J.D. Macbeth, 1973, Risk, return, and equilibrium: Empirical tests, Journal of Political Economy 81, 607–636.

Fama, E.F. and R. Roll, 1968, Some properties of symmetric stable distributions, Journal of the American Statistical Association 63, 817–836.

Fama, E.F. and R. Roll, 1971, Parameter estimates for symmetric stable distributions, Journal of the American Statistical Association 66, 331–338.

Fisher, L., 1966, Some new stock market indexes, Journal of Business, Security Prices: A Supplement 39, 191–225.

Granger, C.W.J. and O. Morgenstern, 1963, Spectral analysis of New York stock market prices, Kyklos 16, 1–25.

Granger, C.W.J. and O. Morgenstern, 1970, Predictability of stock market prices (D.C. Heath and Co., Lexington, MA).

Hartley, H.O., 1955, Communications on Pure and Applied Mathematics 8, 47–55.

Hsu, D., R.B. Miller and D.W. Wichern, 1974, On the stable Paretian behavior of stock-market prices, Journal of the American Statistical Association 69, 108–113.

Mandelbrot, B., 1963, The variation of certain speculative prices, Journal of Business 36, 394–419.

Mandelbrot, B., 1967, The variation of some other speculative prices, Journal of Business 40, 393–413.

Officer, R.R., 1972, The distribution of stock returns, Journal of the American Statistical Association 67, 807–812.

Officer, R.R., 1975, Seasonality in Australian capital markets: Market efficiency and empirical issues, Journal of Financial Economics 2, 29–51.

Press, S.J., 1967, A compound events model for security prices, Journal of Business 40, 317–335.

Shiskin, J., 1972, Systematic aspects of stock price fluctuations, in: J. Lorie and R. Brealey, eds., Modern developments in investment management (Praeger, New York).

Teichmoller, J., 1971, A note on the distribution of stock price changes, Journal of the American Statistical Association 66, 282–284.

Wachtel, S.B., 1942, Certain observations on seasonal movements in stock prices, Journal of Business 15, 184–193.

Wilcoxon, F. and R.A. Wilcox, 1964, Some rapid approximate statistical procedures (Lederle Laboratories, Pearl River).

Winer, B.J., 1962, Statistical principles in experimental design (McGraw-Hill, New York).

Zinbarg, E.D., 1964, The stock market's seasonal pattern, Financial Analysts Journal 20, 53.

Name Index

Ackley, G. 111, 260
Admati, A.R. 581, 598
Albrecht, S. 327
Aldous, D. 605
Amsler, C. 37
Anderson, T.W. 45, 47
Ariel, R.A. 581, 584, 592
Arrow, K.J. 111, 197, 389
Auberman, G. 371

Bachelier, L. 429
Baesel, J.B. 411
Ball, R. 288, 301, 317, 355, 356, 358, 359, 371, 378, 380, 383, 389, 463, 481, 522, 580, 581
Banz, R. 476, 477, 528, 560, 571, 640
Bartlett, M.S. 693
Basu, S. 389, 463, 476, 528
Bathke, A. 305, 309, 333
Baun, P.A. 385
Bawa, V.S. 477
Beaver, W. 390, 391
Beebower, G. 411
Bernard, V. 302, 305, 311, 315, 316, 321, 329, 332–5, 357, 377
Bewley, T.F. 99
Bhandari, L. 385
Billingsley, P. 80
Black, F. 4, 30, 341, 464, 465, 467, 481, 485, 486, 527, 529, 557, 582, 599, 628–30
Blanchard, O. 38, 253, 254, 260
Blume, M. 398, 454, 486, 642
Bonin, J.M. 679, 682
Bowers, J. 580, 581
Box, G.E.P. 233, 685
Bradley, M. 555
Branch, B. 576, 640, 642, 644
Brealey, R. 253, 258
Breeden, D. 105
Brennan, M.J. 485
Brock, W.A. 235
Brown, L. 301, 305, 309, 327
Brown, P. 288, 333, 481, 522, 560, 561, 574
Burns, A. 106

Campbell, J.Y. 4, 14, 16, 23, 31, 91, 92, 99, 407
Chambers, A. 332

Chan, K.C. 352, 355, 368
Chari, V. 317, 357, 378
Chen, A.H. 701
Chen, N. 352, 605
Chopra, N. 598
Cochran, W.G. 698
Cochrane, J.C. 95, 96
Cohen, K. 432, 442
Cohn, R. 203
Conover, W.J. 689, 691
Cootner, P.H. 239, 680
Copeland, B. 189, 190
Cornell, B. 528
Cowles, A. 10, 112, 499
Cross, R. 580, 581

Dann, L. 555
De Bondt, W. 96, 208, 222, 338–40, 343, 349, 355, 371, 383, 384, 388, 391, 392, 395, 398, 402, 430, 435, 437, 454
De Long, J.B. 96, 407, 430
Deaton, A. 255
Diba, B. 97
Dickey, D.A. 12, 144, 150
Dimson, E. 356, 562, 563, 566, 575, 648
Dreman, D.N. 389
Dunn, P. 500
Durlauf, S.N. 69, 76, 89, 91
Dyl, E.A. 644, 648

Easton, P. 334
Elton, E. 500
Engle, R.F. 14
Epstein, L.G. 99, 100

Fama, E.F. 5, 23, 31, 110, 177, 204, 239, 244, 321, 338, 341, 355, 391, 404, 440, 455, 465, 468, 481, 567, 629, 630, 680, 692, 695, 697, 700
Fischer, S. 204
Fisher, L. 285, 432, 441, 482
Flavin, M.A. 3, 66, 73, 180, 211, 253, 254
Flood, R.P. 22, 31, 96, 272
Foster, D.F. 581
Foster, G. 301, 305, 314, 320, 327, 328, 331, 333

Freeman, R. 302, 303, 316, 329, 333, 334
French, K.R. 5, 23, 31, 338, 341, 440, 455, 567, 580, 581, 654
Friedman, M. 160
Friend, I. 486
Fuller, W.A. 12, 144, 145, 150, 256

Gibbons, M.R. 567, 580, 581, 654
Goetzmann, W. 500, 501, 513, 519, 522
Gordon, M.J. 4, 7
Graham, B. 394
Granger, C.W. 14, 107, 164, 242, 679, 682, 683
Grether, D.M. 388
Griffin, P. 305, 333
Grinblatt, M. 500, 502, 506, 516
Grossman, H. 97
Grossman, S.J. 19, 37, 50, 78, 97, 98, 117, 124, 125, 127, 128, 139, 272
Gruber, M. 500

Hall, R.E. 69, 76, 89, 91, 104, 235
Hand, J.R. 334, 379
Hannan, E.J. 262
Hansen, L.P. 5, 19, 95, 153, 256, 259, 260, 262, 263, 272
Harlow, W. 327
Harris, L. 580
Hartley, H.O. 691
Hatanaka, M. 107
Haugen, R.A. 598
Hendricks, D. 500–502, 513, 516, 523
Hess, P.J. 567, 580, 581, 654
Hirsch, Y. 640
Hodrick, R.J. 22, 31, 96, 272
Hsu, D. 693
Husic, F. 642

Ibbotson, R.G. 139, 358, 382, 466, 511, 500, 501, 513, 519, 522
Ippolito, R. 500

Jaffe, J. 580, 581
Jagannathan, R. 95, 357, 378
Jarrow, R. 390
Jegadeesh, N. 371, 454
Jenkins, G. 233, 685
Jensen, M.C. 201, 341, 358, 481, 486, 499, 501, 527, 528, 628–30, 698
Joerding, W. 80
Johnston, J. 484
Jones, C.P. 301, 580
Joy, O.M. 301

Kahneman, D. 197, 338, 388, 389

Kandel, S. 371
Kang, H. 146
Kaplan, P. 22, 31, 96, 272
Keim, D.B. 330, 398, 399, 567, 577, 578, 580, 640, 642
Keynes, J.M. 96, 110, 179, 253, 388
Kim, E.H. 701
Kim, M. 455
Kinney, W.R. 567, 577
Kleidon, A.W. 10, 30, 66, 72, 78, 82, 84, 154, 180, 187, 211, 253, 254, 268, 269, 389, 560, 561, 574
Klein, R.W. 477
Kon, S.J. 701
Kormendi, R. 334
Koski, J.L. 80
Kothari, S.P. 317, 355, 356, 358, 359, 371, 378, 380, 383
Krasker, W. 61
Kreps, D.M. 99
Kritzman, M. 500
Kyle, A.S. 407

La Civita, C.J. 104, 228, 231, 235
Lakonishok, J. 580, 581, 586, 598
Landsman, W.R. 390, 391
Lanstein, R. 671, 675
Latane, H.A. 301
Leamer, E. 190, 205, 604, 607
Leftwich 327
Lehmann, B.N. 418, 430, 435, 630–32, 637
LeRoy, S.F. 30, 37, 38, 66, 72, 77, 81, 83, 86, 89, 93, 94, 98, 104, 131, 132, 155, 171, 203, 210, 227, 228, 230, 231, 235, 237, 253, 260, 430
Levi, M.D. 470, 581
Lintner, J. 154, 184, 219, 481
Lipe, R. 334
Litzenberger, R. 301, 463, 465, 528
Lo, A.W. 432, 433, 442, 454
Long, J. 203, 528, 555
Lookabill, L. 327
Lorek, K. 305, 309, 333
Lorie, J.H. 11
Lucas, R. 104, 171, 228, 230, 271, 430

MacBeth, J. 321, 465, 468, 481, 628, 630, 680, 698, 700
MacKinlay, A.C. 432, 433, 442, 454
Mandelbrot, B. 689
Mankiw, N.G. 30, 76, 86, 96, 212
Markowitz 219
Marsh, P. 356

Marsh, T.A. 5, 11, 30, 88, 204, 211, 223, 253, 254, 268, 560, 561, 574
Mattey, J. 30
Mayers, D. 649
McCallum, B. 259
McEnally, R. 301
McKeown, J. 327
Meese, R. 30
Mehra, R. 98–100
Merton, R.C. 5, 11, 30, 88, 204, 206, 211, 219, 223, 253, 254, 268, 338, 581, 605, 637
Michener, R.W. 98
Miller, M.H. 111, 131, 219, 245
Miller, R.B. 693
Mitchell, W. 106
Modest, D. 630–32, 637
Modigliani, F. 111, 131, 196, 203, 209, 219, 245
Morgenstern, O. 679, 682, 683
Moses, E.A. 679, 682
Myers, S. 253, 258

Nelson, C.R. 135, 144, 455
Nelson, D.B. 385
Newey, W.K. 263, 457

O'Brien, P. 333
Ofer, A.R. 357, 378
Officer, R.R. 567, 679, 681, 682, 687, 692, 693
Ohlson, J.A. 205, 390
Olsen, C. 301, 317, 331
Ou, J. 304, 334

Pakes, A. 155
Parke, W.R. 30, 86, 89, 93, 94
Patel, J. 500–502, 513, 516, 523
Pearce, D.K. 580
Penman, S.H. 205, 304, 332, 334, 390, 598
Perron, P. 12
Pesandro, J. 37
Pettit 488
Pfleiderer, P. 581, 598
Phillips, P.C.B. 12
Phillips, S.M. 646
Pierce, D.A. 164
Plosser, C.I. 135, 144
Porter, R.D. 37, 38, 66, 72, 77, 81, 104, 131, 132, 155, 203, 210, 227, 228, 237, 253
Porteus, E.L. 99
Poterba, J.M. 5, 304, 376, 402, 430
Prescott, E.C. 98–100
Priest, W. 411

Quinn, B.G. 262

Ramaswamy, K. 463, 465, 528
Reid, K. 671, 675
Reinganum, M.R. 368, 398, 476, 528, 560, 563, 566, 571, 640
Rendleman, R.J. 301
Rentzler, J. 500
Richardson, M. 455
Ritter, J.R. 598
Roberts, H.V. 134
Rock, K. 581, 598
Rogalski, R. 584
Roll, R. 368, 399, 445, 466, 468, 528, 562, 566, 575, 578, 605, 692, 695
Romer, D. 30, 76, 86, 96, 212
Rosenberg, B. 671, 675, 677
Ross, S. 582, 605, 634
Rozeff, M. 305, 309, 567, 577
Rubinstein, M. 171
Rudd, A. 584, 671, 677
Russell, T. 390

Samuelson, P. 179, 191, 198, 200, 204, 219, 222, 242
Sargent, T.J. 16, 256, 260, 262
Scholes, M. 4, 341, 441, 465, 467, 485, 486, 562, 575, 628–30, 648, 698
Schultz, P. 581
Schwert, G.W. 5, 398
Scott, L. 89
Shapiro, M.D. 30, 76, 86, 96, 212
Sharpe, W.F. 154, 219, 481
Shea, G.S. 76, 87
Shefrin, H.M. 402, 430
Shevlin, T. 301, 317, 331
Shiller, R.J. 4, 14, 16, 18, 19, 22, 23, 30, 31, 37–9, 49, 50, 52, 54, 61, 66, 71, 77, 78, 81, 83, 91–3, 96, 97, 99, 104, 111–13, 116, 117, 124, 125, 127–9, 131, 133, 137, 139, 142, 150, 153, 155, 160, 163, 179, 180, 182, 188, 198, 203, 207, 210, 212, 218, 227, 228, 233, 253, 254, 261, 268, 270, 272–4, 389, 402
Shishkin, J. 682
Shleifer, A. 381, 407, 430
Shows, G. 411
Sims, C.A. 402
Singleton, K.J. 5, 37, 39, 45, 49, 55, 56, 77, 97, 153, 227, 231, 232, 259, 262, 263, 272
Sinquefield, R.A. 139, 466, 511
Smidt, S. 581, 586, 598
Smith, C.W. 646
Stambaugh, R.F. 5, 30, 398, 580
Startz, R. 455
Statman, M. 402, 430

Stattman, D. 476
Stock, J.H. 14, 154
Stoll, H.R. 561, 646, 650
Stroyny, A.L. 385
Summers, L.H. 5, 14, 196, 200, 206, 211, 260, 270, 304, 376, 402, 407, 430, 440
Sunier, A.M. 385
Sweeney, R.J. 418

Thaler, R. 96, 208, 222, 338–40, 343, 349, 355, 371, 383, 384, 390, 402, 430, 435, 437, 454
Theisen, R. 500
Thomas, J. 302, 305, 311, 315, 316, 329, 332–5, 357, 377
Thorp, E. 411
Tinic, S. 327, 584
Tirole, J. 113, 130, 197, 222
Titman, S. 371, 500, 502, 506, 516
Tobin, J. 111, 219
Treynor, J. 426, 481
Tse, S. 302, 303, 316, 329, 333, 334
Tversky, A. 197, 338, 388, 389

Van Horne, J.C. 196
Vermaelen, T. 555
Vishny, R.W. 381

Viswanathan, S. 581

Wachtel, S.B. 576, 682, 693
Waldmann, R.J. 407, 430
Watson, M. 38, 253, 254, 260
Watts, R.L. 301, 305, 315, 327, 331
Weil, P. 100
West, K.D. 30, 66, 85, 86, 97, 133, 212, 255, 261, 263, 457
Westerfield, R. 488, 580, 581
Whaley, R.E. 561, 646, 650
Wichern, D.W. 693
Wiggins, J.B. 333
Wilcox, R.A. 691
Wilcoxon, F. 691
Williams, J. 389, 566, 575, 648
Wilson, J.W. 580
Woodward, S.E. 171

Yang, S.S. 609

Zarowin, P. 355, 364, 380
Zeckhauser, R. 500–502, 513, 516, 523
Zin, S.E. 99, 100
Zinbarg, E.D. 682, 693
Zmijewski, M. 305, 333, 334